INSIGHT
MATHEMATICS
AUSTRALIAN CURRICULUM FOR NSW

STAGES 5.2/5.3

10

JOHN LEY
MICHAEL FULLER

OXFORD
UNIVERSITY PRESS
AUSTRALIA & NEW ZEALAND

OXFORD

UNIVERSITY PRESS

Oxford University Press is a department of the University of Oxford.
It furthers the University's objective of excellence in research,
scholarship, and education by publishing worldwide. Oxford is a
registered trademark of Oxford University Press in the UK and in
certain other countries.

Published in Australia by
Oxford University Press
253 Normanby Road, South Melbourne, Victoria 3205, Australia

© John Ley, Michael Fuller 2015

The moral rights of the author have been asserted

First published 2015

Reprinted 2015

National Library of Australia Cataloguing-in-Publication data
Oxford Insight Mathematics 10, Stages 5.2/5.3 : Australian
Curriculum for NSW / John Ley, Michael Fuller.
ISBN 978 019 552276 1 (paperback)

For secondary school students.
Mathematics–Study and teaching (Secondary).
Mathematics–New South Wales–Textbooks.
510.76

Reproduction and communication for educational purposes
The Australian *Copyright Act 1968* (the Act) allows a maximum of
one chapter or 10% of the pages of this work,
whichever is the greater, to be reproduced and/
or communicated by any educational institution
for its educational purposes provided that
the educational institution (or the body that
administers it) has given a remuneration notice to
Copyright Agency Limited (CAL) under the Act.

For details of the CAL licence for educational institutions contact:

Copyright Agency Limited
Level 15, 233 Castlereagh Street
Sydney NSW 2000
Telephone: (02) 9394 7600
Facsimile: (02) 9394 7601
Email: info@copyright.com.au

Edited and proofread by Marta Veroni
Technical artwork by Rhonda Idczak and Paulene Meyer
Typeset by Idczak Enterprises
Printed by Golden Cup Printing Co. Ltd

*Links to third party websites are provided by Oxford in good faith and
for information only. Oxford disclaims any responsibility for the materials
contained in any third party website referenced in this work.*

CONTENTS

12 Graphical representation
Number & Algebra — 277

13 Properties of geometrical figures
Measurement & Geometry — 323

Cumulative review chapters 10–13 — 343

14 Data analysis
Statistics & Probability — 345

15 Polynomials
Number & Algebra — 365

16 Circle geometry
Measurement & Geometry — 401

Cumulative review chapters 14–16 — 443

OXFORD

INSIGHT

MATHEMATICS

AUSTRALIAN CURRICULUM FOR NSW

10

STUDENT BOOKS

Peerless maths content designed to support deep understanding of mathematical concepts and development of skills. Written for the Mathematics Syllabus of the Australian Curriculum in New South Wales.

obook
assess

- Diagnostic tools aid student understanding.
- Teachers can manage class progress, set tests, and plan instruction to meet individual and whole-class needs.

PROFESSIONAL SUPPORT

Guided progress through the Australian Curriculum so teachers can drive student learning.

SYLLABUS GRID

Chapter	Name	Outcomes	NSW Syllabus references	AC references
1	Review of Year 9			AC
2	Algebra	MA5.2-1WM, MA5.2-3WM, MA5.2-6NA	5.2 N&A Algebraic techniques, 5.2 N&A Equations (part)	ACMNA213, ACMNA230, ACMNA232
3	Linear relationships	MA5.1-1WM, MA5.1-3WM, MA5.1-6NA, M5.2-1WM, MA5.2-3WM, MA5.2-9NA	5.1 N&A Linear relationships, 5.2 N&A Linear relationships	ACMNA238, ACMNA294
4	Geometrical proofs	MA5.2-1WM, MA5.2-2WM, MA5.2-3WM, MA5.2-14MG	5.2 M&G Properties of geometrical figures	ACMMG220, ACMMG243, ACMMG244
5	Bivariate data analysis	MA5.2-1WM, MA5.2-3WM, MA5.2-16SP	5.2 S&P Bivariate data analysis	ACMSP251, ACMSP252
CR 2–5	**Cumulative review chapters 2–5**			
6	Financial mathematics	MA5.2-1WM, MA5.2-2WM, MA5.2-3WM, MA5.2-4NA	5.2 N&A Financial mathematics	ACMNA229
7	Binomial expressions and quadratics	MA5.2-1WM, MA5.2-3WM, MA5.2-6NA, MA5.3-1WM, MA5.3-5NA	5.2 N&A Algebraic techniques	ACMNA233, ACMNA241, ACMNA269
8	Box plots	MA5.2-1WM, MA5.2-3WM, MA5.2-15SP	5.2 S&P Single variable data analysis	ACMSP227, ACMSP248, ACMSP249, ACMSP250
9	Non-linear relationships	MA5.2-1WM, MA5.2-3WM, MA5.2-10NA	5.2 N&A Non-linear relationships	ACMNA239, ACMNA296
CR 6–9	**Cumulative review chapters 6–9**			
10	Equations	MA5.3-1WM, MA5.3-2WM, MA5.3-3WM, MA5.3-7NA	5.3 N&A Equations	ACMNA233, ACMNA269
11	Further trigonometry	MA5.3-1WM, MA5.3-2WM, MA5.3-3WM, MA5.3-15MG	5.3 M&G Trigonometry and Pythagoras' theorem	ACMMG274, ACMMG276
12	Graphical representation	MA 5.3-1WM, MA5.3-2WM, M5.3-3WM, MA5.3-4NA, MA5.3-9NA	5.3 N&A Ratios and rates, 5.3 N&A Non-linear relationships	ACMNA208, ACMNA267
13	Properties of geometrical figures	MA5.3-1WM, MA5.3-2WM, MA5.3-3WM, MA5.3-16MG	5.3 M&G Properties of geometrical figures	ACMMG243, ACMMG244
CR 10–13	**Cumulative review chapters 10–13**			
14	Data analysis	MA5.3-1WM, MA5.3-2WM, MA5.3-3WM, MA5.3-18SP, MA5.3-19SP	5.3 S&P Single variable data analysis, 5.3 S&P Bivariate data analysis	ACMSP277, ACMSP278, ACMSP279
15	Polynomials	MA5.3-1WM, MA5.3-2WM, MA5.3-3WM, MA5.3-10NA	5.3 N&A Polynomials	ACMNA266, ACMNA268
16	Circle geometry	MA5.3-1WM, MA5.3-2WM, MA5.3-3WM, MA5.3-17MG	5.3 M&G Circle geometry	ACMMG272
CR 14–16	**Cumulative review chapters 14–16**			

1

Review of Year 9

This chapter reviews the Year 9 component of the mathematics syllabus.

After completing this chapter you should be able to:

- apply index laws to simplify algebraic expressions and evaluate arithmetic expressions
- collect and analyse data and the symmetry of data distributions
- use scientific notation to write large and small numbers, convert units and understand measurement error
- solve financial problems involving earning and spending money
- calculate area, surface area and volume
- determine theoretical probabilities and perform probability calculations
- apply trigonometry to solve problems including angles of elevation and depression

- perform calculations involving similar figures
- determine midpoint, length and distance, and graph straight lines and non-linear graphs
- use direct and inverse proportion to solve problems
- solve linear equations, inequalities and simultaneous linear equations
- perform calculations in non-right-angled triangles
- simplify expressions involving surds
- calculate surface area and volume of pyramids, cones and spheres
- work with functions, inverse functions and logarithms.

A Indices

1 Write each in index form.

a $2 \times 2 \times 2 \times 2 \times 2$

b $5 \times 5 \times 5 \times 5 \times 5$

2 Write the base of each number.

a 9^7

b 5^{11}

3 Write each number in expanded form.

a 5^3

b 6^7

4 Use a calculator to evaluate each number.

a 2^9

b 6^5

5 State whether the following are true or false.

a $3^4 \times 2^7 = 6^{11}$

b $8^{10} \div 4^2 = 2^5$

6 Simplify each of the following, leaving the answer in index form.

a $5^{12} \times 5^{16}$

b $(4^5)^2$

c $2^8 \div 2^5$

d $7^6 \times 7$

e $5^6 \times 5^3 \div 5^9$

7 Write the meaning of:

a 2^{-6}

b $5^{\frac{1}{2}}$

c $11^{\frac{1}{3}}$

8 Evaluate:

a 5^{-2}

b $16^{\frac{1}{2}}$

c $8^{\frac{1}{3}}$

d 17^0

9 Simplify:

a $y^{10} \times y^5$

b $k^{11} \div k^6$

c $(p^7)^3$

d $\dfrac{t^7 \times t^7}{t^3 \times t^5}$

e $(5m^4)^2$

f $3a^5b^3 \times 2ab^7$

10 Evaluate:

a v^0

b $6v^0$

c $(6v)^0$

d $6v^0 + 1$

11 Write the meaning of:

a $x^{\frac{1}{2}}$

b $5x^{\frac{1}{2}}$

c $(5x)^{\frac{1}{2}}$

d $x^{\frac{1}{3}}$

e $5x^{\frac{1}{3}}$

12 Write the meaning of:

a z^{-3}

b $3z^{-3}$

c $(3z)^{-3}$

13 Simplify:

a $y^{-3} \times y^7$

b $e^6 \div e^{-3}$

c $(n^{-4})^4$

d $6b^{-2} \times 3b^8$

e $4k^{-5} \div 2k^{-5}$

14 State whether the following are true or false.

a $4q^0 = 4$

b $a^6 \div a^8 = a^2$

c $6m^5 \div 2m^5 = 3m$

d $5b^{-2} = \dfrac{5}{b^2}$

e $4q^{\frac{1}{2}} = 2\sqrt{q}$

15 Expand:

  a $6(2v - 4w)$ **b** $a^3(2a^2 + 3a)$ **c** $-3(5x + 2)$

16 Expand and simplify:

  a $6(m - 2) + 5(2m + 5)$ **b** $4(3a - b) - (2a - b)$

B Collecting and analysing data

Exercise 1B

1 The table below shows the monthly and annual rainfall for Sydney (Observatory Hill) from 2002 to 2011. Measurements are to the nearest millimetre.

Rainfall for Sydney (mm)

Year	J	F	M	A	M	J	J	A	S	O	N	D	Annual
2002	98	348	45	68	93	28	24	20	22	6	32	75	860
2003	14	59	132	192	349	76	58	43	6	103	109	60	1200
2004	51	129	101	33	8	39	44	153	60	234	67	76	995
2005	68	125	154	33	48	79	63	2	51	43	125	25	816
2006	121	51	40	10	40	177	140	86	192	17	45	74	994
2007	45	108	65	180	10	511	67	152	41	27	170	123	1499
2008	57	258	63	147	3	127	90	44	99	67	73	54	1083
2009	25	128	61	153	126	130	53	6	16	180	13	67	956
2010	36	239	51	30	168	147	115	27	42	85	130	83	1154
2011	54	18	192	206	136	94	282	52	72	37	148	78	1369

  a In this time period, in which year was the annual rainfall:

     i highest?   **ii** lowest?

  b How much rain fell in:

     i July 2006?   **ii** June 2007?

    iii October 2011?

  c Which month had the highest rainfall in:

     i 2006?   **ii** 2011?

  d Which month had the lowest rainfall in:

     i 2005?   **ii** 2008?

  e Which year had the wettest:

     i February?   **ii** June?

    iii October?

  f Which year had the driest:

     i January?   **ii** June?

    iii December?

2 State whether the shape of each distribution is symmetrical, positively skewed, negatively skewed or bimodal.

a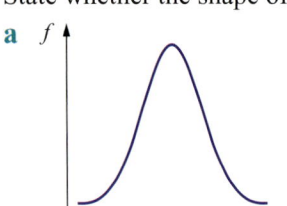
Score

b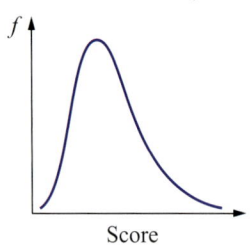
Score

c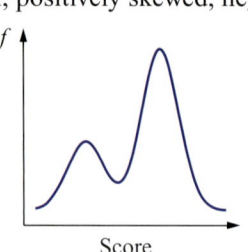
Score

d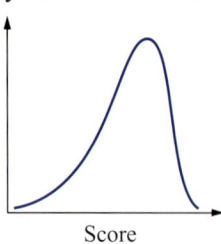
Score

3 The numbers of goals per match scored by two soccer teams are shown in the tables below.

Team A

Number of goals	Number of matches
0	6
1	8
2	4
3	0
4	2

Team B

Number of goals	Number of matches
0	3
1	5
2	6
3	4
4	2

  a Display this information in:
    i a back-to-back histogram
    ii a parallel dot plot.
  b Comment on the shape of each distribution.
  c Compare the mean, median and range for these two distributions.
  d Which team do you think performed better?

C Numbers of any magnitude

Exercise 1C

1 Write the following numbers in scientific notation.
  a 23 000 000 000
  b 0.000 052

2 Write the following as ordinary numbers.
  a 9.8×10^7
  b 3.7×10^{-9}

3 Explain why $4 \times 10^5 \neq 4^5$.

4 Use your calculator to evaluate the following, leaving the answer in scientific notation.
  a $(3.4 \times 10^4) \times (4.8 \times 10^9)$
  b $(5.6 \times 10^{10}) \div (3.5 \times 10^5)$
  c $(4 \times 10^9)^5$
  d $\sqrt{2.25 \times 10^{16}}$

5 Write the following numbers in order from smallest to largest.
  $3.8 \times 10^{15}, 4.6 \times 10^{13}, 7.7 \times 10^{-16}, 3.1 \times 10^{-12}$

6 Write the value of the digit 7 in each of the following numbers.
  a 753.6
  b 1407.2
  c 76.45
  d 7564

7 Round:

    a 3470 to the nearest hundred   **b** 7956 to the nearest ten

    c 37.5 to the nearest whole number   **d** 69 900 to the nearest thousand.

8 Round 7.2681 to:

    a 1 decimal place   **b** 2 decimal places   **c** 3 decimal places.

9 Round:

    a 4.288 correct to 2 decimal places   **b** 39.97 correct to 1 decimal place.

10 A number was rounded to the nearest 10 and the answer was 50.

    a What is the smallest the number could have been?

    b What is the largest the number could have been? Discuss.

    c Write a mathematical statement that shows the range of possible numbers.

11 Write the first significant figure in each of the following numbers.

    a 160   **b** 3.201   **c** 0.006 51

12 Round 67.30591 to the following number of significant figures.

    a 1   **b** 2   **c** 3   **d** 4   **e** 5

13 How many significant figures are there in each of the following numbers?

    a 957   **b** 0.03   **c** 7.500   **d** 0.0035   **e** 142 000

14 Explain the difference between measurements of 4.65 m and 4.650 m.

15 How many nanowatts in 3.6 milliwatts?

16 Convert 43 000 metres to:

    a kilometres   **b** megametres.

17 The time taken for a student to complete a task in an aptitude test was measured to be 21 s.

    a Find the limit of reading of the measuring instrument used.

    b Determine the greatest possible error in the measurement.

    c What are the limits of accuracy of the measurement?

    d Write a mathematical statement that shows the range of values within which the true time lies.

18 The length and breadth of a rectangle were measured as 8 cm and 10 cm to the nearest centimetre.

    a Calculate the perimeter of the rectangle using these measurements.

    b Write down the greatest possible error in each of these measurements.

    c Hence find the limits of accuracy of the length and the breadth.

    d Calculate the lower and upper limits of the true perimeter.

    e Find the maximum error in the answer in part **a**.

19 The length and breadth of a rectangle were measured to be 12.6 cm and 7.9 cm. Give a reasonable estimate of the area of this rectangle using the level of accuracy of the measurements.

D Financial mathematics

Exercise 1D

1 Dan earns $423.76 per week. How much does he earn per:
   a fortnight?   b year?   c month?

2 Convert a salary of $54 700 p.a. to the equivalent salary per:
   a week   b fortnight   c month.

3 Olivia works a 36-hour week and is paid $25.40 per hour. How much does she earn for a week in which she works an additional 6 hours at time-and-a-half and 2 hours at double time?

4 Terry earns $710 per week. He is entitled to 4 weeks annual leave and receives an additional holiday loading of 17.5%. Calculate his total pay for this holiday period.

5 Joanne sews buttons on shirts in a clothing factory. She is paid $0.33 per shirt. Calculate her income for a week in which she completed the following number of shirts: Monday 172, Tuesday 189, Wednesday 203, Thursday 194 and Friday 188.

6 Benita sells printers. She is paid a retainer of $180 per week plus a commission of 1.5% of sales. How much does she earn in a week in which her sales are $33 240?

7 Dennis works as a casual in a coffee shop. He gets paid $19.40 for any hours worked from Monday to Friday, $24.27 per hour for Saturdays and $25.36 for Sundays. Calculate how much he earns for a week in which he works 10 hours between Monday and Friday, 4 hours on Saturday and 6 hours on Sunday.

8 John's gross weekly income is $752 per week. The deductions from his salary each week are tax $126, superannuation $36.78, health insurance $41.20 and savings $50. Calculate his take-home pay each week.

9 Calculate the simple interest on $15 000 if it is invested at 6% p.a. for:
   a 3 years   b 15 months.

10 An electrical goods store offers a discount of 14% for cash purchases. Find the cash price of a toaster marked at $67.

11 List the advantages and disadvantages of using a credit card to purchase goods.

12 An outdoor furniture setting costing $1788 can be bought on terms for $300 deposit and 24 monthly instalments of $90.04.
   a Calculate the cost of buying the furniture on terms.
   b How much interest is paid?

13 A washing machine costing $1598 can be bought on the following terms: deposit $200, the balance to be repaid over 2 years by 24 equal monthly repayments. Simple interest is charged on the balance at 15% p.a. Calculate:
   a the balance owing
   b the interest charged on the balance owing
   c the monthly repayment.

14 Use the table below to calculate the monthly repayments on a loan of $17 000 for 5 years at 10.5% p.a.

Amount per $1000 borrowed

Loan term (months)	Annual interest rate								
	10.0%	10.5%	11.0%	11.5%	12.0%	12.5%	13.0%	13.5%	14.0%
12	87.9159	88.1486	88.3817	88.6151	88.8488	89.0829	89.3173	89.5520	89.7871
18	60.0571	60.2876	60.5185	60.7500	60.9820	61.2146	61.4476	61.6811	61.9152
24	46.1449	46.3760	46.6078	46.8403	47.0735	47.3073	47.5418	47.7770	48.0129
30	37.8114	38.0443	38.2781	38.5127	38.7481	38.9844	39.2215	39.4595	39.6984
36	32.2672	32.5204	32.7387	32.9760	33.2143	33.4536	33.6940	33.9353	34.1776
42	28.3168	28.5547	28.7939	29.0342	29.2756	29.5183	29.7621	30.0071	30.2532
48	25.3626	25.6034	25.8455	26.0890	26.3338	26.5800	26.8275	27.0763	27.3265
54	23.0724	23.3162	23.5615	23.8083	24.0566	24.3064	24.5577	24.8104	25.0647
60	21.2470	21.4939	21.7424	21.9926	22.2444	22.4979	22.7531	23.0098	23.2683

15 A-One Car Hire Co. charges $70 per day all up with unlimited kilometres to rent a new Corolla. B-One Car Rentals charges $52 per day plus 12 cents per kilometre travelled. Which company is cheaper if you are likely to travel the following distances each day?

   a 60 km   **b** 100 km   **c** 150 km   **d** 500 km

16 Calculate the GST included in the price of a pair of shoes costing $149, price including GST.

E Area, surface area and volume

Exercise 1E

1 Complete the following.

   a 5.13 ha = ___ m^2 **b** 4 cm^2 = ___ mm^2 **c** 2700 cm^2 = ___ m^2

2 Find the area of these shapes.

   a   **b**   **c**

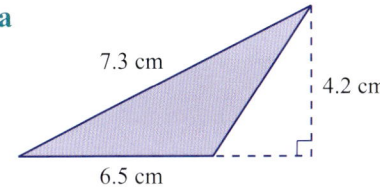
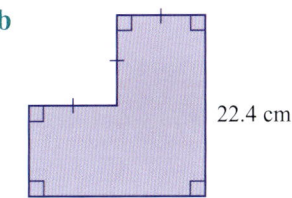
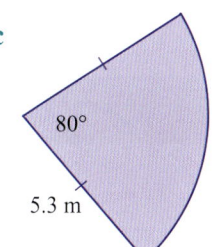

3 Find the shaded area of each shape.

   a   **b**

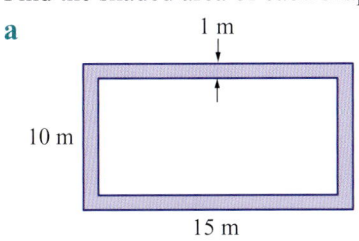
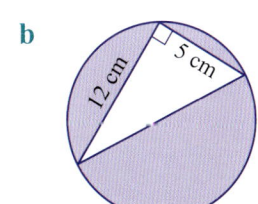

4 Name the solid whose net is shown.

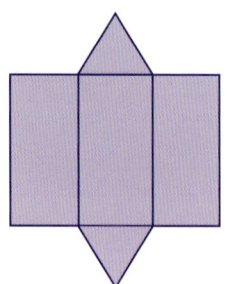

5 Calculate the surface area of each prism.

a

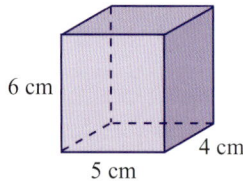

6 cm
4 cm
5 cm

b

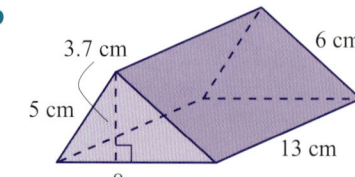

3.7 cm
5 cm
6 cm
13 cm
8 cm

6 A closed metal tank, with the dimensions shown, is to be constructed. What area of metal is required for the tank?

2.9 m
4.3 m
3.6 m

7 Find the surface area and volume of this closed cylinder.

7 cm
5 cm

8 Find the volumes of the following solids.

a

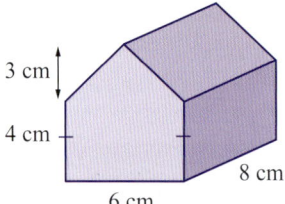

3 cm
4 cm
8 cm
6 cm

b

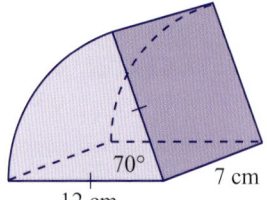

70°
7 cm
12 cm

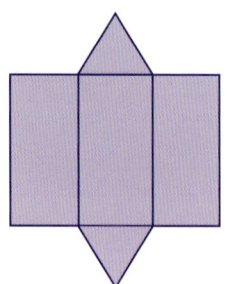

F Probability

1 Four hundred drivers were randomly selected and asked the country in which their car was manufactured. The results are shown in the table.
  a Complete the table.
  b Using this data, estimate the probability that another driver chosen at random will own a car manufactured in Australia.
  c Estimate the probability that the driver's car has been manufactured in Japan.

Country	Frequency	Relative frequency	Percentage
Australia	185		
Japan	93		
Korea	72		
Germany	44		
Other	6		

2 A poker die has faces A, K, Q, J, 10, 9 and is rolled once. Determine the probability of getting:

   a a Q   **b** a number   **c** an A or a K.

3 A game is played with a normal six-sided die. Comment on the statement:

   'I need a 6 to start a game; therefore, the probability that I will start on my first roll is $\frac{1}{6}$.'

4 Kristina rolled a normal six-sided die six times. She did not throw a 6. Kristina concluded that the probability of obtaining a 6 was 0. Why is she wrong? How many 6s would be expected in six throws of the die?

5 A hat contains 5 red, 7 white and 8 blue tickets. A ticket is selected at random from the hat. Determine the probability that the ticket is:

   a red   **b** blue   **c** white   **d** not blue.

6 The Venn diagram represents the number of students in a class who have black hair and brown eyes. What is the probability that a student chosen at random from this class will have:

   a black hair and brown eyes?

   b black hair or brown eyes but not both?

   c black hair or brown eyes or both?

   d neither black hair nor brown eyes?

   e black hair but not brown eyes?

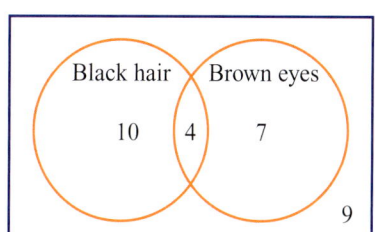

7 The table shows the number of students in a class who study history and art.

	Study art	Do not study art	
Study history	8	12	20
Do not study history	6	7	13
	14	19	33

Find the probability that a student chosen at random from this class will study:

   a history or art or both   **b** history or art but not both

   c art and history   **d** neither history nor art

   e art but not history.

8 A bag contains 4 red balls, 3 blue balls and 2 white balls. A spinner has the numbers 1 to 5 on its 5 equal sectors. The spinner is spun and a ball is chosen at random from the bag. Find the probability of getting:

   a a 5 and a blue ball   **b** an odd number and a red ball

   c an even number and a white ball.

9 Three coins are tossed. What is the probability of getting:

   a 3 tails?   **b** 2 heads and a tail, in that order?

   c 2 heads and a tail, in any order?   **d** at least one tail?

10 A box contains 8 red balls, 5 white balls and 3 black balls. Two balls are selected at random.

   a The first ball is replaced before the second ball is selected.

   b The first ball is *not* replaced before the second ball is selected.

   Find the probability of selecting:

      i 2 red balls   **ii** 2 white balls

     iii a black and a white ball, in any order   **iv** a red and a white ball, in any order

      v at least 1 white ball.

G Right-angled trigonometry

Exercise 1G

1 Write the expressions for sin α, cos α, tan α, sin β, cos β and tan β for each of the following.

a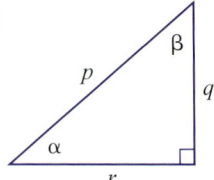

b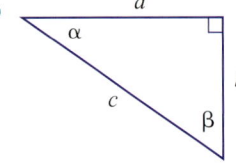

c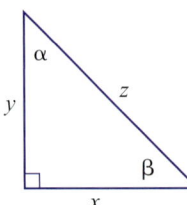

d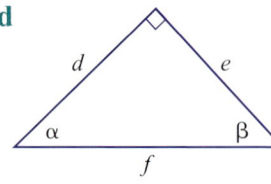

2 Find the length of the side marked *x* to 3 significant figures.

a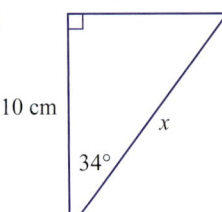

b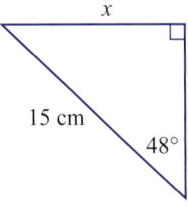

c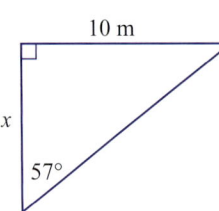

d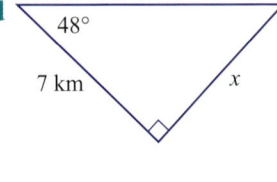

3 Find the value of θ to the nearest minute.

a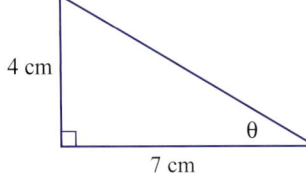

b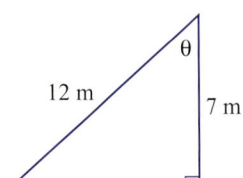

c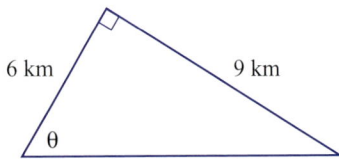

4 Solve the following problems using trigonometry.

a Find all the sides and angles in the given triangle.

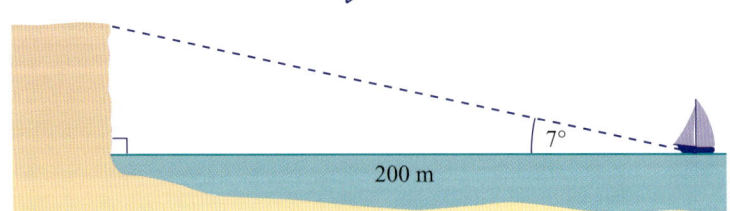

b The diagram shows that the angle of elevation of the top of a cliff from a boat 200 m out to sea is 7°. Calculate the height of the cliff above the boat.

c The angle of depression from the top of a cliff 210 m above sea level to a boat is 48°. Calculate the distance of the boat from the cliff.

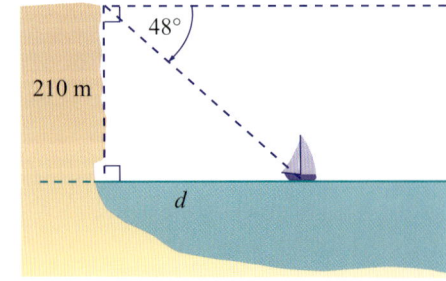

5 Solve the following problems.

    a To measure the width of a river, a surveyor finds a point *B* directly opposite a landmark *T*, such as a building, on the bank on the other side of the river. He then moves 20 m along the bank at right angles to *BT* to a point *A*. With a theodolite he measures ∠*BAT* as 72°11′. Calculate the width of the river to the nearest metre.

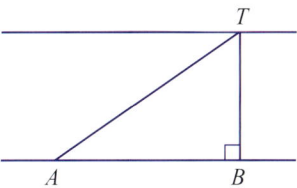

    b An isosceles triangle has sides 9 cm, 9 cm and 8 cm long. Find the measure of the base angles of the triangle to the nearest minute.

    c From the top of a vertical cliff 50 m high, the angle of depression to a boat straight out to sea is 17°. How far is the boat from the foot of the cliff, to the nearest metre?

    d Danielle travels 14 km west and 8 km south. Find the distance and bearing she is from her starting position.

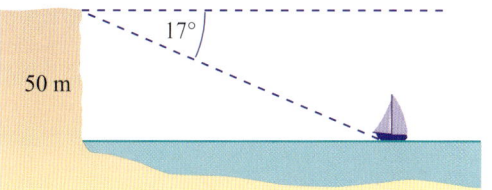

H   Similarity

Exercise 1H

1 **a** Enlarge this figure using an enlargement factor of 2 and *O* as the centre of enlargement.

    b Label the vertices of the enlarged figure and name the pairs of corresponding sides in the similar figures.

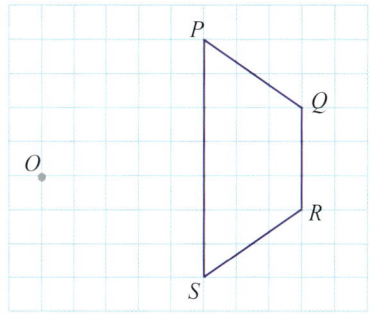

2 Each pair of figures is similar. Find the scale factor and the value of the pronumeral.

  a

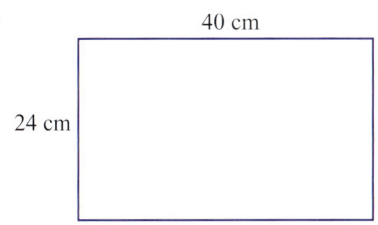

  b

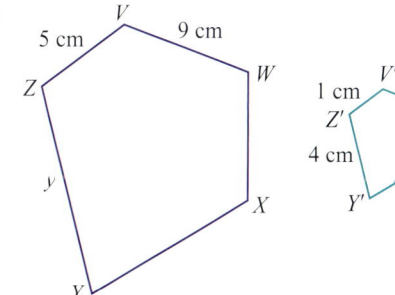

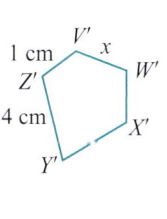

3 In this pair of similar triangles, find the value of the pronumeral.

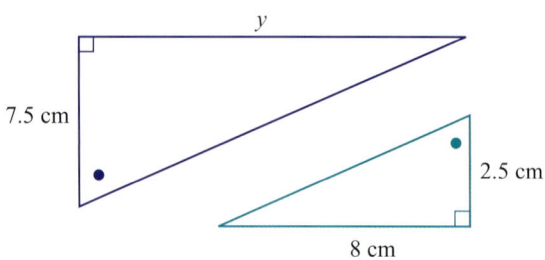

7.5 cm

y

2.5 cm

8 cm

4 In △STU, which side corresponds to:
  a MN?
  b NL?
  c ML?

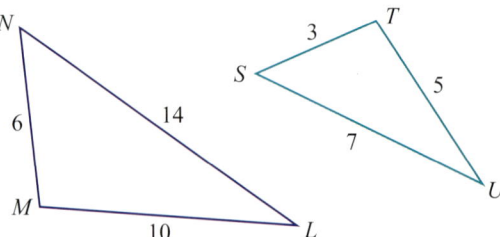

5 Use the information given to determine whether or not the following pairs of figures are similar. If they are similar, state the enlargement factor.

  a

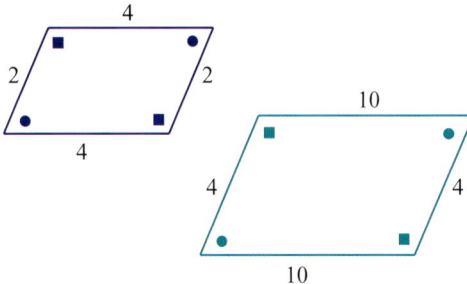

  b

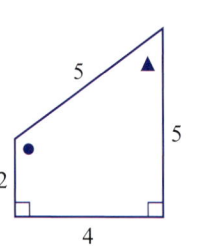 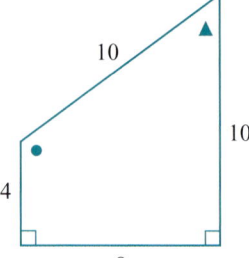

6 a Name the matching (corresponding) sides in these similar triangles.
  b Hence find the enlargement factor.

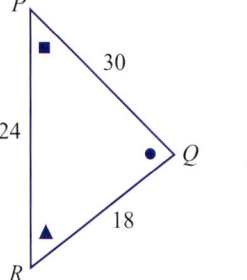 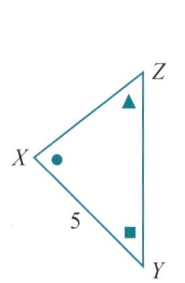

7 Find the enlargement factor and hence the length of the unknown sides in these pairs of similar triangles.

  a

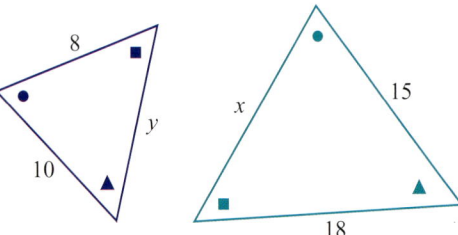

  b

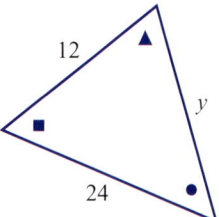 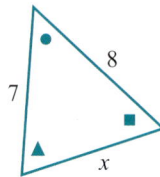

8 For these similar figures, find the enlargement factor and hence the length of the unknown side.

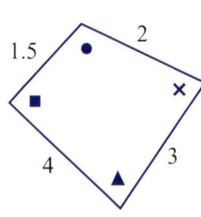 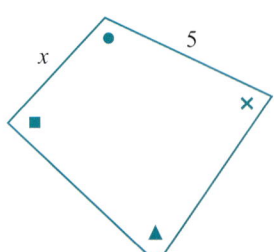

I Linear and non-linear relationships

Exercise 1I

1 By drawing a diagram and plotting the points, find the midpoint of the line joining these points.

   a (4, 3) and (12, 3)   **b** (2, 3) and (2, 9)

   c (4, 1) and (8, 10)   **d** (−4, 3) and (6, −1)

2 Using Pythagoras' theorem, find the distance between these pairs of points.

   a (4, 3) and (10, 5)   **b** (−5, 5) and (2, 8)

3 In this diagram, draw a right-angled triangle and find the gradient of the line.

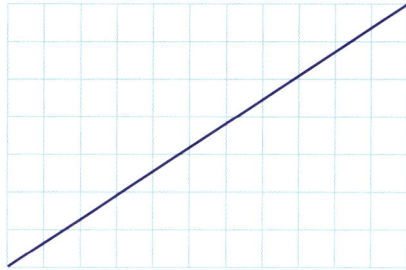

4 Find the gradient of the line passing through these pairs of points.

   a (−3, −2) and (6, 4)   **b** (−3, 6) and (7, 5)

5 Find the gradient of this line.

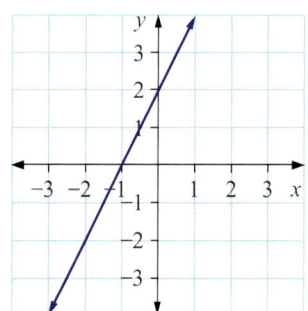

6 Draw a sketch of each of these lines.

   a $y = 4$ **b** $y = -3$

   c $y = x + 1$ **d** $y = 7 - 3x$

   e $x + y = 6$ **f** $x - y = 1$

7 Does the point (4, −3) lie on the line $y = 3x - 15$? Explain your answer.

8 Draw a neat sketch of the relation $y = x^2$.

9 A circle has centre (0, 0) and radius $\sqrt{7}$ units. Sketch the circle and write its equation.

J Proportions and rates

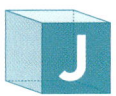

Exercise 1J

1 Convert:

   a 4 mL/min to L/day   **b** 50 km/h to m/s

2 Convert:

   a 6.3 c/s to $/h   **b** 7 m/s to km/h

3 Determine whether the following quantities are in direct proportion, inverse proportion or neither.

  a the radius of a circle and the area of the circle

  b the time taken to lay a brick wall and the number of bricklayers (assuming they all work at the same rate)

  c the thickness of a book and the number of pages (ignore the cover)

4 Do the following graphs show direct proportion, inverse proportion or neither?

a 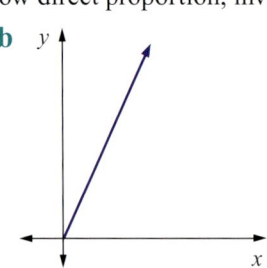   **b** 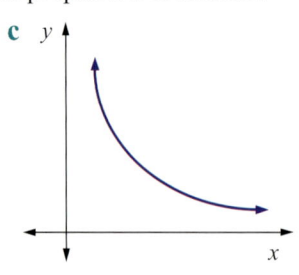   **c** 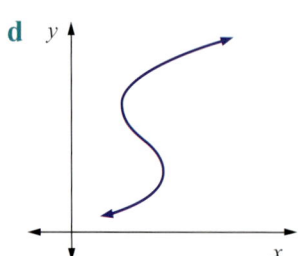   **d**

5 Determine whether or not the variables in the table are in direct linear proportion.

a

x	4	9	15
y	3.2	7.2	12

b

x	5	16	18
y	12.5	40	45

6 Determine whether or not the variables in these equations are in direct linear proportion.

  a $y = 1.36k$ **b** $P = \dfrac{3M}{7}$

7 Use the graph converting Australian dollars (A\$) into euros (€) to convert:

  a A\$400 to euros

  b €120 to A\$

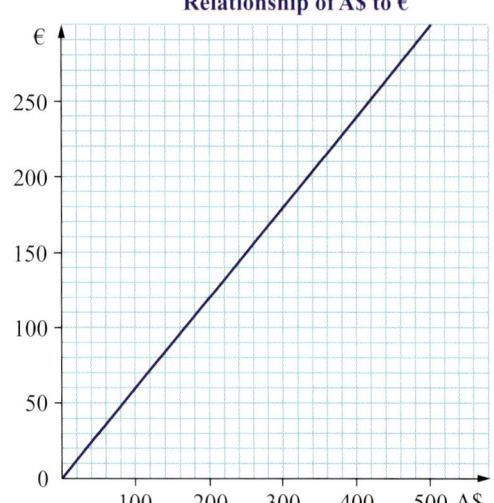

Relationship of A\$ to €

8 Given that the variables in the following table are in direct linear proportion, calculate the missing values.

x	5	4	
y	6		7.2

K   Equations and inequalities

Exercise 1K

1 Solve for x.

  a $3x - 2 = 7$ **b** $4 - 7x = 4$ **c** $\dfrac{x}{5} = -3$

  d $\dfrac{x}{7} + 3 = -5$ **e** $4x - 7 = 7x + 3$ **f** $\dfrac{3x - 2}{5} = 4$

2 If $y = \dfrac{3x - 5}{2}$ find:

   a y when $x = \dfrac{1}{3}$ **b** x when $y = \dfrac{7}{2}$

3 If $y = 6 - 5(4 - x)$, find x when $y = 0$.

4 Solve:

   a $-2(4x + 3) = 17$ **b** $7(3t + 1) = t - 4$ **c** $7(3p - 7) = 4(1 - p)$

   d $x - 5(2x + 1) - 3 = 2$ **e** $\dfrac{4}{3} = \dfrac{x}{7}$ **f** $\dfrac{1}{4}(3x - 1) = -11$

   g $\dfrac{3 - 4x}{3} = \dfrac{x + 5}{4}$ **h** $\dfrac{3x - 4}{3} - \dfrac{2 - 4x}{5} = 1$ **i** $\dfrac{x + 1}{5} + x = \dfrac{3 - x}{3} + 2$

5 Solve these problems.

   a   When 12 is added to twice a number, the answer is 10. Find the number.

   b   If a number is decreased by 3 then multiplied by 5, the result is 1 more than three times the number. Find the number.

6 The velocity of an object is given by $v^2 = u^2 + 2as$.

   a   Find v when $u = 10$, $a = -5$ and $s = 2$.

   b   Find u when $v = 20$, $a = 5$ and $s = 12$.

7 Solve:

   a $x - 4 > 5$ **b** $-3x > 12$ **c** $4 - 3x \leqslant -7$

   d $\dfrac{x}{3} + 3 \geqslant 0$ **e** $\dfrac{4 - 3x}{2} \geqslant 3$ **f** $6 - x \geqslant 5 - 4(x - 1)$

8 **a**   What equation results when $3x - 7y = 5$ is multiplied by -3?

   b   At what point does the line $y = 3x - 5$ meet the x-axis?

   c   If $x = -4$, find y given that $2x - y = 8$.

   d   What equation results when $4x - 3y = 6$ and $3x + 5y = 14$ are added?

9 **a**   On the same set of axes graph the lines with equations $y = x + 5$ and $y = -4x - 5$.

   b   Hence solve the equations $y = x + 5$ and $y = -4x - 5$ simultaneously.

10 **a**   Solve $x = 5 - y$ and $3x - 7y = -25$ simultaneously using the substitution method.

    b   Solve $3x - 2y = 14$ and $4x + 3y = -4$ simultaneously using the elimination method.

11 **a**   Two chocolate frogs and one lollipop cost a total of $1.05, and three chocolate frogs and two lollipops cost $1.70. Find the cost if I buy one chocolate frog and one lollipop.

    b   Four cricket balls and three tennis balls weigh a total of 1060 g. Two cricket balls and five tennis balls weigh 740 g. Find the weight of each type of ball.

12 Explain why the pair of simultaneous equations $x + 2y = 7$ and $x + 2y = 9$ has no solution.

L Further trigonometry

1 Find the length of the side marked *x* correct to 3 significant figures.

a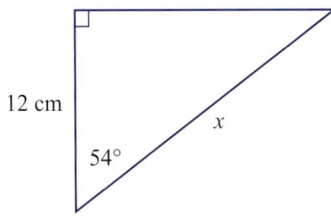

b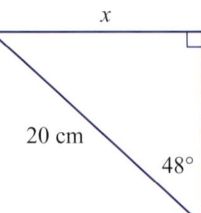

2 Find θ to the nearest minute.

a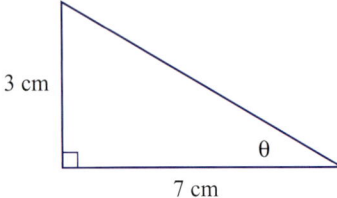

b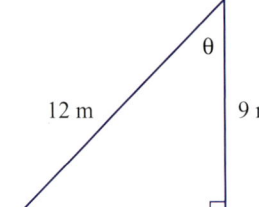

c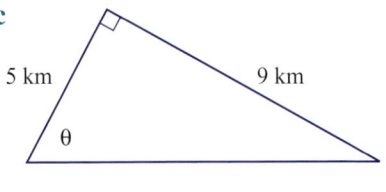

3 Solve these problems using trigonometry.
   a A boat sails 40 km on a bearing 136°T. How far south is it from the starting point?
   b Town A is 185 km south of town B. Town C is 225 km west of town B. Find the bearing and distance of town C from town A to the nearest whole number.

4 Find the exact value of:
   a sin 30°   **b** cos 30°   **c** tan 60°   **d** sin 45°

5 Use the sine rule to find:
   a *x* to the nearest metre

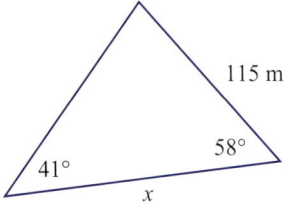

   b α to the nearest degree.

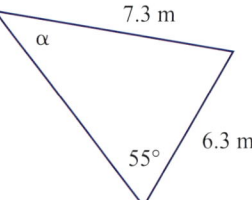

6 Use the cosine rule to find:
   a *x* to the nearest metre

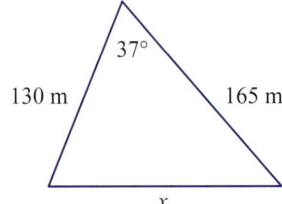

   b α to the nearest degree.

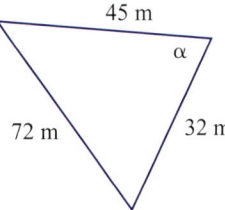

7 Two forest fire stations are 50 km apart. One is due north of the other and they report a fire at 143°T and 58°T respectively. Find the distance from each station to the fire.

M Surds and indices

Exercise 1M

1 Find, where possible:
  a the square root of 64   **b** $\sqrt{64}$ **c** $-\sqrt{64}$ **d** $\sqrt{-64}$ **e** $\sqrt{0}$

2 Show that the following are rational numbers, by expressing them in the form $\frac{a}{b}$.
  a $3\frac{1}{2}$ **b** 5   **c** 0.43   **d** $0.\dot{6}$

3 Convert the following rational numbers to decimals.
  a $\frac{3}{8}$ **b** 53%   **c** $\frac{1}{3}$ **d** $5\frac{1}{4}$

4 Determine whether the following real numbers are rational or irrational.
  a -5.3 **b** $\sqrt{11}$ **c** $\sqrt{49}$ **d** $\sqrt{\frac{7}{6}}$ **e** $\sqrt{\frac{9}{16}}$

5 Simplify:
  a $(\sqrt{5})^2$ **b** $(3\sqrt{5})^2$ **c** $\sqrt{7} \times \sqrt{5}$ **d** $3\sqrt{5} \times 6\sqrt{3}$

6 Express in simplest form:
  a $\sqrt{27}$ **b** $\sqrt{54}$ **c** $\sqrt{27} \times \sqrt{3}$ **d** $\sqrt{8} \times \sqrt{10}$

7 Express in the form $\sqrt{n}$:
  a $2\sqrt{11}$ **b** $4\sqrt{5}$

8 Simplify:
  a $\sqrt{\frac{9}{25}}$ **b** $\sqrt{\frac{11}{9}}$ **c** $\sqrt{1\frac{7}{9}}$ **d** $\sqrt{6\frac{1}{4}}$
  e $\frac{\sqrt{18}}{\sqrt{3}}$ **f** $\frac{\sqrt{54}}{\sqrt{6}}$ **g** $\frac{\sqrt{24}}{\sqrt{8}}$

9 Write true or false:
  a $\sqrt{10^2} = 10$ **b** $5\sqrt{3} = \sqrt{15}$ **c** $\sqrt{54} = 6\sqrt{3}$
  d $\sqrt{2} \times \sqrt{18} = 6$ **e** $\frac{\sqrt{20}}{4} = \sqrt{5}$ **f** $\sqrt{9\frac{1}{4}} = 3\frac{1}{2}$

10 Simplify:
  a $4\sqrt{2} + 5\sqrt{2} - 12\sqrt{2}$ **b** $3\sqrt{5} - 6\sqrt{5} - 4\sqrt{5}$
  c $\sqrt{45} - \sqrt{80}$ **d** $7\sqrt{6} + \sqrt{24}$

11 State whether the following are true or false. Explain your answer.
  a $\sqrt{7} + \sqrt{5} = \sqrt{12}$ **b** $\sqrt{27} - \sqrt{12} = \sqrt{15}$ **c** $6\sqrt{6} - 5\sqrt{6} = 1$

12 Simplify:
  a $2\sqrt{12} \times 7\sqrt{3}$ **b** $5\sqrt{6} \times 2\sqrt{3}$ **c** $4 \times 7\sqrt{2}$
  d $\sqrt{3}(\sqrt{7} - \sqrt{3})$ **e** $4\sqrt{5}(2\sqrt{3} - 3\sqrt{5})$ **f** $(2\sqrt{7} + \sqrt{3})(\sqrt{7} - 2\sqrt{3})$
  g $(2\sqrt{6} - 3)^2$ **h** $(\sqrt{5} + \sqrt{7})^2$ **i** $(2\sqrt{11} + 3\sqrt{5})^2$

13 Rationalise the denominator.

a $\dfrac{1}{\sqrt{3}}$

b $\dfrac{\sqrt{7}}{3\sqrt{5}}$

14 a Expand and simplify $(\sqrt{3} + \sqrt{5})(\sqrt{3} - \sqrt{5})$.

b Hence rationalise the denominator of $\dfrac{1}{\sqrt{3} - \sqrt{5}}$.

15 Write as a surd:

a $n^{\frac{1}{2}}$

b $n^{\frac{1}{3}}$

c $n^{\frac{5}{3}}$

d $n^{\frac{3}{4}}$

16 Write the following in index form.

a $\sqrt{m}$

b $\sqrt[3]{w}$

c $\sqrt{t^3}$

17 Evaluate:

a $64^{\frac{1}{2}}$

b $81^{\frac{3}{4}}$

c $25^{\frac{3}{2}}$

18 Write $\left(\dfrac{2}{5}\right)^{-1}$ as a fraction.

N Surface area and volume

Exercise 1N

1 Find the volumes of the following solids to the nearest whole number.

a
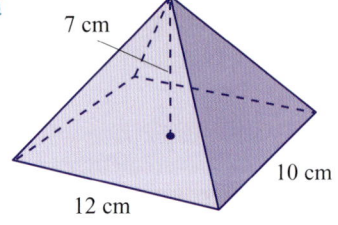
7 cm, 10 cm, 12 cm

b
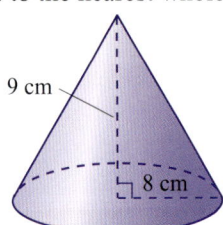
9 cm, 8 cm

c
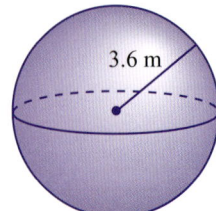
3.6 m

d
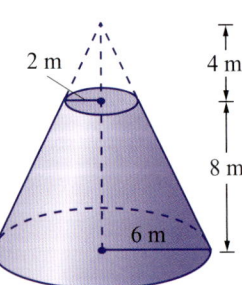
2 m, 4 m, 8 m, 6 m

e
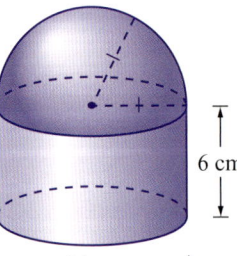
6 cm, 14 cm

f
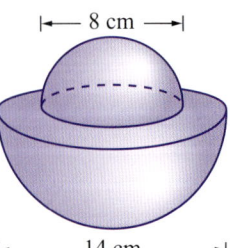
8 cm, 14 cm

2 Find the surface areas of the following solids to the nearest whole number.

a
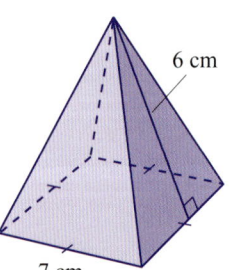
6 cm, 7 cm

b
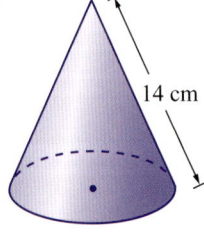
14 cm, 15 cm

c
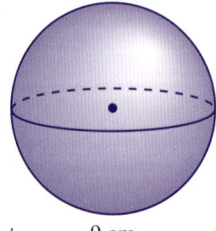
9 cm

d
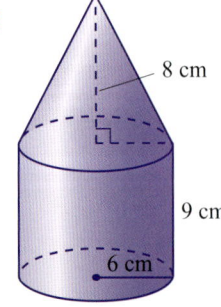
8 cm, 9 cm, 6 cm

3 The volume of a cone with radius 6 cm is 320.4 cm³. What is the height of the cone?

4 The surface area of a sphere is 669.7 cm². Calculate its volume to the nearest cm³.

0 Functions and logarithms

Exercise 10

1 State whether the following sets of ordered pairs are functions.

   a $(-2, 2), (-1, 5), (0, 1), (2, 6)$ **b** $(3, 1), (3, 2), (4, 3), (1, 4)$

2 State whether the following graphs are functions.

   a 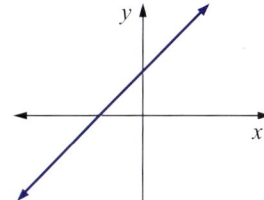   **b** 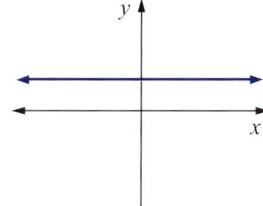   **c**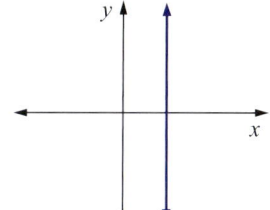

3 Sketch the graphs of two relations that are:

   a functions   **b** not functions.

4 Consider $f(x) = 3x + 5$.

   a Evaluate:

      i $f(-2)$ **ii** $f(0)$ **iii** $f(3) - f(2)$

   b Find expressions for:

      i $f(2k)$ **ii** $f(2k + 1)$ **iii** $\dfrac{f(x) - f(1)}{x - 1}$

   c Find x if $f(x) = 15$.

5 Write the domain and range of the following relations.

   a 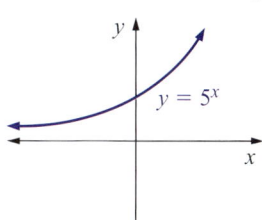   **b** 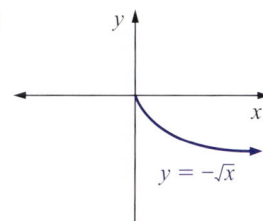   **c**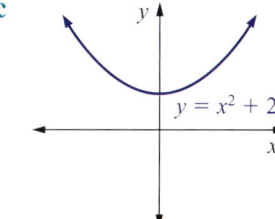

6 a Determine the inverse of the function $f(x) = \dfrac{x - 5}{3}$.

   b Evaluate $f(2)$ and $f^{-1}(f(3))$.

   c Sketch $y = f(x)$, $y = f^{-1}(x)$ and $y = x$ on the same diagram.

7 Copy the graphs of the functions below and on each diagram sketch the graph of the inverse function.

a
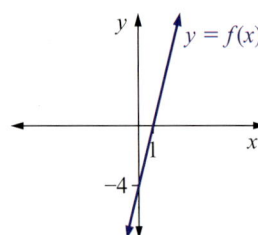

b
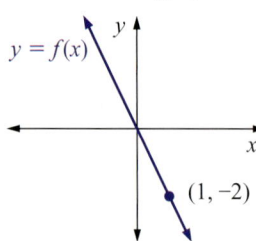

8 Which of the following functions do *not* have an inverse function?

A
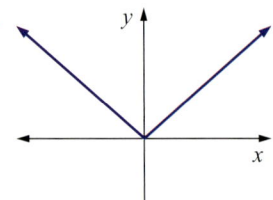

B
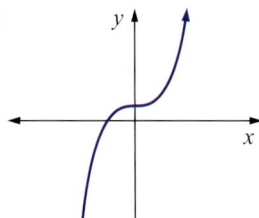

C
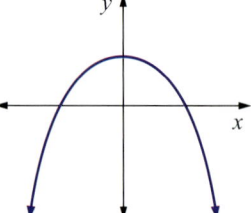

9 Explain the restrictions that need to be placed on the graph of $y = x^2 + x - 6$ with vertex $(-\frac{1}{2}, -6\frac{1}{4})$ to make it a function. Sketch the function and its inverse.

10 a Write $625 = 5^4$ as a logarithmic statement.

 b Write $\log_2 4\sqrt{2} = 2.5$ in index form.

11 Find:

 a $\log_4 32$

 b $\log_2 2\sqrt{2}$

12 Find x when:

 a $\log_{36} x = \frac{1}{2}$

 b $\log_x 125 = 3$

13 Expand:

 a $\log 2xy^3$

 b $\log \frac{x^2}{\sqrt{y}}$

14 Given $\log_a 3 = 0.565$ and $\log_a 5 = 0.827$, evaluate:

 a $\log_a 0.6$

 b $\log_a \sqrt{75}$

15 Evaluate:

 a $\log_{11} 11$

 b $\log_{15} 1$

16 Simplify:

 a $\log 3x + 4\log y$

 b $\frac{1}{2}\log x - 2\log y$

17 Simplify and evaluate the following.

 a $\log_{35} 7 + \log_{35} 5$

 b $\log_3 72 - \log_3 8$

18 Solve:

 a $\log_a 2x - \log_a 5 = \log_a 3$

 b $\log_a (x + 1) + \log_a 3 = \log_a (x + 18)$

19 Solve $4^x = 19$.

20 On the same axes, sketch graphs of $y = 10^x$, $y = \log_{10} x$ and $y = x$.

2

Algebra

This chapter deals with algebraic fractions and using the distributive law to expand and factorise algebraic expressions.

After completing this chapter you should be able to:

▶ perform the four operations with algebraic fractions including those with pronumerals in the denominator and those with binomial numerators

▶ apply the distributive law to the expansion of algebraic expressions and collect like terms where appropriate

▶ factorise algebraic expressions by taking out the highest common algebraic factor.

NSW Syllabus references: 5.2 N&A Algebraic techniques, 5.2 N&A Equations (part)
Outcomes: MA5.2-1WM, MA5.2-3WM, MA5.2-6NA
Number & algebra – ACMNA213, ACMNA230, ACMNA232

Diagnostic test

1 $5a - 2b + 3a - 4b =$

   A $2a - 6b$ **B** $8a - 2b$

   C $8a - 6b$ **D** $8a + 2b$

2 $7x \times 3y =$

   A $73xy$ **B** $21xy$

   C $10xy$ **D** x^7y^3

3 $\dfrac{12m}{8} =$

   A $4m$ **B** $\dfrac{3m}{8}$ **C** $\dfrac{3m}{2}$ **D** $\dfrac{3}{2}$

4 $3m^4n^2 \times 4m^5n^3 =$

   A $12m^9n^5$ **B** $12m^{20}n^6$

   C $7m^9n^5$ **D** $7m^{20}n^6$

5 $\dfrac{a^7b^4}{a^3b} =$

   A $(ab)^{24}$ **B** $(ab)^7$ **C** $\dfrac{a^7}{3b^4}$ **D** a^4b^3

6 $(3y^5)^3 =$

   A $3y^{15}$ **B** $3y^8$

   C $27y^{15}$ **D** $27y^8$

7 $(4p)^0 =$

   A 1 **B** 4 **C** 0 **D** $4p$

8 $-5(2z - 3) =$

   A $-7z + 2$ **B** $-7z + 15$

   C $-10z + 15$ **D** $-10z - 15$

9 $6 + 4(a + 3) =$

   A $4a + 18$ **B** $4a + 9$

   C $10a + 30$ **D** $10a + 3$

10 When fully factorised $18x - 24y =$

   A $2(9x - 12y)$ **B** $3(6x - 8y)$

   C $6(3x - 24y)$ **D** $6(3x - 4y)$

The diagnostic test questions refer to outcomes ACMNA190, ACMNA191, ACMNA192 and ACMNA212. **AC**

NUMBER & ALGEBRA

 # A Algebraic fractions

An algebraic fraction is one in which the numerator or denominator or both contain pronumerals.

For the numerical fraction $\frac{3}{4}$, the denominator (4) indicates the number of equal parts into which the whole has been divided and the numerator (3) indicates the number of these equal fractional parts.

In the algebraic fraction $\frac{5a}{9b}$, the denominator indicates that the whole has been divided into $9b$ equal parts and the numerator indicates that there are $5a$ of these equal parts.

For the fraction $\frac{9b}{5a}$, the denominator indicates that the whole has been divided into $5a$ equal parts and the numerator indicates that there are $9b$ of these equal parts.

The reciprocal of a fraction is the number by which the fraction must be multiplied to give a result of 1.

For example, $\frac{3}{4} \times \frac{4}{3} = 1$. Hence $\frac{4}{3}$ is the reciprocal of $\frac{3}{4}$ (and $\frac{3}{4}$ is the reciprocal of $\frac{4}{3}$).

We say that $\frac{3}{4}$ and $\frac{4}{3}$ are reciprocals of each other.

As $\frac{5a}{9b} \times \frac{9b}{5a} = 1$, $\frac{5a}{9b}$ and $\frac{9b}{5a}$ are reciprocals of each other.

● EXAMPLE 1

Complete the following equivalent fractions.

a $\dfrac{4}{5} = \dfrac{\square}{35}$ **b** $\dfrac{3n}{7} = \dfrac{\square}{14}$ **c** $\dfrac{5x}{y} = \dfrac{\square}{3y}$ **d** $\dfrac{3a}{4b^2} = \dfrac{\square}{12b^7}$

	Solve	Think	Apply
a	$\dfrac{4}{5} = \dfrac{28}{35}$	As $5 \times 7 = 35$, $\dfrac{4}{5} \times \dfrac{7}{7} = \dfrac{28}{35}$	Multiply the numerator and the denominator by the same number.
b	$\dfrac{3n}{7} = \dfrac{6n}{14}$	As $7 \times 2 = 14$, $\dfrac{3n}{7} \times \dfrac{2}{2} = \dfrac{6n}{14}$	
c	$\dfrac{5x}{y} = \dfrac{15x}{3y}$	As $y \times 3 = 3y$, $\dfrac{5x}{y} \times \dfrac{3}{3} = \dfrac{15x}{3y}$	
d	$\dfrac{3a}{4b^2} = \dfrac{9ab^5}{12b^7}$	As $4b^2 \times 3b^5 = 12b^7$, $\dfrac{3a}{4b^2} \times \dfrac{3b^5}{3b^5} = \dfrac{9ab^5}{12b^7}$	Multiply the numerator and the denominator by the same algebraic term.

Exercise 2A

1 Complete the following equivalent fractions.

a $\dfrac{2y}{5} = \dfrac{\square}{15}$ **b** $\dfrac{4m}{3} = \dfrac{\square}{6}$ **c** $\dfrac{5a}{2} = \dfrac{\square}{12}$ **d** $\dfrac{5m}{2n} = \dfrac{\square}{6n}$

e $\dfrac{3t}{4w} = \dfrac{\square}{16w}$ **f** $\dfrac{8}{5q} = \dfrac{\square}{30q}$ **g** $\dfrac{6x}{5y} = \dfrac{\square}{5yz}$ **h** $\dfrac{3a}{4b} = \dfrac{\square}{4b^2}$

i $\dfrac{7m}{9n} = \dfrac{\square}{18np}$ **j** $\dfrac{2u}{3w} = \dfrac{\square}{15wx}$ **k** $\dfrac{5u}{4bc} = \dfrac{\square}{8b^2c^3}$ **l** $\dfrac{7w}{6xy^2z} = \dfrac{\square}{18x^2y^4z^5}$

EXAMPLE 2

Reduce each fraction to its simplest form.

a $\dfrac{36}{48}$ b $\dfrac{9t}{12}$ c $\dfrac{6ab}{9a}$ d $\dfrac{10a^4}{8a^2}$ e $\dfrac{3ab^4}{9a^2b^3}$

	Solve	Think	Apply
a	$\dfrac{36}{48} = \dfrac{^3\cancel{36}}{^4\cancel{48}} = \dfrac{3}{4}$	Divide the numerator and the denominator by the HCF of 36 and 48.	Divide the numerator and the denominator by their highest common factor (HCF).
b	$\dfrac{9t}{12} = \dfrac{^3\cancel{9t}}{^4\cancel{12}} = \dfrac{3t}{4}$	Divide the numerator and the denominator by the HCF of 9t and 12.	
c	$\dfrac{6ab}{9a} = \dfrac{^2\cancel{6ab}}{^3\cancel{9a}} = \dfrac{2b}{3}$	Divide the numerator and the denominator by the HCF of 6ab and 9a. This is equivalent to dividing the numerator and the denominator by the HCF of 6 and 9 and the HCF of ab and a.	
d	$\dfrac{10a^4}{8a^2} = \dfrac{^5\cancel{10a^4}^{a^2}}{^4\cancel{8a^2}} = \dfrac{5a^2}{4}$	Divide the numerator and the denominator by the HCF of $10a^4$ and $8a^2$. This is equivalent to dividing the numerator and the denominator by the HCF of 10 and 8 and the HCF of a^4 and a^2.	
e	$\dfrac{3ab^4}{9a^2b^3} = \dfrac{^1\cancel{3ab^4}^b}{^3\cancel{9a^2b^3}^a} = \dfrac{b}{3a}$	Divide the numerator and the denominator by the HCF of $3ab^4$ and $9a^2b^3$. This is equivalent to dividing the numerator and the denominator by the HCF of 3 and 9, the HCF of a and a^2 and the HCF of b^3 and b^4.	

2   Reduce each fraction to its simplest form.

a $\dfrac{6x}{12}$ b $\dfrac{5t}{20}$ c $\dfrac{10y}{15}$ d $\dfrac{9b}{12}$

e $\dfrac{6a}{9a}$ f $\dfrac{3p}{10p}$ g $\dfrac{8a}{4ab}$ h $\dfrac{12pq}{9q}$

i $\dfrac{8x^5}{6x^2}$ j $\dfrac{9ab^2}{15ab}$ k $\dfrac{4x^3}{6x^4}$ l $\dfrac{6a^3b^4}{21ab^6}$

EXAMPLE 3

Simplify the following.

a $\dfrac{5}{6} + \dfrac{3}{8}$ b $\dfrac{2t}{3} + \dfrac{4t}{5}$ c $\dfrac{7k}{10} - \dfrac{k}{5}$ d $2y - \dfrac{4y}{5}$

	Solve	Think	Apply
a	$\dfrac{5}{6} + \dfrac{3}{8} = \dfrac{20}{24} + \dfrac{9}{24}$ $= \dfrac{29}{24}$ $= 1\dfrac{5}{24}$	LCD = 24 $\dfrac{5}{6} \times \dfrac{4}{4} = \dfrac{20}{24}$ and $\dfrac{3}{8} \times \dfrac{3}{3} = \dfrac{9}{24}$	Find the lowest common denominator (LCD) of the fractions. Change both fractions to equivalent fractions with this denominator.

EXAMPLE 3 CONTINUED

	Solve	Think	Apply
b	$\dfrac{2t}{3} + \dfrac{4t}{5} = \dfrac{10t}{15} + \dfrac{12t}{15}$ $= \dfrac{22t}{15}$	$LCD = 15$ $\dfrac{2t}{3} \times \dfrac{5}{5} = \dfrac{10t}{15}$ and $\dfrac{4t}{5} \times \dfrac{3}{3} = \dfrac{12t}{15}$	Find the LCD of the fractions. Change both fractions to equivalent fractions with this denominator. Simplify the result if possible.
c	$\dfrac{7k}{10} - \dfrac{k}{5} = \dfrac{7k}{10} - \dfrac{2k}{10}$ $= \dfrac{5k}{10} = \dfrac{k}{2}$	$LCD = 10$ $\dfrac{k}{5} \times \dfrac{2}{2} = \dfrac{2k}{10}$	
d	$2y - \dfrac{4y}{5} = \dfrac{10y}{5} - \dfrac{4y}{5}$ $= \dfrac{6y}{5}$	$LCD = 5$ $\dfrac{2y}{1} \times \dfrac{5}{5} = \dfrac{10y}{5}$	

3 Simplify the following.

a $\dfrac{5x}{11} + \dfrac{4x}{11}$ **b** $\dfrac{5n}{6} + \dfrac{2n}{3}$ **c** $\dfrac{7m}{8} - \dfrac{m}{3}$ **d** $\dfrac{5k}{6} + \dfrac{3k}{4}$

e $\dfrac{7b}{8} - \dfrac{b}{4}$ **f** $\dfrac{3a}{5} + \dfrac{a}{10}$ **g** $k + \dfrac{2k}{3}$ **h** $\dfrac{4z}{5} - \dfrac{2z}{3}$

i $4t - \dfrac{7t}{8}$ **j** $\dfrac{2x}{5} - \dfrac{3x}{10}$ **k** $\dfrac{7x}{3} - \dfrac{2x}{5}$ **l** $\dfrac{5t}{7} + \dfrac{9t}{14}$

EXAMPLE 4

Simplify the following.

a $\dfrac{2}{3a} + \dfrac{4}{5a}$ **b** $\dfrac{5k}{4m} - \dfrac{2k}{3m}$

	Solve	Think	Apply
a	$\dfrac{2}{3a} + \dfrac{4}{5a} = \dfrac{10}{15a} + \dfrac{12}{15a}$ $= \dfrac{22}{15a}$	$LCD = 15a$ $\dfrac{2}{3a} \times \dfrac{5}{5} = \dfrac{10}{15a}$ and $\dfrac{4}{5a} \times \dfrac{3}{3} = \dfrac{12}{15a}$	Find the LCD of the fractions. Change both fractions to equivalent fractions with this denominator.
b	$\dfrac{5k}{4m} - \dfrac{2k}{3m} = \dfrac{15k}{12m} - \dfrac{8k}{12m}$ $= \dfrac{7k}{12m}$	$LCD = 12m$ $\dfrac{5k}{4m} \times \dfrac{3}{3} = \dfrac{15k}{12m}$ and $\dfrac{2k}{3m} \times \dfrac{4}{4} = \dfrac{8k}{12m}$	

4 Simplify the following.

a $\dfrac{3}{x} + \dfrac{1}{2x}$ **b** $\dfrac{5}{3a} - \dfrac{3}{2a}$ **c** $\dfrac{7}{4y} + \dfrac{3}{5y}$ **d** $\dfrac{9}{2z} - \dfrac{5}{6z}$

e $\dfrac{2a}{3b} + \dfrac{4a}{b}$ **f** $\dfrac{5m}{3n} - \dfrac{2m}{7n}$ **g** $\dfrac{2xy}{5z} + \dfrac{8xy}{9z}$ **h** $\dfrac{6a}{5c} - \dfrac{5b}{6c}$

i $\dfrac{3a}{5c} - \dfrac{2b}{7c}$ **j** $\dfrac{5p}{7q} - \dfrac{3r}{14q}$ **k** $\dfrac{3x}{2z} + \dfrac{5y}{7z}$ **l** $\dfrac{6r}{11c} - \dfrac{3t}{4c}$

NUMBER & ALGEBRA

EXAMPLE 5

Simplify the following.

a $\dfrac{10}{9} \times \dfrac{18}{25}$ **b** $\dfrac{4m}{3} \times \dfrac{2n}{5}$ **c** $3y \times \dfrac{2z}{9}$ **d** $\dfrac{4b}{9} \times \dfrac{15}{8ab}$

	Solve	Think	Apply
a	$\dfrac{10}{9} \times \dfrac{18}{25} = \dfrac{{}^2\cancel{10}}{\cancel{9}} \times \dfrac{{}^2\cancel{18}}{{}^5\cancel{25}}$ $= \dfrac{2}{1} \times \dfrac{2}{5}$ $= \dfrac{4}{5}$	The HCF of 10 and 25 is 5 and the HCF of 9 and 18 is 9. Divide the numerator and denominator by 5 and 9. Multiply the resulting numerators and denominators.	Simplify by dividing the numerator and the denominator by any common factors, then multiply the resulting numerators and denominators.
b	$\dfrac{4m}{3} \times \dfrac{2n}{5} = \dfrac{8mn}{15}$	$\dfrac{4m}{3} \times \dfrac{2n}{5} = \dfrac{4m \times 2n}{3 \times 5}$	
c	$3y \times \dfrac{2z}{9} = \dfrac{{}^{\cancel{3}}y}{1} \times \dfrac{2z}{{}^3\cancel{9}}$ $= \dfrac{y}{1} \times \dfrac{2z}{3}$ $= \dfrac{2yz}{3}$	The HCF of 3 and 9 is 3. Divide the numerator and denominator by 3. Multiply the resulting numerators and denominators.	
d	$\dfrac{4b}{9} \times \dfrac{15}{8ab} = \dfrac{\cancel{4b}}{{}^3\cancel{9}} \times \dfrac{{}^5\cancel{15}}{{}^2\cancel{8ab}}$ $= \dfrac{1}{3} \times \dfrac{5}{2a}$ $= \dfrac{5}{6a}$	The HCF of 4 and 8 is 4, the HCF of 9 and 15 is 3, and the HCF of b and ab is b. Divide the numerator and denominator by 3, 4 and b. Multiply the resulting numerators and denominators.	

5 Simplify the following.

a $\dfrac{3m}{5} \times \dfrac{10n}{7}$ **b** $\dfrac{2k}{9} \times \dfrac{6n}{5}$ **c** $\dfrac{4w}{3} \times \dfrac{9z}{8}$ **d** $\dfrac{8a}{5} \times \dfrac{15b}{16}$

e $\dfrac{3t}{5} \times \dfrac{10}{9u}$ **f** $\dfrac{5y}{3} \times \dfrac{9}{2y}$ **g** $\dfrac{7}{2z} \times \dfrac{3z}{14}$ **h** $\dfrac{2ab}{3} \times \dfrac{6}{5b}$

i $\dfrac{8mn}{9} \times \dfrac{5}{3m}$ **j** $\dfrac{3k}{15m} \times \dfrac{5n}{9p}$ **k** $\dfrac{6pq}{5r} \times \dfrac{25r}{3q}$ **l** $\dfrac{12ab}{5c} \times \dfrac{10c^2}{3a}$

NUMBER & ALGEBRA

Simplify the following.

a $\dfrac{5}{8} \div \dfrac{3}{4}$ b $\dfrac{2a}{3} \div \dfrac{6b}{7}$ c $\dfrac{4}{5m} \div \dfrac{10}{3m}$ d $\dfrac{5pq}{8} \div \dfrac{3pr}{2q}$

	Solve	Think	Apply
a	$\dfrac{5}{8} \div \dfrac{3}{4} = \dfrac{5}{{}^{2}8} \times \dfrac{\cancel{4}}{3}$ $= \dfrac{5}{2} \times \dfrac{1}{3}$ $= \dfrac{5}{6}$	The reciprocal of $\dfrac{3}{4}$ is $\dfrac{4}{3}$.	To divide by a fraction, multiply by its reciprocal.
b	$\dfrac{2a}{3} \div \dfrac{6b}{7} = \dfrac{2a}{3} \times \dfrac{7}{{}^{3}6b}$ $= \dfrac{a}{3} \times \dfrac{7}{3b}$ $= \dfrac{7a}{9b}$	The reciprocal of $\dfrac{6b}{7}$ is $\dfrac{7}{6b}$.	
c	$\dfrac{4}{5m} \div \dfrac{10}{3m} = \dfrac{{}^{2}4}{5m} \times \dfrac{3m}{{}^{5}10}$ $= \dfrac{2}{25} \times \dfrac{3}{5}$ $= \dfrac{6}{25}$	The reciprocal of $\dfrac{10}{3m}$ is $\dfrac{3m}{10}$.	
d	$\dfrac{5pq}{8} \div \dfrac{3pr}{2q} = \dfrac{5pq}{{}^{4}8} \times \dfrac{2q}{3pr}$ $= \dfrac{5q}{4} \times \dfrac{q}{3r}$ $= \dfrac{5q^2}{12r}$	The reciprocal of $\dfrac{3pr}{2q}$ is $\dfrac{2q}{3pr}$.	

6 Simplify the following.

a $\dfrac{2x}{3} \div \dfrac{8y}{5}$ b $\dfrac{3a}{2} \div \dfrac{6b}{7}$ c $\dfrac{5p}{3} \div \dfrac{10q}{9}$

d $\dfrac{7}{5v} \div \dfrac{3}{10v}$ e $\dfrac{16}{9w} \div \dfrac{8}{3w}$ f $\dfrac{6k}{5} \div \dfrac{7k}{2}$

g $\dfrac{4m}{3} \div \dfrac{2m}{5}$ h $\dfrac{7}{2m} \div \dfrac{m}{8}$ i $\dfrac{4xy}{3} \div \dfrac{2xz}{5}$

j $\dfrac{9p}{10km} \div \dfrac{6p}{5m}$ k $\dfrac{7mn}{p} \div \dfrac{m^2}{p^2}$ l $\dfrac{5xy}{7} \div \dfrac{3xy}{14}$

7 Simplify the following.

a $\dfrac{15x^6}{10x^3}$ b $\dfrac{9x^2y}{3xy}$ c $\dfrac{3mn}{9m^2n}$

d $\dfrac{5a^2}{3} \times \dfrac{6}{2a}$ e $\dfrac{2x^5}{5z^3} \times \dfrac{7z}{6x^9}$ f $\dfrac{a^2b^4}{8} \times \dfrac{12}{a^2b^2}$

g $\dfrac{4m^3}{3n^7} \div \dfrac{5m^8}{6n^2}$ h $\dfrac{3x^2}{8y^5} \div \dfrac{15x^3}{4y}$ i $\dfrac{p^5q^4}{6} \div \dfrac{p^2q^2}{9}$

j $\dfrac{5a}{3bc} - \dfrac{3a}{2bc}$ k $\dfrac{6}{7x^2} + \dfrac{3}{2x^2}$ l $\dfrac{3}{a^2} + \dfrac{5}{a}$

B The distributive law

The distributive law is used to expand algebraic expressions involving grouping symbols.

$$a(b \pm c) = ab \pm ac$$

● EXAMPLE 1

Expand and then simplify the following.

a $3(y + 7)$ b $5w(2w - 3z)$ c $2a^2(3a^4 + 7b)$

	Solve	Think	Apply
a	$3(y + 7) = 3y + 21$	$3(y + 7) = 3 \times y + 3 \times 7$	Use the distributive law to expand and then simplify.
b	$5w(2w - 3z) = 10w^2 - 15wz$	$5w(2w - 3z) = 5w \times 2w - 5w \times 3z$	
c	$2a^2(3a^4 + 7b) = 6a^6 + 14a^2b$	$2a^2(3a^4 + 7b) = 2a^2 \times 3a^4 + 2a^2 \times 7b$	

Exercise 2B

1 Expand and then simplify the following.

a $4(t + 8)$ b $3a(2a - 4)$ c $6k(3k - 4m)$

d $5m^2(2m^3 + 8n)$ e $2p^3(6p^5 - q^2)$ f $4a^2(3a^7 + 2a^3b)$

g $6x^2(3x^5 - 2x^3)$ h $7b^4(3b^5 + 6b^8)$ i $3xy^2(4x^2y^3 - 2xy)$

j $5m^3n^2(2mn^5 + 3m^2n^4)$ k $2a(3a - 4b + 7)$ l $5y^2(2y^2 - 3y - 6)$

● EXAMPLE 2

Expand and then simplify the following.

a $-4(5a + 3b)$ b $-2(3x - 7y)$ c $-(4m + 3n)$

d $-5a(4a - 8b)$ e $-3w^2(2w^3 + 5w^4z)$

	Solve	Think	Apply
a	$-4(5a + 3b)$ $= -20a - 12b$	$-4(5a + 3b) = -4 \times 5a + (-4) \times 3b$ $= -20a + (-12b)$ $= -20a - 12b$	Use the distributive law to expand and then simplify. *Adding $-12b$ is the same as subtracting $12b$.* ❗
b	$-2(3x - 7y)$ $= -6x + 14y$	$-2(3x - 7y) = -2(3x + (-7y))$ $= -2 \times 3x + (-2) \times (-7y)$ $= -6x + 14y$ Or $-2(3x - 7y) = -2 \times 3x - (-2) \times 7y$ $= -6x - (-14y)$	*Subtracting $7y$ is the same as adding $-7y$.* ❗ *Subtracting $-14y$ is the same as adding $14y$.* ❗
c	$-(4m + 3n)$ $= -4m - 3n$	$-(4m + 3n) = -1 \times (4m + 3n)$ $= -1 \times 4m + (-1) \times 3n$ $= -4m + (-3n)$ $= -4m - 3n$	

EXAMPLE 2 CONTINUED

	Solve	Think	Apply
d	$-5a(4a - 8b)$ $= -20a^2 + 40ab$	$-5a(4a - 8b) = -5a(4a + (-8b))$ $\qquad\qquad = -5a \times 4a + (-5a) \times (-8b)$ $\qquad\qquad = -20a^2 + 40ab$	Use the distributive law to expand and then simplify.
e	$-3w^2(2w^3 + 5w^4z)$ $= -6w^5 - 15w^6z$	$-3w^2(2w^3 + 5w^4z)$ $= -3w^2 \times 2w^3 + (-3w^2) \times 5w^4z$ $= -6w^5 + (-15w^6z)$ $= -6w^5 - 15w^6z$	

2 Expand and then simplify the following.

a $-5(6t + 7)$	**b** $-4(3w - z)$	**c** $-(7a + 9b)$
d $-(5v - 2w)$	**e** $-3a(2b + 8c)$	**f** $-2p(3q - 9r)$
g $-5x(2x + 3y)$	**h** $-4m(5m - 7n)$	**i** $-10z^4(2z^3 + 4z^5)$
j $-3m^3(4m^5 - 2m^2n)$	**k** $-6x^4(5x^7 + 2x^5y^2)$	**l** $-2a^2b(3a^3b^2 - 5a^6b^4)$

EXAMPLE 3

Expand and then simplify the following.

a $3(a + 2) + 7$

b $3 + 2(3n - 5)$

	Solve	Think	Apply
a	$3(a + 2) + 7$ $= 3a + 6 + 7$ $= 3a + 13$	$3(a + 2) + 7$ $= 3 \times a + 3 \times 2 + 7$ Multiply before adding. $= 3a + 13$ Collect like terms.	Expand (multiply) first and then collect like terms.
b	$3 + 2(3n - 5)$ $= 3 + 6n - 10 = -7 + 6n$ or $\qquad\qquad = 6n - 7$	$3 + 2(3n - 5)$ $= 3 + 2 \times 3n - 2 \times 5$ Multiply before adding. $= -7 + 6n$ or $6n - 7$ Collect like terms.	

3 Expand and then simplify the following.

a $4(a + 3) + 6$	**b** $2(3b - 12) + 12$	**c** $3(4w + 2) - 7$
d $5(2y - 3) - 2y$	**e** $6(3z - 1) + 4z$	**f** $10x + 2(4x + 3)$
g $12b + 2(3b - 5)$	**h** $13 + 4(y + 5)$	**i** $4w + 3(2w - 4)$
j $16 + 5(4e - 6)$	**k** $10a + 3(2a + 9)$	**l** $5(3c - 2) + 4c$

EXAMPLE 4

Expand and simplify $5 - 2(4y - 3)$.

Solve	Think	Apply
$5 - 2(4y - 3) = 5 - 8y + 6$ $\qquad\qquad\quad = 11 - 8y$ or $\qquad\qquad\quad = -8y + 11$	$5 - 2(4y - 3)$ $= 5 - 2 \times (4y - 3)$ Multiply before adding. $= 5 - 8y + 6$ Collect like terms. $= 11 - 8y$	Expand (multiply) first and then collect like terms.

4 Expand and simplify:
    a $12 - 2(a + 5)$ **b** $8 - 3(y - 2)$
    c $9 - 4(b + 3)$ **d** $7v - 2(v - 6)$
    e $20w - 3(2w + 5)$ **f** $2 - 5(3t - 4)$
    g $4 - 3(5x + 2)$ **h** $10k - 2(3k - 1)$
    i $5z - 3(3 + 4z)$ **j** $3 - 10(1 - 2w)$
    k $12a - 3(2a + 5)$ **l** $15 - 4(3x - 2)$

● EXAMPLE 5

Expand and simplify $4(2m - 3) + 3(m - 2)$.

Solve	Think	Apply
$4(2m - 3) + 3(m - 2)$ $= 8m - 12 + 3m - 6$ $= 11m - 18$	$4(2m - 3) + 3(m - 2)$ $= 4 \times (2m - 3) + 3 \times (m - 2)$ Multiply first. $= 8m - 12 + 3m - 6$ $= 8m + 3m - 12 - 6$ Collect like terms. $= 11m - 18$	Expand (multiply) first and then collect like terms.

5 Expand and simplify:
    a $5(2k + 3) + 3(k - 2)$ **b** $2(6m + 7) + 3(m - 1)$
    c $4(2p - 1) + 2(3p + 5)$ **d** $3(3a + 2) + 4(a - 3)$
    e $2(5x - 3) + 5(3x - 1)$ **f** $3(4y - 2) + (2y + 7)$
    g $(6v - 1) + 3(5 - 2v)$ **h** $4(2y + 3x) + 2(5x - 3y)$
    i $7(2a - 3b) + 3(4b + 3a)$ **j** $3a(6 + 2a) + 4a(3a - 5)$

● EXAMPLE 6

Expand and simplify the following.
    a $2(3p + 4q) - 4(2p - 3q)$ **b** $3(4m - 1) - (m + 4)$

	Solve	Think	Apply
a	$2(3p + 4q) - 4(2p - 3q)$ $= 6p + 8q - 8p + 12q$ $= -2p + 20q$ or $20q - 2p$	$2(3p + 4q) - 4(2p - 3q)$ $= 2 \times (3p + 4q) - 4 \times (2p - 3q)$ $= 6p + 8q - 8p + 12q$ Multiply first. $= 6p - 8p + 8q + 12q$ Collect like terms. $= -2p + 20q$	Expand (multiply) first and then collect like terms.
b	$3(4m - 1) - (m + 4)$ $= 12m - 3 - m - 4$ $= 11m - 7$	$3(4m - 1) - (m + 4)$ $= 3 \times (4m - 1) - 1 \times (m + 4)$ $= 12m - 3 - m - 4$ Multiply first. $= 12m - m - 3 - 4$ Collect like terms. $= 11m - 7$	

6 Expand and simplify:

   a $3(2k + 5) - 2(k + 3)$ **b** $5(w + 4) - 3(w - 2)$

   c $2(6t + 1) - 3(t + 4)$ **d** $3(5z - 1) - (2z + 5)$

   e $2(a + 5) - 4(a - 1)$ **f** $5(d - 3) - 3(1 + 2d)$

   g $4(y + 3x) - (2x - 7y)$ **h** $3(2a - 3b) - (3b + 2a)$

   i $2q(q - 5) - 4(q - 5)$ **j** $4z(3z + 2) - (1 - z)$

7 Expand and simplify:

   a $4x(3x + y) + 2x(5x - 2y)$ **b** $5m(4m - 3n) - 2m(9m - 2n)$

   c $3a^2(4a^3 - b^4) + 2a^2(5a^3 + 3b^4)$ **d** $2y^3(5y^2 + 3y^4) - 4y^2(2y^2 - y^4)$

   e $5a^2b(2a^3b^2 - 3ab^3) - 4a^2b(3a^3b^2 - 4ab^3)$ **f** $3x^2(2x^2 + 5y^3) - 7x^2(3x^3 + 2xy^3)$

● EXAMPLE 7

Simplify the following.

a $\dfrac{p}{3} + \dfrac{p + 2}{4}$ **b** $\dfrac{5m - 3}{6} - \dfrac{3m - 1}{9}$

	Solve	Think	Apply
a	$\dfrac{p}{3} + \dfrac{p + 2}{4}$ $= \dfrac{4p + 3(p + 2)}{12}$ $= \dfrac{4p + 3p + 6}{12}$ $= \dfrac{7p + 6}{12}$	$\text{LCD} = 12$ $\dfrac{p}{3} + \dfrac{p + 2}{4}$ $= \dfrac{4p}{12} + \dfrac{3(p + 2)}{12}$ $= \dfrac{4p + 3(p + 2)}{12}$	Find the lowest common denominator of the fractions. Change both fractions to equivalent fractions with this denominator and simplify.
b	$\dfrac{5m - 3}{6} - \dfrac{3m - 1}{9}$ $= \dfrac{3(5m - 3) - 2(3m - 1)}{18}$ $= \dfrac{15m - 9 - 6m + 2}{18}$ $= \dfrac{9m - 7}{18}$	$\text{LCD} = 18$ $\dfrac{5m - 3}{6} - \dfrac{3m - 1}{9}$ $= \dfrac{3(5m - 3)}{18} - \dfrac{2(3m - 1)}{18}$ $= \dfrac{3(5m - 3) - 2(3m - 1)}{18}$	

8 Simplify the following.

   a $\dfrac{m}{3} + \dfrac{m + 5}{4}$ **b** $\dfrac{4p - 3}{5} - \dfrac{2p}{7}$ **c** $\dfrac{k + 4}{3} + \dfrac{k - 2}{5}$

   d $\dfrac{2x + 5}{4} - \dfrac{x + 3}{8}$ **e** $\dfrac{3y - 5}{4} + \dfrac{2y - 7}{10}$ **f** $\dfrac{9w}{10} - \dfrac{2w - 5}{3}$

   g $\dfrac{2x + 3y}{6} + \dfrac{5x - 2y}{12}$ **h** $\dfrac{5a - b}{9} - \dfrac{2a - 5b}{12}$ **i** $\dfrac{2a + 3c}{6} - \dfrac{3a - 5c}{18}$

C Factorising algebraic expressions

When expanded
$$5(2y + 7) = 5 \times 2y + 5 \times 7$$
$$= 10y + 35$$

Reversing the process
$$10y + 35 = 5 \times 2y + 5 \times 7$$
$$= 5(2y + 7)$$

This second process is called factorising (or factoring).

To factorise, or factor, an algebraic expression means to write it as the product of its factors. Reversing the distributive law gives:

$$ab \pm ac = a(b \pm c)$$

EXAMPLE 1

Factorise these expressions.

a $10z + 16$ **b** $15m - 20n$

	Solve	Think	Apply
a	$10z + 16 = 2(5z + 8)$	The HCF $=$ of $10z$ and $16 = 2$. $10z = 2 \times 5z$ and $16 = 2 \times 8$ Hence $10z + 16 = 2 \times 5z + 2 \times 8$ $\qquad = 2 \times (5z + 8)$ $\qquad = 2(5z + 8)$	Factorise each term using the highest common factor as one factor and apply the distributive law.
b	$15m - 20n = 5(3m - 4n)$	The HCF of $15m$ and $20n = 5$. $15m = 5 \times 3m$ and $20n = 5 \times 4n$ Hence $15m - 20n = 5 \times 3m - 5 \times 4n$ $\qquad = 5 \times (3m - 4n)$ $\qquad = 5(3m - 4n)$	

Exercise 2C

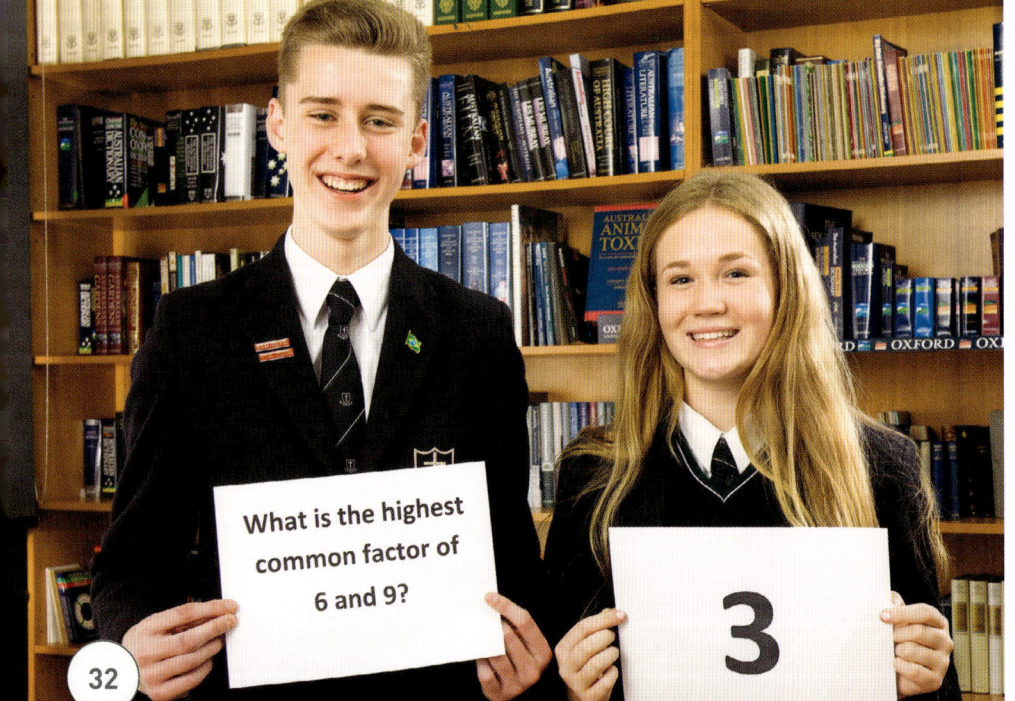

What is the highest common factor of 6 and 9?

3

1 Factorise these expressions.

  a $14s + 10$

  b $9y - 6$

  c $8k + 12b$

  d $15w - 25z$

  e $12 + 9k$

  f $24p - 18q$

  g $6x + 3y + 9z$

  h $24a - 12b - 18c$

EXAMPLE 2

Factorise the following by finding the highest negative common factor.

a $-4m + 6$ **b** $-8k - 12m$

	Solve	Think	Apply
a	$-4m + 6 = -2(2m - 3)$	The highest negative common factor of $-4m$ and $6 = -2$. $-4m = -2 \times 2m$ and $6 = -2 \times (-3)$ Hence $-4m + 6 = -2 \times 2m + (-2) \times (-3)$ $\qquad\qquad\qquad = -2 \times (2m + (-3))$ $\qquad\qquad\qquad = -2(2m - 3)$	Factorise each term using the highest negative common factor as one factor and apply the distributive law.
b	$-8k - 12m = -4(2k + 3m)$	The highest negative common factor of $-8k$ and $-12m = -4$. $-8k = -4 \times 2k$ and $-12m = -4 \times 3m$ Hence $-8k - 12m = -8k + (-12m)$ $\qquad\qquad\qquad = -4 \times 2k + (-4) \times 3m$ $\qquad\qquad\qquad = -4(2k + 3m)$	

2 Factorise the following by finding the highest negative common factor.

     a $-6t + 8$ **b** $-5k - 10$ **c** $-8p + 20q$

     d $-12x - 15y$ **e** $-16 + 8p$ **f** $-18 - 24w$

EXAMPLE 3

Factorise the following.

a $pq + pr$ **b** $6mn - 4m$ **c** $12k^2 + 8k$

	Solve	Think	Apply
a	$pq + pr = p(q + r)$	The HCF of pq and $pr = p$. $pq = p \times q$ and $pr = p \times r$ Hence $pq + pr = p \times q + p \times r$ $\qquad\qquad\quad = p(q + r)$	Factorise each term using the highest common factor as one factor and apply the distributive law.
b	$6mn - 4m = 2m(3n - 2)$	The HCF of 6 and 4 = 2 and the HCF of mn and $m = m$. Hence the HCF of $6mn$ and $4m = 2m$. $6mn = 2m \times 3n$ and $4m = 2m \times 2$ Hence $6mn - 4m = 2m \times 3n - 2m \times 2$ $\qquad\qquad\qquad = 2m(3n - 2)$	
c	$12k^2 + 8k = 4k(3k + 2)$	The HCF of 12 and 8 = 4 and the HCF of k^2 and $k = k$. Hence the HCF of $12k^2$ and $8k = 4k$. $12k^2 = 4k \times 3k$ and $8k = 4k \times 2$ Hence $12k^2 + 8k = 4k(3k + 2)$	

3 Factorise the following.

a $8pq - 12pr$
b $p^2 + 3p$
c $9ab + 6b$
d $x^2 - 7x$
e $12mn - 16n$
f $2k^2 + 4k$
g $6km - 8m^2$
h $10z^2 - 5z$
i $15ab + 3a^2$
j $24t^2 - 18tw$
k $x^2 + 5xy$
l $2bc - b^2$
m $7pq + 5pr + 11ps$
n $4ab + 6bc - 10bd$
o $21xy - 3x + 9x^2$

4 **a** State whether the following statements are true or false.

   i $12ab + 16a = 2(6ab + 8a)$
   ii $12ab + 16a = 4(3ab + 4a)$
   iii $12ab + 16a = 4a(3b + 4)$

  b An algebraic expression is said to be fully factorised when the highest common factor is used. Which of the statements above shows that the expression has been fully factorised? (*Note:* An expression that has been factorised by using a common factor that is not the HCF is said to be partially factorised.)

5 State whether the following expressions are partially or fully factorised.

a $16xy + 20x = 4x(4y + 5)$
b $18mn - 12n = 3n(6m - 4)$
c $3a^2 + 6a = a(3a + 6)$
d $12pq + 9p^2 = 3p(4q + 3p)$

● EXAMPLE 4

Factorise the following.

a $7a^3 + 4a^5$
b $15p^2q^3 - 12pq^4$

	Solve	Think	Apply
a	$7a^3 + 4a^5 = a^3(7 + 4a^2)$	HCF of 7 and 4 = 1 HCF of a^3 and a^5 = a^3 Hence HCF of $7a^3$ and $4a^5$ = a^3 $7a^3 = a^3 \times 7,\ 4a^5 = a^3 \times 4a^2$ Hence $7a^3 + 4a^5 = a^3 \times 7 + a^3 \times 4a^2$ $\qquad\qquad = a^3(7 + 4a^2)$	Factorise each term using the highest common factor as one factor and apply the distributive law.
b	$15p^2q^3 - 12pq^4 = 3pq^3(5p - 4q)$	HCF of 15 and 12 = 3 HCF of p^2 and p = p HCF of q^3 and q^4 = q^3 Hence HCF of $15p^2q^3$ and $12pq^4 = 3pq^3$ $15p^2q^3 = 3pq^3 \times 5p,\ 12pq^4 = 3pq^3 \times 4q$ Hence $15p^2q^3 - 12pq^4 = 3pq^3(5p - 4q)$	

6 Factorise the following.

a $6t^4 + 7t^2$
b $8k^{10} - 12k^5$
c $16n^7 + 24n^9$
d $14w^5 + 8w^3$
e $20k^6 - 15k^2$
f $9a^3b^5 + 8a^5b^2$
g $7x^3y^8 + 5x^4y^5$
h $9a^5b^6 - 3a^3b^8$
i $18m^4n^2 - 9m^3n^5$
j $30x^5y^7 - 20x^3y^7$
k $15x^4y^3 - 3x^5 + 9x^2$
l $16m^2n^7 + 8m^4n^3 - 12m^6n^4$

Language in mathematics

1 Four of the words in the following list have been spelt incorrectly. Find these words and write the correct spelling.

reduse, simplify, subistute, aply, numerator, equivalant

2 Complete the following words used in this chapter by replacing the vowels:

a f__ct__r__s__

b r__c__pr__c__l

c __q__ __v__l__nt

d __lg__br__ __c

3 Using examples, explain the meaning of each term.

a reciprocal

b highest common factor

c lowest common denominator

d full and partial factorisation

4 Explain the difference between the expressions $\dfrac{5x}{2y}$ and $\dfrac{2y}{5x}$.

Terms

algebraic	common	denominator	distributive law	equivalent	expand
expression	factor	factorise	fraction	numerator	parentheses
reciprocal	reduce	reverse	simplify		

Check your skills

1 If $\dfrac{2a}{3b} = \dfrac{\square}{6ab}$, the missing number is:

A $4a$ **B** $4a^2$ **C** $4ab$ **D** $4a^2b$

2 $\dfrac{4x}{3} - \dfrac{3x}{5} =$

A $\dfrac{x}{2}$ **B** $\dfrac{-x}{3}$ **C** $\dfrac{17x}{15}$ **D** $\dfrac{11x}{15}$

3 $\dfrac{2}{3w} + \dfrac{3}{4w} =$

A $\dfrac{5}{7w}$ **B** $\dfrac{17}{12w}$ **C** $\dfrac{17w}{12}$ **D** $\dfrac{17}{12w^2}$

4 $\dfrac{4t}{5v} \div \dfrac{3v}{2t} =$

A $\dfrac{6t^2}{8v^2}$ **B** $\dfrac{8t^2}{15v^2}$ **C** $\dfrac{6}{5}$ **D** $\dfrac{8}{15}$

5 $-4a(a - 7) =$

A $-4a^2 + 28a$ **B** $-4a^2 - 28a$ **C** $4a^2 + 28a$ **D** $4a^2 - 28a$

6 $4(3k - 2) + 5(2k + 9) =$

A $22k + 53$ **B** $22k + 37$ **C** $2k + 53$ **D** $2k + 37$

7 $\dfrac{4q + 1}{5} - \dfrac{q + 3}{4} =$

A $3q - 2$ **B** $\dfrac{11q + 4}{20}$ **C** $\dfrac{11q - 11}{20}$ **D** $\dfrac{11q + 19}{20}$

8 When factorised fully $-12w - 8 =$

    A $-4(3w + 2)$ **B** $-4(3w - 2)$ **C** $-4(3w - 8)$ **D** $-4(3w + 8)$

9 When factorised fully $4x^2 - 6x =$

    A $2x^2(2x^2 - 3)$ **B** $2(2x^2 - 3x)$ **C** $x(4x - 6)$ **D** $2x(2x - 3)$

If you have any difficulty with these questions, refer to the examples and questions in the sections listed in the table.

Question	1–4	5–7	8, 9
Section	A	B	C

2A   Review set

1 Complete to make equivalent fractions.

    a $\dfrac{5k}{3} = \dfrac{\square}{15}$ **b** $\dfrac{4x}{5y} = \dfrac{\square}{30y}$ **c** $\dfrac{2a}{3b} = \dfrac{\square}{12b^2}$

2 Reduce these fractions to the simplest form.

    a $\dfrac{16k}{48}$ **b** $\dfrac{6a}{4ab}$ **c** $\dfrac{8x^3y^2}{10xy^3}$

3 Simplify:

    a $\dfrac{4t}{3} - \dfrac{5t}{8}$ **b** $w + \dfrac{2w}{3}$ **c** $\dfrac{3}{x} + \dfrac{1}{2x}$

4 Simplify:

    a $\dfrac{4d}{5} \times \dfrac{3e}{7}$ **b** $\dfrac{5b}{9} \times \dfrac{27}{10ab}$ **c** $\dfrac{2w}{3} \div \dfrac{8w}{9}$ **d** $\dfrac{4mn}{3p} \div \dfrac{8m}{pq}$

5 Expand and simplify the following where possible.

    a $4x(3x + 2)$ **b** $2p^4(3p^2 - 7q)$ **c** $-6(3x^2 - 2y)$

    d $5(2v - 3) + 7$ **e** $12 - 3(7 - 2x)$ **f** $3(2p + 5q) + 4(3p - 2q)$

6 Simplify:

    a $\dfrac{x + 2}{5} - \dfrac{x + 3}{6}$ **b** $\dfrac{3a}{2} + \dfrac{5a - 1}{7}$

7 Factorise:

    a $3xy + 12y^2$ **b** $-8m - 10$

    c $15x - 9xy - 6x^2$ **d** $8m^3n^2 - 6m^2n^3$

2B   Review set

1 Complete the following to make equivalent fractions.

    a $\dfrac{7t}{4} = \dfrac{\square}{20}$ **b** $\dfrac{5x}{2y} = \dfrac{\square}{10y}$ **c** $\dfrac{4m}{3n} = \dfrac{\square}{12n^2}$

2 Reduce these fractions to the simplest form.

    a $\dfrac{15p}{18}$ **b** $\dfrac{4mn}{6mnp}$ **c** $\dfrac{10k^2m^2}{15km^4}$

3 Simplify:

a $\dfrac{4p}{5} + \dfrac{3p}{4}$

b $\dfrac{12k}{5} - 2k$

c $\dfrac{1}{3x} + \dfrac{4}{5x}$

4 Simplify:

a $\dfrac{3w}{4} \times \dfrac{5w}{2}$

b $\dfrac{5m}{7n} \times \dfrac{14n}{25}$

c $\dfrac{4z}{5} \div \dfrac{8z}{15}$

d $\dfrac{8a^3b^2}{9c} \div \dfrac{2ab}{21}$

5 Expand and simplify where possible.

a $5k(2k - 7m)$

b $3d^2(4d^2 - 7e)$

c $-4m(3m - 7)$

d $6(4z + 3) - 15$

e $7a - 3a(2a - 5)$

f $5(3x - 2y) - 2(x + 5y)$

6 Simplify:

a $\dfrac{2x - 1}{3} - \dfrac{4x - 3}{2}$

b $\dfrac{4k}{3} + \dfrac{6k - 4}{5}$

7 Factorise:

a $-8k - 12$

b $7a^2 + 3ab$

c $12ab - 9 + 6b^2$

d $12x^4y^3 - 16x^2y$

2C Review set

1 Complete the following to make equivalent fractions.

a $\dfrac{7m}{4} = \dfrac{\square}{16}$

b $\dfrac{2k}{m} = \dfrac{\square}{9mn}$

c $\dfrac{4w}{3z} = \dfrac{\square}{3z^2}$

2 Reduce these fractions to the simplest form.

a $\dfrac{8k}{15k}$

b $\dfrac{6p}{26pq}$

c $\dfrac{30a^4b^3}{20ab^2}$

3 Simplify:

a $\dfrac{6k}{7} - \dfrac{3k}{5}$

b $3t + \dfrac{2t}{3}$

c $\dfrac{2}{5w} + \dfrac{3}{4w}$

4 Simplify:

a $\dfrac{7a}{2b} \times \dfrac{3c}{5d}$

b $\dfrac{6p}{5q} \times \dfrac{15q}{4}$

c $\dfrac{3ab}{4} \div \dfrac{7a}{8}$

d $\dfrac{4p^2}{3q^2} \div \dfrac{2p}{q}$

5 Expand and simplify where possible.

a $3s(2s - 1)$

b $7q^2(4q - 5p)$

c $-6a(2a + 5)$

d $19 - 2(5e - 6)$

e $3a(2a + 4b - 5c)$

f $5z(z - 2) + 3z(1 + z)$

6 Simplify:

a $\dfrac{7z}{8} + \dfrac{4z - 2}{3}$

b $\dfrac{5x - 3}{2} - \dfrac{2x + 1}{4}$

7 Factorise:

    a $-24d - 16e$

    b $6pq + 16p^2$

    c $9a^3b^4 - 12ab^3$

    d $2x^3y - 6x^2y + 4xy$

2D   Review set

1 Complete to make equivalent fractions.

    a $\dfrac{3h}{5} = \dfrac{\square}{20}$

    b $\dfrac{2ab}{3} = \dfrac{\square}{18}$

    c $\dfrac{4x}{3y} = \dfrac{\square}{6xy}$

2 Reduce these fractions to simplest form.

    a $\dfrac{24}{36p}$

    b $\dfrac{18xy}{20x}$

    c $\dfrac{10m^4n^5}{5mn^3}$

3 Simplify:

    a $\dfrac{2k}{7} + \dfrac{3k}{4}$

    b $\dfrac{2p}{3} - \dfrac{5p}{6}$

    c $\dfrac{8}{3w} + \dfrac{6}{5w}$

4 Simplify:

    a $\dfrac{2}{3a} \times \dfrac{5}{7b}$

    b $\dfrac{7w}{4z} \times \dfrac{8}{21w}$

    c $\dfrac{4e}{3} \div \dfrac{5e}{6}$

    d $\dfrac{3a^2b}{4c} \div \dfrac{9ab}{2c}$

5 Expand and simplify where possible.

    a $7d(d - 3e)$

    b $10k(4k + 9m)$

    c $-2p^2(3p^2 + q)$

    d $7 + 3(6z - 2)$

    e $4a(3 + 2a) - a(3a + 2)$

    f $3x^2(7 - 2x + 4x^2)$

6 Simplify:

    a $\dfrac{4w - 1}{6} + \dfrac{2w + 5}{12}$

    b $\dfrac{2x + 3y}{6} - \dfrac{x - 2y}{5}$

7 Factorise:

    a $-15q + 12$

    b $12abc + 6bc$

    c $28x + 14x^2 - 7x^3$

    d $a^3b^3 - a^2b^2$

3

Linear relationships

This chapter deals with distance, midpoint and gradient formulas and the use and application of various forms of the equation of the straight line.

After completing this chapter you should be able to:

▶ use the distance, midpoint and gradient formulas

▶ apply the formulas to worded coordinate geometrical problems

▶ graph straight lines in $y = mx + b$ form

▶ find the equation of a straight line

▶ rearrange equations of straight lines into various forms

▶ sketch straight lines given their intercepts

▶ demonstrate that two lines are perpendicular if the product of their gradients is -1

▶ find the equation of a line parallel or perpendicular to a given line.

NSW Syllabus references: 5.1 N&A Linear relationships, 5.2 N&A Linear relationships
Outcomes: MA5.1-1WM, MA5.1-3WM, MA5.1-6NA, M5.2-1WM, MA5.2-3WM, MA5.2-9NA
Number & algebra – ACMNA238, ACMNA294

Diagnostic test

1 The midpoint of the join of (4, 3) and (10, 3) is:

A (14, 6)   **B** (6, 3)

C (7, 3)   **D** (6, 6)

2 The midpoint of the join of $(-3, -5)$ and $(-3, 11)$ is:

A $(-6, 6)$ **B** $(-3, 6)$

C $(-6, 3)$ **D** $(-3, 3)$

3 The midpoint of the join of (1, 4) and (8, 0) is:

A (9, 4)   **B** (7, 4)

C $(4\frac{1}{2}, 2)$ **D** $(3\frac{1}{2}, 2)$

4 The midpoint of the join of $(-5, 1)$ and $(7, -5)$ is:

A $(1, -2)$ **B** $(2, -4)$

C (6, 6)   **D** (6, 3)

5 The distance between points (7, 1) and (2, 9) is:

A $\sqrt{89}$ **B** $\sqrt{181}$

C $\sqrt{39}$ **D** $\sqrt{39}$

6 The distance between points $(-5, 7)$ and $(4, -5)$ is:

A $\sqrt{63}$ **B** 15

C 5   **D** $\sqrt{21}$

7 The slope of *MN* is:

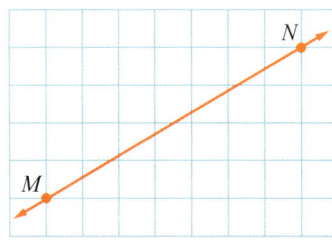

A $+3$ **B** -3

C $\frac{4}{7}$ **D** $\frac{7}{4}$

8 The gradient of the join of $A(-5, -1)$ and $B(3, 5)$ is:

A $+\frac{3}{4}$ **B** $-\frac{3}{4}$

C $+\frac{4}{3}$ **D** $-\frac{4}{3}$

9 The gradient of this line is:

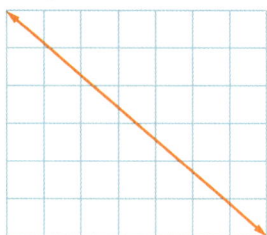

A $\frac{6}{7}$ **B** $\frac{7}{6}$

C $-\frac{6}{7}$ **D** $-\frac{7}{6}$

10 The gradient of the join of $A(-5, 9)$ and $B(7, 5)$ is:

A $+\frac{1}{3}$ **B** $-\frac{1}{3}$

C $+3$ **D** -3

11 The gradient of this line is:

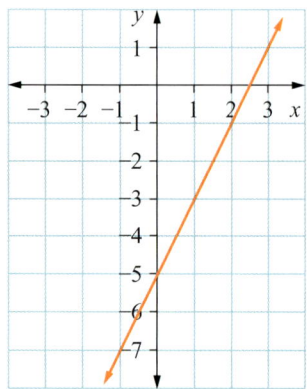

A $+2$ **B** -2

C $+\frac{1}{2}$ **D** $-\frac{1}{2}$

12 The equation of this line is:

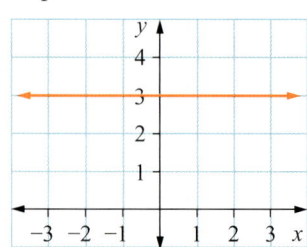

A $y = 3$ **B** $x = 3$

C $y = 3x$ **D** $x = 3y$

NUMBER & ALGEBRA

13 Complete this table of values to determine that the graph of $y = -2x + 1$ is:

x	-2	0	2
y			

A

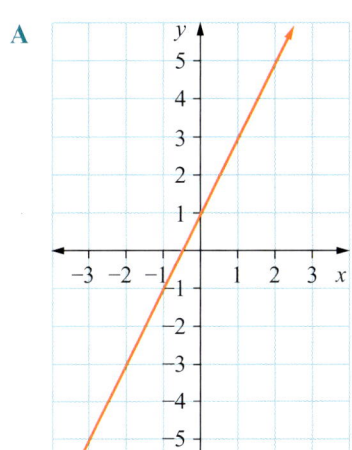

B

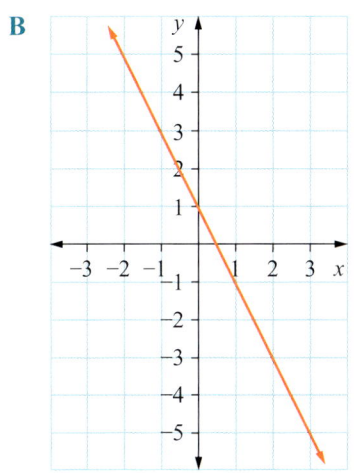

C

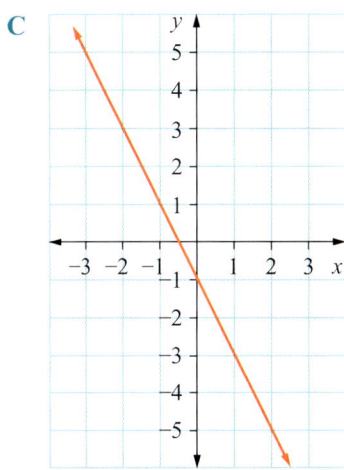

D

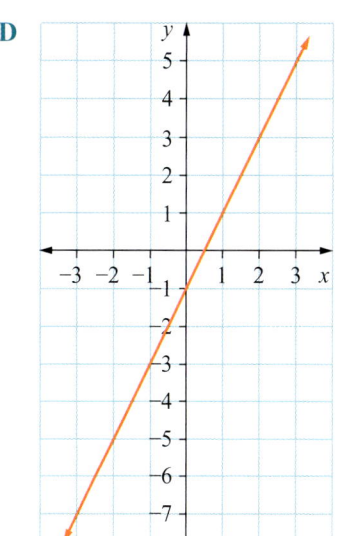

14 By completing this table of values for each equation, determine that the equation of this graph is:

x	-2	0	2
y			

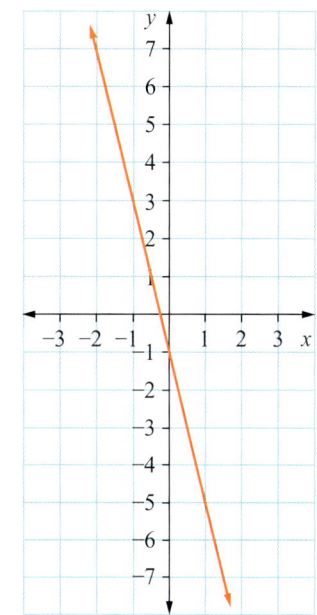

A $y = 3x - 1$ **B** $y = -3x + 1$

C $y = 4x - 1$ **D** $y = -4x - 1$

15 The line containing the point $(2, -2)$ is:

A $y = 3x - 8$ **B** $y = -3x - 3$

C $y = 4x + 14$ **D** $y = -4x - 11$

The diagnostic test questions refer to outcomes ACMNA214, ACMNA215, ACMNA239, ACMNA294 and ACMNA296. (AC)

NUMBER & ALGEBRA

Investigation 1 Distance formula

The purpose of this investigation is to develop a formula to find the distance between the two points $A(x_1, y_1)$ and $B(x_2, y_2)$.

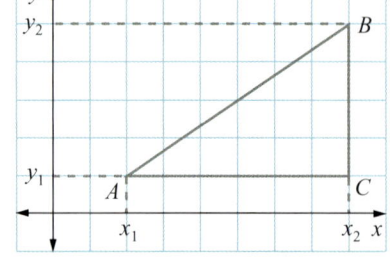

1 Use the graph to find an expression involving y_2 and y_1 for the length BC.

2 Use the graph to find an expression involving x_2 and x_1 for the length AC.

3 Use Pythagoras' rule to find an expression for d, the length AB.

4 Confirm that the distance formula is $d = \sqrt{(x_2 - x_1)^2 + (y_2 - y_1)^2}$.

5 Check the formula by showing that the distance between $(-1, 4)$ and $(5, 2)$ is $\sqrt{40}$ units. Use $(-1, 4)$ for (x_1, y_1) and $(5, 2)$ for (x_2, y_2).

6 Show that the choice for (x_1, y_1) and (x_2, y_2) does not affect the outcome by using $(5, 2)$ for (x_1, y_1) and $(-1, 4)$ for (x_2, y_2) to show the distance is $\sqrt{40}$ units.

7 Use the distance formula to find the distance between the following pairs of points.
  a $(4, 5)$ and $(-6, 3)$
  b $(-5, -3)$ and $(2, -7)$
  c $(0, 0)$ and $(14, 4)$
  d $(-11, 13)$ and $(2, -5)$

8 Lianna uses the formula $d = \sqrt{(x_1 - x_2)^2 + (y_1 - y_2)^2}$ to find the distance between two points.
  a Show that this formula works for the points $(-5, -3)$ and $(2, -7)$.
  b Expand the expression $(x_1 - x_2)^2 + (y_1 - y_2)^2$.
  c Expand the expression $(x_2 - x_1)^2 + (y_2 - y_1)^2$.
  d Explain why both formulas work.

9 Complete the following. In the distance formula:
  a d stands for ____ b x_1 is ____ c x_2 is ____ d y_1 is ____ e y_2 is ____

A Distance, midpoint and gradient review

EXAMPLE 1

Use the distance formula to find the distance between the points $T(2, 6)$ and $U(5, 1)$.

Solve	Think	Apply
$d = \sqrt{(x_2 - x_1)^2 + (y_2 - y_1)^2}$ $= \sqrt{(5 - 2)^2 + (1 - 6)^2}$ $= \sqrt{3^2 + (-5)^2}$ $= \sqrt{9 + 25}$ $= \sqrt{34}$ units	Use $x_1 = 2$, $y_1 = 6$ and $x_2 = 5$, $y_2 = 1$ and substitute.	Choose a point to be (x_1, y_1) and the other (x_2, y_2). It does not matter which is chosen as (x_1, y_1).

1 Use the distance formula to find the distance between these pairs of points.

   a $A(-2, 3)$ and $B(5, 4)$ **b** $A(0, 4)$ and $B(3, 6)$

   c $A(0, 3)$ and $B(6, 4)$ **d** $C(1, 1)$ and $D(6, -2)$

   e $P(1, -2)$ and $Q(-4, 3)$ **f** $W(2, 4)$ and $X(-3, -4)$

● EXAMPLE 2

Use the midpoint formula to find the midpoint of the line segment joining $A(-4, 3)$ and $B(8, -2)$.

Solve	Think	Apply
Midpoint $= \left(\dfrac{x_1 + x_2}{2}, \dfrac{y_1 + y_2}{2}\right)$ $= \left(\dfrac{-4 + 8}{2}, \dfrac{3 + (-2)}{2}\right)$ $= (2, \frac{1}{2})$ The midpoint is $(2, \frac{1}{2})$.	Let A be (x_1, y_1), so $x_1 = -4$, $y_1 = 3$, and B be (x_2, y_2), so $x_2 = 8$, $y_2 = -2$.	The x-coordinate of the midpoint of an interval is the average of the x-values of the endpoints. Similarly the y-coordinate is the average of the y-values.

2 Use the midpoint formula to find the midpoint of the join of:

   a $(2, 3)$ and $(6, 9)$ **b** $(-2, 6)$ and $(8, -1)$

   c $(-5\frac{1}{2}, 4\frac{1}{2})$ and $(7, -1)$ **d** $(-5, -6)$ and $(2, 4)$

● EXAMPLE 3

The midpoint of $A(2, 5)$ and $B(x_2, y_2)$ is $(4, -1)$. Find the coordinates of B.

Solve	Think	Apply
$x = \dfrac{x_1 + x_2}{2}$ $4 = \dfrac{2 + x_2}{2}$ $8 = 2 + x_2$ $x_2 = 6$ $y = \dfrac{y_1 + y_2}{2}$ $-1 = \dfrac{5 + y_2}{2}$ $-2 = 5 + y_2$ $y_2 = -7$ B has coordinates $(6, -7)$.	Let the midpoint be (x, y), then $x = \dfrac{x_1 + x_2}{2}$ and $y = \dfrac{y_1 + y_2}{2}$. Subtract 2 from both sides. Substitute the values: $(x, y) = (4, -1)$, $(x_1, y_1) = (2, 5)$ Subtract 5 from both sides.	When finding one of the endpoints, set the endpoint as (x_2, y_2) and substitute the values into the formula.

3 The midpoint of $A(3, -2)$ and $B(x_2, y_2)$ is $(5, -4)$. Find the coordinates of B.

4 The midpoint of XY is $(-3, 5)$. X has coordinates $(2, 7)$. Find the coordinates of Y.

5 a **i** Find values for the vertical rise and horizontal run as shown in the triangle.

  ii Calculate the gradient using gradient $= \dfrac{\text{rise}}{\text{run}}$.

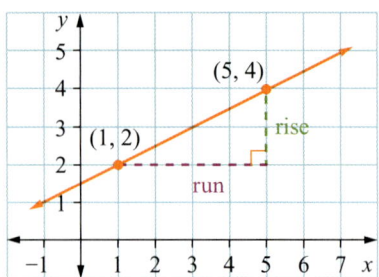

b **i** Copy the diagram shown on the right.

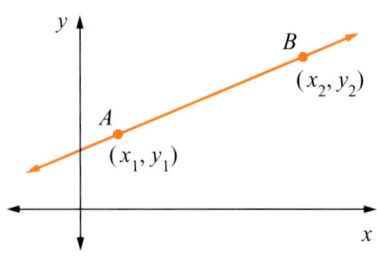

  ii Draw in the triangle as shown.

  iii If A is (x_1, y_1) and B is (x_2, y_2) then from the diagram:
  rise $= y_2 - y_1$ and run $= x_2 - x_1$
  The vertical rise from A to B is $y_2 - y_1$
  (the difference between the y-coordinates).
  The horizontal run from A to B is $x_2 - x_1$
  (the difference between the x-coordinates).
  The symbol for gradient is m. Complete: $m = \dfrac{y_2 - \square}{\square - \square}$

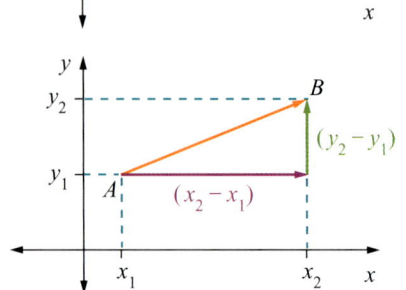

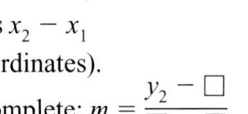

● EXAMPLE 4

Use the gradient formula to find the slope of the line passing through $A(4, 7)$ and $B(7, 3)$.

Solve	Think	Apply
$m = \dfrac{y_2 - y_1}{x_2 - x_1}$ $= \dfrac{3 - 7}{7 - 4}$ $= -\dfrac{4}{3}$	$A(4, 7)$ is (x_1, y_1) $B(7, 3)$ is (x_2, y_2)	Choose one point as (x_1, y_1) and the other as (x_2, y_2).

6 Use the gradient formula to find the slope of the line passing through A and B.

  a $A(2, 3)$ and $B(5, 8)$ **b** $A(4, -1)$ and $B(2, 7)$
  c $A(-3, 2)$ and $B(4, 2)$ **d** $A(-2, 5)$ and $B(0, 6)$
  e $A(-1, -2)$ and $B(-3, -7)$ **f** $A(3, 1)$ and $B(3, 5)$
  g $A(4, 0)$ and $B(6, 0)$ **h** $A(-1, -2)$ and $B(3, -1)$
  i $A(4, 3)$ and $B(-4, -1)$ **j** $A(-1, -4)$ and $B(-2, -3)$

7 Angus wants to the use formula $m = \dfrac{y_1 - y_2}{x_1 - x_2}$ to find gradient. He says that if the expression $\dfrac{y_2 - y_1}{x_2 - x_1}$ is multiplied on the top and bottom by -1, the formulas are equal.

  a Test both formulas on the points $A(2, 3)$ and $B(-7, 5)$.
  b Explain why Angus is correct.

Insight Mathematics 10 stages 5.2/5.3 Australian Curriculum

B Graphing lines

Tables of values can be used to plot points that give the graphs of equations of straight lines. Recall from Year 9 that graphs with positive gradients go *uphill*, and graphs with negative gradients go *downhill*.

EXAMPLE 1

Draw the graph of the lines with these equations.

a $y = x + 3$ **b** $y = -\frac{1}{2}x$ **c** $y = 2x - 1$

Using a table of values will help.

Solve	Think	Apply
a 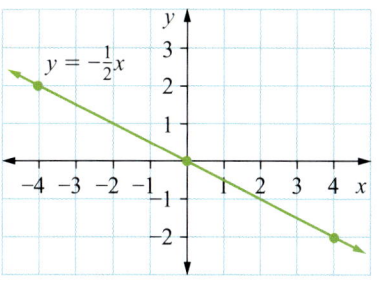	$y = x + 3$ 	**x**	−3	−2	0	2	3	 **y**	0	1	3	5	6	 $x = -3$ $y = -3 + 3 = 0$ $x = -2$ $y = -2 + 3 = 1$	When graphing these equations, the line is extended past the plotted points with an arrow on each end to show that it continues in both directions. Write the equation on the line. It is only necessary to use two points, but it is advisable to use at least three points.

a

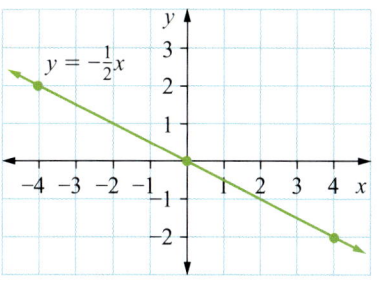

$y = x + 3$

x	−3	−2	0	2	3
y	0	1	3	5	6

$x = -3$
$y = -3 + 3 = 0$
$x = -2$
$y = -2 + 3 = 1$

b

$y = -\frac{1}{2}x$

x	−4	−2	0	2	4
y	2	1	0	−1	−2

$x = -4$
$y = -\frac{1}{2}(-4) = 2$
$x = -2$
$y = -\frac{1}{2}(-2) = 1$

c

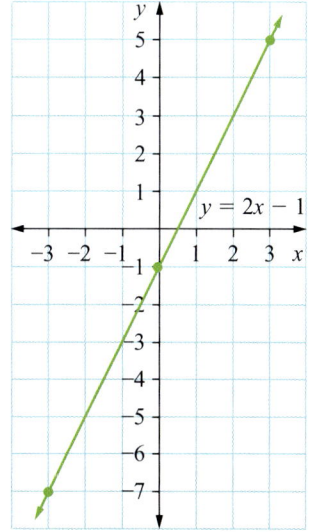

$y = 2x - 1$

x	−3	−2	0	2	3
y	−7	−5	−1	3	5

$x = -3$
$y = 2(-3) - 1 = -7$
$x = -2$
$y = 2(-2) - 1 = -5$

When graphing these equations, the line is extended past the plotted points with an arrow on each end to show that it continues in both directions. Write the equation on the line. It is only necessary to use two points, but it is advisable to use at least three points.

NUMBER & ALGEBRA

1 Complete each table of values below using the rule provided. Plot each set of ordered pairs on separate axes and draw the straight line through the points.

a $y = x + 1$

x	-2	-1	0	1	2
y					

b $y = x - 1$

x	-2	-1	0	1	2
y					

c $y = -x - 2$

x	-2	-1	0	1	2
y					

d $y = 3x - 1$

x	-2	-1	0	1	2
y					

e $y = 2x + 2$

x	-2	-1	0	1	2
y					

f $y = -\frac{1}{2}x + 1$

x	-2	-1	0	1	2
y					

g $y = -2x + 8$

x	-2	-1	0	1	2
y					

h $y = 1 - 3x$

x	-2	-1	0	1	2
y					

2 Consider the straight lines in question **1**.
a Write a list of the equations with a positive gradient.
b Write a list of the equations with a negative gradient.
c What is the difference between these groups of equations?
d Without drawing the graph, state whether each of these equations has a positive or a negative gradient.

   i $y = 2x - 1$ **ii** $y = -3x + 4$ **iii** $y = 5 - 7x$

   iv $y = 3 + 2x$ **v** $y = 7x - 1$ **vi** $y = -5x + 2$

3 When making up a table of values from rules, I unfortunately mixed them up. Can you sort out which graph belongs to which table of values?

a

x	-4	-2	0	2	4
y	-2	-1	0	1	2

A $y = 2x$

b

x	0	1	2	3	4
y	0	2	4	6	8

B $y = -x$

c

x	-4	-2	0	1	3
y	-2	0	2	3	5

C $y = \frac{1}{2}x$

d

x	-2	0	1	2	3
y	4	2	1	0	-1

D $y = x + 2$

e

x	-3	-2	-1	0	1
y	3	2	1	0	-1

E $y = 2 - x$

Investigation 2 Gradients and intercepts

A graphics calculator could be used in this investigation.

1 a On the same number plane draw the graphs of:

$y = 2x$, $y = 2x + 1$, $y = 2x + 2$, $y = 2x + 3$

   b What do you notice about the gradients of these lines?

   c Write the coordinates of the y-intercept of each line. What do you notice about the y-intercept and the equation of the line?

2 a On the same number plane draw the graphs of:

$y = 2x + 1$, $y = 3x + 1$, $y = 5x + 1$, $y = x + 1$

   b What do you notice about the gradients of these lines? Compare the gradient with the coefficient of x.

   c What do you notice about the y-intercept of each line? How is this shown in the equation?

3 a Sketch the line $y = 3x - 2$.

   b Change the gradient to 4 and sketch the new line.

   c Is the new line parallel to $y = 3x - 2$? Explain.

4 a Sketch the line $y = 3x - 1$.

   b What equation will give a line parallel to $y = 3x - 1$ but with a y-intercept of 2?

   c Sketch the line.

C Straight line $y = mx + b$ form

From Investigation 2 it can be seen that:

- if a straight line has gradient m and y-intercept b, it has equation $y = mx + b$
- if two straight lines have the same gradient, they are parallel.

EXAMPLE 1

a Find the equation of the line with gradient -3 and y-intercept 2.

b Sketch the line.

	Solve	Think	Apply
a	$y = -3x + 2$	As $m = -3$ and $b = 2$, the equation is $y = -3x + 2$.	Substitute the m and b values into the equation $y = mx + b$.
b		Plot the point $(0, 2)$. As the gradient is -3, the line slopes downhill with a rise of 3 and a run of -1.	Using a rise of -3 and a run of 1 would give the same graph.

a Find the equation of the line with gradient 4 and y-intercept -3.
b Sketch the line.

	Solve	Think	Apply
a	$y = 4x - 3$	As $m = 4$ and $b = -3$, the equation is $y = 4x - 3$.	Substitute the m and b values into the equation $y = mx + b$.
b		Plot the point $(0, -3)$. As the gradient is $+4$, the line slopes uphill with a rise of 4 and a run of 1.	To check the graph, substitute an x-value into the equation; that point should lie on the line.

Exercise 3C

1 Find the equation of the line with:
   a gradient 2 and y-intercept 7
   b gradient 4 and y-intercept -6
   c gradient -3 and y-intercept -1
   d gradient -2 and y-intercept 2
   e gradient -2 and y-intercept 6
   f gradient 1 and y-intercept 3
   g gradient 3 and y-intercept 0
   h gradient -1 and y-intercept 2.

2 Sketch each of the lines in question **1**.

a Find the equation of the line with gradient $-\frac{2}{3}$ and y-intercept 1.
b Sketch the line.

	Solve	Think	Apply
a	$y = -\frac{2}{3}x + 1$	As $m = -\frac{2}{3}$ and $b = 1$, the equation is $y = -\frac{2}{3}x + 1$.	Substitute the m and b values into the equation $y = mx + b$.
b		Plot the point $(0, 1)$. As the gradient is $-\frac{2}{3}$, the line slopes downhill with a rise of -2 and a run of 3.	Using a rise of 2 and a run of -3 would give the same graph.

3 Find the equation of the line with:

a gradient $-\frac{3}{4}$ and y-intercept 1

b gradient $\frac{2}{3}$ and y-intercept 2

c gradient $\frac{2}{3}$ and y-intercept -1

d gradient $\frac{4}{5}$ and y-intercept -2

e gradient $-\frac{1}{3}$ and y-intercept 4

f gradient $-\frac{1}{4}$ and y-intercept -1

g gradient $\frac{2}{5}$ and y-intercept 0

h gradient $-\frac{2}{5}$ and y-intercept 4.

4 Sketch each of the lines in question **3**.

EXAMPLE 4

Find the gradient of the given line.

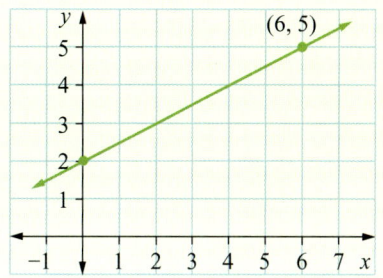

Solve	Think	Apply
Gradient $= \dfrac{\text{rise}}{\text{run}}$ $= \dfrac{3}{6}$ $= \dfrac{1}{2}$	Draw a right-angled triangle, labelling the rise and run.	Any two points can be chosen to find the gradient. The gradient formula can be used.

5 Find the gradient of the following lines.

a

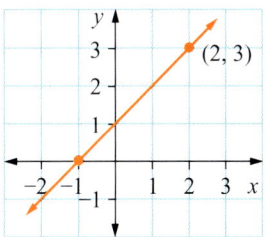

b

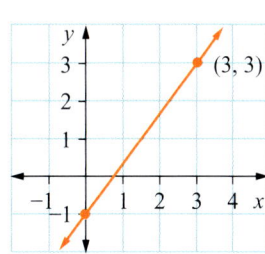

c

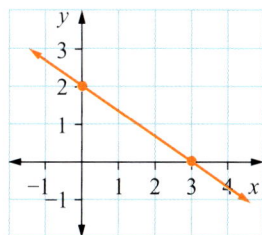

d

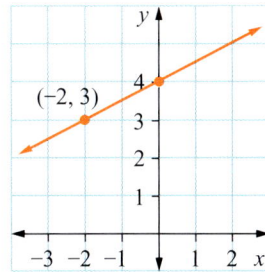

e

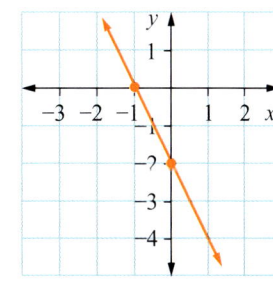

f

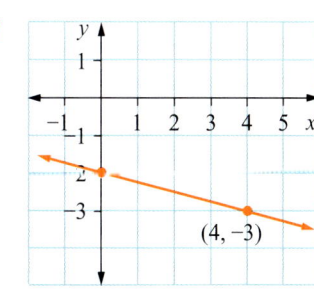

6 Draw the graph of the lines with the following equations.

a $y = \frac{1}{2}x + 2$ **b** $y = 2x + 1$ **c** $y = -x + 3$

d $y = -3x + 2$ **e** $y = -\frac{1}{2}x$ **f** $y = -2x - 2$

g $y = \frac{3}{2}x$ **h** $y = \frac{2}{3}x + 2$ **i** $y = -\frac{3}{4}x - 1$

7 Write the gradient and y-intercept of each of the lines in question **6**.

● EXAMPLE 5

Find the equation of this straight line.

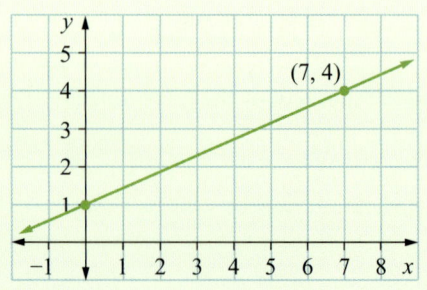

Solve	Think	Apply
Gradient $= \dfrac{\text{rise}}{\text{run}}$ $= \dfrac{3}{7}$ y-intercept is 1. The equation is $y = \frac{3}{7}x + 1$.	Draw a right-angled triangle, labelling the rise and run. *(graph with rise = 3, run = 7, point (7, 4))*	The gradient formula and the points (0, 1) and (7, 4) could be used.

---

8 Find the equation of the lines in question **5**.

9 The equations of three lines are $y = 3x + 1$, $y = 2x + 1$, $y = 3x - 2$.

   a Without sketching the lines, which two lines are parallel? Why?

   b Sketch all three lines on the same number plane. What do you notice?

   c Which of the above three lines would have something in common with these lines? Explain your answers.

     i $y = 2x + 4$ **ii** $y = 5x - 2$

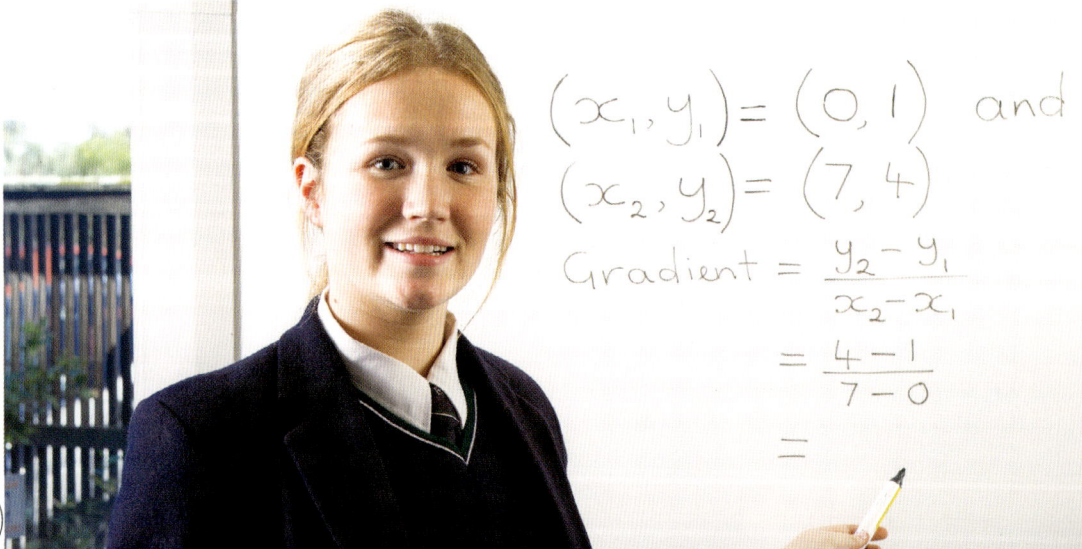

Rewrite the equation $4x - 3y - 12 = 0$ in the form $y = mx + b$. Hence find the gradient and y-intercept.

Solve	Think	Apply
$4x - 3y - 12 = 0$ $4x - 12 = 3y$ $3y = 4x - 12$ $y = \frac{4}{3}x - 4$ Gradient is $m = \frac{4}{3}$ and y-intercept is -4.	Add $3y$ to both sides. Swap sides. Divide both sides by 3.	Use equation-solving techniques to rearrange the terms. $4x - 3y - 12 = 0$ is called the general form of an equation of a straight line and will be examined later in this chapter.

10 Rewrite the following equations in $y = mx + b$ form and hence find the gradient and y-intercept.

    a $x + 2y - 4 = 0$ **b** $3x + 2y - 24 = 0$ **c** $2x - y + 4 = 0$

    d $4x - 2y - 6 = 0$ **e** $5x + 2y + 10 = 0$ **f** $3x + 2y - 8 = 0$

    g $4x - y - 6 = 0$ **h** $3x - 2y + 17 = 0$ **i** $8x - 2y - 7 = 0$

D **Equations of lines**

The equation of a line can be determined if we know:

- the gradient of the line, and
- the coordinates of a point on the line.

If a straight line has gradient m and passes through the point with coordinates (x_1, y_1), then its equation is

$$y - y_1 = m(x - x_1) \text{ and } \frac{y - y_1}{x - x_1} = m$$

Proof

Suppose $P(x, y)$ is any point on the line with gradient m.
Equating the slopes gives:

$$\frac{y - y_1}{x - x_1} = m$$

or $y - y_1 = m(x - x_1)$

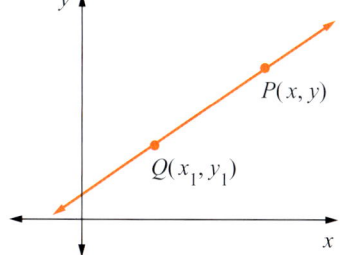

Find the equation of the line that has a gradient of 4 and passes through $(-1, 2)$.

Solve	Think	Apply
$y - 2 = 4(x - (-1))$ $\quad\quad = 4(x + 1)$ $\quad\quad = 4x + 4$ The equation is $y = 4x + 4$.	The equation of the line is $y - y_1 = m(x - x_1)$ where $(x_1, y_1) = (-1, 2)$ and $m = 4$.	The point–gradient formula is a rearrangement of the gradient formula.

Exercise 3D

1 Find the equation of the line:

a with gradient 3 and passing through $(2, -3)$

b with gradient -2 and passing through $(-4, 2)$

c with gradient $-\frac{1}{2}$ and passing through $(7, 4)$

d with gradient 5 and passing through $(2, -5)$

e with gradient $\frac{1}{3}$ and passing through $(3, 7)$

f with gradient $-\frac{1}{2}$ and passing through $(-5, -2)$

g with gradient $-1\frac{1}{2}$ and passing through $(3, 4)$

h with gradient 6 and passing through $(0, 0)$

i with gradient 4 and passing through $(-\frac{1}{2}, 1\frac{1}{2})$

j with gradient 0 and passing through $(5, 4)$.

EXAMPLE 2

Use $y = mx + b$ to find the equation of the line that has a gradient of 3 and passes through $(-3, 5)$.

Solve	Think	Apply
$y = mx + b$ $5 = 3(-3) + b$ $\quad = -9 + b$ $14 = b$ The equation is $y = 3x + 14$.	$y = 3x + b$ as $m = 3$. We substitute $x = -3$ and $y = 5$ as $(-3, 5)$ lies on the line.	The equation can be found using $y = mx + b$. It can also be found using $y - y_1 = m(x - x_1)$.

2 Find the equation of the line that has:

a a gradient of 2 and passing through $(3, -4)$

b a gradient of 1 and passing through $(5, -2)$

c a gradient of -3 and passing through $(8, -2)$

d a gradient of -2 and passing through $(-4, -4)$

e a gradient of 5 and passing through $(3, 0)$

f a gradient of $\frac{1}{2}$ and passing through $(6, 8)$

g a gradient of $-\frac{1}{3}$ and passing through $(0, 5)$

h a gradient of 8 and passing through $(0, 0)$

i a gradient of $\frac{1}{3}$ and passing through $(9, 9)$

j a gradient of 0 and passing through $(6, 2)$.

EXAMPLE 3

Find the equation of the line that passes through the points $A(-1, 5)$ and $B(2, -3)$.

Solve	Think	Apply
$m = \dfrac{y_2 - y_1}{y_2 - x_1}$ $\quad = \dfrac{-3 - 5}{2 - (-1)}$ $\quad = -\dfrac{8}{3}$ $y - 5 = -\dfrac{8}{3}(x - (-1))$ $\quad = -\dfrac{8}{3}(x + 1)$ $\quad y = -\dfrac{8}{3}x - \dfrac{8}{3} + 5$ The equation is $y = -\dfrac{8}{3}x + \dfrac{7}{3}$ or $y = -\dfrac{8}{3}x + 2\dfrac{1}{3}$.	First find the gradient of AB using $(-1, 5)$ for (x_1, y_1) and $(2, -3)$ for (x_2, y_2). Then find the equation of the line using $y - y_1 = m(x - x_1)$. Add 5 to both sides.	$B(2, -3)$ could have been used as (x_1, y_1) to give the same equation.

3 Find the equation of the line passing through the following pairs of points.

a $A(2, 3)$ and $B(4, 7)$

b $A(0, 2)$ and $B(-2, 4)$

c $A(-1, -3)$ and $B(5, -5)$

d $A(6, 3)$ and $B(4, 1)$

e $A(5, -2)$ and $B(2, -5)$

f $P(0, 0)$ and $Q(3, 5)$

g $P(-3, 5)$ and $Q(1, -2)$

h $L(-3, -2)$ and $M(0, 4)$

i $X(2, 2)$ and $Y(-3, -1)$

j $X(0, 6)$ and $Y(-4, 0)$

● EXAMPLE 4

Find the equation of the line that cuts the y-axis at 3 and the x-axis at -2.

Solve	Think	Apply
$m = \dfrac{y_2 - y_1}{x_2 - x_1}$ $= \dfrac{0 - 3}{-2 - 0}$ $= \dfrac{-3}{-2} = \dfrac{3}{2}$ $m = \dfrac{3}{2}, b = 3$ $\therefore y = \dfrac{3}{2}x + 3$ The equation is $y = \dfrac{3}{2}x + 3$.	The y-axis is cut when $x = 0$, thus $(0, 3)$ is one point. The x-axis is cut when $y = 0$, thus $(-2, 0)$ is the other point. Use $y = mx + b$ with $m = \frac{3}{2}$ and $b = 3$.	Once the gradient is found then $y = mx + b$ can be used to find the equation. The equation can also be found using $y - y_1 = m(x - x_1)$.

---

4 Find the equation of the line:

a cutting the y-axis at -4 and the x-axis at 2

b cutting the y-axis at 7 and the x-axis at -2

c cutting the y-axis at -5 and the x-axis at -3

d with y-intercept -3 and x-intercept 2.

Investigation 3 Intercept form of the equation of a line

1 The x-intercept of a line is $(a, 0)$ and the y-intercept is $(0, b)$.

a Calculate the gradient of the line joining these two points.

b Find the equation of the line using the gradient and the point $(a, 0)$.

c Repeat using the gradient and the point $(0, b)$.

d Show that the point $(a, 0)$ lies on the line $\dfrac{x}{a} + \dfrac{y}{b} = 1$.

e Show that the point $(0, b)$ lies on the line $\dfrac{x}{a} + \dfrac{y}{b} = 1$.

f Without calculating, write the equation of the line with x-intercept $(2, 0)$ and y-intercept $(0, 3)$.

g Use the points from part **f** and the equations from parts **b** and **c** to show that the equation of the line with x-intercept $x = a$ and y-intercept $y = b$ is $\dfrac{x}{a} + \dfrac{y}{b} = 1$.

2 Repeat Exercise 3D question **4**. Check that your solutions are correct by rearranging the equation.

E General form of a straight line equation

The general form of the equation of a straight line is:

$Ax + By + C = 0$ where A, B and C are all integers and $A \geqslant 0$.

● **EXAMPLE 1**

Write each equation in general form.

a $y = 3x - 1$

b $y = -\frac{2}{3}x + 4$

	Solve	Think	Apply
a	$y = 3x - 1$ $0 = 3x - y - 1$ $3x - y - 1 = 0$	Subtract y from both sides. Swap sides.	Rearrange using the usual equation-solving techniques. The coefficient of x must be positive and all values integers.
b	$y = -\frac{2}{3}x + 4$ $0 = -\frac{2}{3}x - y + 4$ $\quad = -2x - 3y + 12$ $-2x - 3y + 12 = 0$ $2x + 3y - 12 = 0$	Subtract y from both sides. Multiply both sides by 3. Swap sides. Multiply by -1 so that $A \geqslant 0$.	

Exercise 3E

1 Write the following equations in general form.

a $y = 2x + 1$

b $y = 5x - 2$

c $y = 2x + 5$

d $y = -2x - 5$

e $y = -3x + 4$

f $y = \frac{1}{2}x + 2$

g $y = -\frac{1}{2}x - 5$

h $y = -\frac{2}{3}x - 3$

i $y = -\frac{3}{4}x - \frac{2}{3}$

j $\frac{2}{3}y = \frac{1}{4}x + 1$

k $y = \frac{1}{2}x - \frac{3}{4}$

l $\frac{1}{5}y = x + \frac{1}{2}$

● **EXAMPLE 2**

Rewrite the equation $4x - 3y - 12 = 0$ in the form $y = mx + b$ and hence find the gradient and y-intercept.

Solve	Think	Apply
$4x - 3y - 12 = 0$ $4x - 12 = 3y$ $3y = 4x - 12$ $y = \frac{4}{3}x - 4$ Gradient is $m = \frac{4}{3}$ and y-intercept is -4.	Add $3y$ to both sides. Swap sides. Divide both sides by 3.	The variable y needs to be the subject with a coefficient of 1.

2 Rewrite each equation in $y = mx + b$ form and hence find the gradient and y-intercept.

a $x + 2y - 4 = 0$ **b** $3x + 2y - 24 = 0$ **c** $2x - y + 4 = 0$

d $4x - 2y - 6 = 0$ **e** $5x + 2y + 10 = 0$ **f** $3x + 2y - 8 = 0$

g $4x - y - 6 = 0$ **h** $3x - 2y + 17 = 0$ **i** $8x - 2y - 7 = 0$

3 Find b for the points below, which lie on the line with the given equation.

a $(2, b)$ $x + 2y = -4$ **b** $(-1, b)$ $3x - 4y = 6$

c $(b, 4)$ $5x + 2y = 1$ **d** $(b, -3)$ $4x - y = 8$

● EXAMPLE 3

Find the x- and y-intercepts of the line with equation $4x - 3y - 12 = 0$.

Solve	Think	Apply
$4x - 3(0) - 12 = 0$ $4x - 12 = 0$ $4x = 12$ $x = 3$ The x-intercept is 3. $4(0) - 3y - 12 = 0$ $-3y - 12 = 0$ $-3y = 12$ $y = -4$ The y-intercept is -4.	The x-intercept is when $y = 0$. The y-intercept is when $x = 0$.	Substitute 0 for y and then solve the resulting linear equation. Substitute 0 for x and then solve the resulting linear equation.

4 Find the x- and y-intercepts of the following lines.

a $x + 2y - 8 = 0$ **b** $3x + 2y - 12 = 0$ **c** $2x - y + 6 = 0$

d $3x - 2y - 36 = 0$ **e** $5x + 2y + 20 = 0$ **f** $3x + 2y - 5 = 0$

g $4x - y - 5 = 0$ **h** $3x - 2y + 15 = 0$ **i** $9x - 2y - 5 = 0$

● EXAMPLE 4

Draw the graph of the line with equation $5x - 3y - 15 = 0$.

Solve	Think	Apply
The y-intercept is -5. The x-intercept is 3. 	Find the x- and y-intercepts. When $x = 0$ $5(0) - 3y - 15 = 0$ $-3y - 15 = 0$ $-3y = 15$ $y = -5$ When $y = 0$ $5x - 3(0) - 15 = 0$ $5x - 15 = 0$ $5x = 15$ $x = 3$	Use a third point as a check. Try $x = 1$. $5(1) - 3y - 15 = 0$ $5 - 3y - 15 = 0$ $-3y - 10 = 0$ $-3y = 10$ $y = -\dfrac{10}{3}$ $(1, -\dfrac{10}{3})$ is on the line.

5 Find the *x*- and *y*-intercepts and then draw the graph of the line for each equation.

- **a** $x + 2y - 8 = 0$
- **b** $3x - y - 6 = 0$
- **c** $2x - 3y - 4 = 0$
- **d** $4x + 3y - 8 = 0$
- **e** $x + y - 5 = 0$
- **f** $x - y + 5 = 0$
- **g** $3x - 4y - 12 = 0$
- **h** $5x + 2y + 10 = 0$
- **i** $x - 2y = 0$
- **j** $2x - 5y - 5 = 0$

Investigation 4 Graphs of lines

1 a On the same number plane draw the straight lines with these equations.
$$y = 2x, y = 2x + 1, y = 2x - 3, y = 2x - 1$$
b What do you notice about these lines?

2 a On the same number plane draw the straight lines with these equations.
$$y = -3x + 1, 3x + y - 2 = 0, 6x + 2y + 3 = 0$$
b What do you notice about these three lines?
c Rewrite the second and third equations in $y = mx + b$ form and find their gradients.

3 Complete the following.
Straight lines are _____ if their _____ are equal.

Use a graphics calculator.

4 a On the same number plane draw the straight lines with equations.
$$y = 2x + 1 \text{ and } y = -\frac{1}{2}x + 2.$$
b What do you notice about these lines?

5 a On the same number plane draw the straight lines with equations $y = 3x - 1$ and $x + 3y - 6 = 0$.
b What do you notice about these lines?
c Rewrite $x + 3y - 6 = 0$ in $y = mx + b$ form and find the gradient.

6 Complete the following.
Straight lines are _____ if the product of their gradients is _____.

 **F** **Parallel and perpendicular lines**

From Investigation 4 it can be seen that if two straight lines have gradients m_1 and m_2 then:
- the lines are parallel if $m_1 = m_2$
- the lines are perpendicular if $m_1 \times m_2 = -1$.

EXAMPLE 1

a Find the equation of the line parallel to the line $y = -5x - 7$ and passing through the point $(2, 3)$.

b Find the equation of the line parallel to the line $3x - 6y + 8 = 0$ and passing through the point $(-1, -2)$.

	Solve	Think	Apply
a	$y = -5x + b$ $3 = -5(2) + b$ $\quad = -10 + b$ $b = 13$ The equation is $y = -5x + 13$.	$m = -5$, as the lines are parallel. Substitute $(2, 3)$.	Parallel lines have equal gradients. Find the gradient by inspection or calculation then use $y = mx + b$ or $y - y_1 = m(x - x_1)$.
b	Use $y - y_1 = m(x - x_1)$ with $m = \frac{1}{2}$ and $(-1, -2)$ for (x_1, y_1). $y - (-2) = \frac{1}{2}(x - (-1))$ $\quad y + 2 = \frac{1}{2}(x + 1)$ $\quad\quad y = \frac{1}{2}x + \frac{1}{2} - 2$ The equation is $y = \frac{1}{2}x - 1\frac{1}{2}$.	Rearrange $3x - 6y + 8 = 0$ into $y = mx + b$ form to find the gradient. $3x + 8 = 6y$ $\frac{3x}{6} + \frac{8}{6} = y$ $y = \frac{1}{2}x + \frac{4}{3}$ $m = \frac{1}{2}$	

Exercise 3F

1 Which of the following pairs of lines are parallel?

A $y = 3x + 1$
  $y = 3x - 5$

B $y = 2x - 1$
  $y = 2x$

C $y = 5x + 3$
  $y = 3x + 5$

D $y = 4x - 3$
  $y = 4 - 3x$

E $y = 2x - 5$
  $2x - y + 4 = 0$

F $y = -x - 5$
  $x - 2y + 3 = 0$

G $4x - 3y + 5 = 0$
  $3x + 4y + 2 = 0$

H $2x + 3y - 2 = 0$
  $2x + 3y - 5 = 0$

I $3x - 2y - 5 = 0$
  $y = \frac{2}{3}x + 3$

2 Find the equation of the line:

a parallel to the line $y = 2x - 5$ and passing through the point $(1, 4)$

b parallel to the line $y = -7x - 2$ and passing through the point $(-5, -2)$

c parallel to the line $y = -\frac{1}{2}x + 5$ and passing through the origin

d parallel to the line $5x - 7y + 3 = 0$ and passing through the point $(2, -3)$

e passing through $(-1, -3)$ and parallel to the line passing through the points $(1, 5)$ and $(3, 6)$

f with y-intercept -2 and parallel to the line segment joining $(-7, 5)$ and the origin.

EXAMPLE 2

a Is the line $y = 3x - 5$ perpendicular to the line $2x + 6y + 9 = 0$?

b What is the gradient of the line perpendicular to the line $5x - 2y + 4 = 0$?

c Find the equation of the line passing through $(6, -3)$ and perpendicular to the line $y = -\frac{2}{3}x + 4$.

	Solve	Think	Apply
a	$2x + 6y + 9 = 0$ $6y = -2x - 9$ $y = \dfrac{-2x}{6} - \dfrac{9}{6}$ $y = -\dfrac{1}{3}x - \dfrac{3}{2}$ $2x + 6y + 9 = 0$ has gradient $m_2 = -\dfrac{1}{3}$. $y = 3x - 5$ has gradient $m_1 = 3$. The lines are perpendicular.	Rearrange $2x + 6y + 9 = 0$ into $y = mx + b$ form. Divide both sides by 6. $m_1 \times m_2 = 3 \times -\dfrac{1}{3} = -1$	Lines with gradients m_1 and m_2 are perpendicular if $m_1 \times m_2 = -1$.
b	$5x - 2y + 4 = 0$ $5x + 4 = 2y$ $\dfrac{5x}{2} + \dfrac{4}{2} = y$ $y = \dfrac{5}{2}x + 2$ so $m = \dfrac{5}{2}$ The perpendicular line has gradient $-\dfrac{2}{5}$.	Rearrange $5x - 2y + 4 = 0$ into $y = mx + b$ form. Divide both sides by 2. $5x - 2y + 4 = 0$ has gradient $m_1 = \dfrac{5}{2}$. $m_1 \times m_2 = \dfrac{5}{2} \times -\dfrac{2}{5} = -1$	
c	$y = \dfrac{3}{2}x + b$ $-3 = \dfrac{3}{2}(6) + b$ $= 9 + b$ $\therefore b = -12$ The equation of the line is $y = \dfrac{3}{2}x - 12$.	$y = -\dfrac{2}{3}x + 4$ has gradient $m_1 = -\dfrac{2}{3}$. The gradient of the perpendicular line $m_2 = \dfrac{3}{2}$. $m_1 \times m_2 = -\dfrac{2}{3} \times \dfrac{3}{2} = -1$ Substitute $(6, -3)$ into $y = \dfrac{3}{2}x + b$.	

3 Which of the following pairs of lines are perpendicular?

A $y = 2x - 5$
   $y = 2x$

B $y = -3x + 5$
   $y = \frac{1}{3}x - 2$

C $y = 4x + 7$
   $y = -4x + 3$

D $y = \frac{2}{5}x - 1$
   $y = -\frac{5}{2}x - 1$

E $3x - 4y + 5 = 0$
   $4x + 3y - 2 = 0$

F $7x + 5y + 3 = 0$
   $5y - 7x = 0$

4 Find the gradients of the lines perpendicular to the given lines.

a $y = -\frac{3}{5}x + 2$

b $y = 7x - 2$

c $y = \frac{3}{2}x - 5$

d $y = -\frac{4}{5}x - 7$

e $3x - 2y + 1 = 0$

f $5x - 7y + 7 = 0$

5 Find the equation of the line:

a perpendicular to $y = 5x - 2$ and passing through $(-3, 2)$

b perpendicular to $y = -\frac{1}{4}x + 7$ and passing through $(0, 5)$

c passing through the origin and perpendicular to $y = \frac{3}{4}x + \frac{1}{3}$

d passing through $(-2, 5)$ and perpendicular to $3x - 4y + 12 = 0$

e with y-intercept 7 and perpendicular to $5x + 2y - 7 = 0$

f passing through $(-2, -5)$ and perpendicular to the line segment joining $(2, 3)$ and $(5, -3)$

g passing through the origin and perpendicular to the line segment joining $(3, 0)$ and $(0, -5)$.

6 a Find the equation of all lines that are perpendicular to $y = \frac{1}{2}x - 3$.

b Find the equation of all lines that are parallel to $y = 3x - 2$.

c Write the equation of all lines parallel to $3x - 5y + 6 = 0$.

d Write the equation of all lines perpendicular to $5x - 3y + 7 = 0$.

7 a Find the equations of three lines that are perpendicular to $3x - 4y + 8 = 0$.

b Write the equations of these lines in general form.

c What do you notice?

8 a Find the equations of three lines that are parallel to $2x - 7y + 3 = 0$.

b Write the equations of these lines in general form.

c What do you notice?

9 Write the equation of all lines:

a parallel to $7x - 5y + 6 = 0$

b perpendicular to $7x - 5y + 6 = 0$.

G Further coordinate geometry

EXAMPLE 1

The triangle ABC has vertices $A(-2, 0)$, $B(2, 1)$ and $C(1, -3)$.

a Find the length of the sides AB, BC and AC using the distance formula.

b Classify $\triangle ABC$ as scalene, isosceles or equilateral. Give a reason.

	Solve	Think	Apply
a	$d = \sqrt{(x_2 - x_1)^2 + (y_2 - y_1)^2}$ $d_{AB} = \sqrt{(2 - (-2))^2 + (1 - 0)^2}$ $\quad = \sqrt{4^2 + 1^2}$ $\quad = \sqrt{17}$ $d_{BC} = \sqrt{(1 - 2)^2 + (-3 - 1)^2}$ $\quad = \sqrt{(-1)^2 + (-4)^2}$ $\quad = \sqrt{17}$ $d_{AC} = \sqrt{(1 - (-2))^2 + (-3 - 0)^2}$ $\quad = \sqrt{3^2 + (-3)^2}$ $\quad = \sqrt{18}$ $AB = \sqrt{17}$, $BC = \sqrt{17}$ and $AC = \sqrt{18}$	d_{AB} represents the distance AB. Substitute $(-2, 0)$ for (x_1, y_1) and $(2, 1)$ for (x_2, y_2). d_{BC} represents the distance BC. Substitute $(2, 1)$ for (x_1, y_1) and $(1, -3)$ for (x_2, y_2). d_{AC} represents the distance AC. Substitute $(-2, 0)$ for (x_1, y_1) and $(1, -3)$ for (x_2, y_2).	Calculate each of the sides using the given points. Using the notation d_{AB} allows the delineation of each side for comparison purposes.
b	$\triangle ABC$ is an isosceles triangle.	Two sides are equal to $\sqrt{17}$ and the third is $\sqrt{18}$.	Use the side lengths to classify the triangle.

1 The triangle PQR has vertices $P(1, 0)$, $Q(3, 1)$ and $R(0, 4)$.
   a Find the length of each side.
   b Classify $\triangle PQR$ as scalene, isosceles or equilateral. Give a reason.

2 Classify $\triangle LMN$ with vertices $L(-2, -1)$, $M(0, 3)$ and $N(4, 1)$ as scalene, isosceles or equilateral. Give a reason for your answer.

3 Triangle ABC has $A(-1, 4)$, $B(2, -1)$ and $C(5, 2)$ as vertices. Find the length of the line segment from A to the midpoint of BC.

4 a By finding the equation of line AB and substituting the point C show that points $A(2, 1)$, $B(-2, -11)$ and $C(4, 7)$ all lie on a straight line.
   b Show that the points $A(-3, 13)$, $B(3, 1)$ and $C(4, -1)$ all lie on the same straight line.

5 Line segments AB and CD bisect each other at T.
   a Using A and B, find the coordinates of the midpoint T.
   b Use the midpoint T and the point D to find the coordinates of C.

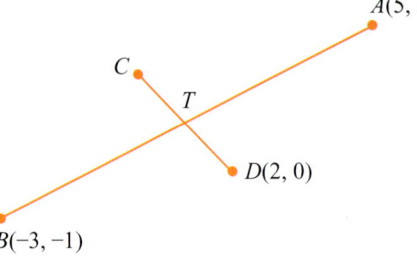

6 $ABCD$ is a parallelogram. Use the fact that the diagonals of the parallelogram bisect each other to find the coordinates of D.

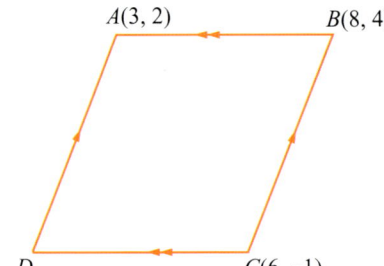

7 The triangle XYZ has vertices $X(1, 2)$, $Y(2, 5)$ and $Z(4, 1)$.
   a Find the length of each of the sides XY, YZ and XZ.
   b Use Pythagoras' rule to decide if $\triangle XYZ$ is right angled. Give a reason for your answer.
   c Find the gradient of the sides XY, YZ and XZ.
   d Two lines are perpendicular, that is they meet at right angles, if the product of their gradients is -1. Multiply each pair of gradients together to find the pair that gives -1.
   e Use the gradients to decide if $\triangle XYZ$ is right angled. Give a reason for your answer.

8 Is the triangle with vertices $D(-2, -1)$, $E(1, -1)$ and $F(-2, 3)$ right angled? Give a reason for your answer.

9 The triangle PQR has vertices $P(-2, 5)$, $Q(3, -1)$ and $R(-4, -7)$.
   a Find the coordinates of S, the midpoint of PQ.
   b Find the coordinates of T, the midpoint of PR.
   c Show that the length of QR is twice the length of ST.

10 The quadrilateral $PQRS$ has vertices $P(2, 4)$, $Q(5, 1)$, $R(-1, -2)$ and $S(-4, 1)$.
   a Prove that $PQRS$ is a parallelogram by showing that:
      i the opposite sides are equal
      ii the diagonals bisect each other because they have the same midpoint.
   b i Find the gradient of each side.
      ii Is $PQRS$ a rectangle; that is, are the sides perpendicular?
   c Is $PQRS$ a rhombus; that is, are all sides equal?

Language in mathematics

1 Rearrange these words to form a sentence.

   a run over Gradient rise is

   b y-intercept b is symbol for the

   c is the m gradient symbol for

   d ordinates Midpoint average of is the the

   e theorem distance Pythagoras' The to is formula related

   f $y = mx + b$ straight line gradient–intercept form is the a of

2 Complete these glossary terms by adding the vowels.

   a __q__ __t__ __n**   **b** f__rm__l__   **c** gr__d__ __nt

   d p__r__ll__l   **e** v__rt__c__l r__s__   **f** h__r__z__nt__l r__n

3 Use every third letter to find a sentence.

```
D F T E D W V G O H U L I O I K J N H G E F D S A S A E R R T G E B N P M
I E K J R G T P Q A E Z S N W E D R F I D C C S H U K O L P L A D U R I O
I D E F A S T F V H B K E N J P M H R K I O L O D P O U T U C X Y T T T O
R R F E E T D D H F F E X F I V H R N P G O I R Y T A E D D S V I H U E K
A N E D T A S S C F I V G S F D N E S E A E G A E A A E T D R I F G V H N
E M J O T G N A X E H U A J K N U P D Z C T V B H M K E L P Y I O A U Y R
U I E I J P H G A I E R E T A R E L E T L R T E A S L C V I B H F N G T D
S H F G E H N I M J R I K G U Y R T R A E D D E D I S W E A D N A S T C V
S B N A N N R M M E S S E R R Q A A U S S A Q W L
```

Terms

average	distance formula	equation	formula	general form
gradient	gradient–intercept form	graph	horizontal run	intercept
linear relationship	midpoint	parallel	perpendicular	point
Pythagoras' theorem	rearrange	sketch	straight line	tables of values
vertical rise	x-intercept	y-intercept		

Check your skills

1 The distance between the points (5, 3) and (1, 7) is:

   A $\sqrt{16}$ **B** $\sqrt{32}$ **C** $\sqrt{136}$ **D** $\sqrt{8}$

2 The distance between points (−5, 8) and (6, −2) is:

   A $\sqrt{11}$ **B** $\sqrt{21}$ **C** $\sqrt{37}$ **D** $\sqrt{221}$

3 The midpoint of the join of (5, 5) and (9, 5) is:

   A (14, 5)   **B** (7, 5)   **C** (4, 10)   **D** (4, 0)

4 The midpoint of the join of (2, −4) and (2, 8) is:

   A (2, 2)   **B** (2, 4)   **C** (0, 12)   **D** (4, 4)

5 The midpoint of the join of (−1, 3) and (7, 1) is:

   A (3, 2)   **B** (8, 2)   **C** (8, 4)   **D** (4, 2)

NUMBER & ALGEBRA

6 The midpoint of the join of $(-6, 3)$ and $(5, -9)$ is:

   A $(-1, -6)$ **B** $(-\frac{1}{2}, -3)$ **C** $(\frac{1}{2}, 3)$ **D** $(-5\frac{1}{2}, 6)$

7 The midpoint of PQ is $(4, -3)$. If P has coordinates $(7, 2)$ then the coordinates of Q are:

   A $(5\frac{1}{2}, -\frac{1}{2})$ **B** $(-10, 7)$ **C** $(1, -8)$ **D** $(1\frac{1}{2}, -\frac{1}{2})$

8 The gradient of the line passing through the points $(4, 3)$ and $(-5, 7)$ is:

   A $\frac{9}{4}$ **B** -10 **C** $-\frac{1}{10}$ **D** $-\frac{4}{9}$

9 The formula for gradient is:

   A $m = \dfrac{x_2 - x_1}{y_2 - y_1}$ **B** $m = \dfrac{y_2 + y_1}{x_2 + x_1}$ **C** $m = \dfrac{y_2 - y_1}{x_2 - x_1}$ **D** $m = \dfrac{x_2 + x_1}{y_2 + y_1}$

10 The length of the line segment from $(1, 3)$ to the midpoint of $(-5, 3)$ and $(3, -1)$ is:

   A $\sqrt{8}$ **B** $\sqrt{36}$ **C** $\sqrt{20}$ **D** $\sqrt{80}$

11 By using this table, the graph of $y = 2x - 1$ is:

x	-2	0	2
y			

A
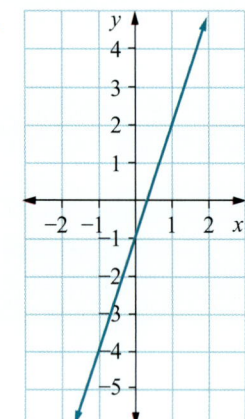

B
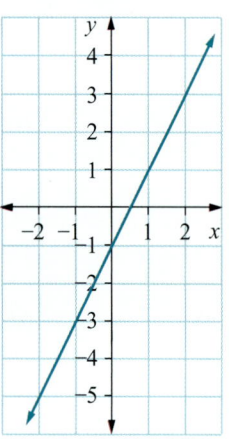

C
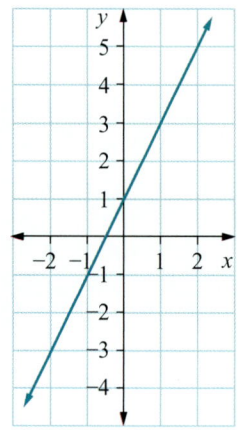

D
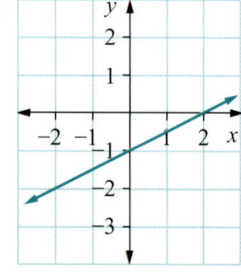

12 By completing this table of values for each equation, the equation of this graph is:

x	-2	0	2
y			

   A $y = 3x - 1$ **B** $y = -3x + 1$

   C $y = 4x - 1$ **D** $y = -4x - 1$

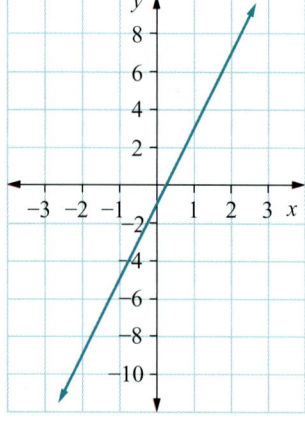

13 The equation of the line corresponding to the values in the table is:

x	-4	-3	-2	-1	0	1	2	3	4
y	7	5	3	1	-1	-3	-5	-7	-9

   A $y = 2x - 1$ **B** $y = -2x - 1$ **C** $y = x + 3$ **D** $y = -x + 3$

NUMBER & ALGEBRA

14 The equation of the line with gradient -3 and y-intercept 5 is:

   A $y = -3x + 5$ **B** $y = 5x - 3$ **C** $x = -3y + 5$ **D** $x = 5y - 3$

15 The equation of the line shown at right is:

   A $y = -x - 3$ **B** $y = -x + 3$

   C $y = x + 3$ **D** $y = x - 3$

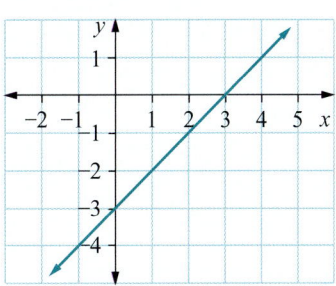

16 The equation $4x - 5y + 20 = 0$ in gradient–intercept form is:

   A $5y = 4x + 20$ **B** $y = \dfrac{4x}{5} + 4$ **C** $y = -\dfrac{4x}{5} - 20$ **D** $x - \dfrac{5y}{4} + 5 = 0$

17 The equation of the line passing through $(-2, -6)$ with gradient 2 is:

   A $y = 2x + 3$ **B** $y = 2x - 7$ **C** $y = 2x - 2$ **D** $y = 2x + 7$

18 The equation of the line passing through $A(-4, 5)$ and $B(2, -13)$ is:

   A $y = -x - 1$ **B** $y = x + 5$ **C** $y = -3x - 7$ **D** $y = -x + 1$

19 The equation of the line cutting the y-axis at -4 and the x-axis at $+5$ is:

   A $y = \dfrac{4x}{5} - 4$ **B** $y = -\dfrac{4x}{5} - 4$ **C** $y = \dfrac{5x}{4} - 4$ **D** $y = -\dfrac{5x}{4} - 4$

20 The equation of the line shown on the right is:

   A $y = 3x - 3$ **B** $y = -3x - 3$

   C $y = -x + 3$ **D** $y = 2x - 3$

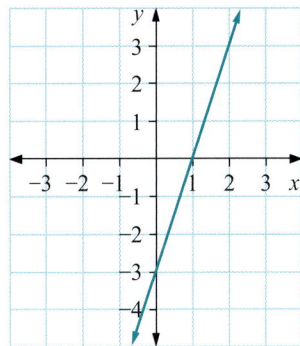

21 The point $(a, 1)$ lies on the line $y = 3x - 2$, so the value of a is:

   A 0   **B** 1

   C 2   **D** 3

22 In general form $y = \frac{1}{2}x - \frac{4}{3}$ is:

   A $6y - 3x + 8 = 0$ **B** $3x - 6y - 8 = 0$ **C** $3x + 2y - 4 = 0$ **D** $\frac{1}{2}x - y - \frac{4}{3} = 0$

23 When written in gradient–intercept form, the equation $3x + 2y + 8 = 0$ is:

   A $2y = 3x + 4$ **B** $3x - 2y = -8$ **C** $y = -\dfrac{3x}{2} + 8$ **D** $y = -\dfrac{3x}{2} - 4$

24 The x- and y-intercepts of $4x + 3y - 12 = 0$ are:

   A 4 and -3 **B** 3 and 4   **C** -4 and 3   **D** -3 and 4

25 A line parallel to $y = -3x + 1$ is:

   A $y = \frac{1}{3}x + 1$ **B** $y = -\frac{1}{3}x + 1$ **C** $y = -3x + 3$ **D** $y = -x + 3$

26 A line perpendicular to $3x + 5y + 7 = 0$ is:

    A $3x + 5y - 2 = 0$ **B** $3x - 5y - 7 = 0$ **C** $3x + 5y + 7 = 0$ **D** $y = \frac{5x}{3} + 2$

If you have any difficulty with these questions, refer to the examples and questions in the sections listed in the table.

Question	1–10	11, 12	13–16	17–21	22–24	25, 26
Section	A	B	C	D	E	F

3A   Review set

1 For the points $A(3, -1)$ and $B(-5, 0)$, find:

  a the distance AB **b** the midpoint of AB **c** the gradient of AB.

2 The midpoint of $A(4, 2)$ and $B(x, y)$ is $(-2, 7)$. Find the coordinates of B.

3 Find the fourth vertex of the parallelogram $ABCD$ for $A(-7, 11)$, $B(6, 5)$ and $C(3, 8)$.

4 a Complete the following table of values for $y = 2x + 3$.

x	-3	-2	-1	0	1	2	3
y							

  b Plot the resulting ordered pairs on a set of coordinate axes and draw the straight line through the points.

  c Does the point $(-10, -17)$ lie on the line?

5 a Write the equation of the line with y-intercept -2 and gradient -3.

  b Sketch the line.

6 a Write the equation of the line with gradient $\frac{2}{3}$ and y-intercept -1.

  b Sketch the line.

7 a Consider the straight line shown on the right. Calculate the gradient.

  b Find the y-intercept.

  c Write the equation of the line.

8 a Write the equation $3x - 2y + 12 = 0$ in the form $y = mx + b$.

  b Sketch the line.

9 For the points $A(3, -1)$ and $B(-5, 0)$, find:

  a the gradient of AB

  b the equation of the line through A and B

  c the x- and y-intercepts of the line AB

  d the equation of the line perpendicular to AB passing through A

  e the equation of the line parallel to AB passing through the point $(3, 0)$.

10 a Write $3y = 4x - 7$ in general form.

  b Write the equation of the line passing through $(-4, 7)$ and $(2, 6)$ in general form.

  c Sketch the line $3x - 4y + 12 = 0$.

11 a Find k if $2x + ky = 5$ is perpendicular to $x - 3y = 11$.

  b $A(-1, 3)$, $B(2, 4)$ and $C(t, -1)$ are collinear. Find t.

1 For the points $A(0, 0)$ and $B(-7, 4)$, find:
   a the distance AB **b** the midpoint of AB **c** the gradient of AB.

2 The triangle ABC has vertices $A(1, 1)$, $B(5, 3)$ and $C(3, -1)$. Find the length of each side and classify the triangle as scalene, isosceles or equilateral.

3 **a** Complete this table of values for $y = -5x + 7$.

x	-3	-2	-1	0	1	2	3
y							

    b Sketch $y = -5x + 7$.

4 **a** Write the equation of the line with y-intercept 3 and gradient -2.
    b Sketch the line.

5 Find the equation of this straight line shown on the right.

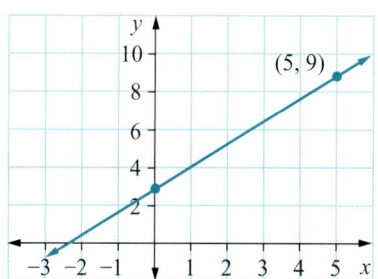

6 Find the equation of the line passing through $M(-4, 2)$ and $N(3, 7)$.

7 Find the equation of the line passing through $(-4, 5)$ and perpendicular to $3x - 2y + 7 = 0$.

8 Write $y = -\frac{2}{3}x - 4$ in general form.

9 Find the equation of the perpendicular bisector of the join of $(-2, 3)$ and $(4, 5)$.

1 For the points $P(-6, 3)$ and $QB(-1, -5)$, find:
   a the distance PQ **b** the midpoint of PQ **c** the gradient of PQ.

2 The midpoint of $L(x, y)$ and $M(0, -1)$ is $(3, -4)$. Find the coordinates of L.

3 Find the coordinates of D for parallelogram $ABCD$ if $A(-2, 3)$, $B(1, 7)$ and $C(5, 1)$ are vertices.

4 **a** Complete the following table of values for $y = -3x + 2$.

x	-3	-2	-1	0	1	2	3
y							

    b Plot the resulting ordered pairs on a set of coordinate axes and draw the straight line through the points.
    c Does the point $(-5, 17)$ lie on the line?

5 **a** Write the equation of the line with gradient 4 and y-intercept -2.
    b Sketch the line.

6 **a** Write the equation of the line with gradient $-\frac{3}{4}$ and y-intercept -2.
    b Sketch the line.

7 Consider the straight line on the right.

    a Calculate the gradient.

    b Find the y-intercept.

    c Write the equation of the line.

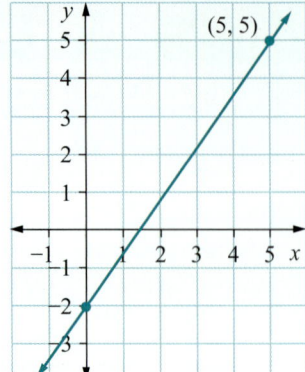

8 **a** Write the equation $5x - 4y + 20 = 0$ in the form $y = mx + b$.

    b Sketch the line.

9 For the points $P(-6, 3)$ and $Q(-1, -5)$, find:

    a the gradient of PQ

    b the equation of the line through P and Q

    c the x- and y-intercepts of the line PQ

    d the equation of the line perpendicular to PQ and passing through Q

    e the equation of the line parallel to PQ and passing through the origin.

10 **a** Write $4x - 7y + 8 = 0$ in gradient–intercept form.

    b Find the equation of the line passing through $(4, -2)$ and the origin in general form.

    c Sketch the line $6x - 7y + 9 = 0$.

3D   Review set

1 For the points $A(-3, 5)$ and $B(2, 4)$, find:

    a the distance AB **b** the midpoint of AB **c** the gradient of AB.

2 The triangle LMN has vertices $L(2, 3)$, $M(3, 6)$ and $N(5, 2)$.

    a Calculate the length of each side.

    b Determine whether $\triangle LMN$ is right-angled. Give a reason for your answer.

3 **a** Complete the table of values for $y = -\frac{1}{2}x + 3$.

    b Sketch $y = -\frac{1}{2}x + 3$.

    c What is the gradient and y-intercept of $y = -\frac{1}{2}x + 3$?

x	-4	-2	0	2	4
y					

4 **a** Write the equation of the line with gradient 2 and y-intercept -8.

    b Sketch the line.

5 Find the equation of the straight line shown on the right.

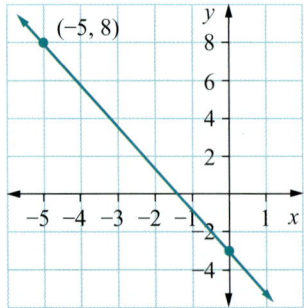

6 **a** Write the equation of the line with gradient 3 and passing through $(-2, 4)$.

    b Find the equation of the line parallel to $3x - 5y = 8$ and passing through the origin.

7 Write $y = -\frac{3x}{4} + 2$ in general form.

8 Does the point $(1, 4)$ lie on the line $3x - 5y + 2 = 0$? Explain your answer.

4

Geometrical proofs

This chapter deals with the use of logical reasoning, including congruence and similarity, to complete numerical and theoretical exercises involving geometrical figures.

At the end of this chapter you should be able to:

- ▶ formulate proofs involving congruent triangles and angle properties
- ▶ explain similarity and develop the minimum conditions for triangles to be similar
- ▶ apply logical reasoning, including the use of congruence and similarity,

- to proofs and numeral exercises involving plane shapes
- ▶ find the sum of the interior and exterior angles of polygons
- ▶ find the size of interior and exterior angles of regular polygons.

NSW Syllabus references: 5.2 M&G Properties of geometrical figures
Outcomes: MA5.2-1WM, MA5.2-2WM, MA5.2-3WM, MA5.2-14MG
Measurement & geometry – ACMMG220, ACMMG243, ACMMG244

Diagnostic test

1 The value of x is:

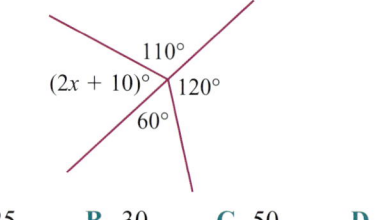

A 25 **B** 30 **C** 50 **D** 55

2 $\angle MKL$ equals:

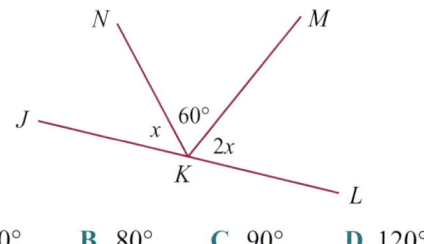

A 40° **B** 80° **C** 90° **D** 120°

3 The value of x is:

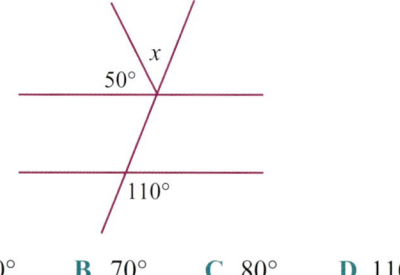

A 60° **B** 70° **C** 80° **D** 110°

4 The value of x is:

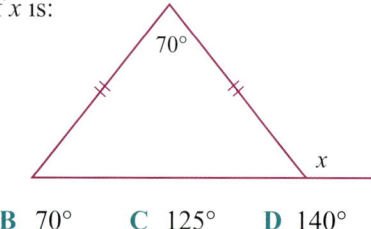

A 55° **B** 70° **C** 125° **D** 140°

5 The values of x and y in this diagram are:

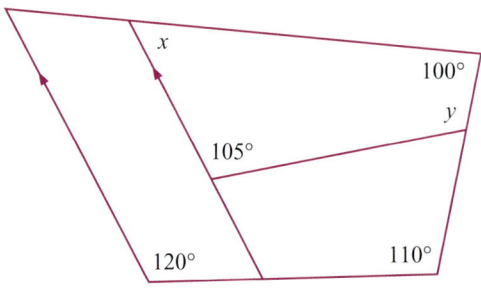

A $x = 45°, y = 110°$ **B** $x = 45°, y = 125°$
C $x = 30°, y = 110°$ **D** $x = 30°, y = 125°$

6 The transformation that could not have been used to produce this pair of congruent figures is:

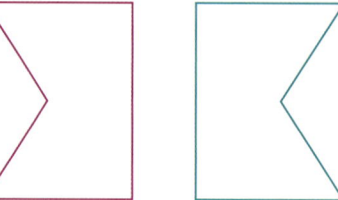

A reflection
B reflection and translation
C rotation
D translation

7 The triangles shown below are congruent. The correct statement of congruency is:

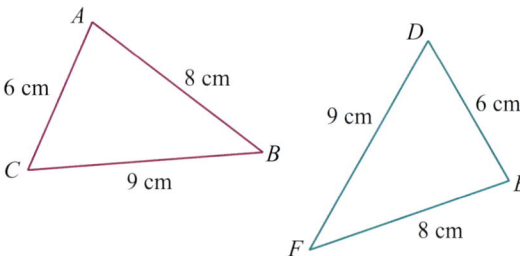

A $\triangle ABC \equiv \triangle DEF$
B $\triangle ABC \equiv \triangle EFD$
C $\triangle ABC \equiv \triangle FDE$
D $\triangle CBA \equiv \triangle DEF$

8 $\triangle ABC$ has been enlarged to $\triangle KLM$ using P as the centre of enlargement. $PA = 24$ mm and $AK = 32$ mm. The enlargement factor is:

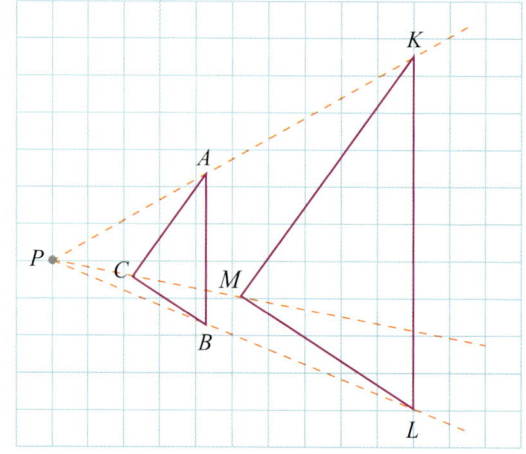

A $\dfrac{4}{3}$ **B** $\dfrac{3}{4}$ **C** $\dfrac{7}{3}$ **D** $\dfrac{3}{7}$

9 The figures that are similar are:

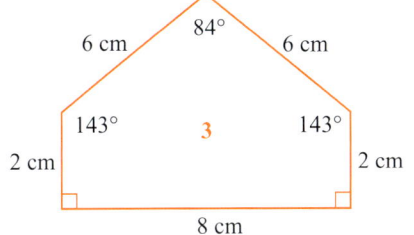

A 1 and 2
B 2 and 3
C 1 and 3
D 1, 2 and 3

10 These triangles are similar.

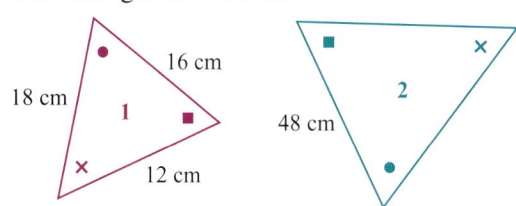

The enlargement factor from triangle 1 to triangle 2 is:

A $2\frac{2}{3}$ B 3   C 4   D 4.8

11 Which of the following statements is not true?

A Congruent figures are identical in all respects except for position.
B Congruent figures have the same shape and the same size.
C Similar figures have the same size but different shape.
D Similar figures have the same shape but not necessarily the same size.

The diagnostic test questions refer to outcomes ACMMG141, AMMG163, AMMG164, AMMG166, AMMG200 and AMMG220.

A Reasoning in geometry

In this section geometrical facts, properties and relationships are applied to proofs and numerical exercises involving diagrams and plane shapes, with appropriate reasons.

● EXAMPLE 1

Find x, giving reasons.

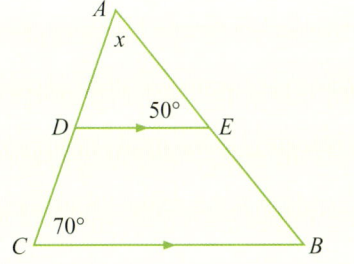

Solve/Think		Apply
$\angle ADE = \angle ACB = 70°$	(Corresponding angles and $DE \cdot CB$.)	The diagram contains triangles and parallel lines. Look for appropriate properties of these to use.
$x + 70° + 50° = 180°$	(Angle sum of a triangle is 180°.)	
$x + 120° = 180°$		
$x = 60°$		

1 Find the values of the pronumerals in the following diagrams, giving reasons.

a

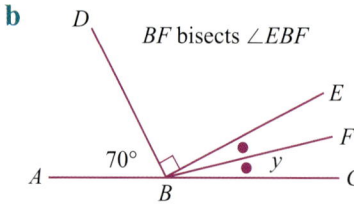

b

BF bisects ∠EBF

c

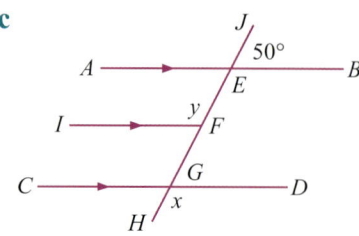

d

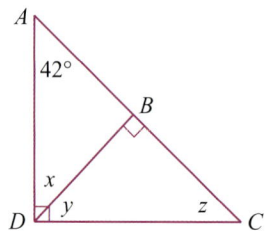

e

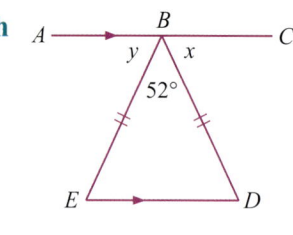

f

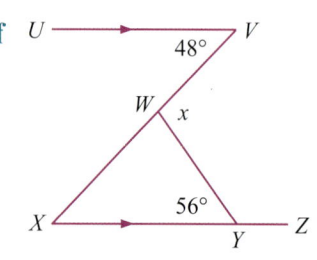

g

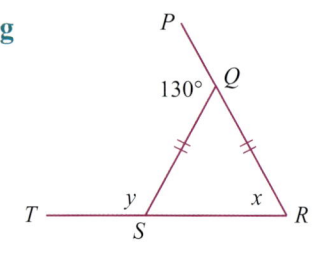

h

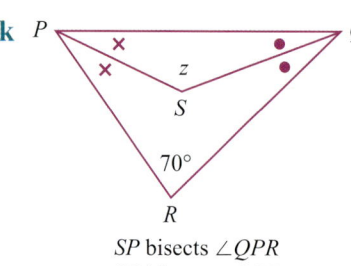

i

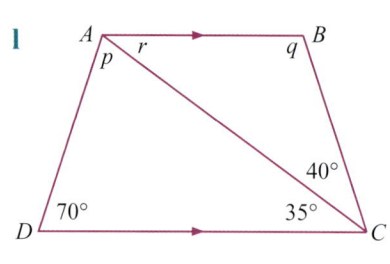

j

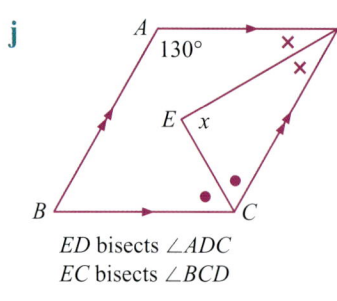

ED bisects ∠ADC
EC bisects ∠BCD

k

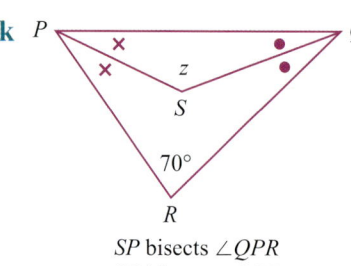

SP bisects ∠QPR
SQ bisects ∠PQR

l

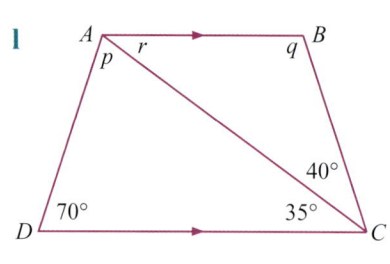

EXAMPLE 2

Given that ∠EGB = ∠CHF, prove that AB ∥ CD.

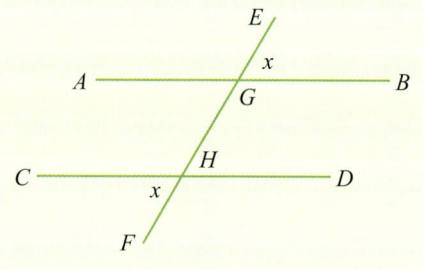

Solve/Think	Apply
∠AGH = ∠EGB = x　　　(vertically opposite angles)	Use the properties of
Hence ∠CHF = ∠AGH = x	intersecting lines and
∴ AB ∥ CD　　　(corresponding angles on lines AB and CD)	parallel lines.

MEASUREMENT & GEOMETRY

2 **a** Given $x + y = 180°$. Prove that $PR \parallel US$.

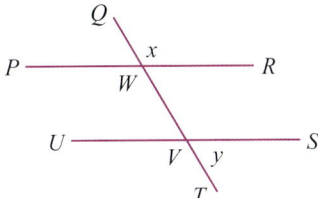

b Prove that TUQ is a straight line.

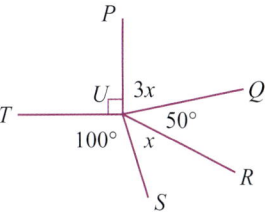

c ABC is a straight line. PB bisects $\angle ABD$. QB bisects $\angle DBC$. Prove that $\angle PBQ = 90°$.

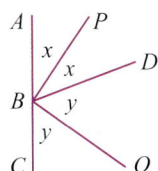

d $PQ \parallel CB$. Prove $a + b + c = 180°$; that is, the sum of the interior angles of a triangle is 180°.

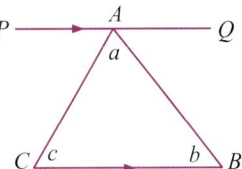

e $BP \parallel CA$. Prove that $z = x + y$.

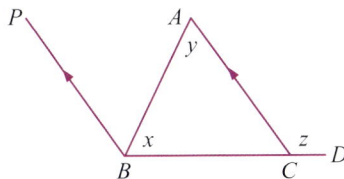

f $QR = QS$ and $TQ \parallel SR$. Prove that TQ bisects $\angle PQS$.

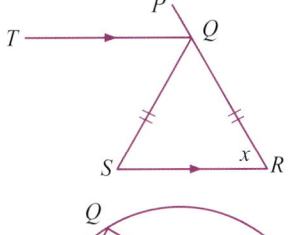

g O is the centre in a semicircle. Q is any point on the circumference. Prove that $\angle PQR = 90°$.
Hint: Draw the radius OQ.

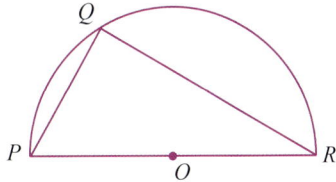

B Congruent triangles

Congruent triangles have the same size and shape; that is, they have three pairs of equal matching sides and three pairs of equal matching angles. They are formed by performing one or more of the transformations translation, rotation or reflection. It is not necessary to show that all matching sides and angles are equal to prove congruency. The four sets of minimum conditions used are known as the congruency tests for triangles.

Tests for congruent triangles

1 If three sides of one triangle are equal to three sides of another triangle, then the two triangles are congruent. (SSS)

2 If two sides and the included angle of one triangle are equal to two sides and the included angle of another triangle, then the two triangles are congruent. (SAS)

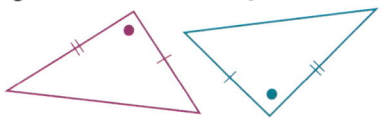

3 If two angles and one side of a triangle are equal to two angles and the matching side of another triangle, then the triangles are congruent. (AAS)

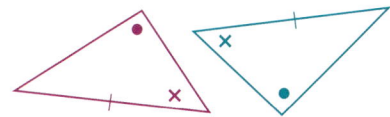

4 If the hypotenuse and a second side of a right-angled triangle are equal to the hypotenuse and a second side of another, then the triangles are congruent. (RHS)

 **EXAMPLE 1**

State the congruency test used to show that the following pairs of triangles are congruent.

a
7 cm, 9 cm, 10 cm — 9 cm, 7 cm, 10 cm

b
45°, 55°, 6 cm — 6 cm, 55°, 45°

c
7 cm, 50°, 9 cm — 7 cm, 50°, 9 cm

d
7 cm, 12 cm — 12 cm, 7 cm

	Solve	Think	Apply
a	SSS	There are three pairs of equal sides.	Look for pairs of equal matching sides and angles that will satisfy one of the congruency tests.
b	AAS	There are two pairs of equal angles and the pair of equal sides are matching sides.	
c	SAS	There are two pairs of equal sides and the angles included by these sides are equal.	
d	RHS	The hypotenuse and a second side of the first right-angled triangle are equal to the hypotenuse and a second side of the second right-angled triangle.	

Exercise 4B

1 State the congruency test used to show that the following pairs of triangles are congruent. (Diagrams are not drawn to scale.)

a
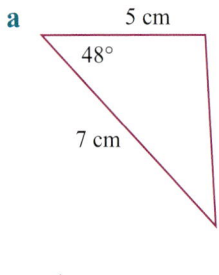

b
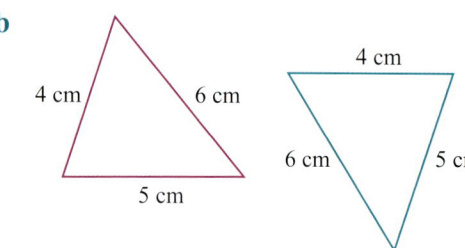

c
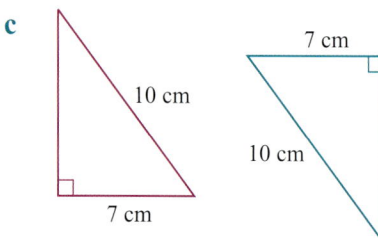

d
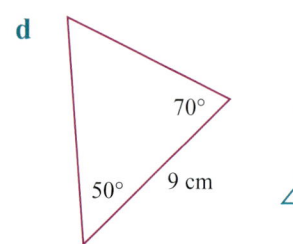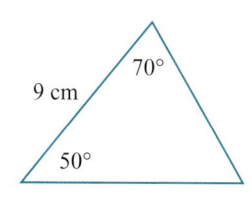

e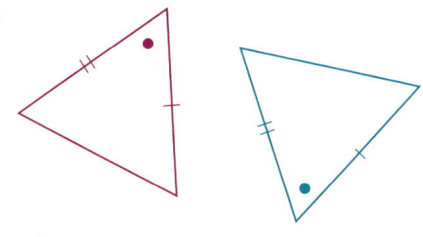

f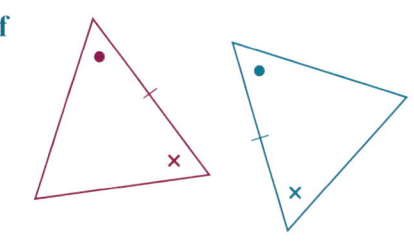

g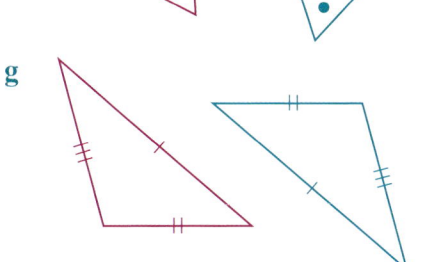

h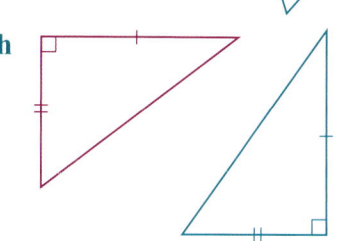

EXAMPLE 2

State why the following pairs of triangles are not congruent.

a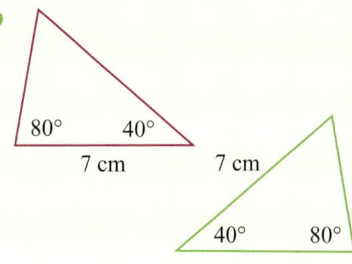

b

c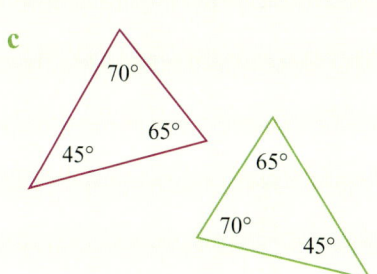

	Solve/Think	Apply
a	The 65° angle in the second triangle is not the included angle.	For the SAS test to apply, both the angles must be included by the pairs of equal sides.
b	The equal sides are not matching sides in the triangles.	For the AAS test to apply, the pair of equal sides must be matching (or corresponding) sides.
c	Three pairs of equal angles do not necessarily make the triangles congruent. These triangles have the same shape but not necessarily the same size.	If two triangles have three pairs of equal angles, then they have the same shape but not necessarily the same size.

2 State why the following pairs of triangles are not congruent.

a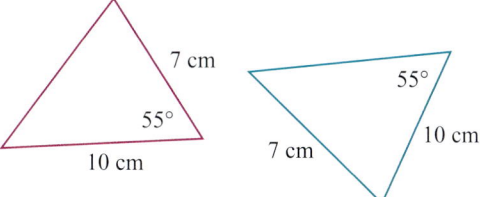

b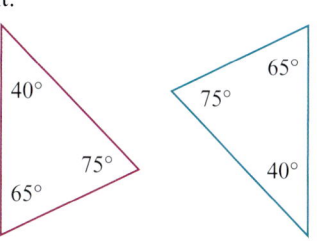

c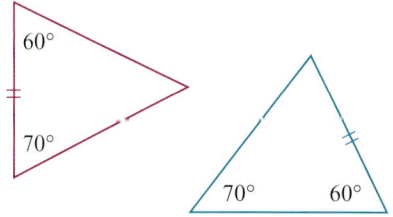

d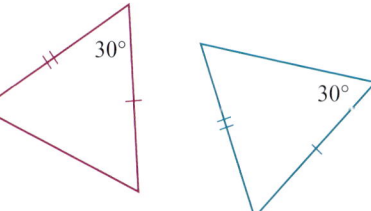

MEASUREMENT & GEOMETRY

3 Which triangles are congruent? Give a reason. (Diagrams are not to scale and all lengths are in centimetres.)

a

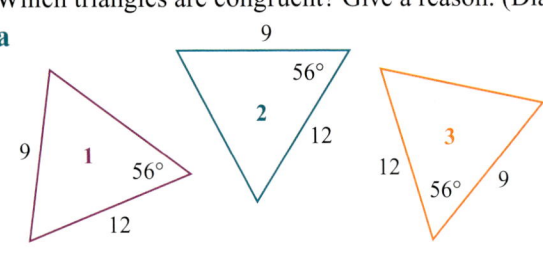

b

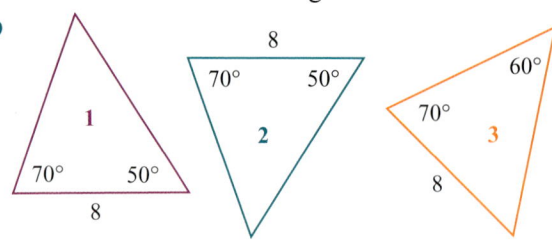

c

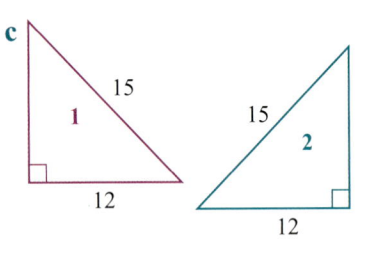 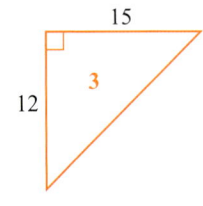

d

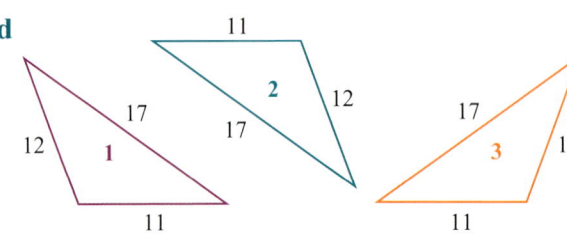

e

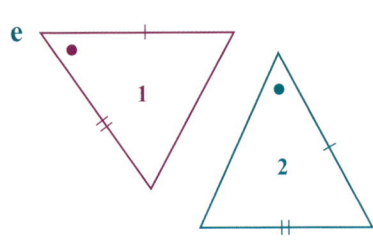 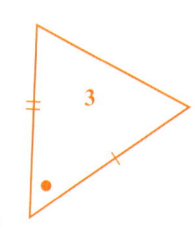

f

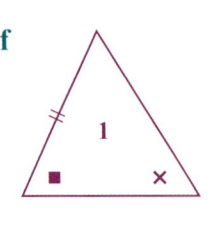 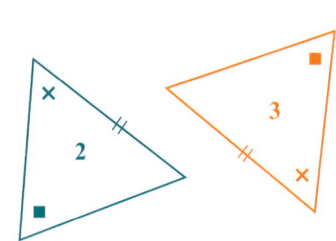

EXAMPLE 3

State why the following pairs of triangles are congruent and find the values of the pronumerals.

a

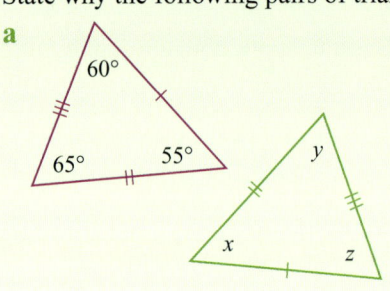

b

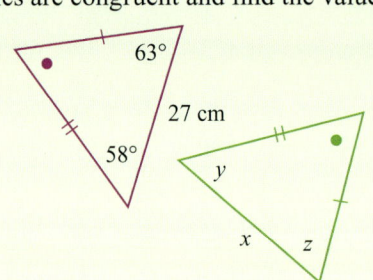

c

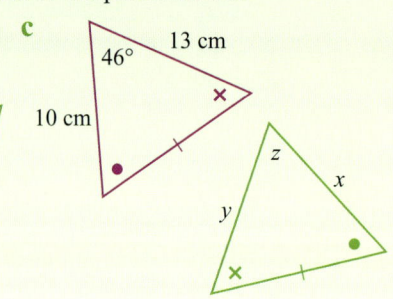

	Solve	Think	Apply
a	SSS: $x = 55°$, $y = 65°$, $z = 60°$	There are three pairs of equal sides. Matching angles are opposite matching sides; hence, x and 55°, y and 65°, and z and 60° are pairs of matching angles.	Use one of the congruency tests to show that the triangles are congruent. The remaining pairs of matching angles and sides are then equal.
b	SAS: $x = 27$ cm, $y = 58°$, $z = 63°$	There are two pairs of equal sides and the angles included by these sides are equal. x and 27 cm are a pair of matching sides, and y and 58°, and z and 63° are pairs of matching angles.	
c	AAS: $x = 10$ cm, $y = 13$ cm, $z = 46°$	There are two pairs of equal angles and the pair of equal sides are matching sides.	

4 State why the following pairs of triangles are congruent and find the values of the pronumerals.

a
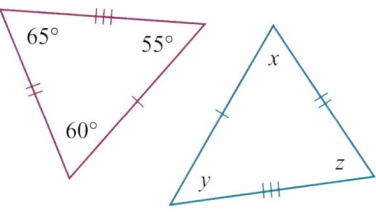

b
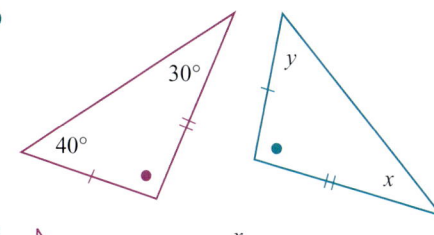

c
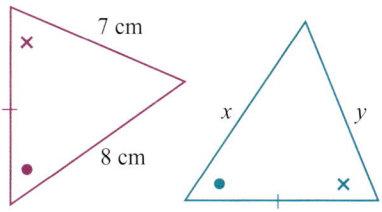

d
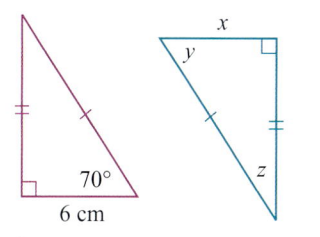

e
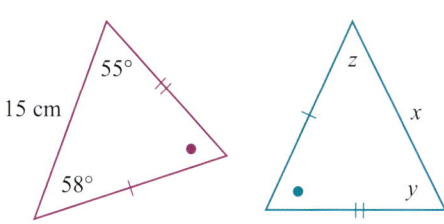

f
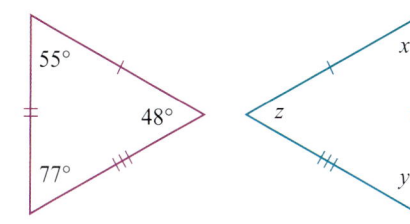

g
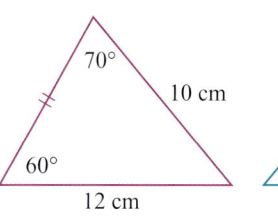

h
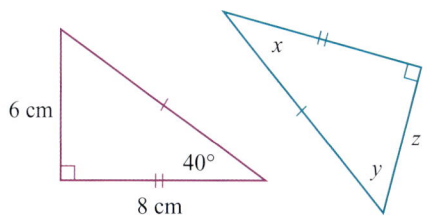

C Formal proofs of congruent triangles

EXAMPLE 1

AC and *BD* are straight lines that intersect at *P* such that *AP = PD* and *BP = PC*.
Prove that:
a $\triangle ABP \equiv \triangle DCP$
b $AB = DC$
c $\angle BAP = \angle CDP$

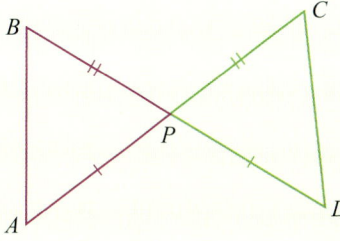

 ≡ is the symbol for congruency. It is read as 'is congruent to'.

	Solve		Think	Apply
a	$AP = DP$ (given) $BP = CP$ (given) $\angle APB = \angle DPC$ (Vertically opposite angles are equal.) Hence $\triangle ABP \equiv \triangle DCP$ (SAS)		Data is the information given about the triangles, either on the diagram or listed. There are two pairs of equal sides and the angles included by these sides are equal.	Look for pairs of equal matching sides and angles that will satisfy one of the congruency tests.
b	$AB = DC$ (Matching sides in congruent $\triangle$s are equal.)			
c	$\angle BAP = \angle CDP$ (Matching angles in congruent $\triangle$s are equal.)			

1 Prove the following.

a $\triangle ACD \equiv \triangle ACB$

b $\angle DAC = \angle BAC$

c $\angle ADC = \angle ABC$

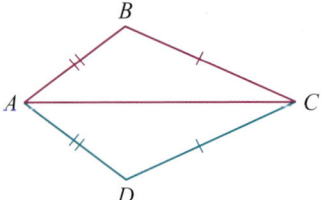

2 Prove the following.

a $\triangle ABP \equiv \triangle DCP$

b $BP = PC$

c $AB = DC$

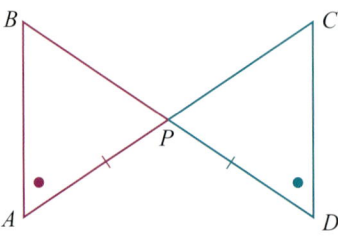

3 Prove the following.

a $\triangle ABP \equiv \triangle CDP$

b $AP = PC$

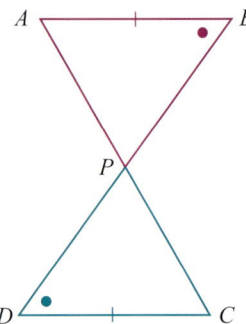

4 $ABCD$ is a rectangle and $DE = CE$. Prove the following.

a $\triangle AED \equiv \triangle BEC$

b E is the midpoint of AB (that is $AE = EB$).

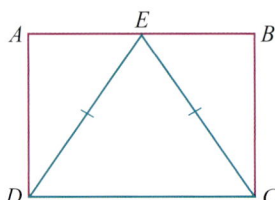

5 Prove the following.

a $\triangle PTQ \equiv \triangle STR$

b $PQ = SR$

c $\angle PQT = \angle SRT$

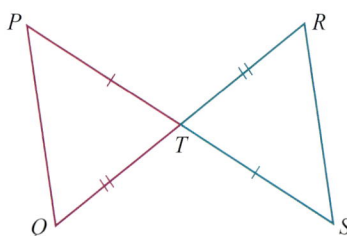

6 PQS is an isosceles triangle with $PS = PQ$ and $PR \perp SQ$.
Prove the following.

a $\triangle PRS \equiv \triangle PRQ$ **b** $\angle PSR = \angle PQR$

c $SR = QR$ **d** $\angle SPR = \angle QPR$

e Complete the following two properties of isosceles
triangles which have been proven above.

    i The angles opposite the equal sides of an isosceles triangle _____.

    ii A line drawn from the vertex of an isosceles triangle and
perpendicular to its base bisects the _____ and the _____ of
the triangle.

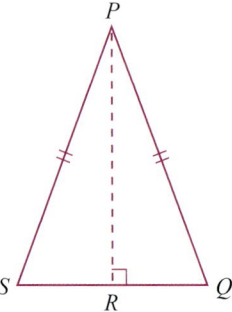

7 $\angle ADC = \angle ABC$ and $AC \perp DB$. Prove the following.

   a $\triangle ACD \equiv \triangle ACB$

   b $\triangle ABD$ is an isosceles triangle.

   c Complete the following: If two angles of a triangle are equal, then the sides opposite these angles are _____; that is, it is an _____ triangle.

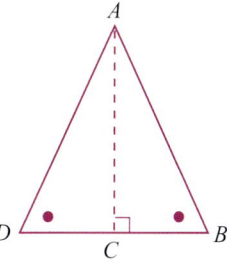

8 $WZ = WX$ and Y is the midpoint of ZX ($ZY = YX$). Prove the following.

   a $\triangle WZY \equiv \triangle WXY$

   b $\angle WYZ = \angle WYX$

   c $\angle WYZ = 90°$ and $\angle WYX = 90°$

   d $\angle ZWY = \angle XWY$

   e Complete: A line drawn from the vertex of an isosceles triangle to the midpoint of its base is _____ to the base and _____ the angle at the vertex.

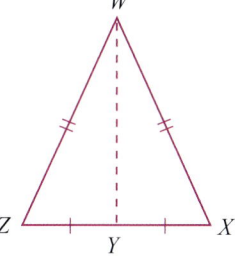

9 An equilateral triangle is one with three sides of equal length.

   a Are all equilateral triangles isosceles triangles?

   b $\triangle ABC$ is an equilateral triangle. Using the properties of isosceles triangles, complete the following.

   $AC = AB$ so $\angle C = \angle$____.

   $AB = BC$ so $\angle C = \angle$____.

   Hence $\angle C = \angle$____ $= \angle$____; that is, the three angles of an equilateral triangle are _____.

   c Prove that each angle of an equilateral triangle is $60°$.

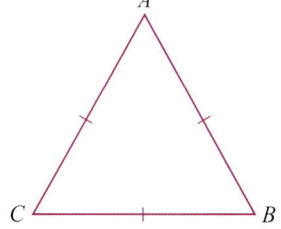

10 $ABCD$ is a parallelogram. ($AB \cdot DC$ and $AD \cdot BC$)

   Prove the following.

   a $\triangle ABC \equiv \triangle CDA$ **b** $AB = DC$

   c $AD = BC$ **d** $\angle B = \angle D$

   e Complete:

   i The opposite sides of a parallelogram _____.

   ii The opposite angles of a parallelogram _____.

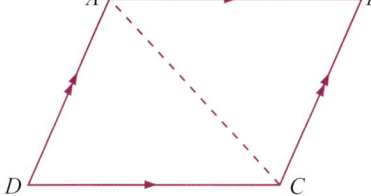

11 $PQRS$ is a parallelogram. The diagonals intersect at T.

   Using the result of question **10**, prove the following.

   a $\triangle PQT \equiv \triangle RST$.   **b** $PT = RT$

   c $QT = ST$

   d Complete: The diagonals of a parallelogram _____.

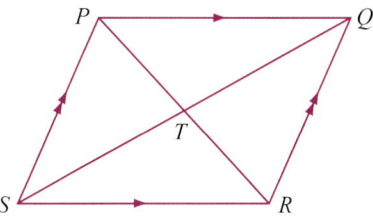

12 The diagram shows the rectangle $ABCD$ with $\triangle ADC$ and $\triangle BCD$ drawn separately. Prove the following.

   a $\triangle ADC \equiv \triangle BCD$ **b** $AC = BD$

   c Complete: The diagonals of a rectangle are _____.

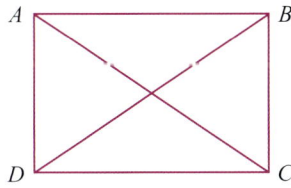 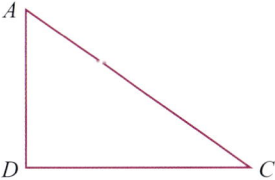 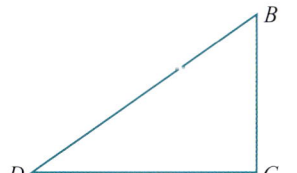

13 *ABCD* is a rhombus (a parallelogram with all sides equal).
The diagonals intersect at *E*. Prove the following.

   a Using the result from question **11** part **d**, $\triangle ADE \equiv \triangle ABE$.

   b $\angle AED = \angle AEB = 90°$

   c $\angle DAE = \angle BAE$

   d Complete:

      i The diagonals of a rhombus intersect at ____.

      ii The diagonals of a rhombus ____ the angles of the rhombus.

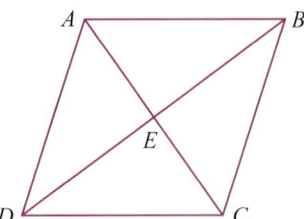

14 *ABCDE* is a regular pentagon (that is all sides and angles equal).

   a Prove that *AC* = *AD*.

   b Hence prove that all the diagonals are equal in length.

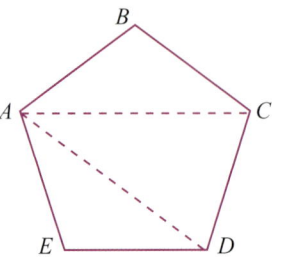

 D # Similar triangles

Two triangles are congruent if they have exactly the same shape and size.
If the shape is identical, but not the size, two triangles are similar.

 'In proportion' means 'in the same ratio'.

If two triangles are similar, then they have three pairs of angles that are equal and three pairs of matching sides that are in proportion. Conversely, if two triangles have three pairs of angles that are equal and three pairs of matching sides that are in proportion, then the triangles are similar.

Investigation 1 Similar triangles

 The matching sides in similar triangles are opposite pairs of equal angles.

1 a Using a protractor, draw two equiangular triangles (two triangles with two pairs of equal angles).
Note: If two pairs of angles are equal, the third pair must also be equal. An example is shown.

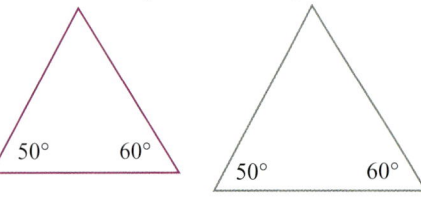

   b Measure the lengths of the sides of the triangles to the nearest millimetre.

   c Complete the statements:

      i $\dfrac{\text{longest side of the large triangle}}{\text{longest side of the small triangle}} = $ ____

      ii $\dfrac{\text{shortest side of the large triangle}}{\text{shortest side of the small triangle}} = $ ____

      iii $\dfrac{\text{other side of the large triangle}}{\text{other side of the small triangle}} = $ ____

   d If two triangles are equiangular, are the lengths of their matching sides in proportion?

   e If two triangles are equiangular, are they similar?

MEASUREMENT & GEOMETRY

2 a Using a ruler and a pair of compasses, draw a triangle with sides 3.5 cm, 4.5 cm and 5.5 cm.
b Draw another triangle with sides 7 cm, 9 cm and 11 cm.
c Measure the angles of both triangles to the nearest degree.
d What is the ratio of the lengths of the matching sides?
e What is the enlargement factor?
f If two triangles have their sides in the same ratio, are they equiangular?
g If two triangles have their sides in the same ratio, are they similar?

3 a Draw a triangle with sides 3 cm and 4 cm, making the angle between these sides 50°.
b Draw another triangle with sides 6 cm and 8 cm and the included angle 50°.
c Measure the angles of both triangles to the nearest degree. Are these triangles equiangular?
d Measure the length of the third side of each triangle. Are the lengths of the three pairs of matching sides in proportion?
e Are these triangles similar?
f Draw another triangle with sides 6 cm and 8 cm, and an angle that is not the included angle 50°.
g By measuring the other angles and side of this triangle, determine whether or not it is similar to the first two triangles.
h If two triangles have two pairs of sides in proportion and a pair of angles equal, are they similar?

4 a Draw a right-angled triangle with hypotenuse 6 cm and one other side 4 cm.
b Draw another right-angled triangle with hypotenuse 9 cm and one other side 6 cm.
c Measure the angles of both triangles. Are these triangles equiangular?
d Measure the length of the third side of each triangle. Are the lengths of the three pairs of matching sides in proportion?
e Are these triangles similar?

From Investigation 1 it can be seen that it is not necessary to show that there are three pairs of equal angles and three pairs of matching sides in proportion for two triangles to be similar. There are four sets of minimum conditions that can be used. These four tests for similar triangles are listed below.

Tests for similar triangles

1 If two angles of one triangle are equal to two angles of another triangle, then the two triangles are similar.

2 If the three sides of one triangle are proportional to three sides of another triangle, then the triangles are similar.

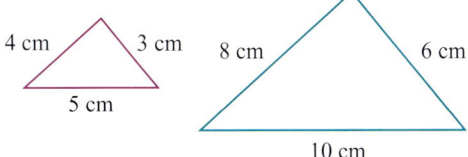

3 If two sides of one triangle are proportional to two sides of another triangle and the included angles are equal, then the triangles are similar.

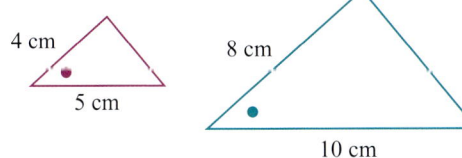

4 If the hypotenuse and a second side of a right-angled triangle are proportional to the hypotenuse and a second side of another right-angled triangle, then the triangles are similar.

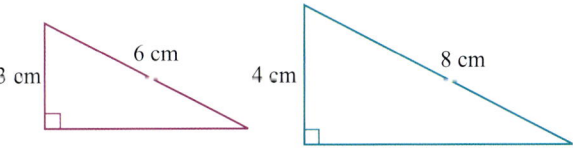

EXAMPLE 1

State the test used to show that the following pairs of triangles are similar. (Diagrams are not to scale and all lengths are in centimetres.)

a 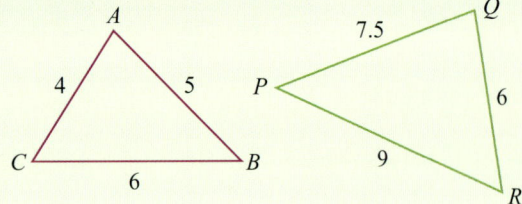 **b**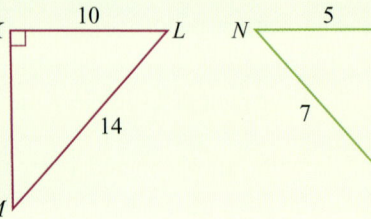

c 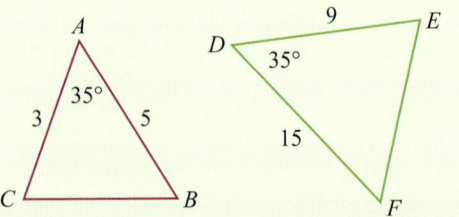 **d**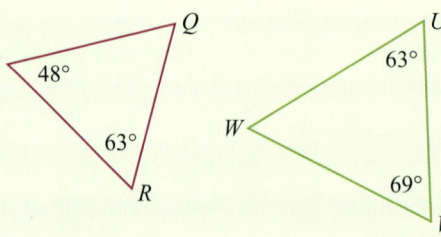

	Solve	Think	Apply
a	Test 2: There are three pairs of sides in proportion.	$\dfrac{PR}{BC} = \dfrac{QR}{AC} = \dfrac{PQ}{BA} = 1.5$ Start with the ratio of the longest sides in the two triangles, then the shortest sides, then the other pair of sides.	Look for pairs of equal angles and pairs of matching sides in proportion that will satisfy one of the tests for similarity.
b	Test 4: The hypotenuse and a second side of right-angled $\triangle ONP$ are proportional to the hypotenuse and a second side of right-angled $\triangle KLM$.	$\dfrac{ON}{KL} = \dfrac{NP}{LM} = 0.5$ $\angle O = \angle K = 90°$	
c	Test 3: Two sides of $\triangle FDE$ are proportional to two sides of $\triangle BAC$ and the included angles are equal.	$\dfrac{DF}{AB} = \dfrac{DE}{AC} = 3$ $\angle FDE = $ included $\angle BAC$	
d	Test 1: Two angles of $\triangle PQR$ are equal to two angles of $\triangle UVW$.	$\angle U = \angle R$ $\angle W = 48°$ (Angle sum of $\triangle UVW = 180°$.) Hence $\angle W = \angle P$	

Exercise 4D

1 State the test used to show that the following pairs of triangles are similar. (All lengths are in centimetres.)

a 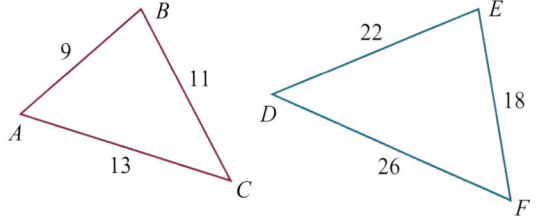 **b**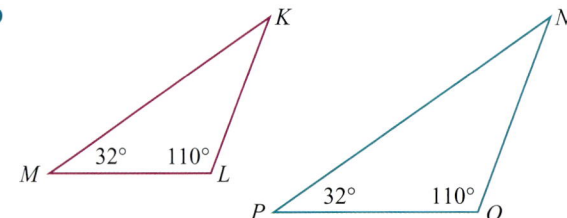

c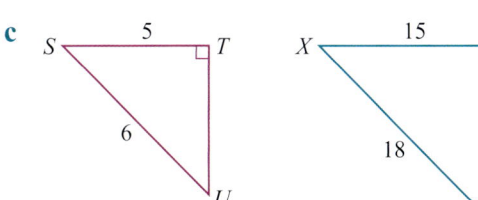

d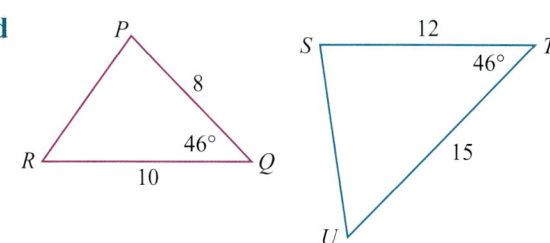

e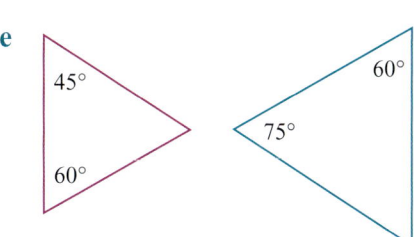

f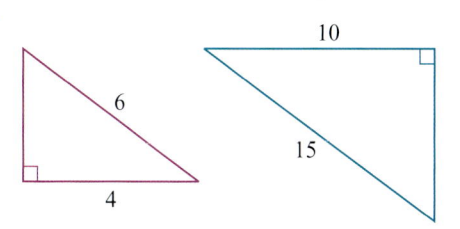

g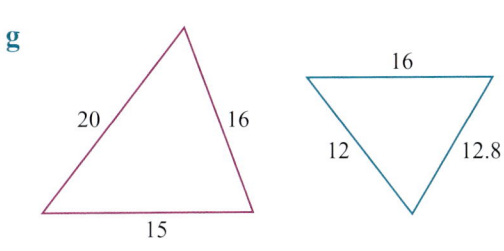

h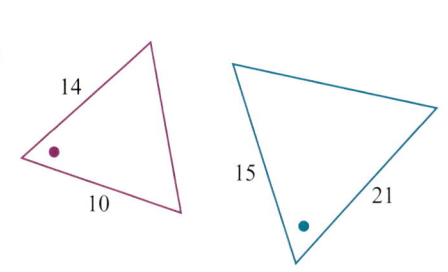

EXAMPLE 2

State why the following pairs of triangles are not similar. (Diagrams are not to scale and all lengths are in centimetres.)

a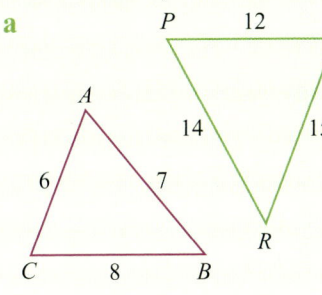

b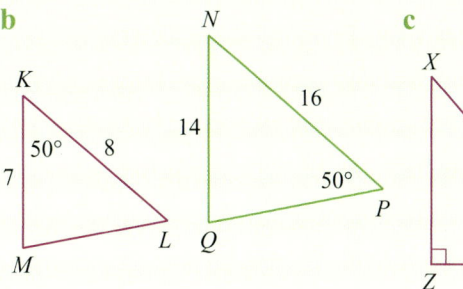

c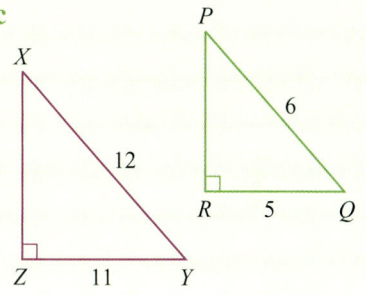

	Solve	Think	Apply
a	Only two pairs of sides are in proportion.	$\dfrac{PR}{AB} = \dfrac{PQ}{AC} = 2$ but $\dfrac{QR}{CB} = \dfrac{15}{8} \neq 2$	Check that all conditions of the test are satisfied.
b	$\angle P$ is not included by the sides in proportion.	$\dfrac{NP}{KL} = \dfrac{NQ}{KM} = 2$ but $\angle P$ is not included by the sides NP and NQ.	
c	The proportion of the second sides of the triangles is not the same as the proportion of the hypotenuses of the triangles.	$\angle R = \angle Z = 90°$ $\dfrac{PQ}{XY} = \dfrac{6}{12} = 0.5$ but $\dfrac{RQ}{ZY} = \dfrac{5}{11} \neq 0.5$ $\therefore \dfrac{PQ}{XY} \neq \dfrac{RQ}{ZY}$	

2 State why the following pairs of triangles are not similar.

a

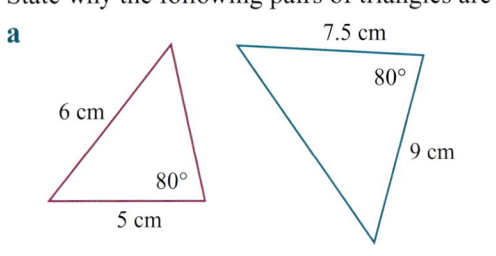

b

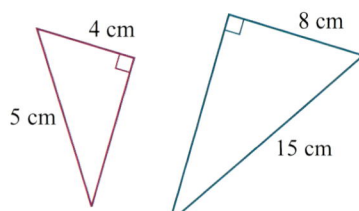

c

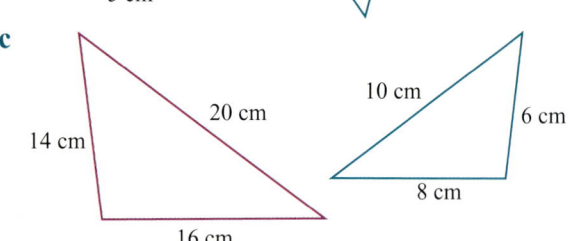

d

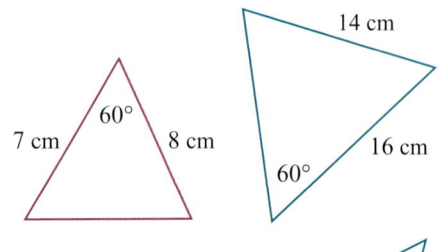

e

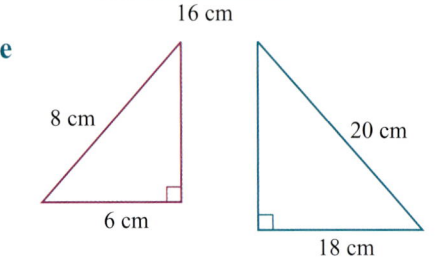

f

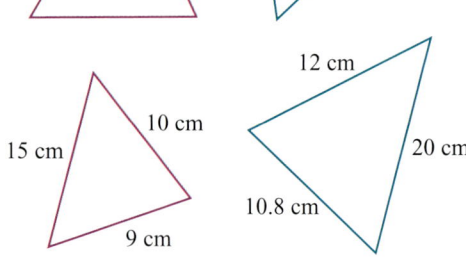

EXAMPLE 3

Determine whether the following pairs of triangles are similar.

a

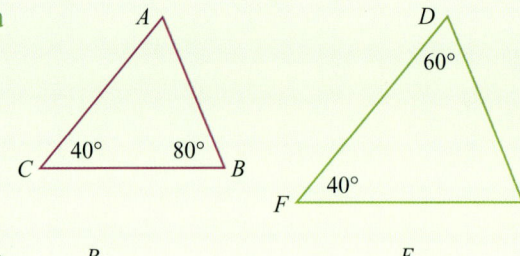

b

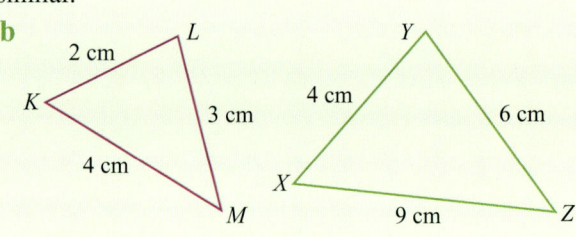

c

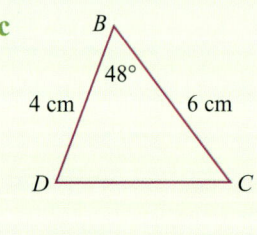
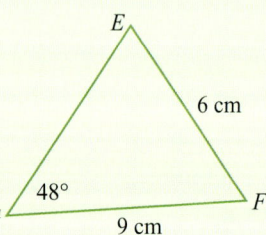

d

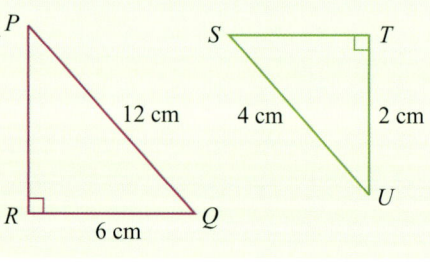

	Solve	Think	Apply
a	$\angle A = 60°$ or $\angle E = 80°$: Hence $\triangle ABC \, ||| \, \triangle DEF$. The triangles are similar.	$\angle A = 60°$ (Angle sum of $\triangle ABC = 180°$.) or $\angle E = 80°$ (Angle sum of $\triangle DEF = 180°$.) Two pairs of equal angles.	Look for pairs of equal angles and pairs of matching sides in proportion that will satisfy one of the four tests for similar triangles.
b	$\dfrac{XY}{KL} = \dfrac{4}{2} = 2$ $\dfrac{YZ}{LM} = \dfrac{6}{3} = 2$ but $\dfrac{XZ}{KM} = \dfrac{9}{4} \neq 2$ The triangles are not similar.	It is not possible to find three pairs of matching sides that are in proportion.	||| is the symbol for similarity. It is read as 'is similar to'.

EXAMPLE 3 CONTINUED

	Solve	Think	Apply
c	$\dfrac{BD}{EF} = \dfrac{BC}{GF} = \dfrac{2}{3}$ $\angle DBC = \angle EGF$ but $\angle EGF$ is not the angle included by EF and GF. The triangles are not similar.	Two pairs of sides are in proportion but the equal angles are not both the included angles.	Look for pairs of equal angles and pairs of matching sides in proportion that will satisfy one of the four tests for similar triangles.
d	$\angle PRQ = \angle STU \ (= 90°)$ $\dfrac{PQ}{SU} = \dfrac{RQ}{TU} = \dfrac{3}{1}$ Hence $\triangle PQR \parallel\mid\mid \triangle SUT.$	The triangles are right-angled. The hypotenuse and a second side of the right-angled triangle are proportional to those of the other right-angled triangle.	

3 Determine whether the following pairs of triangles are similar. Give reasons. (Diagrams are not drawn to scale. All lengths are in centimetres.)

a
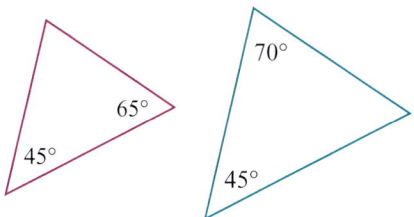

b
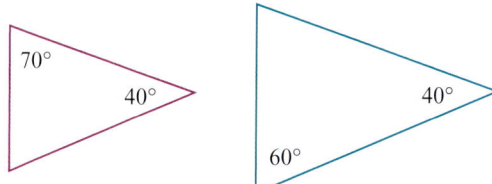

c
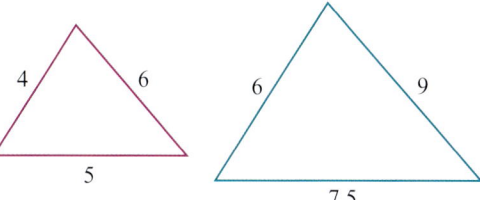

d
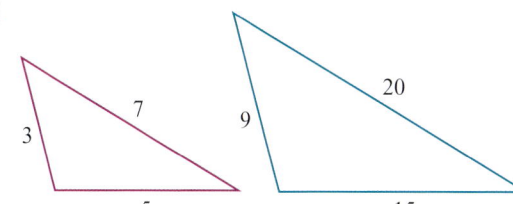

e
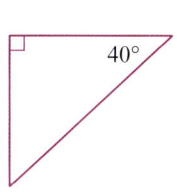

f
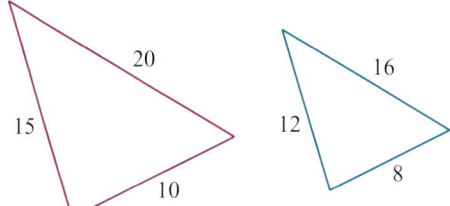

g
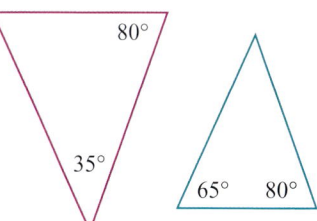

h
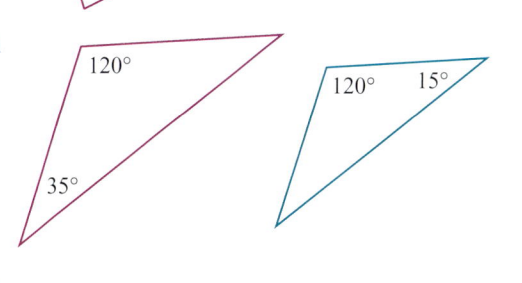

i
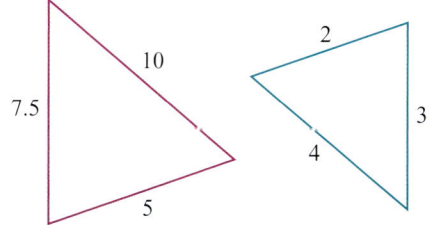

j
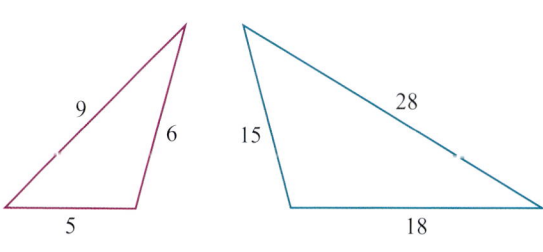

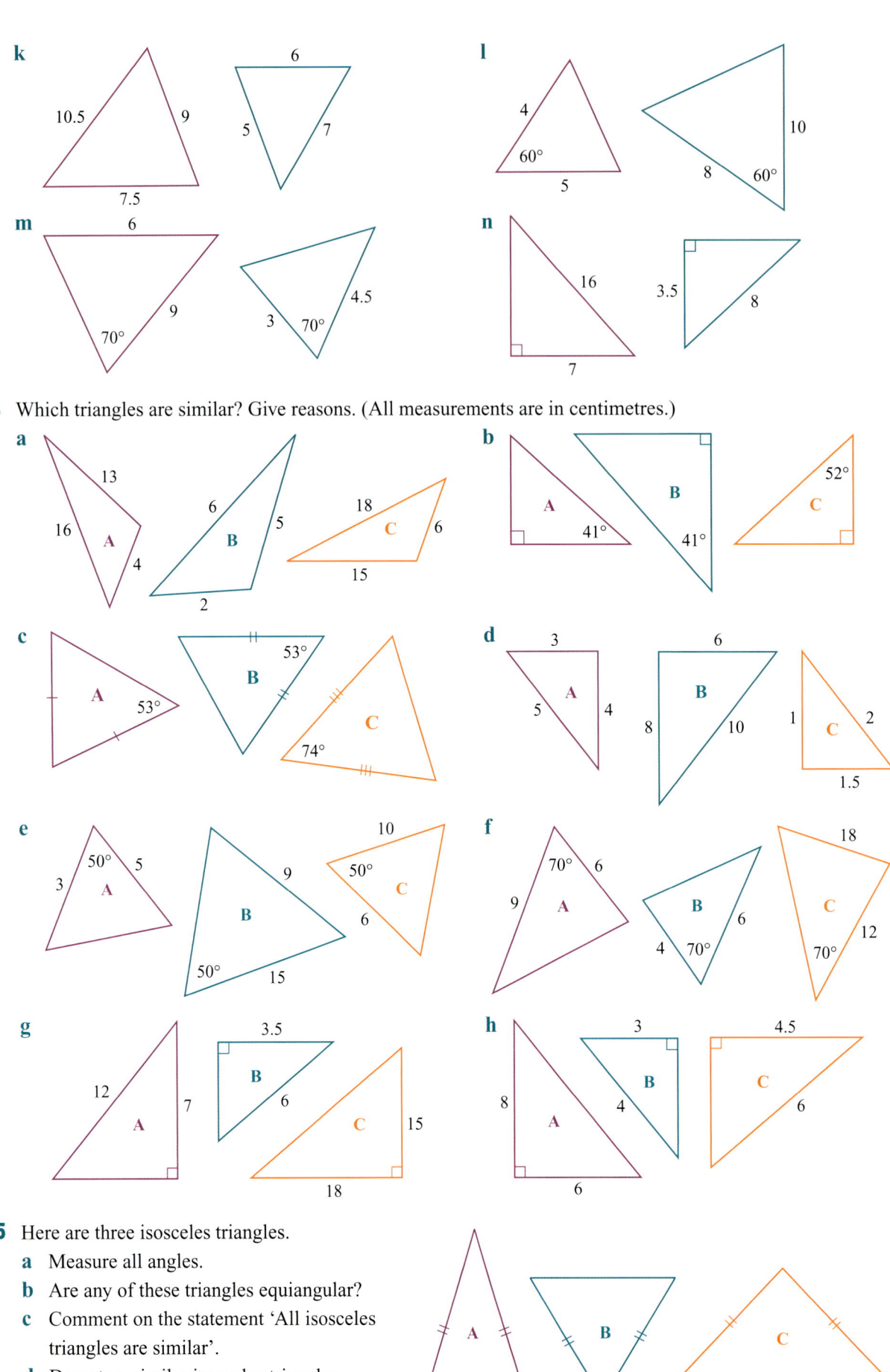

k

l

m

n

4 Which triangles are similar? Give reasons. (All measurements are in centimetres.)

a

b

c

d

e

f

g

h

5 Here are three isosceles triangles.
   a Measure all angles.
   b Are any of these triangles equiangular?
   c Comment on the statement 'All isosceles triangles are similar'.
   d Draw two similar isosceles triangles.

EXAMPLE 4

Find the lengths of the unknown sides in this pair of similar triangles.

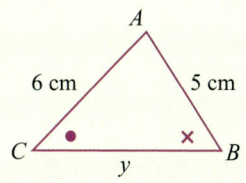

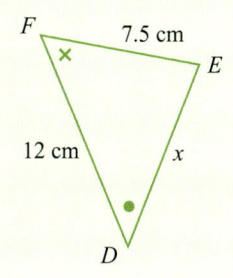

Solve	Think	Apply
Method 1 To find x: $k = \dfrac{7.5}{5} = 1.5$ $x = 1.5 \times 6 = 9$ To find y: $k = \dfrac{5}{7.5} = \dfrac{2}{3}$ $y = \dfrac{2}{3} \times 12 = 8$ $\therefore x = 9$ cm and $y = 8$ cm	*Method 1* To find x: EF and AB are a pair of matching sides. $k = \dfrac{EF}{AB} = \dfrac{7.5}{5} = 1.5$ The length of each side in the second triangle is 1.5 times the length of its matching side in the first triangle. Hence $DE = k \times CA$. To find y: AB and EF are a pair of matching sides. $k = \dfrac{AB}{EF} = \dfrac{5}{7.5} = \dfrac{2}{3}$ The length of each side in the first triangle is $\dfrac{2}{3}$ times the length of its matching side in the second triangle. Hence $CB = k \times DF$.	*Method 1* Find the scale factor, k, using a known pair of matching sides. Apply this scale factor to the side corresponding to the unknown side.
Method 2 $\dfrac{x}{6} = \dfrac{7.5}{5}$ $x = 6 \times \dfrac{7.5}{5} = 9$ $\dfrac{y}{12} = \dfrac{5}{7.5}$ $y = 12 \times \dfrac{5}{7.5} = 8$ $\therefore x = 9$ cm and $y = 8$ cm	*Method 2* AB and EF, BC and DF, CA and DE are pairs of corresponding sides in the two triangles. Take the ratio of each pair in the same order.	*Method 2* Identify the pairs of corresponding sides and equate their ratios in the appropriate order.

6 Find the lengths of the unknown sides in the following pairs of similar triangles.

a

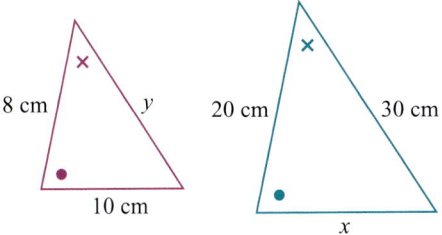

b

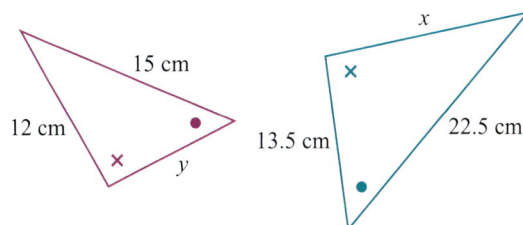

c

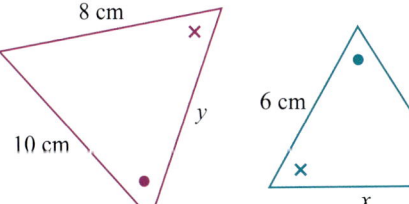

d

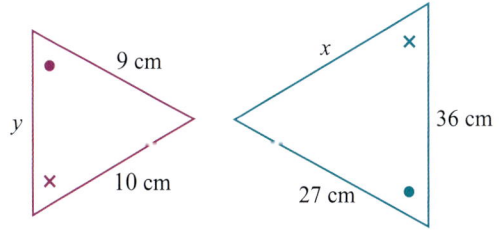

e
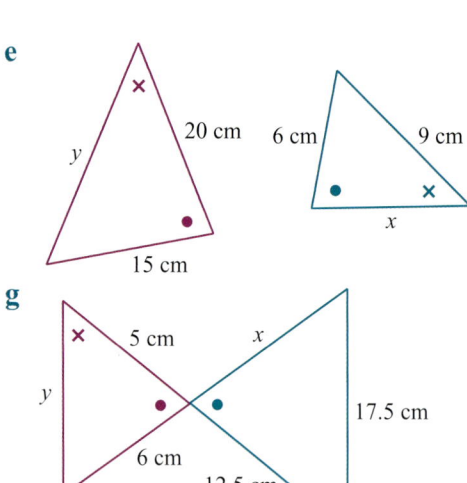

20 cm
6 cm
9 cm
y
x
15 cm

f
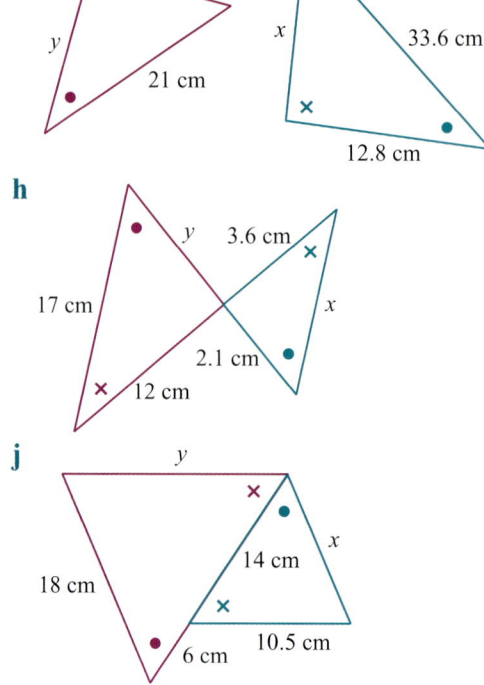

15 cm
y
21 cm
x
33.6 cm
12.8 cm

g

5 cm x
y
17.5 cm
6 cm
12.5 cm

h

y 3.6 cm
17 cm
2.1 cm
x
12 cm

i

20 cm
y
x
10 cm
8 cm   27.5 cm

j

y
14 cm
x
18 cm
10.5 cm
6 cm

● EXAMPLE 5

Find the length of the unknown side in the following pair of similar triangles.

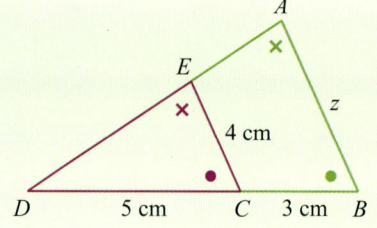

A
E
4 cm
z
D 5 cm C 3 cm B

Solve	Think	Apply
	Draw △ABD and △ECD separately. E A 4 cm z D 5 cm C D 8 cm B	Draw the similar triangles separately.
Method 1 $k = \dfrac{8}{5}$ $z = \dfrac{8}{5} \times 4$ $= 6.4$ cm	*Method 1* DB and DC are a pair of corresponding sides. Hence $k = \dfrac{DB}{DC} = \dfrac{8}{5}$. AB and EC are corresponding sides. Hence $AB = k \times EC$.	*Method 1* Find the scale factor using a known pair of matching sides. Apply this factor to the side corresponding to the unknown side.
Method 2 $\dfrac{z}{4} = \dfrac{8}{5}$ $z = 4 \times \dfrac{8}{5}$ $= 6.4$ cm	*Method 2* AB and EC, DB and DC are pairs of corresponding sides. Hence $\dfrac{AB}{EC} = \dfrac{DB}{DC}$.	*Method 2* Identify the pairs of matching sides and equate their ratios in the appropriate order.

MEASUREMENT & GEOMETRY

7 Find the length of the unknown side in the following pairs of similar triangles.

a

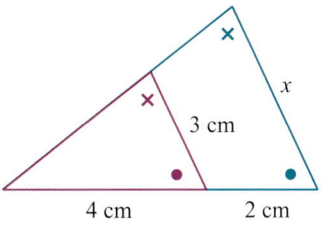

3 cm
x
4 cm
2 cm

b

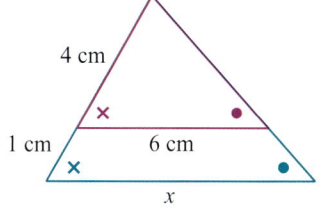

4 cm
1 cm
6 cm
x

c

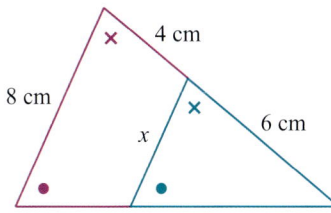

4 cm
8 cm
x
6 cm

d

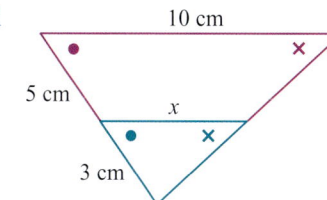

10 cm
5 cm
x
3 cm

e

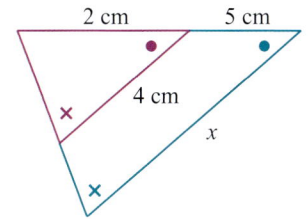

2 cm
5 cm
4 cm
x

f

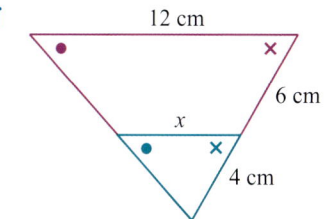

12 cm
6 cm
x
4 cm

g

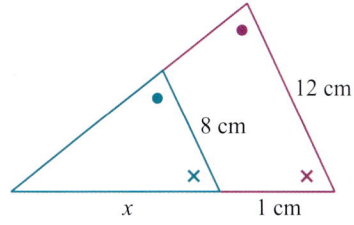

12 cm
8 cm
x
1 cm

h

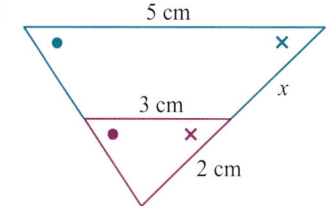

5 cm
3 cm
x
2 cm

EXAMPLE 6

When a 30 cm ruler stands vertically on the ground it casts a shadow 25 cm long. At the same time a flagpole casts a shadow of length 7 m.

a Name a pair of similar triangles, giving reasons for your answer.

b What is the height of the flagpole?

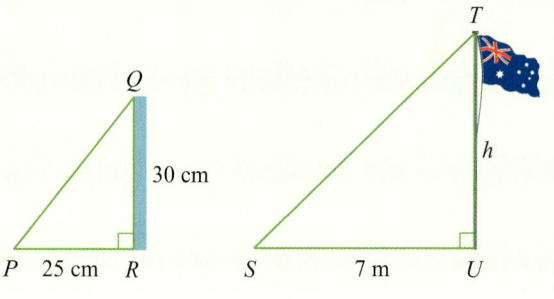

	Solve	Think	Apply
a	$\angle U = \angle R$ and $\angle S = \angle P$ $\triangle STU \,|||\, \triangle PQR$ because two angles of one triangle are equal to two angles of the other triangle.	$\angle U = \angle R = 90°$ as the ruler and the flagpole are vertical to the ground. $\angle TSU = \angle QPR$ as the sun's rays make the same angle with the ground.	Look for pairs of equal angles and pairs of matching sides in proportion that will satisfy one of the four tests for similar triangles.
b	$\dfrac{h}{30} = \dfrac{700}{25}$ $h = 30 \times \dfrac{700}{25}$ $= 840$ cm or 8.4 m	TU and QR, SU and PR are pairs of matching sides in similar triangles. Hence $\dfrac{TU}{QR} = \dfrac{SU}{PR}$. Change measurements to the same units.	Identify the pairs of corresponding sides and equate their ratios in the appropriate order.

8 On a sunny day the shadow cast by a tree is 8.4 m long. At the same time the shadow cast by a 30 cm ruler is 45 cm long.

   a Name a pair of similar triangles, giving reasons for your answer.

   b What is the height of the tree?

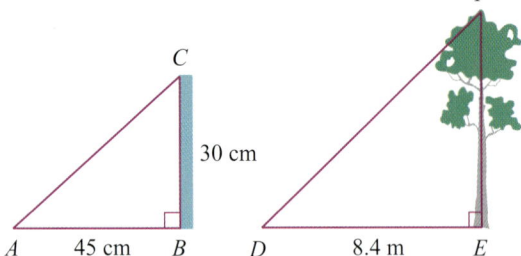

9 A fence surrounding a football field is 1.2 m high. At a certain time of the day the shadow of the fence was 1.8 m long and the shadow of the goalposts was 13.5 m long.

   a Name a pair of similar triangles, giving reasons for your answer.

   b What is the height of the goalposts?

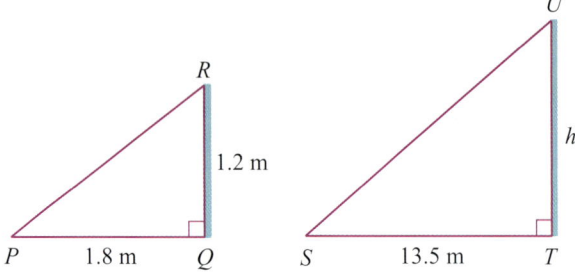

10 When a man of height 170 cm stands 8 m from the base of a street light his shadow is 2 m long.

   a Name a pair of similar triangles, giving reasons.

   b What is the height of the light above the ground?

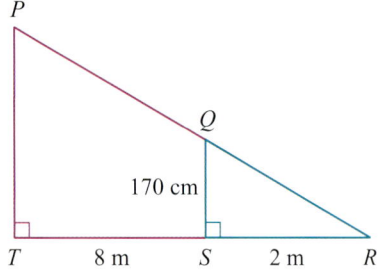

11 A ramp for a BMX track is to be built with two vertical supports *VY* and *WX*. The dimensions are shown in the diagram.

   a Name a pair of similar triangles, giving reasons.

   b Calculate the length of the inner support (*VY*).

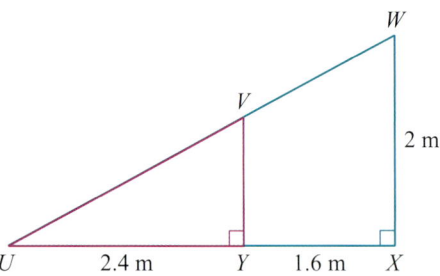

12 A cone has a vertical height of 10 cm and radius 4 cm. The top of this cone is sliced off at a height of 7 cm above its base. What will be the radius of the circular cross-section cut off?

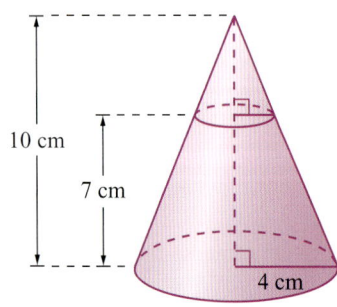

MEASUREMENT & GEOMETRY

 **E** # Polygons

A polygon is a plane shape with straight sides. Polygons are named according to the number of sides. The simplest polygon is a triangle, which has an interior angle sum of 180°. A quadrilateral has four sides and an angle sum of 360°.

 ## EXAMPLE 1

Find the sum of the interior angles of a heptagon.

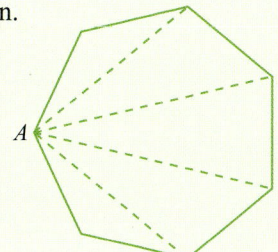

A heptagon and a septagon are different terms meaning a seven-sided figure.

Solve	Think	Apply
Choose one vertex and draw all the diagonals from it. Sum of interior angles = 5 × 180° = 900°	A heptagon is a polygon with 7 sides. The diagonals divide the heptagon into five triangles. The sum of the interior angles of the heptagon is equal to the sum of the interior angles of the five triangles.	Choose any vertex and draw all the diagonals from it. The sum of the interior angles of the polygon is equal to the sum of the interior angles of the triangles formed.

Exercise 4E

1 a Draw any pentagon (5-sided polygon) and label one of its vertices *A*.
   b Draw all the diagonals from *A*.
   c Find the interior angle sum of the pentagon.

2 Repeat question **2** with different polygons, drawing diagonals from one vertex only. Complete the table below. Example 1 shows this for the heptagon.

Polygon	Number of sides	Number of triangles	Angle sum of polygon
Quadrilateral	4	2	2 × 180° = 360°
Pentagon	5		
Hexagon			
Heptagon	7	5	5 × 180° = 900°
Octagon			
Nonagon			
Decagon			
n-gon			

3 Complete the following statement:

The sum of the measure of the interior angles of any *n*-sided polygon is _____ × 180°.

● EXAMPLE 2

Find the size of each interior angle of a regular dodecagon.

A dodecagon has 12 sides.

Solve	Think	Apply
Sum of angles = (12 − 2) × 180° = 1800° Each angle = 1800° ÷ 12 = 150°	Sum of angles of dodecagon = (12 − 2) × 180°. A regular polygon has all its sides and interior angles equal.	Find the sum of the interior angles and then divide by the number of equal interior angles.

---

4 Find the size of each interior angle in these regular polygons.

  a pentagon   **b** hexagon   **c** heptagon

  d octagon   **e** nonagon   **f** decagon

5 A regular polygon has 24 sides.

  a Find the sum of the interior angles.

  b Find the size of each interior angle.

● EXAMPLE 3

Find *x*, giving reasons for your answers.

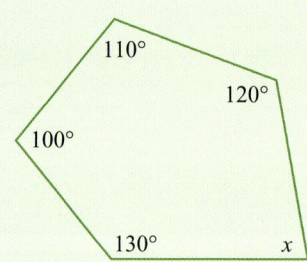

Solve	Think	Apply

Angle sum of polygon = 3 × 180° = 540°
 x + 130° + 100° + 110° + 120° = 540°
          x + 460° = 540°
              x = 80°
	Angle sum of an *n*-gon is
	 (*n* − 2) × 180°.
	 This is a pentagon so the angle sum = 3 × 180°
	 = 540°.
		Find the sum of the angles of the polygon. Form an equation from which the value of the pronumeral can be found.

---

6 Find the value of *x* in these pentagons. Give a reason for your answer.

  a   **b**   **c**

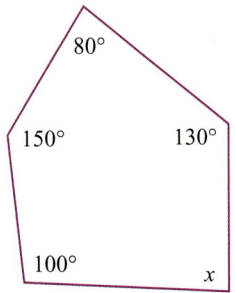 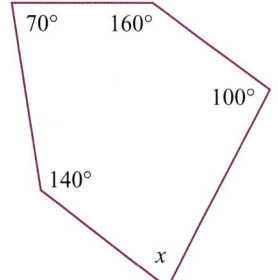 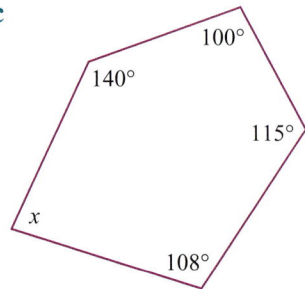

7 a Find the angle sum of a hexagon.

b Find the value of *x* in these hexagons.

i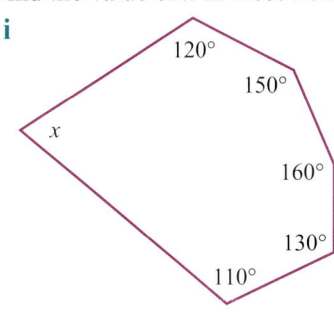

ii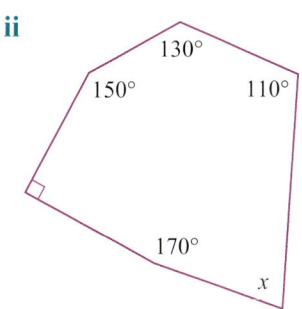

iii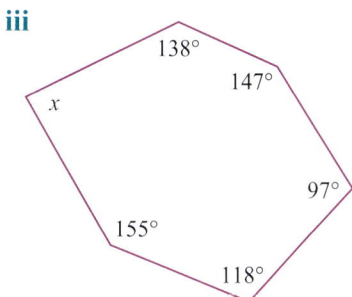

8 Find *x*, giving a brief reason.

a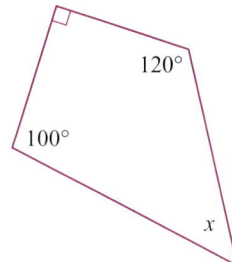

b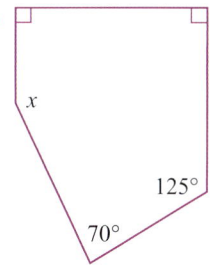

c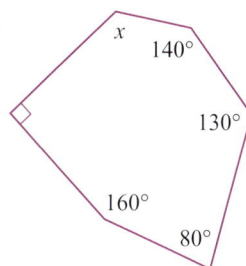

d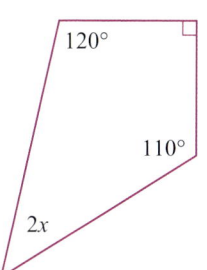

e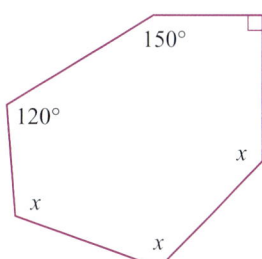

f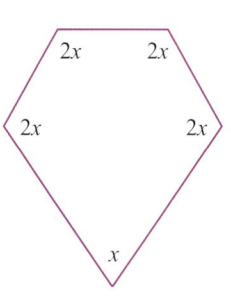

g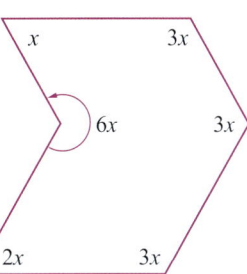

h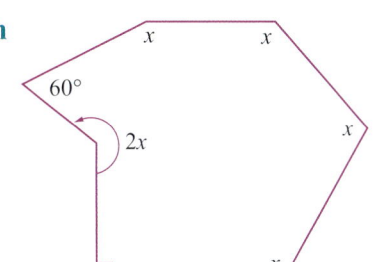

i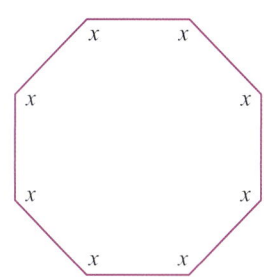

9 A pentagon has three right angles and two other equal angles. Find the size of each of these two equal angles.

10 A hexagon has two right angles and all other angles equal. Find the size of each of the equal angles.

Investigation 2 Exterior angle sum

The exterior angles of a polygon are formed by extending each side in the same order, as shown in the diagram. Each exterior angle is the angle between the extended side and the side that is adjacent to it.

1 The five exterior angles of a pentagon are shown. As this is a regular pentagon all exterior angles are equal.
   a Measure the exterior angles.
   b Find the sum of the five exterior angles.

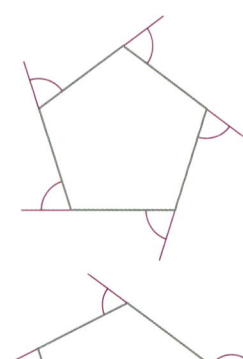

2 A non-regular pentagon is shown opposite.
   a Measure the five exterior angles.
   b Find the sum of the exterior angles.

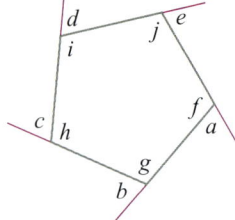

3 a Draw a hexagon.
   b Measure the exterior angles.
   c Find the sum of the exterior angles.

4 a Draw an octagon.
   b Measure the exterior angles.
   c Find the sum of the exterior angles.

5 Complete the following.
   The sum of the exterior angles of any polygon is ____.

6 Complete the following.
   a i $(a + f) = $ ___   ii $(b + g) = $ ___
   b The sum of the exterior and interior angles is
      $(a + f) + (b + g) + (c + h) + (d + i) + (e + j) = 5 \times$ ___.
   c The sum of the interior angles is $f + g + h + i + j = 3 \times$ ___.
   d The sum of the exterior angles is ____.

EXAMPLE 4

a Find the size of each exterior angle of a regular decagon.
b Hence, find the size of each interior angle.
c Find the angle sum of a decagon.

	Solve	Think	Apply
a	Exterior angle $= \dfrac{360°}{10}$ $= 36°$	From Investigation 2, the sum of the exterior angles of any polygon is 360°. A regular decagon has 10 equal exterior angles.	Exterior angle $= \dfrac{360°}{n}$ where n is the number of equal exterior angles (number of equal sides).
b	Each interior angle $= 180° - 36° = 144°$	The sum of each interior angle and its exterior angle is 180°.	Interior angle $= 180° -$ exterior angle.
c	Angle sum $= 144° \times 10$ $= 1440°$	A regular decagon has 10 equal interior angles.	Multiply the size of each interior angle by the number of angles.

11 **a** Find the size of each exterior angle of a regular octagon.

    b Use the exterior angle to find the size of the interior angle. Give a reason for the answer.

    c Hence, find the angle sum of an octagon.

12 **a** Find the size of each exterior angle of a regular 20-sided polygon.

    b Find the size of each interior angle.

    c Hence, find the angle sum of a 20-sided polygon.

● EXAMPLE 5

a The measure of each exterior angle of a regular polygon is 12°. How many sides does this polygon have?

b An irregular polygon has one exterior angle of 80° and all the others are 7°. How many sides does this polygon have?

	Solve	Think	Apply
a	$12° = \dfrac{360°}{n}$ $n = \dfrac{360°}{12°} = 30$ The polygon has 30 sides.	Each exterior angle $= \dfrac{360°}{n}$ where n is the number of sides. Substitute exterior angle $= 12°$.	Use $n = \dfrac{360°}{\text{angle size}}$
b	$80° + (n-1) \times 7° = 360°$ $80° + 7°(n-1) = 360°$ $7°(n-1) = 280°$ $n - 1 = 40$ $n = 41$ The polygon has 41 sides.	Let n equal the number of sides. If one exterior angle is 80°, then the other $(n-1)$ exterior angles are each 7°.	The sum of the exterior angles of any polygon is 360°.

13 Each exterior angle of a regular polygon is 15°. Find the number of sides of the polygon.

14 Find the number of sides in regular polygons with these exterior angles.

    a 10°   **b** 18°   **c** 24°   **d** 90°

15 An irregular polygon has one exterior angle of 100° and all others 13°. How many sides does it have?

16 Find the number of sides in an irregular polygon with:

    a one exterior angle of 60° and all others 10°   **b** one exterior angle of 120° and all others 12°

    c one exterior angle of 45° and all others 15°.

17 An irregular polygon has two exterior angles twice the size of the others. If the other exterior angles are 15°, find the number of sides.

18 An irregular polygon has two exterior angles twice the size of the others. If the other exterior angles are 20°, find the number of sides.

Language in mathematics

1 Explain why all congruent triangles are similar but not all similar triangles are congruent.

2 Define and list all the properties of these triangles.
   a isosceles triangles
   b equilateral triangles

3 What is the meaning of the term 'equiangular'? Are all equiangular figures similar?

4 If two angles of a triangle are equal to two angles of another, explain why the remaining third pair of angles must be equal.

5 a Explain why $\triangle ABC$ is not congruent to $\triangle ADC$.
   b What extra piece of information would make them congruent?

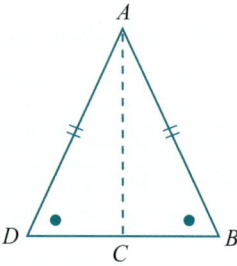

6 Define the exterior angle of a polygon.

7 Write two equivalent formulas for the sum of the interior angles of a polygon. Explain the meaning of any pronumerals used.

8 ABCDE is a diagram of a pentagonal-shaped field. The sides have been produced as shown. Cherie stands at A facing P, turns and walks to B. She then turns and walks to C, turns and walks to D, turns and walks to E and then turns and walks back to A. To complete this circuit, through what angle has Cherie walked?

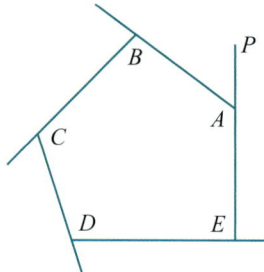

Terms

bisect	congruent	congruency	enlargement	equilateral	exterior
included	interior	isosceles	matching	parallelogram	polygon
proportional	similar	similarity	vertices	vertex	

Check your skills

1 The following is the setting out used to find the value of the pronumeral z in the diagram.
   $x = 20°$ (_____)
   $y = 20°$ (_____)
   $\therefore z = 40°$ (_____)

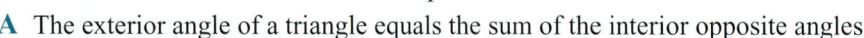

The reason that is not used in the above proof is:
   A The exterior angle of a triangle equals the sum of the interior opposite angles.
   B A straight angle is 180°.
   C The angles opposite the equal sides in an isosceles triangle are equal.
   D Vertically opposite angles are equal.

2 The congruency test used to show that these triangles are congruent is:

A SSS B SAS
C AAS D RHS

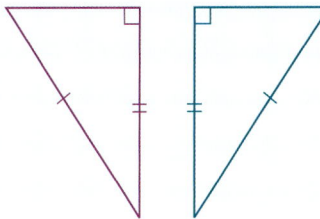

3 The congruency test used to show that these triangles are congruent is:

A SSS B SAS
C AAS D RHS

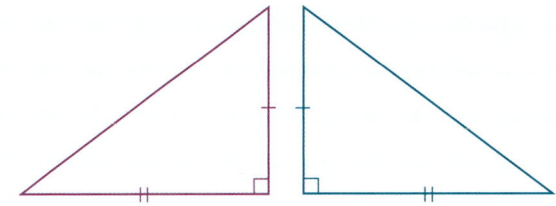

4 The triangles that are congruent are:

A 1 and 2 B 2 and 3
C 1 and 3 D 1, 2 and 3

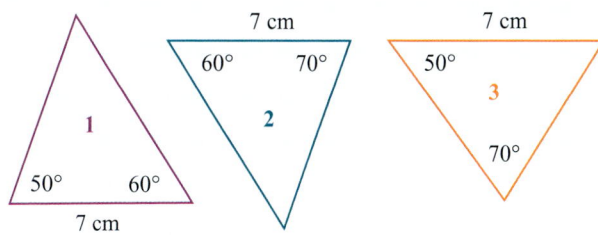

5 The value of the pronumeral in this pair of congruent triangles is:

A 45° B 55°
C 80° D 35°

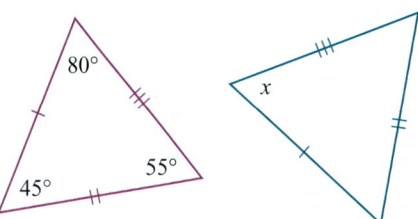

6 The value of the pronumeral in this pair of congruent triangles is:

A 5 cm B 6 cm
C 7 cm D 18 cm

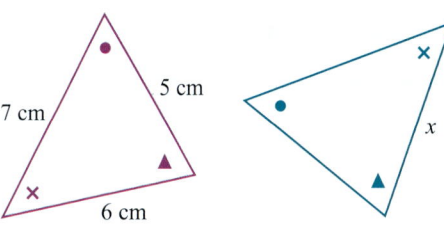

7 In $\triangle ABC$ and $\triangle ADC$:

$$AB = AD \qquad (\underline{\quad})$$
$$AC = \underline{\quad} \qquad (\text{common})$$
$$\angle BAC = \angle DAC \qquad (\text{given})$$
$$\therefore \triangle ABC \equiv \triangle ADC \qquad (\underline{\quad})$$

The missing statements in the above proof are:

A given, AC, SAS B isosceles triangle, AC, SAS
C given, AB, SSS D isosceles triangle, AB, SAS

8 The similar triangles are:

A 1 and 2 B 2 and 3
C 1 and 3 D 1, 2 and 3

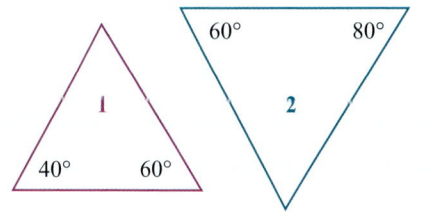
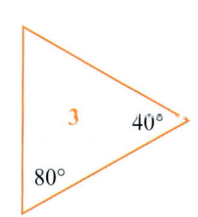

9 The similar triangles are:

A 1 and 2   B 2 and 3

C 1 and 3   D 1, 2 and 3

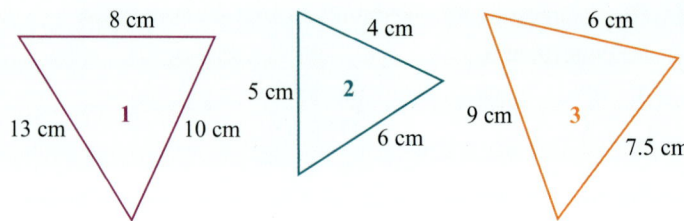

10 The similar triangles are:

A 1 and 2   B 2 and 3

C 1 and 3   D 1, 2 and 3

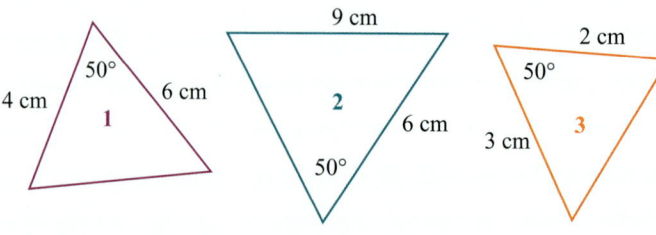

11 The similar triangles are:

A 1 and 2   B 2 and 3

C 1 and 3   D 1, 2 and 3

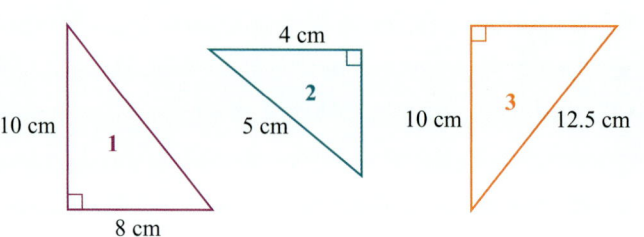

12 These triangles are similar. The enlargement factor (from 1 to 2) is:

A 2   B 3

C 2.4   D 14

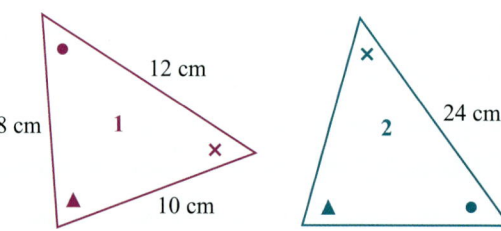

13 The values of the pronumerals in these similar triangles are:

A $x = 15, y = 31.5$ B $x = 15, y = 14$

C $x = 6\frac{2}{3}, y = 31.5$ D $x = 6\frac{2}{3}, y = 14$

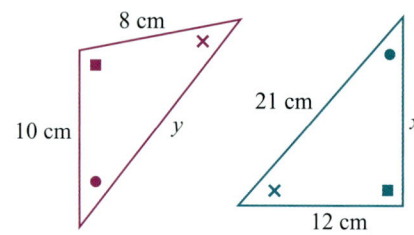

14 The statement about these triangles that is correct is:

A $\dfrac{x}{a} = \dfrac{y}{b}$ B $\dfrac{x}{b} = \dfrac{y}{a}$

C $\dfrac{x}{c} = \dfrac{y}{a}$ D $\dfrac{x}{c} = \dfrac{y}{b}$

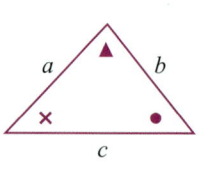 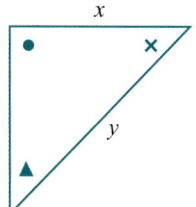

15 The angle sum of an eight-sided polygon is:

A 540°   B 720°   C 900°   D 1080°

16 A ten-sided polygon is called a:

A pentagon   B nonagon   C decagon   D hexagon

17 A regular polygon with 24-sides has interior angle size of:

A 3960°   B 165°   C 4320°   D 180°

18 The value of x in this figure is:

A 145°   B 235°

C 325°   D 35°

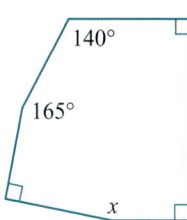

19 A heptagon has three right angles and the other angles are all equal. The size of the equal angles is:

A 900°   B 112.5°   C 157.5°   D 247.5°

20 The exterior angle of a 30-sided regular polygon is:

A 12°   B 168°   C 360°   D 5040°

21 An irregular polygon has one exterior angle of 100° and all others 13°. The number of sides of this polygon is:

A 20   B 21   C 30   D 113

If you have any difficulty with these questions, refer to the examples and questions in the sections listed in the table.

Question	1	2–6	7	8–14	15–21
Section	A	B	C	D	E

4A   Review set

1 $AE \parallel CF$. AE bisects $\angle DAB$. Prove, giving reasons, that $AB = AC$.

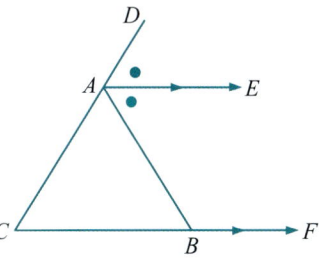

2 State the congruency test used to show that the following triangles are congruent.

a
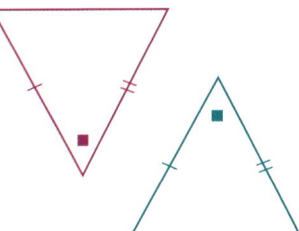

b
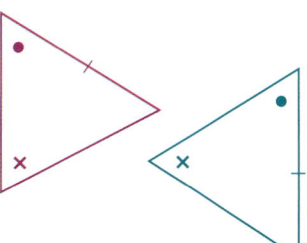

c
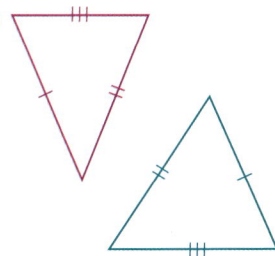

3 State why the following pairs of figures are not congruent.

a
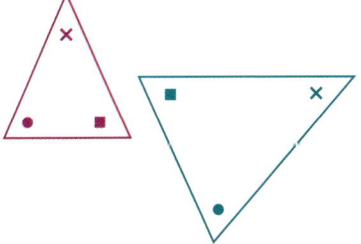

b
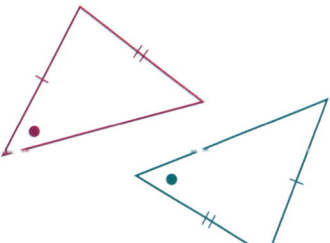

c
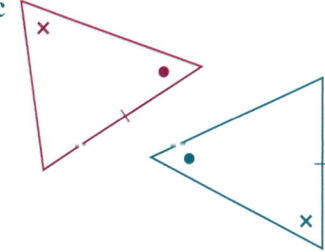

4 Which triangles are congruent? Give a reason for your answer.

a

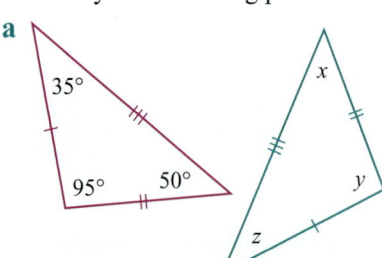 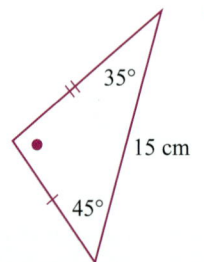

b

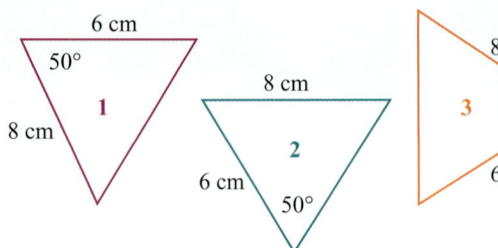 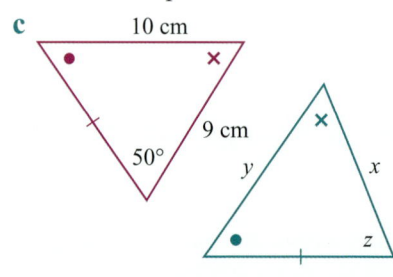

5 State why the following pairs of triangles are congruent and hence find the values of the pronumerals.

a

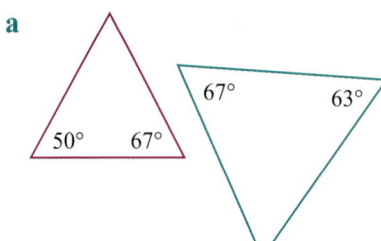

b

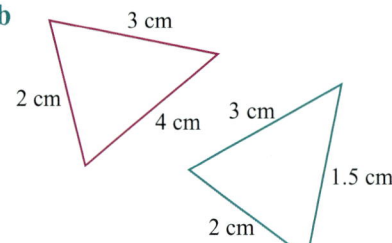

c

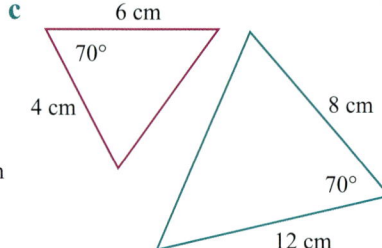

6 Complete the proofs that $\triangle PQT \equiv \triangle RQS$ and $PQ = RQ$.

a In $\triangle PQT$ and $\triangle RQS$:

$$PT = \underline{\quad} \qquad \text{(given)}$$
$$\angle PTQ = \angle RSQ \qquad (\underline{\quad})$$
$$\angle PQT = \angle RQS \qquad (\underline{\quad})$$
$$\therefore \triangle PQT \equiv \triangle RQS \qquad (\underline{\quad})$$

b $\therefore PQ = RQ \qquad (\underline{\quad})$

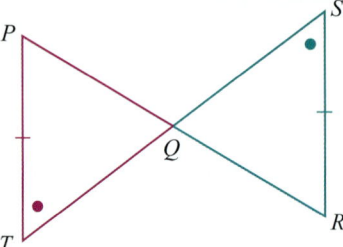

7 State with reasons whether or not the following pairs of triangles are similar.

a

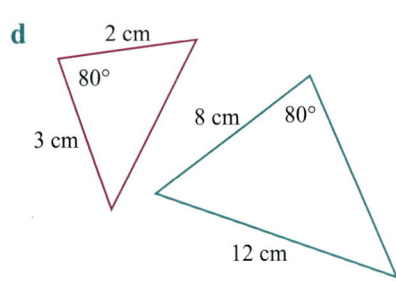

b

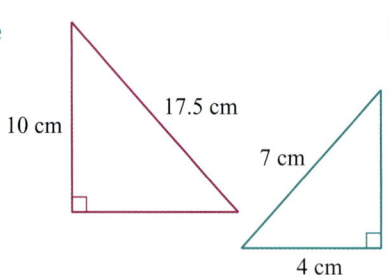

c

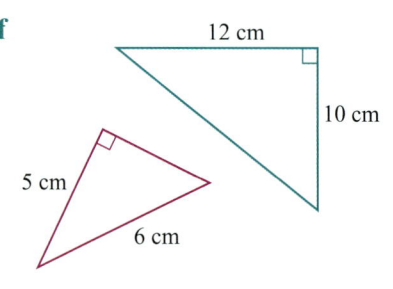

d

e

f

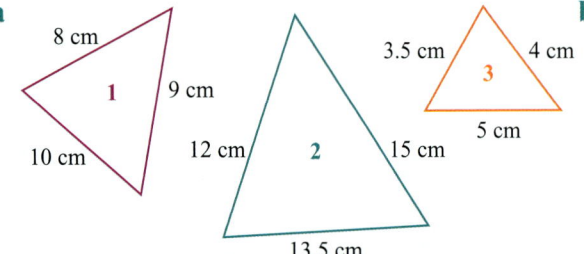

8 Which triangles are similar? State the test used.

a

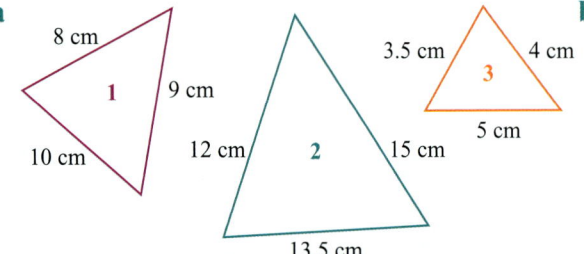

b

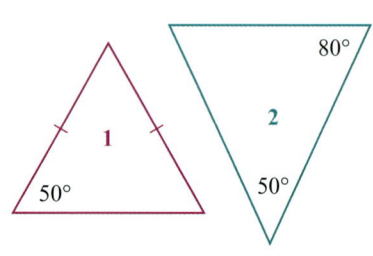

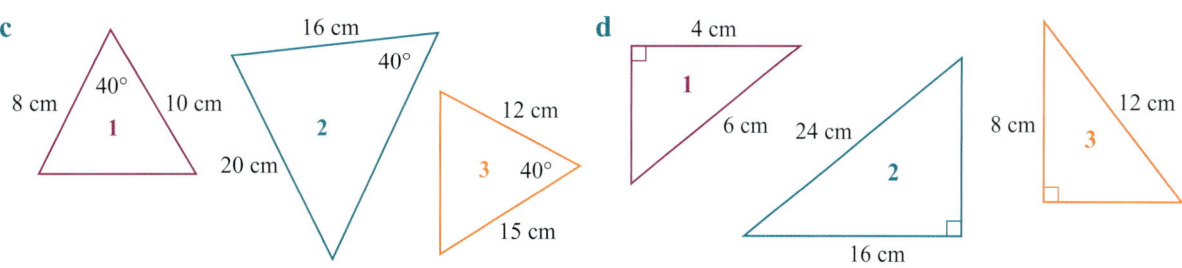

c

d

9 Find the enlargement factor and hence the length of the unknown sides in these pairs of similar triangles.

a
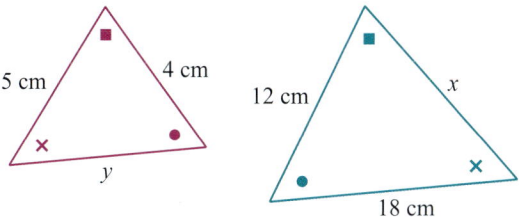

b
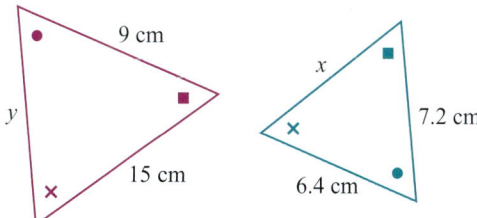

10 Use the ratios of matching sides to find the length of the unknown sides in these pairs of similar triangles.

a
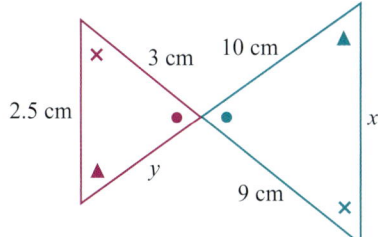

b
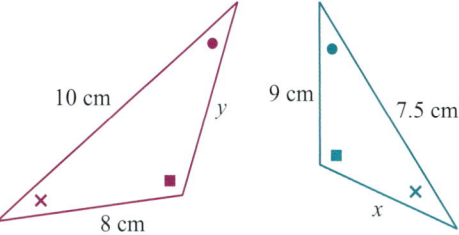

11 **a** Draw a hexagon.
   b Draw all the diagonals from one vertex.
   c Find the angle sum of a hexagon.

12 Find x, giving a reason for your answer.

a
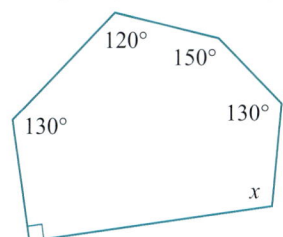

b
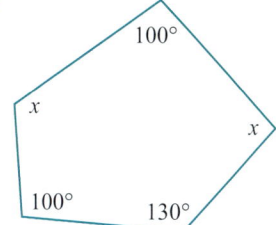

13 Consider a regular octagon.
   a What is the size of each interior angle?   **b** What is the sum of the exterior angles?

14 A regular polygon has exterior angles $10°$.
   a How many sides does it have?   **b** What is the sum of the interior angles?

4B   Review set

1 $AB = AC$ and $DC = DE$. Prove with reasons that $AB \parallel DE$.

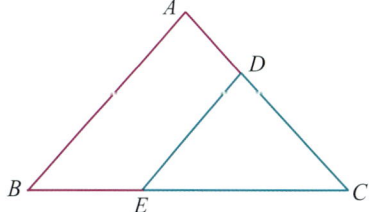

2 State the congruency test used to show that the following triangles are congruent.

a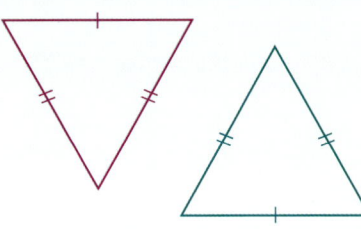

b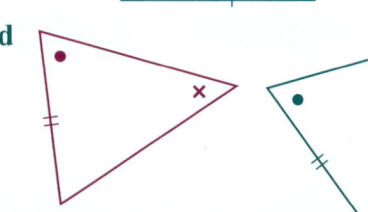

c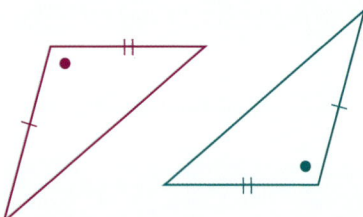

d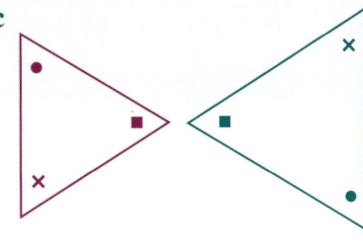

3 State why the following pairs of figures are not congruent.

a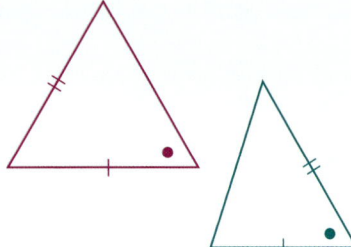

b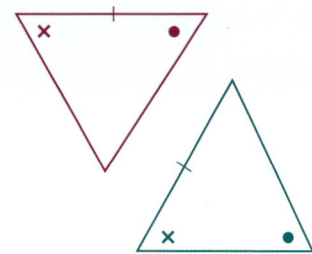

c

4 Which triangles are congruent? Give a reason for your answer.

a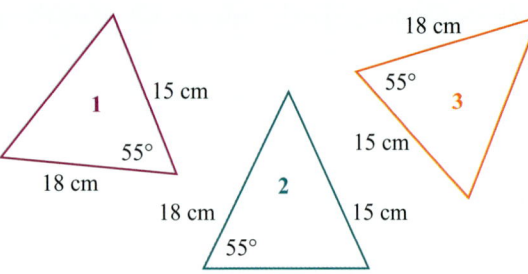

b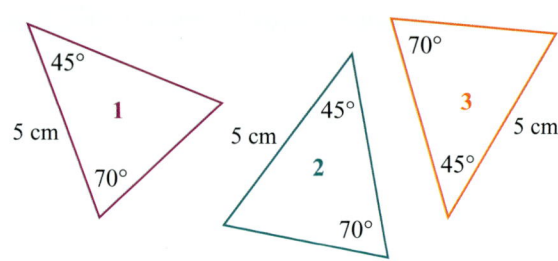

5 State why the following pairs of triangles are congruent. Hence find the values of the pronumerals.

a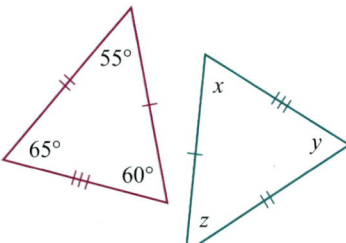

b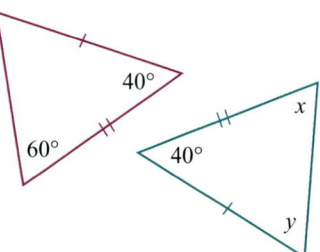

c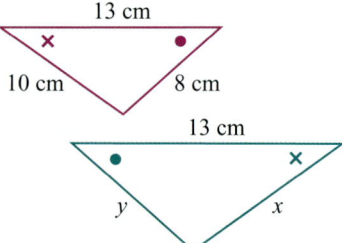
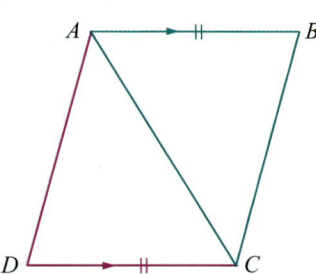

6 Complete the proofs that $\triangle ABC \equiv \triangle CDA$ and $AD = CB$.

  a In $\triangle ABC$ and $\triangle CDA$:

      $AB = $ ____   (given)

      $AC = $ ____   (common)

     $\angle BAC = \angle DCA$ (____)

    $\therefore \triangle ABC \equiv \triangle CDA$ (____)

  b $\therefore AD = $ ____   (matching sides of congruent triangles)

7 State with reasons whether or not the following pairs of triangles are similar.

a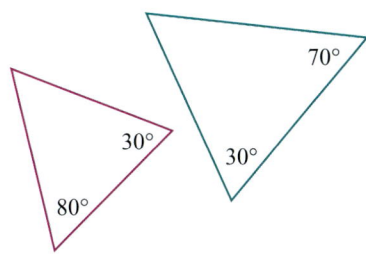

b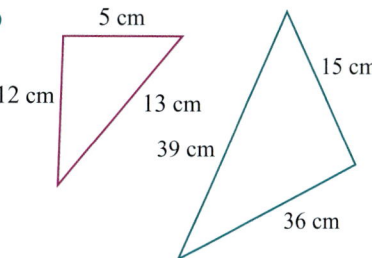

c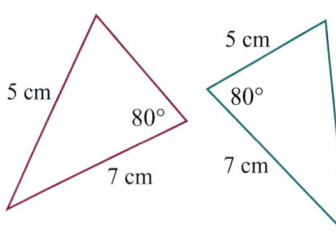

d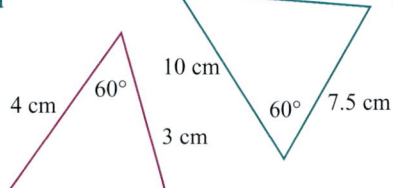

e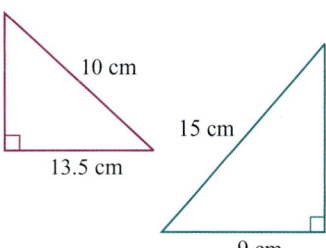

f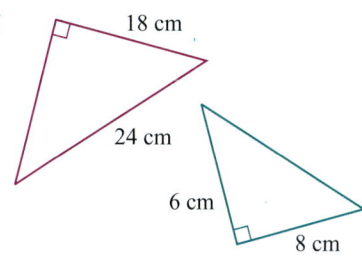

8 Which triangles are similar? State the test used.

a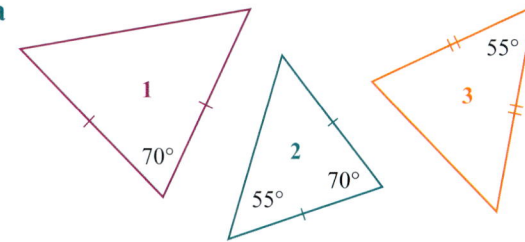

b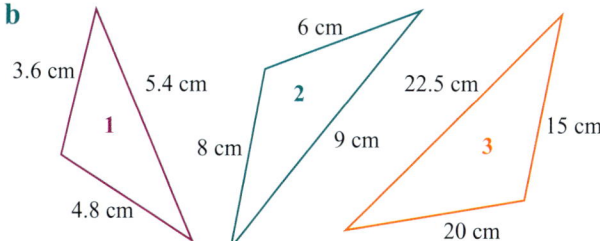

c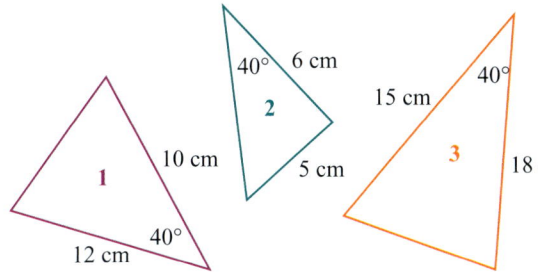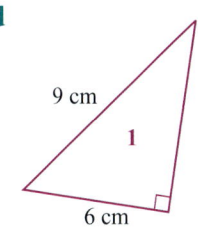

d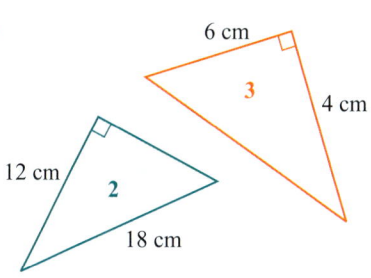

9 Find the enlargement factor and hence the length of the unknown sides in these pairs of similar triangles.

a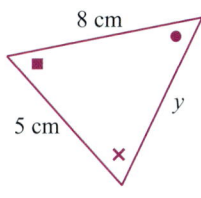

b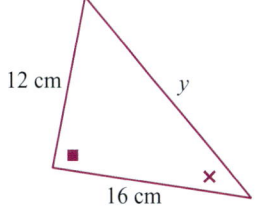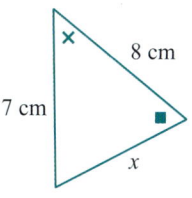

10 Use proportion to find the length of the unknown sides in these pairs of similar triangles.

a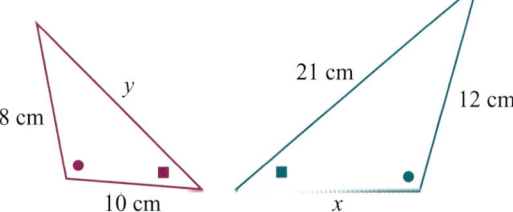

b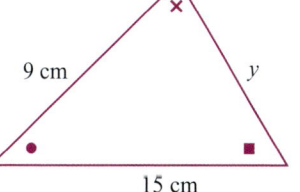

11 **a** Find the angle sum of a dodecagon (12 sides).
   b Find the size of each interior angle of a regular dodecagon.

12 Find x, giving a reason for your answer.

a

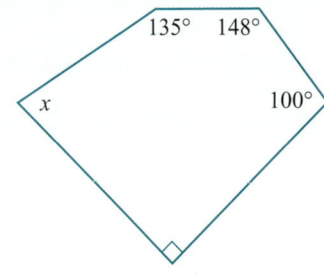

135° 148° 100° x

b

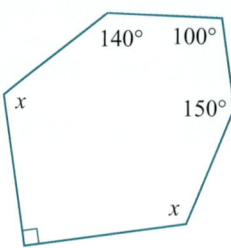

140° 100° 150° x x

13 A nine-sided figure has three right angles and all other angles equal. What is the measure of each of these equal angles?

14 **a** Find the size of each exterior angle of a 25-sided regular polygon.
b Find the size of each interior angle.
c Hence, find the angle sum of a 25-sided polygon.

4C   Review set

1 *IF* bisects $\angle BFG$ and *IG* bisects $\angle FGD$. Prove that $\angle FIG = 90°$.

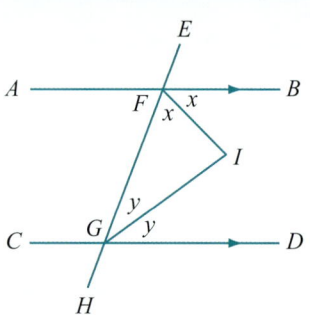

2 State the congruency test used to show that the following pairs of triangles are congruent.

a

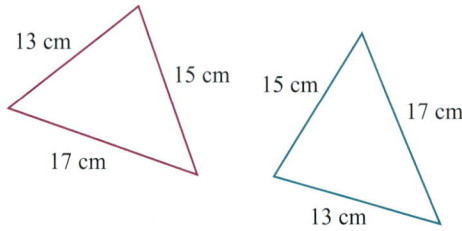

13 cm 15 cm 15 cm 17 cm 17 cm 13 cm

b

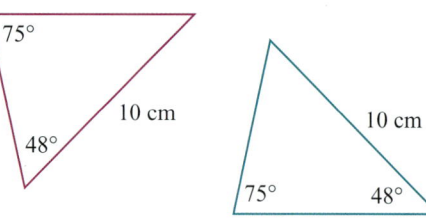

75° 10 cm 48° 75° 48° 10 cm

c

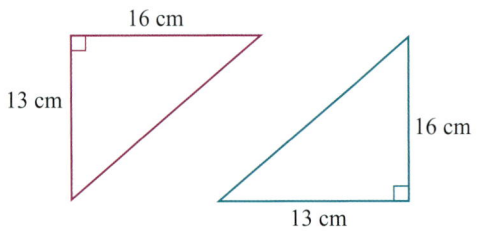

16 cm 13 cm 16 cm 13 cm

d

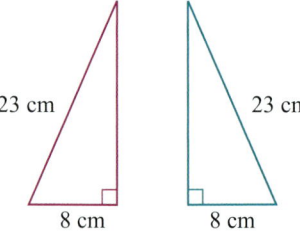

23 cm 23 cm 8 cm 8 cm

3 State why the following pairs of triangles are not congruent.

a

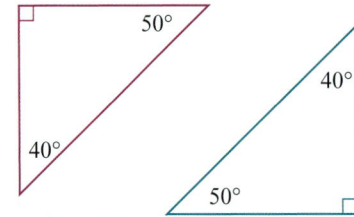

50° 40° 40° 50°

b

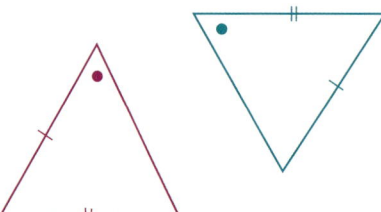

4 Which triangles are congruent. Give a reason for your answer.

a

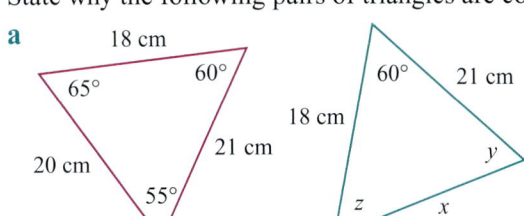

b

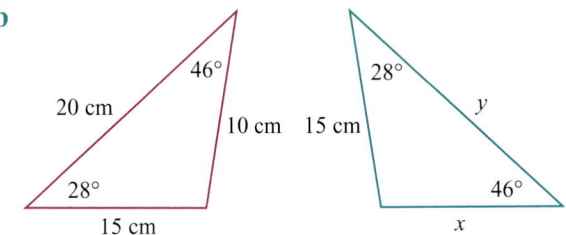

5 State why the following pairs of triangles are congruent and find the values of the pronumerals.

a

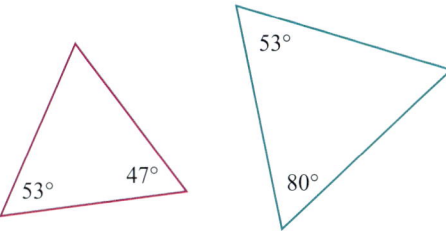

b

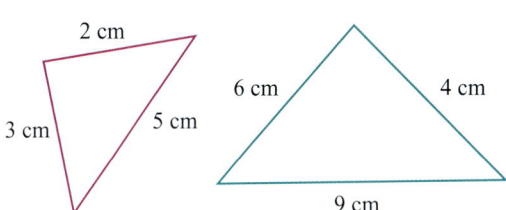

6 $PQ = RS$. $\angle PQS = \angle QSR = 90°$. Prove the following.

a $\triangle PQS \equiv \triangle RSQ$

b $PS = RQ$

c $PS \parallel RQ$

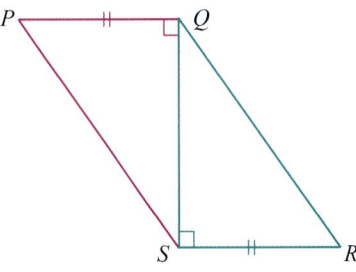

7 State with reasons whether or not the following triangles are similar.

a

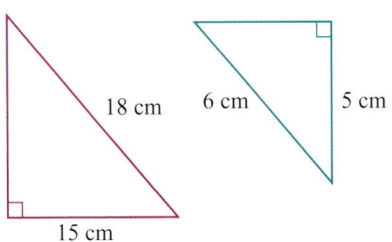

b

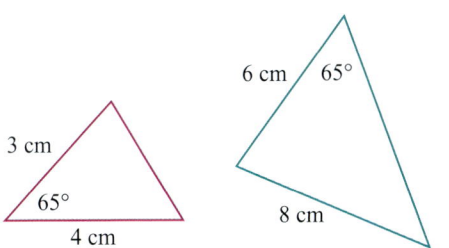

c

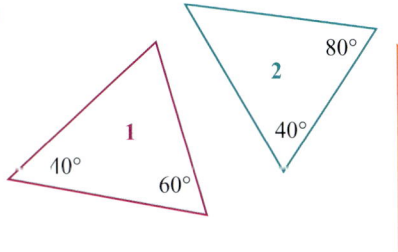

d

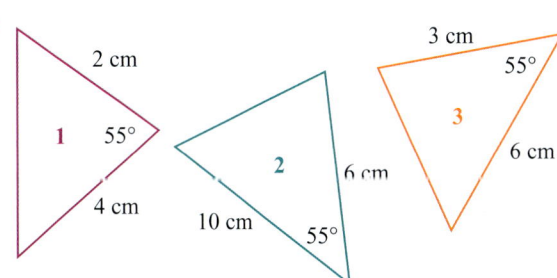

8 Which triangles are similar? State the test used.

a

b

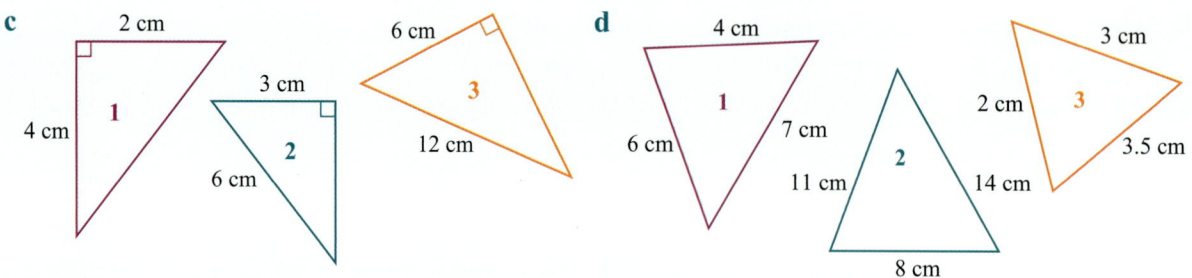

c 2 cm · 3 cm · 4 cm · 6 cm · 6 cm · 12 cm · (triangles 1, 2, 3)

d 4 cm · 6 cm · 7 cm · 11 cm · 8 cm · 2 cm · 14 cm · 3 cm · 3.5 cm · (triangles 1, 2, 3)

9 Find the lengths of the unknown sides in the following pairs of similar triangles.

a
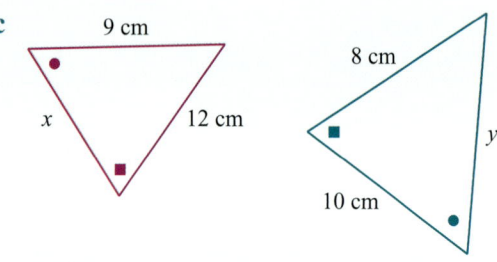
7 cm · y · 6 cm · 12.5 cm · 15 cm · x

b
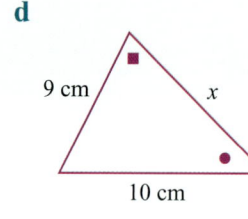
8 cm · y · 12 cm · 7.5 cm · x · 10 cm

c
9 cm · x · 12 cm · 8 cm · y · 10 cm

d
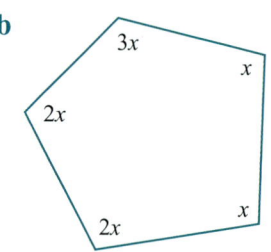
9 cm · x · 10 cm · 25 cm · y · 20 cm

10 A regular polygon has 36 sides.
  a Find the sum of the interior angles.
  b Find the size of each interior angle.

11 Find x, giving a reason for your answer.

a
120° · 115° · 150° · 168° · x · 135°

b
3x · x · 2x · 2x · x

12 A regular pentagon has two right angles and all other angles equal. Find the size of the equal angles.

13 Find the size of the exterior angle in a regular 30-sided figure.

4D   Review set

1 △ABC is right-angled at A. DA = DC. Prove that DA = DB.
Hint: Let ∠ACD = x.

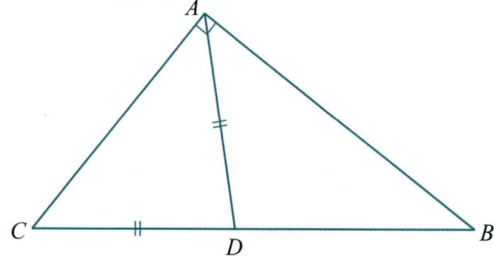

2 State the congruency test used to show that the following pairs of triangles are congruent.

a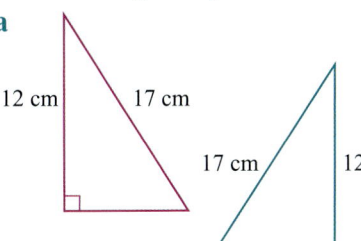

b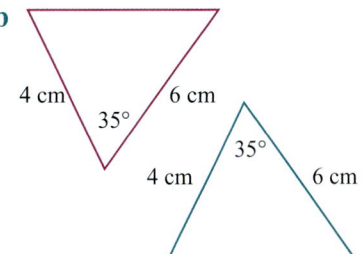

c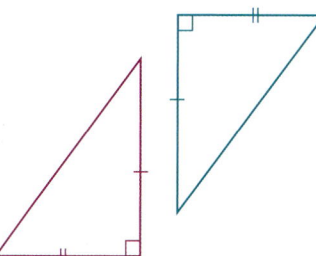

3 State why the following pairs of triangles are not congruent.

a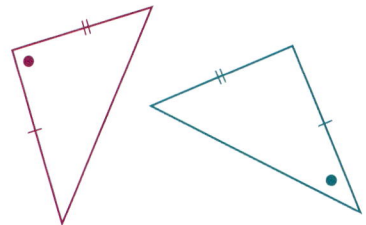

b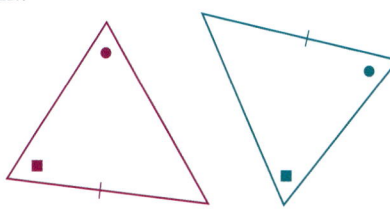

4 Which triangles are congruent? Give a reason for your answer.

a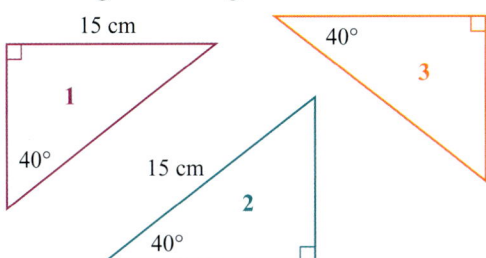

b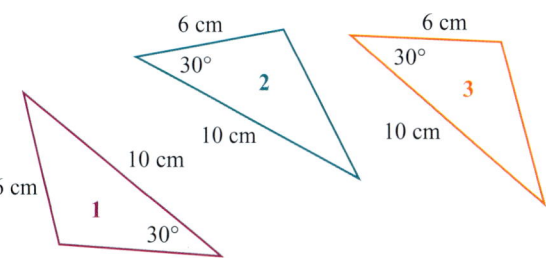

5 State why the following pairs of triangles are congruent and find the values of the pronumerals.

a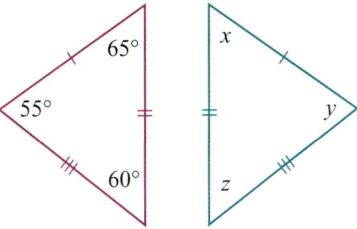

b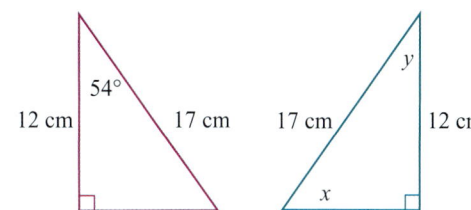

6 Prove the following.

a $\triangle BED \equiv \triangle CFD$

b $\triangle ABC$ is isosceles.

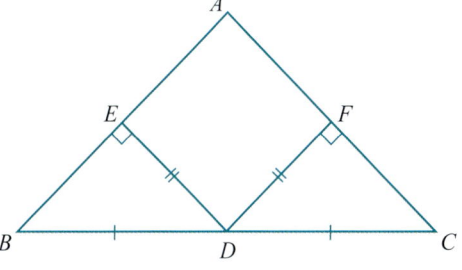

7 State with reasons whether or not the following triangles are similar.

a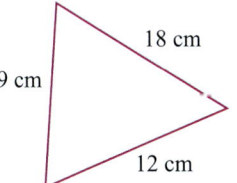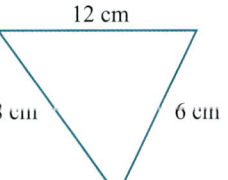

b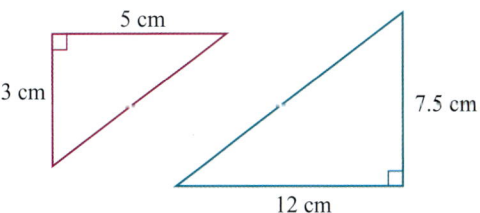

c

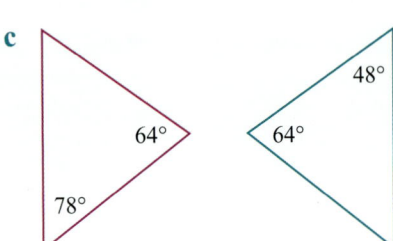

d

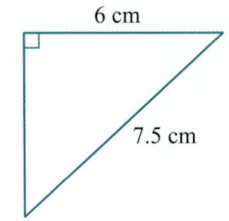

8 Which triangles are similar? State the test used.

a

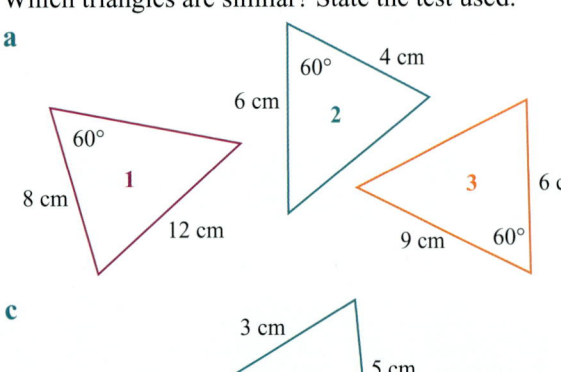

b

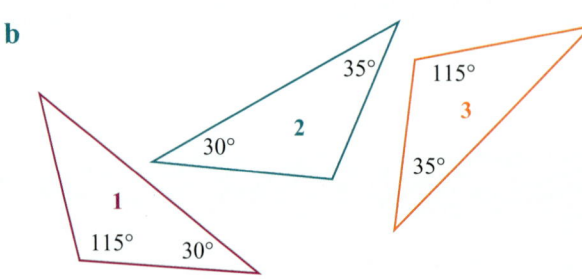

c

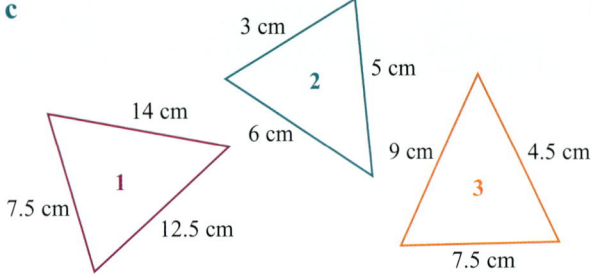

d

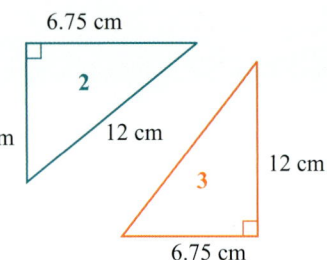

9 Find the lengths of the unknown sides in the following pairs of similar triangles.

a   **b**   **c**

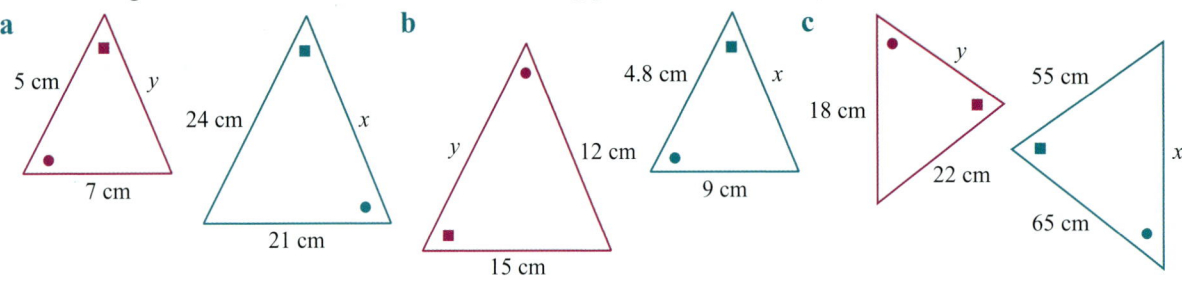

10 a Draw a pentagon.

  b Draw all diagonals from one vertex.

  c What is the angle sum of a pentagon?

11 Find *x*, giving a reason for your answer.

a

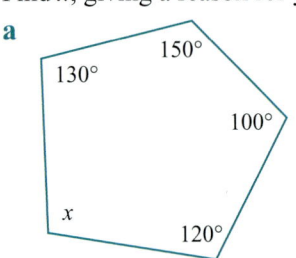

b

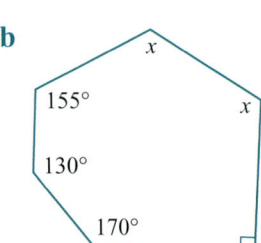

12 A hexagon has three right angles and all other angles equal. Find the size of the equal angles.

13 Find the size of the exterior angle in a regular octagon.

5

Bivariate data analysis

This chapter deals with the analysis of bivariate data.

After completing this chapter you should be able to:

▸ recognise the difference between dependent and independent variables

▸ distinguish bivariate data from single variable data

▸ describe bivariate data where the independent variable is time

▸ construct a scatter plot with and without technology

▸ describe informally the strength and direction of the relationship between two variables

▸ make predictions from a scatter plot

▸ find the equation of a line of best fit.

NSW Syllabus references: 5.2 S&P Bivariate data analysis
Outcomes: MA5.2-1WM, MA5.2-3WM, MA5.2-16SP
STATISTICS & PROBABILITY – ACMSP251, ACMSP252

Diagnostic test

1 For the straight line shown below, when $y = 4$, $x =$

A 5   **B** $5\frac{1}{2}$ **C** 7   **D** 2

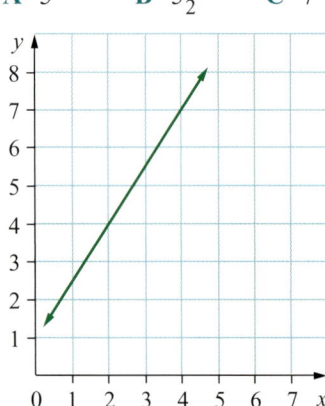

2 The point that does not lie on the line $y = \frac{1}{2}x - 3$ is:

A $(4, -1)$ **B** $(-4, -5)$

C $(3, -1\frac{1}{2})$ **D** $(-3, 1\frac{1}{2})$

3 If the point $(-2, 3)$ lies on the line $y = -x + c$ then the value of c is:

A 5   **B** -5 **C** 1   **D** -1

4 The gradient of the line joining the points $P(2, -1)$ and $Q(-3, 14)$ is:

A $\frac{1}{3}$ **B** $-\frac{1}{3}$ **C** 3   **D** -3

5 The equation of the line joining the points P and Q in question **4** is:

A $y = \frac{1}{3}x - 1\frac{2}{3}$ **B** $y = -\frac{1}{3}x - \frac{1}{3}$

C $y = 3x - 7$ **D** $y = -3x + 5$

6 The equation of the line passing through $(-2, 3)$ with gradient 2 is:

A $y = 2x + 3$ **B** $y = 2x - 7$

C $y = 2x - 2$ **D** $y = 2x + 7$

7 The equation of the line passing through $K(-3, 2)$ and $L(4, -5)$ is:

A $y = -x - 1$ **B** $y = x + 5$

C $y = 3x - 7$ **D** $y = -x + 1$

8 The equation of the line cutting the y-axis at 4 and the x-axis at -5 is:

A $y = \frac{4}{5}x + 4$ **B** $y = -\frac{4}{5}x + 4$

C $y = \frac{5}{4}x + 4$ **D** $y = -\frac{5}{4}x + 4$

9 The equation of this line is:

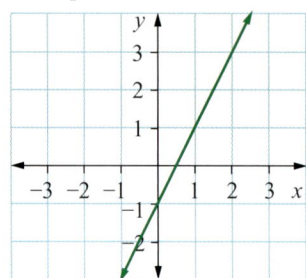

A $y = \frac{2}{3}x - 1$ **B** $y = \frac{3}{2}x - 1$

C $y = -x + 3$ **D** $y = 2x - 1$

10 The value of a if $(a, -2)$ lies on the line $y = 3x - 2$ is:

A 0   **B** 1   **C** 2   **D** 3

11 In general form $y = \frac{1}{2}x - \frac{2}{3}$ is:

A $6y - 3x + 4 = 0$ **B** $3x - 6y - 4 = 0$

C $3x + 2y - 2 = 0$ **D** $\frac{1}{2}x - y - \frac{2}{3} = 0$

12 When written in gradient–intercept form the equation $3x - 2y + 8$ is:

A $2y = 3x + 4$ **B** $3x - 2y = -8$

C $y = \frac{3}{2}x + 4$ **D** $y = \frac{3}{2}x + 8$

13 The x- and y-intercepts of $3x - 4y - 12 = 0$ are:

A 4 and -3 **B** 3 and -4

C -4 and 3   **D** -3 and 4

The diagnostic test questions refer to outcomes ACMNA215, ACMNA238 and ACMNA294. (AC)

A Variables

Variables are quantities that vary or change in value. In practical situations the value of one variable usually depends on the value of another. For example, the number of people waiting at a bus stop depends on the time of day. The first variable, number of people waiting at the bus stop, is called the **dependent variable** and the second, time of day, the **independent variable**.

When graphing the relationship between two variables, the independent variable is placed on the horizontal axis and the dependent variable on the vertical axis.

● EXAMPLE 1

Consider the statements below.
  i State the variables being compared.
  ii Decide which variable is the dependent variable to be graphed on the vertical axis.
a The height of a burning candle decreases with time.
b The bigger the hall, the more people can attend the concert.

		Solve	Think	Apply
a	**i**	The height of the candle and the time	The height of the candle depends on the length of time it has been burning. The length of time the candle has been burning does not depend on the height of the candle.	State the two variables being compared and determine which variable is dependent on the value of the other.
	ii	The height of the candle		
b	**i**	The size of hall and the number of people	The number of people who can attend the concert depends on the size of the hall. The size of the hall does not depend on the number of people attending a concert.	
	ii	The number of people		

Exercise 5A

1 Consider the statements below.
  i State the variables being compared.
  ii Decide which variable is the dependent variable to be graphed on the vertical axis.
a The weight of a baby increases with age.
b The value of a diamond increases with its weight.
c The share of a lottery prize decreases as the number of winners increases.
d The more goods sold, the greater the commission.
e The more hours worked, the greater the income.
f For a fixed distance, the higher the average speed the shorter the time.
g The more income earned, the more tax paid.
h The greater the speed, the greater the distance it takes to stop.

B Bivariate numerical data

Single variable data analysis examines one variable only; for example, the length of an arm. The data can be analysed using measures of central tendency (mean, mode, median) and measures of spread (for example range).

Bivariate data analysis compares two variables; for example, the length of an arm and height. The data can be graphed using one variable as the dependent variable and the other as the independent variable. One of the most frequent uses of these graphs is a comparison of a quantity over time, where time is the independent variable. These are sometimes referred to as time series.

EXAMPLE 1

The All Ordinaries Price Index is a measure of the collective value of share prices on the Australian Stock Exchange. This graph shows the end of month values of the index for 2012.

a   In which month(s) was the index:
   i   highest?
   ii lowest?
b   Describe the trend for this year.

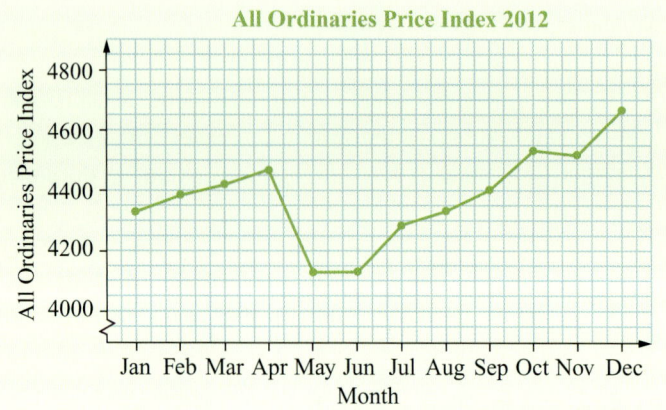

		Solve	Think	Apply
a	**i**	December	Find the highest and lowest points of the graph.	Determine the highest and lowest points on the graph.
	ii	May and June		
b		The index increased steadily until April, dropped for May and June, then gradually increased until it reached its highest value in December.	The trend was upwards until April, then downwards until June, then steadily upwards to the December value.	Look for downwards, horizontal and upwards trends in the graph.

Exercise 5B

1   This graph shows the monthly values of the All Ordinaries Price Index for 2013.

a   In which month(s) was the index:
   i   highest?
   ii lowest?
b   Describe the trend for this year.
c   Compare the value of the index in 2012 and 2013.

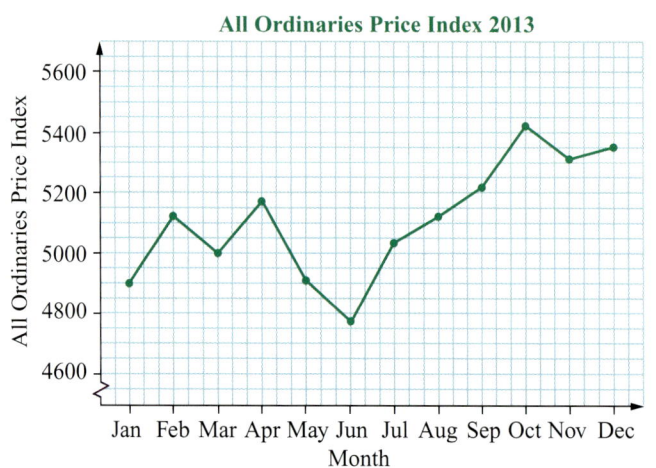

2 The graph shows the percentage of Australians who had private health insurance cover in the years 1994 to 2012.

   a What percentage of the population had private cover in:

   i 1996?   **ii** 2006?

   b Comment on the trends.

   c During this time period, the government introduced a 30% rebate on private health insurance to encourage more people to take out private cover. From the graph, state the year in which this might have happened.

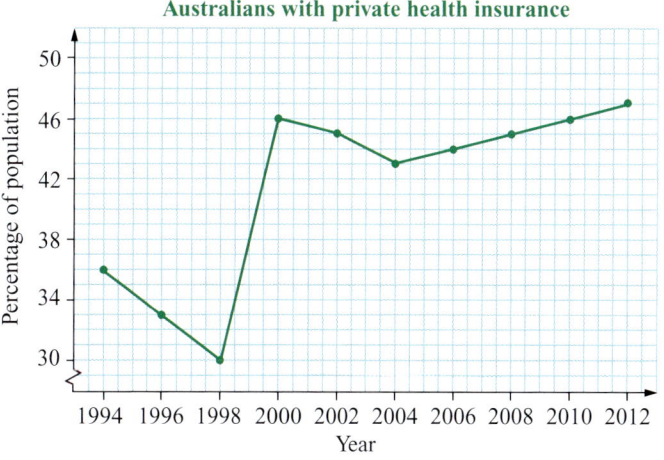
Australians with private health insurance

3 The graph shows the six-monthly exchange rates for the Australian dollar (A$) against the US dollar ($US) and the euro (€) from March 2009 to 2014.

   a How many US dollars was the Australian dollar worth in:

   i September 2009?

   ii March 2014?

   b How many euros was the Australian dollar worth in:

   i March 2010?

   ii September 2012?

   c Which currency exchange rate varied more over this time period?

   d When did the A$ reach its maximum value compared with the $US? What was this value?

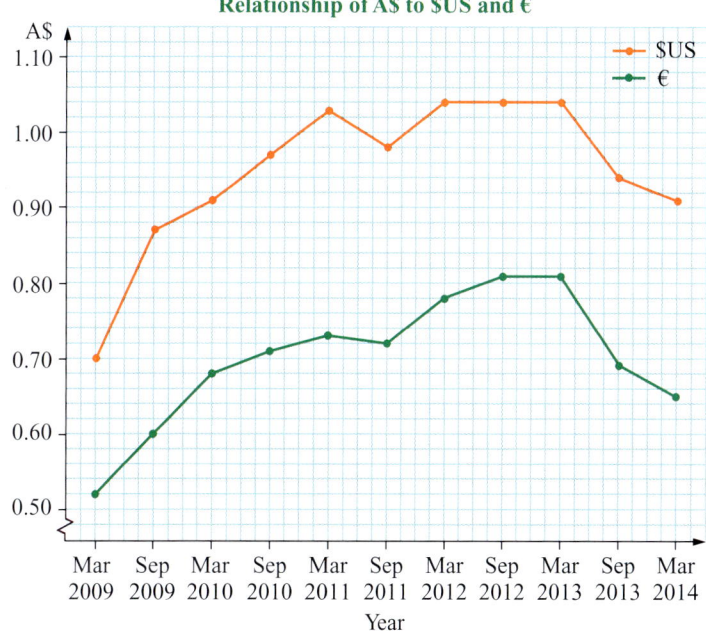
Relationship of A$ to $US and €

   e When did the A$ reach its maximum value compared with the euro? What was this value?

   f What was the biggest fall in the exchange rate with the $US in this time period? When did this occur?

   g Did the biggest fall in the exchange rate with the euro also occur at this time?

   h Give a brief description of the change in the exchange rates over this time period.

4 **a** The table shows the price from 2008 to 2013 paid by milk processing companies in New South Wales to dairy farmers for the milk they produced. Draw a graph using time as the independent variable. Comment on any trends in the price paid over this period.

Year	2008	2009	2010	2011	2012	2013
Price (c/L)	48.6	52.4	48.7	48.3	47.4	46.4

   b This table shows the average price paid for milk across Australia for the same period. Draw a graph of these prices on the same axes as in part **a**. Compare the price paid in New South Wales with the average price paid in Australia.

Year	2008	2009	2010	2011	2012	2013
Price (c/L)	49.6	42.4	37.3	43.2	42.0	40.2

5 This table shows the mean monthly maximum temperatures (°C) in Sydney and Melbourne for 2012.

Month	J	F	M	A	M	J	J	A	S	O	N	D
Sydney	26	26	25	24	21	18	18	20	23	23	24	26
Melbourne	27	27	24	22	17	14	15	15	19	21	23	26

    a On the same axes draw graphs showing the maximum temperatures in each city. Use time as the independent variable.

    b Which city had the colder winter?

    c   **i** In which city did the biggest fall occur from one month to the next?

       ii What was the size of this fall?

    d   **i** In which city did the biggest increase occur from one month to the next?

       ii What was the size of this increase?

    e Comment on the shape of these graphs, giving possible reasons.

6 This table shows the mean monthly rainfall (mm) in Sydney and Melbourne for 2012.

Month	J	F	M	A	M	J	J	A	S	O	N	D
Sydney	139	111	270	187	37	244	56	19	24	29	52	45
Melbourne	29	60	59	51	83	72	59	53	39	29	37	30

    a On the same axes draw graphs showing the monthly rainfall in each city. Use time as the independent variable.

    b Which city was the wetter in 2012?

    c In Sydney, which month(s) was/were the:

       i driest?   **ii** wettest?

    d In Melbourne, which month(s) was/were the:

       i driest?   **ii** wettest?

    e Which city had the wetter winter?

    f Comment on the shape of the graphs. Are there any trends?

7 The graph shows the number of short-term visitor arrivals to Australia for the years 2003 to 2013. The majority of these arrivals are tourists.

    a How many visitors arrived in:

       i 2005?   **ii** 2012?

    b   **i** When was the largest increase in the number of visitors from one year to the next?

       ii What was this increase?

    c   **i** Were there any decreases in number of visitors from one year to the next?

       ii When did this occur?

       iii The global financial crisis (GFC) had a significant effect on the number of visitors to Australia. From the graph, in which year do you think the GFC occurred?

    d Comment on any trends evident in the graph.

Short-term visitor arrivals in Australia (2003–2013)

8 a The graph below shows the number of immigrants to Australia for 2001 to 2013. How many arrived in:

    i 2001?   **ii** 2011?

b In which year was the number of immigrants:

    i highest?   **ii** lowest?

c Between which years was there the largest increase in the number of immigrants?

d Between which years was there the largest decrease in the number of immigrants?

e Comment on the shape of the graph and any trends that are evident.

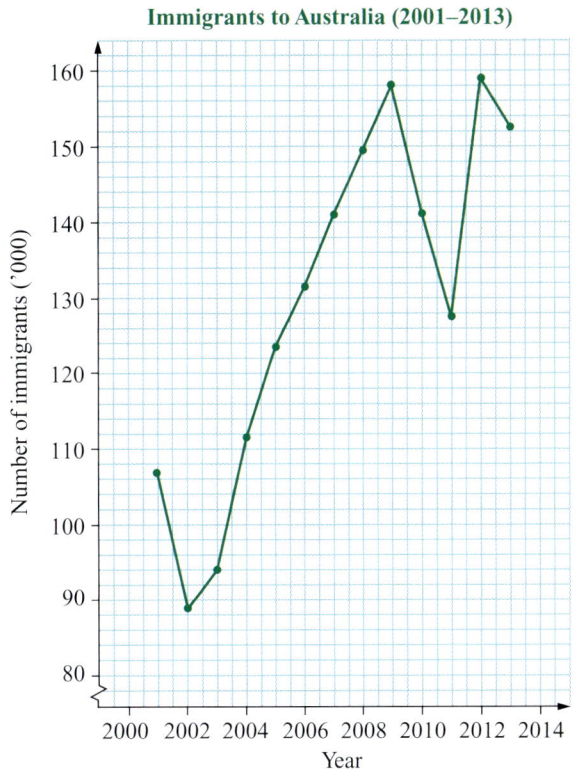

Immigrants to Australia (2001–2013)

Investigation 1 Variables

Investigate a topic of interest for which graphs of one variable against another can be plotted. Represent the dependent numerical variable against the independent variable, in an appropriate graphical form. For example, plot retail sales, the number of building approvals or job advertisements in your state, city or town against time.

Describe the changes in the dependent variable over time and suggest reasons for these changes with reference to relevant national or international events.

 C   # Scatter plots

The aim of many statistical investigations is to determine whether there is a relationship, or association, between the two variables being investigated. For example, medical researchers might be interested in the relationship, if any, between the dose of a drug and the number of patients cured. A business might be interested in the relationship, if any, between the amount of money spent on advertising and an increase in sales.

In this section we will investigate a way of illustrating bivariate data so that a relationship, if it exists, can be identified. A simple method to illustrate numerical data relating two variables is to plot the data as ordered pairs. The resulting diagram is known as a scatter plot (or scattergram).

EXAMPLE 1

The heights and weights of 10 students were measured and the results listed in the table.

Student	1	2	3	4	5	6	7	8	9	10
Height (cm)	179	165	160	179	152	168	168	165	166	166
Weight (kg)	60	55	58	67	48	64	61	52	65	55

a Illustrate this data on a scatter plot.

b Draw a trend line if it exists.

c Determine whether there is a possible relationship between the variables.

	Solve	Think	Apply
a **b**	**Height versus weight** (scatter plot: Weight (kg) vs Height (cm))	Points are plotted as ordered pairs with height as the independent variable and weight as the dependent variable. In this case a line can be drawn that roughly passes through this set of points.	You can use a spreadsheet to plot the data. *Step1:* Put the data in a table. *Step 2:* Highlight the table. *Step 3:* Click on Chart from the menu bar. *Step 4:* Choose x–y Scatter from Chart type.
c	There is a trend that as height increases so does weight, but the scatter of the points from the trend line indicates only a weak link between the variables.	There does not appear to be a mathematical connection between the variables that would allow the weight of a student to be predicted accurately from their height.	This line is called a 'line of best fit'. There are different methods of finding the line of best fit, but in this section we will approximate it by drawing a general trend line that has approximately half the points above it and half below it.

Analysing scatter plots

If the points on a scatter plot are scattered at random, as shown in graph A below, there is no relationship between the variables.

If the points are scattered along a straight line as shown in graphs B and C below, there is a linear relationship between the variables.

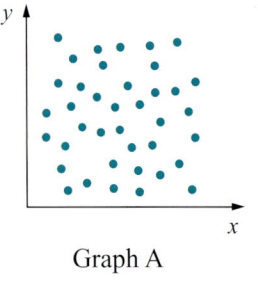

Graph A

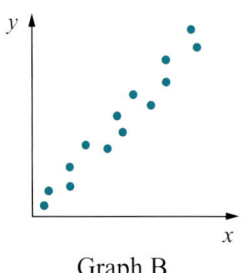

Graph B

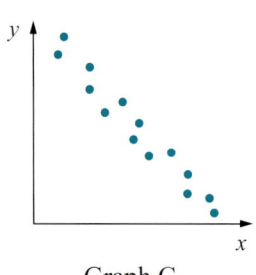

Graph C

If there is an upwards trend, that is the trend line slopes up from left to right as in graph B, there is a positive relationship between the variables. For a positive relationship, large values of one variable, x, are associated with large values of another variable, y, and small values of the variable x are associated with small values of the variable y.

If there is a downwards trend, that is the trend line slopes down from left to right as in graph C, there is a negative relationship between the variables. For a negative relationship, large values of variable x are associated with small values of the variable y, and small values of variable x are associated with large values of variable y.

Further, the association can be classified as strong or weak.
- If the points are closely spread about the trend line, as in graph D, the association is strong or high.
- If there is a trend, but the points are widely scattered about the trend line, as in graph E, the association is weak or low.

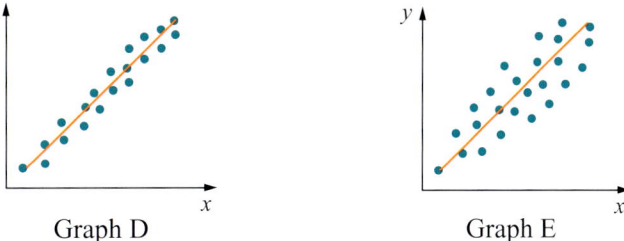

Graph D   Graph E

EXAMPLE 2

Classify these scatter plots for the strength and direction of the relationship between the variables.

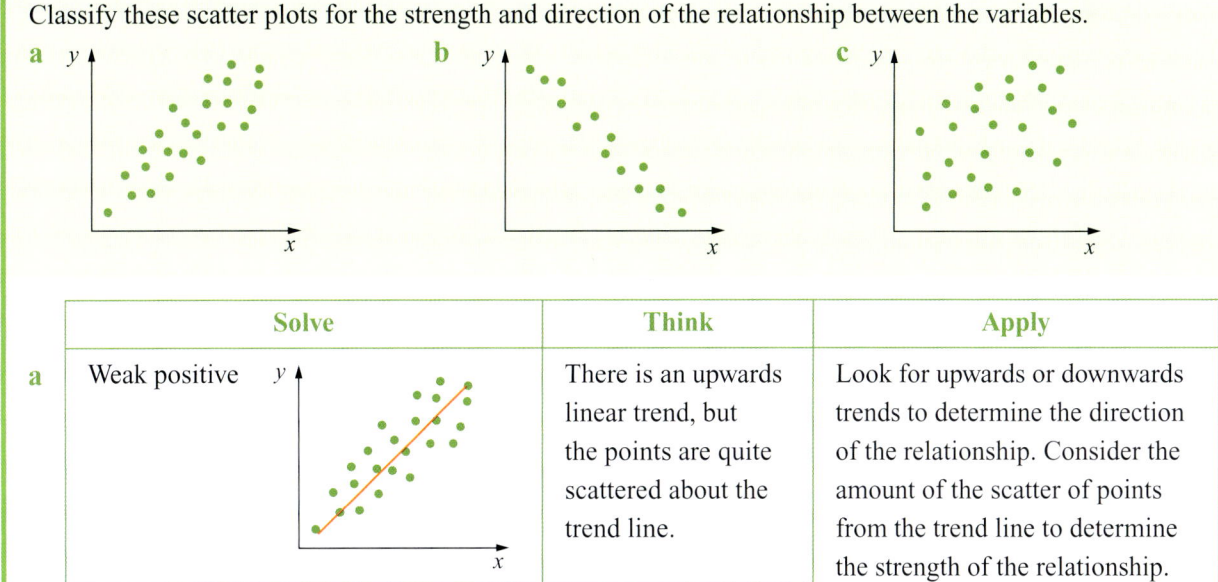

	Solve	Think	Apply
a	Weak positive	There is an upwards linear trend, but the points are quite scattered about the trend line.	Look for upwards or downwards trends to determine the direction of the relationship. Consider the amount of the scatter of points from the trend line to determine the strength of the relationship. Randomly scattered points indicate no relationship between the variables.
b	Strong negative	There is a downwards linear trend with some spread, but with the points quite close to the trend line.	*The strength of the relationship between two variables is called correlation.*
c	No association	The points are randomly scattered on the number plane. There is no upwards or downwards trend.	

1 For the scatter plots drawn below, classify the strength and direction of the relationship between the variables.

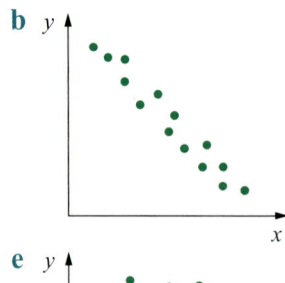

2 For each set of bivariate data given in the tables below:
    i draw a scatter plot
    ii determine the strength and direction of the relationship between the variables.

a

x	0.5	1	1.5	2	2.5	3	3.5	4
y	1.3	1.7	2.1	2.6	2.5	3	3.5	3.8

b

x	1	2	3	4	5	6	7	8
y	5	2.5	3	3.5	2	1	3	1

3 Draw a scatter plot for two variables that have:
    a a strong positive relationship
    b a weak negative relationship
    c no relationship
    d a weak positive association
    e a strong negative association.

● **EXAMPLE 3**

This scatter plot shows the English marks and History marks for a group of students. A line of best fit has been drawn for these points. Use the line to predict:
a the History marks for a student who scores 70 in English
b the English mark for a student who scores 50 in History.

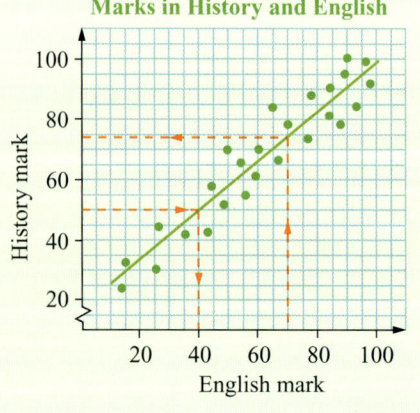

Marks in History and English

	Solve	Think	Apply
a	74	Draw a vertical line from 70 on the English axis to meet the line of best fit. From this point, draw a horizontal line to meet the History axis. Read off the mark, about 74, which is the predicted History mark for a student who scores 70 in English.	Locate the point on the line with the given x-coordinate (English mark) and read off the y-coordinate (History mark) of the point.

EXAMPLE 3 CONTINUED

	Solve	Think	Apply
b	40	Draw a horizontal line from 50 on the History axis to meet the line of best fit. From this point, draw a vertical line to meet the English axis. Read off the mark, 40, which is the predicted English mark for a student who scores 50 in History.	Find the appropriate *x*-coordinate (English mark) using the line of best fit.

4 This scatter plot shows the marks in Mathematics and Science for a group of students. A line of best fit has been drawn for these points. Use the line of best fit to predict:

a the Science mark of a student who scored the following in Mathematics

    i 65   **ii** 72   **iii** 84

b the Mathematics mark of a student who scored the following in Science

    i 70   **ii** 76   **iii** 89

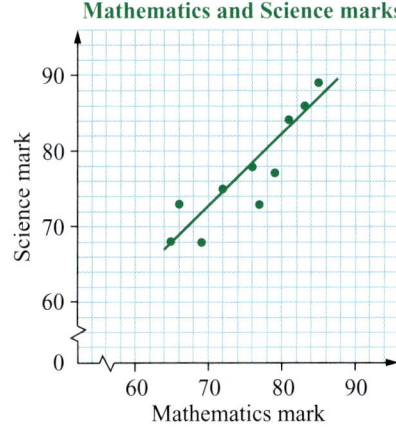

Mathematics and Science marks

5 The scatter plot shows the amount of fertiliser applied (in kg/m²) and the number of flowers produced per square metre in an experimental garden. A line of best fit has been drawn for these points. Use the line of best fit to predict:

a the number of flowers produced by applying these amounts of fertiliser

    i 0.32 kg/m²   **ii** 0.63 kg/m²

b the amount of fertiliser needed to produce these numbers of flowers/m²

    i 25/m²   **ii** 70/m²

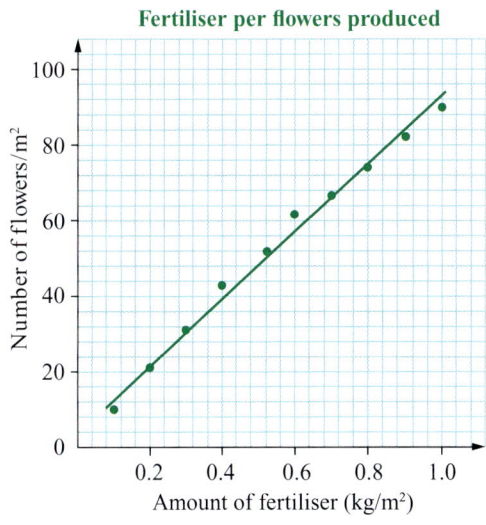

Fertiliser per flowers produced

6 The scatter plot shows the results of a survey of the annual income of a group of people who work in the city and the amount they spent on entertainment. A line of best fit has been drawn for these points. Use the line of best fit to predict:

a the amount spent on entertainment by a person who has an annual income of

    i $55 000   **ii** $75 000

    iii $110 000

b the annual income of a person who spends the following amount on entertainment

    i $5000   **ii** $9500   **iii** $14 500

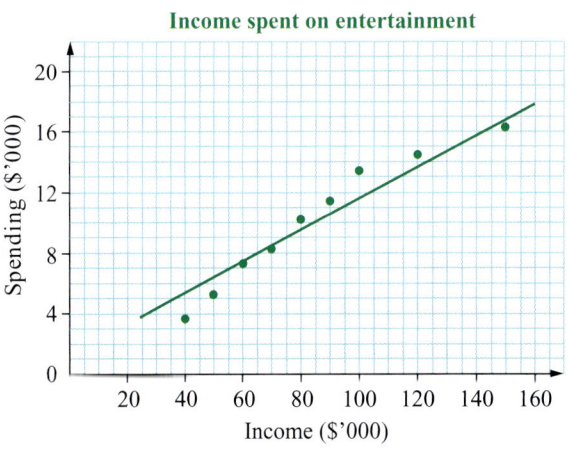

Income spent on entertainment

STATISTICS & PROBABILITY

EXAMPLE 4

x	65	66	69	70	72	74	76	81	84	85
y	67	72	69	74	77	73	78	83	85	88

a Draw a scatter plot for the data given in the table above.
b Determine the strength and direction of the relationship between the variables.
c Draw a line of best fit on the scatter plot.
d Use the line of best fit to predict the value of:
   i y when $x = 80$ ii x when $y = 75$.

	Solve	Think	Apply
a		Plot as points on a number plane.	Plot the points, draw a line of best fit and use the line to make the predictions.
b	Strong positive relationship	There is a strong, linear upwards trend.	
c	A line of best fit is drawn on the scatter plot in part **a**.	Draw a general trend line that has approximately half the points above it and half the points below it.	
d	i When $x = 80$, $y = 82$. ii When $y = 75$, $x = 73$.	Read the values off the line of best fit.	

7

x	84	66	63	74	69	78	71	62
y	53	72	74	65	70	55	66	75

a Draw a scatter plot for the data given in the table above.
b Determine the strength and direction of the relationship between the variables.
c Draw a line of best fit on the scatter plot.
d Use the line of best fit to predict the value of:
   i y when $x = 70$ ii x when $y = 60$.

8 The data in the table below shows the age and value of a sample of a particular brand of car.

Age (years)	1	1	2	2	3	3	3	4	4	5	5	5	6	6
Value ('000)	27	26	25	25.5	22.5	23	22	18	17.5	14	15	16	13	11.5

  a Draw a scatter plot for the data given in the table.
  b Determine the strength and direction of the relationship between the variables.
  c Draw a line of best fit on the scatter plot.
  d Use the line of best fit to predict:
      i the value of a car of this brand after $3\frac{1}{2}$ years   **ii** the age of a car with a value of $15\,000.

● EXAMPLE 5

x	5	6	7	8	9	10	11	12	13
y	8	10	12	13	14	16	18	22	22

  a Draw a scatter plot for the data given in the table above.
  b Draw a line of best fit on the scatter plot.
  c Find the equation of the line of best fit.
  d Use the equation to predict the value of:
      i y when $x = 15$ **ii** x when $y = 20$.

	Solve/Think	Apply
a **b**	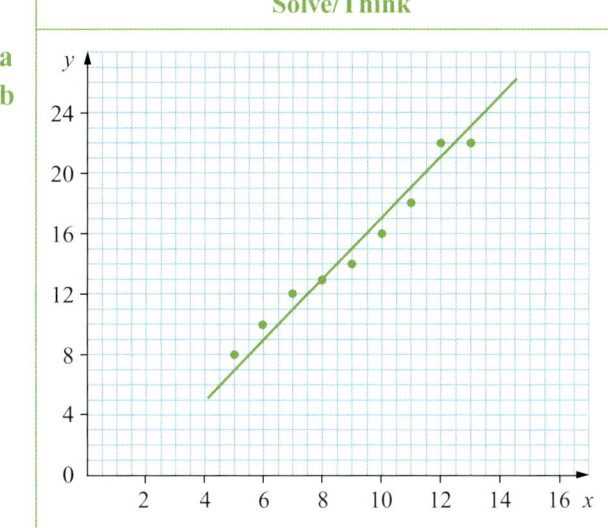	Plot as points on a number plane.
c	The points $(5, 7)$ and $(13, 23)$ lie on this line. Gradient of line $= \dfrac{23 - 7}{13 - 5} = 2$ Equation is of the form $y = 2x + c$. As the point $(5, 7)$ lies on the line: $7 = 2 \times 5 + c$ $7 = 10 + c$ $c = -3$ The equation of the line of best fit is $y = 2x - 3$.	Choose any two suitable points on the line of best fit. Use these points to express the equation in the form $y = mx + c$.
d	**i** When $x = 15$, $y = 27$. **ii** When $y = 20$, $x = 11.5$.	Substitute the given values into the equation and solve to find the unknown.

9

x	1	2	3	4	5	6	7	8
y	14	14	10	10	6	5	4	1

a Draw a scatter plot for the data given in the table above.
b Draw a line of best fit on the scatter plot.
c Find the equation of the line of best fit.
d Use the equation to predict the value of:
    i y when $x = 10$ ii x when $y = 12$.

10 The data in the table shows a comparison of the fitness level of a group of 16-year-old females, measured on a scale of 1 to 20, and the number of hours spent each week playing sport.

Time (h)	1	1	2	2	3	4	5	8	10	15	18	20
Fitness level	3	2	4	3	5	5	6	9	10	15	17	19

a Draw a scatter plot for the data given in the table above.
b Determine the strength and direction of the relationship between the variables.
c Draw a line of best fit on the scatter plot.
d Find the equation of the line of best fit.
e Use the equation to predict:
    i the fitness level of a student who plays sport for 12 hours per week
    ii the hours of sport a student would need to play each week to attain a fitness level of 16.

Investigation 2 Investigating data

1 Investigate a matter of interest that involves two numerical variables such as height versus arm span, hand span, shoe size or head circumference.
a Draw a scatter plot for the data (with or without the use of technology).
b Determine the strength and direction of the relationship, if any, between the variables.
c Draw a line of best fit on the scatter plot.
d Find the equation of the line of best fit.

Language in mathematics

1 Explain the following, giving examples:
  a the difference between bivariate data and single variable data
  b the meaning of the terms 'dependent variable' and 'independent variable'.

2 Why are line graphs the most appropriate method of representing data collected over time?

3 a What is meant by a 'line of best fit'?
  b For what purpose is a line of best fit used?

Terms

association	bivariate	correlation	dependent	independent	line of best fit
relationship	scatter plot	time series	trend	trend line	variable

Check your skills

1 Which statement is correct for 'the number of people waiting at the station during the day'?
  A The number of people waiting at the station is the independent variable.
  B The time of day is the independent variable.
  C The time of day would be placed on the vertical axis.
  D The number of people waiting at the station would be placed on the horizontal axis.

The graph below shows the number of short-term visitor arrivals to Australia for the years 2003 to 2013. Use the graph to answer questions **2** and **3**.

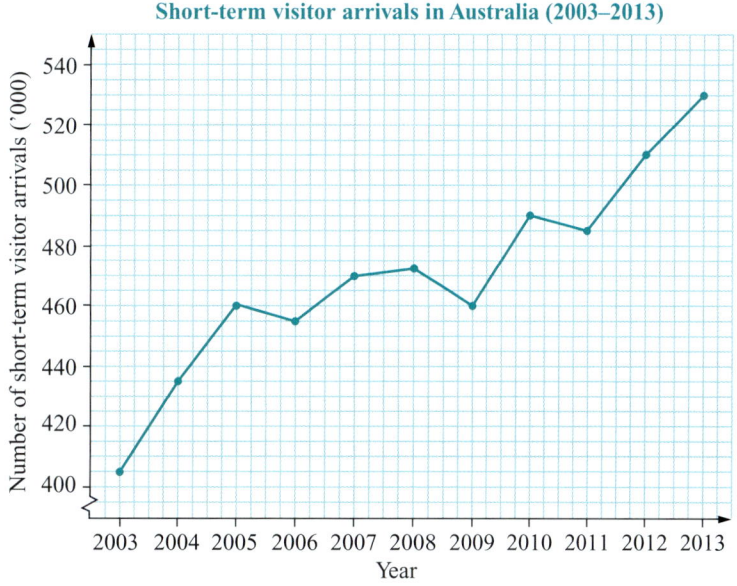

2 Which statement is true for the number of visitors?
  A The largest increase in the number of visitors occurred between 2008 and 2009.
  B The number of visitors increased between years on three occasions.
  C The largest increase in visitors was from 2011 to 2012.
  D The number of visitors decreased between years on three occasions.

3 The number of short-term visitor arrivals was approximately the same in the years:

  A 2005 and 2006
  B 2007 and 2008
  C 2009 and 2010
  D 2011 and 2012

4 The graph shows the value of the US dollar ($US) in terms of the Australian dollar (A$).

The months with the highest and lowest values are:

  A May 2012 and November 2014
  B January 2013 and December 2014
  C July 2012 and January 2014
  D September 2012 and January 2014

5 The scatter plot below that shows a weak negative relationship between the variables is:

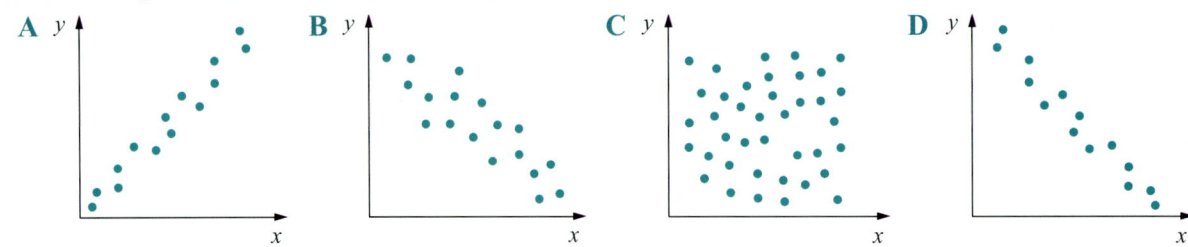

6 This scatter plot shows that the relationship between the variables is:

  A strong positive
  B weak positive
  C no relationship
  D strong negative

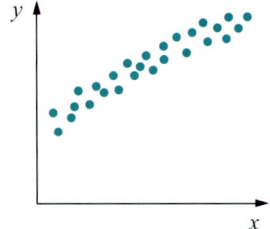

7 The diagram that illustrates a line of best fit for the data graphed in the scatter plot is:

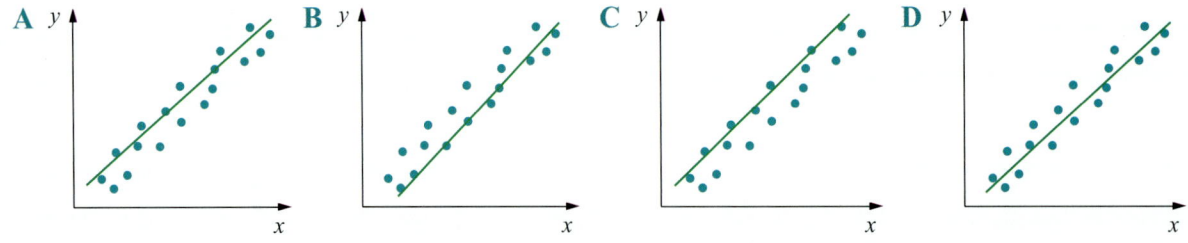

8 Using the line of best fit in the diagram, the value of x when $y = 3.5$ is:

A 1.3   B 1.7

C 6.3   D 7.3

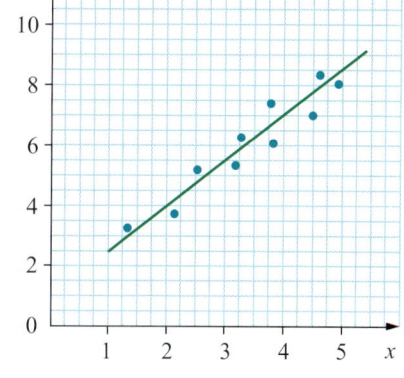

9 The equation of the line of best fit in the diagram using the information given is:

A $y = 0.6x + 0.2$

B $y = 0.6x + 0.52$

C $y = \frac{5}{3}x - \frac{13}{15}$

D $y = \frac{5}{3}x - \frac{1}{3}$

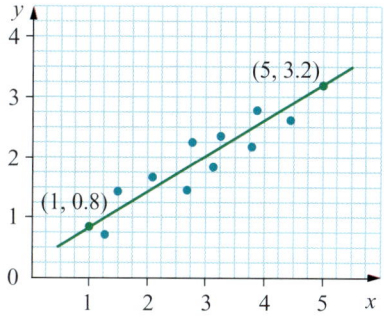

If you have any difficulty with these questions, refer to the examples and questions in the sections listed in the table.

Question	1	2–4	5–9
Section	A	B	C

5A   Review set

1 Consider the statements below.

     i State the variables being compared.

     ii Decide which variable is the dependent variable to be graphed on the vertical axis.

   a The fewer people there are, the bigger the slice of cake.

   b The older a car is, the lower its value.

2 The graph shows the exchange rates of the Australian dollar (A$) against the British pound (GBP) from March 2010 to December 2013.

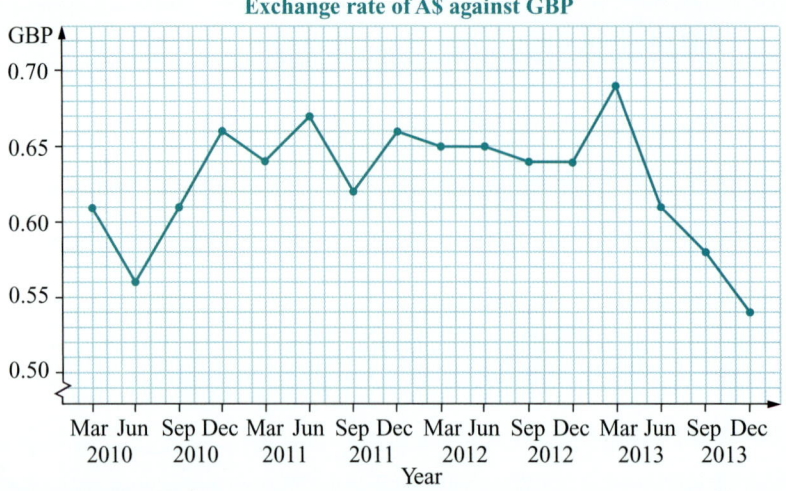

a How many British pounds was the Australian dollar worth in:
   i September 2010?   **ii** March 2011?   **iii** June 2012?
b When was the (A$) worth more than 0.65 GBP?
c **i** When did the (A$) reach its maximum value compared with the GBP in this time period?
   ii What was this value?
d What was the biggest fall in the exchange rate with the GBP in this time period?
e When did this occur?
f Comment on any trends in the change in the exchange rates over this time period.

3 Classify the strength and direction of the relationship between the variables shown on the scatter plots below.

a 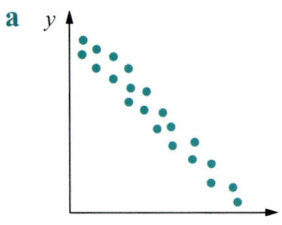   **b** 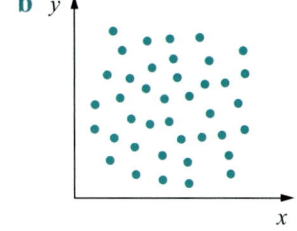   **c**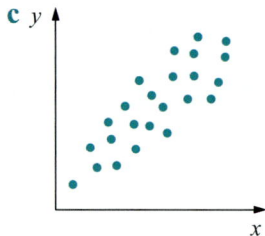

4

x	10	15	20	25	30	35	40	45	50
y	11	17	22	26	33	38	42	46	52

a Draw a scatter plot for the data given in the table above.
b Determine the strength and direction of the relationship between the variables.
c Draw a line of best fit on the scatter plot.
d Find the equation of the line of best fit.
e Use the equation to predict the value of:
   i y when $x = 32$ **ii** x when $y = 24$

1 Consider the statements below.

  i State the variables being compared.

  ii Decide which variable is the dependent variable to be graphed on the vertical axis.

  a The greater the speed of the car, the greater the distance it takes to stop.

  b The more alcohol consumed, the lower the ability to drive.

2 The graph shows the six-monthly dividends per share paid by the Commonwealth Bank (CBA) from April 2009 to April 2014.

  a What was the dividend paid in:

    i April 2010?

    ii October2011?

    iii April 2013?

  b **i** What was the maximum dividend paid in this time interval?

    ii When did this occur?

  c In which six-monthly period did the dividend paid have the:

    i largest increase?

    ii largest decrease?

  d Give a brief description of the change in the dividends paid over this time period.

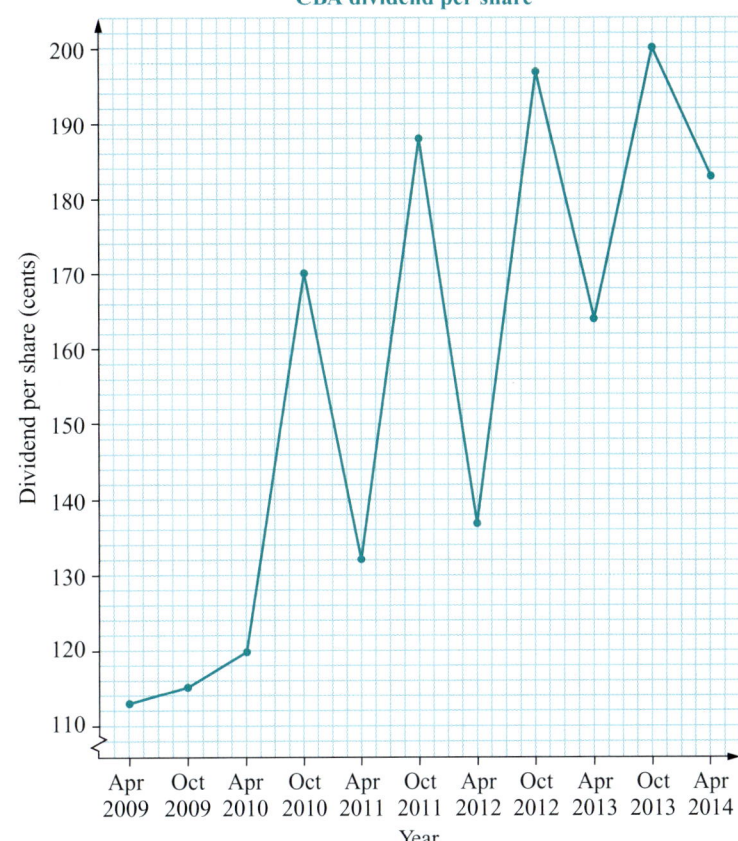

CBA dividend per share

3 Classify the strength and direction of the relationship between the variables shown on the scatter plots below.

  a 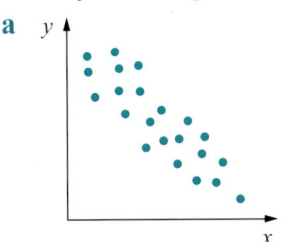 **b** 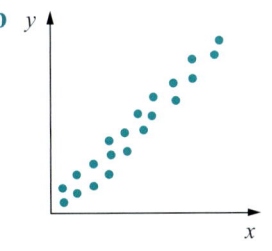 **c**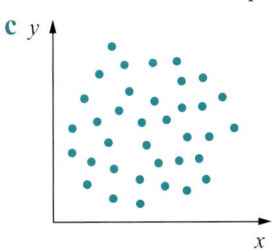

4

x	5	6	7	8	9	10	11	12	13	14
y	35	33	28	27	22	22	15	13	10	7

  a Draw a scatter plot for the data given in the table above.

  b Determine the strength and direction of the relationship between the variables.

  c Draw a line of best fit on the scatter plot.

  d Find the equation of the line of best fit.

  e Use the equation to predict the value of:

    i y when $x = 15$

    ii x when $y = 20$

1 Consider the statements below.

   i State the variables being compared.

   ii Decide which variable is the dependent variable to be graphed on the vertical axis.

   a The more police cars on the road, the fewer accidents occur.

   b As the radius of a sphere increases, its volume also increases.

2 The graph shows the number of people working in the mining industry in Australia for the years 1992 to 2012.

   a Approximately how many people were employed in:

   i 1994?

   ii 2001?

   iii 2009?

   b **i** What was the lowest number of people employed in this time period?

   ii When did this occur?

   c Estimate when the 'mining boom' began in Australia.

   d Comment on any trends in the change of employment over this time period.

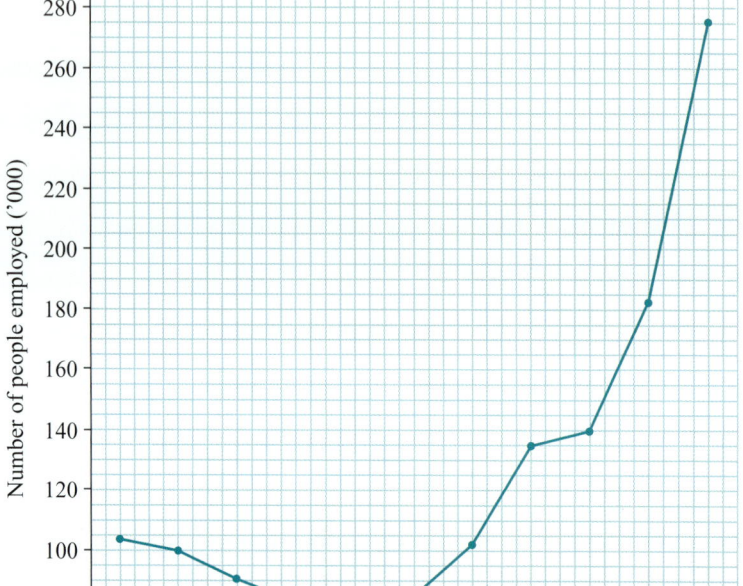

People employed in the mining industry

3 Classify the strength and direction of the relationship between the variables shown on the scatter plots below.

a
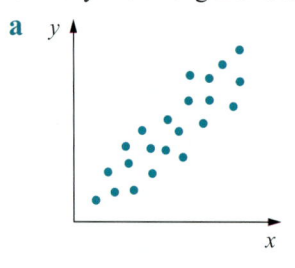

b
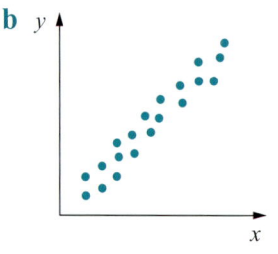

c
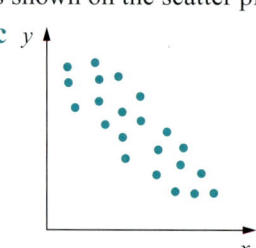

4

x	10	12	16	22	26	29	33	37	42	49
y	2.6	2.7	3	3.4	3.5	3.9	4.0	4.1	4.5	4.8

   a Draw a scatter plot for the data given in the table above.

   b Determine the strength and direction of the relationship between the variables.

   c Draw a line of best fit on the scatter plot.

   d Find the equation of the line of best fit.

   e Use the equation to predict the value of:

   i y when $x = 30$

   ii x when $y = 3.2$

1 Consider the statements below.

    i State the variables being compared.

    ii Decide which variable is the dependent variable to be graphed on the vertical axis.

  a The greater the speed, the shorter the travel time.

  b The more rainy days, the greater the number of umbrellas sold.

2 The graph shows the number of people living in a town for the years 2000 to 2012.

  a What was the population of the town in:

    i 2002?

    ii 2005?

    iii 2012?

  b **i** What was the lowest population in this period of time?

    ii When did this occur?

  c A new mine opened near this town in the time period shown. When does the graph indicate that this occurred?

  d Give a brief description of the change in population over this time period.

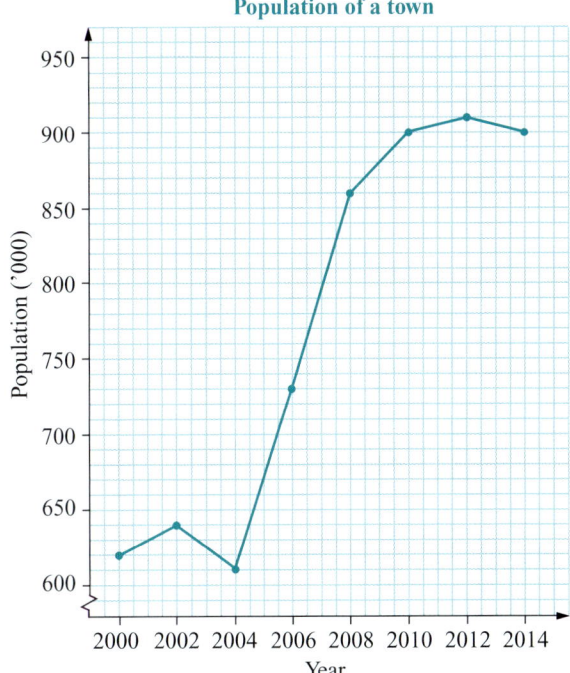
Population of a town

3 Classify the strength and direction of the relationship between the variables shown on the scatter plots below.

  a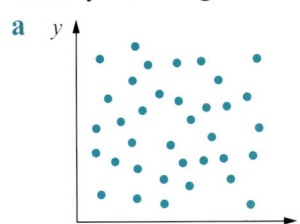

  b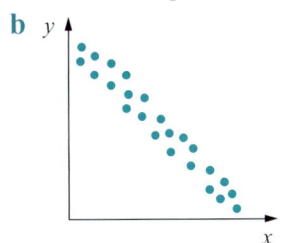

  c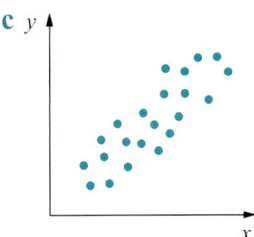

4

x	10	20	30	40	50	60	70	80
y	2.1	2.0	1.8	1.7	1.5	1.3	1.0	0.9

  a Draw a scatter plot for the data given in the table above.

  b Determine the strength and direction of the relationship between the variables.

  c Draw a line of best fit on the scatter plot.

  d Find the equation of the line of best fit.

  e Use the equation to predict the value of:

    i y when $x = 25$

    ii x when $y = 1.6$.

1 **a** Complete to make equivalent fractions.

    i $\dfrac{3k}{5} = \dfrac{\square}{15}$
    ii $\dfrac{5x}{4y} = \dfrac{\square}{28y}$
    iii $\dfrac{3a}{2b} = \dfrac{\square}{12b^2}$

  b Reduce to simplest form.

    i $\dfrac{18p}{15}$
    ii $\dfrac{6mn}{4mnp}$
    iii $\dfrac{15km^4}{12k^2m^2}$

  c Simplify:

    i $\dfrac{6k}{5} - \dfrac{3k}{7}$
    ii $2t + \dfrac{3t}{2}$
    iii $\dfrac{4}{5w} + \dfrac{7}{3w}$

  d Simplify:

    i $\dfrac{4z}{7w} \times \dfrac{21w}{8}$
    ii $\dfrac{3}{4e} \div \dfrac{6}{5e^2}$

  e Expand and simplify:

    i $3(5x - 7) + 4$
    ii $4(2p - 3q) + 5(6p - 7q)$

  f Factorise:

    i $-16d + 24e$
    ii $16pq^2 + 6p^2q$

    iii $9ab - 12bc + 6b^2$
    iv $12x^4y^3 - 16x^2y$

2 **a** For the points $L(-3, 5)$ and $M(1, -3)$ find the following.

    i the distance LM
    ii the midpoint of LM
    iii the gradient of LM

  b **i** Complete the table of values for $y = 2x - 3$.

x	-3	-2	-1	0	1	2	3
y							

    ii Plot the ordered pairs on a set of coordinate axes. Draw the straight line graph through the points.

  c **i** Find the equation of the line with gradient 3 and y-intercept -4.

    ii Sketch the line.

  d Consider the straight line shown on the right.

    i Find the gradient.

    ii State the y-intercept.

    iii Write the equation of the line.

  e **i** Write the equation $3x + 2y - 6 = 0$ in the form $y = mx + b$.

    ii Sketch the line.

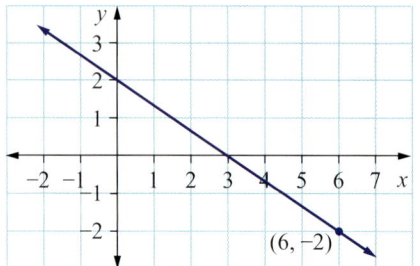

3 **a** State the congruency test used to show that these triangles are congruent.

  b State why the following pair of triangles is not congruent.

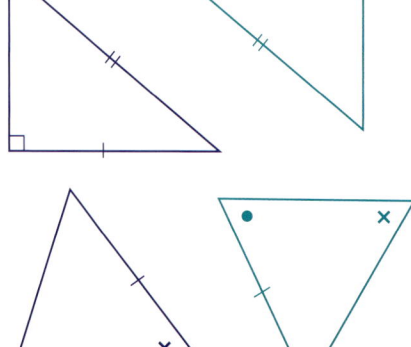

c Which triangles are congruent? Give a reason for your answer.

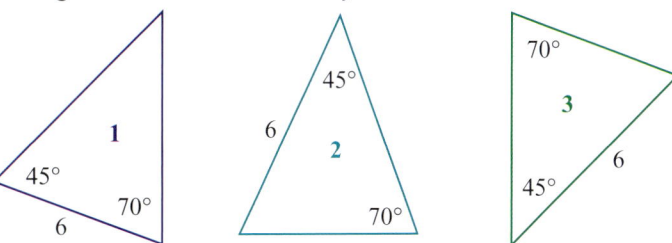

d State the congruency test showing that the following pair of triangles is congruent, and hence find the values of the pronumerals.

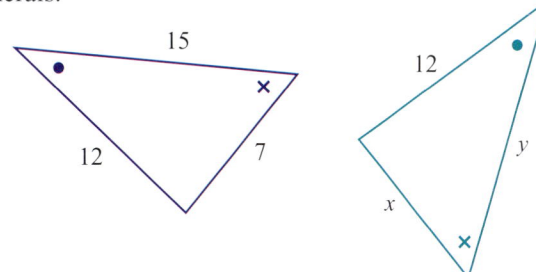

e Determine whether or not the following triangles are similar. If they are similar, state the test used.

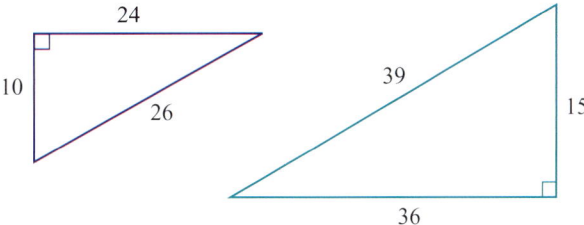

f Find the enlargement factor and hence the length of the unknown sides in these similar triangles.

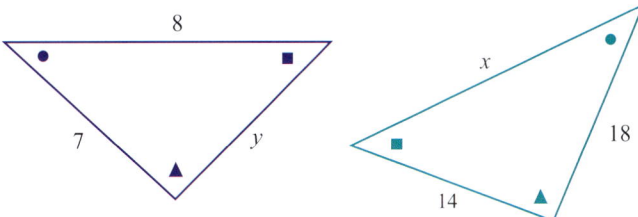

4 a Find the angle sum of a 9-sided polygon.

b How many sides has a hexagon?

c Find the interior angle size of a regular polygon with 24 sides.

d Find the value of x in this diagram.

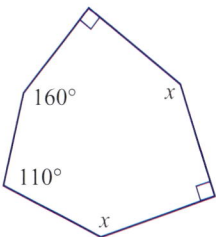

e An octagon has two right angles and all the other angles are equal. Find the size of the equal angles.

f Find the exterior angle of a 20-sided regular polygon.

g Find the number of sides of an irregular polygon that has one exterior angle of 110° and all other 10°.

5 a Consider this statement: 'The more sunny days, the greater the amount of sunscreen sold'.

    i State the variables being compared.

    ii Decide which is the dependent variable to be graphed on the vertical axis.

b For the scatter plots classify the strength and direction of the relationship between the variables.

    i 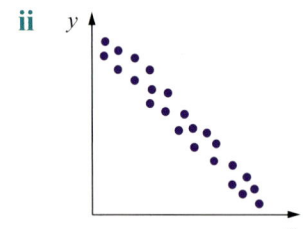   **ii** 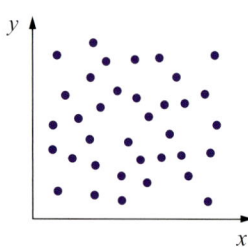   **iii**

6 The graph shows the six-monthly dividends for a share.

    a What was the dividend paid in

      i February 2010?

      ii August 2011?

      iii February 2013?

    b **i** What was the maximum dividend paid in this time interval?

      ii When did this occur?

    c In which six-monthly period was there the biggest:

      i gain in the dividend paid?

      ii decrease in the dividend paid?

    d Give a brief description of the change in the dividends paid over this time period?

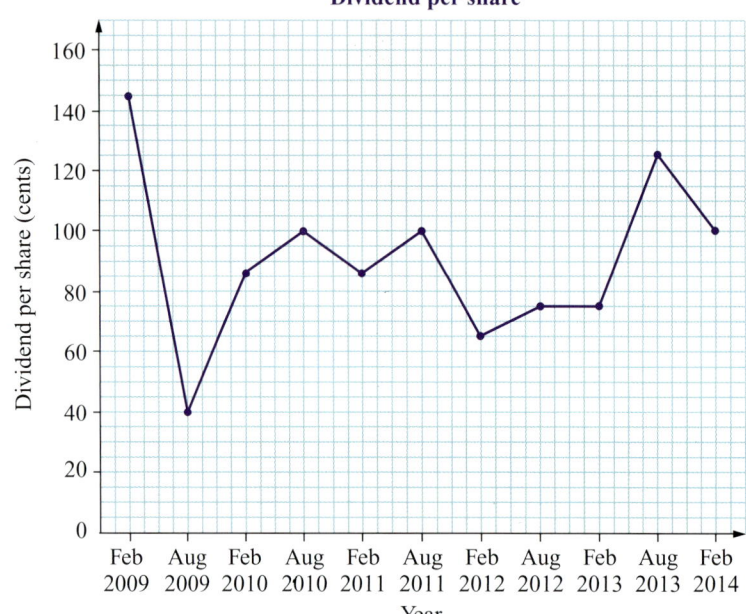

7

x	15	16	17	18	19	20	21	22	23	24
y	42	40	35	34	29	29	22	20	17	14

    a Draw a scatter plot for the data given in the table.

    b Determine the strength and direction of the relationship between the variables.

    c Draw a line of best fit on the scatter plot.

    d Find the equation of the line of best fit.

    e Use the equation to find the value of:

      i y when $x = 26$ **ii** x when $y = 27$

6

Financial mathematics

This chapter deals with solving problems involving compound interest and depreciation.

After completing this chapter you should be able to:

▶ calculate compound interest by repeated multiplication and using a table

▶ use the compound interest formula
▶ calculate depreciation using the compound interest formula.

NSW Syllabus references: 5.2 N&A Financial mathematics
Outcomes: MA5.2-1WM, MA5.2-2WM, MA5.2-3WM, MA5.2-4NA
Number & algebra –ACMNA229

Diagnostic test

1 The percentage of this shape that is shaded is:

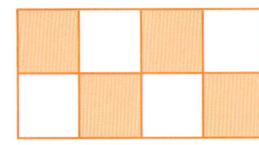

   A $\frac{1}{2}$ B 50%   C 0.5   D $\frac{4}{8}$%

2 41% expressed as a fraction is:

   A $4\frac{1}{10}$ B 0.41   C 0.041   D $\frac{41}{100}$

3 125% expressed as a simplified fraction is:

   A $1\frac{1}{4}$ B $\frac{125}{100}$ C $1\frac{25}{100}$ D $\frac{25}{20}$

4 $8\frac{1}{5}$% expressed as a decimal is:

   A 0.0082   B 0.082

   C 0.82   D 8.2

5 $\frac{4}{5}$ expressed as a percentage is:

   A 20%   B 40%

   C 60%   D 80%

6 3.56 expressed as a percentage is:

   A 356%   B 35.6%

   C 3.56%   D 0.356%

7 $270 expressed as a percentage of $300 is:

   A 90%   B 111.1%

   C 11.1%   D 10%

8 330 mL expressed as a percentage of 2L is:

   A 16500%   B 1650%

   C 165%   D 16.5%

9 12% of 90 km is:

   A 10.8 km   B 12.2 km

   C 14.6 km   D 18.3 km

10 $12\frac{1}{2}$% of 400 m is:

   A 0.05 m   B 0.5 m   C 5 m   D 50 m

11 The simple interest on $2490 at 4.5% p.a. for 5 years is:

   A $112.05   B $2602.05

   C $560.25   D $3050.25

12 Michelle invested $3000 for 4 years and earned $780 in interest. The annual rate of interest was:

   A 26%   B 6.5%   C 1.04%   D 4%

Use the values $x = 4$ and $y = 5$ for questions **13** to **15**.

13 The value of $3xy$ is:

   A 345   B 17   C 12   D 60

14 The value of $3x - 2y$ is:

   A 2   B 9   C 50   D 24

15 The value of $2x^2$ is:

   A 64   B 32   C 576   D 16

16 If $y = 6$ the value of $\frac{5y}{2}$ is:

   A 28   B 15   C 35   D 53

17 If $k = 5$ the value of $3(k + 2)$ is:

   A 21   B 17   C 37   D 11

18 Given $k = 5$, the value of $\frac{k + 10}{5}$ is:

   A 11   B 3   C 7   D 10

The diagnostic test questions refer to outcomes ACMNA157 and ACMNA176. (AC)

 # A Compound interest

If the interest earned each year on an investment is reinvested, the size of the principal on which interest is calculated increases each year. Hence the amount of interest earned also increases. This is called **compound interest**.

EXAMPLE 1

$6000 is invested for 3 years at 5% p.a. interest, compounded yearly.

a Calculate the value of the investment after 3 years.

b What is the total amount of interest earned?

'Compounded yearly' means that the interest is reinvested each year.

Solve	Think/Apply
a After 3 years, balance = $6615 + $330.75 = $6945.75	For the 1st year, the principal is $6000. 1st year interest = 5% of $6000 = $\frac{5}{100} \times \$6000 = \$300$ For the 2nd year, the principal is $6000 + $300 = $6300. 2nd year interest = 5% of $6300 = $\frac{5}{100} \times \$6300 = \$315$ For the 3rd year, the principal is $6300 + $315 = $6615. 3rd year interest = 5% of $6615 = $\frac{5}{100} \times \$6615 = \$330.75$ Hence, the balance after 3 years = $6615 + $330.75 = $6945.75. We can set this out in a table.
b Total interest earned = $6945.75 − $6000 (or $300 + $315 + $330.75) = $945.75	The total interest earned is the value of the investment at the end of the term minus the initial principal (amount invested), or the sum of all the interest payments.

Year	Principal	Interest (at 5%)	Balance at end of year
1st	$6000	$300	$6300
2nd	$6300	$315	$6615
3rd	$6615	$330.75	**a** $6945.75
	Total	**b** $945.75	

Exercise 6A

1 $5000 is invested for 3 years at 4% p.a. interest, compounded yearly. Use the table method above to calculate:

a the value of the investment after 3 years

b the total amount of interest earned.

2 $9000 is invested for 3 years at 2% p.a. interest, compounded yearly.

a Calculate the value of the investment after 3 years.

b What is the total amount of interest earned.

3 $8400 is invested for 3 years at 6% p.a. interest, compounded yearly.

    a Calculate the value of the investment after 3 years.

    b What is the total amount of interest earned?

● EXAMPLE 2

This example uses the constant multiplier method for the data in Example 1.   *The number 1.05 is called*
$6000 is invested for 3 years at 5% p.a. interest, compounded yearly.   *a constant multiplier.*

a Calculate the value of the investment after 3 years.

b What is the total amount of interest earned?

	Solve	Think	Apply
a	The value of the investment after 3 years is $6945.75.	Balance at the end of the 1st year = principal + 5% of principal = 100% of $6000 + 5% of $6000 or 105% of $6000 $= \dfrac{105}{100} \times \$6000 = 1.05 \times \$6000 = \$6300$ Balance at the end of the 2nd year = principal + 5% of principal = 100% of $6300 + 5% of $6300 or 105% of $6300 = 1.05 × $6300 = $6615 Balance at the end of the 3rd year = principal + 5% of principal = 100% of $6615 + 5% of $6615 or 105% of $6615 = 1.05 × $6615 = $6945.75	The balance at the end of each year can be found by repeated multiplication by a constant multiplier. In this case $\dfrac{105}{100} = 1.05.$
b	Total interest earned = $6945.75 − $6000 = $945.75	Total interest earned is the principal at the end of the term minus the initial principal, or the sum of all the interest payments.	

● EXAMPLE 3

a Find the amount to which $8600 grows in 3 years at 4% p.a. interest, compounded yearly.

b Hence calculate the total amount of interest earned over the 3 years.

	Solve	Think	Apply
a	The value of the investment after 3 years is $9673.83.	Constant multiplier = 100% + 4% = $\dfrac{104}{100}$ = 1.04 Balance at end of 1st year = $8600 × 1.04 = $8944 Balance at end of 2nd year = $8944 × 1.04 = $9301.76 Balance at end of 3rd year = $9301.76 × 1.04 = $9673.83	The principal is multiplied by as many of the constant multipliers as there are years.
b	Interest earned = $9673.83 − $8600 = $1073.83	Total interest earned is the principal at the end of the term minus the initial principal.	

4 a Use the constant multiplier method to find the amount to which $5000 grows in 3 years at 4% p.a. interest, compounded yearly.

b What is the total amount of interest earned?

5 a Calculate the amount to which $12 000 grows in 3 years at 5% p.a. interest, compounded yearly.

b What is the total amount of interest earned?

6 Complete the table below to find:

a the amount to which $25 000 grows in 3 years at 3% p.a. interest, compounded yearly

b the total amount of interest earned.

Year	Principal	Balance at end of year
1st	$25 000	$25 000 × 1.03 = $25 750
2nd	$25 750	$25 750 × 1.03 = ___
3rd		

7 Use a table like the one in question **6** to find:

a the amount to which $16 000 grows in 2 years at 8% p.a. interest, compounded yearly

b the total amount of interest earned.

8 Use a table to find:

a the amount to which $5800 grows in 3 years at 4.5% p.a. interest, compounded yearly

b the total amount of interest earned.

9 $14 200 is invested for 2 years at 2.9% p.a., interest compounded yearly.

a Calculate the value of the investment after 2 years.

b What is the total amount of interest earned?

10 $16 000 is invested for 3 years at 7.2% p.a. interest, compounded annually.

a Calculate the value of the investment after 3 years.

b What is the total amount of interest earned?

11 a Calculate the amount to which $11 000 will grow in 3 years if it is invested at 8% p.a.:

　i simple interest

　ii compound interest.

b Which method of calculating interest produces the greater amount and by how much?

12 a Calculate the amount to which $30 000 will grow in 4 years if it is invested at 5.6% p.a.:

　i simple interest

　ii compound interest.

b Which method of calculating interest produces the greater amount and by how much?

Investigation 1 Compound interest formula

Complete the following to calculate the amount to which $5000 will grow if invested for 10 years at 7% p.a. interest, compounding yearly.

Balance at end of 1st year = $5000 × 1.07

Balance at end of 2nd year = ($5000 × 1.07) × 1.07 = $5000 × 1.07^2

Balance at end of 3rd year = ($5000 × 1.07^2) × 1.07 = $5000 × _____

Balance at end of 4th year = ($5000 × 1.07^3) × 1.07 = _____

Balance at end of 5th year = ($5000 × 1.07^4) × 1.07 = _____

Balance at end of 6th year = ($5000 × 1.07^5) × 1.07 = _____

Balance at end of 7th year = ($5000 × 1.07^6) × 1.07 = _____

Balance at end of 8th year = ($5000 × 1.07^7) × 1.07 = _____

Balance at end of 9th year = ($5000 × 1.07^8) × 1.07 = _____

Balance at end of 10th year = $5000 × $1.07^{\square}$

In general, the amount A to which P will grow if invested for n years at r% p.a. compound interest is given by:

$$A = P(1 + R)^n \text{ where } R = \frac{r}{100}$$

This is known as the **compound interest formula**.

B Compound interest formula

From Investigation 1 the compound interest formula was found to be:

$$A = P(1 + R)^n$$

where P is the initial amount invested (principal)

$R = \frac{r}{100}$ and r is the percentage interest rate per compounding period

n is the number of compounding periods

A is the final amount (includes principal and interest).

● EXAMPLE 1

Use the compound interest formula to calculate:
a the amount to which $10 000 grows if invested for 8 years at 4.5% p.a. compound interest
b the amount of interest earned over this period.

	Solve	Think	Apply
a	$A = \$10\,000\left(1 + \dfrac{4.5}{100}\right)^8$ $= \$10\,000(1.045)^8$ $= \$14\,221.01$	$P = 10\,000$ $r = 4.5$ $n = 8$	Substitute the values into the compound interest formula $A = P(1 + R)^n$. The amount is always the original amount plus interest.
b	Interest $= \$14\,221.01 - \$10\,000$ $= \$4221.01$	Subtract the original amount invested.	

1 Use the compound interest formula to calculate:

    a the amount to which $6000 grows if it is invested for 5 years at 3% p.a. compound interest

    b the amount of interest earned over this period.

2 Use the compound interest formula to calculate:

    a the amount to which $18 000 grows if it is invested for 7 years at 6% p.a. compound interest

    b the amount of interest earned over this period.

3 a If I invest $25 000 at 6.5% p.a. compound interest, how much will I have in 10 years time?

    b Calculate the amount of interest earned over this period.

4 a If I invest $5000 at 4.7% p.a. compound interest, how much will I have in 8 years time?

    b Calculate the amount of interest earned over this period.

EXAMPLE 2

Use the compound interest formula to calculate the amount to which $10 000 grows if it is invested for 5 years at 9% p.a. interest, compounded:

    a monthly   **b** quarterly   **c** six-monthly.

	Solve	Think	Apply
a	$A = \$10\,000\left(1 + \dfrac{0.75}{100}\right)^{60}$ $= \$10\,000(1.0075)^{60}$ $= \$15\,656.81$	In this case the time period is monthly. Hence $r = \dfrac{9}{12}\% = 0.75\%$ per month and $n = 5 \times 12 = 60$ months.	The compound interest formula $A = P(1 + R)^n$ where $R = \dfrac{r}{100}$, can be adapted for this question by using r as the interest rate per time period and n as the number of time periods. *Note:* The more often the interest is reinvested, the greater the final value of the investment.
b	$A = \$10\,000\left(1 + \dfrac{2.25}{100}\right)^{20}$ $= \$10\,000(1.0225)^{20}$ $= \$15\,605.09$	The time period is quarterly. Hence $r = \dfrac{9}{4}\% = 2.25\%$ per quarter and $n = 5 \times 4 = 20$ quarters.	
c	$A = \$10\,000\left(1 + \dfrac{4.5}{100}\right)^{10}$ $= \$10\,000(1.045)^{10}$ $= \$15\,529.69$	The time period is six-monthly. Hence $r = \dfrac{9}{2}\% = 4.5\%$ per 6 months and $n = 5 \times 2 = 10$ six-monthly periods.	

5 Use the compound interest formula to calculate the amount to which $10 000 grows if it is invested for 3 years at 12% p.a. interest, compounded:

    a monthly   **b** quarterly   **c** six-monthly

6 Use the compound interest formula to calculate the amount to which $5000 grows if it is invested for 4 years at 6% p.a. interest, compounded:

    a monthly   **b** quarterly   **c** six-monthly

7 a Use the compound interest formula to calculate the amount to which $20 000 grows if it is invested for 5 years at 3% p.a. interest, compounded:

      i monthly   **ii** quarterly   **iii** six-monthly

    b Calculate the amount of interest earned in each case of part **a**. Which time period of compounding (reinvesting) gives the greatest amount of interest?

8 $5000 is invested at the following terms. Which investment will earn the greatest amount of interest?

    A 6% p.a. interest for 4 years, compounded yearly

    B 6% p.a. interest for 4 years, compounded six-monthly

    C 6% p.a. interest for 4 years, compounded quarterly

    D 6% p.a. interest for 4 years, compounded monthly

    E 6% p.a. interest for 4 years, simple interest

EXAMPLE 3

Cash advances, up to a certain limit, can be obtained using a credit card. In these cases compound interest is charged daily from the time the cash is withdrawn. Calculate the interest charged on a cash advance of $400 for 27 days when the annual interest rate is 16%.

Solve	Think	Apply
$A = \$400\left(1 + \left(\frac{16}{365} \div 100\right)\right)^{27}$ $= \$404.76$ (to the nearest cent) Interest charged $= \$404.76 - \$400 = \$4.76$	Use the compound interest formula: daily interest rate $= \frac{16}{365}\%$	Divide the percentage rate by 365 to make it daily, then by 100 to make it a decimal.

9 Calculate the interest charged on credit card cash advances with these annual interest rates.

    a $600 for 19 days at 16%   **b** $350 for 22 days at 16%   **c** $200 for 25 days at 19%

    d $500 for 15 days at 21%   **e** $400 for 13 days at 14%

C   Compound interest calculations

At times the final amount of an investment is given and calculations are used to find the principal, the time period or the interest rate.

EXAMPLE 1

Calculate how much money (principal) must be invested at 4% p.a. interest compounding annually to have $10 000 at the end of 3 years.

Solve	Think	Apply
$10\ 000 = P(1 + 0.04)^3$ $\qquad = P(1.04)^3$ $\frac{10\ 000}{(1.04)^3} = P$ $\qquad P = \$8889.96$	$A = P(1 + R)^n$ Substitute the values into the compound interest formula. As the interest compounds annually, $R = 0.04$ and $n = 3$.	Carefully check the compounding period. Substitute the answer into the formula to check.

1 Calculate the amount that must be invested at 6% p.a. interest compounding annually to have $4000 at the end of 5 years.

2 Calculate the amount that must be invested at 7% p.a. interest compounding annually to have $6000 at the end of 4 years.

3 Calculate the amount that must be invested at 2.5% p.a. interest compounding annually to have $1000 at the end of 7 years.

4 Calculate the amount that must be invested at 3.6% p.a. interest compounding annually to have $800 at the end of 6 years.

5 Calculate the amount that must be invested at 1.8% p.a. interest compounding annually to have $400 at the end of 10 years.

EXAMPLE 2

Calculate how much money must be invested at 6% p.a. interest compounding quarterly to have $5000 after 2 years.

Solve	Think	Apply
$5000 = P(1 + 0.015)^8$ $\quad\quad = P(1.015)^8$ $\dfrac{5000}{(1.015)^8} = P$ $P = \$4438.56$	$A = P(1 + R)^n$ The investment compounds quarterly. Divide 0.06 by 4 to obtain R. Multiply 2 by 4 to obtain n.	Calculate the values of R and n. In general, R is divided by the number of compounding periods per annum and n is multiplied.

6 Calculate the amount that must be invested at 8% p.a. interest compounding quarterly to have $3000 at the end of 3 years.

7 Calculate the amount that must be invested at 3.2% p.a. interest compounding quarterly to have $7000 at the end of 8 years.

8 Calculate the amount that must be invested at 8% p.a. interest compounding quarterly to have $3000 at the end of 6 years.

9 Calculate the amount that must be invested at 6% p.a. interest compounding monthly to have $500 at the end of 6 years.

10 Calculate the amount that must be invested at 4.8% p.a. interest compounding monthly to have $1200 at the end of 5 years.

11 Calculate the amount that must be invested at 2.4% p.a. interest compounding monthly to have $10 000 at the end of 8 years.

12 Calculate the amount that must be invested at 5.1% p.a. interest compounding monthly to have $450 at the end of 3 years.

EXAMPLE 3

What annual compound interest rate is required to increase $2000 to $2500 over 5 years?

Solve	Think	Apply
$2500 = 2000(1 + R)^5$ $\dfrac{2500}{2000} = (1 + R)^5$ $1.25 = (1 + R)^5$ $\sqrt[5]{1.25} = (1 + R)$ $1.0456\ldots = 1 + R$ $\therefore R = 0.0456\ldots \approx 0.046$ The interest rate required is 4.6% p.a.	$A = P(1 + R)^n$ Substitute the values. As the compounding period is annual, $n = 5$. $R = \dfrac{r}{100}$ so $r = R \times 100$	Substitute the values and solve the resulting equation. The value of R is for that compounding time period.

13 What annual compound interest rate is required to increase $1000 to $1200 over 4 years?

14 What annual compound interest rate is required to increase $500 to $800 over 6 years?

15 What annual compound interest rate is required to increase $3500 to $4000 over 4 years?

16 What annual compound interest rate is required to increase $200 to $300 over 8 years?

17 What annual compound interest rate is required to increase $450 to $500 over 3 years?

EXAMPLE 4

What interest rate compounding monthly is required to increase $500 to $700 over 3 years?

Solve	Think	Apply
$700 = 500(1 + R)^{36}$ $\dfrac{700}{500} = (1 + R)^{36}$ $1.4 = (1 + R)^{36}$ $\sqrt[36]{1.4} = 1 + R$ $1.009\ 39 = 1 + R$ $R = 0.009\ 39$ $r = 0.00939 \times 12 \times 100$ $= 11.27\%$ p.a. The interest rate required is 11.27% p.a.	$A = P(1 + R)^n$ $A = 700,\ P = 500$ 3 years is 36 months so $n = 36$. Subtract 1 from both sides. This is R for 1 month. Multiply R by 12 to make the rate annual. Multiply by 100 to make it a percentage.	Substitute the values and calculate. The number of time periods depends on the frequency of compounding the interest. The value of R is in terms of the compounding period.

18 What interest rate compounding monthly is required to increase $900 to $1200 over 6 years?

19 What interest rate compounding monthly is required to increase $8000 to $10 000 over 5 years?

20 What interest rate compounding monthly is required to increase $100 to $125 over 4 years?

21 What interest rate compounding quarterly is required to increase $400 to $450 over 3 years?

22 What interest rate compounding quarterly is required to increase $900 to $1200 over 6 years?

23 What interest rate compounding half yearly is required to increase $1000 to $1300 over 8 years?

• EXAMPLE 5

The amount of $7300 is obtained when $6000 is invested at 5% interest, compounding annually. Use guess, check and refine to calculate the value of n.

Solve	Think	Apply
$A = P(1 + R)^n$ $7300 = 6000(1.05)^n$ $6000(1.05)^3 = \$6945.75$ $6000(1.05)^6 = \$8040.57$ $6000(1.05)^4 = \$7293.04$ The time is approximately 4 years.	Substitute the values into the compound interest formula. Try $n = 3$ too small Try $n = 6$ too big Try $n = 4$ very close	Try different values for n. If the value is less, then use a bigger value of n.

24 The amount of $2020 is obtained when $1500 is invested at 5.1% p.a. interest, compounding annually. Use guess, check and refine to calculate the value of n.

25 The amount of $2700 is obtained when $2000 is invested at 3.4% p.a. interest, compounding annually. Use guess, check and refine to calculate the value of n.

26 The amount of $800 is obtained when $600 is invested at 4.2% p.a. interest, compounding annually. Use guess, check and refine to calculate the value of n.

• EXAMPLE 6

How long would it take to obtain $1000 if $600 is invested at 4.8% p.a. interest, compounding monthly? Use the guess, check and refine method. Give the answer to the nearest month.

Solve	Think	Apply
$A = P(1 + R)^n$ $1000 = 600(1 + 0.004)^n$ $600(1.004)^{100} = \$894$ $600(1.004)^{150} = \$1091.96$ $600(1.004)^{130} = \$1008.17$ $600(1.004)^{128} = \$1000.15$ Thus $n = 128$ The time is 10 years and 8 months.	Substitute using $R = 0.048 \div 12 = 0.004$ Try $n = 100$ too small Try $n = 150$ too big Try $n = 130$ very close Try $n = 128$ correct Thus $n = 128$ months or 10 years 8 months.	The value of n will be approximate and may take many attempts to obtain the correct value.

27 The amount of $600 is obtained when $550 is invested at 3.2% p.a. interest, compounding quarterly. Use guess, check and refine to calculate the value of n.

28 The amount of $1400 is obtained when $1300 is invested at 5% p.a. interest, compounding quarterly. Use guess, check and refine to calculate the value of n.

29 The amount of $820 is obtained when $750 is invested at 3.6% p.a. interest, compounding monthly. Use guess, check and refine to calculate the value of *n*.

30 The amount of $5100 is obtained when $5000 is invested at 2.4% p.a. interest, compounding monthly. Use guess, check and refine to calculate the value of *n*.

Investigation 2 Using a spreadsheet

The following spreadsheets can be used for compound interest calculations. Enter the formulas as shown to perform the calculations. Use the spreadsheets to confirm the answers to the questions in Exercise 6C.

1 This spreadsheet can be used to calculate the final amount of an investment when the principal, interest rate and time period are known.

	A	B	C	D
1	Compound interest calculator			
2	Principal	Interest rate as a percentage	Number of years	Number of compounding periods per year
3	8889.96	6	3	1
4				
5	Final amount			
6	=A3*(1+B3/(100*D3))^(C3*D3)			

2 This spreadsheet can be used to calculate the interest rate required to achieve a final amount of an investment when the principal and time period are known.

	A	B	C	D
1	Compound interest calculator			
2	Principal	Final amount	Number of years	Number of compounding periods per year
3	2000	2500	5	1
4				
5	Interest rate	Annual rate as a percentage		
6	=(B3/A3)^(1/C3)-1	=D3*A6*100		

3 This spreadsheet can be used to calculate the time period required to achieve a final amount of an investment when the principal and time period are known. Enter the formulas for this spreadsheet and then fill down until the amount required is shown. The number in column A shows the number of time periods.

	A	B	C	D
1	Compound interest calculator			
2	Principal	Final amount	Interest rate as a percentage	Number of compounding periods per year
3	5000	5100	2.4	1
4				
5	Time period	Amount		
6	1	=$A$3*(1+$C$3/($D$3*100))^A6		Fill down A7 and B7 until the amount is located.
7	=A6+1	=$A$3*(1+$C$3/($D$3*100))^A7		

D Depreciation

Many items such as cars, machinery and computers lose value over time because of wear and tear from usage, becoming out of date, and so on. This loss is called **depreciation**.

EXAMPLE 1

a A farm tractor depreciates each year by 20% of its value at the start of the year. Calculate the value after 3 years of a new tractor that costs $35 000.

b Find the amount the tractor has been depreciated over the 3 years.

	Solve	Think	Apply
a	Value after 1 year = 80% of $35 000 = $28 000 Value after 2 years = 80% of $28 000 = $22 400 Value after 3 years = 80% of $22 400 = $17 920	As the tractor loses 20% of its value each year, its value at the end of the year will be 100% − 20% = 80% of its value at the start of the year.	Depreciation is similar to compound interest except that the 'interest' is subtracted, thus reducing the value.
b	Amount of depreciation = $35 000 − $17 920 = $17 080	Subtract the depreciated value from the original cost.	

Exercise 6D

1 a Calculate the value after 3 years of a new car that costs $30 000 and depreciates by 20% of its value at the start of each year.

b Find the amount of depreciation over the 3 years.

2 a Calculate the value after 2 years of a new car that costs $25 000 and depreciates by 18% of its value at the start of each year.

b Find the amount of depreciation over the 2 years.

3 a Calculate the value after 3 years of a new computer that costs $4000 and depreciates by 25% of its value at the start of each year.

b Find the amount of depreciation over the 3 years.

EXAMPLE 2

a A new car that costs \$35 000 depreciates by 22% of its value at the start of each year. Calculate the value after 3 years.

b Find the amount of depreciation over the 3 years

	Solve	Think/Apply
a	$V = P(1 - R)^n$ $= \$35\,000\left(1 - \dfrac{22}{100}\right)^3$ $= \$16\,609$ to the nearest dollar	The compound interest formula can be adapted for these calculations as follows. $V = P(1 - R)^n$ where V is the depreciated value, P is original value, R is the rate of depreciation per year and n is the number of years.
b	Amount of depreciation $= \$35\,000 - \$16\,609$ $= \$18\,391$	Subtract the depreciated value from the original amount.

4 a Calculate the value after 3 years of a new forklift that costs \$48 000 and depreciates by 25% of its value at the start of each year.

b What is the amount of depreciation over the 3 years?

5 a Calculate the value after 5 years of a photocopier that costs \$21 000 and depreciates by 18% of its value at the start of each year.

b What is the amount of depreciation over the 5 years?

6 a Calculate the value after 2 years of a computer that costs \$2500 and depreciates by 16% of its value at the start of each year.

b What is the amount of depreciation over the 2 years?

7 a Calculate the present value of office furniture purchased 6 years ago for \$11 900 if the rate of depreciation is 15% p.a.

b How much has the furniture depreciated in value?

8 a What is the current value of a security system installed 5 years ago for \$17 600 if the rate of depreciation is 28% p.a?

b How much has the security system depreciated in value?

EXAMPLE 3

The purchase price of a new grand piano is $32 000. It depreciates by 15% of its value at the start of each year. Use the guess and refine method to find how long it will take for the piano to depreciate in value to $16 000.

Solve	Think	Apply
$V = P(1 - R)^n$ $= \$32\,000\left(1 - \dfrac{15}{100}\right)^n$ $= \$32\,000(0.85)^n$ $V = \$32\,000(0.85)^3$ $= \$19\,652$ $V = \$32\,000(0.95)^4$ $= \$16\,704$ $V = \$32\,000(0.85)^5$ $= \$14\,199$ The piano is worth $16 000 after approximately 4 years.	Use the depreciation formula to find the value of the piano after n years. Substitute the values. Try $n = 3$ too high Try $n = 4$ close Try $n = 5$ too low	The value of n will be approximate and may take many attempts to obtain the correct or a close value. *Use the guess, check and refine method.*

9 The purchase price of a new boat is $28 000. It depreciates by 20% of its value at the start of each year. Use the guess and refine method to find how long it will take for the boat to depreciate in value to $11 000.

10 The purchase price of a new motor bike is $36 000. It depreciates by 22% of its value at the start of each year. Use the guess and refine method to find how long it will take for the motor bike to be worth half its original price.

11 A bicycle courier purchases a bicycle for $3250. It depreciates at 25% p.a. Use the guess and refine method to find how long it will take for the bicycle to depreciate in value to $1000.

Language in mathematics

1 Using examples, explain the difference between simple interest and compound interest.

2 Complete the following words by replacing the vowels.
   a pr__nc__p__l
   b m__n__m__m
   c __nv__stm__nt
   d m__lt__pl__ __r
   e r__p__ym__nt

3 Three of the following words have been spelt incorrectly. Write these words with their correct spelling.
   a quorterly
   b constant
   c depresiation
   d intrest
   e reducible
   f purchase

Terms

annually	balance	compound interest	constant multiplier	depreciation	equivalent
interest	investment	principal	quarterly	reducible	repayment

Check your skills

1 The calculations for $5000 invested for 3 years at 4% p.a. interest compounded yearly are set out in the table.

Year	Principal	Interest (at 4%) p.a.	Balance at end of year
1st	$5000	$200	x
2nd	$5200	y	$5408
3rd	$5408	$216.32	$5624.32

The amounts missing from the table above are:
   A $x = \$5000, y = \$200$
   B $x = \$5000, y = \$208$
   C $x = \$5200, y = \$208$
   D $x = \$5200, y = \$200$

2 The calculations for the amount to which $24 000 grows in 3 years at 6.5% p.a. interest compounded yearly are set out in the table.

Year	Principal	Balance at end of year
1st	$24 000	$24\,000 \times x = \$25\,560$
2nd	$25 560	$\$25\,560 \times 1.065 = \$27\,221.40$
3rd	$27 221.40	$= \$y$

The amounts missing from the table above are:
   A $x = 0.065, y = 28\,990.79$
   B $x = 0.065, y = 1769.39$
   C $x = 1.065, y = 28\,990.79$
   D $x = 1.065, y = 1769.39$

3 $12 000 is invested for 3 years at 4.5% p.a. interest, compounded yearly. The amount of interest earned is:
   A $13 693.99
   B $1693.99
   C $1620
   D $13 620

4 The amount to which an investment of $9000 grows if it is invested for 7 years at 3% p.a. interest compounded yearly is:
   A $9000(1 + 0.07)^3$
   B $9000(1 + 0.03) \times 7$
   C $\$(9000 + (1 + 0.03)^7)$
   D $9000(1 + 0.03)^7$

5 The amount of interest earned when $15 000 is invested for 12 years at 6% p.a. interest compounded yearly is (to the nearest dollar):

   A $30 183   **B** $29 607   **C** $10 800   **D** $15 183

6 The amount to which an investment of $10 000 grows if invested for 4 years at 3% p.a. interest compounded monthly is:

   A $10 100.38   **B** $11 273.28   **C** $32 714.90   **D** $41 322.52

7 The interest charged on a credit card cash advance of $500 for 18 days if the annual interest rate is 24% and compound interest is charged daily is (to the nearest cent):

   A $120   **B** $0.33   **C** $5.92   **D** $5.95

8 If $6000 is invested at 4% p.a. interest for 7 years, the investment will earn the greatest amount when the interest is compounded:

   A yearly   **B** six-monthly   **C** quarterly   **D** monthly

9 The amount of money that must be invested at 8% p.a. interest compounding quarterly to have $5000 at the end of 3 years is:

   A $1986   **B** $3942   **C** $3969   **D** $54 712

10 A new car that costs $28 000 depreciates by 22% of its value at the start of each year. Its value after 5 years is:

   A $\{28\,000(1 + 0.22) \times 5\}$ **B** $\{28\,000(1 - 0.22) \times 5\}$

   C $28\,000(1 + 0.22)^5$ **D** $28\,000(1 - 0.22)^5$

11 The amount of depreciation over 3 years of a computer that costs $18 000 and depreciates by 28% of its value at the start of the year is (to the nearest dollar):

   A $15 120   **B** $11 282   **C** $6718   **D** $2880

If you have any difficulty with these questions, refer to the examples and questions in the sections listed in the table.

Question	1, 2	3–8	9	10, 11
Section	A	B	C	D

6A   Review set

1 $8000 is invested for 3 years at 7% p.a. interest, compounded (reinvested) yearly.

   a Calculate the value of the investment after 3 years.

   b What is the total amount of interest earned?

2 Complete the table below to calculate:

   a the amount to which $30 000 grows in 3 years at 4% p.a. interest, compounded yearly

   b the total amount of interest earned.

Year	Principal	Balance at end of year
1st	$30 000	$30 000 × 1.04 = $31 200
2nd	$31 200	$31 200 × 1.04 = $_____
3rd	$_____	$_____

3 a Calculate the amount to which $25 000 will grow in 4 years if it is invested at 6.5% p.a.:

    i simple interest   **ii** compound interest.

  b Which method of calculating interest produces the greater amount, and by how much?

4 Use the compound interest formula to calculate:

  a the amount to which $12 000 grows if it is invested for 6 years at 7.5% p.a. compound interest

  b the amount of interest earned over this period.

5 Calculate the amount to which $6000 grows if it is invested for 4 years at 9% p.a. interest, compounded:

  a monthly   **b** quarterly   **c** six-monthly.

6 Calculate the compound interest charged when using a credit card for a cash advance of $800 for 19 days if the annual interest rate is 21% and interest is charged daily.

7 Calculate the amount that must be invested at 5.5% p.a. interest compounding annually to have $3000 at the end of 4 years.

8 a Calculate the value after 3 years of a new yacht that costs $34 000 and depreciates by 22% of its value at the start of each year.

  b Find the amount of depreciation over the 3 years.

9 Use the depreciation formula to find the value after 3 years of a computer that costs $3499 and depreciates by 22% of its value at the start of each year.

10 The purchase price of a new car is $29 000. It depreciates by 20% of its value at the start of each year. Use the guess and refine method to find how long it will take for the car to depreciate in value to $12 000.

6B   Review set

1 $6500 is invested for 3 years at 4.9% p.a. interest, compounded (reinvested) yearly.

  a Calculate the value of the investment after 3 years.

  b What is the total amount of interest earned?

2 Complete the table below to find:

  a the amount to which $20 000 grows in 3 years at 6% p.a. interest, compounded yearly

  b the total amount of interest earned.

Year	Principal	Balance at end of year
1st	$20 000	$20 000 × 1.06 = $21 200
2nd	$21 200	$21 200 × 1.06 = $_____
3rd	$_____	$_____

3 a Calculate the amount to which $15 000 will grow in 5 years if it is invested at 4.5% p.a.:

    i simple interest   **ii** compound interest.

  b Which method of calculating interest produces the greater amount, and by how much?

4 Use the compound interest formula to calculate:

  a the amount to which $8000 grows if it is invested for 6 years at 3.5% p.a. compound interest

  b the amount of interest earned over this period.

5 Calculate the amount to which $10 000 grows if it is invested for 3 years at 8% p.a. and interest is compounded:
    a monthly   **b** quarterly   **c** six-monthly.

6 Calculate the compound interest charged when using a credit card for a cash advance of $500 for 15 days if the annual interest rate is 28% and interest is charged daily.

7 Calculate the amount that must be invested at 3.6% p.a. interest compounding monthly to have $700 at the end of 5 years.

8 **a** Calculate the value after 3 years of a new piece of farm machinery that costs $36 000 and depreciates by 19% of its value at the start of each year.
    b What is the amount of depreciation over the 3 years?

9 Use the depreciation formula to find the value after 3 years of a photocopier that costs $7899 and depreciates by 23% of its value at the start of each year.

10 The purchase price of office furniture is $25 600. It depreciates by 18% of its value at the start of each year. Use the guess and refine method to find how long it will take for the furniture to depreciate in value to $12 000.

6C   Review set

1 $9500 is invested for 3 years at 3.6% p.a. interest, compounded (reinvested) yearly.
    a Calculate the value of the investment after 3 years.
    b What is the total amount of interest earned?

2 Complete the table below to find:
    a the amount to which $12 000 grows in 3 years at 4.8% p.a. interest, compounded yearly
    b the total amount of interest earned.

Year	Principal	Balance at end of year
1st	$12 000	$12 000 × 1.048 = $12 576
2nd	$12 576	$12 576 × 1.048 = $_____
3rd	$_____	$_____

3 **a** Calculate the amount to which $6000 will grow in 5 years if it is invested at 7.2% p.a.:
       i simple interest   **ii** compound interest.
    b Which method of calculating interest produces the greater amount, and by how much?

4 Use the compound interest formula to calculate:
    a the amount to which $5000 grows if it is invested for 8 years at 4.5% p.a. compound interest
    b the amount of interest earned over this period.

5 Calculate the amount to which $8000 grows if it is invested for 3 years at 6% p.a. and interest is compounded:
    a monthly   **b** quarterly   **c** six-monthly.

6 Calculate the compound interest charged when using a credit card for a cash advance of $600 for 22 days if the annual interest rate is 25% and interest is charged daily.

7 What annual compound interest rate is required to increase $3000 to $3800 over 6 years?

8 a Calculate the value after 4 years of a new tractor that costs $38 000 and depreciates by 24% of its value at the start of each year.

b Find the amount of depreciation over the 4 years.

9 Use the depreciation formula to find the value after 3 years of a printer that costs $3500 and depreciates by 28% of its value at the start of each year.

10 The purchase price of a new car is $31 400. It depreciates by 19% of its value at the start of each year. Use the guess and refine method to find how long it will take for the car to depreciate in value to $13 500.

6D   Review set

1 $4500 is invested for 3 years at 5.5% p.a. interest, compounded (reinvested) yearly.

a Calculate the value of the investment after 3 years.

b What is the total amount of interest earned?

2 Complete the table below to find:

a the amount to which $13 000 grows in 3 years at 5.2% p.a. interest, compounded yearly

b the total amount of interest earned.

Year	Principal	Balance at end of year
1st	$13 000	$13 000 × 1.052 = $13 676
2nd	$13 676	$13 676 × 1.052 = $_____
3rd	$_____	$_____

3 a Calculate the amount to which $9000 will grow in 5 years if it is invested at 3.8% p.a.:

   i simple interest   **ii** compound interest.

b Which method of calculating interest produces the greater amount, and by how much?

4 Use the compound interest formula to calculate:

a the amount to which $5000 grows if it is invested for 6 years at 4.2% p.a. compound interest

b the amount of interest earned over this period.

5 Calculate the amount to which $30 000 grows if it is invested for 4 years at 6% p.a. and interest is compounded:

a monthly   **b** quarterly   **c** six-monthly.

6 Calculate the compound interest charged when using a credit card for a cash advance of $700 for 25 days if the annual interest rate is 28% and interest is charged daily.

7 What interest rate compounding monthly is required to increase $1200 to $1500 over 3 years?

8 a Calculate the value after 3 years of a new robot that costs $29 500 and depreciates by 23% of its value at the start of each year.

b Find the amount of depreciation over the 3 years.

9 Use the depreciation formula to find the value after 3 years of a bottling machine that costs $19 600 and depreciates by 23% of its value at the start of each year.

10 The purchase price of a new car is $31 400. It depreciates by 18% of its value at the start of each year. Use the guess and refine method to find how long it will take for the car to depreciate in value to $14 000.

7

Binomial expressions and quadratics

This chapter deals with expanding binomial products, factorising quadratic expressions and solving simple quadratic equations.

After completing this chapter you should be able to:

▶ expand quadratic expressions
▶ solve simple quadratic equations
▶ factorise binomial products

▶ factorise quadratic trinomial expressions
▶ simplify expressions by factorising.

NSW Syllabus references: 5.2 N&A Algebraic techniques
Outcomes: MA5.2-1WM, MA5.2-3WM, MA5.2-6NA, MA5.3-1WM, MA5.3-5NA
Number & algebra – ACMNA233, ACMNA241, ACMNA 269

Diagnostic test

1. The diagram shows 2 cups and 3 marbles.

   If there are y marbles in each cup, an expression for the total number of marbles is:

   A $2 \times y + 3$ **B** $3 \times y + 2$

   C $2 \times y + 3 \times y$ **D** $2(3 + y)$

2. The value of $4 \times p - 2$ when $p = 5$ is:

   A 43   **B** 18   **C** 12   **D** 5

3. The expression that does not simplify to $36m$ is:

   A $36 \times m$ **B** $3 \times 6 \times m$

   C $6 \times 6 \times m$ **D** $4 \times 9 \times m$

4. When $x = 3$ and $y = 8$, the value of $4xy$ is:

   A 438   **B** 20   **C** 152   **D** 96

5. The expressions that is not equivalent to $\dfrac{2r}{3p}$ is:

   A $2r \div 3p$ **B** $2 \times r \div 3p$

   C $2 \times r \div (3 \times p)$ **D** $3p \div 2r$

6. When $t = 4$, the value of $\dfrac{3t + 8}{4}$ is:

   A 5   **B** $10\frac{1}{2}$ **C** 9   **D** $\frac{11}{4}$

7. The missing numbers in the pattern 3, 7, __, 15, __, 23 are:

   A 11 and 27   **B** 10 and 18

   C 10 and 19   **D** 11 and 19

8. $5a + 7a + 3 =$

   A $12a^2 + 3$ **B** $12a + 3$

   C $15a$ **D** $15a^2$

9. $-8g \times 4m =$

   A -32 **B** $-32gm$

   C $4gm$ **D** $-84gm$

10. $6ab \div 18b =$

    A $\dfrac{a}{3}$ **B** $3a$ **C** $3ab^2$ **D** $\dfrac{3}{a}$

11. $\dfrac{6k}{11} + \dfrac{4k}{11} =$

    A $\dfrac{10k}{22}$ **B** $\dfrac{5k}{11}$ **C** $\dfrac{2k}{11}$ **D** $\dfrac{10k}{11}$

12. $\dfrac{2x}{3} + \dfrac{x}{5} =$

    A $\dfrac{3x}{8}$ **B** $\dfrac{2x^2}{15}$ **C** $\dfrac{13x}{15}$ **D** $\dfrac{2x^2}{8}$

13. When expanded $a(x - y) =$

    A $x - ay$ **B** $ax - ay$

    C $ax - y$ **D** $ax - a^2y$

14. When expanded $6(2m - 5) =$

    A $8m - 11$ **B** $12m - 5$

    C $12m - 30$ **D** $2m - 30$

15. When factorised $15x - 20 =$

    A $5(3x - 20)$ **B** $5(3x - 4)$

    C $x(15 - 20)$ **D** $-5x$

16. When $m = 5$ and $n = -3$, the value of the expression $3m - 2n$ is:

    A 9   **B** 2   **C** -19 **D** 21

17. By inspection, the value of the pronumeral if $x + 9 = 10$ is:

    A 19   **B** -1 **C** 1   **D** -19

18. The value of T in the equation $3T = -9$ is:

    A -3 **B** 0   **C** $\frac{1}{3}$ **D** 3

19. The value of G in the equation $\dfrac{5G - 2}{7} = 3$ is:

    A $3\frac{4}{5}$ **B** $4\frac{3}{5}$ **C** $4\frac{4}{5}$ **D** $3\frac{3}{5}$

20. The value of m in the equation $3m - 9 = 5m + 5$ is:

    A 2   **B** -7 **C** -2 **D** 7

21. When $x = 7$, $y = -3$ and $z = 0$, the value of the expression $z(4x - 2y)$ is:

    A 34   **B** 6   **C** 22   **D** 0

22. Given $s = p^3 + \sqrt{m^2 - n}$, the value of s when $p = 5$, $m = 4$ and $n = 12$ is:

    A 18   **B** 58   **C** 127   **D** 156

23. An equation using x as the number for: 'Four times a certain number is added to ten and the result is eighteen' is:

    A $40 + x = 18$ **B** $4x + 10 = 18$

    C $4(x + 10) = 18$ **D** $40x + 10 - 18$

The diagnostic test questions refer to outcomes ACMNA190, ACMNA191, ACMNA192, ACMNA234, ACMNA235 and ACMNA240. **AC**

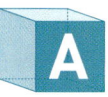 **A** # Quadratic expressions

Quadratic expressions are of the form $ax^2 + bx + c$ where x is a variable and a, b and c are constants, with $a \neq 0$.

EXAMPLE 1

A rectangle has length 4 cm more than its breadth. Write an expression for the area.

Solve	Think	Apply
$A = (x + 4) \times x$ $\quad = x(x + 4)$ $\quad = x^2 + 4x$ cm²	$x + 4$ x Let the breadth be x cm. Then the length is $(x + 4)$ cm. Area = length × breadth	Define the first variable and then obtain an expression for the second variable.

Exercise 7A

1 A rectangle has length 6 cm more than its breadth. Write an expression for the area.

2 A rectangle has length 5 cm more than its breadth. Write an expression for the area.

3 A rectangle has length 3 cm more than its breadth. Write an expression for the area.

4 A triangle has perpendicular height 3 cm more than its base length. Write an expression for the area.

5 What is an expression for the area of the rectangle with sides $(x + 3)$ and $(x + 1)$?

6 What is an expression for the area of the triangle with base $(x + 7)$ and height $(x + 2)$?

EXAMPLE 2

Expand and simplify the expression for the area of a rectangle with sides $(x + 3)$ and $(x + 2)$.

Solve	Think	Apply
Area $= (x + 3)(x + 2)$ $\quad = x(x + 2) + 3(x + 2)$ $\quad = x^2 + 2x + 3x + 6$ $\quad = x^2 + 5x + 6$	$\begin{array}{c|c|c} & x & +3 \\ \hline x & x^2 & +3x \\ \hline +2 & +2x & +6 \end{array}$	Use a diagram to find the four terms.

7 Expand and simplify the expression for the area of a rectangle with these sides.

   a $(x + 5)$ and $(x + 1)$ **b** $(x + 7)$ and $(x + 2)$ **c** $(x + 3)$ and $(x + 8)$

● EXAMPLE 3

Expand and simplify the following.

   a $(x + 3)(x - 5)$ **b** $(x - 2)(x - 1)$ **c** $(x - 5)(x + 7)$

	Solve	Think/Apply
a	$(x + 3)(x - 5) = x(x - 5) + 3(x - 5)$ $= x^2 - 5x + 3x - 15$ $= x^2 - 2x - 15$	Split the first bracket then multiply each term by the second bracket. Simplify your answer.
b	$(x - 2)(x - 1) = x(x - 1) - 2(x - 1)$ $= x^2 - x - 2x + 2$ $= x^2 - 3x + 2$	
c	$(x - 5)(x + 7) = x(x + 7) - 5(x + 7)$ $= x^2 + 7x - 5x - 35$ $= x^2 + 2x - 35$	

8 Expand and simplify the following.

   a $(x + 4)(x + 2)$ **b** $(x - 3)(x + 2)$ **c** $(x + 6)(x - 2)$

   d $(x + 4)(x - 3)$ **e** $(x - 5)(x + 3)$ **f** $(x + 9)(x - 5)$

   g $(x - 10)(x + 3)$ **h** $(x - 4)(x - 7)$ **i** $(x + 7)(x - 1)$

   j $(x - 3)(x - 2)$ **k** $(x - 6)(x - 9)$ **l** $(x - 12)(x - 3)$

● EXAMPLE 4

If $x = 3$ and $y = -2$, find the value of:

   a $3x^2 - 2x + 5$ **b** $(x + 2)(y + 3)$ **c** $(3x - 2)(x + 5)$

	Solve	Think/Apply
a	$3x^2 - 2x + 5 = 3(3)^2 - 2(3) + 5$ $= 26$	Substitute the values then evaluate the equation.
b	$(x + 2)(y + 3) = (3 + 2)(-2 + 3)$ $= (5)(1)$ $= 5$	
c	$(3x - 2)(x + 5) = (3(3) - 2)(3 + 5)$ $= (7)(8)$ $= 56$	

9 If $x = 4$ and $y = -3$, find the value of:

   a $2x^2 - 3x + 1$ **b** $4x^2 + 2x - 1$ **c** $y^2 - 3y + 5$

   d $4y^2 - 7y - 2$ **e** $5x^2 - 7x + 1$ **f** $(x + 3)(y - 2)$

   g $(x - 5)(x + 2)$ **h** $(y - 3)(y + 5)$ **i** $(3x - 7)(2x + 1)$

   j $(4x + 1)(3y - 2)$ **k** $(5x - 2)(3x + 1)$ **l** $(8y - 2)(y + 1)$

EXAMPLE 5

Expand and simplify the following.

a $(2x - 5)(x + 3)$ b $(5x - 7)(2x + 5)$ c $(3x + 2)(2x - 1)$

	Solve	Think/Apply
a	$(2x - 5)(x + 3) = 2x(x + 3) - 5(x + 3)$ $\qquad = 2x^2 + 6x - 5x - 15$ $\qquad = 2x^2 + x - 15$	Split the first bracket and multiply the second bracket by each item. Collect like terms.
b	$(5x - 7)(2x + 5) = 5x(2x + 5) - 7(2x + 5)$ $\qquad = 10x^2 + 25x - 14x - 35$ $\qquad = 10x^2 + 11x - 35$	
c	$(3x + 2)(2x - 1) = 3x(2x - 1) + 2(2x - 1)$ $\qquad = 6x^2 - 3x + 4x - 2$ $\qquad = 6x^2 + x - 2$	

10 Expand and simplify the following.

a $(2x + 3)(x - 1)$ b $(2x - 5)(x - 8)$ c $(3x - 5)(x - 5)$

d $(3x + 2)(3x - 5)$ e $(2x + 9)(3x - 2)$ f $(4x - 5)(4x + 5)$

g $(4x + 1)(3x - 1)$ h $(2x - 5)(3x - 2)$ i $(2x + 3)(4x - 5)$

j $(7x - 2)(7x + 2)$ k $(5x - 3)(2x - 5)$ l $(4x + 1)(3x - 5)$

11 Expand and simplify the following.

a $3x + (x - 5)(x + 2)$ b $6x + (2x - 1)(3x + 4)$ c $(x + 2)(x - 7) - 2x$

d $(x + 5)(x + 2) - 5x$ e $(3x - 7)(x - 2) + 5x$ f $(4x - 2)(x + 3) - 4x^2 + 2$

g $4 - (x - 3)(x + 2)$ h $7x - (2x + 1)(x - 5)$ i $6x - (x - 2)(2x - 3)$

Investigation 1 Using substitution

Rachel and Diana have different answers to the same question.

Rachel has $(3x - 2)(4x + 7) = 12x^2 + 13x - 14$.

Diana has $(3x - 2)(4x + 7) = 12x^2 + 25x - 14$.

Answer the following questions to determine who is correct.

1 Substitute $x = 1$ and evaluate these three expressions.

a $(3x - 2)(4x + 7)$ b $12x^2 + 13x - 14$ c $12x^2 + 25x - 14$

2 Who is correct, Rachel or Diana?

3 Robert substitutes $x = 0$ into the three expressions in question **1** and decides that both Rachel and Diana are correct.

a Evaluate each expression when $x = 0$.

b Explain the flaw in Robert's reasoning.

4 How can you ensure your substitution will work?

NUMBER & ALGEBRA

Investigation 2 Square numbers

1 Find 3×3 and -3×-3. Compare the answers.

2 Find:

   a 4×4 and -4×-4 **b** 5×5 and -5×-5

   c -6×-6 and 6×6 **d** -10×-10 and 10×10

3 What do you notice about the answers to each part in question **2**?

4 The solution to the equation $x^2 = 49$ is found by finding a number that when multiplied by itself gives 49. What are the two answers?

5 The solution to $x^2 = 64$ is $x = 8$ or -8. Explain why there are two answers.

6 Are there always two answers to $x^2 = c$ where c is a number? Explain, considering c as positive or negative.

B Simple quadratic equations

From Investigation 2 it can be seen that there are two solutions to the equation $x^2 = c$ where $c > 0$.

This equation is called a **quadratic equation** because the variable x has a power of 2.

EXAMPLE 1

Solve the following.

  a $x^2 = 25$ **b** $x^2 = 169$

	Solve	Think/Apply
a	$x^2 = 25$ $x = \pm\sqrt{25}$ $= \pm 5$	Find the square root of both sides. Use the $\pm$ symbol to indicate that there is a positive and a negative answer.
b	$x^2 = 169$ $x = \pm\sqrt{169}$ $= \pm 13$	$\pm$ is the symbol for 'plus or minus'.

Exercise 7B

1 Solve the following.

  a $x^2 = 9$ **b** $x^2 = 16$ **c** $x^2 = 64$ **d** $x^2 = 144$

  e $x^2 = 49$ **f** $x^2 = 121$ **g** $x^2 = 36$ **h** $x^2 = 81$

  i $x^2 = 100$ **j** $x^2 = 4$ **k** $x^2 = 225$ **l** $x^2 = 289$

EXAMPLE 2

Solve the following.

a $x^2 = 10$ **b** $x^2 = 43$

	Solve	Think/Apply
a	$x^2 = 10$ $x = \pm\sqrt{10}$ $= \pm 3.16$ (2 decimal places)	Find the square root of both sides. There is always a positive and a negative answer so we use $\pm$.
b	$x^2 = 43$ $x = \pm\sqrt{43}$ $= \pm 6.56$ (2 decimal places)	

2 Solve the following, giving the answers to 2 decimal places.

    a $x^2 = 12$ **b** $x^2 = 51$ **c** $x^2 = 19$ **d** $x^2 = 47$

    e $x^2 = 83$ **f** $x^2 = 28$ **g** $x^2 = 68$ **h** $x^2 = 91$

    i $x^2 = 193$ **j** $x^2 = 200$ **k** $x^2 = 39$ **l** $x^2 = 17$

EXAMPLE 3

Solve the following.

a $5x^2 = 80$ **b** $3x^2 = 75$

	Solve	Think	Apply
a	$5x^2 = 80$ $x^2 = 16$ $x = \pm\sqrt{16}$ $= \pm 4$	Divide both sides by 5. Find the square root of both sides.	You can only find the square root of both sides when x^2 is a number.
b	$3x^2 = 75$ $x^2 = 25$ $x = \pm\sqrt{25}$ $= \pm 5$	Divide both sides by 3. Find the square root of both sides.	

Quadratic equations have two answers. **!**

3 Solve the following.

    a $2x^2 = 18$

    b $5x^2 = 180$

    c $8x^2 = 72$

    d $3x^2 = 48$

    e $7x^2 = 175$

    f $10x^2 = 160$

    g $7x^2 = 252$

    h $6x^2 = 294$

    i $4x^2 = 676$

NUMBER & ALGEBRA

EXAMPLE 4

Solve the following.

a $9x^2 = 25$ **b** $81x^2 = 49$

	Solve	Think	Apply
a	$9x^2 = 25$ $x^2 = \dfrac{25}{9}$ $x = \pm\sqrt{\dfrac{25}{9}}$ $= \pm\dfrac{5}{3}$	Divide both sides by 9. Find the square root of the numerator and the denominator.	You can only find the square root of both sides when x^2 is a number.
b	$81x^2 = 49$ $x^2 = \dfrac{49}{81}$ $x = \pm\sqrt{\dfrac{49}{81}}$ $= \pm\dfrac{7}{9}$	Divide both sides by 9. Find the square root of the numerator and the denominator.	

4 Solve the following.

a $4x^2 = 49$ **b** $100x^2 = 81$ **c** $25x^2 = 16$

d $81x^2 = 16$ **e** $49x^2 = 144$ **f** $121x^2 = 64$

g $144x^2 = 49$ **h** $81x^2 = 100$ **i** $36x^2 = 169$

EXAMPLE 5

Solve the following.

a $3x^2 = 21$ **b** $5x^2 = 12$

	Solve	Think	Apply
a	$3x^2 = 21$ $x^2 = 7$ $x = \pm\sqrt{7}$ $= \pm2.65$ (2 decimal places)	Divide both sides by 3. Find the square root of both sides.	If the number is not a square number use a calculator for an approximation.
b	$5x^2 = 12$ $x^2 = \dfrac{12}{5}$ $x = \pm\sqrt{\dfrac{12}{5}}$ $= \pm1.55$ (2 decimal places)	Divide both sides by 5. Find the square root of both sides.	

5 Solve, giving answers to 2 decimal places if necessary.

a $7x^2 = 56$ **b** $4x^2 = 12$ **c** $11x^2 = 66$

d $13x^2 = 47$ **e** $7x^2 = 18$ **f** $5x^2 = 23$

EXAMPLE 6

Solve $4x^2 - 5 = 20$.

Solve	Think	Apply
$4x^2 - 5 = 20$		The last step is to find the square root.
$4x^2 = 25$	Add 5 to both sides.	
$x^2 = \dfrac{25}{4}$	Divide both sides by 4.	
$x = \pm\dfrac{\sqrt{25}}{\sqrt{4}} = \pm\dfrac{5}{2}$	Take the square root of both sides.	

6 Solve, leaving the answer as a fraction if necessary.

    a $9x^2 - 8 = 56$ **b** $4x^2 + 3 = 52$ **c** $81x^2 + 7 = 107$ **d** $49x^2 - 20 = 5$

C Binomial products

A **binomial product** is the product of expressions that each have two terms, such as $(x + 1)(x + 3)$.

Perfect squares expansion

$$
\begin{aligned}
(a + b)^2 &= (a + b)(a + b) \\
&= a(a + b) + b(a + b) \\
&= a^2 + ab + ba + b^2 \\
&= a^2 + 2ab + b^2
\end{aligned}
$$

So $\qquad (a + b)^2 = a^2 + 2ab + b^2$

and similarly $\quad (a - b)^2 = a^2 - 2ab + b^2$

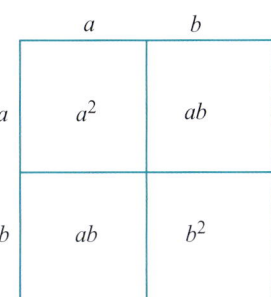

Difference of two squares expansion

$$
\begin{aligned}
(a + b)(a - b) &= a(a - b) + b(a - b) \\
&= a^2 - ab + ba - b^2 \\
&= a^2 - b^2
\end{aligned}
$$

So $\qquad (a + b)(a - b) = a^2 - b^2$

EXAMPLE 1

Expand and simplify the following.

    a $(x + 5)^2$ **b** $(x - 3)^2$ **c** $(4x - 5)^2$

	Solve	Think/Apply
a	$(x + 5)^2 = x^2 + 2 \times x \times 5 + 5^2$ $\qquad\qquad = x^2 + 10x + 25$	Use the perfect square expansion. Make sure the middle term is calculated correctly. The last term is always positive.
b	$(x - 3)^2 = x^2 - 2 \times x \times 3 + 3^2$ $\qquad\qquad = x^2 - 6x + 9$	
c	$(4x - 5)^2 = (4x)^2 - 2 \times 4x \times 5 + 5^2$ $\qquad\qquad\quad = 16x^2 - 40x + 25$	

NUMBER & ALGEBRA

1 Expand the following perfect squares.

a $(x + 2)^2$ b $(x + 6)^2$ c $(y + 10)^2$ d $(3x + 1)^2$

e $(2x + 3)^2$ f $(4a + 5)^2$ g $(5x + 4)^2$ h $(3y + 2)^2$

i $(4 + 3x)^2$ j $(1 + 2x)^2$ k $(5 + 2x)^2$ l $(4 + 5x)^2$

2 Expand the following perfect squares.

a $(x - 2)^2$ b $(x - 6)^2$ c $(y - 9)^2$ d $(3x - 1)^2$

e $(2x - 3)^2$ f $(5a - 4)^2$ g $(3x - 4)^2$ h $(4y - 1)^2$

i $(5 - 2x)^2$ j $(1 - 3x)^2$ k $(5 - 3x)^2$ l $(4 - 2x)^2$

3 Expand these perfect squares.

a $(x + 5)^2$ b $(x - 5)^2$ c $(2x - 7)^2$

d $(2x + 7)^2$ e $(3x - 5)^2$ f $(4x + 3)^2$

g $(5 + 2x)^2$ h $(3 - 7x)^2$ i $(3 - 11x)^2$

EXAMPLE 2

Expand the following using the difference of two squares.

a $(x + 5)(x - 5)$ b $(2x - 3)(2x + 3)$

	Solve	Think/Apply
a	$(x + 5)(x - 5) = x^2 - 5^2$ $= x^2 - 25$	Use the difference of two squares expansion. There is no middle term and the second term is always negative.
b	$(2x - 3)(2x + 3) = (2x)^2 - (3)^2$ $= 4x^2 - 9$	

4 Expand and simplify using the difference of two squares.

a $(x + 3)(x - 3)$ b $(x + 4)(x - 4)$

c $(x + 6)(x - 6)$ d $(x - 10)(x + 10)$

e $(x + 1)(x - 1)$ f $(2x - 5)(2x + 5)$

g $(3x - 2)(3x + 2)$ h $(5x + 1)(5x - 1)$

i $(7x + 8)(7x - 8)$ j $(11x - 9)(11x + 9)$

5 Expand and simplify using one of the rules.

a $(x - 10)^2$ b $(x + 7)^2$

c $(x + 8)(x - 8)$ d $(x + 11)(x - 11)$

e $(x + 4)(x + 4)$ f $(x - 7)(x + 7)$

g $(x - 7)^2$ h $(x - 12)(x + 12)$

i $(x + 12)(x + 12)$ j $(x + 3)(x + 3)$

NUMBER & ALGEBRA

EXAMPLE 3

Complete the following expressions.

a $(x + 5)^2 = x^2 + \square x + \square$ **b** $(x - \square)^2 = x^2 - 8x + \square$ **c** $(y + \square)^2 = y^2 + 5y + \square$

	Solve	Think	Apply
a	$(x + 5)^2 = x^2 + \square x + \square$ $= x^2 + 10x + 25$	The coefficient of x is the 'twice the product' term, so $2 \times 1 \times 5 = 10$. The constant term is the second term squared, so $5^2 = 25$.	These expressions are based on the perfect square expansions $(x + y)^2 = x^2 + 2xy + y^2$ and $(x - y)^2 = x^2 - 2xy + y^2$.
b	$(x - \square)^2 = x^2 - 8x + \square$ $(x - 4)^2 = x^2 - 8x + 16$	The coefficient of x must be halved: $-8 \div 2 = -4$ The constant term is thus $(-4)^2 = 16$.	
c	$(y + \square)^2 = y^2 + 5y + \square$ $(y + \frac{5}{2})^2 = y^2 + 5y + \frac{25}{4}$	The coefficient of y must be halved: $5 \div 2 = \frac{5}{2}$ The constant term is thus $\left(\frac{5}{2}\right)^2 = \frac{25}{4}$.	

6 Complete the following expressions.

a $(x + 3)^2 = x^2 + \square x + \square$

b $(x - 7)^2 = x^2 - 14x + \square$

c $(x - 2)^2 = x^2 \_\_ \square + \square$

d $(x - \square)^2 = x^2 - 6x + \square$

e $(x - \square)^2 = x^2 - 10x + \square$

f $(x + \square)^2 = x^2 + 12x + \square$

g $(x + \square)^2 = x^2 \_\_ \square + 49$

h $(x + \square)^2 = x^2 + 18x + \square$

EXAMPLE 4

What number needs to be added to these expressions to complete the square?

a $x^2 + 4x$ **b** $x^2 - 7x$

	Solve	Think	Apply
a	$x^2 + 4x$ $x^2 + 4x + \square = (x + \square)^2$ 4 needs to be added. The expression is $x^2 + 4x + 4$.	Constant term $= \left(\frac{4}{2}\right)^2 = 4$	Halve the coefficient of x and square it to find the constant term.
b	$x^2 - 7x$ $x^2 - 7x + \square = (x - \square)^2$ $\frac{49}{4}$ needs to be added. The expression is $x^2 - 7x + \frac{49}{4}$.	Constant term $= \left(-\frac{7}{2}\right)^2 = \frac{49}{4}$	

7 What number needs to be added to complete the square in the following expressions?

a $x^2 + 6x$ **b** $x^2 + 10x$ **c** $x^2 - 8x$

d $x^2 - 4x$ **e** $x^2 + 12x$ **f** $x^2 - 18x$

g $x^2 + 7x$ **h** $x^2 + 15x$ **i** $x^2 - 3x$

j $x^2 - 9x$ **k** $x^2 - x$ **l** $x^2 + x$

D | Common factors review

Factorisation is the reverse process of expansion.

As $3(x + 2) = 3x + 6$, then factorisation of $3x + 6 = 3(x + 2)$.

Remove the highest common factor (HCF). ❗

● EXAMPLE 1

Factorise the following fully by removing the HCF.

a $10x + 5$ b $4x^2 - 2x$ c $p^2q - q^2p$

	Solve	Think	Apply
a	$10x + 5 = 5(2x + 1)$	The HCF is 5.	To factorise completely, always remove the HCF factor.
b	$4x^2 - 2x = 2x(2x - 1)$	The HCF is $2x$.	
c	$p^2q - q^2p = pq(p - q)$	The HCF is pq.	Check the factorising by expanding your answer.

Exercise 7D

1 Factorise the following fully.

a $3a - 3b$ b $5m + 10n$ c $pq - qr$

d $x^2 - 5x$ e $4x^2 + x$ f $15x + 3x^2$

g $pq - 3q^2$ h $2\pi R - 2\pi r$ i $6x^2y - 18xy^2$

j $28p^2a - 21pa$ k $9x^2y + 27xy$ l $3pqr - 15p^2q$

Take care when removing a negative sign. ❗

2 Factorise the following fully, removing the negative factor.

a $-3a - 3b$ b $-4x^2 - 2x$ c $-8a + 4b$

d $-4 - 8b$ e $-3 - x$ f $-18x^2 + 9x$

● EXAMPLE 2

Factorise the following fully.

a $6R + xR + yR$ b $9x + 18xy + 12x^2$

c $4(x - 1) + y(x - 1)$ d $x(y + 3) - (y + 3)$

	Solve	Think	Apply
a	$6R + xR + yR = R(6 + x + y)$	The HCF is R.	To factorise completely always remove the common factor, which may be a term such as $(x - 1)$.
b	$9x + 18xy + 12x^2 = 3x(3 + 6y + 4x)$	The HCF is $3x$.	
c	$4(x - 1) + y(x - 1) = (x - 1)(4 + y)$	The HCF is $(x - 1)$.	
d	$x(y + 3) - (y + 3) = (y + 3)(x - 1)$	The HCF is $(y + 3)$.	Check the factorising by expanding your answer.

3 Factorise the following fully.

a $6B + aB + cB$

b $4R - xR + yR$

c $7x + 14xy - 3xz$

d $8x^2 - 24xy + 16xyz$

e $4(x - 2) + y(x - 2)$

f $3(x - 1) + y(x - 1)$

g $a(x + 1) + 3(x + 1)$

h $x(x - 4) - (x - 4)$

i $3(p - 3) + x(p - 3) + y(p - 3)$

j $x(a + 1) - (a + 1) - y(a + 1)$

● EXAMPLE 3

Factorise the following fully.

a $3x + 6 + xy + 2y$

b $4x - 4 + xz - z$

	Solve	Think	Apply
a	$3x + 6 + xy + 2y = 3(x + 2) + y(x + 2)$ $= (x + 2)(3 + y)$	Factorise 3 from one pair and y from the other. The common factor is $(x + 2)$.	Factorise in pairs first if there is not a common factor. It might be necessary to try factorising different pairs.
b	$4x - 4 + xz - z = 4(x - 1) + z(x - 1)$ $= (x - 1)(4 + z)$	Factorise 4 from one pair and z from the other. The common factor is $(x - 1)$.	

---

4 Factorise the following fully.

a $4x + 2 + 2x^2 + x$

b $3x - 3 + xz - z$

c $xy + 5y + 3x + 15$

d $xy - 2y + 4x - 8$

e $x^2 - 7x + xy - 7y$

f $4x - x^2 + 4y - xy$

g $xy + 3x - 2y - 6$

h $2xy - 8x + 5y - 20$

i $3xy - 7y + 12x - 28$

j $3x + 3t - x^2 - xt$

k $3a + ac - 3b - bc$

l $3x^2 + 3xy - 2x - 2y$

m $4 + 4y - 3x - 3xy$

n $6a - 5ay + 6b - 5by$

o $4p - 3p^2 - 4q + 3pq$

E Difference of two squares factorisation

Recall that $(x + y)(x - y) = x^2 - y^2$, so the factorisation of $x^2 - y^2$ is $(x + y)(x - y)$.

This is the difference of two squares factorisation, and can be shown in a diagram.

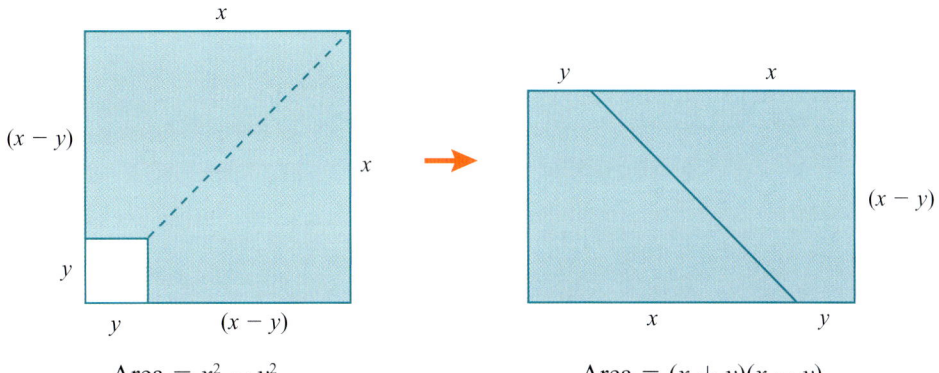

Area $= x^2 - y^2$ Area $= (x + y)(x - y)$

Thus: $x^2 - y^2 = (x + y)(x - y)$

EXAMPLE 1

Factorise the following.

a $x^2 - 9$ **b** $4y^2 - 9$ **c** $4x^2 - 25$

	Solve	Think/Apply
a	$x^2 - 9 = (x + 3)(x - 3)$	Use the difference of two squares factorisation, taking the square root of each term.
b	$4y^2 - 9 = (2y + 3)(2y - 3)$	
c	$4x^2 - 25 = (2x + 5)(2x - 5)$	

Exercise 7E

1 Factorise the following fully.

a $x^2 - 4$ **b** $y^2 - 9$ **c** $z^2 - 16$

d $a^2 - 9$ **e** $c^2 - 25$ **f** $x^2 - y^2$

g $a^2 - c^2$ **h** $m^2 - n^2$ **i** $4x^2 - 1$

j $9x^2 - 4$ **k** $9x^2 - 1$ **l** $16y^2 - 9$

m $25y^2 - 16x^2$ **n** $100x^2 - 81y^2$ **o** $64a^2 - 25b^2$

EXAMPLE 2

Evaluate the following using the difference of two squares factorisation.

a $101^2 - 99^2$ **b** $(4.8)^2 - (2.8)^2$

	Solve	Think/Apply
a	$101^2 - 99^2 = (101 + 99)(101 - 99)$ $= (200)(2)$ $= 400$	Use the difference of two squares to make the calculation easier.
b	$(4.8)^2 - (2.8)^2 = (4.8 + 2.8)(4.8 - 2.8)$ $= (7.6)(2)$ $= 15.2$	

2 Evaluate using the difference of two squares factorisation.

a $301^2 - 299^2$ **b** $201^2 - 199^2$ **c** $105^2 - 95^2$

d $(3.5)^2 - (2.5)^2$ **e** $(9.4)^2 - (9.3)^2$ **f** $856^2 - 855^2$

3 Factorise the following.

a $x^4 - y^4$ **b** $a^4 - b^4$ **c** $p^4 - q^4$

d $16a^4 - 81b^4$ **e** $81a^4 - b^4$ **f** $16x^4 - 625y^4$

g $(p - q)^2 - (p + q)^2$ **h** $(a + b)^2 - (a - b)^2$ **i** $(2x - 3y)^2 - (2x + 3y)^2$

F Perfect squares factorisation

As $(x + y)^2 = (x + y)(x + y) = x^2 + 2xy + y^2$, the factorisation of $x^2 + 2xy + y^2$ is $(x + y)^2$.

Similarly $(x - y)^2 = (x - y)(x - y)$
$\qquad\qquad\quad = x^2 - 2xy + y^2$

So the factorisation of $x^2 - 2xy + y^2$ is $(x - y)^2$.

The sign of the coefficient of the x term has the sign inside the bracket.

● EXAMPLE 1

Factorise the following.

a $x^2 + 4x + 4$

b $x^2 - 6x + 9$

Take the square root of the constant term.

	Solve	Think	Apply
a	$x^2 + 4x + 4 = x^2 + 4x + 4$ $\qquad\qquad\quad = (x + 2)^2$	Square root of 4 is 2 and $2 \times 2 = 4$.	The coefficient of x must be double the square root of the constant term.
b	$x^2 - 6x + 9 = (x - 3)^2$	Square root of 9 is 3 and $2 \times 3 = 6$.	

Exercise 7F

1 Factorise the following.

a $x^2 + 10x + 25$ **b** $x^2 - 20x + 100$ **c** $x^2 + 18x + 81$

d $x^2 - 16x + 64$ **e** $x^2 - 14x + 49$ **f** $x^2 + 22x + 121$

g $y^2 - 6y + 9$ **h** $y^2 + 2y + 1$ **i** $x^2 - 24x + 144$

j $p^2 - 8p + 16$ **k** $m^2 + 6m + 9$ **l** $a^2 - 10a + 25$

● EXAMPLE 2

Factorise the following.

a $4x^2 + 12x + 9$

b $9x^2 - 30x + 25$

	Solve	Think/Apply
a	$4x^2 + 12x + 9$ $\sqrt{4} = 2, \sqrt{9} = 3$ $2 \times 3 \times 2 = 12$ Thus $4x^2 + 12x + 9 = (2x + 3)^2$	Find the square root of the coefficient of x^2. Find the square root of the constant term. Check that the product of these square roots multiplied by 2 is the coefficient of x.
b	$9x^2 - 30x + 25$ $\sqrt{9} = 3, \sqrt{25} = 5$ $2 \times 3 \times 5 = 30$ Thus $9x^2 - 30x + 25 = (3x - 5)^2$	*The square root of the constant term must be positive.*

2 Factorise the following.

a $4x^2 + 20x + 25$ **b** $25x^2 + 60x + 36$ **c** $16x^2 - 72x + 81$

d $9x^2 - 48x + 64$ **e** $121x^2 - 132x + 36$ **f** $81x^2 + 90x + 25$

g $49x^2 + 140x + 100$ **h** $25x^2 - 20x + 4$ **i** $4x^2 + 44x + 121$

j $49x^2 - 42x + 9$ **k** $9x^2 - 30x + 25$ **l** $100x^2 - 180x + 81$

● EXAMPLE 3

Factorise the following.

a $x^2 + 2xy + y^2$

b $a^2 - 2ab + b^2$

	Solve	Think/Apply
a	$x^2 + 2xy + y^2 = (x + y)^2$	These are both perfect squares.
b	$a^2 - 2ab + b^2 = (a - b)^2$	

---

3 Factorise the following.

a $p^2 + 2pq + q^2$ **b** $m^2 - 2mn + n^2$ **c** $r^2 + 2rt + t^2$

d $d^2 - 2dp + p^2$ **e** $n^2 - 2nt + t^2$ **f** $r^2 + 2ry + y^2$

g $a^2 - 2ab + b^2$ **h** $y^2 + 2xy + x^2$ **i** $z^2 + 2zw + w^2$

G Quadratic trinomials

First expand $(x + a)(x + b)$.

$$(x + a)(x + b) = x(x + b) + a(x + b)$$
$$= x^2 + bx + ax + ab$$
$$= x^2 + (a + b)x + ab$$

So, the factorisation of $x^2 + (a + b)x + ab = (x + a)(x + b)$.

The sum of the numbers a and b is the coefficient of the term x and the product of the numbers a and b is the constant term.

● EXAMPLE 1

Factorise the following.

a $x^2 + 5x + 6$ **b** $x^2 + 7x + 10$ **c** $x^2 + 7x + 12$

	Solve	Think	Apply
a	$x^2 + 5x + 6 = (x + 3)(x + 2)$	Two numbers that add to give 5 and have a product of 6 are 3 and 2.	The constant term is the product of a and b and the sign indicates adding or subtracting.
b	$x^2 + 7x + 10 = (x + 5)(x + 2)$	Two numbers that add to give 7 and have a product of 10 are 5 and 2.	
c	$x^2 + 7x + 12 = (x + 4)(x + 3)$	Two numbers that add to give 7 and have a product of 12 are 4 and 3.	

NUMBER & ALGEBRA

1 Fully factorise the following.

- **a** $x^2 + 8x + 7$
- **b** $x^2 + 8x + 12$
- **c** $x^2 + 13x + 12$
- **d** $x^2 + 10x + 9$
- **e** $x^2 + 10x + 24$
- **f** $x^2 + 13x + 30$
- **g** $x^2 + 11x + 30$
- **h** $x^2 + 12x + 20$
- **i** $x^2 + 9x + 20$
- **j** $x^2 + 9x + 18$
- **k** $x^2 + 19x + 18$
- **l** $x^2 + 13x + 42$

● EXAMPLE 2

Factorise the following.

- **a** $x^2 - 4x + 3$
- **b** $x^2 - 8x + 12$

	Solve	Think	Apply
a	$x^2 - 4x + 3 = (x - 3)(x - 1)$	Two numbers whose sum is -4 and product is 3 are -3 and -1.	A positive constant term has both factors with the same sign.
b	$x^2 - 8x + 12 = (x - 6)(x - 2)$	Two numbers whose sum is -8 and product is 12 are -6 and -2.	

2 Fully factorise the following.

- **a** $x^2 - 6x + 5$
- **b** $x^2 - 8x + 7$
- **c** $x^2 - 12x + 11$
- **d** $x^2 - 6x + 8$
- **e** $x^2 - 9x + 8$
- **f** $x^2 - 7x + 10$
- **g** $x^2 - 11x + 10$
- **h** $x^2 - 8x + 15$
- **i** $x^2 - 16x + 15$
- **j** $x^2 - 9x + 14$
- **k** $x^2 - 15x + 14$
- **l** $x^2 - 11x + 24$

● EXAMPLE 3

Factorise the following.

- **a** $x^2 - 3x - 10$
- **b** $x^2 + x - 6$

	Solve	Think	Apply
a	$x^2 - 3x - 10 = (x - 5)(x + 2)$	Two numbers whose sum is -3 and product is -10 are -5 and 2.	A negative constant term has factors with different signs.
b	$x^2 + x - 6 = (x + 3)(x - 2)$	Two numbers whose sum is 1 and product is -6 are 3 and -2.	

3 Fully factorise the following.

- **a** $x^2 + 7x - 8$
- **b** $x^2 + 3x - 10$
- **c** $x^2 + x - 2$
- **d** $x^2 + x - 42$
- **e** $x^2 + 4x - 12$
- **f** $x^2 - 11x - 12$
- **g** $x^2 - 5x - 24$
- **h** $x^2 + 5x - 24$
- **i** $x^2 + 4x - 21$
- **j** $x^2 - 20x - 21$
- **k** $x^2 + 17x - 60$
- **l** $x^2 + 3x - 54$

4 Fully factorise the following.

- **a** $x^2 + 19x + 18$
- **b** $x^2 - 7x - 18$
- **c** $x^2 + 17x - 18$
- **d** $x^2 + 15x + 54$
- **e** $x^2 + 53x - 54$
- **f** $x^2 - 25x - 54$
- **g** $x^2 - 16x + 64$
- **h** $x^2 + 12x - 64$
- **i** $x^2 - 30x - 64$
- **j** $x^2 + 2x - 35$
- **k** $x^2 + 7x - 30$
- **l** $x^2 - 15x + 50$

H # Further quadratic trinomials

There are several methods for factorising trinomials of the form $ax^2 + bx + c$ where $a \neq 1$. The method used in this book is given in Example 1.

● **EXAMPLE 1**

Factorise the following.

a $2x^2 + x - 3$ **b** $3x^2 + 16x + 5$ **c** $5x^2 + 13x - 6$

	Solve	Think	Apply
a	$2x^2 + x - 3 = \dfrac{(2x + 3)(2x - 2)}{2}$ $= \dfrac{(2x + 3)2(x - 1)}{2}$ $= (2x + 3)(x - 1)$	$2 \times -3 = -6$ Thus we need two numbers with a product of -6 and a sum of $+1$. These are 3 and -2. Take out the common factor and cancel with the denominator.	Place the coefficient of x^2 together with x at the beginning of each bracket and divide the whole expression by this coefficient to maintain equality.
b	$3x^2 + 16x + 5 = \dfrac{(3x + 15)(3x + 1)}{3}$ $= \dfrac{3(x + 5)(3x + 1)}{3}$ $= (x + 5)(3x + 1)$	$3 \times 5 = 15$ Thus we need two numbers with a product of 15 and a sum of 16. These are 15 and 1. Take out the common factor and cancel with the denominator.	
c	$5x^2 + 13x - 6 = \dfrac{(5x + 15)(5x - 2)}{5}$ $= \dfrac{5(x + 3)(5x - 2)}{5}$ $= (x + 3)(5x - 2)$	$5 \times -6 = -30$ Thus we need two numbers with a product of -30 and a sum of $+13$. These are 15 and -2. Take out the common factor and cancel with the denominator.	

Exercise 7H

1 Fully factorise the following.

a $2x^2 + 5x + 3$	**b** $2x^2 - 9x - 5$	**c** $3x^2 + 5x - 2$	**d** $3x^2 - 5x - 2$
e $2x^2 + 7x + 5$	**f** $2x^2 + 3x - 2$	**g** $7x^2 + 9x + 2$	**h** $2x^2 + 3x - 5$
i $5x^2 - 14x - 3$	**j** $5x^2 + 2x - 3$	**k** $5x^2 - 8x + 3$	**l** $11x^2 - 9x - 2$

2 Fully factorise the following.

a $2x^2 + 5x - 12$	**b** $3x^2 - 7x - 6$	**c** $3x^2 + 7x + 4$	**d** $2x^2 - 3x - 9$
e $3x^2 + 13x + 4$	**f** $3x^2 - 17x + 10$	**g** $3x^2 + 8x + 4$	**h** $5x^2 - 13x - 6$
i $3x^2 + 10x - 8$	**j** $2x^2 + 17x - 9$	**k** $2x^2 + 9x - 18$	**l** $2x^2 + 11x - 21$

3 Fully factorise the following.

a $2x^2 + 9x - 35$	**b** $3x^2 + 5x - 12$	**c** $5x^2 - 8x + 3$	**d** $3x^2 - x - 2$
e $5x^2 - 29x + 20$	**f** $7x^2 + 15x + 2$	**g** $11x^2 - 52x - 15$	**h** $7x^2 - 61x + 40$
i $5x^2 - 52x + 63$	**j** $5x^2 + 11x - 12$	**k** $3x^2 + 13x + 12$	**l** $2x^2 + 5x - 3$

EXAMPLE 2

Fully factorise the following.

a $6x^2 - 13x - 5$ b $12x^2 - 5x - 2$

	Solve	Think	Apply
a	$6x^2 - 13x - 5 = \dfrac{(6x - 15)(6x + 2)}{6}$ $= \dfrac{3(2x - 5)2(3x + 1)}{6}$ $= (2x - 5)(3x + 1)$	$6 \times -5 = -30$ Thus we need two numbers with a product of -30 and a sum of -13. These are -15 and 2. Factorise each bracket then cancel.	Place the coefficient of x^2 together with x at the beginning of each bracket and divide the whole expression by this coefficient to maintain equality.
b	$12x^2 - 5x - 2 = \dfrac{(12x - 8)(12x + 3)}{12}$ $= \dfrac{4(3x - 2)3(4x + 1)}{12}$ $= (3x - 2)(4x + 1)$	$12 \times -2 = -24$ Thus we need two numbers with a product of -24 and a sum of -5. These are -8 and 3. Factorise each bracket then cancel.	

4 Fully factorise the following.

a $8x^2 + 14x + 3$ b $15x^2 + x - 2$ c $21x^2 + 17x + 2$ d $6x^2 + 5x + 1$

e $6x^2 + 19x + 3$ f $10x^2 + 17x + 3$ g $14x^2 + 37x + 5$ h $21x^2 - 62x - 3$

i $4x^2 + 4x + 1$ j $10x^2 + x - 2$ k $9x^2 - 12x + 4$ l $3x^2 + 14x + 8$

5 Fully factorise the following.

a $6x^2 - 7x - 3$ b $4x^2 - 23x + 15$ c $9x^2 - 6x - 8$ d $12x^2 - 23x + 5$

e $12x^2 - 7x - 10$ f $12x^2 - 79x - 35$ g $10x^2 + 19x - 15$ h $20x^2 - 31x - 7$

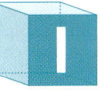

Miscellaneous factorisation

When solving miscellaneous equations the following order of factorising is useful:

1 Take out a common factor.   **2** Use the difference of two squares.

3 Factorise the quadratic trinomial.   **4** Group in pairs.

EXAMPLE 1

Factorise the following.

a $3x^2 - 12$ b $2x^2 - 10x + 12$ c $x^4 - 9x^2$

	Solve	Think	Apply
a	$3x^2 - 12 = 3(x^2 - 4)$ $= 3(x + 2)(x - 2)$	Common factor is 3 then use difference of two squares.	Always look for the common factor first.
b	$2x^2 - 10x + 12 = 2(x^2 - 5x + 6)$ $= 2(x \quad 3)(x - 2)$	Common factor of 2 first then use quadratic trinomial.	
c	$x^4 - 9x^2 = x^2(x^2 - 9)$ $= x^2(x + 3)(x - 3)$	Common factor of x^2 first then use difference of two squares.	

1 Fully factorise the following.

  a $3x^2 + 2x$ **b** $x^2 - 81$ **c** $2p^2 + 8$

  d $3b^2 - 75$ **e** $2x^2 - 32$ **f** $n^4 - 4n^2$

  g $x^2 - 8x - 9$ **h** $d^2 + 6d - 7$ **i** $3x^2 - 108$

  j $2g^2 - 12g - 110$ **k** $4a^2 - 9d^2$ **l** $4t + 8t^2$

  m $12 - 11x - x^2$ **n** $5a^2 - 5a - 10$ **o** $2c^2 - 8c + 6$

  p $x^4 - x^2$ **q** $d^4 + 2d^3 - 3d^2$ **r** $b^2 + 3b - 28$

  s $a^3b^2 - ab^2$ **t** $x^2 - x - 6$ **u** $x^3 + 4x^2 + 4x$

  v $9x^4 - 4x^2$ **w** $x^2 + 8x - 9$ **x** $-2a^2 - 12a - 18$

2 Fully factorise the following.

  a $14 - x^2 - 5x$ **b** $x^2 + 14x + 49$ **c** $4a^3 - 4ab^2$

  d $18x - 2x^3$ **e** $ab + ac - 2a$ **f** $a^2b^2 - 2ab$

  g $4x^2 - 2x^3$ **h** $x^3y - 4xy$ **i** $(a + b)^2 - 9$

  j $(x + 2)^2 - 4$ **k** $4x^4 - 64$ **l** $(x - 2)y - (x - 2)z$

  m $(x + 1)a + (x + 1)b$ **n** $x^4 - a^4$ **o** $(x - y)a + (x - y)$

  p $x(x + 2) + 3(x + 2)$ **q** $x^3 + x^2 + x + 1$ **r** $x^3 + 2x^2 + x + 2$

3 Where possible, fully factorise the following miscellaneous expressions.

  a $3x^2 + 9x$ **b** $4x^2 - 1$ **c** $5x^2 - 15x$

  d $3x - 5x^2$ **e** $x^2 + 3x - 40$ **f** $x^2 - 16$

  g $x^3 + 2x^2$ **h** $x^2 - 9$ **i** $3x^3 + 6x$

  j $3x^2 - 12$ **k** $3x^3 + 6x^2$ **l** $x^2 + 10x + 25$

  m $x^2 - x - 6$ **n** $4x^2 + 8x$ **o** $9x^2 - 25$

  p $x^2 - 16x + 39$ **q** $7x^2 - 21x$ **r** $2x^2 - 50$

  s $9x - 18x^2$ **t** $8x^2 - 12x$ **u** $4x^2 + 4x - 3$

  v $13x^2 - 52x$ **w** $x^2 + 2x - 3$ **x** $x^3 - 9x$

4 Where possible, fully factorise the following miscellaneous expressions.

  a $x^3 + x^2 + x$ **b** $x^2 - 17x - 60$

  c $3x^2 - 27$ **d** $x^2 - 2x - 8$

  e $x^2 + 4x + 4$ **f** $6x^2 + 5x - 6$

  g $x^2 - 5x + 6$ **h** $36x^2 + 25$

  i $4x^2 - 8x - 60$ **j** $3x^2 - 42x + 99$

  k $x^2 + 11x + 30$ **l** $49x^2 - 1$

  m $x^2 - 7x + 12$ **n** $x^2 + 6x - 16$

  o $x^2 - 5x - 24$ **p** $x^2 - 8x + 16$

  q $x^2 - 9x + 14$ **r** $x^2 + 13x + 36$

  s $x^2 - 9x - 36$ **t** $x^2 + 7x - 18$

  u $x^2 - 10x + 25$ **v** $3x^2 + 6x - 72$

  w $4x^2 - 4x - 48$ **x** $(2x + 1)^2 - 9$

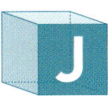 **J** # Factorising more complex expressions

To simplify algebraic expressions with numerators and denominators, first factorise all expressions fully.
Then simplify the expression by cancelling as appropriate.

 EXAMPLE 1

Factorise and simplify the following.

a $\dfrac{x^2 - x - 6}{x - 3}$

b $\dfrac{x^2 - 16}{8x - 32}$

	Solve	Think	Apply
a	$\dfrac{x^2 - x - 6}{x - 3} = \dfrac{(x - 3)(x + 2)}{(x - 3)}$ $= x + 2$	Factorise the quadratic first. Cancel the common factor $(x - 3)$.	Factorise the numerator and the denominator first. If a linear factor is in the fraction, put brackets around it so that the entire factor is cancelled.
b	$\dfrac{x^2 - 16}{8x - 32} = \dfrac{(x + 4)(x - 4)}{8(x - 4)}$ $= \dfrac{x + 4}{8}$	Factorise the difference of two squares in the numerator and take out the common factor in the denominator. Cancel $(x - 4)$.	

Exercise 7J

1 Factorise and simplify the following.

a $\dfrac{x^2 + 2x}{x^2 - 4}$

b $\dfrac{3x + x^2}{9 - x^2}$

c $\dfrac{3x^2 - 9x}{x^2 - 2x - 3}$

d $\dfrac{x^2 + 2x + 1}{x^2 - 1}$

e $\dfrac{2x^2 + 6x - 8}{x^2 - x - 20}$

f $\dfrac{x^2 + 6x + 9}{x^2 - 5x - 24}$

g $\dfrac{3x^2 - 12}{14 - 5x - x^2}$

h $\dfrac{2x^2 + 6x - 36}{12 + 8x - 4x^2}$

EXAMPLE 2

Factorise and simplify the following.

a $\dfrac{2y - 4}{5} \times \dfrac{10y}{y^2 - 2y}$

b $\dfrac{x^2 - 9}{x + 5} \div \dfrac{x^2 + 4x + 3}{x^2 + 6x + 5}$

	Solve	Think	Apply
a	$\dfrac{2y - 4}{5} \times \dfrac{10y}{y^2 - 2y} = \dfrac{2(y - 2)}{5} \times \dfrac{10y}{y(y - 2)}$ $= 4$	Factorise the numerator and the denominator. Cancel any common factors.	Only cancel terms in brackets or in front of brackets.
b	$\dfrac{x^2 - 9}{x + 5} \div \dfrac{x^2 + 4x + 3}{x^2 + 6x + 5}$ $= \dfrac{(x + 3)(x - 3)}{(x + 5)} \div \dfrac{(x + 3)(x + 1)}{(x + 5)(x + 1)}$ $= \dfrac{(x + 3)(x - 3)}{(x + 5)} \times \dfrac{(x + 5)(x + 1)}{(x + 3)(x + 1)}$ $= x - 3$	Factorise the numerator and the denominator. For division invert the second fraction and multiply. Cancel any common factors.	

2 Factorise and simplify the following.

a $\dfrac{3x - 6}{7} \times \dfrac{14x}{x^2 - 2x}$

b $\dfrac{2x^2 + 10x}{4x} \times \dfrac{6}{3x + 15}$

c $\dfrac{x^2 - 16}{4x - 16} \div \dfrac{x^2 + 5x + 4}{2x + 2}$

d $\dfrac{x^2 + 8x + 15}{x^2 - 25} \div \dfrac{4x + 12}{x^2 - 5x}$

e $\dfrac{7x + 7}{x^2 - x - 2} \times \dfrac{x^2 + x - 6}{5x + 15}$

f $\dfrac{2x^2 - 10x}{3x^2 - 9x} \div \dfrac{x^2 - 2x - 15}{x^2 - 9}$

g $\dfrac{x^2 - 4}{x^2 + 2x - 8} \div \dfrac{x + 2}{x^2 + 3x - 4}$

h $\dfrac{x^2 + 2x}{x + 4} \times \dfrac{3x - 15}{x^2 - 3x - 10}$

● EXAMPLE 3

Factorise and simplify the following.

a $\dfrac{2}{x^2 + 2x} - \dfrac{3}{x^2 - 4}$

b $\dfrac{4}{x^2 - 3x - 10} + \dfrac{3}{2x - 10}$

Solve	Think/Apply
a $\dfrac{2}{x^2 + 2x} - \dfrac{3}{x^2 - 4}$ $= \dfrac{2}{x(x + 2)} - \dfrac{3}{(x - 2)(x + 2)}$ $= \dfrac{2}{x(x + 2)} \times \dfrac{(x - 2)}{(x - 2)} - \dfrac{3}{(x - 2)(x + 2)} \times \dfrac{(x)}{(x)}$ $= \dfrac{2(x - 2) - 3x}{x(x + 2)(x - 2)}$ $= \dfrac{2x - 4 - 3x}{x(x + 2)(x - 2)}$ $= \dfrac{-x - 4}{x(x + 2)(x - 2)}$	Factorise the denominators. Find a common denominator and express both fractions over the common denominator. Combine into a single fraction then simplify if possible.
b $\dfrac{4}{x^2 - 3x - 10} + \dfrac{3}{2x - 10}$ $= \dfrac{4}{(x - 5)(x + 2)} + \dfrac{3}{2(x - 5)}$ $= \dfrac{4}{(x - 5)(x + 2)} \times \dfrac{(2)}{(2)} + \dfrac{3}{2(x - 5)} \times \dfrac{(x + 2)}{(x + 2)}$ $= \dfrac{8 + 3(x + 2)}{2(x - 5)(x + 2)}$ $= \dfrac{3x + 14}{x(x - 5)(x + 2)}$	

3 Factorise and simplify the following.

a $\dfrac{3}{x^2 + 3x} - \dfrac{4}{x^2 - 9}$

b $\dfrac{2}{x^2 - 16} + \dfrac{5}{4x - 16}$

c $\dfrac{2}{x^2 - 4x - 12} + \dfrac{3}{x^2 - 6x}$

d $\dfrac{4}{3x - 12} - \dfrac{2}{x^2 - 3x - 4}$

e $\dfrac{2}{x^2 - 2x} - \dfrac{1}{x^2 + 5x - 14}$

f $\dfrac{7}{x^2 - 7x + 10} + \dfrac{3}{x^2 - 2x}$

g $\dfrac{1}{x^2 - 25} + \dfrac{1}{x^2 - 6x + 5}$

h $\dfrac{4}{x^2 - 3x} - \dfrac{2}{x^2 - 9}$

Sir William Rowan Hamilton (1805–1865)

William Rowan Hamilton was born in Dublin in 1805, the son of a solicitor. His ability was evident early on, and by 13 years of age he had managed to learn 13 different languages. This mastery of languages helped him to become one of the few great mathematicians with a facility for involved mental calculations. In 1823 Hamilton entered Trinity College in Dublin and was appointed to the post of Andrew's Professor of Astronomy and Royal Astronomer to Ireland while still an undergraduate. In 1827 he moved to Dunsink Observatory just outside Dublin. Hamilton continued his work in physics, astronomy and algebra, and in 1835 was knighted for his contribution to science. In the same year he discovered quaternions—a very important step in the development of modern algebra. He continued to work on quaternion theory and spent the last 20 years of his life as a recluse.

The result of his research *The Elements of Quaternions* was published after his death in 1866. He was honoured by many foreign academics for his contributions in each of his fields of interest.

1   **a**   How old was Hamilton when he became Professor of Astronomy and Royal Astronomer to Ireland?
  b   For what was he knighted? When?
  c   How old was Hamilton when he moved to Dunsink?
  d   What were Hamilton's main interests?
  e   What is a recluse?

2   Rearrange these words to form sentences.
  a   opposite Expanding is factorising of the
  b   highest Always factor factorise common possible the using
  c   brackets brackets the the by in outside Multiply term all terms the the

3   Use every third letter to find a sentence.

```
H K T Q T O F G C Y U H F D E S A C E E K R R A T L F A C A B T C I E T Q W O O
P R D F I Z T S N H A Z Y S K N O J T L P B U A C T B E I R S O A A N I O Y P R
O D T U G T C H Y A E R N A X E V T I N H T M O H Q Q E A E R F E E G E X T T P
H J A A A N C V D B G Y E D O Y H U K H R A R A T I N O I S B K W C D E X S R W
E O R G R H J S K M U N B B G F S D Q T E H I O L T F X U F G T U U E E U A N J
N A D U T H M U J B W Q E A S R C T I B U N N I T O P O F D T G H H T E E A E Q
S H U N Y E F G S J K T E R I T H O A S N F G A Y U N I O D L L T A S H C F E V
Y A N U N M I S O L W W C E E V R T N T Y J O I E S A S E D F E G H I J K F L O
T T R H Q A E Z X Y C V A B N R M K E H J E G F Q S A U Q W A E R L
```

Terms

algebra	binomial product	common factor	difference of two squares	expand
expression	grouping in pairs	factorise	perfect square	quadratic equation
solve	substitution	trinomial		

Check your skills

1 $(x + 7)(x - 5) =$
  A $x^2 - 35$ **B** $x^2 + 2x - 35$ **C** $x^2 + 2x + 2$ **D** $2x + 2$

2 $(4x - 3)(2x + 5) =$
  A $8x^2 + 14x - 15$ **B** $8x^2 + 6x - 15$ **C** $6x + 2$ **D** $8x^2 + 26x - 15$

3 $4x - (2x + 1)(x - 3) =$

A $-2x^2 - x - 3$ **B** $-2x^2 - x + 3$ **C** $-2x^2 + 9x + 3$ **D** $-2x^2 + 9x - 3$

4 A solution to $3x^2 = 12$ is:

A $x = +\sqrt{12}$ **B** $x = -\sqrt{12}$ **C** $x = 4$ **D** $x = -2$

5 $(y - 5)^2 =$

A $y^2 - 25$ **B** $y^2 + 25$ **C** $y^2 - 5x + 25$ **D** $y^2 - 10x + 25$

6 $(5x - 3)^2 =$

A $25x^2 - 9$ **B** $5x^2 - 9$ **C** $25x^2 - 30x + 9$ **D** $25x^2 - 30x - 9$

7 $(3x - 2)(3x + 2) =$

A $3x - 2$ **B** $9x^2 - 4$ **C** $9x^2 - 12x - 4$ **D** $9x^2 - 12x + 4$

8 If $(x - \square)^2 = x^2 - \triangle x + 16$ then:

A $\square = 4, \triangle = 8$ **B** $\square = 16, \triangle = 8$ **C** $\square = 256, \triangle = 128$ **D** $\square = 16, \triangle = 4$

9 When factorised, $3x^2 - 6x =$

A $-3x$ **B** $-3x^3$ **C** $3x(x - 2)$ **D** $3(x^2 - 2x)$

10 When factorised, $px + 3q - 3p - qx =$

A $(p - q)(x - 3)$ **B** $pq(3 - x)$ **C** $(p - 3)(x - q)$ **D** cannot be factorised

11 When factorised, $x^2 - y^2 =$

A $(x - y)(x + y)$ **B** $(x - y)^2$ **C** $(x + y)^2$ **D** $2(x - y)$

12 When factorised, $4p^2 - 25q^2 =$

A $(2p - 5q)^2$ **B** $(2p - 5q)(2p + 5q)$ **C** $(4p - 25q)(4p + 25q)$ **D** $(4p - 25q)^2$

13 When factorised, $x^2 - 10x + 25 =$

A $(x + 5)(x - 5)$ **B** $(x + 5)^2$ **C** $(x - 10)^2$ **D** $(x - 5)^2$

14 When factorised, $81x^2 - 198x + 121 =$

A $(9x + 11)(9x - 11)$ **B** $(9x - 11)^2$ **C** $(81x + 11)^2$ **D** $(81x - 121)^2$

15 When factorised, $x^2 + 4x - 21 =$

A $(x + 7)(x - 3)$ **B** $(x - 7)(x + 4)$ **C** $(x + 2)(x - 1)$ **D** $(x - 21)(x + 1)$

16 When factorised, $5x^2 - 7x - 6 =$

A $(5x - 3)(x + 2)$ **B** $(5x + 1)(x - 6)$ **C** $(5x + 3)(x - 2)$ **D** $(5x - 1)(x + 6)$

17 When factorised, $8x^2 + 5x - 3 =$

A $(4x - 1)(2x + 3)$ **B** $(8x + 3)(x - 1)$ **C** $(4x + 1)(2x - 3)$ **D** $(8x - 3)(x + 1)$

18 When factorised, $16x^2 - 4 =$

A $(4x - 2)(4x + 2)$ **B** $4(2x + 1)(2x - 1)$ **C** $4(4x^2 - 1)$ **D** $4(x + 1)(x - 1)$

19 When simplified $\dfrac{x^2 - 12x + 35}{3x - 15} =$

A $\dfrac{x^2 - 4x + 7}{-3}$ **B** $\dfrac{x - 7}{3}$ **C** $x^2 - 9x + 20$ **D** $\dfrac{x - 5}{3}$

20 When simplified, $\dfrac{7}{x^2 - 7x + 10} - \dfrac{2}{x^2 - 5x} =$

A $\dfrac{5}{(x^2 - 7x + 10)(x^2 - 5x)}$

B $\dfrac{7x^2 - 33x - 4}{x(x - 5)(x - 2)}$

C $\dfrac{5x + 4}{x(x - 5)(x - 2)}$

D $\dfrac{7x^2 - 37x - 4}{x(x - 5)(x - 2)}$

If you have any difficulty with these questions, refer to the examples and questions in the sections listed in the table.

Question	1–3	4	5–8	9, 10	11, 12	13, 14	15	16, 17	18	19, 20
Section	A	B	C	D	E	F	G	H	I	J

7A   Review set

1 Expand and simplify:

  a $4 - (5x + 3)$
      b $3(x - 5) - 2$
      c $n(n + 2) - 2n(n - 1)$

2 Solve the following.

  a $x^2 = 12$
      b $5x^2 = 9$

3 Expand and simplify if possible.

  a $(x + 5)(x - 3)$
      b $(2x - 7)(3x - 8)$
      c $(x - 8)^2$

  d $(3x - 4)^2$
      e $(x - 2)(x + 2)$
      f $(3x - 5)(3x + 5)$

4 **a** Evaluate $3x^2 - 5x + 8$ when $x = 3$.

  b What number must be added to these expressions to complete the square?

    i $x^2 - 6x$
          ii $x^2 + 11x$

5 Factorise fully:

  a $7x + 14$
    b $8x^2y - 20xy$
    c $3x - 9 + xy - 3y$
    d $4y^2 - 25$

  e $x^2 + 7x - 8$
    f $3x^2 + 11x - 4$
    g $x^4 - 16x^2$
    h $-2x^2 + 2x + 24$

6 Factorise and simplify:

  a $\dfrac{x^2 + x - 6}{x - 2}$
    b $\dfrac{x^2 - 9}{4x + 12} \times \dfrac{2x + 4}{x^2 - x - 6}$
    c $\dfrac{2}{x^2 - 4x} + \dfrac{3}{x^2 - 16}$

7B   Review set

1 Expand and simplify:

  a $-3 - 2(3x - 1)$
      b $4(2x - 3) - 5x$
      c $p(p + 7) - 3p(4 - p)$

2 Solve the following.

  a $x^2 = 16$
      b $5x^2 = 2$

3 Expand and simplify if possible.

  a $(x + 2)(x - 11)$
      b $(3x - 8)(4x - 3)$
      c $(x + 4)^2$

  d $(8x - 5)^2$
      e $(x - 3)(x + 3)$
      f $(5x - 3)(5x + 3)$

4 **a** Evaluate $2x^2 - 9x + 5$ when $x = -2$.

  b What number must be added to these expressions to complete the square?

    i $x^2 + 10x$
          ii $x^2 - 9x$

NUMBER & ALGEBRA

5 Factorise fully:

a $3a - 9$

b $12xy + 18x^2$

c $2xy - 6x + 7y - 21$

d $16y^2 - 25$

e $x^2 - 3x + 2$

f $6x^2 - 7x - 5$

g $9x^4 - 16x^2$

h $x^3 + 3x^2 + x + 3$

6 Factorise and simplify:

a $\dfrac{x^2 - 9}{6x - 18}$

b $\dfrac{x^2 - 3x - 4}{8x - 32}$

c $\dfrac{1}{x^2 + 7x + 10} - \dfrac{3}{x^2 - 4}$

7C   Review set

1 Expand and simplify:

a $4 - (3x - 2)$

b $2(x + 3) - 4$

c $y(y + 2) - 3y(y + 4)$

2 Why doesn't the equation $3x^2 = -5$ have a solution?

3 Expand and simplify if possible.

a $(x - 3)(x + 4)$

b $(2x - 5)(3x - 7)$

c $(x - 4)^2$

d $(4p - 5)^2$

e $(x - 3)(x + 3)$

f $(4x - 3)(4x + 3)$

4 **a** Use $x = 3$ to show that $6x^2 - x - 2 = (3x - 2)(2x + 1)$.

b Complete: $x^2 - 4x + \square = (x - 2)^2$.

5 Factorise:

a $5x + 10$

b $3x^2 - 6xy$

c $2x - 4 + 3xy - 6y$

d $9x^2 - 100$

e $x^2 - x - 12$

f $3x^2 + 16x + 5$

g $x^3 - 16x$

h $-3x^2 - 21x + 24$

6 Simplify:

a $\dfrac{x^2 - x - 20}{x - 5}$

b $\dfrac{x^2 - 4}{x^2 + x - 6} \times \dfrac{3x^2 - 15x}{x^2 - 3x - 10}$

c $\dfrac{4}{x^2 - 9} - \dfrac{5}{x^2 + 3x}$

7D   Review set

1 Expand and simplify:

a $2x - 2(4x - 7)$

b $3(7 - 4x) - 3x$

c $m(m - 4) - 3m(6 - m)$

2 Solve:

a $x^2 = 25$

b $7x^2 = 9$

3 Expand and simplify if possible.

a $(x - 2)(x + 11)$

b $(3x - 7)(4x + 2)$

c $(y + 3)^2$

d $(6z - 5)^2$

e $(x - 9)(x + 9)$

f $(6x - 5)(6x + 5)$

4 **a** Use $x = -1$ to show that $10x^2 - x - 3 = (5x - 3)(2x + 1)$.

b Complete: $x^2 + \square + 9 = (x - 3)^2$

5 Factorise:

a $3x - 15$

b $12xy - 8yz$

c $xp + 2x - yp - 2y$

d $16x^2 - 25$

e $x^2 + 4x - 21$

f $5x^2 + 7x - 6$

g $6x^2 - 11x - 10$

h $2x^3 - 18x$

i $-15x - 20y + 10z$

6 Simplify:

a $\dfrac{x^2 + 5x - 14}{2x + 14}$

b $\dfrac{x^2 - 25}{3x^2 + 15x} \div \dfrac{x^2 - 4x - 5}{x^2 + x}$

c $\dfrac{2}{x^2 - 5x} - \dfrac{3}{x^2 - 25}$

8

Box plots

This chapter deals with the construction and interpretation of box plots.

At the end of this chapter you should be able to:

- find the upper and lower extremes, the median, and the upper and lower quartiles for sets of numerical data
- calculate the range and interquartile range
- compare the relative merits of range and interquartile range as measures of spread
- construct a box plot using the median, upper and lower quartiles, and upper and lower extremes of a set of data

- compare two or more sets of data using parallel box plots
- determine quartiles from data displayed in histograms and dot plots and use these to draw box plots
- identify skewed and symmetrical sets of data displayed in histograms and dot plots
- evaluate survey data reported in the digital media and elsewhere.

NSW Syllabus references: 5.2 S&P Single variable data analysis
Outcomes: MA5.2-1WM, MA5.2-3WM, MA5.2-15SP
Statistics & probability – ACMSP227, ACMSP248, ACMSP249, ACMSP250

Diagnostic test

Use the table below to answer questions **1** to **4**.

Score	5	6	7	8	9	10
Frequency	4	7	12	17	11	5

1 The mean of the data in the table is closest to:

    A 7   **B** 7.7   **C** 8   **D** 7.5

2 The median of the data in the table is closest to:

    A 17   **B** 7.7   **C** 8   **D** 7.5

3 The mode of the data in the table is closest to:

    A 17   **B** 7.7   **C** 8   **D** 7.5

4 The cumulative frequency for the score of 8 is:

    A 40   **B** 17   **C** 8   **D** 23

5 The ogive is the:

    A frequency polygon

    B frequency histogram

    C cumulative frequency polygon

    D cumulative frequency histogram

Use this cumulative frequency histogram and polygon to answer questions **6** and **7**.

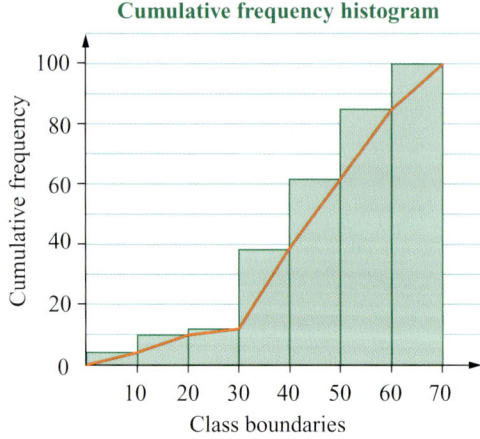

Cumulative frequency histogram

6 The cumulative frequency for the 40–49 class is:

    A 61   **B** 44.5   **C** 26

    D It is impossible to determine without the exact scores.

7 An estimate for the median is closest to:

    A 40–49 class   **B** 50   **C** 45

    D It is impossible to determine without the exact scores.

8 Which frequency distribution table represents the following scores?

12, 30, 38, 49, 13, 28, 33, 17, 21, 31, 23, 32, 25, 26, 39, 36, 42, 46, 36, 50, 48, 32, 45, 57, 43, 51, 49, 53, 42, 33

A

x	f
10–19	3
20–29	6
30–39	9
40–49	8
50–59	4

B

x	f
10–19	3
20–29	5
30–39	10
40–49	8
50–59	4

C

x	f
10–19	4
20–29	5
30–39	9
40–49	9
50–59	3

D

x	f
10–19	4
20–29	4
30–39	10
40–49	7
50–59	5

9 The class centre for the 32–38 class is:

    A 32   **B** 38   **C** 70   **D** 35

Use this table to answer questions **10** to **12**.

Class	Class centre	Frequency	fx
10–16		3	
17–23		15	
24–30		8	
31–37		12	
38–44		5	

10 The class centre for the 38–44 class is:

    A 84   **B** 41   **C** 5   **D** 10–44

11 The mean for the data is closest to:

    A 27   **B** 10   **C** 8.6

    D It is impossible to determine without the exact scores.

12 The modal class is:

    A 24–30   **B** 17–23

    C 24–30   **D** 31–37

The diagnostic test questions refer to outcomes ACMSP170 and ACMSP171.

STATISTICS & PROBABILITY

A Mean, mode, median and range

This section reviews the three measures of central tendency, mean, mode and median, and the measure of spread or range.

Mean

The **mean** is the statistical term most thought of when the word 'average' is used. The mean of a set of scores is calculated by adding all the scores and dividing this sum by the number of scores. $\bar{x}$ is the symbol used to represent the mean.

For example, for the scores 3, 7, 8, 9 and 9:

$$\bar{x} = \frac{3 + 7 + 8 + 9 + 9}{5} = \frac{36}{5} = 7.2$$

Mode

The **mode** is the score that occurs most often; that is, it is the score with the highest frequency. It is the most commonly occurring score. For example, for the scores 3, 7, 8, 9 and 9, the mode is 9 (as it occurs more frequently that any other score).

A set of scores may be **bimodal**; that is, have two modes. For example, 2, 3, 3, 3, 4, 4, 4, 5, 6, 8 is bimodal as it has two modes; namely, 3 and 4.

Median

The **median** of a set of scores is the middle score (or the average of the two middle scores) after the scores have been arranged in ascending order (that is from smallest to largest).

- For an *odd number* of scores, there is one middle score.
  If there are n scores in ascending order, the median is the value of the score in the $\left(\dfrac{n + 1}{2}\right)$th position.
  For example, for the scores 7, 9, 3, 9, 8, the ascending order is 3, 7, 8, 9, 9.

$$n = 5, \text{ so } \frac{n + 1}{2} = 3$$

  The median is the 3rd score; that is, the median is 8.

 There are two numbers below the median and two numbers above the median.

- For an *even number* of scores, there are two middle scores so the median is not always one of the scores.
  For example, consider the scores 4, 7, 9, 6, 5, 9, 3, 7.
  The ascending order is   3   4   5   6   7   7   9   9
  　　　　　　　　　　　　　　1st　2nd　3rd　4th　5th　6th　7th　8th

 There are four scores below the median and four scores above the median.

  As $n = 8$, the median is the number midway between the 4th and 5th scores.
  The median $= \dfrac{6 + 7}{2}$ (the average of the 4th and 5th scores) = 6.5.

Range

The range of a set of data is a measure of its spread. It is found by subtracting the lowest score from the highest score.

$$\text{Range} = \text{highest score} - \text{lowest score}$$

Consider these two data sets:

　　Set A: 3, 5, 7, 9, 11
　　Set B: 1, 2, 3, 4, 5, 6, 7, 8, 9, 10, 11, 12, 13

Both sets have a mean of 7. However, set B is obviously more spread out and the range highlights this fact.

For set A: range $= 11 - 3 = 8$
For set B: range $= 13 - 1 = 12$

EXAMPLE 1

For the scores 12, 13, 14, 14, 14, 15, 16, find the:

a mean   **b** mode   **c** median   **d** range.

	Solve	Think	Apply
a	Mean = 14	$\text{Mean} = \dfrac{12 + 13 + 14 + 14 + 14 + 15 + 16}{7} = \dfrac{98}{7}$ $\bar{x} = 14$	Use the definitions for mean, mode, median and range to find these measures.
b	Mode = 14	As 14 occurs more frequently than any other score, the mode = 14.	
c	Median = 14	To find the median, arrange the scores in ascending order. Find the middle score by crossing out equal numbers of scores from each end. 12 13 14 (14) 14 15 16 Median = 14	
d	Range = 4	Range = highest score − lowest score = 16 − 12 = 4	

EXAMPLE 2

For the scores 110, 106, 114, 109, 114, 107, find the:

a mean   **b** mode   **c** median   **d** range.

	Solve	Think	Apply
a	Mean = 110	$\text{Mean} = \dfrac{110 + 106 + 114 + 109 + 114 + 107}{6} = \dfrac{660}{6}$ $\bar{x} = 110$	Use the definitions for mean, mode, median and range to find these measures.
b	Mode = 114	As 114 occurs more frequently than any other score, the mode = 114.	
c	Median = 109.5	To find the median, first arrange the scores in ascending order. Cross out scores from each end until there are two numbers left. The median is the average of them. 106 107 (109) (110) 114 114 $\text{Median} = \dfrac{109 + 110}{2} = 109.5$	
d	Range = 8	Range = 114 − 106 = 8	

Exercise 8A

1 Find the mean of the following sets of data. Answer to 1 decimal place if necessary.

   a 1, 3, 4, 5, 8, 8, 9   **b** 1, 2, 2, 3, 4, 5, 6, 8, 9   **c** 10, 12, 13, 15, 16

   d 20, 20, 20, 23, 25, 27   **e** 51, 52, 54, 55, 57, 57, 58, 59   **f** 0, 0, 1, 3, 3, 3, 5, 6, 6, 7, 8, 9

   g 105, 101, 104, 101, 101, 102   **h** 3, 4, 9, 5, 1, 8, 3, 2, 0   **i** 6, 4, 5, 8, 9, 3, 5, 5, 4, 9

Insight Mathematics 10 stages 5.2/5.3 Australian Curriculum

2 Find the mode, if there is one, of the scores in question **1**.

A set of scores with two modes is called bimodal.

3 Find the median of the scores in question **1**.

4 Find the range of the scores in question **1**.

5 The number of lollies in 10 packets were 15, 18, 17, 15, 16, 14, 15, 18, 16, 19. Find the:
   a range
   b mean number of lollies per packet
   c modal number of lollies per packet
   d median number of lollies per packet.

6 **a** **i** Find the mean of the first eight counting numbers: 1, 2, 3, 4, 5, 6, 7, 8.
      ii Subtract 3 from each of the first eight counting numbers and then find the mean of these numbers.
      iii How has the mean changed?
   b **i** Add 20 to each of the first eight counting numbers and then find the mean of these numbers.
      ii How has the mean changed?
   c **i** Find the median of the first eight counting numbers.
      ii Add 3 to each of the first eight counting numbers and then find the median of these numbers.
      iii How has the median changed?
   d **i** Find the range of the first eight counting numbers.
      ii Add 3 to each of the first eight counting numbers and find the range.
      iii What has happened to the range?

7 A shoe store had a special on women's running shoes and sold the following sizes: 6, 10, 4, 7, 8, 7, 6, 5, 7, 8, 7, 5, 6, 4, 3, 7.

The average female shoe size is 7. This refers to the mode not the mean.

   a Find the:
     i range
     ii mean
     iii mode
     iv median.
   b Which of the mean, mode and median would be of most use to the shop owner?

8 The Lighthouse Lamp Company has a total of 30 employees whose annual salaries are listed below.

1 general manager	$260 000
1 marketing manager	$100 000
1 accountant	$120 000
1 engineer	$100 000
1 warehouse manager	$100 000
15 production workers	$50 000 each
10 tradespeople	$60 000 each

   a What is the total annual wages bill for this company?
   b Calculate the mean wage for the employees.
   c How many employees earn:
     i less than this mean wage?
     ii more than this mean wage?
   d What is the median wage?
   e What is the modal wage?
   f In a wage determination case for the employees of this company, which measure of central tendency would you use to support your argument if you were the representative for:
     i the general manager?
     ii the production workers?
   g Which measure of central tendency is the most appropriate to represent the wages of the employees of this company? Give reasons for your answer.

9 a Find the mean and median of these scores:
15, 16, 16, 17, 19, 20, 430.

b Find the mean and median leaving out the score 430.

c The score 430 is called an **outlier** score because it is an extremely large score compared with all the other scores. An outlier can also be a very small score when compared with the other scores. Which measure, mean or median, is most affected by the outlier?

10 A batsman's scores for six innings are 55, 73, 96, 88, 34, 64.

a Find the mean and median.

b In his next innings he scores 0 runs. Find the new mean and median.

c In cricket a score of 0 is called a 'duck'. For this batsman's scores, what statistical name would you give the score of 0?

d Is the mean or median most affected by the score of 0?

● EXAMPLE 3

The mean of five scores is 12.2. What is the sum of the scores?

Solve/Think	Apply
Let S = sum of scores $\dfrac{S}{5} = 12.2$ $S = 12.2 \times 5 = 61$ The sum of the scores is 61.	Substitute the given information into the formula: Mean = $\dfrac{\text{sum of scores}}{\text{number of scores}}$ Solve the resulting equation.

11 a The mean of eight scores is 7.5. What is the sum of the scores?

b The mean of nine scores is 11.6. What is the sum of the scores?

c While on an outback trip, Bill drove, on average, 262 km per day for a period of 12 days. How far did Bill drive in total while on the trip?

d The mean monthly sales of a clothing store is $15 467. Calculate the total sales of the store for the year.

● EXAMPLE 4

Find x if 10, 7, 3, 6 and x have a mean of 8.

Solve/Think	Apply
$\dfrac{10 + 7 + 3 + 6 + x}{5} = 8$ $\dfrac{26 + x}{5} = 8$ $26 + x = 40$ $x = 14$	Write an algebraic expression for the sum of the scores and then substitute the given information into the formula. Mean = $\dfrac{\text{sum of scores}}{\text{number of scores}}$ Solve the resulting equation.

12 a Find x if 8, 11, 5, 7 and x have a mean of 8.

b Find x if 3, 15, 7, 9, 11 and x have a mean of 10.

c Find x if 5, 9, 11, 12, 13, 14, 17 and x have a mean of 12.

d Find a, given that 3, 0, a, a, 4, a, 6, a and 3 have a mean of 4.

e Over the complete assessment period, Jenny averaged 35 out of a possible 40 marks for her eight Mathematics tests. However, when checking her files, she could only find seven of the tests. For these she scored 29, 36, 32, 38, 35, 34 and 39. Can you determine how many marks she scored for the eighth test?

● EXAMPLE 5

A cricketer played 12 innings and had a mean of 38.5 runs. He then scored 12 and 71 runs in the next two innings. Find the cricketer's new mean number of runs.

Solve/Think	Apply
Let S = sum of scores $$\frac{S}{12} = 38.5$$ $$S = 462$$ New mean $= \dfrac{462 + 12 + 71}{14}$ $\qquad = \dfrac{545}{14} \approx 38.9$	Find the sum of the scores for the first 12 innings. Use this to determine the sum of the cricketer's 14 scores. Calculate the mean of these 14 scores. *There are 12 + 2 = 14 scores in total.* ❗

13 a A netballer played 14 matches and had a mean of 16.5 goals per game. In the next two matches she threw 21 goals and 24 goals. Calculate her new mean.

b A cricketer played 11 matches and had a mean of 23 runs per game. In the next two games she scored 41 and 35 runs. Calculate her new mean.

c A tennis player averaged 8 aces per match in her first six matches. In the next three matches she served 6, 11 and 13 aces. Calculate her new average.

14 A sample of 12 measurements has a mean of 16.5, and a sample of 15 measurements has a mean of 18.6. What is the mean of all 27 measurements?

15 Fifteen of 31 measurements are below 10 cm and 12 measurements are above 11 cm. Find the median if the other four measurements are 10.1 cm, 10.4 cm, 10.7 cm and 10.9 cm.

16 The mean and the median of a set of nine measurements are both 12. If seven of the measurements are 7, 9, 11, 13, 14, 17 and 19, find the other two measurements.

17 Write your own group of seven scores for which the following measure of central tendency is not appropriate.

a the mean   **b** the mode   **c** the median

18 Write a group of seven scores for which:

a the mean is less than the median   **b** the mean is greater than the median

c the mean and the median are equal   **d** the mean, the mode and the median are equal.

Summary: choosing the appropriate measure

The mean, mode and median can be used to indicate the middle of a set of numbers. Which of these values is the most appropriate measure to use will depend on the type of data under consideration. For example, when reporting on shoe sizes stocked by a shoe store, the average or mean size would be a useless measure of the stock. In this case, the mode would be the most useful measure.

When selecting which of the three measures of central tendency to use as a representative figure for a set of data, you should keep the following advantages and disadvantages of each measure in mind.

Mean

- The mean's main advantage is that it is commonly used, easy to understand and easy to find.
- The mean's main disadvantage is that it is affected by extreme values within a set of data and may give a distorted impression of the data. For example, consider the data set 4, 6, 7, 8, 19, 111. The total of these six numbers is 155, so the mean is approximately 25.8. Is 25.8 a representative figure for the data? The outlier of 111 has distorted the mean in this case.

Mode

- The mode's main advantage is that it is the most usual or typical value within a set of data.
- The mode has an advantage over the mean in that it is not affected by extreme values contained in the data.
- The mode's main disadvantage is that it does not take into account all the values within the data. For example, the mode for the scores 2, 2, 2, 5, 5, 7, 8, 8, 9, 9, 10, 11, 12, 12 is 2. This is not representative of the rest of the data.

Median

- The median's main advantage is that it is easily calculated and is the middle value of the data.
- Unlike the mean, the median is not affected by extreme values.
- The median's main disadvantage is that it ignores all values outside the middle range. For example, the median of the scores 1, 1, 2, 2, 3, 104, 108, 110, 135 is 3, but this is not necessarily representative of the sample.

B Quartiles

The median divides a set of data into two parts with an equal number of scores in each.

In the same way, a set of data can be divided into four parts with an equal number of scores in each. These scores are called quartiles. Each set of data then has three quartiles, the lower, the middle (called the median) and the upper, usually denoted as Q_1, Q_2 and Q_3 respectively.

- The median (Q_2) is the middle score. It divides the data into two equal groups.
- The upper quartile (Q_3) is the middle score of the upper group.
- The lower quartile (Q_1) is the middle score of the lower group.
- The interquartile range (IQR) = upper quartile − lower quartile, or IQR = $Q_3 - Q_1$.

For a large number of scores:
- 25% of the scores $< Q_1$ and 75% of the scores $> Q_1$
- 50% of the scores $< Q_2$ and 50% of the scores $> Q_2$
- 75% of the scores $< Q_3$ and 25% of the scores $> Q_3$.

Hence the interquartile range is a measure of the spread of the middle 50% of the data. It is often a better measure of dispersion (the spread of the scores) than the range because it is not affected by outliers in the data.

EXAMPLE 1

Find the lower, middle and upper quartiles of these scores and then find the interquartile range.

21   22   22   23   25   26   27

Solve/Think	Apply
There are seven scores so the median is the fourth score $\left(\frac{7+1}{2} = 4\right)$. 21 22 22 23 25 26 27 $\uparrow$ Q_2 The median is 23. The data is divided into two parts each with three scores. 21 22 22 ㉓ 25 26 27 $\uparrow$ $\uparrow$ $\uparrow$ Q_1 Q_2 Q_3 Cross out in each half to find the quartiles: $Q_1 = 22$ and $Q_3 = 26$. Interquartile range $= Q_3 - Q_1$ $= 26 - 22 = 4$	Divide the scores into two parts with equal numbers of scores in each by finding the median. The median is the middle quartile. The lower quartile is the middle score of the lower group. The upper quartile is the middle score of the upper group.

Exercise 8B

1 For the scores 19, 20, 22, 27, 28, 30, 31, find:
  a the median
  c the upper quartile
  b the lower quartile
  d the interquartile range.

2 For the scores below, find:
  i the median
  iii the upper quartile
  ii the lower quartile
  iv the interquartile range.
  a 1, 3, 4, 7, 9, 10, 11
  b 14, 14, 15, 16, 16, 18, 19, 19, 20, 20, 21

EXAMPLE 2

Find the lower, middle and upper quartiles for these scores, and then find the interquartile range.

3   3   4   4   5   5   5   6   8   10

Solve/Think	Apply
There are ten scores, so the median is the average of the 5th and 6th scores. 3 3 4 4 5 | 5 5 6 8 10 Median is $Q_2 = \frac{5+5}{2} = 5$ The median divides the scores into two equal groups of five scores. 3 3 4 4 5 | 5 5 6 8 10 $\uparrow$ $\uparrow$ $\uparrow$ Q_1 Q_2 Q_3 Cross out in each half to find the quartiles: $Q_1 = 4$ and $Q_3 = 6$. Interquartile range $= Q_3 - Q_1$ $= 6 - 4 = 2$	Find the upper and lower quartiles and hence the interquartile range.

3 For the scores below, find:

    i the median   **ii** the lower quartile

    iii the upper quartile   **iv** the interquartile range.

  a 8, 8, 9, 10, 11, 11, 11, 11, 14, 15   **b** 15, 17, 20, 22, 22, 24

  c 12, 12, 15, 16, 17, 20, 21, 23, 25, 25, 27, 27   **d** 13, 15, 19, 25, 28, 31, 42, 45

4 Find the interquartile range for the following scores.

  a 15, 16, 16, 20, 22, 23, 25   **b** 11, 13, 13, 14, 14, 15, 18

  c 30, 32, 35, 35, 35, 37, 38   **d** 2, 3, 3, 4, 5, 5, 6, 7

  e 50, 50, 52, 55, 55, 57, 57, 58, 60, 60   **f** 15, 15, 16, 17, 17, 18, 20, 21, 21, 22

  g 23, 23, 23, 24, 25, 26, 28, 28, 29, 32   **h** 33, 35, 38, 42, 43, 44, 52, 53, 55, 58, 61, 64, 66, 67

  i 11, 12, 14, 18, 18, 20, 22, 25, 25, 26, 30   **j** 46, 50, 50, 53, 54, 54, 58, 58, 58, 60, 62, 62, 66, 66

EXAMPLE 3

Find the interquartile range for the following scores.

  a 30, 32, 32, 33, 35, 40, 41, 42, 45   **b** 9, 5, 7, 11, 10, 4, 14, 7

Solve/Think	Apply
a Find the median by crossing off from each end.	Find the upper and lower quartiles and hence the interquartile range.
~~30~~ ~~32~~ ~~32~~ ~~33~~ 35 ~~40~~ ~~41~~ ~~42~~ ~~45~~	
Median = 35	
The middle score in the set 30, 32, 32, 33 is $Q_1 = \dfrac{32 + 32}{2} = 32$	
The middle score in the set 40, 41, 42, 45 is $Q_3 = \dfrac{41 + 42}{2} = 41.5$	
Interquartile range = $41.5 - 32 = 9.5$	
b Arrange in ascending order to find the median.	
~~4~~ ~~5~~ ~~7~~ 7 9 ~~10~~ ~~11~~ ~~14~~	
Median = $\dfrac{7 + 9}{2} = 8$	
The middle score in the set 4, 5, 7, 7 is $Q_1 = \dfrac{5 + 7}{2} = 6$	
The middle score in the set 9, 10, 11, 14 is $Q_3 = \dfrac{10 + 11}{2} = 10.5$	
Interquartile range = $10.5 - 6 = 4.5$	

5 Find the interquartile range for the following scores.

  a 42, 45, 45, 48, 53, 61, 64, 68, 71   **b** 170, 170, 170, 185, 188, 189, 194, 196, 203

  c 2, 3, 5, 8, 8, 8, 9, 9, 9, 11, 15, 17, 18   **d** 15, 17, 20, 23, 28, 35, 42, 44

  e 95, 102, 95, 89, 92, 103, 90, 98   **f** 5, 2, 3, 9, 7, 11, 1, 5, 7, 13

EXAMPLE 4

Find the interquartile range from this stem-and-leaf plot.

Stem	Leaf
4	2 4 6
5	0 3 7 7 9 9
6	1 3 4 5 9
7	0 2 4 7
8	1 5 5 6 7

EXAMPLE 5 CONTINUED

Solve/Think	Apply
There are 23 scores so the median is the 12th score. Alternatively cross off the numbers to find the median. The median is 64. There are 11 scores above the median and 11 scores below the median. The lower quartile is the 6th score; that is, 57. The upper quartile is the 12th + 6 = 18th score; that is, 77. Interquartile range = 77 − 57 = 20	Find the upper and lower quartiles and hence the interquartile range.

6 Find the interquartile range from these stem-and-leaf plots.

a

Stem	Leaf
7	1 1 2 2 3 3 7 8 9
8	2 3 3 6 8 8

b

Stem	Leaf
10	4 5 6 8 9
11	2 2 2 3 5 6 8 8 9
12	0 0 2 2 5 6 7 7
13	1 1 1 6

c

Stem	Leaf
85	5 8 4 5 3 4 2
86	1 2 1 1 1 2 3 4 7 6
87	2 3 4 8 4 5 1 3 6 9 9
88	5 3 6 8 7 4 3 0 3

For part c put in order first.

7 Consider the scores 8, 8, 9, 10, 12, 14, 148.

a Determine:

   i the range   **ii** the interquartile range.

b Explain why the interquartile range is a better measure of spread than the range for this set of data.

C   Box plots

A box plot uses five especially selected numbers to display information about numerical scores in a graphical form. The numbers used are the extremes (the highest and lowest scores), the median (the middle score) and the upper and lower quartiles. These five numbers make up the five-number summary.

A box plot is used to show the range and middle half of ranked data. Ranked data is numerical data such as numbers. The middle half of the data is represented by the box. The highest and lowest scores are joined to the box by straight lines. The regions above the upper quartile and below the lower quartile each contain 25% of the data.

The five-number summary is shown in the diagram.

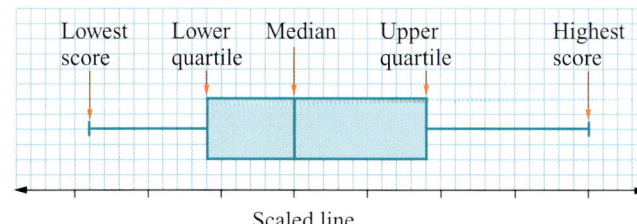

EXAMPLE 1

From this box plot, find the following.

a i highest score
   ii lowest score
   iii range of the scores
b median
c i upper quartile   ii lower quartile   iii interquartile range

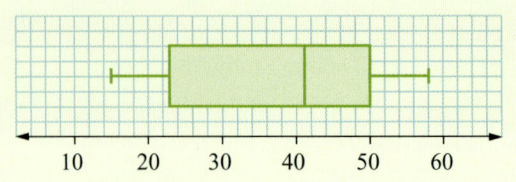

	Solve/Think	Apply
a i	Highest score = 58	Read the values of the quartiles and extremes from the box plot. Calculate the range and interquartile range from these values.
ii	Lowest score = 15	*Note:* From these results we can say that:
iii	Range = 58 − 15 = 43	• The bottom 25% of the scores take values from 15 up to, but less than, 23.
b	Median = 41	• The top 25% of the scores take values from, but not including, 50 up to 58.
c i	Q_3 = 50	• The middle 50% of the scores lie between 23 and 50.
ii	Q_1 = 23	The median is closer to the upper quartile than to the lower
iii	Interquartile range = 50 − 23 = 27	quartile, so the top half of the scores are clustered closer to the median than the bottom half.

Exercise 8C

1 From the box plots shown below, find the following.

    i highest score   **ii** lowest score   **iii** range of the scores   **iv** median
    v upper quartile   **vi** lower quartile   **vii** interquartile range

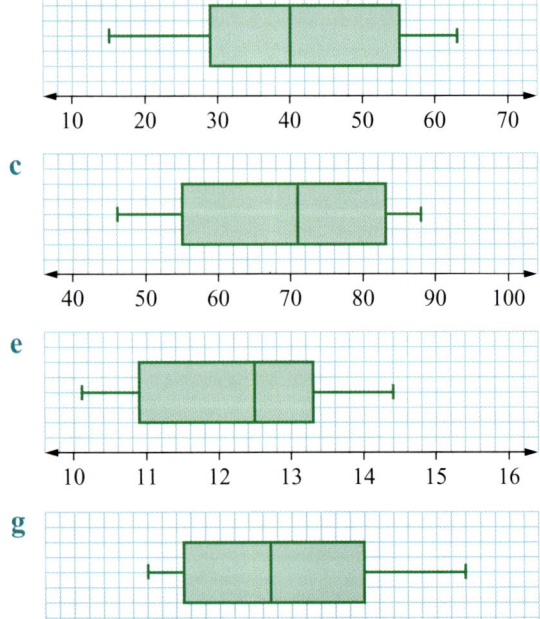

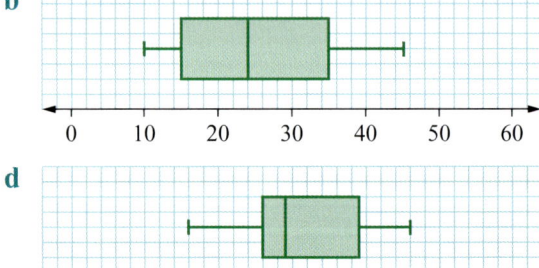

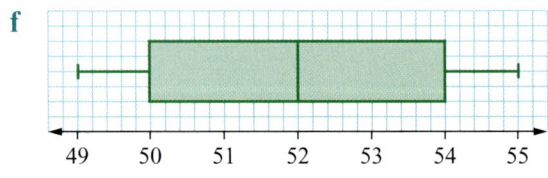

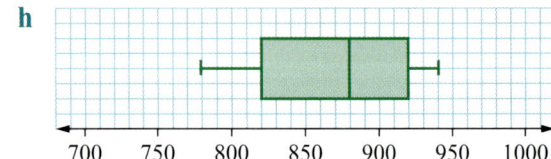

EXAMPLE 2

Draw a box plot for ranked data with highest score 65, lowest score 42, median 58, upper quartile 60 and lower quartile 49.

Solve/Think	Apply
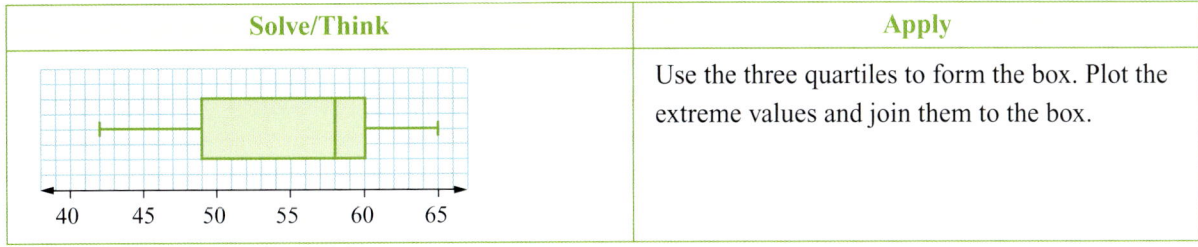	Use the three quartiles to form the box. Plot the extreme values and join them to the box.

2 Draw box plots for ranked data with the following values.

	Highest score	Lowest score	Median	Upper quartile	Lower quartile
a	40	15	28	32	23
b	153	130	141	148	139
c	28	6	10	18	7
d	83	71	78	80	73
e	9	1	5	7	3

EXAMPLE 3

Draw a box plot for the scores 21, 22, 22, 23, 25, 26, 27.

Solve	Think	Apply
	Median is 23. Upper quartile is 26. Lower quartile is 22. Highest score is 27. Lowest score is 21.	Determine the values of the quartiles and extremes. Draw the box plot.

3 Draw box plots for the following scores.
   a 34, 35, 36, 36, 37, 38, 39, 39, 39, 40
   b 4, 5, 8, 8, 10, 12, 12, 14, 15, 19
   c 21, 21, 23, 24, 24, 24, 26, 28, 30
   d 89, 90, 92, 95, 95, 98, 102, 103
   e 18, 20, 22, 23, 25, 29, 30, 30, 30, 31
   f 1, 3, 4, 4, 5, 5, 5, 7, 11, 15

EXAMPLE 4

Construct a box plot for the data in this stem-and-leaf plot.

Stem	Leaf
4	2 4 6
5	0 3 7 7 9 9
6	1 3 4 5 9
7	0 2 4 7
8	1 5 5 6 7

Solve	Think	Apply
	There are 23 leaves and hence 23 scores. So median = 12th score = 64 Q_1 (lower quartile) = 6th score = 57 Q_3 (upper quartile) = 18th score = 77 Highest score = 87, lowest score = 42	Determine the values of the quartiles and extremes. Draw the box plot.

4 Draw box plots for the data in the following stem-and-leaf plots.

a

Stem	Leaf
2	1 1 3 5 6 8 8
3	2 2 3 3 3 4 5 6 8
4	0 0 3 4 4 4 5 5 7 7 8
5	5 5 6 8

b

Stem	Leaf
10	8 8 9
11	1 1 2 3 3 3 4 4 5 8 8 9
12	0 2 2 3 4 4 4 5 5 8 8 8 9
13	0 0 0 1 1

c

Stem	Leaf
7	1 1 2 3 3 3 7 8 9
8	2 2 2 3 5 6 8 8 9
9	5 5 5 5 6 6 6 9 9

d

Stem	Leaf
5	1 1 2 3 3 4 5 6 6 7 7 8
6	0 1 2 3 4 4 5 5 8 8
7	2 3 4 5 5 5 6 7 8 8

e

Stem	Leaf
33	7 7 7 7
34	3 4 4 5 5 5 5 6 9
35	0 0 3 7 7 8 8 9
36	0 1 2 3 3 4 7 7 9
37	1 1 1 2

f

Stem	Leaf
21	0 3 3 3 4 5 6 7 8
22	1 1 1 1 2 2 3 4 6 7
23	2 3 4 4 5 5 8
24	1 2 3 3 4 4 5 6 8 9 9

EXAMPLE 5

Draw a box plot for the data in this frequency distribution table.

Score	Frequency	Cumulative frequency
0	1	1
1	3	4
2	4	8
3	3	11
4	3	14
5	7	21
6	4	25
7	5	30
8	1	31
9	1	32

EXAMPLE 5 CONTINUED

Solve	Think	Apply
	As there are 32 scores, the median is the average of the 16th and 17th scores. $$\text{Median} = \frac{\text{16th score} + \text{17th score}}{2}$$ $$= \frac{5 + 5}{2} = 5$$ There are 16 scores above and 16 scores below the median. The 16th score is found by looking for the first score in the cumulative frequency column that is equal to or greater than 16. Go across from this value to find the score required, in this case 5. All other scores are found in this way. The lower quartile is the average of the 8th and 9th scores. $$Q_1 = \frac{\text{8th score} + \text{9th score}}{2}$$ $$= \frac{2 + 3}{2} = 2.5$$ The upper quartile is the average of the 24th and 25th scores. $$Q_3 = \frac{\text{24th score} + \text{25th score}}{2}$$ $$= \frac{6 + 6}{2} = 6$$ Highest score = 9 Lowest score = 0	If it is not given, complete a cumulative frequency column to determine the values of the quartiles and extremes. Draw the box plot.

5 Copy these tables and add a cumulative frequency column. Calculate the necessary information and draw a box plot for each data set.

a

Score	Frequency
12	20
13	18
14	15
15	15
16	17
17	15

b

Score	Frequency
53	15
54	30
55	13
56	3
57	9
58	30

c

Score	Frequency
110	5
111	22
112	26
113	25
114	17
115	5

d

Score	Frequency
32	6
33	8
34	9
35	13
36	9
37	3
38	2

STATISTICS & PROBABILITY

e	Score	Frequency
	47	4
	48	7
	49	12
	50	21
	51	10
	52	6

f	Score	Frequency
	0	1
	1	2
	2	3
	3	4
	4	2
	5	5
	6	4

D Comparing data sets

EXAMPLE 1

Two data sets are shown in these parallel box plots.
a Describe any similarities in the data sets.
b Compare the range of set A with that of set B.
c For which data set is the middle 50% clustered more closely to the median?
d In which data set is the top 50% of scores more closely clustered to the median?

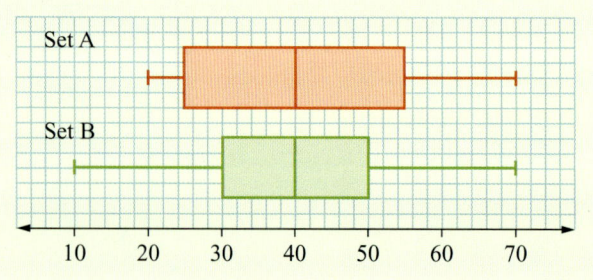

	Solve	Think	Apply
a	The greatest score and the median are the same for both data sets.	Greatest score of both is 70. Median of both is 40.	Use the known proportion of values between the quartiles as well as the extreme values to analyse the data.
b	The range of set A is less than the range of set B.	Range of set A $= 70 - 20 = 50$. Range of set B $= 70 - 10 = 60$. Set B has the greater spread of scores.	
c	Set B	IQR of set A $= 55 - 25 = 30$. IQR of set B $= 50 - 30 = 20$. The spread of scores about the median is less for set B than set A.	
d	Set B	As the top 50% of scores are spread over the same interval, the scores between Q_2 and Q_3 will show any clustering. Q_3 is closer to the median for set B than for set A. The 25% of scores between Q_2 and Q_3 (and hence the top 50%) for set B are closer to their median.	

Exercise 8D

1 A class has eight assessment tasks over a year. The parallel box plots show a summary of the marks for the assessments for two students, Jamie and Maryanne.

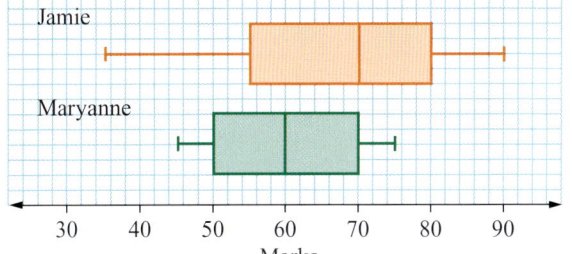

  a **i** Who scored the highest mark?
  ii Who scored the lowest mark?
  b **i** What was the range of marks for each student?
  ii Who had the greater spread of marks?
  c **i** What was the interquartile range of marks for each student?
  ii Whose marks were the more consistent?
  d Who had more marks over 70?
  e Assuming each assessment task had the same weighting, who do you think finished the year with the higher overall assessment? Give reasons for your answer.

2 These parallel box plots show the life span of two brands of light globes ($\times$ 100 hours).

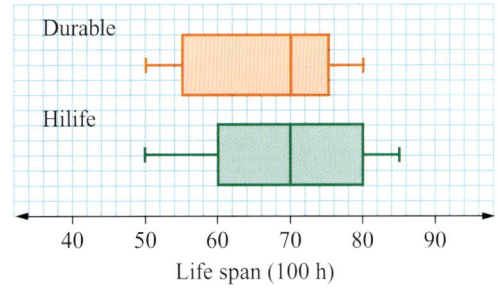

  a Describe any similarities in the data.
  b Which brand had the globe with the:
   i greatest life span? **ii** shortest life span?
  c **i** What was the range of life spans for each brand?
  ii Which brand had the greater spread of life spans?
  d **i** What was the interquartile range for each brand?
  ii What does this indicate about the middle 50% of life spans for each brand?
  e Which brand lasts longer? Give reasons for your answer.

3 A new Toyota Corolla and Mazda 3 were each taken for ten test drives over the same routes. These parallel box plots show a summary of the fuel consumption, in L/100 km, of each vehicle over these routes.

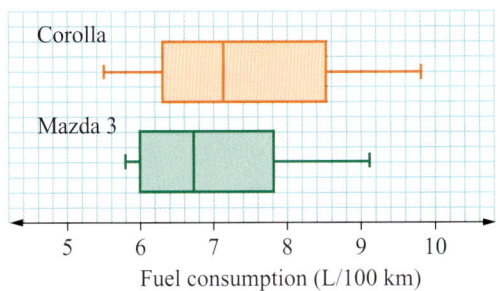
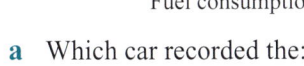

  a Which car recorded the:
   i highest fuel consumption?
   ii lowest fuel consumption?
  b Which car had the greater range of results?
  c Which car demonstrated the more consistent fuel consumption over all routes? Give a reason.
  d Which car used less than 7 L/100 km more often?
  e Which car had the better overall fuel consumption. Give reasons.

EXAMPLE 2

The histogram shows the number of days in a month on which students in a Year 10 class were absent. Draw a box plot for this data

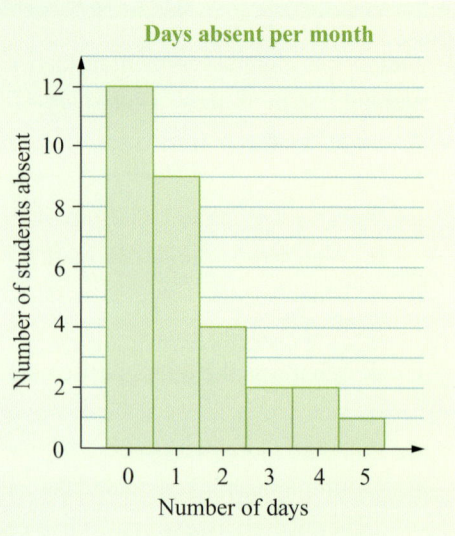

Days absent per month

	Solve		Think	Apply

The frequency of each score can be found from the histogram and put in a frequency distribution table. Add a cumulative frequency column.

Number of days	Number of students absent	Cumulative frequency
0	12	12
1	9	21
2	4	25
3	2	27
4	2	29
5	1	30

From the cumulative frequency column:

$$Q_2 = \frac{15\text{th} + 16\text{th scores}}{2} = 1$$

$Q_1 = 8\text{th score} = 0$

$Q_3 = 23\text{rd score} = 2$

Lowest score = 0

Highest score = 5

Apply

Put the information shown in the histogram into a frequency distribution table and add a cumulative frequency column. Use the cumulative frequency column to find the quartiles and add the extreme scores to make a five-number summary for the data. Draw the box plot.

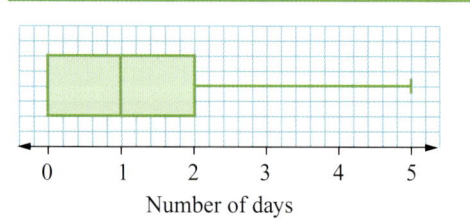

Number of days

4 The histogram shows the marks scored by a class in a test. Draw a box plot for this data.

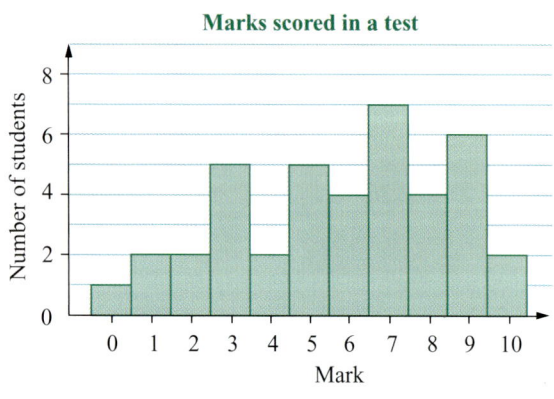

Marks scored in a test

5 The dot plot shows the maximum daily temperatures for February. Draw a box plot for this information.

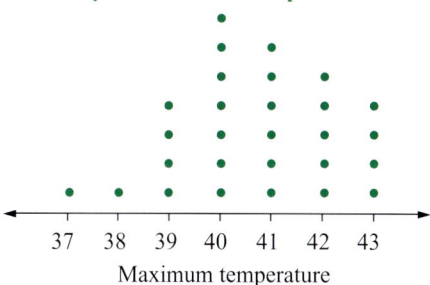

Maximum temperature

EXAMPLE 3

i Draw a box plot for the data shown in each of the histograms below.

ii Describe and compare the features of each histogram and its corresponding box plot.

a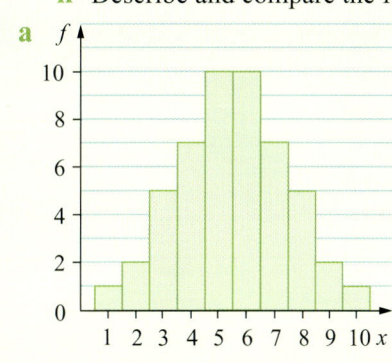

b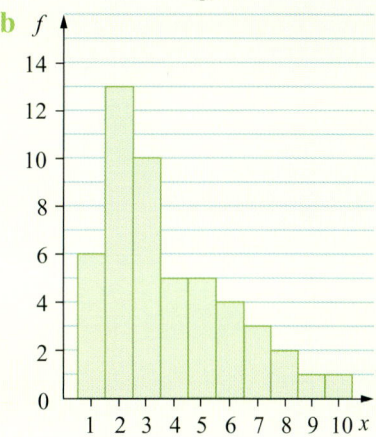

c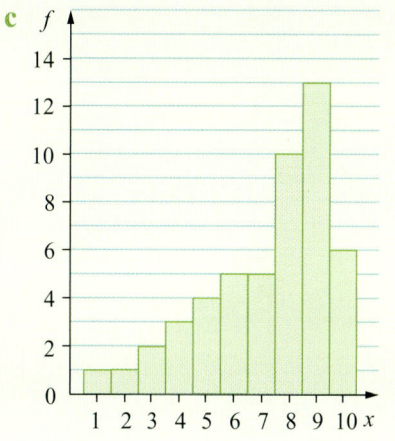

	Solve	Think	Apply
a **i**	From the histogram: So the box plot is: 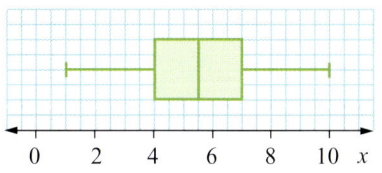	Using the information from the histogram, first compile a cumulative frequency table. Determine the position of the box and the relative spread between the quartiles and extremes in the box plot. For this data: $\text{Median} = \dfrac{25\text{th} + 26\text{th scores}}{2}$ $= \dfrac{5 + 6}{2}$ $= 5.5$ Upper quartile is 38th score $= 7$ Lower quartile is 13th score $= 4$ Highest score $= 10$ Lowest score $= 1$ Q_1 and Q_3 are equally spaced from the median. The lowest and highest scores are equally spaced from Q_1 and Q_3 respectively.	Put the information shown in the histogram into a frequency distribution table and add a cumulative frequency column. Use the cumulative frequency column to find the quartiles and add the extreme scores to make a five-number summary for the data. Draw the box plot.

Table within cell **a i**:

x	f	cf
1	1	1
2	2	3
3	5	8
4	7	15
5	10	25
6	10	35
7	7	42
8	5	47
9	2	49
10	1	50

STATISTICS & PROBABILITY

EXAMPLE 3 CONTINUED

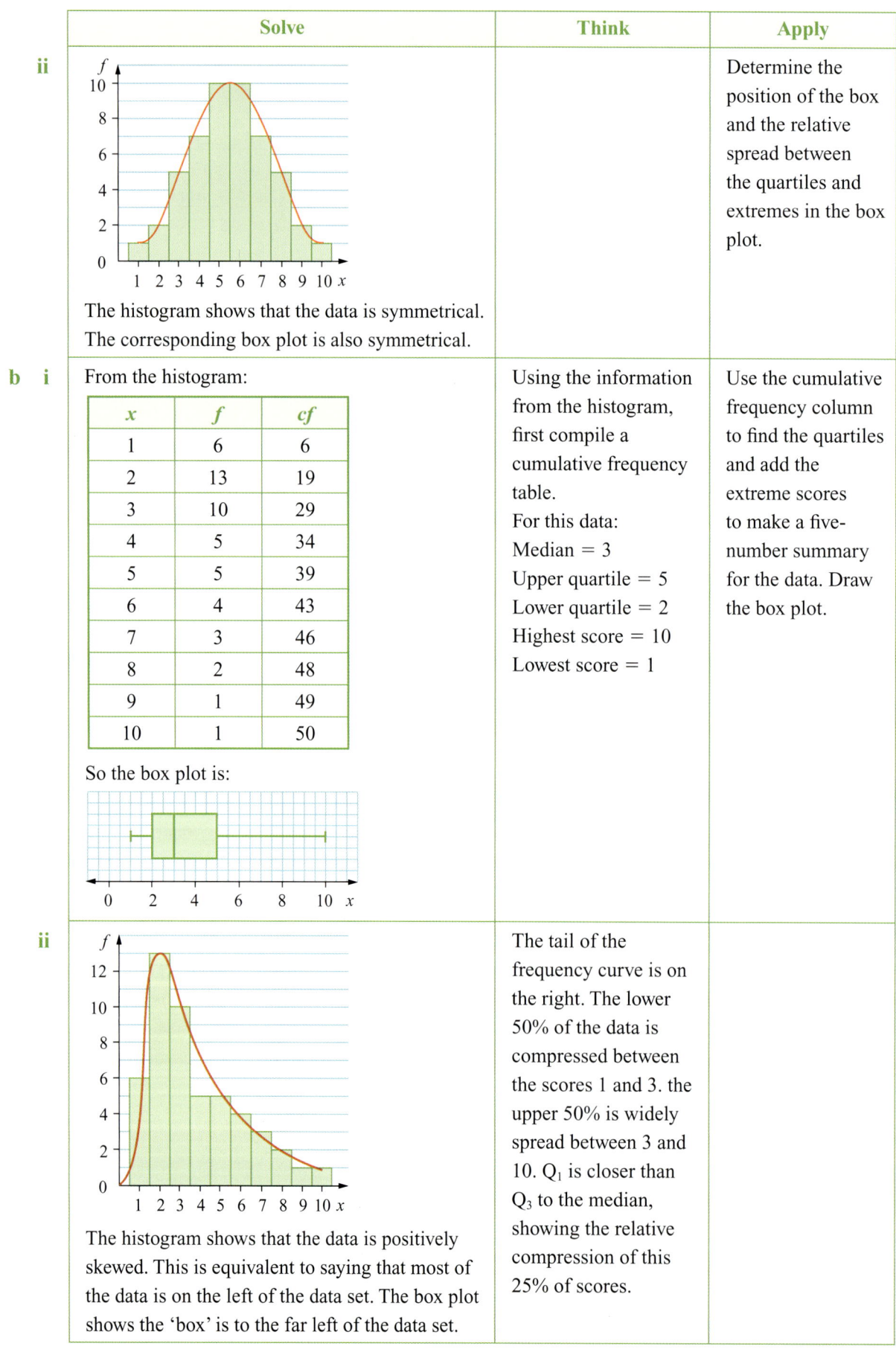

		Solve	Think	Apply
ii		The histogram shows that the data is symmetrical. The corresponding box plot is also symmetrical.		Determine the position of the box and the relative spread between the quartiles and extremes in the box plot.

b i From the histogram:

x	f	cf
1	6	6
2	13	19
3	10	29
4	5	34
5	5	39
6	4	43
7	3	46
8	2	48
9	1	49
10	1	50

So the box plot is:

Think: Using the information from the histogram, first compile a cumulative frequency table.
For this data:
Median = 3
Upper quartile = 5
Lower quartile = 2
Highest score = 10
Lowest score = 1

Apply: Use the cumulative frequency column to find the quartiles and add the extreme scores to make a five-number summary for the data. Draw the box plot.

ii The histogram shows that the data is positively skewed. This is equivalent to saying that most of the data is on the left of the data set. The box plot shows the 'box' is to the far left of the data set.

Think: The tail of the frequency curve is on the right. The lower 50% of the data is compressed between the scores 1 and 3. the upper 50% is widely spread between 3 and 10. Q_1 is closer than Q_3 to the median, showing the relative compression of this 25% of scores.

	Solve	Think	Apply
c i	From the histogram:	Using the information from the histogram, first compile a cumulative frequency table. For this data: Median = 8 Upper quartile = 9 Lower quartile = 6 Highest score = 10 Lowest score = 1	Use the cumulative frequency column to find the quartiles and add the extreme scores to make a five-number summary for the data. Draw the box plot.

From the histogram:

x	f	cf
1	1	1
2	1	2
3	2	4
4	3	7
5	4	11
6	5	16
7	5	21
8	10	31
9	13	44
10	6	50

So the box plot is:

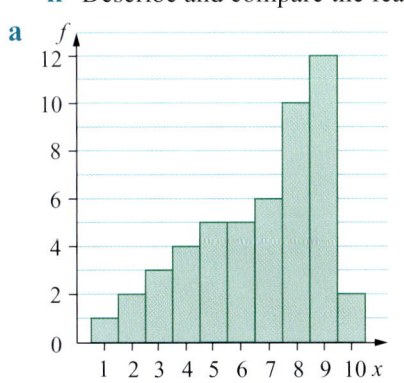

	Solve	Think	Apply
ii	The histogram shows that the data is negatively skewed. The corresponding box plot shows the 'box' is to the far right of the data set.	The tail of the frequency curve is on the left as most of the data is on the right of the data set. The upper 50% of the data is compressed between the scores 8 and 10. The lower 50% is widely spread between 1 and 8. Also Q_3 is closer than Q_1 to the median, showing the relative compression of this 25% of scores.	Determine the position of the box and the relative spread between the quartiles and extremes in the box plot.

6 i Draw a box plot for the data shown in each of the histograms below.

    ii Describe and compare the features of each histogram and its corresponding box plot.

a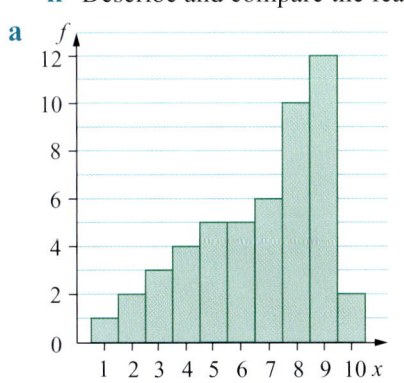

b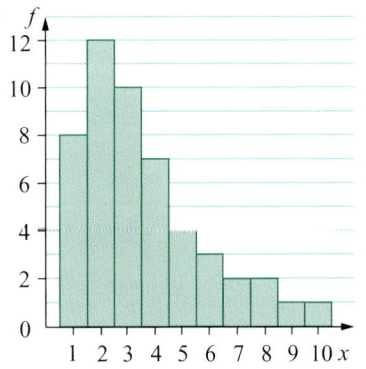

c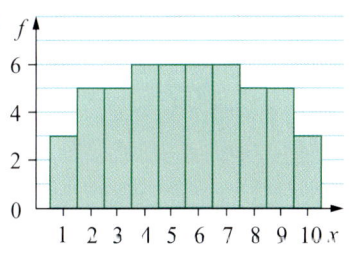

7 Match each histogram or dot plot with its corresponding box plot.

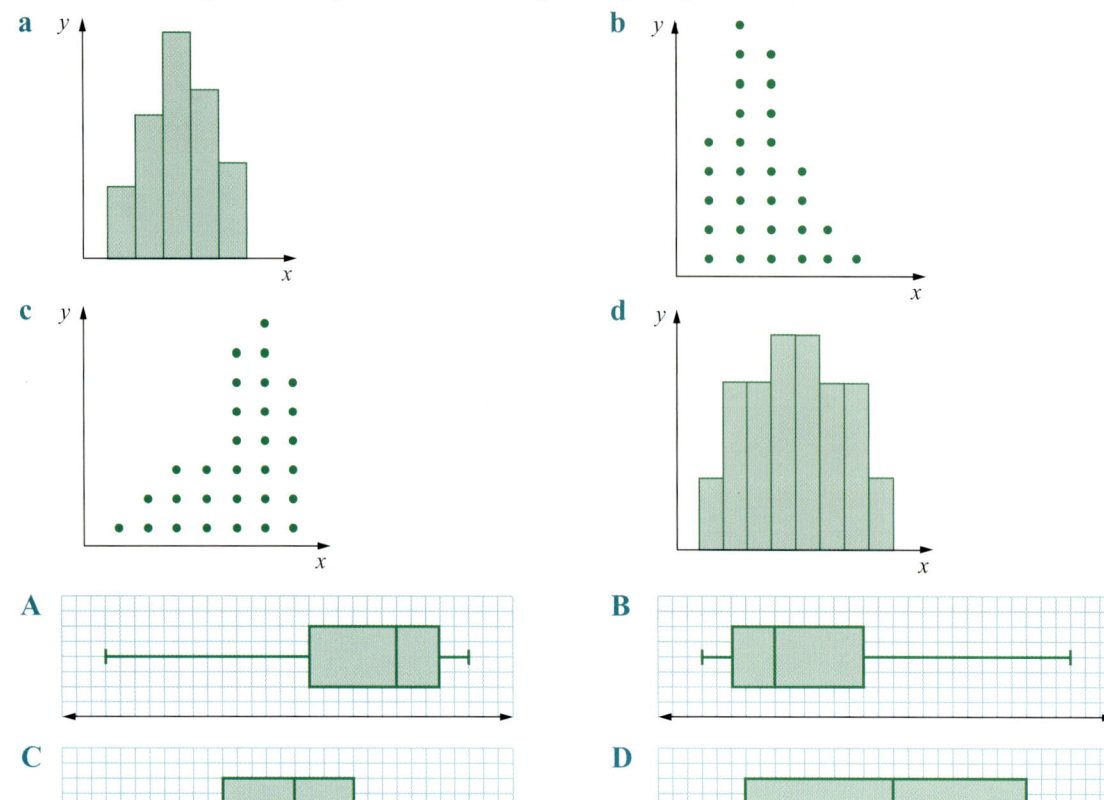

a y

b y

c y

d y

A

B

C

D

Investigation 1 Statistical reports in the media

1 Investigate survey data reported in the digital media and elsewhere to critically evaluate the reliability and validity of the source of the data and its usefulness. Describe bias that may exist due to the way in which the data was obtained. These are questions to consider:

   a Who instigated and/or funded the research?

   b Is the sample being used representative of the population?

   c Is the sample big enough?

   d Do the questions contain bias?

   e Is the research recent?

Language in mathematics

1 Insert vowels to complete these terms

    a m__ __n   **b** q__ __rt_l   **c** sk_w_d d_str_b_t_ _n

    d _pp_r q_ _rt_l_   **e** b_x pl_ts

2 **a** Describe the difference between the range and the interquartile range of a set of scores.

    b When would it be better to use the interquartile range rather than the range?

3 Rearrange these words to form a sentence. The first word has a capital letter.

    a by is range The unaffected outliers interquartile

    b spread a is The of measure range

    c score middle median order in the The is when arranged scores are the

4 Use every third letter to reveal a sentence about statistics.

```
E F T G T H H Y E U J M I K E A S A D F N E F A K G N Q E D D C M V G E B
H D P O I I U A Y T N T G A H J R K K E L L M O O E I I A W S S C F U B G
R Y A E X G S E T O U T F Y E C Q T E A V N E F T H R R J K A E D L W S T
Q A E Z X N D F D B H E J U N T G C B N Y M K W L O H O I I I U L U Y E T
R T Q W H S D E R V R G B A H N N J U G Y T E T S A F E N E C D E T I E D
N E T T I Y E A S R D V Q G T U Q B A J O R R F T D G I B M L A E E T G R
R F A E D N S E G E T E V H A U I R Y T E E W M S Q E A Z A X V S D F U G
W R Q X E C T S Y N O M I F R F S A G P C T R Q Z E X C A V G D H J T I K
H I O E O L I U Y N W E T F G E B H R U J Q M W U S Y A T O R D V T Q S I
C G L J I E L I R P O A T T N R E G C E E S E I A E S Q S T C V H H Y E I
U O T R N F H L E I Y O P M E D E C E A V E S F E U R G R T H E J K O A S
F S A S E S P E A R S E E D E A F E D R G T H J H Q S A A Z T C G I U O S
J K N R F O B T T H J A E D F N J F O I E O K C O L T P O E U Y D E R B F
G Y V F O E R U S D T V R L T H I U K E O I R L I S
```

Terms

bimodal	box plots	data sets	five-number summary	highest score
interquartile range	lower quartile	lowest score	mean	median
mode	normal distribution	outlier	quartile	range
skewed distribution	upper quartile			

Check your skills

1 The mean of the scores 8, 11, 11, 12, 14, 15, 15, 15, 16, 17, 20 is:

    A 15   **B** 14   **C** 12   **D** 11

2 The range of the scores 8, 11, 11, 12, 14, 15, 15, 15, 16, 17, 20 is:

    A 15   **B** 14   **C** 12   **D** 11

3 The median of the scores 8, 11, 11, 12, 14, 15, 15, 15, 16, 17, 20 is:

    A 15   **B** 14   **C** 12   **D** 11

4 The mode of the scores 8, 11, 11, 12, 14, 15, 15, 15, 16, 17, 20 is:

   A 15   **B** 14   **C** 12   **D** 11

5 The mean of 11, 15, 16, 19, 21 and x is 17. The value of x is:

   A 20   **B** 21   **C** 16.4   **D** 10

Use the scores 15, 16, 17, 18, 18, 18, 20, 21, 21, 25 to answer questions **6** to **8**.

6 The lower quartile is:

   A 25   **B** 21   **C** 17   **D** 15

7 The upper quartile is:

   A 21   **B** 18   **C** 17   **D** 10

8 The interquartile range is:

   A 10   **B** 18   **C** 5   **D** 4

Use the information in this box plot to answer questions **9** to **11**.

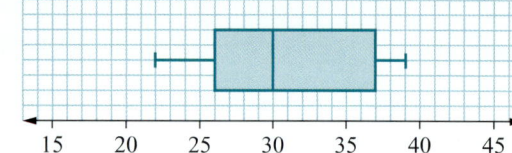

9 The range is:

   A 39   **B** 17

   C 11   **D** 30

10 The median is:

   A 39   **B** 17   **C** 11   **D** 30

11 The interquartile range is:

   A 39   **B** 17   **C** 11   **D** 30

Use the data in this stem-and-leaf plot to answer questions **12** to **14**.

Stem	Leaf
4	8 8 9
5	1 3 5 5 8
6	1 1 2 4 6 7 7 8 9 9
7	1 2 2 2 3 5 5 6 6 7 7 7 9
8	0 3 6 6 6 6 7 8 8 9 9
9	1 2 3 6 7 8 8 8

12 The median is:

   A 86   **B** 75.5

   C 65   **D** 50

13 The interquartile range is:

   A 50   **B** 86

   C 21   **D** 11

14 The lowest and highest scores are:

   A 48 and 98   **B** 65 and 86   **C** 0 and 9   **D** 48 and 75

15 For the parallel box plots shown on the right, which statement is not true?

   A The range is the same for both data sets.

   B The interquartile range is the same for both data sets.

   C The median of set X is greater than the median of set Y.

   D Both data sets are symmetrical.

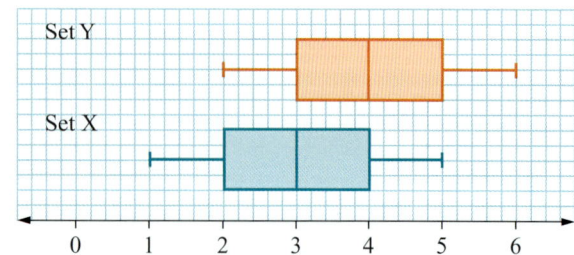

16 The box plot that best matches the given dot plot is:

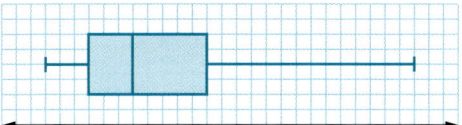

A

B

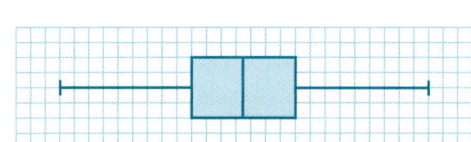

C

D

17 The histogram that best matches this box plot is:

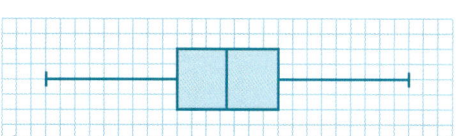

A

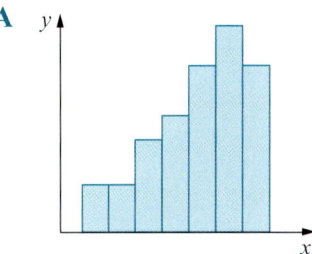

B

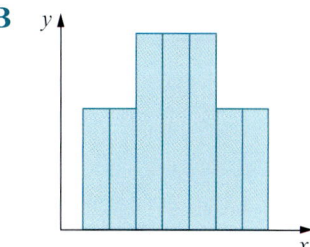

C

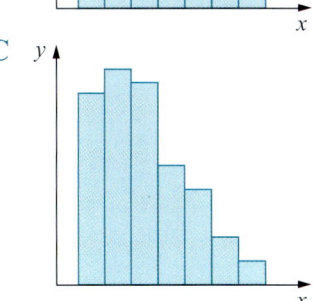

D

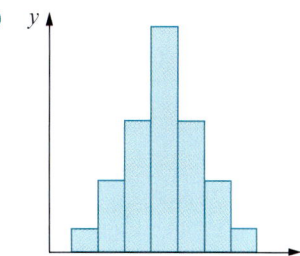

If you have any difficulty with these questions, refer to the examples and questions in the sections listed in the table.

Question	1–5	6–8	9–14	15–17
Section	A	B	C	D

8A   Review set

1 For the scores 6, 7, 7, 9, 10, 11, 14, find:

  a the mean

  b the median

  c the range

  d the interquartile range.

2 Find x when the mean of 7, 12, 18, 16 and x is 15.

3 From the box plot shown, find:

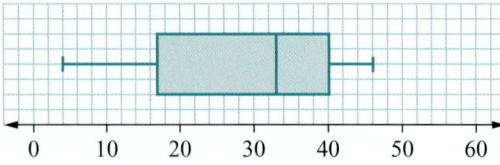

    a the highest score   **b** the lowest score

    c the range   **d** the median

    e the upper quartile   **f** the lower quartile

    g the interquartile range.

4 The diagram shows parallel box plots for the data in sets A and B.

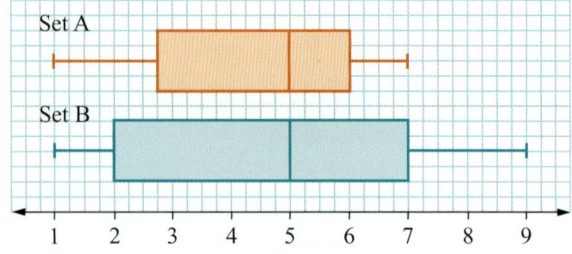

    a What are the similarities between these sets of data?

    b Which data set has the greater range?

    c Which data set has the greater spread of the middle 50% of its scores?

    d Compare the spread of the lower 50% of scores in each data set.

    e If the box plots represent the marks of two classes on a test, which class do you think was more consistent?

8B   Review set

1 For the scores 2, 4, 6, 9, 9, 10, find:

    a the mean   **b** the median

    c the range   **d** the interquartile range.

2 **a** The mean of six scores is 14. What is the sum of the scores?

    b If 11, 15, 12, 11, 8 and x have a mean of 13, find x.

3 **a** Find the range of the scores in these frequency distribution tables.

    b What is the interquartile range?

i

Score	Frequency
9	6
10	5
11	9
12	11
13	3
14	6

ii

Score	Frequency
25	6
26	10
27	10
28	13
29	6
30	2

4 Draw box plots for the following data sets.

    a 3, 4, 7, 7, 9, 11, 11, 13, 14, 18

b

Score	Frequency
15	18
16	16
17	13
18	13
19	15
20	13

    c

Stem	Leaf
6	3 3 3 3
7	3 4 4 5 5 5 6 6 8
8	0 0 2 5 5 9 9 9
9	0 1 3 3 3 4 7 7 9
10	3 3 3 4

STATISTICS & PROBABILITY

5 **a** Draw a box plot for the data shown in the histogram.

  b Describe how the features of the histogram are shown in the corresponding box plot.

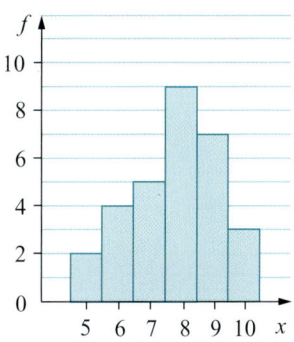

8C   Review set

1 For the scores 11, 11, 12, 13, 15, 15, 15, 16, 19, 20, 21, 21, find:

  a the mean   **b** the median

  c the range   **d** the interquartile range.

2 Find x when the mean of 17, 22, 38, 36 and x is 30.

3 From the box plot, find:

  a the highest score   **b** the lowest score

  c the range   **d** the median

  e the upper quartile   **f** the lower quartile

  g the interquartile range.

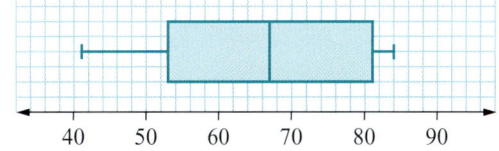

4 **a** Find the range and interquartile range for the scores in this frequency distribution table.

  b Draw a histogram for the scores in the table.

  c Comment on the shape of the distribution.

Score	Frequency
16	4
17	6
18	8
19	15
20	23
21	14

5 Select the data set in the box plot that best matches the given histogram or dot plot.

a
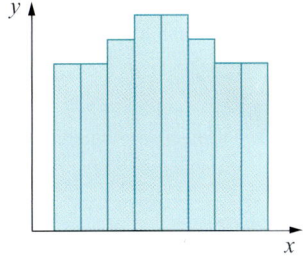

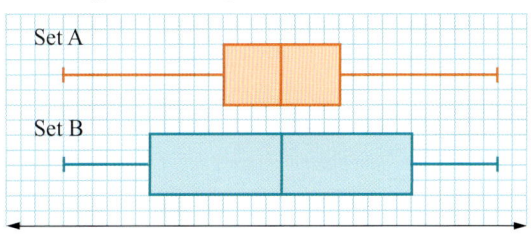

b
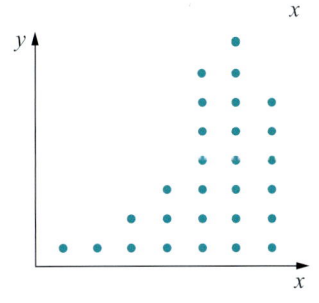

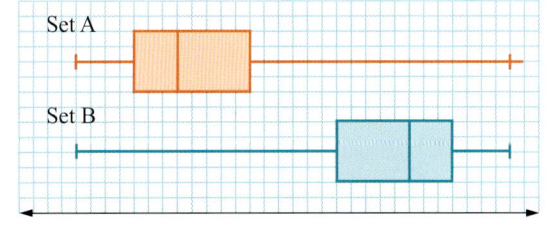

1 For the scores 65, 61, 64, 61, 61, 62, find:

   a the mean   **b** the median

   c the range   **d** the interquartile range.

2 a If 9, 6, 2, 5 and x have a mean of 7, find x.

   b The mean of eight scores is 5.25. What is the sum of the scores?

3 a For this stem-and-leaf plot, find:

     i the mean   **ii** the range

     iii the median   **iv** the interquartile range.

   b Is this distribution symmetrical or skewed? Explain.

Stem	Leaf
4	1 2 2 3
5	2 4 6 9 9
6	1 3 4 5 5 6 7 7 8
7	0 0 2 3 3 3 8
8	5 6 7 9
9	0 1 2

4 Draw box plots for the following data sets.

   a 1, 1, 3, 4, 5, 5, 5, 6, 7, 10, 11

   b

Score	Frequency
21	23
22	28
23	15
24	31
25	12

   c

Stem	Leaf
18	1 2 3 3 5 6 7 8
19	1 1 1 1 2 2 3 6 6 7 9
20	1 3 4 5 6 6 7 8
21	0 0 0 1 3 4 5 9

5 The box plot shows the mean daily maximum temperatures in Sydney and Melbourne for the month of January. Compare and describe the features of the weather illustrated by these displays.

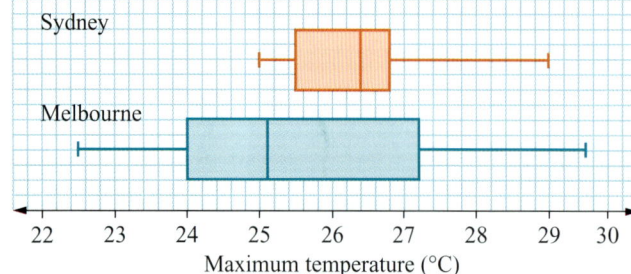

9

Non-linear relationships

This chapter deals with the graphs of simple non-linear relationships.

After completing this chapter you should be able to:

- graph parabolic relationships of the form $y = ax^2 + c$
- determine the x-coordinate of a point on a parabola given its y-coordinate
- sketch, compare and describe the features of simple exponential curves
- recognise and describe equations that represent circles with centre the origin and radius r
- sketch circles of the form $x^2 + y^2 = r^2$
- identify graphs and equations of straight lines, parabolas, circles and exponentials
- match the graphs of straight lines, parabolas, circles and exponentials to the appropriate equations
- sort and classify different types of graphs.

NSW Syllabus references: 5.2 N&A Non-linear relationships
Outcomes: MA5.2-1WM, MA5.2-3WM, MA5.2-10NA
Number & algebra – ACMNA239, ACMNA296

Diagnostic test

1 The equation of the line with gradient $\frac{2}{3}$ and y-intercept -5 is:

A $y = -5x + \frac{2}{3}$ **B** $y = 5x - \frac{2}{3}$

C $y = \frac{2}{3}x + 5$ **D** $y = \frac{2}{3}x - 5$

2 The graph of $y = 2x - 2$ is:

A   **B**

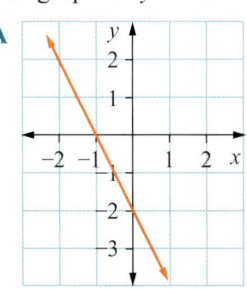 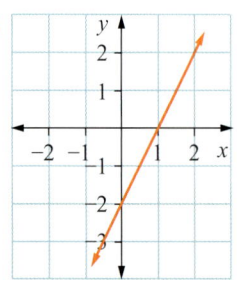

C   **D**

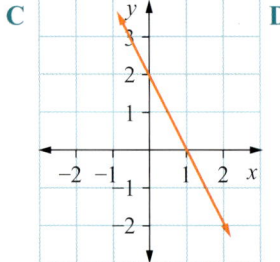 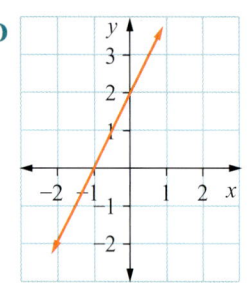

3 The graph of the straight line $x - 2y - 8 = 0$ has:

A gradient $= -2$ and y-intercept $= -8$

B gradient $= 2$ and y-intercept $= 8$

C gradient $= \frac{1}{2}$ and y-intercept $= -4$

D gradient $= -\frac{1}{2}$ and y-intercept $= 4$

4 The equation of the line graph is:

A $y = 2x - 3$

B $y = -2x + 3$

C $y = \frac{1}{3}x - 3$

D $y = -\frac{1}{3}x - 3$

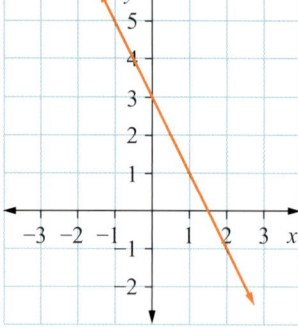

5

x	-2	-1	0	1	2
y	-8	-5	-2	1	4

The equation of the line that passes through the points in the table is:

A $y = -4x$ **B** $y = -4x - 1$

C $y = x - 2$ **D** $y = 3x - 2$

6 The y-coordinate of the point on the curve $y = 2x^2 - 3x + 1$ with x-coordinate -2 is:

A 15   **B** 6   **C** 0   **D** -4

7 The value of $(-2)^{-3}$ is:

A 6   **B** -8 **C** $\frac{1}{8}$ **D** $-\frac{1}{8}$

8 The distance of the point $(8, 15)$ from the origin is:

A 23 units   **B** 17 units

C 15 units   **D** 7 units

The diagnostic test questions refer to outcome ACMNA193, ACMNA214, ACMNA215 and ACMNA294. **(AC)**

A The parabola

This exercise explores some of the properties of the parabola. A parabola is a graph of the form $y = ax^2 + bx + c$ and is either a $\cup$ or $\cap$ shaped curve. The turning point is called the vertex of the parabola.

Graphics calculators may be used to help draw the graphs.

Exercise 9A

1 **a** Complete this table of values for the parabola $y = x^2$.
   b Graph $y = x^2$.

x	-4	-3	-2	-1	0	1	2	3	4
y									

   c Write the coordinates of the vertex of the parabola.

2 **a** On the same number plane, graph:

   i $y = x^2$, $y = 2x^2$, $y = \frac{1}{2}x^2$ **ii** $y = x^2$, $y = 3x^2$, $y = 4x^2$, $y = \frac{1}{4}x^2$

   b Comment on the effect of the coefficient of x^2 on the graph of $y = ax^2$.

3 Graph $y = -x^2$ by first completing the table.

x	-4	-3	-2	-1	$-\frac{1}{2}$	0	$\frac{1}{2}$	1	2	3	4
y											

4 **a** On the same number plane, graph:

   i $y = -x^2$, $y = -2x^2$, $y = -3x^2$ **ii** $y = -x^2$, $y = -\frac{1}{2}x^2$, $y = -\frac{1}{3}x^2$

   b Comment on the effect of the coefficient of x^2 on the graph of $y = -ax^2$.

5 **a** On the same number plane, graph $y = x^2$, $y = x^2 + 1$, $y = x^2 + 3$.
   b Write the coordinates of the vertex of each parabola.
   c Comment on the effect of the constant term on the graph of $y = x^2 + c$.

6 **a** On the same number plane, graph $y = x^2$, $y = x^2 - 3$, $y = x^2 - 5$.
   b Write the coordinates of the vertex of each parabola.
   c Comment on the effect of the constant term on the graph of the parabola.

7 **a** On the same number plane, graph $y = -x^2$, $y = -x^2 + 2$, $y = -x^2 - 2$.
   b Write the coordinates of the vertex of each parabola.
   c Comment on the effect of the constant term on the graph of the parabola.

8 **a** On the same number plane, graph $y = 2x^2$, $y = 2x^2 + 2$, $y = 2x^2 - 2$.
   b Write the coordinates of the vertex of each parabola.
   c Comment on the effect of the constant term on the graph of the parabola.

9 Find the equation of the graph with the same shape as $y = x^2$ but with vertex:
   a $(0, -1)$ **b** $(0, 1)$ **c** $(0, -3)$ **d** $(0, -5)$ **e** $(0, 4\frac{1}{2})$

NUMBER & ALGEBRA

10 The sketch shows the new position of the graph of $y = \pm x^2$ after it has been translated up or down. Write the equation of each new parabola.

a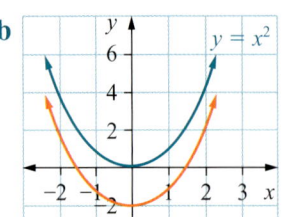

b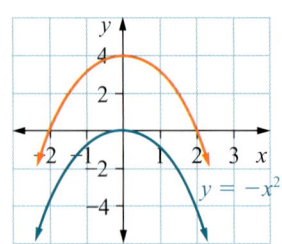

c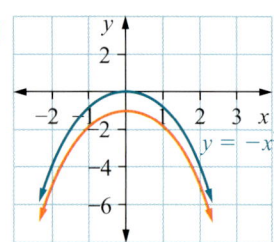

d

11 Match the following equations with the parabolas drawn below.

a $y = 5x^2$

b $y = \frac{1}{3}x^2$

c $y = -4x^2$

d $y = -\frac{1}{2}x^2$

e $y = 3x^2 + 1$

f $y = -2x^2 - 3$

A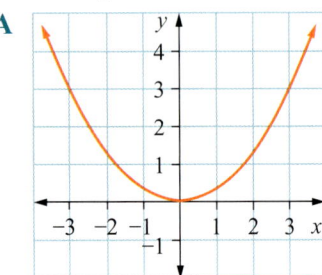

B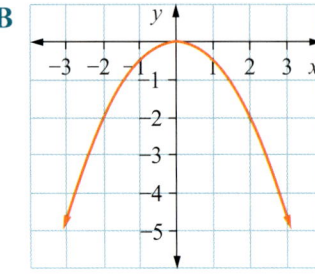

C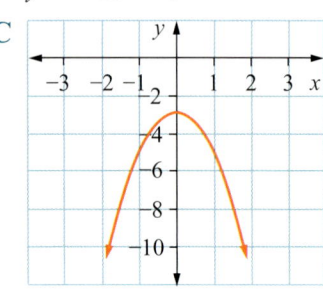

D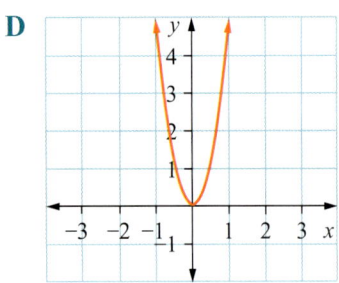

E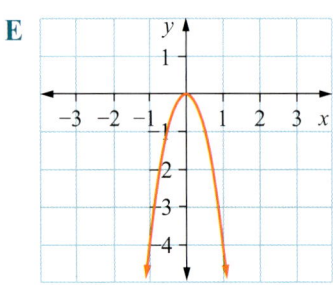

F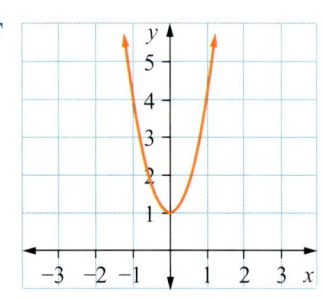

EXAMPLE 1

Find the x-coordinate(s) of the point(s) on the parabola $y = 2x^2 - 7$ whose y-coordinate is 5.

Solve	Think	Apply
$5 = 2x^2 - 7$ $12 = 2x^2$ $x^2 = 6$ $x = \pm\sqrt{6}$	Substitute $y = 5$ into $y = 2x^2 - 7$. For $x^2 = 6$ there are two solutions, $\sqrt{6}$ and $-\sqrt{6}$, written $\pm\sqrt{6}$. The sketch of the graph shows that there are two points on the parabola whose y-coordinate is 5.	Substitute the given y-coordinate into the equation of the parabola, solve the resulting equation.

NUMBER & ALGEBRA

12 Find the x-coordinate(s) of the point(s) on the parabola:

a $y = x^2 - 7$ whose y-coordinate is 3

b $y = 2x^2 - 3$ whose y-coordinate is 11

c $y = 3x^2 + 1$ whose y-coordinate is 4

d $y = 4x^2 - 5$ whose y-coordinate is 4

e $y = 2x^2 + 7$ whose y-coordinate is 57

f $y = 7x^2 - 9$ whose y-coordinate is 5.

Investigation 1 Parabolas

The parabola with equation of the form $y = (x - b)^2 + c$ can be drawn by starting with $y = x^2$.

1 a To sketch $y = (x - 3)^2 + 1$ first sketch $y = x^2$.

   i Translate the graph across so that the vertex is at $(3, 0)$.

   ii Translate the graph up 1 unit.

b Where is the vertex now?

2 a To sketch $y = (x + 3)^2 - 1$ first sketch $y = x^2$.

   i Translate the graph across so that the vertex is at $(-3, 0)$.

   ii Translate the graph down 1 unit.

b Where is the vertex now?

3 Sketch the following parabolas starting with $y = x^2$.

a $y = (x - 2)^2 + 3$

b $y = (x + 2)^2 + 2$

c $y = (x - 3)^2 + 2$

d $y = (x + 5)^2 - 3$

e $y = (x + 1)^2 - 3$

f $y = (x - 2)^2 - 1$

4 Sketch the following parabolas starting with $y = -x^2$.

a $y = -(x + 1)^2 + 1$

b $y = -(x + 2)^2 - 2$

c $y = -(x - 2)^2 + 3$

d $y = -(x - 4)^2 + 3$

5 Complete the following for the graph $y = (x - b)^2 + c$. Use up, down, left or right.

a If $b > 0$, the graph of $y = x^2$ is moved _____.

b If $b < 0$, the graph of $y = x^2$ is moved _____.

c If $c > 0$, the graph of $y = x^2$ is moved _____.

d If $c < 0$, the graph of $y = x^2$ is moved _____.

6 A parabola has vertex at $(1, -8)$ and cuts the x-axis at $(3, 0)$. Find its equation.

Start with $y = a(x - b)^2 + c.$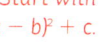

7 Repeat question **6** for the following parabolas.

a vertex $(-2, -27)$ and passing through $(1, 0)$

b vertex $(-2, -20)$ and passing through $(0, 0)$

c vertex $(2, 5)$ and passing through $(3, 0)$

d vertex $(1, 4)$ and passing through $(2, 0)$

B Exponential graphs

Exponential graphs have the variable x in the power of the equation, which makes them different from all other graphs in this chapter. The general form of an exponential graph is $y = a^x$ where a is a constant.

Exercise 9B

1 **a** Complete this table of values for $y = 2^x$.

x	-3	-2	-1	0	1	2	3	4
y								

    b Graph the values from the table.

    c Are there any negative values for y? Explain.

    d What happens to the value of y as x gets:

      i larger (consider $x = 5, 10, 20, \ldots$)?   **ii** smaller (consider $x = -5, -10, -20, \ldots$)?

    e An asymptote is a straight line that a curve approaches (gets closer to) but does not cross. This curve has an asymptote. What is its equation?

2 **a** Using the x-values in question **1**, complete a similar table of values for $y = 3^x$.

    b Graph $y = 3^x$.

    c Compare $y = 3^x$ and $y = 2^x$. Discuss common features.

    d Use your answer to part **c** to predict the shape of the graph of $y = 5^x$.

3 **a** Complete this table of values for $y = 2^{-x}$.

x	-3	-2	-1	0	1	2	3	4
y								

    b Use the table of values to graph $y = 2^{-x}$.

    c Describe the features of the graph, comparing with $y = 2^x$.

    d What happens to the value of y as x gets:

      i larger (consider $x = 5, 10, 20, \ldots$)?   **ii** smaller (consider $x = -5, -10, -20, \ldots$)?

    e State the asymptote. How is it different from that for $y = 2^x$?

4 **a** Sketch $y = -2^x$, noting that it is the negative of $y = 2^x$; that is, the sign of each y-value is the opposite of that for $y = 2^x$.

    b Describe the features of the graph of $y = -2^x$.

5 **a** Sketch $y = -2^{-x}$.

    b Compare this graph with $y = 2^{-x}$, noting similarities and differences.

6 Without completing a table of values, sketch each set of graphs on the same number plane.

    a $y = 3^x$ and $y = 5^x$ **b** $y = 3^x$ and $y = 3^{-x}$

    c $y = 3^x$ and $y = -3^x$ **d** $y = 5^x, y = 5^{-x}, y = -5^{-x}$ and $y = -5^x$

7 Sketch each set of graphs on the same number plane.

    a $y = 2^x, y = 2^x + 2, y = 2^x - 2$ **b** $y = -3^x, y = -3^x + 2, y = -3^x - 2$

    c $y = 2^{-x}, y = 2^{-x} + 3, y = 2^{-x} - 3$ **d** $y = -2^{-x}, y = -2^{-x} + 2, y = -2^{-x} - 3$

8 **a** What is the value of y when $x = 0$ for:

      i $y = a^x$?   **ii** $y = a^{-x}$?

    What common feature of the graphs of $y = a^x$ does this illustrate?

    b What is the value of y when $x = 0$ for:

      i $y = -a^x$?   **ii** $y = -a^{-x}$?

    What common feature of the graphs of $y = -a^x$ does this illustrate?

EXAMPLE 1

Find the *x*-coordinate of the point on the graph of $y = 6^x$ whose *y*-coordinate is 216.

Solve	Think	Apply
$6^x = 216$ Try $x = 1, 6^1 = 6$ $x = 2, 6^2 = 36$ $x = 3, 6^3 = 216$ If the *y*-coordinate $= 216$, the *x*-coordinate $= 3$.	Substitute $y = 216$ into the equation $y = 6^x$.	Substitute the value of the *y*-coordinate into the equation of the curve and solve the resulting equation by trial and error.

9 Find, by trial and error, the *x*-coordinate of the given points on the following curves.

  a $y = 3^x$ whose *y*-coordinate $= 81$ **b** $y = 2^x$ whose *y*-coordinate $= 32$

  c $y = 5^x$ whose *y*-coordinate $= 125$ **d** $y = 10^x$ whose *y*-coordinate $= 1\ 000\ 000$

Investigation 2 Circles

1 The point (5, 12) lies on the circumference of a circle with centre $O(0, 0)$.

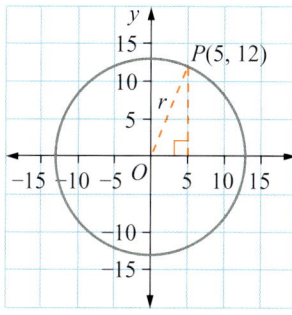

  a Using the right-angled triangle shown in the diagram, find the radius, r, of the circle.

  b Show that $Q(-5, 12)$ and $R(0, -13)$ also lie on the circumference of this circle; that is, show that $OQ = OR = OP$.

  c Write down the coordinates of three other points that lie on the circumference of this circle.

  d If $T(x, y)$ lies on the circumference, show that $x^2 + y^2 = 169$.

  e Verify that the equation of the circle centre $O(0, 0)$ and radius r units is $x^2 + y^2 = r^2$.

C Circles

Investigation 2 showed that the equation of the circle with centre the origin O and radius r units is $x^2 + y^2 = r^2$.

EXAMPLE 1

Find the radius of the circle with equation $x^2 + y^2 = 9$. Sketch the graph.

Solve/Think	Apply
$r^2 = 9$ $r = \sqrt{9}$ $= 3$ (radius > 0)	When the equation of a circle is in the form $x^2 + y^2 = r^2$, the radius is r.

1 Find the radius and draw a sketch of the following circles.

    a $x^2 + y^2 = 64$ **b** $x^2 + y^2 = 81$ **c** $x^2 + y^2 = = 36$

    d $x^2 + y^2 = 144$ **e** $x^2 + y^2 = 100$ **f** $x^2 + y^2 = 20$

    g $x^2 + y^2 = \frac{9}{4}$ **h** $9x^2 + 9y^2 = 1$ **i** $16x^2 + 16y^2 = 9$

2 Write the equation of the circle with centre $(0, 0)$ and radius:

    a 3 units   **b** 15 units   **c** 1.5 units   **d** $\sqrt{7}$ units

3 Write the equation of the following circles.

    a 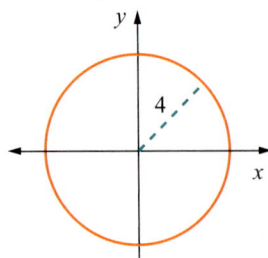   **b** 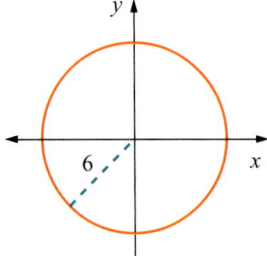   **c**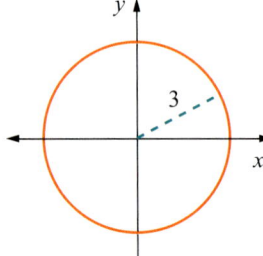

    d 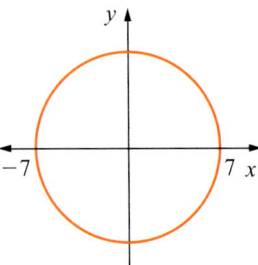   **e** 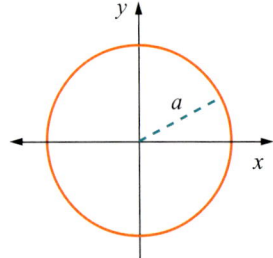   **f**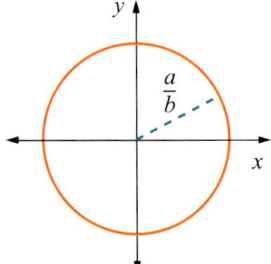

4 Show that the equation of a circle with centre $(0, 0)$ and radius $\sqrt{\frac{5}{2}}$ is $4x^2 + 4y^2 = 5$.

EXAMPLE 2

Find the equation of the circle with its centre at the origin and $(-5, 6)$ on its circumference.

Solve/Think	Apply
Let the equation of the circle be $x^2 + y^2 = r^2$. As the point $(-5, 6)$ lies on the circle $(-5)^2 + 6^2 = r^2$ $61 = r^2$ $r = \sqrt{61}$ Hence the equation of the circle is $x^2 + y^2 = 61$.	Let the equation of the circle be $x^2 + y^2 = r^2$. Substitute the coordinates of the given point into this equation to find r^2.

5 Find the equation of the circles, centre the origin, with the following points on their circumference.

    a $(2, 5)$ **b** $(-6, -3)$ **c** $(7, -5)$ **d** $(0, 8)$ **e** $(-1, -1)$

6 Which of the following equations represent circles with centre the origin?

    A $x^2 + y^2 = 1$ **B** $x^2 = 3 - y^2$ **C** $x^2 - y^2 = 25$ **D** $\dfrac{x^2 + y^2}{3} = 3$

    E $\dfrac{x^2}{2} + \dfrac{y^2}{3} = 1$ **F** $\dfrac{x^2}{5} - \dfrac{y^2}{2} = 1$ **G** $\dfrac{x^2}{5} + \dfrac{y^2}{5} = 1$ **H** $(x - 3)^2 + y^2 = 25$

    I $x = \pm\sqrt{9 - y^2}$ **J** $y = \pm\sqrt{1 - x^2}$ **K** $y = \sqrt{16 - x^2}$ **L** $y = -\sqrt{4 - x^2}$

D Miscellaneous graphs

This section explores the connection between algebraic and graphical representations of straight lines, parabolas, exponential curves and circles. A summary of each type follows.

Straight lines

These are the graphs of equations of the form $y = mx + b$.
They are straight lines with gradient m and y-intercept of b.

$y = 2x + 1$ has gradient $= 2$ and y-intercept $= 1$.

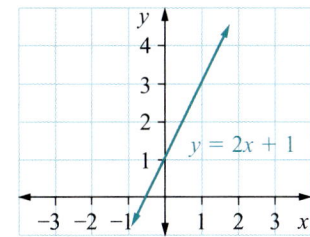

Parabolas

These are graphs of equations of the form $y = ax^2 + bx + c$ where c is the y-intercept.

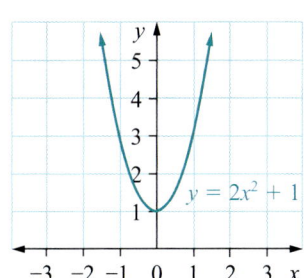

Exponential curves

These are graphs of equations of the form $y = a^x$ where a is a constant.
They all pass through the point $(0, 1)$.

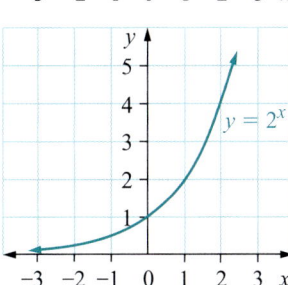

Circles

These are graphs of equations of the form $x^2 + y^2 = r^2$.
The centre of the circle is $(0, 0)$ and the radius is r.

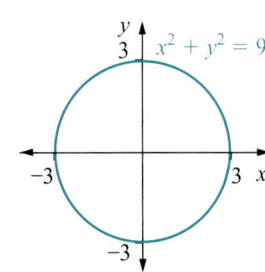

Exercise 9D

1 Test the point on each graph to decide which of these parabolas have equation $y = 2x^2$.

A
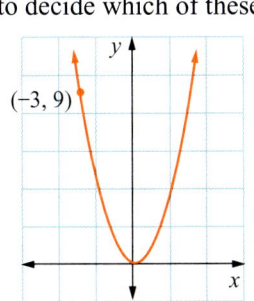
$(2, 8)$

B
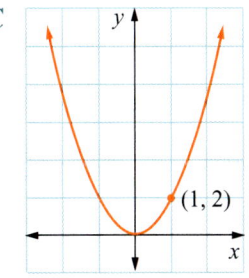
$(-3, 9)$

C
$(1, 2)$

D
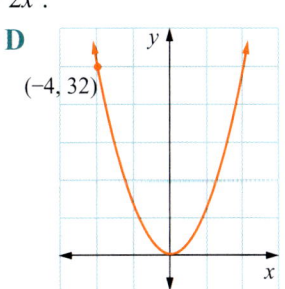
$(-4, 32)$

NUMBER & ALGEBRA

2 Test a point on each graph to decide which of these straight lines have equation $y = 3 - x$.

A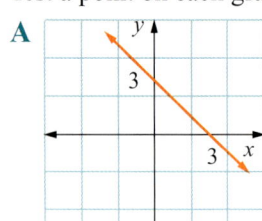

B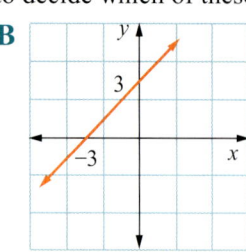

C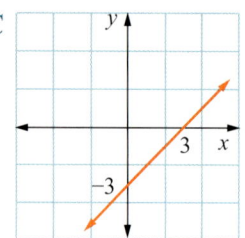

D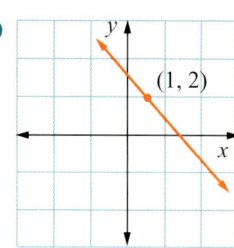

3 Test a point on each graph to decide which of these circles has equation $x^2 + y^2 = 16$.

A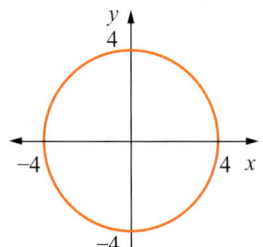

B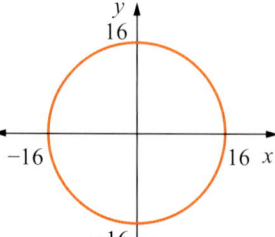

4 Test a point on each graph to decide which of these exponential graphs is $y = 3^x$.

A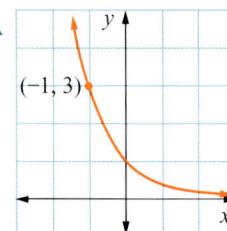

B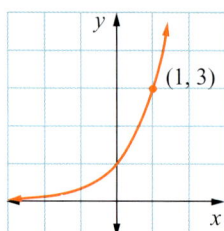

C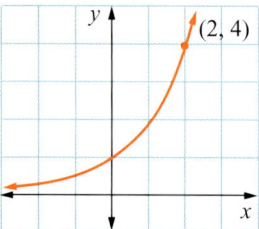

5 Determine which of the following could be the graph of:

a $y = 2^x$

A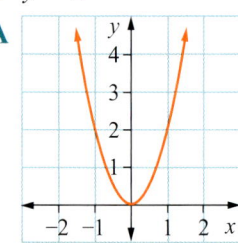

B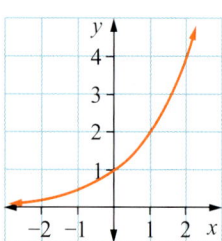

C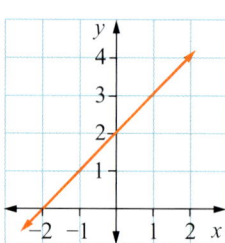

D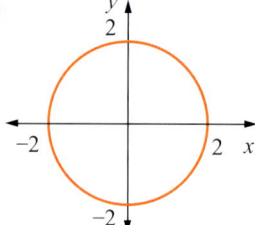

b $y = 2x^2 - 1$

A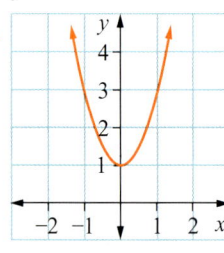

B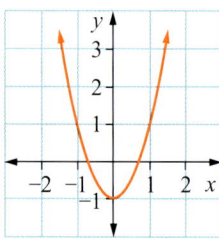

C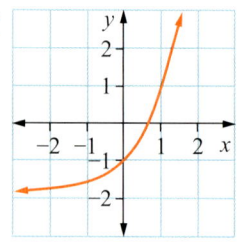

D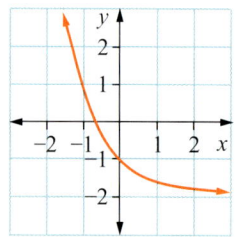

c $x^2 + y^2 = 2$

A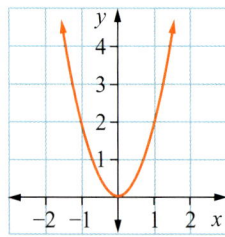

B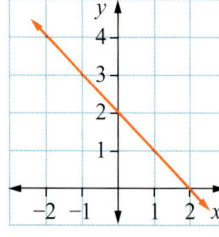

C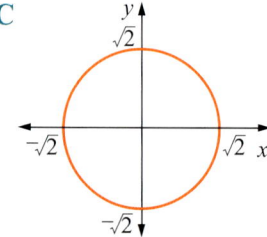

D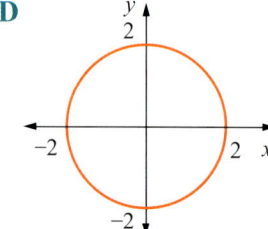

6 Match the following equations with the graphs below.

a $y = 2 - x$ **b** $y = 2x$ **c** $y = x^2$ **d** $y = 2^x$

A 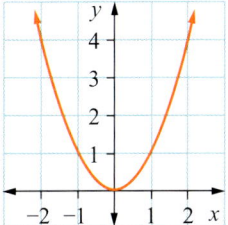   B   C 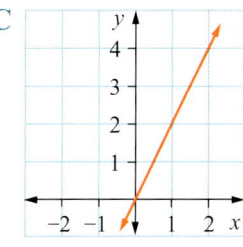   D

7 Match the following equations with the graphs below.

a $y = 2x^2$ **b** $y = 6$ **c** $x^2 + y^2 = 4$

d $y = x + 1$ **e** $y = x$ **f** $y = 2^{-x}$

A 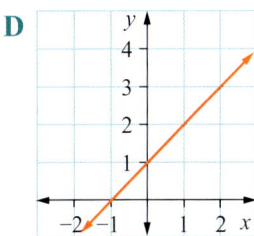   B 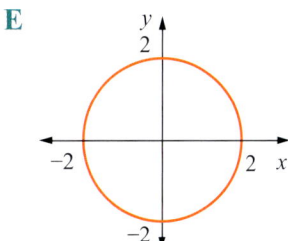   C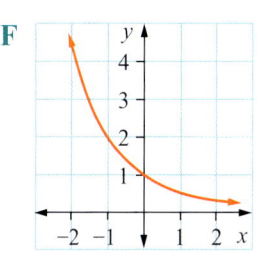

D 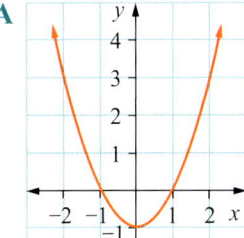   E 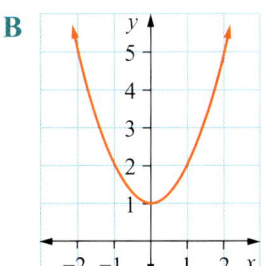   F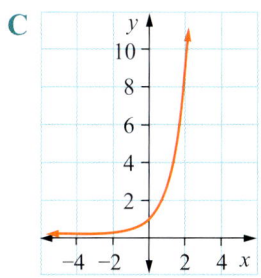

8 Match the following equations with the graphs below.

a $y = 3^x$ **b** $x^2 + y^2 = 25$ **c** $y = x^2 + 1$

d $y = x + 2$ **e** $y = x^2 - 1$ **f** $y = 1 - x^2$

A   B   C

D 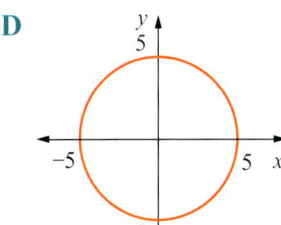   E 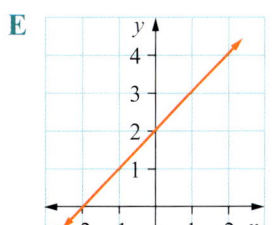   F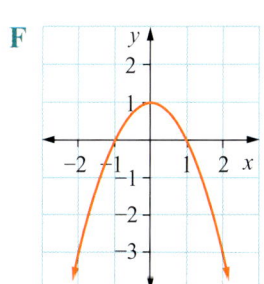

Language in mathematics

Benoit Mandelbrot (1924–2010)

Benoit Mandelbrot was largely responsible for the present interest in fractal geometry. He showed how fractals can occur in many different places in both mathematics and nature.

Mandelbrot was born in Poland in 1924 into a family with a very academic tradition. As a young boy, he was introduced to mathematics by his two uncles. The family emigrated to France in 1936. Mandelbrot attended school in Paris until the start of World War II, when his family moved to the country. The war, the constant threat of poverty and the need to survive often kept him away from school. Mandelbrot now attributes much of his success to this unconventional education.

After completing his studies in France, Mandelbrot went to the United States where he studied further and later worked for IBM and Harvard University. With the aid of computer graphics, he was able to discover some of the most beautiful fractals known today. To do this he had to develop not only new mathematical ideas, but also some of the first computer programs to print graphics.

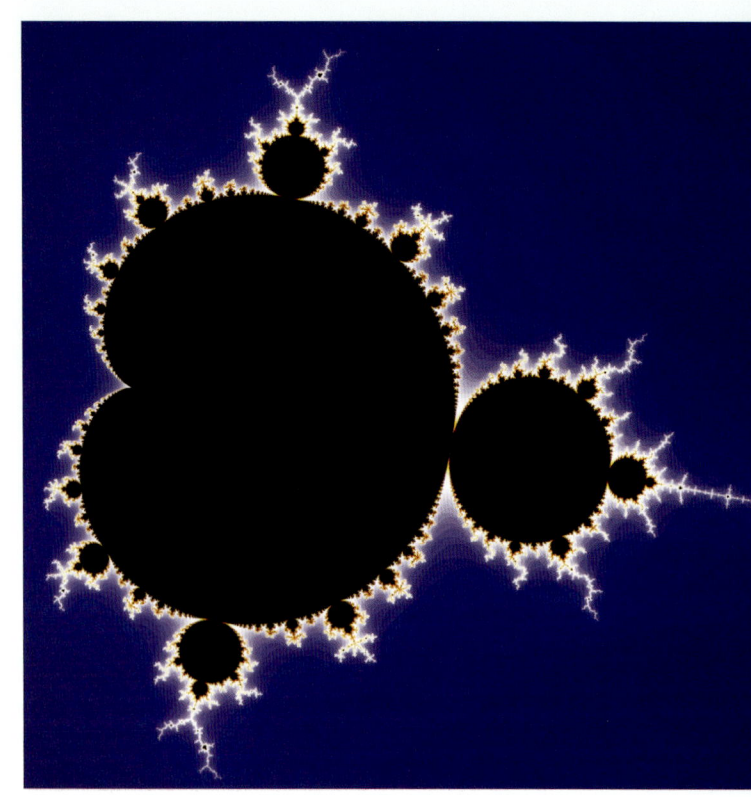

The Mandelbrot set is a connected set of points that are generated through an iteration on quadratic polynomials of the form $y = x^2 + c$. (Iteration means to repeat a process over and over again.) This gives a sequence, or list, of values. This sequence of values must remain within a certain distance of the origin forever to be in the Mandelbrot set, otherwise the pattern does not continue.

The same pattern is repeated over and over, with the size decreasing after each iteration. In this picture the Mandelbrot set is shown in black and as you zoom in on the picture the shapes and patterns are repeated indefinitely.

Fractals occur in physics in the description of the behaviour of turbulence, as the foundations of what is now known as chaotic systems, in economics in the behaviour of the stock exchange, and in the growth of mammalian cells. In the garden, the difference between the flower heads of broccoli and cauliflower can be exactly characterised in fractal theory.

Mandelbrot received numerous honours and prizes in recognition of his remarkable achievements.

1 Answer these questions based on the notes on Benoit Mandelbrot.
   a How old was Mandelbrot when the family moved to France?
   b To what does he attribute his success?
   c What is it about a sequence that make it a Mandelbrot set?
   d In your own words, define an iteration and give an example.
   e Investigate some fractals other than the Mandelbrot set.

2 Rearrange these words to form a sentence.
   a is a graph A with parabola x^2
   b moves constant up or term a graph down parabola The the of

NUMBER & ALGEBRA

3 Use every third letter to complete a sentence.

S D T H T H W U E R B G M O R A D A N O P P Q H R G S T H O U O F S C E T R X F
U P O W O A C N V U E P O N Q E T D U I T E A F Y L K G S A S A D R N T T D U X
P G S A I O R E R A A S B F G O J K L O I A Y T S R E A W Q R Q A E Z S B C D O
R F T T H H J U C I K U O L R P O V I S E A Z S S X W D C I C F T G B H H N T J
M H K L E L P E O K X I J P U H O Y G N T F E R D N E S T W Q I W E A T U L O P
A L G S D E A T U N F S U A G M H B B D E E Y U R R G T S E O F T T G U H K O E
D T P H D O J H W S D E G S R H T O H S F K U X T C A D T N I U D Y G T R D H W
A E C F P B H A I Y R S A A C A B G F O J Y L K G A N G A U E S A G X G A T H R
O A R T U J H Y H E T G P F H O H F W J F E J R R I R O A A F V F T H M W K P O

Terms

asymptote	circle	circumference	coefficient	constant term	equation
exponential	graph	linear	number plane	parabola	parabolic
radius	quadratic relationship		square	straight line	symmetrical
variable	vertex				

Check your skills

1 The graphs drawn have equations:

   A $y = x^2$ and $y = x^2 + 2$

   B $y = x^2$ and $y = -x^2$

   C $y = x^2$ and $y = 3x^2$

   D $y = -x^2$ and $y = -x^2 + 2$

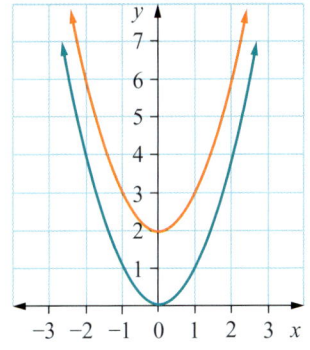

2 The graph with the same shape as $y = x^2$ and vertex (0, 5) has equation:

   A $y = x^2 + 5$ **B** $y = -x^2 + 5$ **C** $y = -x^2 - 5$ **D** $y = x^2 - 5$

3 The graph of $y = 3x^2 - 2$ could be:

   A 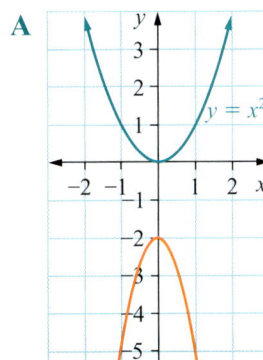   **B** 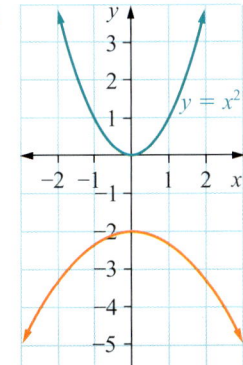   **C** 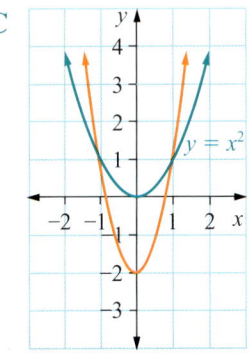   **D**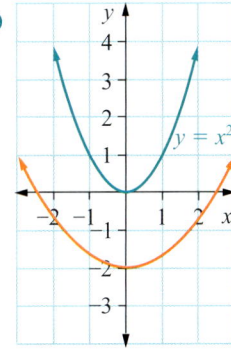

4 The x-coordinates of the points on $y = 2x^2 - 5$ with y-coordinate $y = 7$ are:

   A $\pm\sqrt{12}$ **B** $\pm\sqrt{6}$ **C** $\pm\sqrt{5}$ **D** $\pm\sqrt{2}$

5 The y-intercept of the parabola $y = x^2 - 3x + 7$ is:

   A -7 **B** 7   **C** -3 **D** 1

6 The graph of $y = -3^x$ is:

A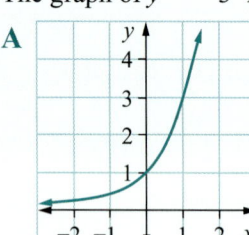
B
C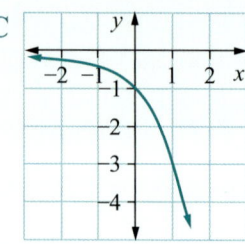
D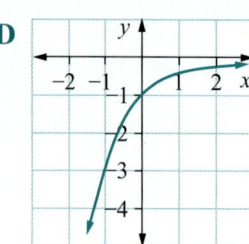

7 The equation of the exponential curve shown is:

A $y = 2^x$ B $y = 2^{-x}$

C $y = 5^x$ D $y = 5^{-x}$

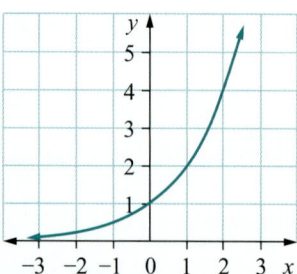

8 Which of the following could be the graph of $y = 4^x$?

A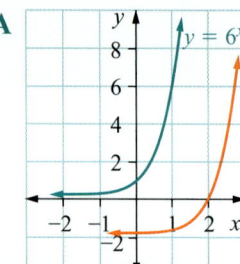
B
C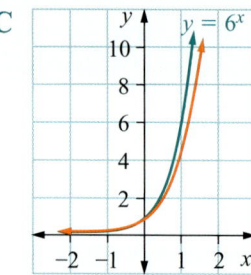
D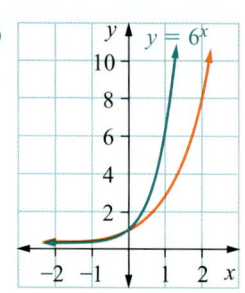

9 The x-coordinate of the point on the graph of $y = 3^x$ with y-coordinate $= 243$ is:

A 2   B 3   C 4   D 5

10 The radius of the circle $x^2 + y^2 = 16$ is:

A 16   B 8   C 4   D 2

11 The equation of the circle shown is::

A $x^2 + y^2 = 9$ B $x^2 + y^2 = 16$

C $x^2 + y^2 = 25$ D $x^2 + y^2 = 49$

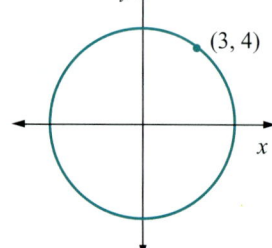

If you have any difficulty with these questions, refer to the examples and questions in the sections listed in the table.

Question	1–5	6–9	10–11
Section	A	B	C

9A   Review set

1 On the same number plane, sketch graphs of:

a $y = x^2$ b $y = 3x^2$ c $y = \frac{1}{2}x^2$ d $y = x^2 + 3$

2 Find the x-coordinate(s) of the point(s) on the following parabolas.

a $y = 3x^2 - 1$ with y-coordinate $= 5$ b $y = 2x^2 + 3$ with y-coordinate $= 21$

3 On the same number plane, sketch graphs of:

  a $y = 3^x$ **b** $y = 3^{-x}$ **c** $y = -3^x$

  d $y = -3^{-x}$ **e** $y = 3^x + 1$

4 Find the x-coordinate of the point on the graph of $y = 2^x$ that has y-coordinate $= 16$.

5 Write the equation of the circle with centre at the origin and a radius of:

  a 5 units   **b** $\sqrt{5}$ units

6 Find the equation of the circle with centre the origin and passing through the point $(5, 7)$.

7 Match each of the following equations with the graphs below.

  a $y = 3 - x$ **b** $y = -2x^2$ **c** $y = 4x^2 - 1$

  d $y = 5^{-x}$ **e** $y = 3^x + 1$ **f** $x^2 + y^2 = 1$

A 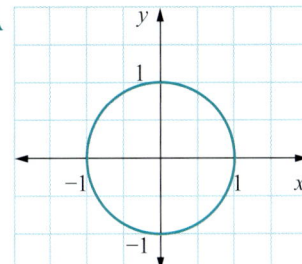   **B** 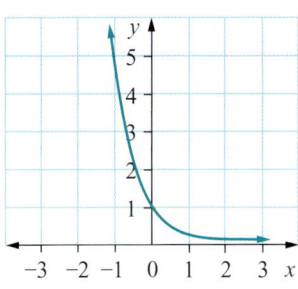   **C**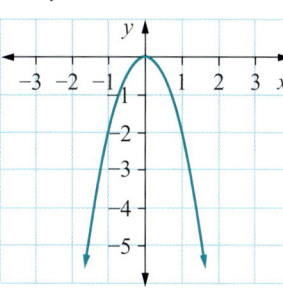

D 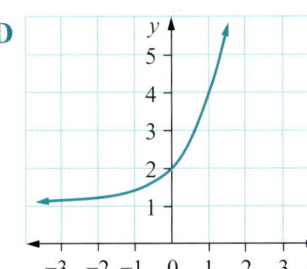   **E** 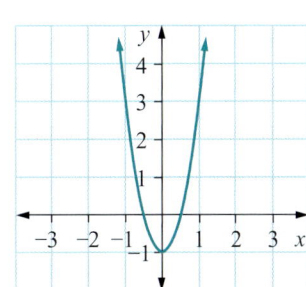   **F**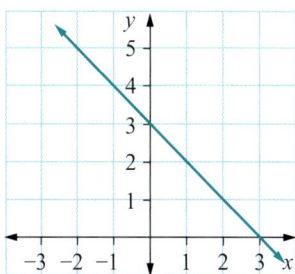

9B   Review set

1 On the same number plane sketch graphs of:

  a $y = -x^2$ **b** $y = -2x^2$

  c $y = -\frac{1}{2}x^2$ **d** $y = -x^2 - 3$

2 Find the x-coordinate(s) of the point(s) on the following parabolas.

  a $y = 4x^2 + 1$ with y-coordinate $= 37$

  b $y = 2x^2 - 3$ with y-coordinate $= 17$

3 On the same number plane, sketch graphs of:

  a $y = 2^x$ **b** $y = 2^{-x}$ **c** $y = -2^x$

  d $y = -2^{-x}$ **e** $y = 2^x - 1$

4 Find the x-coordinate of the point on the graph of $y = 3^x$ which has y-coordinate $= 81$.

5 Write the equation of the circle with centre at the origin and a radius of:

  a 4 units   **b** $\sqrt{3}$ units

6 Find the equation of the circle with centre the origin and passing through the point $(5, 12)$.

7 Match each of the following equations with the graphs below.

a $y = 2x - 4$ **b** $y = -3x^2$ **c** $y = 2x^2 + 5$

d $y = -5^{-x}$ **e** $y = 5^x - 1$ **f** $x^2 + y^2 = 7$

A
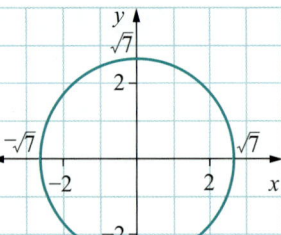

B
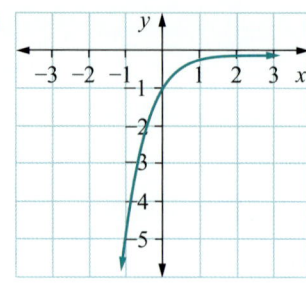

C
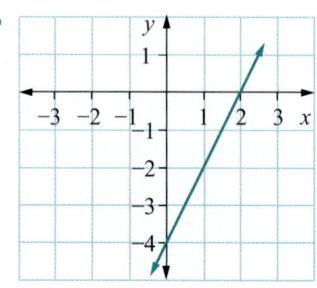

D
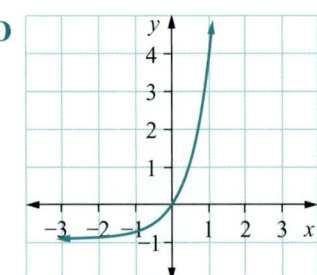

E
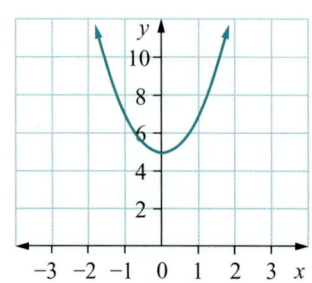

F
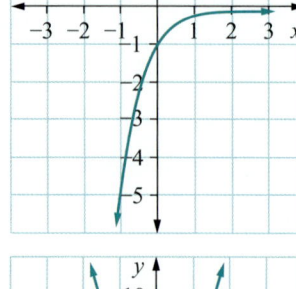

9C   Review set

1 On the same number plane sketch graphs of:

a $y = x^2$ **b** $y = -3x^2$ **c** $y = -\frac{2}{3}x^2$ **d** $y = 2x^2 + 2$

2 Find the x-coordinate(s) of the point(s) on the following parabolas.

a $y = x^2 + 11$ with y-coordinate $= 47$

b $y = 5x^2 + 17$ with y-coordinate $= 42$

3 On the same number plane, sketch graphs of:

a $y = 4^x$ **b** $y = 4^{-x}$ **c** $y = -4^x$

d $y = -4^x + 3$ **e** $y = -4^x - 2$

4 Find the x-coordinate of the point on the graph of $y = 10^x$ that has y-coordinate $= 100\ 000$.

5 Write the equation of the circle with centre at the origin and a radius of:

a 10 units **b** $\sqrt{10}$ units

6 Find the equation of the circle with centre the origin and passing through the point (16, 30).

7 Match each of the following equations with the graphs shown.

a $x + y + 1 = 0$ **b** $y = -\frac{1}{3}x^2$ **c** $y = -x^2 + 4$

d $y = -4^{-x}$ **e** $y = 4^x + 3$ **f** $x^2 + y^2 = 81$

A
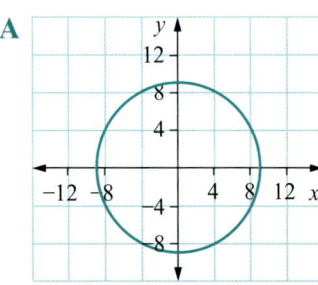

B
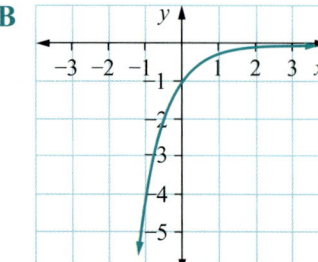

C
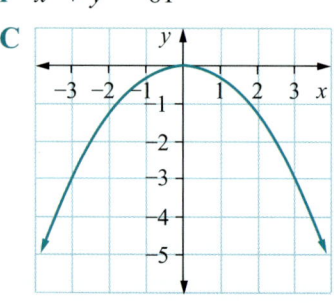

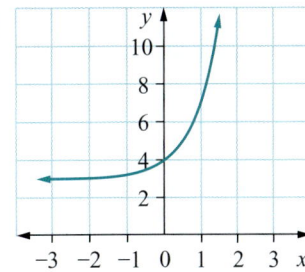
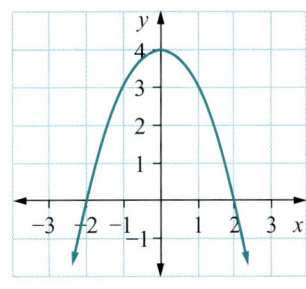
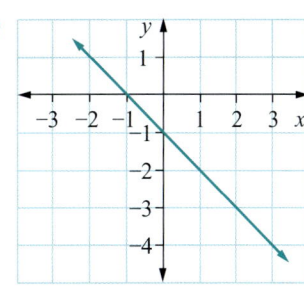

9D   Review set

1 On the same number plane sketch graphs of:

  a $y = -x^2$ **b** $y = -3x^2$

  c $y = -\frac{3}{2}x^2$ **d** $y = -x^2 + 2$

2 Find the x-coordinate(s) of the point(s) on the following parabolas.

  a $y = 2x^2 - 13$ with y-coordinate $= 19$

  b $y = 3x^2 + 9$ with y-coordinate $= 21$

3 On the same number plane, sketch graphs of:

  a $y = 3^x + 2$ **b** $y = 3^x - 2$ **c** $y = -3^x + 2$

  d $y = -3^{-x} + 2$ **e** $y = -3^x - 2$

4 Find the x-coordinate of the point on the graph of $y = 2^x$ which has y-coordinate $= 128$.

5 Write the equation of the circle with centre at the origin and a radius of:

  a 7 units   **b** $\sqrt{\frac{3}{2}}$ units

6 Find the equation of the circle with centre the origin and passing through the point $(-4, 8)$.

7 Match each of the following equations with the graphs below.

  a $x + 2y - 4 = 0$ **b** $y = 2x^2 + 3$ **c** $y = -2x^2 - 3$

  d $y = -2^{-x} + 1$ **e** $y = -2^x - 1$ **f** $x^2 + y^2 = 144$

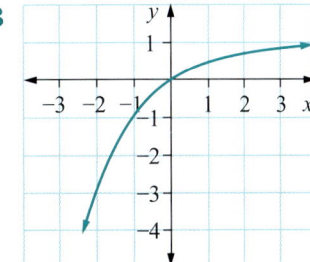
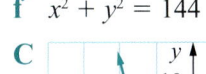
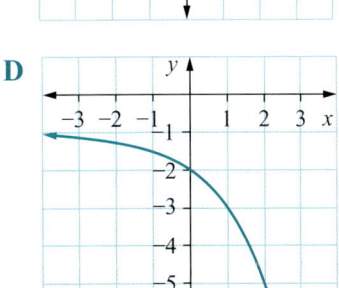
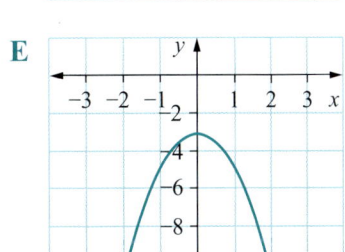
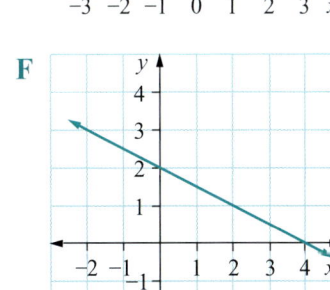

1 a $3600 is invested for 3 years at 3.9% p.a. interest, compounding yearly.

    i Calculate the value of the investment after 3 years.

    ii What is the total amount of interest earned?

b **i** Calculate the amount to which $20 000 grows in 3 years at 6% p.a. interest, compounded yearly.

    ii What is the total amount of interest earned?

Year	Principal	Balance at end of year
1st	$20 000	$20 000 × 1.06 = $21 200
2nd	$21 200	$21 200 × 1.06 = $____
3rd	$____	$____

c Calculate the amount to which $15 000 will grow in 5 years if invested at 4.5% p.a. at:

    i simple interest   **ii** compound interest.

    iii Which method of calculating interest produces the greater amount, and by how much?

d Calculate the amount to which $15 000 will grow in 5 years if it is invested at 8% p.a. and interest is compounded:

    i monthly   **ii** quarterly   **iii** six-monthly.

e Calculate the compound interest charged on a credit card cash advance of $500 for 17 days if the annual interest rate is 28% and the interest is charged daily.

f **i** Calculate the value after 4 years of a new car that costs $38 000 and depreciates by 19% of its value at the start of each year.

    ii What is the amount of depreciation over the 4 years?

g The purchase price of a new car is $25 700. It depreciates by 18% of its value each year. Use the guess and refine method to find how long it will take for the car to depreciate in value to $12 000.

2 a Expand and simplify $2y(y + 2) - 3y(4 - 3y)$.

b Expand and simplify these expressions if possible.

    i $(x + 2)(x - 5)$ **ii** $(3x - 4)(2x - 7)$ **iii** $(x + 1)^2$

    iv $(3r - 4p)^2$ **v** $(x - 2)(x + 2)$ **vi** $(3x - 1)(3x + 1)$

c Complete $x^2 - 4x + \square = (x - \triangle)^2$.

d Factorise:

    i $3x - 9$ **ii** $4x^2 + 12xy$ **iii** $2x - 6 + 3xy - 9y$

    iv $x^2 - 36$ **v** $16x^2 - 25$ **vi** $x^2 - 7x + 10$

    vii $x^2 + x - 20$ **viii** $6x^2 - 13x - 5$ **ix** $4x^2 - 11x + 6$

e Simplify:

    i $\dfrac{x^2 + 2x - 35}{x^2 - 25} \times \dfrac{2x + 10}{x^2 + 7x}$ **ii** $\dfrac{2}{x^2 - 3x} - \dfrac{5}{x^2 - 9}$

3 For the scores 12, 17, 11, 12, 15, 16, 16, 16, 17, find the:

    a mean (to 2 decimal places)   **b** mode   **c** median

    d range   **e** upper quartile   **f** lower quartile

    g interquartile range.

4 a 8, 3, 12, 7 and x have a mean of 9. Find x.

b The mean of eight scores is 27. What is the sum of scores?

c The mean of eight scores is 27. If a score of 18 is added, find the new mean.

5 Here are scores in a frequency distribution table.

a Find the:

   i mean   **ii** mode

   iii median   **iv** range

   v upper quartile   **vi** lower quartile

   vii interquartile range.

b Draw a box plot for the data.

c Draw a histogram for the data.

Score	Frequency
4	8
5	3
6	0
7	2
8	9
9	12
10	6

6 Here are scores in a frequency distribution table.

a Draw a box plot for the data.

b Is the distribution symmetrical? Explain your answer.

Score	Frequency
9	1
10	4
11	11
12	6
13	12
14	1

7 a For this stem-and-leaf plot, find the:

   i mean (to 1 decimal place)   **ii** median

   iii mode   **iv** range.

b Is this distribution normal or skewed? Explain.

c Draw a box plot for this information.

Stem	Class B
11	0 8 9
12	1 2 2 2 2 3 4 5 6
13	2 3 4 4 4 5 5 5 6 7 8 9
14	0 1 2 2 5 8 8 9
15	3 5 7 7
16	1 9

8 Two box plots are shown.

a Describe any similarities in the data.

b Compare the range of set A and set B.

c For which set of scores is the middle 50% clustered more closely to the median?

d In which data set is the top 50% of scores more closely clustered to the median?

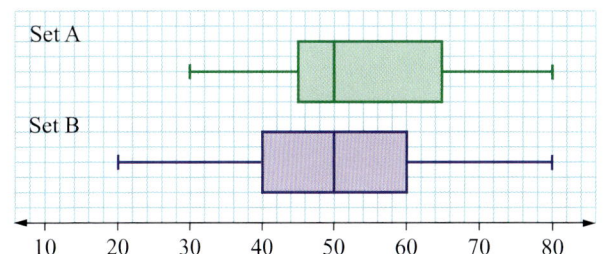

9 Consider this table of values.

x	0	1	2	3	4	5	6
y	-2	-1	2	7	14	23	34

a Plot the points and sketch the graph.

b What kind of graph is this?

10 Match the following equations with their graphs.

a $y = x^2$ **b** $y = 3x + 1$ **c** $y = 5$

d $y = x^2 - 2$ **e** $x^2 + y^2 = 9$ **f** $y = 5^x$

A
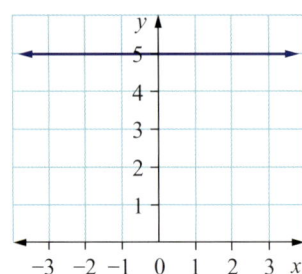

B
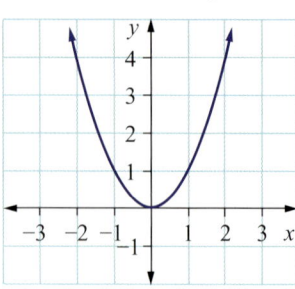

C
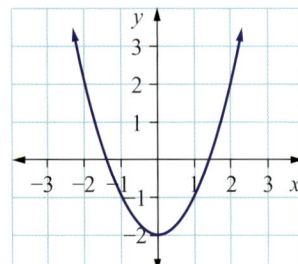

D
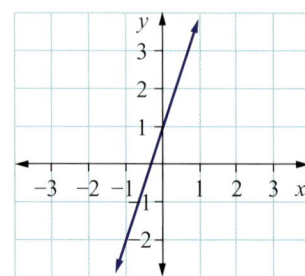

E
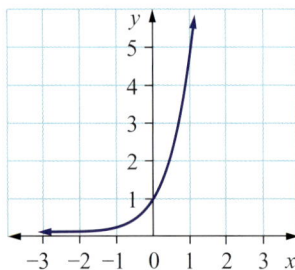

F
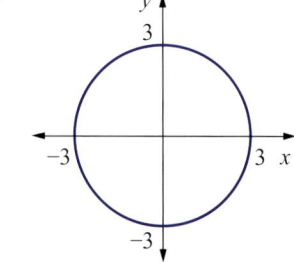

11 a Consider the parabola $y = x^2 + 5x + 4$.
   i Find the y-intercept.
   ii Find the x-intercepts.
   iii Sketch the graph.
   iv Write the coordinates of the vertex.

   b **i** Find the length of the radius and sketch the circle $x^2 + y^2 = 81$.
   ii What is the equation of a circle with centre the origin and radius $\frac{3}{4}$?

   c On the same number plane sketch the graphs of $y = 3^x$ and $y = 5^x$.

12 a On the same number plane sketch the graphs of $y = 2^x$, $y = 2^x + 1$ and $y = 2^x - 1$.

   b Find the x-coordinate of the point(s) on the parabola $y = 3x^2 - 13$ with a y-coordinate of 5.

   c Find the x-coordinate of the point on the graph $y = 3^x$ with a y-coordinate of 81.

   d **i** Find the equation of the circle with its centre the origin and passing through the point $(2, 5)$.
   ii Sketch the circle.

10

Equations

This chapter deals with linear, quadratic, simultaneous and literal equations, inequalities and non-linear simultaneous equations.

After completing this chapter you should be able to:

▶ solve linear equations
▶ expand and factorise 'special products' that result in quadratics
▶ solve quadratic equations by factorising, completing the square and applying the quadratic formula
▶ solve problems involving quadratic equations

▶ solve non-linear simultaneous equations
▶ solve simple cubic equations
▶ solve and rearrange literal equations
▶ solve equations reducible to quadratics.

NSW Syllabus references: 5.3 N&A Equations
Outcomes: MA5.3-1WM, MA5.3-2WM, MA5.3-3WM, MA5.3-7NA
Number & algebra – ACMNA233, ACMNA269

Diagnostic test

1. $15a - a =$
   - A 15
   - B 14
   - C $15a$
   - D $14a$

2. $3a - 2b + 4a =$
   - A $-a - 2b$
   - B $-a + 2b$
   - C $7a - 2b$
   - D $5a^2b$

3. $5 - (2x - 3) =$
   - A $8 - 2x$
   - B $2 - 2x$
   - C $-2x - 2$
   - D $5 + x$

4. $y(y - 7) - 2y(4 - y) =$
   - A $-y^2 - 15y$
   - B $y^2 - 15y$
   - C $3y^2 - 15y$
   - D $3y^2 - y$

5. $\dfrac{t}{3} - \dfrac{t}{5} =$
   - A 0
   - B -2
   - C $\dfrac{2t}{15}$
   - D $2t$

6. $\dfrac{a}{3} + a =$
   - A $\dfrac{2a}{3}$
   - B $\dfrac{4a}{3}$
   - C $\dfrac{a^2}{3}$
   - D $\dfrac{2a^2}{3}$

7. $3y - 4x - \dfrac{2y}{3} + \dfrac{3x}{4} =$
   - A $\dfrac{-5y + 5x}{12}$
   - B $\dfrac{28y - 39x}{12}$
   - C $\dfrac{7y - 13x}{12}$
   - D $\dfrac{y - x}{12}$

8. $(x - 3)(x + 5) =$
   - A $x^2 - 15$
   - B $x^2 + 2x - 15$
   - C $2x + 2$
   - D $x^2 - 2x - 15$

9. $(3x - 5)(2x + 3) =$
   - A $6x^2 - x - 15$
   - B $6x^2 + 5x - 15$
   - C $6x^2 - x - 2$
   - D $6x^2 + 5x - 2$

10. $7x - (3x - 1)(x + 2) =$
    - A $3x^2 + 12x - 2$
    - B $-3x^2 + 12x - 2$
    - C $-3x^2 + 3x + 2$
    - D $-3x^2 + 2x + 2$

11. $(x - 3)^2 =$
    - A $x^2 - 9$
    - B $x^2 + 9$
    - C $x^2 - 6x + 9$
    - D $x^2 + 6x - 9$

12. $(5 - 3x)^2 =$
    - A $25 - 3x^2$
    - B $25 - 9x^2$
    - C $25 - 15x + 9x^2$
    - D $25 - 30x + 9x^2$

13. $(5x - 1)(5x + 1) =$
    - A $25x^2 - 1$
    - B $25x^2 + 1$
    - C $25x^2 - 10x + 1$
    - D $25x^2 + 10x - 1$

14. If $(x - \square)^2 = x^2 - 8x + \triangle$ then:
    - A $\square = 8; \triangle = 64$
    - B $\square = 4; \triangle = 16$
    - C $\square = 2; \triangle = 4$
    - D $\square = \sqrt{8}; \triangle = 8$

15. When factorised, $pq - 5p^2 =$
    - A $-4p^2$
    - B $p(q - 5p)$
    - C $pq(1 - 5p)$
    - D Cannot be factorised.

16. When factorised, $4x + 4t - x^2 - xt =$
    - A $(4 - x)(x + t)$
    - B $(4 - x)(4 - t)$
    - C $x(4 - x - t) + 4t$
    - D $3x - 3t$

17. When factorised, $m^2 - 4n^2 =$
    - A $(m - 4n)(m + 4n)$
    - B $(m - 4n)^2$
    - C $(m - 2n)^2$
    - D $(m + 2n)(m - 2n)$

18. When factorised, $81x^2 - 16y^2 =$
    - A $(9x - 2y)(9x + 2y)$
    - B $(9x - 4y)(9x + 4y)$
    - C $(3x - 2y)(3x + 2y)$
    - D $(9x - 4y)^2$

19. When factorised, $x^2 - 18x + 81 =$
    - A $(x + 9)(x - 9)$
    - B $(x + 9)^2$
    - C $(x - 18)^2$
    - D $(x - 9)^2$

20. When factorised, $16x^2 - 40x + 25 =$
    - A $(16x - 25)^2$
    - B $(16x + 25)^2$
    - C $(4x - 5)^2$
    - D $(4x + 5)^2$

21 When factorised, $x^2 - 7x + 10 =$
 A $(x - 5)(x - 2)$
 B $(x + 5)(x + 2)$
 C $(x - 10)(x - 1)$
 D $(x + 10)(x + 1)$

22 When factorised, $3x^2 + x - 10 =$
 A $(3x + 1)(x - 10)$
 B $(3x + 5)(x + 2)$
 C $(3x - 1)(x + 10)$
 D $(3x - 5)(x + 2)$

23 When factorised, $12x^2 + 5x - 2 =$
 A $(4x - 1)(3x + 2)$
 B $(12x + 1)(x - 2)$
 C $(4x + 1)(3x - 2)$
 D $(12x - 1)(x + 2)$

24 When factorised, $x^3 + x^2 - 12x =$
 A $x(x^2 + x - 12)$
 B $x(x - 3)(x + 4)$
 C $x(x + 12)(x + 1)$
 D $x^2(x + 1) - 12x$

25 When simplified, $\dfrac{x^2 + 5x - 14}{2x + 14} =$
 A $x^2 + 3x$ B $x(x + 3)$
 C $x - 1$ D $\dfrac{x - 2}{2}$

26 When simplified, $\dfrac{3}{x^2 + 2x} - \dfrac{5}{x^2 - 4} =$
 A $\dfrac{-2(x + 3)}{x(x + 2)(x - 2)}$ B $\dfrac{-2x^2 - 10x - 12}{(x^2 + 2x)(x^2 - 4)}$
 C $\dfrac{-2}{2x - 4}$ D $\dfrac{-2}{2x^2 + 2x - 4}$

The diagnostic test questions refer to outcome ACMNA193 and ACMNA233.

A Linear equations

When we solve equations with pronumerals on both sides, it may be necessary not only to add and subtract numbers from both sides, but also to add and subtract pronumerals from both sides. The first step is to add or subtract the pronumerals to move them to one side. It doesn't matter which side. Next add or subtract to move the numbers to the other side of the equation.

EXAMPLE 1

Solve these equations.
a $5x + 2 = 3x - 5$
b $5(x + 1) - 2(x - 2) = 7$

	Solve	Think	Apply
a	$5x + 2 = 3x - 5$ $2x + 2 = -5$ $2x = -7$ $x = -\dfrac{7}{2}$ $= -3\dfrac{1}{2}$	Subtract $3x$ from both sides. Subtract 2 from both sides. Divide both sides by 2.	Add or subtract the same pronumeral or number on both sides of the equation and simplify until the pronumeral equals a number.
b	$5(x + 1) - 2(x - 2) = 7$ $5x + 5 - 2x + 4 = 7$ $3x + 9 = 7$ $3x = 2$ $x = -\dfrac{2}{3}$	Expand brackets. Collect 'like' terms. Subtract 9 from both sides. Divide both sides by 3.	

1 Solve the following.

   a $x - 3 = 5x + 8$ **b** $3 + x = 17 + 5x$

   c $11 - 3x = 2 - x$ **d** $5a + 3 = a - 2$

   e $4 - 3s = 2s + 19$ **f** $7x - 4 = 3 + 4x$

2 Solve the following for x.

   a $3(x + 2) - 7 = 8$ **b** $2(x + 1) + 3(x - 1) = 7$

   c $4(2x - 1) + 3 = 0$ **d** $11 - 2(x - 1) = 5$

   e $5x - 4(4 - x) = x + 3$ **f** $4 - x = 5 - 2(x + 1)$

   g $2(x - 1) = 2 - (3 - x)$ **h** $x + 7(4 - x) = 5x + 3(x - 1)$

EXAMPLE 2

Solve the following for x.

a $\dfrac{3x + 1}{2} = x - 1$ **b** $\dfrac{3x - 1}{5} = \dfrac{2x}{7}$

	Solve	Think	Apply
a	$\dfrac{3x + 1}{2} = x - 1$ $3x + 1 = 2(x - 1)$ $3x + 1 = 2x - 2$ $3x - 2x + 1 = -2$ $x + 1 = -2$ $x = -3$	Multiply both sides by 2. Expand. Subtract $2x$ from both sides. Subtract 1 from both sides.	When multiplying both sides of an equation by the same expression we sometimes need to use brackets.
b	$\dfrac{3x - 1}{5} = \dfrac{2x}{7}$ $35\left(\dfrac{3x - 1}{5}\right) = 35\left(\dfrac{2x}{7}\right)$ $7(3x - 1) = 5(2x)$ $21x - 7 = 10x$ $11x - 7 = 0$ $11x = 7$ $x = \dfrac{7}{11}$	Multiply both sides by 35. Cancel and expand. Subtract $10x$ from both sides. Add 7 to both sides. Divide both sides by 11.	

3 Solve the following for x.

   a $\dfrac{2x + 1}{3} = x - 1$ **b** $\dfrac{4x + 1}{2} = x - 2$ **c** $\dfrac{3x - 2}{4} = 5 - 2x$

   d $\dfrac{2x + 1}{3} = x - 4$ **e** $\dfrac{3x + 1}{4} = x - 2$ **f** $\dfrac{3x + 2}{5} = \dfrac{x - 1}{3}$

   g $\dfrac{1 - x}{2} = \dfrac{x + 2}{5}$ **h** $\dfrac{x + 1}{4} = \dfrac{x}{3}$ **i** $\dfrac{2x - 1}{6} = \dfrac{3x}{5}$

   j $\dfrac{x + 1}{2} = \dfrac{2x - 3}{5}$ **k** $\dfrac{2x + 5}{3} = x + 7$ **l** $\dfrac{2x + 7}{3} = x - 4$

EXAMPLE 3

Solve the following for x.

a $\dfrac{2x + 1}{3} - \dfrac{x - 2}{2} = 5$

b $\dfrac{x}{5} - 3 = \dfrac{3x + 4}{8}$

	Solve	Think	Apply
a	$\dfrac{2x + 1}{3} - \dfrac{x - 2}{2} = 5$ $6\left(\dfrac{2x + 1}{3}\right) - 6\left(\dfrac{x - 2}{2}\right) = 30$ $2(2x + 1) - 3(x - 2) = 30$ $4x + 2 - 3x + 6 = 30$ $x + 8 = 30$ $x = 22$	LCD is 6. Multiply both sides by 6.	When either the LHS or RHS of a fraction equation has more than one term, we solve it by multiplying both sides of the equation by the lowest common denominator (LCD).
b	$\dfrac{x}{5} - 3 = \dfrac{3x + 4}{8}$ $40\left(\dfrac{x}{5}\right) - 120 = 40\left(\dfrac{3x + 4}{8}\right)$ $8x - 120 = 5(3x + 4)$ $= 15x + 20$ $8x - 15x = 20 + 120$ $-7x = 140$ $x = -20$	LCD is 40. Multiply both sides by 40.	

4 Solve the following for x.

a $\dfrac{x}{2} + \dfrac{x}{5} = 3$

b $\dfrac{x}{2} - \dfrac{2x}{3} = \dfrac{5}{7}$

c $\dfrac{3x}{2} - \dfrac{x}{8} = 12$

d $\dfrac{x}{3} + \dfrac{x - 1}{4} = 0$

e $\dfrac{x}{4} + \dfrac{2x + 1}{6} = 0$

f $\dfrac{x + 2}{3} + \dfrac{3x - 1}{5} = 1\frac{1}{2}$

g $\dfrac{2x + 3}{5} - \dfrac{x + 4}{2} = -3$

h $\dfrac{x - 2}{3} - 2 = \dfrac{2x + 1}{16}$

i $\dfrac{2x + 5}{3} - \dfrac{3x - 4}{7} = 4$

j $\dfrac{4x - 3}{7} - \dfrac{x + 2}{3} = \dfrac{1}{4}$

k $\dfrac{2x - 3}{5} - \dfrac{x + 7}{3} = \dfrac{1}{4}$

l $\dfrac{2x - 7}{3} - \dfrac{5 - 4x}{2} = \dfrac{2}{5}$

m $\dfrac{6x - 5}{4} - \dfrac{7 - 8x}{3} = \dfrac{1}{2}$

n $\dfrac{7x + 3}{5} - \dfrac{8x + 1}{3} = \dfrac{2}{3}$

o $\dfrac{5x - 3}{2} - \dfrac{7x - 5}{5} = \dfrac{3}{10}$

B Quadratic equations review

This section revises special products, factorising and the solution of simple quadratic equations from Chapter 7.

Perfect square expansion

$(a + b)^2 = a^2 + 2ab + b^2$

$(a - b)^2 = a^2 - 2ab + b^2$

Difference of two squares expansion

$(a + b)(a - b) = a^2 - b^2$

EXAMPLE 1

Expand and simplify the following.

a $(x - 4)^2$　　　　　**b** $(x + 3)^2$　　　　　**c** $(3x - 4)^2$

	Solve	Think/Apply
a	$(x - 4)^2 = x^2 - 2 \times x \times 4 + 4^2$ $= x^2 - 8x + 16$	Use the perfect square expansion. Make sure that the middle term is calculated correctly. The last term is always positive.
b	$(x + 3)^2 = x^2 + 2 \times x \times 3 + 3^2$ $= x^2 + 6x + 9$	
c	$(3x - 4)^2 = (3x)^2 - 2 \times 3x \times 4 + 4^2$ $= 9x^2 - 24x + 16$	

Exercise 10B

1 Expand and simplify the following.

a $(x + 4)^2$　　　　　**b** $(x - 6)^2$　　　　　**c** $(x + 10)^2$

d $(y - 5)^2$　　　　　**e** $(3x - 2)^2$　　　　　**f** $(5x - 8)^2$

EXAMPLE 2

Expand using the difference of two squares.

a $(x - 3)(x + 3)$　　　　　　　　**b** $(5x - 7)(5x + 7)$

	Solve	Think/Apply
a	$(x - 3)(x + 3) = x^2 - 3^2$ $= x^2 - 9$	Use the difference of two squares expansion. There is no middle term. The second term is always negative.
b	$(5x - 7)(5x + 7) = (5x)^2 - (7)^2$ $= 25x^2 - 49$	

---

2 Expand the following using the difference of two squares.

a $(x - 5)(x + 5)$　　　　**b** $(x - 2)(x + 2)$　　　　**c** $(x - 7)(x + 7)$

d $(2x - 3)(2x + 3)$　　　**e** $(5x - 2)(5x + 2)$　　　**f** $(7x - 1)(7x + 1)$

NUMBER & ALGEBRA

3 Expand the following.

   a $(x - 8)(x + 8)$ **b** $(x - 7)^2$ **c** $(3x - 2)(3x + 2)$

   d $(4x - 7)^2$ **e** $(7x + 3)^2$ **f** $(2x - 7)(2x + 7)$

● EXAMPLE 3

Complete the following expressions.

a $(x + 3)^2 = x^2 + \square + \square$ **b** $(x - \square)^2 = x^2 - 12x + \square$

c $(y + \square)^2 = y^2 + 7y + \square$

	Solve	Think	Apply
a	$(x + 3)^2 = x^2 + \square + \square$ $= x^2 + 6x + 9$	The coefficient of x is the 'twice the product' term: $2 \times 1 \times 3 = 6$ The constant term is the second term squared: $3^2 = 9$	These expressions are based on the perfect square expansions $(x + y)^2 = x^2 + 2xy + y^2$ and $(x - y)^2 = x^2 - 2xy + y^2$.
b	$(x - \square)^2 = x^2 - 12x + \square$ $(x - 6)^2 = x^2 - 12x + 36$	The coefficient of x must be halved: $-12 \div 2 = -6$ The constant term is the second term squared: $(-6)^2 = 36$	
c	$(y + \square)^2 = y^2 + 7y + \square$ $\left(y + \dfrac{7}{2}\right)^2 = y^2 + 7y + \dfrac{49}{4}$	The coefficient of y must be halved: $7 \div 2 = \dfrac{7}{2}$ The constant term is the second term squared: $\left(\dfrac{7}{2}\right)^2 = \dfrac{49}{4}$	

4 Complete the following expressions.

   a $(x + 2)^2 = x^2 + \square x + \square$ **b** $(x - \square)^2 = x^2 - 6x + \square$

   c $(x - 5)^2 = x^2 \underline{\quad} \square + \square$ **d** $(x - \square)^2 = x^2 - 14x + \square$

   e $(x + \square)^2 = x^2 \underline{\quad} \square + 64$ **f** $(x + \square)^2 = x^2 + 32x + \square$

● EXAMPLE 4

What number needs to be added to complete the square?

a $x^2 + 6x$ **b** $x^2 - 5x$

	Solve	Think	Apply
a	$x^2 + 6x$ $x^2 + 6x + \underline{\quad} = (x + \underline{\quad})^2$ $\therefore 9$ must be added.	Constant term $= \left(\dfrac{6}{2}\right)^2 = 9$	Halve the coefficient of x and square it to find the constant term.
b	$x^2 - 5x$ $x^2 - 5x + \underline{\quad} = (x - \underline{\quad})^2$ $\therefore \dfrac{25}{4}$ must be added.	Constant term $= \left(-\dfrac{5}{2}\right)^2 = \dfrac{25}{4}$	

5 What number needs to be added to complete the square in the following expressions?

   a $x^2 + 8x$ **b** $x^2 + 14x$ **c** $x^2 - 6x$ **d** $x^2 - 8x$

   e $x^2 + 18x$ **f** $x^2 - 20x$ **g** $x^2 + 5x$ **h** $x^2 + 17x$

   i $x^2 - 5x$ **j** $x^2 - 7x$ **k** $x^2 - x$ **l** $x^2 + x$

● EXAMPLE 5

Fully factorise the following expressions.

   a $x^2 - 25$ **b** $4y^2 - 25$ **c** $9x^2 - 16$

	Solve	Think/Apply
a	$x^2 - 25 = (x + 5)(x - 5)$	Take the square root of each term and use the difference of two terms factorisation.
b	$4y^2 - 25 = (2y + 5)(2y - 5)$	
c	$9x^2 - 16 = (3x + 4)(3x - 4)$	

6 Fully factorise the following.

   a $x^2 - 4$ **b** $z^2 - 16$ **c** $c^2 - 25$ **d** $a^2 - c^2$

   e $4x^2 - 1$ **f** $9x^2 - 4$ **g** $25y^2 - 16x^2$ **h** $100x^2 - 81y^2$

● EXAMPLE 6

Factorise the following.

   a $x^2 + 5x + 6$ **b** $x^2 + 7x + 12$

   c $x^2 - 8x + 12$ **d** $x^2 + x - 6$

	Solve	Think	Apply
a	$x^2 + 5x + 6 = (x + 3)(x + 2)$	Two numbers that add to 5 and whose product is 6 are 3 and 2.	The sum of the numbers is the coefficient of x and the product of the numbers is the constant term.
b	$x^2 + 7x + 12 = (x + 4)(x + 3)$	Two numbers that add to 7 and whose product is 12 are 4 and 3.	If the constant term is positive, both factors have the same sign.
c	$x^2 - 8x + 12 = (x - 6)(x - 2)$	Two numbers that add to -8 and whose product is 12 are -6 and -2.	If the constant is negative, the numbers must be opposite in sign.
d	$x^2 + x - 6 = (x + 3)(x - 2)$	Two numbers that add to 1 and whose product is -6 are 3 and -2.	

7 Factorise the following.

   a $x^2 + 10x + 9$ **b** $x^2 - 9x + 8$ **c** $x^2 - 7x + 10$

   d $x^2 - 11x + 10$ **e** $x^2 - 8x + 15$ **f** $x^2 + 4x - 21$

   g $x^2 - 20x - 21$ **h** $x^2 - 17x - 60$ **i** $x^2 + 3x - 54$

   j $x^2 + 53x - 54$ **k** $x^2 - 25x - 54$ **l** $x^2 - 16x + 64$

   m $x^2 + 12x - 64$ **n** $x^2 - 30x - 64$ **o** $x^2 + 2x - 35$

   p $x^2 + 7x - 30$ **q** $x^2 - 15x + 50$ **r** $x^2 - 9x - 22$

   s $x^2 + 34x - 35$ **t** $x^2 - x - 72$ **u** $x^2 - 17x + 72$

EXAMPLE 7

Fully factorise the following expressions.

a $2x^2 + x - 15$ **b** $5x^2 - 18x - 8$ **c** $15x^2 + 7x - 2$

	Solve	Think	Apply
a	$2x^2 + x - 15 = \dfrac{(2x + 6)(2x - 5)}{2}$ $= \dfrac{2(x + 3)(2x - 5)}{2}$ $= (x + 3)(2x - 5)$	$2 \times -15 = -30$ Thus we need two numbers with a product of -30 and a sum of $+1$; that is, 6 and -5. Factorise the common factor of 2 from the second bracket and cancel.	Place the coefficient of x^2 together with x at the beginning of each bracket and divide the whole expression by this coefficient to maintain equality. Multiply the coefficient of x^2 by the constant term. Use that number to find the factors.
b	$5x^2 - 18x - 8 = \dfrac{(5x - 20)(5x + 2)}{5}$ $= \dfrac{5(x - 4)(5x + 2)}{5}$ $= (x - 4)(5x + 2)$	$5 \times -8 = -40$ Thus we need two numbers with a product of -40 and a sum of -18; that is, -20 and 2. Factorise the common factor of 5 from the first bracket and cancel.	
c	$15x^2 + 7x - 2 = \dfrac{(15x + 10)(15x - 3)}{15}$ $= \dfrac{5(3x + 2)3(5x - 1)}{15}$ $= (3x + 2)(5x - 1)$	$15 \times -2 = -30$ Thus we need two numbers with a product of -30 and a sum of $+7$; that is, 10 and -3. Factorise the common factor of 5 from the first bracket and 3 from the second bracket. Cancel 3 and 5 with the denominator of 15.	

8 Fully factorise the following.

a $2x^2 + 7x - 4$ **b** $3x^2 - 5x - 2$ **c** $4x^2 + 3x - 10$

d $5x^2 - 13x + 6$ **e** $6x^2 + 28x - 10$ **f** $3x^2 + 8x - 35$

g $4x^2 - 13x - 35$ **h** $10x^2 - 17x - 6$ **i** $8x^2 + 3x - 5$

j $11x^2 + 13x - 18$ **k** $6x^2 - 7x - 3$ **l** $15x^2 + 4x - 4$

m $8x^2 - 18x - 5$ **n** $12x^2 + 4x - 5$ **o** $12x^2 + 25x - 7$

p $21x^2 - 8x - 5$ **q** $36x^2 - 5x - 1$ **r** $22x^2 + 3x - 7$

C | Solve quadratic equations by factorising

EXAMPLE 1

Solve the following equations.

a $3x^2 = 7$ **b** $5x^2 = 9$

	Solve	Think	Apply
a	$3x^2 = 7$ $x^2 = \dfrac{7}{3}$ $x = \pm\sqrt{\dfrac{7}{3}}$	Take the square root of both sides.	Make x^2 the subject of the equation and take the square root of both sides. Remember that there are two answers, one positive and one negative.
b	$5x^2 = 9$ $x^2 = \dfrac{9}{5}$ $x = \pm\sqrt{\dfrac{9}{5}}$ $= \pm\dfrac{3}{\sqrt{5}}$	Use $\sqrt{9} = 3$ to simplify the answer.	

Exercise 10C

1 Solve the following equations.

a $5x^2 = 7$ **b** $3x^2 = 11$ **c** $2x^2 = 7$ **d** $4x^2 = 5$

e $9x^2 = 7$ **f** $11x^2 = 25$ **g** $6x^2 = 25$ **h** $4x^2 = 3$

EXAMPLE 2

Solve these equations.

a $(y - 2)^2 = 9$ **b** $(x + 3)^2 = 16$

	Solve	Think	Apply
a	$y - 2 = \pm 3$ $y = +3 + 2 = 5$ and $y = -3 + 2 = -1$ $\therefore y = -1$ or 5	Take the square root of both sides, giving $y - 2$ and ± 3. Solve the two resulting linear equations.	This technique can only be used if there are two quantities equal to each other. If there were any terms on LHS outside the bracket then this method could not be used.
b	$x + 3 = \pm 4$ $x = +4 - 3 = 1$ and $x = -4 - 3 = -7$ $\therefore x = -7$ or 1	Take the square root of both sides, giving $(x + 3)$ and ± 4. Solve the two resulting linear equations.	

2 Solve the following quadratic equations.

a $(x - 3)^2 = 25$

b $(y + 5)^2 = 9$

c $(x + 2)^2 = 16$

d $(y + 7)^2 = 49$

e $(x - 1)^2 = 36$

f $(x - 5)^2 = 49$

EXAMPLE 3

Solve the following quadratic equations by factorising.

a $3x^2 + 6x = 0$

b $x^2 - 8x + 12 = 0$

c $x^2 + 2x - 15 = 0$

	Solve	Think	Apply
a	$3x^2 + 6x = 0$ $3x(x + 2) = 0$ $3x = 0$ or $x + 2 = 0$ $\therefore x = 0$ or -2	Factorise by taking out the common factor of $3x$.	When we solve quadratic equations, if $a \times b = 0$ then $a = 0$, $b = 0$ or $a = b = 0$.
b	$x^2 - 8x + 12 = 0$ $(x - 6)(x - 2) = 0$ $x - 6 = 0$ or $x - 2 = 0$ $x = 6$ or 2	Factorise using the factors of 12 that add to give 8 (6 and 2).	
c	$x^2 + 2x - 15 = 0$ $(x + 5)(x - 3) = 0$ $x + 5 = 0$ or $x - 3 = 0$ $\therefore x = -5$ or 3	Factorise using the factors of 15 whose sum is 2 (5 and -3).	

3 Solve the following quadratic equations by factorising.

a $4x^2 + 12x = 0$

b $7x^2 - 21x = 0$

c $x^2 - 5x = 0$

d $x^2 - 3x - 4 = 0$

e $x^2 + 5x + 4 = 0$

f $x^2 + 2x - 24 = 0$

g $x^2 + 7x + 10 = 0$

h $x^2 - 5x + 4 = 0$

i $x^2 + 10x + 25 = 0$

j $x^2 + 7x - 18 = 0$

k $x^2 + 11x - 60 = 0$

l $x^2 - 11x + 24 = 0$

m $x^2 - 12x + 36 = 0$

n $x^2 + 14x - 15 = 0$

o $x^2 + 8x + 12 = 0$

p $x^2 + 6x - 27 = 0$

EXAMPLE 4

Solve the following quadratic equations by factorising.

a $3x^2 - 17x + 20 = 0$

b $2x^2 + 7x - 15 = 0$

c $6x^2 + x - 2 = 0$

	Solve	Think/Apply
a	$3x^2 - 17x + 20 = 0$ $(3x - 5)(x - 4) = 0$ $3x - 5 = 0$ or $x - 4 = 0$ $3x - 5$ or $x = 4$ $\therefore x = \frac{5}{3}$ or 4	Use the techniques from Section 10B to factorise each quadratic. Use the fact that if $a \times b = 0$ then either $a = 0$ or $b = 0$ or both.

EXAMPLE 4 CONTINUED

Solve	Think/Apply
b $2x^2 + 7x - 15 = 0$ $(2x - 3)(x + 5) = 0$ $2x - 3 = 0$ or $x + 5 = 0$ $2x = 3$ or $x = -5$ $\therefore x = \frac{3}{2}$ or -5	Use the techniques from Section 10B to factorise each quadratic. Use the fact that if $a \times b = 0$ then either $a = 0$ or $b = 0$ or both.
c $6x^2 + x - 2 = 0$ $(3x + 2)(2x - 1) = 0$ $3x + 2 = 0$ or $2x - 1 = 0$ $3x = -2$ or $2x = 1$ $\therefore x = -\frac{2}{3}$ or $\frac{1}{2}$	

4 Solve the following quadratic equations by factorising.

a $2x^2 + 5x + 3 = 0$ b $3x^2 - 5x - 2 = 0$ c $7x^2 + 9x + 2 = 0$

d $5x^2 + 2x - 3 = 0$ e $3x^2 - 7x - 6 = 0$ f $3x^2 + 13x + 4 = 0$

g $5x^2 - 13x - 6 = 0$ h $2x^2 + 9x - 18 = 0$ i $21x^2 + 17x + 2 = 0$

j $10x^2 + 17x + 3 = 0$ k $4x^2 + 4x + 1 = 0$ l $3x^2 + 14x + 8 = 0$

m $3x^2 + 7x + 4 = 0$ n $5x^2 - 14x - 3 = 0$ o $11x^2 - 9x - 2 = 0$

EXAMPLE 5

Rearrange the following equations to form quadratics and solve by factorising.

a $x^2 = 15 - 2x$ b $\dfrac{x^2 - 12}{x} = 4$ c $3x^2 = 2 - x$

Solve	Think/Apply
a $x^2 = 15 - 2x$ $x^2 + 2x - 15 = 0$ $(x + 5)(x - 3) = 0$ $x + 5 = 0$ or $x - 3 = 0$ $\therefore x = -5$ or 3	Use normal algebra and equation rules to rearrange the quadratic equation. Solve as in the previous examples.
b $\dfrac{x^2 - 12}{x} = 4$ $x^2 - 12 = 4x$ $x^2 - 4x - 12 = 0$ $(x - 6)(x + 2) = 0$ $x - 6 = 0$ or $x + 2 = 0$ $\therefore x = 6$ or -2	
c $3x^2 = 2 - x$ $3x^2 + x - 2 = 0$ $(3x - 2)(x + 1) = 0$ $3x - 2 = 0$ or $x + 1 = 0$ $3x = 2$ or $x = -1$ $\therefore x = \frac{2}{3}$ or -1	

5 Rearrange the following equations to form quadratics and solve by factorising.

a $x^2 + 1 = 2x$ **b** $x^2 = 20 + x$ **c** $x^2 + 2 = 3x$

d $8 = x^2 + 7x$ **e** $x^2 = 24 - 5x$ **f** $x^2 = 10x - 16$

g $\dfrac{x^2 - 20}{x} = 19$ **h** $\dfrac{x^2}{4} = x + 8$ **i** $\dfrac{x^2 + 1}{x} = 2$

6 Rearrange the following equations to form quadratics and solve by factorising.

a $2x^2 + 5 = 11x$ **b** $21x^2 = 62x + 3$ **c** $3x^2 = 17x - 20$

d $6x^2 + 13x = 5$ **e** $2x^2 = 7x - 5$ **f** $5x^2 = 13x + 6$

g $3x^2 + 2x = 8$ **h** $\dfrac{7x}{2} = 18 - 2x^2$ **i** $\dfrac{2x + 1}{x} = 3x$

D Completing the square

Another method of solving quadratic equations is by completing the square.

This uses the expansions:

$$(x + y)^2 = x^2 + 2xy + y^2$$
$$(x - y)^2 = x^2 - 2xy + y^2$$

 EXAMPLE 1

Solve the following quadratics by completing the square.

a $x^2 + 4x - 12 = 0$ **b** $x^2 - 6x + 8 = 0$

	Solve	Think	Apply
a	$x^2 + 4x - 12 = 0$ $x^2 + 4x = 12$ $x^2 + 4x + \left(\dfrac{4}{2}\right)^2 = 12 + \left(\dfrac{4}{2}\right)^2$ $x^2 + 4x + (2)^2 = 12 + (2)^2$ $(x + 2)^2 = 16$ $x + 2 = \pm\sqrt{16}$ $= \pm 4$ $x = -2 \pm 4$ $= -2 + 4 \text{ or } -2 - 4$ $\therefore x = 2 \text{ or } x = -6$	Rearrange to put the x terms on the LHS. Add the constant to both sides. Complete the square.	Complete the square by adding the third term found by squaring half the coefficient of x.
b	$x^2 - 6x + 8 = 0$ $x^2 - 6x = -8$ $x^2 - 6x + \left(\dfrac{6}{2}\right)^2 = -8 + \left(\dfrac{6}{2}\right)^2$ $x^2 - 6x + (3)^2 = -8 + 3^2$ $(x - 3)^2 = 1$ $x - 3 = \pm 1$ $x = 3 \pm 1$ $= 3 + 1 \text{ or } 3 - 1$ $\therefore x = 4 \text{ or } x = 2$	Rearrange to put the x terms on the LHS. Add the constant to both sides. Complete the square.	

NUMBER & ALGEBRA

Reminders

- If $x^2 = k$ then
  $$x = \pm\sqrt{k} \qquad \text{if } k > 0$$
  $$x = 0 \qquad \text{if } k = 0$$
  $$\text{no solutions exist} \qquad \text{if } k < 0$$

- If $k > 0$ and $(x - a)^2 = k$, then $x - a = \pm\sqrt{k}$.
  If $k > 0$ and $(x + a)^2 = k$, then $x + a = \pm\sqrt{k}$.

- $\sqrt{ab} = \sqrt{a} \times \sqrt{b}$ and $\sqrt{\dfrac{a}{b}} = \dfrac{\sqrt{a}}{\sqrt{b}} =$ for $a > 0, b > 0$.

Exercise 10D

1 Solve the following quadratics by completing the square. All answers are integers.

a $x^2 + 8x - 9 = 0$ **b** $x^2 + 4x - 5 = 0$

c $x^2 - 10x + 9 = 0$ **d** $x^2 + 2x - 35 = 0$

e $x^2 + 6x - 27 = 0$ **f** $x^2 - 6x - 16 = 0$

● EXAMPLE 2

Solve the following quadratic equations by completing the square.

a $x^2 + 8x + 3 = 0$ **b** $x^2 - 10x - 2 = 0$

	Solve	Think	Apply
a	$x^2 + 8x + 3 = 0$ $x^2 + 8x = -3$ $x^2 + 8x + \left(\dfrac{8}{2}\right)^2 = -3 + \left(\dfrac{8}{2}\right)^2$ $x^2 + 8x + (4)^2 = -3 + (4)^2$ $(x + 4)^2 = 13$ $x + 4 = \pm\sqrt{13}$ $x = -4 \pm \sqrt{13}$	Halve 8 to get 4 and add 4^2 to both sides. Solve by taking the square root of both sides.	Complete the square, then solve the resulting quadratic equality. Note that only one side needs $\pm$ to the square root.
b	$x^2 - 10x - 2 = 0$ $x^2 - 10x = 2$ $x^2 - 10x + \left(-\dfrac{10}{2}\right)^2 = 2 + \left(-\dfrac{10}{2}\right)^2$ $x^2 - 10x + (-5)^2 = 2 + (-5)^2$ $(x - 5)^2 = 27$ $x - 5 = \pm\sqrt{27}$ $= \pm 3\sqrt{3}$ $x = 5 \pm 3\sqrt{3}$	Halve -10 to get -5 and add $(-5)^2$ to both sides. Solve by taking the square root of both sides. Note that $\sqrt{27} = \sqrt{3 \times 9} = 3\sqrt{3}$.	

2 Solve the following quadratic equations by completing the square.

a $x^2 + 4x + 1 = 0$ **b** $x^2 - 2x - 5 = 0$

c $x^2 - 6x + 2 = 0$ **d** $x^2 - 8x - 3 = 0$

e $x^2 - 10x + 8 = 0$ **f** $x^2 + 12x - 7 = 0$

EXAMPLE 3

Solve the following quadratics by completing the square.

a $x^2 + 5x - 3 = 0$ **b** $x^2 - 7x + 8 = 0$

	Solve	Think	Apply
a	$x^2 + 5x - 3 = 0$ $x^2 + 5x = 3$ $x^2 + 5x + \left(\dfrac{5}{2}\right)^2 = 3 + \left(\dfrac{5}{2}\right)^2$ $\left(x + \dfrac{5}{2}\right)^2 = 3 + \dfrac{25}{4} = \dfrac{37}{4}$ $x + \dfrac{5}{2} = \pm\sqrt{\dfrac{37}{4}}$ $x = -\dfrac{5}{2} \pm \dfrac{\sqrt{37}}{2} = \dfrac{-5 \pm \sqrt{37}}{2}$	Halve 5 to get $\dfrac{5}{2}$ and add $\left(\dfrac{5}{2}\right)^2$ to both sides. Solve by taking the square root of both sides.	These expressions have a fraction for the constant term. The process is the same but the answer has a surd and factors as well.
b	$x^2 - 7x + 8 = 0$ $x^2 - 7x = -8$ $x^2 - 7x + \left(-\dfrac{7}{2}\right)^2 = -8 + \left(-\dfrac{7}{2}\right)^2$ $\left(x - \dfrac{7}{2}\right)^2 = -8 + \dfrac{49}{4} = \dfrac{17}{4}$ $x - \dfrac{7}{2} = \pm\sqrt{\dfrac{17}{4}}$ $x = \dfrac{7}{2} \pm \dfrac{\sqrt{17}}{2} = \dfrac{7 \pm \sqrt{17}}{2}$	Halve -7 to get $-\dfrac{7}{2}$ and add $\left(-\dfrac{7}{2}\right)^2$ to both sides. Solve by taking the square root of both sides.	

3 Solve the following quadratic equations by completing the square.

a $x^2 + 3x - 1 = 0$ **b** $x^2 - 5x + 2 = 0$ **c** $x^2 + 7x + 3 = 0$

d $x^2 - x - 3 = 0$ **e** $x^2 + 9x - 3 = 0$ **f** $x^2 - 7x - 4 = 0$

EXAMPLE 4

Solve the following quadratic equations by completing the square.

a $2x^2 - 8x - 3 = 0$ **b** $3x^2 - 6x - 5 = 0$

	Solve	Think	Apply
a	$2x^2 - 8x - 3 = 0$ $2x^2 - 8x = 3$ $x^2 - 4x = \dfrac{3}{2}$ $x^2 - 4x + \left(\dfrac{4}{2}\right)^2 = \dfrac{3}{2} + \left(\dfrac{4}{2}\right)^2$ $x^2 - 4x + (2)^2 = \dfrac{3}{2} + (2)^2$ $(x - 2)^2 = \dfrac{3}{2} + 4 = \dfrac{11}{2}$ $x - 2 = \pm\sqrt{\dfrac{11}{2}} \times \dfrac{\sqrt{2}}{\sqrt{2}}$ $x = 2 \pm \dfrac{\sqrt{22}}{2} = \dfrac{4 \pm \sqrt{22}}{2}$	Divide both sides by 2. Halve 4 to get 2 and add 2^2 to both sides. Solve by taking the square root of both sides.	The coefficient of x must be divided by the coefficient of x^2 before halving and squaring to add the constant term to both sides.

NUMBER & ALGEBRA

EXAMPLE 4 CONTINUED

Solve	Think	Apply
b $3x^2 - 6x - 5 = 0$ $3x^2 - 6x = 5$ $x^2 - 2x = \dfrac{5}{3}$ $x^2 - 2x + \left(-\dfrac{2}{2}\right)^2 = \dfrac{5}{3} + \left(-\dfrac{2}{2}\right)^2$ $x^2 - 2x + (-1)^2 = \dfrac{5}{3} + (-1)^2$ $(x-1)^2 = \dfrac{5}{3} + 1 = \dfrac{8}{3}$ $x - 1 = \pm\sqrt{\dfrac{8}{3}} \times \dfrac{\sqrt{3}}{\sqrt{3}}$ $x = 1 \pm \dfrac{\sqrt{24}}{3}$ $= \dfrac{3 \pm 2\sqrt{6}}{3}$	Divide both sides by 3. Halve 2 to get 1 and add $(-1)^2$ to both sides. Solve by taking the square root of both sides.	The coefficient of x must be divided by the coefficient of x^2 before halving and squaring to add the constant term to both sides.

4 Solve the following quadratic equations by completing the square.

a $2x^2 - 5x + 1 = 0$ **b** $3x^2 + 4x - 5 = 0$

c $5x^2 - 7x - 1 = 0$ **d** $4x^2 - 11x + 1 = 0$

e $3x^2 - 3x - 7 = 0$ **f** $4x^2 - 7x - 3 = 0$

Investigation 1 Quadratic equations

One technique for solving quadratic equations is a process that uses guess, check and refine. Spreadsheets can also be used.

1 Solve $x^2 + x - 12 = 0$ using guess, check and refine.
  a Complete this table. Use a spreadsheet if possible.
  b What do you notice about the values of the numbers close to the answers?

2 Examine the quadratic equation $8x^2 - 10x - 3 = 0$.
  a Draw a similar table using the same x-values.
  b The roots are not integers. Between which two integers do the answers lie?
  c Use a table involving decimal numbers to refine your guesses.

3 Complete:
  If the sign of the quadratic changes from one integer value to another then a solution is _____.

x	$x^2 + x - 12$
-5	
-4	
-3	
-2	
-1	
0	
1	
2	
3	
4	

Extension

4 Investigate the 'halving the interval' rule for solving quadratic equations or equations with powers of x greater than 2.

E The quadratic formula

When the completing the square technique is applied to the general quadratic equation $ax^2 + bx + c = 0$, the resulting formula is called 'the quadratic formula' and is used to solve any quadratic equation that has solutions.

Consider $ax^2 + bx + c = 0$.

$$ax^2 + bx = -c$$ Rearrange to get the x terms on the LHS.

$$\frac{ax^2}{a} + \frac{bx}{a} = \frac{-c}{a}$$ Divide by the coefficient of x^2.

$$x^2 + \frac{b}{a}x = \frac{-c}{a}$$

$$x^2 + \frac{b}{a}x + \left(\frac{b}{2a}\right)^2 = \frac{-c}{a} + \left(\frac{b}{2a}\right)^2$$ Halve the coefficient of x and complete the square.

$$\left(x + \frac{b}{2a}\right)^2 = \frac{-c}{a} + \frac{b^2}{4a^2}$$

$$= \frac{-4ac + b^2}{4a^2}$$

$$= \frac{b^2 - 4ac}{4a^2}$$

$$x + \frac{b}{2a} = \pm\sqrt{\frac{b^2 - 4ac}{4a^2}}$$

$$= \pm\frac{\sqrt{b^2 - 4ac}}{2a}$$

$$x = -\frac{b}{2a} \pm \frac{\sqrt{b^2 - 4ac}}{2a}$$

$$= \frac{-b \pm \sqrt{b^2 - 4ac}}{2a}$$

So, if $ax^2 + bx + c = 0$ then $x = \dfrac{-b \pm \sqrt{b^2 - 4ac}}{2a}$, which is known as the quadratic formula.

EXAMPLE 1

Solve the following equations using the quadratic formula.

a $x^2 - 5x + 2 = 0$ **b** $3x^2 - 7x - 5 = 0$

	Solve	Think/Apply
a	$x^2 - 5x + 2 = 0 \therefore a = 1, b = -5, c = 2$ $x = \dfrac{-(-5) \pm \sqrt{(-5)^2 - 4(1)(2)}}{2(1)}$ $= \dfrac{5 \pm \sqrt{25 - 8}}{2}$ $= \dfrac{5 \pm \sqrt{17}}{2}$	Find the values of a, b and c. Substitute these into the quadratic formula: $x = \dfrac{-b \pm \sqrt{b^2 - 4ac}}{2a}$
b	$3x^2 - 7x - 5 = 0 \therefore a = 3, b = -7, c = -5$ $x = \dfrac{-(-7) \pm \sqrt{(-7)^2 - 4(3)(-5)}}{2(3)}$ $= \dfrac{7 \pm \sqrt{49 + 60}}{6}$ $= \dfrac{7 \pm \sqrt{109}}{6}$	

1 Solve the following equations using the quadratic formula.

a $x^2 - 5x + 3 = 0$ **b** $x^2 + 7x - 4 = 0$ **c** $x^2 + 3x - 1 = 0$

d $x^2 + 5x - 7 = 0$ **e** $x^2 - 7x + 2 = 0$ **f** $x^2 + 9x - 5 = 0$

g $2x^2 - 7x - 8 = 0$ **h** $3x^2 + 3x - 5 = 0$ **i** $7x^2 + 11x + 3 = 0$

j $5x^2 - x - 2 = 0$ **k** $5x^2 - 5x - 6 = 0$ **l** $8x^2 - x - 1 = 0$

2 **a** Solve the quadratic equation $x^2 - 14x + 24 = 0$ by factorising.

     b Solve the equation by completing the square.

     c Solve the equation by using the quadratic formula.

     d Which method was the easiest? Explain.

3 Repeat question **2** for the quadratic $4x^2 - 58x - 30 = 0$.

4 **a** Apply the quadratic formula to the equation $x^2 - 3x + 4 = 0$. What do you notice?

     b How many solutions does the equation $x^2 - 3x + 4$ have?

     c What test could you use to show that an equation has no solution?

5 **a** Apply the quadratic formula to the equation $x^2 - 6x + 9 = 0$. What do you notice?

     b How many solutions does $x^2 - 6x + 9 = 0$ have?

     c Complete the square to solve $x^2 - 6x + 9 = 0$. What do you notice?

     d Factorise $x^2 - 6x + 9 = 0$. What do you notice?

     e What test could you use to show that a quadratic equation has only one solution?

Investigation 2 The discriminant

Some features of the quadratic formula were discovered from Exercise 10E. The expression under the square root in the quadratic formula, $b^2 - 4ac$, determines the number of solutions for the quadratic equation. This is called the **discriminant** and has symbol Δ.

- If $\Delta = b^2 - 4ac > 0$ there are two solutions for the quadratic equation.

- If $\Delta = b^2 - 4ac = 0$ there are two equal solutions.

- If $\Delta = b^2 - 4ac < 0$ there are no real solutions.

1 Consider the quadratic equation $x^2 - 4x + 7 = 0$.

     a Calculate the discriminant.

     b How many solutions are there for the equation $x^2 - 4x + 7 = 0$?

     c Complete the square to try and solve $x^2 - 4x + 7 = 0$. What happens? How does this show there are no solutions?

2 Consider the equation $x^2 - 4x + 4 = 0$.

     a Calculate the discriminant.

     b How many solutions are there to $x^2 - 4x + 4 = 0$? Are they the same or different?

     c Complete the square to solve $x^2 - 4x + 4 = 0$. What is/are the solutions?

        Note that $(x - 2)^2 = 0$ has two solutions $+(x - 2) = 0$ and $-(x - 2) = 0$; both give $x = 2$ as the solution.

     d Complete the following.

        If the discriminant, $b^2 - 4ac$, equals _____ then the quadratic is a _____ square.

3 Without solving, determine the number of solutions of each of these quadratic equations.

a $x^2 - 3x + 5 = 0$ b $x^2 + 7x - 4 = 0$

c $x^2 - 6x + 9 = 0$ d $x^2 + 5x + 10 = 0$

e $x^2 - 5x - 3 = 0$ f $x^2 - 10x + 25 = 0$

g $4x^2 - 4x + 1 = 0$ h $6x^2 + 5x - 9 = 0$

F Worded quadratic problems

When solving problems resulting in quadratic equations, it is important to check that any solutions make sense in the context of the question.

EXAMPLE 1

When the square of a number is decreased by 5, the result is 4 times the number. Find the number.

Solve	Think	Apply
$n^2 - 5 = 4n$ $n^2 - 4n - 5 = 0$ $(n - 5)(n + 1) = 0$ $n = -1$ or 5 The number is -1 or 5.	Let the number be n. The square of the number is n^2 and decreasing by 5 is subtraction: $n^2 - 5$.	Check that the solutions make sense in the context of the question.

EXAMPLE 2

Twice the number squared is 7 more than five times the number. Find the number.

Solve	Think	Apply
$2n^2 - 5n - 7 = 0$ $\dfrac{(2n - 7)(2n + 2)}{2} = 0$ $(2n - 7)(n + 1) = 0$ $2n - 7 = 0$ or $n + 1 = 0$ $2n = 7$ or $n = -1$ $n = \dfrac{7}{2}$ or $n = -1$ So the number is $3\frac{1}{2}$ or -1.	If the number is n then $2n^2 = 7 + 5n$. Factorise the quadratic to solve.	Choose the best method to solve the quadratic. If the factors are hard to find then use the quadratic formula.

Exercise 10F

1 When a number is squared, it is 12 more than eleven times the number. Find the number.

2 When a number is subtracted from its square, the result is 20. Find the number.

3 When a number is subtracted from its square, the result is 30. Find the number.

4 Find a number that when squared is 2 less than three times the number.

5 Twice a number squared is 5 more than nine times the number. Find the number.

6 Three times a number squared is 8 more than twice the number. Find the number.

EXAMPLE 3

A rectangle has length 4 cm more than its breadth. Find the dimensions of the rectangle given that its area is 96 cm².

Solve	Think	Apply
$96 = (x + 4) \times x$ $\quad = x^2 + 4x$ $x^2 + 4x = 96$ $x^2 + 4x - 96 = 0$ $(x + 12)(x - 8) = 0$ $\therefore x = 8$ or -12 cm The breadth cannot be -12 cm. Therefore the breadth $= 8$ cm and the length $= 12$ cm.	$x + 4$ x [rectangle diagram] Area $=$ length $\times$ breadth Let the breadth be x cm, then the length is $(x + 4)$ cm. As the breadth cannot be -12, $x = 8$. So breadth $= 8$ cm and length $= 8 + 4$ cm.	A quadratic equation will usually have two solutions. Make sure any solution makes sense in the context of the question.

7 A rectangle has length 6 cm more than its breadth. Find the dimensions of the rectangle given that its area is 112 cm².

8 Natalie is 3 years younger than one brother and 8 years younger than her other brother. The product of her brothers' ages is equal to 50. How old is Natalie?

9 The formula for the sum of an arithmetic series is $S = \frac{n}{2}[2a + (n - 1)d]$. Find the value of n if $a = 5$, $d = 4$ and $S = 945$.

10 Repeat question **9** using $a = 3$, $d = -5$ and $S = -1425$.

G Higher-order equations

There are many methods for solving quadratic equations but few methods exist for solving equations of higher order. Sometimes, following substitution, equations can be reduced to quadratic equations and subsequently solved.

EXAMPLE 1

Use the substitution $u = x^2$ to solve the equation $x^4 - 5x^2 - 36 = 0$.

Solve	Think	Apply
$x^4 - 5x^2 - 36 = 0$ becomes $u^2 - 5u - 36 = 0$ $(u - 9)(u + 4) = 0$ $u = 9$ or -4 Solution is $x = \pm 3$.	Replace x^2 with u and $x^4 = (x^2)^2$ with u^2. Solve by factorising. Replace u with x^2. Thus $x^2 = 9$ or $x^2 = -4$. $x^2 = -4$ has no solution.	Although there were two values for u only one value can be used with x^2. There was the potential for four solutions but in this case there were only two solutions.

Exercise 10G

1 Solve these equations by substituting $u = x^2$ and factorising.

  a $x^4 - x^2 - 12 = 0$ **b** $x^4 - 13x^2 + 36 = 0$ **c** $x^4 - 13x^2 - 48 = 0$

  d $x^4 + 4x^2 - 5 = 0$ **e** $x^4 - 5x^2 + 4 = 0$ **f** $x^4 - 7x^2 - 18 = 0$

  g $x^4 - 12x^2 + 35 = 0$ **h** $x^4 - x^2 - 6 = 0$ **i** $x^4 - 26x^2 + 25 = 0$

Investigation 3 Higher-order quadratic equations

1 a Factorise $x^2 - x - 6$.   **b** Solve $x^2 - x - 6 = 0$.

2 a Substitute $(x + 1)$ for x in the expression $x^2 - x - 6$. Simplify the expression to show it is $x^2 + x - 6$.

  b Factorise and solve $x^2 + x - 6 = 0$. Compare your answer with question **1** part **b**.

3 a Factorise and solve $x^2 - 8x - 20 = 0$.

  b Substitute $x + 1$ for x in $x^2 - 8x - 20 = 0$, simplify, factorise and solve.

  c Compare your answers for parts **a** and **b**.

4 a Factorise and solve $x^2 - 7x + 12 = 0$.

  b Substitute $x + 2$ for x in $x^2 - 7x + 12 = 0$, simplify, factorise and solve.

  c Compare your answers for parts **a** and **b**.

5 a Factorise and solve $x^2 - 4x - 21 = 0$.

  b Without factorising, write the solutions for the following quadratics. Check your solutions.

    i $(x + 1)^2 - 4(x + 1) - 21 = 0$ **ii** $(x - 1)^2 - 4(x - 1) - 21 = 0$

    iii $(x + 3)^2 - 4(x + 3) - 21 = 0$ **iv** $(x - 5)^2 - 4(x - 5) - 21 = 0$

6 Solve these equations

  a $(x + 3)^2 - 15(x + 3) + 50 = 0$ **b** $(x - 1)^2 + 7(x - 1) - 30 = 0$

  c $(x + 2)^2 - 30(x + 2) - 64 = 0$ **d** $2(x + 1)^2 + 5(x + 1) + 3 = 0$

  e $2(x - 2)^2 + 11(x - 2) - 21 = 0$ **f** $2(x - 5)^2 + 3(x - 5) - 20 = 0$

H Non-linear simultaneous equations

When we solved linear simultaneous equations we employed two methods: substitution and elimination. When solving all other types of simultaneous equations we use the substitution method.

EXAMPLE 1

Solve simultaneously the linear equations $y = 5x - 2$ and $y = 3 - 2x$.

Solve	Think	Apply
$5x - 2 = 3 - 2x$ $5x + 2x - 2 = 3$ $7x - 2 = 3$ $7x = 5$ $x = \dfrac{5}{7}$ $y = 5\left(\dfrac{5}{7}\right) - 2 = \dfrac{11}{7}$ $\therefore x = \dfrac{5}{7}$ and $y = \dfrac{11}{7}$	Let the equations equal each other. Solve the resulting equation. Substitute $x = \dfrac{5}{7}$ into $y = 5x - 2$. Substitute to find the second value.	You can substitute into either equation to find the other solution. Substitute both into the other equation to check.

Exercise 10H

1 Solve these equations simultaneously.

   a $y = 2x - 5$ and $y = 4x + 2$ **b** $y = -4x + 3$ and $y = 3x - 5$

   c $y = 6 - 3x$ and $y = 5x + 2$ **d** $y = 3x - 5$ and $y = 5x - 7$

EXAMPLE 2

Solve the equations $y = x^2 + 5x - 5$ and $y = 2x + 5$ simultaneously.

Solve	Think	Apply
$x^2 + 5x - 5 = 2x + 5$ $x^2 + 5x - 2x - 5 - 5 = 0$ $x^2 + 3x - 10 = 0$ $(x + 5)(x - 2) = 0$ $x = 2$ or -5 When $x = 2$, $y = 2(2) + 5 = 9$ When $x = -5$, $y = 2(-5) + 5 = -5$ $(2, 9)$ and $(-5, -5)$ are the two solutions.	Let the equations equal each other. Rearrange to equal 0. Solve the quadratic. Substitute each into $y = 2x + 5$. The values for x will give two points.	There are two solutions to the quadratic equation. Substitute into either equation to find the y values.

2 Solve these equations simultaneously.

   a $y = x^2 + 8x - 14$ and $y = 5x - 4$ **b** $y = x^2 - x + 9$ and $y = 2x + 7$

   c $y = x^2 + x - 24$ and $y = -3x - 3$ **d** $y = x^2 + 10x - 22$ and $y = 3x + 8$

   e $y = x^2 - 3x - 24$ and $y = 5x - 4$ **f** $y = x^2 + 6x - 56$ and $y = 9x - 2$

EXAMPLE 3

Solve the equations $y = \dfrac{8}{x}$ and $y = x + 7$ simultaneously.

Solve	Think	Apply
$x + 7 = \dfrac{8}{x}$	Let the equations equal each other.	Solve these equations in the same way.
$x(x + 7) = \dfrac{8}{x} \times x$	Multiply both sides by x.	Note: $x = 0$ cannot be a
$x^2 + 7x = 8$	Expand and subtract 8 from both	solution as $y = \dfrac{8}{0}$ is not
$x^2 + 7x - 8 = 0$	sides.	defined. Any other value
$(x + 8)(x - 1) = 0$	Factorise and solve.	of x is possible.
$\qquad x = 1$ or -8		
$\qquad y = 8$ or -1	Substitute to find the values of y.	
$(1, 8)$ and $(-8, -1)$ are the solutions.		

3 Solve these equations simultaneously.

a $y = x + 5$ and $y = \dfrac{6}{x}$

b $y = x + 7$ and $y = \dfrac{-12}{x}$

c $y = x + 2$ and $y = \dfrac{15}{x}$

d $y = x + 3$ and $y = \dfrac{10}{x}$

e $y = x - 12$ and $y = \dfrac{-20}{x}$

f $y = x + 10$ and $y = \dfrac{11}{x}$

EXAMPLE 4

Solve the equations $y = x^2$ and $y = 5x - 8$ simultaneously if possible.

Solve	Think	Apply
$x^2 = 5x - 8$	Let the equations equal each other.	If there is no solution
$x^2 - 5x + 8 = 0$	Rearrange to equal 0.	to the simultaneous
$x = \dfrac{5 \pm \sqrt{25 - 4(1)(8)}}{2}$	It cannot be factorised, so use the quadratic formula:	equations then the graphs would not
$= \dfrac{5 \pm \sqrt{-7}}{2}$	$x = \dfrac{-b \pm \sqrt{b^2 - 4ac}}{2a}$	intersect.
There is no solution.	with $a = 1$, $b = -5$ and $c = 8$.	
	$\sqrt{b^2 - 4ac} = \sqrt{25 - 32} = \sqrt{-7}$	
	The discriminant is <0, so the equation has no solution.	

4 Determine which pairs of simultaneous equations have solutions and which do not.

a $y = x^2$ and $y = 3x - 10$

b $y = x^2$ and $y = 2x - 5$

c $y = x^2$ and $y = x + 6$

d $y = x^2$ and $y = -2x - 7$

Investigation 4 Simultaneous equations

Graphic calculators or graphing software can be used for this investigation.

1 Draw the graph of $y = x^2$ using x-values between -3 and 3.

2 On the same axes draw the line $y = x$.

3 From your graphs, find the points of intersection of the two graphs.

4 The x-values are the solutions of the two equations simultaneously. Solve $y = x^2$ and $y = x$ algebraically to check the graphical solution.

5 Solve the simultaneous equations from Exercise 10H question **2** by drawing each pair of graphs. Note that it is important to substitute the values into each equation to check their accuracy.

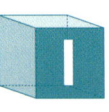

1 Simple cubic equations

Unlike quadratic equations, which usually have two solutions, cubic equations of the form $x^3 = a$ have only one real solution. There is always one solution.

EXAMPLE 1

Solve the following.
a $x^3 = 125$ **b** $x^3 = -27$

	Solve	Think	Apply
a	$x^3 = 125$ $x = \sqrt[3]{125}$ $\quad = 5$	Take the cube root of both sides.	If unsure of the value, use the $\sqrt[3]{}$ button on the calculator. Cubic equations always have one real solution.
b	$x^3 = -27$ $x = \sqrt[3]{-27}$ $\quad = -3$	The cube root of a negative is a negative.	

Exercise 10I

1 Solve the following.
  a $x^3 = 8$ **b** $x^3 = -64$ **c** $x^3 = 216$
  d $x^3 = 27$ **e** $x^3 = -1000$ **f** $x^3 = -125$

EXAMPLE 2

Solve the following.

a $8x^3 = 27$ **b** $5x^3 = 8$

	Solve	Think	Apply
a	$8x^3 = 27$ $x^3 = \dfrac{27}{8}$ $x = \sqrt[3]{\dfrac{27}{8}}$ $= \dfrac{3}{2}$	Divide both sides by 8. Find the cube root of 27 and 8.	If the cube root is an integer then find it. If it is not an integer, then either leave as a cube root or find a decimal approximation.
b	$5x^3 = 8$ $x^3 = \dfrac{8}{5}$ $= \sqrt[3]{\dfrac{8}{5}} = \dfrac{2}{\sqrt[3]{5}}$ ≈ 1.2	Divide both sides by 5. $\sqrt[3]{8} = 2$ but $\sqrt[3]{5}$ is not an integer value.	

2 Solve the following.

a $27x^3 = 8$ **b** $125x^3 = -27$ **c** $27x^3 = 125$ **d** $8x^3 = 216$

e $5x^3 = 27$ **f** $7x^3 = 8$ **g** $8x^3 = 31$ **h** $7x^3 = 11$

J Literal equations

A literal equation does not have a specific numeral solution. It is the rearrangement of a formula.

EXAMPLE 1

Make x the subject of $y = mx + b$.

Solve	Think	Apply
$y = mx + b$ $mx + b = y$ $mx = y - b$ $x = \dfrac{y - b}{m}$	Swap sides. Subtract b from both sides. Dividing both sides by m.	Always check if there are restrictions on any values. Zero cannot be a denominator. *m ≠ 0, as dividing by zero is meaningless.* ❗

Exercise 10J

1 Rearrange the equation to make x the subject.

a $p + x = q$ **b** $rx = t$ **c** $3x + b = d$

d $a = mx + b$ **e** $bx + cy = t$ **f** $4 - mx = y$

g $p - qx = r$ **h** $l - x = m + c$ **i** $3 = t - mx$

2 Make y the subject.

a $a + by = c$

b $p + qy = r$

c $xy - p = r$

d $a - b = cy$

e $x - ky = t$

f $c = 4 - ry$

g $a + by + r = 0$

h $k = r - py$

i $r + px = t - qy$

● EXAMPLE 2

Make x the subject of $ax + b = cx + 5$.

Solve	Think	Apply
$ax + b = cx + 5$ $ax - cx + b = 5$ $ax - cx = 5 - b$ $x(a - c) = 5 - b$ $x = \dfrac{5 - b}{a - c}$	Subtract cx from both sides. Subtract b from both sides. Factorise. Divide both sides by $a - c$.	If dividing by $(a - c)$, then $a - c \neq 0$; that is $a \neq c$.

3 Make x the subject.

a $bx + c = dx + 3$

b $ax + d = 3x + c$

c $px - r = qx + z$

d $rx - t = 4 - px$

e $3x + b = t - qx$

f $b - x = c + dx$

● EXAMPLE 3

Make y the subject.

a $a = \dfrac{5}{y}$

b $\dfrac{b}{y} = \dfrac{y}{c}$

	Solve	Think	Apply
a	$a = \dfrac{5}{y}$ $ay = 5$ $y = \dfrac{5}{a}$	Multiply both sides by y then solve.	*Note: $a \neq 0$.* ❗
b	$\dfrac{b}{y} = \dfrac{y}{c}$ $y^2 = bc$ $y = \pm\sqrt{bc}$	Multiply both sides by y and c then rearrange.	We cannot find the square root of a negative number. The values under the square root must be positive. *Note: $bc \geqslant 0$.* ❗

4 Make y the subject.

a $t = \dfrac{x}{y}$

b $\dfrac{b}{y} = c$

c $\dfrac{5}{b} = \dfrac{7}{y}$

d $\dfrac{y}{x} = \dfrac{z}{y}$

e $\dfrac{r}{y} = \dfrac{y}{s}$

f $\dfrac{p}{y} = \dfrac{y}{2q}$

g $\dfrac{y}{t} = \dfrac{a + z}{y}$

h $\dfrac{3y}{z} = \dfrac{p}{y}$

i $\dfrac{z}{y} = \dfrac{3y}{p + q}$

5 Make z the subject.

a $az + bx = d$

b $\dfrac{8}{z} = \dfrac{x}{y}$

c $\dfrac{3}{z} = \dfrac{z}{y}$

d $xz + by = cz - d$

e $4 = y - xz$

f $\dfrac{m}{z} = \dfrac{z}{p - q}$

g $4 - z = p$

h $pz + e = d - rz$

i $\dfrac{z}{4} = \dfrac{x + y}{z}$

● EXAMPLE 4

a Make u the subject of $v^2 = u^2 + 2as$.

b Make a the subject of $P = \dfrac{c}{x - a}$.

	Solve	Think	Apply
a	$v^2 = u^2 + 2as$ $u^2 + 2as = v^2$ $u^2 = v^2 - 2as$ $u = \pm\sqrt{v^2 - 2as};\ v^2 \geqslant 2as$	Swap sides. Subtract $2as$ from both sides. Take the square root of both sides.	Check for zero in the denominator or a negative under the square root. Note $v^2 - 2as$ must be $\geqslant 0$ for $\sqrt{v^2 - 2as}$ to exist.
b	$P = \dfrac{c}{x - a};\ x \neq a$ $P(x - a) = c$ $Px - Pa = c$ $-Pa = c - Px$ $Pa = Px - c$ $a = \dfrac{Px - c}{P};\ P \neq 0$	Multiply both sides by $(x - a)$. Expand and rearrange. Subtract Px from both sides.	

---

6 a Make b the subject of $V = Ibh$.

b Make a the subject of $F = ma$.

c Make h the subject of $A = \frac{1}{2}bh$.

d Make R the subject of $I = \dfrac{PRN}{100}$.

e Make y the subject of $P = \frac{1}{2}h(x + y)$.

f Make r the subject of $C = 2\pi r$.

g Make c the subject of $E = mc^2$.

h Make h the subject of $A = \pi r^2 + 2\pi rh$.

i Make d the subject of $T = a + (n - 1)d$.

j Make r the subject of $S = \dfrac{a}{1 - r}$.

k Make v the subject of $E = \frac{1}{2}mv^2$.

l Make a the subject of $s = ut + \frac{1}{2}at^2$.

m Make a the subject of $v^2 = u^2 + 2as$.

n Make x the subject of $y = 3x^2$.

o Make d the subject of $S = \frac{n}{2}(2a + (n - 1)d)$.

Language in mathematics

1. Complete these glossary terms by inserting the vowels.

   a. _q _ _ t _ _ n

   b. q _ _ dr _ t _ c

   c. s _ l _ t _ _ n

   d. s _ m _ lt _ n _ _ _ s

2. Rearrange these words to form a sentence.

   a. have solution one equations Linear

   b. can Quadratic solutions two have equations

   c. simultaneous substitution equations solved Non-linear must be by

3. Use every third letter to complete a sentence.

   A S Q E D U R T A Y Y D G B R N E A A S T E I I O I C H G E C D Q V G U H T A
   U J T I O I A E O Z X N Z W S E R C T Y A U I N O D B E T E I T S U T O O T L
   A T V A T E E S D E F B E G Y E H F E K A E L C E W T E Q O E A R A D I A F S
   A G I A H N A T G E E C A A O C V M G H P O P L P O E Q W T S E I T E N F V G
   C G T H I H O P E L K S J Y Q F S U A E A T E R C T E B E A T N N Y M D U K T
   E C H W S E A S Q Z D U F T A Q U D A R R I O A C E T C T I C U C R V F A D O
   C I R P B M W C U R T L U J A M A I E T F I O T I T H I E E I S Q I W U S I A
   I S D H T R O O A E E T C R I T H C E E F A A O T T R I I M H G U N R L N E A
   N E I D G S E T U S S S E F E S S D A R A T H N T T D S S T E E H O O E L Y R
   V R E A S I C E S T H N N E O X E S S Q U A R R A T D A Y T A H H H R E H E N
   D F T B N H C E E F T Q Y H U J I A K X D W A R D R A G T T Y U I O I C C C C
   C C O A A U O O L L I D A S H H R A G D V A T E J E B I R E F H E A F N R G F
   E R A E T C T R T T U O O I R I O I Y R S S S E E E D

Terms

algebra	discriminant	equation	expression	factor
factorising	fraction	linear	literal equation	non-linear
quadratic	quadratic equation	quadratic formula	simultaneous equation	solution
substitution	value	variable		

Check your skills

1. The solution to $\dfrac{3x - 2}{5} = \dfrac{3x}{2}$ is:

   A $x = -\dfrac{2}{9}$ **B** $x = -\dfrac{4}{9}$ **C** $x = \dfrac{2}{9}$ **D** $x = -\dfrac{2}{21}$

2. The solution to $\dfrac{3x - 5}{2} - \dfrac{4 - 2x}{3} = -4$ is:

   A $x = \dfrac{43}{5}$ **B** $x = \dfrac{43}{13}$ **C** $x = -\dfrac{1}{13}$ **D** $x = \dfrac{3}{5}$

3. The expansion of $(x + 5)^2$ is:

   A $x^2 - 25$ **B** $x^2 + 25$ **C** $x^2 + 5x + 25$ **D** $x^2 + 10x + 25$

4. The expansion of $(3x - 2)^2$ is:

   A $3x^2 - 4$ **B** $9x^2 - 6x + 4$ **C** $9x^2 - 12x + 4$ **D** $9x^2 - 4$

5 The expansion of $(x - 3)(x + 3)$ is:

A $x^2 + 9$

B $x^2 - 9$

C $x^2 + 3x + 9$

D $x^2 - 6x + 9$

6 The expansion of $(5 - x)(5 + x)$ is:

A $x^2 - 25$

B $25 - x^2$

C $25 - 10x + x^2$

D $25 - 5x + x^2$

7 The number needed to complete the square of $x^2 - 3x$ is:

A $\frac{3}{2}$

B $\frac{9}{4}$

C $\frac{81}{10}$

D any number

8 When factorised $d^2 - a^2$ is:

A $(d - a)(d - a)$

B $(d - a)(d + a)$

C $(d - a)^2$

D $d^2 - 2ad + d^2$

9 When factorised $x^2 + x - 12$ is:

A $(x - 4)(x + 3)$

B $(x + 4)(x - 3)$

C $(x - 6)(x + 2)$

D $(x + 6)(x - 2)$

10 When factorised $10x^2 - 17x + 3$ is:

A $(5x + 3)(2x + 1)$

B $(5x + 1)(2x + 3)$

C $(5x - 1)(2x + 3)$

D $(5x - 1)(2x - 3)$

11 The solutions of $5x^2 = 9$ are:

A $x = \pm\dfrac{3}{\sqrt{5}}$

B $x = \pm\dfrac{\sqrt{3}}{5}$

C $x = \pm\sqrt{9}$

D $x = \pm\sqrt{45}$

12 The solutions of $3x^2 - 9x = 0$ are:

A 0 and 3

B 0 and -3

C 0 and 9

D -3 and 9

13 The solutions of $x^2 - 7x - 18 = 0$ are:

A -9 and 2

B 9 and -2

C 6 and -3

D -6 and 3

14 The solutions of $3x^2 - 7x + 4 = 0$ are:

A 1 and 4

B -1 and -4

C -1 and $-\frac{4}{3}$

D 1 and $\frac{4}{3}$

15 The solutions to $\dfrac{x^2 - 12}{x} = -4$ are:

A -6 or 2

B 6 or -2

C 0 or $\sqrt{12}$

D -4 or -3

16 The constant term that needs to be added to solve $x^2 - 4x - 2 = 0$ by completing the square is:

A 2

B 16

C 4

D 8

17 The solutions to $x^2 + 5x + 3 = 0$ are:

A $\dfrac{-5 \pm \sqrt{13}}{2}$

B $\dfrac{5 \pm \sqrt{13}}{2}$

C $\dfrac{-5 \pm \sqrt{37}}{2}$

D $\dfrac{5 \pm \sqrt{37}}{2}$

18 The solutions to $3x^2 + 3x - 7 = 0$ are:

A $\dfrac{3 + \sqrt{93}}{6}$

B $\dfrac{-3 \pm \sqrt{93}}{6}$

C $\dfrac{3 \pm \sqrt{93}}{3}$

D $\dfrac{3 \pm \sqrt{93}}{3}$

19 Four times a number squared is 8 more than fourteen times the number. The quadratic equation to find the number is:

A $4x^2 + 14x + 8 = 0$ **B** $x^2 - 14x + 8 = 0$

C $x^2 + 14x - 8 = 0$ **D** $4x^2 - 14x - 8 = 0$

20 The solutions to $x^4 - 29x^2 + 100$ are:

A $x = 4$ and 25 only   **B** $x = \pm 4$ and ± 25

C $x = \pm 2$ and ± 5 **D** $x = \pm 2$ only

21 The quadratic equation that must be used to solve $y = 3x^2 - 2x - 14$ and $y = 4x - 13$ is:

A $3x^2 - 6x - 1 = 0$ **B** $3x^2 + 6x + 27 = 0$

C $3x^2 + 6x - 1 = 0$ **D** $3x^2 - 6x - 27 = 0$

22 The solution to $5x^3 = 8$ is:

A $x = \dfrac{2}{\sqrt[3]{5}}$ **B** $x = \pm\dfrac{2}{\sqrt[3]{5}}$ **C** $x = \dfrac{8}{5}$ **D** $x = \pm\dfrac{8}{5}$

23 When $r + xy + t = 0$ is rearranged to make x the subject, the result is:

A $x = \dfrac{t - r}{y}$ **B** $x = \dfrac{-r - t}{y}$ **C** $x = \dfrac{r + t}{y}$ **D** $y = \dfrac{t - r}{x}$

24 When y is made the subject of $P = \frac{1}{3}h(x + y)$, the result is:

A $y = P - \frac{1}{3}hx$ **B** $y = \dfrac{3P}{h} - x$ **C** $y = \dfrac{3P - x}{h}$ **D** $y = \dfrac{P - \frac{1}{3}h}{x}$

If you have any difficulty with these questions, refer to the examples and questions in the sections listed in the table.

Question	1–2	3–10	11–15	16	17–18	19	20	21	22	23, 24
Section	A	B	C	D	E	F	G	H	I	J

10A   Review set

1 Solve:

a $x - 2 = 5 - 3x$ **b** $4(x - 5) - 3(x + 1) = 7$

c $\dfrac{3x - 2}{5} = \dfrac{4x}{3}$ **d** $\dfrac{2x - 5}{3} - \dfrac{x - 4}{2} = -3$

2 When a number is subtracted from 15 the result is 4 more than the number. Find the number.

3 Expand and simplify where possible.

a $(x - 3)^2$ **b** $(5x - 7)^2$ **c** $(x + 2)(x - 2)$

4 What number needs to be added to $x^2 - 9x$ to complete the square?

5 Factorise:

a $x^2 - 9$ **b** $a^2 - r^2$ **c** $25y^2 - 16n^2$

d $x^2 - 5x + 6$ **e** $x^2 + 3x - 10$ **f** $5x^2 - 8x + 3$

6 Solve:

a $x^2 + 20x + 36 = 0$ **b** $3x^2 - 5x - 3 = 0$ **c** $8x^3 = 27$

7 When the square of a number is decreased by 20 the result is eight times the number. Find the number.

8 Solve simultaneously $y = x^2 - 5x - 15$ and $y = 3x + 5$.

9 Solve $x^4 - 5x^2 + 6 = 0$.

10 Make x the subject.
    a $y = mx + b$ **b** $r - qx = px + t$

11 Make y the subject of $A = \dfrac{h}{2}(x + y)$.

10B   Review set

1 Solve:
    a $3x - 5 = 7x + 1$ **b** $3(x - 3) - 4(5 - 2x) = 9$
    c $\dfrac{1 - 5x}{3} = \dfrac{2x + 1}{5}$ **d** $\dfrac{4x - 5}{3} - \dfrac{2x + 1}{2} = -3$

2 Expand and simplify where possible.
    a $(2x + 1)^2$ **b** $(x - 5)(x + 5)$ **c** $(5x - 11)(5x + 11)$

3 Factorise:
    a $x^2 - 81$ **b** $p^2 - q^2$ **c** $64n^2 - 25y^2$
    d $x^2 - 9x + 8$ **e** $x^2 + 3x - 18$ **f** $6x^2 - x - 15$

4 Solve $7x^3 = 125$.

5 Solve by completing the square $x^2 + 4x - 2 = 0$.

6 Solve:
    a $x^2 + x - 20 = 0$ **b** $5x^2 - 3x - 7 = 0$ **c** $\dfrac{x^2 - 5}{x} = 4$

7 Solve simultaneously $y = x^2 + 15x + 13$ and $y = 3x - 7$.

8 Solve $x^4 - 12x^2 + 11 = 0$.

9 Make x the subject of:
    a $3 + rx = a + b$ **b** $\dfrac{p}{x} = \dfrac{x}{r}$

10C   Review set

1 Solve:
    a $5 - 2x = 7 + 5x$ **b** $7(2x - 5) + 3(1 - 5x) = 0$
    c $\dfrac{2x + 1}{4} = \dfrac{5x - 1}{3}$ **d** $\dfrac{3x - 7}{5} - \dfrac{4x - 1}{2} = -3$

2 Expand and simplify where possible.
    a $(x + 5)^2$ **b** $(7x - 4)^2$ **c** $(3x + 2)(3x - 2)$

3 What number needs to be added to $x^2 + 4x$ to complete the square?

4 Factorise:

   a $9 - a^2$
               b $r^2 - t^2$
               c $x^2 + 6x + 9$

   d $x^2 + 2x - 15$
         e $2x^2 + 15x - 8$
         f $5x^2 + 11x + 2$

5 Solve:

   a $6x^2 + 7x - 5 = 0$
                         b $3x^2 - 5x - 1 = 0$

6 Twice a number squared is 15 more than the number. Find the number.

7 Solve simultaneously $y = 3x^2 + 8x - 10$ and $y = 2x - 1$.

8 Solve $125x^3 = -8$.

9 Make x the subject of:

   a $b + cx = y$
                         b $cx + d = ex - 5$

10 Make R the subject of $A = \pi(R^2 - r^2)$.

10D   Review set

1 Solve:

   a $4x - 5 = 7x - 4$
                       b $3(4x - 5) - 2 = 5(1 - 7x)$

   c $\dfrac{4 - 2x}{5} = \dfrac{3x - 5}{7}$
               d $\dfrac{4x - 2}{5} - \dfrac{3x + 1}{2} = -7$

2 Solve $8x^3 = 27$.

3 Expand, writing the answer in simplest form.

   a $(7 - 3x)^2$
             b $(4 - x)(4 + x)$
           c $(8x - 3)(3 + 8x)$

4 Factorise:

   a $16 - x^2$
              b $r^2 - t^2$
               c $81n^2 - 49t^2$

   d $x^2 + 8x + 15$
         e $x^2 - 8x - 20$
         f $8x^2 - 10x + 3$

5 Solve $x^4 - 5x^2 + 4 = 0$.

6 Solve by completing the square $x^2 - 6x - 4 = 0$.

7 Solve:

   a $x^2 - 7x + 12 = 0$
          b $4x^2 - 7x + 1 = 0$
         c $3x^2 - 8 = -2x$

8 Solve simultaneously $y = 2x^2 + 8x + 9$ and $y = 5x + 8$.

9 Make x the subject of:

   a $p + qx = a - by$
                   b $a - x = b + dx$

11

Further trigonometry

This chapter deals with Pythagoras' theorem in three-dimensional space, and angles of any magnitude.

At the end of this chapter you should be able to:

- ▶ solve problems involving the lengths of edges and diagonals in three-dimensional objects
- ▶ solve problems involving right-angled triangles in three dimensions with and without a given diagram
- ▶ graph and compare trigonometric curves

- ▶ use the unit circle
- ▶ investigate graphs of sine, cosine and tangent functions for angles of any magnitude
- ▶ use $\sin A = \sin (180° - A)$, $\cos A = -\cos (180° - A)$ and $\tan A = -\tan (180° - A)$, where $0° \leqslant A \leqslant 90°$.

NSW Syllabus references: 5.3 M&G Trigonometry and Pythagoras' theorem
Outcomes: MA5.3-1WM, MA5.3-2WM, MA5.3-3WM, MA5.3-15MG
Measurement & geometry – ACMMG274, ACMMG276

Diagnostic test

1 The tangent ratio is the ratio of:

A $\dfrac{\text{adjacent}}{\text{hypotenuse}}$
B $\dfrac{\text{opposite}}{\text{adjacent}}$

C $\dfrac{\text{adjacent}}{\text{opposite}}$
D $\dfrac{\text{opposite}}{\text{hypotenuse}}$

2 In this triangle $\sin \theta$ is:

A $\dfrac{12}{9}$ **B** $\dfrac{9}{12}$

C $\dfrac{9}{15}$ **D** $\dfrac{12}{15}$

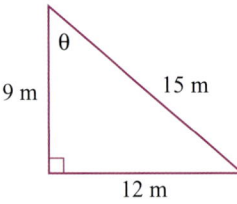

3 Correct to 4 decimal places, $\tan 53°18'$ is:

A 0.5976   **B** 0.8018
C 0.6018   **D** 1.3416

4 If $\cos \theta = \frac{5}{7}$ then, to the nearest minute, $\theta =$

A 44°25'   **B** 44°24'
C 45°35'   **D** 45°36'

5 In the triangle, to the nearest minute, $\theta =$

A 38°29'
B 38°30'
C 38°3'
D 51°30'

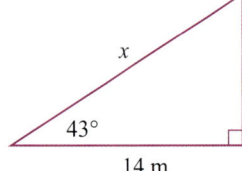

6 To 1 decimal place, $x =$

A 20.5 m
B 19.1 m
C 19.2 m
D 15.0 m

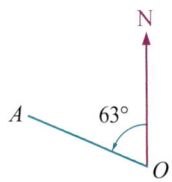

7 The true bearing of A from O in the diagram is:

A 063°T
B 117°T
C 297°T
D 63°N

8 A ship sails 57 km from a port A on a bearing of 298°T. The distance the ship is west of its starting point is:

A 50.3 km   **B** 64.6 km
C 107.2 km   **D** 121.4 km

9 A town X is 73 km east and 113 km south of town Y. The bearing of X from Y is closest to:

A 32°52'   **B** 57°8'
C 122°52'   **D** 147°8'T

10 When $\sin \theta = 0.3842$, the value of θ is closest to:

A 157°24'   **B** 67°24'
C 21°1'   **D** none of these

11 The exact value of x in this triangle is:

A $\dfrac{\sqrt{3}}{2}$ m

B $4\sqrt{3}$ m

C 4 m

D $4\sqrt{2}$ m

12 The area of this triangle is closest to:

A 6.1 km²
B 17.3 km²
C 12.0 km²
D 14.1 km²

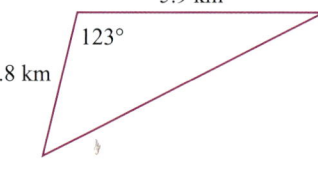

13 The length of AC is closest to:

A 9.6 cm
B 33.6 cm
C 8.7 cm
D 37.3 cm

14 The value of θ in this triangle is closest to:

A 2°47'
B 11°46'
C 29°57'
D 78°14'

15 The value of x is closest to:

A 427 cm
B 20.7 cm
C 16.8 cm
D 11.3 cm

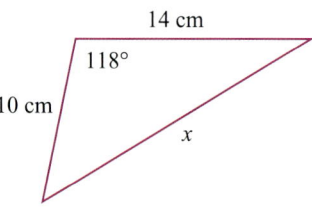

16 The value of θ is closest to:

A 36°51′

B 51°48′

C 81°6′

D 128°12′

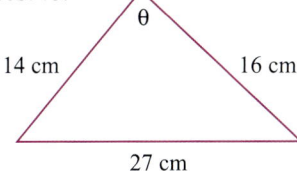

18 The size of ∠*BAC* is:

A 30°   B 70°   C 42°   D 48°

19 The bearing of the ship from its starting point is:

A 90°T   B 102°T

C 108°T   D 130°T

The following description and diagram refer to questions **17** to **19**.

A ship sails 85 km from *A* to *B* on a bearing of 060°T. It then turns and sails 120 km to *C* on a bearing of 130°T.

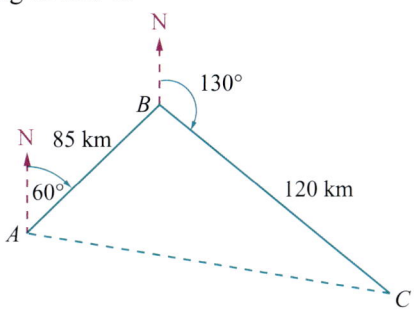

This diagram refers to questions **20** and **21**.

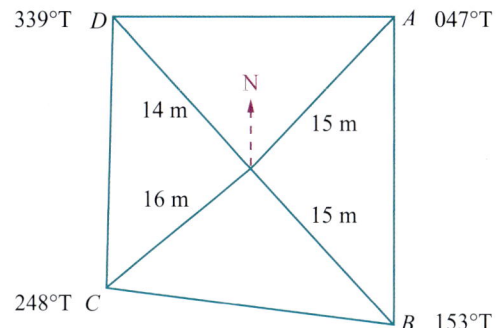

17 The size of ∠*ABC* and the distance of the ship from the starting point are:

A 110°, 169 km   B 110°, 28 602 km

C 170°, 204 km   D 170°, 41 715 km

20 The perimeter of this field is closest to:

A 83 m   B 84 m

C 85 m   D 43 m

21 The area of this field is closest to:

A 1748 m²   B 437 m²

C 438 m²   D 439 m²

The diagnostic test questions refer to outcomes ACMMG223, ACMMG224 and ACMMG241.

A   Three-dimensional objects

● EXAMPLE 1

This rectangular prism has side lengths 2 cm, 3 cm and 5 cm, as shown in the diagram. Calculate the length of *AC* and hence the length of *AF* in surd form.

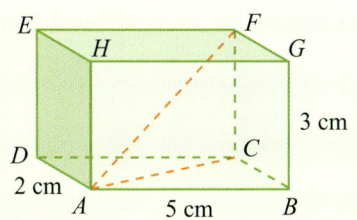

Solve	Think	Apply
$AC^2 = 5^2 + 2^2 = 29$ $AC = \sqrt{29}$ $AF^2 = AC^2 + FC^2$ $\quad = (\sqrt{29})^2 + 3^2$ $\quad = 29 + 9 = 38$ $AF = \sqrt{38}$ cm	$\triangle ABC$ is right angled at B. $AC^2 = AB^2 + BC^2$ $\triangle ACF$ is right angled at C. $AC = \sqrt{29}, FC = 3$	Identify the right angles and then apply Pythagoras' theorem in each right-angled triangle.

1 A rectangular prism has side lengths 3 cm, 4 cm and 8 cm. Calculate the length of *DB* and hence the length of *EB* in surd form.

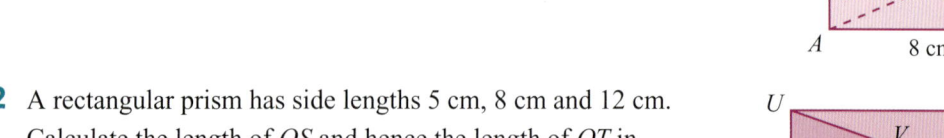

2 A rectangular prism has side lengths 5 cm, 8 cm and 12 cm. Calculate the length of *QS* and hence the length of *QT* in surd form.

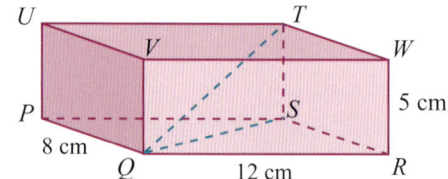

3 A rectangular prism has side lengths 5 cm, 7 cm and 10 cm. Calculate the length *EB* in surd form.

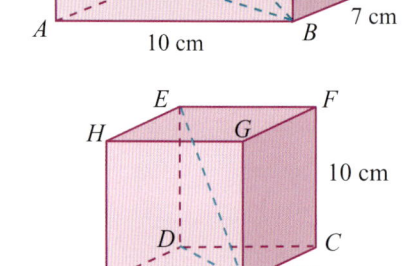

4 A cube has side length 10 cm. Calculate the length *EB* in surd form.

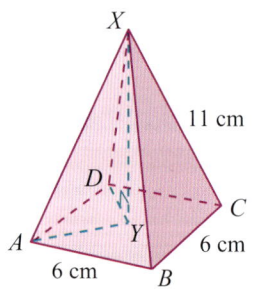

5 A square pyramid has square base *ABCD* with side length 6 cm. The lengths *AX*, *BX*, *CX* and *DX* are 11 cm each.
a Calculate length *AC* in surd form.
b Given that $AY = \frac{1}{2}AC$, calculate *XY* in surd form.

6 A square pyramid has base *ABCD* with side lengths 10 cm. The lengths *AX*, *BX*, *CX* and *DX* are each 15 cm. Calculate *XY* in surd form.

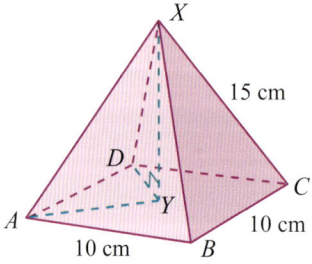

7 A triangular prism is shown.

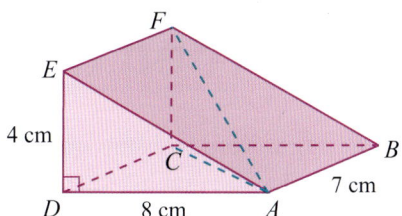

   a Calculate length AC in surd form.

   b Calculate length AF in surd form.

8 A triangular prism is shown. Calculate length AF in surd form.

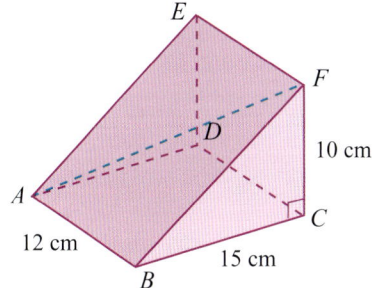

● **EXAMPLE 2**

The rectangular prism has dimensions 5 cm, 8 cm and 11 cm, as shown in the diagram.

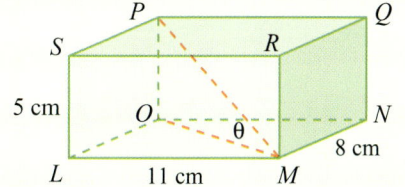

   a Calculate length OM.

   b Calculate, θ, the angle between the line PM and the plane $LMNO$.

	Solve	Think	Apply
a	$OM^2 = 8^2 + 11^2 = 185$ $OM = \sqrt{185}$ cm	Use Pythagoras' theorem in $\triangle OLM$.	Divide the solid into right-angled triangles and use Pythagoras' theorem or trigonometry.
b	$\tan \theta = \dfrac{5}{\sqrt{185}}$ $\theta = 20°11'$	In $\triangle OMP$, relative to θ: opposite side = 5 cm adjacent side = $\sqrt{185}$ cm	

---

9 This rectangular prism has side lengths 4 cm, 7 cm and 12 cm as shown.

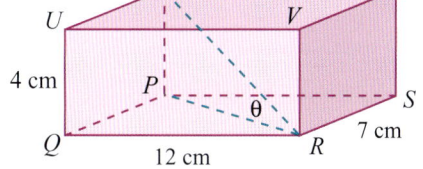

   a Calculate the length PR.

   b Calculate, θ, the angle between the line RT and the plane $PQRS$.

10 A triangular prism is shown.

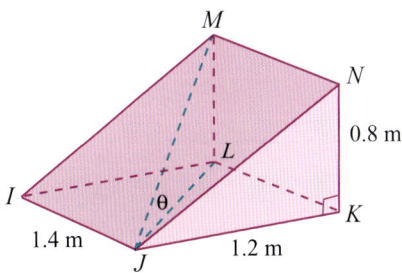

   a Calculate the length JL.

   b Calculate the angle JM makes with the plane $IJKL$.

11 Calculate $\angle TQS$ for the rectangular prism in question **2**.

12 a Calculate $\angle DBE$ for the cube in question **4**.

   b Is this angle the same for all cubes? Explain.

13 Calculate $\angle XAY$ for the square pyramid in question **6**.

14 Calculate $\angle FAC$ for the triangular prism in question **8**.

MEASUREMENT & GEOMETRY

B Worded three-dimensional problems

When solving worded problems it is essential to first draw a diagram showing all the information. It may be necessary to perform multiple calculations to answer the question.

● EXAMPLE 1

From a point X due south of the top of a tower 150 m tall on level ground, the angle of elevation of the top of the tower is 28°. From a point Y due east of the tower, the angle of elevation of the top of the tower is 33°, as shown in the diagram. Calculate the distance XY to the nearest metre.

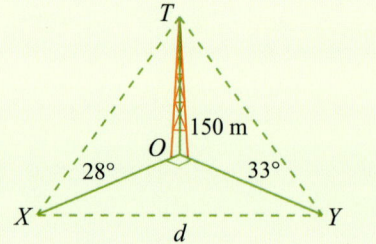

Solve	Think	Apply
$\tan 28° = \dfrac{150}{OX}$ $OX = \dfrac{150}{\tan 28°} = 282.11$ m $\tan 33° = \dfrac{150}{OY}$ $OY = \dfrac{150}{\tan 33°} = 230.98$ m $XY^2 = (282.11)^2 + (230.98)^2$ $XY = 365$ m	Find distance OX using trigonometry in $\triangle XOT$. Find distance OY using trigonometry in $\triangle YOT$. Use Pythagoras' rule in $\triangle XOY$. *Note:* South and east are perpendicular.	Separate the triangles that involve the top of the object from the triangle on the ground. Sometimes the right angles do not look accurate, so check the information and label any right angles on the diagram.

Exercise 11B

1 From a point X due south of a tower 200 m tall on level ground, the angle of elevation of the top of the tower is 41°. From a point Y due east of the tower, the angle of elevation of the top of the tower is 37°, as shown in the diagram. Calculate the distance XY to the nearest metre.

2 From a point X due south of a tower 180 m tall on level ground, the angle of elevation of the top of the tower is 18°. From a point Y east of the tower, the angle of elevation of the top of the tower is 23°, as shown in the diagram. Calculate the distance XY to the nearest metre.

3 From a point A due north of a flagpole 80 m tall on level ground, the angle of elevation of the top of the flagpole is 38°. From a point B due west of the flagpole, the angle of elevation of the top of the flagpole is 47°.
   a Complete the diagram.
   b Calculate the distance AB to the nearest metre.

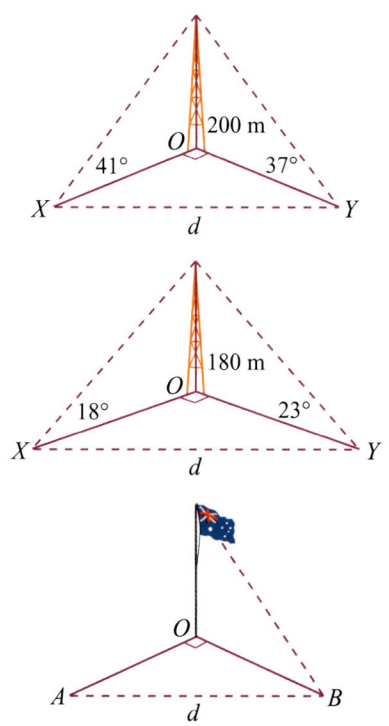

MEASUREMENT & GEOMETRY

4 From a point C due north of a tree 120 m tall on level ground, the angle of elevation of the top of the tree is 51°. From the point D due east of the tree, the angle of elevation of the top of the tree is 37°.

   a Draw a diagram showing this information.

   b Calculate the distance CD to the nearest metre.

5 **a** Two boats at sea are both observing the same lighthouse, which is at a height of 220 m above sea level. From boat A the bearing of the lighthouse is 040°T and the angle of elevation is 12°. From boat B the bearing of the lighthouse is 310°T and the angle of elevation is 17°. Complete this diagram.

   b Show that $\angle AOB$ is 90°.

   c Calculate the distances OA and OB and hence the distance AB.

   d Calculate $\angle OAB$ and hence the bearing of boat B from boat A.

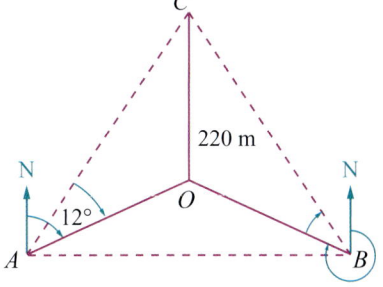

6 Two boats at sea are both observing the same lighthouse, which is at a height of 520 m above sea level. From boat A the bearing of the lighthouse is 067°T and the angle of elevation is 15°. From boat B the bearing of the lighthouse is 337°T and the angle of elevation is 9°.

   a Calculate the distance between the boats.

   b Calculate the bearing of boat B from boat A.

7 Two boats are observed from a lighthouse 350 m above sea level. Boat X is on a bearing of 138°T and at an angle of depression of 23°. Boat Y is on a bearing of 228°T and at an angle of depression of 16°.

   a Draw a diagram showing this information.

   b Calculate the distance between boat X and boat Y.

   c Calculate the bearing of boat Y from boat X.

Extension

8 Two boats at sea are observing the same lighthouse, which is at a height of 370 m above sea level. From the lighthouse, the bearing of boat A is 121°T and the bearing of boat B is 237°T. The angle of elevation of the lighthouse from boat A is 17° and from boat B is 21°.

   a Draw a diagram showing this information.

   b Calculate the distances of each boat from the foot of the lighthouse.

   c Use the cosine rule to calculate the distance between the two boats.

   d Calculate the bearing of boat B from boat A.

9 A surveyor, S, standing on the bank of a river is directly opposite the base, B, of a tree BT of height h m. From a point R, 11 m upstream from S, the angle of elevation of the top of the tree is 27°. From a point P, 18 m downstream from S, the angle of elevation of the top of the tree is 23°. Given that the tree is on the edge of the river and that PSR is a straight line, calculate the width w m of the river.

Investigation 1 Trigonometry and the number plane

1 This diagram shows a straight line passing through the origin with a right-angled triangle drawn to it.

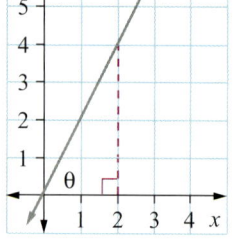

   a Use the diagram to find the gradient of the line.
   b From the diagram, write an expression for tan θ.
   c What do you notice about the expression for tan θ and the gradient?
   d Given the symbol for gradient is *m*, complete *m* = ___ θ.
   e Find the value of θ.

2 Use this diagram to answer the questions.

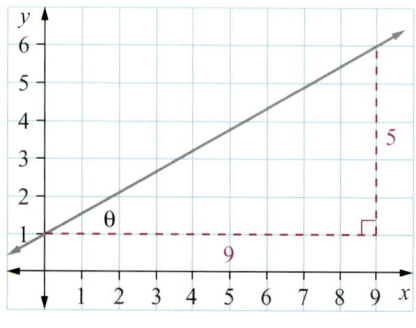

   a What is the gradient of the line?
   b Find an expression for tan θ.
   c Find the value of θ to the nearest minute.
   d Complete: The angle made by a line and the *x*-axis can be found using ____.

3 Find the angle these lines make with the axis.
   a $y = 5x - 2$
   b $y = \frac{1}{2}x$
   c $y = 4x - 1$
   d $y = \frac{1}{3}x - 2$
   e $3x - 5y - 4 = 0$
   f $2x - 7y + 1 = 0$

C Angles greater than 90°

Trigonometry can be extended to non-right-angled triangles. Angles between 0° and 180° will be examined; that is, both acute and obtuse angles will be examined.

Acute angle   Obtuse angle

● EXAMPLE 1

Find the value of the following correct to 4 decimal places.
   a sin 65°
   b cos 173°15′
   c tan 116.6°

	Solve	Think/Apply
a	sin 65° = 0.9063	Check the correct use of your calculator to evaluate trigonometric functions. Usually either 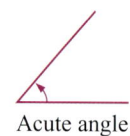 or 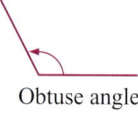 is used for degrees and minutes.
b	cos 173°15′ = −0.9931	
c	tan 116.6° = −1.9970	

Exercise 11C

1 Use a calculator to find these value correct to 4 decimal places.
   a sin 80°
   b cos 121°
   c tan 101°
   d cos 11°15′
   e tan 171.3°
   f cos 144.3°
   g cos 91°12′
   h sin 115°18′
   i cos 135.9°
   j tan 111°11′
   k sin 59°15′
   l tan 175°8′

MEASUREMENT & GEOMETRY

2 a Complete the following table of values for $y = \sin \theta$. Give the values correct to 2 decimal places.

θ	0°	10°	20°	30°	40°	50°	60°	70°	80°	90°
y										

θ	100°	110°	120°	130°	140°	150°	160°	170°	180°
y									

b Plot the points from part **a** to draw the graph of $y = \sin \theta$ for θ between 0° and 180°.

c Look at the values of sin 20° and sin 160°. What do you notice?

d Look at the values of sin 30° and sin 150°. What do you notice?

e Complete: $\sin \theta = \sin (180 - \underline{})$.

3 a Complete the following table of values for $y = \cos \theta$. Give the values correct to 2 decimal places.

θ	0°	10°	20°	30°	40°	50°	60°	70°	80°	90°
y										

θ	100°	110°	120°	130°	140°	150°	160°	170°	180°
y									

b Plot the points from part **a** to draw the graph of $y = \cos \theta$ for θ between 0° and 180°.

c Look at the values of cos 20° and cos 160°. What do you notice?

d Look at the values of cos 30° and cos 150°. What do you notice?

e Complete: $\cos \theta = -\cos (180 - \underline{})$.

EXAMPLE 2

Find the value of θ to the nearest minute.

a $\cos \theta = 0.4312$ **b** $\cos \theta = -0.5318$

c $\sin \theta = 0.2713 \ (0° < \theta < 90°)$ **d** $\sin \theta = 0.2713 \ (90° < \theta < 180°)$

	Solve	Think	Apply
a	$\cos \theta = 0.4312$ $\theta = 64°27'$	The value of cos θ is positive, so the angle is acute.	The three trigonometric ratios sine, cosine and tan are positive for acute angles. Tan and cosine are negative if the angle is obtuse. But sine is positive for both acute and obtuse angles, and further information is required when determining the angle.
b	$\cos \theta = -0.5318$ $\theta = 122°8'$	The value of cos θ is negative, so the angle is obtuse.	
c	$\sin \theta = 0.2713 \ (0° < \theta < 90°)$ $\theta = 15°44'$	The angle is restricted to acute.	
d	$\sin \theta = 0.2713$ $\therefore \theta = 15°44'$ But $90° < \theta < 180°$, so it is obtuse. $\therefore \theta = 180° - 15°44'$ $\quad\ = 164°16'$	The angle is restricted to obtuse, so the acute angle given must be subtracted from 180°.	

4 Find the value of θ. All angles are obtuse.

   a $\cos \theta = -0.9312$ **b** $\cos \theta = -0.4718$ **c** $\sin \theta = 0.4113$

   d $\sin \theta = 0.2771$ **e** $\sin \theta = 0.6643$ **f** $\sin \theta = 0.8118$

Investigation 2 The unit circle

The unit circle is a circle centre (0, 0) with radius 1 unit, as shown in the diagram.

A radius inclined at $\theta°$ to the x-axis is drawn to meet the circle at the point $P(x, y)$. The perpendicular PQ is drawn from the x-axis to P as shown.

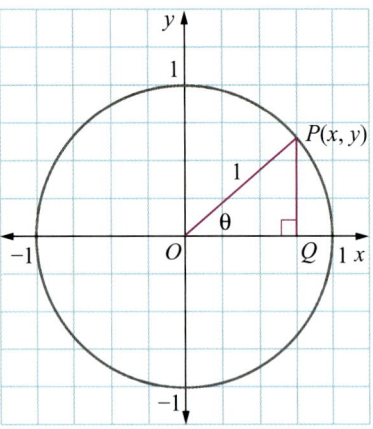

1 The length $PQ = y$ units. What is the length OQ?

2 In $\triangle OPQ$, $\sin \theta = \dfrac{PQ}{OP} = \dfrac{y}{1} = y$.

Complete: In $\triangle OPQ$, $\cos \theta =$ ___ $=$ ___ $=$ ___

Therefore P has coordinates (____, $\sin \theta$).

In quadrant 1, as shown, the coordinates of P are both positive.

A triangle congruent to OPQ is drawn as shown. The quarter circle containing the $\triangle OP'Q'$ is called quadrant 2.

3 Given that the coordinates of P' are $(-x, y)$, use $x = \cos \theta$ and $y = \sin \theta$ to write the coordinates of P' in terms of $\sin \theta$ and $\cos \theta$.

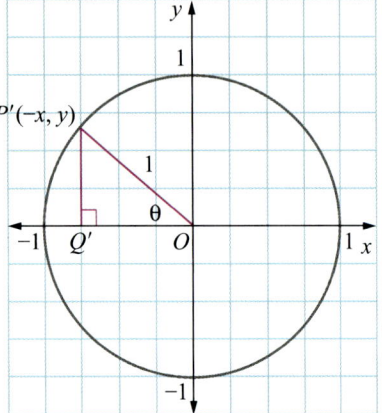

Another triangle congruent to $\triangle OPQ$ is drawn in quadrant 3. Here the coordinates of P'' are $(-x, -y)$.

4 Complete: $\cos \theta =$ ____, $\sin \theta =$ ____.

P'' has coordinates (____, $-\sin \theta$).

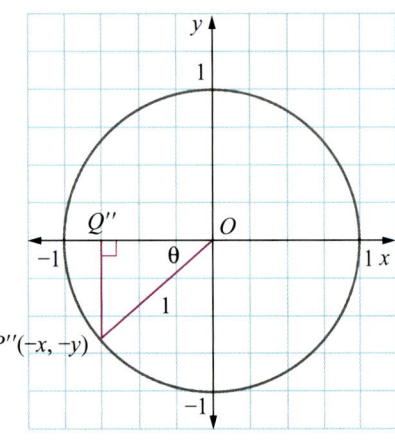

A third triangle congruent to $\triangle OPQ$ is drawn in quadrant 4. Here the coordinates of P''' are $(x, -y)$.

5 Complete: ____ $= y$, $\cos \theta =$ ____.

Therefore P''' has coordinates (____, ____).

D # Trigonometric graphs

The relationships for obtuse angles were examined in Year 9 and in Investigation 2.

Recall that for $0° \leqslant \theta \leqslant 90°$ these were:

$$\sin \theta = \sin (180° - \theta) \qquad \cos \theta = -\cos (180° - \theta) \qquad \tan \theta = -\tan (180° - \theta)$$

Obtuse angles are in quadrant 2 and it was determined that $\sin \theta > 0$ and $\cos \theta < 0$.

Using $\tan \theta = \dfrac{\sin \theta}{\cos \theta}$ it can be determined that in quadrant 2 $\tan \theta < 0$.

This indicates that only the sine ratio is positive in quadrant 2.

Extending this into quadrant 3, where the angle is $(180° + \theta)$, the results are:

$$\sin \theta = -\sin (180° + \theta) \qquad \cos \theta = -\cos (180° + \theta) \qquad \tan \theta = +\tan (180° + \theta)$$

This indicates that only the tan ratio is positive in quadrant 3.

In quadrant 4 the angle is $(360° - \theta)$. The results are:

$$\sin \theta = -\sin (360° - \theta) \qquad \cos \theta = \cos (360° - \theta) \qquad \tan \theta = -\tan (360° - \theta)$$

This indicates that only the cosine ratio is positive in quadrant 4.

These facts are summarised in the quadrant diagram. Remember them using ASTC, which is sometimes given the phrase 'All stations To Central'.

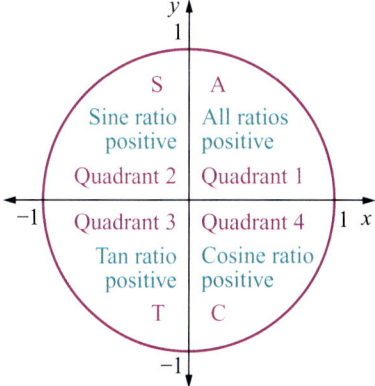

Trigonometric graphs are cyclic. This means that the same graph repeats over and over. The number of degrees needed for one complete cycle is called the period of the graph. The sine graph has a period of 360°.

Exercise 11D

1 a Complete the following table of values for $y = \sin \theta$. Give the values correct to 1 decimal place.

θ	0°	30°	60°	90°	120°	150°	180°	210°	240°	270°	300°	330°	360°
y													

b Plot the points and draw the graph of $y = \sin \theta$ for θ between 0° and 360°.

c Examine the graph for θ between 180° and 270°. What do you notice about all the values of $\sin \theta$ in this range? How does this compare with the expected sign of $\sin \theta$ in quadrant 3?

d For θ between 270° and 360°, what is the sign of $\sin \theta$ and how does this compare with the expected sign of $\sin \theta$ in quadrant 4?

2 a Complete this table of values for $y = \cos \theta$. Write the expected sign of $\cos \theta$ using the ASTC rule first before calculating the values.

θ	0°	30°	60°	90°	120°	150°	180°	210°	240°	270°	300°	330°	360°
y													

b Plot the points and draw the graph of $y = \cos \theta$ for θ between 0° and 360°.

c Compare the graphs of $y = \sin \theta$ and $y = \cos \theta$ and write three similarities and three differences.

3 Complete this table of values for $y = \tan\theta$. Write the expected sign of $\tan\theta$ using the ASTC rule first before calculating the values. Note that there are no values for $\tan 90°$ and $\tan 270°$, as $\cos\theta = 0$ for these values and division by 0 is not permitted. There are asymptotes at these values, similar to hyperbolic graphs.

θ	0°	30°	60°	90°	120°	150°	180°	210°	240°	270°	300°	330°	360°
y													

b Complete the graph of $y = \tan\theta$ by plotting the points between 90° and 360°.

c Compare the graph of $y = \tan\theta$ with the graphs of $y = \sin\theta$ and $y = \cos\theta$. Write three similarities and three differences.

d The part of the graph between 90° and 270° is a complete tan graph, which means the period of the tan graph is 180° (it repeats every 180°). Use this fact to complete the other two parts to draw the graph $y = \tan\theta$ for θ between $-90°$ and 450°.

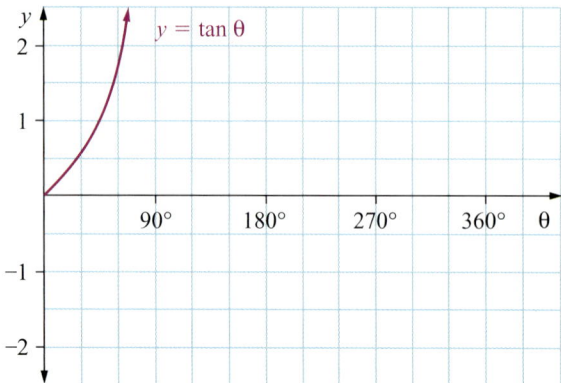

4 a The graph of $y = \sin\theta$ has been drawn for θ between 0° and 720°. Compare this with the graph in question **1**. Describe what you notice.

b The graph of $y = \sin\theta$ repeats every 360°. This is the period of the graph. How many complete sine graphs are there?

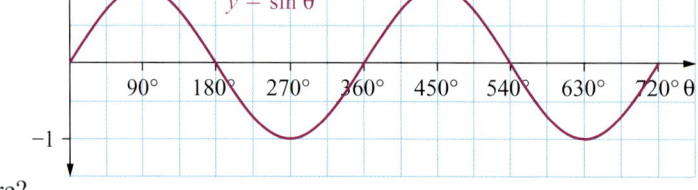

c Without calculating any values, extend the graph of $y = \sin\theta$ to 1080°.

d Without calculating any values, extend the graph of $y = \sin\theta$ to $-360°$.

5 Given that the period of the cosine graph is 360°, draw the graph of $y = \cos\theta$ for values of θ between $-720°$ and 720°.

6 Use the tidal chart to answer the questions below.

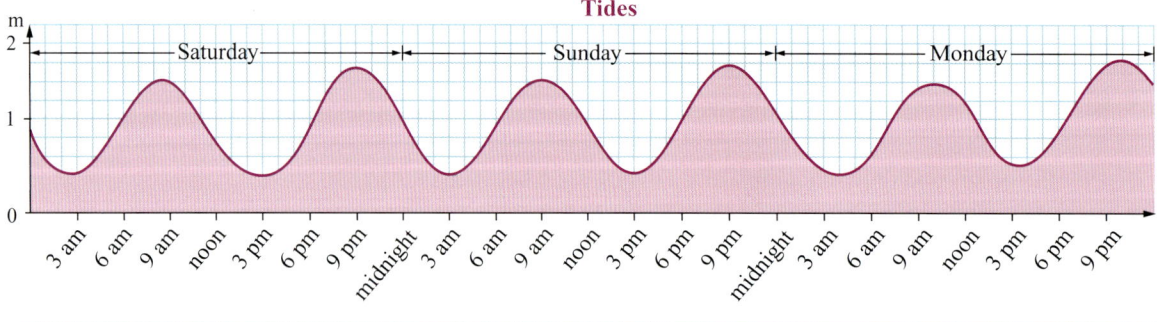

2:30 am	8:34 am	2:40 pm	8:54 pm	3:06 am	9:10 am	3:09 pm	9:26 pm	3:45 am	9:46 am	3:39 am	10:00 pm
0.4 m	1.5 m	0.4 m	1.6 m	0.4 m	1.5 m	0.4 m	1.7 m	0.4 m	1.4 m	0.5 m	1.7 m

Tides information: • Port Stephens: + 5 min • Jervis Bay: + 8 min • Port Hacking: + 8 min

a How many low tides occur each day?

b How many high tides occur each day?

c Which trigonometric graph does the tide chart resemble?

d For Saturday between noon and midnight, what were the lowest and highest values for the tide height?

e What is the approximate period of the tide chart graph?

7 The diagram on the right and the graph below show the motion of a swinging pendulum.

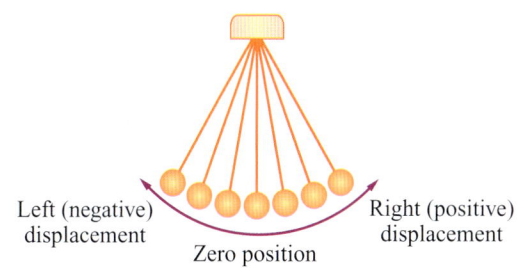

Left (negative) displacement — Zero position — Right (positive) displacement

   a What trigonometric graph does this resemble?

   b What is the period of the graph?

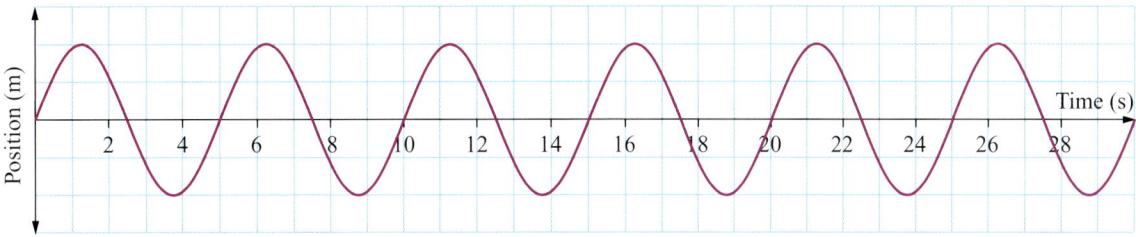

8 The table shows the average monthly temperature for a particular city over 2 years.

Month	Jan	Feb	Mar	Apr	May	Jun	Jul	Aug	Sep	Oct	Nov	Dec
Temperature (°C)	23	22	20	17	12	11	10	11	12	14	18	22

Month	Jan	Feb	Mar	Apr	May	Jun	Jul	Aug	Sep	Oct	Nov	Dec
Temperature (°C)	24	24	22	16	13	11	10	11	13	15	18	21

   a Plot these points or use a spreadsheet to draw a graph displaying this data.

   b Which trigonometric graph does this resemble?

   c What is the period of this graph?

   d What is the difference between the highest and lowest values?

   e Is this city in the Northern Hemisphere or the Southern Hemisphere? Explain.

9 A nocturnal animal is studied over the course of a year. The time that it commences its evening activity on the first day of each month is recorded in the table.

Month	Jan	Feb	Mar	Apr	May	Jun	Jul	Aug	Sep	Oct	Nov	Dec
Time started (h)	2000	1900	1800	1740	1645	1600	1650	1700	1800	1840	1950	2000

   a Plot and draw a smooth graph through the points.

   b Describe the type of graph.

   c What is the period of the graph?

   d What is the difference between the highest and lowest values?

10 The table shows the average monthly temperature for Sydney in 2012 and 2013.

Month	Jan	Feb	Mar	Apr	May	Jun	Jul	Aug	Sep	Oct	Nov	Dec
Temperature (°C)	28	26	24	23	21	17	15	18	21	23	24	26

Month	Jan	Feb	Mar	Apr	May	Jun	Jul	Aug	Sep	Oct	Nov	Dec
Temperature (°C)	28	26	24	23	21	17	15	18	21	23	24	26

  a Plot these points or use a spreadsheet to draw a graph displaying this data.
  b Which trigonometric graph does this resemble?
  c What is the period of this graph?
  d What is the difference between the highest and lowest values?

Investigation 3 Sine and cosine graphs

The unit circle can be used directly to draw the graphs of sine θ and cos θ.

From Investigation 2, and using the unit circle, the coordinates of P, a point on the unit circle, can be expressed as $P(\cos \theta, \sin \theta)$. Using this fact and the unit circle, the graphs of $\sin \theta$ and $\cos \theta$ can be drawn.

$y = \sin \theta$

1 **a** Draw a circle with radius 3 cm. This will be the unit circle.
    b Using a protractor draw angles in increments of 30°, as shown in the diagram. Add the 45° and 135° lines.

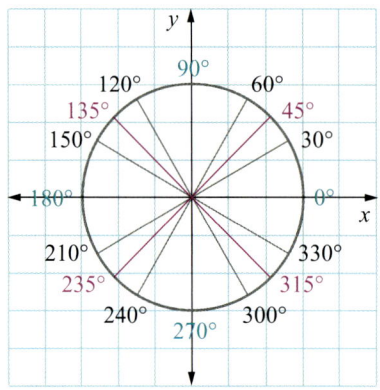

2 Extend the x-axis and mark off the angles on the axis, as shown.

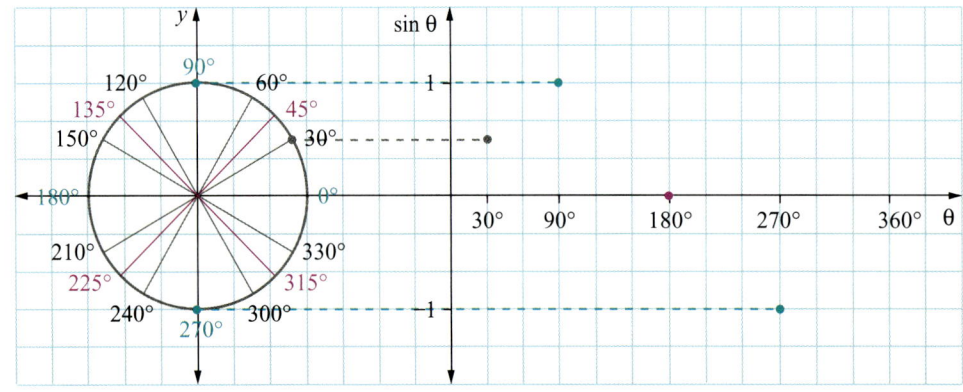

  a Draw a line across at 30° from the circle and intersect that with the 30° mark on the x-axis. This is a point on the graph.
  b Repeat with all the other angles. Some have been done for you.

3 Draw the graph of $y = \sin \theta$.

$y = \cos \theta$

4 The graph of $\cos \theta$ can be drawn in a similar manner using the fact that the x-coordinate of P is equal to $\cos \theta$. Use this diagram to graph $y = \cos \theta$. Some values have been completed for you.

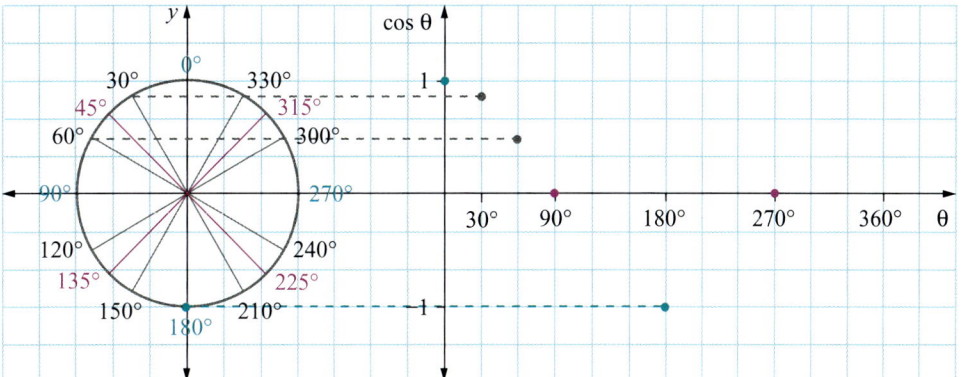

E Using the unit circle

From the previous investigations you would have seen a link between the unit circle and the graphs of $\sin \theta$ and $\cos \theta$. This diagram shows points on a unit circle drawn every 30°.

As the points on the unit circle have the coordinates $(\cos \theta, \sin \theta)$, these values can be used to determine the values of $\cos \theta$ and $\sin \theta$ for any size angle.

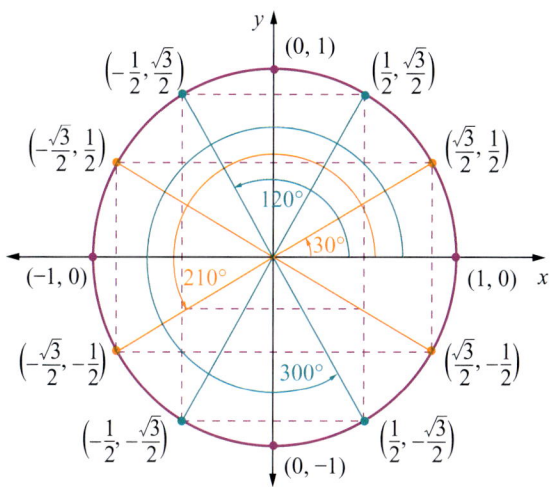

EXAMPLE 1

Use the diagram of the unit circle to find the value of:
a $\sin 210°$ b $\cos 300°$ c $\cos 120°$

	Solve	Think	Apply
a	$\sin 210° = -\dfrac{1}{2}$	Rotate anticlockwise to 210°. The value for $\sin \theta$ is the y-coordinate.	Angles are made in an anticlockwise direction starting at the positive x-axis. Rotate the appropriate number of degrees to find the value of $x = \cos \theta$ and $y = \sin \theta$.
b	$\cos 300° = \dfrac{1}{2}$	Rotate clockwise to 300°. The value for $\cos \theta$ is the x-coordinate.	
c	$\cos 120° = -\dfrac{1}{2}$	Rotate clockwise to 120°. The value for $\cos \theta$ is the x-coordinate.	

1 Use the unit circle diagram to find these values.

   a sin 150°   **b** cos 210°   **c** sin 240°

   d cos 330°   **e** sin 120°   **f** cos 300°

   g sin 60°   **h** cos 30°   **i** sin 330°

● EXAMPLE 2

Use the unit circle diagram to find the values of sin 150° and cos 150°. Hence find the value of tan 150°.

Solve	Think	Apply
$\sin 150° = \dfrac{1}{2}$ $\cos 150° = -\dfrac{\sqrt{3}}{2}$ $\tan 150° = \dfrac{\frac{1}{2}}{-\frac{\sqrt{3}}{2}} = -\dfrac{1}{\sqrt{3}}$	Use the y-coordinate at 150°. Use the x-coordinate at 150°. Use $\tan \theta = \dfrac{\sin \theta}{\cos \theta}$.	To calculate the value of $\tan \theta$, first find $\sin \theta$ and $\cos \theta$. Use $\tan \theta = \dfrac{\sin \theta}{\cos \theta}$.

2 Use the unit circle diagram to find these values.

   a **i** sin 120°   **ii** cos 120°   **iii** tan 120°

   b **i** sin 210°   **ii** cos 210°   **iii** tan 210°

   c **i** sin 300°   **ii** cos 300°   **iii** tan 300°

3 Find these values.

   a tan 150°   **b** tan 240°   **c** tan 330°

● EXAMPLE 3

Use the unit circle diagram to find all the angles between 0° and 360° that have:

   a $\cos \theta = \dfrac{\sqrt{3}}{2}$ **b** $\sin \theta = -\dfrac{1}{2}$

	Solve	Think	Apply
a	$\cos \theta = \dfrac{\sqrt{3}}{2}$ $\theta = 30°$ and 330°	Look on the unit circle for an x-value of $\dfrac{\sqrt{3}}{2}$.	Use the fact that the coordinates on the unit circle are $(\cos \theta, \sin \theta)$ to find the values.
b	$\sin \theta = -\dfrac{1}{2}$ $\theta = 210°$ and 330°	Look on the unit circle for a y-value of $-\dfrac{1}{2}$.	

4 Use the unit circle diagram to find all the angles between 0° and 360° that have:

   a $\sin \theta = \dfrac{1}{2}$ **b** $\cos \theta = -\dfrac{\sqrt{3}}{2}$ **c** $\sin \theta = \dfrac{\sqrt{3}}{2}$

   d $\cos \theta = \dfrac{1}{2}$ **e** $\sin \theta = -\dfrac{\sqrt{3}}{2}$ **f** $\cos \theta = -\dfrac{1}{2}$

Language in mathematics

1 Rearrange these words in sentences.
   a a straight equal gradient to of line is The tan θ
   b one positive in ratio is The quadrants and sine two
   c three quadrants in negative cosine The ratio is two and
   d calculations Three-dimensional ratio usually use the tan problems part as a of the
   e period $y = \sin \theta$ The of graph is 360° the
   f asymptotes of vertical The $y = \tan \theta$ graph has

Terms

acute angle	angle of depression	angle of elevation	bearing	gradient
obtuse angle	period	rectangular prism	surd	trigonometry

Check your skills

Use this diagram to answer questions **1** and **2**.

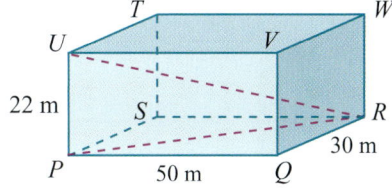

1 The length *PR* is closest to:
   A 80 m   **B** 60 m
   C 40 m   **D** 20 m

2 The length *UR* is closest to:
   A 85 m   **B** 65 m   **C** 45 m   **D** 25 m

3 The angle *PRU* is closest to:
   A 40°   **B** 31°   **C** 25°   **D** 21°

4 From a point *X* due south of a tower 145 m tall on level ground, the angle of elevation of the top of the tower is 38°. From the point *Y* due east of the tower, the angle of elevation of the top of the tower is 33°, as shown in the diagram. The distance *XY* to the nearest metre is:
   A 290 m   **B** 250 m
   C 220 m   **D** 190 m

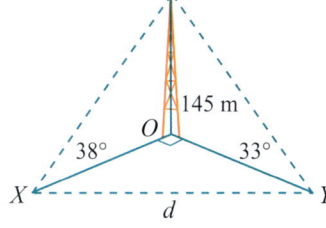

5 cos 130° =
   A sin 130°   **B** cos 50°   **C** −cos 50°   **D** sin 50°

6 The graph of $y = \sin \theta$ is:
   A 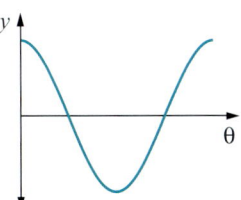   **B** 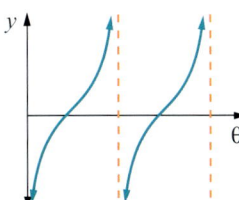   **C** 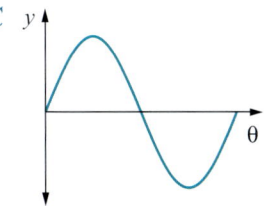   **D** none of these

MEASUREMENT & GEOMETRY

Use the unit circle diagram to answer questions **7** to **10**.

7 The value of sin 210° is:

   A $\frac{1}{2}$ **B** $-\frac{1}{2}$

   C $\frac{\sqrt{3}}{2}$ **D** $-\frac{\sqrt{3}}{2}$

8 The value of cos 330° is:

   A $\frac{1}{2}$ **B** $-\frac{1}{2}$

   C $\frac{\sqrt{3}}{2}$ **D** $-\frac{\sqrt{3}}{2}$

9 The value of tan 150° is:

   A $\frac{1}{\sqrt{3}}$ **B** $-\frac{1}{\sqrt{3}}$

   C $\sqrt{3}$ **D** $-\sqrt{3}$

10 A solution to $\sin\theta = \frac{\sqrt{3}}{2}$ is:

   A 60°   **B** 150°   **C** 240°   **D** 330°

If you have any difficulty with these questions, refer to the examples and questions in the sections listed in the table.

Question	1–3	4	5	6	7–10
Section	A	B	C	D	E

11A   Review set

1 A rectangular prism has side lengths 8 cm, 13 cm and 20 cm. Calculate the length *EB* in surd form.

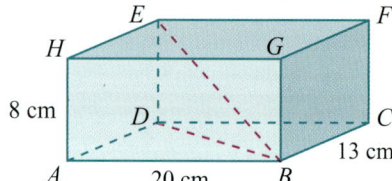

2 A triangular prism is shown.

   a Calculate the length *JL*.

   b Calculate the angle that the line *JM* makes with the plane *IJKL*.

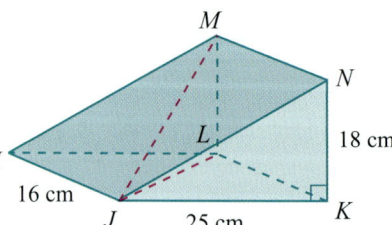

3 From a point *A* due north of a flagpole 130 m tall on level ground, the angle of elevation of the top of the flagpole is 33°. From point *B* due west of the flagpole, the angle of elevation of the top of the flagpole is 42°.

   a Complete the diagram.

   b Calculate the distance *AB*.

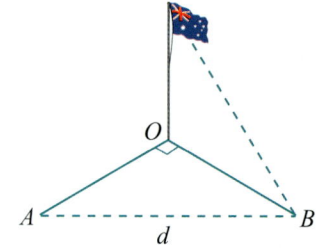

4 Find θ.

   a $\cos θ = -0.8651$ **b** $\sin θ = 0.3318$

5 Draw the graph of $y = \tan θ$ for $-360° \leqslant θ \leqslant 360°$.

6 What is the exact value of $\cos 210°$?

11B   Review set

1 A triangular prism is shown. Calculate length *AF* in surd form.

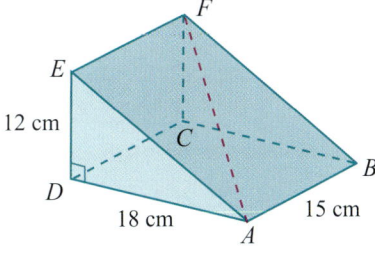

2 A rectangular prism has side lengths 7 cm, 9 cm and 15 cm as shown.

   a Calculate the length *QS*.

   b Calculate, θ, the angle made between the line *US* and the plane *PQRS*.

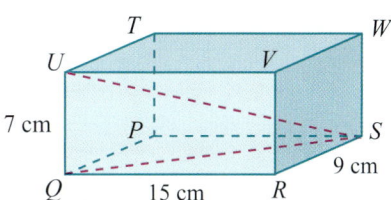

3 From a point *C* due south of a tree, *T*, 70 m tall on level ground, the angle of elevation of the top of the tree is 62°. From a point *D* due east of the tree, the angle of elevation of the top of the tree is 41°.

   a Draw a diagram showing this information.

   b Calculate the distance *CD* to the nearest metre.

4 Calculate the obtuse angle θ for which $\sin θ = 0.3127$.

5 Draw the graph of $y = \sin θ$ for $-360° \leqslant θ \leqslant 360°$.

6 What is the exact value of $\tan 240°$?

11C   Review set

1 A pyramid has square base *ABCD* with side length 8 cm. The lengths *AX*, *BX*, *CX* and *DX* are each 15 cm.

   a Calculate length *AC* in surd form.

   b Given that $AY = \frac{1}{2}AC$, calculate *XY* in surd form.

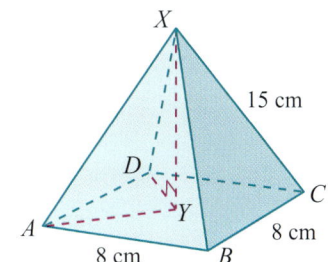

2 A triangular prism is shown.

   a Calculate the length *EC*.

   b Calculate the angle that the line *BE* makes with the plane *EFCD*.

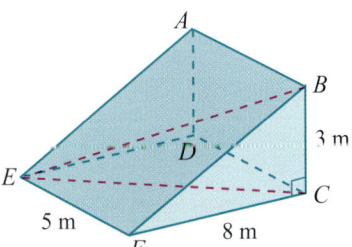

MEASUREMENT & GEOMETRY

3 Two boats at sea observe the same lighthouse at a height of 350 m above sea level. From boat A the bearing of the lighthouse is 045°T and the angle of elevation is 15°. From boat B the bearing of the lighthouse is 315°T and the angle of elevation is 16°.

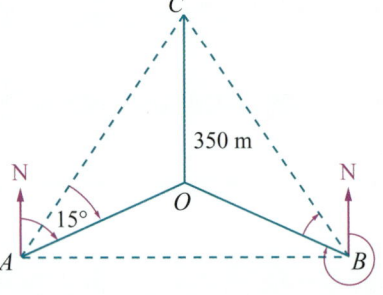

  a Complete this diagram.
  b Show that $\angle AOB$ is 90°.
  c Calculate the distances OA and OB and hence AB.
  d Calculate $\angle OAB$ and hence the bearing of boat B from boat A.

4 Calculate θ for which $\cos\theta = 0.7142$.

5 Draw the graph of $y = \cos\theta$ for $0° \leqslant \theta \leqslant 720°$.

6 What is the exact value of $\sin 330°$?

11D   Review set

1 A cube has side length 13 cm. Calculate the length EB in surd form.

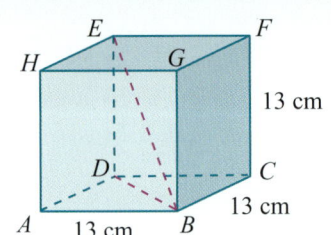

2 A rectangular prism has side lengths 10 cm, 17 cm and 20 cm as shown.

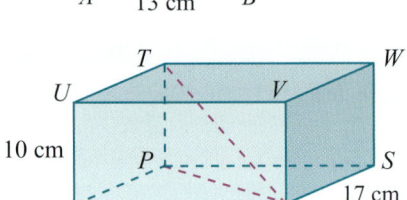

  a Calculate the length PR.
  b Calculate, θ, the angle made between the line RT and the plane $PQRS$.

3 From a point X due south of a tower 310 m tall on level ground, the angle of elevation of the top of the tower is 21°. From a point Y due east of the tower, the angle of elevation of the top of the tower is 24°, as shown in the diagram. Calculate the distance XY to the nearest metre.

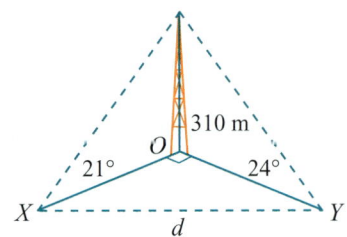

4 Calculate θ for which $\sin\theta = 0.8631$ and $90° < \theta < 180°$.

5 Draw the trigonometric graph that has a period of 180° and has asymptotes, for $0° \leqslant \theta \leqslant 360°$.

6 What is the exact value of θ for which $\sin\theta = -\dfrac{1}{2}$?

12

Graphical representation

This chapter deals with the relationship between graphs and equations corresponding to simple rate problems and with the interpretation and sketching of parabolas, hyperbolas, circles and exponential functions and their transformations.

After completing this chapter you should be able to:

▶ interpret graphs showing the rate of increase or decrease of a variable

▶ sketch a graph from a simple description

▶ find the x- and y-intercepts, the equation of the axis of symmetry and the coordinates of the vertex of a parabola of the form $y = ax^2 + bx + c$

▶ sketch and describe transformations of the parabola $y = x^2$

▶ sketch and describe transformations of the hyperbola $y = \dfrac{1}{x}$

▶ recognise and describe equations of circles with centre (h, k) and radius r

▶ sketch and describe transformations of exponential curves

▶ identify and name different types of graphs from their equations

▶ determine a possible equation from a given graph

▶ sketch and interpret cubics and other graphs and their transformations

▶ determine the points of intersection of a line with a parabola, hyperbola or circle graphically and algebraically.

NSW Syllabus references: 5.3 N&A Ratios and rates, 5.3 N&A Non-linear relationships
Outcomes: MA 5.3-1WM, MA5.3-2WM, M5.3-3WM, MA5.3-4NA, MA5.3-9NA
Number & algebra – ACMNA208, ACMNA267

Diagnostic test

1 The graphs drawn have equations:

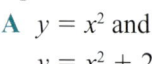

  A $y = x^2$ and
     $y = x^2 + 2$

  B $y = x^2$ and $y = -x^2$

  C $y = x^2$ and $y = 3x^2$

  D $y = x^2$ and $y = -x^2 + 2$

2 The graph with the same shape as $y = x^2$ and which passes through $(0, -3)$ has equation:

  A $y = x^2 + 3$ B $y = x^2 - 3$

  C $y = -x^2 + 3$ D $y = -x^2 - 3$

3 The graph of $y = -\frac{1}{3}x^2 - 2$ is:

A 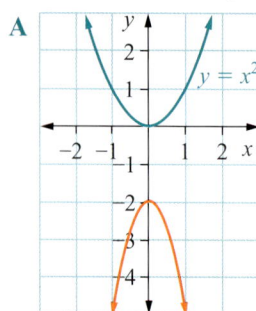 B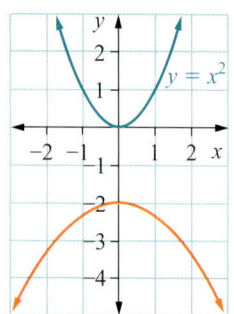

C 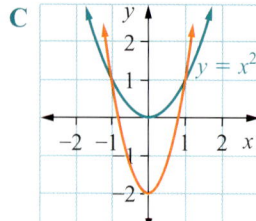 D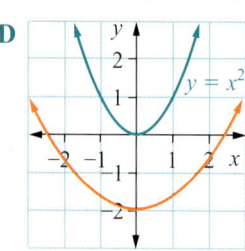

4 The x-coordinates of the points on $y = 2x^2 - 7$ with y-coordinate $y = 3$ are:

  A $\pm\sqrt{10}$ B $\pm\sqrt{5}$ C ± 2 D $\pm\sqrt{2}$

5 The y-intercept of parabola $y = x^2 - 6x - 9$ is:

  A -6 B 6 C 9 D -9

6 The graph of $y = -5^{-x}$ is:

A 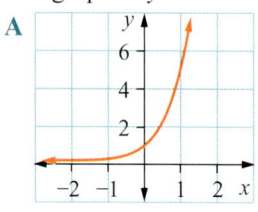 B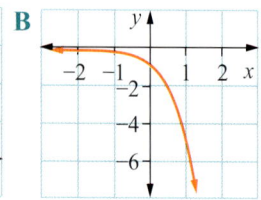

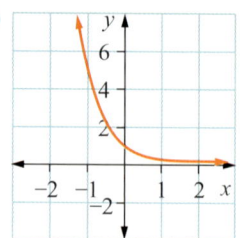

7 The equation of the exponential curve shown is:

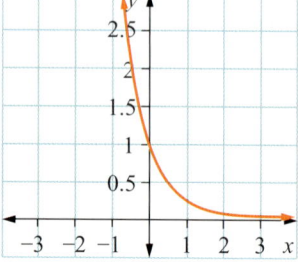

  A $y = 2^x$

  B $y = 2^{-x}$

  C $y = 4^x$

  D $y = 4^{-x}$

8 The graph of $y = 2^x$ is:

A 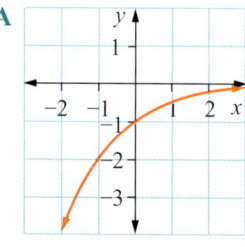 B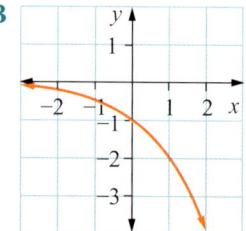

C 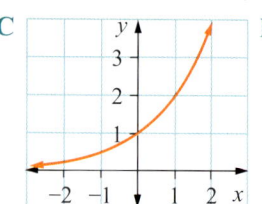 D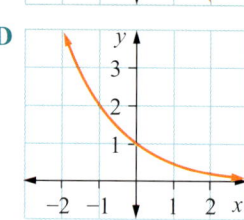

9 The x-coordinate of the point on the graph of $y = 2^x$ with y-coordinate $= 32$ is:

  A 3   B 4   C 5   D 6

10 The radius of the circle $x^2 + y^2 = 64$ is:

  A 16   B 8   C 4   D 2

11 The equation of the circle shown is:

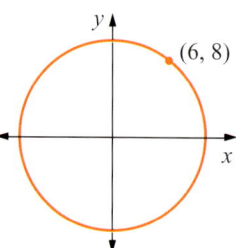

  A $x^2 + y^2 = 36$

  B $x^2 + y^2 = 64$

  C $x^2 + y^2 = 100$

  D $x^2 + y^2 = 10$

The diagnostic test questions refer to outcome ACMNA239 and ACMNA296. (AC)

A Interpreting distance–time graphs

A distance–time graph shows the relative position at different times of a person or object as it moves. The position is indicated by the distance of the person or object from a starting point.

In Year 7 you should have discovered that on a distance–time graph consisting of straight line segments:

- The slope of the line segment indicates the speed of the object.
- The steeper the line segment, the greater the speed of the object.
- The horizontal sections indicate that the object is not moving.
- A positive gradient indicates that the distance from the origin is increasing.
- A negative gradient indicates that the distance from the origin is decreasing.

Exercise 12A

1 This graph represents the journeys of four motorists.
  a For the time intervals shown, which motorist was stationary?
  b For the time intervals shown, which motorist travelled the:
     i fastest?
     ii slowest?

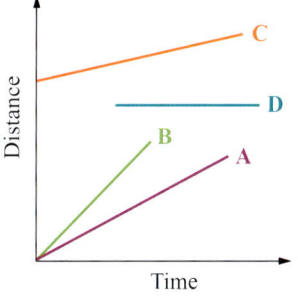

2 The graph represents the trips made by three cyclists.

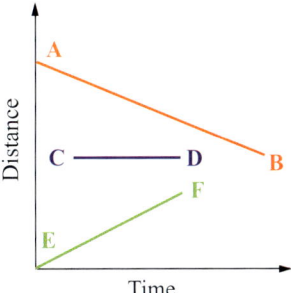

Which line segment indicates that the cyclist's distance from the origin is:
  a not changing?
  b increasing?
  c decreasing?

3 The graph shows the journey of a motorist. State the time interval(s) that represent(s) these situations.
  a The motorist was stationary.
  b The motorist was travelling the fastest.
  c The motorist was travelling the slowest.
  d The motorist's distance from home was increasing.
  e The motorist's distance from home was decreasing.

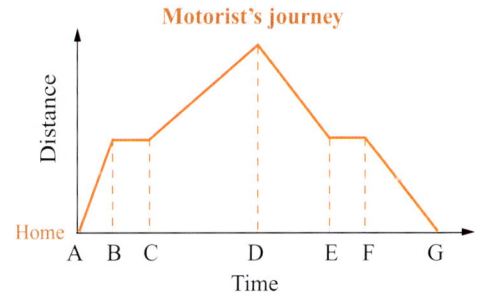

Motorist's journey

4 Pete drew the distance–time graph shown to represent a trip made by a cyclist. Unfortunately Pete made an error. Explain why Pete's graph is not possible.

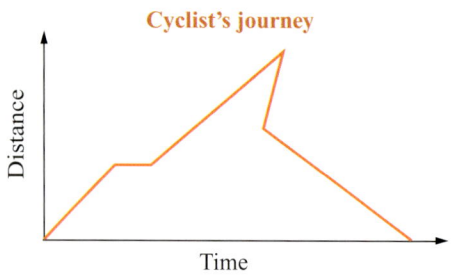

5 Which of these graphs do not represent distance–time graphs?

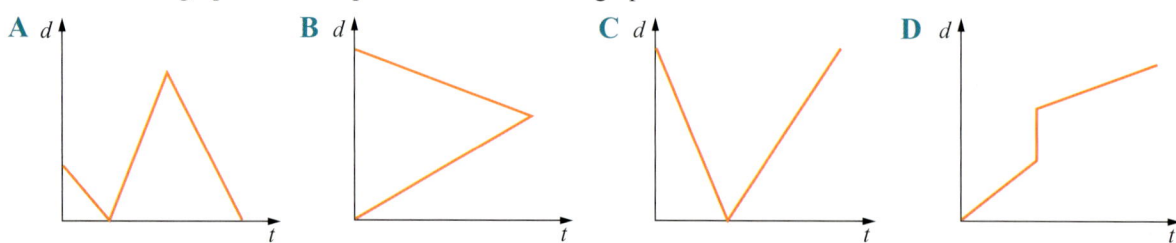

6 Match each of these descriptions to one of the graphs below.
   a I left home and travelled at a constant speed for the entire journey.
   b I returned home travelling at a constant speed.
   c I waited for my friend to arrive and then we travelled home at a constant speed.
   d I waited for my friend to arrive and then we completed the journey at a constant speed.

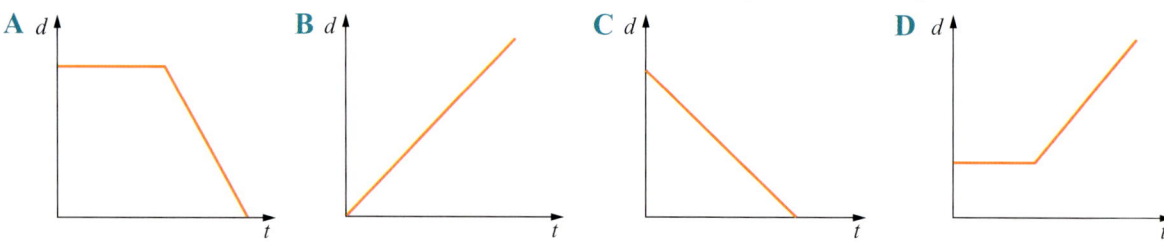

7 Match each of these descriptions to one of the graphs shown.
   a Ashya left school and walked home.
   b Her brother Rob left at the same time and rode his bike home.
   c Their sister Jane talked to a friend for a short time and then caught the bus home from school.

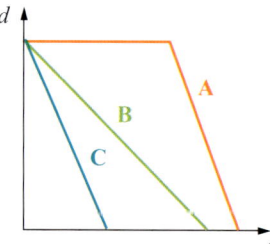

EXAMPLE 1

Each graph below is part of a distance–time graph.

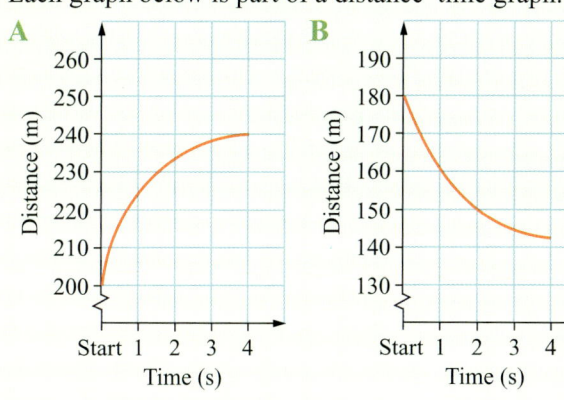

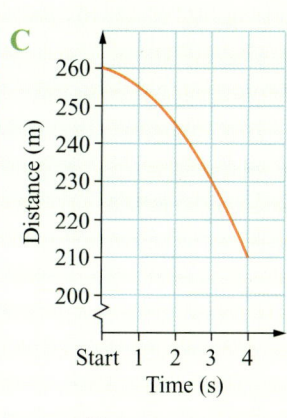

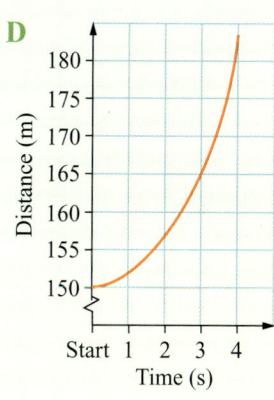

a In the first second of observation, how far did the car travel?

b How far did the car travel in the:

   i second second?   **ii** third second?   **iii** fourth second?

c Describe how distance is changing over this four-second period.

d How is the steepness of the curve related to how distance from the origin is changing?

	Solve/Think	Apply
A a	The car travelled 25 m.	When interpreting rate of change (how a quantity varies with time) it is useful to match the following curve shape with its description.
b	**i** 8 m **ii** 5 m **iii** 2 m	
c	Distance increases at a decreasing rate.	
B a	The car travelled 20 m.	
b	**i** 10 m **ii** 5 m **iii** 3 m	
c	Distance decreases at a decreasing rate.	
C a	The car travelled 5 m.	
b	**i** 10 m **ii** 15 m **iii** 20 m	
c	Distance decreases at an increasing rate.	
D a	The car travelled 2 m.	
b	**i** 5 m **ii** 8 m **iii** 18 m	
c	Distance increases at an increasing rate.	
d	The steeper the curve at a point on it the more quickly distance is changing at that time.	

Apply column diagrams:

Constant rate: not changing

Increasing at a constant rate

Increasing at an increasing rate: slowly at first then more quickly

Increasing at a decreasing rate: quickly at first then more slowly

Decreasing at a constant rate

Decreasing at an increasing rate: slowly at first then more quickly

Decreasing at a decreasing rate: quickly at first then more slowly

8 Match each of the statements below to one of the distance–time graphs.

   a Distance increases slowly at first and then more quickly.

   b Distance increases quickly at first and then more slowly.

   c Distance increases at a constant rate.

   d Distance decreases slowly at first and then more quickly.

   e Distance decreases quickly at first and then more slowly.

   f Distance decreases at a constant rate.

A 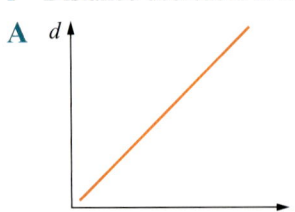   **B** 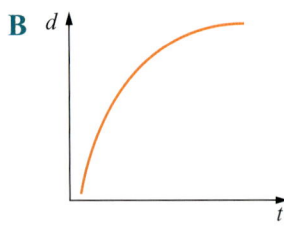   **C**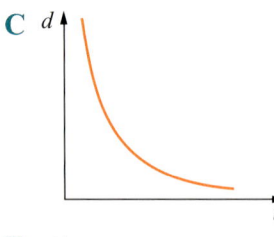

D 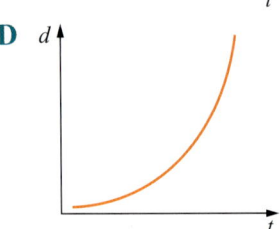   **E** 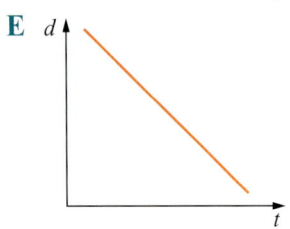   **F**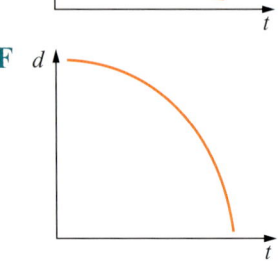

9 Copy the distance–time graphs below and label any parts of the graph where the distance travelled is:

   A increasing at an increasing rate   **B** increasing at a decreasing rate

   C increasing at a constant rate   **D** decreasing at an increasing rate

   E decreasing at a decreasing rate   **F** decreasing at a constant rate.

a 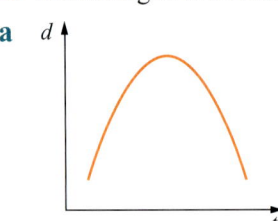   **b** 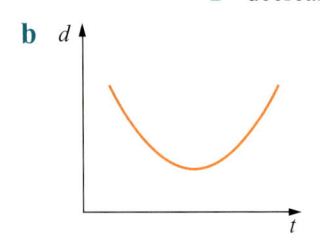   **c**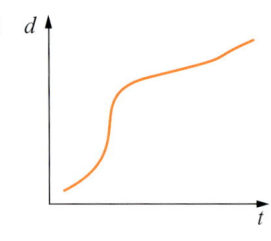

d 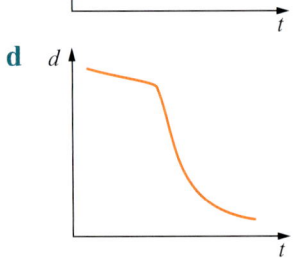   **e**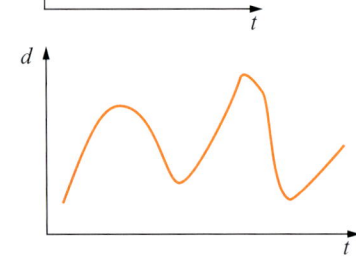

10 Describe, with the terms used in questions **8** and **9**, what is happening in each distance–time graph.

a 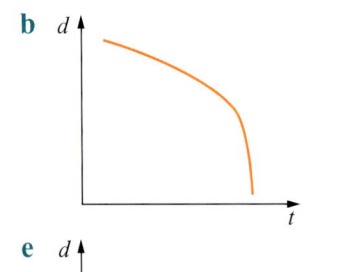   **b** 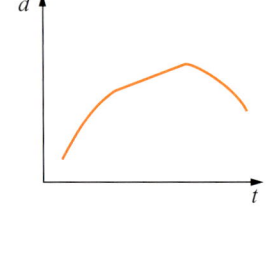   **c**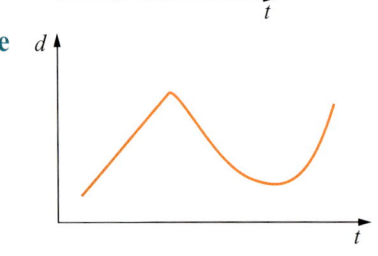

d 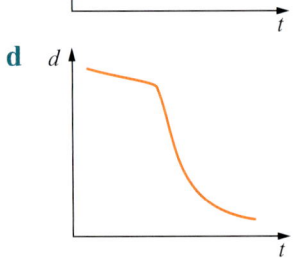   **e**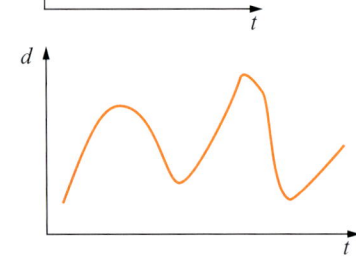

11 Sketch distance–time graphs that match the following descriptions.
   - **a** Distance is increasing at an increasing rate.
   - **b** Distance is increasing at a decreasing rate.
   - **c** Distance is increasing at a constant rate.
   - **d** Distance is decreasing at an decreasing rate.
   - **e** Distance is decreasing at a increasing rate.
   - **f** Distance is decreasing at a constant rate.
   - **g** Distance is not changing.

12 a A bus starts its journey 120 km from a city and travels towards the city at an average speed of 30 km/h. Complete the table and draw a distance–time graph to show where the bus was at different times.

Time (h)	0	$\frac{1}{2}$	1	$1\frac{1}{2}$	2	$2\frac{1}{2}$	3	$3\frac{1}{2}$	4
Distance from city (km)	120	105	90						

   b Another bus starts from the same place 1 hour after the first and travels at the same speed along the same road. Complete the table below and show the position of this bus on the graph in part **a**. Note that time is measured from the departure of the first bus.

Time (h)	0	$\frac{1}{2}$	1	$1\frac{1}{2}$	2	$2\frac{1}{2}$	3	$3\frac{1}{2}$	4
Distance from city (km)	120	120	120	105					

   c A third bus leaves the same place 2 hours after the first and travels at 60 km/h along the same road. Complete the table below and show the position of this bus on the graph in part **a**.

Time (h)	0	$\frac{1}{2}$	1	$1\frac{1}{2}$	2	$2\frac{1}{2}$	3	$3\frac{1}{2}$	4
Distance from city (km)	120	120	120	120	120	90			

   d At what time does the third bus overtake the other two buses?

13 Draw distance–time graphs to illustrate the following situations.
   - **a** David moves away from the traffic lights gradually increasing his speed until he is travelling at 60 km/h.
   - **b** At the start of the bicycle race, Helen sprints to get to the front of the pack of riders and then maintains a constant speed.
   - **c** Ahmet is driving at a constant speed and then applies the brakes hard to stop when a dog runs onto the road in front of him.
   - **d** Katherine is driving at a steady speed and applies the brakes gradually to stop at the traffic lights.
   - **e** Chai Li is driving at the maximum legal speed in a 50 km/h zone and then gradually increases her speed up to the allowable maximum when she enters a 70 km/h zone.
   - **f** Martin is driving along the freeway at 80 km/h, he increases his speed quickly to overtake another car and then drops his speed back to 80 km/h again.

B Describing graphs

● **EXAMPLE 1**

The graph shows the number of people at a bus stop on a typical weekday. Describe in words how the number of people varies with time.

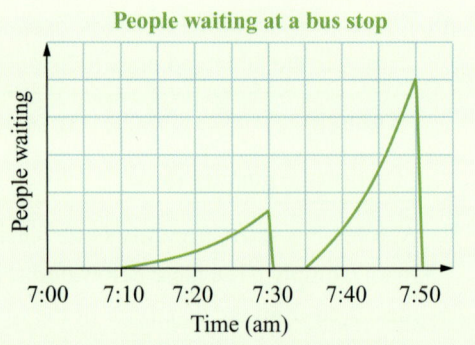

People waiting at a bus stop

Solve/Think	Apply
There were no people waiting at the bus stop from 7:00 am to 7:10 am, but from 7:10 am the number of people waiting increased at an increasing rate until 7.30 am when it decreased rapidly back to 0. This is when the first bus arrived and the people got on the bus. The bus stop was then empty until 7:35 am. The number of people waiting then increased at an increasing rate, more quickly than before, until 7:50 am when the next bus arrived and the people boarded this bus.	Interpret sections of the graph as increasing or decreasing at an increasing or decreasing rate.

Exercise 12B

1 The graph shows the number of people waiting on a platform at a railway station one morning.

   a Describe in words how the number of people varies for this time interval.

   b How often do trains arrive during this time interval?

   c For approximately how long does each train stop at this station?

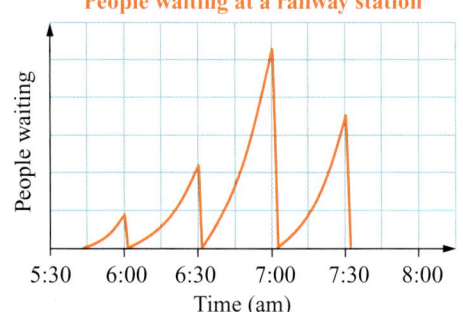

People waiting at a railway station

2 The graph shows the number of cans of soft drink in the vending machine of a school canteen.

   a Describe in words how the number of cans varies during the day.

   b When do you think the recess and lunch breaks occur in this school?

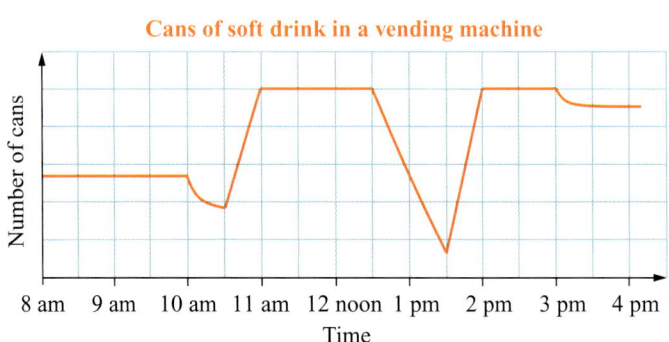

Cans of soft drink in a vending machine

NUMBER & ALGEBRA

3 The graph shows the number of cars that pass through a suburban intersection on Sunday and Monday.

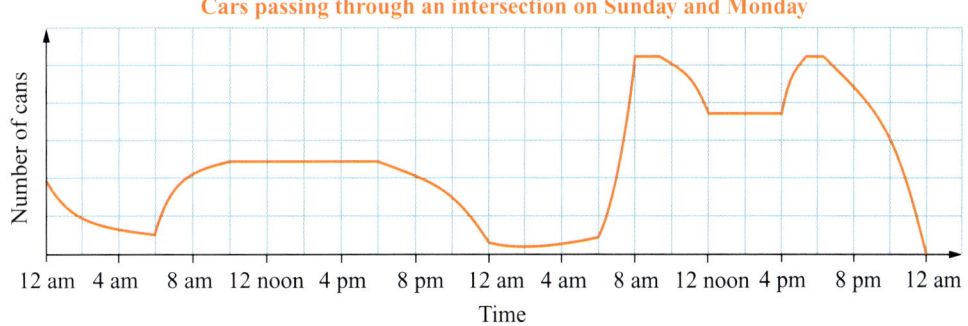

Cars passing through an intersection on Sunday and Monday

a Describe in words how the number of cars varies over these two days.

b What do you think the two peaks on the graph represent?

4 Match each graph below with one of these stories.

    a Jenny climbs a hill at a steady speed and then runs down the hill stopping as quickly as possible.

    b Peter starts slowly and increases his speed until he is running as fast as possible then gradually slows.

    c Danielle gradually increases her speed and when at full speed continues to run.

    d Brook walks for a while then jogs for a while then runs for a while.

A
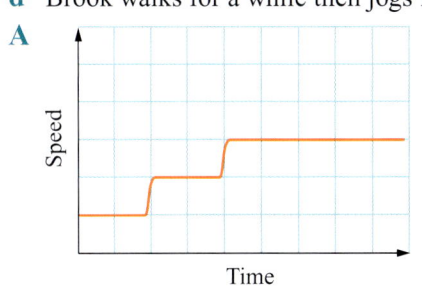

B
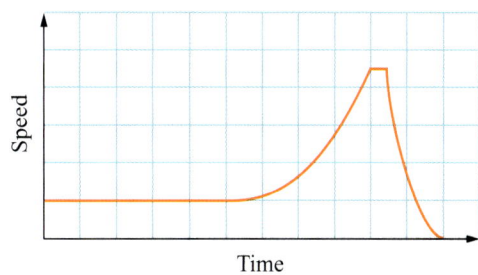

C
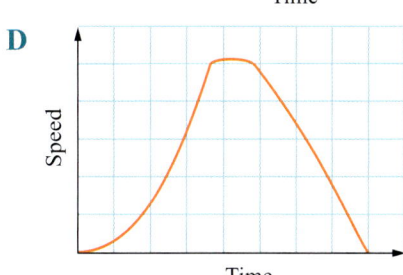

D

5 **a** A racing car travels around each of the three circuits shown. The graphs below show the speed of the car on the second lap of each of these circuits. Match each graph with a circuit.

i
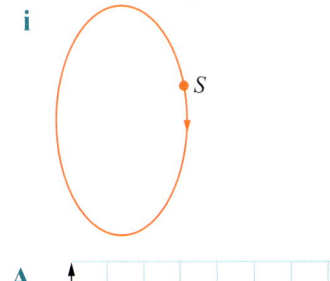

ii
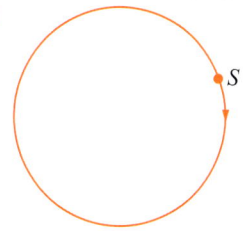

iii
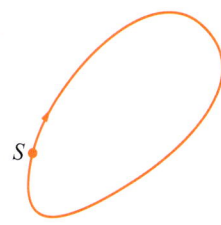

A
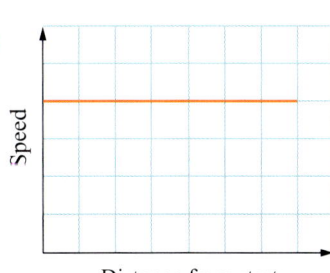
Distance from start

B
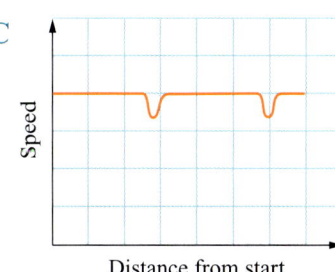
Distance from start

C

Distance from start

NUMBER & ALGEBRA

b Draw graphs to show the speed of a racing car as it travels around the second lap of each of the following circuits.

i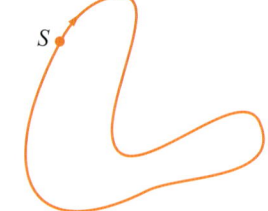

ii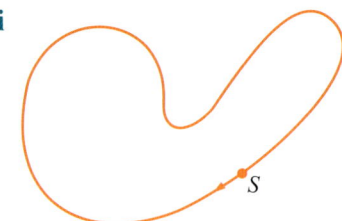

iii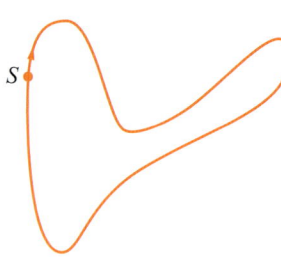

6 Draw graphs to illustrate the following statements. (Be sure to label the axes.)
  a Although prices are still rising, they are rising at a slower rate than in the previous 6 months.
  b The temperature of a cup of coffee decreases quickly at first and then more slowly until it reaches room temperature.
  c The level of pollution in the atmosphere of a large city is increasing at an increasing rate.
  d The population of a town increased rapidly when a new factory opened and then it remained steady.
  e The weight of a baby decreased slightly after its birth and then increased at an increasing rate.
  f When radioactive material decays, the amount of material present decreases at a decreasing rate.
  g When a passenger liner travelling at 20 knots turns off its motor, the speed of the ship decreases at a decreasing rate.
  h The amount of interest earned increases at an increasing rate when money is invested at 8% p.a., interest, compounding monthly.

7 a The amount of the drug quodine in the bloodstream after taking a tablet decreases quickly at first and then more slowly. The effect wears off completely after about 5 hours. Draw a graph to illustrate this.
  b Draw a graph to show the level of quodine in the bloodstream over a 12-hour period if one tablet is taken every 4 hours.

8 a Water is poured into the container shown at a steady rate. Which of these graphs could represent the height of the water in the container as it is filled?

A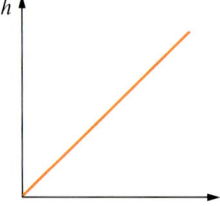

B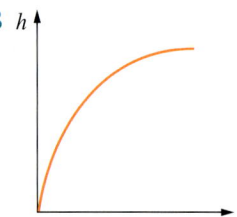

C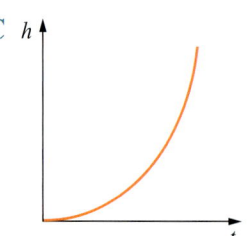

D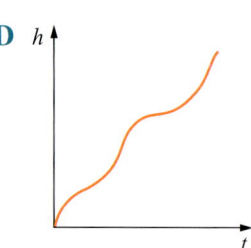

  b The following containers are filled with water at a constant rate. Draw graphs to show how the height of water in each container increases with time.

i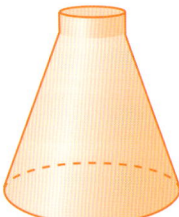

ii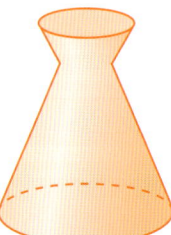

iii

iv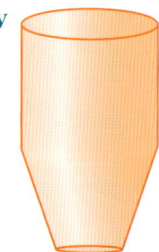

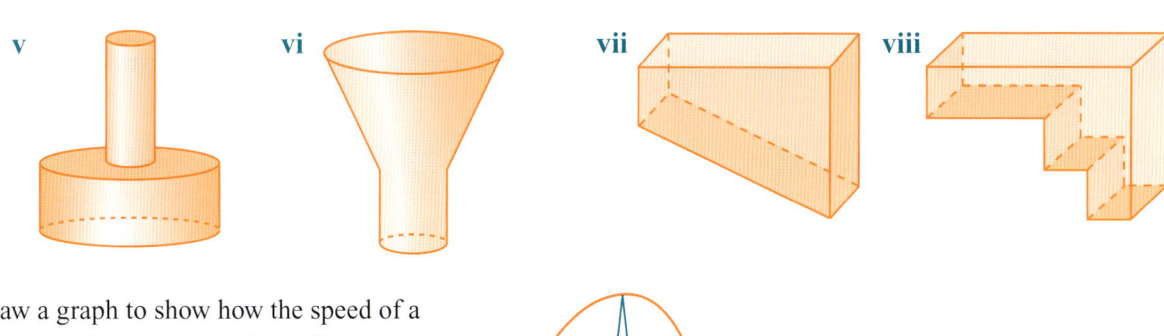

v   vi   vii   viii

9 Draw a graph to show how the speed of a
car on a roller coaster varies as it travels
along this part of its circuit.

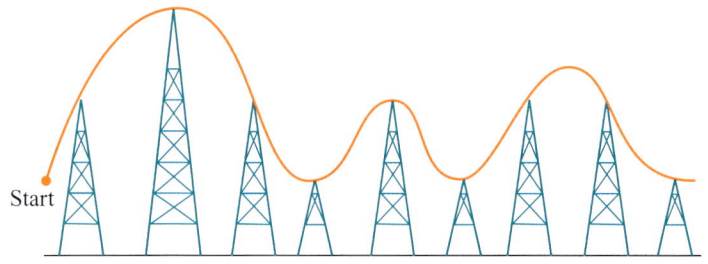

Start

10 a A chalk mark is put on the top of a tyre (position 1) as shown and
the tyre rolled along the ground. Which of the following graphs
could represent the height of the chalk mark above the ground?

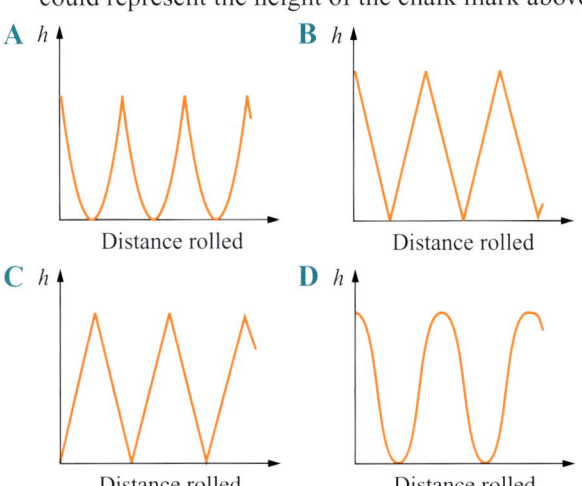

A h

Distance rolled

B h

Distance rolled

C h

Distance rolled

D h

Distance rolled

1

3

2

b Draw a graph to show the height of the chalk mark above the ground if the tyre starts at:
  i position 2   **ii** position 3

11 Draw graphs to show the height above the ground
of cars A, B and C on the Ferris wheel as it turns
clockwise at a constant rate, if they start in the
positions shown.

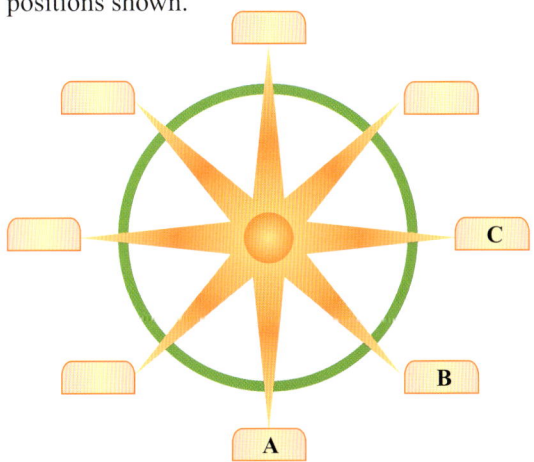

C

B

A

Investigation 1 Modelling motion

This is a practical activity for the class. Have a member of the class move along a 50 m tape for 30 s using a variety of activities that involve a constant rate.

You will need: 50 m measuring tape, stopwatch, markers (such as flags or witches' hats)

Here are some possible activities for the mover:

Walk slowly for 30 s.

Walk quickly for 30 s.

Walk for 10 s, stop for 10 s, walk (at the same rate) for 10 s.

Walk for 10 s, jog for 10 s, walk for 10 s.

Walk for 10 s, stop for 10 s, walk back to the start.

Stop for 10 s, walk slowly for 10 s, jog for 10 s.

Start walking slowly and then speed up until reaching the end of the tape.

Run at an increasing then decreasing speed.

Start at the other end of the tape and repeat some of the above activities.

1 Lay a 50 m measuring tape out in a straight line.
   a Appoint a member of the class as the timekeeper to call out the time every 5 s.
   b Appoint a member of the class as the 'mover', who moves along the tape according to the instructions given.
   c Appoint six other members of the class to mark the position of the mover every 5 s.

2 Record the distance of the mover from the start at fixed time intervals in a table like the one below.

Time (s)	5	10	15	20	25	30
Distance (m)						

3 Draw a distance–time graph to represent each situation using the values recorded in your table.

C The parabola

Parabola is the name given to the graph of an equation of the form $y = ax^2 + bx + c$ where a, b and c are constants.

Exercise 12C

1 a Complete the table below and draw the graph of the parabola $y = 2x^2 - 6x + 7$.

x	-1	0	1	2	3	4
y						

b Complete the table below and draw the graph of the parabola $y = -2x^2 - 4x + 6$.

x	-4	-3	-2	-1	0	1	2
y							

● EXAMPLE 1

A parabola has equation $y = x^2 - 5x + 6$.
a Find the y-intercept(s).
b Find the x-intercept(s).

	Solve	Think	Apply
a	$y = x^2 - 5x + 6$ Put $x = 0$: $y = 0^2 - 5 \times 0 + 6 = 6$ The y-intercept is 6.	The y-intercept is the point where the curve cuts the y-axis. This point has its x-coordinate $= 0$. Substitute $x = 0$ into the equation of the parabola. The parabola cuts the y-axis at the point $(0, 6)$.	To find the y-intercept(s) of any curve substitute $x = 0$ into its equation.
b	$y = x^2 - 5x + 6$ Put $y = 0$: $0 = x^2 - 5x + 6$ $(x - 2)(x - 3) = 0$ $x = 2, 3$ The x-intercepts are $x = 2$ and $x = 3$.	The x-intercept is the point where the curve cuts the x-axis. This point has its y-coordinate $= 0$. Substitute $y = 0$ into the equation of the parabola and factorise. The parabola cuts the x-axis at the points $(2, 0)$ and $(3, 0)$.	To find the x-intercept(s) of any curve substitute $y = 0$ into its equation.

2 Find the x- and y-intercepts of the following parabolas.

a $y = x^2 - 3x - 10$ **b** $y = x^2 + 5x - 14$

c $y = 8 - 2x - x^2$ **d** $y = 18 - 7x + x^2$

e $y = 2x^2 - x - 3$ **f** $y = 2 + 5x - 3x^2$

EXAMPLE 2

A parabola has equation $y = x^2 - 3x - 10$.

a Find the x- and y-intercepts.

b Find the equation of the axis of symmetry.

c Find the coordinates of the vertex.

d Sketch the parabola.

	Solve	Think	Apply
a	The y-intercept is $y = -10$. The x-intercepts are $x = -2$ and $x = 5$.	If $x = 0$, $y = -10$. If $y = 0$: $x^2 - 3x - 10 = 0$ $(x + 2)(x - 5) = 0$ $x = -2, 5$	To find the x- and y-intercepts, substitute $y = 0$ and $x = 0$ respectively into the equation of the parabola.
b	x-intercepts are at $(-2, 0)$ and $(5, 0)$. Midpoint of the interval joining these points is: $\left(\dfrac{-2 + 5}{2}, \dfrac{0 + 0}{2}\right)$ or $\left(\dfrac{3}{2}, 0\right)$ The equation of the axis of symmetry is $x = \dfrac{3}{2}$.	The axis of symmetry will be a line parallel to the y-axis and passing through the midpoint of the interval joining the x-intercepts. The equation of the line through the point $(\frac{3}{2}, 0)$ and parallel to the y-axis is $x = \frac{3}{2}$.	The axis of symmetry of a parabola of the form $y = ax^2 + bx + c$ is parallel to the y-axis (perpendicular to the x-axis). Find the equation of the line through the midpoint of the interval joining the x-intercepts and parallel to the y-axis.
c	If $x = \dfrac{3}{2}$ $y = \left(\dfrac{3}{2}\right)^2 - 3\left(\dfrac{3}{2}\right) - 10 = -\dfrac{49}{4}$ The vertex is point $\left(\dfrac{3}{2}, -\dfrac{49}{4}\right)$.	Substitute $x = \frac{3}{2}$ into the equation of the parabola to find the y-coordinate.	The axis of symmetry passes through the vertex V of the parabola and has the same x-coordinate for all points. Substitute the axis of symmetry equation into the equation of the parabola.
d		Sketch the parabola showing the x- and y-intercepts, the axis of symmetry and the vertex.	*Note:* The vertex of a parabola is often referred to as the turning point. A curve is concave up at a point if it lies above the tangent at that point, such as at point P, and is concave down at a point if it lies below the curve at that point, such as at point R. If the constant $a > 0$, the parabola is $\cup$ shaped, it is concave up. If the constant $a < 0$, the parabola is $\cap$ shaped, it is concave down.

3 For each of the following parabolas:

    i Find the equation of the axis of symmetry.

    ii Find the coordinates of the vertex.

    iii Sketch the parabola.

  a $y = x^2 + x - 6$ **b** $y = x^2 + 2x - 15$

  c $y = 2x^2 + x - 6$ **d** $y = 3x^2 - 13x - 10$

● EXAMPLE 3

Describe the features of the parabola $y = -x^2 + 2x + 3$.

Solve/Think	Apply
If $x = 0$, $y = 3$ If $y = 0$, $-x^2 + 2x + 3 = 0$ $\qquad -(x^2 - 2x - 3) = 0$ $\qquad\quad x^2 - 2x - 3 = 0$ $\qquad\quad (x + 1)(x - 3) = 0$ $\qquad\qquad\qquad x = -1, 3$ Axis of symmetry is $x = \dfrac{-1 + 3}{2} = 1$. If $x = 1$, $y = -1 + 2 + 3 = 4$. The vertex is the point $(1, 4)$. The parabola $y = -x^2 + 2x + 3$ has y-intercept 3 and x-intercepts -1 and 3. The equation of its axis of symmetry is $x = 1$. The coordinates of its vertex are $(1, 4)$. As $a < 0$, the curve is concave down. 	Find the x- and y-intercepts, the axis of symmetry and the vertex. Determine if the curve is concave up or down.

4 Describe the features of these parabolas.

  a $y = -x^2 + 2x + 8$ **b** $y = -x^2 - 5x - 6$

  c $y = 3 - x - 2x^2$ **d** $y = 2 + 5x - 3x^2$

5 a Sketch the graphs of $y = x^2 + 5x - 6$ and $y = 2x^2 + 10x - 12$ on the same set of axes.

  b Describe the similarities between the parabolas.

  c Describe the similarities between the equations.

● EXAMPLE 4

A parabola cuts the x-axis at $x = -2$ and $x = 4$. Write a possible equation of the parabola.

Solve	Think	Apply
$y = (x + 2)(x - 4)$ $y = x^2 - 2x - 8$ is a possible equation.	When $y = 0$, $x = -2, 4$. Hence the factors of $y = 0$ are $(x + 2)$ and $(x - 4)$.	If the x-intercepts are h and k then a possible equation is $y = (x - h)(x - k)$.

Note: There are many parabolas that have the x-intercepts -2 and 4 (and hence axis of symmetry $x = 1$), as shown in the diagram.

From the graph it can be seen that:

$y = 2(x^2 - 2x - 8)$ or $y = 2x^2 - 4x - 16$ and

$y = -(x^2 - 2x - 8)$ or $y = -x^2 + 2x + 8$

also satisfy the required condition.

In fact, any equation of the form $y = a(x^2 - 2x - 8)$ will satisfy the required condition.

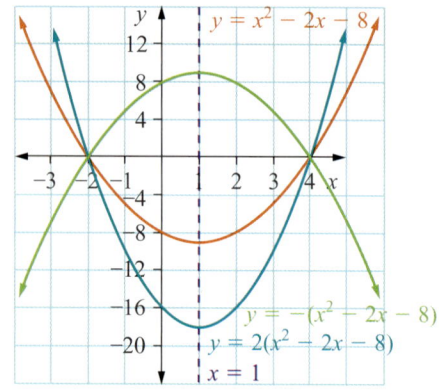

6 Write three possible equations of a parabola that cuts the x-axis at:

a $x = 2$ and $x = 4$ **b** $x = -3$ and $x = 2$

c $x = -5$ and $x = -2$

Axis of symmetry of a parabola

The equation of the axis of symmetry of the parabola $y = ax^2 + bx + c$ is $x = \dfrac{-b}{2a}$.

Following is the proof.

First find the x-intercepts: if $y = 0$, $ax^2 + bx + c = 0$

From the quadratic formula: $x = \dfrac{-b \pm \sqrt{b^2 - 4ac}}{2a}$

The x-intercepts are at $\left(\dfrac{-b + \sqrt{b^2 - 4ac}}{2a}, 0\right)$ and $\left(\dfrac{-b - \sqrt{b^2 - 4ac}}{2a}, 0\right)$.

The midpoint of the interval joining these two points is:

$$\left(\dfrac{\dfrac{-b + \sqrt{b^2 - 4ac}}{2a} + \dfrac{-b - \sqrt{b^2 - 4ac}}{2a}}{2}, \dfrac{0 + 0}{2}\right) = \left(\dfrac{-b + \sqrt{b^2 - 4ac} + -b - \sqrt{b^2 - 4ac}}{4a}, 0\right)$$

$$= \left(\dfrac{-2b}{4a}, 0\right) = \left(\dfrac{-b}{2a}, 0\right)$$

The equation of the axis of symmetry is $x = \dfrac{-b}{2a}$.

EXAMPLE 5

Sketch the graph of $y = x^2 - 4x + 5$.

Solve/Think	Apply
Using the previous method: if $x = 0$, $y = 5$ if $y = 0$, $x^2 - 4x + 5 = 0$ This equation has no solutions because $\Delta < 0$. Hence the parabola has no x-intercepts and we cannot find the axis of symmetry. But it can be shown that for $y = ax^2 + bx + c$, the equation of the axis of symmetry is $x = -\dfrac{b}{2a}$. Using this information, the equation of the axis of symmetry is: $x = -\dfrac{b}{2a} = -\dfrac{-4}{2 \times 1} = 2$ If $x = 2$, $y = (2)^2 - 4(2) + 5 = 1$. Thus the vertex is the point $(2, 1)$. So we can sketch $y = x^2 - 4x + 5$. 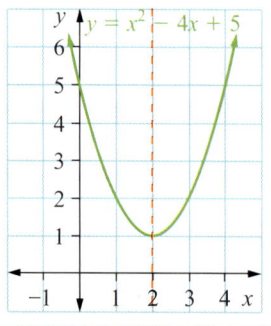	If the parabola does not cross the x-axis it either lies completely above or completely below the x-axis as shown. 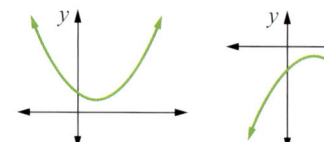 If the x-intercepts cannot be found, use $x = -\dfrac{b}{2a}$ for the equation. *Note:* $x = -\dfrac{b}{2a}$ is the equation of the axis of symmetry of the parabola whether or not the x-intercepts can be found.

7 Sketch the following parabolas showing the y-intercept, the axis of symmetry and the vertex.

   a $y = x^2 - 2x + 3$ **b** $y = 2x^2 + 4x + 8$ **c** $y = -x^2 - 2x - 5$

   d $y = -2x^2 - 4x - 12$ **e** $y = 3x^2 - 4x + 4$ **f** $y = -4x^2 + 6x - 5$

Using technology, or otherwise, investigate the following graphs.

8 **a**   Draw graphs of $y = 3x^2$, $y = -7x^2$, $y = 1.5x^2$, $y = 0.6x^2$.

    b   Describe each of the curves as concave up or concave down.

    c   What is the effect of the sign of the constant a on the concavity of the parabola $y = ax^2$?

9 **a**   Sketch graphs of $y = x^2$, $y = 3x^2$ and $y = 0.6x^2$ on the same axes.

      i   What is the effect of the magnitude of the constant a on the graph of $y = ax^2$?

      ii   Describe the similarities and differences between the graphs of $y = x^2$ and $y = 3x^2$.

      iii   Describe the similarities and differences between the graphs of $y = x^2$ and $y = 0.6x^2$.

    b   Sketch graphs of $y = -x^2$, $y = -2x^2$ and $y = -\frac{1}{3}x^2$ on the same axes.

      i   What is the effect of the magnitude of the constant a on the graph of $y = -ax^2$?

      ii   Describe the similarities and differences between the graphs of $y = -x^2$ and $y = -2x^2$.

      iii   Describe the similarities and differences between the graphs of $y = -x^2$ and $y = -\frac{1}{3}x^2$.

10 **a**   Sketch graphs of $y = x^2$, $y = x^2 + 5$, $y = x^2 - 4$ on the same axes.

      i   What is the effect of the constant c on the graph of $y = x^2 + c$?

      ii   Describe the similarities and differences between the graphs of $y = x^2$ and $y = x^2 + 5$.

    b   Sketch graphs of $y = -x^2$, $y = -x^2 + 7$, $y = -x^2 - 6$ on the same axes.

      i   What is the effect of the constant c on the graph of $y = -x^2 + c$?

      ii   Describe the similarities and differences between the graphs of $y = -x^2$ and $y = -x^2 - 9$.

11 **a**   Describe the similarities and differences between $y = x^2$ and the following graphs.

      i $y = 2x^2 - 3$ **ii** $y = 0.4x^2 + 7$

    b   Describe the similarities and differences between $y = -x^2$ and the following graphs.

      i $y = -5x^2 + 1$ **ii** $y = -0.7x^2 - 8$

12 **a**   Sketch graphs of $y = x^2$, $y = (x - 1)^2$, $y = (x - 3)^2$, $y = (x - 4)^2$ on the same axes.

      i   For each of the graphs, what is the equation of the axis of symmetry and the coordinates of the vertex?

      ii   What is the effect of the constant b on the graph of $y = (x - b)^2$?

      iii   Without graphing, write the equation of the axis of symmetry and the coordinates of the vertex of the parabola $y = (x - 9)^2$.

    b   Sketch graphs of $y = x^2$, $y = (x + 1)^2$, $y = (x + 2)^2$, $y = (x + 5)^2$ on the same axes.

      i   For each of the graphs, what is the equation of the axis of symmetry and the coordinates of the vertex?

      ii   What is the effect of the constant b on the graph of $y = (x + b)^2$?

      iii   Without graphing, write the equation of the axis of symmetry and the coordinates of the vertex of the parabola $y = (x + 7)^2$.

13 **a**   Sketch graphs of $y = x^2$, $y = (x - 3)^2 + 2$, $y = (x + 4)^2 - 5$ on the same axes.

    b   For each of the graphs, what is the equation of the axis of symmetry and the coordinates of the vertex?

    c   Without graphing, write the equation of the axis of symmetry and the coordinates of the vertex of the parabola $y = (x - 8)^2 - 5$.

NUMBER & ALGEBRA

EXAMPLE 6

Consider each of the following parabolas.

   i What transformation of $y = x^2$ is required to produce the parabola?

   ii Hence find the concavity.

   iii Find the equation of the axis of symmetry.

   iv Find the coordinates of the vertex.

a $y = -12x^2$ **b** $y = 0.3x^2 + 7$ **c** $y = (x + 5)^2$ **d** $y = (x - 6)^2 - 1$

Solve/Think		Apply
a i The graph of $y = -12x^2$ is the graph of $y = x^2$ reflected in the x-axis and made narrower. **ii** Concave down **iii** $x = 0$ **iv** $(0, 0)$	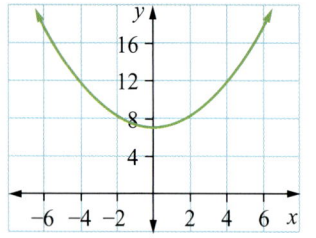	The magnitude of a determines the width of the parabola. • If $0 < a < 1$, then $y = ax^2$ is wider than $y = x^2$. • If $a > 1$, then $y = ax^2$ is narrower than $y = x^2$. • If $a > 0$, the curve is concave up. • If $a < 0$, the curve is concave down. The curve $y = -ax^2$ is the reflection of $y = ax^2$ in the x-axis. For $y = x^2 + c$, the effect of the constant c is to translate the graph of $y = x^2$ up c units when $c > 0$ and down c units when $c < 0$. For $y = (x - b)^2$, the effect of the constant b is to translate the graph of $y = x^2$ by b units to the right when $b > 0$ and b units to the left when $b < 0$.
b i The graph of $y = 0.3x^2 + 7$ is the graph of $y = x^2$ made wider and translated up 7 units. **ii** Concave up **iii** $x = 0$ **iv** $(0, 7)$	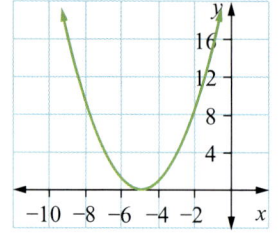	
c i The graph of $y = (x + 5)^2$ is the graph of $y = x^2$ translated 5 units to the left. **ii** Concave up **iii** $x = -5$ **iv** $(-5, 0)$	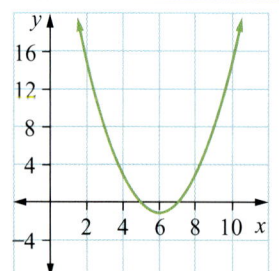	
d i The graph of $y = (x - 6)^2 - 1$ is the graph of $y = x^2$ translated 6 units to the right and 1 unit down. **ii** Concave up **iii** $x = 6$ **iv** $(6, -1)$		

14 Consider the following parabolas.

   i What transformation of the graph of $y = x^2$ is required to produce the parabola?

   ii Hence find the concavity.

   iii Find the equation of the axis of symmetry.

   iv Find the coordinates of the vertex.

a $y = -10x^2$ **b** $y = 8x^2 - 3$ **c** $y = \frac{5}{8}x^2 + 4$

d $y = (x - 15)^2$ **e** $y = (x + 11)^2$ **f** $y = (x - 5)^2 + 1$

g $y = (x + 7)^2 - 9$ **h** $y = -(x - 3)^2 + 5$ **i** $y = \frac{1}{2}(x - 1)^2 - 3$

15 The following graphs are transformations of the parabola $y = x^2$. Determine the equation of each using the information shown.

a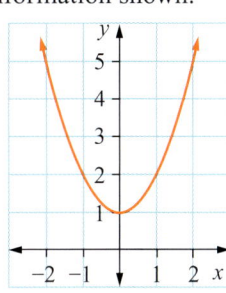

b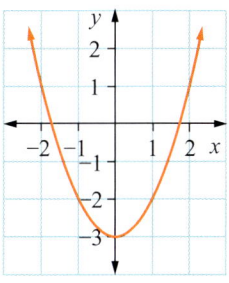

c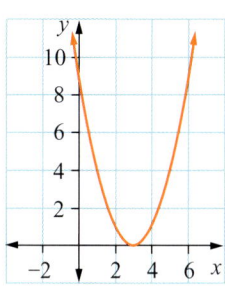

d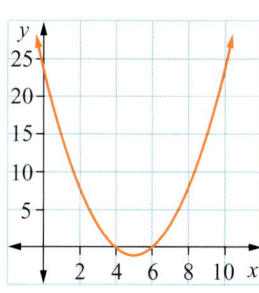

e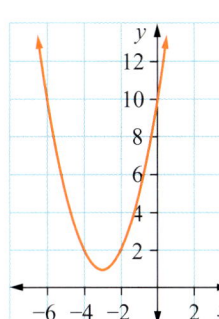

f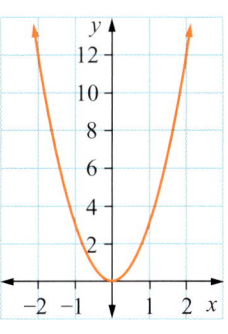

g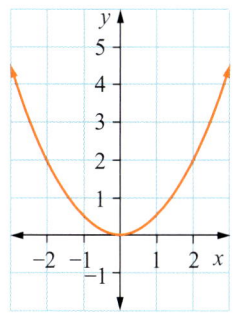

h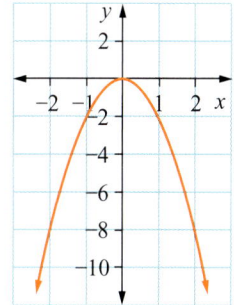

EXAMPLE 7

Find the equation of the axis of symmetry and the coordinates of the vertex of each parabola by first completing the square on x.

a $y = x^2 - 6x + 7$

b $y = x^2 + 7x + 15$

	Solve	Think	Apply
a	$y = x^2 - 6x + 7$ $= (x^2 - 6x + 9) + 7 - 9$ $= (x - 3)^2 - 2$ Axis of symmetry is $x = 3$. Coordinates of vertex are $(3, -2)$.	$y = x^2 - 6x + 7$ can be written as $y = (x^2 - 6x + \square) + 7 - \square$ where $\square$ is the number that must be added to $x^2 - 6x$ to make it a perfect square. $\square = \left(\frac{1}{2} \times \text{coefficient of } x\right)^2$ $= \left(\frac{1}{2} \times -6\right)^2 = (-3)^2 = 9$	Complete the square on x to write the equation of the parabola in the form $y = (x + h)^2 + k$. The axis of symmetry is then $x = -h$ and
b	$y = x^2 + 7x + 15$ $= x^2 + 7x + \frac{49}{4} + 15 - \frac{49}{4}$ $= \left(x + \frac{7}{2}\right)^2 + 2\frac{3}{4}$ Axis of symmetry is $x = -\frac{7}{2}$. Coordinates of vertex are $\left(-3\frac{1}{2}, 2\frac{3}{4}\right)$.	$y = x^2 + 7x + 15$ can be written as $y = (x^2 + 7x + \square) + 15 - \square$ where $\square$ is the number that must be added to $x^2 + 7x$ to make it a perfect square. $\square = \left(\frac{1}{2} \times \text{coefficient of } x\right)^2$ $= \left(\frac{1}{2} \times 7\right)^2 = \left(\frac{7}{2}\right)^2$ $= \frac{49}{4}$ or $12\frac{1}{4}$	the vertex is $(-h, k)$. *Note:* Whatever amount we add to the expression, we must also subtract the same amount to ensure that the expressions are equivalent.

16 Find the equation of the axis of symmetry and the coordinates of the vertex of the following parabolas, by completing the square on x.

a $y = x^2 - 4x + 2$

b $y = x^2 + 10x - 6$

c $y = x^2 - 3x + 4$

d $y = x^2 + 5x - 1$

e $y = x^2 - 9x + 5$

f $y = x^2 + 8x$

EXAMPLE 8

Determine a quadratic expression of the form $y = ax^2 + c$ that will generate the following number patterns.

a

x	0	1	2	3	4	5
y	1	2	5	10	17	26

b

x	0	1	2	3	4	5
y	-1	1	7	17	31	49

	Solve	Think	Apply
a	If $x = 0$, $y = 1$, hence $1 = a \times 0^2 + c$ $\qquad 1 = c$ Thus $y = ax^2 + 1$. If $x = 1$, $y = 2$, hence $2 = a \times 1^2 + 1$ $\qquad 2 = a + 1$ $\qquad a = 1$ The expression is $y = x^2 + 1$.	Assume $y = ax^2 + c$. Substitute the value of y when $x = 0$. This produces the value of c. Substitute any other value of x and y from the table.	Assume $y = ax^2 + c$. Substitute the value of y when $x = 0$ to find the value of c. Substitute any other value of x and y from the table to find a.
b	If $x = 0$, $y = -1$, hence $-1 = 0^2 + c$ $\qquad -1 = c$ Thus $y = ax^2 - 1$. If $x = 1$, $y = 1$, hence $1 = a \times 1^2 - 1$ $\qquad 1 = a - 1$ $\qquad a = 2$ The expression is $y = 2x^2 - 1$.	Assume $y = ax^2 + c$. Substitute $y = -1$ when $x = 0$. Substitute $y = 1$ when $x = 1$.	

17 Determine a quadratic expression of the form $y = ax^2 + c$ that will generate these number patterns.

a

x	0	1	2	3	4	5
y	-1	0	3	8	15	24

b

x	0	1	2	3	4	5
y	0	-3	-12	-27	-48	-75

c

x	0	1	2	3	4	5
y	1	3	9	19	33	51

d

x	0	1	2	3	4	5
y	10	9	6	1	-6	-15

EXAMPLE 9

Determine a quadratic expression of the form $y = x^2 + bx + c$ that will generate the number pattern in the table.

x	0	1	2	3	4	5
y	3	-1	-3	-3	-1	3

Solve	Think	Apply
If $x = 0$, $y = 3$, hence $3 = 0^2 + b \times 0 + c$ so $c = 3$. Thus $y = x^2 + bx + 3$. If $x = 1$, $y = -1$. Hence: $-1 = 1^2 + b \times 1 + 3$ $\qquad -1 = 1 + b + 3$ $\qquad\quad b = -5$ The expression is $y = x^2 - 5x + 3$.	Assume $y = x^2 + bx + c$. Substitute $y = 3$ when $x = 0$. Substitute $y = -1$ when $x = 1$.	Assume $y = x^2 + bx + c$. Substitute the value of y when $x = 0$ to find the value of c. Substitute any other value of x and y from the table to find b.

18 Determine a quadratic expression of the form $y = x^2 + bx + c$ that will generate these number patterns.

a

x	0	1	2	3	4	5
y	-2	-2	0	4	10	18

b

x	0	1	2	3	4	5
y	1	-1	-1	-1	5	11

c

x	0	1	2	3	4	5
y	2	0	0	2	6	12

d

x	0	1	2	3	4	5
y	1	7	15	25	37	51

D The hyperbola

Hyperbola is the name given to the graph of an equation of the form $y = \dfrac{k}{x}$. This equation may be written $xy = k$.

EXAMPLE 1

a Complete the following table and draw the graph of $y = \dfrac{1}{x}$.

x	-4	-3	-2	-1	$-\frac{1}{2}$	$-\frac{1}{4}$	$-\frac{1}{8}$	$\frac{1}{8}$	$\frac{1}{4}$	$\frac{1}{2}$	1	2	3	4
y														

b What happens at $x = 0$? Is it possible for y to equal 0?

c What happens to the value of y as x gets very large? (Consider the value of y for $x = 10, 100, 1000, \ldots$)

d What happens to the value of y as x gets closer and closer to 0 approaching from the right? (Consider the value of y for $x = \frac{1}{10}, \frac{1}{100}, \frac{1}{1000}, \ldots$)

e What happens to the value of y as x gets smaller? Consider the value of y for $x = -10, -100, -1000, \ldots$)

f What happens to the value of y as x gets closer and closer to 0 approaching from the left? (Consider the value of y for $x = -\frac{1}{10}, -\frac{1}{100}, -\frac{1}{1000}, \ldots$)

g An asymptote is a line that the curve gets closer and closer to but never crosses. Write the equations of the two asymptotes of this graph.

h Draw the lines $y = x$ and $y = -x$ on the same axes. Does the curve reflect onto itself in these lines? Write the equations of the two axes of symmetry of the hyperbola.

	Solve	Think/Apply

a

x	-4	-3	-2	-1	$-\frac{1}{2}$	$-\frac{1}{4}$	$-\frac{1}{8}$	$\frac{1}{8}$	$\frac{1}{4}$	$\frac{1}{2}$	1	2	3	4
y	$-\frac{1}{4}$	$-\frac{1}{3}$	$-\frac{1}{2}$	-1	-2	-3	-8	8	4	2	1	$\frac{1}{2}$	$\frac{1}{3}$	$\frac{1}{4}$

The graph of an equation of the form $y = \frac{1}{x}$ is called a hyperbola.

The hyperbola $y = \frac{1}{x}$ consists of two separate branches. The asymptotes (the lines the curve gets closer and closer to but never touches) of the hyperbola $y = \frac{1}{x}$ are $y = 0$ and $x = 0$.

The axes of symmetry are $y = x$ and $y = -x$.

b

There is no point on the curve that has an x-coordinate $= 0$.

There is no point on the curve with a y-coordinate $= 0$.

If $x = 0$, $y = \frac{1}{0}$, which is undefined.

If $y = 0$, $0 = \frac{1}{x}$.

There is no value of x that makes this statement true.

c

y approaches the value 0.

As x gets larger, y gets closer to 0 (but is never equal to 0).

x	10	100	1000
y	$\frac{1}{10}$	$\frac{1}{100}$	$\frac{1}{1000}$

d

y gets very large.

As x gets closer to 0 from the right, y gets larger.

x	$\frac{1}{10}$	$\frac{1}{100}$	$\frac{1}{1000}$
y	10	100	1000

e

y approaches 0.

As x gets smaller, y gets closer to 0.

x	-10	-100	-1000
y	$-\frac{1}{10}$	$-\frac{1}{100}$	$-\frac{1}{1000}$

f

y gets very small.

As x gets closer to 0 from the left, y gets smaller.

x	$-\frac{1}{10}$	$-\frac{1}{100}$	$-\frac{1}{1000}$
y	-10	-100	-1000

g

$y = 0$ and $x = 0$

Both branches of the curve get closer and closer to the x- and y-axes but never cross them. The equations of the x- and y-axes are $y = 0$ and $x = 0$ respectively.

h

The curve reflects onto itself (see the graphs in part **a**). The axes of symmetry are $y = x$ and $y = -x$.

The curve reflects onto itself in the lines $y = x$ and $y = -x$.

1 a Complete the following table and draw the graph of $y = -\frac{1}{x}$.

x	-4	-3	-2	-1	$-\frac{1}{2}$	$-\frac{1}{4}$	$-\frac{1}{8}$	$\frac{1}{8}$	$\frac{1}{4}$	$\frac{1}{2}$	1	2	3	4
y														

b What happens at $x = 0$?

c Is it possible for y to equal 0?

d What happens to the value of y as x gets very large? (Consider the value of y for $x = 10, 100, 1000, \ldots$)

e What happens to the value of y as x gets closer and closer to 0 approaching from the right?

(Consider the value of y for $x = \frac{1}{10}, \frac{1}{100}, \frac{1}{1000}, \ldots$)

f What happens to the value of y as x gets smaller? (Consider the value of y for $x = -10, -100, -1000, \ldots$)

g What happens to the value of y as x gets closer and closer to 0 approaching from the left?

(Consider the value of y for $x = -\frac{1}{10}, -\frac{1}{100}, -\frac{1}{1000}, \ldots$)

h An asymptote is a line the curve gets closer and closer to but never crosses. Write the equations of the two asymptotes of this hyperbola.

i Write the equations of the two axes of symmetry of the hyperbola.

Using technology, or otherwise, investigate the following graphs.

2 a Sketch graphs of $y = \frac{1}{x}, y = \frac{6}{x}, y = \frac{10}{x}, y = \frac{0.2}{x}, y = \frac{0.7}{x}$ on the same axes.

b What is the effect of the magnitude of the constant k on the graph of $y = \frac{k}{x}$?

c What are the equations of the asymptotes of the above hyperbolas?

d What are the equations of the axes of symmetry of the above hyperbolas?

3 a Sketch the graphs of $y = \frac{1}{x}, y = -\frac{2}{x}, y = -\frac{3}{x}, y = -\frac{5}{x}$ on the same axes.

b What is the effect of the sign of the constant k on the graph of $y = \frac{k}{x}$?

c What are the equations of the asymptotes of the above hyperbolas?

d What are the equations of the axes of symmetry of the above hyperbolas?

4 a On the same axes sketch these graphs:

   i $y = \frac{1}{x}$ **ii** $y = \frac{1}{x} + 3$ **iii** $y = \frac{1}{x} - 3$

b What is the effect of the constant c on the graph of $y = \frac{1}{x} + c$?

c What are the equations of the asymptotes of the above hyperbolas?

d Without graphing, write the equations of the asymptotes of these hyperbolas.

   i $y = \frac{1}{x} + 5$ **ii** $y = \frac{3}{x} - 4$ **iii** $y = -\frac{2}{x} + 1$

5 a On the same axes sketch these graphs:

   i $y = \frac{1}{x}$ **ii** $y = \frac{1}{x - 3}$ **iii** $y = \frac{1}{x - 5}$ **iv** $y = \frac{1}{x + 1}$ **v** $y = \frac{1}{x + 2}$

b What is the effect of the constant b on the graph of $y = \frac{1}{x + b}$?

c What are the equations of the asymptotes of the above hyperbolas?

d Without graphing, write the equations of the asymptotes of these hyperbolas.

   i $y = \frac{1}{x - 7}$ **ii** $y = \frac{1}{x + 3}$ **ii** $y = \frac{-5}{x - 2}$ **iv** $y = \frac{-1}{x + 4}$

EXAMPLE 2

Consider the following hyperbolas.
  i What transformation of the graph of $y = \frac{1}{x}$ is required to produce the hyperbola?
  ii Hence find the equations of the asymptotes.
  iii Find the equations of the axes of symmetry.

a $y = -\dfrac{10}{x}$ **b** $y = \dfrac{1}{x} + 4$ **c** $y = \dfrac{1}{x+7}$

Solve/Think		Apply
a **i** The graph $y = -\dfrac{10}{x}$ is $y = \dfrac{1}{x}$ reflected in the x-axis and is further out from the asymptotes. **ii** $y = 0, x = 0$ **iii** $y = x, y = -x$	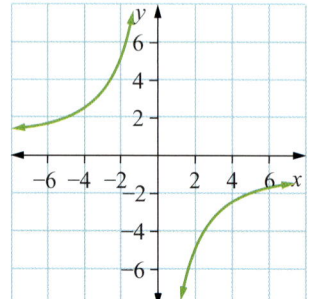	For the graph of $y = \dfrac{k}{x-a} + c$, the graph of $y = \dfrac{1}{x}$ is: • translated a units to the right and c units up, • moved further from the asymptotes if $k > 1$ (or $k < -1$) • moved closer to the asymptotes if $0 < k < 1$ (or $-1 < k < 0$). The asymptotes are $x = a$ and $y = c$.
b **i** The graph of $y = \dfrac{1}{x} + 4$ is $y = \dfrac{1}{x}$ translated 4 units up. **ii** $y = 4, x = 0$ **iii** $y = x + 4, y = -x + 4$	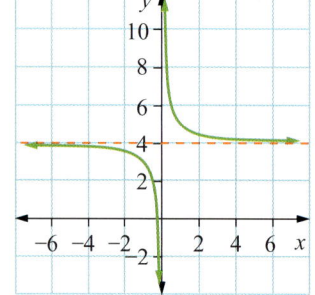	
c **i** The graph of $y = \dfrac{1}{x+7}$ is $y = \dfrac{1}{x}$ translated 7 units to the left. **ii** $y = 0, x = -7$ **iii** $y = x + 7, y = -x - 7$	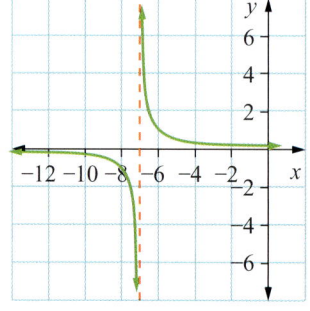	

6 Consider the following hyperbolas.
  i What transformation of the graph of $y = \frac{1}{x}$ is required to produce the hyperbola?
  ii Hence find the equations of the asymptotes.
  iii Find the equations of the axes of symmetry.

a $y = -\dfrac{9}{x}$ **b** $y = \dfrac{1}{x} + 8$ **c** $y = \dfrac{1}{x+5}$

d $y = \dfrac{1}{x} - 7$ **e** $y = \dfrac{1}{x-6}$ **f** $y = -\dfrac{1}{x} + 5$

g $y = \dfrac{-1}{x-2}$ **h** $y = \dfrac{6}{x} - 7$ **i** $y = \dfrac{-2}{x+12}$

7 The following graphs are transformations of the hyperbola $y = \frac{1}{x}$. Determine the equation of each.

a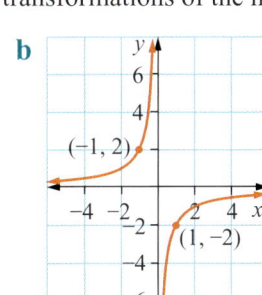

b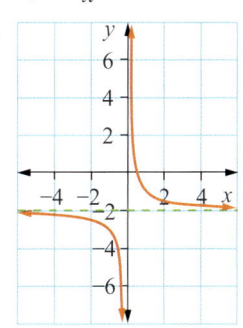

c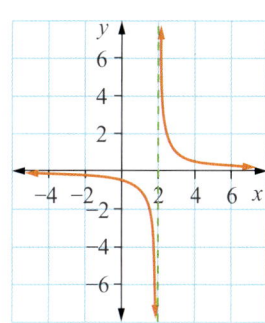

d

E The circle

The equation of the circle with centre $(0, 0)$ and radius r is $x^2 + y^2 = r^2$.

Exercise 12E

1 Write the equation of the circle with centre at the origin and radius:

    a 5   **b** $\sqrt{7}$ **c** $\frac{5}{4}$

2 What is the radius of each circle?

    a $x^2 + y^2 = 9$ **b** $x^2 + y^2 = 10$ **c** $x^2 + y^2 = \frac{25}{49}$ **d** $x^2 + y^2 = \frac{7}{4}$ **e** $9x^2 + 9y^2 = 16$

● EXAMPLE 1

a Using technology, or otherwise, sketch graphs of:

    i $(x - 1)^2 + (y - 3)^2 = 4$ **ii** $(x + 1)^2 + (y + 3)^2 = 9$ **iii** $(x - 2)^2 + (y + 5)^2 = 1$

b What are the coordinates of the centre and the radius of each of these circles?

c What transformation of the graph of $x^2 + y^2 = r^2$ is required to produce these circles?

d Write the coordinates of the centre and the radius of the circle $(x + 7)^2 + (y - 5)^2 = 49$.

Solve/Think	Apply
a **i** 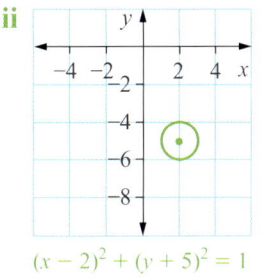 **ii** **iii** 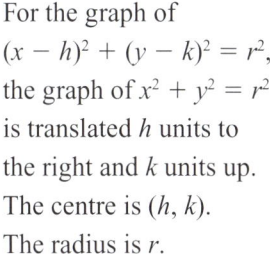 $(x - 1)^2 + (y - 3)^2 = 4$ $(x + 1)^2 + (y + 3)^2 = 9$ $(x - 2)^2 + (y + 5)^2 = 1$	For the graph of $(x - h)^2 + (y - k)^2 = r^2$, the graph of $x^2 + y^2 = r^2$ is translated h units to the right and k units up. The centre is (h, k). The radius is r.
b **i** $(1, 3)$, $r = 2$ **ii** $(-1, -3)$, $r = 3$ **iii** $(2, -5)$, $r = 1$	

c   **i** Translation 1 unit right and 3 units up
    ii Translation 1 unit left and 3 units down
    iii Translation 2 units right and 5 units down	

d $(-7, 5)$, $r = 7$	

3 a Using technology, or otherwise, sketch these graphs on the same axes.

  i $(x - 4)^2 + (y - 2)^2 = 25$ **ii** $(x + 3)^2 + (y + 7)^2 = 4$ **iii** $(x - 6)^2 + (y + 8)^2 = 100$

b What are the coordinates of the centre and the radius of each of these circles.

c What transformation of the graph of $x^2 + y^2 = r^2$ is required to produce these circles?

4 Write the coordinates of the centre and the radius of these circles.

  a $(x - 7)^2 + (y - 5)^2 = 49$ **b** $(x + 7)^2 + (y + 5)^2 = 49$ **c** $(x - 7)^2 + (y + 5)^2 = 49$

  d $(x + 7)^2 + (y - 5)^2 = 49$ **e** $(x + 4)^2 + (y - 9)^2 = 36$ **f** $(x - 10)^2 + (y + 5)^2 = 81$

  g $x^2 + (y - 5)^2 = 1$ **h** $(x + 9)^2 + y^2 = 16$

5 Write the equation of the circle with:

  a centre $(4, 5)$, radius $= 2$ **b** centre $(-2, -4)$, radius $= 5$

  c centre $(3, -2)$, radius $= 6$ **d** centre $(-1, 4)$, radius $= 3$

  e centre $(0, 2)$, radius $= 1$ **f** centre $(-5, 0)$, radius $= 7$

● EXAMPLE 2

Find the coordinates of the centre and the radius of the circle $x^2 + y^2 - 4x + 6y + 9 = 0$.

Solve/Think	Apply
$x^2 + y^2 - 4x + 6y + 9 = 0$ can be written as $x^2 - 4x + y^2 + 6y = -9$ Completing the square on x and y: $(x^2 - 4x + 4) + (y^2 + 6y + 9) = -9 + 4 + 9$ *Note:* Whatever has been added to the left-hand side of the equation must also be added to the right-hand side. $(x - 2)^2 + (y + 3)^2 = 4$ Coordinates of centre are $(2, -3)$, radius $= 2$ units	Rearrange the equation so that the x terms are together, the y terms are together and the constant is on the right-hand side. Complete the square on x and on y. Add to the right-hand side of the equation whatever has been added to the left-hand side. This rearranges the equation to the form $(x - h)^2 + (y - k)^2 = r^2$.

---

6 Find the coordinates of the centre and the radius of these circles.

  a $x^2 + y^2 + 2x - 8y - 8 = 0$ **b** $x^2 + y^2 - 10x - 6y + 33 = 0$

  c $x^2 + y^2 + 14x + 2y + 1 = 0$ **d** $x^2 + y^2 - 20x + 96 = 0$

  e $x^2 + y^2 - 12y + 20 = 0$ **f** $2x^2 + 2y^2 - 6x - 2y - 13 = 0$ *Divide both sides by 2.*

● EXAMPLE 3

a Write the equation of the circle with centre $(-5, 7)$ and radius 11.

b Express the equation in the general form.

	Solve/Think	Apply
a	$(x - -5)^2 + (y - 7)^2 = 11^2$ or $(x + 5)^2 + (y - 7)^2 = 121$	The equation of the circle with centre (h, k) and radius r is $(x - h)^2 + (y - k)^2 = r^2$. This is known as the centre–radius form of the equation of a circle.
b	Expanding the above equation gives: $x^2 + 10x + 25 + y^2 - 14y + 49 = 121$ $x^2 + y^2 + 10x - 14y - 47 = 0$	Expand and collect like terms. This is known as the general form of the equation of a circle.

NUMBER & ALGEBRA

7 Write the equation of the circle in centre–radius and general form given the centre and radius.

   a centre is $(3, 6)$, radius $= 5$ **b** centre is $(-4, 3)$, radius $= 1$

   c centre is $(7, -4)$, radius $= 3$ **d** centre is $(-6, -7)$, radius $= 4$

• EXAMPLE 4

a Determine whether the following points lie inside, on, or outside the circle $x^2 + y^2 = 25$.

   i $(-1, 3)$ **ii** $(4, 4)$ **iii** $(3, -4)$

b Determine whether the following points lie inside, on, or outside the circle $(x - 2)^2 + (y + 3)^2 = 16$.

   i $(3, 1)$ **ii** $(-2, -3)$ **iii** $(1, -2)$

		Solve/Think	Think	Apply
a		Radius $= 5$ units and the centre is $(0, 0)$.	Use the distance formula:	Calculate the
	i	Distance of the point $(-1, 3)$ from the centre of the circle is $d = \sqrt{(-1)^2 + 3^2} = \sqrt{10}$. As $d < 5$, the point lies inside the circle.	$d = \sqrt{(x_1 - x_2)^2 + (y_1 - y_2)^2}$	distance, d, of the point from the centre of the circle of radius r.
	ii	Distance of the point $(4, 4)$ from the centre of the circle is $d = \sqrt{4^2 + 4^2} = \sqrt{32}$. As $d > 5$, the point lies outside the circle.		• If $d < r$, the point lies inside the circle.
	iii	Distance of the point $(-3, 4)$ from the centre of the circle is $d = \sqrt{(-3)^2 + 4^2)} = \sqrt{25} = 5$. As $d = 5$, the point lies on the circle.		• If $d = r$, the point lies on the circumference of the circle.
b		Radius $= 4$ units and the centre is $(2, -3)$.	Use the distance formula:	• If $d > r$, the point lies outside the circle.
	i	Distance of the point $(3, 1)$ from the centre of the circle is $d = \sqrt{(3 - 2)^2 + (1 - (-3))^2} = \sqrt{17}$. As $d > 4$, the point lies outside the circle.	$d = \sqrt{(x_1 - x_2)^2 + (y_1 - y_2)^2}$	
	ii	Distance of the point $(-2, -3)$ from the centre of the circle is $d = \sqrt{(-2 - 2)^2 + (-3 - (-3))^2}$ $= \sqrt{16} = 4$. As $d = 4$, the point lies on the circle.		
	iii	Distance of the point $(1, -2)$ from the centre of the circle is $d = \sqrt{(1 - 2)^2 + (-2 - (-3))^2} = \sqrt{2}$. As $d < 4$, the point lies inside the circle.		

8 **a** Determine whether the following points lie inside, on, or outside the circle $(x - 1)^2 + (y + 4)^2 = 9$.

     i $(2, 1)$ **ii** $(2, -3)$ **iii** $(1, -1)$

  b Determine whether the following points lie inside, on, or outside the circle $(x + 3)^2 + (y - 5)^2 = 36$.

     i $(-3, -1)$ **ii** $(-2, -3)$ **iii** $(2, 9)$

  c Determine whether the following points lie inside, on, or outside the circle $(x - 4)^2 + y^2 = 25$.

     i $(3, -2)$ **ii** $(1, -4)$ **iii** $(-2, 2)$

  d Determine whether the following points lie inside, on, or outside the circle $(x - 5)^2 + (y + 4)^2 = 49$.

     i $(8, 2)$ **ii** $(0, 4)$ **iii** $(5, 3)$

F Exponential graphs

Graphs of equations of the form $y = a^x$, where a is a constant, are called exponential curves. The graph passes through the point $(0, 1)$ and $y = 0$ is its asymptote.

● EXAMPLE 1

a Using technology, or otherwise, sketch these exponential graphs on the same axes.

    i $y = 2^x$ ii $y = 2^x + 1$ iii $y = 2^x + 5$

    iv $y = 2^x - 4$ v $y = 2^x - 7$

b What transformation of the graph of $y = 2^x$ will produce each of these graphs?

c Write the equation of the asymptote of each graph.

d Write the coordinates of the y-intercept of each graph.

Solve/Think	Apply
a *[Graph showing curves $y = 2^x + 5$, $y = 2^x + 1$, $y = 2^x$, $y = 2^x - 4$, $y = 2^x - 7$ on axes from -4 to 4 on x-axis and -8 to 12 on y-axis]*	The graph of $y = a^x + c$ is the graph of $y = a^x$ translated: • c units up, if $c > 0$ • c units down, if $c < 0$. The asymptote is $y = c$. The coordinates of the y-intercept are $(0, c + 1)$.

b   ii Translation 1 unit up
   iii Translation 5 units up
   iv Translation 4 units down
   v Translation 7 units down	

c   i $y = 0$ ii $y = 1$
   iii $y = 5$ iv $y = -4$
   v $y = -7$	

d   i $(0, 1)$ ii $(0, 2)$
   iii $(0, 6)$ iv $(0, -3)$
   v $(0, -6)$	

Exercise 12F

1 a Sketch these graphs on the same axes.

    i $y = 3^x$ ii $y = 3^x + 4$ iii $y = 3^x - 5$

  b Write the equation of the asymptote of each graph.

  c Write the coordinates of the y-intercept of each graph.

EXAMPLE 2

a Using technology, or otherwise, sketch these exponential graphs on the same axes.

  i $y = 2^x$ **ii** $y = 2^{-x}$

  iii $y = 2^{-x} + 3$ **iv** $y = 2^{-x} - 4$

b What transformation of the graph of $y = 2^x$ will produce each of these graphs?

c Write the equation of the asymptote of each graph.

d Write the coordinates of the y-intercept of each graph.

Solve/Think	Apply
a	The graph of $y = a^{-x}$ is the reflection of $y = a^x$ in the y-axis. Its asymptote is $y = 0$ and it passes through the point $(0, 1)$. The graph of $y = a^{-x} + c$ is the graph of $y = a^{-x}$ translated: • c units up, if $c > 0$ • c units down, if $c < 0$. The asymptote is $y = c$. The coordinates of the y-intercept are $(0, c + 1)$. *Note:* $2^{-x} = (2^{-1})^x = \left(\frac{1}{2}\right)^x$.

b   **ii** Reflection in the y-axis.
 	
    iii Reflection in the y-axis and translation up 3 units.
 	
    iv Reflection in y-axis and translation down 4 units.	

c **i** $y = 0$ **ii** $y = 0$ **iii** $y = 3$ **iv** $y = -4$	Thus the graph of $y = 2^{-x}$ is the same as the graph of $y = \left(\frac{1}{2}\right)^x$.
d **i** $(0, 1)$ **ii** $(0, 1)$ **iii** $(0, 4)$ **iv** $(0, -3)$	

2 **a** Sketch these graphs on the same axes.

  i $y = 5^{-x}$ **ii** $y = 5^{-x} - 3$ **iii** $y = 5^{-x} + 2$

b What transformation of the graph of $y = 5^x$ will produce each of these graphs?

c Write the equation of the asymptote of each graph.

d Write the coordinates of the y-intercept of each graph.

3 **a** Using technology, or otherwise, sketch these graphs on the same axes.

  i $y = 2^{x-1}$ **ii** $y = 2^{x-3}$

  iii $y = 2^{x+2}$ **iv** $y = 2^{x+5}$

b What transformation of the graph of $y = 2^x$ will produce each of these graphs?

c Write the equation of the asymptote of each graph.

d Write the coordinates of the y-intercept of each graph.

e What is the effect of the constant b on the graph of $y = 2^{x-b}$?

4 **a** Sketch these graphs on the same axes.

  i $y = 3^x$ **ii** $y = 3^{x-2}$ **iii** $y = 3^{x+3}$

b Write the equation of the asymptote of each graph.

c Write the coordinates of the y-intercept of each graph.

EXAMPLE 3

a Using technology, or otherwise, sketch these graphs.

 i $y = 2^{x-2} + 3$ ii $y = 2^{x+2} - 3$

b What transformation of the graph of $y = 2^x$ will produce each of these graphs?

c Write the equation of the asymptote of each graph.

d What is the affect of the constants b and c on the graph of $y = 2^{x-b} + c$?

Solve/Think		Apply
a i ii		For the graph of $y = a^{x-b} + c$, the graph of $y = a^x$ is translated: • b units to the right if $b > 0$, or b units to the left if $b < 0$ • c units up if $c > 0$ or c units down if $c < 0$. The equation of the asymptote is $y = c$.
b i $b = 2$ so translated 2 units right. $c = 3$ so translated 3 units up. ii $b = -2$ so translated 2 units left. $c = -3$ so translated 3 units down.		
c i $y = 3$ ii $y = -3$		
d The constants b affects how far the graph is translated right or left. The constants c affects how far the graph is translated up or down.		

5 a Sketch graphs of:

 i $y = 2^{x-4} + 1$ ii $y = 2^{x+2} - 3$

 iii $y = 3^{x-2} - 4$ iv $y = 5^{x+3} + 6$

 b Write the equation of the asymptote of each graph.

G Other graphs

Exercise 12G

1 Using technology, or otherwise, investigate the following graphs.

 a i Draw graphs of $y = x^3$, $y = 2x^3$, $y = 4x^3$, $y = \frac{1}{2}x^3$, $y = 0.2x^3$ on the same axes.

  ii What is the effect of the magnitude of the constant a on the graph of $y = ax^3$?

 b i Draw graphs of $y = x^3$, $y = -x^3$, $y = 2x^3$, $y = -2x^3$, $y = \frac{1}{2}x^3$, $y = -\frac{1}{2}x^3$ on the same axes.

  ii What is the effect of the sign of the constant a on the graph of $y = ax^3$?

 c i Draw graphs of $y = 2x^3$, $y = 2x^3 + 4$, $y = 2x^3 - 3$ on the same axes.

  ii What is the effect of the constant d on the graph of $y = ax^3 + d$?

 d i Draw graphs of $y = x^3$, $y = (x - 1)^3$, $y = (x + 2)^3$ on the same axes.

  ii What is the effect of the constant r on the graph of $y = (x - r)^3$?

2 Draw neat sketches, showing the main features of these graphs.

a $y = 0.4x^3$

b $y = -0.4x^3$

c $y = x^3 + 2$

d $y = x^3 - 4$

e $y = -x^3 + 1$

f $y = -2x^3 - 2$

g $y = (x + 1)^3$

h $y = 2(x + 1)^3$

i $y = (x - 3)^3 + 1$

j $y = (x + 4)^3 - 2$

● EXAMPLE 1

Consider the graph of $y = (x - 3)(x - 1)(x + 2)$.

a Find the x-intercepts.

b Find the y-intercept.

c Draw a neat sketch of the curve.

d On the same axes draw these graphs.

   i $y = 2(x - 3)(x - 1)(x + 2)$ **ii** $y = \frac{1}{2}(x - 3)(x - 1)(x + 2)$ **iii** $y = -(x - 3)(x - 1)(x + 2)$

	Solve/Think	Apply
a	If $y = 0$, $(x - 3)(x - 1)(x + 2) = 0$. The x-intercepts are $x = 3, 1, -2$. The curve passes through the points $(3, 0)$, $(1, 0)$ and $(-2, 0)$.	Find the x- and y-intercepts and draw a smooth curve through these points. Use the fact that if $a \times b \times c = 0$
b	If $x = 0$, $y = (0 - 3)(0 - 1)(0 + 2) = 6$. The y-intercept is $y = 6$. The curve passes through the point $(0, 6)$.	then $a = 0$, $b = 0$, or $c = 0$. The graph of the equation $y = a(x - r)(x - s)(x - t)$ has x-intercepts r, s and t.
c	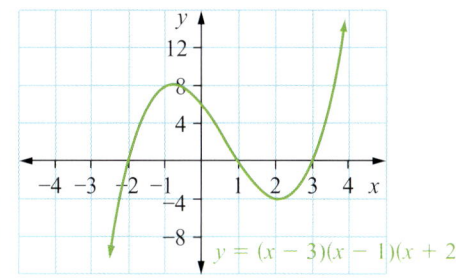	The value of a makes the curve steeper (if $a > 1$), or less steep (if $0 < a < 1$), between the x-intercepts. If $a < 0$, the curve is reflected in the x-axis.
d	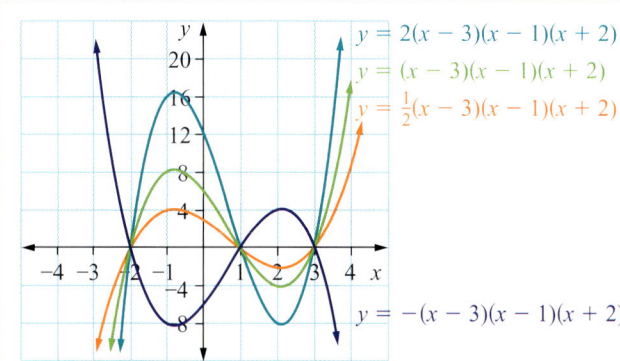	

3 Draw neat sketches of the curves.

a $y = (x - 2)(x + 1)(x + 3)$

b $y = 2(x - 2)(x + 1)(x + 3)$

c $y = \frac{1}{2}(x - 2)(x + 1)(x + 3)$

d $y = -(x - 2)(x + 1)(x + 3)$

e $y = (x - 5)(x - 2)(x + 3)$

f $y = 2(x + 1)(x + 2)(x + 3)$

g $y = (x - 2)(x - 4)(x - 5)$

h $y = -x(x - 2)(x + 4)$

4 Using technology, or otherwise, investigate the following graphs.
  a **i** Draw graphs of $y = 2x^2$, $y = 2x^3$, $y = 2x^4$, $y = 2x^5$, $y = 2x^6$ on the same axes.
      ii Describe the effect of n being odd or even on the shape of $y = ax^n$.
  b **i** Draw graphs of $y = 0.5x^4$, $y = 0.5x^4 + 3$, $y = 0.5x^4 - 3$ on the same axes.
      ii Describe the effect of the constant k on the graph $y = ax^n + k$
  c **i** Draw graphs of $y = x^5$, $y = (x - 2)^5$, $y = (x + 1)^5$ on the same axes.
      ii Describe the effect of the constant r on the graph of $y = a(x - r)^n$.

5 Draw neat sketches of these graphs.
  a $y = x^7$
  b $y = -x^6$
  c $y = x^4 + 2$
  d $y = x^5 - 4$
  e $y = 3(x - 2)^5$
  f $y = 2(x + 2)^6$
  g $y = (x - 4)^4 + 2$
  h $y = -(x - 1)^3 - 1$

6 State whether the graphs of the following equations are straight lines, parabolas, hyperbolas, circles or exponential functions.
  a $x^2 + y^2 = 4$
  b $y = (x - 3)^2 - 4$
  c $y = 4$
  d $y = 3^x + 4$
  e $y = x^2 + 3x - 4$
  f $y = 3x - 4$
  g $y = \dfrac{3}{x - 4}$
  h $y = 3^{x-4}$
  i $(x + 4)^2 + (y - 4)^2 = 1$

7 Match each of the graphs below with the following equations.
  a $y = 5^x + 5$
  b $y = 5 - x$
  c $y = 5 - x^2$
  d $y = \dfrac{1}{x - 5}$
  e $x^2 + y^2 = 5$
  f $y = (x - 5)^2$
  g $y = 5$
  h $(x - 5)^2 + (y + 5)^2 = 25$
  i $y = -5^{-x}$
  j $y = x^5$
  k $y = x(x - 5)(x + 5)$
  l $y = 0.5x^2$

A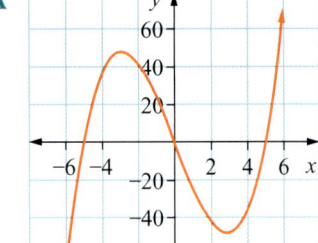

B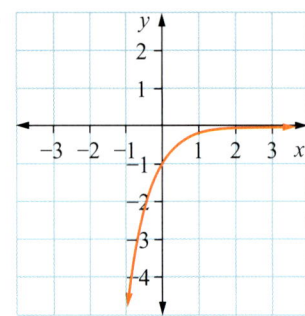

C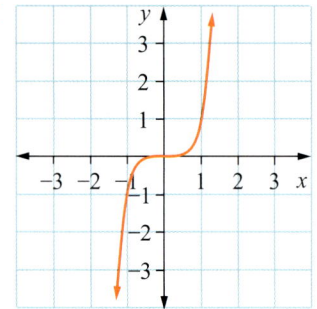

D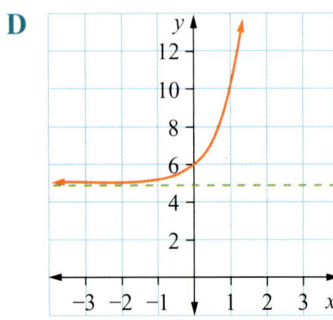

E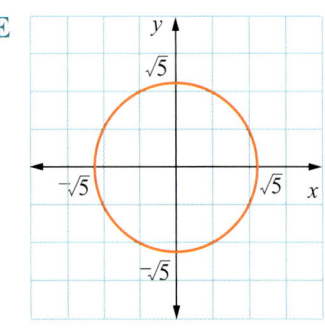

F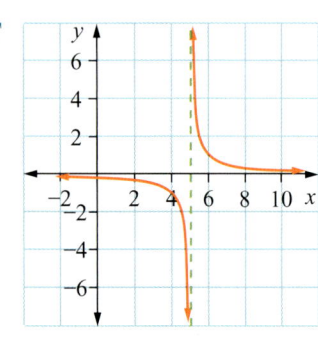

G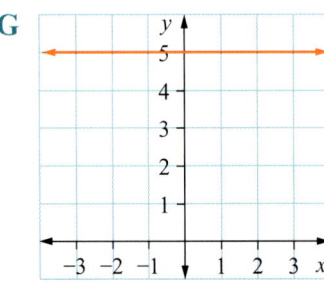

H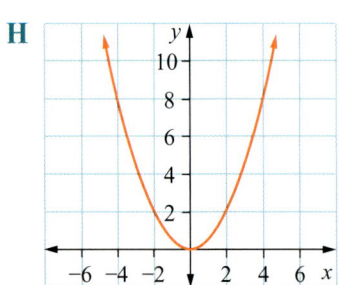

I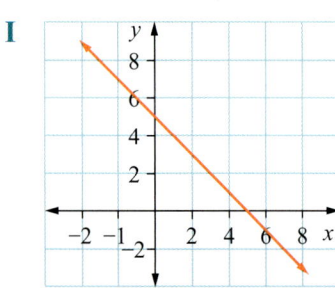

NUMBER & ALGEBRA

J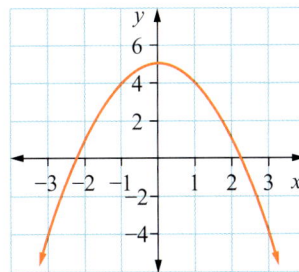

K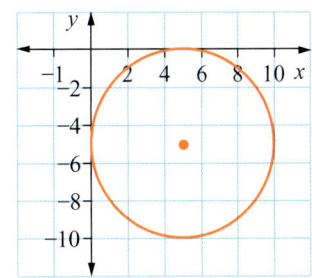

L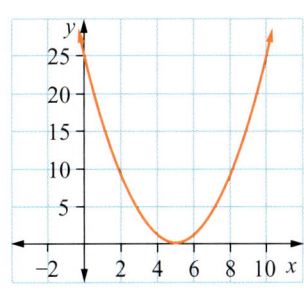

EXAMPLE 2

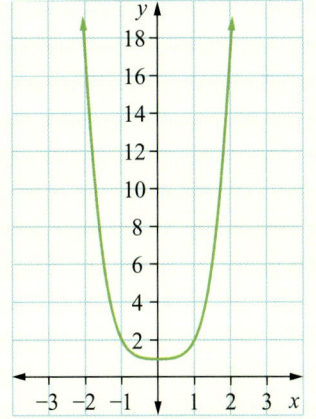

a Use the graph to complete the table below.

x	-2	-1	0	1	2
y					

b What do you notice about the values of y when $x = \pm 2, \pm 1$?

c Is the curve symmetrical about the y-axis? (Is the y-axis an axis of symmetry of the curve?)

d Determine the equation of the curve given that it is of the form $y = x^4 + c$.

e Calculate the values of y for $x = \pm 3, x = \pm 4, x = \pm 5$. What do you notice?

	Solve	Think	Apply
a	<table><tr><td>x</td><td>-2</td><td>-1</td><td>0</td><td>1</td><td>2</td></tr><tr><td>y</td><td>17</td><td>2</td><td>1</td><td>2</td><td>17</td></tr></table>	Read the appropriate coordinates from the graph.	A curve is symmetrical about the y-axis if the values of y are the same for $x = \pm k$.
b	If $x = \pm 2, y = 17$. If $x = \pm 1, y = 2$. The values of y are the same for $x = \pm k$.	Read the values from the table.	
c	Yes	The curve reflects on to itself using the y-axis.	
d	Substitute $(0, 1)$ into $y = x^4 + c$ $\qquad\qquad 1 = 0^4 + c$ $\qquad\qquad c = 1$ The equation of curve is $y = x^4 + 1$.	The point $(0, 1)$ lies on the curve, so its coordinates satisfy the equation.	
e	If $x = \pm 3, y = 82$ If $x = \pm 4, y = 257$ If $x = \pm 5, y = 626$ The values of y are the same for $x = \pm k$.	Use the equation found in part **d** to calculate the values of y.	

8 a i Use the graph to complete the table below.

x	-3	-2	-1	0	1	2	3
y							

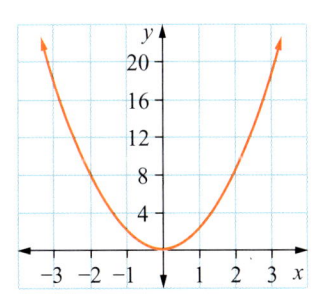

   ii What do you notice about the values of y when $x = \pm 3, \pm 2, \pm 1$?

   iii Is the curve symmetrical about the y-axis? (Is the y-axis an axis of symmetry of the curve?)

b **i** Use the graph to complete the table below.

x	-3	-2	-1	0	1	2	3
y							

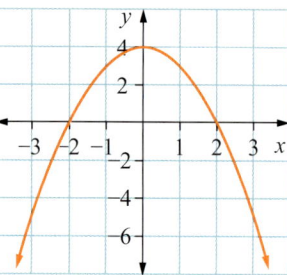

ii What do you notice about the values of y when $x = \pm 3$, ± 2, ± 1?

iii Is the curve symmetrical about the y-axis? (Is the y-axis an axis of symmetry of the curve?)

9 Determine algebraically whether the following curves are symmetrical about the y-axis.

a $y = 3x^2$ **b** $y = x^2 - 5$ **c** $y = 5 - x^2$

d $y = x^2 + 1$ **e** $y = x^2 + x$ **f** $y = x^3$

g $y = -2x^6$ **h** $y = 3x^4$ **i** $y = \dfrac{1}{x}$

j $y = 2^x$ **k** $y = 2^x + 2^{-x}$ **l** $y = \sqrt{25 - x^2}$

H Points of intersection of curves

EXAMPLE 1

Find the point(s) of intersection of these curves.

a $y = x^2 + 5x - 5$ and $y = 2x + 5$ **b** $y = \dfrac{4}{x}$ and $y = x + 3$

	Solve	Think	Apply
a	$x^2 + 5x - 5 = 2x + 5$ $x^2 + 3x - 10 = 0$ $(x + 5)(x - 2) = 0$ $\qquad\qquad x = -5, 2$ If $x = -5$, $y = -5$. If $x = 2$, $y = 9$. Points of intersection are $(-5, -5)$ and $(2, 9)$.	Replace y in the second equation by the expression for y in the first. Solve for x. Substitute $x = -5$ into $y = 2x + 5$ or $y = x^2 + 5x - 5$. $y = 2(-5) + 5$ or $y = (-5)^2 + 5(-5) - 5)$ $y = -5$ Substitute $x = 2$ into $y = 2x + 5$. $y = 2 \times 2 + 5 = 9$	The points of intersection can be found algebraically by solving the pair of equations simultaneously, using the substitution method. The solutions are the x- and y-coordinates of the points of intersection.
b	$\dfrac{4}{x} = x + 3$ $4 = x(x + 3)$ $\quad = x^2 + 3x$ $x^2 + 3x - 4 = 0$ $(x + 4)(x - 1) = 0$ $\qquad\qquad x = -4, 1$ If $x = -4$, $y = -4 + 3 = -1$. If $x = 1$, $y = 1 + 3 = 4$. Points of intersection are $(-4, -1)$ and $(1, 4)$.	Replace y in the second equation by the expression for y in the first. Solve for x. Substitute $x = -4$ into $y = x + 3$ or $y = \dfrac{4}{x}$: $y = -4 + 3$ or $y = \dfrac{4}{-4}$ $y = -1$ Substitute $x = 1$ into $y = x + 3$: $y = 1 + 3 = 4$	

Exercise 12H

1 **a** Find algebraically the point(s) of intersection of the curves.
   - **i** $y = x^2 + 8x - 14$ and $y = 5x - 4$
   - **ii** $y = x^2 - x + 9$ and $y = 2x + 7$
   - **iii** $y = 6x^2 + 19x - 7$ and $y = 4$
   - **iv** $y = 2x^2 - 5x - 8$ and $y = 2x + 7$
   - **v** $y = \dfrac{16}{x}$ and $y = x$
   - **vi** $y = \dfrac{-8}{x}$ and $y = x - 6$
   - **vii** $y = \dfrac{6}{x + 3}$ and $y = x - 2$
   - **viii** $y = \dfrac{-3}{x - 1}$ and $y = x - 5$
   - **ix** $x^2 + y^2 = 18$ and $y = x$
   - **x** $x^2 + y^2 = 10$ and $y = \frac{1}{2}(x + 5)$

   b Draw graphs to confirm your answers for parts **i**, **v**, **vii**, **ix** and **x**.

   c Which method, algebraic or graphical, was easier to use to find the points of intersection? Justify your choice.

● EXAMPLE 2

Find the point of intersection of the parabola $y = x^2$ and the straight line $y = x + 5$.

Solve/Think	Apply
Algebraically $x^2 = x + 5$ $x^2 - x - 5 = 0$ This quadratic equation does not factorise, but does have solutions since $\Delta > 0$. The quadratic formula could be used to find the solutions, but the graphs of these equations are quite simple to draw, so it may be more efficient to graph the equations and locate the points of intersection on the graphs. *Graphically* $y = x^2$ <table><tr><td>**x**</td><td>−3</td><td>−2</td><td>−1</td><td>1</td><td>1</td><td>2</td><td>3</td></tr><tr><td>**y**</td><td>9</td><td>4</td><td>1</td><td>0</td><td>1</td><td>4</td><td>9</td></tr></table> $y = x + 5$ <table><tr><td>**x**</td><td>−1</td><td>0</td><td>2</td></tr><tr><td>**y**</td><td>4</td><td>5</td><td>7</td></tr></table> Points of intersection are $(-1.8, 3.2)$ and $(2.8, 7.8)$ 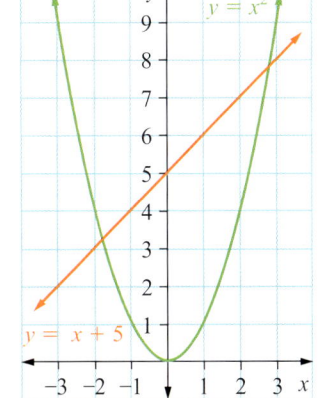	If, when solving the equations algebraically, the resulting quadratic equation does not factorise, and if the graphs are simple to draw, it may be more efficient to find the points of intersection graphically.

2 Choose a suitable method to find the point(s) of intersection of the following curves. Justify your choice of method.
   - **a** $y = x^2$ and $y = 4x - 1$
   - **b** $y = 2x^2$ and $y = x + 2$
   - **c** $y = \dfrac{1}{x}$ and $y = x + 3$
   - **d** $y = \dfrac{2}{x}$ and $y = x - 4$
   - **e** $x^2 + y^2 = 4$ and $y = x + 1$
   - **f** $(x - 1)^2 + (y - 2)^2 = 25$ and $y = x$

Language in mathematics

1 Use the following words to complete the statement below:
   depends, dependent, vertical, independent, change, horizontal
   a Variables are quantities whose values _____ or vary. In practical situations the value of one variable usually _____ on the value of another; for example, the number of people waiting at a bus stop depends on the time of day.
   b The first variable is called the _____ variable and the second is called the _____ variable.
   c When graphing the relationship between two variables, the independent variable is placed on the _____ axis and the dependent variable on the _____ axis.

2 Use a dictionary to explain the difference in meaning between these terms.
   a dependent and dependant
   b stationery and stationary

3 Draw graphs to show the meaning of these phrases.
   a increasing at an increasing rate
   b increasing at a decreasing rate
   c decreasing at an increasing rate
   d decreasing at a decreasing rate

4 The graph shows the amount of money in Alison's purse in a particular week. Write a story to explain the shape of the graph.

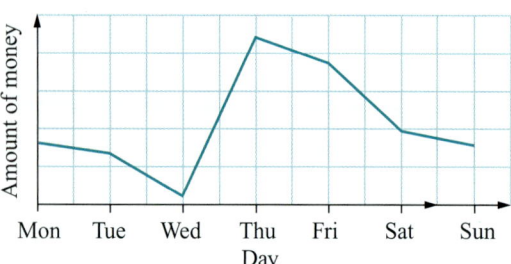

5 At the beginning of the period the noise level in the classroom increases as the students enter. When the teacher arrives in the room the level of noise drops quickly and the students get out their maths books. The teacher asks for quiet while she explains the work to be done. The students then work quietly. Halfway through the lesson the teacher gives the class a problem and asks them to work in groups to solve it. Each group reports its findings. At the end of the period the class is dismissed and the students leave the room. Draw a graph that illustrates how the noise level in the classroom changes during this period.

Terms

asymptote	axis of symmetry	circle	centre	concavity	
completing the square	constant	gradient	horizontal	hyperbola	hyperbolic
illustrate	interpret	intercept	interval	parabola	parabolic
radius	relative	stationary	steady	steadily	straight
turning point	variable	vertex			

NUMBER & ALGEBRA

Check your skills

1 If a variable is increasing at an increasing rate then it:

   A increases slowly at first and then more quickly   **B** increases quickly at first and then more slowly

   C increases at a constant rate   **D** increases before it decreases

2 The graph that shows that distance is decreasing at a decreasing rate is:

  A 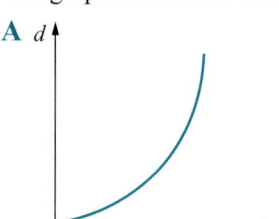 **B** 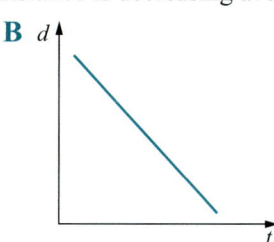 **C** 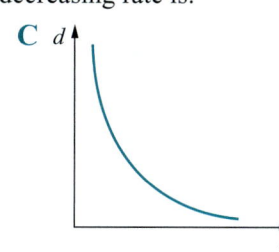 **D**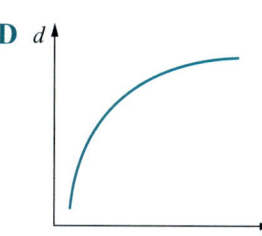

3 At the start of a 100 m race, Helen sprints to the front and then maintains a constant speed for about 20 m. As she tries to increase her speed again, she loses her footing and falls. The graph that could represent this situation is:

  A 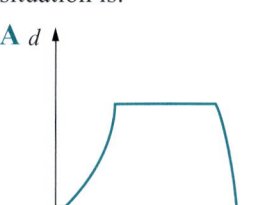 **B** 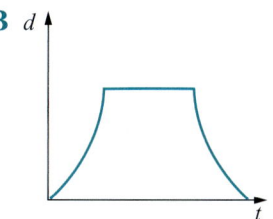 **C** 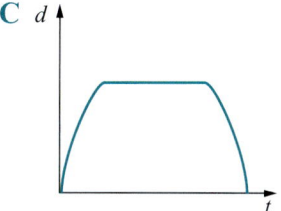 **D**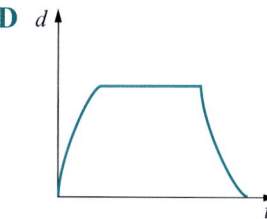

4 A racing car travels around the circuit shown. The graph that could represent the speed of the car as it travels around the second lap of the race is:

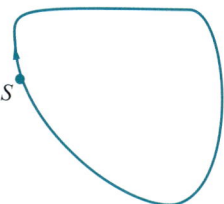

  A 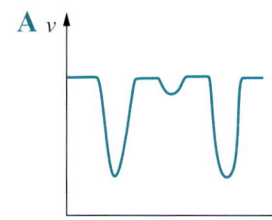 **B** 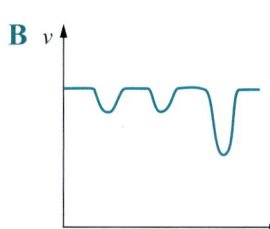 **C** 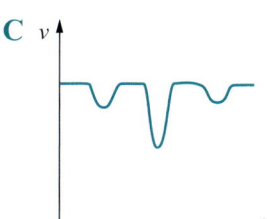 **D**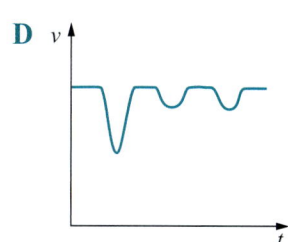

5 Water is poured into the container at a steady rate. The graph that could represent the height of the water in the container as it is filled is:

  A 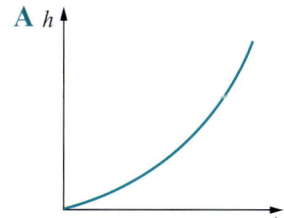 **B** 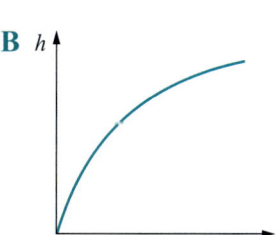 **C** 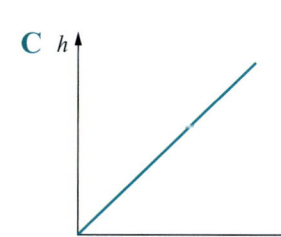 **D**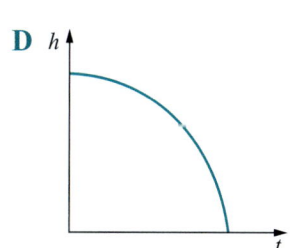

6 For the parabola $y = -x^2 + 2x + 35$ the x-intercepts are:

    A $5, -7$ **B** $-5, -7$ **C** $5, 7$ **D** $-5, 7$

7 For the parabola $y = -x^2 + 2x + 35$ the equation of the axis of symmetry is:

    A $x = 1$ **B** $x = -1$ **C** $x = 6$ **D** $x = -6$

8 A parabola cuts the x-axis at $x = -2$ and $x = 4$. The equation that could not be an equation of the parabola is:

    A $y = x^2 + 2x - 8$ **B** $y = -x^2 + 2x + 8$

    C $y = 2x^2 + 4x - 16$ **D** $y = 3x^2 + 2x - 24$

9 For the parabola $y = x^2 + 2x - 6$, the coordinates of the vertex are:

    A $(1, -3)$ **B** $(-1, -7)$ **C** $(2, 2)$ **D** $(-2, -6)$

10 The graph that could be the graph of $y = (x + 2)^2 - 3$ is:

    A 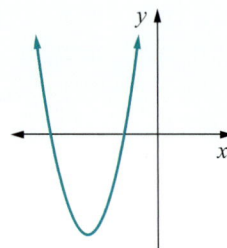   **B** 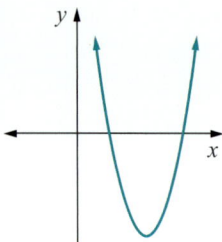   **C** 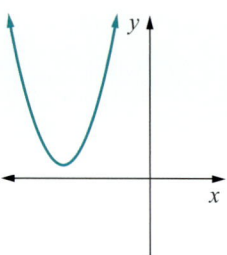   **D**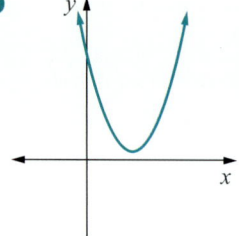

11 The equation of the parabola shown is:

    A $y = -6x^2$ **B** $y = 6x^2$

    C $y = -3x^2$ **D** $y = 3x^2$

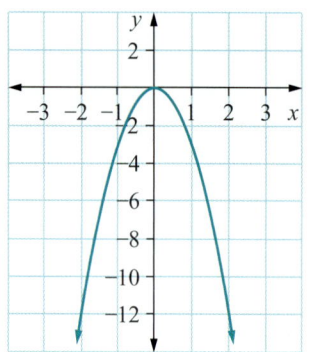

12 A quadratic equation of the form $y = x^2 + bx + c$ that will generate the number pattern in the table is:

x	0	1	2	3	4	5
y	-1	-2	-1	2	7	14

    A $y = -x^2 + 2x - 1$ **B** $y = -x^2 - 2x - 1$

    C $y = x^2 + 2x - 1$ **D** $y = x^2 - 2x - 1$

13 Completing the square will transform $y = x^2 - 10x + 3$ to:

    A $y = (x - 5)^2 - 22$ **B** $y = (x - 5)^2 + 28$

    C $y = (x - 10)^2 - 97$ **D** $y = (x - 10)^2 + 103$

14 The graph that could be the graph of $y = \dfrac{2}{x-3}$ is:

A 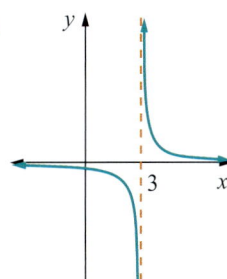   **B** 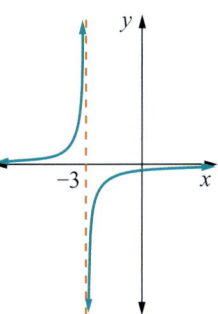   **C** 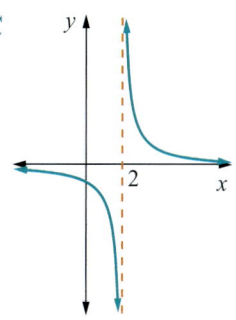   **D**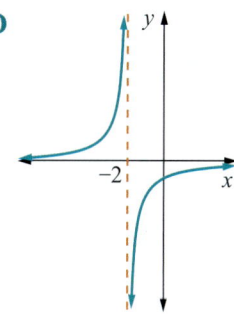

15 The equation of the hyperbola shown is:

A $y = -\dfrac{2}{x}$ **B** $y = -\dfrac{1}{4x}$

C $y = -\dfrac{4}{x}$ **D** $y = \dfrac{4}{x}$

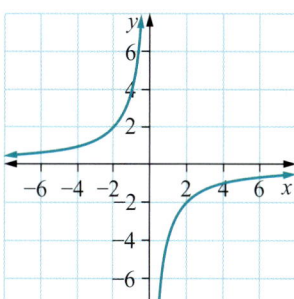

16 The point that lies inside the circle $(x + 2)^2 + (y - 1)^2 = 9$ is:

A $(3, -1)$ **B** $(-1, 3)$

C $(-4, -3)$ **D** $(4, -1)$

17 The centre and radius of the circle $x^2 + y^2 - 4x - 6y - 3 = 0$ are:

A $(2, 3), r = 4$ **B** $(2, 3), r = \sqrt{3}$

C $(-2, -3), r = 4$ **D** $(-2, -3), r = \sqrt{3}$

18 The graph that could be the graph of $y = -4^{-x}$ is:

A 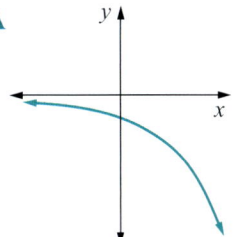   **B** 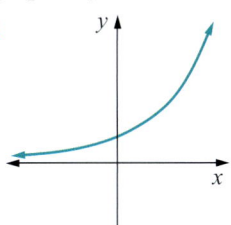   **C** 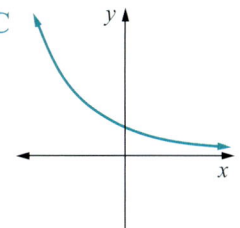   **D**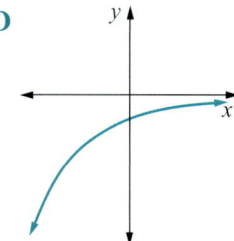

19 A possible equation for the graph shown is:

A $y = 4x^3$ **B** $y = -4x^3$

C $y = 2x^3$ **D** $y = -2x^3$

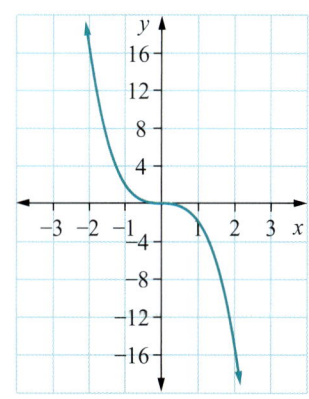

20 The x-intercepts of the graph of $y = 2(x + 1)(x - 2)(x - 3)$ are:

    A $1, -2, -3$ **B** $2, -4, -6$ **C** $-1, 2, 3$ **D** $-2, 4, 6$

21 The equation that has a graph that is symmetrical about the y-axis is:

    A $y = x^2 + 4x$ **B** $y = -4x^4$ **C** $y = 4x^3$ **D** $y = \dfrac{4}{x}$

22 The points of intersection of the graphs of $y = \dfrac{10}{x}$ and $y = x - 3$ are:

    A $(2, 5)$ and $(-5, 2)$ **B** $(2, 5)$ and $(5, 2)$

    C $(2, -5)$ and $(5, -2)$ **D** $(-2, -5)$ and $(5, 2)$

If you have any difficulty with these questions, refer to the examples and questions in the sections listed in the table.

Question	1–2	3–5	6–13	14, 15	16, 17	18	19–21	22
Section	A	B	C	D	E	F	G	H

12A   Review set

1 The graph below that shows that distance is increasing at a decreasing rate is:

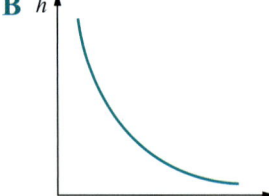 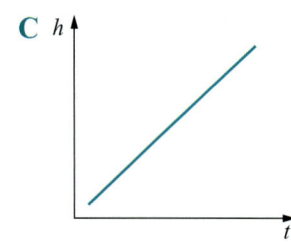 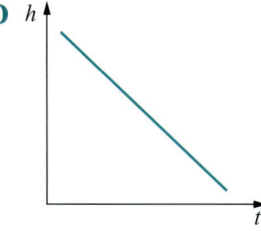

2 Draw graphs to represent the following situations.

    a Although prices are still rising, they are rising at a slower rate than in the previous 6 months.

    b The temperature of boiled water decreases quickly at first and then more slowly until it reaches room temperature.

3 The following containers are filled with water at a constant rate. Draw graphs to show how the height of water increases with time.

    a 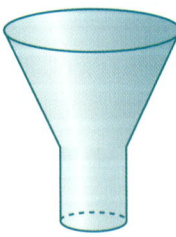   **b**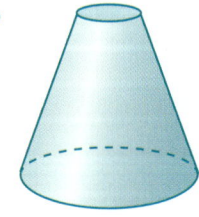

4 A racing car travels around the circuit shown. Draw a graph to represent the speed of the car as it travels around the second lap of the race.

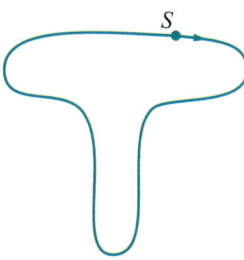

5 Consider the parabola $y = x^2 - x - 12$.

   a Find the x- and y-intercepts.

   b Find the equation of the axis of symmetry.

   c What are the coordinates of the vertex?

   d Sketch the curve.

6 **a** Sketch graphs of:

      i $y = x^2$ **ii** $y = 4x^2$ **iii** $y = x^2 - 3$

      iv $y = (x + 1)^2$ **v** $y = (x - 2)^2 + 5$

   b Write the coordinates of the vertex of each of the above graphs.

7 Find a quadratic equation of the form $y = ax^2 + c$ that will generate the number pattern in the table.

x	0	1	2	3	4	5
y	-3	-1	5	15	29	47

8 Consider the graph of $y = \dfrac{1}{x - 2} + 3$.

   a Find the equations of the asymptotes.

   b What are the equations of the axes of symmetry?

9 Write the equation of each circle, in general form.

   a centre $(0, 0)$ and radius $= \sqrt{8}$ **b** centre $(5, -6)$ and radius $= 10$

10 Find the centre and radius of the circle $x^2 + y^2 - 8x + 4y + 11 = 0$.

11 Sketch graphs of:

   a $y = 4^x$ **b** $y = -4^x$ **c** $y = 4^{-x}$ **d** $y = -4^{-x}$

12 Match each of the given equations with the graphs below.

   a $y = x^3$ **b** $y = 0.2x^3$ **c** $y = x^3 - 1$ **d** $y = (x - 1)^3$

A 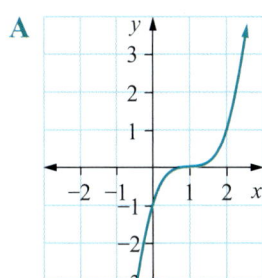   **B** 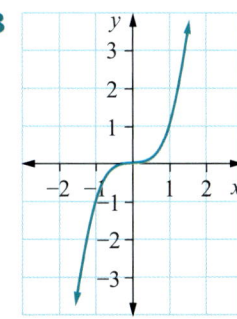   **C** 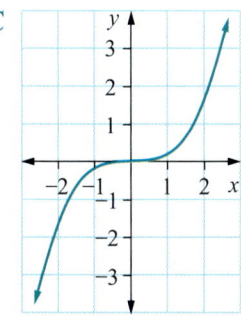   **D**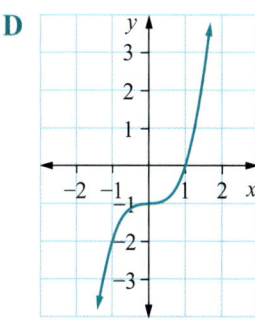

13 Consider the graph of $y = (x + 1)(x + 2)(x + 4)$.

   a Find the x- and y-intercepts.

   b Sketch the curve.

14 Find the points of intersection of $y = \dfrac{24}{x}$ and $y = x - 2$.

1 The graph that shows that distance is increasing at an increasing rate is:

A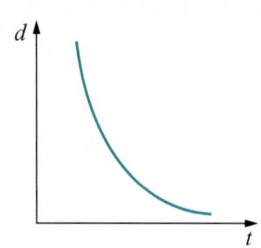

2 Draw graphs to represent the following situations.
  a Although prices are still falling, they are falling at a slower rate than in the previous 6 months.
  b When a refrigerator is turned off, the temperature increases slowly at first and then more quickly until it reaches room temperature.

3 The following containers are filled with water at a constant rate. Draw graphs to show how the height of water increases with time.

  a

  b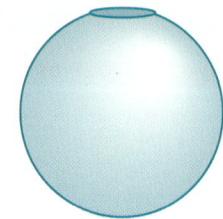

4 A racing car travels around the circuit shown. Draw a graph to represent the speed of the car as it travels around the second lap of the race.

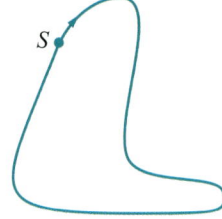

5 Consider the parabola $y = x^2 + 5x + 2$.
  a Find the y-intercept.
  b Find the equation of the axis of symmetry.
  c What are the coordinates of the vertex?
  d Sketch the curve.

6 Match each of the given equations with the graphs below.
  a $y = 2x^2$ **b** $y = 0.2x^2$ **c** $y = x^2 + 2$ **d** $y = (x - 2)^2$

  A 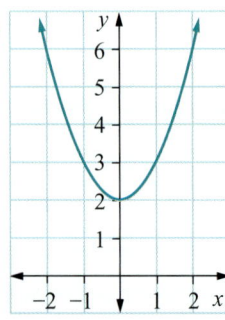   **B** 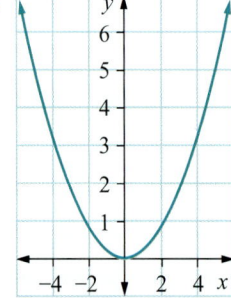   **C** 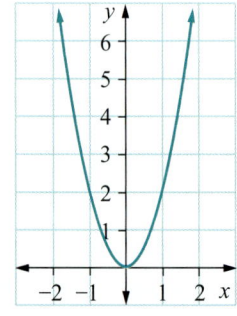   **D**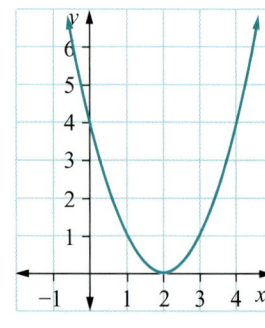

7 **a** Sketch graphs of:

  i $y = \dfrac{1}{x}$ **ii** $y - \dfrac{1}{x}$ **iii** $y = \dfrac{1}{x} + 4$ **iv** $y = \dfrac{1}{x - 4}$

  b Write the equations of the asymptotes of each curve.

8 Write the coordinate of the centre and the radius of these circles.

  a $2x^2 + 2y^2 = 16$ **b** $(x + 5)^2 + (y - 2)^2 = 9$

  c $x^2 + y^2 + 10x - 12y + 60 = 0$

9 Determine whether the point $(-1, 1)$ lies inside, on or outside the circle $(x + 2)^2 + (y + 1)^2 = 10$.

10 Which of the following have graphs that are symmetrical about the y-axis?

  A $y = 3x^2$ **B** $y = 3x$ **C** $y = 3 - x^2$ **D** $y = 2 - x^3$

11 Match each of the given equations with the graphs below.

  a $y = 5^x$ **b** $y = 5^x + 3$ **c** $y = 5^{-x}$ **d** $y = 5^{x-3}$

A 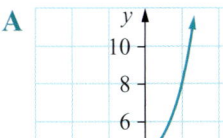 **B** 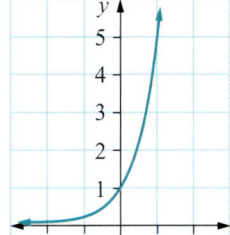 **C** 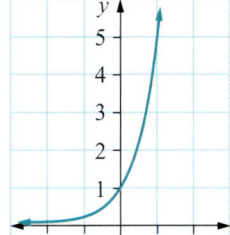 **D**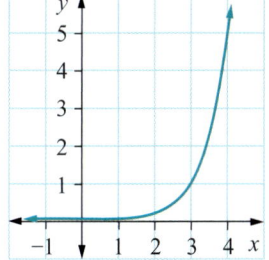

12 Sketch graphs of:

  a $y = x^3$ **b** $y = 3x^3$ **c** $y = \dfrac{1}{2}x^3$ **d** $y = x^3 - 5$ **e** $y = (x - 5)^3$

13 Consider the graph of $y = (x + 1)(x + 2)(x + 3)$.

  a Find the x- and y-intercepts.

  b Sketch the curve.

14 Find the point of intersection of the graphs of $y = x^2$ and $y = 28 - 3x$.

12C **Review set**

1 The graph that shows that the quantity Q is decreasing at an increasing rate is:

A 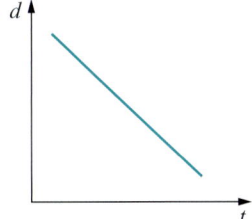 **B** 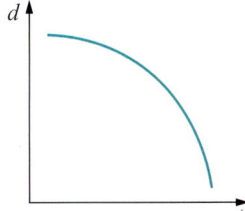 **C** 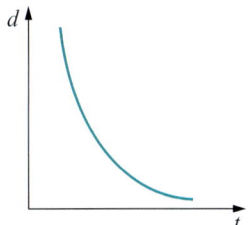 **D**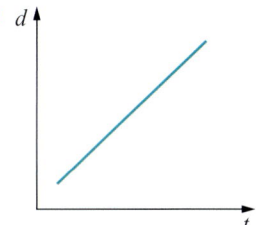

2 Draw graphs to represent the following situations.

  a Unemployment is increasing but at a slower rate than in the previous quarter (of a year).

  b The mass of radioactive material in a reactor decreases quickly at first but then more slowly.

3 The following containers are filled with water at a constant rate. Draw graphs to show how the height of the water increases with time.

a

b

4 Consider the parabola $y = -x^2 - 3x + 28$.
  a Find the x- and y-intercepts.
  b Find the equation of the axis of symmetry.
  c What are the coordinates of the vertex?
  d Sketch the curve.

5 a Sketch graphs of:
  i $y = 4x^2$
  ii $y = 0.4x^2$
  iii $y = x^2 + 6$
  iv $y = (x - 6)^2$
  v $y = (x + 5)^2 - 2$
  b Write the coordinates of the vertex of each of the above graphs.

6 Find a quadratic equation of the form $y = x^2 + bx + c$ that will generate the number pattern in the table.

x	0	1	2	3	4	5
y	3	2	3	6	11	18

7 Consider the graph of $y = \dfrac{1}{x + 2} - 7$.
  a Find the equations of the asymptotes.
  b What are the equations of the axes of symmetry?

8 Write the equation of the circle, in general form, with:
  a centre $(0, 0)$ and radius $1\frac{1}{2}$
  b centre $(4, -6)$ and radius $\sqrt{5}$

9 Find the centre and radius of the circle $4x^2 + 4y^2 + 16x - 12y + 9 = 0$.

10 Sketch graphs of:
  a $y = 6^x$
  b $y = 6^x - 6$
  c $y = 6^{x-6}$

11 Match each of the given equations with the graphs below.
  a $y = x^3$
  b $y = 3^x$
  c $y = \dfrac{3}{x}$
  d $y = 3x^2$

A
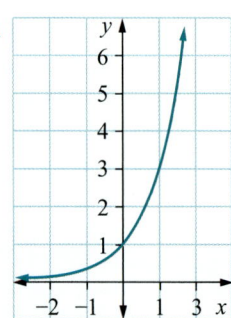

B
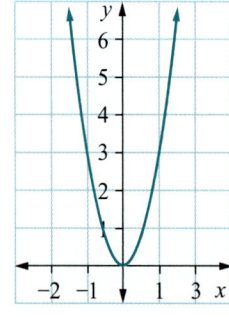

C
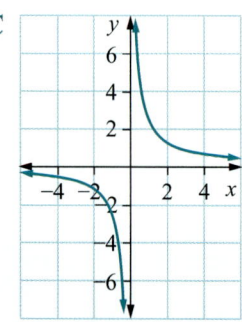

D
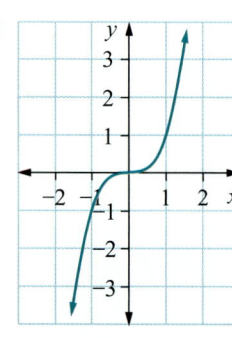

12 State whether the following equations represent straight lines, parabolas, hyperbolas, circles or exponential curves.

  a $x^2 + y^2 = 5$ **b** $y = 5 - x^2$ **c** $y = 5 - x$ **d** $y = \dfrac{1}{x - 5}$ **e** $y = 5^x$

13 Consider the graph $y = x(x + 2)(x - 5)$.

  a Find the x- and y-intercepts.

  b Sketch the curve.

14 Find the points of intersection of $y = 2x^2 + 7x - 15$ and $y = 2x - 3$.

12D   Review set

1 The graph that shows that distance is decreasing at an decreasing rate is:

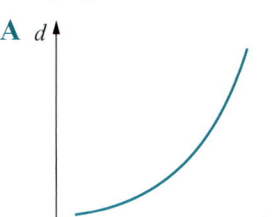   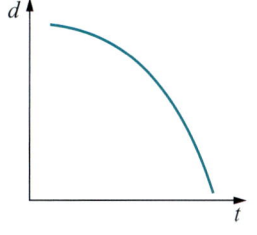   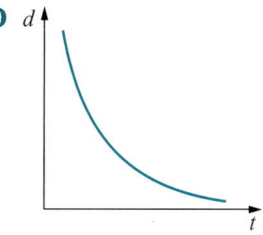

2 Draw graphs to represent the following situations.

  a The population of a country town is slowly decreasing at a constant rate but increases quickly at first and then more slowly when a new mine opens in the area.

  b The number of bacteria in a culture increases slowly at first but then more quickly.

3 A racing car travels around the circuit shown. Draw a graph to represent the speed of the car as it travels around the second lap of the race.

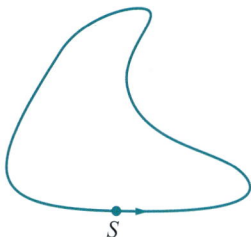

4 Consider the parabola $y = -x^2 - 2x - 7$.

  a Find the y-intercept.

  b Find the equation of the axis of symmetry.

  c What are the coordinates of the vertex?

  d Sketch the curve.

5 Match each of the given equations with the graphs below.

  a $y = 3x^2$ **b** $y = 0.3x^2$ **c** $y = x^2 - 3$ **d** $y = (x - 3)^2$

A 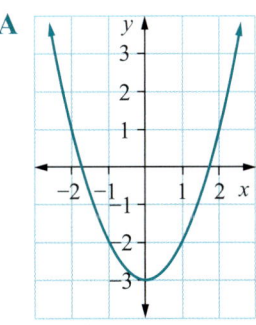 **B** 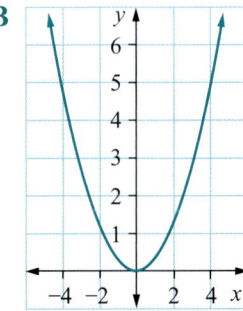 **C** 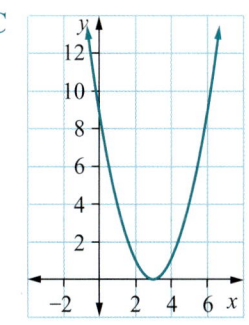 **D**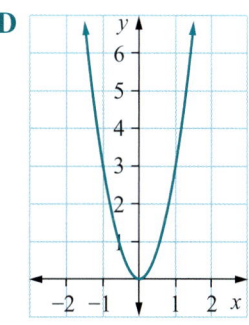

6 **a** Sketch graphs of:

    i $y = \dfrac{4}{x}$ **ii** $y = -\dfrac{4}{x}$ **iii** $y = \dfrac{4}{x} + 4$ **iv** $y = \dfrac{4}{x - 4}$

    b Write the equations of the asymptotes of each curve.

7 Write the coordinates of the centre and the radius of these circle.

    a $3x^2 + 3y^2 = 18$ **b** $(x - 8)^2 + (y + 7)^2 = 13$ **c** $x^2 + y^2 + 10x - 24 = 0$

8 Determine if the point $(3, -4)$ lies inside, on or outside the circle $(x + 1)^2 + (y + 7)^2 = 25$.

9 Which of the following have graphs that are symmetrical about the y-axis?

    A $y = x^5$ **B** $y = 5x^2$ **C** $y = 5 + x^2$ **D** $y = 5 - x^3$

10 Match each of the given equations with the graphs below.

    a $y = 2^x$ **b** $y = 2^x - 3$ **c** $y = 2^{-x}$ **d** $y = 2^{x-3}$

A 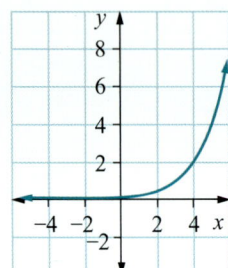   **B** 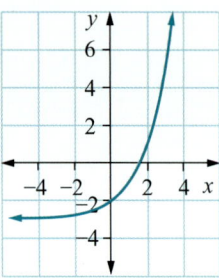   **C** 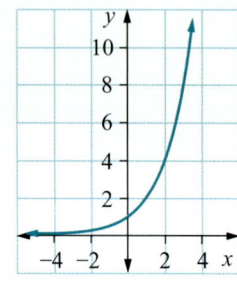   **D**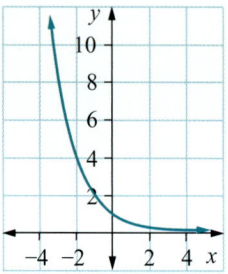

11 Sketch graphs of:

    a $y = x^3$ **b** $y = -x^3$ **c** $y = -x^3 + 2$ **d** $y = x^3 - 3$ **e** $y = (x - 3)^3$

12 State whether the following equations represent straight lines, parabolas, hyperbolas, circles or exponential curves.

    a $y = 7^x$ **b** $y = 7x$ **c** $y = 7x^2$ **d** $y = \dfrac{1}{x - 7}$ **e** $y^2 = 7 - x^2$

13 Consider the graph $y = (x - 2)(x + 2)(x + 4)$.

    a Find the x- and y-intercepts.

    b Sketch the curve.

    c On the same axes sketch the graph of $y = -(x - 2)(x + 2)(x + 4)$.

14 Find the point of intersection of the graphs of $y = x$ and $(x + 3)^2 + (y - 1)^2 = 9$.

13

Properties of geometrical figures

This chapter deals with the application of congruency and similarity to proofs and numerical exercises involving plane shapes.

At the end of this chapter you should be able to:

▶ write formal proofs of the similarity of triangles

▶ use the relationship between the dimensions of similar figures to find their areas and volumes

▶ prove the properties of special quadrilaterals using their formal definitions

▶ prove and apply theorems and properties related to quadrilaterals.

NSW Syllabus references: 5.3 M&G Properties of geometrical figures
Outcomes: MA5.3-1WM, MA5.3-2WM, MA5.3-3WM, MA5.3-16MG
Measurement & geometry – ACMMG243, ACMMG244

Diagnostic test

1 The congruency test used to show that these triangles are congruent is:

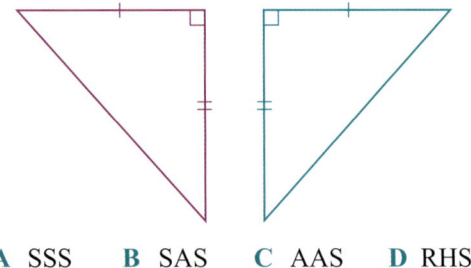

A SSS **B** SAS **C** AAS **D** RHS

2 The congruency test used to show that these triangles are congruent is:

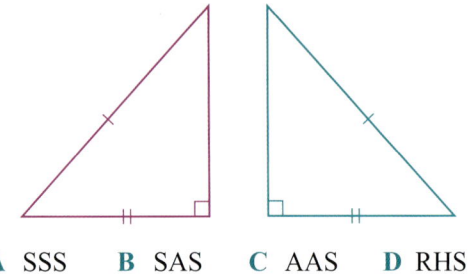

A SSS **B** SAS **C** AAS **D** RHS

3 The congruent triangles are:

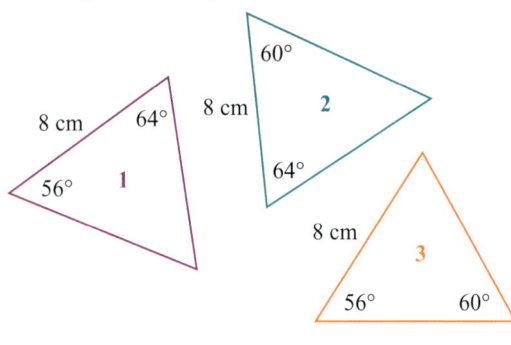

A 1, 2 **B** 2, 3 **C** 1, 3 **D** 1, 2, 3

4 The value of x in this pair of congruent triangles is:

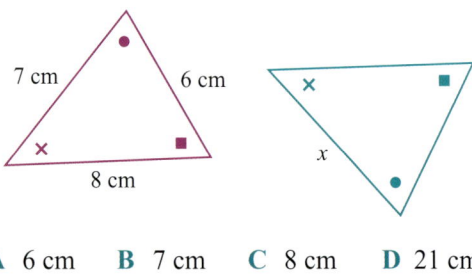

A 6 cm **B** 7 cm **C** 8 cm **D** 21 cm

5 The similar triangles are:

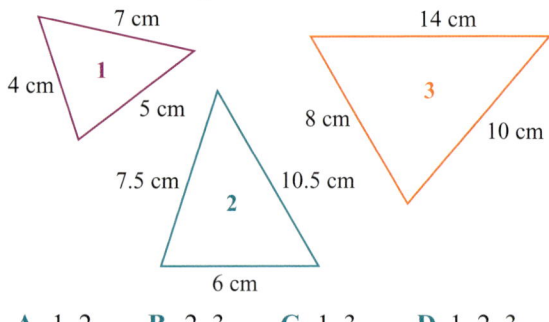

A 1, 2 **B** 2, 3 **C** 1, 3 **D** 1, 2, 3

6 The similar triangles are:

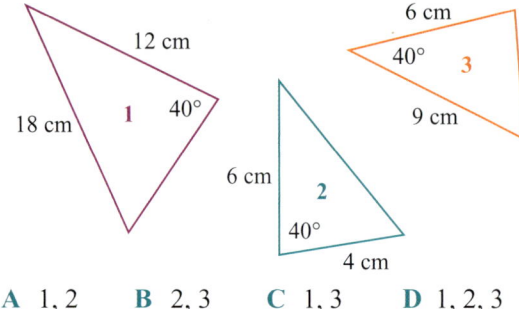

A 1, 2 **B** 2, 3 **C** 1, 3 **D** 1, 2, 3

7 The values of x and y are:

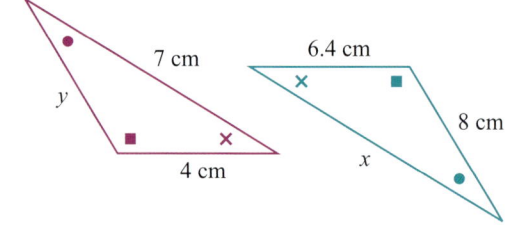

A $x = 11.2$ cm, $y = 5$ cm
B $x = 6.4$ cm, $y = 4$ cm
C $x = 4.75$ cm, $y = 12.8$ cm
D $x = 11.2$ cm, $y = 12.8$ cm

8 The value of h is:

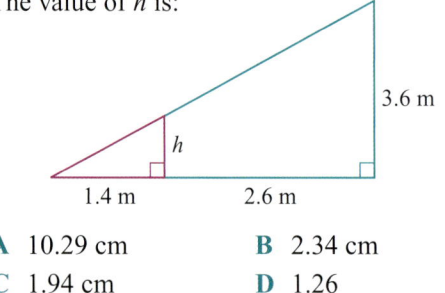

A 10.29 cm **B** 2.34 cm
C 1.94 cm **D** 1.26

The diagnostic test questions refer to outcomes ACMMG201, ACMMG202 and ACMMG221.

A   Formal proofs of similar triangles

EXAMPLE 1

Prove that the following pairs of triangles are similar.

a

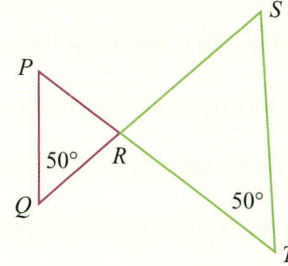

b

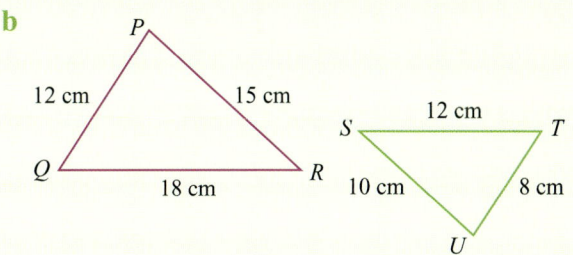

Solve/Think	Apply
a In $\triangle PQR$ and $\triangle STR$: $\angle PQR = \angle STR$ (given) $\angle PRQ = \angle SRT$ (Vertically opposite angles are equal.) $\therefore \triangle PRQ \,\|\|\, \triangle SRT$ (Two angles of one $\triangle$ equal two angles of the other $\triangle$.)	Look for pairs of equal angles and matching sides that satisfy one of the four tests for similar triangles.
b In $\triangle PRQ$ and $\triangle UST$: $\dfrac{PQ}{TU} = \dfrac{PR}{SU} = \dfrac{QR}{ST} \left(= \dfrac{3}{2}\right)$ $\therefore \triangle PRQ \,\|\|\, \triangle UST$ (Three pairs of sides are in proportion.)	

Exercise 13A

1 Prove that the following pairs of triangles are similar.

   a $\triangle ABC$ and $\triangle EDC$

   b $\triangle PQT$ and $\triangle RQS$

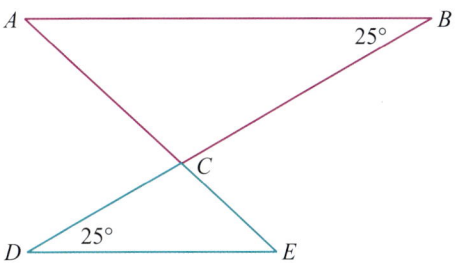

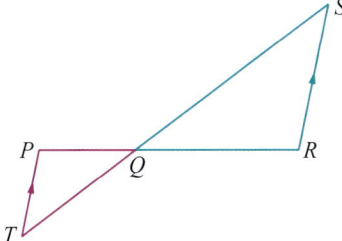

   c $\triangle XYZ$ and $\triangle WUV$

   d $\triangle NKL$ and $\triangle MNL$

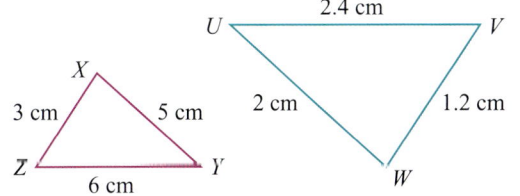

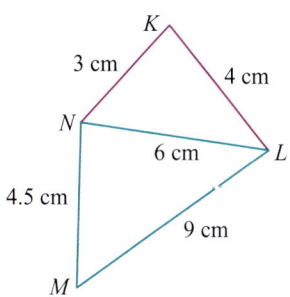

MEASUREMENT & GEOMETRY

e △*ABE* and △*CBD*

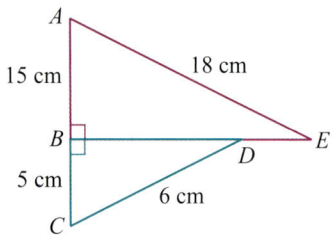

f △*PQR* and △*RST*

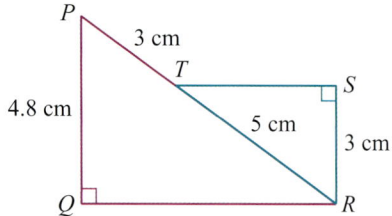

g △*ABC* and △*EDF*

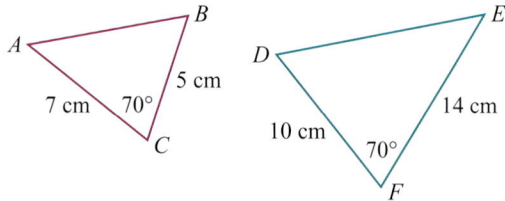

h △*KLO* and △*MLN*

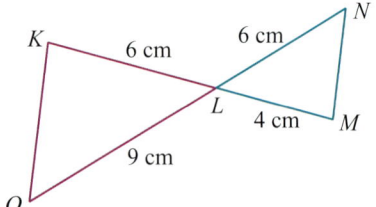

● EXAMPLE 2

Prove that △*PQR* ⫴ △*TQS* and hence find the value of the pronumeral.

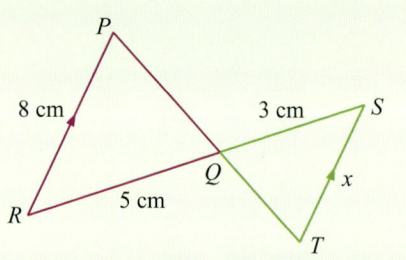

Solve/Think	Apply
In △*PQR* and △*TQS*: ∠*PQR* = ∠*TQS* (Vertically opposite angles are equal.) ∠*RPQ* = ∠*STQ* (Alternate angles and *PR* ∥ *ST*.) ∴ △*PQR* ⫴ △*TQS* (Two angles of one △ equal two angles of the other △.) Hence $\dfrac{x}{8} = \dfrac{3}{5}$ (Matching sides of similar △s are in proportion.) $x = 4\dfrac{4}{5}$ or 4.8 cm	Look for pairs of equal angles and matching sides that satisfy one of the four tests for similar triangles. In similar triangles the matching sides are in proportion. Solve the resulting equation.

---

2 Prove that the following pairs of triangles are similar and hence find the value of the pronumeral.

a

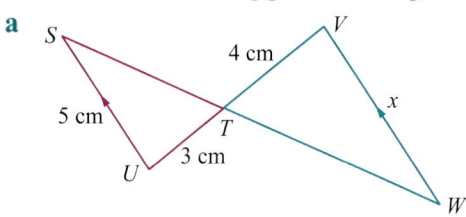

b

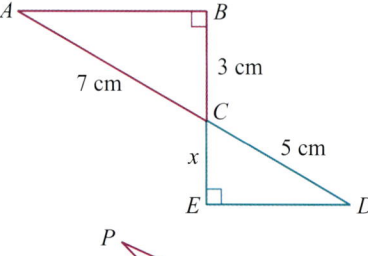

c

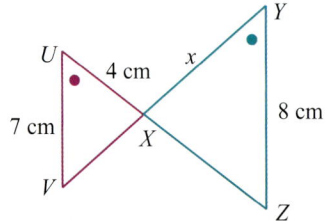

d

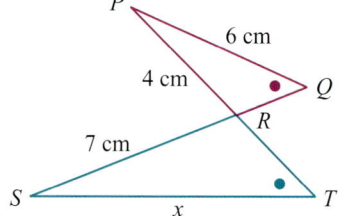

EXAMPLE 3

Prove that $\triangle ADE \,|||\, \triangle ABC$ and hence find the value of the pronumeral.

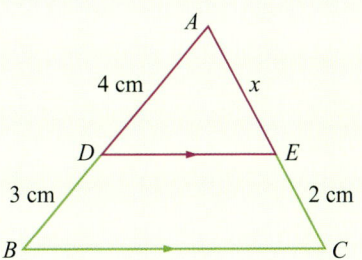

Solve/Think	Apply
In $\triangle ADE$ and $\triangle ABC$: $\angle ADE = \angle ABC$ (Corresponding angles and $DE \,\|\, BC$.) $\angle DAE = \angle BAC$ (common angle) $\therefore \triangle ADE \,|||\, \triangle ABC$ ((Two angles of one $\triangle$ equal two angles of the other $\triangle$.) Hence $\dfrac{x}{x+2} = \dfrac{4}{7}$ (Matching sides of similar $\triangle$s are in proportion.) $\qquad 7x = 4(x+2)$ $\qquad\quad = 4x + 8$ $\qquad 3x = 8$ $\qquad\ x = 2\frac{2}{3}$ cm	Look for pairs of equal angles and matching sides that satisfy one of the four tests for similar triangles. In similar triangles the matching sides are in proportion. Solve the resulting equation.

3 Prove that $ADE \,|||\, \triangle ABC$ and determine the value of the pronumeral.

a

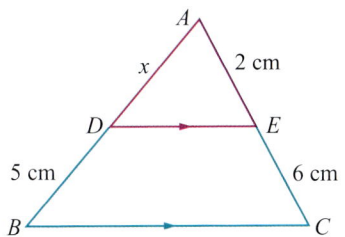

b

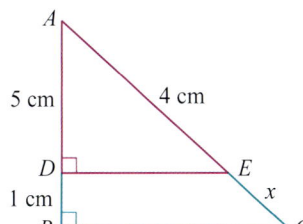

4 Prove that the given pair of triangles is similar and determine the value of the pronumeral.

a $\triangle ABC$ and $\triangle EBD$

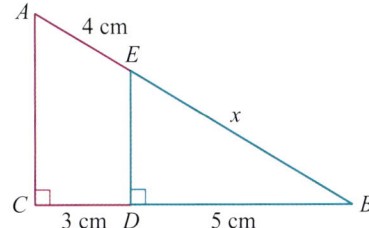

b $\triangle KLM$ and $\triangle PLQ$

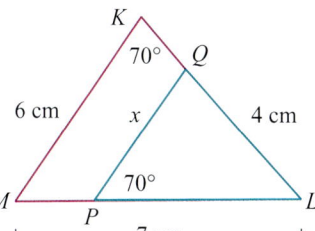

c $\triangle XVU$ and $\triangle XZY$

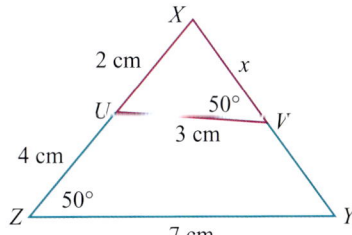

d $\triangle ABC$ and $\triangle EBD$

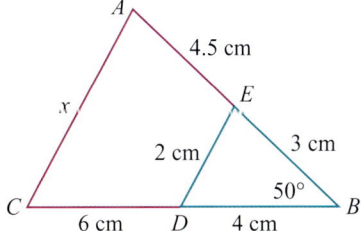

MEASUREMENT & GEOMETRY

e △*VYU* and △*XYZ*

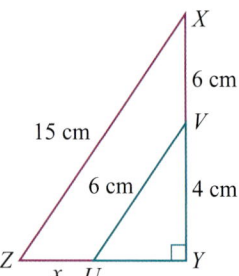

f △*PQR* and △*STR*

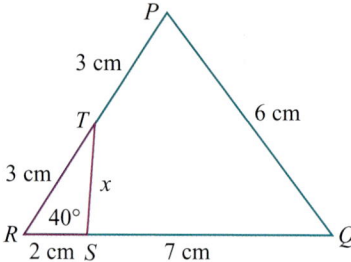

5 *D* and *E* are the midpoints of *AC* and *AB* respectively.
  a Prove that △*ADE* ||| △*ACB*.
  b Hence prove that:
  i $DE \parallel CB$ **ii** $DE = \frac{1}{2}CB$

You have proved that the interval joining the midpoint of two sides of a triangle is parallel to the third side and half its length.

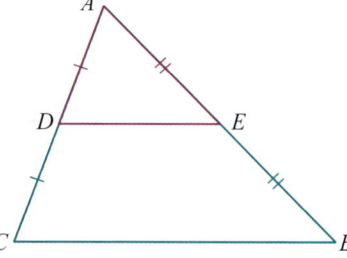

6 *D* is the midpoint of *AC* and *DE* || *CB*.
  a Prove that △*ADE* ||| △*ACB*.
  b Hence prove that *E* is the midpoint of *AB*.

You have proved that the line through the midpoint of a side of a triangle parallel to another side bisects the third side.

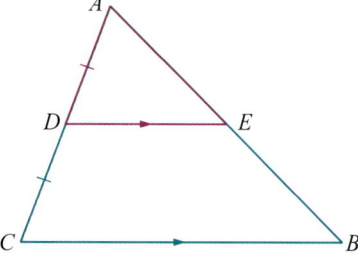

7 **a** Find the size of angles *SPR*, *RPQ* and *PQR* in terms of α.
  b Hence prove that △*SRP* ||| △*PRQ* ||| △*SPQ*.

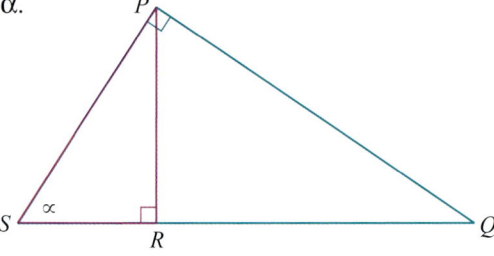

8 Using the results of question **7**, find the value of the pronumeral in the following diagrams.

a

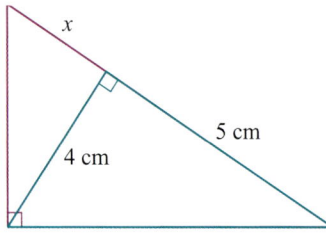

b

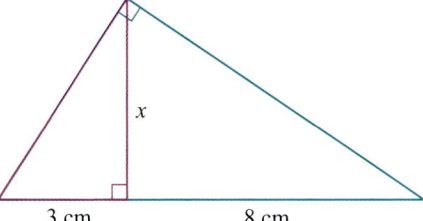

c

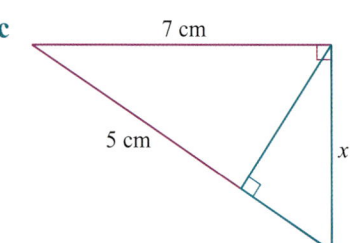

d

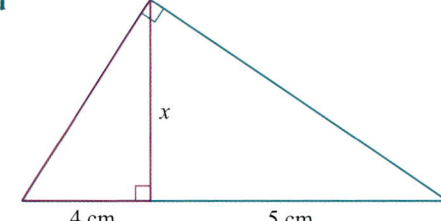

B Area and volume of similar figures

This section investigates the relationship between the sides and the areas and volumes of similar figures.

EXAMPLE 1

$\triangle ABC$ has been enlarged to $\triangle DEF$ using a scale factor $k = 3$.

$\triangle ABC$ and $\triangle DEF$ are similar with

$\dfrac{DE}{AB} = \dfrac{EF}{BC} = \dfrac{DF}{AC} \left(= \dfrac{DQ}{AP}\right) = \dfrac{3}{1}.$

a Calculate the lengths of FE and DQ.

b Calculate the ratio $\dfrac{\text{area } \triangle DEF}{\text{area } \triangle ABC}$.

c Express this ratio in the form $k^{\square} : 1$ or $\dfrac{k^{\square}}{1}$.

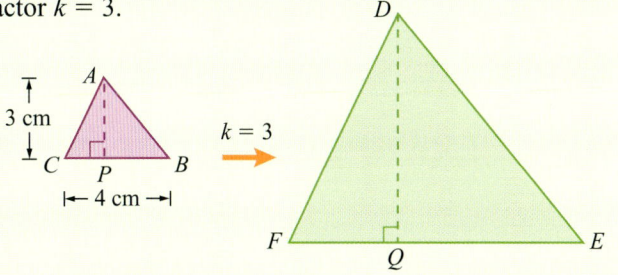

	Solve	Think	Apply
a	$FE = 3 \times CB = 3 \times 4 = 12$ cm $DQ = 3 \times AP = 3 \times 3 = 9$ cm	$FE = k \times CB$ $DQ = 3 \times AP$	Calculate the scaled dimensions of the enlarged triangle and calculate the ratio of the areas.
b	$\dfrac{\text{Area } \triangle DEF}{\text{Area } \triangle ABC} = \dfrac{\frac{1}{2} \times 12 \times 9}{\frac{1}{2} \times 4 \times 3} = \dfrac{54}{6} = \dfrac{9}{1}$	Area of a triangle $= \frac{1}{2}bh$	
c	$\dfrac{9}{1} = \dfrac{3^2}{1}$ so ratio of areas is $3^2 : 1$.	$9 = 3^2$	

Example 1 indicates that if the sides of two similar triangles are in the ration $k : 1$, their areas are in the ratio $k^2 : 1$.

EXAMPLE 2

$\triangle DEF$ and $\triangle ABC$ are similar and the area of $\triangle ABC = 17$ cm². Calculate the area of $\triangle DEF$ when:

a $k = 2$

b $k = \dfrac{4}{5}$

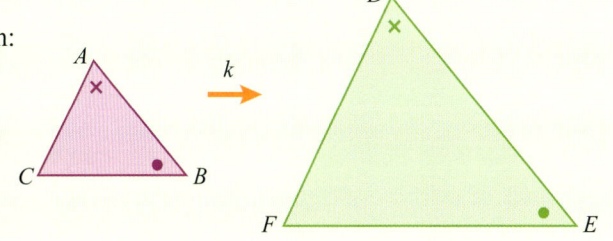

	Solve	Think	Apply
a	$\dfrac{\text{Area } \triangle DEF}{17} = \dfrac{2^2}{1}$ $\text{Area } \triangle DEF = \dfrac{2^2}{1} \times 17 = 68$ cm²	From Example 1: $\dfrac{\text{Area } \triangle DEF}{\text{Area } \triangle ABC} = \dfrac{2^2}{1}$	If the sides of two similar triangles are in the ratio $k : 1$, their areas are in the ratio $k^2 : 1$.
b	$\dfrac{\text{Area } \triangle DEF}{17} = \dfrac{\left(\frac{4}{5}\right)^2}{1}$ $\text{Area } \triangle DEF = \dfrac{\left(\frac{4}{5}\right)^2}{1} \times 17 = 10.88$ cm²	From Example 1: $\dfrac{\text{Area } \triangle DEF}{\text{Area } \triangle ABC} = \dfrac{\left(\frac{4}{5}\right)^2}{1}$	

MEASUREMENT & GEOMETRY

Exercise 13B

1 $\triangle DEF$ and $\triangle ABC$ are similar and the area of $\triangle ABC = 24$ cm². Calculate the area of $\triangle DEF$ when:

a $k = 3$ **b** $k = \frac{5}{4}$ **c** $k = \frac{3}{4}$ **d** $k = 2.2$

2 $\triangle PQR$ and $\triangle XYZ$ are similar and the area of $\triangle PQR = 80$ cm².

a Find the scale factor.

b Hence find the area of $\triangle XYZ$.

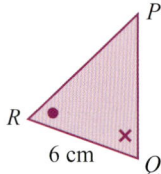
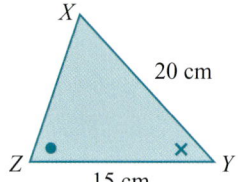

EXAMPLE 3

$\triangle PQR$ has been enlarged to $\triangle STU$ using a scale factor $k = 1.6$.
If the area of $\triangle STU = 20$ cm², find the area of $\triangle PQR$.

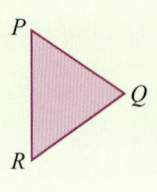
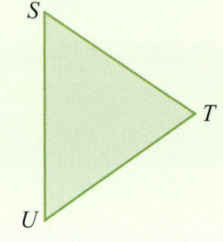

Solve	Think	Apply
$\dfrac{20}{\text{Area } \triangle PQR} = \dfrac{1.6^2}{1}$ $20 = 1.6^2 \times \text{area } \triangle PQR$ $\dfrac{20}{1.6^2} = \text{area } \triangle PQR$ Area $\triangle PQR = 7.8125$ cm² Or scale factor from $\triangle STU$ to $\triangle PQR$ is $\dfrac{1}{1.6}$. Hence $\dfrac{\text{Area } \triangle PQR}{20} = \dfrac{\left(\frac{1}{1.6}\right)^2}{1}$ Area $\triangle PQR = \left(\dfrac{1}{1.6}\right)^2 \times 20 = 7.8125$ cm²	$\dfrac{\text{Area } \triangle STU}{\text{Area } \triangle PQR} = \dfrac{1.6^2}{1}$ Solve the resulting equation. Or if the scale factor from $\triangle PQR$ to $\triangle STU$ is k, the scale factor from $\triangle STU$ to $\triangle PQR$ is $\dfrac{1}{k}$. Solve the resulting equation.	If the sides of two similar triangles are in the ratio $k : 1$, their areas are in the ratio $k^2 : 1$.

---

3 $\triangle ABC$ has been enlarged to $\triangle DEF$ using a scale factor k.
The area of $\triangle DEF = 96$ cm². Calculate the area of $\triangle ABC$ when:

a $k = 2$ **b** $k = 1.5$

c $k = \frac{2}{5}$ **d** $k = \frac{13}{4}$

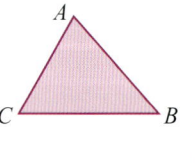
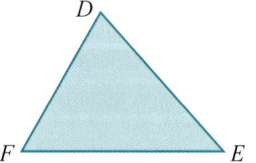

4 $\triangle ABC$ has been enlarged to $\triangle DEF$ using a scale factor k.
Complete the following to find the area of $\triangle DEF$.

$$\frac{\text{Area } \triangle DEF}{\text{Area } \triangle ABC} = \frac{\frac{1}{2} \times DE \times FE \times \sin E}{\frac{1}{2} \times AB \times CB \times \sin \square}$$

$$= \frac{DE \times FE}{AB \times CB} \qquad (\angle E = \angle \underline{\quad})$$

$$= \frac{(k \times AB) \times (k \times \square)}{AB \times CB} = \frac{\square}{1} \qquad (DE = k \times AB \text{ and } FE = k \times \underline{\quad})$$

Or area $\triangle DEF = \underline{\quad} \times$ area $\triangle ABC$

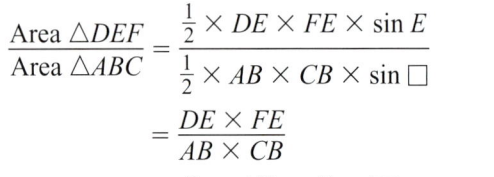
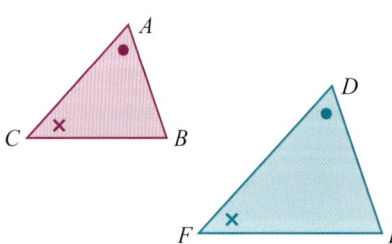

The result from question **4.** can be extended to any two similar figures. Consider these two similar polygons whose sides are in the ratio $k : 1$.

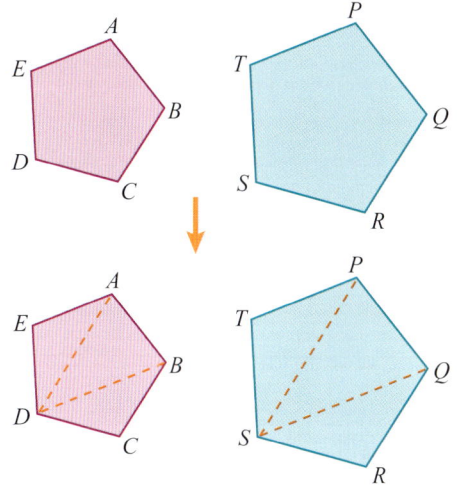

The pentagons can be dissected into triangles, as shown.
Area $\triangle PST = k^2 \times$ area $\triangle ADE$
Area $\triangle PQS = k^2 \times$ area $\triangle ABD$
Area $\triangle QRS = k^2 \times$ area $\triangle BCD$
Hence area $\triangle PST +$ area $\triangle PQS +$ area $\triangle QRS$
$\qquad = k^2 \times$ (area $\triangle ADE +$ area $\triangle ABD +$ area $\triangle BCD$)
Area pentagon $PQRST = k^2 \times$ area pentagon $ABCDE$

5 Use the information given to find the unknown area for each pair of similar figures.

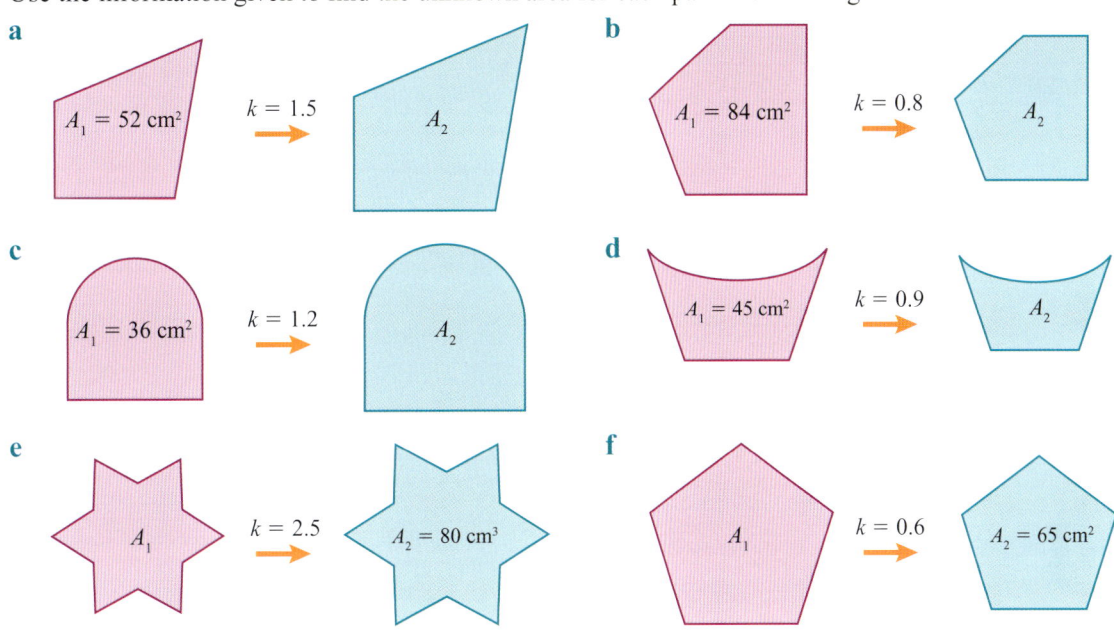

a $A_1 = 52$ cm^2 $k = 1.5$ A_2

b $A_1 = 84$ cm^2 $k = 0.8$ A_2

c $A_1 = 36$ cm^2 $k = 1.2$ A_2

d $A_1 = 45$ cm^2 $k = 0.9$ A_2

e A_1 $k = 2.5$ $A_2 = 80$ cm^3

f A_1 $k = 0.6$ $A_2 = 65$ cm^2

6 A map is drawn to a scale of 1 : 1000.
   a The area of a nature reserve is 3.6 ha. What will be its area on the map?
   b The area on the map of a school and its playgrounds is 96 cm^2. What is its actual area?

EXAMPLE 4

The first rectangular prism has been enlarged by a scale factor of $k = 4$.

a What is the length, breadth and height of the second rectangular prism?

b Calculate this ratio: $\dfrac{\text{volume of second prism}}{\text{volume of first prism}}$

c Express this ratio in the form $k^{\square} : 1$.

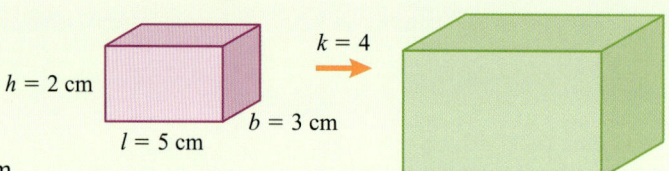

$h = 2$ cm
$l = 5$ cm
$b = 3$ cm
$k = 4$

	Solve	Think	Apply
a	Length = 20 Breadth = 12 Height = 8	Each dimension of the enlarged prism is $k \times$ the matching dimension of the first.	Calculate the scaled dimensions of the enlarged solid and calculate the ratio of the volumes. Express the ratio as a power of k.
b	$\dfrac{\text{Volume of second prism}}{\text{Volume of first prism}} = \dfrac{20 \times 12 \times 8}{5 \times 3 \times 2}$ $= \dfrac{64}{1}$	Volume of rectangular prism $= l \times b \times h$	
c	$\dfrac{64}{1} = \dfrac{4^3}{1}$ so ratio of volumes $= 4^3 : 1$	$64 = 4^3$	

Example 4 is an illustration of the general property that if two similar solids have their dimensions in the ratio $k : 1$, then their volumes are in the ratio $k^3 : 1$.

EXAMPLE 5

Cylinder 2 is an enlargement of cylinder 1 by a scale factor $k = 2.4$. If the volume of the first cylinder is 110 cm³, find the volume of the second.

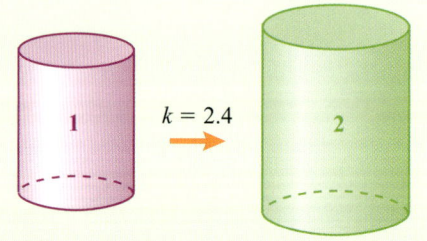

1     $k = 2.4$ 2

Solve	Think	Apply
$\dfrac{V_2}{110} = \dfrac{2.4^3}{1}$ $V_2 = 2.4^3 \times 110 = 1520.64$ cm³	$\dfrac{\text{Volume of cylinder 2}}{\text{Volume of cylinder 1}} = \dfrac{k^3}{1}$	If two similar solids have their dimensions in the ratio $k : 1$ then their volumes are in the ratio $k^3 : 1$.

7 Given that the following pairs of solids are similar, find the unknown volume using the information given.

a

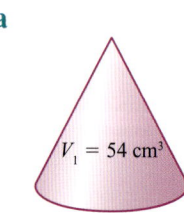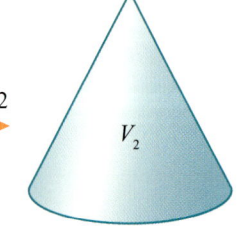

$V_1 = 54$ cm³ $k = 2$ V_2

b

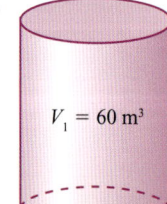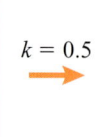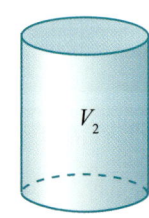

$V_1 = 60$ m³ $k = 0.5$ V_2

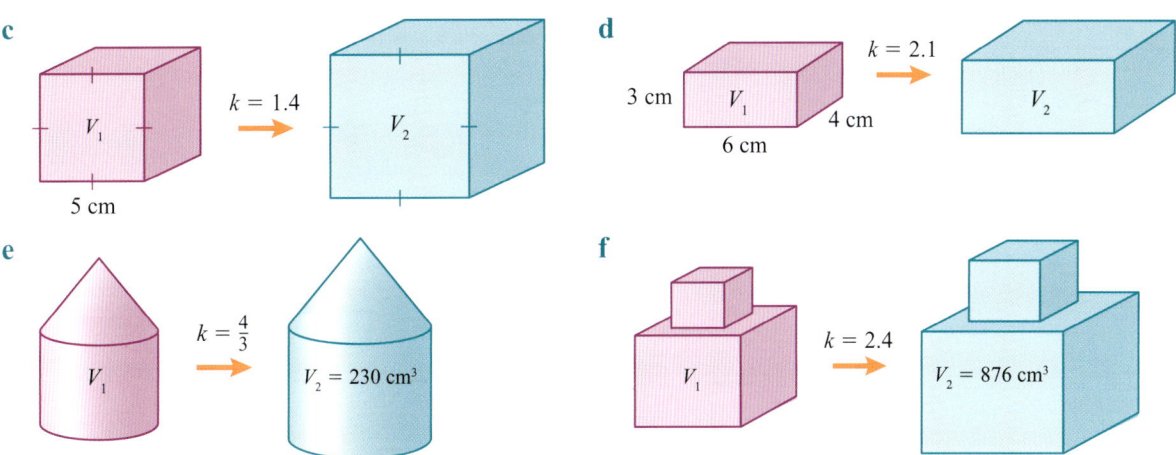

8 a The matching lengths of two similar prisms are 2 cm and 5 cm.
 i Write the scale factor from the smaller to the larger prism.
 ii If the volume of the smaller prism is 63 cm³, what is the volume of the larger prism?
 b The matching sides of two similar solids are in the ratio 3 : 4.
 i Write the scale factor from the larger to the smaller solid.
 ii If the volume of the larger solid is 384 cm³, what is the volume of the smaller solid?

9 The surface area and volume of a solid are 350 cm² and 480 cm³ respectively. The solid is enlarged using a scale factor $k = 1.8$. Calculate the surface area and volume of the larger solid.

10 The matching dimensions of two similar solids are in the ratio 3 : 5.
 a If the surface area of the smaller solid is 270 cm², what is the surface area of the larger solid?
 b If the volume of the smaller solid is 405 cm³, what is the volume of the larger solid?

11 A statue has a surface area and volume of 1.8 m² and 0.12 m³ respectively. A scale model is made with dimensions in the ratio 1 : 20. Find the surface area and volume of the scale model.

12 A box holds exactly 360 ball bearings. If all the dimensions of the box are doubled, how many ball bearings would it hold?

13 The ratio of the area of a field on a scale drawing to its actual area is 1 : 2500. What is the ratio of the dimensions of the field on the diagram to its actual dimensions?

14 A model is made of a statue and the volumes of the statue and its model are in the ratio 27 : 1.
   a What is the ratio of the height of the statue to the height of the model?
   b What is the ratio of the surface areas?

15 A solid metal ball is melted down and made into similar balls with $\frac{1}{5}$ the radius. How many smaller solid balls can be made?

16 A cylindrical tank is four times the diameter and four times the height of a small can. If the large tank contains juice, how many of the cans could be filled?

17 A dog uses moisture evaporation from its tongue to regulate its body temperature. This is not effective for large animals. Consider what would happen if a dog's dimensions were increased by a factor of 10.
   a By what factor would its volume be increased?
   b By what factor would the surface area of its tongue be increased?
   c By what further factor would its tongue's surface area need to be increased to keep up with the increase in its volume?
   d What effect would this have on the animal?

C Quadrilaterals

Definitions

A **trapezium** is a quadrilateral with one pair of opposite sides parallel.

A **parallelogram** is a quadrilateral with both pairs of opposite sides parallel.

A **rhombus** is a parallelogram with two adjacent sides equal in length.

A **rectangle** is a parallelogram with one angle a right angle.

A **square** is a rectangle with two adjacent sides equal.

Exercise 13C

1 When is:

   a a parallelogram a rectangle?   **b** a rectangle a square?

   c a parallelogram a rhombus?   **d** a rhombus a square?

2 Which of the following are true?

   a Squares have all the properties of rectangles.

   b Rectangles have all the properties of squares.

   c Parallelograms have all the properties of rectangles.

   d Rectangles have all the properties of parallelograms.

   e Squares have all the properties of parallelograms.

   f Rhombi have all the properties of parallelograms.

   g Rhombi have all the properties of rectangles.

   h Parallelograms have all the properties of rhombi.

   i Squares have all the properties of rhombi.

3 **a** Give reasons why a square is a rhombus, but a rhombus is not necessarily a square.

   b Give reasons why a rhombus is a parallelogram, but a parallelogram is not necessarily a rhombus.

4 Using the previous definitions and congruency of triangles, prove the following.

   a The opposite sides of a parallelogram are equal.

   b The opposite angles of a parallelogram are equal.

   c The diagonals of a parallelogram bisect each other.

5 Using the previous definitions, prove the following.

   a All the angles of a rectangle are 90°.

   b The diagonals of a rectangle are equal.

6 Using the previous definitions, prove the following.

   a All the sides of a rhombus are equal.

   b The diagonals of a rhombus intersect at right angles.

   c The diagonals of a rhombus bisect the angles of the rhombus.

7 Using the previous definitions, prove that all the sides of a square are equal.

8 Complete the following table to summarise the properties of the special quadrilaterals.

	Parallelogram	Rhombus	Rectangle	Square
Both pairs of opposite sides parallel	√			
Both pairs of opposite sides equal	√			
Both pairs of opposite angles equal	√			
All angles 90°				
All sides equal				
Diagonals bisect each other	√			
Diagonals intersect at right angles				
Diagonals equal				
Diagonals bisect angles of quadrilateral				

9 Find the value of the pronumerals in the following diagrams, giving reasons.

a *PQRS* is a parallelogram and $QS = 15$ cm.

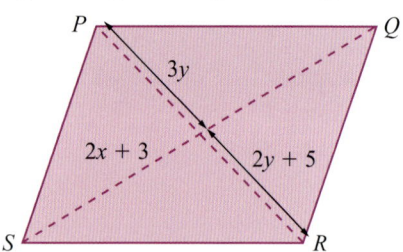

b *ABCD* is a rectangle.

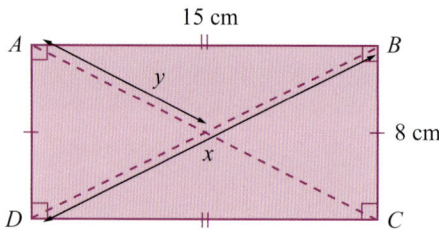

c *KLMN* is a rhombus.

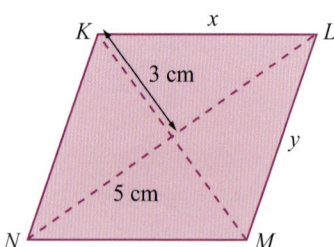

d *WXYZ* is a square.

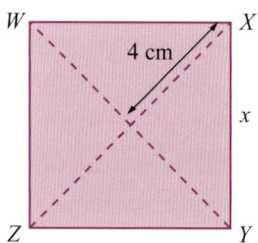

e *ABCD* is a parallelogram. *DC* is produced to *P* such that *CP* = *PB*.

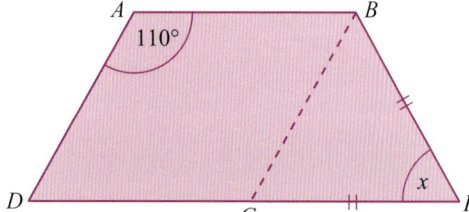

f *PQRS* is a rhombus. *SR* is produced to *X* such that *QR* = *RX*.

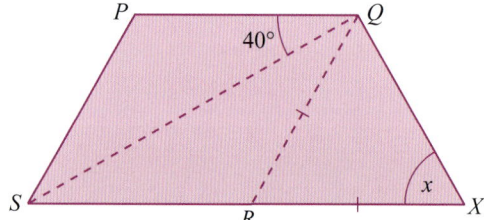

10 a Complete the following proof to show that if both pairs of opposite angles of a quadrilateral are equal, the quadrilateral is a parallelogram.

Data: ∠*A* = ∠*C* and ∠*B* = ∠*D*

Aim: To prove that *ABCD* is a parallelogram.

Proof: Let ∠*A* = *x* and ∠*B* = *y* then:

∠*C* = ∠*A* = *x*   (given)

∠*D* = ∠____ = ____   (given)

x + *y* + *x* + *y* = ____   (Angle sum of a quadrilateral is ____°.)

2*x* + 2*y* = ____

____(*x* + *y*) = ____

x + *y* = ____

∠*A* + ∠____ = ____°

Hence *AB* ‖ ____   (A pair of co-interior angles are supplementary.)

Also ∠*A* + ∠____ = 180°

Hence *AD* ‖ ____   (____)

∴ *ABCD* is a parallelogram.   (Both pairs of ____.)

b Prove that if both pairs of opposite sides of a quadrilateral *ABCD* are equal, the quadrilateral is a parallelogram.

c Prove that if all sides of a quadrilateral *ABCD* are equal then the quadrilateral is a rhombus.

MEASUREMENT & GEOMETRY

11 Given $PQ = SR$ and $PQ \parallel SR$, prove that $PQRS$ is a parallelogram.

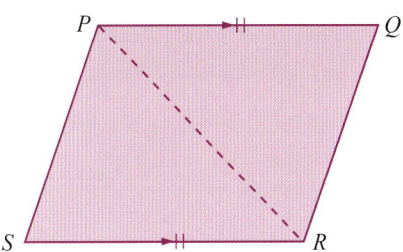

12 Given than $PQRS$ is a parallelogram and $PX = RY$, prove that $SX = QY$.

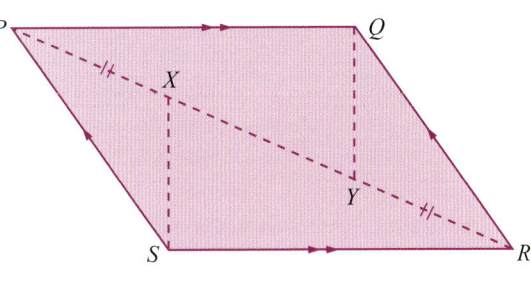

13 Given that $PQRS$ is a parallelogram and $QX = SY$, prove that $SX = QY$.

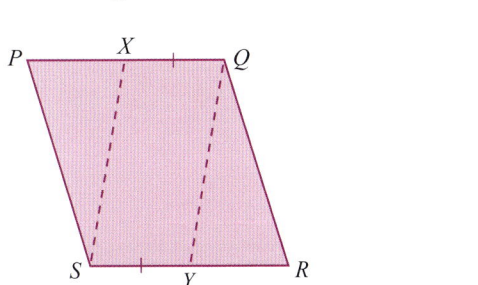

14 $ABCD$ is a parallelogram. The diagonal AC is produced so that $AY = CX$. Prove that $BXDY$ is a parallelogram.

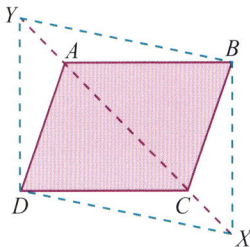

15 If the diagonals of a quadrilateral $ABCD$ are equal and bisect each other, prove that it is a rectangle.

Language in mathematics

1 Write in words the four tests for similar triangles.

2 Explain the relationship between the areas and volumes of similar figures.

3 Explain why:
   a a rhombus is a parallelogram but a parallelogram is not necessarily a rhombus
   b a square is a rhombus but a rhombus is not necessarily a square.

4 List all the properties of the diagonals of these quadrilaterals.
   a parallelogram   b rectangle   c rhombus   d square

5 Draw a flowchart to show the relationship between the special quadrilaterals: trapezium, parallelogram, rhombus, rectangle and square.

Terms

congruent	congruence	parallelogram	quadrilateral	rectangle
rhombus	similar	similarity	square	trapezium

Check your skills

1 Complete the following proof.
In $\triangle CDE$ and $\triangle CBA$:
$\angle DCE = \angle BCA$ (Vertically opposite angles are equal.)
$\dfrac{CE}{\square} = \dfrac{CD}{\square} (= \underline{\quad})$

$\therefore \triangle CDE \parallel\!\parallel\!\parallel \triangle CBA$ (Two pairs of sides in proportion and the included angles equal.)
The missing parts in the proof, in order, are:

A $CB, CA, \dfrac{3}{4}$ **B** $CA, CB, \dfrac{3}{2}$ **C** $CD, AC, \dfrac{1}{2}$ **D** $CA, CE, 2$

2 The value of x in the diagram is:
   A 2.5   **B** 7.5
   C 10   **D** 12.5

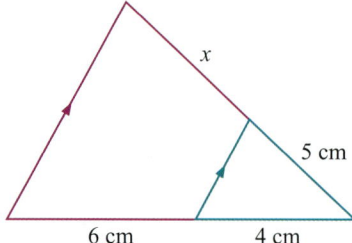

3 The quadrilateral $PQRS$ has been enlarged to $TUVW$ using a scale factor of $k = 2.4$. If the area of $PQRS$ is 36 cm², then the area of $TUVW$ is:
   A 15 cm²   **B** 86.4 cm²
   C 207.36 cm²   **D** 497.664 cm²

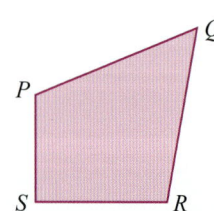
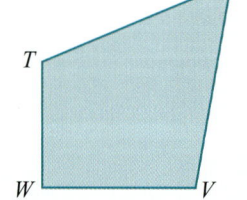

MEASUREMENT & GEOMETRY

4 The solids shown are similar with AB and PQ a pair of matching sides. The volume of the larger solid is:

A 98 cm³ **B** 137.2 cm³
C 192.08 cm³ **D** 527.07 cm³

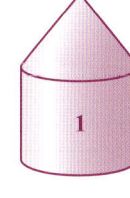

5 The ratio of the surface areas of the similar solids shown is given by $\dfrac{\text{SA of solid 2}}{\text{SA of solid 1}} = \dfrac{729}{64}$

The ratio $\dfrac{\text{volume of solid 2}}{\text{volume of solid 1}}$ is:

A $\dfrac{19\,683}{512}$ **B** $\dfrac{81}{16}$

C $\dfrac{27}{8}$ **D** $\dfrac{9}{4}$

6 The statement that is not true is:

A All squares are rhombi. **B** All squares are rectangles.
C All rhombi are parallelograms. **D** All rectangles are squares.

7 The property that is not true for a rhombus is:

A The diagonals bisect each other. **B** The diagonals are equal.
C The diagonals are perpendicular. **D** The diagonals bisect the vertex angles.

8 $ABCD$ is a rhombus with $BD = 20$ cm. The values of x and y respectively are:

A 56°, 8.5 **B** 56°, 3.5
C 34°, 8.5 **D** 34°, 3.5

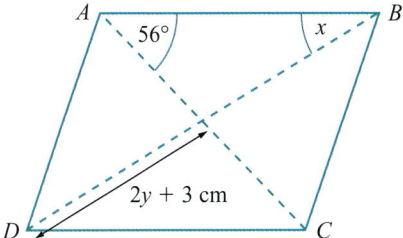

If you have any difficulty with these questions, refer to the examples and questions in the sections listed in the table.

Question	1, 2	3–5	6–8
Section	A	B	C

13A   Review set

1 $\triangle PQR \;|||\; \triangle STU$. XP bisects $\angle RPQ$ and YS bisects $\angle UST$.

a Prove $\triangle PXR \;|||\; \triangle SYU$.

b Prove $\dfrac{PX}{SY} = \dfrac{PQ}{ST}$.

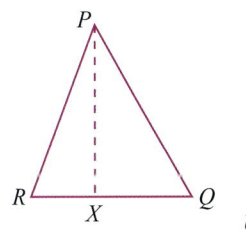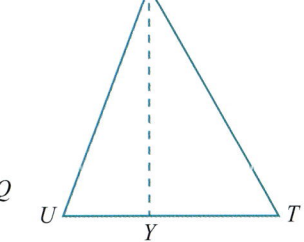

2 BD is perpendicular to AC, CE is perpendicular to AB, $EF = 3$ cm, $BF = 4$ cm and $FD = 7$ cm.
  a Prove $\triangle EFB \;|||\; \triangle DFC$.
  b Find the value of x.

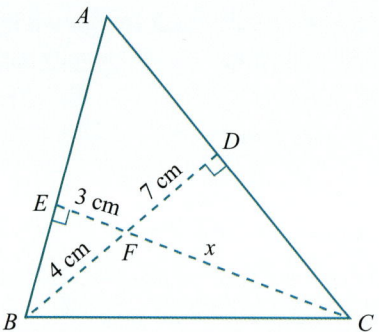

3 a The quadrilateral $ABCD$ has been enlarged to $EFGH$ using a scale factor of 1.8. If the area of $ABCD$ is 68 cm², calculate the area of $EFGH$.
  b The first rectangular prism has been enlarged to form the second prism. AB and XY are a pair of matching sides.
   i What is the enlargement factor?
   ii Calculate the volume of the second prism.

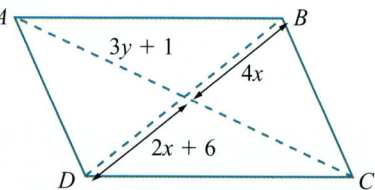
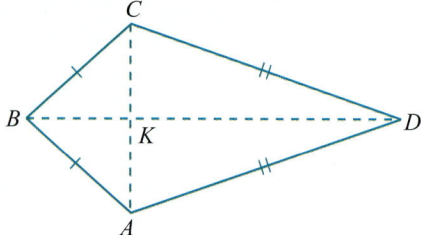

4 State whether the following are true or false.
  a All squares are rectangles.
  b All rhombi are squares.

5 $ABCD$ is a parallelogram and $AC = 20$ cm. Find the values of the pronumerals.

6 $ABCD$ is a kite (a quadrilateral with two pairs of adjacent sides equal).
  a Prove $\triangle ABD \equiv \triangle CBD$.
  b Prove $\triangle ABK \equiv \triangle CBK$.
  c Prove BD bisects AC at right angles.

13B   Review set

1 a Prove $\triangle ADE \;|||\; \triangle ABC$.
  b Prove $DE \parallel BC$.

2 a Prove $\triangle ADE \;|||\; \triangle ABC$.
  b Find the values of x and y.

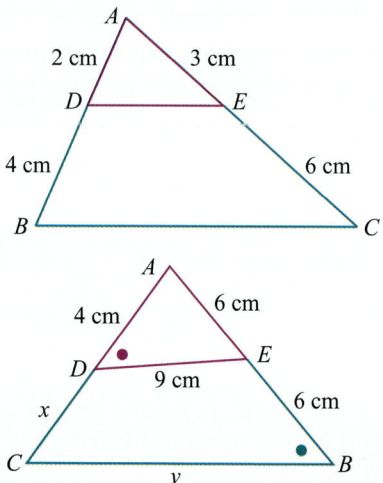

3 The first solid has been enlarged to the second using a scale factor of 2.4.

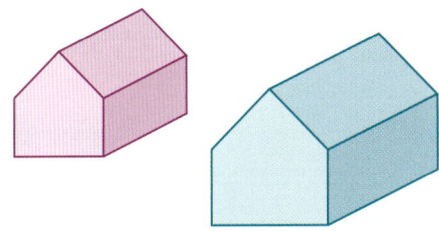

    a If the surface area of the first solid is 236 cm², what is the surface area of the second?

    b If the volume of the first solid is 315 cm³, what is the volume of the second?

4 State whether the following are true or false.

    a All rectangles are parallelograms.
    b All rectangles are squares.
    c All squares are rhombi.

5 *PQRS* is a rhombus and angle *PQR* = 70°. Find the values of the pronumerals.

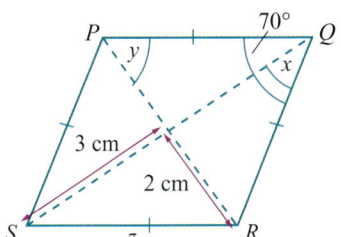

6 **a** Prove that the opposite angles of a parallelogram are equal.

    b Prove that if the opposite angles of a quadrilateral are equal then the quadrilateral is a parallelogram.

13C Review set

1 **a** Prove that $\triangle ABC \;|||\; \triangle DBE$.

    b Hence find *x*.

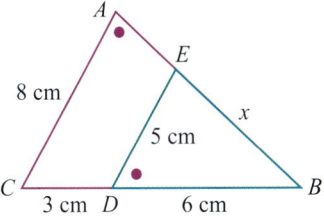

2 *D* and *E* are the midpoints of *AB* and *AC* respectively.

    a Prove *DE* ∥ *BC*.

    b Prove $DE = \frac{1}{2}BC$.

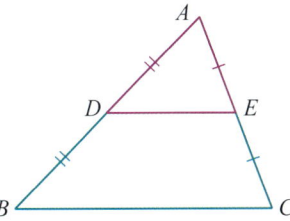

3 A model is made of a statue and the ratio of their volumes is 1 : 27.

    a Find the ratio of the height of the model to the height of the statue.

    b If the surface area of the statue is 0.216 m², what is the surface area of the model?

4 *ABCD* is a parallelogram. *AX* bisects ∠*CAB*. Find the value of *x*.

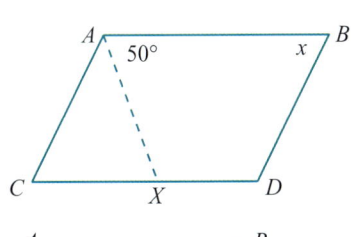

5 *ABDE* is a rectangle. *EF* = *DC*. Prove that *AF* = *BC*.

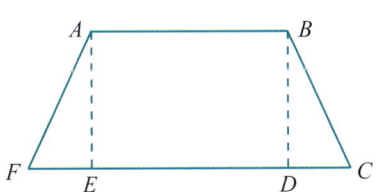

MEASUREMENT & GEOMETRY

6 $ABCD$ is a square. X is the midpoint of AB and Y is the midpoint of BC. Prove that $XD = YA$.

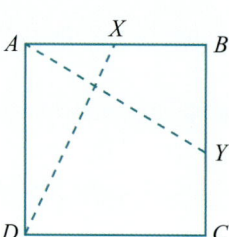

13D   Review set

1 **a** Prove $\triangle PQR \;|||\; \triangle TQS$.
　b Hence find the value of x.

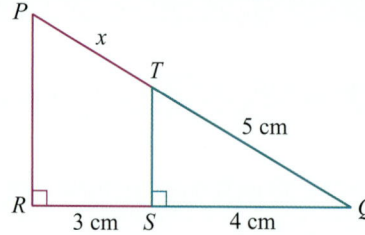

2 D is the midpoint of AB and $DE \parallel BC$.
Prove E is the midpoint of AC.

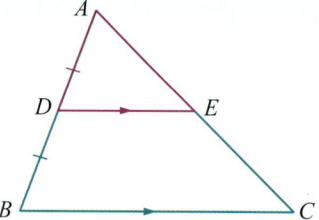

3 A box in the shape of a rectangular prism holds 600 ball bearings. If all the dimensions of the prism were doubled, how many ball bearings would it hold?

4 $PQRS$ is a rhombus. QK bisects $\angle SQR$. $\angle KQR = x$.
Prove that $\angle PQR = 4x$ and $\angle QKR = 3x$.

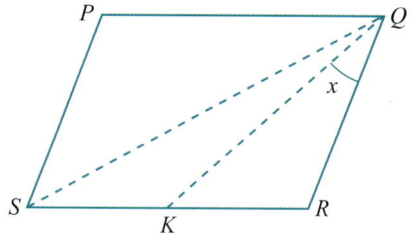

5 $ABCD$ and $AEFD$ are parallelograms. EA bisects angle BAD.
Find the values of the pronumerals.

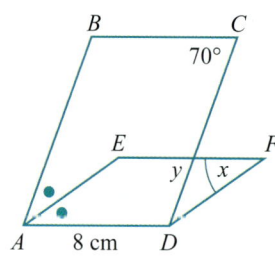

6 $ABEF$ and $BCDE$ are parallelograms. BE is produced to G.
Prove:
　a $\angle ABC = \angle FED$
　b $\triangle ABC \equiv \triangle FED$
　c $ACDF$ is a parallelogram.

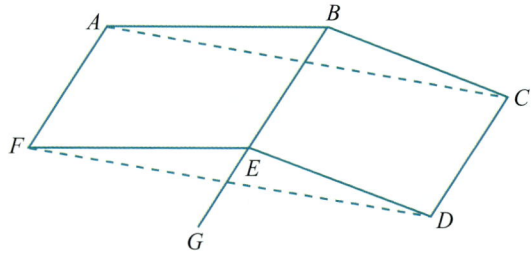

1 a Solve the following.

   i $4x + 2 = 8x - 1$

   ii $4(x - 5) - 3(2 - 7x) = 1$

   iii $\dfrac{5x + 4}{3} = \dfrac{1 - 3x}{2}$

   iv $\dfrac{3x - 2}{3} - \dfrac{2x + 5}{5} = -4$

b Expand and simplify.

   i $(3x - 2)^2$

   ii $(x - 4)(x + 4)$

   iii $(3x - 7)(3x + 7)$

c Factorise:

   i $x^2 - 64$

   ii $r^2 - t^2$

   iii $81p^2 - 25q^2$

   iv $x^2 - 8x + 7$

   v $x^2 + 3x - 10$

   vi $6x^2 - 7x - 5$

d Solve:

   i $5x^3 = 64$

   ii $x^4 - 11x^2 + 10 = 0$

e Solve $x^2 - 8x - 7 = 0$ by completing the square.

f Solve $y = 2x^2 - 3x - 11$ and $y = -10x + 4$ simultaneously.

g Make x the subject of each equation.

   i $l + mx = p - qy$

   ii $b + x = p - ex$

2 a A triangular prism is shown at right.

   i Calculate the length EC.

   ii Calculate the angle the line BE makes with the plane $EFCD$.

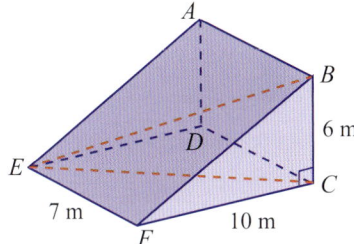

b **i** From a point C due south of a tree, T, 40 m tall on level ground, the angle of elevation of the top of the tree is 22°. From the point D due east of the tree, the angle of elevation of the top of the tree is 31°. Draw a diagram showing this information.

   ii Calculate the distance CD to the nearest metre.

c Two boats at sea observe the same lighthouse, which is at a height of 600 m above sea level. From boat A the bearing of the lighthouse is 045°T and the angle of elevation is 15°. From boat B the bearing of the lighthouse is 315°T and the angle of elevation is 16°.

   i Complete the diagram.

   ii Show that $\angle AOB$ is 90°.

   iii Calculate distances OA and OB, and hence AB.

   iv Calculate $\angle OAB$ and hence the bearing of boat B from boat A.

d Find the value of θ to the nearest minute if $90° \leqslant \theta \leqslant 180°$ and

   i $\cos \theta = -0.6135$

   ii $\sin \theta = 0.6321$

e Draw the graph of $y = \sin \theta$ for $0° \leqslant \theta \leqslant 720°$.

f What is the exact value of:

   i $\sin 300°$?

   ii $\cos 240°$?

   iii $\tan 150°$?

3 a Which of the graphs below shows that distance is decreasing at a decreasing rate?

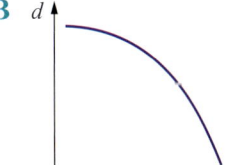 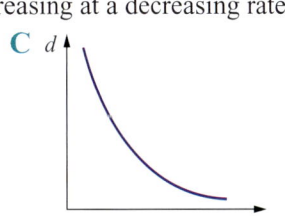 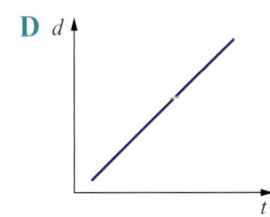

b Draw graphs to represent the following situations.

    i Unemployment is increasing at a faster rate than in the previous quarter (of a year).

    ii The number of bacteria in a culture increases quickly at first then more slowly.

c The following containers are filled with water at a constant rate. Draw graphs to show how the height of water increases with time.

    i    **ii**

d Consider the parabola $y = -x^2 - 4x - 3$.

    i Find the x- and y-intercepts.   **ii** Find the equation of the axis of symmetry.

    iii What are the coordinates of the vertex?   **iv** Sketch the curve.

e Sketch these graphs showing all points of interest.

    i $y = \dfrac{1}{x - 3}$ **ii** $y = x^2 + 6$ **iii** $(x + 3)^2 - (y - 1)^2 = 16$

    iv $y = (x - 4)^2 + 2$ **v** $y = 5^x$ **vi** $y = \dfrac{5}{x} + 5$

f Find the centre and radius of the circle with equation $x^2 + y^2 - 6x + 4y - 12 = 0$.

g Consider the graph of $y = (x - 4)(x + 3)(x - 1)$.

    i Find the x- and y-intercepts.   **ii** Sketch the curve.

    iii On the same axes sketch the graph of $y = -(x - 4)(x + 3)(x - 1)$.

h Find the point(s) of intersection of the graphs $y = x^2$ and $y = 12x - 35$.

4 a **i** Prove $\triangle PQR \;|||\; \triangle TQS$.

    ii Hence find the value of x.

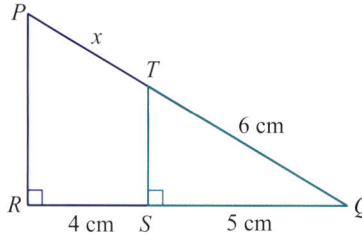

b $DE \parallel BC$.

    i Prove that $\triangle ADE \;|||\; \triangle ABC$.

    ii Given that $AD = DB$, prove that $DE = \frac{1}{2}BC$.

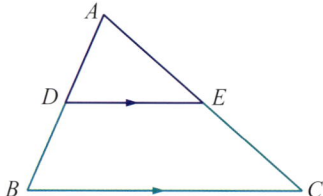

c A model is made of a water tank and the ratio of their volumes is $1 : 1000$.

    i Find the ratio of the height of the model to the height of the structure.

    ii If the surface area of the water tank is 220 m^2, what is the surface area of the model?

d $PQRS$ is a parallelogram. QX bisects $\angle PQR$. Find the value of x and y.

e $ABDE$ is a rectangle. $AF = BC$. Prove that $EF = DC$.

14

Data analysis

This chapter deals with finding standard deviation, comparing data sets and using technology to construct a line of best fit.

At the end of this chapter you should be able to:

► investigate the standard deviation of a small set of data

► find standard deviation using technology

► use the mean and standard deviation to compare sets of data

► compare the merits of the range, interquartile range and standard deviation as a measure of spread

► use technology to construct a line of best fit for bivariate data

► use line of best fit for interpolation and extrapolation.

NSW Syllabus references: 5.3 S&P Single variable data analysis, 5.3 S&P Bivariate data analysis
Outcomes: MA5.3-1WM, MA5.3-2WM, MA5.3-3WM, MA5.3-18SP, MA5.3-19SP
Statistics & probability – ACMSP277, ACMSP278, ACMSP279

Diagnostic test

Use the scores 4, 4, 5, 7, 8, 8, 8, 9 and 10 to answer questions **1** to **4**.

1 The mean of the scores is:
  A 8   **B** 7   **C** 6   **D** 5

2 The range of the scores is:
  A 8   **B** 7   **C** 6   **D** 5

3 The median of the scores is:
  A 8   **B** 7   **C** 6   **D** 5

4 The mode of the scores is:
  A 8   **B** 7   **C** 6   **D** 5

5 The mean of 13, 15, 16, 19, 21 and x is 17. The value of x is:
  A 16   **B** 16.8   **C** 84   **D** 18

Use the scores 21, 21, 23, 25, 25, 26, 28, 30, 31 and 32 to answers questions **6** to **8**.

6 The lower quartile is:
  A 21   **B** 23   **C** 30   **D** 11

7 The upper quartile is:
  A 21   **B** 23   **C** 30   **D** 11

8 The interquartile range is:
  A 11   **B** 5.5   **C** 9   **D** 7

Answer questions **9** to **11** using this box plot.

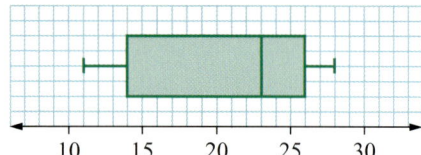

9 The range is:
  A 28   **B** 17   **C** 12   **D** 11

10 The median is:
  A 28   **B** 26   **C** 23   **D** 14

11 The interquartile range is:
  A 28   **B** 17   **C** 12   **D** 11

Use the data in this stem-and-leaf plot to answer questions **12** to **14**.

Stem	Leaf
1	8 8 9
2	1 3 5 5 6 7 8 8
3	0 0 0 4 6 7 7 8 9 9
4	1 2 2 2 3 5 5 9
5	0 3 6 6 6
6	1 2 3 6

12 The median is:
  A 8   **B** 38.5   **C** 8.5   **D** 39

13 The lower and upper quartiles are:
  A 28 and 49   **B** 18 and 66
  C 27 and 50   **D** 26 and 53

14 The lowest and highest scores are:
  A 28 and 49   **B** 18 and 66
  C 27 and 50   **D** 26 and 53

The diagnostic test questions refer to outcomes ACMSP171 and ACMSP248.

STATISTICS & PROBABILITY

A # Standard deviation

The range and interquartile range have already been used to measure the spread of a set of scores. The range can be unreliable as it depends on only two scores, the highest and lowest scores. It is thus greatly affected by outliers. Also, it does not provide any information about how the scores are spread between these two values.

The interquartile range is not affected by outliers, but again relies on only two values, the upper and lower quartiles. It is a measure of the spread of the middle 50% of the scores.

Another more commonly used measure of spread, whose value depends on the value of every score in the data set, is the standard deviation. The standard deviation may be calculated using the formula:

$$\sigma_n = \sqrt{\frac{\Sigma(x - \bar{x})^2}{n}}$$

where σ_n is the standard deviation, x is the score, $\bar{x}$ is the mean and n is the number of scores.

The standard deviation is a measure of the distance of each score from the mean. For example, consider two sets of scores: set A is 1, 2, 5, 8, 9 and set B is 4, 4, 5, 6, 6. Each data set has a mean of 5, but the standard deviation of set A is 3.2 and of set B is 0.9. By observation, the scores in set A are much more spread out than those in set B. The standard deviation gives this information. The scores in set B are close to the mean, have a small standard deviation and are described as being more consistent.

EXAMPLE 1

Use the formula to calculate the standard deviation of the scores 6, 6, 6, 8, 9 and 10.

Solve	Think	Apply
$\bar{x} = \frac{45}{6} = 7.5$ 	Score (x)	$x - \bar{x}$	$(x - \bar{x})^2$	 6 | 6 − 7.5 = −1.5 | 2.25 6 | 6 − 7.5 = −1.5 | 2.25 6 | 6 − 7.5 = −1.5 | 2.25 8 | 8 − 7.5 = 0.5 | 0.25 9 | 9 − 7.5 = 1.5 | 2.25 10 | 10 − 7.5 = 2.5 | 6.25 $\Sigma(x - \bar{x})^2 = 15.5$ $\sigma_n = \sqrt{\frac{15.5}{6}}$ $= \sqrt{2.583} = 1.61$	To calculate the standard deviation using the formula $\sigma_n = \sqrt{\frac{\Sigma(x - \bar{x})^2}{n}}$: • Find the deviation of each score from the mean $(x - \bar{x})$. • Square the deviations $(x - \bar{x})^2$. • Find the mean of the squares $\frac{\Sigma(x - \bar{x})^2}{n}$. • Find the square root. *Note:* The mean of the deviations is always 0. Squaring the deviations changes them to positive values before taking the mean. This is why we take the square root of the squares of the deviations.	The standard deviation is a measure of the distance of each score from the mean. The lower the standard deviation, the closer the scores are to the mean.

Exercise 14A

1 Use the formula to calculate the standard deviation for the following small sets of data.

   a 5, 6, 6, 6, 7   **b** 2, 4, 6, 8, 10

   c 5, 8, 8, 10, 12   **d** 6, 6, 7, 7, 8, 9, 10, 11

EXAMPLE 2

Find the standard deviation for the scores 12, 13, 14, 14, 14, 15 and 16 using a calculator.

Solve/Think	Apply
Set the calculator to statistics mode, enter the score and use the σ_n or σ_x key to give the standard deviation. Check your calculator instructions for the correct method. Possible steps for a Sharp calculator are: *Step 1:* **2ndF** **MODE** DRG 1 to set statistics mode. *Step 2:* **2ndF** **DEL** to clear the calculator. *Step 3:* 12 **M+** 13 **M+** 14 **M+** **M+** **M+** 15 **M+** 16 **M+** enters the data. To enter three scores of 14, press the **M+** button three times after entering 14. *Step 4:* Press **RCL** **σx** for the standard deviation. $\sigma_n = 1.2$ (1 decimal place). *Step 5:* Press **2ndF** **MODE** DRG 0 to return to normal. Possible steps for a Casio calculator are: *Step 1:* **MODE** 1 to set to statistics mode. *Step 2:* **SHIFT** **AC** to clear the statistics memory. *Step 3:* 12 **M+** 13 **M+** 14 **M+** **M+** **M+** 15 **M+** 16 **M+** enters the data. To enter three scores of 14, press the **M+** button three times after entering 14. *Step 4:* Press **SHIFT** **σx** for the standard deviation. $\sigma_n = 1.2$ (1 decimal place).	Use the appropriate steps on a calculator. Make sure that the statistics memory is cleared before the next calculation.

2 Use a calculator to find the standard deviation of these sets of scores. Remember to clear the statistics memory between questions. Give the answers correct to 2 decimal places.
   a   25, 26, 27, 28, 29, 33
   b   89, 91, 92, 89, 91, 88
   c   239, 248, 253, 254, 245, 250, 253, 258
   d   7, 5, 9, 9, 3, 3

EXAMPLE 3

Find the mean and standard deviation of the scores 21, 22, 22, 22, 24, 26 and 26.

Solve/Think	Apply
Pressing the appropriate keys for the mean, $\bar{x}$: $\bar{x} = 23.3$ (1 decimal place) Following the calculator steps in Example 2 above: $\sigma_n = 1.9$ (1 decimal place)	Use the appropriate steps on a calculator.

3 Use your calculator to find the mean and standard deviation of these scores correct to 1 decimal place.
   a   3, 5, 6, 6, 8, 2, 9, 7, 8, 8, 9, 8
   b   35, 38, 40, 42, 38, 39, 41, 44, 41, 38

EXAMPLE 4

Find the mean and standard
deviation for the scores in this table.

Score	Frequency
20	5
21	7
22	13
23	8
24	11

Solve/Think	Apply
The calculator steps are the same as in Example 2 except for Step 3. Sharp calculator: *Step 3:* 20 STO 5 M+ 21 STO 7 M+ 22 STO 13 M+ 23 STO 8 M+ 24 STO 11 M+ Casio calculator: *Step 3:* 20 × 5 M+ 21 × 7 M+ 22 × 13 M+ 23 × 8 M+ 24 × 11 M+ $\bar{x} = 22.3$, $\sigma_n = 1.3$	Use the appropriate steps on a calculator.

4 Consider the scores 20, 22, 25, 25, 25, 28, 30.

  a Calculate the mean and standard deviation.

  b **i** An additional score of 25 is added to the data set. Recalculate the mean and standard deviation.

    ii What is the effect of adding another score equal to the mean?

  c **i** An additional score of 22 is added to the original data set. Recalculate the mean and standard deviation.

    ii What is the effect of adding another score less than the mean?

  d **i** An additional score of 28 is added to the original data set. Recalculate the mean and standard deviation.

    ii What is the effect of adding another score greater than the mean?

  e **i** An additional score of 70 is added to the original data set. Recalculate the mean and standard deviation.

    ii What is the effect of adding an outlier score?

  f Repeat part **e** for a score of 1.

5 Find the mean and standard deviation for these scores.

a

Score	Frequency
8	6
9	5
10	2
11	4
12	3

b

Score	Frequency
121	4
122	6
123	11
124	3
125	1

EXAMPLE 5

Using class centres, find the mean and standard deviation of the following grouped data.

Class	Frequency
6–10	2
11–15	5
16–20	7
21–25	6
26–30	4

Solve	Think	Apply
<table><tr><th>Class</th><th>Class centre</th><th>Frequency</th></tr><tr><td>6–10</td><td>8</td><td>2</td></tr><tr><td>11–15</td><td>13</td><td>5</td></tr><tr><td>16–20</td><td>18</td><td>7</td></tr><tr><td>21–25</td><td>23</td><td>6</td></tr><tr><td>26–30</td><td>28</td><td>4</td></tr></table> $\bar{x} = 19.04$, $\sigma_n = 5.95$	Enter the data into a calculator as in Example 4, using the class centres as the scores.	Find the class centres and use these as the scores. The centre of the class interval a–b is $\dfrac{a + b}{2}$.

6 Grouped data uses the class centre in a calculation of the mean and standard deviation. Use the class centre to find the mean and standard deviation of the following.

a
Class	Frequency
1–5	3
6–10	5
11–15	9
16–20	6
21–25	2
26–30	1

b
Class	Frequency
1–10	8
11–20	11
21–30	14
31–40	12
41–50	6

c
Class	Frequency
0–9	3
10–19	14
20–29	17
30–39	12
40–49	8

d
Class	Frequency
18–23	8
24–29	19
30–35	23
36–41	15
42–47	6

7 a Find the range, mean and standard deviation for the scores 15, 16, 16, 16, 17, 18 and 21.
  b Add 5 to each of the scores and calculate the range, mean and standard deviation.
  c Subtract 8 from each of the scores and calculate the range, mean and standard deviation.
  d What effect does adding or subtracting a constant to each of the scores have on the range, mean and standard deviation?

8 a Find the range, mean and standard deviation for the scores 8, 8, 9, 10, 10, 10, 11, 12, 12, 13.

b Multiply each of the scores by 3 and find the range, mean and standard deviation.

c Divide the scores by 5 and find the range, mean and standard deviation.

d What effect does multiplying or dividing each of the scores by a constant have on the range, median and standard deviation?

9 A sprinter has recorded her times over 100 m for 10 races. The mean is 12.7 s and the standard deviation is 0.52. It was found that the timer made an error of 0.1 s on every race time recorded. Each time was recorded 0.1 s longer than it should have been. State the correct mean and standard deviation.

EXAMPLE 6

The histograms show three data sets A, B and C. Which data set has the highest:

i mean?　　　　　　　　**ii** range?　　　　　　　　**iii** standard deviation?

	Solve	Think	Apply
a	Data set C has the highest mean.	In data sets A and B, the histograms are symmetrical about the score 4. Hence their mean = 4. The data in set C is skewed to the right; that is, there are more high scores. Hence the mean > 4.	The mean of a symmetrical distribution is at the centre of the data set. If the distribution is skewed such that there is more data on the right (negatively skewed), then there are more high scores and hence the mean will be to the right of the data set. If the distribution is skewed such that there is more data on the left (positively skewed), then there are more low scores and hence the mean will be to the left of the data set.
b	Data set B has the highest range.	Range of A = 2 Range of B = 4 Range of C = 2	Range = highest score − lowest score
c	Data set B has the highest standard deviation.	The data in B is spread further from the mean. (Or, the data in A and C is clustered more closely about the mean.)	The further the scores are spread from the mean the greater the standard deviation. The closer the scores are clustered about the mean the lower the standard deviation.

10 Which data set has the highest:

  i mean?   **ii** range?   **iii** standard deviation?

a   **A** 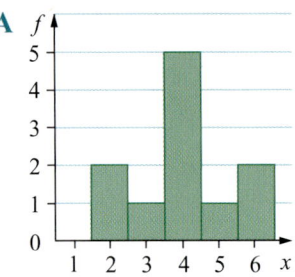   **B** 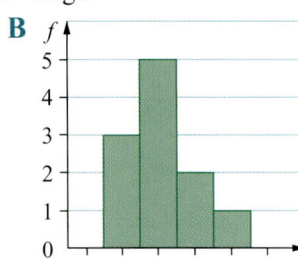   **C**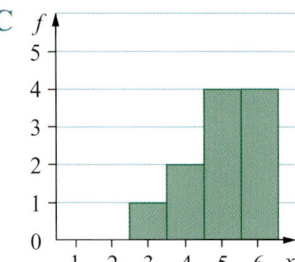

b   **A** 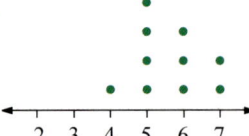   **B** 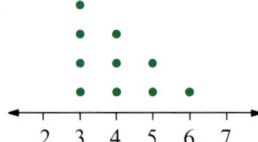   **C**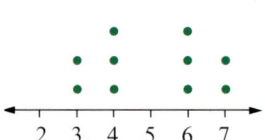

11 Consider the data sets shown below.

   A 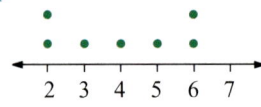   **B** 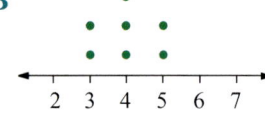   **C**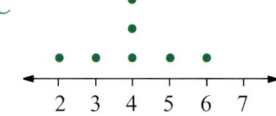

   D 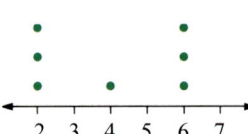   **E** 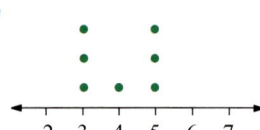   **F**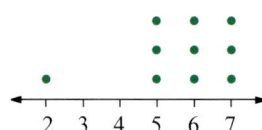

  a   Which set has the highest:

      i mean?   **ii** range?   **iii** standard deviation?

  b   Sets A to E have a mean of 4. Explain why.

  c   **i** What is the range of sets A, C and D?

     ii Do sets A, C and D have the same standard deviation?

     iii What is the range of sets B and E?

     iv Do sets B and E have the same standard deviation?

      v Do all sets with the same range have the same standard deviation?

  d   Does the set with the highest range have the highest standard deviation?

12 **a**   Find the range, mean and standard deviation for each of the following three sets of scores.

i

Score	Frequency
12	9
13	9
14	9
15	9
16	9

ii

Score	Frequency
12	9
13	6
14	3
15	6
16	9

iii

Score	Frequency
12	3
13	6
14	9
15	6
16	3

  b   Compare the range of each set of scores.

  c   Compare the mean of each set of scores.

  d   Compare the standard deviation of each set of scores.

  e   Draw frequency histograms or dot plots to see the distribution of scores in each set of data.

STATISTICS & PROBABILITY

13 Complete the following statements based on these two histograms using the same scale. Use equal to, greater than or less than to fill the gaps.

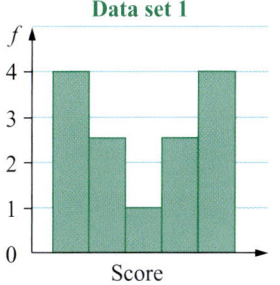
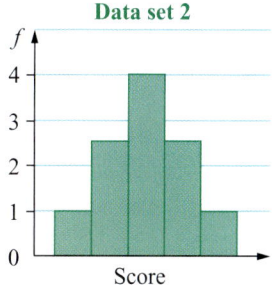

a The mean of data set 1 is _____ the mean of data set 2.

b The range of data set 1 is _____ the range of data set 2.

c The standard deviation of data set 1 is _____ the standard deviation of data set 2.

14 The results of a test out of 20 are 4, 9, 10, 11, 11, 12, 13, 13, 15, 16, 17, 18, 19 and 20.

a Calculate the mean and standard deviation.

b Calculate the mean plus twice the standard deviation.

c Calculate the mean minus twice the standard deviation.

d The answers to parts **b** and **c** give a range of values that are within two standard deviations of the mean. Which score(s) are outside this range?

15 The times (in minutes) taken by Jack to get to school each day over 2 weeks are 21, 23, 24, 25, 25, 29, 31, 34, 37 and 41.

a Calculate the mean and standard deviation.

b Calculate the mean plus the standard deviation.

c Calculate the mean minus the standard deviation.

d The values from parts **b** and **c** give an upper and lower limit for the time Jack takes to get to school. Calculate the percentage of times that are within these limits.

Investigation 1 Errors in data

1 a The eleven members of the school cricket team were weighed. Their weights in kilograms are 67, 49, 53, 65, 58, 71, 166, 56, 59 and 62. What statistical comment can be made for the weight 166 kg?

b What do you think the weight should be? Why?

c Calculate the mean and standard deviation:

   i using all ten scores

   ii using nine scores, omitting the error score

   iii changing the incorrect score and using ten scores.

2 The members of the debating team have their heights measured. The measurements in metres are 1.45, 1.36, 1.65, 0.24, 1.28, 1.84, 3.75, 1.61, 1.35 and 1.29.

a Comment on the heights. Are there any errors? Explain your answer.

b What should the values probably be for the heights you think are errors? Explain.

c Which scores would you use to calculate the mean and standard deviation? Why?

d Calculate the mean and standard deviation appropriate for these measurements. Explain your choice.

B Comparing two data sets

This section uses the skills developed in Section A to make comparisons between data sets.

Use the following table to answer questions **1** and **2**.

Mean maximum temperature (°C) in January

Year	Sydney	Melbourne	Brisbane	Adelaide
2004	27.6	24.6	31.5	25.9
2005	26.6	26.5	30.2	29.1
2006	27.0	27.7	30.6	31.9
2007	26.4	27.9	29.8	29.6
2008	26.0	27.9	28.9	31.0
2009	27.6	28.6	30.1	32.0
2010	27.6	27.5	31.1	31.4
2011	27.4	26.5	29.6	30.6
2012	26.1	27.4	28.7	31.1
2013	27.6	27.3	30.5	30.4

1 a Calculate the mean and standard deviation for Sydney and Melbourne in January.
  b Which city has the more consistent temperature in January? Explain.

2 a Calculate the mean and standard deviation for Brisbane and Adelaide in January.
  b Which city has the more consistent temperature in January? Explain.
  c Find the range and interquartile range for each city. What do these measures show about consistency?

3 Here are two lists of scores.

List 1: 4, 5, 6, 7, 9, 11   List 2: 2, 5, 6, 6, 9, 14

  a Calculate the mean for each list. What does the mean show?
  b Calculate the standard deviation of each list. In which list are the scores clustered more closely about the mean?
  c Calculate the range for each list. What does the range show?
  d Calculate the interquartile range for each list. What conclusion about consistency can be made using the interquartile range?

4 The back-to-back stem-and-leaf plot shows the times taken to travel to school by a sample of 15 students from a city school and a country school.

  a For each school, calculate the:
     i mean   **ii** range
     iii standard deviation.
  b Which school do you think is the city school? Explain.
  c Comment on the spread of travel times for each school.

School A Leaf	Stem	School B Leaf
8	0	
7 6 5	1	8 9
9 8 7 2 2 0	2	4 6 7
9 5 3 1	3	5 8 8 9
0	4	0 2 3 5 7
	5	1

5 Stuart and Greg play 9 holes of golf. Their scores are listed in the table below.

Hole	1	2	3	4	5	6	7	8	9	Total
Stuart	4	7	5	2	4	7	3	6	7	45
Greg	3	5	4	2	3	7	3	5	14	46

a For each player, calculate the:
    i mean   **ii** standard deviation   **iii** range   **iv** interquartile range.

b Statistically the lower the standard deviation the more consistent the score. Based on the standard deviation, which golfer was more consistent?

c **i** Greg scored 14 on the 9th hole. What statistical term might be given to this score?
    ii Which measure of spread was not affected by this score of 14?

d The golfer with the lowest score on a hole is the winner of that hole.
    i Who won the most holes?
    ii Did the statistically more consistent golfer win the most holes? Explain your answer.

6 The marks scored by Lleyton and Rodger in their eight Mathematics tests are shown below.

Test	1	2	3	4	5	6	7	8
Lleyton	85	84	94	87	85	78	91	57
Rodger	84	83	89	86	91	75	89	82

a Find the total mark scored by each student.

b Calculate the mean and standard deviation for each student. Comment on the spread and consistency of marks.

c In how many tests did Lleyton score more marks than Rodger?

d Compare and comment on the:
    i range   **ii** interquartile range.

e Which student's performance was more consistent? Explain.

f The Mathematics prize will be given to the better of these two students.
    i Present an argument for Lleyton to win the prize.
    ii Present an argument for Rodger to win the prize.
    iii Who should receive the prize? Why?

7 Alicia scored 75 in English and 62 in Mathematics.
a Based on the marks only, in which subject did she perform better?
b The mean score for the whole class was 70 for English and 60 for Mathematics. In which subject would you say Alicia performed better? Why?
c The standard deviation was 10 for English and 2 for Mathematics. In which subject would you say Alicia performed better? Explain.
d Give an example of when the mean score would be sufficient to determine the better mark in two subjects.

8 Georgina and Benjamin were comparing their classes' results in the half-yearly History test. For Georgina's class the mean was 68 and the range was 54. For Benjamin's class the mean was also 68 but the range was 18.
a Make some comments about the results for the two classes.
b This is a histogram for Georgina's class. Using the same scale, draw a possible histogram for Benjamin's class. Explain your answer.

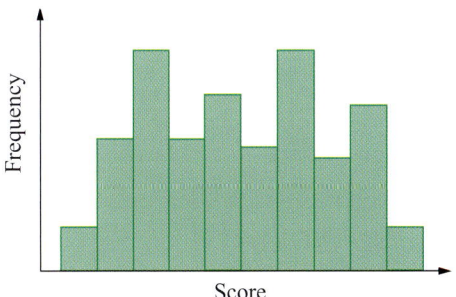

C Line of best fit

There are a number of methods used by statisticians to draw a line of best fit. The method shown in Chapter 5 involves estimating, by eye, a trend line that is placed so that roughly the same number of points are above it as below it. This is not a very exact method, but is suitable for simple examples. Two of the most common methods used by statisticians are 'the least squares regression line' and the 'three-median regression line'. The equations for both these lines are quite complex and are better determined using technology.

Using a line of best fit to predict what might happen between known data values is called **interpolation**. To predict what might happen beyond known data values is called **extrapolation**.

EXAMPLE 1

The heights and weights of 16 members of the Waratah 2014 rugby team are displayed in the table.

Height	185	182	184	192	185	197	193	192	202	193	182	194	186	190	195	182
Weight	94	98	90	98	93	110	100	110	119	103	89	114	91	102	109	101

a Enter this data into a spreadsheet and draw a scatter plot. Add the trendline (least squares line of best fit) and show the equation.

b Use the line of best fit to estimate the weight of a player with height

   i 188 cm

   ii 210 cm.

	Solve	Think	Apply
a	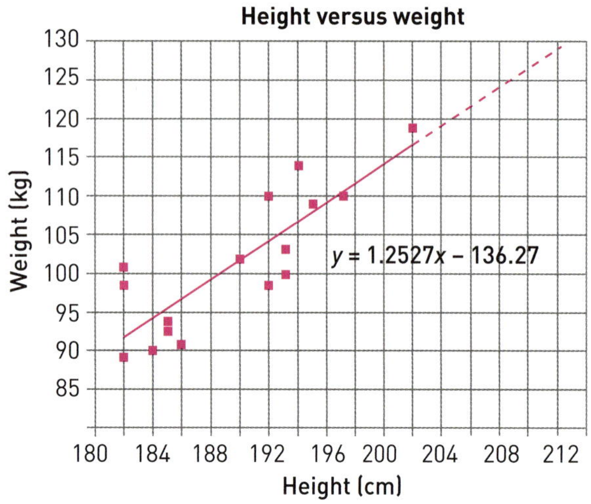 **Height versus weight** (scatter plot, Weight (kg) vs Height (cm)) $y = 1.2527x - 136.27$	Enter data into the spreadsheet in two columns. Insert the scatterplot graph. From the Insert menu, select Scatterplot then the first scatterplot type. From the Chart tools, select Linear Trendline. Right click on the line and select Format Trendline from the drop-down menu. Check the Display equation on chart box.	The least squares line of best fit is a straight line that is fitted to the data such that it minimises the square of the distance of each point from the line. The equation is found using technology. In part **b ii** be careful when extrapolating, as an extended trendline may not be accurate outside the data set.
b	i The estimated weight of a player with height 188 cm is 99 kg. ii The estimated weight of a player with height 210 cm is 126 kg.	Draw a vertical line up from 188 cm on the x-axis to the graph and across to the weight axis. Extend the line of best fit and draw a line up from 210 cm on the x-axis to the graph and across to the weight axis.	

Exercise 14C

1 The heights and weights of 19 members of the Sydney Swans 2014 team are displayed in the table.

Height (cm)	191	187	183	192	181	196	194	188	192	178
Weight (kg)	100	88	82	94	81	103	94	86	100	78

Height (cm)	171	188	179	202	181	183	181	201	183
Weight (kg)	75	96	85	104	81	83	77	104	86

  a Enter this data into a spreadsheet and draw a scatter plot.

  b Add the trendline (least squares line of best fit) and show the equation.

  c Use the line of best fit to estimate the weight of a player with height 188 cm.

  d Use the line of best fit to estimate the weight of a player with height 210 cm.

  e Use the line of best fit to estimate the height of a player with weight 75 kg.

2 The population of koalas over a period of 10 years is shown in the table. The time is measured in years from the start of 2000; that is, $t = 1$ is the start of 2001, $t = 2$ is the start of 2002, etc.

Time (year)	1	2	3	4	5	6	7	8	9	10
Population	8000	7400	6900	6500	6100	5600	4900	4500	4100	3400

  a Enter this data into a spreadsheet and draw a scatter plot.

  b Add the trendline (least squares line of best fit) and show the equation.

  c Use the line of best fit to estimate the population after 3.5 years.

  d Use the line of best fit to estimate when the population will be 4700.

  e Use the line of best fit to estimate the time when the population of koalas will be 0.

3 The table shows the number of hours of study and the test scores of 10 students.

Hours of study	2	20	10	3	5	2	15	13	10	8
Test score	70	85	92	68	72	82	88	79	75	81

  a Enter this data into a spreadsheet and draw a scatter plot.

  b Add the trendline (least squares line of best fit) and show the equation.

  c Use the line of best fit to estimate the test score for a student who spends 17 hours studying.

  d Use the line of best fit to estimate the number of hours of study that will obtain a test score of 90.

  e What comment can be made on the reliability of this scatter plot?

4 The number of shots and the handicaps of 12 golfers are displayed in the table.

Handicap	5	28	13	15	4	10	22	27	29	33	17	19
Shots	78	106	88	87	73	86	96	102	100	112	89	80

a Enter this data into a spreadsheet and draw a scatter plot.

b Add the trendline (least squares line of best fit) and show the equation.

c Use the line of best fit to estimate the number of shots played by a golfer with a handicap of 20.

d Use the line of best fit to estimate the handicap of a player who plays 82 shots.

● EXAMPLE 2

Use a scientific calculator to find the equation of the least squares regression line for the data in the table.

Income ($'000)	10	12	16	22	26	29	33	37	42	49
Expenditure ($'000)	2.5	2.8	3	3.3	3.6	3.8	3.9	4.1	4.5	4.9

For most scientific calculators, the least squares regression line is usually expressed in the form $y = A + Bx$.

Solve/Think	Apply
First put the calculator in REG mode (regression mode). On a CASIO fx-82TL press **MODE** 3 I for linear regression. To enter the data from the table, press: 10 **,** 2.5 **DT** 12 **,** 2.8 **DT** 16 **,** 3 **DT** 22 **,** 3.3 **DT** 26 **,** 3.6 **DT** 29 **,** 3.8 **DT** 33 **,** 3.9 **DT** 37 **,** 4.1 **DT** 42 **,** 4.5 **DT** 49 **,** 4.9 **DT** To obtain the linear coefficients A and B, press: **SHIFT** $A = 2.15$ (2 decimal places) **SHIFT** $B = 0.05$ (2 decimal places) The equation of the regression line for this data is $y = 2.15 + 0.05x$, where x represents income and y represents expenditure.	Use the appropriate steps on your calculator.

5 Use your calculator to find the equation of the least squares regression line for the data in the tables below.

a

x	100	120	125	140	170	180	190	210	220	240
y	90	85	100	90	100	115	105	125	110	120

b

x	10	14	20	22	28	35	38	43	47
y	9	15	16	13	24	20	29	22	27

c

x	86	95	100	90	96	105	94	98	110	100	93
y	120	74	20	104	46	50	80	96	10	25	100

6 a Draw a scatterplot for the data in the table below.

x	8	14	17	17	22	27	30	33
y	11	14	20	16	22	29	28	35

  b i Draw, by eye, a line of best fit; that is, draw is a line so that approximately half the points are above it and half the points are below it.

  ii Find the equation of this line.

  c Use a spreadsheet or calculator to find the equation of the least squares line of best fit.

  d Use the equations in parts **b** and **c** to predict the value of y when x is:

  i 18   **ii** 45

  e Another method used to find a line of best fit is known as the three-median regression line. For the data in the table, the equation of the three-median regression line is found to be $y = 0.9x + 1.6$. Use this equation to find the values of y when x is:

  i 18   **ii** 45

  f Compare and comment on the values obtained by the three different lines of best fit used in this question.

7 Repeat question **6** for the data in the table below. The equation of the three-median regression line for this data is $y = 0.4x + 6.8$.

x	5	10	14	15	24	27	32	33
y	10	11	12	14	15	17	20	20

Investigation 2 Reports of studies in the digital media

1 Investigate and evaluate the appropriateness of sampling methods and sample size used in reports in which statements about a population are based on a sample.

2 Critically review surveys, polls and media reports. Consider the sampling techniques used and the wording of questions used to collect data. Can you find any misrepresentation of data?

3 Investigate the use of statistics and associated probabilities in shaping decisions made by governments and companies; for example, the setting of insurance policies or the use of demographic data to determine where and when various facilities may be built.

4 Use Australian census data to identify issues in your local area or state or territory and suggest implications of this data for future planning.

Language in mathematics

1 Explain the difference between these terms.

   a range and interquartile range   **b** interpolation and extrapolation

2 Explain how to find the standard deviation of a data set using:

   a the formula   **b** a scientific calculator   **c** a graphics calculator.

3 Describe the effect, if any, on the standard deviation of adding a data value to the set of data, such as adding a data value equivalent to the mean, or adding a data value greater than or less than one standard deviation from the mean.

4 Describe the effect, if any, on the standard deviation of altering all the data by adding the same number to or subtracting the same number from each score, or by multiplying each score or dividing each score by the same number.

Terms

extrapolation	interpolation	interquartile range	least squares regression line
line of best fit	outlier	range	scatterplot
standard deviation	three-median regression line		trend line

Check your skills

1 The standard deviation of the scores 8, 11, 11, 12, 14, 15, 15, 15, 16, 17, 20 is:

   A 15   **B** 12   **C** 3   **D** 2

2 A set of scores has a mean of 12, a range of 16 and a standard deviation of 2.4. Each score has 2 subtracted from it. The statement that is correct for these scores is:

   A Mean = 12, range = 14, standard deviation = 4

   B Mean = 14, range = 16, standard deviation = 2.4

   C Mean = 10, range = 16, standard deviation = 4

   D Mean = 10, range = 16, standard deviation = 2.4

3 The mean and standard deviation of the scores in the frequency distribution table are:

   A 25 and 17   **B** 25 and 1.3

   C 63 and 4   **D** 15 and 1.3

Score	Frequency
23	11
24	15
25	17
26	12
27	8

4 The statement that is true for the scores in these two lists is:

     List A: 1, 5, 7, 8, 9   List B: 4, 4, 6, 8, 8

   A The scores in list B are more consistent than the scores in list A.

   B The scores in list A are more consistent than the scores in list B.

   C The mean of the scores in list B is greater than the mean of the scores in list A.

   D The mean of the scores in list A is greater than the mean of the scores in list B.

5 A Science test has a mean of 65 and standard deviation of 5. A History test has a mean of 50 and standard deviation of 2. Euginie scores 67 in Science and 60 in History. The statement that is true is:

    A The Science mark is better than the History mark because it is higher.

    B The Science mark is better than the History mark because it has a higher standard deviation.

    C The History mark is better that the Science mark because it is more standard deviations from the mean.

    D The History mark is better that the Science mark because the standard deviation for Science is larger.

This graph is a scatterplot, with a line of best fit, of the Mathematics and Science marks for a group of students. Use the graph to answer questions **6** and **7**.

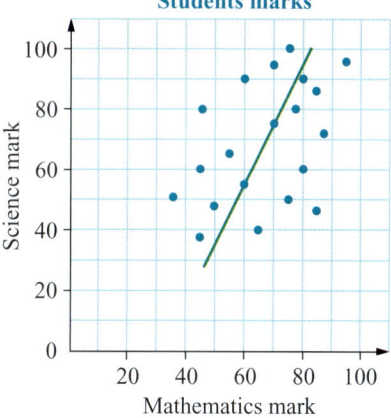

6 The Science mark for a student who scores 70 in Mathematics is:

    A 60   **B** 65

    C 70   **D** 75

7 The Mathematics mark of a student who scores 55 in Science is:

    A 50   **B** 55

    C 60   **D** 65

8 The table shows the distance travelled in 1000 km versus the servicing costs in $1000 for a motor vehicle.

Distance ('000 km)	50	100	180	200	230	270	330	350	400
Cost ($'000)	3.2	4.1	4.4	6	7.3	8.5	9.1	9.8	13.5

The equation of the least squares line of best fit is:

    A $y = 33.6x - 11.2$ **B** $y = 0.027x + 0.95$

    C $y = 0.45x + 231$ **D** $y = 0.03x + 234$

If you have any difficulty with these questions, refer to the examples and questions in the sections listed in the table.

Question	1–3	4, 5	6–8
Section	A	B	C

14A   Review set

1 a For the scores 6, 7, 7, 9, 10, 11, 14 find the:

    i mean   **ii** standard deviation

    iii range   **iv** interquartile range.

  b 5 is added to each of the above scores. Recalculate the:

    i mean   **ii** standard deviation

    iii range   **iv** interquartile range.

  c Each of the scores in part **a** is multiplied by 5. Recalculate the:

    i mean   **ii** standard deviation

    iii range   **iv** interquartile range.

2 Which of these data sets has the greatest:

   a mean?   **b** range?   **c** standard deviation?

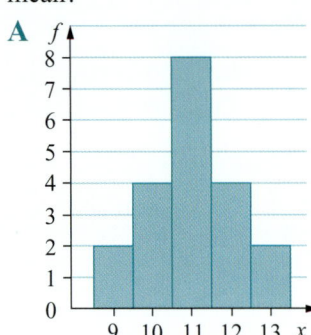 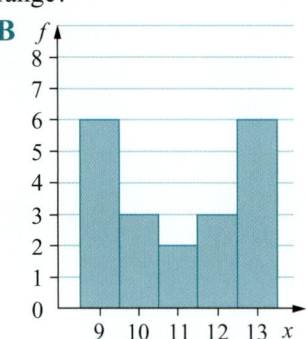 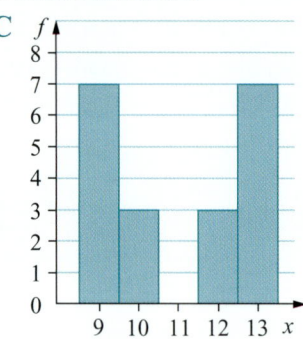

3 Which of these data sets has the greatest:

   a mean?   **b** range?   **c** standard deviation?

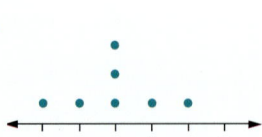 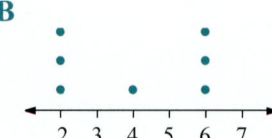 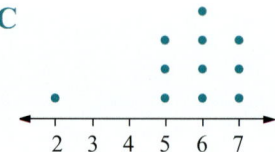

4 a Enter the data in the table below into a spreadsheet and draw a scatterplot.

x	10	20	30	40	50	60	70	80
y	2.2	1.9	1.8	1.8	1.4	1.3	0.9	0.8

   b Determine the equation of the line of best fit.

   c Use the line of best fit to predict:

      i the value of y when $x = 35$ **ii** the value of x when $y = 1$

14B   Review set

1 a For the scores in the frequency distribution table, find the:

     i mean   **ii** standard deviation

     iii range   **iv** interquartile range.

Score	9	10	11	12	13	14	25
Frequency	6	5	9	11	3	5	1

   b The outlier (25) is replaced by the score 15. For these scores find the:

     i mean   **ii** standard deviation

     iii range   **iv** interquartile range.

   c Which measures have been affected by the outlier?

2 Which of these data sets has the greatest:

   a mean?   **b** range?   **c** standard deviation?

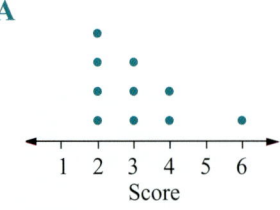 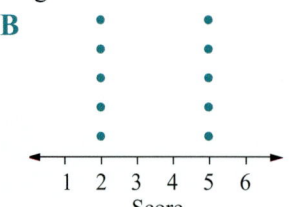 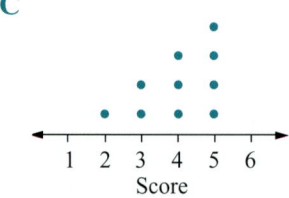

3 Complete the following statements based on the two histograms drawn below. Use equal to, greater than or less than to fill the gaps.

a The mean of data set 1 is _____ the mean of data set 2.

b The range of data set 1 is _____ the range of data set 2.

c The standard deviation of data set 1 is _____ the standard deviation of data set 2.

Data set 1

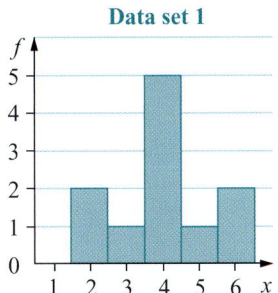

Data set 2

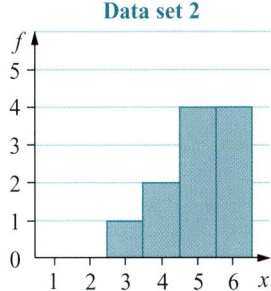

4 The assessments of a group of students in Visual Arts and their results on a creativity test are shown in the table.

Art assessment	68	74	72	85	51	64	51	82	78	66
Creativity score	15	17	15	19	12	14	13	18	16	16

a Enter the data into a spreadsheet and draw a scatterplot. Display the line of best fit.

b Determine the equation of the least squares line of best fit.

c Predict the creativity test score of a student who scores 60 in Visual Arts.

14C Review set

1 a For the scores 2, 4, 4, 5, 6, 6, 7, 8 find the:

    i mean   **ii** standard deviation

    iii range   **iv** interquartile range.

  b 4 is subtracted from each of the above scores. Recalculate the:

    i mean   **ii** standard deviation

    iii range   **iv** interquartile range.

  c Each of the scores in part **a** is divided by 2. Recalculate the:

    i mean   **ii** standard deviation

    iii range   **iv** interquartile range.

2 Which of these data sets has the greatest:

  a mean?   **b** range?   **c** standard deviation?

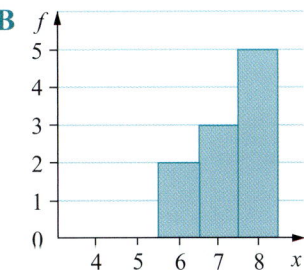

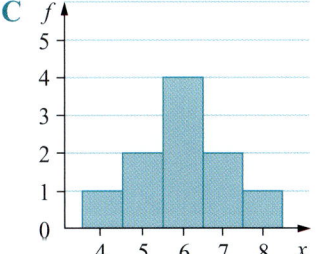

3 The results of a survey of 10 tertiary students comparing their annual income and the amount of money they spend on entertainment is shown in the table.

Income ($'000)	10	12	16	22	26	29	33	37	42	44
Entertainment ($'000)	2.5	2.8	3	3.3	3.6	3.8	3.9	4.1	4.5	4.9

  a Enter the data into a spreadsheet and draw a scatterplot.
  b Determine the equation of the line of best fit.
  c Use the line of best fit to predict:
    i the amount spent on entertainment when income is $20 000
    ii the average income of a student who spends $4700 annually on entertainment.

14D Review set

1 a For the scores in the stem-and-leaf plot, find the:
  i mean
  ii standard deviation
  iii range
  iv interquartile range.
b If the outlier 61 is ignored, calculate the new:
  i mean
  ii standard deviation
  iii range
  iv interquartile range.

Stem	Leaf
0	6 8 9
1	2 3 5 6 6 8
2	1 1 4 6
3	2 5
6	1

2 Which of these data sets has the greatest:
a mean?
b range?
c standard deviation?

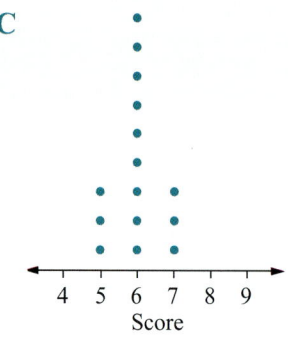

3 A survey of the business records of a holiday resort show the daily running costs associated with the number of guests staying at the hotel.

Number of guests	20	30	40	50	60	70	80	90	100
Cost ($'000)	6.6	7.3	8.1	9.1	9.7	10.7	11.3	12.1	13

  a Enter the data into a spreadsheet and draw a scatterplot.
  b Determine the equation of the line of best fit.
  c Use the line of best fit to predict:
    i the daily running cost when 65 people are staying at the resort
    ii the number of people staying at the resort when the running cost is $12 000.

15

Polynomials

This chapter deals with the algebra of polynomials and sketching polynomials.

After completing this chapter you should be able to:

▶ recognise polynomial expressions and perform algebraic operations with polynomials

▶ apply the remainder and factor theorems to polynomial functions

▶ sketch linear, quadratic and cubic polynomial functions

▶ determine the effect of single, double and triple roots of a polynomial equation on the shape of a curve.

NSW Syllabus references: 5.3 N&A Polynomials
Outcomes: MA5.3-1WM, MA5.3-2WM, MA5.3-3WM, MA5.3-10NA
Number & algebra – ACMNA266, ACMNA268

Diagnostic test

1 The expansion of $(x - 5)^2$ is:

   A $x^2 - 25$ **B** $x^2 + 25$

   C $x^2 - 5x + 25$ **D** $x^2 - 10x + 25$

2 The expansion of $(3x + 2)^2$ is:

   A $3x^2 + 4$ **B** $9x^2 + 6x + 4$

   C $9x^2 + 12x + 4$ **D** $9x^2 + 4$

3 The expansion of $(x - 2)(x + 2)$ is:

   A $x^2 - 4$ **B** $x^2 + 4$

   C $x^2 + 2x + 4$ **D** $x^2 - 4x + 4$

4 The expansion of $(5 - 2x)(5 + 2x)$ is:

   A $4x^2 - 25$ **B** $25 - 4x^2$

   C $25 - 10x + 4x^2$ **D** $25 - 20x + 4x^2$

5 The number needed to complete the square of $x^2 - 9x$ is:

   A 9 **B** $\dfrac{9}{2}$

   C $\dfrac{81}{4}$ **D** any number

6 When factorised $c^2 - a^2$ is:

   A $(c - a)(c - a)$ **B** $(c - a)(c + a)$

   C $(c - a)^2$ **D** $c^2 - 2ac + c^2$

7 When factorised $x^2 - x - 12$ is:

   A $(x - 4)(x + 3)$ **B** $(x + 4)(x - 3)$

   C $(x - 6)(x + 2)$ **D** $(x + 6)(x - 2)$

8 When factorised $10x^2 + 17x + 3$ is:

   A $(5x + 3)(2x + 1)$ **B** $(5x - 1)(2x + 3)$

   C $(5x + 1)(2x + 3)$ **D** $(5x - 1)(2x - 3)$

9 The solutions of $5x^2 = 3$ are:

   A $x = \pm\dfrac{3}{5}$ **B** $x = \pm\sqrt{\dfrac{3}{5}}$

   C $x = \pm\sqrt{15}$ **D** $x = \pm\sqrt{3}$

10 The solutions of $3x^2 + 9x = 0$ are:

   A 0 and 3 **B** 0 and -3

   C 0 and 9 **D** -3 and 9

11 The solutions of $x^2 + 7x - 18 = 0$ are:

   A -9 and 2 **B** 9 and -2

   C 6 and -3 **D** -6 and 3

12 The solutions of $3x^2 + 7x + 4 = 0$ are:

   A 1 and 4 **B** -1 and -4

   C -1 and $-\dfrac{4}{3}$ **D** 1 and $\dfrac{3}{4}$

13 The solutions of $\dfrac{x^2 - 12}{x} = 4$ are:

   A -6 or 2 **B** 6 or -2

   C 0 or $\sqrt{12}$ **D** -4 or -3

14 The constant term that needs to be added to solve $x^2 - 10x - 2 = 0$ by completing the square is:

   A -5 **B** 5 **C** 25 **D** -25

15 The solutions to $x^2 - 5x + 3 = 0$ are:

   A $\dfrac{-5 \pm \sqrt{13}}{2}$ **B** $\dfrac{5 \pm \sqrt{13}}{2}$

   C $\dfrac{-5 + \sqrt{37}}{2}$ **D** $\dfrac{5 \pm \sqrt{37}}{2}$

16 The solutions to $4x^2 - 3x - 8 = 0$ are:

   A $\dfrac{3 \pm \sqrt{137}}{8}$ **B** $\dfrac{-3 \pm \sqrt{94}}{8}$

   C $\dfrac{-3 \pm \sqrt{137}}{4}$ **D** $\dfrac{3 \pm \sqrt{94}}{4}$

The diagnostic test questions refer to outcomes ACMMG233, ACMMG241 and ACMMG269.   **(AC)**

A # Curve sketching

For the following investigations students will require the use of a graphics calculator and/or graphics software. If these are not available, the use of a suitable table of values or a spreadsheet is recommended.

Investigation 1 The graph of $y = x^n$

1 a Sketch the following graphs by completing the table below and choosing a suitable scale.

   i $y = x^2$ **ii** $y = x^3$ **iii** $y = x^4$ **iv** $y = x^6$

x	-2.5	-2.0	-1.5	-1.0	-0.5	0	0.5	1.0	1.5	2.0	2.5
y											

  b Describe the difference between the shapes of graphs with an even index and those with an odd index.
  c What are the x- and y-intercepts of each of the curves?
  d What happens to the value of y as:
     i $x \to +\infty$ (x gets very large and positive)?   **ii** $x \to -\infty$ (x get very large and negative)?
  e Is there a value of:
     i y for every value of x?   **ii** x for every value of y?

2 Consider the points $P(-3, 81)$ and $Q(3, 81)$ on the curve $y = x^4$. Join PQ and let N be the point where it cuts the y-axis.

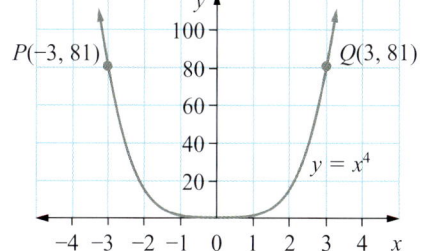

  a **i** Is PQ perpendicular to the y-axis?
     ii Is $PN = NQ$? Give reasons.
  b What transformation will map P onto Q?
  c Can we always find pairs of points on this curve for which part **b** will be true? Give two examples.
  d Hence, what kind of symmetry does this curve have?

3 Consider the points $P(-2, -8)$ and $Q(2, 8)$ on the curve $y = x^3$.
  a Find the coordinates of the midpoint of the interval PQ.
  b Draw a sketch showing the points P and Q and join POQ.
  c What transformation will map P onto Q?
  d Can we always find pairs of points on this curve for which part **c** will be true? Give two examples.
  e Hence, what kind of symmetry does this curve have?

Summary

The graph of $y = x^n$ always passes through the origin. Graph A is **concave up** for all values of x and has line symmetry about the y-axis; that is, the y-axis is the axis of symmetry of the graph.

Graph B is **concave up** where $x > 0$ and **concave down** where $x < 0$. It has point symmetry (of order 2) about the origin; that is, any point on the graph when rotated through $180°$ about the origin will also lie on the graph.

Graph A: n is even. 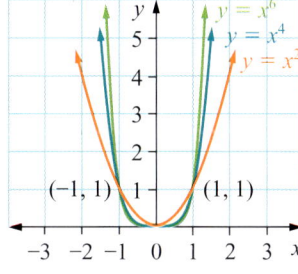   Graph B: n is odd.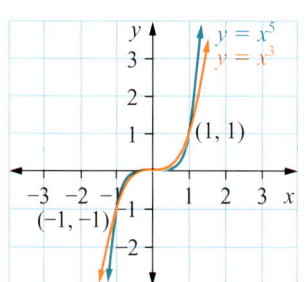

Investigation 2 The graph of $y = ax^n$

1 On the same diagram, sketch graphs of:

  a   **i** $y = x^2$ **ii** $y = 2x^2$ **iii** $y = 3x^2$ **iv** $y = \frac{1}{2}x^2$ **v** $y = \frac{1}{3}x^2$

  b   **i** $y = x^3$ **ii** $y = 2x^3$ **iii** $y = 3x^3$ **iv** $y = \frac{1}{2}x^3$ **v** $y = \frac{1}{3}x^3$

  c   Describe in words the effect of the constant a on the graph of $y = ax^n$, when compared with the graph of $y = x^n$.

2 Match each graph below with its correct equation.

  a $y = x^4$ **b** $y = 5x^4$ **c** $y = \frac{1}{2}x^4$ **d** $y = \frac{1}{6}x^4$

A 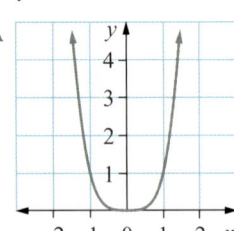   B 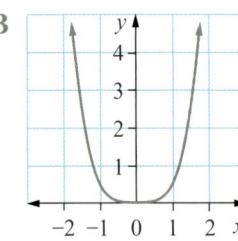   C 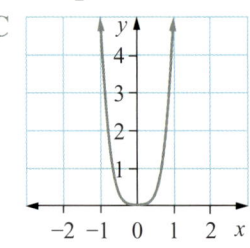   D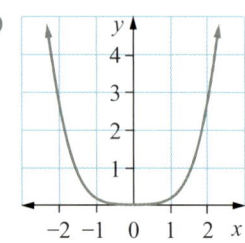

3 This is a sketch of $y = x^7$. Copy this graph and on the same axes draw the graphs of:

  a $y = \frac{2}{3}x^7$ **b** $y = 3x^7$

  c $y = \frac{5}{4}x^7$ **d** $y = 10x^7$

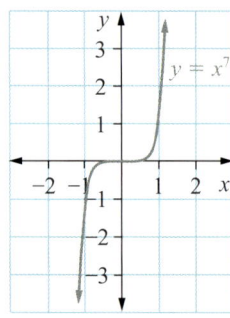

Summary

For the graph of $y = ax^n$, where n is a positive integer, the effect of the constant a is to:

- compress the curve $y = x^n$ horizontally and make it steeper when $a > 1$
- stretch the curve $y = x^n$ horizontally and make it less steep when $0 < a < 1$.

We will investigate negative values of a later in this chapter.

Investigation 3 The graph of $y = ax^n + k$

1   **a**   On the same axes for $-2 \leqslant x \leqslant 2$, sketch graphs of:

       i $y = 2x$ **ii** $y = 2x + 3$ **iii** $y = 2x - 3$

     b   Write the gradient and y-intercept of each line.

2   **a**   On the same axes for $-2 \leqslant x \leqslant 2$, sketch graphs of:

       i $y = 3x^2$ **ii** $y = 3x^2 + 2$ **iii** $y = 3x^2 - 1$

     b   For each curve:

       i   state the y-intercepts

       ii   state the equation of the axis of symmetry

       iii   find the coordinates of the vertex.

3   **a**   On the same axes for $-2 \leqslant x \leqslant 2$, sketch graphs of:

       i $y = x^3$ **ii** $y = x^3 + 1$ **iii** $y = x^3 - 2$

     b   Write the y-intercept of each curve.

4 Given the graph of a function $y = ax^n$, describe in words how to sketch the graph of $y = ax^n + k$.

5 This is a sketch of the function $y = x^4$. Match each graph below with its correct equation.

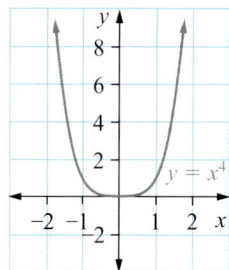

a $y = x^4 - 5$ b $y = x^4 + 1$

c $y = x^4 - 7$ d $y = x^4 + 5$

A 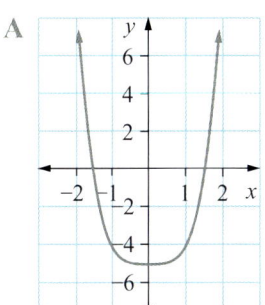   **B** 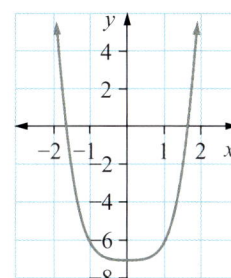   **C** 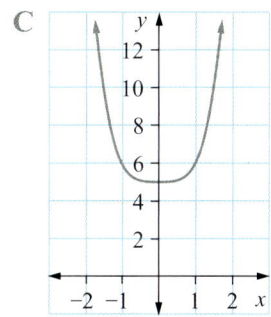   **D**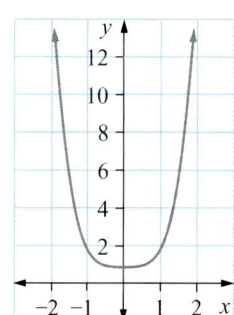

6 This is a sketch of $y = 2x^5$. Copy this graph and on the same axes draw the graphs of:

a $y = 2x^5 + 3$ b $y = 2x^5 - 1$

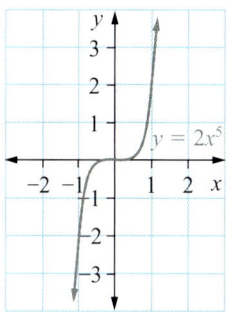

Summary

For $y = ax^n + k$, the effect of the constant k is to:

• translate the graph of $y = ax^n$ vertically k units up when $k > 0$

• translate the graph of $y = ax^n$ vertically k units down when $k < 0$.

Investigation 4 The graph of $y = a(x - b)^n$

1 **a** Sketch graphs of:

   i $y = 2x$ **ii** $y = 2(x - 1)$ **iii** $y = 2(x + 1)$

   b Write the gradient and y-intercept of each line.

   c Find the x-intercept of each line.

   d What would be the gradient and x-intercept of $y = 2(x - 15)$?

2 **a** Sketch graphs of the following functions on the same axes.

i $y = 3x^2$	for $-3 \leqslant x \leqslant 3$	**ii** $y = 3(x - 1)^2$ for $-2 \leqslant x \leqslant 4$
iii $y = 3(x - 2)^2$	for $1 \leqslant x \leqslant 5$	**iv** $y = 3(x + 1)^2$ for $-4 \leqslant x \leqslant 2$
v $y = 3(x + 2)^2$	for $-1 \leqslant x \leqslant 1$	**vi** $y = 3(x - 5)^2$ for $2 \leqslant x \leqslant 8$

   b For each curve find the:

   i x- and y-intercepts   **ii** equation of the axis of symmetry

   iii coordinates of the vertex.

   c What would be the coordinates of the vertex of each of these functions?

   i $y = 3(x - 14)^2$ **ii** $y = 3(x + 17)^2$

3 a Sketch graphs of the following functions on the same axes.

   i $y = 2x^3$ for $-2 \leqslant x \leqslant 2$ **ii** $y = 2(x - 1)^3$ for $-1 \leqslant x \leqslant 3$

   iii $y = 2(x - 2)^3$ for $0 \leqslant x \leqslant 4$ **iv** $y = 2(x + 1)^3$ for $-3 \leqslant x \leqslant 1$

   v $y = 2(x + 2)^3$ for $-4 \leqslant x \leqslant 0$

 b What is the x-intercept for each of these curves?

 c Using only the results of parts **a** and **b**, can you sketch these graphs on your diagram?

   i $y = 2(x - 10)^3$ **ii** $y = 2(x + 9)^3$

4 Given the graph of a function $y = ax^n$, describe how to sketch the graph of $y = a(x - b)^n$.

5 A sketch of the function $y = 3x^4$ is given. Match each graph below with its correct equation.

 a $y = 3(x - 1)^4$ **b** $y = 3(x + 1)^4$

 c $y = 3(x + 3)^4$ **d** $y = 3(x - 5)^4$

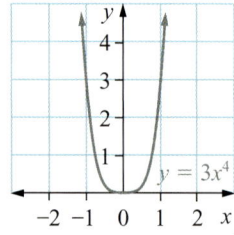

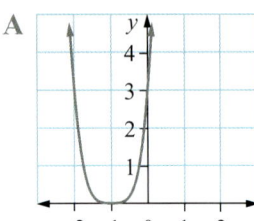   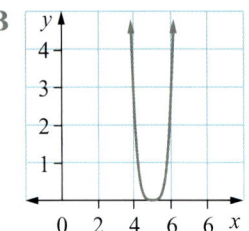   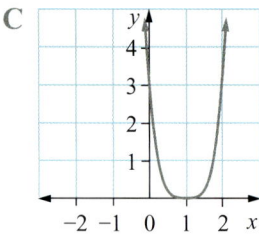   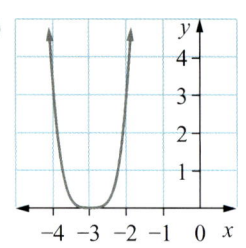

6 On the same axes draw sketches of:

 a $y = x^5$ **b** $y = (x - 4)^5$ **c** $y = (x + 3)^5$ **d** $y = \left(x + \frac{3}{2}\right)^5$

Summary

For $y = a(x - b)^n$ the effect of the constant b on $y = ax^n$ is to:

- translate the graph of $y = f(x)$ horizontally b units to the right when $b > 0$
- translate the graph of $y = f(x)$ horizontally b units to the left when $b < 0$.

Investigation 5 The graph of $y = -f(x)$

1 On the same axes sketch the graphs of:

 a $y = 2x^3$ and $y = -2x^3$ **b** $y = 3x^4$ and $y = -3x^4$

 c $y = x^3 + 1$ and $y = -(x^3 + 1)$ **d** $y = 3(x - 1)^2$ and $y = -3(x - 1)^2$

2 Describe in words the relationship between the graphs of $y = f(x)$ and $y = -f(x)$.

3 Match each of the following graphs with its correct equation.

 a $y = 4x^2$ **b** $y = -4x^2$ **c** $y = x^3 - 1$

 d $y = -x^3 + 1$ **e** $y = (x + 2)^6$ **f** $y = -(x + 2)^6$

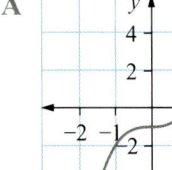   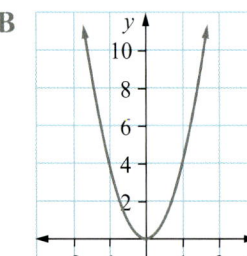   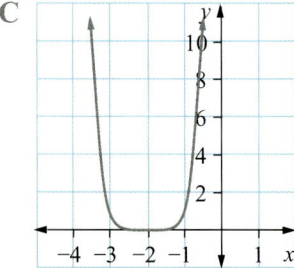

D 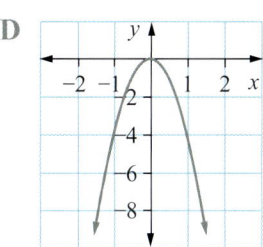 E 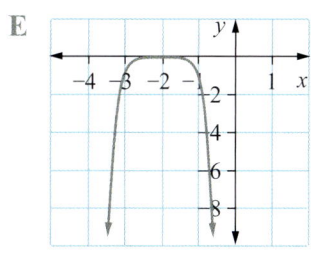 F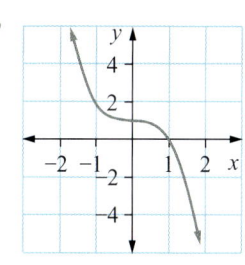

4 On the same diagram, draw freehand sketches of:

    a $y = x^4$ and $y = -x^4$ **b** $y = 5x^2$ and $y = -5x^2 + 7$ **c** $y = (x - 2)^3$ and $y = -(x - 2)^3$

Summary

The graph of $y = -f(x)$ is the reflection of the graph of $y = f(x)$ in the x-axis.

Exercise 15A

1 Sketch graphs of the following functions on the same axes.

	i	**ii**	**iii**	**iv**	**v**
a	$y = x^2$	$y = 4x^2$	$y = x^2 + 4$	$y = 4x^2 - 1$	$y = (x - 4)^2$
b	$y = x^3$	$y = x^3 - 8$	$y = (x - 8)^3$	$y = 2(x - 8)^3$	$y = (x - 8)^3 + 1$
c	$y = x^4$	$y = -x^4$	$y = -x^4 + 3$	$y = -(x + 3)^4$	$y = -(x + 3)^4 - 1$
d	$y = x^5$	$y = -2x^5$	$y = -2x^5 - 1$	$y = -(x - 1)^5$	$y = -2(x - 1)^5$

EXAMPLE 1

Sketch the following functions. Show graphically and describe in words the relationship of each function to the graph of $y = x^2$.

a $y = 3x^2 - 1$ **b** $y = -\frac{1}{5}(x + 7)^2 + 4$

	Solve	**Think**	**Apply**
a	*(graph of $y = 3x^2 - 1$ and $y = x^2$)*	This is the graph of $y = x^2$ compressed horizontally and translated 1 unit down.	Begin with $y = x^2$ and apply each change to produce the new graph.
b	*(graph of $y = -\frac{1}{5}(x + 7)^2 + 4$ and $y = x^2$)*	$y = -\frac{1}{5}(x + 7)^2 + 4$ $= -\left(\frac{1}{5}(x + 7)^2 - 4\right)$ This is the graph of $y = x^2$ stretched horizontally, translated 7 units to the left, translated vertically 4 units down and then reflected in the x-axis.	

2 Sketch the following functions. Show graphically and describe the relationship of each function to $y = x^2$.

   a $y = 5x^2$ **b** $y = \frac{3}{4}x^2$ **c** $y = x^2 - 8$

   d $y = x^2 + 5$ **e** $y = (x - 4)^2$ **f** $y = 2(x - 4)^2$

   g $y = (x + 7)^2$ **h** $y = \frac{1}{3}(x + 7)^2$ **i** $y = -5x^2$

   j $y = -\frac{3}{4}x^2$ **k** $y = -(x^2 - 8)$ **l** $y = -x^2 - 5$

   m $y = -(x - 4)^2$ **n** $y = -\frac{1}{3}(x + 6)^2$ **o** $y = (x - 1)^2 + 5$

   p $y = -(x - 1)^2 - 5$ **q** $y = (x + 2)^2 - 1$ **r** $y = -(x + 2)^2 + 1$

   s $y = 3(x - 6)^2 - 3$ **t** $y = -3(x - 6)^2 + 3$

3 Which of the following could be the graph of each function?

   a $y = (x - 1)^3 - 5$

     A 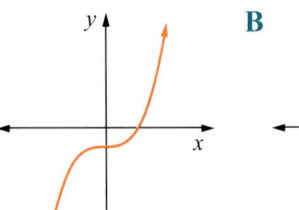   **B** 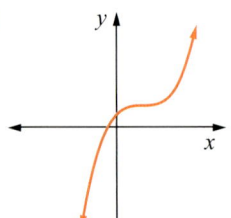   **C** 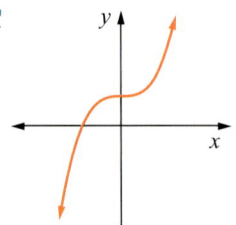   **D**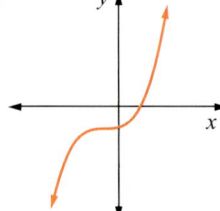

   b $y = (x + 2)^3 + 4$

     A 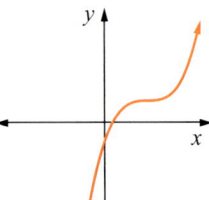   **B** 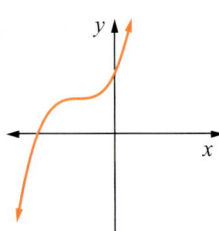   **C** 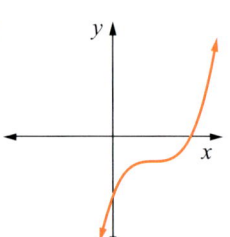   **D**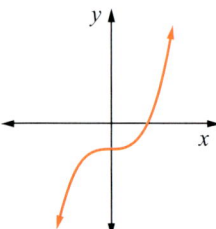

   c $y = -(x - 3)^4$

     A 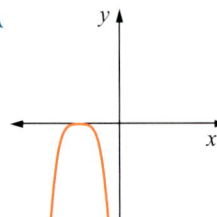   **B** 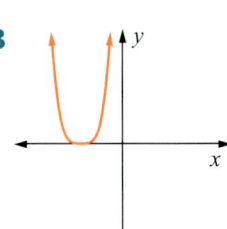   **C** 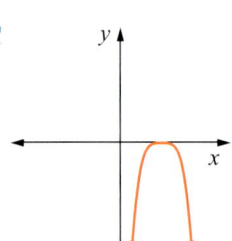   **D**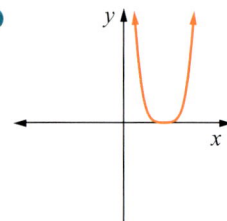

   d $y = (x + 1)^5 - 2$

     A 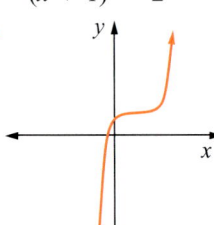   **B** 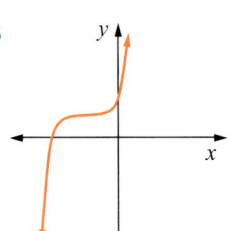   **C** 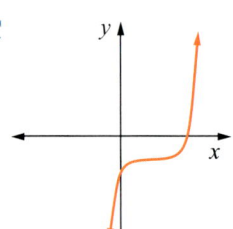   **D**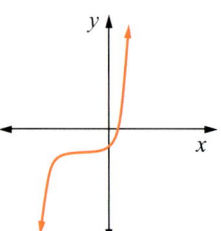

   e $y = -(x + 1)^3 + 3$

     A 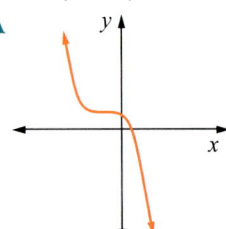   **B** 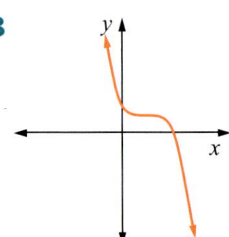   **C** 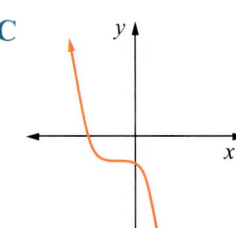   **D**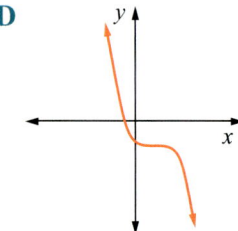

EXAMPLE 2

Use the graph of $y = f(x)$ given to sketch graphs of:

a $y = 3f(x)$
b $y = f(x) + 3$
c $y = f(x - 3)$
d $y = -f(x)$

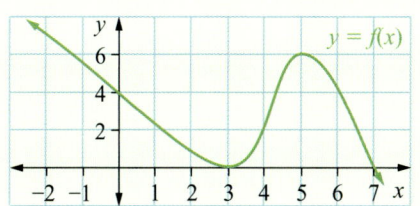

	Solve	Think	Apply
a		All points move three times further away from the *x*-axis.	Use the results from Investigations 1–5 to transform the original graph of $f(x)$ to produce the required graphs.
b		All points move up 3 units.	
c		All points move 3 units to the right.	
d		All points are reflected in the *x*-axis.	

4 Use the graph of $y = f(x)$ given and grid paper to sketch graphs of:

a $y = 2f(x)$
b $y = f(x) + 2$
c $y = f(x - 2)$
d $y = f(x + 2)$
e $y = -f(x)$

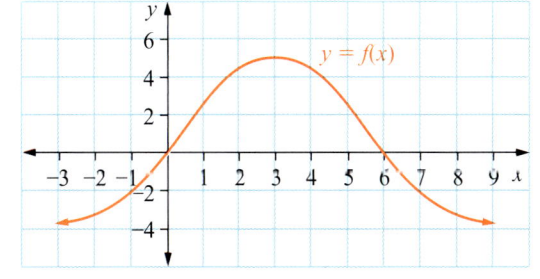

5 Use the graph of $y = f(x)$ given and grid paper to draw neat sketches of:

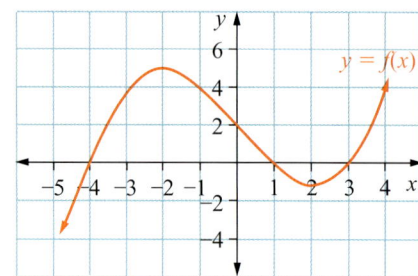

a $y = 3f(x)$ 　　　　　　**b** $y = f(x) + 3$
c $y = f(x - 3)$ 　　　　　**d** $y = f(x + 3)$
e $y = -f(x)$

6 Without sketching, explain the similarities and differences between the curves $y = x^3 + x^2 + x$ and $y = x^3 + x^2 + x + 1$.

B Symmetry about the *y*-axis

● EXAMPLE 1

a On the same diagram sketch the graphs of $y = f(x)$ and $y = f(-x)$ given:
　　i $f(x) = 2x^3$ 　　　　　**ii** $f(x) = x^3 + 1$ 　　　　　**iii** $f(x) = (x - 2)^4$
b Study the symmetry of the three graphs from part **a** and then describe in words the relationship between the graphs of $y = f(x)$ and $y = f(-x)$.

	Solve	Think	Apply
a i	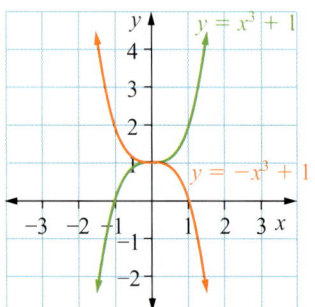	$f(x) = 2x^3$ so $f(-x) = 2(-x)^3$ 　　　　$= -2x^3$	The graph of $y = f(-x)$ is the reflection of $y = f(x)$ in the *y*-axis.
ii	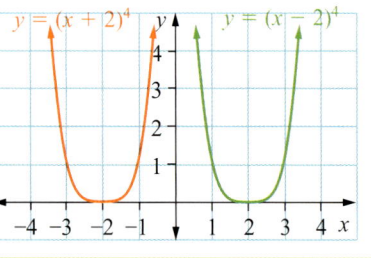	$f(x) = x^3 + 1$ so $f(-x) = (-x)^3 + 1$ 　　　　$= -x^3 + 1$	
iii		$f(x) = (x - 2)^4$ so $f(-x) = (-x - 2)^4$ 　　　　$= (-1(x + 2))^4$ 　　　　$= (-1)^4(x + 2)^4$ 　　　　$= (x + 2)^4$	
b	The graphs $f(x)$ and $f(-x)$ are reflections of each other in the *y*-axis.		

NUMBER & ALGEBRA

● EXAMPLE 2

Given the graph of $y = f(x)$, sketch $y = f(-x)$.

a

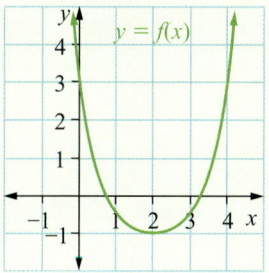

b

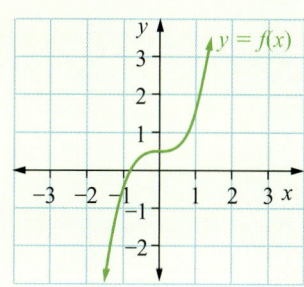

Solve	Think	Apply
a 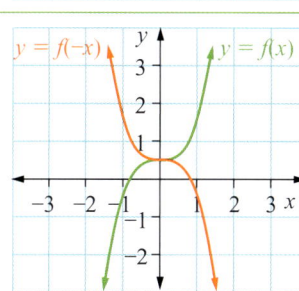	Reflect each curve in the y-axis.	The graphs $f(x)$ and $f(-x)$ intersect at the same point on the y-axis.
b 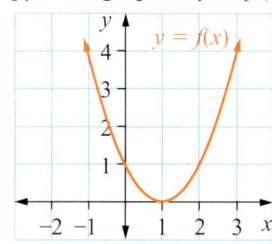		

Exercise 15B

1 Copy each graph of $y = f(x)$ and sketch $y = f(-x)$ on the same axes.

a

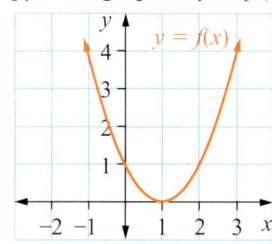

b

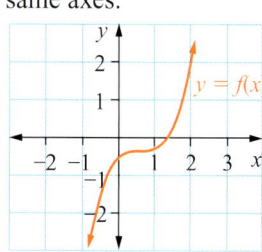

c

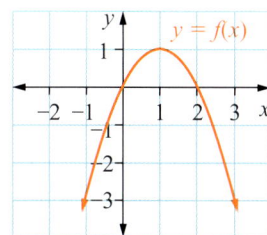

d

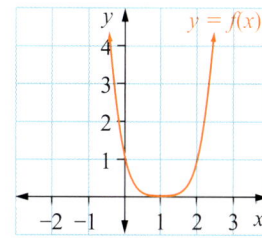

2 On the same diagram, sketch the graphs of $y = f(x)$ and $y = f(-x)$.

  a $f(x) = -(x + 1)^2$ **b** $f(x) = -x^3 + 1$ **c** $f(x) = (x + 1)^3$ **d** $f(x) = (x - 1)^4$

EXAMPLE 3

For each of the functions given:

  i   Sketch $y = f(x)$ and $y = f(-x)$.
  ii Explain graphically what happens and why.
  iii Determine $f(-x)$. What do you notice?

a $f(x) = x^4$

b $f(x) = x^2 - 1$

	Solve/Think	Apply
a i	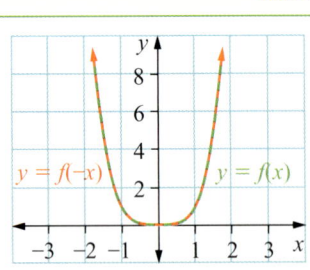	If $f(-x) = f(x)$ then the graph of $y = f(x)$ is symmetrical about the y-axis.
ii	$y = f(x)$ is symmetrical about the y-axis, so when it is reflected in the y-axis it reflects onto itself.	
iii	$f(-x) = (-x)^4 = x^4$ $\therefore f(-x) = f(x)$	
b i	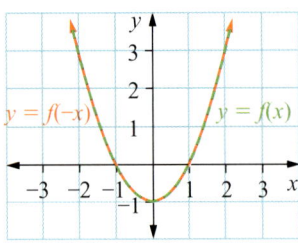	
ii	$y = f(x)$ is symmetrical about the y-axis, so when it is reflected in the y-axis it reflects onto itself.	
iii	$f(-x) = (-x)^2 - 1 = x^2 - 1$ $\therefore f(-x) = f(x)$	

EXAMPLE 4

Determine whether the graphs of the following functions are symmetrical about the y-axis.

a $f(x) = -7x^2$

b $f(x) = x^2 - 5x + 1$

	Solve	Think/Apply
a	$f(-x) = -7(-x)^2 = -7x^2$ $f(-x) = f(x)$ $\therefore y = f(x)$ is symmetrical about the y-axis.	Substitute $-x$ for x. If $f(-x) = f(x)$ then the graph is symmetrical about the y-axis. It is called an even function.
b	$f(-x) = (-x)^2 - 5(-x) + 1 = x^2 + 5x + 1$ $f(-x) \neq f(x)$ $\therefore y = f(x)$ is not symmetrical about the y-axis.	An even polynomial function has all powers of x even.

NUMBER & ALGEBRA

3 Determine whether the graphs of the following functions are symmetrical about the y-axis.

a $f(x) = 5x^2$

b $f(x) = 2x^3$

c $f(x) = -6x^{10}$

d $f(x) = x^2 + 7$

e $f(x) = 3x^4 - 1$

f $f(x) = x^3 + 1$

g $f(x) = x^2 + x$

h $f(x) = x^4 + x^2$

i $f(x) = x^2 - 2x + 3$

j $f(x) = 5x^6 - 7x^4 + 3x^2 + 2$

C Polynomials

A polynomial expression is one of the form:
$$a_n x^n + a_{n-1} x^{n-1} + a_{n-2} x^{n-2} + \ldots + a_2 x^2 + a_1 x + a_0$$
where n is a non-negative integer (a positive integer or zero).

The **degree** of the polynomial is the highest power of x in the expression; that is, the value of n.

The **leading term** is the first term when the terms are written in descending powers of x.

The **leading coefficient** is the coefficient of the leading term. If the leading coefficient is 1 then the polynomial is said to be **monic**.

The **constant term** is the term containing x^0.

The function P defined by $P(x) = a_n x^n + a_{n-1} x^{n-1} + a_{n-2} x^{n-2} + \ldots + a_2 x^2 + a_1 x + a_0$ is called a **polynomial function** of degree n.

EXAMPLE 1

Which of the following expressions are polynomials? Give reasons for your answers.

a $5x^3 - 7x^2 + 2x + 1$

b 25

c $x^2 - 5x + \dfrac{3}{x} - 2$

d $2x^4 - 6x^3 + 7\sqrt{x} + 1$

	Solve	Think	Apply
a	Yes	The powers of all terms in x are integers greater than or equal to zero, so it is a polynomial.	Polynomials must have positive integer powers.
b	Yes	$25 = 25x^0$; it is a polynomial of degree zero.	
c	No	It contains the term $\dfrac{3}{x} = 3x^{-1}$, which has a negative index.	
d	No	It contains a term $7\sqrt{x} = 7x^{\frac{1}{2}}$, which has a fractional index.	

Exercise 15C

1 State whether or not the following expressions are polynomials. Give reasons for your answers.

a $7x^3 - 4x^2 + \dfrac{1}{2}$

b $x^2 - \dfrac{2}{x^2} + 1$

c $\dfrac{x^4 + x^2 - 1}{3}$

d $\dfrac{3}{2x^3 - 4x^2 + 5x - 2}$

e $-9\sqrt{x}$

f $3^x - 2^x + 1$

EXAMPLE 2

For each of the following polynomials, state:

 i the degree   **ii** the leading term   **iii** the leading coefficient
 iv the constant term   **v** whether the polynomial is monic.
a $15x^3 + 7x^2 - 8x - 3$ **b** $3x - 7x^2 + x^4$

		Solve	Think/Apply
a	**i**	Degree = 3	The degree is the highest power.
	ii	Leading term = $15x^3$	The leading term is the term with the highest power of x.
	iii	Leading coefficient = 15	A monic polynomial has the leading coefficient equal to 1.
	iv	Constant term = -3	
	v	$15x^3 + 7x^2 - 8x - 3$ is not a monic polynomial.	
b	**i**	Degree = 4	Rearrange the terms in descending powers of x, such as $x^4 - 7x^2 + 3x$ in part **b**.
	ii	Leading term = x^4	$3x - 7x^2 + x^4$ is a monic polynomial as the leading coefficient = 1.
	iii	Leading coefficient = 1	
	iv	Constant term = 0	
	v	$3x - 7x^2 + x^4$ is a monic polynomial.	

Note: 2, -3 and 11 are examples of polynomials of degree zero since $2 = 2x^0$, $-3 = -3x^0$, $11 = 11x^0$ and so on. These are sometimes called constant polynomials. However, the constant polynomial 0 (that is, a polynomial with all its coefficients zero) is called the zero polynomial and is considered to have no degree.

2 For each of the following polynomials state:

 i the degree   **ii** the leading term   **iii** the leading coefficient
 iv the constant term   **v** whether the polynomials is monic.
 a $3x^5 - 2x^3 + 7x + 11$ **b** $-7 - 5x + x^2$ **c** $\frac{1}{3}x^3 + \frac{1}{2}x^2 + x - 1$
 d $4x - 2x^3 + 5x^2 - 1$ **e** $3x + 2$ **f** 5

EXAMPLE 3

If $P(x) = x^3 - 2x^2 + 5x + 1$, find the value of $P(-2)$ and $P(0)$.

Solve	Think	Apply
$P(-2) = (-2)^3 - 2(-2)^2 + 5(-2) + 1$ $\quad = -25$ $P(0) = 0^3 - 2 \times 0^2 + 5 \times 0 + 1$ $\quad = 1$	$P(-2)$ is the value of the polynomial when $x = -2$. Substitute $x = -2$. Substitute $x = 0$.	Substitute the value of x and calculate.

3 For each polynomial function find the values indicated.
 a $P(x) = 3x^2 - 7x + 1$ find $P(0)$, $P(1)$, $P(-2)$
 b $Q(x) = 25x - 27$ find $Q(-1)$, $Q(1)$, $Q(0)$
 c $R(x) = 3x^6$ find $R(2)$, $R(-3)$, $R(0)$

4 For each polynomial given evaluate $P(10)$.

   a $P(x) = 7x + 3$

   b $P(x) = 8x^2 + 5x + 6$

   c $P(x) = 2x^3 + 4x^2 + 6x + 1$

   d $P(x) = 3x^4 + 2x^3 + 4x^2 + 5x + 9$

   e $P(x) = 9x^5 + 7x^4 + 6x^3 + 5x^2 + 8x + 4$

   f $P(x) = 5x^3 + 2x^2 + 3$

   g $P(x) = x^4 + 3x^2$

   h $P(x) = x^3 + x + 1$

5 a   **i** Evaluate $P(x) = 2x - 1$ for $x = 1, 2, 3, \ldots$; that is, find $P(1), P(2), P(3), \ldots$

      ii Which well known sequence of numbers is formed?

   b Evaluate $Q(x) = x^2$ for $x = 1, 2, 3, \ldots$

   c Evaluate $H(x) = 2x^3$ for $x = 1, 2, 3, \ldots$

6 Can you find a polynomial $P(x)$ that would generate the following number patterns for $x = 1, 2, 3, 4, \ldots$?

   a 2, 4, 6, 8, …

   b 2, 5, 10, 17, …

   c 1, 8, 27, 64, …

   d 2, 5, 8, 11, …

   e 5, 8, 11, 14, …

   f 1, 4, 9, 16, …

7 Find the polynomial function $P(x)$ given the following information.

   a Degree = 1, leading coefficient = 3, constant term = 5

   b Degree = 1, leading coefficient = 2, $P(1) = 3$

   c Degree = 2, monic, constant term = 1, $P(2) = 13$

   d Leading term = $4x^3$, constant term = 1, $P(1) = 9$, $P(-1) = -5$

   e Degree = 3, leading coefficient = 2, $P(0) = 1$, $P(1) = 0$, $P(2) = 1$

D   The algebra of polynomials

Polynomials can be added, subtracted and multiplied using the laws of algebra learnt in previous work.

Addition and subtraction of polynomials

EXAMPLE 1

a Find the sum of the polynomials $P(x) = 4x^3 - 3x^2 + 7x - 1$ and $Q(x) = 2x^3 + 6x^2 - 2x - 5$.

b Find the difference $P(x) - Q(x)$.

	Solve	Think	Apply
a	$P(x) + Q(x)$ $= (4x^3 - 3x^2 + 7x - 1) + (2x^3 + 6x^2 - 2x - 5)$ $= (4x^3 + 2x^3) + (-3x^2 + 6x^2) + (7x - 2x) + (-1 - 5)$ $= 6x^3 + 3x^2 + 5x - 6$	The working could be set out as: $\quad 4x^3 - 3x^2 + 7x - 1$ $+\ 2x^3 + 6x^2 - 2x - 5$ $\overline{\quad 6x^3 + 3x^2 + 5x - 6}$	Writing one polynomial under the other makes calculation easier. Ensure terms with the same power are under each other.
b	$P(x) - Q(x)$ $= (4x^3 - 3x^2 + 7x - 1) - (2x^3 + 6x^2 - 2x - 5)$ $= 4x^3 - 3x^2 + 7x - 1 - 2x^3 - 6x^2 + 2x + 5$ $= 2x^3 - 9x^2 + 9x + 4$	Also: $\quad 4x^3 - 3x^2 + 7x - 1$ $-\ 2x^3 + 6x^2 - 2x - 5$ $\overline{\quad 2x^3 - 9x^2 + 9x + 4}$	

If $P(x)$ and $Q(x)$ are polynomial expressions then:

   the *sum* $P(x) + Q(x)$ and the *difference* $P(x) - Q(x)$ are also polynomial expressions.

NUMBER & ALGEBRA

1 a Find the sum $P(x) + Q(x)$ and the difference $P(x) - Q(x)$ of the polynomials given.

  i $P(x) = 3x^2 - 5x + 2$, $Q(x) = x^2 + 7x - 3$

  ii $P(x) = x^3 - 2x^2 + 3x + 7$, $Q(x) = 2x^3 + 3x^2 - 5x + 2$

  iii $P(x) = 2x^3 + 9x^2 + 8x + 1$, $Q(x) = 6x^2 - 5x - 3$

  iv $P(x) = 3x^4 + 2x^3 - 3x^2 + 4x - 2$, $Q(x) = 2x^4 + 3x^3 - 7x^2 + 5x - 11$

  v $P(x) = x^4 + 9x^3 + 7x^2 - 4x + 9$, $Q(x) = 4x^3 - 8x^2 - 15$

b How is the degree of $P(x) \pm Q(x)$ related to the degree of $P(x)$ and $Q(x)$ for these polynomials?

c Will the result of part **b** be true for all polynomials $P(x)$ and $Q(x)$? Discuss. (For example, consider what happens if the leading terms of $P(x)$ and $Q(x)$ are opposites.)

2 Given $P(x) = x^3 - 3x^2 + 10x - 11$, $Q(x) = x^3 + 8x^2 - 7x + 3$ and $R(x) = 12x^2 + 15x - 1$ find:

a $P(x) + Q(x) - R(x)$	**b** $P(x) - Q(x) + R(x)$
c $P(x) - Q(x) - R(x)$	**d** $-P(x) + Q(x) - R(x)$
e $-P(x) - Q(x) - R(x)$	**f** $P(x) + Q(x) + R(x)$

Multiplication of polynomials

EXAMPLE 2

Given $P(x) = 3x - 2$ and $Q(x) = x^3 + 7x^2 - 5x + 8$, find $P(x) \times Q(x)$.

Solve	Think	Apply
$P(x) \times Q(x)$ $= (3x - 2)(x^3 + 7x^2 - 5x + 8)$ $= 3x(x^3 + 7x^2 - 5x + 8)$ $\quad - 2(x^3 + 7x^2 - 5x + 8)$ $= 3x^4 + 21x^3 - 15x^2 + 24x$ $\quad - 2x^3 - 14x^2 + 10x - 16$ $= 3x^4 + 19x^3 - 29x^2 + 34x - 16$	The working can be set out as follows: $\qquad x^3 + 7x^2 - 5x + 8$ $\times \qquad\qquad\qquad 3x - 2$ $\overline{\qquad -2x^3 - 14x^2 + 10x - 16}$ $+ \quad 3x^4 + 21x^3 - 15x^2 + 24x$ $\overline{\quad 3x^4 + 19x^3 - 29x^2 + 34x - 16}$	If $P(x)$ and $Q(x)$ are polynomials, then the product $P(x) \times Q(x)$ is also a polynomial.

3 Find the product of the polynomials $P(x)$ and $Q(x)$.

  a $P(x) = x + 5$, $Q(x) = x^2 - 3x + 7$

  b $P(x) = 2x + 1$, $Q(x) = x^3 + x^2 + 2x + 3$

  c $P(x) = 1 - 5x$, $Q(x) = 7x^2 + 21x - 3$

  d $P(x) = 4x + 3$, $Q(x) = 2x^3 + 5x^2 - 7x + 1$

  e $P(x) = 1 - 6x$, $Q(x) = x^3 - 2x^2 + 4x - 9$

4 Describe in words how the degree of $P(x) \times Q(x)$ is related to the degree of $P(x)$ and $Q(x)$.

5 Find the following products.

a $(x^2 + x + 1)(x^3 + 2x^2 - 3x - 5)$	**b** $(2x^2 - 3x + 4)(3x^3 + 4x^2 - 1)$
c $(x^2 + 3x + 2)^2$	**d** $(x - 3)(2x + 1)(x^2 - 3x - 4)$
e $(x + 5)(x - 2)(3x + 1)(4x - 3)$	**f** $(x - 2)(x - 5)(2x + 1)(3x - 1)$

E Division of polynomials

Before undertaking the division of polynomials, it is best to consider the method for long division of integers.

● EXAMPLE 1

Divide 385 by 18.

Solve	Think	Apply
$\begin{array}{r} 2\ 1 \\ 18\overline{)3\ 8\ 5} \\ -\ 3\ 6 \\ \hline 2\ 5 \\ -\ 1\ 8 \\ \hline 7 \end{array}$ $385 \div 18 = 21$ r 7	The result of the long division algorithm may be expressed as $385 \div 18 = 21$ with a remainder of 7; that is, $385 \div 18 = 21$ r 7 or $385 = 18 \times 21 + 7$	In the long division process, dividend $=$ divisor $\times$ quotient $+$ remainder: 385 is called the dividend. 18 is called the divisor. 21 is called the quotient. 7 is called the remainder.

● EXAMPLE 2

Divide 17 368 by 34 and write the result in the form 17 368 = 34 $\times$ quotient + remainder.

Solve	Think	Apply
$\begin{array}{r} 5\ 1\ 0 \\ 34\overline{)1\ 7\ 3\ 6\ 8} \\ -\ 1\ 7\ 0 \\ \hline 3\ 6 \\ -\ \ \ 3\ 4 \\ \hline 2\ 8 \end{array}$ $17\ 368 = 34 \times 510 + 28$	So $17\ 368 \div 34 = 510$ r 28 or $17\ 368 = 34 \times 510 + 28$.	The division process continues until the dividend is less than the divisor. The number left is the remainder.

● EXAMPLE 3

Use the long division algorithm from Examples 1 and 2 to divide the polynomial $3x^2 - 11x + 2$ by $x - 1$. Express the result in the form dividend = divisor $\times$ quotient + remainder.

Solve	Think	Apply
$\begin{array}{r} 3x - 8 \\ x - 1\overline{)3x^2 - 11x + 2} \\ -\ (3x^2 - 3x) \\ \hline -8x + 2 \\ -\ \ (-8x + 8) \\ \hline -6 \end{array}$ $3x^2 - 11x + 2$ $= (x - 1)(3x - 8) + (-6)$	Divide x into $3x^2$. $3x \times (x - 1)$ Subtract. Bring down the 2. Divide x into $-8x$. $-8 \times (x - 1)$ Subtract. Express the result as dividend $=$ divisor $\times$ quotient $+$ remainder.	Each term in the quotient is obtained by dividing the leading term of the divisor (x) into the leading term of the dividend, first $3x^2$ and then $-8x$ in this example. *Note:* Degree of remainder $<$ degree of divisor.

EXAMPLE 4

Divide $8x^3 + 4x^2 + 12x - 5$ by $2x + 1$ and express the result in this form:

$8x^3 + 4x^2 + 12x - 5 = (2x + 1) \times Q(x) + R$

Solve	Think	Apply
$$\begin{array}{r} 4x^2 \qquad\quad + 6 \\ 2x+1{\overline{\smash{\big)}\,8x^3 + 4x^2 + 12x - 5}} \\ \underline{-\,(8x^3 + 4x^2)\qquad\qquad\quad} \\ 12x - 5 \\ \underline{-\qquad\qquad\quad (12x + 6)} \\ -11 \end{array}$$ $8x^3 + 4x^2 + 12x - 5$ $= (2x + 1)(4x^2 + 6) + (-11)$	Divide $2x$ into $8x^2$. Subtract. Bring down $12x - 5$. Divide $2x$ into $12x$. Subtract. *Note:* Degree of remainder $<$ degree of divisor.	1 If we use the long division algorithm to divide one polynomial $P(x)$ by another $D(x)$, we get a unique quotient $Q(x)$ and a unique remainder $R(x)$ such that $P(x) = D(x) \times Q(x) + R(x)$ where the degree $R(x) <$ degree $D(x)$. 2 If $D(x)$ is degree 1 (linear polynomial), degree $R(x) < 1$. Degree $R(x) = 0$ or $R(x) = $ a constant $= R$.

Exercise 15E

1 Complete the following.

a
$$\begin{array}{r} 2\square 7 \\ 15{\overline{\smash{\big)}\,3\,8\,6\,4}} \\ \underline{-\,3\,0} \\ 8\square \\ \underline{-\,\,7\,5} \\ 1\,1\,4 \\ \underline{-\,\square\square\square} \\ 9 \end{array}$$

b
$$\begin{array}{r} 2x^2 - \square + 2 \\ 3x - 2{\overline{\smash{\big)}\,6x^3 - 7x^2 + 8x - 5}} \\ \underline{-\,(6x^3 - 4x^2)\qquad\qquad\quad} \\ \square + 8x \\ \underline{-\quad(-3x^2 + 2x)} \\ 6x - \square \\ \underline{-\quad(6x - 4)} \\ \square \end{array}$$

2 Perform the following divisions and express each result in this form:

dividend $=$ divisor $\times$ quotient $+$ remainder

a $12\,564 \div 28$

b $92\,156 \div 18$

c $(3x^2 - 11x - 10) \div (x + 5)$

d $(-2x^2 + 10x - 3) \div (x + 1)$

e $(x^3 + 2x^2 - 8x - 6) \div (x - 2)$

f $(3x^3 - 4x^2 + 3x + 2) \div (x + 3)$

g $(x^4 + 4x^3 - 3x^2 + 2x - 1) \div (x - 1)$

h $(2x^3 + x^2 - 4x - 7) \div (2x - 3)$

i $(3x^3 + 4x^2 - x + 7) \div (3x - 2)$

j $(2x^4 - 3x^3 + 6x^2 + 2x + 5) \div (2x + 1)$

NUMBER & ALGEBRA

Insight Mathematics 10 stages 5.2/5.3 Australian Curriculum

By dividing prove that $x - 2$ is a factor of $2x^3 + x^2 - 8x - 4$.

Hence express $2x^3 + x^2 - 8x - 4$ as the product of three linear factors.

Solve	Think/Apply
$$\begin{array}{r} 2x^2 + 5x + 2 \\ x - 2 \overline{)\, 2x^3 + x^2 - 8x - 4} \\ -\,(2x^3 - 4x^2) \\ \hline 5x^2 - 8x \\ -\quad (-5x^2 - 10x) \\ \hline 2x - 4 \\ -\qquad (2x - 4) \\ \hline 0 \end{array}$$ $2x^3 + x^2 - 8x - 4 = (x - 2)(2x^2 + 5x + 2)$ $\qquad\qquad\qquad\qquad = (x - 2)(2x + 1)(x + 2)$	As the remainder is zero, $(x - 2)$ is a factor of $2x^3 + x^2 - 8x - 4$. Factorise the quadratic.

3 For each of the following, show by division that the first polynomial is a factor of the second polynomial.

a $x + 2, x^3 + 5x^2 + 5x - 2$ **b** $2x - 1, 2x^3 - x^2 + 2x - 1$

c $x + 1, x^3 + 3x^2 + 3x + 1$ **d** $3x + 4, 3x^3 + 10x + 11x + 4$

e $x - 2, x^4 + x^3 - 8x^2 + 5x - 2$ **f** $x + 2, x^4 - x^3 - 9x^2 + 3x + 18$

4 Express each polynomial $P(x)$ as the product of three linear factors given that $h(x)$ is one of these factors.

a $P(x) = x^3 + 4x^2 + x - 6, h(x) = x - 1$ **b** $P(x) = 2x^3 - 5x^2 - x + 6, h(x) = 2x - 3$

c $P(x) = 2x^3 - 15x^2 + 22x + 15, h(x) = x - 5$ **d** $P(x) = 4x^3 + 12x^2 - x - 3, h(x) = x + 3$

e $P(x) = 8x^3 + 36x^2 + 54x + 27, h(x) = 2x + 3$ **f** $P(x) = 8x^3 - 12x^2 + 6x - 1, h(x) = 2x - 1$

5 Find the quotient and remainder for each of the following divisions.

a $(3x^3 - 2x^2 - 27x - 18) \div (3x - 2)$ **b** $(-6x^3 + x^2 + 4x + 3) \div (2x + 1)$

c $(5x^3 + 7x - 4) \div (x - 3)$ **d** $(x^3 - 1) \div (x + 1)$

e $(6x^3 - 5x^2 - 2) \div (2x - 1)$ **f** $(x^4 - a^4) \div (x - a)$

g $(4x^3 - 7x^2 + 2x - 3) \div (x^2 + 2x - 1)$ **h** $(2x^3 + 5x^2 + 11x - 1) \div (x^2 - x + 3)$

F   The remainder theorem

When $2x^3 - 5x^2 + 8x - 10$ is divided by $x - 3$ we get a quotient of $2x^2 + x + 11$ and a remainder of 23; that is, if $P(x) = 2x^3 - 5x^2 + 8x - 10$ then $P(x) = (x - 3)(2x^2 + x + 11) + 23$.

If we substitute $x = 3$ into this statement then:

$$P(3) = (3 - 3)(2(3)^2 + (3) + 11) + 23$$
$$= 0 \times 32 + 23$$
$$= 23$$

So $P(3)$ is the remainder when $P(x)$ is divided by $(x - 3)$.

This is a particular example of a general result known as the **remainder theorem**.

The remainder theorem states that:

If the polynomial $P(x)$ is divided by $(x - a)$ until a constant remainder is obtained, then the remainder is $P(a)$.

Proof: Let $Q(x)$ be the quotient and $R(x)$ the remainder when $P(x)$ is divided by $(x - a)$.

Note: Degree $R(x) <$ degree $(x - a)$, so degree $R(x) < 1$ and $R(x)$ must be a constant.

$$P(x) = (x - a)Q(x) + R$$
$$P(a) = (a - a)Q(a) + R \qquad \text{Substitute } x = a.$$
$$= 0 \times Q(a) + R$$
$$= R$$

Thus the remainder $R = P(a)$.

● EXAMPLE 1

Find the remainder when $2x^3 - 5x^2 + 7x - 4$ is divided by the following:

a $x - 2$ **b** $x + 2$

	Solve	Think	Apply
a	Let $P(x) = 2x^3 - 5x^2 + 7x - 4$, so remainder $= P(2)$. Remainder $= 2(2)^3 - 5(2)^2 + 7(2) - 4$ $\qquad = 6$	Substitute $x = 2$ and evaluate.	To find the remainder when $P(x)$ is divided by $(x - a)$ evaluate $P(a)$.
b	Let $P(x) = x + 2 = x - (-2)$, so the remainder is $P(-2)$. Remainder $= 2(-2)^3 - 5(-2)^2 + 7(-2) - 4$ $\qquad = -54$	Substitute $x = -2$ and evaluate.	

Exercise 15F

1 Use the remainder theorem to find the remainder when the first polynomial is divided by the second.

a $2x + 7, x + 1$

b $3x^2 + 12x - 28, x - 1$

c $5x^2 - 11x - 31, x - 4$

d $x^3 - 4x^2 + 3x + 1, x + 1$

e $-x^3 + 2x^2 - 7x - 13, x + 5$

f $2x^3 + 7x^2 - 10x - 5, x - 3$

g $-4x^3 - x^2 + x + 1, x + 2$

h $x^4 + x^3 - 2x^2 - 4x + 3, x + 2$

i $3x^4 - 5x^3 - 6x^2 + 8x - 6, x - 2$

j $2x^4 - 25x^3 + 71x^2 - 56x + 35, x$

2 **a** When $P(x) = ax^2 - 8x + 3$ is divided by $x - 7$ the remainder is 45. Find a.

   b When $F(x) = x^3 + 5x^2 + kx + 1$ is divided by $x + 5$ the remainder is 31. Find k.

   c When $Q(x) = ax^3 + bx^2 + x - 1$ is divided by $(x - 1)$ the remainder is -3, and when divided by $(x + 2)$ the remainder is -39. Find a and b.

3 Find the remainder when $P(x)$ is divided by $g(x)$.

   a $P(x) = x^3 + 5x^2 + 3x - 6$, $g(x) = x + 2$ **b** $P(x) = x^3 - 2x^2 - 5x + 6$, $g(x) = x - 3$

   c Comment on the meaning of the results in parts **a** and **b**.

G The factor theorem

If, when $P(x)$ is divided by $(x - a)$, the remainder is zero, then $(x - a)$ is a factor of $P(x)$.

So if $P(a) = 0$ then $(x - a)$ is a factor of $P(x)$.

● EXAMPLE 1

Show that $x - 3$ is a factor of $x^3 - 4x^2 + x + 6$.

Solve	Think	Apply
Let $P(x) = x^3 - 4x^2 + x + 6$ then $P(3) = 27 - 36 + 3 + 6 = 0$ $\therefore x - 3$ is a factor of $P(x)$.	Substitute $x = 3$ into $P(x)$.	If $P(a) = 0$ then $(x - a)$ is a factor of $P(x)$.

Exercise 15G

1 Verify that the first polynomial is a factor of the second.

   a $x - 1, 3x^3 + 5x^2 - 4x - 4$ **b** $x + 1, 4x^3 + 3x^2 + 9x + 10$

   c $x - 2, 2x^3 + 3x^2 - 18x + 8$ **d** $x + 2, 2x^4 + 2x^3 + x^2 + x - 2$

   e $x + 4, 2x^3 + 3x^2 - 12x + 32$ **f** $x - 3, 3x^4 - 9x^3 + 5x^2 - 7x - 24$

● EXAMPLE 2

Find all the linear factors of the polynomial $P(x) = x^3 + 6x^2 + 11x + 6$.

Solve	Think	Apply
$\begin{array}{r} x^2 + 5x + 6 \\ x + 1 \overline{)\,x^3 + 6x^2 + 11x + 6} \\ -(x^3 + x^2) \\ \hline 5x^2 + 11x \\ -\ (5x^2 + 5x) \\ \hline 6x + 6 \\ -\ (6x + 6) \\ \hline 0 \end{array}$ $P(x) = (x + 1)(x + 2)(x + 3)$	The factors of the constant term 6 are ± 1, ± 2, ± 3 and ± 6, so we try $P(\pm 1)$, $P(\pm 2)$, $P(\pm 3)$ and $P(\pm 6)$ until we find a factor. $P(1) = 1 + 6 + 11 + 6 \neq 0$ $\therefore x - 1$ is not a factor. $P(-1) = -1 + 6 - 11 + 6 = 0$ $\therefore x + 1$ is a factor. We can find the other factors by factorising the quotient: $(x^2 + 5x + 6) = (x + 2)(x + 3)$	Once a single linear factor of a cubic is found then polynomial division gives a quadratic that can be factorised.

2 Use the factor theorem to find all the linear factors of the following polynomials.

a $x^3 + 3x^2 - 6x - 8$ b $x^3 - 7x + 6$

c $x^3 + 3x^2 - 16x + 12$ d $x^3 + 6x^2 + 12x + 8$

e $x^3 + 6x^2 - x - 6$ f $x^3 + 3x^2 - 10x - 24$

g $x^3 - 7x^2 + 36$ h $x^4 + x^3 - 3x^2 - 4x - 4$

i $x^4 + 2x^3 - 3x^2 - 4x + 4$ j $2x^3 - 13x^2 - 13x + 42$

3 a If $x - 3$ is a factor of $6x^3 + kx^2 + 2x + 3$, find the value of k.

b If $P(x) = x^3 + ax^2 + bx - 6$ is divisible by $(x + 1)$ and $(x - 2)$, find the values of a and b.

c $(x + 1)$ is a factor of $f(x) = x^3 + mx^2 + nx - 3$, and when $f(x)$ is divided by $(x + 3)$ the remainder is -24. Find m and n.

d Find the values of a and b if $(x - 1)$ is a factor of $g(x) = ax^4 - 5x^3 + b$, and when $g(x)$ is divided by $(x + 2)$ the remainder is 135.

e Find the values of k and m if $P(x) = x^3 + kx^2 - 12x + m$ is divisible by $x^2 - x - 6$.

4 a If n is a positive integer, show that $(x - a)$ is always a factor of $x^n - a^n$.

b Is $(x + a)$ always a factor of $x^n + a^n$? Discuss and explain.

H Polynomial equations

Previously we have solved polynomial equations of degree 1 (linear equations) and of degree 2 (quadratic equations). Polynomial equations of degree 3 or higher can be difficult to solve, but in some cases we can use the factor theorem to help us.

EXAMPLE 1

Solve $x^3 + 5x^2 - 12x - 36 = 0$.

Solve	Think	Apply
$\begin{array}{r} x^2 + 3x - 18 \\ \hline x + 2)\overline{\smash{)}x^3 + 5x^2 - 12x - 36} \\ -\ (x^3 + 2x^2) \\ \hline 3x^2 - 12x \\ -\quad (3x^2 + 6x) \\ \hline -18x - 36 \\ -\quad (-18x - 36) \\ \hline 0 \end{array}$ $P(x) = (x + 2)(x^2 + 3x - 18)$ $= (x + 2)(x - 3)(x + 6)$ Thus $x = -2, 3, -6$	Let $P(x) = x^3 + 5x^2 - 12x - 36$. To find the factors of $P(x)$ try $P(\pm 1)$, $P(\pm 2)$, and so on. $P(1) = 1 + 5 - 12 - 36 \neq 0$ $P(-1) = -1 + 5 + 12 - 36 \neq 0$ $P(2) = 8 + 20 - 24 - 36 \neq 0$ $P(-2) = -8 + 20 + 24 - 36$ $= 0$ $\therefore (x + 2)$ is a factor of $P(x)$. We can find the other factors by factorising the quotient: $x^2 + 3x - 18 = (x - 3)(x + 6)$	Any value of x that makes the value of $P(x)$ equal to zero is called a zero of the polynomial. The zeros of the polynomial $P(x) = x^3 + 5x^2 - 12x - 36$ are -2, 3 and -6.

● EXAMPLE 2

Solve $x^3 - 2x^2 - 2x - 3 = 0$.

Solve	Think	Apply
$$\begin{array}{r} x^2 + x + 1 \\ x - 3\overline{)\,x^3 - 2x^2 - 2x - 36} \\ -(x^3 - 3x^2) \\ \hline x^2 - 2x \\ -\quad(x^2 - 3x) \\ \hline x - 3 \\ -\quad(-x - 3) \\ \hline 0 \end{array}$$ $x = 3$ or $x^2 + x + 1 = 0$ $\therefore x = 3$ is the only solution.	Let $f(x) = x^3 - 2x^2 - 2x - 3$ $f(1) = 1 - 2 - 2 - 3 \neq 0$ $f(-1) = -1 - 2 + 2 - 3 \neq 0$ $f(3) = 27 - 18 - 6 - 3 = 0$ $\therefore (x - 3)$ is a factor of $f(x)$. $x^3 - 2x^2 - 2x - 3 = 0$ $\therefore (x - 3)(x^2 + x + 1) = 0$ If the quadratic does not factorise, use the quadratic formula to solve. $x = \dfrac{-1 \pm \sqrt{1 - 4}}{2}$ has no solutions.	If the polynomial $f(x) = x^3 - 2x^2 - 2x - 3$ has only one zero (3), it follows that the zeros of the polynomial $P(x)$ are the solutions of the polynomial equation $P(x) = 0$. A quadratic equation has no real roots if the discriminant $\Delta = b^2 - 4ac < 0$. In this case $\Delta = -3$.

Exercise 15H

1 Solve the following polynomial equations.

 a $x^3 - 3x^2 - 10x + 24 = 0$ **b** $x^3 + 7x^2 + 7x - 15 = 0$

 c $x^3 + 10x^2 = 24x$ **d** $x^3 + 9x^2 + 26x + 24 = 0$

 e $2x^3 - 3x^2 = 11x - 6$ **f** $x^3 = 3x^2 - 3x + 1$

 g $x^3 + 6x^2 + 7x + 2 = 0$ **h** $x^3 + 2x^2 - 6x = 4$

 i $x^4 + x^3 - 3x^2 - 4x - 4 = 0$ **j** $x^4 + 2x^3 - 4x^2 - 7x - 2 = 0$

2 A box is to be built with a square base and height 2 cm more than the length of the base.

 a Write an expression for the volume of the box.

 b If the volume is to be 45 cm³, find a polynomial equation from which the dimensions of the box can be found.

 c Find the dimensions that will give this volume.

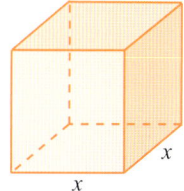

3 Four identical squares are cut from the corners of a rectangular sheet of metal 10 cm × 8 cm. The sides are folded along the dotted lines to form a rectangular box, as shown.

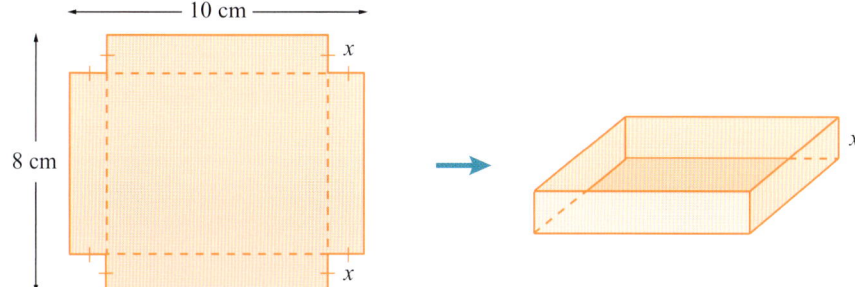

 a Find an expression for the volume of the box.

 b Find the side length of the square that should be cut from each corner if the volume is to be 48 cm³.

 c Hence find the dimensions of the rectangular box with this volume.

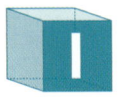

Sketching polynomials

We sketched some simple polynomials in Section 15A. We now extend this to more general examples.

EXAMPLE 1

Find the zeros of the polynomial function $y = (x + 3)(x + 1)(x - 2)$ and hence sketch its graph.

Solve	Think	Apply
(graph of $y = (x+3)(x+1)(x-2)$ with x-intercepts at -3, -1, 2 and y-intercept at -6)	Let $y = 0$: $x = -3, -1$ and 2 are the x-intercepts. Let $x = 0$: $y = -6$ is the y-intercept. As $x \to +\infty, y \to +\infty$ $x \to -\infty, y \to -\infty$	If the leading term is positive, then a cubic graph looks similar to $y = x^3$ as $x \to \pm\infty$.

Exercise 15I

1 Sketch these polynomials.

  a $y = (x + 5)(x + 2)(x + 1)$ **b** $y = -2(x + 3)(x - 2)(x - 3)$ **c** $y = x(x + 4)(x - 3)$

  d $y = x(x - 2)(x - 5)(x + 1)$ **e** $y = (4 - x)(x - 3)(x - 1)(x + 2)$

EXAMPLE 2

Find the zeros of the polynomial function $P(x) = 6x^3 + 5x^2 - 2x - 1$. Hence sketch the graph of $y = P(x)$.

Solve	Think/Apply
$\begin{array}{r} 6x^2 - x - 1 \\ x + 1 \overline{)\, 6x^3 + 5x^2 - 2x - 1} \\ -\underline{(6x^3 + 6x^2)} \\ -x^2 - 2x \\ -\underline{(-x^2 - x)} \\ -x - 1 \\ -\underline{(-x - 1)} \\ 0 \end{array}$ (graph of $y = 6x^3 + 5x^2 - 2x - 1$ with x-intercepts at -1, $\frac{1}{3}$, $\frac{1}{2}$ and y-intercept -1)	$P(x) = 6x^3 + 5x^2 - 2x - 1$ $P(1) = 6 + 5 - 2 - 1 \neq 0$ $P(-1) = -6 + 5 + 2 - 1 = 0$ $\therefore (x + 1)$ is a factor. $P(x) = (x + 1)(6x^2 - x - 1)$ $\quad\quad = (x + 1)(2x - 1)(3x + 1)$ The zeros of the polynomial are $-1, \frac{1}{2}, -\frac{1}{3}$. $\therefore$ The x-intercepts are $-1, \frac{1}{2}, -\frac{1}{3}$. Let $x = 0$: $y = -1$ *Note:* This is the constant term of $P(x)$. As $x \to +\infty, y \to +\infty$ $\quad\quad x \to -\infty, y \to -\infty$ We put all this information together to sketch the graph.

Notes:

1 The graphs of polynomial functions are continuous curves; that is, they have no gaps in them, as there is a value of y for every value of x.

2 For very large positive values of x (as $x \to +\infty$) and for very large negative values of x (as $x \to -\infty$) the value of y approximately equals the value of the leading term. Hence the sign of the leading term of a polynomial determines whether $y \to \pm\infty$ as $x \to \pm\infty$.

3 In Examples 1 and 2, y is a polynomial function of degree 3. A polynomial of degree 3 can have no more than three linear factors, therefore it can have no more than three zeros. In general, a polynomial of degree n can have no more than n zeros.

2 Use the factor theorem to find the zeros of the following polynomials and hence sketch each function.

a $P(x) = x^3 + 2x^2 - x - 2$ b $P(x) = x^3 + 2x^2 - 5x - 6$

c $P(x) = x^3 + 3x^2 - 70x$ d $P(x) = x^3 + 9x^2 + 26x + 24$

e $P(x) = -x^3 + 5x^2 + 4x - 20$ f $P(x) = x^4 - 19x^2 + 30x$

g $P(x) = -x^4 - 3x^3 - x^2 + 3x + 2$ h $P(x) = x^4 - 2x^3 - 15x^2$

 J Significance of double and triple roots

● EXAMPLE 1

a Give an example of a polynomial equation of degree 2 with:
  i two distinct (different roots)
  ii one distinct root
  iii no roots.

b Sketch the graph of each of the corresponding polynomial functions.

	Solve	Think/Apply
a i	$(x + 1)(x - 2) = 0$ $\therefore x^2 - x - 2 = 0$ The roots are $x = -1$ and 2.	• The polynomial equation $(x + 1)(x - 2) = 0$ has two distinct roots and the graph of the polynomial function $y = (x + 1)(x - 2)$ cuts the x-axis in two distinct points.
ii	$(x + 1)^2 = 0$ or $(x + 1)(x + 1) = 0$ $\therefore x^2 + 2x + 1 = 0$ Roots are $x = -1$ and -1, so the distinct root is $x = -1$. -1 is called a double root of the equation.	• The polynomial equation $(x + 1)^2 = 0$ has a double root at $x = -1$ and the graph of $y = (x + 1)^2$ touches the x-axis at $x = -1$; that is, the x-axis is a tangent to the curve at $x = -1$.
iii	$x^2 + 1 = 0$ has no roots.	• The polynomial equation $x^2 + 1 = 0$ has no (real) roots ($x^2 = -1$ has no solution) and the graph of $y = x^2 + 1$ does not cut the x-axis.
b	**i** 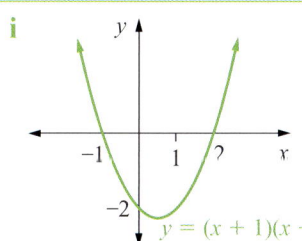	**ii** 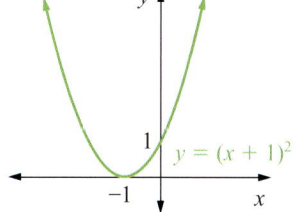 **iii** 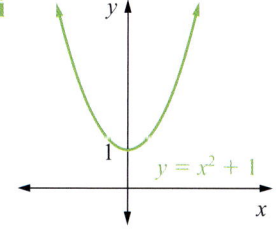

Graphically the case of a double root (two equal roots) may be considered as the limiting position as two distinct roots approach each other, as shown.

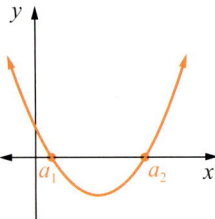 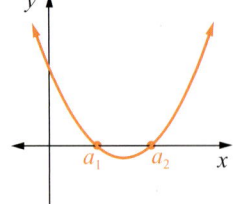 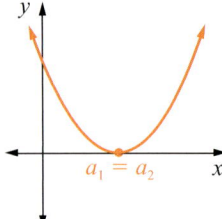

Exercise 15J

1 a Give an example of a polynomial of degree 0.
 b Sketch the graph of the corresponding function.
 c How many zeros does the polynomial have?

2 a Give an example of a polynomial of degree 1.
 b Sketch the graph of the corresponding function.
 c How many zeros does the polynomial have?
 d Can a polynomial of degree 1 have no zeros?

3 a What is the maximum number of zeros a polynomial of degree 2 can have?
 b Give an example of a polynomial of degree 2 with:
  i two distinct zeros   **ii** one distinct zero   **iii** no zeros
 c Sketch the corresponding polynomial function.

4 a What is the maximum number of zeros a polynomial of degree 3 can have?
 b Can a polynomial of degree 3 have no zeros?
 c Sketch an example of a polynomial of degree 3 with the following number of distinct zeros.
  i 3   **ii** 2   **iii** 1
 d Give an example of a polynomial equation of degree 3 with the following number of distinct zeros.
  i 3   **ii** 2   **iii** 1

EXAMPLE 2

Sketch the following polynomial functions.
 a $y = (x + 1)(x - 2)(x - 3)$ **b** $y = (x + 1)^2(x - 2)$ **c** $y = (x + 1)^3$

Solve	Think/Apply
a 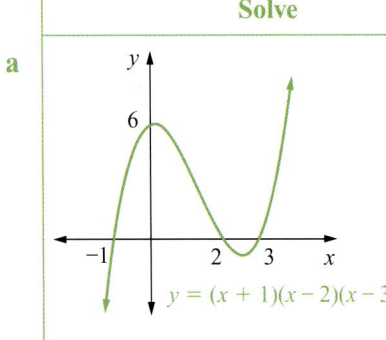	$y = 0$ has three distinct roots: $x = -1, 2$ and 3. These are the x-intercepts. Let $x = 0$: $y = (+1)(-2)(-3) = 6$ This is the y-intercept. The leading term (after expanding) will be x^3. $\therefore$ As $x \to +\infty, y \to +\infty$ and as $x \to -\infty, y \to -\infty$

EXAMPLE 2 CONTINUED

	Solve	Think/Apply
b	$y = (x + 1)^2(x - 2)$	$y = 0$ has three roots $x = -1, -1$ and 2 (from $(x + 1)(x + 1)(x - 2) = 0$), but these are not all distinct. Distinct roots are $x = -1$ and 2. These are the x-intercepts. As -1 is a double root of the equation, the graph will touch the x-axis at $x = -1$; that is, the x-axis is a tangent to the curve at $x = -1$. Let $x = 0$: $y = -2$. The leading term is x^3. $\therefore$ As $x \to +\infty$, $y \to +\infty$ and as $x \to -\infty$, $y \to -\infty$
c	$y = (x + 1)^3$	$y = 0$ has three roots $x = -1, -1$ and -1 (from $(x + 1)(x + 1)(x + 1) = 0$), but these are obviously all equal. The distinct root is $x = -1$. This is the only x-intercept. -1 is called a triple root of the equation. Let $x = 0$: $y = 1$. The leading term is x^3. $\therefore$ As $x \to +\infty$, $y \to +\infty$ and as $x \to -\infty$, $y \to -\infty$. *Note:* When $x = -1.1$, $y < 0$ and when $x = -0.9$, $y > 0$. So y changes sign as the curve passes through $x = -1$; that is, the curve cuts the x-axis at $x = -1$. Remember this is the curve $y = x^3$ translated 1 unit to the left.

Graphically, the case of a triple root (three equal roots) may be considered as the limiting position as three distinct roots approach each other, as shown below.

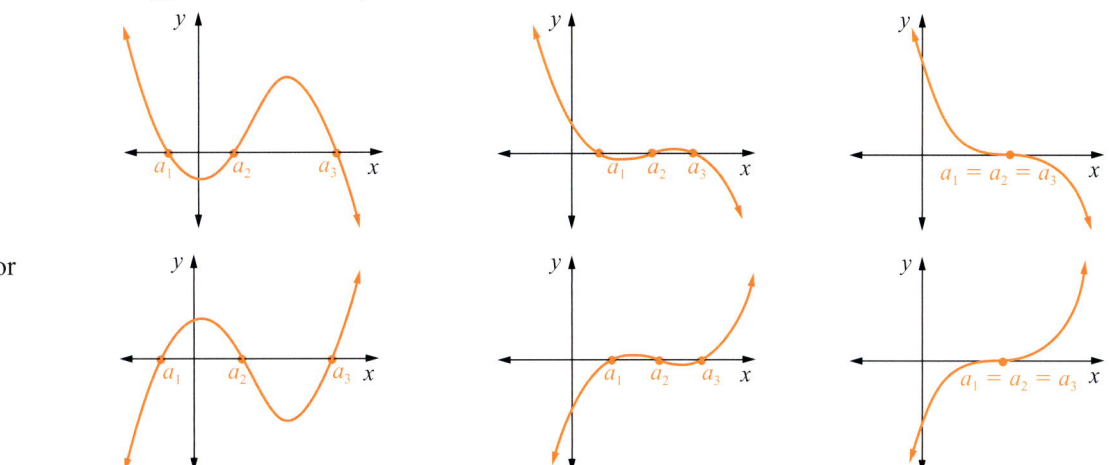

or

Note that the concavity of the curve changes as we pass through the triple root from left to right along the curve. A curve is concave up at a point if it lies above the tangent at that point, and is concave down at a point if it lies below the tangent at that point.

These curves are concave up at the points P and Q.   These curves are concave down at the points R and S.

In Example 2 parts **a**, **b** and **c**, the polynomials are of degree 3 with 3, 2 and 1 distinct zeros, respectively. The question arises as to whether it is possible for a polynomial of degree 3 to have no zeros.

Consider the following argument.

Let $y = ax^3 + bx^2 + cx + d$. For x very large, positive or negative, the graph approaches $y = ax^3$.

If $a > 0$, as $x \to +\infty$, $y \to +\infty$ and as $x \to -\infty$, $y \to -\infty$.

As y is a continuous function, the curve must cut the x-axis at least once.

If $a < 0$, as $x \to +\infty$, $y \to -\infty$ and as $x \to -\infty$, $y \to +\infty$.

Again, as y is a continuous function the curve must cut the x-axis at least once; that is, any polynomial function of degree 3 must cut the x-axis at least once. Hence a polynomial of degree 3 must have at least one zero.

The same argument can be used for any polynomial of odd degree.

Summary

1 To sketch $y = P(x)$:
- Find the x-intercepts by finding the zeros of $P(x)$.
- Find the y-intercept by putting $x = 0$. This is the constant term of $P(x)$.

2 The significance of double and triple roots:
- If the equation $P(x) = 0$ has a double root at $x = a$, then the x-axis is a tangent to the curve $y = P(x)$ at $x = a$.
- If $P(x) = 0$ has a triple root at $x = b$, then the curve cuts the x-axis and changes concavity at $x = b$.

3 If $P(x)$ is of degree n, then at most it can have n zeros.

4 If $P(x)$ is of odd degree, then it has at least one zero.

EXAMPLE 3

Sketch the function $y = (x + 1)^3(x - 2)^2(x + 3)$.

Solve	Think/Apply
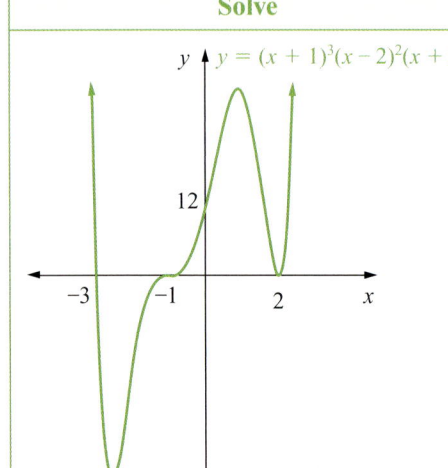	Zeros are -3, -1 and 2 with a double root at $x = 2$. $\therefore$ The x-axis is a tangent to the curve at $x = 2$. There is a triple root at $x = -1$. The curve cuts the x-axis at $x = -1$ and changes concavity at this point. Let $x = 0$: $y = (1)^3(-2)^2(3) = 12$ The y-intercept $= 12$. The leading term is x^6. $\therefore$ As $x \to +\infty$, $y \to +\infty$ and as $x \to -\infty$, $y \to +\infty$.

5 Sketch the following polynomials.

a $y = (x + 1)(x - 2)^2$

b $y = (x + 2)^3$

c $y = (x + 2)(x - 3)^3$

d $y = -x^2(x - 1)^3$

e $y = x^3(x - 1)^2$

f $y = -x^3(x - 2)^2(x + 3)$

6 Use the factor theorem to find the zeros of the following polynomials and hence sketch each function.

 a $P(x) = 2x^3 - 18x^2 + 30x + 50$
 b $P(x) = x^3 - 3x - 2$
 c $P(x) = -x^3 + 2x^2 - x$
 d $P(x) = x^4 + x^3$
 e $P(x) = -x^3 + 6x^2 - 12x + 8$
 f $P(x) = x^4 - x^3 - 3x^2 + 5x - 2$

7 Write an equation that could represent the following polynomials and sketch the corresponding polynomial functions.

 a **i** degree = 1, single root at $x = 3$, constant term = -6
   ii degree = 1, single root at $x = 3$, constant term = $+6$
 b **i** degree = 2, single roots at $x = -1, 4$, constant term = -4
   ii degree = 2, single roots at $x = -1, 4$, constant term = $+4$
 c degree = 2, double root at $x = 3$, leading coefficient = -2
 d degree = 3, single roots at $x = -1, 0, 1$, monic
 e degree = 3, single root at $x = -2$, double root at $x = 1$, monic
 f degree = 3, triple root at $x = 4$, leading coefficient = 2
 g degree = 4, single root at $x = -3$, triple root at $x = 2$, constant term = -24
 h degree = 4, double root at $x = -2$, double root at $x = 2$, monic

8 **a** Produce your own sketch of a polynomial function.
 b Describe the main features of your sketch to another student so that they can reproduce your sketch without looking at it.
 c Compare your graph with that of your partner. Are they identical? Discuss any differences.
 d Swap roles and repeat parts **a** to **c**.

9 **a** Sketch $y = (x + 2)(x - 4)$ showing the x-intercepts, the y-intercept and the coordinates of the turning point.
 b Use your sketch in part **a** to help you sketch:
   i $y = 2(x + 2)(x - 4)$
   ii $y = \frac{1}{2}(x + 2)(x - 4)$
   iii $y = (x + 2)(x - 4) + 1$
   iv $y = (x + 2)(x - 4) - 2$
   v $y = -(x + 2)(x - 4)$
   vi $y = (-x + 2)(-x - 4)$ (*Note: $y = P(-x)$*)

10 A sketch of $y = P(x)$ is given.
 a Use it to sketch the following polynomials.
   i $y = 2P(x)$
   ii $y = \frac{1}{2}P(x)$
   iii $y = P(x) + 2$
   iv $y = P(x) - 1$
   v $y = -P(x)$
   vi $y = P(x - 2)$
   vii $y = P(-x)$

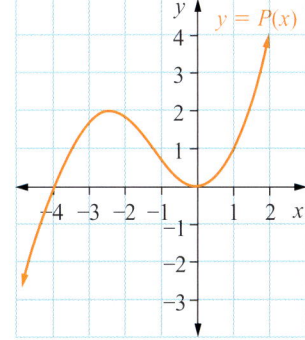

 b Describe in words the relationship between the graph of $y = P(x)$ and the graph of each of the polynomials in part **a**.

11 Using a graphics calculator, sketch $y = x^3 + x^2 + x + 1$ and $y = x^3 + x^2 + x$. Discuss the similarities and differences in the graphs.

Language in mathematics

1. Describe the effect on the graph of $y = x^n$ of including a constant k as follows.

   a $y = kx^n$
   b $y = x^n + k$
   c $y = (x - k)^n$

2. Describe line symmetry and point symmetry by reference to graphs of $y = x^n$.

3. Describe the relationship between these graphs.

   a $y = x^n$ and $y = -x^n$
   b $y = x^n$ and $y = (-x)^n$

4. Consider these terms.

   a translate
   b function

      i State their mathematical meaning.
      ii Write their ordinary English meaning.

5. Explain in your own words the meaning of the following terms.

   a coefficient
   b concave
   c distinct
   d infinity

6. Define the following terms.

   a polynomial
   b degree
   c leading term
   d leading coefficient
   e constant term
   f monic polynomial

7. Using an example of the long division algorithm, define the terms 'divisor', 'dividend', 'quotient' and 'remainder'.

8. Three of the words below are spelt incorrectly. Give the correct spelling for these words.

   compress, factoor, triple, significance, algebracally, skech

Terms

algebraically	algorithm	compress	concave	constant
coordinates	degree of polynomial	distinct	dividend	divisor
double root	function	graphically	horizontally	infinity
intercept	intersection	leading coefficient	leading term	monic
polynomial	quotient	reflection	relationship	remainder
significant	sketch	stretch	symmetry	transformation
translate	triple root	unique	vertically	zero

Check your skills

1. Given the graph of $y = ax^n$, which of the following statements could not be true?

   A n is even.
   B n is odd.
   C a is positive.
   D The curve is symmetrical about O.

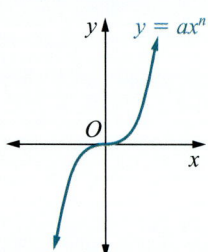

2 This is the graph of $y = x^n$. Which of the following could be the graph of $y = 2x^n - 1$?

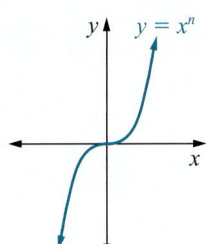

A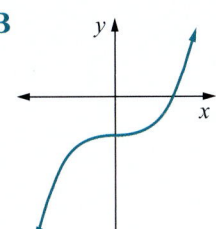

B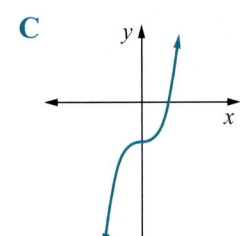

C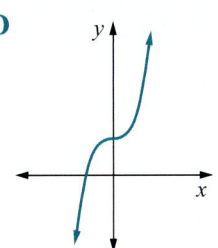

D

3 Which of the following could be the graph of $y = (x + 2)^4$?

A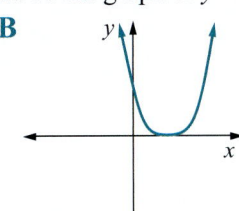

B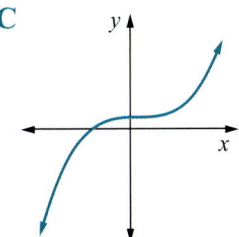

C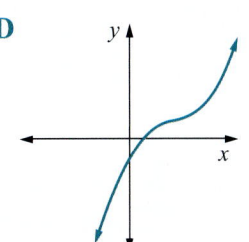

D

4 Which of the following could be the graph of $y = -(x - 1)^4 + 2$?

A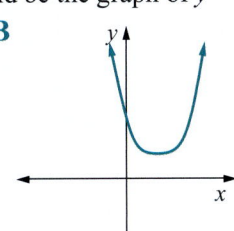

B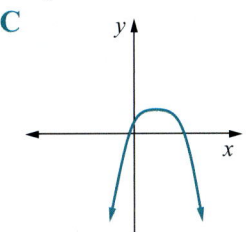

C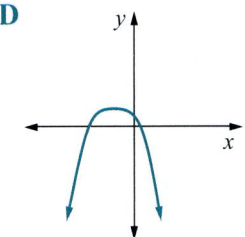

D

5 Given $y = f(x)$, which of the following could be the graph of $y = -f(x)$?

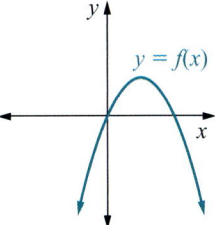

A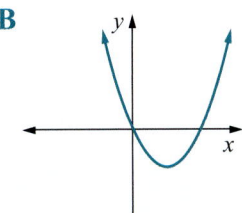

B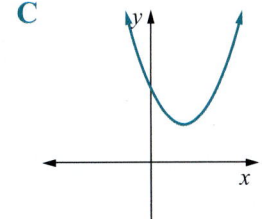

C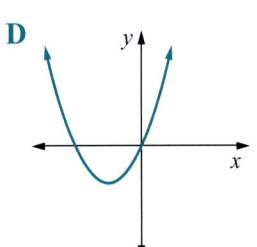

D

6 Which of the following is not symmetrical about the y-axis?

A $y = 3x^{10}$ **B** $y = -3x^{10}$ **C** $y = 3x^{10} + 1$ **D** $y = 3x^{10} + x^3$

7 Which of the following expressions is not a polynomial?

A $\dfrac{1}{2x^3 + 3x^2 - 4x + 5}$　　**B** $x^4 + x^2 + 1$　　　　**C** 15　　　　　　**D** $x + 3$

8 A polynomial $P(x)$ with degree = 2, constant term = 2 and $P(-1) = 4$ could be:

A $2x^2 + 2x$　　　　**B** $x^2 - x + 2$　　　　**C** $x^2 + 2$　　　　**D** $x^2 + x + 2$

9 Which of the statements below is always true?

　　i The degree of the $P(x) \pm Q(x)$ equals the degree of $P(x)$ or $Q(x)$, whichever is the greater.

　　ii The degree of $P(x) \times Q(x)$ equals the degree of $P(x)$ multiplied by the degree of $Q(x)$.

A i only　　　　　　**B ii** only　　　　　　**C** both **i** and **ii**　　　　**D** neither **i** nor **ii**

10 When $x^3 - 4x^2 - 5x + 6$ is divided by $x - 2$ the quotient is:

A $x^2 + 2x - 1$　　　**B** $x^2 - 6x - 17$　　　**C** $x^2 + 6x + 7$　　　**D** $x^2 - 2x - 9$

11 When $P(x) = 2x^3 - 4x^2 + 3x + 2$ is divided by $(x + 3)$ the remainder is:

A -97　　　　　　**B** -25　　　　　　**C** 11　　　　　　**D** 83

12 If $(x - 1)$ and $(x + 2)$ are factors of $P(x) = 3x^3 + ax^2 + bx + 4$, then the values of a and b are respectively:

A 3 and -10　　　　**B** 3 and -4　　　　**C** 1 and -8　　　　**D** 1 and 8

13 Which of the following could be the graph of $y = (3 - x)(x + 2)(x - 1)$?

A　　　　　　　　**B**　　　　　　　　**C**　　　　　　　　**D**

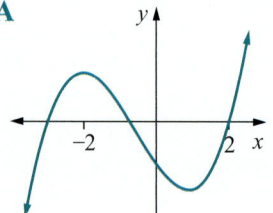　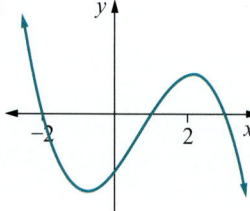　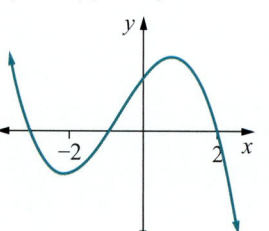　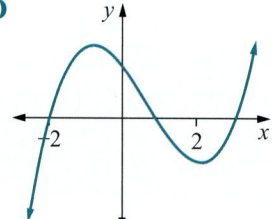

14 Which of the statements below is always true?

　　i If $P(x)$ is of degree n, then $P(x)$ has n zeros.

　　ii If $P(x)$ is of odd degree, then $P(x)$ has at least one zero.

A i only　　　　　　**B ii** only　　　　　　**C** both **i** and **ii**　　　　**D** neither **i** nor **ii**

15 Which of the following could be the graph of $y = (x - 1)^2(x + 2)^3$?

A　　　　　　　　**B**　　　　　　　　**C**　　　　　　　　**D**

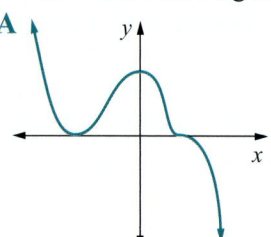　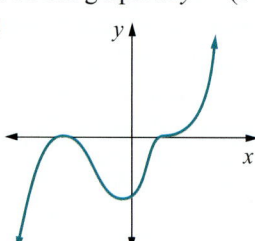　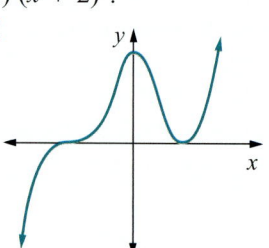　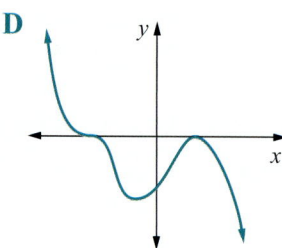

If you have any difficulty with these questions, refer to the examples and questions in the sections listed in the table.

Question	1–5	6	7, 8	9	10	11	12	13	14	15
Section	A	B	C	D	E	F	G	H	I	J

1 On the same diagram, draw neat sketches of:

a   **i** $y = x^2$ **ii** $y = 3x^2$ **iii** $y = \frac{1}{2}x^2$ **iv** $y = -x^2$

b   **i** $y = x^2$ **ii** $y = x^2 + 3$ **iii** $y = x^2 - 3$

c   **i** $y = x^2$ **ii** $y = (x - 2)^2$ **iii** $y = (x + 1)^2$

d   **i** $y = x^2$ **ii** $y = 2x^2 - 1$

e   **i** $y = x^2$ **ii** $y = (x - 1)^2 - 3$

f   **i** $y = x^2$ **ii** $y = -(x + 1)^2 + 2$ **iii** $y = -\frac{1}{2}(x + 1)^2 + 2$

2 Use the graph of $y = f(x)$ given to draw neat sketches of:

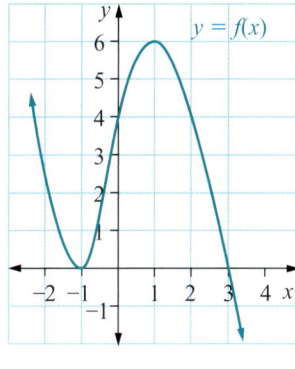

a $y = 2f(x)$ b $y = f(x) + 2$

c $y = f(x - 2)$ d $y = f(x + 2)$

e $y = -f(x)$ f $y = f(-x)$

3 Determine whether the following functions are symmetrical about the y-axis.

a $f(x) = -3x^2$ b $f(x) = 2x^3$ c $f(x) = x^2 - 2x + 3$

4 State whether or not the following are polynomials.

a $4x^3 - 3x^2 + 7x + \frac{2}{3}$ b $x^2 + 3x + \frac{2}{x}$ c 3 d $3^x + 2^x + 5$

5 For each of the following polynomials state:

     i   the degree   **ii**   the leading term   **iii**   the leading coefficient

     iv   the constant term   **v**   whether or not the polynomial is monic.

a $2x^3 - 5x^2 - 7x - 2$ b $4x + 2x^3 - 2x^5$

6 Given $P(x) = 2x^3 - x^2 + 7$ and $Q(x) = x^3 + 3x^2 - 4x - 2$, find:

a $P(x) + Q(x)$ b $P(x) - Q(x)$

7 The degree of $P(x) + Q(x)$ equals the degree of $P(x)$ or $Q(x)$, whichever is the greater.
This statement is true:

   A   never   **B**   sometimes   **C**   always

8 Given $P(x) = x - 1$ and $Q(x) = 4x^3 + 2x^2 - 3x + 5$, find:

a $P(x) \times Q(x)$

b $Q(x) \div P(x)$ Express the result in the form $Q(x) = P(x) \times A(x) + R$.

9 a   Find the remainder when $x^3 - 2x^2 - 5x + 1$ is divided by $x - 2$.

   b   When $P(x) = kx^2 - 5x + 3$ is divided by $(x + 1)$, the remainder is 20. Find k.

10 a   Show that $x - 2$ is a factor of $P(x) = x^3 + 3x^2 - 4x - 12$.

    b   Hence find all the linear factors of $P(x)$.

    c   State the zeros of $y = P(x)$.

    d   Draw a neat sketch of $y = P(x)$.

11 Sketch the following polynomials.

a $y = (x - 1)^2(x + 2)^3$ b $y = -(x + 3)^3(x - 2)^2$

1 On the same diagram, draw neat sketches of:

a   i $y = x^3$ ii $y = 2x^3$ iii $y = \frac{1}{2}x^3$ iv $y = -x^3$

b   i $y = x^3$ ii $y = x^3 + 1$ iii $y = x^3 - 2$

c   i $y = x^3$ ii $y = (x - 1)^3$ iii $y = (x + 2)^3$

d   i $y = x^3$ ii $y = 3x^3 + 1$

e   i $y = x^3$ ii $y = (x - 2)^3 - 1$

f   i $y = x^3$ ii $y = -(x - 1)^3 + 2$ iii $y = -\frac{1}{2}(x - 1)^3 + 2$

2 Use the graph of $y = f(x)$ given to draw neat sketches of:

a $y = 2f(x)$ b $y = f(x) + 2$

c $y = f(x - 2)$ d $y = f(x + 2)$

e $y = -f(x)$ f $y = f(-x)$

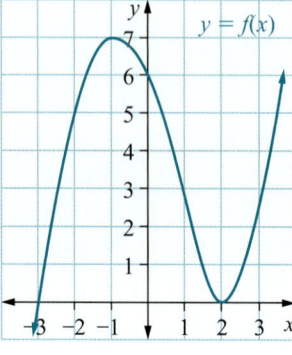

3 Determine whether the following functions are symmetrical about the y-axis.

a $f(x) = -4x^3$ b $f(x) = x^4 + x^2$ c $f(x) = x^4 + x^2 - 1$

4 State whether or not the following are polynomials.

a $1 + 4x + x^2 + x^3$ b $x^3 + \sqrt{x^3}$ c 42 d $\dfrac{2}{x^2 + 8x + 11}$

5 For each of the following polynomials state:

     i   the degree   ii   the leading term   iii   the leading coefficient

     iv   the constant term   v   whether or not the polynomial is monic.

a $3 + 2x - x^2 + 5x^3$ b $x^4 + 2x^3 + 3x^2 + 4x + 5$

6 Given $P(x) = 4x^3 + 7x^2 - 2x + 11$ and $Q(x) = -2x^3 + x^2 + 7x - 4$, find:

a $P(x) + Q(x)$ b $P(x) - Q(x)$

7 How is the degree of $P(x) \pm Q(x)$ related to the degree of $P(x)$ and $Q(x)$?

8 Given $P(x) = x + 2$ and $Q(x) = x^3 + 6x^2 - 4x + 5$, find:

a $P(x) \times Q(x)$

b $Q(x) \div P(x)$ Express the result in the form $Q(x) = P(x) \times A(x) + R$.

9 a   Find the remainder when $2x^3 + 4x^2 - 11x + 3$ is divided by $x + 1$.

b   When $P(x) = x^3 + kx^2 - 2x - 1$ is divided by $x - 2$, the remainder is 6. Find k.

10 a   Show that $(x + 1)$ is a factor of $P(x) = x^3 + 2x^2 - 11x - 12$.

b   Hence find all the linear factors of $P(x)$.

c   State the zeros of $y = P(x)$.

d   Draw a neat sketch of $y = P(x)$.

11 Sketch the following polynomials.

a $y = (x + 2)^3(x - 3)^2$ b $y = -(x - 1)^3(x + 2)^2$

1 On the same diagram, draw neat sketches of:

a **i** $y = x^4$ **ii** $y = 2x^4$ **iii** $y = \frac{1}{3}x^4$ **iv** $y = -x^4$

b **i** $y = x^4$ **ii** $y = x^4 + 1$ **iii** $y = x^4 - 2$

c **i** $y = x^4$ **ii** $y = (x - 3)^4$ **iii** $y = (x + 3)^4$

d **i** $y = x^4$ **ii** $y = 2x^4 - 3$

e **i** $y = x^4$ **ii** $y = (x - 1)^4 + 2$

f **i** $y = x^4$ **ii** $y = -(x + 1)^4 + 1$ **iii** $y = -3(x + 1)^4 - 1$

2 Use the graph of $y = f(x)$ given to draw neat sketches of:

a $y = 2f(x)$ **b** $y = f(x) + 2$

c $y = f(x - 2)$ **d** $y = f(x + 2)$

e $y = -f(x)$ **f** $y = f(-x)$

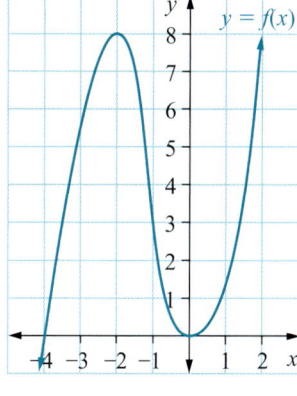

3 Determine whether the following functions are symmetrical about the y-axis.

a $f(x) = 2x^{10}$ **b** $f(x) = x^3 - x + 1$ **c** $f(x) = x^4 - x^2$

4 State whether or not the following are polynomials.

a $x + \sqrt{x} + 1$ **b** $\frac{1}{2}x^3 - \frac{2}{3}x^2 + \frac{4}{5}x - \frac{1}{4}$ **c** $3x + \frac{3}{x}$ **d** 14

5 For each of the following polynomials state:

   i the degree   **ii** the leading term   **iii** the leading coefficient

   iv the constant term   **v** whether or not the polynomial is monic.

a $1 - x + x^2 - 2x^3$ **b** $x^4 - 6x^2 + 3$

6 Given $P(x) = 4x^3 + x^2 - 5x + 7$ and $Q(x) = 3x^3 - 7x^2 - 11x - 12$ find:

a $P(x) + Q(x)$ **b** $P(x) - Q(x)$

7 The degree of $P(x) + Q(x)$ equals the degree of $P(x)$ plus the degree of $Q(x)$. This statement is true:

A never   **B** sometimes   **C** always

8 Given $P(x) = x - 2$ and $Q(x) = 3x^3 - 4x^2 + 9x - 3$, find:

a $P(x) \times Q(x)$

b $Q(x) \div P(x)$ Express the result in the form $Q(x) = P(x) \times A(x) + R$.

9 **a** Find the remainder when $2x^3 + 11x^2 - 8x + 3$ is divided by $x + 2$.

   b When $P(x) = x^3 - kx^2 + 4x - 3$ is divided by $x - 1$, the remainder is 10. Find k.

10 **a** Show that $(x + 3)$ is a factor of $P(x) = x^3 - 13x - 12$.

   b Hence find all the linear factors of $P(x)$.

   c State the zeros of $y = P(x)$.

   d Draw a neat sketch of $y = P(x)$

11 Sketch the following polynomials.

a $y = x^2(x - 2)^3$ **b** $y = -x^3(x + 1)^2$

1 On the same diagram, draw neat sketches of:

a **i** $y = x^5$ **ii** $y = 2x^5$ **iii** $y = \frac{1}{3}x^5$ **iv** $y = -x^5$

b **i** $y = x^5$ **ii** $y = x^5 + 3$ **iii** $y = x^5 - 3$

c **i** $y = x^5$ **ii** $y = (x - 2)^5$ **iii** $y = (x + 2)^5$

d **i** $y = x^5$ **ii** $y = 3x^5 - 1$

e **i** $y = x^5$ **ii** $y = (x - 1)^5 + 2$

f **i** $y = x^5$ **ii** $y = -(x + 1)^5 - 3$ **iii** $y = -\frac{1}{2}(x + 1)^5 - 3$

2 Use the graph of $y = f(x)$ given to draw neat sketches of:

a $y = 2f(x)$ **b** $y = f(x) + 2$

c $y = f(x - 2)$ **d** $y = f(x + 2)$

e $y = -f(x)$ **f** $y = f(-x)$

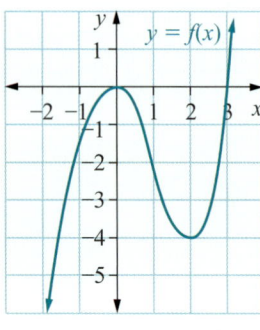

3 Determine whether the following functions are symmetrical about the y-axis.

a $f(x) = 4x^2$ **b** $y = -3x^4$ **c** $y = x^4 - 3x^2$

4 State whether or not the following are polynomials.

a $\frac{5}{8}x^2 - \frac{3}{5}x + \frac{2}{3}$ **b** $x + \frac{1}{\sqrt{x}}$ **c** $\frac{1}{x^3 + x^2 - x - 1}$ **d** 21

5 For each of the following polynomials state:

  i the degree   **ii** the leading term   **iii** the leading coefficient

  iv the constant term   **v** whether or not the polynomial is monic.

a $x^4 + 3x^2 - 1$ **b** $1 - 2x + 3x^2 - 4x^3$

6 Given $P(x) = x^4 + 3x^3 - 2x^2 + 3x - 11$ and $Q(x) = -2x^3 + x^2 - 4x + 10$ find:

a $P(x) + Q(x)$ **b** $P(x) - Q(x)$

7 The degree of $P(x) \times Q(x)$ equals the degree of $P(x)$ multiplied by the degree of $Q(x)$.

This statement is true:

A never   **B** sometimes   **C** always

8 Given $P(x) = x + 3$ and $Q(x) = x^3 - 12x^2 + 5x - 3$, find:

a $P(x) \times Q(x)$

b $Q(x) \div P(x)$ Express the result in the form $Q(x) = P(x) \times A(x) + R$.

9 **a** Find the remainder when $P(x) = 2x^3 - x^2 + x - 4$ is divided by $x + 3$.

  b When $P(x) = kx^3 - 2x^2 + 2x - 1$ is divided by $(x + 2)$, the remainder is 1. Find k.

10 **a** Show that $x + 3$ is a factor of $P(x) = x^3 - 2x^2 - 9x + 18$.

  b Hence find all the linear factors of $P(x)$.

  c State the zeros of $y = P(x)$.

  d Draw a neat sketch of $y = P(x)$.

11 Sketch the following polynomials.

a $y = (x + 2)^2(x - 1)^2$ **b** $y = (x + 1)^3(x - 3)^2$

16

Circle geometry

This chapter deals with applying reasoning to prove circle theorems and to solve problems.

After completing this chapter you should be able to:

▶ identify and name parts of a circle

▶ use terminology associated with angles in circles

▶ identify the arc on which an angle at the centre or the circumference stands

▶ demonstrate that at any point on a circle there is a unique tangent and that this tangent is perpendicular to the radius at the point of contact

▶ prove and apply theorems involving chord, angle, tangent and secant properties of circles.

NSW Syllabus references: 5.3 M&G Circle geometry
Outcomes: MA5.3-1WM, MA5.3-2WM, MA5.3-3WM, MA5.3-17MG
Measurement & geometry – ACMMG272

Diagnostic test

1 This diagram shows:

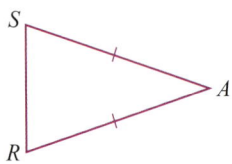

- **A** line *J*
- **B** interval *J*
- **C** line *JK*
- **D** interval *JK*

2 This diagram shows:

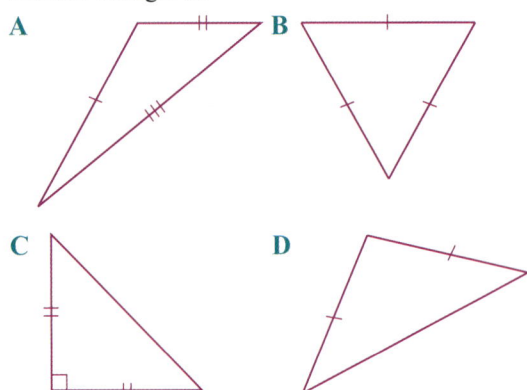

- **A** △*SAR*
- **B** an isosceles triangle
- **C** a triangle with two equal sides
- **D** all of the above

3 The diagram that shows an obtuse-angled scalene triangle is:

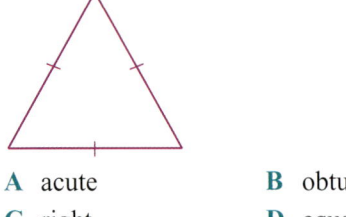

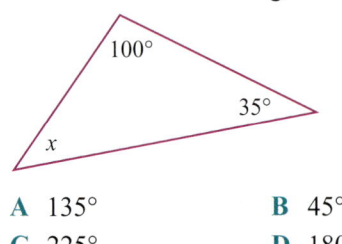

4 The angle name for this triangle is:

- **A** acute
- **B** obtuse
- **C** right
- **D** equal

5 The value of *x* in the diagram is:

- **A** 135°
- **B** 45°
- **C** 225°
- **D** 180°

6 The value of *y* in the diagram is:

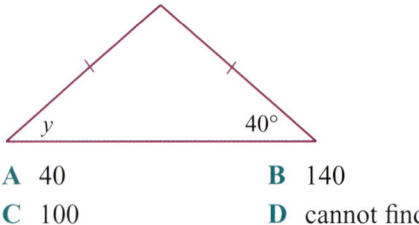

- **A** 40
- **B** 140
- **C** 100
- **D** cannot find

7 The value of *z* in the diagram is:

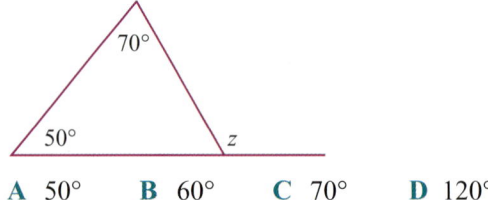

- **A** 50°
- **B** 60°
- **C** 70°
- **D** 120°

8 A convex quadrilateral has:
- **A** all sides equal
- **B** all angles equal
- **C** all diagonals inside the figure
- **D** all of the above properties

9 A quadrilateral with equal diagonals is a:
- **A** rhombus
- **B** rectangle
- **C** parallelogram
- **D** kite

10 A quadrilateral with adjacent sides equal is a:
- **A** rhombus
- **B** rectangle
- **C** parallelogram
- **D** trapezium

11 The value of *a* in this diagram is:

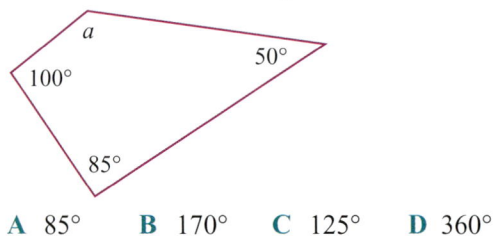

- **A** 85°
- **B** 170°
- **C** 125°
- **D** 360°

12 A quadrilateral with more than one axis of symmetry is a:
- **A** rhombus
- **B** parallelogram
- **C** trapezium
- **D** kite

13 The only difference between two congruent figures is:
- **A** angle size
- **B** side length
- **C** area
- **D** orientation

MEASUREMENT & GEOMETRY

14 The transformation that would not result in a pair of congruent figures is:

A rotating   B reflecting
C translating   D halving all sides

15 The polygon that does not give congruent shapes when cut along the dotted line is:

A    B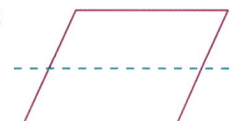

C 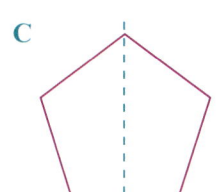   D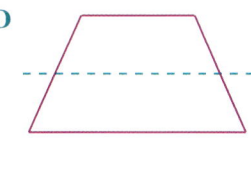

16 The correct congruence statement for these two triangles is:

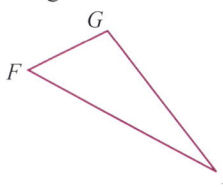 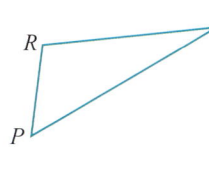

A $\triangle GDF \equiv \triangle PRT$ B $\triangle DGF \equiv \triangle TPR$
C $\triangle GDF \equiv \triangle RPT$ D $\triangle GDF \equiv \triangle RTP$

17 The single transformation that superimposes these two congruent figures is:

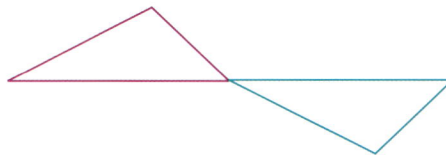

A reflection   B rotation
C translation   D none of these

18 The only property of two similar figures that is the same in both is:

A angle size   B side length
C area   D orientation

19 The similarity statement for these two similar figures is:

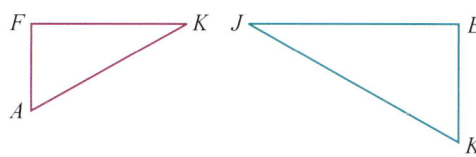

A $\triangle AFK \,|||\, \triangle JEK$ B $\triangle AFK \,|||\, \triangle JKE$
C $\triangle AFK \,|||\, \triangle KEJ$ D $\triangle AFK \,|||\, \triangle EKJ$

20 This pair of figures is similar. The scale factor and value of x are:

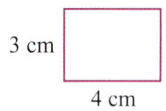   

A $k = 2, x = 6$ cm   B $k = 2, x = 3$ cm
C $k = 1\frac{1}{2}, x = 6$ cm   D $k = 1\frac{1}{2}, x = 3$ cm

21 This pair of figures is similar. The values of a and b are:

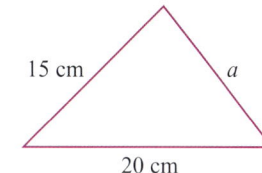   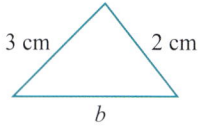

A $a = \frac{2}{5}, b = 100$ B $a = 10, b = 100$
C $a = \frac{2}{5}, b = 4$ D $a = 10, b = 4$

The diagnostic test questions refer to outcomes ACMMG220 and ACMMG221.

 **A** ## Circle terminology

Exercise 16A

1 a Draw diagrams and identify the following parts of a circle.

i radius	**ii** diameter	**iii** circumference	**iv** chord
v centre	**vi** minor arc	**vii** major arc	**viii** semicircle
ix minor sector	**x** major sector	**xi** secant	**xii** minor segment
xiii major segment	**xvi** tangent		

b Share your diagrams with others in the group and make a summary in your exercise book.

EXAMPLE 1

Given interval *AB* and point *P*, *A* is joined to *P* and *B* to *P* to form $\angle APB$.
$\angle APB$ is the angle subtended by the interval *AB* at the point *P*.
On a circle, mark the angle $\angle APB$ subtended by the chord *AB* at
the point *P*.

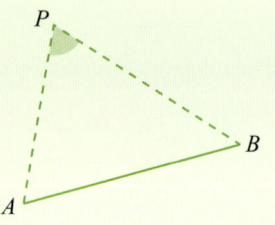

Solve	Think/Apply
	Draw a circle. Mark a chord *AB* and mark a point *P* on the circumference. Join *A* to *P* and *B* to *P* to form $\angle APB$. $\angle APB$ is the angle subtended by the chord *AB* at the point *P*. As *P* is also on the circumference we say that $\angle APB$ is an angle subtended by the chord *AB* at the circumference.

2 Name two angles subtended by:
a chord *AB* at the circumference
b chord *XY* at the circumference
c chord *AY* at the circumference
d chord *BX* at the circumference.

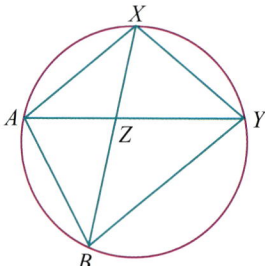

3 Copy this diagram. *O* is the centre of the circle. Draw and name the angle subtended at the centre by each of these chords.
a *AB*   **b** *CD*   **c** *EF*

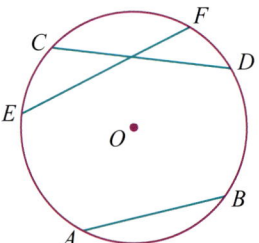

4 Name the chord that subtends each of these angles.

   a ∠EOD   **b** ∠CAB   **c** ∠ABC

   d ∠EFA   **e** ∠EDC

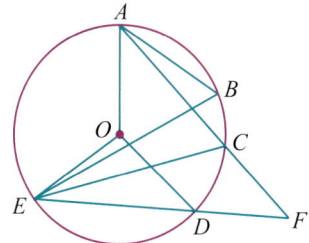

5 Name the angle subtended by the chord *AB* at the circumference in:

   a the major segment

   b the minor segment.

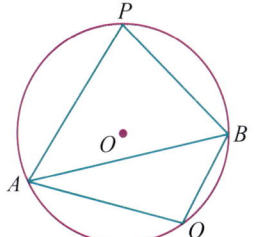

6 Name two angles subtended by the chord *XY* at the circumference in:

   a the major segment

   b the minor segment.

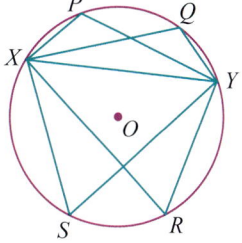

EXAMPLE 2

Draw a diagram of a circle and mark the angle at *P* standing on the arc *AB*. Also mark the angle at the centre *O* standing on the arc *AB*.

Solve	Think/Apply
	Draw a circle. Mark an arc *AB*, the centre *O* and a point *P* on the circumference. Draw ∠*APB* and ∠*AOB*. ∠*APB* is the angle at *P* standing on the arc *AB*. (This is the same as the angle subtended by the chord *AB* at *P*.) ∠*AOB* is the angle at the centre *O* standing on the arc *AB*. (This is the same as the angle subtended by the chord *AB* at *O*.)

---

7 **a** Name the angle at the centre subtended by the arc *PS*.

   b Name an angle at the circumference on the arc *PS*.

   c Name two angles standing on the arc *QR*.

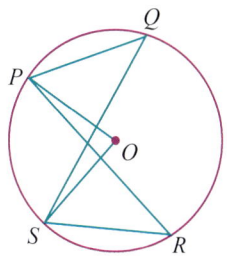

8 **a** Name two angles subtended at the circumference by the minor arc *AB*.

   b Name two angles standing on the major arc *AB*.

   c Name two angles in the same segment as ∠*AQB* and standing on the arc *AB*.

   d Name an angle in the same segment as ∠*ATB* and standing on the arc *AB*.

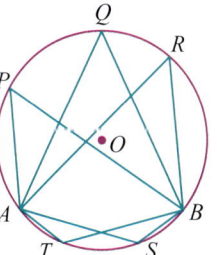

9 Identify the minor or major arc on which each of these angles stands.

   a $\angle BEC$ **b** $\angle EDC$ **c** $\angle ABE$

   d $\angle ECB$ **e** $\angle EDA$

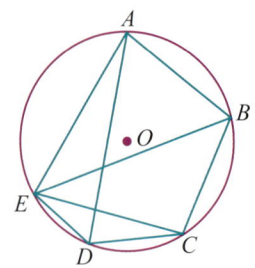

B Chord properties of a circle

Exercise 16B

1 **a** In a circle draw two chords, AB and CD, of the same length. Join the endpoints of each chord to the centre O, as shown on the right. Measure the angles AOB and COD.

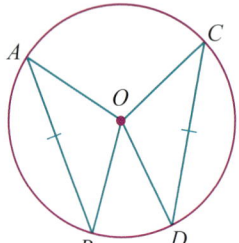

   b Using a set square, measure the distance of each chord from the centre.

   c Compare your results with those of the rest of the class.

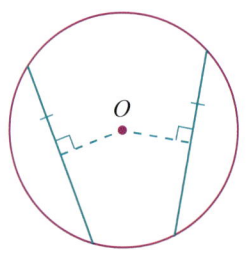

2 Complete the following proofs.

   a *Data:* $AB = CD$, O is the centre of the circle.

      Aim: To prove $\angle AOB = \angle COD$.

      Proof: In $\triangle AOB$ and $\triangle COD$:

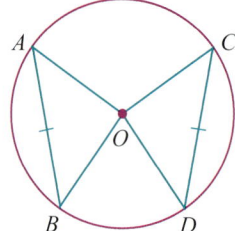

$$
\begin{aligned}
AB &= AC &&\text{(given)}\\
AO &= \underline{\ \ \ } &&(\underline{\ \ \ \ \ \ })\\
BO &= \underline{\ \ \ } &&(\underline{\ \ \ \ \ \ })\\
\therefore \triangle AOB &\equiv \triangle COD &&(\underline{\ \ \ \ \ \ })\\
\text{Hence } \angle AOB &= \underline{\ \ \ } &&(\underline{\ \ \ \ \ \ })
\end{aligned}
$$

    Also $\angle ABO = \angle CDO$ (Matching angles in congruent $\triangle$s are equal.)

            We will need this in part **b**.

   b *Data:* $AB = CD$, and OP and OQ are perpendiculars from O to AB and CD respectively.

      Aim: To prove $OP = OQ$.

      Proof: In $\triangle OPB$ and $\triangle OQD$:

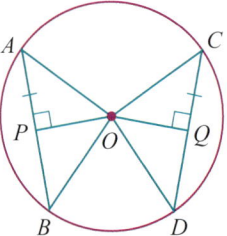

$$
\begin{aligned}
\angle OPB &= \angle OQD = 90° &&\text{(given)}\\
\angle OBP &= \underline{\ \ \ } &&\text{(from part }\mathbf{a})\\
BO &= \underline{\ \ \ } &&(\underline{\ \ \ \ \ \ })\\
\therefore \triangle OPB &\equiv \triangle OQD &&(\underline{\ \ \ \ \ \ })\\
\therefore OP &= OQ &&(\underline{\ \ \ \ \ \ })
\end{aligned}
$$

    From parts **a** and **b** we can conclude that:

    Chords of equal length in a circle subtend equal angles at the centre and are equidistant from the centre.

3 Draw any chord *AB* in a circle with centre *O*. Using a set square, draw the perpendicular *OP* from *O* to the chord *AB*. Measure the lengths of *AP* and *PB*. Compare your results with the class.

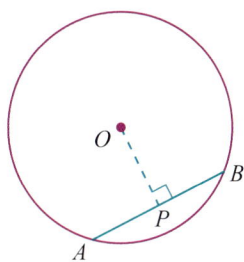

4 a *O* is the centre of a circle and *OP* ⊥ chord *AB*.

    i Prove that △*OAP* ≡ △*OBP*.

    ii Hence deduce that *PA* = *PB*; that is, prove the following.

    The perpendicular drawn from the centre of a circle to a chord bisects the chord.

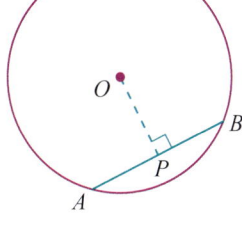

b Prove the converse of the theorem in part **a**; that is, given *M* is the midpoint of chord *AB*, prove that *OM* ⊥ chord *AB*.

    The line from the centre of a circle to the midpoint of a chord is perpendicular to the chord.

c From parts **a** and **b** it follows that *O*, the centre of the circle, is on the perpendicular bisector of the chord *AB*.

    The perpendicular bisector a chord passes through the centre of the circle.

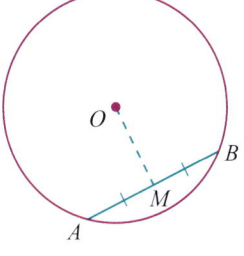

5 a *P* is a point on the perpendicular bisector of *AB*.

    i Prove △*APM* ≡ △*BPM*.

    ii *PA* = *PB*

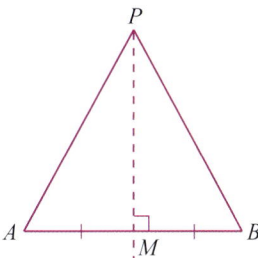

b Complete the following.

    Data: *A*, *B* and *C* are three non-collinear points. *PQ* and *MN* are the perpendicular bisectors of *AB* and *BC* respectively. *X* is the point of intersection of *PQ* and *MN*.

    Aim: To prove that *X* is the centre of the circle that passes through *A*, *B* and *C*.

    Proof: As *X* is on the perpendicular bisectors of *AB* and *BC*, then *XA* = ___ and *XB* = ___; that is, *XA* = ___ = ___.

    ∴ *A*, *B*, *C* are equidistant from ___ so *X* is the centre of the circle that passes through ___.

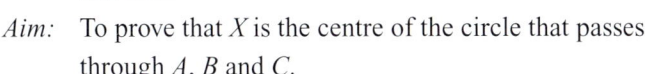

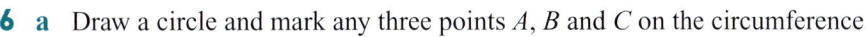

Given any three non-collinear points, the point of intersection of the perpendicular bisectors of any two sides of the triangle formed by the three points is the centre of a circle through all three points.

6 a Draw a circle and mark any three points *A*, *B* and *C* on the circumference.

b Construct the perpendicular bisectors of *AB* and *BC*.

c Mark the position of *O*, the centre of the circle.

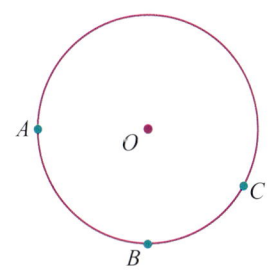

7 Draw these circles and, by construction, find the centre of each.

  a circle of radius 1.5 cm   **b** circle of radius 2 cm

8 Draw any two intersecting circles. Join the centres *P* and *Q*.
Draw the common chord *AB*.

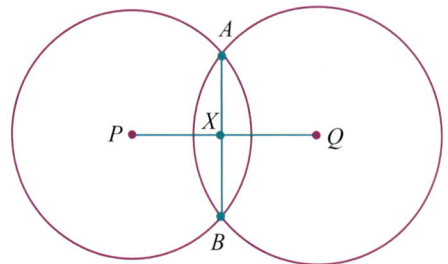

  a Measure the lengths of *XA* and *XB*.
  b Measure the angle *AXQ*.
  c Discuss your results with the class.

9 *Data: P and Q are the centres of the circles. AB is the common
     chord. X is the point of intersection of PQ and AB.*
  a **i** Prove that △*PAQ* ≡ △*PBQ*.
     ii List all the equal angles in these two triangles.
  b **i** Prove that △*XAQ* ≡ △*XBQ*.
     ii Hence prove that *XA* = *XB* and ∠*AXQ* = ∠*BXQ* = 90°.

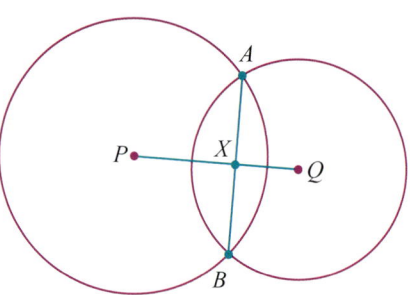

  ***When two circles intersect, the line joining their centres
  bisects their common chord at right angles.***

C Using chord properties

EXAMPLE 1

Find the value of the pronumerals.

a 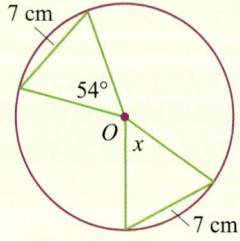   **b** 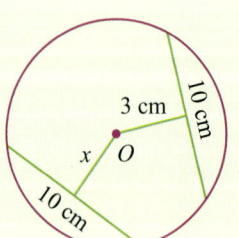   **c**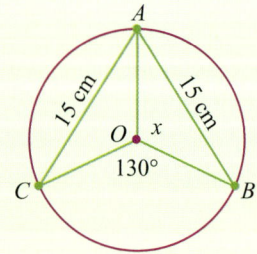

	Solve	Think	Apply
a	$x = 54°$	Equal chords subtend equal angles at the centre.	Examine all the data and determine the appropriate theorem.
b	$x = 3$ cm	Equal chords are equidistant from the centre.	
c	$\angle AOC = x$ $x + x + 130° = 360°$ $\therefore x = 115°$	Equal chords subtend equal angles at the centre. Angles at a point add to 360°.	

MEASUREMENT & GEOMETRY

Exercise 16C

1 Find the values of the pronumerals in these circles. O is the centre.

a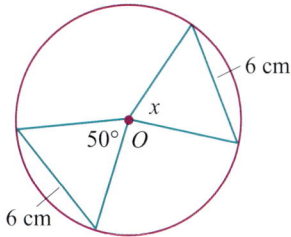

b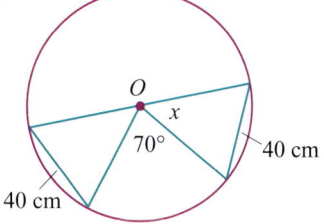

c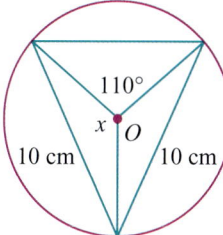

d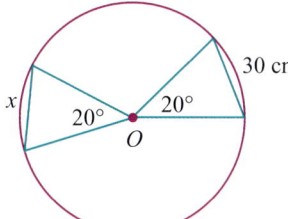

e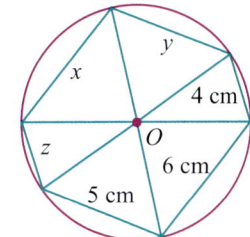

f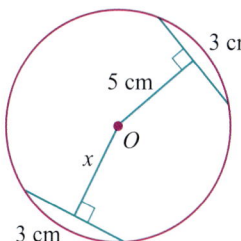

g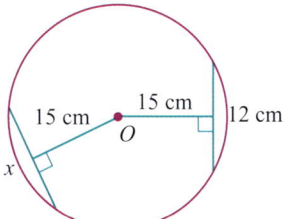

h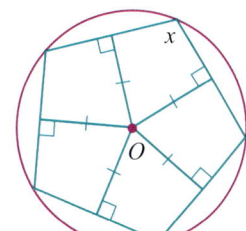

i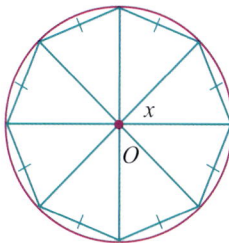

j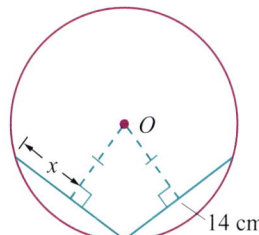

k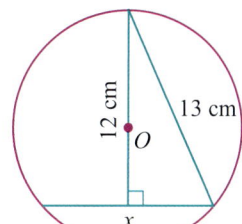

l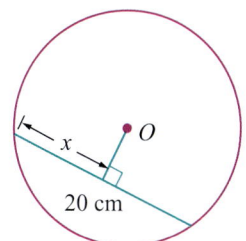

EXAMPLE 2

P and Q are the centres of circles. $\angle PAX = 60°$, $AX = 5$ cm and $XQ = 12$ cm. Find the value of the pronumerals.

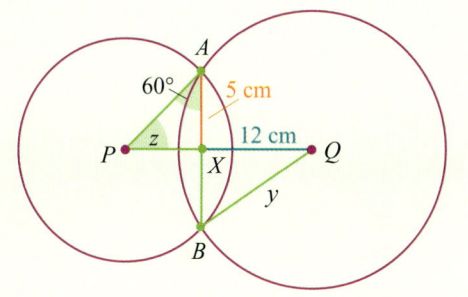

Solve	Think	Think/Apply
$\angle AXP = 90°$ $\therefore z = 30°$ $XB = XA = 5$ cm $y^2 = 5^2 + 12^2 = 169$ $\therefore y = 13$ cm	The line joining the centres of intersecting circles bisects the common chord at right angles. Angle sum of a triangle $= 180°$. Pythagoras' theorem	When looking for sides check to see if the triangle is right-angled.

2 In the diagrams below, P and Q are the centres of the circles. Find the values of the pronumerals.

a

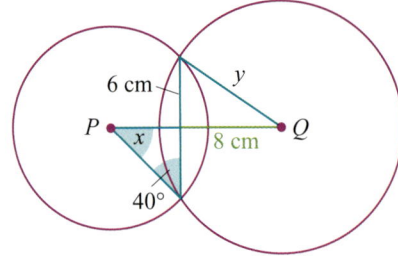

b

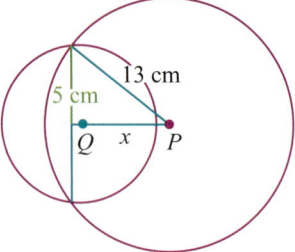

3 In the circle on the right, $AN = 18$ cm and $NB = 8$ cm. Find the length of PQ.

4 The figure shows two concentric circles, centre O. $OL = 13$ cm, $OK = 15$ cm and $LM = 10$ cm. Find KN.

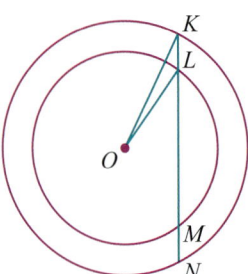

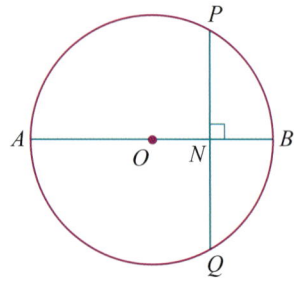

5 A hemispherical bowl has a diameter of 10 cm. Water is poured into the bowl until its surface is 3 cm below the top of the bowl as shown. Find the diameter of the water surface.

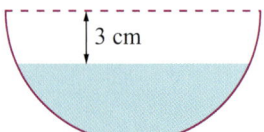

6 OP is perpendicular to the chord AB. If $AB = 14$ cm and $PQ = 1$ cm, find the radius of the circle.

7 If a chord of length 100 mm is 120 mm from the centre of a circle, find the radius of the circle.

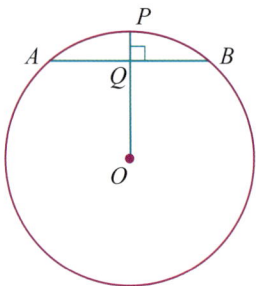

8 A chord 8 cm long is drawn in a circle of radius 6 cm. What is the distance of the chord from the centre?

D Angle properties of a circle

Exercise 16D

O is the centre of the circle in all diagrams.

1 Consider the following diagrams.
  i State the size of the angle at the circumference standing on the arc AB ($\angle ACB$).
  ii Find the size of the angle at the centre standing on the arc AB ($\angle AOB$).

a

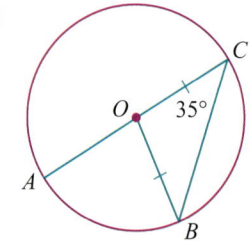

b

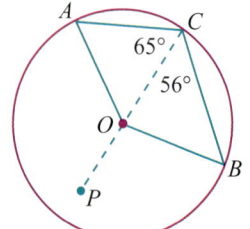

c

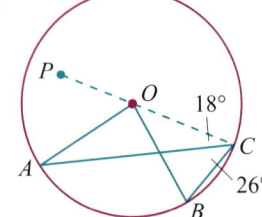

2 a Draw a circle and mark the position of the centre O and any three points A, B and P on the circumference, as shown.

b Measure the size of the angle subtended at the centre by the arc AB.

c Measure the angle subtended at P by the arc AB.

d Discuss your results with the class.

3 Complete the following general proofs.

a *Data:* O is the centre of the circle.

Aim: To prove $\angle AOB = 2 \times \angle ACB$.

Proof: Let $\angle ACO = x$ and $\angle OCB = y$.

In $\triangle AOC$:

$$\angle OAC = \angle OCA \qquad (_____)$$
$$= x$$

Now $\angle POA = \_\_\_ + \_\_\_$ (Exterior angle of a $\triangle$ equals the sum of interior opposite angles.)

$$= 2x$$

Similarly $\angle POB = 2y$

$$\therefore \angle AOB = 2x + 2y$$
$$= 2(\_\_\_)$$
$$= 2 \times \angle ACB$$

The angle at the centre of a circle is double the angle at the circumference, standing on the same arc.

b *Data:* O is the centre of the circle.

Aim: To prove $\angle AOB = 2 \times \angle ACB$.

Proof: Let $\angle ACO = x$ and $\angle OCB = y$.

Show that $\angle POA = 2x$ and $\angle POB = 2y$.

Now $\angle AOB = \angle POB - \angle POA$

$$= \_\_\_$$
$$= 2(y - x)$$

But $\angle ACB = \_\_\_$

$$\therefore \angle AOB = 2 \times \angle ACB$$

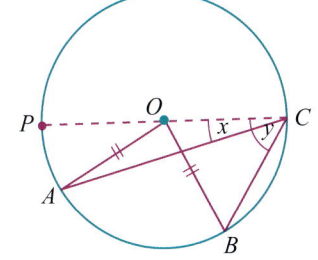

The angle at the centre of a circle is double the angle at the circumference, standing on the same arc.

● EXAMPLE 1

Find x using the results from question **3**.

a

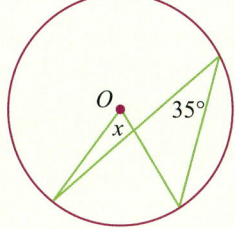

b

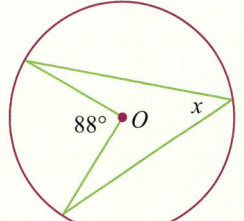

c

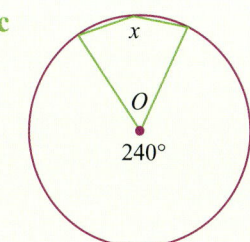

	Solve	Think/Apply
a	$x = 2 \times 35° = 70°$	The angle at the centre is double the angle at the circumference, standing on the same arc.
b	$88° = 2 \times x$ $\quad x - 44°$	
c	$240° = 2 \times x$ $\quad x = 120°$	

4 Find *x* using the results of question **3**.

a
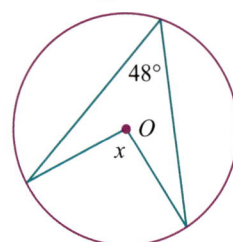

b
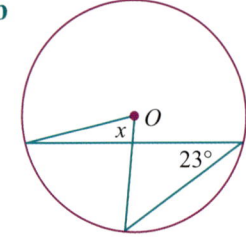

c
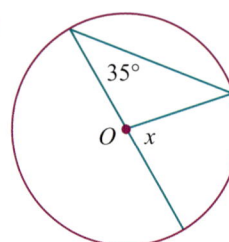

d
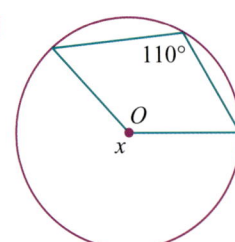

e
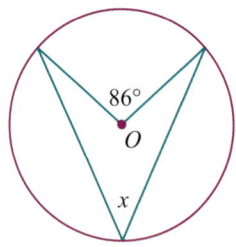

f
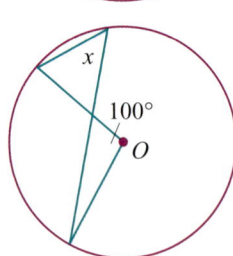

5 Find *x* in each of the following diagrams. Give reasons for your answers.

a
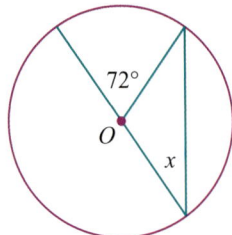

b
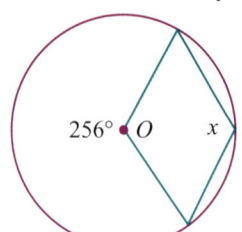

c
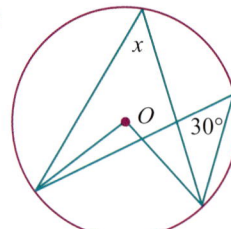

d
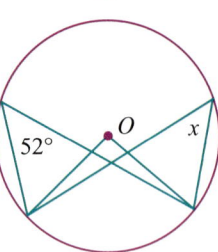

e
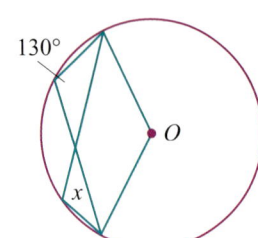

f
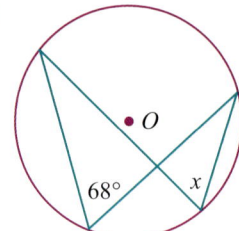

6 a Draw a circle and mark the position of any four points *A*, *B*, *P* and *Q* as shown.

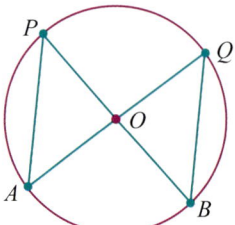

   i Measure the angle subtended at *P* by the arc *AB*.

   ii Measure the angle subtended at *Q* by the arc *AB*.

   iii Discuss your results with the class.

b Complete the following proof.

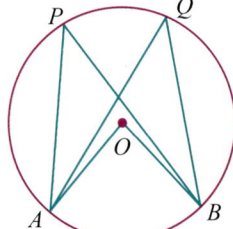

Data: *O* is the centre of the circle.

Aim: To prove $\angle APB = \angle AQB$.

Proof: $\angle APB = \frac{1}{2} \times \angle AOB$ (_____)

$\angle AQB = \frac{1}{2} \times$ ____   (_____)

$\therefore \angle APB = \angle AQB$

Angles at the circumference of a circle, standing on the same arc, are equal.

This result is often stated as:

Angles in the same segment of a circle are equal.

EXAMPLE 2

Find the values of these pronumerals.

a
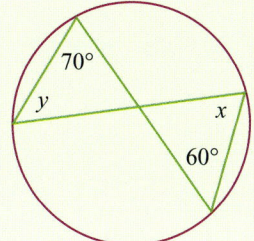

b
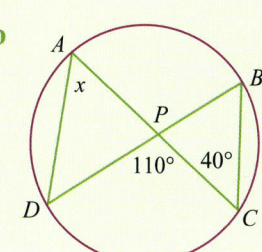

	Solve	Think	Apply
a	$x = 70°, y = 60°$	∠s in the same segment are equal.	This is often stated as angles at the circumference of a circle, standing on the same arc are equal.
b	$\angle ADB = 40°$ $\angle CPD = \angle PAD + \angle ADP$ $110° = x + 40°$ $\therefore x = 70°$	∠s in the same segment are equal. Exterior angle of △ = sum of interior opposite angles.	

7 Find the values of the pronumerals.

a
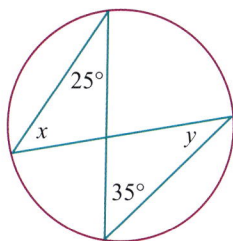

b
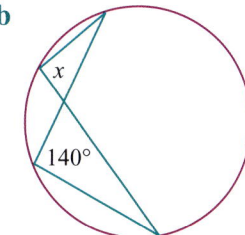

c
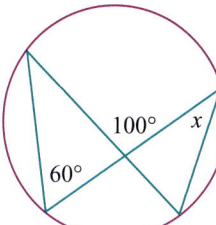

d
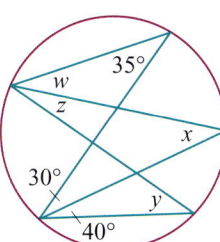

e
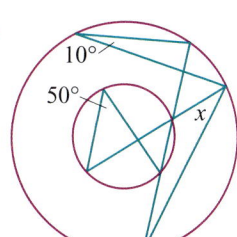

f
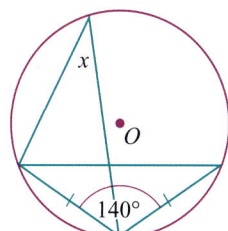

8 a In a circle draw a diameter AB. Join the endpoints of AB to any point P on the circumference. Measure the size of $\angle APB$.

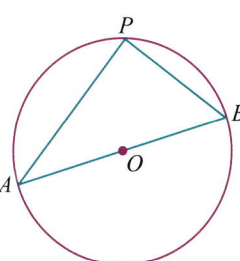

b **i** Name the angle at the centre standing on the arc AB.
ii What is the size of this angle?
iii Name the angle at the circumference standing on the arc AB.
iv State the size of this angle.

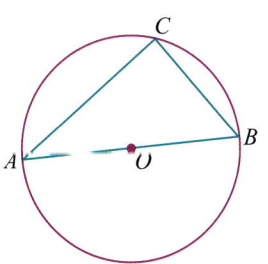

MEASUREMENT & GEOMETRY

c Complete the following proof.

Data: AB is a diameter and O is the centre.

Aim: To prove $\angle ACB = 90°$.

Proof: $\angle AOB = 2 \times \angle ACB$ (_____)

But $\angle AOB = $ ___ °   (_____)

     $2 \times \angle ACB = $ ___ °

       $\therefore \angle ACB = 90°$

The angle in a semicircle is a right angle.

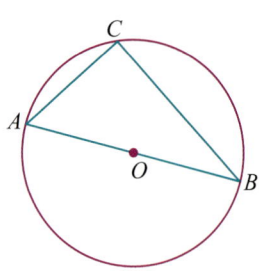

d Prove the above theorem using the properties of isosceles triangles. Let $\angle OAC = x$ and $\angle OBC = y$.

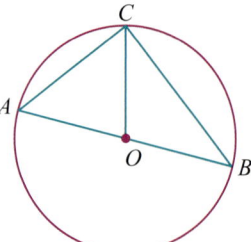

● EXAMPLE 3

Find the values of these pronumerals.

a

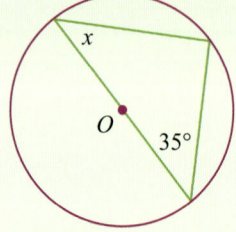

b

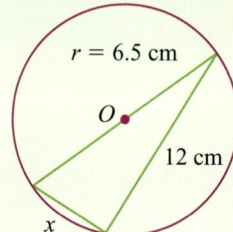

Solve	Think/Apply
a $x + 35° + 90° = 180°$ $x = 55°$	Look for a right angle. The angle in a semicircle is a right angle.

b $x^2 + 12^2 = 13^2$
    $x^2 + 144 = 169$
         $x^2 = 25$
        $x = 5$ cm	

9 Find the values of the pronumerals.

a

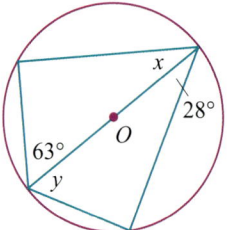

b

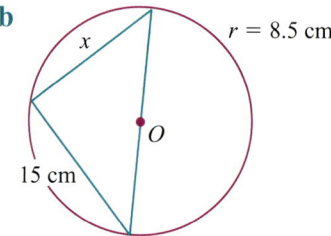

10 a Draw a circle using a template.

   b Use a set square to find the end points of a diameter and draw the diameter.

   c Repeat part **b** to find another diameter and hence the centre of the circle.

   d Explain why the method is valid.

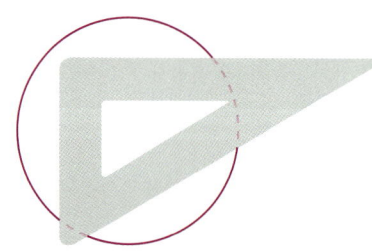

MEASUREMENT & GEOMETRY

11 a Join any four points A, B, C and D that lie on the circumference of a circle to form a quadrilateral.

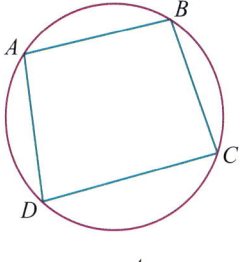

  i Measure the size of all the interior angles of the quadrilateral.

  ii What do you notice about the sum of these angles?

  $\angle BAD$ and $\angle BCD$

  $\angle ABC$ and $\angle ADC$

  iii Discuss your results with the class.

b Giving reasons, find the size of:

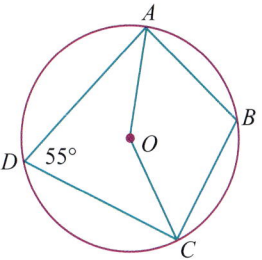

  i $\angle AOC$ **ii** reflex $\angle AOC$

  iii $\angle ABC$ **iv** $\angle ADC + \angle ABC$

  v $\angle DAB + \angle DCB$

Concyclic points are points through which a circle can be drawn. Any three non-collinear points are concyclic (see Exercise 16B, question **5**).

If the four vertices of a quadrilateral lie on a circle then it is known as a **cyclic quadrilateral**.

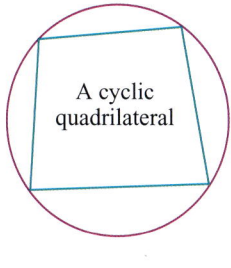

A cyclic quadrilateral

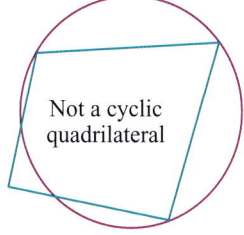

Not a cyclic quadrilateral

c Complete the following proof.

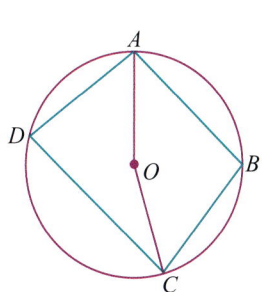

Data: $ABCD$ is a cyclic quadrilateral.

Aim: **i** To prove $\angle ADC + \angle ABC = 180°$.

     ii To prove $\angle DAB + \angle DCB = 180°$.

Proof: **i** $\angle AOC = 2 \times \angle ADC$ (_____)

        reflex $\angle AOC = 2 \times$ ___   (_____)

But $\angle AOC +$ reflex $\angle AOC =$ ___   (_____)

   $2 \times (\angle ADC + \angle ABC) = 360°$

     $\therefore \angle ADC + \angle ABC =$ ___

   ii $\angle ABC + \angle BCD + \angle CDA + \angle DAB = 360°$ (_____)

       $\therefore \angle BCD + \angle DAB + 180° = 360°$ (using the result from part **i**)

         $\angle BCD + \angle DAB =$ ___

The opposite angles of a cyclic quadrilateral are supplementary.

● EXAMPLE 4

Find the values of the pronumerals.

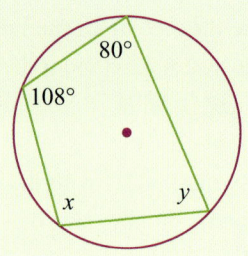

Solve	Think/Apply
$x + 80° = 180°$ $x = 100°$ $y + 108° = 180°$ $y = 72°$	Opposite angles of a cyclic quadrilateral are supplementary.

12 Find the values of the pronumerals.

a
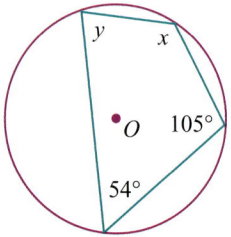

b
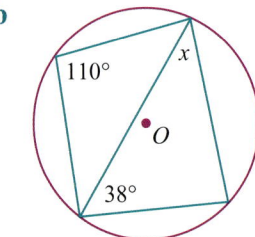

13 a Draw a cyclic quadrilateral *ABCD* and produce *DC* to *E*.
  i Measure angles *DAB* and *BCE*.
  ii Discuss your results with the class.

b Find the value of *x* and *y*.
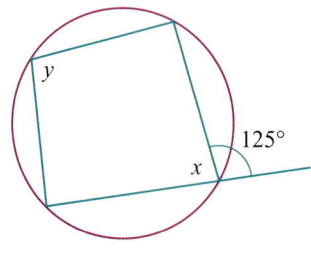

c Complete the following proof.
  Data: *ABCD* is a cyclic quadrilateral. *CB* is produced to *P*.
  Aim: To prove $\angle ABP = \angle ADC$.
  Proof: Let $\angle ABP = x$
    $\angle ABC = $ ___   (*CBP* is a straight line.)
    $\angle ADC = $ ___   (_____)
    $\therefore \angle ABP = \angle ADC$

  An exterior angle at a vertex of a cyclic quadrilateral is equal to the interior opposite angle.

EXAMPLE 5

Find the values of the pronumerals.

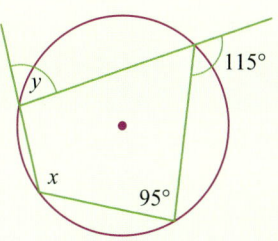

Solve	Think	Think/Apply
$x = 115°$	The exterior angle of a cyclic quadrilateral	Make sure the quadrilateral
$y = 95°$	equals the interior opposite angle.	is cyclic.

14 Find the value of x.

a

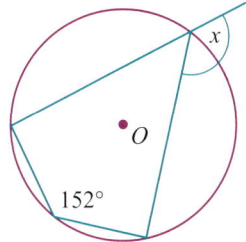

b

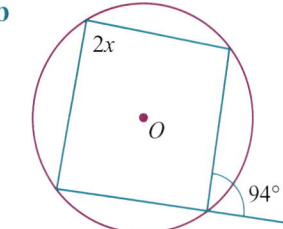

15 Find the values of the pronumerals.

a

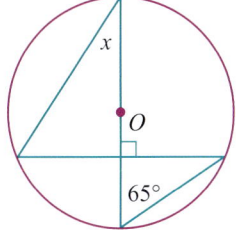

b

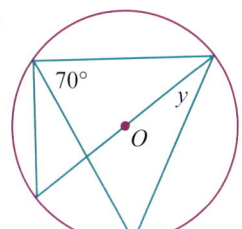

c

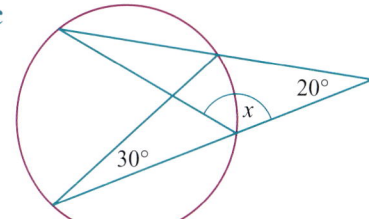

d

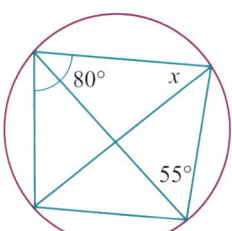

e

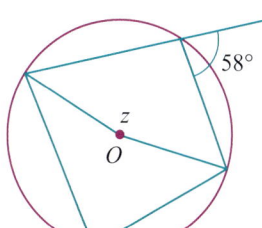

f

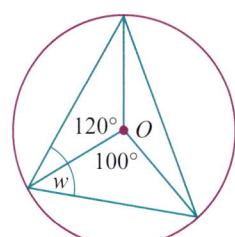

g

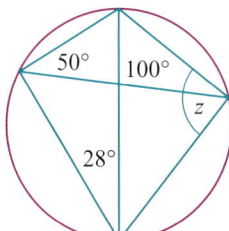

h

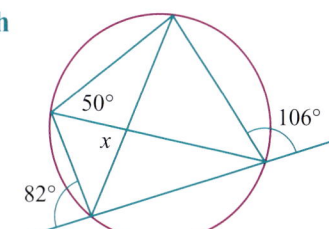

i

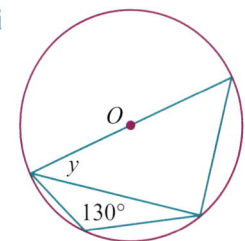

16 a Complete the following proof.

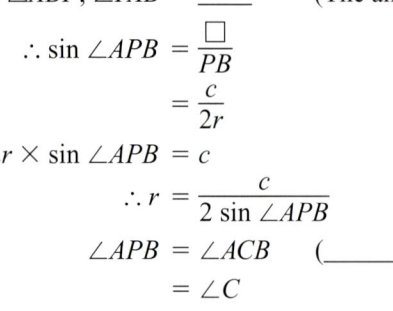

Data: O is the centre of the circumcircle of $\triangle ABC$. Let $OB = r$.

Using the usual triangle notation, let the lengths $AB = c$,

$BC = a$ and $CA = b$.

Construction: Draw the diameter BOP and join AP.

Aim: To find the radius, r, of the circumcircle.

Proof: In $\triangle ABP$, $\angle PAB = $ _____   (The angle in a semicircle is a right angle.)

$$\therefore \sin \angle APB = \frac{\square}{PB}$$

$$= \frac{c}{2r}$$

$$\therefore 2r \times \sin \angle APB = c$$

$$\therefore r = \frac{c}{2 \sin \angle APB}$$

But $\angle APB = \angle ACB$ (_____)

$$= \angle C$$

$$\therefore r = \frac{c}{2 \sin C}$$

b Use $\triangle BCP$ to show that $r = \dfrac{a}{2 \sin A}$

c Draw diameter AOQ and show that $r = \dfrac{b}{2 \sin B}$

d Use parts **a**, **b** and **c** to derive the sine rule for any triangle ABC.

Extension

Questions **17** and **18** are examples of what is known as an **indirect proof**. In an indirect proof we assume the conclusion to be false and show that this assumption leads to a contradiction. Hence the original conclusion must be true.

17 a *Data: ABCD* is a quadrilateral in which the opposite angles are supplementary.

Aim: To prove that A, B, C and D lie on a circle (i.e. *ABCD* is a cyclic quadrilateral).

Construction: A circle can be drawn through any three non-collinear points, so we draw the circle through A, B and C and *assume that D does not lie on this circle*. Two cases arise:

Case 1

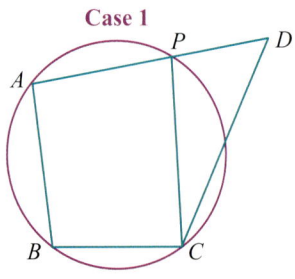

D outside circle

Case 2

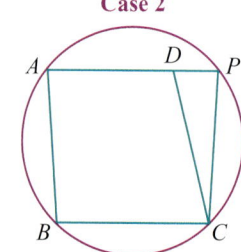

D inside circle

Read and discuss the following proof for case 1. When you understand all the concepts involved complete the proof for case 2.

Case 1: Let P be the point where the circle cuts AD and let $\angle ABC = x$.

Proof: $\angle ADC = 180° - x$ (given)

$\angle APC = 180° - x$ (Opposite angles of a cyclic quadrilateral are supplementary.)

$\therefore \angle ADC = \angle APC$

But $\angle APC = \angle ADC + \angle DCP$ (Exterior angle of a $\triangle$ equals the sum of interior opposite angles.)

$\therefore \angle ADC = \angle ADC + \angle DCP$

This is impossible and thus the original assumption that D does not lie on the circle is false; that is, A, B, C and D are concyclic points.

Case 2: Let *P* be the point where the circle cuts *AD* produced and let ∠*ABC* = *x*.

Complete the proof. We have proved that:

If the opposite angles of a quadrilateral are supplementary, then the quadrilateral is cyclic.

b Determine whether or not the following quadrilaterals are cyclic. Give reasons for your answer.

i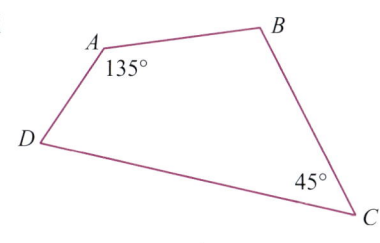

ii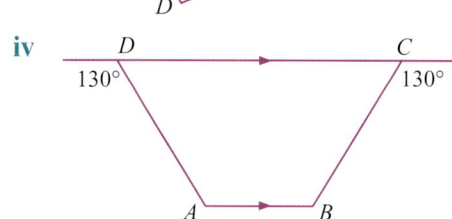

iii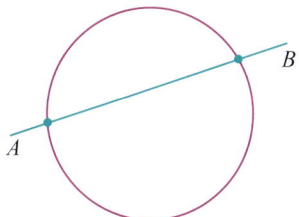

iv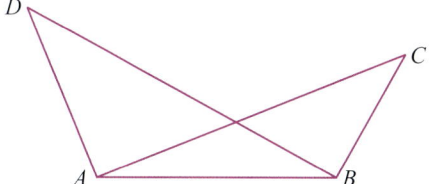

c Which of the special quadrilaterals can always have a circle drawn through their vertices?

18 Use the method of indirect proof to prove the following.
If an interval subtends equal angles at two points on the same side of the interval, then the two points and the two endpoints of the interval are concyclic; that is, if ∠*ADB* = ∠*ACB* then *ABCD* is a cyclic quadrilateral.

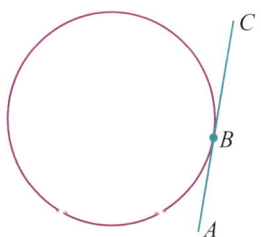

E Tangents and secants

A **secant** is a straight line that intersects a circle at two distinct points. For example, *AB* is a secant.

A **tangent** is a straight line that intersects (or touches) a circle at one point only. For example, *ABC* is a tangent.

The point of intersection, *B*, is called the **point of contact** of the tangent with the circle. Only one tangent can be drawn through a given point on a circle.

Exercise 16E

1 a Draw a circle and a radius *OB*. At *B* draw the tangent *ABC*. Measure the size of ∠*OBC*.

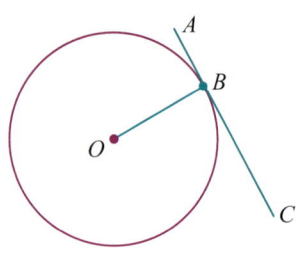

b Draw any tangent *PQR* to a circle. Join the centre to the point of contact. Measure the size of ∠*OQR*.

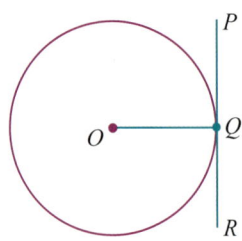

From question **1** we infer that:

A tangent to a circle is perpendicular to the radius drawn to the point of contact.

● EXAMPLE 1

PT is a tangent to the circle. *O* is the centre. Find the values of the pronumerals.

a

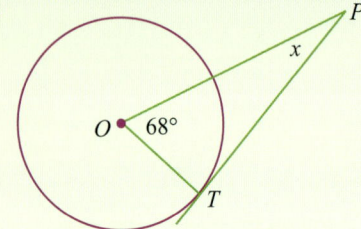

b

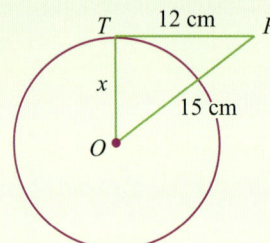

	Solve	Think	Apply
a	$x + 68° + 90° = 180°$ $x = 22°$	A tangent to a circle is perpendicular to the radius drawn to the point of contact.	Although there are many theorems resulting in right angles do not assume angles are 90°.
b	$x^2 + 12^2 = 15^2$ $x^2 + 144 = 225$ $x^2 = 81$ $x = 9$ cm		

2 *PT* is a tangent to the circle. *O* is the centre. Find the values of the pronumerals.

a

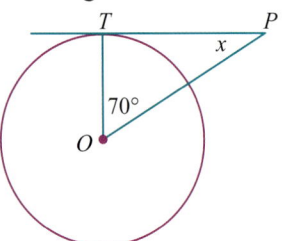

b

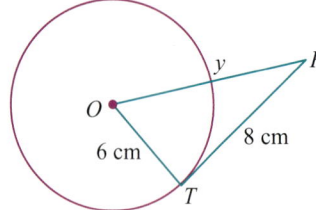

c

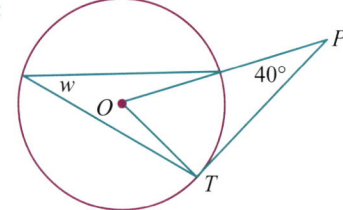

d

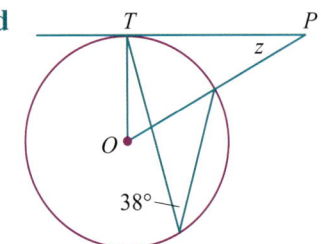

e

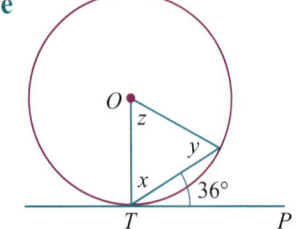

f

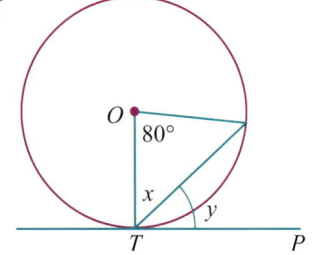

MEASUREMENT & GEOMETRY

g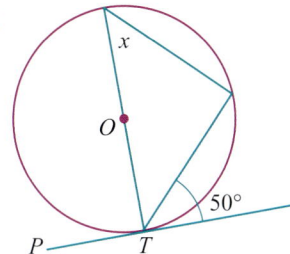

h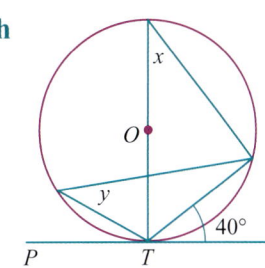

i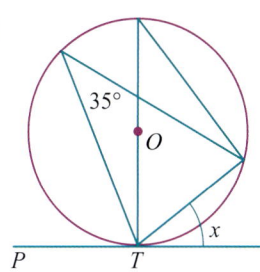

j The concentric circles with centre O have radii 6 cm and 8 cm. AB is a chord of the larger circle and a tangent to the smaller circle. Calculate the length of AB.

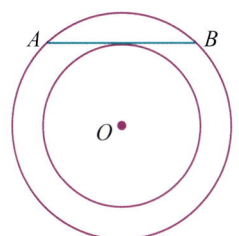

3 a Draw a circle of radius 30 mm. Mark the centre O and any point T on the circle. Using a straight edge and compasses only, construct the tangent at T.

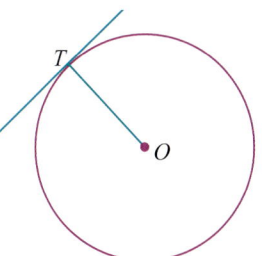

b Draw a circle of radius 30 mm and mark the centre O. Using a set square, draw all the tangents to the circle from an external point P.

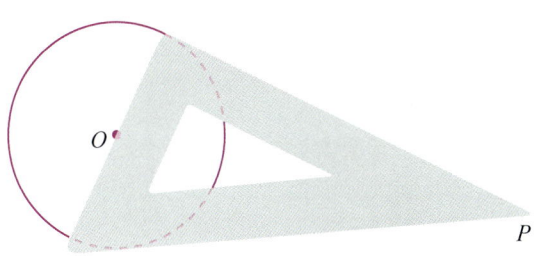

c i Draw a circle of radius 30 mm and mark the centre O. Mark any external point P. Bisect OP at M and draw the circle with centre M and radius $= MO$. Draw PT and explain why it is a tangent. Draw the other tangent from P.

  ii Draw a circle with centre O. Use the method of part **i** to construct the tangents to this circle from any external point.

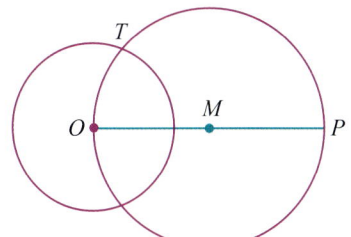

d Draw a circle using a template. Find the centre of the circle using tangents. Explain how your method works.

e Draw a circle of radius 25 mm. Construct the smallest square that contains this circle.

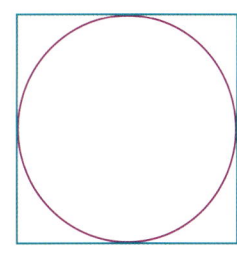

f Draw any line AB and mark a point O above the line. Construct a circle with centre O such that AB is a tangent to this circle.

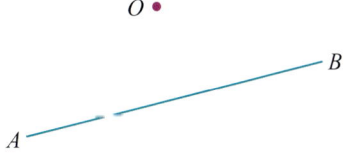

The length of a tangent from an external point P to a circle is defined to be the distance from P to the point of contact of the tangent.

4 Find the length of the tangent *PT*.

a

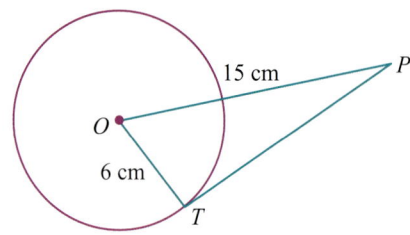

15 cm

P

O

6 cm

T

b

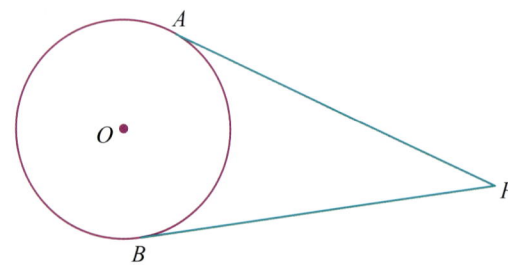

T

P

4 cm

24 cm

O

c Find the length of the tangent to a circle of radius 10 cm from a point *P* if P is 35 cm from the centre.

5 a Draw the tangents *PA* and *PB* to any circle from the point *P*. Measure the lengths of *PA* and *PB*.

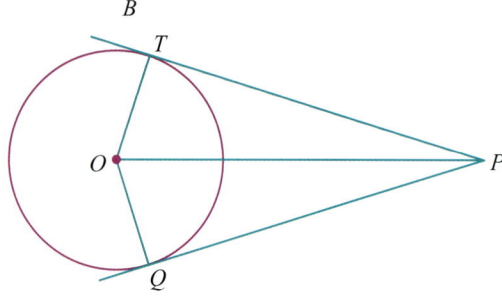

A

O

P

B

b *PT* and *PQ* are the tangents from *P* to a circle with centre *O*.

  i Prove $\triangle PTO \equiv \triangle PQO$.

  ii Hence prove *PT* = *PQ*.

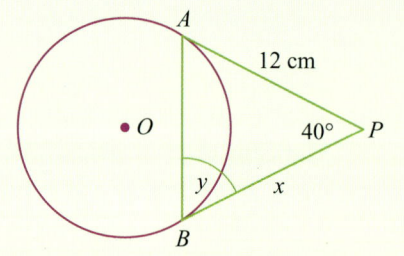

T

O

P

Q

Two tangents drawn to a circle from an external point are equal in length.

● EXAMPLE 2

PA and PB are tangents and O is the centre of a circle. Find the values of the pronumerals.

A

12 cm

O

40° *P*

y

x

B

Solve	Think/Apply
$x = 12$ cm $2y + 40° = 180°$ $2y = 140°$ $\therefore y = 70°$	Two tangents drawn to a circle from an external point are equal in length. $\triangle ABP$ is isosceles so the base angles are equal.

6 a *PA* and *PB* are tangents to the circle with centre *O*. Find the values of the pronumerals.

  i

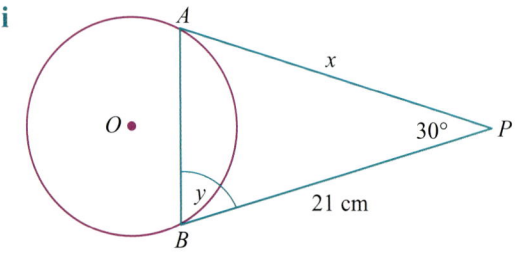

A

x

O

30° *P*

y

21 cm

B

  ii

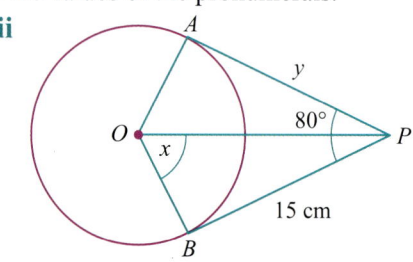

A

y

80°

O

x

P

15 cm

B

iii

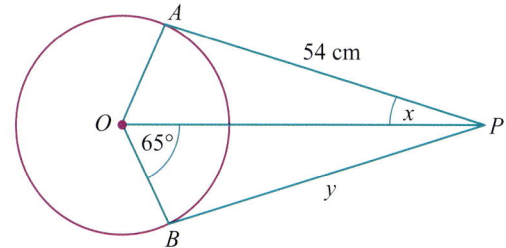

iv

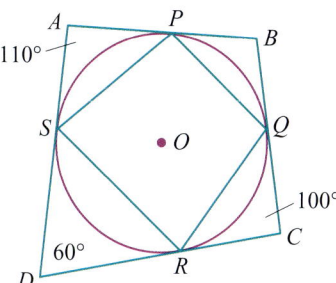

b The circle touches the sides of the quadrilateral *ABCD* at *P*, *Q*, *R* and *S* as shown. Find the angles of the quadrilateral *PQRS*.

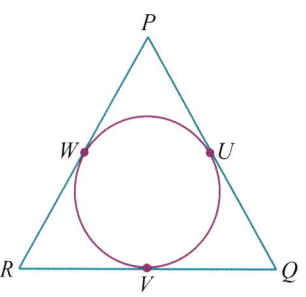

c *PQ*, *QR* and *RP* are tangents. If *PR* = 9 cm, *RW* = 5 cm and *RQ* = 12 cm, find *PQ*.

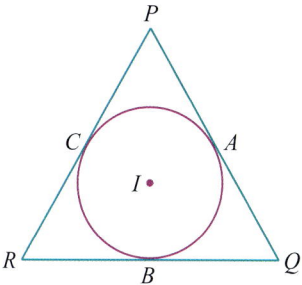

d *I* is the incentre of △*PQR*. *RQ* = 8 cm, *PR* = 9 cm and *PQ* = 7 cm. Find *RB*.

7 a Find the values of the pronumerals, given that *PQ* is a tangent.

i

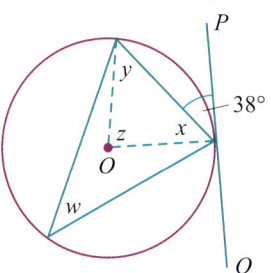

ii

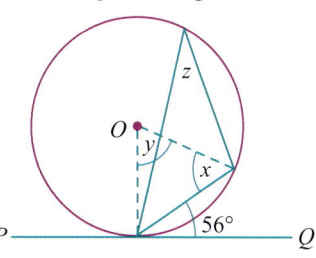

iii

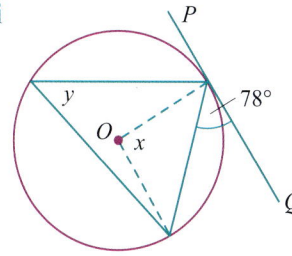

iv

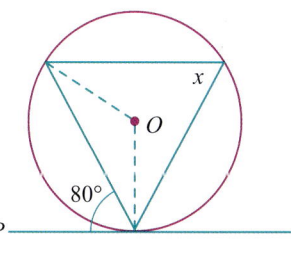

v

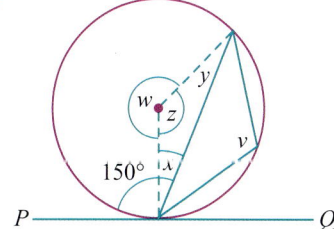

vi

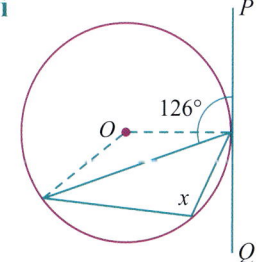

b Complete the following proof.

Data: *PQ* is a tangent to the circle with centre *O*.

Aim: To prove ∠*BCQ* = ∠*CAB*.

Proof: Join *CO* and *BO*. Let ∠*BCQ* = *x*.

∠*OCB* = ___ (A tangent to a circle is perpendicular to the radius.)

∠*OBC* = 90° − *x* (_____)

∠*COB* = ___ (Angle sum of a triangle is 180°.)

∠*BAC* = ___ (The angle at the centre of a circle is double the angle at the circumference.)

∴ ∠*BCQ* = ∠*CAB*

The angle between a tangent and a chord drawn to the point of contact is equal to the angle in the alternate segment. The chord BC divides the circle into two segments. ∠BCQ is in the minor segment while ∠CAB is in the alternate or other (major) segment.

● EXAMPLE 3

Find the values of the pronumerals. *PQ* is a tangent.

a

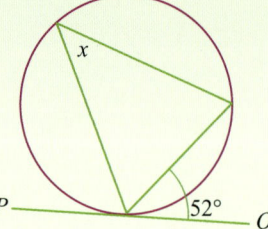

b

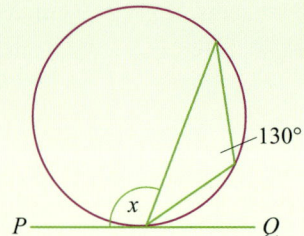

	Solve	Think	Apply
a	*x* = 52°	Alternate segment theorem.	Angles cannot be in the same segment.
b	*x* = 130°		

8 Find the values of the pronumerals.

a

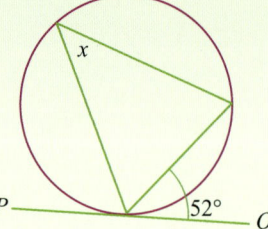

55°, *x*

b

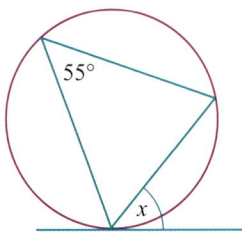

x, 136°

c

55°, *y*, 130°, *x*

d

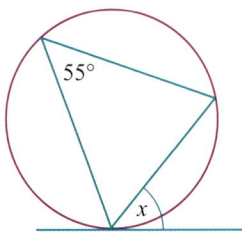

x, 70°

e

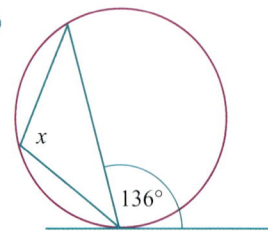

100°, *x*, 36°

f

49°, 75°, *x*, *y*

g

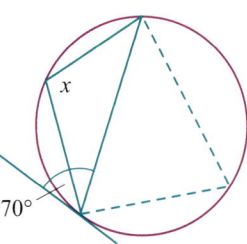

O, 48°, *x*

h

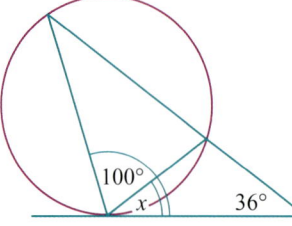

70°, *x*, 85°

i

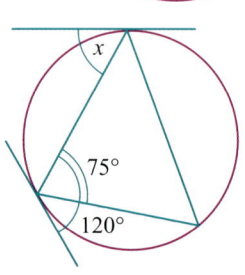

x, 75°, 120°

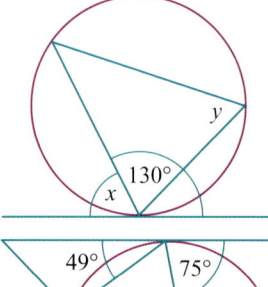

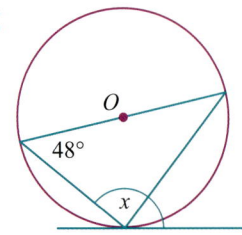

A **common tangent** to two circles is a straight line that touches both circles. Four cases arise as outlined below.

1 *AB* and *CD* are known as direct common tangents.

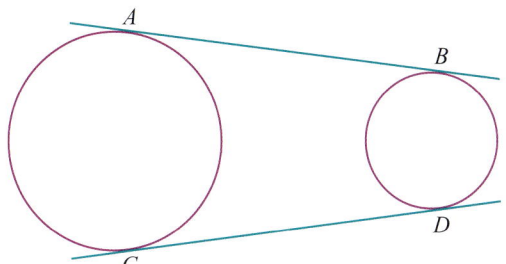

2 *PQ* and *RS* are indirect common tangents.

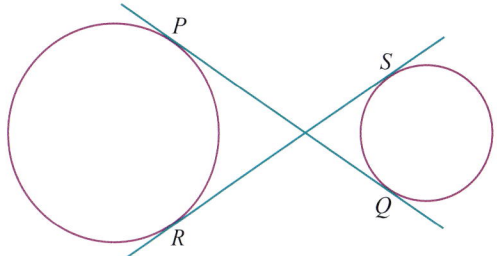

3 *PQ* is a common tangent to two circles that touch externally.

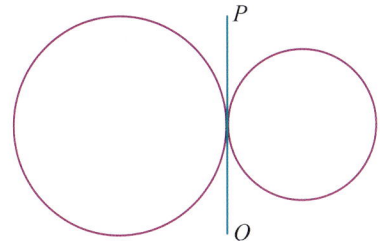

4 *PQ* is a common tangent to two circles that touch internally.

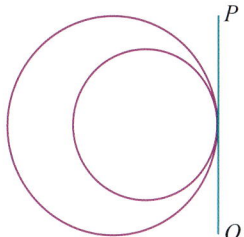

9 Two circles of radii 2 cm and 7 cm have their centres 13 cm apart. Find the length of the direct common tangent *PQ*.

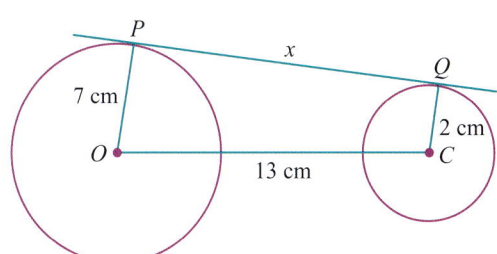

10 a Draw two circles with centres *C* and *O* that touch externally at the point *P*. Join *CP* and *OP*. Is *CPO* a straight line?

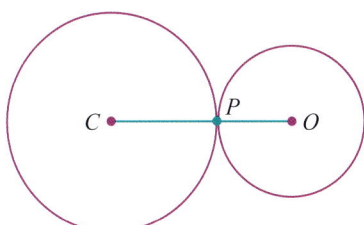

b Complete the following proof.
  Data: *KPL* is the common tangent to two circles with centres *O* and *C* that touch externally at *P*.
  Aim: To prove *C*, *P* and *O* are collinear.
  Proof: $\angle KPO = \_\_\_°$ (A tangent to a circle is perpendicular to the radius at the point of contact.)
    $\angle KPC = \_\_\_°$ (_____)
    $\therefore \angle CPO = \_\_\_°$
    $\therefore CPO$ is a straight line; that is, *C*, *P* and *O* are collinear.

c *KPL* is a common tangent to the two circles with centres *C* and *O* that touch internally at *P*. Prove that *C*, *O* and *P* are collinear.

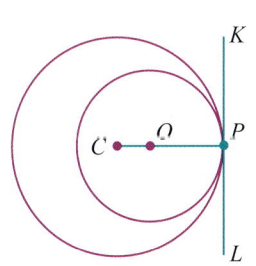

From parts **b** and **c** we conclude:

When two circles touch, their centres and the point of contact are collinear.

11 a Draw two chords that intersect at *P*. Measure the lengths of the intervals *AP*, *PB*, *CP* and *PD*. Calculate:

   i *AP* × *PB*   **ii** *CP* × *PD*

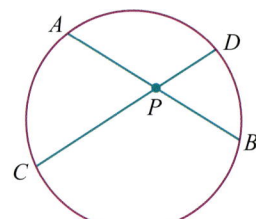

b *AB* and *CD* are two chords of a circle that intersect at *P*.

   i Prove that △*APD* is similar to △*CPB*.

   ii Write down all the equal ratios of sides in these two triangles.

   iii Hence show that *AP* × *PB* = *DP* × *PC*.

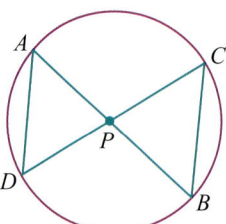

The products of the intercepts of two intersecting chords of a circle are equal.

● EXAMPLE 4

Find the value of *x*.

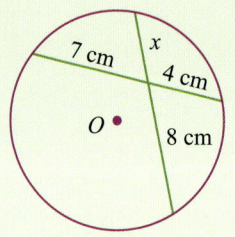

Solve	Think/Apply	Think/Apply
$x \times 8 = 7 \times 4$ $8x = 28$ $x = 3.5$	Use the product of intercepts rule.	Use the values for the intercepts not the entire chords.

12 a Find *x*.

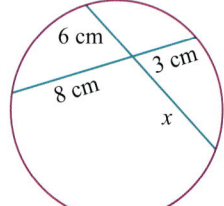

b Find *x*.

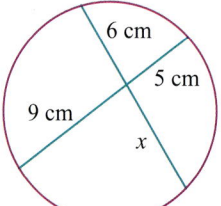

c Find *x*.

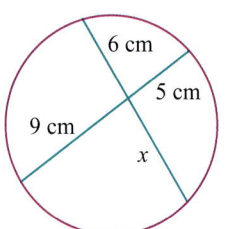

d *PQ* = 24 cm
   XQ = 8 cm
   XL = 10 cm
   Find *KX*.

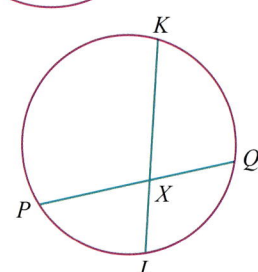

e *AB* = 40 cm
   PD = 25 cm
   CD bisects *AB*.
   Find *CP*.

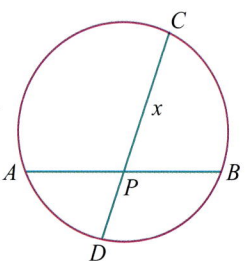

f Find *x*.

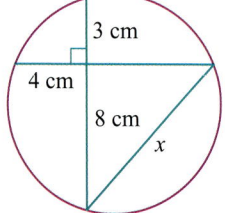

13 a Draw the tangent *PT* and the secant *PQR*. Measure the
lengths of the intervals *PT*, *PR* and *PQ*. Calculate:

  i PT^2 **ii** $PR \times PQ$

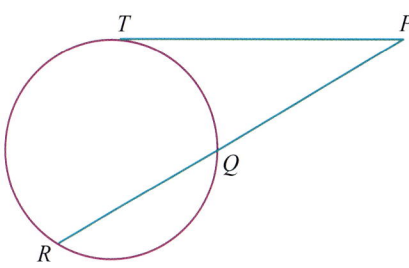

b Complete the following proof.

Data: *TP* is a tangent to the circle.

Aim: To prove $TP^2 = TA \times TB$.

Proof: In $\triangle PTB$ and $\triangle ATP$:

  $\angle TPB = \underline{\hspace{1cm}}$ (The angle between a chord and a tangent is
  equal to the angle in the alternate segment.)

  $\angle PTB = \angle ATP$ $(\underline{\hspace{1cm}})$

  $\therefore \triangle PTB$ is similar to $\triangle ATP$. $(\underline{\hspace{1cm}})$

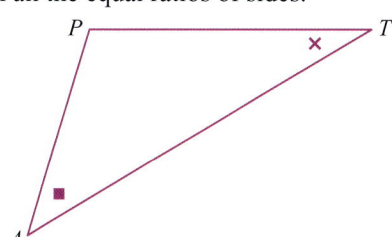

Let us separate and redraw these triangles. Write down all the equal ratios of sides.

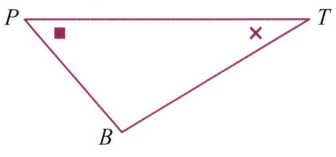

$$\frac{AP}{PB} = \frac{TP}{TB} = \frac{TA}{TP}$$

$\therefore TP^2 = TA \times TB$

The square of the length of a tangent from an external point equals the product of the intercepts of any secant from the point.

● EXAMPLE 5

$PT = 7$ cm and $PB = 5$ cm. Find *AB*.

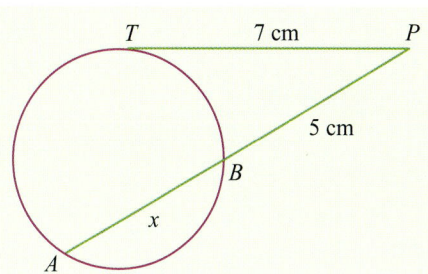

Solve	Think/Apply	Think/Apply
$7^2 = 5(5 + x)$	$PT^2 = PB \times PA$	Label the unknown as x and add
$49 = 25 + 5x$	Let $AB = x$ then $PA = x + 5$.	or subtract to find the required
$24 = 5x$		lengths.
$x = 4.8$		

---

14 a $TA = 8$ cm
$TB = 2$ cm
Find *TP*.

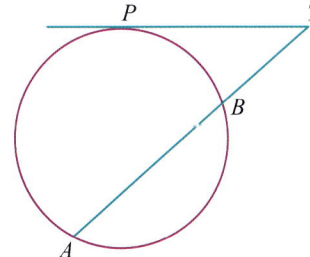

b $CA = 12$ cm
$CB = 3$ cm
Find *CD*.

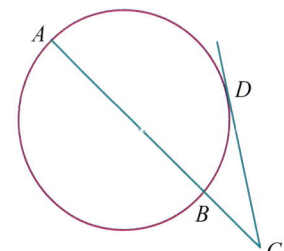

c $QP = 10$ cm
$QR = 5$ cm
Find QS and RS.

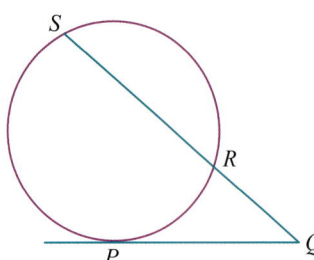

d $LK = 12$ cm
$LN = 16$ cm
Find LM and MN.

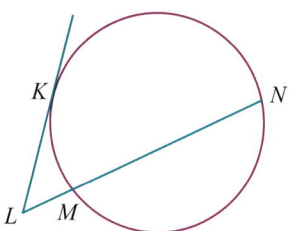

e Find x.

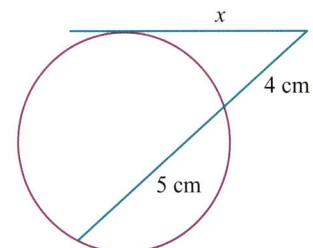

f Find x.

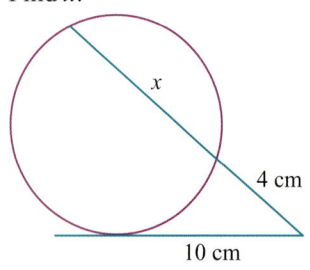

g Find x.

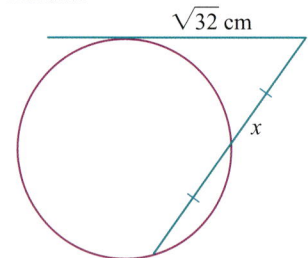

15 A person of height h metres stands on the surface of Earth, which is assumed to be a sphere of radius R.

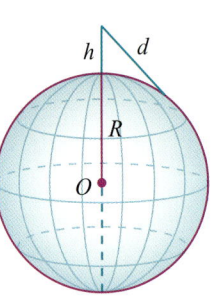

  a Show that the distance, d, to the horizon is given by $d = \sqrt{h^2 + 2hR}$.
  b Calculate the distance across level ground to the horizon that can be seen by a person of height 1.8 m. Use $R = 6400$ km.
  c The formula in part **a** is often given as $d \approx \sqrt{2hR}$. Use this formula to calculate the distance to the horizon seen by a person of height 1.8 m.
  d Explain why this second formula gives the same answer as the first for many cases.

16 a Draw two secants, PAB and PCD, to a circle from an external point P.
  Measure the lengths of the intervals PA, PB, PC and PD.
  Calculate:
  i $PA \times PB$
  ii $PC \times PD$

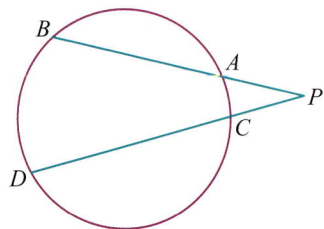

MEASUREMENT & GEOMETRY

b $TP = 12$ cm, $TB = 6$ cm and $TC = 18$ cm. Find TA and TD.
Is $TA \times TB = TC \times TD$?

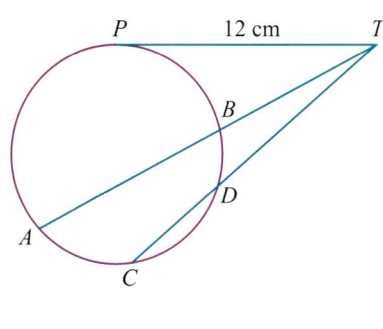

c $SQ = 10$ cm, $SR = 40$ cm and $SV = 16$ cm. Find SW.
Is $SQ \times SR = SV \times SW$?

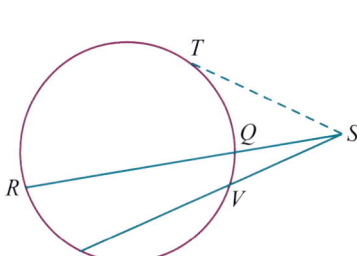

d Complete the following proof.
Data: AB and CD are two secants that meet at T.
Aim: To prove $TB \times TA = TD \times TC$.
Construction: Draw the tangent TP.
Proof: $\quad TP^2 = TB \times TA \qquad$ (_____)
$\quad\quad$ also $\quad TP^2 =$ _____ $\qquad$ (_____)
$\quad\quad \therefore TB \times TA = TD \times TC$

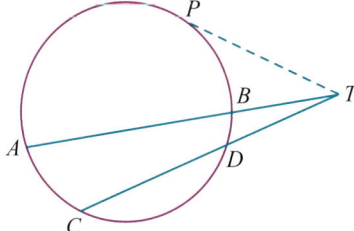

The products of the intercepts of two intersecting secants to a circle from an external point are equal.

● EXAMPLE 5

Find the value of x.

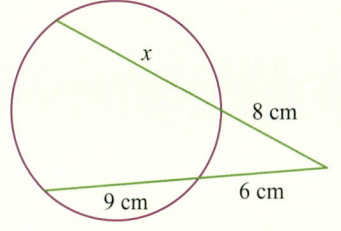

Solve	Think/Apply	Think/Apply
$8 \times (8 + x) = 6(6 + 9)$ $64 + 8x = 90$ $8x = 26$ $x = 3.25$ cm	Add or subtract values as required.	Do not confuse tangents and secants.

17 Find the value of the pronumerals.

a

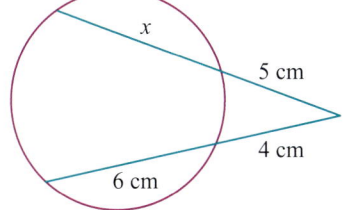

b

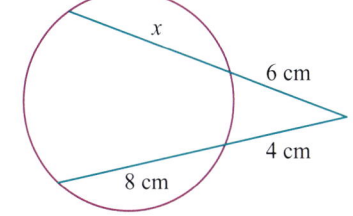

c

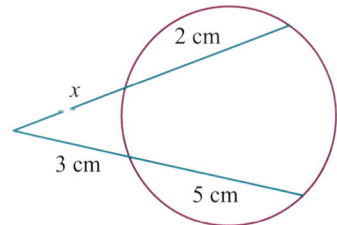

d

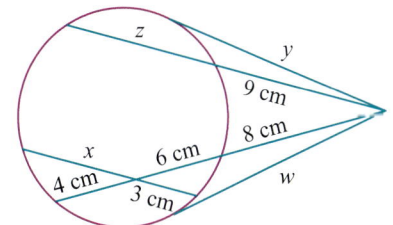

F Proofs using circle theorems

Exercise 16F

1 Prove that if two chords subtend equal angles at the centre of a circle then they are equal in length.

2 Prove that if two chords are equidistant from the centre of a circle then the chords are equal in length.

3 **a** Prove that $\triangle BTD$ is similar to $\triangle CTA$.
   b Hence prove that $TA \times TB = TC \times TD$.

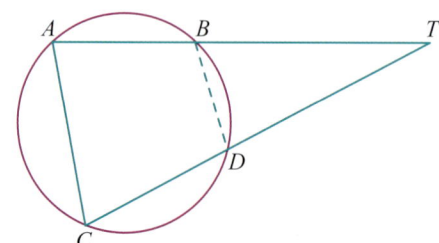

4 O is the centre of the two concentric circles. $ABCD$ is a straight line. Prove that $AB = CD$.

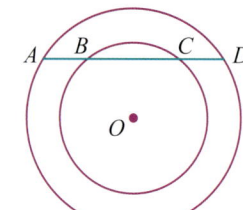

5 PQ and RS are two equal chords of a circle with centre O. K and L are the midpoints of PQ and RS respectively. Prove that $\angle PKL = \angle KLR$.

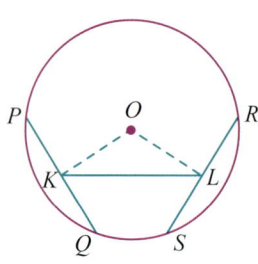

6 P and Q are the centres of the circles that intersect at K and L. AKC is parallel to PQ. Prove that $AC = 2 \times PQ$.

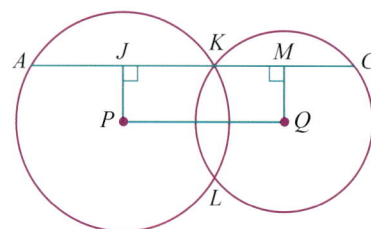

7 AB and CD are parallel chords of a circle with centre O. $AP \perp CD$ and $BQ \perp CD$.
   a Prove that $CP = QD$.   **b** Prove that $AC = BD$.

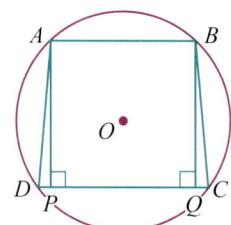

8 O is the centre of the circle and $AB = AC$. Prove that $\angle COB = 4 \times \angle OBA$.

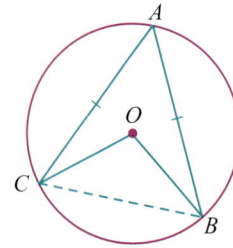

9 *PQRS* is a cyclic quadrilateral. *PQ* has been produced to *T* such that *PTRS* is a parallelogram. Prove that △*QRT* is isosceles.

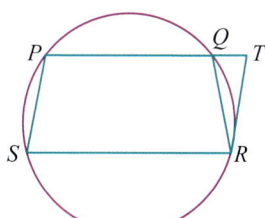

10 *AC* and *BC* are equal chords and *CD* is a tangent. Prove that *AB* ∥ *CD*.

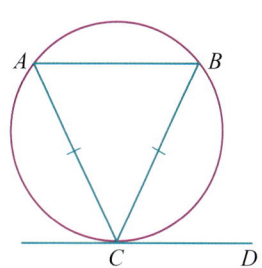

11 *PQ* is a tangent, *QTS* is a straight line and *NQ* ∥ *RS*. Prove that ∠*QRS* = ∠*QTR*.

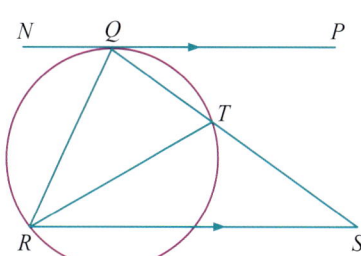

12 *AB* and *CD* are chords that intersect at *P*. If *AC* ∥ *DB*, prove that ∠*CPB* = 2 × ∠*BDC*.

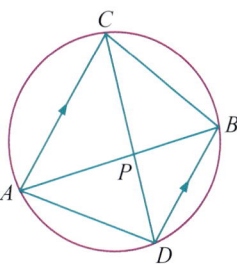

13 Given that *AT* = *PT*, prove that *AP* ∥ *QB*.

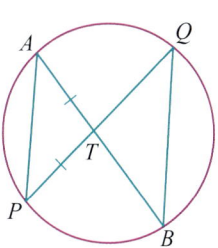

14 Given that *AP* = *DP*, prove that *CP* = *BP*.

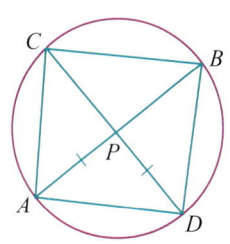

15 Prove that ∠*KSM* = ∠*RLM*.

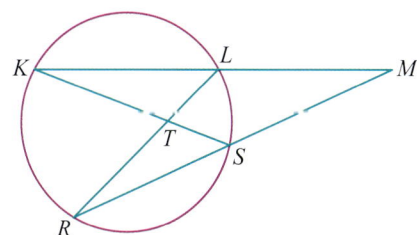

16 If $BE \parallel AD$, prove that $CA = CD$.

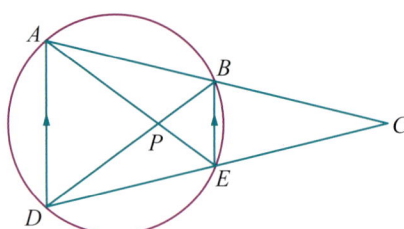

17 If QS bisects $\angle PQR$ and $\angle PSR$, prove that $\angle QRS = \angle QPS = 90°$.

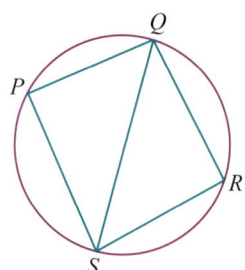

18 The two circles intersect at B and D. AB is a diameter and ABC and ADE are straight lines. Prove that $\angle ACE = 90°$.

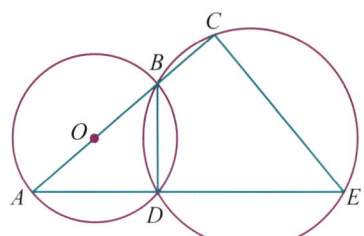

19 O is the centre of the larger circle and OX is a diameter of the inner circle that touches the larger circle at X. XY is a chord that cuts the inner circle at P. Prove that $XP = PY$.

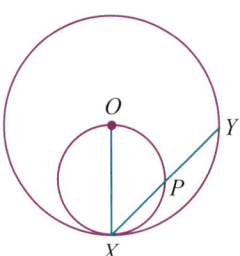

20 O is the centre of the circle and $\angle OPQ = \angle PRQ$. Prove that $\angle POQ = 90°$.

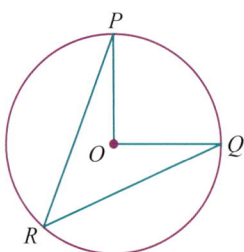

21 ABC and ADE are chords of a circle with centre O. They are also tangents at B and D to a concentric circle as shown. Prove that $AB = BC$.

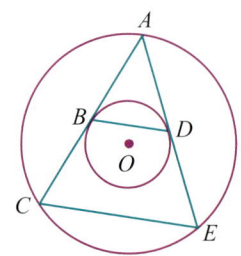

22 O is the centre of the circle. $\angle AOC = 90°$ and CD is a tangent. Prove that $CD = CB$.

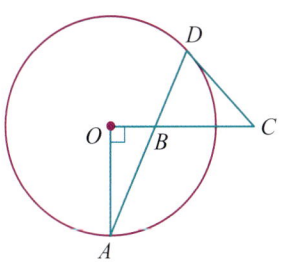

23 $\triangle PQR$ is inscribed in a circle. The tangents at R and Q meet at T. Prove that $RT = QT$.

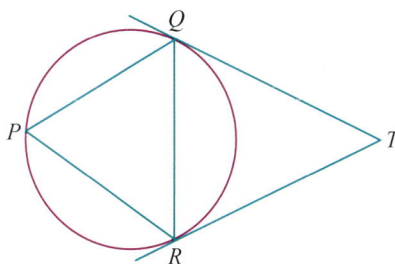

24 PQ is a tangent to a circle with centre O and PB bisects $\angle QBA$. Prove that $\angle PQB = 90°$.

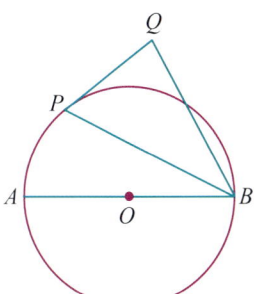

25 The two circles touch externally at X. P is any point on the common tangent. Prove that the tangents PQ and PT are equal in length.

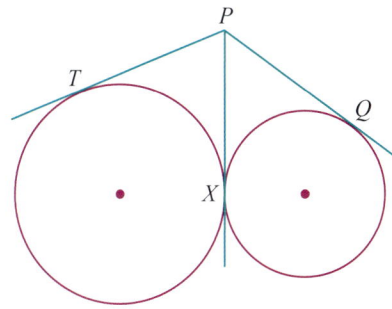

26 $PQ = PR$ and $VW \parallel QR$. Prove that $VWRQ$ is a cyclic quadrilateral.

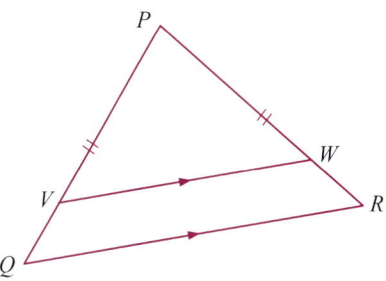

27 TP is a tangent and $PA = 3 \times PT$. Prove that $AB = 8 \times PB$.

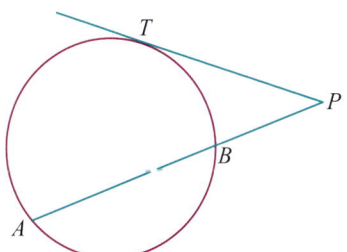

Language in mathematics

1 Name an angle that is:

  a subtended at the circumference by the chord *PQ*

  b subtended by the chord *QR* at the centre

  c standing on the arc *SR*

  d subtended at the circumference by the chord *QS* in the major segment

  e subtended at the circumference by the chord *QS* in the minor segment

  f in the same segment as ∠*STR*.

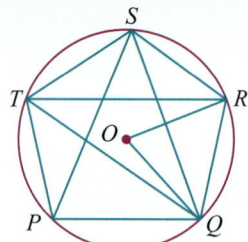

2 Draw a circle and mark any four points *A*, *B*, *C* and *D* on the circumference. On your diagram draw an angle:

  a subtended at the circumference by the chord *AB*

  b subtended by the chord *BC* at the centre

  c standing on the arc *AC*

  d subtended at the circumference by the chord *BC* in the major segment

  e subtended at the circumference by the chord *AC* in the minor segment

  f in the same segment as ∠*ADB*.

3 Explain in your own words the meaning of these terms.

  a collinear points   **b** concyclic points   **c** a cyclic quadrilateral

4 Explain the difference in meaning between these terms.

  a sector and segment   **b** supplementary angles and complementary angles

  c alternate and alternative

5 Draw diagrams to illustrate the following.

  a the point of contact of a tangent   **b** the perpendicular bisector of an interval

  c a point equidistant from two lines   **d** an exterior angle of a cyclic quadrilateral

6 Three of the words in the following list are spelt incorrectly. Find these words and write the correct spelling:

  vertex, diametre, tangent, interior, circumfrence, intersept

Terms

arc	bisector	centre	chord	circle	circumference
collinear	concyclic	cyclic	diameter	equidistant	exterior
intercept	interior	intersect	major	minor	non-collinear
perpendicular	quadrilateral	radius	secant	sector	segment
semicircle	subtend	supplementary	tangent	vertex	vertices

Check your skills

1 The statement that is not correct is:

  A *A* is a tangent   **B** *B* is a sector

  C *C* is a segment   **D** *D* is a chord

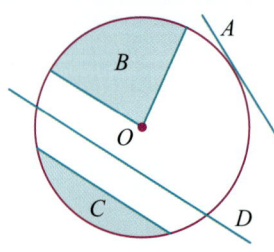

2 The angle at the circumference standing on the arc *BC* is:

  A ∠*BDC*   **B** ∠*BCD*

  C ∠*BEC*   **D** ∠*BCE*

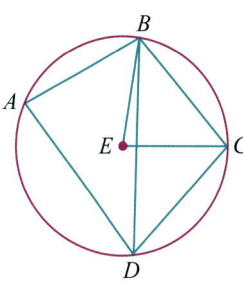

3 The values of the pronumerals are:

  A $x = 35°, y = 9$ cm   **B** $x = 35°, y = 4$ cm

  C $x = 55°, y = 9$ cm   **D** $x = 55°, y = 4$ cm

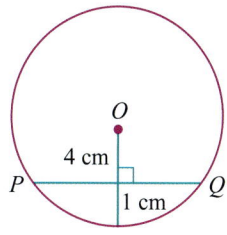

4 The length of the chord *PQ* is:

  A 5 cm   **B** 6 cm

  C 8 cm   **D** 10 cm

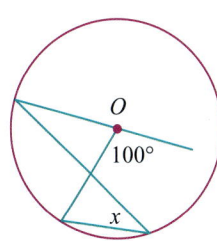

5 *C* and *O* are the centres of the circles. *PR* = 6 cm, *RO* = 8 cm and ∠*PCR* = 35°. The values of *x* and *y* are:

  A $x = 55°, y = 6$ cm   **B** $x = 35°, y = 10$ cm

  C $x = 55°, y = 10$ cm   **D** $x = 35°, y = 6$ cm

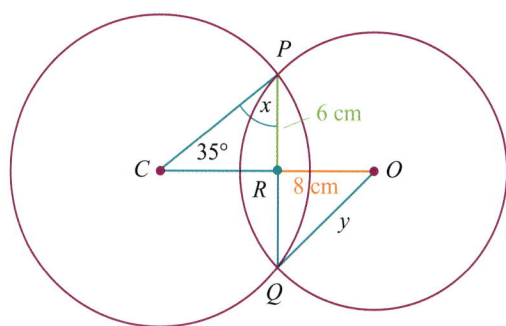

6 The value of *x* is:

  A 40°   **B** 50°

  C 100°   **D** 160°

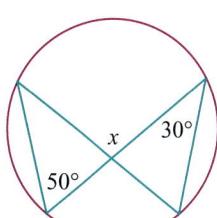

7 The value of *x* is:

  A 60°   **B** 80°

  C 100°   **D** 160°

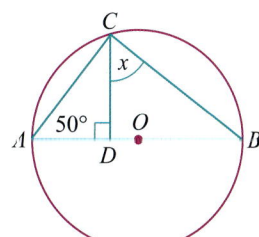

8 *AOB* is a diameter and *CD* ⊥ *AB*.
The value of *x* is:

  A 25°   **B** 40°

  C 50°   **D** 90°

9 The values of x and y are:

  A $x = 100°, y = 80°$ **B** $x = 55°, y = 40°$

  C $x = 70°, y = 100°$ **D** $x = 90°, y = 120°$

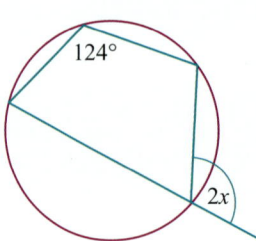

10 The value of x is:

  A 28°   **B** 56°

  C 62°   **D** 124°

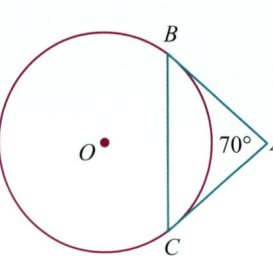

11 PT is a tangent and O is the centre. The value of x is:

  A 25°   **B** 40°

  C 50°   **D** 80°

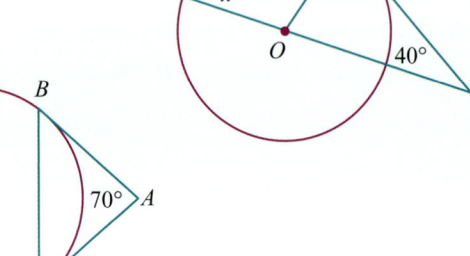

12 AB and AC are tangents and O is the centre. The size of $\angle ACB$ is:

  A 20°   **B** 55°

  C 70°   **D** 90°

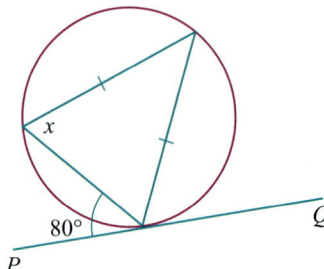

13 PQ is a tangent. The value of x is:

  A 10°   **B** 50°

  C 80°   **D** 100°

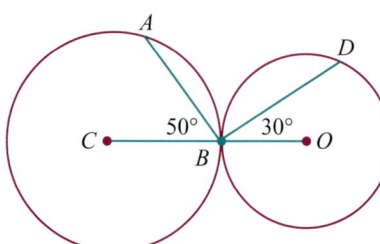

14 The two circles with centres C and O touch externally at B. The size of $\angle ABD$ is:

  A 80°   **B** 90°

  C 100°   **D** 140°

15 AB and CD are chords that intersect at P. The value of x is:

  A 3 cm   **B** 8 cm

  C 12 cm   **D** 24 cm

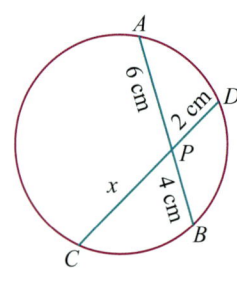

16 The length of the tangent PT is:

  A 4 cm   **B** 8 cm

  C 16 cm   **D** 48 cm

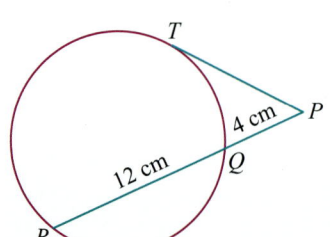

17 The value of x is:

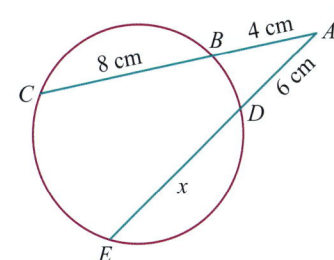

A 2

B $5\frac{1}{3}$

C 6

D 10

If you have any difficulty with these questions, refer to the examples and questions in the sections listed in the table.

Question	1, 2	3–5	6–10	11–17
Section	A	C	D	E

16A   Review set

1 Copy the following diagrams and label as many parts as possible.

a

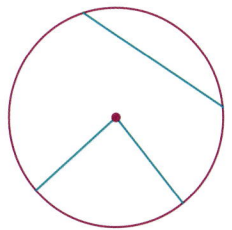

b

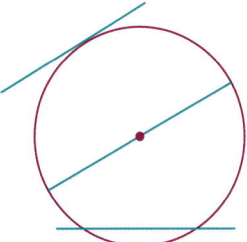

2 Name an angle that is:

a subtended by the chord AB at the circumference

b subtended at the centre by the chord AB

c standing on the arc BC

d subtended by the chord CE at the circumference in the minor segment.

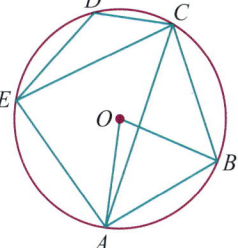

3 Find the values of the pronumerals. O is the centre.

a

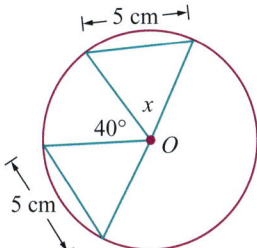

b

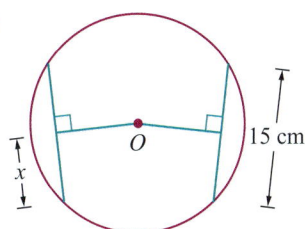

c

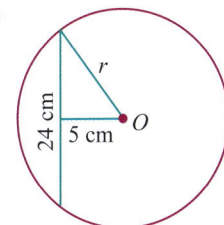

4 Find the values of the pronumerals. P and Q are the centres of the circles.

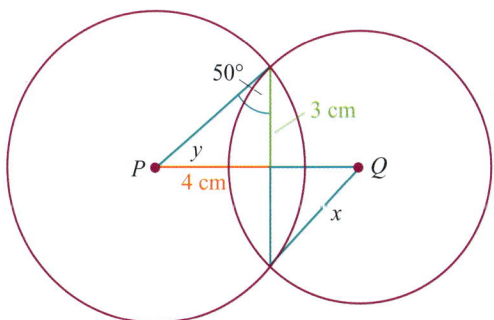

MEASUREMENT & GEOMETRY

5 Find the values of the pronumerals. O is the centre of each circle.

a

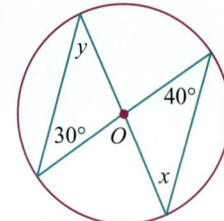

b

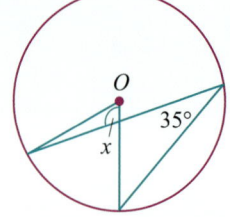

c

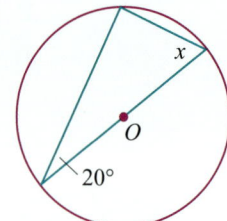

d

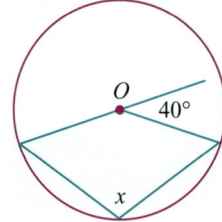

e

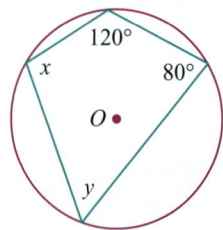

f

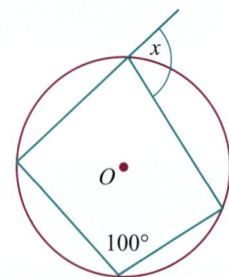

6 Find the values of the pronumerals.

a O is the centre.
   PT is a tangent.

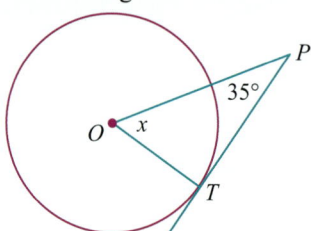

b O is the centre.
   PT and PU are tangents

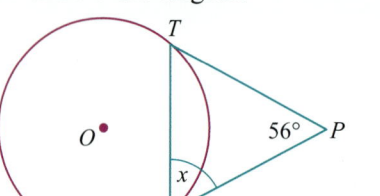

c PT is a tangent.

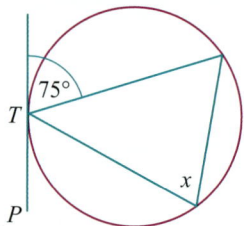

d C and O are the centres.
   P is the point of contact of
   the circles.

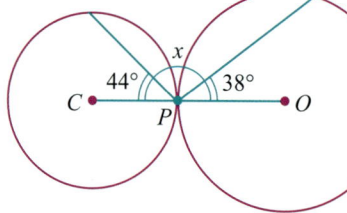

e

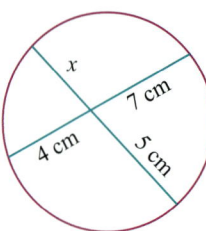

f

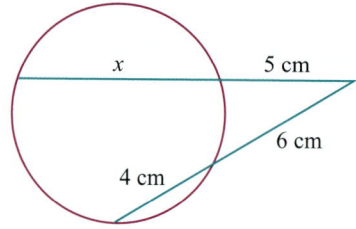

16B   Review set

1 Draw diagrams and identify the following parts of a circle:
   centre, radius, minor sector, major sector, tangent, secant, chord, arc, diameter, semicircle, segment

2 Name an angle that is:
   a subtended by the chord AB at the circumference
   b subtended at the centre by the chord AB
   c standing on the arc ED
   d subtended by the chord DB at the circumference, in the minor segment.

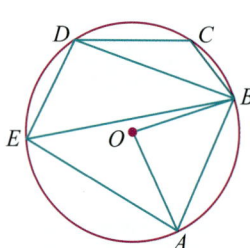

3 Find the values of the pronumerals. *O* is the centre.

a
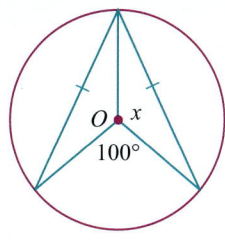

b
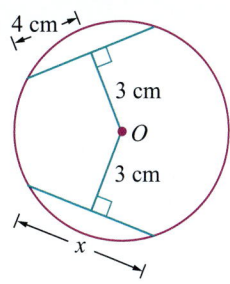

c
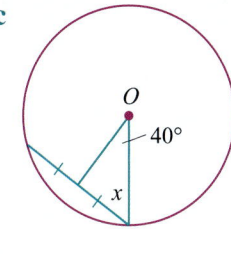

4 Find the values of the pronumerals. *P* and *Q* are the centres of the circles.

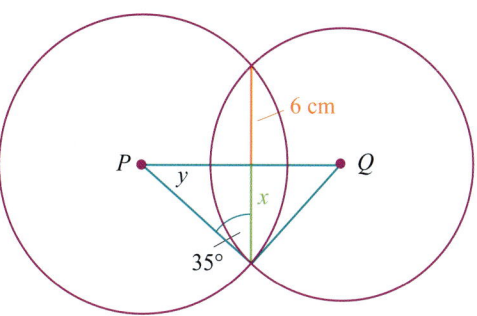

5 Find the values of the pronumerals. *O* is the centre.

a
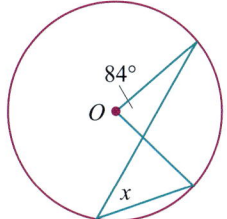

b
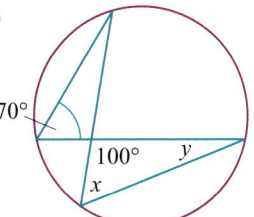

c
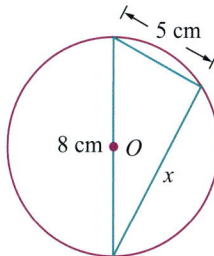

d
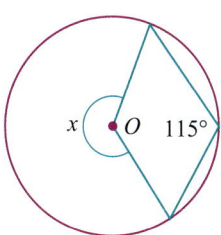

e
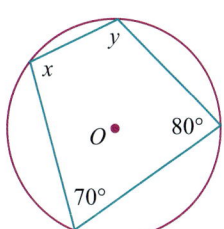

f
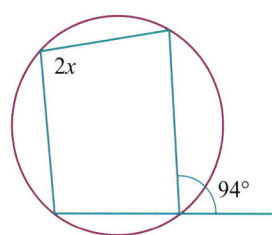

6 Find the values of the pronumerals.

a *O* is the centre. *PT* is a tangent.
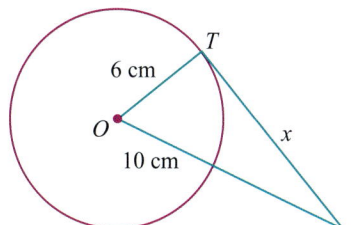

b *PQ* and *PR* are tangents.
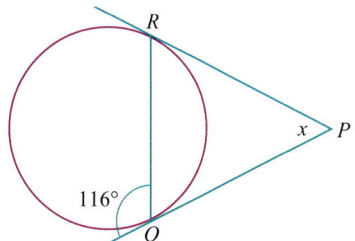

c *PT* is a tangent.
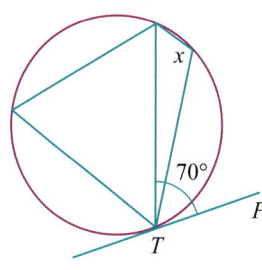

d
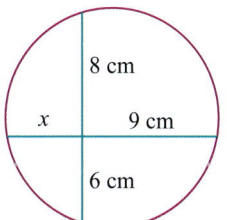

e *PT* is a tangent.
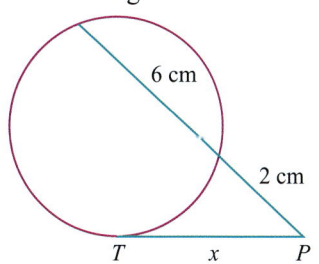

f
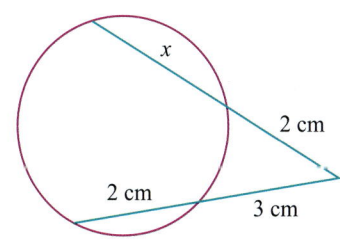

1 Copy the diagrams and label as may parts as you can.

a

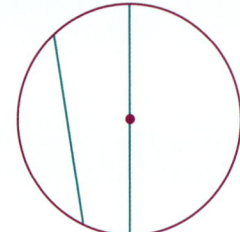

b

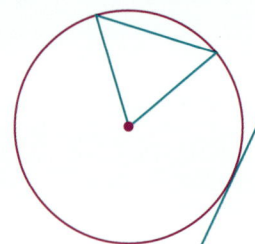

2 Name an angle that is:

    a subtended by the chord *PQ* at the circumference

    b subtended at the centre by the chord *QR*

    c standing on the arc *RS*

    d subtended by the chord *SP* at the circumference in the minor segment.

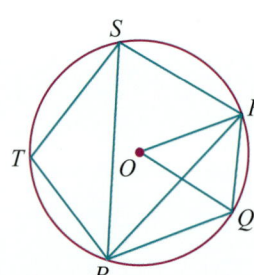

3 Find the values of the pronumerals. *O* is the centre of each circle.

a

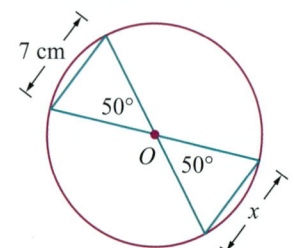

b

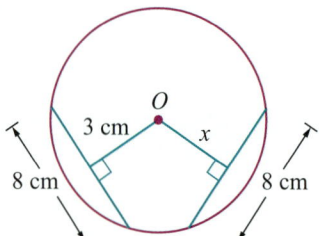

c

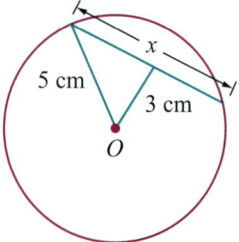

4 Find the values of the pronumerals.
    P and *Q* are the centres of the circles.

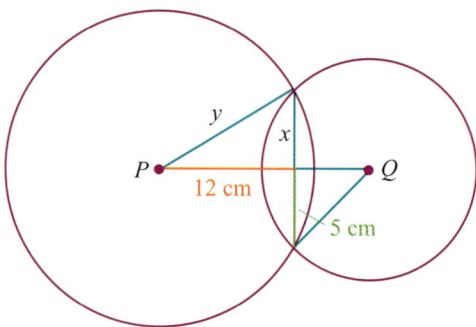

5 Find the values of the pronumerals. *O* is the centre of each circle.

a

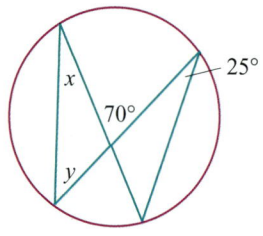

b

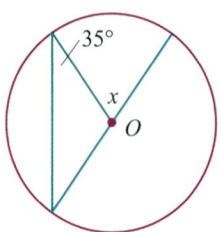

c

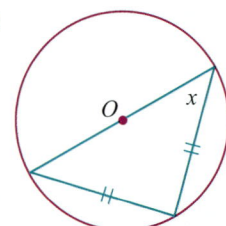

d

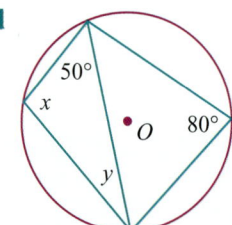

e

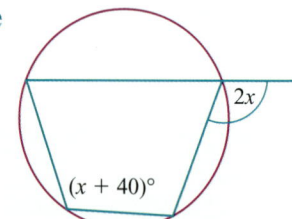

f

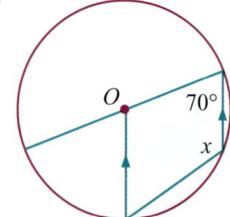

6 Find the values of the pronumerals.

a O is the centre of the circle. PT is a tangent.

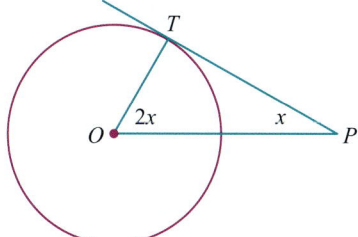

b AP and AQ are tangents.

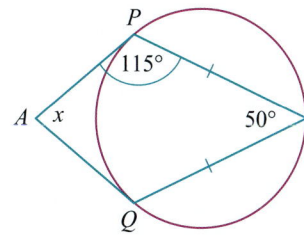

c PT is a tangent.

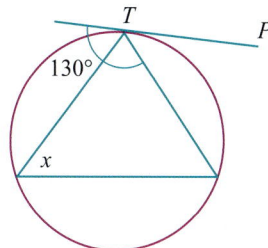

d C and O are the centres. P is the point of contact of the circles.

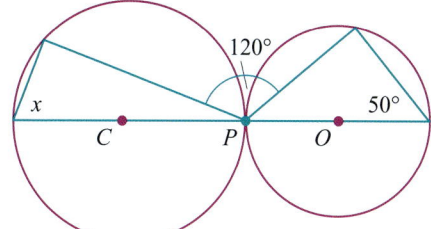

e

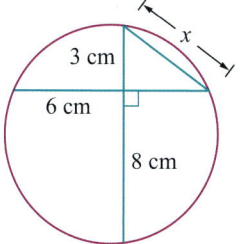

f

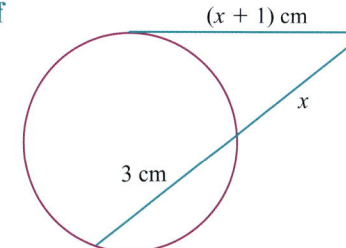

g

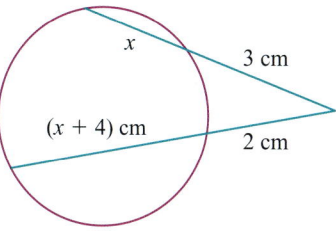

16D   Review set

1 Draw diagrams and label the following parts of a circle:

chord, minor arc, major arc, minor segment, major segment, semicircle, diameter, tangent, secant, sector

2 Name an angle that is:

a subtended at the circumference by the chord JK

b subtended by the chord JK at the centre

c standing on the arc MN

d subtended by the chord KM at the circumference in the minor segment.

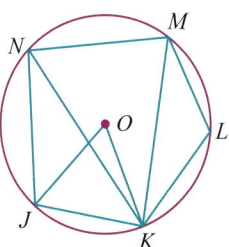

3 Find the values of the pronumerals. O is the centre of each circle.

a

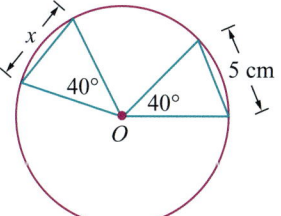

b

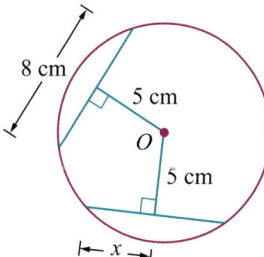

c

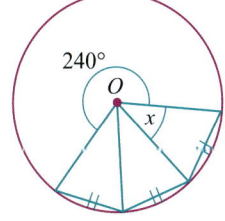

MEASUREMENT & GEOMETRY

4 Find the values of the pronumerals. *P* and *Q* are the centres of the circles.

5 Find the values of the pronumerals. *O* is the centre of the circle.

a

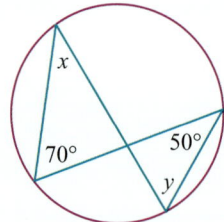

b

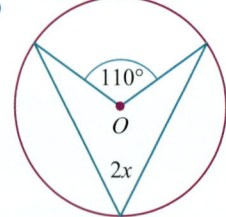

c

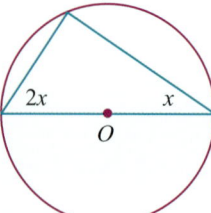

d

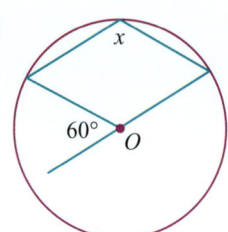

e

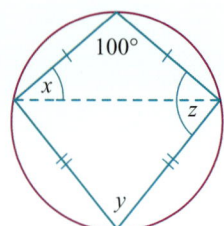

f

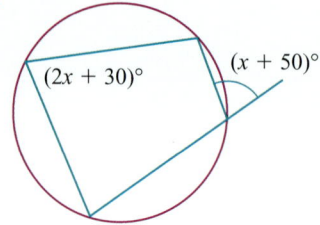

6 Find the values of the pronumerals. *O* is the centre of the circle.

a *PT* is a tangent.

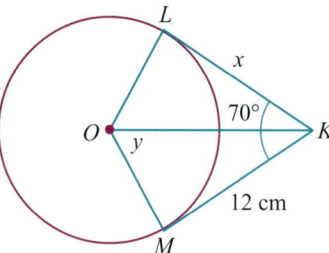

b *KL* and *KM* are tangents.

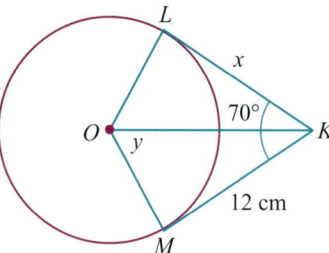

c *PT* is a tangent.

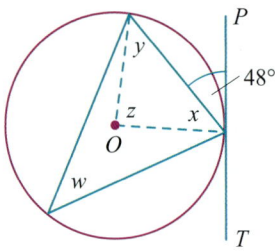

d *C* and *O* are the centres. *P* is the point of contact of the circles.

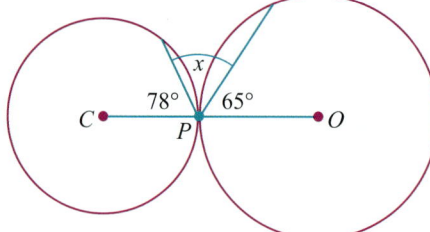

e

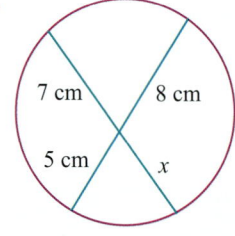

f *PT* is a tangent.

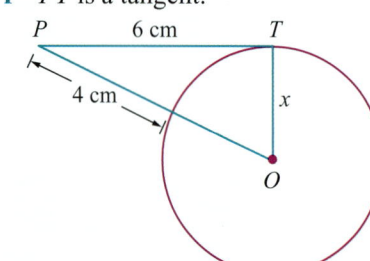

g

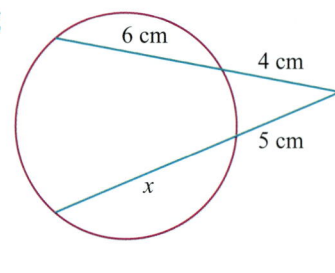

1 a For the scores 3, 5, 5, 6, 7, 7, 8 and 9, calculate the:

   i mean   **ii** standard deviation

   iii range   **iv** interquartile range.

b If 2 is subtracted from each score in part **a**, calculate the new:

   i mean   **ii** standard deviation

   iii range   **iv** interquartile range.

c If each of the scores in part **a** is multiplied by 3, calculate the new:

   i mean   **ii** standard deviation

   iii range   **iv** interquartile range.

2 The results of a survey comparing the annual income and the amount of money spent on entertainment by 10 university students is shown in the table.

Income ($'000)	11	13	17	22	25	30	32	38	41	53
Entertainment ($'000)	1.8	2.5	3.2	3.5	3.7	3.7	3.8	4.2	4.6	5.7

a Use a spreadsheet to draw a scatterplot and a line of best fit.

b Determine the equation of the line of best fit.

c Use the line of best fit to predict:

   i the amount spent on entertainment when the income is $20 000

   ii the average income of a student who spends $4000 on entertainment.

3 a On the same diagram, sketch graphs of:

$$y = x^4 \qquad y = x^4 + 3 \qquad y = (x - 2)^4 \qquad y = -(x + 1)^4 - 2$$

b Use the graph of $y = f(x)$ given to draw neat sketches of:

   i $y = 2f(x)$ **ii** $y = f(x) + 2$

   iii $y = f(x - 2)$ **iv** $y = f(x + 2)$

   v $y = -f(x)$ **vi** $y = f(-x)$

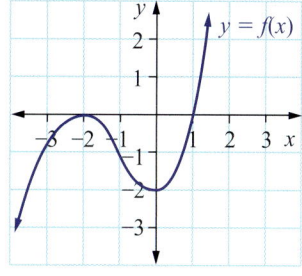

c Determine whether the following functions are symmetrical about the y-axis.

   i $f(x) = 3x^4$ **ii** $f(x) = -2x^3$ **iii** $f(x) = x^5 - 3x^3$

d Explain why $y = 2x^2 + \sqrt{x}$ is not a polynomial.

e For the polynomial $1 - 2x^2 + 5x^3 + 2x^7$ state:

   i the degree   **ii** the leading term   **iii** the leading coefficient

   iv the constant term   **v** whether or not the polynomial is monic.

f Given $P(x) = 2x^4 - 3x^2 + 5x - 1$ and $Q(x) = 3x^3 + 2x^2 - 7x - 8$, find:

   i $P(x) + Q(x)$ **ii** $P(x) - Q(x)$

g Given $P(x) = x - 2$ and $Q(x) = x^3 - 8x^2 + 7x + 2$, find:

   i $P(x) \times Q(x)$

   ii $Q(x) \div P(x)$. Express the result in the form $Q(x) = P(x) \times A(x) + R$.

h Find the remainder when $Q(x) = 3x^4 - 2x^3 + 8x - 7$ is divided by $x + 2$.

i
  i Show that $x + 5$ is a factor of $P(x) = x^3 + 4x^2 - 11x - 30$.

  ii Hence find all the linear factors of $P(x)$.

  iii State the zeros of $y = P(x)$.

  iv Draw a neat sketch of $y = P(x)$.

j Sketch the following polynomials:

  i $y = (x + 2)^2(x - 3)^2$ **ii** $y = (x + 1)^3(x - 2)^2$ **iii** $y = x^2(x + 5)^3$

4 a Draw diagrams and identify the following parts of a circle.

  i chord   **ii** minor arc   **iii** major segment

  iv semicircle   **v** diameter   **vi** tangent

  vii secant   **viii** sector   **ix** radius

b Find the values(s) of the pronumerals. Give a reason. O is the centre circle.

i

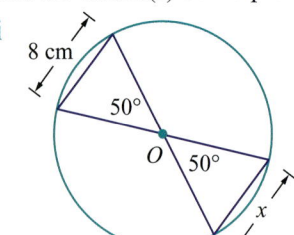

ii

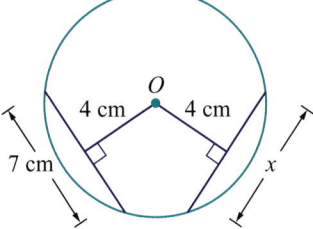

iii

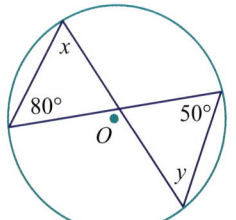

iv

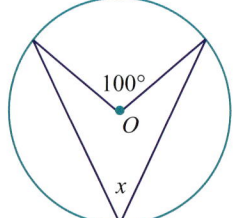

v PT is a tangent.

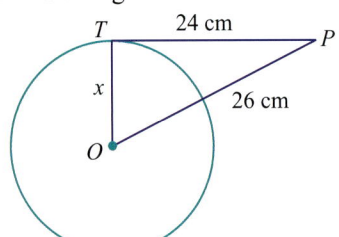

vi PA and PB are tangents.

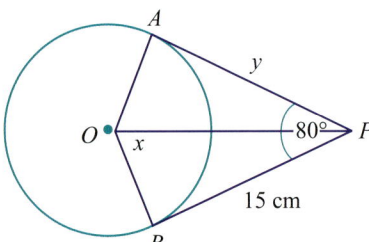

vii

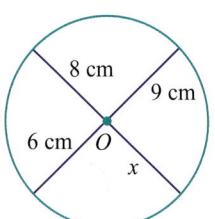

viii PT is a tangent.

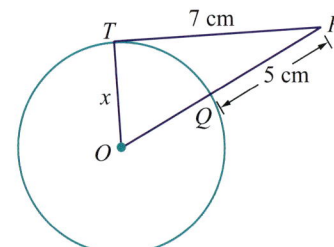

CHAPTER 1 REVIEW OF YEAR 9

Exercise 1A

1 a 2^5 **b** 5^5

2 a base = 9   **b** 5

3 a $5 \times 5 \times 5$ **b** $6 \times 6 \times 6 \times 6 \times 6 \times 6 \times 6$

4 a 512   **b** 7776

5 a False   **b** False

6 a 5^{28} **b** 4^{10} **c** 2^3

d 7^7 **e** $5^0 = 1$

7 a $\dfrac{1}{2^6}$ **b** $\sqrt{5}$ **c** $\sqrt[3]{11}$

8 a $\dfrac{1}{25}$ **b** 4   **c** 2   **d** 1

9 a y^{15} **b** k^5 **c** p^{21}

d t^6 **e** $25m^8$ **f** $6a^6b^{10}$

10 a 1   **b** 6   **c** 1   **d** 7

11 a $\sqrt{x}$ **b** $5\sqrt{x}$ **c** $\sqrt{5x}$ **d** $\sqrt[3]{x}$ **e** $5\sqrt[3]{x}$

12 a $\dfrac{1}{z^3}$ **b** $\dfrac{3}{z^3}$ **c** $\dfrac{1}{27z^3}$

13 a y^4 **b** e^9 **c** $n^{-16} = \dfrac{1}{n^{16}}$

d $18b^6$ **e** 2

14 a True   **b** False   **c** False

d True   **e** False

15 a $12v - 24w$ **b** $2a^5 + 3a^4$ **c** $-15x - 6$

16 a $16m + 13$ **b** $10a - 3b$

Exercise 1B

1 a i 2007   **ii** 2005

b i 140 mm   **ii** 511 mm   **iii** 37 mm

c i September   **ii** July

d i August   **ii** May

e i 2002   **ii** 2007   **iii** 2004

f i 2003   **ii** 2002   **iii** 2005

2 a Symmetrical   **b** Positively skewed

c Bimodal   **d** Negatively skewed

3 a i

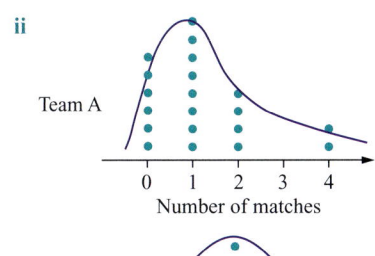

ii

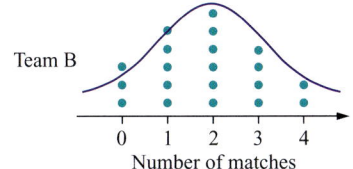

b Team A: positively skewed; team B: symmetrical

c Team A: mean = 1.2, median = 1, range = 4
Team B: mean = 1.85, median = 2, range = 4
Team B has a larger mean and median, indicating that it scored more goals than team A. Ranges are equal.

d Team B performed better with more goals and higher mean number of goals per match.

Exercise 1C

1 a 2.3×10^{10} **b** 5.2×10^{-5}

2 a 98 000 000   **b** 0.000 000 003 7

3 $4 \times 10^5 = 400\,000$ and
$4^5 = 4 \times 4 \times 4 \times 4 \times 4 = 1024$

4 a 1.632×10^{14} **b** 1.6×10^5

c 1.024×10^{48} **d** 1.5×10^8

5 7.7×10^{-16}, 3.1×10^{-12}, 4.6×10^{13}, 3.8×10^{15}

6 a 700   **b** 7   **c** 70   **d** 7000

7 a 3500   **b** 7960   **c** 38   **d** 70 000

8 a 7.3   **b** 7.27   **c** 7.268

9 a 4.29   **b** 40.0

10 a 45   **b** <55   **c** $45 \le x < 55$

11 a 1   **b** 3   **c** 6

12 a 70   **b** 67   **c** 67.3   **d** 67.31   **e** 67.306

13 a 3   **b** 1   **c** 4   **d** 2   **e** 3, 4, 5 or 6

14 4.65 m accurate to 1 cm. 4.650 m accurate to 0.1 cm.

15 3.6×10^6 nanowatts

16 a 43 km   **b** 0.043 Mm

17 a 1 s   **b** ±0.5 s

c 20.5 to 21.5 s

d $20.5 \text{ s} \le$ measurement < 21.5 s

18 a 36 cm   **b** ±0.5 cm

c 7.5 to 8.5 cm and 9.5 to 10.5 cm

d 34 cm to 38 cm   **e** ±2 cm

19 Area is 99.54 cm², lower limit of area is 98.5175 cm², upper limit of area is 100.5675 cm², estimate = 99.5 cm²

Exercise 1D

1 a $847.52   **b** $22 035.52   **c** $1836.29

2 a $1051.92   **b** $2103.85   **c** $4558.33

3 $1244.60   **4** $3337

5 $312.18   **6** $678.60

7 $443.24   **8** $498.02

9 a $2700   **b** $1125

10 $57.62

11 *Advantages:* instant purchase, purchase goods without having the cash.
Disadvantages: interest high, impulse buying.

12 a $2460.96   **b** $672.96

13 a $1398   **b** $419.40   **c** $75.73

14 $365.40

15 a B   **b** B   **c** Equal   **d** A

16 $13.55

Exercise 1E

1 a 51 300   **b** 400   **c** 0.27

2 a 13.7 cm²   **b** 326.2 cm²   **c** 19.6 m²

3 a 46 m²   **b** 103 cm²

4 Triangular prism

5 a 148 cm²   **b** 276.6 cm²

6 76.78 m²

7 SA = 527.8 cm², $V = 769.7$ cm³

8 a 264 cm³   **b** 615.8 cm³

Exercise 1F

1 a

Country	Frequency	Relative frequency	Percentage (%)
Australia	185	$\frac{185}{400}$	46.25
Japan	93	$\frac{93}{400}$	23.25
Korea	72	$\frac{72}{400}$	18
Germany	44	$\frac{44}{400}$	11
Other	6	$\frac{6}{400}$	1.5

  b 46.25%   **c** 23.25%

2 a $\frac{1}{6}$ **b** $\frac{2}{6} = \frac{1}{3}$ **c** $\frac{2}{6} = \frac{1}{3}$

3 True in theory.

4 $P(6) = \frac{1}{6}$, so would expect one 6 in six throws.

5 a $\frac{5}{20} = \frac{1}{4}$ **b** $\frac{8}{20} = \frac{2}{5}$ **c** $\frac{7}{20}$ **d** $\frac{3}{5}$

6 a $\frac{4}{30} = \frac{2}{15}$ **b** $\frac{17}{30}$ **c** $\frac{21}{30} = \frac{7}{10}$

  d $\frac{9}{30} = \frac{3}{10}$ **e** $\frac{10}{30} = \frac{1}{3}$

7 a $\frac{26}{33}$ **b** $\frac{18}{33} = \frac{6}{11}$ **c** $\frac{8}{33}$

  d $\frac{7}{33}$ **e** $\frac{6}{33} = \frac{2}{11}$

8 a $\frac{1}{15}$ **b** $\frac{4}{15}$ **c** $\frac{4}{45}$

9 a $\frac{1}{8}$ **b** $\frac{1}{8}$ **c** $\frac{3}{8}$ **d** $\frac{7}{8}$

10 a i $\frac{1}{4}$ **ii** $\frac{25}{256}$ **iii** $\frac{30}{256} = \frac{15}{128}$

  iv $\frac{5}{16}$ **v** $\frac{135}{256}$

  b i $\frac{7}{30}$ **ii** $\frac{1}{12}$ **iii** $\frac{1}{8}$ **iv** $\frac{1}{3}$ **v** $\frac{13}{24}$

Exercise 1G

1 a $\sin \alpha = \frac{q}{p}, \cos \alpha = \frac{r}{p}, \tan \alpha = \frac{q}{r}$

    $\sin \beta = \frac{r}{p}, \cos \beta = \frac{q}{p}, \tan \beta = \frac{r}{q}$

  b $\sin \alpha = \frac{b}{c}, \cos \alpha = \frac{a}{c}, \tan \alpha = \frac{b}{a}$

    $\sin \beta = \frac{a}{c}, \cos \beta = \frac{b}{c}, \tan \beta = \frac{a}{b}$

  c $\sin \alpha = \frac{x}{z}, \cos \alpha = \frac{y}{z}, \tan \alpha = \frac{x}{y}$

    $\sin \beta = \frac{y}{z}, \cos \beta = \frac{x}{z}, \tan \beta = \frac{y}{x}$

  d $\sin \alpha = \frac{e}{f}, \cos \alpha = \frac{d}{f}, \tan \alpha = \frac{e}{d}$

    $\sin \beta = \frac{d}{f}, \cos \beta = \frac{e}{f}, \tan \beta = \frac{d}{e}$

2 a 12.1 cm   **b** 11.1 cm   **c** 6.49 m   **d** 7.77 km

3 a 29°45′   **b** 54°19′   **c** 56°19′

4 a $\theta = 39°, x = 17.6$ m, $y = 21.8$ m

  b The height is 24.6 m.

  c The boat is 189 m from the cliff.

5 a 62 m   **b** 63°37′   **c** 164 m

  d 16.1 km, 240°T

Exercise 1H

1 b PQ and $P'Q'$, QR and $Q'R'$, RS and $R'S'$, PS and $P'S'$

2 a Scale factor $= \frac{3}{8}, x = 9$ cm

  b Scale factor $= \frac{1}{5}, x = \frac{9}{5}$ cm, $y = 20$ cm

3 $y = 24$ cm

4 a TS **b** SU **c** TU

5 a Not similar   **b** Similar; scale factor $= 2$

6 a PQ and YX, QR and XZ, PR and YZ

  b Enlargement factor $= \frac{1}{6}$

7 a Enlargement factor $= \frac{3}{2}, x = 12, y = 12$

  b Enlargement factor $= \frac{1}{3}, x = 4, y = 21$

8 Enlargement factor $= \frac{5}{2}, x = 3.75$

Exercise 1I

1 a $(8, 3)$ **b** $(2, 6)$ **c** $(6, 5\frac{1}{2})$ **d** $(1, 1)$

2 a $\sqrt{40} \approx 6.3$ **b** $\sqrt{58} \approx 7.6$

3 $\frac{7}{11}$

4 a $\frac{2}{3}$ **b** $-\frac{1}{10}$

5 2

6 a 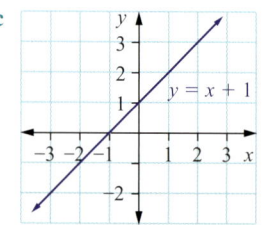   **b**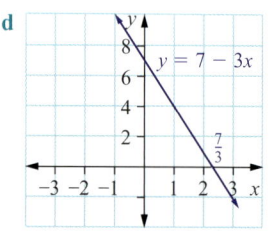

  c 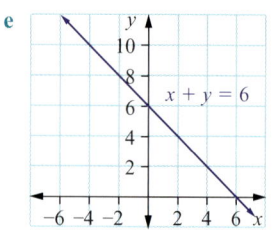   **d**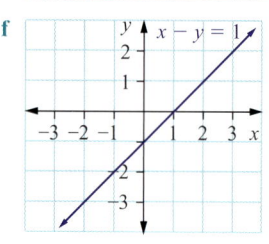

  e 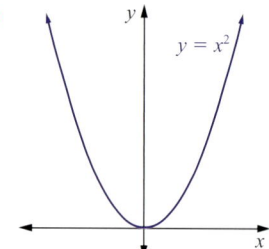   **f**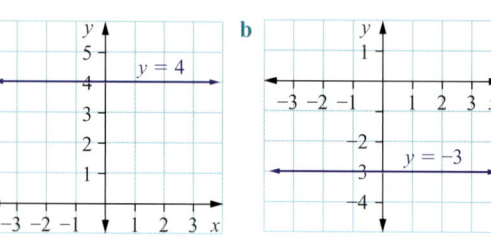

7 Yes since $-3 = 3(4) - 15$

8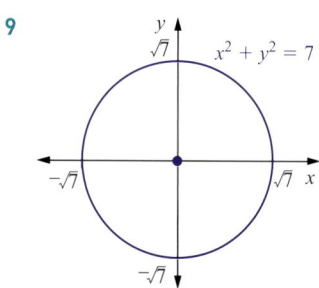

9

Exercise 1J

1 a 5.76 L/day   **b** 13.9 m/s
2 a $226.80/h   **b** 25.2 km/h
3 a Neither   **b** Inverse   **c** Direct
4 a Neither   **b** Direct   **c** Inverse   **d** Neither
5 a Yes   **b** Yes
6 a Yes   **b** Yes
7 a €240   **b** $200
8 $y = 4.8, x = 6$

Exercise 1K

1 a $x = 3$ **b** $x = 0$ **c** $x = -15$
   d $x = -56$ **e** $x = -\frac{10}{3}$ **f** $x = \frac{22}{3}$
2 a $y = -2$ **b** $x = 4$
3 $x = \frac{14}{5}$
4 a $x = -\frac{23}{8}$ **b** $t = -\frac{11}{20}$ **c** $p = \frac{53}{25}$
   d $x = -\frac{10}{9}$ **e** $x = \frac{28}{3}$ **f** $x = -\frac{43}{3}$
   g $x = -\frac{3}{19}$ **h** $x = \frac{41}{27}$ **i** $x = \frac{42}{23}$
5 a -1 **b** 8
6 a $v = \sqrt{80} \approx 8.9$ **b** $u = \sqrt{280} \approx 16.7$
7 a $x > 9$ **b** $x < -4$ **c** $x \geqslant \frac{11}{3}$
   d $x \geqslant -9$ **e** $x \leqslant -\frac{2}{3}$ **f** $x \geqslant 1$
8 a $-9x + 21y = -15$ **b** $x = \frac{5}{3}$
   c $y = -16$ **d** $7x + 2y = 20$
9 a

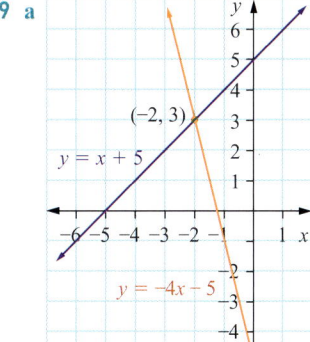

   b $x = -2, y = 3$
10 a $(1, 4)$ **b** $(2, -4)$
11 a 65 cents
   b Tennis ball is 60 g, cricket ball is 220 g.
12 The lines are parallel.

Exercise 1L

1 a 20.4 cm   **b** 14.9 cm
2 a 29°12′   **b** 41°25′   **c** 60°57′
3 a 28.8 km   **b** 309°T, 291 km
4 a $\frac{1}{2}$ **b** $\frac{\sqrt{3}}{2}$ **c** $\sqrt{3}$ **d** $\frac{1}{\sqrt{2}}$
5 a 173 m   **b** 45°
6 a 99 m   **b** 138°
7 42.6 km and 30.2 km

Exercise 1M

1 a 8   **b** 8   **c** -8
   d No answer   **e** 0
2 a $\frac{7}{2}$ **b** $\frac{5}{1}$ **c** $\frac{43}{100}$ **d** $\frac{2}{3}$

3 a 0.375   **b** 0.53   **c** $0.\dot{3}$ **d** 5.25
4 a Rational   **b** Irrational   **c** Rational
   d Irrational   **e** Rational
5 a 5   **b** 45   **c** $\sqrt{35}$ **d** $18\sqrt{15}$
6 a $3\sqrt{3}$ **b** $3\sqrt{6}$ **c** 9   **d** $4\sqrt{5}$
7 a $\sqrt{44}$ **b** $\sqrt{80}$
8 a $\frac{3}{5}$ **b** $\frac{\sqrt{11}}{3}$ **c** $\frac{4}{3}$ **d** $\frac{5}{2}$
   e $\sqrt{6}$ **f** 3   **g** $\sqrt{3}$
9 a True   **b** False   **c** False
   d True   **e** False   **f** False
10 a $-3\sqrt{2}$ **b** $-7\sqrt{5}$ **c** $-\sqrt{5}$ **d** $9\sqrt{6}$
11 a False   **b** False   **c** False
12 a 84   **b** $30\sqrt{2}$ **c** $28\sqrt{2}$
   d $\sqrt{21} - 3$ **e** $8\sqrt{15} - 60$ **f** $8 - 3\sqrt{21}$
   g $33 - 12\sqrt{6}$ **h** $12 + 2\sqrt{35}$ **i** $99 + 12\sqrt{55}$
13 a $\frac{\sqrt{3}}{3}$ **b** $\frac{\sqrt{35}}{15}$
14 a -2 **b** $\frac{\sqrt{3} + \sqrt{5}}{-2}$
15 a $\sqrt{n}$ **b** $\sqrt[3]{n}$ **c** $\sqrt[3]{n^5}$ **d** $\sqrt[4]{n^3}$
16 a $m^{\frac{1}{2}}$ **b** $w^{\frac{1}{3}}$ **c** $t^{\frac{3}{2}}$
17 a 8   **b** 27   **c** 125
18 $\frac{5}{2}$

Exercise 1N

1 a 280 cm³   **b** 603 cm³   **c** 195 m³
   d 436 m³   **e** 1642 cm³   **f** 852 cm³
2 a 133 cm²   **b** 507 cm²
   c 254 cm²   **d** 641 cm²
3 8.5 cm   **4** 1630 cm³

Exercise 1O

1 a Yes   **b** No
2 a Yes   **b** Yes   **c** No
4 a i -1 **ii** 5   **iii** 3
   b i $6k + 5$ **ii** $6k + 8$ **iii** 3
   c $x = 3\frac{1}{3}$
5 a x is any real number; y is any real number, $y > 0$
   b Both are real numbers; $x \geqslant 0, y \leqslant 0$
   c x is any real number; y is any real number, $y \geqslant 2$
6 a $3x + 5$
   b $f(2) = -1, f^{-1}(f(3)) = 3$
   c

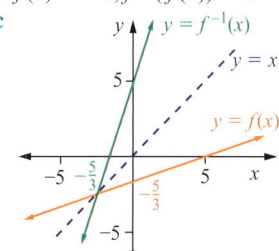

7 a

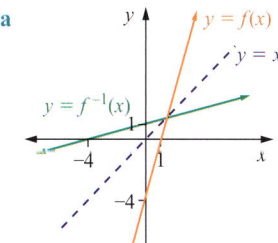

b

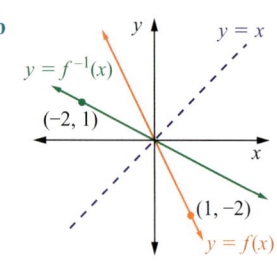

8 **A** and **C** do not have an inverse function.

9 $x \geqslant -\frac{1}{2}$

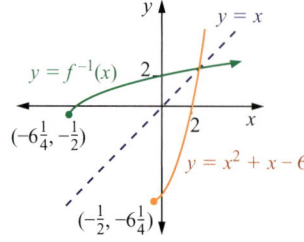

or $x \leqslant -\frac{1}{2}$

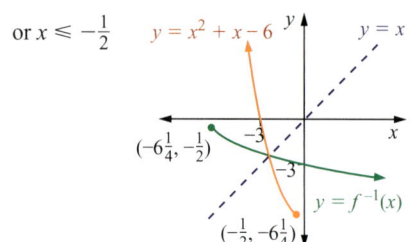

10 a $\log_5 625 = 4$ **b** $2^{2.5} = 4\sqrt{2}$

11 a $\frac{5}{2}$ **b** $\frac{3}{2}$

12 a $x = 6$ **b** $x = 5$

13 a $\log 2 + \log x + 3\log y$ **b** $2\log x - \frac{1}{2}\log y$

14 a -0.262 **b** 1.1095

15 a 1 **b** 0

16 a $\log 3xy^4$ **b** $\log \frac{\sqrt{x}}{y^2}$

17 a 1 **b** 2

18 a $x = 7.5$ **b** $x = 7.5$

19 $x \approx 2.12$

20

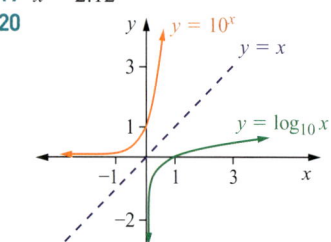

CHAPTER 2 ALGEBRA

Diagnostic test

1 C   **2** B   **3** C   **4** A   **5** D
6 C   **7** A   **8** C   **9** A   **10** D

Exercise 2A

1 a $\frac{6y}{15}$ **b** $\frac{8m}{6}$ **c** $\frac{30a}{12}$ **d** $\frac{15m}{6n}$

e $\frac{12t}{16w}$ **f** $\frac{48}{30q}$ **g** $\frac{6xz}{5yz}$ **h** $\frac{3ab}{4b^2}$

i $\frac{14mp}{18np}$ **j** $\frac{10ux}{15wx}$ **k** $\frac{10abc^2}{8b^2c^3}$ **l** $\frac{21wxy^2z^4}{18x^3y^4z^5}$

2 a $\frac{x}{2}$ **b** $\frac{t}{4}$ **c** $\frac{2y}{3}$ **d** $\frac{3b}{4}$

e $\frac{2}{3}$ **f** $\frac{3}{10}$ **g** $\frac{2}{b}$ **h** $\frac{4p}{3}$

i $\frac{4x^3}{3}$ **j** $\frac{3b}{5}$ **k** $\frac{2}{3x}$ **l** $\frac{2a^2}{7b^2}$

3 a $\frac{9x}{11}$ **b** $\frac{3n}{2}$ **c** $\frac{13m}{24}$ **d** $\frac{19k}{12}$

e $\frac{5b}{8}$ **f** $\frac{7a}{10}$ **g** $\frac{5k}{3}$ **h** $\frac{2z}{15}$

i $\frac{25t}{8}$ **j** $\frac{x}{10}$ **k** $\frac{29x}{15}$ **l** $\frac{19t}{14}$

4 a $\frac{7}{2x}$ **b** $\frac{1}{6a}$ **c** $\frac{47}{20y}$

d $\frac{11}{3z}$ **e** $\frac{14a}{3b}$ **f** $\frac{29m}{21n}$

g $\frac{58xy}{45z}$ **h** $\frac{36a - 25b}{30c}$ **i** $\frac{21a - 10b}{35c}$

j $\frac{10p - 3r}{14q}$ **k** $\frac{21x + 10y}{14z}$ **l** $\frac{24r - 33t}{44c}$

5 a $\frac{6mn}{7}$ **b** $\frac{4kn}{15}$ **c** $\frac{3wz}{2}$ **d** $\frac{3ab}{2}$

e $\frac{2t}{3u}$ **f** $\frac{15}{2}$ **g** $\frac{3}{4}$ **h** $\frac{4a}{5}$

i $\frac{40n}{27}$ **j** $\frac{kn}{9mp}$ **k** $10p$ **l** $8bc$

6 a $\frac{5x}{12y}$ **b** $\frac{7a}{4b}$ **c** $\frac{3p}{2q}$ **d** $\frac{14}{3}$

e $\frac{2}{3}$ **f** $\frac{12}{35}$ **g** $\frac{10}{3}$ **h** $\frac{28}{m^2}$

i $\frac{10y}{3z}$ **j** $\frac{3}{4k}$ **k** $\frac{7np}{m}$ **l** $\frac{10}{3}$

7 a $\frac{3x^3}{2}$ **b** $3x$ **c** $\frac{1}{3m}$ **d** $5a$

e $\frac{7}{15x^4z^2}$ **f** $\frac{3b^2}{2}$ **g** $\frac{8}{5m^5n^5}$ **h** $\frac{1}{10xy^4}$

i $\frac{3p^3q^2}{2}$ **j** $\frac{a}{6bc}$ **k** $\frac{33}{14x^2}$ **l** $\frac{3 + 5a}{a^2}$

Exercise 2B

1 a $4t + 32$ **b** $6a^2 - 12a$

c $18k^2 - 24mk$ **d** $10m^5 + 40m^2n$

e $12p^8 - 2p^3q^2$ **f** $12a^9 + 8a^5b$

g $18x^7 - 12x^5$ **h** $21b^9 + 42b^{12}$

i $12x^3y^5 - 6x^2y^3$ **j** $10m^4n^7 + 15m^5n^6$

k $6a^2 - 8ab + 14a$ **l** $10y^4 - 15y^3 - 30y^2$

2 a $-30t - 35$ **b** $-12w + 4z$

c $-7a - 9b$ **d** $-5v + 2w$

e $-6ab - 24ac$ **f** $-6pq + 18pr$

g $-10x^2 - 15xy$ **h** $-20m^2 + 28mn$

i $-20z^7 - 40z^9$ **j** $-12m^8 + 6m^5n$

k $-30x^{11} - 12x^9y^2$ **l** $-6a^5b^3 + 10a^8b^5$

3 a $4a + 18$ **b** $6b - 12$

c $12w - 1$ **d** $8y - 15$

e $22z - 6$ **f** $18x + 6$

g $18b - 10$ **h** $33 + 4y$

i $10w - 12$ **j** $20e - 14$

k $16a + 27$ **l** $19c - 10$

4 a $2 - 2a$ **b** $14 - 3y$ **c** $-3 - 4b$

d $5v + 12$ **e** $14w - 15$ **f** $22 - 15t$

g $-2 - 15x$ **h** $4k + 2$ **i** $-7z - 9$

j $20w - 7$ **k** $6a - 15$ **l** $23 - 12x$

5 a $13k + 9$ **b** $15m + 11$
  c $14p + 6$ **d** $13a - 6$
  e $25x - 11$ **f** $14y + 1$
  g 14 **h** $22x + 2y$
  i $23a - 9b$ **j** $18a^2 - 2a$

6 a $4k + 9$ **b** $2w + 26$
  c $9t - 10$ **d** $13z - 8$
  e $-2a + 14$ **f** $-d - 18$
  g $11y + 10x$ **h** $4a - 12b$
  i $2q^2 - 14q + 20$ **j** $12z^2 + 9z - 1$

7 a $22x^2$ **b** $2m^2 - 11mn$
  c $22a^5 + 3a^2b^4$ **d** $10y^5 + 6y^7 - 8y^4 + 4y^6$
  e $-2a^5b^3 + a^3b^4$ **f** $6x^4 + 15x^2y^3 - 21x^5 - 14x^3y^3$

8 a $\dfrac{7m + 15}{12}$ **b** $\dfrac{18p - 21}{35}$ **c** $\dfrac{8k + 14}{15}$

  d $\dfrac{3x + 7}{8}$ **e** $\dfrac{19y - 39}{20}$ **f** $\dfrac{7w + 50}{30}$

  g $\dfrac{9x + 4y}{12}$ **h** $\dfrac{14a + 11b}{36}$ **i** $\dfrac{3a + 14c}{18}$

Exercise 2C

1 a $2(7s + 5)$ **b** $3(3y - 2)$
  c $4(2k + 3b)$ **d** $5(3w - 5z)$
  e $3(4 + 3k)$ **f** $6(4p - 3q)$
  g $3(2x + y + 3z)$ **h** $6(4a - 2b - 3c)$

2 a $-2(3t - 4)$ **b** $-5(k + 2)$
  c $-4(2p - 5q)$ **d** $-3(4x + 5y)$
  e $-8(2 - p)$ **f** $-6(3 + 4w)$

3 a $4p(2q - 3r)$ **b** $p(p + 3)$
  c $3b(3a + 2)$ **d** $x(x - 7)$
  e $4n(3m - 4)$ **f** $2k(k + 2)$
  g $2m(3k - 4m)$ **h** $5z(2z - 1)$
  i $3a(5b + a)$ **j** $6t(4t - 3w)$
  k $x(x + 5y)$ **l** $b(2c - b)$
  m $p(7q + 5r + 11s)$ **n** $2b(2a + 3c - 5d)$
  o $3x(7y - 1 + 3x)$

4 a i True   **ii** True   **iii** True
  b iii

5 a Fully   **b** Partially
  c Partially   **d** Fully

6 a $t^2(6t^2 + 7)$ **b** $4k^5(2k^5 - 3)$
  c $8n^7(2 + 3n^2)$ **d** $2w^3(7w^2 + 4)$
  e $5k^2(4k^4 - 3)$ **f** $a^3b^2(9b^3 + 8a^2)$
  g $x^3y^5(7y^3 + 5x)$ **h** $3a^3b^6(3a^2 - b^2)$
  i $9m^3n^2(2m - n^3)$ **j** $10x^3y^7(3x^2 - 2)$
  k $3x^2(5x^2y^3 - x^3 + 3)$ **e** $4m^2n^3(4n^4 + 2m^2 - 3m^4n)$

Language in mathematics

1 reduce, substitute, apply, equivalent

2 a factorise   **b** reciprocal
  c equivalent   **d** algebraic

3 a The reciprocal is the number by which a fraction must be multiplied to equal 1. A fraction multiplied by its reciprocal equals 1.

   For example, $\frac{2}{3}$ is the reciprocal of $\frac{3}{2}$.

  b The highest common factor of two terms is the largest number that divides into the two terms. For example, the HCF of 8 and 12 is 4.

c The lowest common denominator is the smallest number into which the denominators of the fractions added or subtracted divide exactly. For example, the LCD of $\frac{1}{2}$ and $\frac{1}{3}$ is 6 or $\frac{1}{2} + \frac{1}{3} = \frac{3}{6} + \frac{2}{6} = \frac{5}{6}$.

d If the HCF is factorised out of the expression, then the expression is fully factorised. If a common factor, not the HCF, is used the factorisation is only partial.

4 They are reciprocals.

Check your skills

1 B   **2** D   **3** B   **4** B   **5** A
6 B   **7** C   **8** A   **9** D

Review set 2A

1 a $\dfrac{25k}{15}$ **b** $\dfrac{24x}{30y}$ **c** $\dfrac{8ab}{12b^2}$

2 a $\dfrac{k}{3}$ **b** $\dfrac{3}{2b}$ **c** $\dfrac{4x^2}{5y}$

3 a $\dfrac{17t}{24}$ **b** $\dfrac{5w}{3}$ **c** $\dfrac{7}{2x}$

4 a $\dfrac{12de}{35}$ **b** $\dfrac{3}{2a}$ **c** $\dfrac{3}{4}$ **d** $\dfrac{nq}{6}$

5 a $12x^2 + 8x$ **b** $6p^6 - 14p^4q$
  c $-18x^2 + 12y$ **d** $10v - 8$
  e $-9 + 6x$ or $6x - 9$ **f** $18p + 7q$

6 a $\dfrac{x - 3}{30}$ **b** $\dfrac{31a - 2}{14}$

7 a $3y(x + 4y)$ **b** $-2(4m + 5)$
  c $3x(5 - 3y - 2x)$ **d** $2m^2n^2(4m - 3n)$

Review set 2B

1 a $\dfrac{35t}{20}$ **b** $\dfrac{25x}{10y}$ **c** $\dfrac{16mn}{12n^2}$

2 a $\dfrac{5p}{6}$ **b** $\dfrac{2}{3p}$ **c** $\dfrac{2k}{3m^2}$

3 a $\dfrac{31p}{20}$ **b** $\dfrac{2k}{5}$ **c** $\dfrac{17}{15x}$

4 a $\dfrac{15w^2}{8}$ **b** $\dfrac{2m}{5}$ **c** $\dfrac{3}{2} = 1\frac{1}{2}$ **d** $\dfrac{28a^2b}{3c}$

5 a $10k^2 - 35km$ **b** $12d^4 - 21d^2e$
  c $-12m^2 + 28m$ **d** $24z + 3$
  e $22a - 6a^2$ **f** $13x - 20y$

6 a $\dfrac{-8x + 7}{6}$ **b** $\dfrac{38k - 12}{15}$

7 a $-4(2k + 3)$ **b** $a(7a + 3b)$
  c $3(4ab - 3 + 2b^2)$ **d** $4x^2y(3x^2y^2 - 4)$

Review set 2C

1 a $\dfrac{28m}{16}$ **b** $\dfrac{18kn}{9mn}$ **c** $\dfrac{4wz}{3z^2}$

2 a $\dfrac{8}{15}$ **b** $\dfrac{3}{13q}$ **c** $\dfrac{3a^3b}{2}$

3 a $\dfrac{9k}{35}$ **b** $\dfrac{11t}{3}$ **c** $\dfrac{23}{20w}$

4 a $\dfrac{21ac}{10bd}$ **b** $\dfrac{9p}{2}$ **c** $\dfrac{6b}{7}$ **d** $\dfrac{2p}{3q}$

5 a $6s^2 - 3s$ **b** $28q^3 - 35pq^2$
  c $-12a^2 - 30a$ **d** $31 - 10e$
  e $6a^2 + 12ab - 15ac$ **f** $8z^2 - 7z$

6 a $\dfrac{53z - 16}{24}$ **b** $\dfrac{8x - 7}{4}$

7 a $-8(3d + 2e)$ **b** $2p(3q + 8p)$

  c $3ab^3(3a^2b - 4)$ **d** $2xy(x^2 - 3x + 2)$

Review set 2D

1 a $\dfrac{12h}{20}$ **b** $\dfrac{12ab}{18}$ **c** $\dfrac{8x^2}{6xy}$

2 a $\dfrac{2}{3p}$ **b** $\dfrac{9y}{10}$ **c** $2m^3n^2$

3 a $\dfrac{29k}{28}$ **b** $-\dfrac{p}{6}$ **c** $\dfrac{58}{15w}$

4 a $\dfrac{10}{21ab}$ **b** $\dfrac{2}{3z}$ **c** $\dfrac{8}{5} = 1\dfrac{3}{5}$ **d** $\dfrac{a}{6}$

5 a $7d^2 - 21de$ **b** $40k^2 + 90km$

  c $-6p^4 - 2p^2q$ **d** $1 + 18z$

  e $10a + 5a^2$ **f** $21x^2 - 6x^3 + 12x^4$

6 a $\dfrac{10w + 3}{12}$ **b** $\dfrac{4x + 27y}{30}$

7 a $-3(5q - 4)$ **b** $6bc(2a + 1)$

  c $7x(4 + 2x - x^2)$ **d** $a^2b^2(ab - 1)$

CHAPTER 3 LINEAR RELATIONSHIPS

Diagnostic test

1 C	**2** D	**3** C	**4** A	**5** A
6 B	**7** C	**8** A	**9** C	**10** B
11 A	**12** A	**13** B	**14** D	**15** A

Exercise 3A

1 a $\sqrt{50}$ **b** $\sqrt{13}$ **c** $\sqrt{37}$

  d $\sqrt{34}$ **e** $\sqrt{50}$ **f** $\sqrt{89}$

2 a $(4, 6)$ **b** $(3, 2\tfrac{1}{2})$ **c** $(\tfrac{3}{4}, 1\tfrac{3}{4})$ **d** $(-\tfrac{3}{2}, -1)$

3 $(7, -6)$ **4** $(-8, 3)$

5 a **i** Rise $= 2$, run $= 4$ **ii** $m = \dfrac{1}{2}$

  b iii $m = \dfrac{y_2 - y_1}{x_2 - x_1}$

6 a $\dfrac{5}{3}$ **b** -4 **c** 0 **d** $\dfrac{1}{2}$

  e $\dfrac{5}{2}$ **f** undefined   **g** 0 **h** $\dfrac{1}{4}$

  i $\dfrac{1}{2}$ **j** -1

Exercise 3B

1 a $y = x + 1$

x	-2	-1	0	1	2
y	-1	0	1	2	3

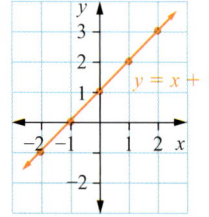

  b $y = x - 1$

x	-2	-1	0	1	2
y	-3	-2	-1	0	1

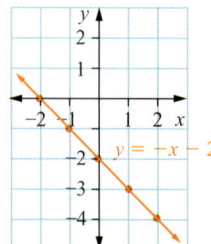

c $y = -x - 2$

x	-2	-1	0	1	2
y	0	-1	-2	-3	-4

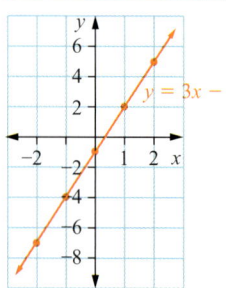

d $y = 3x - 1$

x	-2	-1	0	1	2
y	-7	-4	-1	2	5

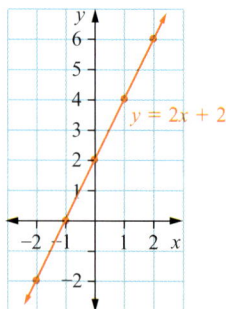

e $y = 2x + 2$

x	-2	-1	0	1	2
y	-2	0	2	4	6

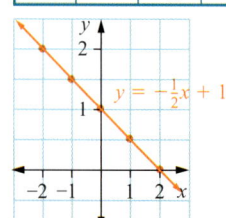

f $y = -\dfrac{1}{2}x + 1$

x	-2	-1	0	1	2
y	2	$1\tfrac{1}{2}$	1	$\tfrac{1}{2}$	0

g $y = -2x + 8$

x	-2	-1	0	1	2
y	12	10	8	6	4

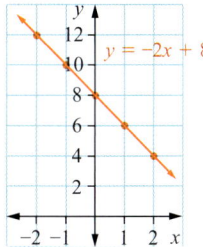

h $y = 1 - 3x$

x	-2	-1	0	1	2
y	7	4	1	-2	-5

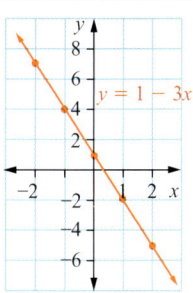

2 a $y = x + 1, y = x - 1, y = 3x - 1, y = 2x + 2$

b $y = -x - 2, y = -\frac{1}{2}x + 1, y = -2x + 8, y = 1 - 3x$

c If the coefficient of x is positive then the gradient is positive, and if the coefficient is negative so too is the gradient.

d i Positive   **ii** Negative   **iii** Negative
   iv Positive   **v** Positive   **vi** Negative

3 a C   **b** A   **c** D   **d** E   **e** B

Exercise 3C

1 a $y = 2x + 7$ **b** $y = 4x - 6$
   c $y = -3x - 1$ **d** $y = -2x + 2$
   e $y = -2x + 6$ **f** $y = x + 3$
   g $y = 3x$ **h** $y = -x + 2$

2 a
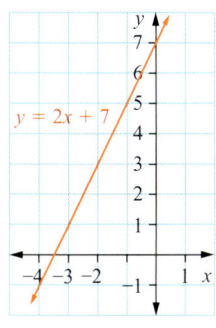
b
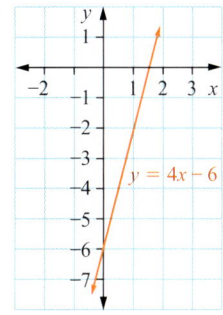

c
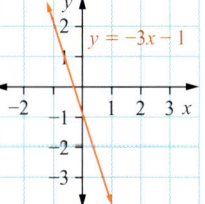
d
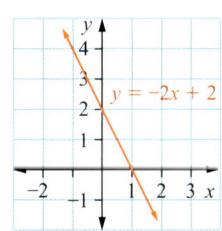

e
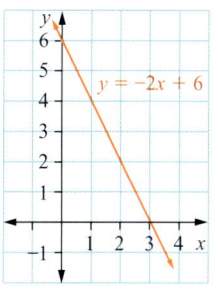
f
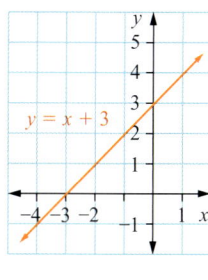

g
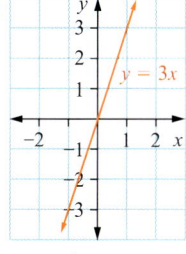
h
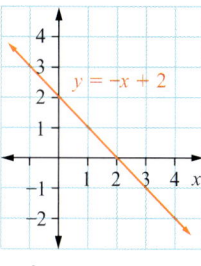

3 a $y = -\frac{3}{4}x + 1$ **b** $y = \frac{2}{3}x + 2$
   c $y = \frac{2}{3}x - 1$ **d** $y = \frac{4}{5}x - 2$
   e $y = -\frac{1}{3}x + 4$ **f** $y = -\frac{1}{4}x - 1$
   g $y = \frac{2}{5}x$ **h** $y = -\frac{2}{5}x + 4$

4 a
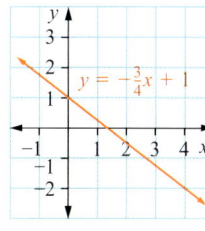
b
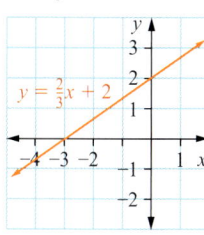

c
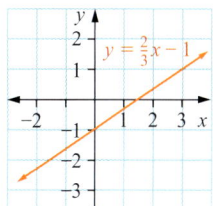
d
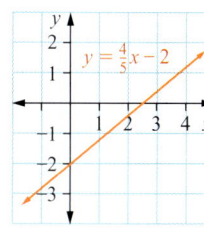

e
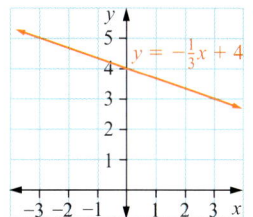
f
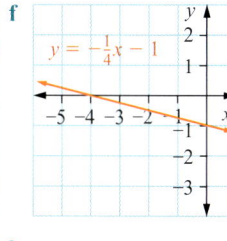

g
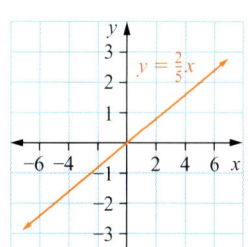
h
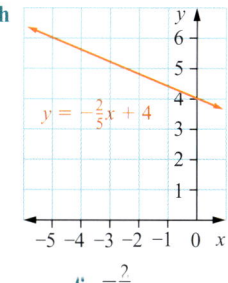

5 a 1   **b** $\frac{4}{3}$ **c** $-\frac{2}{3}$
   d $\frac{1}{2}$ **e** -2 **f** $-\frac{1}{4}$

6 a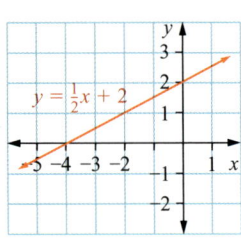

b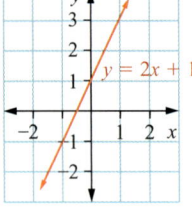

c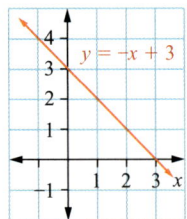

d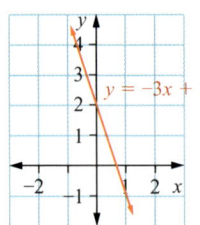

e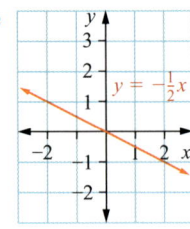

f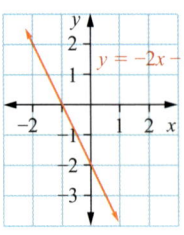

g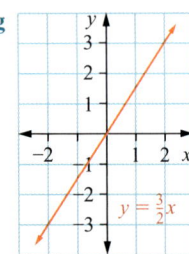

h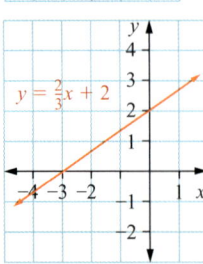

i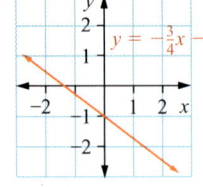

7 a $m = \frac{1}{2}, b = 2$ **b** $m = 2, b = 1$

c $m = -1, b = 3$ **d** $m = -3, b = 2$

e $m = -\frac{1}{2}, b = 0$ **f** $m = -2, b = -2$

g $m = \frac{3}{2}, b = 0$ **h** $m = \frac{2}{3}, b = 2$

i $m = -\frac{3}{4}, b = -1$

8 a $y = x + 1$ **b** $y = \frac{4}{3}x - 1$

c $y = -\frac{2}{3}x + 2$ **d** $y = \frac{1}{2}x + 4$

e $y = -2x - 2$ **f** $y = -\frac{1}{4}x - 2$

9 a $y = 3x + 1$, $y = 3x - 2$; they have the same gradient

b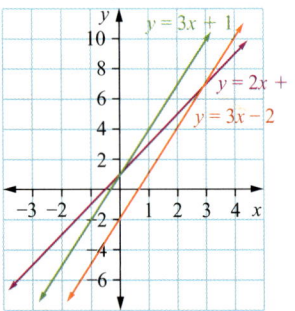

$y = 3x + 1$ and $y = 2x + 1$ have the same y-intercept

c i $y = 2x + 1$, parallel as it has the same gradient

  ii $y = 3x - 2$, as it has the same y-intercept

10 a $y = -\frac{1}{2}x + 2, m = -\frac{1}{2}, b = 2$

b $y = -\frac{3}{2}x + 12, m = -\frac{3}{2}, b = 12$

c $y = 2x + 4, m = 2, b = 4$

d $y = 2x - 3, m = 2, b = -3$

e $y = -\frac{5}{2}x - 5, m = -\frac{5}{2}, b = -5$

f $y = -\frac{3}{2}x + 4, m = -\frac{3}{2}, b = 4$

g $y = 4x - 6, m = 4, b = -6$

h $y = \frac{3}{2}x + 8\frac{1}{2}, m = \frac{3}{2}, b = 8\frac{1}{2}$

i $y = 4x - 3\frac{1}{2}, m = 4, b = -3\frac{1}{2}$

Exercise 3D

1 a $y = 3x - 9$ **b** $y = -2x - 6$

c $y = -\frac{1}{2}x + 7\frac{1}{2}$ **d** $y = 5x - 15$

e $y = \frac{1}{3}x + 6$ **f** $y = -\frac{1}{2}x - 4\frac{1}{2}$

g $y = -\frac{3}{2}x + 8\frac{1}{2}$ **h** $y = 6x$

i $y = 4x + 3\frac{1}{2}$ **j** $y = 4$

2 a $y = 2x - 10$ **b** $y = x - 7$

c $y = -3x + 22$ **d** $y = -2x - 12$

e $y = 5x - 15$ **f** $y = \frac{1}{2}x + 5$

g $y = -\frac{1}{3}x + 5$ **h** $y = 8x$

i $y = \frac{1}{3}x + 6$ **j** $y = 2$

3 a $y = 2x - 1$ **b** $y = -x + 2$

c $y = -\frac{1}{3}x - 3\frac{1}{3}$ **d** $y = x - 3$

e $y = x - 7$ **f** $y = \frac{5}{3}x$

g $y = -\frac{7}{4}x - \frac{1}{4}$ **h** $y = 2x + 4$

i $y = \frac{3}{5}x + \frac{4}{5}$ **j** $y = \frac{3}{2}x + 6$

4 a $y = 2x - 4$ **b** $y = \frac{7}{2}x + 7$

c $y = -\frac{5}{3}x - 5$ **d** $y = \frac{3}{2}x - 3$

Exercise 3E

1 a $2x - y + 1 = 0$ **b** $5x - y - 2 = 0$

c $2x - y + 5 = 0$ **d** $2x + y + 5 = 0$

e $3x + y - 4 = 0$ **f** $x - 2y + 4 = 0$

g $x + 2y + 10 = 0$ **h** $2x + 3y + 9 = 0$

i $9x + 12y + 8 = 0$ **j** $3x - 8y + 12 = 0$

k $2x - 4y - 3 = 0$ **l** $10x - 2y + 5 = 0$

2 a $y = -\frac{1}{2}x + 2, m = -\frac{1}{2}, b = 2$

b $y = -\frac{3}{2}x + 12, m = -\frac{3}{2}, b = 12$

c $y = 2x + 4, m = 2, b = 4$

d $y = 2x - 3, m = 2, b = -3$

e $y = -\frac{5}{2}x - 5, m = -\frac{5}{2}, b = -5$

f $y = -\frac{3}{2}x + 4, m = -\frac{3}{2}, b = 4$

g $y = 4x - 6, m = 4, b = -6$

h $y = \frac{3}{2}x + 8\frac{1}{2}, m = \frac{3}{2}, b = 8\frac{1}{2}$

i $y = 4x - 3\frac{1}{2}, m = 4, b = -3\frac{1}{2}$

3 a -3 **b** $-\frac{9}{4}$ **c** $-\frac{7}{5}$ **d** $\frac{5}{4}$

4 a $8, 4$ **b** $4, 6$ **c** $-3, 6$

d $12, -18$ **e** $-4, -10$ **f** $\frac{5}{3}, \frac{5}{2}$

g $\frac{5}{4}, -5$ **h** $-5, 7\frac{1}{2}$ **i** $\frac{5}{9}, -2\frac{1}{2}$

5 a $x + 2y - 8 = 0$

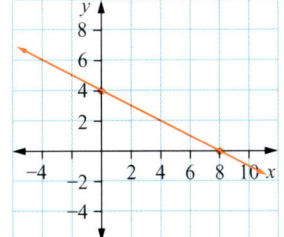

b $3x - y - 6 = 0$

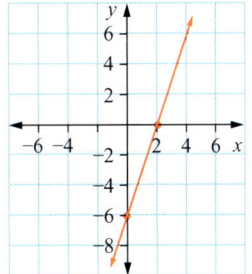

c $2x - 3y - 4 = 0$

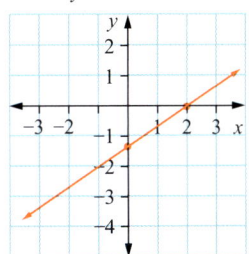

d $4x + 3y - 8 = 0$

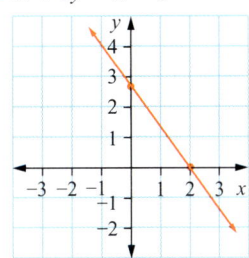

e $x + y - 5 = 0$

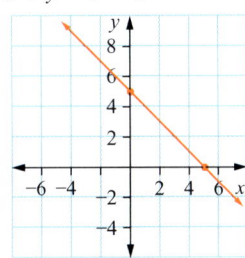

f $x - y + 5 = 0$

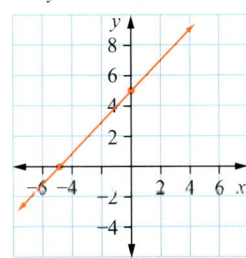

g $3x - 4y - 12 = 0$

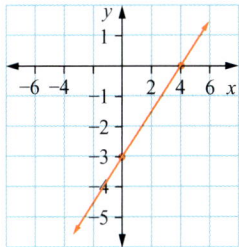

h $5x + 2y + 10 = 0$

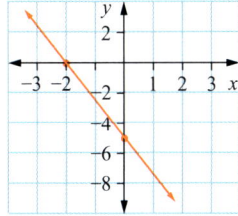

i $x - 2y = 0$

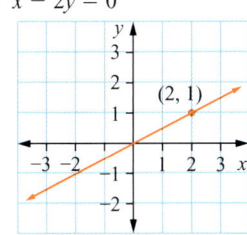

j $2x - 5y - 5 = 0$

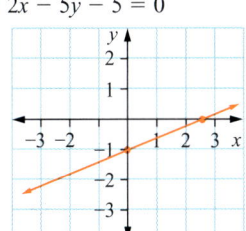

Exercise 3F

1 A, B, E, H

2 a $y = 2x + 2$ **b** $y = -7x - 37$
   c $y = -\frac{1}{2}x$ **d** $5x - 7y - 31 = 0$
   e $y = \frac{1}{2}x - 2\frac{1}{2}$ **f** $y = -\frac{5}{7}x - 2$

3 B, D, E

4 a $\frac{5}{3}$ **b** $-\frac{1}{7}$ **c** $-\frac{2}{3}$
   d $\frac{5}{4}$ **e** $-\frac{2}{3}$ **f** $-\frac{7}{5}$

5 a $y = -\frac{1}{5}x + \frac{7}{5}$ **b** $y = 4x + 5$
   c $y = -\frac{4}{3}x$ **d** $4x + 3y - 7 = 0$
   e $2x - 5y + 35 = 0$ **f** $y = \frac{1}{2}x - 4$
   g $y = -\frac{3}{5}x$

6 a $y = -2x + c$ **b** $y = 3x + c$
   c $3x - 5y + c = 0$ **d** $3x + 5y + c = 0$

7 b $4x + 3y + c = 0$
   c Coefficients of x and y are interchanged and the sign of y is changed.

8 b $2x - 7y + c - 0$
   c Same coefficients of x and y.

9 a $7x - 5y + c = 0$ **b** $5x + 7y + c = 0$

Exercise 3G

1 a $d_{PQ} = \sqrt{5}, d_{QR} = \sqrt{18}, d_{PR} = \sqrt{17}$
  b Scalene as all sides are different lengths.
2 $d_{LM} = \sqrt{20}, d_{MN} = \sqrt{20}, d_{LN} = \sqrt{40}, \triangle LMN$ is isosceles.
3 5.7
4 a $y = 3x - 5$ **b** $y = -2x + 7$
5 a (1, 1) **b** (0, 2)
6 (1, −3)
7 a $d_{XY} = \sqrt{10}, d_{YZ} = \sqrt{20}, d_{XZ} = \sqrt{10}$
  b $\triangle XYZ$ is right angled since $XY^2 + XZ^2 = YZ^2$
  c $m_{XY} = 3, m_{YZ} = -2, m_{XZ} = -\frac{1}{3}$
  d $m_{XY} \times m_{XZ} = -1$
  e Yes, as $m_{XY} \times m_{XZ} = -1$
8 Yes, DE and DF are perpendicular.
9 a $S = (\frac{1}{2}, 2)$ **b** $T = (-3, -1)$
  c $d_{QR} = \sqrt{85}$
  $d_{ST} = \sqrt{\frac{85}{4}} = \frac{1}{2}\sqrt{85}$
  ∴ true
10 a i $d_{PQ} = d_{RS} = \sqrt{18}, d_{QR} = d_{PS} = \sqrt{45}$
  ii Midpoint $PR = (\frac{1}{2}, 1)$
  Midpoint $QS = (\frac{1}{2}, 1)$
  ∴ diagonals bisect
  b i $m_{PQ} = -1, m_{QR} = \frac{1}{2}, m_{RS} = -1, m_{PS} = \frac{1}{2}$
  ii Sides are parallel and non-perpendicular so it is not a rectangle.
  c No

Language in mathematics

1 a Gradient is rise over run.
  b b is the symbol for y-intercept.
  c m is the symbol for gradient.
  d Midpoint is the average of the ordinates.
  e The distance formula is related to Pythagoras' theorem.
  f $y = mx + b$ is the gradient–intercept form of a straight line.
2 a equation **b** formula **c** gradient
  d parallel **e** vertical rise **f** horizontal run
3 Two lines are perpendicular if the product of their gradients is negative one and they are parallel if their gradients are equal.

Check your skills

1 B	**2** D	**3** B	**4** A	**5** A
6 B	**7** C	**8** D	**9** C	**10** A
11 B	**12** C	**13** B	**14** A	**15** D
16 B	**17** C	**18** C	**19** A	**20** A
21 B	**22** B	**23** D	**24** B	**25** C
26 D				

Review set 3A

1 a $\sqrt{65}$ **b** $(-1, -\frac{1}{2})$ **c** $-\frac{1}{8}$
2 (−8, 12) **3** (−10, 14)
4 a $y = 2x + 3$

x	−3	−2	−1	0	1	2	3
y	−3	−1	1	3	5	7	9

b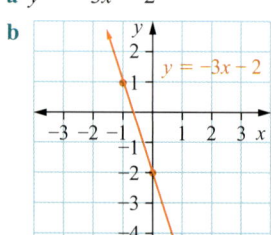

c Yes
5 a $y = -3x - 2$
b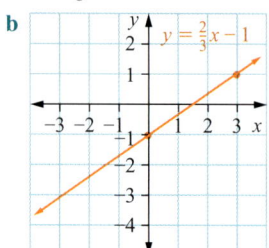

6 a $y = \frac{2x}{3} - 1$
b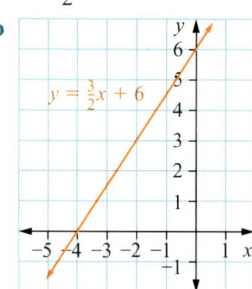

7 a $m = -1$ **b** 2 **c** $y = -x + 2$
8 a $y = \frac{3x}{2} + 6$
b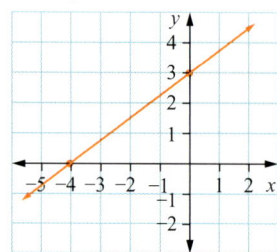

9 a $-\frac{1}{8}$ **b** $y = -\frac{1}{8}x - \frac{5}{8}$
  c x-intercept $= -5$, y-intercept $= -\frac{5}{8}$
  d $y = 8x - 25$ **e** $y = -\frac{1}{8}x + \frac{3}{8}$
10 a $4x - 3y - 7 = 0$ **b** $x + 6y - 38 = 0$
  c $3x - 4y + 12 = 0$

11 a $\frac{2}{3}$ **b** $t = -13$

Review set 3B

1 a $\sqrt{65}$ **b** $(-3\frac{1}{2}, 2)$ **c** $-\frac{4}{7}$

2 $d_{AB} = \sqrt{20}$, $d_{BC} = \sqrt{20}$, $d_{AC} = \sqrt{8}$

  Isosceles since $d_{AB} = d_{BC}$

3 a $y = -5x + 7$

x	-3	-2	-1	0	1	2	3
y	22	17	12	7	2	-3	-8

  b

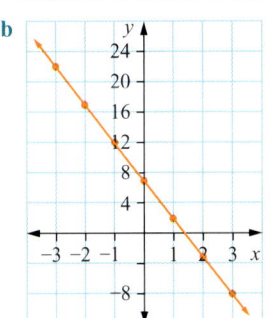

4 a $y = -2x + 3$

  b

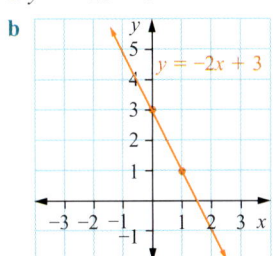

5 $y = \frac{6x}{5} + 3$

6 $5x - 7y + 34 = 0$

7 $3x + 2y + 2 = 0$

8 $2x + 3y + 12 = 0$

9 $y = -3x + 7$

Review set 3C

1 a $\sqrt{89}$ **b** $(-3\frac{1}{2}, -1)$ **c** $-\frac{8}{5}$

2 $(6, -7)$ **3** $(2, -3)$

4 a $y = -3x + 2$

x	-3	-2	-1	0	1	2	3
y	11	8	5	2	-1	-4	-7

  b

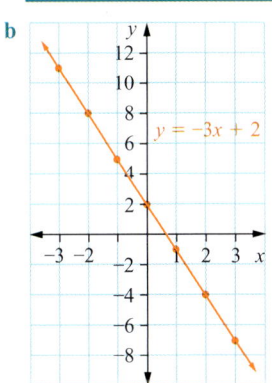

  c Yes

5 a $y = 4x - 2$

  b

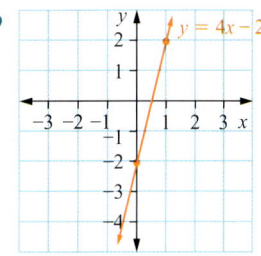

6 a $y = -\frac{3}{4}x - 2$

  b

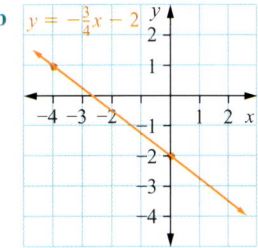

7 a $m = \frac{7}{5}$ **b** -2 **c** $y = \frac{7}{5}x - 2$

8 a $y = \frac{5}{4}x + 5$

  b

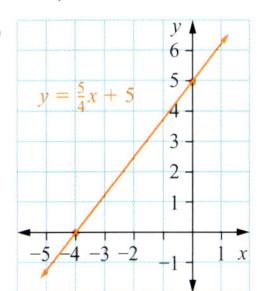

9 a $-\frac{8}{5}$

  b $y = -\frac{8}{5}x - 6\frac{3}{5}$; $8x + 5y + 33 = 0$

  c x-intercept $-4\frac{1}{8}$, y-intercept $-6\frac{3}{5}$

  d $5x - 8y - 35 = 0$ **e** $y = -\frac{8}{5}x$

10 a $y = \frac{4}{7}x + \frac{8}{7}$ **b** $x + 2y = 0$

  c

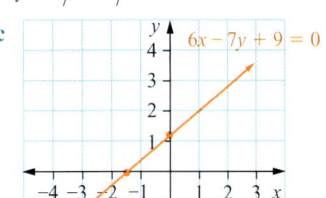

Review set 3D

1 a $\sqrt{26}$ **b** $(-\frac{1}{2}, \frac{9}{2})$ **c** $-\frac{1}{5}$

2 a $d_{LM} = \sqrt{10}$, $d_{MN} = \sqrt{20}$, $d_{LN} = \sqrt{10}$

  b $(\sqrt{10})^2 + (\sqrt{10})^2 = (\sqrt{20})^2$, $\therefore$ right-angled

3 a $y = -\frac{1}{2}x + 3$

x	-4	-2	0	2	4
y	5	4	3	2	1

b

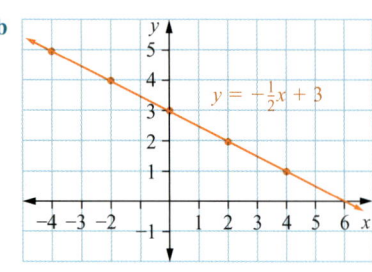

$y = -\frac{1}{2}x + 3$

c Gradient $= -\frac{1}{2}$, y-intercept $= 3$

4 a $y = 2x - 8$

b

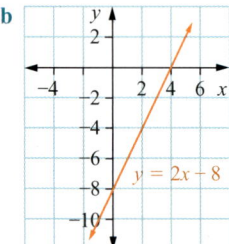

$y = 2x - 8$

5 $y = -\frac{11}{5}x - 3$

6 a $y = 3x + 10$ **b** $3x - 5y = 0$

7 $3x + 4y - 8 = 0$

8 No, as $3(1) - 5(4) + 2 \ne 0$

CHAPTER 4 GEOMETRICAL PROOFS

Diagnostic test

1 B	2 B	3 A	4 C	5 D
6 C	7 B	8 C	9 C	10 B
11 C				

Exercise 4A

1 a $5y = 55°$ (Vertically opposite angles are equal.)
$y = 11°$
$2z = 46°$ (Vertically opposite angles are equal.)
$z = 23°$
$x + 46° + 55° = 180°$ (DPC is a straight line.)
$x = 79°$

b $2y + 90° + 70° = 180°$ (ABC is a straight line.)
$y = 10°$

c $\angle EGD = \angle JEB = 50°$ (Corresponding angles and $AB \parallel CD$.)
$\angle EGD + \angle DGH = 180°$ ($\angle EGH$ is a straight angle.)
$50° + x = 180°$
$x = 130°$
$\angle FGC = \angle HGD = 130°$ (Vertically opposite angles are equal.)
$\angle EFI = \angle FGC$ (Corresponding angles and $IF \parallel CD$.)
$y = 130°$

d $\angle BAE = \angle DEF$ (Corresponding angles and $AB \parallel CD$.)
$2x + 10° = x + 40$
$\therefore x = 30°$
$\angle AEC = \angle DEF$ (Vertically opposite angles are equal.)
$2y - 20° = 70°$
$y = 45°$

e $\angle ABD = 90°$ ($\angle ABC$ is a straight angle.)
$x + 90° + 42° = 180°$ (Angle sum of a $\triangle$ is 180°.)
$x = 48°$
$y = 42°$ ($\angle ADC$ is 90°.)
$z = 48°$ (Angle sum of a $\triangle$ is 180°.)

f $\angle WXY = \angle UVW = 48°$
(Alternate angles and $UV \parallel XZ$.)
$x = 48° + 56° = 104°$ (Exterior angle of a $\triangle$ equals the sum of the interior opposite angles.)

g $\angle QSR = x$ (Angles opposite equal sides of a $\triangle$ are equal.)
$130 = x + x$ (Exterior angle of a $\triangle$ equals the sum of the interior opposite angles.)
$x = 65°$
$y = 115°$ ($\angle TSR = 180°$)

h $\angle BDE = \angle CBD = x$ (Alternate angles and $AC \parallel ED$.)
$\angle DEB = \angle BDE = x$ (Angles opposite equal sides of a $\triangle$ are equal.)
$x + x + 52° = 180°$ (Angle sum of a $\triangle$ is 180°.)
$x = 64°$
$\angle ABE = \angle BED = y$ (Alternate angles and $AC \parallel ED$.)
$y = 64°$

i $3x + 70° + 2x + 90° = 360°$ (Angle sum of a quadrilateral is 360°.)
$5x + 160° = 360°$, $x = 40°$
$\angle ADE + \angle ADC = 180°$ ($\angle CDE$ is a straight angle.)
$y + 80° = 180°$
$y = 100°$

j $\angle ADC = 50°$ (Co-interior angles and $AB \parallel CD$.)
$\angle EDC = 25°$ (ED bisects $\angle ADC$.)
$\angle BCD = 130°$ (Co-interior angles and $AD \parallel BC$.)
$\angle DCE = 65°$ (EC bisects $\angle BCD$.)
$x + 25° + 65° = 180°$ (Angle sum of a $\triangle$ is 180°.)
$x = 90°$

k Let $\angle SPQ = x$ and let $\angle SQP = y$.
$2x + 2y + 70° = 180°$ (Angle sum of a $\triangle$ is 180°.)
$2x + 2y = 110°$
$x + y = 55°$
$x + y + z = 180°$ (Angle sum of a $\triangle$ is 180°.)
$55° + z = 180°$
$z = 125°$

l $p + 70° + 35° = 180°$ (Angle sum of a $\triangle$ is 180°.)
$p = 75°$
$r = 35°$ (Alternate angles and $AB \parallel CD$.)
$q = 180° - 40° - 35°$ (Angle sum of a $\triangle$ is 180°.)
$q = 105°$

2 a $\angle PWV = \angle QWR = x$ (Vertically opposite angles are equal.)
$\angle UVW = \angle SVT = y$ (Vertically opposite angles are equal.)
$\angle PWV + \angle UVW = x + y = 180°$ (given)
$\therefore PR \parallel US$ ($\angle PWV$ and $\angle UVW$ are co-interior and supplementary.)

b $3x + 50° + x + 100° + 90° = 360°$
(Angle sum at a point is 360°.)
$4x + 240° = 360°$
$x = 30°$
$\angle PUQ = 3 \times 30° = 90°$
$\therefore TUQ$ is a straight line.   ($\angle TUP + \angle PUQ = 180°$)

c $2x + 2y = 180°$ (ABC is a straight line.)
$2(x + y) = 180°$
$x + y = 90°$
$\angle PBQ = \angle PBD + \angle DBQ = x + y = 90°$

d $\angle QAB = \angle CBA = b$ (Alternate angles and $PQ \parallel CB$.)
$\angle PAC = \angle BCA = c$ (Alternate angles and $PQ \parallel CB$.)
$\angle PAC + \angle CAB + \angle BAQ = 180°$
(PAQ is a straight line.)
$c + a + b = 180°$

e $\angle PBA = y$ (Alternate angles and $PB \parallel AC$.)
$\angle ACD = \angle PBC$ (Corresponding angles and $PB \parallel AC$.)
$z = x + y$

f $\angle PQT = x$ (Corresponding angles and $TQ \parallel SR$.)
$\angle RSQ = x$ (Angles opposite equal sides of a $\triangle$ are equal.)
$\angle TQS = \angle RSQ = x$ (Alternate angles and $TQ \parallel SR$.)
$\angle PQT = \angle RSQ = x$
TQ bisects $\angle PQS$.

g Join OQ. Let $\angle OPQ = x$ and $\angle ORQ = y$.
In $\triangle OPQ$, $\angle OQP = x$ ($OP = OQ$, radii)
In $\triangle OQR$, $\angle OQR = y$ ($OQ = OR$, radii)
In $\triangle PQR$, $x + x + y + y = 180°$
$2x + 2y = 180°$ (Angle sum of a $\triangle$ is $180°$.)
$x + y = 90°$
$\angle PQR = \angle PQO + \angle OQR = x + y = 90°$

Exercise 4B

1 a SAS   **b** SSS   **c** RHS   **d** AAS
  e SAS   **f** AAS   **g** SSS   **h** SAS

2 a The $55°$ angle in the second triangle is not the included angle.
  b Three pairs of equal angles do not necessarily make the triangles congruent.
  c The equal sides are not matching sides.
  d The $30°$ angle in the second triangle is not the included angle.

3 a 2 and 3 (SAS)   **b** 1, 2 and 3 (AAS)
  c 1 and 2 (RHS)   **d** 1, 2 and 3 (SSS)
  e 1 and 3 (SAS)   **f** 2 and 3 (AAS)

4 a SSS, $x = 60°$, $y = 55°$, $z = 65°$
  b SAS, $x = 30°$, $y = 40°$
  c AAS, $x = 8$ cm, $y = 7$ cm
  d RHS, $x = 6$ cm, $y = 70°$, $z = 20°$
  e SAS, $x = 15$ cm, $y = 55°$, $z = 58°$
  f SSS, $x = 55°$, $y = 77°$, $z = 48°$
  g AAS, $x = 10$ cm, $y = 12$ cm, $z = 50°$
  h RHS, $x = 40°$, $y = 50°$, $z = 6$ cm

Exercise 4C

1 a In $\triangle ACD$ and $\triangle ACB$:
$AD = AB$ (given)
$DC = BC$ (given)
AC is common.
$\therefore \triangle ACD \equiv \triangle ACB$ (SSS)
  b $\angle DAC = \angle BAC$ (Matching angles in congruent $\triangle$s are equal.)
  c $\angle ADC = \angle ABC$ (Matching angles in congruent $\triangle$s are equal.)

2 a In $\triangle ABP$ and $\triangle DCP$:
$\angle BAP = \angle CDP$ (given)
$\angle APB = \angle DPC$ (Vertically opposite angles are equal.)
$AP = DP$ (given)
$\therefore \triangle ABP \equiv \triangle DCP$ (AAS)
  b $BP = CP$ (Matching sides in congruent $\triangle$s are equal.)
  c $AB = DC$ (Matching sides in congruent $\triangle$s are equal.)

3 a In $\triangle ABP$ and $\triangle CDP$:
$\angle ABP = \angle CDP$ (given)
$\angle APB = \angle CPD$ (Vertically opposite angles are equal.)
$AB = CD$ (given)
$\therefore \triangle ABP \equiv \triangle CDP$ (AAS)
  b $AP = CP$ (Matching sides in congruent $\triangle$s are equal.)

4 a In $\triangle AED$ and $\triangle BEC$:
$ED = EC$ (given)
$AD = BC$ (Opposite sides of a rectangle are equal.)
$\angle DAE = \angle EBC$ ($= 90°$, $ABCD$ is a rectangle.)
$\therefore \triangle AED \equiv \triangle BEC$ (RHS)
  b $AE = BE$ (Matching sides in congruent $\triangle$s are equal.)
$\therefore E$ is the midpoint of AB.

5 a In $\triangle PTQ$ and $\triangle STR$:
$PT = ST$ (given)
$QT = RT$ (given)
$\angle PTQ = \angle STR$ (Vertically opposite angles are equal.)
$\therefore \triangle PTQ \equiv \triangle STR$ (SAS)
  b $PQ = SR$ (Matching sides in congruent $\triangle$s are equal.)
  c $\angle PQT = \angle SRT$ (Matching angles in congruent $\triangle$s are equal.)

6 a In $\triangle PRS$ and $\triangle PRQ$:
$PS = PQ$ (given)
$\angle PRS = \angle PRQ$ ($= 90°$, $PR \perp SQ$)
PR is common.
$\therefore \triangle PRS \equiv \triangle PRQ$ (RHS)
  b $\angle PSR = \angle PQR$ (Matching angles in congruent $\triangle$s are equal.)
  c $SR = QR$ (Matching sides in congruent $\triangle$s are equal.)
  d $\angle SPR = \angle QPR$ (Matching angles in congruent $\triangle$s are equal.)
  e **i** The angles opposite the equal sides of an isosceles triangle are equal.
    ii A line drawn from the vertex of an isosceles triangle and perpendicular to its base bisects the base and the vertex angle of the triangle.

7 a In $\triangle ACD$ and $\triangle ACB$:
$\angle ADC = \angle ABC$ (given)
$\angle ACD = \angle ACB$ ($= 90°$, $AC \perp DB$)
AC is common.
$\therefore \triangle ACD \equiv \triangle ACB$ (AAS)
  b $AD = AB$ (Matching sides in congruent $\triangle$s are equal.)
$\therefore ABC$ is an isosceles triangle.
  c If two angles of a triangle are equal, then the sides opposite these angles are equal; that is, it is an isosceles triangle.

8 a In $\triangle WZY$ and $\triangle WXY$:
$WZ = WX$ (given)
$ZY = XY$ (given)
$WY = WY$ (common)
$\therefore \triangle WZY \equiv \triangle WXY$ (SSS)
  b $\angle WYZ = \angle WYX$ (Matching angles in congruent $\triangle$s are equal.)

c $\angle WYZ + \angle WYX = 180°$ ($\angle ZYX$ a straight angle.)
∴ $\angle WYZ = \angle WYX = 90°$

d $\angle ZWY = \angle XWY$ (Matching angles in congruent △s are equal.)

e A line drawn from the vertex of an isosceles triangle to the midpoint of its base is perpendicular to the base and bisects the angle at the vertex.

9 a Yes

b $AC = AB$ so $\angle C = \angle B$
$AB = AC$ so $\angle C = \angle A$.
Hence $\angle C = \angle A = \angle B$; that is, the three angles of an equilateral triangle are equal.

c Let $\angle A = \angle B = \angle C = x$ then
$x + x + x = 180°$
$3x = 180°$
$x = 60°$

10 a In $\triangle ABC$ and $\triangle CDA$:
$\angle BAC = \angle DCA$ (Alternate angles and $AB \parallel DC$.)
$\angle BCA = \angle DAC$ (Alternate angles and $AD \parallel BC$.)
$AC = CA$ (common)
∴ $\triangle ABC \equiv \triangle CDA$ (AAS)

b $AB = DC$ (Matching sides in congruent △s are equal.)

c $AD = BC$ (Matching sides in congruent △s are equal.)

d $\angle B = \angle D$ (Matching angles in congruent △s are equal.)

e i The opposite sides of a parallelogram are equal.
ii The opposite angles of a parallelogram are equal.

11 a In $\triangle PQT$ and $\triangle RST$:
$\angle QPT = \angle SRT$ (Alternate angles and $PQ \parallel SR$.)
$\angle PQT = \angle RST$ (Alternate angles and $PQ \parallel SR$.)
$PQ = RS$ (proven in question **10**)
∴ $\triangle PQT \equiv \triangle RST$ (AAS)

b $PT = RT$ (Matching sides in congruent △s are equal.)

c $QT = ST$ (Matching sides in congruent △s are equal.)

d The diagonals of a parallelogram bisect each other.

12 a In $\triangle ADC$ and $\triangle BCD$:
$AD = BC$ (Opposite sides of a rectangle are equal.)
DC is common.
$\angle ADC = \angle BCD$ (= 90°, $ABCD$ is a rectangle.)
∴ $\triangle ADC \equiv \triangle BCD$ (SAS)

b $AC = BD$ (Matching sides in congruent △s are equal.)

c The diagonals of a rectangle are equal.

13 a In $\triangle ADE$ and $\triangle ABE$:
$AD = AB$ (All sides of a rhombus are equal.)
$DE = BE$ (Diagonals of a parallelogram bisect each other.)
AE is common.
$\triangle ADE \equiv \triangle ABE$ (SSS)

b $\angle AED = \angle AEB$ (Matching angles in congruent △s are equal.)
$\angle AED + \angle AEB = 180°$ ($\angle DEB$ a straight angle.)
∴ $\angle AED = \angle AEB = 90°$

c $\angle DAE = \angle BAE$ (Matching angles in congruent △s are equal.)

d i The diagonals of a rhombus intersect at right angles.
ii The diagonals of a rhombus bisect the angles of the rhombus.

14 a In $\triangle ABC$ and $\triangle AED$:
$AB = AE$ (given)
$BC = ED$ (given)
$\angle ABC = \angle AED$ (given)
∴ $\triangle ABC \equiv \triangle AED$ (SAS)
∴ $AC = AD$ (Matching sides in congruent △s are equal.)

b Similarly:
$\triangle ABC \equiv \triangle CDE$ ∴ $AC = CE$
$\triangle AED \equiv \triangle BCD$ ∴ $AD = BD$
$\triangle ABE \equiv \triangle DCE$ ∴ $BE = CE$
$AC = AD = CE = BD = BE$

Exercise 4D

1 a Test 2 (Three pairs of sides are in proportion.)
b Test 1 (Two pairs of equal angles.)
c Test 4 (The hypotenuse and a second side in each right-angled triangle are in proportion.)
d Test 3 (Two pairs of sides are in proportion and included angles are equal.)
e Test 1 (Two pairs of equal angles.)
f Test 4 (The hypotenuse and a second side in each right-angled triangle are in proportion.)
g Test 2 (Three pairs of sides are in proportion.)
h Test 3 (Two pairs of sides are in proportion and included angles are equal.)

2 a The 80° angle in the first triangle is not included by the sides in proportion.
b The second sides are not in the same proportion as the hypotenuses.
c Only two pairs of sides are in proportion.
d The 60° angle in the second triangle is not the included angle.
e The second sides are not in the same proportion as the hypotenuses.
f Only two pairs of sides are in proportion.

3 a Yes: Test 1 (Two pairs of equal angles.)
b No: Not all pairs of angles are equal.
c Yes: Test 2 (Three pairs of sides are in proportion.)
d No: Only two pairs of sides are in proportion.
e Yes: Test 1 (Two pairs of equal angles.)
f Yes: Test 2 (Three pairs of sides are in proportion.)
g Yes: Test 1 (Two pairs of equal angles.)
h No: Not all pairs of angles are equal.
i Yes: Test 2 (Three pairs of sides are in proportion.)
j No: Only two pairs of sides are in proportion.
k Yes: Test 2 (Three pairs of sides are in proportion.)
l Yes: Test 3 (Two pairs of sides are in proportion and included angles are equal.)
m No: The first 70° angle is not the included angle.
n Yes: Test 4 (The hypotenuse and a second side in each right-angled triangle are in proportion.)

4 a B, C (Test 2)   **b** A, B (Test 1)
c A, C (Test 1 or Test 3)   **d** A, B (Test 2)
e A, C (Test 3)   **f** A, B (Test 3)
g A, B (Test 4)   **h** B, C (Test 4)

5 b No   **c** Not true

6 a $x = 25$ cm, $y = 12$ cm   **b** $x = 18$ cm, $y = 9$ cm
c $x = 3.2$ cm, $y = 15$ cm   **d** $x = 30$ cm, $y = 12$ cm
e $x = 8$ cm, $y = 22.5$ cm   **f** $x = 24$ cm, $y = 8$ cm
g $x = 15$ cm, $y = 7$ cm   **h** $x = 5.1$ cm, $y = 7$ cm
i $x = 25$ cm, $y = 11$ cm   **j** $x = 12.6$ cm, $y = 15$ cm

7 a $x = 4.5$ cm   **b** $x = 7.5$ cm
  c $x = 4.8$ cm   **d** $x = 3.75$ cm
  e $x = 14$ cm   **f** $x = 4.8$ cm
  g $x = 2$ cm   **h** $x = 1\frac{1}{3}$ cm

8 a $\triangle FED \,|||\, \triangle CBA$ $(\angle E = \angle B, \angle D = \angle A)$
  b $h = 5.6$ m

9 a $\triangle UTS \,|||\, \triangle RQP$ $(\angle T = \angle Q, \angle S = \angle P)$
  b $h = 9$ m

10 a $\triangle PRT \,|||\, \triangle QRS$ $(\angle T = \angle S, \angle R = \angle R)$
  b $h = 8.5$ m

11 a $\triangle VYU \,|||\, \triangle WXU$ $(\angle VYU = \angle WXU, \angle U$ is common.$)$
  b $VY = 1.2$ m

12 $r = 1.2$ cm

Exercise 4E

1 a, b 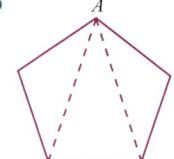   **c** $540°$

A

2

Polygon	Number of sides	Number of triangles	Angle sum of polygon
Quadrilateral	4	2	360°
Pentagon	5	3	540°
Hexagon	6	4	720°
Heptagon	7	5	900°
Octagon	8	6	1080°
Nonagon	9	7	1260°
Decagon	10	8	1440°
n-gon	n	$n - 2$	$(n - 2) \times 180°$

3 $(n - 2)$

4 a $108°$ **b** $120°$ **c** $128\frac{4}{7}°$
  d $135°$ **e** $140°$ **f** $144°$

5 a $3960°$ **b** $165°$

6 a $80°$ **b** $70°$ **c** $77°$

7 a $720°$
  b i $50°$ **ii** $70°$ **iii** $65°$

8 a $x = 50°$ (Angle sum of a quadrilateral is $360°$.)
  b $x = 165°$ (Angle sum of a pentagon is $540°$.)
  c $x = 120°$ (Angle sum of a hexagon is $720°$.)
  d $x = 20°$ (Angle sum of a quadrilateral is $360°$.)
  e $x = 120°$ (Angle sum of a hexagon is $720°$.)
  f $x = 60°$ (Angle sum of a pentagon is $540°$.)
  g $x = 40°$ (Angle sum of a hexagon is $720°$.)
  h $x = 125°$ (Angle sum of a heptagon is $900°$.)
  i $x = 135°$ (Angle sum of an octagon is $1080°$.)

9 $135°$ **10** $135°$

11 a $45°$ **b** $135°$ (Straight line is $180°$.)
  c $1080°$

12 a $18°$ **b** $162°$ **c** $3240°$

13 24 sides

14 a 36 sides   **b** 20 sides
  c 15 sides   **d** 4 sides

15 21 sides

16 a 31 sides   **b** 21 sides   **c** 22 sides

17 22 sides

18 16 sides

Language in mathematics

1 Congruent triangles have the same shape (and size) so they are similar. Similar triangles have the same shape but not necessarily the same size, hence they are not necessarily congruent.

2 a An isosceles triangle has two equal sides.
  Properties:
  Angles opposite equal sides are equal.
  A line from the vertex drawn perpendicular to its base bisects the base and the angle at the vertex.
  A line drawn from the vertex to the midpoint of its base is perpendicular to the base and bisects the angle at the vertex.
  b An equilateral triangle has 3 equal sides.
  Properties:
  All the properties of isosceles triangles. All angles equal $60°$.

3 Two plane figures are equiangular if all the angles of one are equal to all the angles of the other. Yes, they have the same shape.

4 The remaining angle in each triangle is $180°$ minus the sum of the other two angles (which are equal in each triangle).

5 a $AB = AD$, $AC = AC$, $\angle B = \angle D$ but angles B and D are not included by the equal sides.
  b i If $CB = CD$ the triangles would be congruent (SAS or SSS).
    ii If $\angle BAC = \angle DAC$, the triangles would be congruent (AAS).
    iii If $\angle ACB = \angle ACD$, the triangles would be congruent (AAS).

6 The exterior angle of a polygon is formed by extending the sides in the same order. The exterior angle is the angle between the extended side and the side that is adjacent to it.

7 $S = (n - 2) \times 180°$ or $S = n \times 180° - 360°$ where S is the sum of the angles and n is the number of sides of the polygon.

8 $360°$

<table>
<tr><td colspan="5">Check your skills</td></tr>
</table>

1 D	**2** D	**3** B	**4** C	**5** C
6 B	**7** A	**8** D	**9** B	**10** C
11 B	**12** A	**13** B	**14** C	**15** D
16 C	**17** B	**18** A	**19** C	**20** A
21 B				

Review set 4A

1 $\angle ABC = \angle EAB$ (Alternate angles and $AE \parallel CF$.)
  $\angle ACB = \angle DAE$ (Corresponding angles and $AE \parallel CF$.)
  $\therefore \angle ABC = \angle ACB$ ($\angle EAB = \angle DAE$, given)
  $\therefore AB = AC$ (Sides opposite equal angles in a $\triangle$ are equal.)

2 a SAS   **b** AAS   **c** SSS

3 a Three pairs of equal angles do not make two triangles congruent.
  b The equal angles are not the included angles.
  c The equal sides are not matching sides.

4 a 1, 2 (AAS)   **b** 1, 3 (SAS)

5 a SSS, $x = 50°$, $y = 95°$, $z = 35°$
  b SAS, $x = 15$ cm, $y = 45°$, $z = 35°$
  c AAS, $x = 9$ cm, $y = 10$ cm, $z = 50°$

6 a In $\triangle PQT$ and $\triangle RQS$:

| $PT = RS$ | (given) |
| | |

$PT = RS$ (given)
$\angle PTQ = \angle RQS$ (given)
$\angle PQT = \angle QRS$ (Vertically opposite angles are equal.)
$\therefore \triangle PQT \equiv \triangle RQS$ (AAS)

b $PQ = RQ$ (Matching sides in congruent $\triangle$s are equal.)

7 a Yes: Test 1 (Three pairs of equal angles.)

b No: Only two pairs of sides in proportion.

c Yes: Test 3 (Two pairs of sides are in proportion and included angles are equal.)

d No: The 80° angle in the second triangle is not included by the sides in proportion.

e Yes: The hypotenuses and a second side in each right-angled triangle are in proportion.

f No: The sides in proportion do not include the hypotenuses of each triangle.

8 a 1, 2 (Test 2)   **b** 1, 2, 3 (Test 1 or Test 3)
c 1, 3 (Test 3)   **d** 1, 2, 3 (Test 4)

9 a $k = 3$, $x = 15$ cm, $y = 6$ cm
b $k = 0.8$, $x = 12$ cm, $y = 8$ cm

10 a $x = 7.5$ cm, $y = 3.3$ cm   **b** $x = 6$ cm, $y = 12$ cm

11 a, b 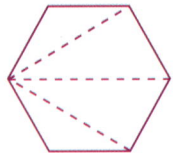   **c** $4 \times 180° = 720°$

12 a $x = 100°$ (Angle sum of a hexagon is 720°.)
b $x = 105°$ (Angle sum of a pentagon is 540°.)

13 a 135°   **b** 360°

14 a 36   **b** 6120°

Review set 4B

1 $\angle DEC = \angle DCE$ ($DC = DE$)
$\angle ABC = \angle ACB$ ($AB = AC$)
$\angle DEC = \angle ABC$ ($\angle DCE = \angle ACB$)
$\therefore AB \parallel DE$ (A pair of corresponding angles are equal.)

2 a SSS   **b** RHS   **c** SAS   **d** AAS

3 a The angle of first triangle is not the included angle.
b The equal sides are not matching sides.
c Three pair of equal angles do not make triangles congruent.

4 a 1, 3 (SAS)   **b** 2, 3 (AAS)

5 a SSS, $x = 60°$, $y = 65°$, $z = 55°$
b SAS, $x = 60°$, $y = 80°$
c AAS, $x = 10$ cm, $y = 8$ cm

6 a $AB = CD$ (given)
$AC = CA$ (common)
$\angle BAC = \angle DCA$ (Alternate angles and $AB \parallel DC$.)
$\therefore \triangle ABC \equiv \triangle CDA$ (SAS)

b $AD = BC$

7 a Yes: Test 1 (Two pairs of equal angles.)
b Yes: Test 2 (Three pairs of sides are in proportion.)
c No: The angle of the first triangle is not the included angle.
d Yes: Test 3 (Two pairs of sides are in proportion and included angles are equal.)
e No: The second sides are not in the same proportion as the hypotenuses
f No: The equal angles are not both the included angles, or, the hypotenuses are not proportional to another pair of sides.

8 a 1, 2 (Test 1)   **b** 1, 2, 3 (Test 2)
c 1, 3 (Test 3)   **d** 1, 2 (Test 4)

9 a $k = 3$, $x = 24$ cm, $y = 6$ cm
b $k = \frac{1}{2}$, $x = 6$ cm, $y = 14$ cm

10 a $x = 15$ cm, $y = 14$ cm   **b** $x = 10$ cm, $y = 12$ cm

11 a 1800°   **b** 150°

12 a $x = 67°$ (Angle sum of a pentagon is 540°.)
b $x = 120°$ (Angle sum of a hexagon is 720°.)

13 165°

14 a 14.4°   **b** 165.6°   **c** 4140°

Review set 4C

1 $\angle BFG + \angle FGD = 180°$
    (Co-interior angles and $AB \parallel CD$.)
$2x + 2y = 180°$
$x + y = 90°$
$\angle FIG = 180° - (x + y)$ (Angle sum of a $\triangle$ is 180°.)
$\angle FIG = 180° - 90° = 90°$

2 a SSS   **b** AAS   **c** SAS   **d** RHS

3 a Three pairs of equal angles do not make triangles congruent.
b The equal angles are not included angles.

4 a 2, 3 (AAS)   **b** 1, 3 (SAS)

5 a SAS, $x = 20$ cm, $y = 55°$, $z = 65°$
b AAS, $x = 10$ cm, $y = 20$ cm

6 a In $\triangle PQS$ and $\triangle RSQ$:
$PQ = RS$ ($= 90°$, given)
QS is common.
$\angle PQS = \angle RSQ$ (given)
$\therefore \triangle PQS \equiv \triangle RSQ$ (SAS)

b $PS = RQ$ (Matching sides in congruent $\triangle$s are equal.)

c $\angle PSQ = \angle RQS$ (Matching angles in congruent $\triangle$s are equal.)
$\therefore PS \parallel RQ$ (Alternate angles are equal.)

7 a Yes: Test 1 (Two pairs of equal angles.)
b No: Only two pairs of sides are in proportion.
c Yes: Test 4 (The hypotenuse and a second side in each right-angled triangle are in proportion.)
d No: The 65° angle in the second triangle is not the included angle.

8 a 1, 2, 3 (Test 1)   **b** 1, 3 (Test 3)
c 2, 3 (Test 4)   **d** 1, 3 (Test 2)

9 a $x = 17.5$ cm, $y = 5$ cm   **b** $x = 15$ cm, $y = 6$ cm
c $x = 15$ cm, $y = 6$ cm   **d** $x = 8$ cm, $y = 22.5$ cm

10 a 6120°   **b** 170°

11 a $x = 32°$ (Angle sum of a hexagon is 720°.)
b $x = 60°$ (Angle sum of a pentagon is 540°.)

12 120°   **13** 12°

Review set 4D

1 In $\triangle ADC$:
$\angle CAD = \angle ACD = x$ ($DC = DA$)
$\therefore \angle DAB = 90° - x$ ($\angle CAB = 90°$)
In $\triangle ABC$:
$\angle C + \angle A + \angle B = 180°$ (Angle sum of a $\triangle$ is 180°.)
$x + 90° + \angle B = 180°$
$x + \angle B = 90°$
$\angle B = 90° - x$
$\therefore \angle B = \angle DAB$
$DA = DB$ (Equal sides opposite equal angles in $\triangle ADB$.)

2 a RHS **b** SAS **c** SAS
3 a The angle in the second triangle is not the included angle.
b The equal sides are not matching sides.
4 a 1, 3 (AAS) **b** 2, 3 (SAS)
5 a SSS, $x = 65°$, $y = 55°$, $z = 60°$
b RHS, $x = 36°$, $y = 54°$
6 a In $\triangle BED$ and $\triangle CFD$:
   $DE = DF$ (given)
   $DB = DC$ (given)
   $\angle BED = \angle CFD$ (given)
   $\therefore \triangle BED \equiv \triangle CFD$ (RHS)
b $\angle B = \angle C$ (Matching angles in congruent $\triangle$s are equal.)
   $\therefore AB = AC$
   $\triangle ABC$ is an isosceles triangle.
7 a Yes: Test 2 (Three pairs of sides are in proportion.)
b No: The sides that include the equal angles are not in proportion.
c No: There is only one pair of equal angles.
d Yes: Test 4 (The hypotenuse and a second side in each right-angled triangle are in proportion.)
8 a 2, 3 (Test 3) **b** 1, 2, 3 (Test 1)
c 2, 3 (Test 2) **d** 1, 2 (Test 4)
9 a $x = 15$ cm, $y = 8$ cm **b** $x = 11.25$ cm, $y = 6.4$ cm
c $x = 45$ cm, $y = 26$ cm
10 a, b 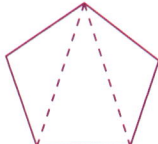 **c** $3 \times 180° = 540°$
11 a $x = 40°$ (Angle sum of a pentagon is 540°.)
b $x = 87.5°$ (Angle sum of a hexagon is 720°.)
12 150° **13** 45°

CHAPTER 5 BIVARIATE DATA ANALYSIS

Diagnostic test

1 D **2** D **3** C **4** D **5** D
6 D **7** A **8** B **9** D **10** A
11 B **12** C **13** A

Exercise 5A

1 a i Weight, age **ii** Weight
b i Value, weight **ii** Value
c i Lottery prize share, number of winners
   ii Lottery prize share
d i Goods sold, commission **ii** Commission
e i Hours worked, income **ii** Income
f i Average speed, time **ii** Time
g i Income earned, tax paid **ii** Tax paid
h i Speed, distance **ii** Distance

Exercise 5B

1 a i October **ii** June
b The index increased from Jan to Feb, decreased from Feb to Mar, increased from Mar to Apr, decreased significantly from Apr to Jun then increased considerably from Jun to Oct, decreasing again in Nov before slightly increasing in Dec.

c For both years there was an upwards trend in the early months of the year, a dip in May–June, followed by another upwards trend.
2 a i 33% **ii** 44%
b Steady decrease from 1994 to 1998, then a significant increase from 1998 to the year 2000, where there was a slight decrease for the next 4 years followed by a steady increase to 2012.
c 1998 or 1999
3 a i $0.87 **ii** $0.91
b i $0.68 **ii** $0.81
c $US
d March 2012 to March 2013; $1.04
e September 2012 to March 2013; $0.81
f $0.10, March–September 2013
g Yes
h The exchange rate for both the $US and the € increased steadily from March 2009 to March 2011. Both decreased in September 2011, then increased to reach maximum values before decreasing steadily from March 2013 to March 2014.

4 a, b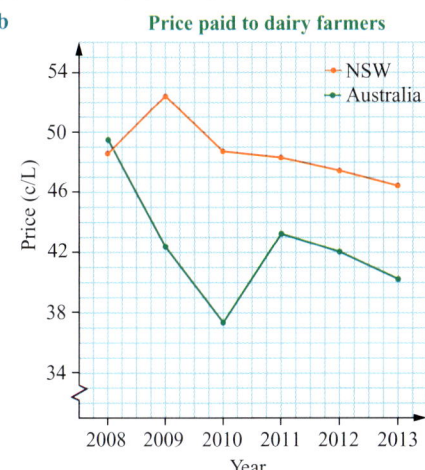

a After an increase in 2009, the price paid to dairy farmers in NSW has been decreasing.
b Overall, the average paid across Australia is significantly less than that paid in NSW; however, the difference in prices was less and more consistent from 2011 to 2013.

5 a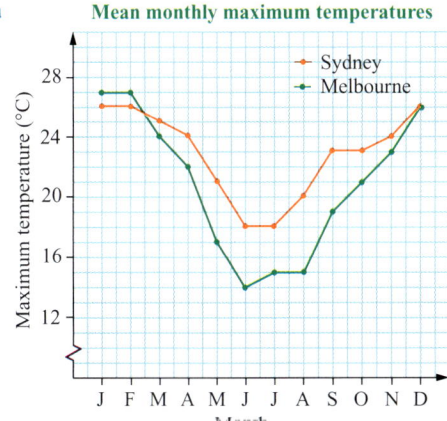

b Melbourne
c i Melbourne **ii** 5° (April to May)
d i Melbourne **ii** 4° (Sept to Oct)

e Both graphs represent a trough. The temperatures at the start and end of the year are high due to the summer weather, and decrease through the colder winter months then increase again in the warmer months. Melbourne had a bigger trough as it had a colder winter.

6 a

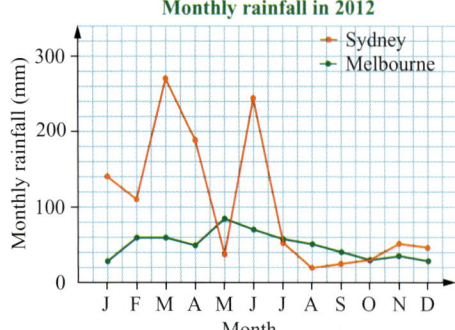

Monthly rainfall in 2012

b Sydney
c i August   **ii** March
d i January and October   **ii** May
e Sydney
f As we would expect, in Melbourne the rainfall increases over the middle of the year (winter) and decreases over the warmer (summer) months. In Sydney larger than expected rainfalls in March, April and June resulted in two large peaks.

7 a i 460 000   **ii** 510 000
b i 2003–04 and 2009–10   **ii** 30 000
c i Yes
  ii 2005–06, 2008–09, 2010–11
  iii 2008–09
d Overall, the graph is increasing steadily over time.

8 a i 107 000   **ii** 127 500
b i 2012   **ii** 2002
c 2011–12   **d** 2001–02 and 2009–10
e Overall, the graph is steadily increasing over time with the exception of significant decreases in 2002, 2010, 2011 and a smaller decrease in 2013.

Exercise 5C

1 a Strong positive   **b** Strong negative
c Weak positive   **d** Weak negative
e No association   **f** Strong negative

2 a i

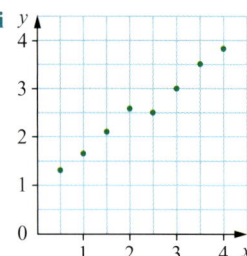

  ii Strong positive
b i

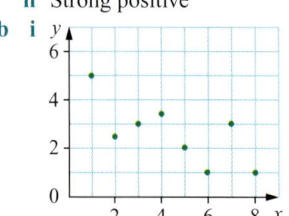

  ii Weak negative

3 a **b**

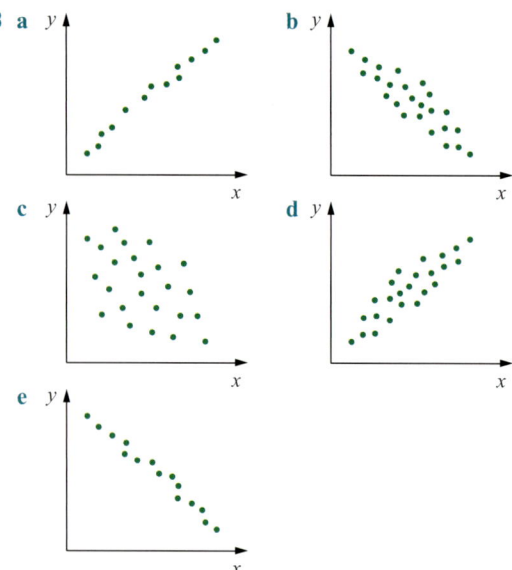

c **d**

e

4 a i 68   **ii** 75   **iii** 86
b i 67   **ii** 74   **iii** 87
5 a i 32/m²   **ii** 60/m²
b i 0.24 kg/m² **ii** 0.74 kg/m²
6 a i $7000   **ii** $9000   **iii** $12 500
b i $35 000   **ii** $80 000   **iii** $130 000
7 a, c

[scatter plot with line of best fit, y-axis 50–75, x-axis 60–85]

b Strong negative
d i 67   **ii** 77
8 a, c

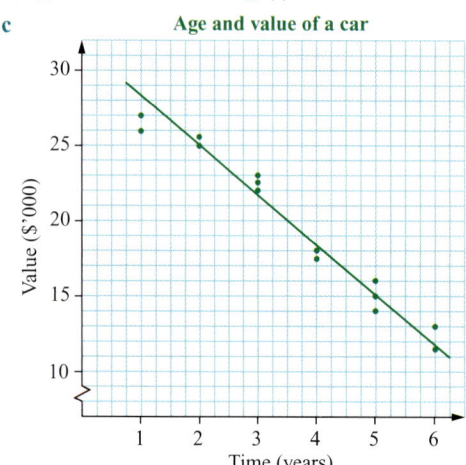

Age and value of a car

b Strong negative
d i $20 000   **ii** 5 years

9 a, b

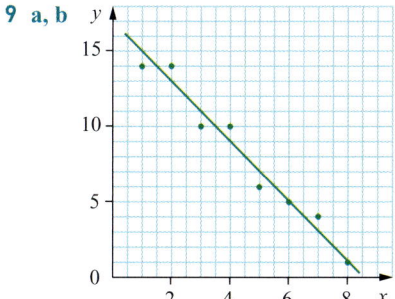

c $y = -2x + 17$

d i -3 **ii** 2.5

10 a, c

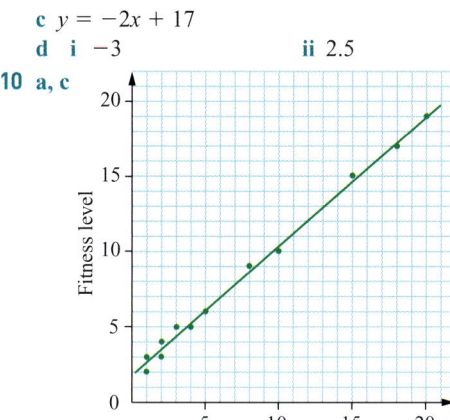

b Strong positive

d Fitness $= 0.85 \times$ time $+ 1.8$

e i 12 **ii** 16.7 h

Language in mathematics

1 a Single variable data analysis examines one variable only; for example, length of foot. Bivariate data compares two variables; for example, length of foot and height.

b The value of the dependent variable will depend on the value of the independent variable. The dependent variable is placed on the y-axis.

2 Line graphs allow a comparison of quantities over time.

3 a The line of best fit is drawn on a scatter plot to give an indication of the relationship between variables.

b The line of best fit enables calculations to be made relating one variable to the other.

Check your skills

1 B	**2** D	**3** B	**4** D	**5** B
6 A	**7** D	**8** B	**9** A	

Review set 5A

1 a i Number of people, size of slice of cake
     ii Size of slice of cake

b i Age of car, value of car   **ii** Value of car

2 a i £0.61   **ii** £0.64   **iii** £0.65

b Dec 2010, June 2011, Dec 2011, Mar 2013

c i Mar 2013   **ii** £0.69

d £0.08   **e** March–June 2013

f The exchange rate increased from June to December 2010. It was relatively steady until December 2012, peaked in March 2013 and has steadily declined since then.

3 a Strong negative   **b** No association

c Weak positive

4 a, c

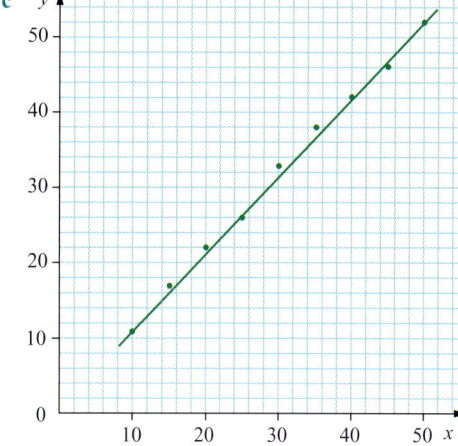

b Strong positive   **d** $y = x + 1.6$

e i 33.6 **ii** 22.4

Review set 5B

1 a i Speed, distance   **ii** Distance

b i Alcohol consumed, driving ability
     ii Driving ability

2 a i $1.20   **ii** $1.88   **iii** $1.64

b i $2.00   **ii** Oct 2013

c i Apr–Oct 2012   **ii** Oct 2011–Apr 2012

d Every 6 months the dividends increase then decrease, over time the amounts are increasing.

3 a Weak negative   **b** Strong positive

c No association

4 a, c

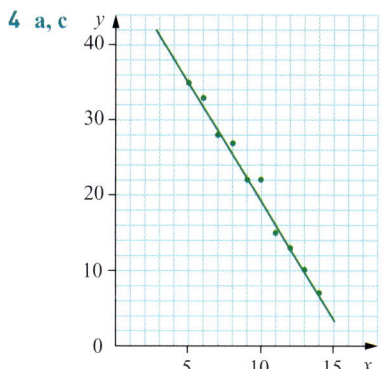

b Strong negative

d $y = -3.2x + 51.4$

e i 3.4 **ii** 9.8

Review set 5C

1 a i Number of police cars, number of accidents
     ii Number of accidents

b i Radius, volume   **ii** Volume

2 a i 100 000   **ii** 80 000
     iii 160 000

b i 75 000   **ii** Year 2000

c 2010

d There was a steady decrease in employment from 1992 to 2000. Employment then started increasing, and continued to increase for the next 12 years.

3 a Weak positive   **b** Strong positive
  c Weak negative

4 a, c

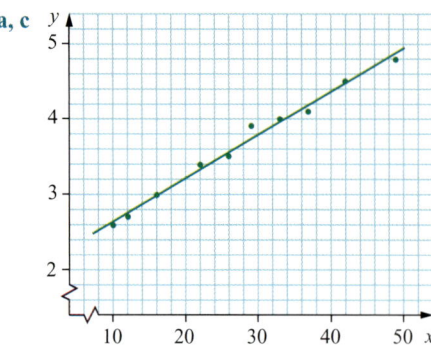

b Strong positive   **d** $y = 0.06x + 2$
e i 3.8   **ii** 20

Review set 5D

1 a i Speed, time   **ii** Time
  b i Number of rainy days, number of umbrellas sold
    ii Number of umbrellas sold
2 a i 640 000   **ii** 670 000
    iii 910 000
  b i 610 000   **ii** 2004
  c 2005–06
  d After a slight decrease in population in 2004, the
    population significantly increased until 2008 when
    the increase in the population slowed down.
3 a No association   **b** Strong negative
  c Weak positive

4 a, c

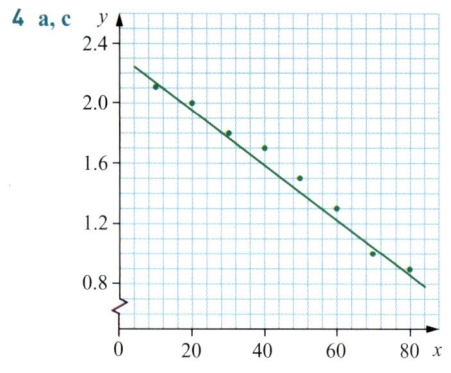

b Strong negative   **d** $y = -0.018x + 2.3$
e i 1.85   **ii** 39

CUMULATIVE REVIEW: 2–5

1 a i $9k$ **ii** $35x$ **iii** $18ab$
  b i $\dfrac{6p}{5}$ **ii** $\dfrac{3}{2p}$ **iii** $\dfrac{5m^2}{4k}$
  c i $\dfrac{27k}{35}$ **ii** $\dfrac{7t}{2}$ **iii** $\dfrac{47}{15w}$
  d i $\dfrac{3z}{2}$ **ii** $\dfrac{5e}{8}$
  e i $15x - 17$ **ii** $38p - 47q$
  f i $-4(4d - 6e)$ or $4(-4d + 6e)$
    ii $2pq(8q + 3p)$
    iii $3b(3a - 4c + 2b)$
    iv $4x^2y(3x^2y^2 - 4)$

2 a i $\sqrt{80}$ **ii** $(-1, 1)$ **iii** -2

  b i

x	-3	-2	-1	0	1	2	3
y	-9	-7	-5	-3	-1	1	3

    ii

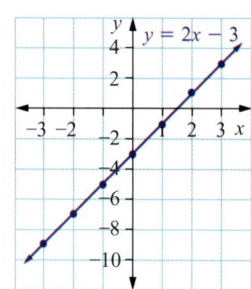

c i $y = 3x - 4$
  ii

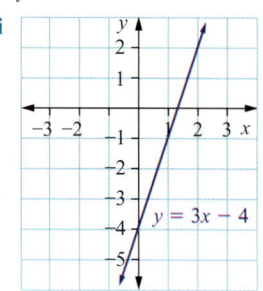

d i $-\dfrac{2}{3}$ **ii** 2
  iii $y = -\dfrac{2}{3}x + 2$
e i $y = -\dfrac{3x}{2} + 3$
  ii

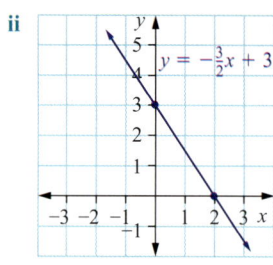

3 a RHS
  b The equal sides are not corresponding.
  c 2 and 3, AAS
  d AAS, $x = 7$, $y = 15$
  e Yes, SSS
  f $k = 2.57$, $x = 20.57$, $y = 5.44$
4 a 1260°   **b** 6   **c** 165°
  d 135°   **e** 150°   **f** 18°
  g 26 sides
5 a i Number of sunny days and amount of sunscreen
    sold
    ii Amount of sunscreen sold
  b i Weak positive   **ii** Negative strong
    iii No association
6 a i 85c   **ii** 100c
    iii 75c
  b i 145c   **ii** Feb 2009
  c i Feb to Aug 2013   **ii** Feb to Aug 2009
  d A large decrease followed by similar dividends until
    a large increase in August 2013.

7 a, c

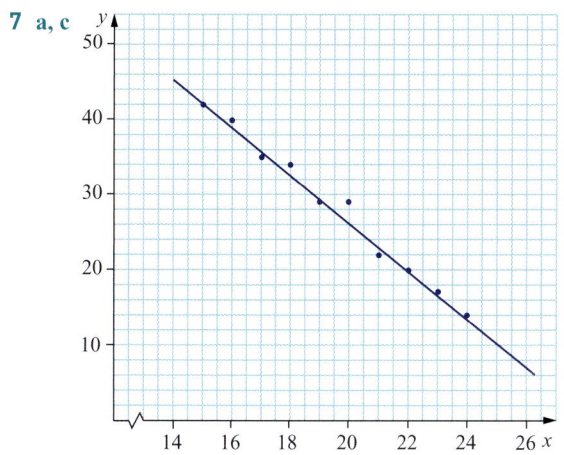

b Strong negative
d $y = -3.2x + 90$
e i 6.8 **ii** 19.7

CHAPTER 6 FINANCIAL MATHEMATICS

Diagnostic test

1 B	**2** D	**3** A	**4** B	**5** D
6 A	**7** A	**8** D	**9** A	**10** D
11 C	**12** B	**13** D	**14** A	**15** B
16 B	**17** A	**18** B		

Exercise 6A

1

Year	Principal	Interest	Balance
1st	$5000	$200	$5200
2nd	$5200	$208	$5408
3rd	$5408	$216.32	$5624.32
		Total	$624.32

a $5624.32 **b** $624.32

2

Year	Principal	Interest	Balance
1st	$9000	$180	$9180
2nd	$9180	$183.60	$9363.60
3rd	$9363.60	$187.27	$9550.87
		Total	$550.87

a $9550.87 **b** $550.87

3

Year	Principal	Interest	Balance
1st	$8400	$504	$8 904
2nd	$8904	$534.24	$9 438.24
3rd	$9438.24	$566.29	$10 004.53
		Total	$1604.53

a $10 004.53 **b** $1604.53
4 a $5624.32 **b** $624.32
5 a $13 891.50 **b** $1891.50

6

Year	Principal	Balance
2nd	$25 750	$26 522.50
3rd	$26 522.50	$27 318.18

a $27 318.18 **b** $2318.18

7

Year	Principal	Balance
2nd	$16 000	$17 280
3rd	$17 280	$18 662.40

a $18 662.40 **b** $2662.40

8

Year	Principal	Balance
1st	$5800	$6061
2nd	$6061	$6333.75
3rd	$6333.75	$6618.76

a $6618.76 **b** $818.76
9 a $15 035.54 **b** $835.54
10 a $19 710.80 **b** $3710.80
11 a i $13 640 **ii** $13 856.83
b Compound interest by $216.83
12 a i $36 720 **ii** $37 305.85
b Compound interest by $585.85

Exercise 6B

1 a $6955.64 **b** $955.64
2 a $27 065.34 **b** $9065.34
3 a $46 928.44 **b** $21 928.44
4 a $7220.10 **b** $2220.10
5 a $14 307.69 **b** $14 257.61 **c** $14 185.19
6 a $6352.45 **b** $6344.93 **c** $6333.85
7 a i $23 232.34 **ii** $23 223.68 **iii** $23 210.82
b i $3232.34 **ii** $3223.68
iii $3210.82; monthly
8 D
9 a $5.02 **b** $3.39 **c** $2.62
d $4.33 **e** $2.00

Exercise 6C

1 $2989.03 **2** $4577.37
3 $841.27 **4** $647.04
5 $334.64 **6** $2365.48
7 $5424.52 **8** $1865.16
9 $349.15 **10** $944.41
11 $8254.65 **12** $386.28
13 4.7% **14** 8.1%
15 3.4% **16** 5.2%
17 3.6% **18** 4.8%
19 4.5% **20** 5.6%
21 3.9% **22** 4.8%
23 3.3% **24** 6 years
25 9 years **26** 7 years
27 11 quarters **28** 6 quarters
29 30 months **30** 10 months

Exercise 6D

1 a $15 360 **b** $14 640
2 a $16 810 **b** $8190
3 a $1687.50 **b** $2312.50
4 a $20 250 **b** $27 750
5 a $7785.54 **b** $13 214.46
6 a $1764 **b** $736
7 a $4488.08 **b** $7411.92
8 a $3405.46 **b** $14 194.54
9 About 4 years **10** About 3 years
11 About 4 years

Language in mathematics

2 a principal   **b** minimum   **c** investment
   d multiplier   **e** repayment
3 a quarterly   **c** depreciation   **d** interest

Check your skills

1 C   **2** C   **3** B   **4** D   **5** D
6 B   **7** D   **8** D   **9** B   **10** D
11 B

Review set 6A

1 a $9800.34   **b** $1800.34
2 a $33 745.92   **b** $3745.92
3 a i $31 500   **ii** $32 161.66
   b Compound by $661.66
4 a $18 519.62   **b** $6519.62
5 a $8588.43   **b** $8565.73
   c $8532.60
6 $8.79   **7** $2421.65
8 a $16 134.77   **b** $17 865.23
9 $1660.46   **10** About 4 years

Review set 6B

1 a $7503.08   **b** $1003.08
2 a $23 820.32   **b** $3820.32
3 a i $18 375   **ii** $18 692.73
   b Compound by $317.73
4 a $9834.04   **b** $1834.04
5 a $12 702.37   **b** $12 682.42
   c $12 653.19
6 $5.78   **7** $584.85
8 a $19 131.88   **b** $16 868.12
9 $3606.15   **10** About 4 years

Review set 6C

1 a $10 563.38   **b** $1063.38
2 a $13 812.27   **b** $1812.27
3 a i $8160   **ii** $8494.25
   b Compound by $334.25
4 a $7110.50   **b** $2110.50
5 a $9573.44   **b** $9564.95
   c $9552.42
6 $9.11   **7** 4.0%
8 a $12 677.63   **b** $25 322.37
9 $1306.37   **10** About 4 years

Review set 6D

1 a $5284.09   **b** $784.09
2 a $15 135.28   **b** 2135.28
3 a i $10 710   **ii** $10 844.99
   b Compound by $134.99
4 a $6399.95   **b** $1399.95
5 a $38 114.67   **b** $38 069 .57
   c $38 003.10
6 $13.55   **7** 7.5%
8 a $13 467.72   **b** $16 032.28
9 $8948.05   **10** About 4 years

CHAPTER 7 BINOMIAL EXPRESSIONS AND QUADRATICS

Diagnostic test

1 A   **2** B   **3** B   **4** D   **5** D
6 A   **7** D   **8** B   **9** B   **10** A
11 D   **12** C   **13** B   **14** C   **15** B
16 D   **17** C   **18** A   **19** B   **20** B
21 D   **22** C   **23** B

Exercise 7A

1 $x^2 + 6x$ **2** $x^2 + 5x$
3 $x^2 + 3x$ **4** $\frac{1}{2}(x^2 + 3x)$
5 $(x + 3)(x + 1)$ **6** $\frac{1}{2}(x + 7)(x + 2)$
7 a $x^2 + 6x + 5$ **b** $x^2 + 9x + 14$
   c $x^2 + 11x + 24$
8 a $x^2 + 6x + 8$ **b** $x^2 - x - 6$
   c $x^2 + 4x - 12$ **d** $x^2 + x - 12$
   e $x^2 - 2x - 15$ **f** $x^2 + 4x - 45$
   g $x^2 - 7x - 30$ **h** $x^2 - 11x + 28$
   i $x^2 + 6x - 7$ **j** $x^2 - 5x + 6$
   k $x^2 - 15x + 54$ **l** $x^2 - 15x + 36$
9 a 21   **b** 71   **c** 23   **d** 55
   e 53   **f** −35   **g** −6   **h** −12
   i 45   **j** −187   **k** 234   **l** 52
10 a $2x^2 + x - 3$ **b** $2x^2 - 21x + 40$
   c $3x^2 - 20x + 25$ **d** $9x^2 - 9x - 10$
   e $6x^2 + 23x - 18$ **f** $16x^2 - 25$
   g $12x^2 - x - 1$ **h** $6x^2 - 19x + 10$
   i $8x^2 + 2x - 15$ **j** $49x^2 - 4$
   k $10x^2 - 31x + 15$ **l** $12x^2 - 17x - 5$
11 a $x^2 - 10$ **b** $6x^2 + 11x - 4$
   c $x^2 - 7x - 14$ **d** $x^2 + 2x + 10$
   e $3x^2 - 8x + 14$ **f** $10x - 4$
   g $-x^2 + x + 10$ **h** $-2x^2 + 16x + 5$
   i $-2x^2 + 13x - 6$

Exercise 7B

1 a $x = \pm3$ **b** $x = \pm4$ **c** $x = \pm8$
   d $x = \pm12$ **e** $x = \pm7$ **f** $x = \pm11$
   g $x = \pm6$ **h** $x = \pm9$ **i** $x = \pm10$
   j $x = \pm2$ **k** $x = \pm15$ **l** $x = \pm17$
2 a $x = \pm3.46$ **b** $x = \pm7.14$ **c** $x = \pm4.36$
   d $x = \pm6.86$ **e** $x = \pm9.11$ **f** $x = \pm5.29$
   g $x = \pm8.25$ **h** $x = \pm9.54$ **i** $x = \pm13.89$
   j $x = \pm14.14$ **k** $x = \pm6.24$ **l** $x = \pm4.12$
3 a $x = \pm3$ **b** $x = \pm6$ **c** $x = \pm3$
   d $x = \pm4$ **e** $x = \pm5$ **f** $x = \pm4$
   g $x = \pm6$ **h** $x = \pm7$ **i** $x = \pm13$
4 a $x = \pm\frac{7}{2}$ **b** $x = \pm\frac{9}{10}$ **c** $x = \pm\frac{4}{5}$
   d $x = \pm\frac{4}{9}$ **e** $x = \pm\frac{12}{7}$ **f** $x = \pm\frac{8}{11}$
   g $x = \pm\frac{7}{12}$ **h** $x = \pm\frac{10}{9}$ **i** $x = \pm\frac{13}{6}$
5 a $x = \pm2.83$ **b** $x = \pm1.73$ **c** $x = \pm2.45$
   d $x = \pm1.90$ **e** $x = \pm1.60$ **f** $x = \pm2.14$
6 a $x = \pm\frac{8}{3}$ **b** $x = \pm\frac{7}{2}$ **c** $x = \pm\frac{10}{9}$
   d $x = \pm\frac{5}{7}$

Exercise 7C

1. a $x^2 + 4x + 4$ b $x^2 + 12x + 36$
   c $y^2 + 20y + 100$ d $9x^2 + 6x + 1$
   e $4x^2 + 12x + 9$ f $16a^2 + 40a + 25$
   g $25x^2 + 40x + 16$ h $9y^2 + 12y + 4$
   i $16 + 24x + 9x^2$ j $1 + 4x + 4x^2$
   k $25 + 20x + 4x^2$ l $16 + 40x + 25x^2$

2. a $x^2 - 4x + 4$ b $x^2 - 12x + 36$
   c $y^2 - 18y + 81$ d $9x^2 - 6x + 1$
   e $4x^2 - 12x + 9$ f $25a^2 - 40a + 16$
   g $9x^2 - 24x + 16$ h $16y^2 - 8y + 1$
   i $25 - 20x + 4x^2$ j $1 - 6x + 9x^2$
   k $25 - 30x + 9x^2$ l $16 - 16x + 4x^2$

3. a $x^2 + 10x + 25$ b $x^2 - 10x + 25$
   c $4x^2 - 28x + 49$ d $4x^2 + 28x + 49$
   e $9x^2 - 30x + 25$ f $16x^2 + 24x + 9$
   g $25 + 20x + 4x^2$ h $9 - 42x + 49x^2$
   i $9 - 66x + 121x^2$

4. a $x^2 - 9$ b $x^2 - 16$ c $x^2 - 36$
   d $x^2 - 100$ e $x^2 - 1$ f $4x^2 - 25$
   g $9x^2 - 4$ h $25x^2 - 1$ i $49x^2 - 64$
   j $121x^2 - 81$

5. a $x^2 - 20x + 100$ b $x^2 + 14x + 49$
   c $x^2 - 64$ d $x^2 - 121$
   e $x^2 + 8x + 16$ f $x^2 - 49$
   g $x^2 - 14x + 49$ h $x^2 - 144$
   i $x^2 + 24x + 144$ j $x^2 + 6x + 9$

6. a $x^2 + 6x + 9$ b $x^2 - 14x + 49$
   c $x^2 - 4x + 4$ d $(x - 3)^2 = x^2 - 6x + 9$
   e $(x - 5)^2 = x^2 - 10x + 25$
   f $(x + 6)^2 = x^2 + 12x + 36$
   g $(x + 7)^2 = x^2 + 14x + 49$
   h $(x + 9)^2 = x^2 + 18x + 81$

7. a 9 b 25 c 16 d 4 e 36 f 81
   g $\frac{49}{4}$ h $\frac{225}{4}$ i $\frac{9}{4}$ j $\frac{81}{4}$ k $\frac{1}{4}$ l $\frac{1}{4}$

Exercise 7D

1. a $3(a - b)$ b $5(m + 2n)$
   c $q(p - r)$ d $x(x - 5)$
   e $x(4x + 1)$ f $3x(5 + x)$
   g $q(p - 3q)$ h $2\pi(R - r)$
   i $6xy(x - 3y)$ j $7ap(4p - 3)$
   k $9xy(x + 3)$ l $3pq(r - 5p)$

2. a $-3(a + b)$ b $-2x(2x + 1)$
   c $-4(2a - b)$ d $-4(1 + 2b)$
   e $-(3 + x)$ f $-9x(2x - 1)$

3. a $B(6 + a + c)$ b $R(4 - x + y)$
   c $x(7 + 14y - 3z)$ d $8x(x - 3y + 2yz)$
   e $(x - 2)(4 + y)$ f $(x - 1)(3 + y)$
   g $(x + 1)(a + 3)$ h $(x - 4)(x - 1)$
   i $(p - 3)(3 + x + y)$ j $(a + 1)(x - 1 - y)$

4. a $(2x + 1)(2 + x)$ b $(x - 1)(3 + z)$
   c $(x + 5)(y + 3)$ d $(x - 2)(y + 4)$
   e $(x - 7)(x + y)$ f $(4 - x)(x + y)$
   g $(y + 3)(x - 2)$ h $(y - 4)(2x + 5)$
   i $(3x - 7)(y + 1)$ j $(3 - x)(x + t)$
   k $(a - b)(3 + c)$ l $(3x - 2)(x + y)$
   m $(4 - 3x)(1 + y)$ n $(6 - 5y)(a + b)$
   o $(4 - 3p)(p - q)$

Exercise 7E

1. a $(x - 2)(x + 2)$ b $(y + 3)(y - 3)$
   c $(z - 4)(z + 4)$ d $(a - 3)(a + 3)$
   e $(c + 5)(c - 5)$ f $(x + y)(x - y)$
   g $(a - c)(a + c)$ h $(m - n)(m + n)$
   i $(2x - 1)(2x + 1)$ j $(3x - 2)(3x + 2)$
   k $(3x + 1)(3x - 1)$ l $(4y - 3)(4y + 3)$
   m $(5y - 4x)(5y + 4x)$ n $(10x - 9y)(10x + 9y)$
   o $(8a - 5b)(8a + 5b)$

2. a 1200 b 800 c 2000
   d 6 e 1.87 f 1711

3. a $(x^2 + y^2)(x + y)(x - y)$
   d $(a^2 + b^2)(a + b)(a - b)$
   c $(p^2 + q^2)(p + q)(p - q)$
   d $(4a^2 + 9b^2)(2a + 3b)(2a - 3b)$
   e $(9a^2 + b^2)(3a + b)(3a - b)$
   f $(4x^2 - 25y^2)(2x + 5y)(2x - 5y)$
   g $-4pq$ h $4ab$ i $-24xy$

Exercise 7F

1. a $(x + 5)^2$ b $(x - 10)^2$
   c $(x + 9)^2$ d $(x - 8)^2$
   e $(x - 7)^2$ f $(x + 11)^2$
   g $(y - 3)^2$ h $(y + 1)^2$
   i $(x - 12)^2$ j $(p - 4)^2$
   k $(m + 3)^2$ l $(a - 5)^2$

2. a $(2x + 5)^2$ b $(5x + 6)^2$
   c $(4x - 9)^2$ d $(3x - 8)^2$
   e $(11x - 6)^2$ f $(9x + 5)^2$
   g $(7x + 10)^2$ h $(5x - 2)^2$
   i $(2x + 11)^2$ j $(7x - 3)^2$
   k $(3x - 5)^2$ l $(10x - 9)^2$

3. a $(p + q)^2$ b $(m - n)^2$ c $(r + t)^2$
   d $(d - p)^2$ e $(n - t)^2$ f $(r + y)^2$
   g $(a - b)^2$ h $(y + x)^2$ i $(z + w)^2$

Exercise 7G

1. a $(x + 7)(x + 1)$ b $(x + 6)(x + 2)$
   c $(x + 12)(x + 1)$ d $(x + 9)(x + 1)$
   e $(x + 6)(x + 4)$ f $(x + 10)(x + 3)$
   g $(x + 6)(x + 5)$ h $(x + 10)(x + 2)$
   i $(x + 5)(x + 4)$ j $(x + 6)(x + 3)$
   k $(x + 18)(x + 1)$ l $(x + 7)(x + 6)$

2. a $(x - 5)(x - 1)$ b $(x - 7)(x - 1)$
   c $(x - 11)(x - 1)$ d $(x - 4)(x - 2)$
   e $(x - 8)((x - 1)$ f $(x - 5)(x - 2)$
   g $(x - 10)(x - 1)$ h $(x - 5)(x - 3)$
   i $(x - 15)(x - 1)$ j $(x - 7)(x - 2)$
   k $(x - 14)(x - 1)$ l $(x - 8)(x - 3)$

3. a $(x + 8)(x - 1)$ b $(x + 5)(x - 2)$
   c $(x + 2)(x - 1)$ d $(x + 7)(x - 6)$
   e $(x + 6)(x - 2)$ f $(x - 12)(x + 1)$
   g $(x - 8)(x + 3)$ h $(x + 8)(x - 3)$
   i $(x + 7)(x - 3)$ j $(x - 21)(x + 1)$
   k $(x + 20)(x - 3)$ l $(x + 9)(x - 6)$

4. a $(x + 18)(x + 1)$ b $(x - 9)(x + 2)$
   c $(x + 18)(x - 1)$ d $(x + 9)(x + 6)$
   c $(x + 54)(x - 1)$ f $(x - 27)(x + 2)$
   g $(x - 8)(x - 8)$ h $(x + 16)(x - 4)$
   i $(x - 32)(x + 2)$ j $(x - 5)(x + 7)$
   k $(x - 3)(x + 10)$ l $(x - 5)(x - 10)$

Exercise 7H

1 a $(2x + 3)(x + 1)$ **b** $(2x + 1)(x - 5)$
 c $(3x - 1)(x + 2)$ **d** $(3x + 1)(x - 2)$
 e $(2x + 5)(x + 1)$ **f** $(2x - 1)(x + 2)$
 g $(7x + 2)(x + 1)$ **h** $(2x + 5)(x - 1)$
 i $(5x + 1)(x - 3)$ **j** $(5x - 3)(x + 1)$
 k $(5x - 3)(x - 1)$ **l** $(11x + 2)(x - 1)$
2 a $(2x - 3)(x + 4)$ **b** $(3x + 2)(x - 3)$
 c $(3x + 4)(x + 1)$ **d** $(2x + 3)(x - 3)$
 e $(3x + 1)(x + 4)$ **f** $(3x - 2)(x - 5)$
 g $(3x + 2)(x + 2)$ **h** $(5x + 2)(x - 3)$
 i $(3x - 2)(x + 4)$ **j** $(2x - 1)(x + 9)$
 k $(2x - 3)(x + 6)$ **l** $(2x - 3)(x + 7)$
3 a $(2x - 5)(x + 7)$ **b** $(3x - 4)(x + 3)$
 c $(5x - 3)(x - 1)$ **d** $(3x + 2)(x - 1)$
 e $(5x - 4)(x - 5)$ **f** $(7x + 1)(x + 2)$
 g $(11x - 3)(x + 5)$ **h** $(7x - 5)(x - 8)$
 i $(5x - 7)(x - 9)$ **j** $(x + 3)(5x - 4)$
 k $(x + 3)(3x + 4)$ **l** $(x + 3)(2x - 1)$
4 a $(4x + 1)(2x + 3)$ **b** $(5x + 2)(3x - 1)$
 c $(7x + 1)(3x + 2)$ **d** $(3x + 1)(2x + 1)$
 e $(6x + 1)(x + 3)$ **f** $(5x + 1)(2x + 3)$
 g $(7x + 1)(2x + 5)$ **h** $(21x + 1)(x - 3)$
 i $(2x + 1)^2$ **j** $(5x - 2)(2x + 1)$
 k $(3x - 2)^2$ **l** $(3x + 2)(x + 4)$
5 a $(2x - 3)(3x + 1)$ **b** $(4x - 3)(x - 5)$
 c $(3x - 4)(3x + 2)$ **d** $(4x - 1)(3x - 5)$
 e $(3x + 2)(4x - 5)$ **f** $(12x + 5)(x - 7)$
 g $(5x - 3)(2x + 5)$ **h** $(4x - 7)(5x + 1)$

Exercise 7I

1 a $x(3x + 2)$ **b** $(x + 9)(x - 9)$
 c $2(p^2 + 4)$ **d** $3(b + 5)(b - 5)$
 e $2(x - 4)(x + 4)$ **f** $n^2(n + 2)(n - 2)$
 g $(x - 9)(x + 1)$ **h** $(d + 7)(d - 1)$
 i $3(x - 6)(x + 6)$ **j** $2(g - 11)(g + 5)$
 k $(2a - 3d)(2a + 3d)$ **l** $4t(1 + 2t)$
 m $-1(x + 12)(x - 1)$ **n** $5(a - 2)(a + 1)$
 o $2(c - 3)(c - 1)$ **p** $x^2(x + 1)(x - 1)$
 q $d^2(d + 3)(d - 1)$ **r** $(b + 7)(b - 4)$
 s $ab^2(a + 1)(a - 1)$ **t** $(x - 3)(x + 2)$
 u $x(x + 2)^2$ **v** $x^2(3x - 2)(3x + 2)$
 w $(x + 9)(x - 1)$ **x** $-2(a + 3)^2$
2 a $-(x + 7)(x - 2)$ **b** $(x + 7)^2$
 c $4a(a + b)(a - b)$ **d** $2x(3 - x)(3 + x)$
 e $a(b + c - 2)$ **f** $ab(ab - 2)$
 g $2x^2(2 - x)$ **h** $xy(x + 2)(x - 2)$
 i $(a + b - 3)(a + b + 3)$ **j** $x(x - 4)$
 k $4(x^2 + 4)(x + 2)(x - 2)$ **l** $(x - 2)(y - z)$
 m $(x + 1)(a + b)$ **n** $(x^2 + a^2)(x + a)(x - a)$
 o $(x - y)(a + 1)$ **p** $(x + 2)(x + 3)$
 q $(x + 1)(x^2 + 1)$ **r** $(x^2 + 1)(x + 2)$
3 a $3x(x + 3)$ **b** $(2x + 1)(2x - 1)$
 c $5x(x - 3)$ **d** $x(3 - 5x)$
 e $(x + 8)(x - 5)$ **f** $(x + 4)(x - 4)$
 g $x^2(x + 2)$ **h** $(x + 3)(x - 3)$
 i $3x(x^2 + 2)$ **j** $3(x + 2)(x - 2)$

 k $3x^2(x + 2)$ **l** $(x + 5)^2$
 m $(x - 3)(x + 2)$ **n** $4x(x + 2)$
 o $(3x - 5)(3x + 5)$ **p** $(x - 13)(x - 3)$
 q $7x(x - 3)$ **r** $2(x + 5)(x - 5)$
 s $9x(1 - 2x)$ **t** $4x(2x - 3)$
 u $(2x - 1)(2x + 3)$ **v** $13x(x - 4)$
 w $(x + 3)(x - 1)$ **x** $x(x + 3)(x - 3)$
4 a $x(x^2 + x + 1)$ **b** $(x - 20)(x + 3)$
 c $3(x + 3)(x - 3)$ **d** $(x - 4)(x + 2)$
 e $(x + 2)^2$ **f** $(3x - 2)(2x + 3)$
 g $(x - 3)(x - 2)$ **h** $36x^2 + 25$
 i $4(x - 5)(x + 3)$ **j** $3(x - 11)(x - 3)$
 k $(x + 6)(x + 5)$ **l** $(7x + 1)(7x - 1)$
 m $(x - 4)(x - 3)$ **n** $(x + 8)(x - 2)$
 o $(x - 8)(x + 3)$ **p** $(x - 4)^2$
 q $(x - 7)(x - 2)$ **r** $(x + 4)(x + 9)$
 s $(x - 12)(x + 3)$ **t** $(x + 9)(x - 2)$
 u $(x - 5)^2$ **v** $3(x + 6)(x - 4)$
 w $4(x - 4)(x + 3)$ **x** $4(x - 1)(x + 2)$

Exercise 7J

1 a $\dfrac{x}{x - 2}$ **b** $\dfrac{x}{3 - x}$ **c** $\dfrac{3x}{x + 1}$

 d $\dfrac{x + 1}{x - 1}$ **e** $\dfrac{2(x - 1)}{x - 5}$ **f** $\dfrac{x + 3}{x - 8}$

 g $\dfrac{-3(x + 2)}{x + 7}$ **h** $\dfrac{-(x + 6)}{2(x + 1)}$

2 a 6 **b** 1 **c** $\dfrac{1}{2}$ **d** $\dfrac{x}{4}$

 e $\dfrac{7}{5}$ **f** $\dfrac{2}{3}$ **g** $x - 1$ **h** $\dfrac{3x}{x + 4}$

3 a $\dfrac{-x - 9}{x(x + 3)(x - 3)}$ **b** $\dfrac{5x + 28}{x(x + 4)(x - 4)}$

 c $\dfrac{5x + 6}{x(x - 6)(x + 2)}$ **d** $\dfrac{4x - 2}{3(x - 4)(x + 1)}$

 e $\dfrac{x + 14}{x(x - 2)(x + 7)}$ **f** $\dfrac{5(2x - 3)}{x(x - 5)(x - 2)}$

 g $\dfrac{2x + 4}{(x + 5)(x - 5)(x - 1)}$ **h** $\dfrac{2x + 12}{x(x - 3)(x + 3)}$

Language in mathematics

1 a 18
 b For his contribution to science, 1835
 c 22
 d Physics, astronomy, algebra
 e Someone who shuns other people
2 a Expanding is the opposite of factorising.
 b Always factorise using the highest possible common factor.
 c Multiply all the terms in the brackets by the term outside the brackets.
3 To check a factor is a solution you can either expand your answer or substitute a number into the question and the answer to see if they are equal.

Check your skills

1 B	2 A	3 C	4 D	5 D
6 C	7 B	8 A	9 C	10 A
11 A	12 B	13 D	14 B	15 A
16 C	17 D	18 B	19 B	20 C

Review set 7A

1 a $-5x + 1$ **b** $3x - 17$ **c** $-n^2 + 4n$

2 a $x = \pm\sqrt{12}$ **b** $x = \pm\sqrt{\dfrac{9}{5}}$

3 a $x^2 + 2x - 15$ **b** $6x^2 - 37x + 56$
c $x^2 - 16x + 64$ **d** $9x^2 - 24x + 16$
e $x^2 - 4$ **f** $9x^2 - 25$

4 a 20
b i 9 **ii** $\dfrac{121}{4}$

5 a $7(x + 2)$ **b** $4xy(2x - 5)$
c $(x - 3)(3 + y)$ **d** $(2y - 5)(2y + 5)$
e $(x + 8)(x - 1)$ **f** $(3x - 1)(x + 4)$
g $x^2(x + 4)(x - 4)$ **h** $-2(x - 4)(x + 3)$

6 a $x + 3$ **b** $\dfrac{1}{2}$ **c** $\dfrac{5x + 8}{x(x - 4)(x + 4)}$

Review set 7B

1 a $-6x - 1$ **b** $3x - 12$ **c** $4p^2 - 5p$

2 a $x = \pm 4$ **b** $x = \pm\sqrt{\dfrac{2}{5}}$

3 a $x^2 - 9x - 22$ **b** $12x^2 - 41x + 24$
c $x^2 + 8x + 16$ **d** $64x^2 - 80x + 25$
e $x^2 - 9$ **f** $25x^2 - 9$

4 a 31
b i 25 **ii** $\dfrac{81}{4}$

5 a $3(a - 3)$ **b** $6x(2y + 3x)$
c $(y - 3)(2x + 7)$ **d** $(4y + 5)(4y - 5)$
e $(x - 2)(x - 1)$ **f** $(3x - 5)(2x + 1)$
g $x^2(3x - 4)(3x + 4)$ **h** $(x^2 + 1)(x + 3)$

6 a $\dfrac{x + 3}{6}$ **b** $\dfrac{x + 1}{8}$
c $\dfrac{-2x - 17}{(x + 5)(x + 2)(x - 2)}$

Review set 7C

1 a $-3x + 6$ **b** $2x + 2$ **c** $-2y^2 - 10y$

2 $\sqrt{\dfrac{-5}{3}}$ has no solution.

3 a $x^2 + x - 12$ **b** $6x^2 - 29x + 35$
c $x^2 - 8x + 16$ **d** $16p^2 - 40p + 25$
e $x^2 - 9$ **f** $16x^2 - 9$

4 a Both expressions equal 49.
b $\square = 4$

5 a $5(x + 2)$ **b** $3x(x - 2y)$
c $(x - 2)(2 + 3y)$ **d** $(3x + 10)(3x - 10)$
e $(x + 3)(x - 4)$ **f** $(3x + 1)(x + 5)$
g $x(x + 4)(x - 4)$ **h** $-3(x + 8)(x - 1)$

6 a $x + 4$ **b** $\dfrac{3x}{x + 3}$
c $\dfrac{-x + 15}{x(x + 3)(x - 3)}$

Review set 7D

1 a $-6x + 14$ **b** $21 - 15x$
c $4m^2 - 22m$

2 a $x = \pm 5$ **b** $x = \pm\dfrac{3}{\sqrt{7}}$

3 a $x^2 + 9x - 22$ **b** $12x^2 - 22x - 14$
c $y^2 + 6y + 9$ **d** $36z^2 - 60z + 25$
e $x^2 - 81$ **f** $36x^2 - 25$

4 a Both expressions equal 8.
b $\square = -6x$

5 a $3(x - 5)$ **b** $4y(3x - 2z)$
c $(x - y)(p + 2)$ **d** $(4x - 5)(4x + 5)$
e $(x - 3)(x + 7)$ **f** $(5x - 3)(x + 2)$
g $(3x + 2)(2x - 5)$ **h** $2x(x + 3)(x - 3)$
i $-5(3x + 4y - 2z)$

6 a $\dfrac{x - 2}{2}$ **b** $\dfrac{1}{3}$ **c** $\dfrac{10 - x}{x(x - 5)(x + 5)}$

CHAPTER 8 BOX PLOTS

Diagnostic test

1 B	2 C	3 C	4 A	5 C
6 A	7 C	8 B	9 D	10 B
11 A	12 B			

Exercise 8A

1 a 5.4 **b** 4.4 **c** 13.2 **d** 22.5 **e** 55.4
f 4.3 **g** 102.3 **h** 3.9 **i** 5.8
2 a 8 **b** 2 **c** none **d** 20 **e** 57
f 3 **g** 101 **h** 3 **i** 5
3 a 5 **b** 4 **c** 13 **d** 21.5 **e** 56
f 4 **g** 101.5 **h** 3 **i** 5
4 a 8 **b** 8 **c** 6 **d** 7 **e** 8
f 9 **g** 4 **h** 9 **i** 6
5 a 5 **b** 16.3 **c** 15 **d** 16
6 a i 4.5 **ii** 1.5 **iii** Reduced by 3
b i 24.5 **ii** Increased by 20
c i 4.5 **ii** 7.5 **iii** Increased by 3
d i 7 **ii** 7 **iii** Unchanged
7 a i 7 **ii** 6.3 **iii** 7 **iv** 6.5
b The mode, as it is the most popular so they need more of that size.
8 a \$2 030 000 **b** \$67 667
c i 25 **ii** 5
d \$55 000 **e** \$50 000
f i Mean **ii** Mode
g Median: half the employees earn more, half earn less.
9 a Mean = 76.1, median = 17
b Mean = 17.2, median = 16.5
c Mean
10 a Mean = 68.3, median = 68.5
b Mean = 58.6, median = 64
c Outlier **d** Mean
11 a 60 **b** 104.4
c 3144 km **d** \$185 604
12 a 9 **b** 15 **c** 15 **d** 5 **e** 37
13 a 17.25 **b** 25.3 (1 decimal place)
c 8.7 (1 decimal place)
14 17.7 (1 decimal place) **15** 10.1 cm
16 12 and 6

Exercise 8B

1 a 27 **b** 20 **c** 30 **d** 10
2 a i 7 **ii** 3 **iii** 10 **iv** 7
b i 18 **ii** 15 **iii** 20 **iv** 5
3 a i 11 **ii** 9 **iii** 11 **iv** 2
b i 21 **ii** 17 **iii** 22 **iv** 5
c i 20.5 **ii** 15.5 **iii** 25 **iv** 9.5
d i 26.5 **ii** 17 **iii** 36.5 **iv** 19.5
4 a 7 **b** 2 **c** 5 **d** 2.5
e 6 **f** 5 **g** 5 **h** 19
i 11 **j** 9

5 a 21   **b** 25   **c** $6\frac{1}{2}$
  d 20   **e** 9   **f** 6
6 a 11   **b** 14   **c** 18.5
7 a i Range = 140   **ii** IQR = 6
  b The outlier of 148 affects the range but not IQR.

Exercise 8C

1 a i 63   **ii** 15   **iii** 48   **iv** 40
    v 55   **vi** 29   **vii** 26
  b i 45   **ii** 10   **iii** 35   **iv** 24
    v 35   **vi** 15   **vii** 20
  c i 88   **ii** 46   **iii** 42   **iv** 71
    v 83   **vi** 55   **vii** 28
  d i 46   **ii** 16   **iii** 30   **iv** 29
    v 39   **vi** 26   **vii** 13
  e i 14.4   **ii** 10.1   **iii** 4.3   **iv** 12.5
    v 13.3   **vi** 10.9   **vii** 2.4
  f i 55   **ii** 49   **iii** 6   **iv** 52
    v 54   **vi** 50   **vii** 4
  g i 254   **ii** 210   **iii** 44   **iv** 227
    v 240   **vi** 215   **vii** 25
  h i 940   **ii** 780   **iii** 160   **iv** 880
    v 920   **vi** 820   **vii** 100

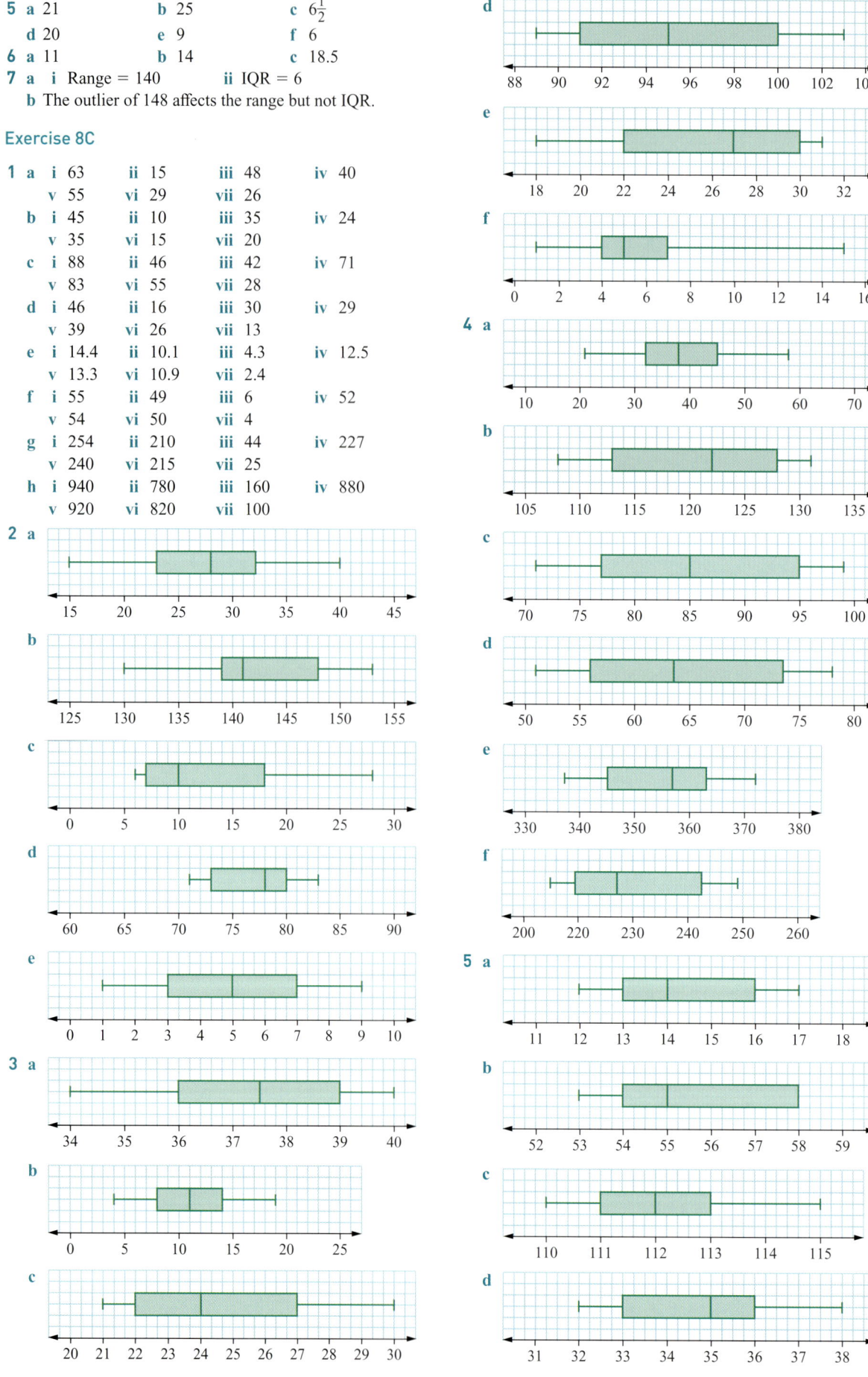

2 a

b

c

d

e

3 a

b

c

4 a

b

c

d

e

f

5 a

b

c

d

e

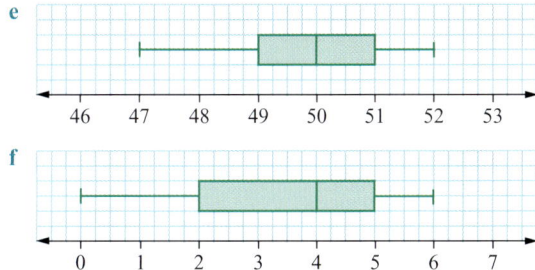

f

Exercise 8D

1 a i Jamie   **ii** Jamie
  b i Jamie = 55, Maryanne = 30   **ii** Jamie
  c i Jamie = 25, Maryanne = 20   **ii** Maryanne
  d Jamie
  e Jamie: the top 75% of marks were higher.
2 a Same minimum scores and same median value
  b i Hilife   **ii** Durable, Hilife
  c i Durable = 3000, Hilife = 3500
    ii Hilife
  d i Durable = 2000, Hilife = 2000
    ii They have the same spread: 50% of the life spans
    are 2000 hours
  e Hilife: Higher values at the 25% and 75% mark
3 a i Corolla   **ii** Corolla
  b Corolla
  c Mazda 3: smaller range and smaller IQR
  d Mazda 3
  e Mazda 3: lower 50% of scores compared to Corolla

4

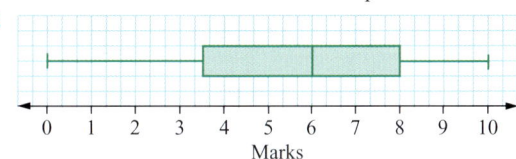

5

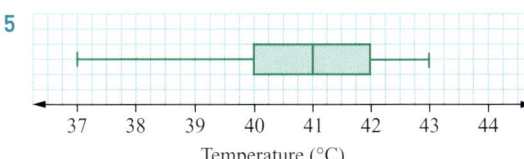

6 a i

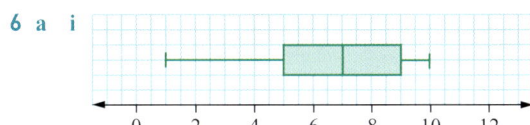

  ii The histogram shows that the data is negatively
  skewed (tail to the left). The corresponding box
  plot also shows that most of the data is to the right
  of the data set. (The upper 50% of the data is
  compressed between 7 and 10, and the lower 50%
  is spread between 1 and 7.)

  b i

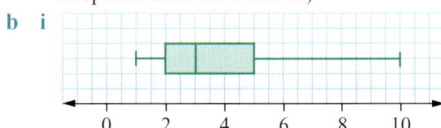

  ii The histogram shows that the data is positively
  skewed (tail to the right). The corresponding box
  plot also shows that most of the data is to the
  left of the data set. (The lower 50% of the data is
  compressed between 1 and 3 and the upper 50% is
  spread between 3 and 10.)

c i

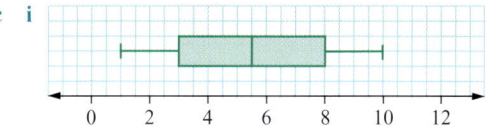

  ii The histogram is symmetrical and bell-shaped, and
  so the box plot is also symmetrical.
7 a C   **b** B   **c** A   **d** D

Language in mathematics

1 a mean   **b** quartile
  c skewed distribution   **d** upper quartile
  e box plots
2 a The range measures the spread of all the data set; the
  interquartile range measures the spread of the middle
  50% of data.
  b Better to use when there are outliers.
3 a The interquartile range is unaffected by outliers.
  b The range is a measure of spread.
  c The median is the middle score when the scores are
  arranged in order.
4 The mean and median are measures of central tendency
  while the range and interquartile range are measures of
  spread. The interquartile range is the only measure of
  spread that is not affected by outliers.

Check your skills

1 B   **2** C   **3** A   **4** A   **5** A
6 C   **7** A   **8** D   **9** B   **10** D
11 C   **12** B   **13** C   **14** A   **15** C
16 B   **17** D

Review set 8A

1 a 9.14   **b** 9   **c** 8   **d** 4
2 22
3 a 46   **b** 4   **c** 42   **d** 33
  e 40   **f** 17   **g** 23
4 a Same minimum value, same median value
  b Set B   **c** Set B
  d The lower 50% of the scores in both sets have the
  same spread. In set A the data is clustered closer to
  the median.
  e Class A, smaller range, smaller IQR: more consistent

Review set 8B

1 a 6.7   **b** 7.5   **c** 8   **d** 5
2 a 84   **b** 21
3 a i 5   **ii** 5
  b i 2   **ii** 2
4 a

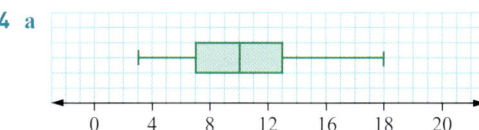

  b

  c

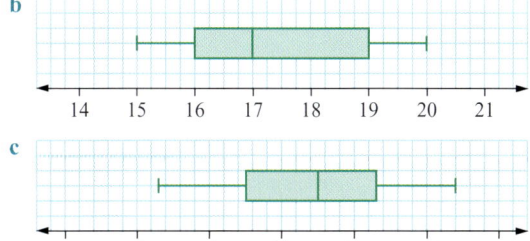

5 a

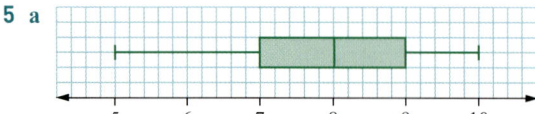

b The histogram shows that the data is negatively skewed (tail to the left). The corresponding box plot also shows that most of the data is to the right of the data set. The upper 50% of the data is between 8 and 10, the lower 50% is between 5 and 8.

Review set 8C

1 a 15.75 **b** 15 **c** 10 **d** 7
2 37
3 a 84 **b** 41 **c** 43 **d** 67
  e 81 **f** 53 **g** 28
4 a 5, 2
  b

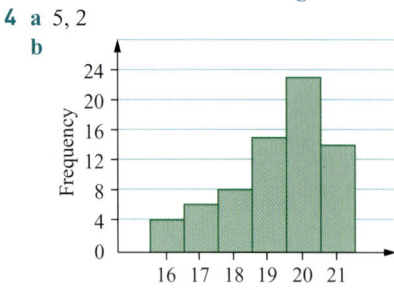

  c Negatively skewed
5 a Set A   **b** Set B

Review set 8D

1 a 62.3 **b** 61.5 **c** 4 **d** 3
2 a 13 **b** 42
3 a i 67.6 **ii** Range = 51
   iii Median = 67 **iv** IQR = 16.5
  b Close to symmetrical, very slight positive skew
4 a

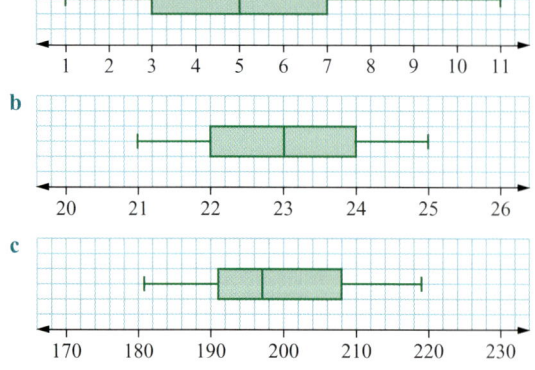

b

c

5 Sydney has a smaller range and IQR indicating that the temperatures over January did not vary as much as they did in Melbourne. Melbourne had more lower temperatures in January.

CHAPTER 9 NON-LINEAR RELATIONSHIPS

Diagnostic test

1 D **2** B **3** C **4** B **5** D
6 A **7** D **8** B

Exercise 9A

1 a

x	-4	-3	-2	-1	0	1	2	3	4
y	16	9	4	1	0	1	4	9	16

b

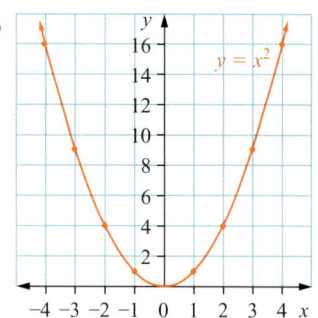

c $(0, 0)$

2 a i

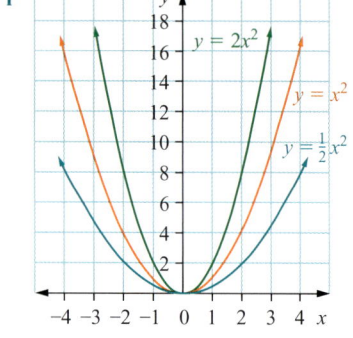

   ii

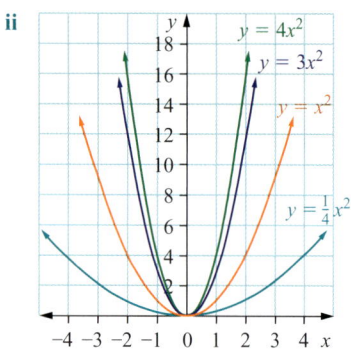

b For $y = ax^2$, the coefficient a affects the width of the parabola. If $a > 1$, the parabola is narrower than $y = x^2$. If $0 < a < 1$, the parabola is wider.

3

x	-4	-3	-2	-1	$-\frac{1}{2}$	0	$\frac{1}{2}$	1	2	3	4
y	-16	-9	-4	-1	$-\frac{1}{4}$	0	$-\frac{1}{4}$	-1	-4	-9	-16

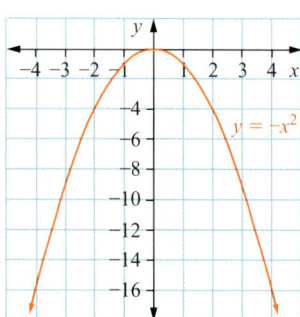

4 a i

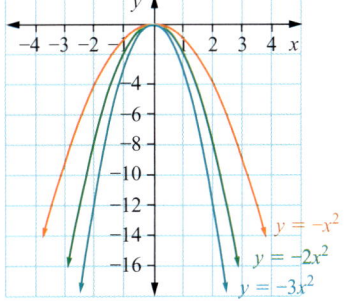

ii

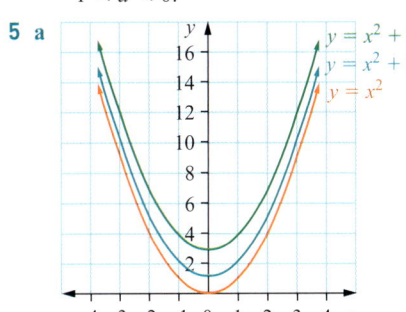

b From question **3**, $y = -x^2$ is the reflection of $y = x^2$ in the x-axis. For $y = ax^2$, the graph is narrower than $y = -x^2$ if $a < -1$ and wider than $y = -x^2$ if $-1 < a < 0$.

5 a

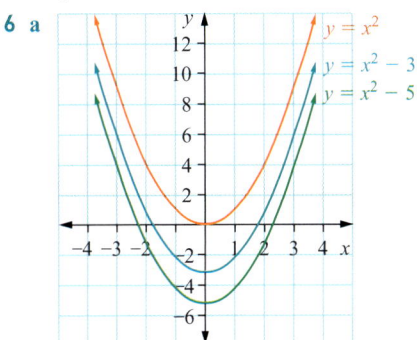

b $(0, 0), (0, 1), (0, 3)$

c The constant c affects the position of the vertex of the parabola. Positive values of c translate the parabola up c units.

6 a

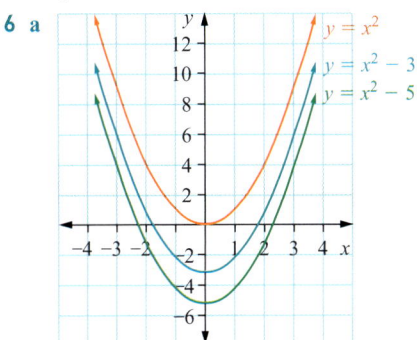

b $(0, 0), (0, -3), (0, -5)$

c The constant c affects the position of the vertex of the parabola. Negative values of c translate the parabola down c units.

7 a

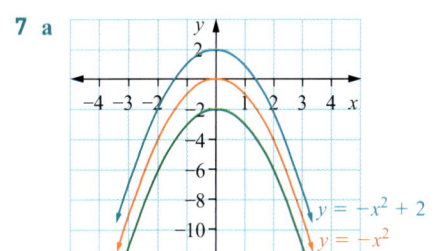

b $(0, 0), (0, 2), (0, -2)$

c The constant c affects the position of the vertex of the parabola. Positive values of c translate the parabola up. Negative values of c translate it down.

8 a

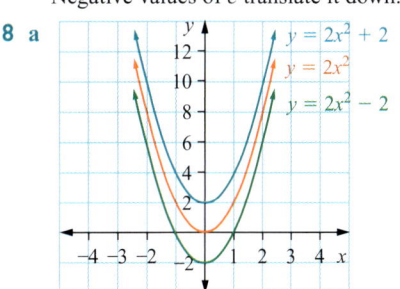

b $(0, 0), (0, 2), (0, -2)$

c The constant c affects the position of the vertex of the parabola. Positive values of c translate the parabola up c units. Negative values of c translate it down.

9 a $y = x^2 - 1$ **b** $y = x^2 + 1$ **c** $y = x^2 - 3$
 d $y = x^2 - 5$ **e** $y = x^2 + 4\frac{1}{2}$

10 a $y = x^2 + 3$ **b** $y = x^2 - 2$
 c $y = -x^2 + 4$ **d** $y = -x^2 - 1$

11 a D **b** A **c** E **d** B **e** F **f** C

12 a $\pm\sqrt{10}$ **b** $\pm\sqrt{7}$ **c** ± 1
 d $\pm 1\frac{1}{2}$ **e** ± 5 **f** $\pm\sqrt{2}$

Exercise 9B

1 a $y = 2^x$

x	-3	-2	-1	0	1	2	3	4
y	$\frac{1}{8}$	$\frac{1}{4}$	$\frac{1}{2}$	1	2	4	8	16

b

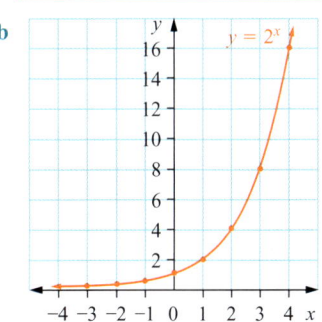

c No, the graph remains above the x-axis. Negative values of x reduce the y-value but it remains positive.

d i y increases   **ii** y approaches 0

e $y = 0$

2 a $y = 3^x$

x	-3	-2	-1	0	1	2	3	4
y	$\frac{1}{27}$	$\frac{1}{9}$	$\frac{1}{3}$	1	3	9	27	81

b

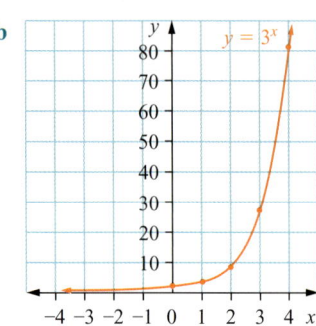

c $y = 3^x$ is steeper and both have asymptote $y = 0$ and pass through $(0, 1)$.

d $y = 5^x$ is steeper than $y = 3^x$.

3 a $y = 2^{-x}$

x	−3	−2	−1	0	1	2	3	4
y	8	4	2	1	$\frac{1}{2}$	$\frac{1}{4}$	$\frac{1}{8}$	$\frac{1}{16}$

b

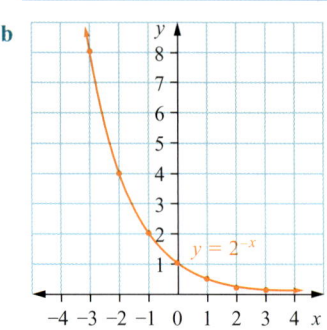

c It is a reflection of $y = 2^x$ in the y-axis.

d **i** y decreases   **ii** y increases

e $y = 0$ but $y \to 0$ as $x \to \infty$.
For $y = 2^x$, $y \to 0$ as $x \to -\infty$.

4 a

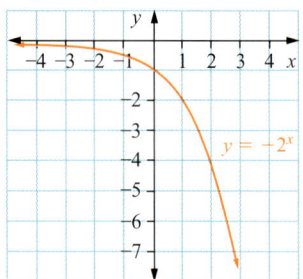

b It is a reflection of $y = 2^x$ in the x-axis. It passes through $(0, -1)$. As x gets larger, y gets smaller, and as x gets smaller y approaches 0.

5 a

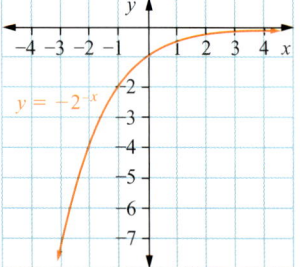

b It is a reflection of $y = 2^{-x}$ in the x-axis. It passes through $(0, -1)$. As x gets larger, y approaches 0, and as x gets smaller, y gets smaller.

6 a

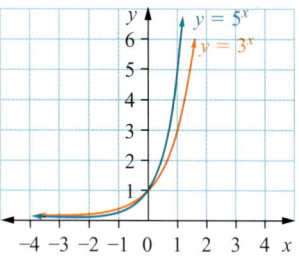

b

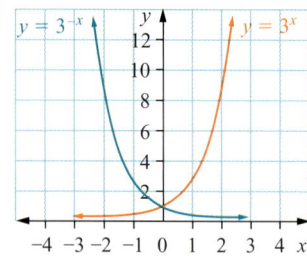

c

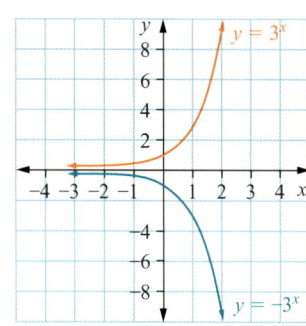

d

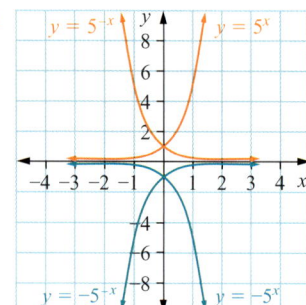

7 a

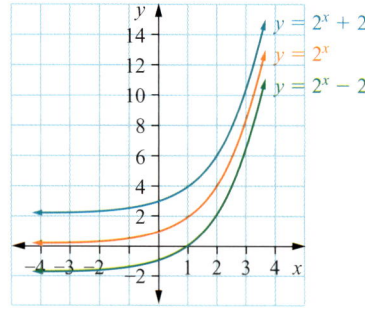

b

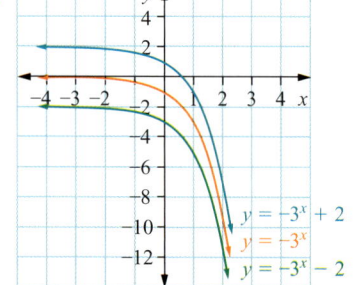

c

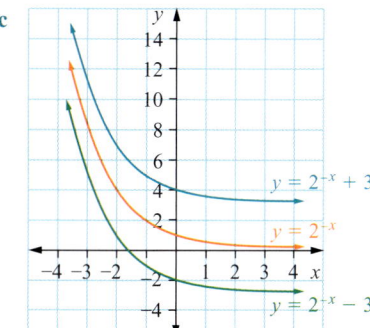

d

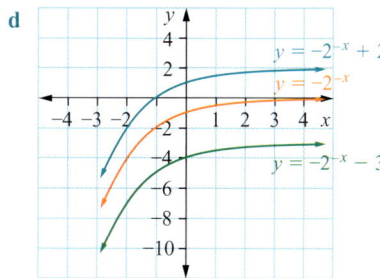

8 a i 1 **ii** 1

All graphs of this type must go through the point $(0, 1)$.

b i -1 **ii** -1

All graphs of this type must go through the point $(0, -1)$.

9 a $x = 4$ **b** $x = 5$

c $x = 3$ **d** $x = 6$

Exercise 9C

1 a $r = 8$ units **b** $r = 9$ units

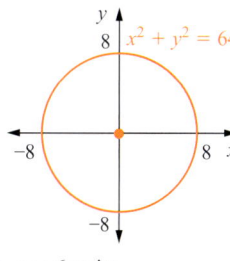 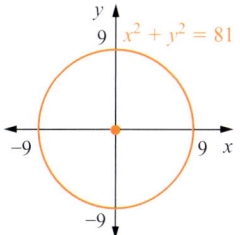

c $r = 6$ units **d** $r = 12$ units

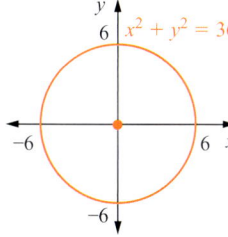 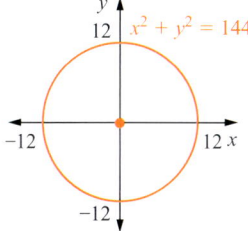

e $r = 10$ units **f** $r = \sqrt{20}$ units

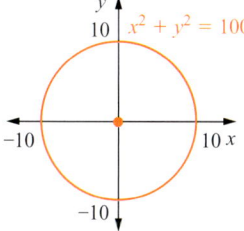 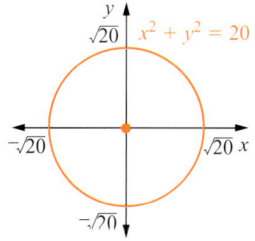

g $r = \frac{3}{2}$ units **h** $r = \frac{1}{3}$ units

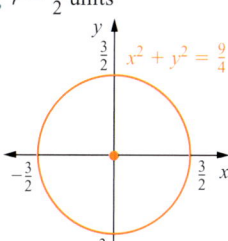 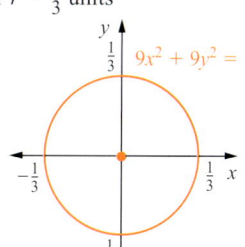

i $r = \frac{3}{4}$ units

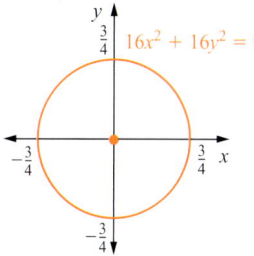

2 a $x^2 + y^2 = 9$ **b** $x^2 + y^2 = 15^2 = 225$

c $x^2 + y^2 = (1.5)^2 = 2.25$ **d** $x^2 + y^2 = 7$

3 a $x^2 + y^2 = 4^2 = 16$ **b** $x^2 + y^2 = 6^2 = 36$

c $x^2 + y^2 = 3^2 = 9$ **d** $x^2 + y^2 = 7^2 = 49$

e $x^2 + y^2 = a^2$ **f** $x^2 + y^2 = \left(\frac{a}{b}\right)^2 = \frac{a^2}{b^2}$

4 $x^2 + y^2 = \left(\frac{\sqrt{5}}{2}\right)^2, x^2 + y^2 = \frac{5}{4}, 4x^2 + 4y^2 = 5$

5 a $x^2 + y^2 = 29$ **b** $x^2 + y^2 = 45$

c $x^2 + y^2 = 74$ **d** $x^2 + y^2 = 64$

e $x^2 + y^2 = 2$

6 A, B, D, G, I, J

Exercise 9D

1 A, C and D **2** A and D

3 A **4** B

5 a B **b** B **c** C

6 a B **b** C **c** A **d** D

7 a C **b** A **c** E

d D **e** B **f** F

8 a C **b** D **c** B

d E **e** A **f** F

Language in mathematics

1 a 12

b To his unconventional education with its interruptions

c The sequence must remain within a certain distance of the origin forever.

2 a A parabola is a graph with x^2.

b The constant term of a parabola moves the graph up or down.

3 The graphs of exponentials and parabolas are both curves with the exponential as a number to the power of x and the parabola as x to the power of two.

Check your skills

1 A **2** A **3** C **4** B **5** B

6 C **7** A **8** C **9** D **10** C

11 C

Review set 9A

1

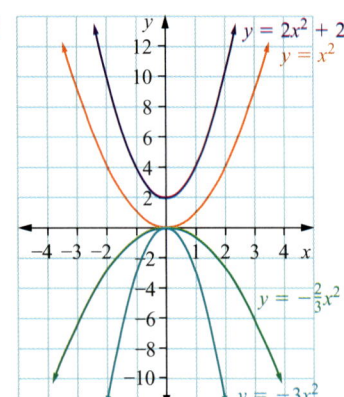

2 a $\pm\sqrt{2}$ **b** ± 3

3

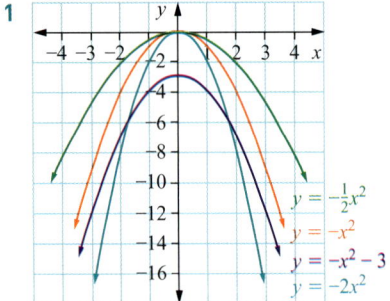

4 $x = 4$

5 a $x^2 + y^2 = 25$ **b** $x^2 + y^2 = 5$

6 $x^2 + y^2 = 74$

7 a F   **b** C   **c** E   **d** B   **e** D   **f** A

Review set 9B

1

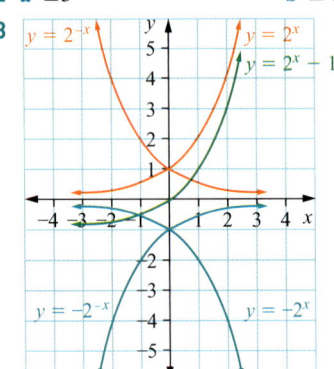

2 a ± 3 **b** $\pm\sqrt{10}$

3

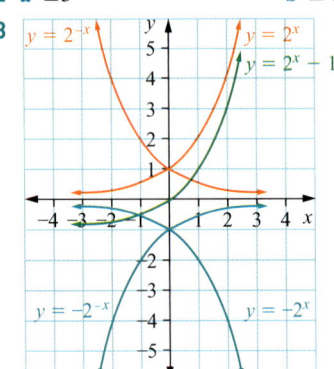

4 $x = 4$

5 a $x^2 + y^2 = 16$ **b** $x^2 + y^2 = 3$

6 a $x^2 + y^2 = 169$

7 a F   **b** C   **c** E   **d** B   **e** D   **f** A

Review set 9C

1

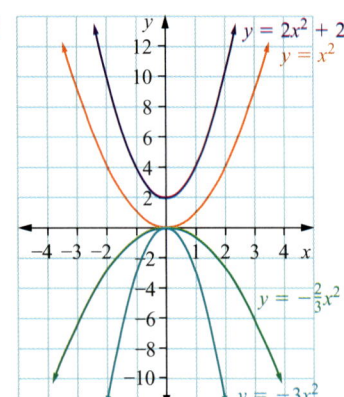

2 a ± 6 **b** $\pm\sqrt{5}$

3

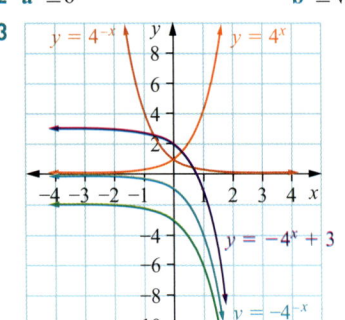

4 $x = 5$

5 a $x^2 + y^2 = 100$ **b** $x^2 + y^2 = 10$

6 $x^2 + y^2 = 1156$

7 a F   **b** C   **c** E   **d** B   **e** D   **f** A

Review set 9D

1

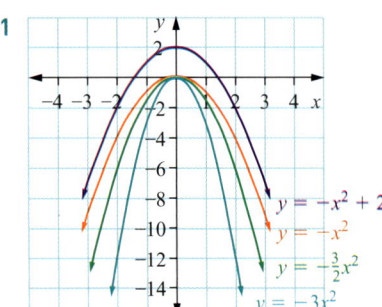

2 a ± 4 **b** ± 2

3

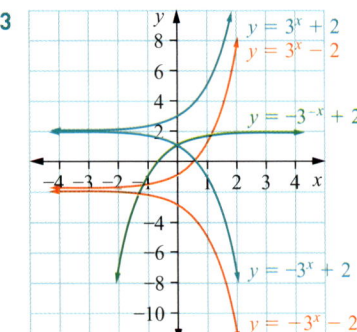

4 $x = 7$

5 a $x^2 + y^2 = 49$ **b** $x^2 + y^2 = \frac{3}{2}$

6 $x^2 + y^2 = 80$

7 a F   **b** C   **c** E   **d** B   **e** D   **f** A

CUMULATIVE REVIEW: 6–9

1 a i $4037.84 **ii** $437.84
  b i $23 820.32 **ii** $3820.32
  c i $18 375 **ii** $18 692.73
   iii Compound interest by $317.73
  d i $22 347.69 **ii** $22 289.21
   iii $22 203.66
  e $6.56
  f i $16 357.75 **ii** $21 642.25
  g About 3.8 years

2 a $11y^2 - 8y$
  b i $x^2 - 3x - 15$ **ii** $6x^2 - 29x + 28$
   iii $x^2 + 2x + 1$ **iv** $9r^2 - 24rp + 16p^2$
   v $x^2 - 4$ **vi** $9x^2 - 1$
  c $x^2 - 4x + 4 = (x - 2)^2$
  d i $3(x - 3)$ **ii** $4x(x + 3y)$
   iii $(x - 3)(3y + 2)$ **iv** $(x + 6)(x - 6)$
   v $(4x - 5)(4x + 5)$ **vi** $(x - 5)(x - 2)$
   vii $(x + 5)(x - 4)$ **viii** $(2x - 5)(3x + 1)$
   ix $(4x - 3)(x - 2)$
  e i $\dfrac{2}{x}$ **ii** $\dfrac{-3(x - 2)}{x(x - 3)(x + 3)}$

3 a 14.67 **b** 16 **c** 16
  d 6 **e** 16.5 **f** 12
  g 4.5

4 a $x = 15$ **b** 216 **c** 26

5 a i 7.525 **ii** 9 **iii** 8 **iv** 6
  v 9 **vi** 5 **vii** 4
  b

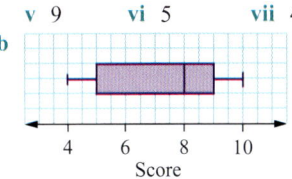

Score

  c

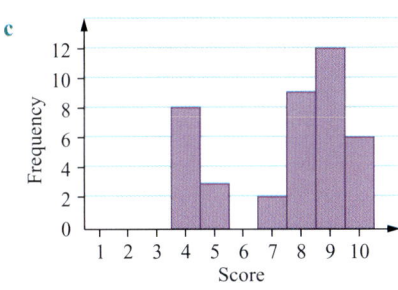

Score

6 a

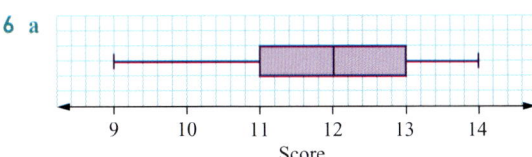

Score

  b Yes, symmetrical (very slight negative skew)

7 a i 136.4 **ii** 135 **iii** 122 **iv** 59
  b Positively skewed
  c

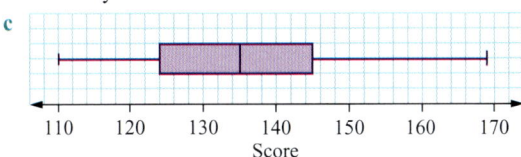

Score

8 a The greatest score, the median and the interquartile
     range are the same in both data sets.
  b Range for set A< range for set B
  c They are the same. **d** Set B

9 a

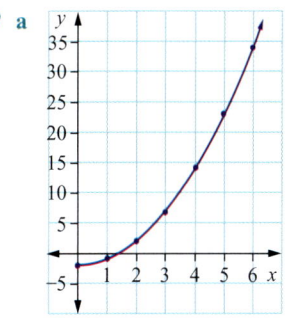

  b It is the right-hand half of a parabola.

10 a B **b** D **c** A **d** C **e** F **f** E

11 a i $y = 4$ **ii** $x = -4$ and -1
   iii

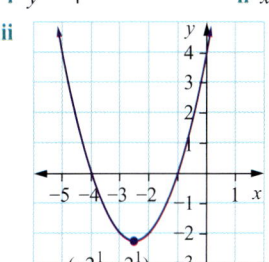

   iv $\left(-2\tfrac{1}{2}, -2\tfrac{1}{4}\right)$
  b i $r = 9$ units
   ii $x^2 + y^2 = \dfrac{9}{16}$

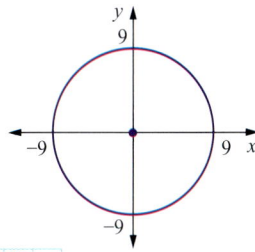

  c

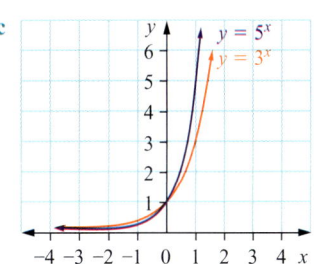

12 a

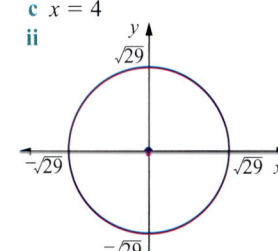

  b $x = \pm\sqrt{6}$ **c** $x = 4$
  d i $x^2 + y^2 = 29$ **ii**

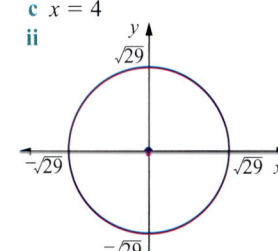

CHAPTER 10 EQUATIONS

Diagnostic test

1 D	**2** C	**3** A	**4** C	**5** C
6 B	**7** B	**8** B	**9** A	**10** D
11 C	**12** D	**13** A	**14** B	**15** B
16 A	**17** D	**18** B	**19** D	**20** C
21 A	**22** D	**23** A	**24** B	**25** D
26 A				

Exercise 10A

1 a $x = -\frac{11}{4}$ **b** $x = -\frac{7}{2}$ **c** $x = \frac{9}{2}$

d $a = -\frac{5}{4}$ **e** $s = -3$ **f** $x = \frac{7}{3}$

2 a $x = 3$ **b** $x = \frac{8}{5}$ **c** $x = \frac{1}{8}$

d $x = 4$ **e** $x = \frac{19}{8} = 2\frac{3}{8}$ **f** $x = -1$

g $x = -1$ **h** $x = \frac{31}{14}$

3 a $x = 4$ **b** $x = -\frac{5}{2} = -2\frac{1}{2}$ **c** $x = 2$

d $x = 13$ **e** $x = 9$ **f** $x = -\frac{11}{4} = 2\frac{3}{4}$

g $x = \frac{1}{7}$ **h** $x = 3$ **i** $x = -\frac{5}{8}$

j $x = -11$ **k** $x = -16$ **l** $x = 19$

4 a $x = \frac{30}{7}$ **b** $x = -4\frac{2}{7}$ **c** $x = \frac{96}{11} = 8\frac{8}{11}$

d $x = \frac{3}{7}$ **e** $x = -\frac{2}{7}$ **f** $x = \frac{31}{28} = 1\frac{3}{28}$

g $x = 16$ **h** $x = 13\frac{1}{10}$ **i** $x = 7\frac{2}{5}$

j $x = 3\frac{11}{20}$ **k** $x = 47\frac{3}{4}$ **l** $x = 1\frac{77}{80}$

m $x = \frac{49}{50}$ **n** $x = -\frac{6}{19}$ **o** $x = \frac{8}{11}$

Exercise 10B

1 a $x^2 + 8x + 16$ **b** $x^2 - 12x + 36$
c $x^2 + 20x + 100$ **d** $y^2 - 10y + 25$
e $9x^2 - 12x + 4$ **f** $25x^2 - 80x + 64$
2 a $x^2 - 25$ **b** $x^2 - 4$
c $x^2 - 49$ **d** $4x^2 - 9$
e $25x^2 - 4$ **f** $49x^2 - 1$
3 a $x^2 - 64$ **b** $x^2 - 14x + 49$
c $9x^2 - 4$ **d** $16x^2 - 56x + 49$
e $49x^2 + 42x + 9$ **f** $4x^2 - 49$
4 a $x^2 + 4x + 4$ **b** $(x - 3)^2 = x^2 - 6x + 9$
c $x^2 - 10x + 25$
d $(x - 7)^2 = x^2 - 14x + 49$
e $(x + 8)^2 = x^2 + 16x + 64$
f $(x + 16)^2 = x^2 + 32x + 256$
5 a 16   **b** 49   **c** 9   **d** 16
e 81   **f** 100   **g** $\frac{25}{4}$ **h** $\frac{289}{4}$
i $\frac{25}{4}$ **j** $\frac{49}{4}$ **k** $\frac{1}{4}$ **l** $\frac{1}{4}$
6 a $(x + 2)(x - 2)$ **b** $(z + 4)(z - 4)$
c $(c + 5)(c - 5)$ **d** $(a + c)(a - c)$
e $(2x - 1)(2x + 1)$ **f** $(3x + 2)(3x - 2)$
g $(5y - 4x)(5y + 4x)$ **h** $(10x - 9y)(10x + 9y)$
7 a $(x + 9)(x + 1)$ **b** $(x - 8)(x - 1)$
c $(x - 5)(x - 2)$ **d** $(x - 10)(x - 1)$
e $(x - 5)(x - 3)$ **f** $(x + 7)(x - 3)$
g $(x - 21)(x + 1)$ **h** $(x - 20)(x + 3)$
i $(x + 9)(x - 6)$ **j** $(x + 54)(x - 1)$

k $(x - 27)(x + 2)$ **l** $(x - 8)^2$
m $(x + 16)(x - 4)$ **n** $(x - 32)(x + 2)$
o $(x + 7)(x - 5)$ **p** $(x + 10)(x - 3)$
q $(x - 10)(x - 5)$ **r** $(x - 11)(x + 2)$
s $(x - 35)(x + 1)$ **t** $(x + 9)(x - 8)$
u $(x - 9)(x - 8)$
8 a $(2x - 1)(x + 4)$ **b** $(3x + 1)(x - 2)$
c $(4x - 5)(x + 2)$ **d** $(5x - 3)(x - 2)$
e $(6x - 2)(x + 5)$ **f** $(3x - 7)(x + 5)$
g $(4x + 7)(x - 5)$ **h** $(10x + 3)(x - 2)$
i $(8x - 5)(x + 1)$ **j** $(11x - 9)(x + 2)$
k $(2x - 3)(3x + 1)$ **l** $(5x - 2)(3x + 2)$
m $(4x + 1)(2x - 5)$ **n** $(6x + 5)(2x - 1)$
o $(3x + 7)(4x - 1)$ **p** $(7x - 5)(3x + 1)$
q $(9x + 1)(4x - 1)$ **r** $(11x + 7)(2x - 1)$

Exercise 10C

1 a $x = \pm\sqrt{\frac{7}{5}}$ **b** $x = \pm\sqrt{\frac{11}{3}}$

c $x = \pm\sqrt{\frac{7}{2}}$ **d** $x = \pm\frac{\sqrt{5}}{2}$

e $x = \pm\frac{\sqrt{7}}{3}$ **f** $x = \pm\frac{5}{\sqrt{11}}$

g $x = \pm\frac{5}{\sqrt{6}}$ **h** $x = \pm\frac{\sqrt{3}}{2}$

2 a $x = -2$ or 8 **b** $y = -8$ or -2
c $x = -6$ or 2 **d** $y = -14$ or 0
e $x = -5$ or 7 **f** $x = -2$ or 12
3 a $x = 0$ or -3 **b** $x = 0$ or 3
c $x = 0$ or 5 **d** $x = 4$ or -1
e $x = -1$ or -4 **f** $x = -6$ or 4
g $x = -2$ or -5 **h** $x = 1$ or 4
i $x = -5$ **j** $x = -9$ or 2
k $x = -15$ or 4 **l** $x = 3$ or 8
m $x = 6$ **n** $x = -15$ or 1
o $x = -2$ or -6 **p** $x = -9$ or 3
4 a $x = -1$ or $-\frac{3}{2}$ **b** $x = 2$ or $-\frac{1}{3}$
c $x = -\frac{2}{7}$ or -1 **d** $x = \frac{3}{5}$ or -1
e $x = -\frac{2}{3}$ or 3 **f** $x = -\frac{1}{3}$ or -4
g $x = 3$ or $-\frac{2}{5}$ **h** $x = \frac{3}{2}$ or -6
i $x = -\frac{1}{7}$ or $-\frac{2}{3}$ **j** $x = -\frac{1}{5}$ or $-\frac{3}{2}$
k $x = -\frac{1}{2}$ **l** $x = -\frac{2}{3}$ or -4
m $x = -\frac{4}{3}$ or -1 **n** $x = -\frac{1}{5}$ or 3
o $x = -\frac{2}{11}$ or 1
5 a $x = 1$ **b** $x = 5$ or -4 **c** $x = 1$ or 2
d $x = 1$ or -8 **e** $x = 3$ or -8 **f** $x = 2$ or 8
g $x = -1$ or 20 **h** $x = 8$ or -4 **i** $x = 1$
6 a $x = \frac{1}{2}$ or 5 **b** $x = -\frac{1}{21}$ or 3
c $x = 4$ or $\frac{5}{3}$ **d** $x = \frac{1}{3}$ or $-\frac{5}{2}$
e $x = \frac{5}{2}$ or 1 **f** $x = -\frac{2}{5}$ or 3
g $x = -2$ or $\frac{4}{3}$ **h** $x = -4$ or $\frac{9}{4}$
i $x = 1$ or $-\frac{1}{3}$

Exercise 10D

1 a $x = 1$ or -9 **b** $x = -5$ or 1
c $x = 1$ or 9 **d** $x = -7$ or 5
e $x = 3$ or -9 **f** $x = -2$ or 8

2 a $-2 \pm \sqrt{3}$ **b** $1 \pm \sqrt{6}$
c $3 \pm \sqrt{7}$ **d** $4 \pm \sqrt{19}$
e $5 \pm \sqrt{17}$ **f** $-6 \pm \sqrt{43}$

3 a $\dfrac{-3 \pm \sqrt{13}}{2}$ **b** $\dfrac{5 \pm \sqrt{17}}{2}$

c $\dfrac{-7 \pm \sqrt{37}}{2}$ **d** $\dfrac{1 \pm \sqrt{13}}{2}$

e $\dfrac{-9 \pm \sqrt{93}}{2}$ **f** $\dfrac{7 \pm \sqrt{65}}{2}$

4 a $\dfrac{5 \pm \sqrt{17}}{4}$ **b** $\dfrac{-2 \pm \sqrt{19}}{3}$

c $\dfrac{7 \pm \sqrt{69}}{10}$ **d** $\dfrac{11 \pm \sqrt{105}}{8}$

e $\dfrac{3 \pm \sqrt{93}}{6}$ **f** $\dfrac{7 \pm \sqrt{97}}{8}$

Exercise 10E

1 a $x = \dfrac{5 \pm \sqrt{13}}{2}$ **b** $x = \dfrac{-7 \pm \sqrt{65}}{2}$

c $x = \dfrac{-3 \pm \sqrt{13}}{2}$ **d** $x = \dfrac{-5 \pm \sqrt{53}}{2}$

e $x = \dfrac{7 \pm \sqrt{41}}{2}$ **f** $x = \dfrac{-9 \pm \sqrt{101}}{2}$

g $x = \dfrac{7 \pm \sqrt{113}}{4}$ **h** $x = \dfrac{-3 \pm \sqrt{69}}{6}$

i $x = \dfrac{-11 \pm \sqrt{37}}{14}$ **j** $x = \dfrac{1 \pm \sqrt{41}}{10}$

k $x = \dfrac{5 \pm \sqrt{145}}{10}$ **l** $x = \dfrac{1 \pm \sqrt{33}}{16}$

2 $x = 2$ or 12; factorising was quickest.

3 $x = -\frac{1}{2}$ or 15, factorise (take out common factor first)

4 a $x = \dfrac{3 \pm \sqrt{-7}}{2}$; negative under $\sqrt{\ }$
b 0 **c** $b^2 - 4ac < 0$

5 a $x = \dfrac{6 \pm \sqrt{0}}{2}$; zero under $\sqrt{\ }$
b 1 **c** perfect square, $(x - 3)^2$
d $(x - 3)^2 = 0$ **e** $b^2 - 4ac = 0$

Exercise 10F

1 12 or -1 **2** 5 or -4
3 6 or -5 **4** 1 or 2
5 $-\frac{1}{2}$ or 5 **6** 2 or $-\frac{4}{3}$
7 8 cm by 14 cm **8** Natalie is 2 years old.
9 21 or -22.5 **10** 25 or -22.8

Exercise 10G

1 a $x = \pm 2$ **b** $x = \pm 3$ or ± 2
c $x = \pm 4$ **d** $x = \pm 1$
e $x = \pm 1, \pm 2$ **f** $x = \pm 3$
g $x = \pm\sqrt{5}, \pm\sqrt{7}$ **h** $x = \pm\sqrt{3}$
i $x = \pm 1$ or ± 5

Exercise 10H

1 a $x = -3\frac{1}{2}, y = -12$ **b** $x = 1\frac{1}{7}, y = -1\frac{4}{7}$
c $x = \frac{1}{2}, y = 4\frac{1}{2}$ **d** $x = 1, y = -2$

2 a $(2, 6)$ and $(-5, -29)$ **b** $(1, 9)$ and $(2, 11)$
c $(3, -12)$ and $(-7, 18)$ **d** $(3, 17)$ and $(-10, -22)$
e $(10, 46)$ and $(-2, -14)$ **f** $(9, 79)$ and $(-6, -56)$

3 a $(1, 6)$ and $(-6, -1)$ **b** $(-3, 4)$ and $(-4, 3)$
c $(3, 5)$ and $(-5, -3)$ **d** $(2, 5)$ and $(-5, -2)$
e $(2, -10)$ and $(10, -2)$ **f** $(-11, -1)$ and $(1, 11)$

4 a No solutions **b** No solutions
c $(-2, 4)$ or $(3, 9)$ **d** No solutions

Exercise 10I

1 a $x = 2$ **b** $x = 4$ **c** $x = 6$
d $x = 3$ **e** $x = -10$ **f** $x = -5$

2 a $x = \frac{2}{3}$ **b** $x = -\frac{3}{5}$ **c** $x = \frac{5}{3}$

d $x = 3$ **e** $x = \dfrac{3}{\sqrt[3]{5}}$ **f** $x = \dfrac{2}{\sqrt[3]{7}}$

g $x = \dfrac{\sqrt[3]{31}}{2}$ **h** $x = \sqrt[3]{\dfrac{11}{7}}$

Exercise 10J

1 a $x = q - p$ **b** $x = \dfrac{t}{r}$ **c** $x = \dfrac{d - b}{3}$

d $x = \dfrac{a - b}{m}$ **e** $x = \dfrac{t - cy}{b}$ **f** $x = \dfrac{4 - y}{m}$

g $x = \dfrac{p - r}{q}$ **h** $x = l - m - c$

i $x = \dfrac{t - 3}{m}$

2 a $y = \dfrac{c - a}{b}$ **b** $y = \dfrac{r - p}{q}$

c $y = \dfrac{r + p}{x}$ **d** $y = \dfrac{a - b}{c}$

e $y = \dfrac{x - t}{k}$ **f** $y = \dfrac{4 - c}{r}$

g $y = \dfrac{-a - r}{b}$ **h** $y = \dfrac{r - k}{p}$

i $y = \dfrac{t - r - px}{q}$

3 a $x = \dfrac{3 - c}{b - d}$ **b** $x = \dfrac{c - d}{a - 3}$

c $x = \dfrac{z + r}{p - q}$ **d** $x = \dfrac{4 + t}{r + p}$

e $x = \dfrac{t - b}{3 + q}$ **f** $x = \dfrac{b - c}{d + 1}$

4 a $y = \dfrac{x}{t}$ **b** $y = \dfrac{b}{c}$

c $y = \dfrac{7b}{5}$ **d** $y = \pm\sqrt{xz}$ where $xz \geqslant 0$

e $y = \pm\sqrt{rs}$ where $rs \geqslant 0$
f $y = \pm\sqrt{2pq}$ where $pq \geqslant 0$
g $y = \pm\sqrt{t(a + z)}$ where $(ta + tz) \geqslant 0$

h $y = \pm\dfrac{\sqrt{pz}}{3}$ where $pz \geqslant 0$

i $y = \pm\dfrac{\sqrt{z(p + q)}}{3}$ where $(zp + zq) \geqslant 0$

5 a $z = \dfrac{d - bx}{a}$ **b** $z = \dfrac{8y}{x}$

c $z = \pm\sqrt{3y}$ where $y \geqslant 0$

d $z = \dfrac{d + by}{c - x}$ **e** $z = \dfrac{y - 4}{x}$

f $z = \pm\sqrt{m(p - q)}$ where $(x + y) \geqslant 0$

g $z = 4 - p$ **h** $z = \dfrac{d - e}{p + r}$

i $z = \pm\sqrt{4(x + y)}$ where $(x + y) \geqslant 0$

6 a $b = \dfrac{V}{lh}$ **b** $a = \dfrac{F}{m}$ **c** $h = \dfrac{2A}{b}$

d $R = \dfrac{100I}{PN}$ **e** $y = \dfrac{2P}{h} - x$ **f** $r = \dfrac{C}{2\pi}$

g $c = \pm\sqrt{\frac{E}{m}}$ where $\frac{E}{m} \geq 0$ and $m \neq 0$

h $h = \frac{A - \pi r^2}{2\pi r}$ **i** $d = \frac{T - a}{n - 1}$

j $r = 1 - \frac{a}{S}$ **k** $v = \pm\sqrt{\frac{2E}{m}}$ where $\frac{E}{m} \geq 0$

l $a = \frac{2(s - ut)}{t^2}$ **m** $a = \frac{v^2 - u^2}{2s}$

n $x = \pm\sqrt{\frac{y}{3}}$ where $y \geq 0$ **o** $d = \frac{2s - 2an}{n(n - 1)}$

Language in mathematics

1 a equation **b** quadratic
  c solution **d** simultaneous
2 a Linear equations have one solution.
  b Quadratic equations can have two solutions.
  c Non-linear simultaneous equations must be solved by substitution.
3 Quadratic equations can be solved by factorising, completing the square and the quadratic formula. If the quadratic formula is used and there is no surd then the quadratic could have been factorised.

Check your skills

1 B	**2** C	**3** D	**4** C	**5** B
6 B	**7** B	**8** B	**9** B	**10** D
11 A	**12** A	**13** B	**14** D	**15** A
16 C	**17** A	**18** B	**19** D	**20** C
21 A	**22** A	**23** B	**24** B	

Review set 10A

1 a $x = \frac{7}{4}$ **b** $x = 30$

  c $x = -\frac{6}{11}$ **d** $x = -20$

2 $x = \frac{11}{2}$

3 a $x^2 - 6x + 9$ **b** $25x^2 - 70x + 49$

  c $x^2 - 4$

4 $\frac{81}{4}$

5 a $(x + 3)(x - 3)$ **b** $(a + r)(a - r)$
  c $(5y - 4n)(5y + 4n)$ **d** $(x - 3)(x - 2)$
  e $(x + 5)(x - 2)$ **f** $(5x - 3)(x - 1)$

6 a $x = -18$ or -2 **b** $x = \frac{5 \pm \sqrt{61}}{6}$

  c $x = \frac{3}{2}$

7 10 or -2 **8** $(-2, 1)$ and $(10, 35)$

9 $x = \pm\sqrt{3}, \pm\sqrt{2}$

10 a $x = \frac{y - b}{m}$ **b** $x = \frac{r - t}{p + q}$

11 $y = \frac{2A}{h} - x$ or $y = \frac{2A - xh}{h}$

Review set 10B

1 a $x = -\frac{3}{2}$ **b** $x = \frac{38}{11}$

  c $x = \frac{2}{31}$ **d** $x = -\frac{5}{2}$

2 a $4x^2 + 4x + 1$ **b** $x^2 - 25$
  c $25x^2 - 121$

3 a $(x + 9)(x - 9)$ **b** $(p + q)(p - q)$
  c $(8n - 5y)(8n + 5y)$ **d** $(x - 1)(x - 8)$
  e $(x + 6)(x - 3)$ **f** $(3x - 5)(2x + 3)$

4 $x = \frac{5}{\sqrt[3]{7}}$

5 $x = -2 \pm \sqrt{6}$

6 a $x = -5$ or 4 **b** $x = \frac{3 \pm \sqrt{149}}{10}$
  c $x = 5$ or -1

7 $(-2, -13)$ and $(-10, -37)$

8 $x = \pm 1, \pm\sqrt{11}$

9 a $x = \frac{a + b - 3}{r}$ **b** $x = \pm\sqrt{pr}$

Review set 10C

1 a $x = -\frac{2}{7}$ **b** $x = -32$

  c $x = \frac{1}{2}$ **d** $x = \frac{3}{2}$

2 a $x^2 + 10x + 25$ **b** $49x^2 - 56x + 16$
  c $9x^2 - 4$

3 4

4 a $(3 - a)(3 + a)$ **b** $(r + t)(r - t)$
  c $(x + 3)^2$ **d** $(x + 5)(x - 3)$
  e $(2x - 1)(x + 8)$ **f** $(5x + 1)(x + 2)$

5 a $x = \frac{1}{2}$ or $-\frac{5}{3}$ **b** $x = \frac{5 \pm \sqrt{37}}{6}$

6 3 or $-\frac{5}{2}$ **7** $(1, 1)$ and $(-3, -7)$

8 $x = -\frac{2}{5}$

9 a $x = \frac{y - b}{c}$ **b** $x = \frac{d + 5}{e - c}$

10 $R = \pm\sqrt{\frac{A}{\pi} + r^2}$ or $R = \pm\sqrt{\frac{A + \pi r^2}{\pi}}$

Review set 10D

1 a $x = -\frac{1}{3}$ **b** $x = \frac{22}{47}$

  c $x = \frac{53}{29}$ **d** $x = \frac{61}{7}$

2 $x = \frac{3}{2}$

3 a $49 - 42x + 9x^2$ **b** $16 - x^2$
  c $64x^2 - 9$

4 a $(4 - x)(4 + x)$ **b** $(r + t)(r - t)$
  c $(9n - 7t)(9n + 7t)$ **d** $(x + 5)(x + 3)$
  e $(x - 10)(x + 2)$ **f** $(4x - 3)(2x - 1)$

5 $x = \pm 1, \pm 2$ **6** $x = 3 \pm \sqrt{13}$

7 a $x = 3$ or 4 **b** $x = \frac{7 \pm \sqrt{33}}{8}$
  c $x = 1\frac{1}{3}$ or -2

8 $(-\frac{1}{2}, \frac{11}{2})$ and $(-1, 3)$

9 a $x = \frac{a - by - p}{q}$ **b** $x = \frac{a - b}{d + 1}$

CHAPTER 11 FURTHER TRIGONOMETRY

Diagnostic test

1 B	**2** D	**3** D	**4** A	**5** B
6 B	**7** C	**8** A	**9** D	**10** A
11 B	**12** C	**13** B	**14** D	**15** B
16 D	**17** A	**18** C	**19** B	**20** B
21 B				

Exercise 11A

1 $DB = \sqrt{80} = 4\sqrt{5}$ cm, $EB = \sqrt{89}$ cm

2 $QS = \sqrt{208} = 4\sqrt{13}$ cm, $QT = \sqrt{233}$ cm

3 $EB = \sqrt{174}$ cm

4 $EB = \sqrt{300} = 10\sqrt{3}$ cm

5 a $AC = \sqrt{72} = 6\sqrt{2}$ cm   **b** $XY = \sqrt{103}$ cm
6 $XY = \sqrt{175} = 5\sqrt{7}$ cm
7 a $AC = \sqrt{113}$ cm   **b** $AF = \sqrt{129}$ cm
8 $AF = \sqrt{469}$ cm
9 a $PR = \sqrt{193}$ cm   **b** 16°
10 a $JL = 1.84$ m   **b** 23°
11 19°
12 a 35°16′
  b Yes; $\tan \theta = \dfrac{\text{side length}}{\text{side length}} \times \sqrt{3} = \dfrac{1}{\sqrt{3}}$ for any side length.
13 $\angle XAY = 61°52′$ **14** $\angle FAC = 27°30′$

Exercise 11B

1 $XY = 351$ m
2 $XY = 698$ m
3 a 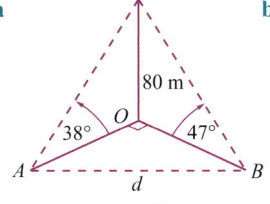   **b** 127 m

4 a 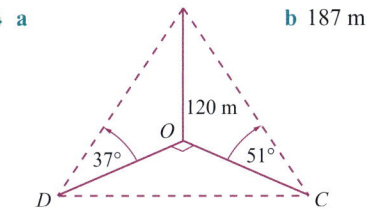   **b** 187 m

5 a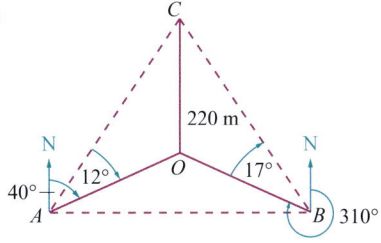

  b $\angle AOB = (360° - 310°) + 40° = 90°$
  c $OA = 1035$ m, $OB = 720$ m, $AB = 1261$ m
  d $\angle OAB = 35°$, bearing $= 075°$T
6 a 3814 m   **b** 126°T
7 a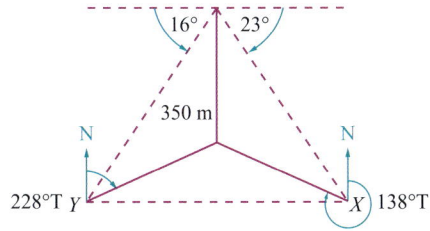

  b $XY = 1473$ m   **c** 262°T
8 a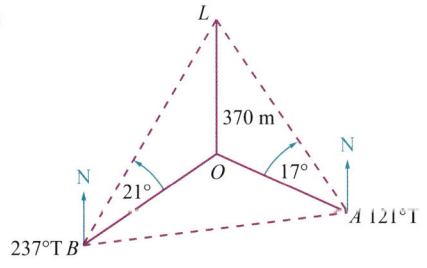

  b Boat A is 1210 m. Boat B is 964 m.
  c 1848 m   **d** 273°T

9

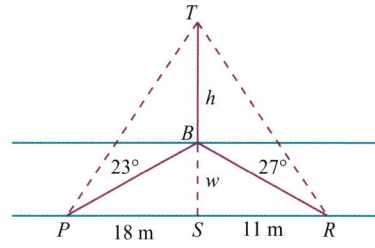

$w = 25$ m

Exercise 11C

1 a 0.9848   **b** −0.5150   **c** −5.1446
  d 0.9808   **e** −0.1530   **f** −0.8121
  g −0.0209   **h** 0.9041   **i** −0.7181
  j −2.5804   **k** 0.8594   **l** −0.0851

2 a

θ	0°	10°	20°	30°	40°	50°	60°
y	0	0.17	0.34	0.5	0.64	0.77	0.87

θ	70°	80°	90°	100°	110°	120°	130°
y	0.94	0.98	1	0.98	0.94	0.87	0.77

θ	140°	150°	160°	170°	180°
y	0.64	0.5	0.34	0.17	0

b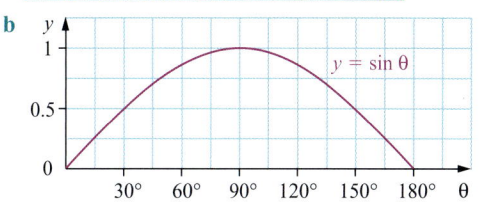

c They are equal.
d They are equal.
e $\sin \theta = \sin(180° - \theta)$

3 a

θ	0°	10°	20°	30°	40°	50°	60°
y	1	0.98	0.94	0.87	0.77	0.64	0.5

θ	70°	80°	90°	100°	110°	120°	130°
y	0.34	0.17	0	−0.17	−0.34	−0.5	−0.64

θ	140°	150°	160°	170°	180°
y	−0.77	−0.87	−0.94	−0.98	−1

b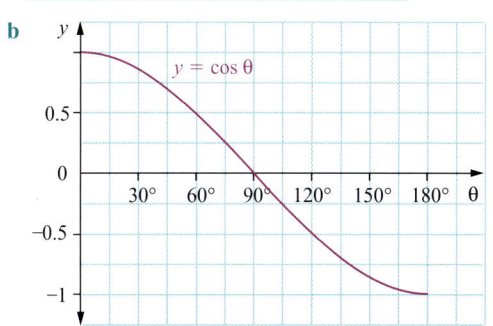

c They are equal in magnitude but opposite in sign.
d They are equal in magnitude but opposite in sign.
e $\cos \theta = -\cos(180° - \theta)$
4 a 158°37′   **b** 118°9′
  c 155°43′   **d** 163°55′
  e 138°22′   **f** 125°44′

Exercise 11D

1 a

θ	0°	30°	60°	90°	120°	150°	180°
y	0	0.5	0.87	1	0.87	0.5	0

θ	210°	240°	270°	300°	330°	360°
y	−0.5	−0.87	−1	−0.87	−0.5	0

b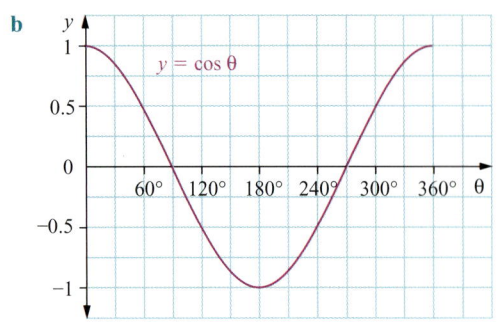

c Expected negative   **d** Expected negative

2 a

θ	0°	30°	60°	90°	120°	150°	180°
y	1	0.87	0.5	0	0.5	0.87	1

θ	210°	240°	270°	300°	330°	360°
y	−0.87	−0.5	−1	−0.5	−0.87	0

b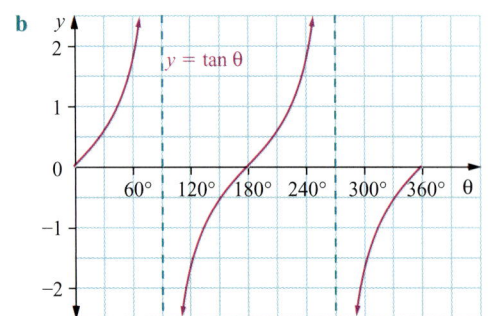

c The sine and cosine graphs have the same shape, period and maximum values. The sine graph starts at 0 and is positive $0° < θ < 180°$. The cosine graph starts at 1 and is positive and negative $0° < θ < 180°$. The sine graph is negative $180° < θ < 360°$ while cosine graph is negative and positive.

3 a

θ	0°	30°	60°	90°	120°	150°	180°
y	0	0.58	1.73	∞	−1.73	−0.58	0

θ	210°	240°	270°	300°	330°	360°
y	0.58	1.73	∞	1.73	0.58	0

b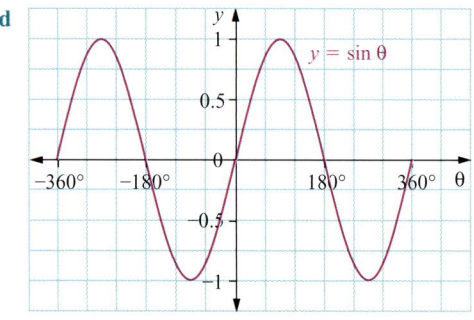

c All graphs are positive in quadrant 1, $0 < θ < 90°$. The tan and sine graphs are negative in quadrant 4, $270° < θ < 360°$. The tan and cosine graphs are both negative while the sine graph is positive in quadrant 2, $90° < θ < 180°$. The tan graph is positive while the sine and cosine graphs are both negative in quadrant 3, $180° < θ < 270°$. The tan graph has asymptotes. The tan period is 180° while the sine and cosine graphs both have a period of 360°.

d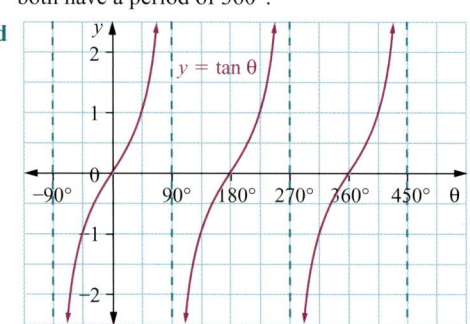

4 a The graph is the same but it is repeated (there are two of them).

b 2

c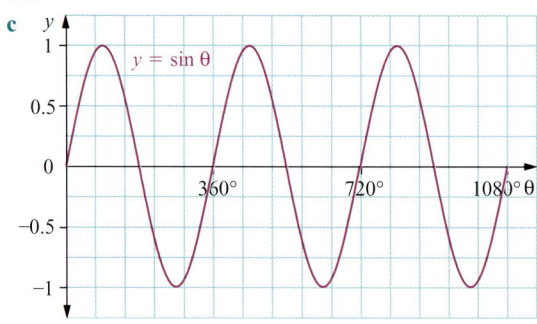

d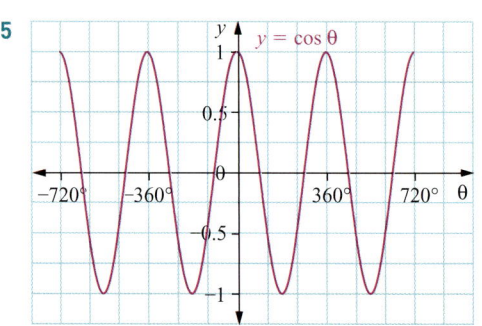

5

6 a 2   **b** 2   **c** Sine or cosine graph

    d 0.4 m and 1.5 m   **e** about 12 h

7 a Sine or cosine graphs   **b** 5 s

8 a

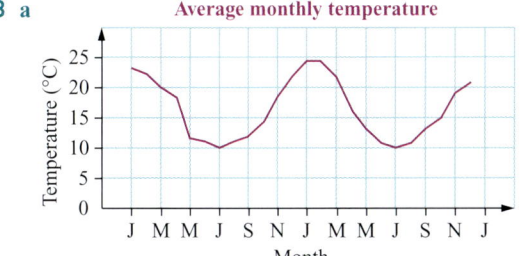

Average monthly temperature

b Cosine graph   **c** 12 months   **d** 14°C
e Southern hemisphere, so winter is in June and summer is in January.

9 a

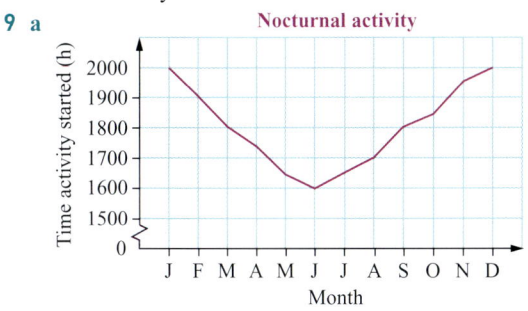

Nocturnal activity

b Cosine graph   **c** 12 months   **d** 4 hours

10 a

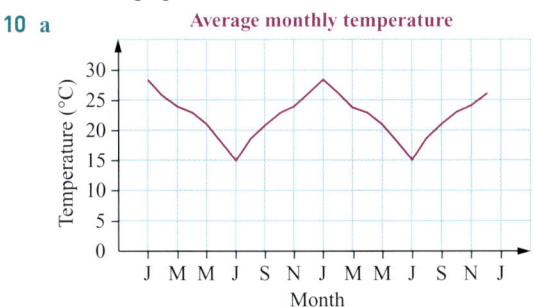

Average monthly temperature

b Cosine graph   **c** 12 months   **d** 13°C

Exercise 11E

1 a $\frac{1}{2}$ **b** $-\frac{\sqrt{3}}{2}$ **c** $-\frac{\sqrt{3}}{2}$ **d** $\frac{\sqrt{3}}{2}$ **e** $\frac{\sqrt{3}}{2}$

f $\frac{1}{2}$ **g** $\frac{\sqrt{3}}{2}$ **h** $\frac{\sqrt{3}}{2}$ **i** $-\frac{1}{2}$

2 a i $\frac{\sqrt{3}}{2}$ **ii** $-\frac{1}{2}$ **iii** $-\sqrt{3}$

b i $-\frac{1}{2}$ **ii** $-\frac{\sqrt{3}}{2}$ **iii** $\frac{1}{\sqrt{3}}$

c i $-\frac{\sqrt{3}}{2}$ **ii** $\frac{1}{2}$ **iii** $-\sqrt{3}$

3 a $-\frac{1}{\sqrt{3}}$ **b** $\sqrt{3}$ **c** $-\frac{1}{\sqrt{3}}$

4 a 30°, 150°   **b** 150°, 210°
c 60°, 120°   **d** 60°, 300°
e 240°, 300°   **f** 120°, 240°

Language in mathematics

1 a The gradient of a straight line is equal to tan θ.
b The sine ratio is positive in quadrants 1 and 2.
c The cosine ratio is negative in quadrants 2 and 3.
d Three-dimensional problems usually use the tan ratio as a part of the calculations.
e The period of the graph $y = \sin θ$ is 360°.
f The graph of $y = \tan θ$ has vertical asymptotes.

Check your skills

1 B   **2** B   **3** D   **4** A   **5** C
6 C   **7** B   **8** C   **9** B   **10** A

Review set 11A

1 $\sqrt{633}$ cm
2 a $\sqrt{881}$ **b** 31°
3 a   **b** 247 m

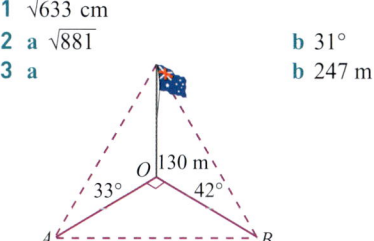

4 a 150°   **b** 19°

5

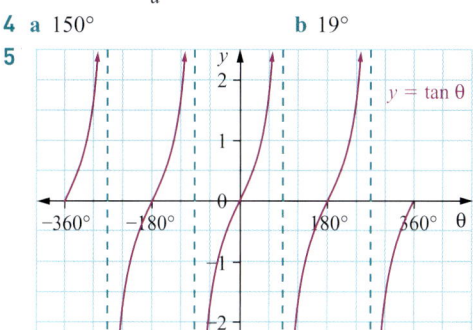

$y = \tan θ$

6 $-\frac{\sqrt{3}}{2}$

Review set 11B

1 $\sqrt{693} = 3\sqrt{77}$ cm
2 a $\sqrt{306}$ **b** 22°
3 a   **b** 88.7 m

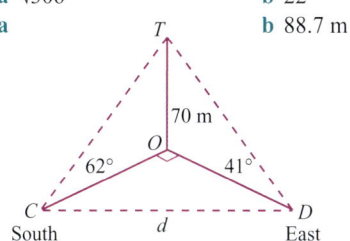

4 162°

5

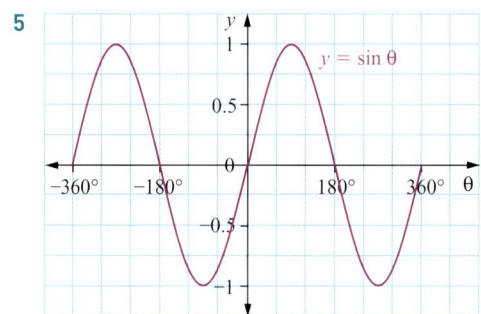

$y = \sin θ$

6 $\sqrt{3}$

Review set 11C

1 a $8\sqrt{2}$ cm   **b** $\sqrt{193}$ cm
2 a $\sqrt{89}$ m   **b** 18°

3 a

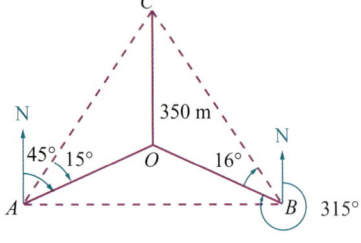

b $315° − 270° = 45°, 45° + 45° = 90°$
c $AO = 1306$ m, $OB = 1221$ m, $AB = 1788$ m
d $\angle OAB = 43°$, bearing = 088°T

4 44°

5

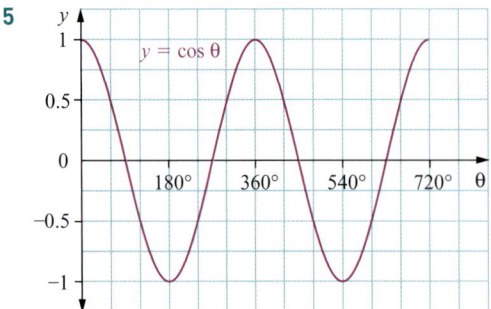

6 $-\frac{1}{2}$

Review set 11D

1 $\sqrt{507} = 13\sqrt{3}$ cm

2 a $\sqrt{689}$ cm **b** 21°

3 a $XY = 1066$ m

4 120°

5

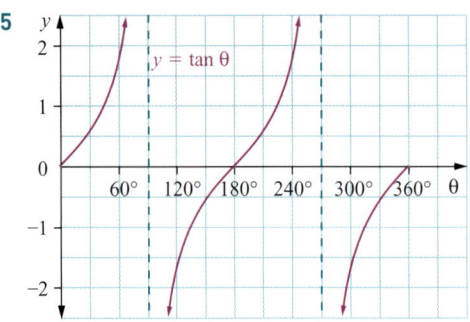

6 $\theta = 210°, 330°$

CHAPTER 12 GRAPHICAL REPRESENTATION

Diagnostic test

1 D	**2** B	**3** B	**4** B	**5** D
6 D	**7** D	**8** C	**9** C	**10** B
11 C				

Exercise 12A

1 a D
  b i B **ii** C
2 a CD **b** EF **c** AB
3 a BC, EF **b** AB **c** CD
  d AB, CD **e** DE, FG
4 Time cannot go backwards.
5 B, D
6 a B **b** C **c** A **d** D
7 a B **b** C **c** A

8 a D **b** B **c** A **d** F **e** C **f** E

9 a 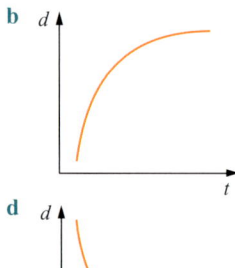 **b**

c **d**

e

10 a The distance travelled increases at a constant rate, then increases at an increasing rate.
  b The distance travelled decreases at an increasing rate, then decreases at an even faster rate.
  c The distance travelled increases at a decreasing rate, then increases at a constant rate, then decreases at an increasing rate.
  d The distance travelled increases at an increasing rate, then increases at a constant rate, then decreases at an increasing rate, then decreases at a constant rate.
  e The distance travelled increases at a constant rate, then decreases at a constant rate, then decreases at a decreasing rate, then increases at an increasing rate.
  Note: For distance to change from increasing to decreasing, the object must stop.

11 a 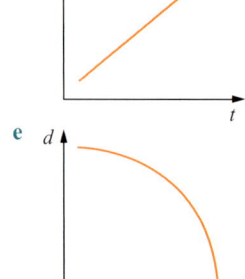 **b**

c **d**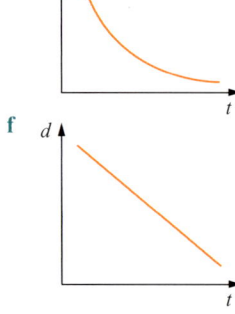

e **f**

g

12 a Bus 1

t	0	$\frac{1}{2}$	1	$1\frac{1}{2}$	2	$2\frac{1}{2}$	3	$3\frac{1}{2}$	4
d	120	105	90	75	60	45	30	15	0

b Bus 2

t	0	$\frac{1}{2}$	1	$1\frac{1}{2}$	2	$2\frac{1}{2}$	3	$3\frac{1}{2}$	4
d	120	120	120	105	90	75	60	45	30

c Bus 3

t	0	$\frac{1}{2}$	1	$1\frac{1}{2}$	2	$2\frac{1}{2}$	3	$3\frac{1}{2}$	4
d	120	120	120	120	120	90	60	30	0

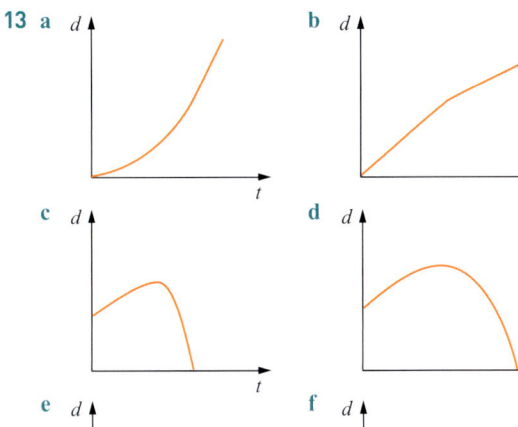

d 1 h after third bus leaves it overtakes the 2nd bus.
4 h after the 3rd bus leaves it catches the 1st bus.

13 a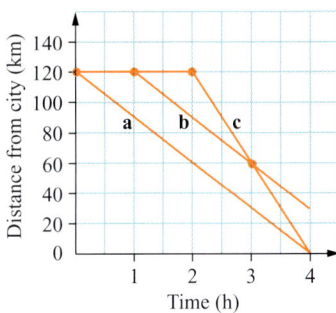

Exercise 12B

1 a The number of people waiting increases at an increasing rate until a train arrives. Then the number waiting decreases rapidly as people board the train.
  b A train arrives every 30 min.
  c Approximately 2 min
2 a The number of cans remains the same until 10 am when it decreases at a decreasing rate. The number of cans then increases at a constant rate as the vending machine is filled, from 10:30 am to 11:00 am. At 12·30 pm the number of cans decreases at a constant rate until 1:30 pm when the machine is refilled at a constant rate. Some cans are removed between 3.00 pm and 3.30 pm.
  b 10:00–10:30 am recess; 12:30–1:30 pm lunch

3 a On Sunday the number of cars passing through the intersection is less than half the number of cars on Monday.
  b Peak hour traffic getting to work and returning home.
4 a B   **b** D   **c** C   **d** A
5 a i C   **ii** B   **iii** A
  b i

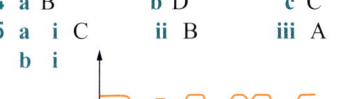

ii

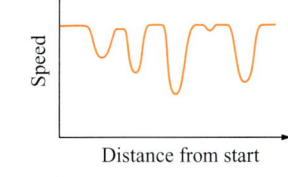

iii

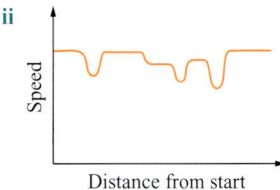

6 a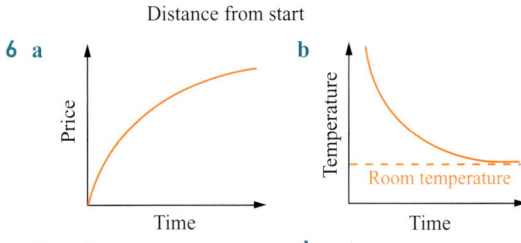

7 a Drug in bloodstream   **b** Drug in bloodstream

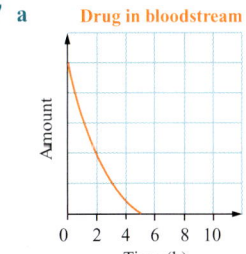
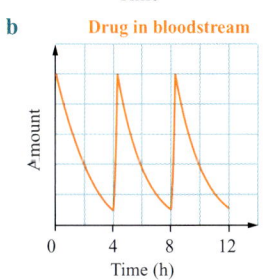

8 a B

b i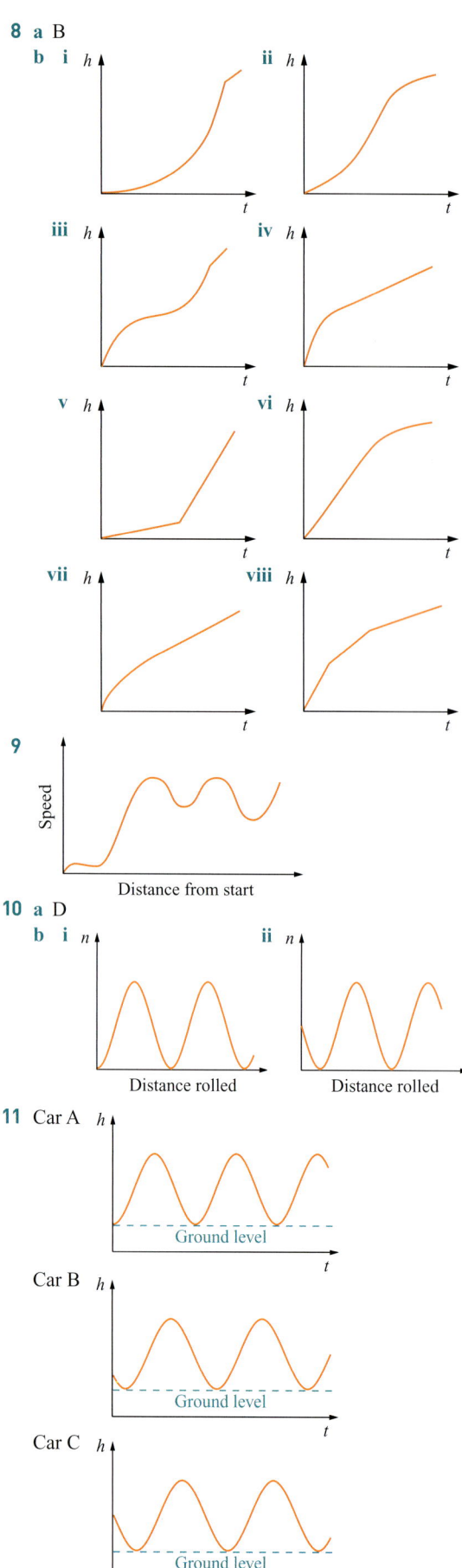

ii

iii

iv

v

vi

vii

viii

9

Speed

Distance from start

10 a D

b i n

ii n

Distance rolled

Distance rolled

11 Car A h

Ground level

Car B h

Ground level

Car C h

Ground level

Exercise 12C

1 a

x	-1	0	1	2	3	4
y	15	7	3	3	7	15

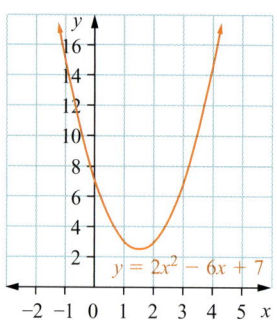

$y = 2x^2 - 6x + 7$

b

x	-4	-3	-2	-1	0	1	2
y	-10	0	6	8	6	0	-10

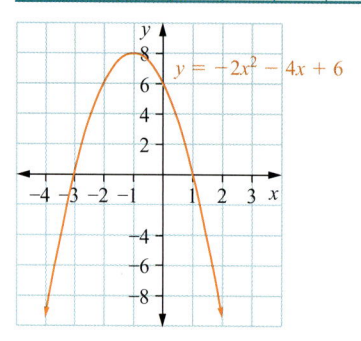

$y = -2x^2 - 4x + 6$

2 a $x = 5, x = -2, y = -10$
b $x = -7, x = 2, y = -14$
c $x = -4, x = 2, y = 8$
d No x-intercepts, $y = 18$
e $x = 1.5, x = -1, y = -3$
f $x = 2, x = -\frac{1}{3}, y = 2$

3 a i $x = -\frac{1}{2}$ **ii** $\left(-\frac{1}{2}, -6\frac{1}{4}\right)$

iii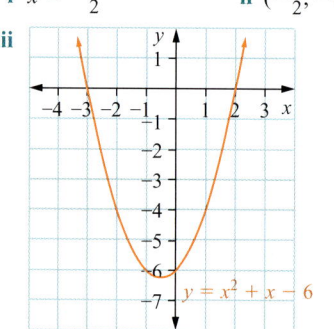

$y = x^2 + x - 6$

b i $x = -1$ **ii** $(-1, -16)$

iii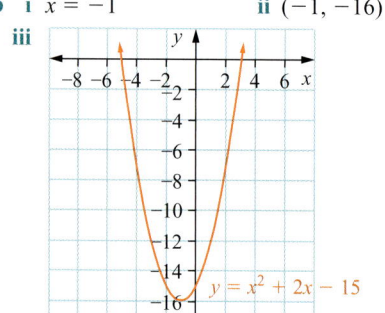

$y = x^2 + 2x - 15$

c **i** $x = -\frac{1}{4}$　　　　**ii** $(-\frac{1}{4}, -6\frac{1}{8})$

iii

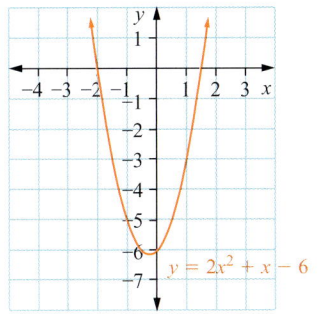

d **i** $x = \frac{13}{6}$　　　　**ii** $-\frac{289}{12}$

iii

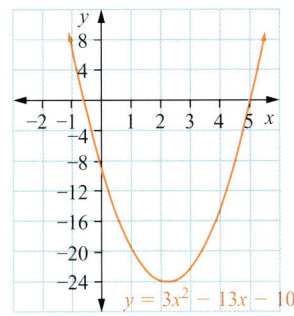

4 **a** The parabola $y = -x^2 + 2x + 8$ has y-intercept 8 and x-intercepts -2 and 4. The equation of its axis of symmetry is $x = 1$ and the coordinates of its vertex are $(1, 9)$. As $a = -1$, the curve is concave down.

b The parabola $y = -x^2 - 5x - 6$ has y-intercept -6 and x-intercepts -3 and -2. The equation of it axis of symmetry is $x = -\frac{5}{2}$ and the coordinates of its vertex are $(-\frac{5}{2}, \frac{1}{4})$. As $a = -1$, the curve is concave down.

c The parabola $y = 3 - x - 2x^2$ has y-intercept 3 and x-intercepts $-\frac{3}{2}$ and 1. The equation of it axis of symmetry is $x = -\frac{1}{4}$ and the coordinates of its vertex are $(-\frac{1}{4}, \frac{25}{8})$. As $a = -2$, the curve is concave down.

d The parabola $y = 2 + 5x - 3x^2$ has y-intercept 2 and x-intercepts 2 and $-\frac{1}{3}$. The equation of it axis of symmetry is $x = \frac{5}{6}$ and the coordinates of its vertex are $(\frac{5}{6}, \frac{49}{12})$. As $a = -3$, the curve is concave down.

5 **a**

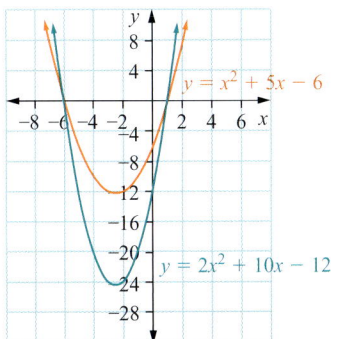

b Both graphs are concave up. They have the same axis of symmetry and the same x-intercepts.

c The second equation is double the first equation; that is, for each x-coordinate, the y-coordinate of the second parabola is double the y-coordinate of the first parabola.

6 Some examples:

a $y = x^2 - 6x + 8$, $y = 2x^2 - 12x + 16$, $y = 3x^2 - 18x + 24$

b $y = x^2 + x - 6$, $y = 2x^2 + 2x - 12$, $y = 3x^2 + 3x - 18$

c $y = x^2 + 7x + 10$, $y = 2x^2 + 14x + 20$, $y = 3x^2 + 21x + 30$

7 **a**

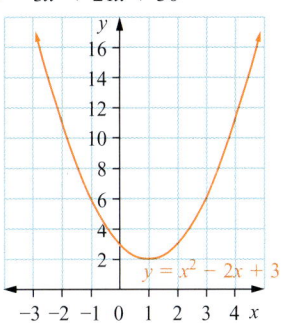

b

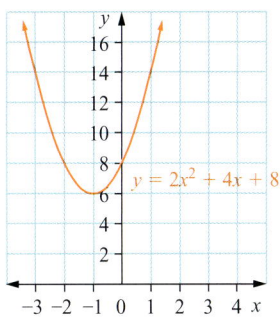

c

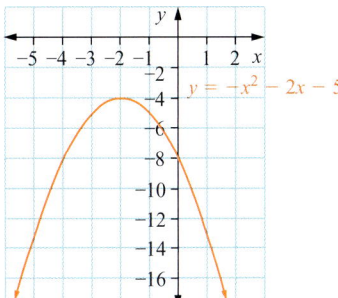

d

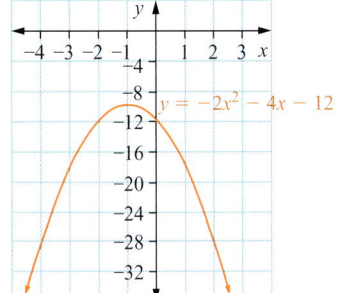

e

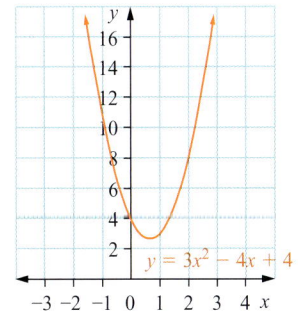

f

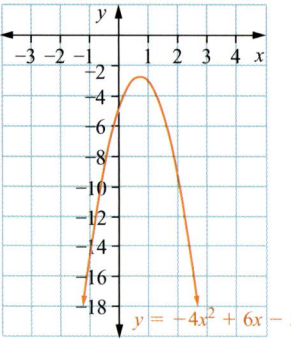

$y = -4x^2 + 6x - 5$

8 a

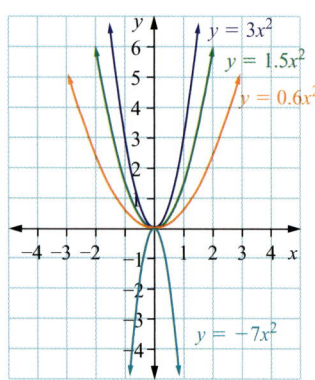

$y = 3x^2$
$y = 1.5x^2$
$y = 0.6x^2$
$y = -7x^2$

b $y = 3x^2$, $y = 1.5\,x^2$ and $y = 0.6\,x^2$ are concave up.
$y = -7x^2$ is concave down.

c If a is negative, parabola is concave down.
If a is positive, parabola is concave up.

9 a

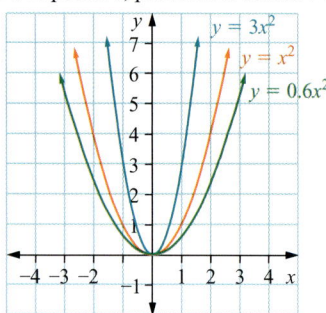

$y = 3x^2$
$y = x^2$
$y = 0.6x^2$

i If $a > 1$, the parabola is narrower than $y = x^2$.
If $0 < a < 1$, the parabola is wider than $y = x^2$.
ii Same axis of symmetry, vertex and shape. Both are concave up.
$y = 3x^2$ is narrower than $y = x^2$.
iii Same axis of symmetry, vertex and shape. Both are concave up.
$y = 0.6x^2$ is wider than $y = x^2$.

b

$y = -\frac{1}{3}x^2$
$y = -x^2$
$y = -2x^2$

i If $a < -1$, the parabola is narrower than $y = -x^2$.
If $-1 < a < 0$, the parabola is wider than $y = -x^2$.

ii Same axis of symmetry, vertex and shape. Both are concave down.
$y = -3x^2$ is narrower than $y = -x^2$.
iii Same axis of symmetry, vertex and shape. Both are concave down.
$y = -\frac{1}{3}x^2$ is wider than $y = -x^2$.

10 a

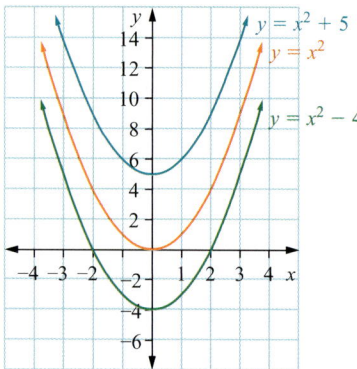

$y = x^2 + 5$
$y = x^2$
$y = x^2 - 4$

i If $c > 0$, the parabola is translated c units up.
If $c < 0$, the parabola is translated c units down.
ii Same axis of symmetry and shape. Both are concave up.
$y = x^2 + 5$ is $y = x^2$ translated 5 units up.

b

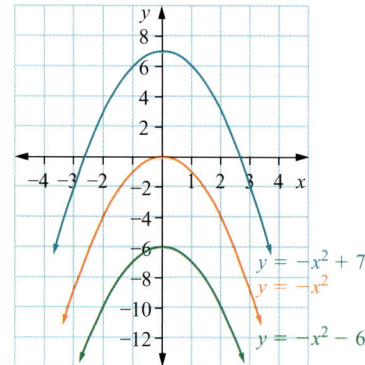

$y = -x^2 + 7$
$y = -x^2$
$y = -x^2 - 6$

i If $c > 0$, the parabola is translated c units up.
If $c < 0$, the parabola is translated c units down.
ii Same axis of symmetry and shape. Both are concave are down.
$y = -x^2 - 9$ is $y = -x^2$ translated 9 units down.

11 a i Both are concave up, $y = 2x^2 - 3$ is narrower than $y = x^2$ and is 3 units below it $y = 2x^2$.
ii Both are concave up, $y = 0.4x^2 + 7$ is wider than $y = x^2$ and is 7 units above $y = 0.4x^2$.

b i Both are concave down, $y = -5x^2 + 1$ is narrower than $y = -x^2$ and is 1 unit above $y = -5x^2$.
ii Both are concave down, $y = -0.7x^2 - 8$ is wider than $y = -x^2$ and is 8 units below $y = -0.7x^2$.

12 a

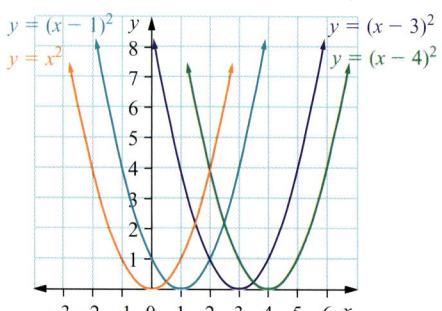

$y = (x - 1)^2$
$y = x^2$
$y = (x - 3)^2$
$y = (x - 4)^2$

i $x = 0, (0, 0); x = 1, (1, 0); x = 3, (3, 0);$
$x = 4, (4, 0)$
ii b translates the graph to the right by b units.
iii $x = 9, (9, 0)$

b
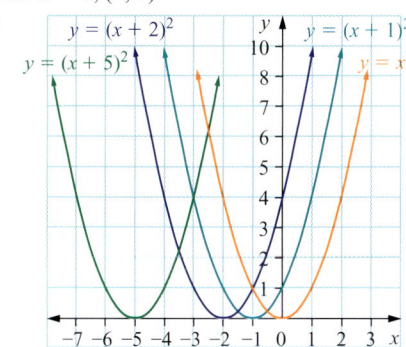

i $x = 0, (0, 0); x = -1, (-1, 0); x = -2, (-2, 0);$
$x = -5, (-5, 0)$
ii b translates the graph to the left by b units.
iii $x = -7, (-7, 0)$

13 a
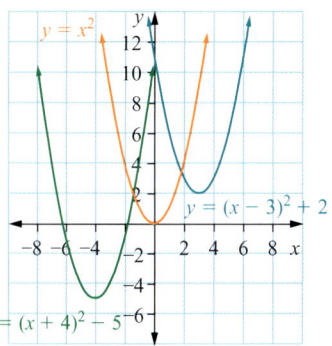

b $x = 0, (0, 0); x = 3, (3, 2); x = -4, (-4, -5)$
c $x = 8, (8, -5)$
14 a **i** Reflected in the x-axis and made narrower
   ii Concave down   **iii** $x = 0$
   iv $(0, 0)$
b **i** Made narrower and translated 3 units down
   ii Concave up   **iii** $x = 0$
   iv $(0, -3)$
c **i** Made wider and translated 4 units up
   ii Concave up   **iii** $x = 0$
   iv $(0, 4)$
d **i** Translated 15 units to the right
   ii Concave up   **iii** $x = 15$
   iv $(15, 0)$
e **i** Translated 11 units to the left
   ii Concave up   **iii** $x = -11$
   iv $(-11, 0)$
f **i** Translated 5 units to the right and 1 unit up
   ii Concave up   **iii** $x = 5$
   iv $(5, 1)$
g **i** Translated 7 units to the left and 9 units down
   ii Concave up   **iii** $x = -7$
   iv $(-7, -9)$
h **i** Reflected in the x-axis, translated 3 units to the
   right and 5 units up
   ii Concave down   **iii** $x = 3$
   iv $(3, 5)$

i **i** Made wider and translated 1 unit to the right and
   3 units down.
   ii Concave up   **iii** $x = 1$
   iv $(1, -3)$
15 a $y = x^2 + 1$ **b** $y = x^2 - 3$
   c $y = (x - 3)^2$ **d** $y = (x - 5)^2 - 1$
   e $y = (x + 3)^2 + 1$ **f** $y = 3x^2$
   g $y = 0.5x^2$ **h** $y = -2x^2$
16 a $x = 2, (2, -2)$ **b** $x = -5, (-5, -31)$
   c $x = 1.5, (1.5, 1.75)$ **d** $x = -2.5, (-2.5, -7.25)$
   e $x = 4.5, (4.5, -15.25)$ **f** $x = -4, (-4, -16)$
17 a $y = x^2 - 1$ **b** $y = -3x^2$
   c $y = 2x^2 + 1$ **d** $y = -x^2 + 10$
18 a $y = x^2 - x - 2$ **b** $y = x^2 - 3x + 1$
   c $y = x^2 - 3x + 2$ **d** $y = x^2 + 5x + 1$

Exercise 12D

1 a

x	-4	-3	-2	-1	$-\frac{1}{2}$	$-\frac{1}{4}$	$-\frac{1}{8}$	$\frac{1}{8}$	$\frac{1}{4}$	1	2	3	4
y	$\frac{1}{4}$	$\frac{1}{3}$	$\frac{1}{2}$	1	2	4	8	-8	-4	-1	$-\frac{1}{2}$	$-\frac{1}{3}$	$-\frac{1}{4}$

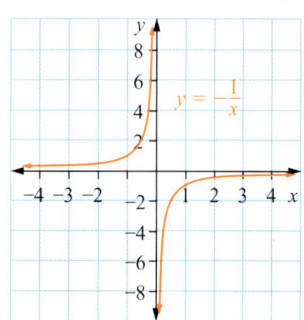

b There is no solution, the graph is undefined at $x = 0$.
c No   **d** y approaches zero.
e y gets smaller.   **f** y approaches zero.
g y gets very large. **h** $x = 0$ $y = 0$
i $y = x$ and $y = -x$
2 a

b If $k > 1$, the hyperbola is moved further away from
the asymptotes.
If $0 < k < 1$, the hyperbola is moved closer to the
asymptotes.
c $x = 0, y = 0$ **d** $y = x, y = -x$

3 a

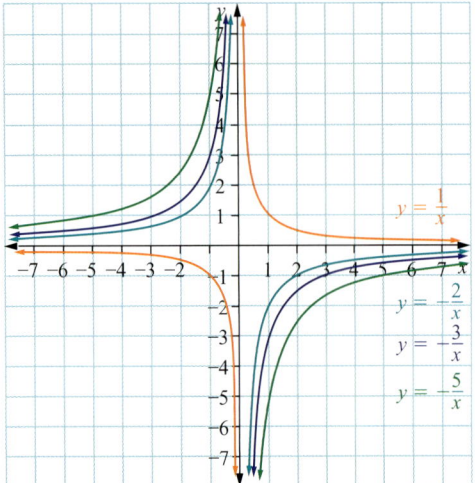

$y = \frac{1}{x}$

$y = \frac{2}{x}$

$y = -\frac{3}{x}$

$y = -\frac{5}{x}$

b If $k > 0$, the branches are in the 1st and 3rd quadrants. If $k < 0$, the branches are in the 2nd and 4th quadrants. Also $y = \pm x$, $y = \pm 2x$, $y = \pm 3x$, etc. are reflections of each other in the x- or y-axes.

c $x = 0, y = 0$ **d** $y = x, y = -x$

4 a

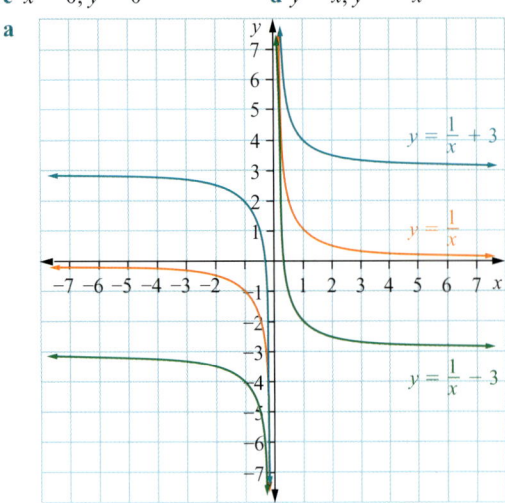

$y = \frac{1}{x} + 3$

$y = \frac{1}{x}$

$y = \frac{1}{x} - 3$

b The constant c translates the graph up or down.

c   **i** $x = 0, y = 0$ **ii** $x = 0, y = 3$

     iii $x = 0, y = -3$

d   **i** $x = 0, y = 5$ **ii** $x = 0, y = -4$

     iii $x = 0, y = 1$

5 a

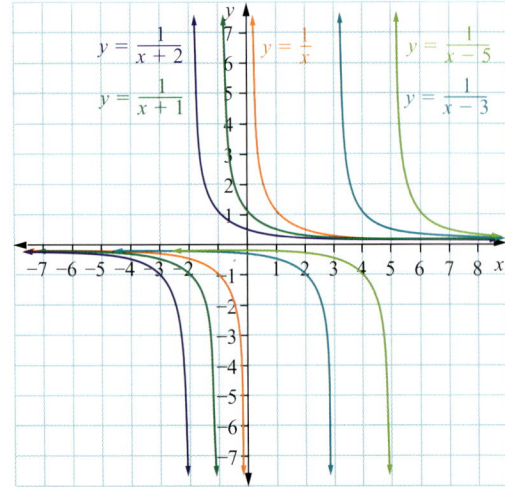

$y = \frac{1}{x + 2}$ $y = \frac{1}{x}$ $y = \frac{1}{x - 5}$

$y = \frac{1}{x + 1}$ $y = \frac{1}{x - 3}$

b The constant b translates the graph to the left or right.

c   **i** $x = 0, y = 0$ **ii** $x = 3, y = 0$

     iii $x = 5, y = 0$ **iv** $x = -1, y = 0$

     v $x = -2, y = 0$

d   **i** $x = 7, y = 0$ **ii** $x = -3, y = 0$

     iii $x = 2, y = 0$ **iv** $x = -4, y = 0$

6 a   **i** A reflection in the x-axis and further out from the asymptotes

     ii $x = 0, y = 0$ **iii** $y = x, y = -x$

b   **i** A translation 8 units up

     ii $x = 0, y = 8$

     iii $y = x + 8, y = -x + 8$

c   **i** A translation 5 units to the left

     ii $x = -5, y = 0$

     iii $y = x + 5, y = -x - 5$

d   **i** A translation 7 units down

     ii $x = 0, y = -7$

     iii $y = x - 7, y = -x - 7$

e   **i** A translation 6 units to the right

     ii $x = 6, y = 0$

     iii $y = x - 6, y = -x + 6$

f   **i** A reflection in the x-axis, translated 5 units up

     ii $x = 0, y = 5$

     iii $y = x + 5, y = -x + 5$

g   **i** A reflection in the x-axis, translated 2 units to the right

     ii $x = 2, y = 0$

     iii $y = x - 2, y = -x + 2$

h   **i** A translation 7 units down and further out from the asymptotes

     ii $x = 0, y = -7$

     iii $y = x - 7, y = -x - 7$

i   **i** Reflected in the x-axis, translated 12 units to the left and further out from the asymptotes

     ii $x = -12, y = 0$

     iii $y = x + 12, y = -x - 12$

7 a $y = \frac{5}{x}$ **b** $y = -\frac{2}{x}$

   c $y = \frac{1}{x} - 2$ **d** $y = \frac{1}{x - 2}$

Exercise 12E

1 a $x^2 + y^2 = 25$ **b** $x^2 + y^2 = 7$ **c** $x^2 + y^2 = \frac{25}{16}$

2 a 3   **b** $\sqrt{10}$ **c** $\frac{5}{7}$ **d** $\frac{\sqrt{7}}{2}$ **e** $\frac{4}{3}$

3 a

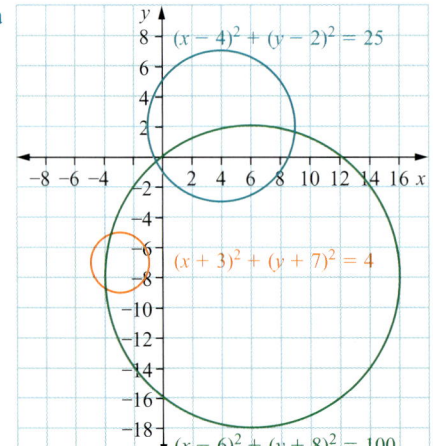

$(x - 4)^2 + (y - 2)^2 = 25$

$(x + 3)^2 + (y + 7)^2 = 4$

$(x - 6)^2 + (y + 8)^2 = 100$

b i $(4, 2), r = 5$ **ii** $(-3, -7), r = 2$
iii $(6, -8), r = 10$
c i A translation 4 units right and 2 units up
ii A translation 3 units left and 7 units down
iii A translation 6 units right and 8 units down
4 a $(7, 5), r = 7$ **b** $(-7, -5), r = 7$
c $(7, -5), r = 7$ **d** $(-7, 5), r = 7$
e $(-4, 9), r = 6$ **f** $(10, -5), r = 9$
g $(0, 5), r = 1$ **h** $(-9, 0), r = 4$
5 a $(x - 4)^2 + (y - 5)^2 = 4$
b $(x + 2)^2 + (y + 4)^2 = 25$
c $(x - 3)^2 + (y + 2)^2 = 36$
d $(x + 1)^2 + (y - 4)^2 = 9$
e $x^2 + (y - 2)^2 = 1$
f $(x + 5)^2 + y^2 = 49$
6 a $(-1, 4), r = 5$ **b** $(5, 3), r = 1$
c $(-7, -1), r = 7$ **d** $(10, 0), r = 2$
e $(0, 6), r = 4$ **f** $(1.5, 0.5), r = 3$
7 a $x^2 + y^2 - 6x - 12y + 20 = 0$
b $x^2 + y^2 + 8x - 6y + 24 = 0$
c $x^2 + y^2 - 14x + 8y + 56 = 0$
d $x^2 + y^2 + 12x + 14y + 69 = 0$
8 a i Outside **ii** Inside **iii** On
b i On **ii** Outside **iii** Outside
c i Inside **ii** On **iii** Outside
d i Inside **ii** Outside **iii** On

Exercise 12F

1 a

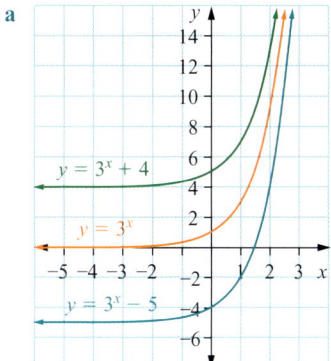

b i $y = 0$ **ii** $y = 4$ **iii** $y = -5$
c i $(0, 1)$ **ii** $(0, 5)$ **iii** $(0, -4)$

2 a

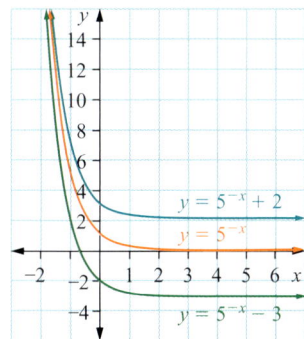

b i $y = 5^{-x}$ is a reflection in the y-axis.
ii $y = 5^{-x} - 3$ is a reflection in the y-axis and a translation down 3 units.
iii $y = 5^{-x} + 2$ is a reflection in the y-axis and a translation up 2 units.
c i $y = 0$ **ii** $y = -3$ **iii** $y = 2$
d i $(0, 1)$ **ii** $(0, -2)$ **iii** $(0, 3)$

3 a

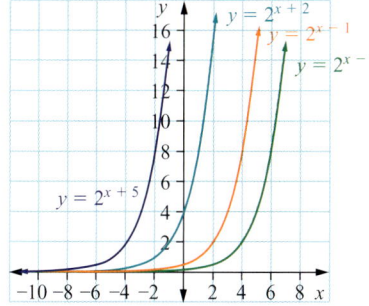

b i A translation 1 unit right
ii A translation 3 units right
iii A translation 2 units left
iv A translation 5 units left
c All asymptotes are $y = 0$.
d i $(0, \frac{1}{2})$ **ii** $(0, \frac{1}{8})$ **iii** $(0, 4)$ **iv** $(0, 32)$
e For $y = a^{x - b}$, if $b > 0$, the graph of $y = a^x$ is translated b units to the right, and if $b < 0$, the graph of $y = a^x$ is translated b units to the left.

4 a

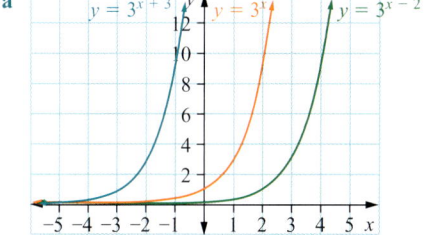

b All asymptotes are $y = 0$.
c i $(0, 1)$ **ii** $(0, \frac{1}{9})$ **iii** $(0, 27)$

5 a

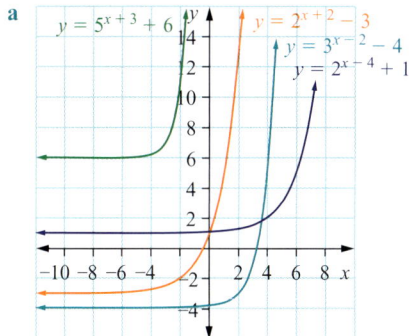

b i $y = 1$ **ii** $y = -3$
iii $y = -4$ **iv** $y = 6$

Exercise 12G

1 a i

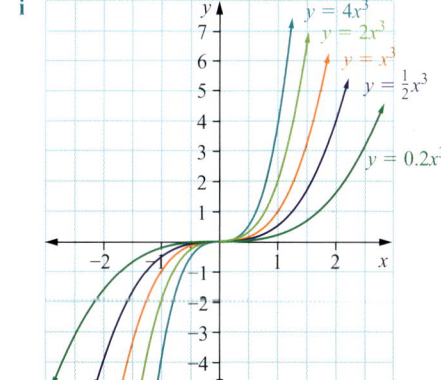

ii If $a > 1$, the graph of $y = ax^3$ is narrower than $y = x^3$. If $0 < a < 1$, the graph of $y = ax^3$ is wider than $y = x^3$.

b **i**
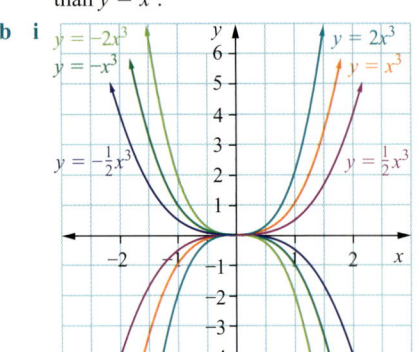

ii The graph is reflected on the y-axis.

c **i**

ii If $d > 0$, the graph of $y = ax^3$ is translated d units up. If $d < 0$, the graph of $y = ax^3$ is translated d units down.

d **i**

ii If $r > 0$, the graph of $y = x^3$ is translated r units to the right. If $r < 0$, the graph of $y = x^3$ is translated r units to the left.

2 a

b

c $y = x^3 + 2$

d $y = x^3 - 4$

e $y = -x^3 + 1$

f $y = -2x^3 - 2$

g $y = (x + 1)^3$

h $y = 2(x + 1)^3$

i $y = (x - 3)^3 + 1$

j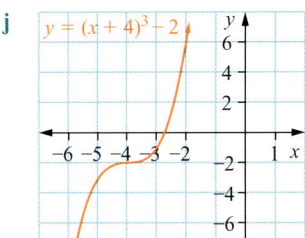
$y = (x + 4)^3 - 2$

3 a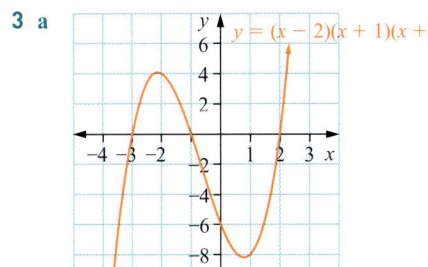
$y = (x - 2)(x + 1)(x + 3)$

b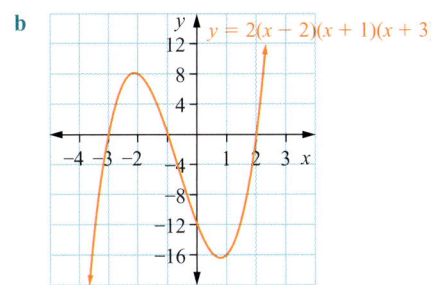
$y = 2(x - 2)(x + 1)(x + 3)$

c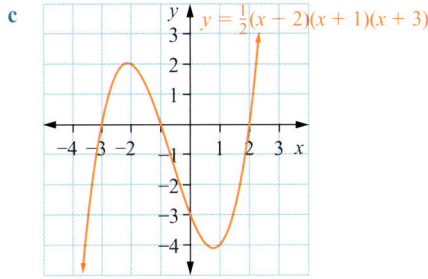
$y = \frac{1}{2}(x - 2)(x + 1)(x + 3)$

d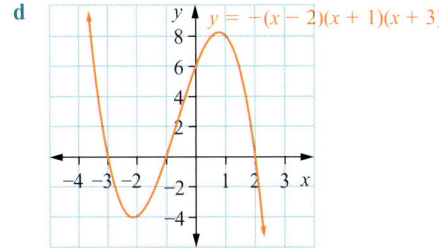
$y = -(x - 2)(x + 1)(x + 3)$

e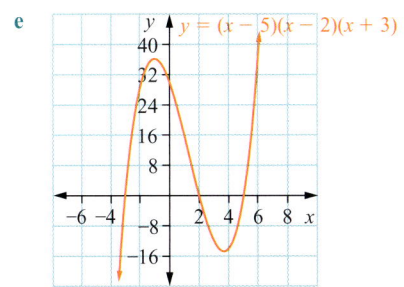
$y = (x - 5)(x - 2)(x + 3)$

f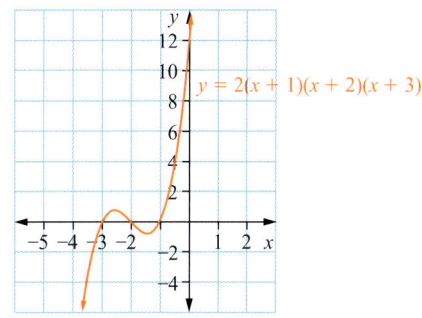
$y = 2(x + 1)(x + 2)(x + 3)$

g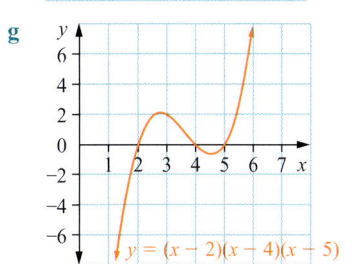
$y = (x - 2)(x - 4)(x - 5)$

h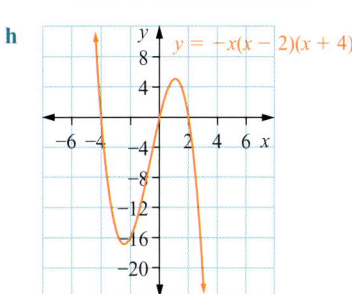
$y = -x(x - 2)(x + 4)$

4 a i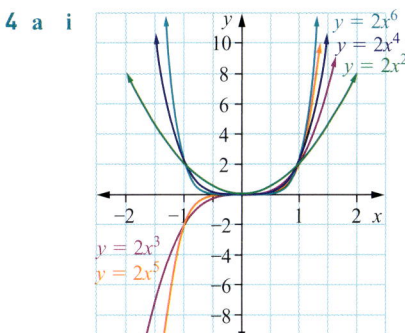
$y = 2x^6$
$y = 2x^4$
$y = 2x^2$
$y = 2x^3$
$y = 2x^5$

ii If n is odd, the graph has rotational symmetry about the origin, like a cubic graph.
If n is even, the graph is symmetrical about the y-axis, similar in shape to a parabola.

b i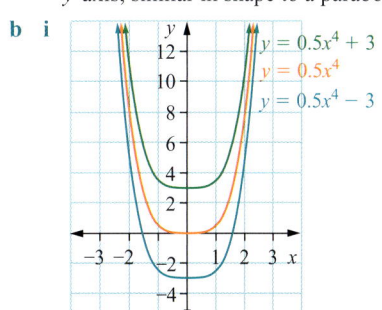
$y = 0.5x^4 + 3$
$y = 0.5x^4$
$y = 0.5x^4 - 3$

ii If $k > 0$, the graph of $y = ax^n$ is translated k units up. If $k < 0$, the graph of $y = ax^n$ is translated k units down.

c i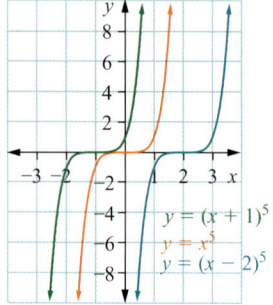

$y = (x + 1)^5$
$y = x^5$
$y = (x - 2)^5$

ii If $r > 0$, the graph of $y = ax^n$ is translated r units to the right.
If $r < 0$, the graph of $y = ax^n$ is translated r units to the left.

5 a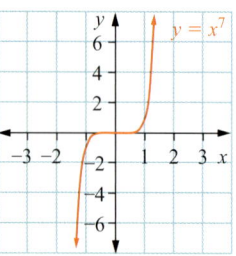

$y = x^7$

b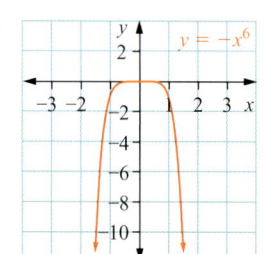

$y = -x^6$

c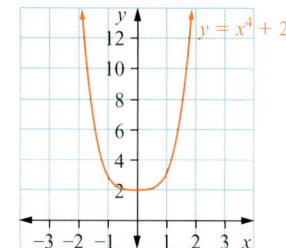

$y = x^4 + 2$

d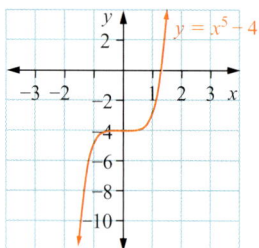

$y = x^5 - 4$

e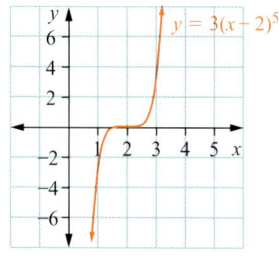

$y = 3(x - 2)^5$

f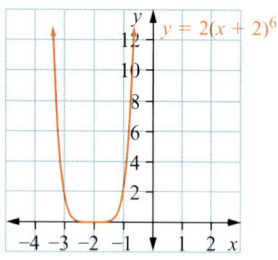

$y = 2(x + 2)^6$

g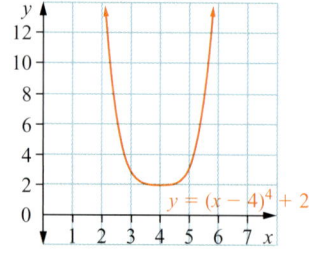

$y = (x - 4)^4 + 2$

h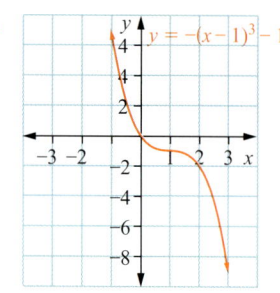

$y = -(x - 1)^3 - 1$

6 a Circle **b** Parabola
c Straight line **d** Exponential
e Parabola **f** Straight line
g Hyperbola **h** Exponential
i Circle

7 a D **b** I **c** J **d** F
e E **f** L **g** G **h** K
i B **j** C **k** A **l** H

8 a i

x	-3	-2	-1	0	1	2	3
y	18	8	2	0	2	8	18

ii They are the same value.
iii Yes

b i

x	-3	-2	-1	0	1	2	3
y	-5	0	3	4	3	0	-5

ii They are the same value.
iii Yes

9 a Yes **b** Yes **c** Yes **d** Yes
e No **f** No **g** Yes **h** Yes
i No **j** No **k** Yes **l** No

Exercise 12H

1 a i $(-5, -29), (2, 6)$ **ii** $(1, 9), (2, 11)$
iii $(-3\frac{2}{3}, 4), (\frac{1}{2}, 4)$ **iv** $(-1.5, 4), (5, 17)$
v $(4, 4), (-4, -4)$ **vi** $(2, -4), (4, -2)$
vii $(-4, -6), (3, 1)$ **viii** $(2, -3), (4, -1)$
ix $(3, 3), (-3, -3)$ **x** $(-3, 1), (1, 3)$

b i

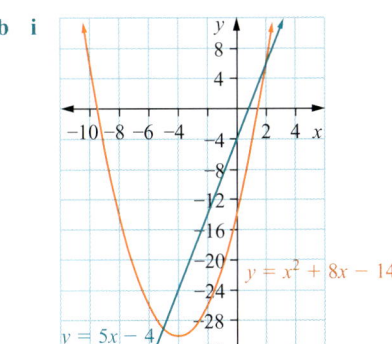

$y = x^2 + 8x - 14$

$y = 5x - 4$

v

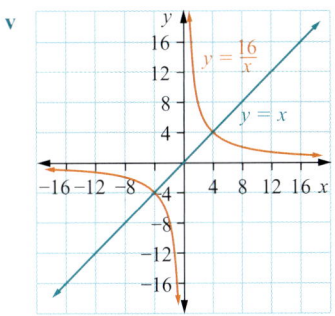

$y = \dfrac{16}{x}$

$y = x$

vii

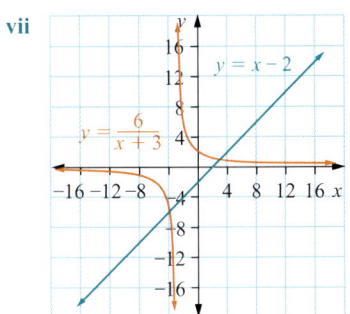

$y = x - 2$

$y = \dfrac{6}{x + 3}$

ix

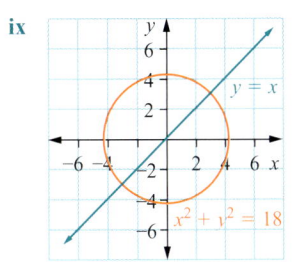

$y = x$

$x^2 + y^2 = 18$

x

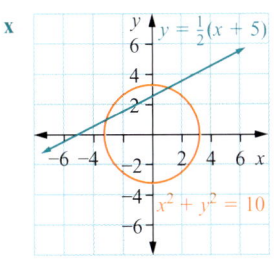

$y = \frac{1}{2}(x + 5)$

$x^2 + y^2 = 10$

2 a $(0.27, 0.072), (3.73, 13.93)$
b $(-0.78, 1.22), (1.28, 3.28)$
c $(-3.3, -0.3), (0.3, 3.3)$
d $(-0.45, -4.45), (4.45, 0.5)$
e $(-1.82, -0.82), (0.82, 1.82)$
f $(-2, -2), (5, 5)$

Language in mathematics

1 a change, depends
   b independent, dependent
   c horizontal, vertical

3 a

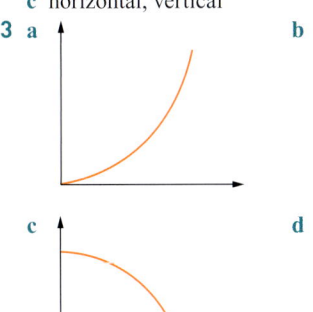

b

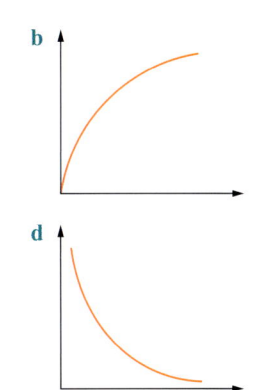

c

d

Check your skills

1 A	**2** C	**3** B	**4** D	**5** B
6 D	**7** A	**8** B	**9** B	**10** A
11 C	**12** D	**13** A	**14** A	**15** C
16 B	**17** A	**18** D	**19** D	**20** C
21 B	**22** D			

Review set 12A

1 A

2 a

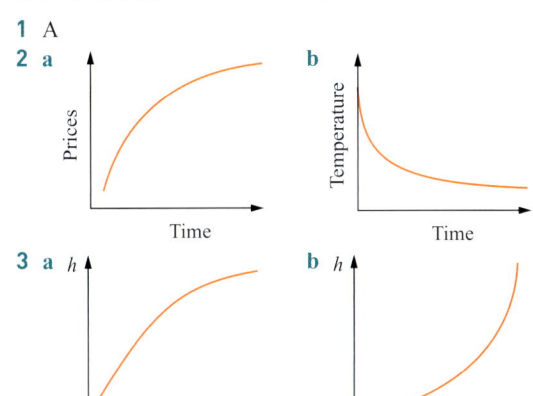

Prices / Time

b

Temperature / Time

3 a h

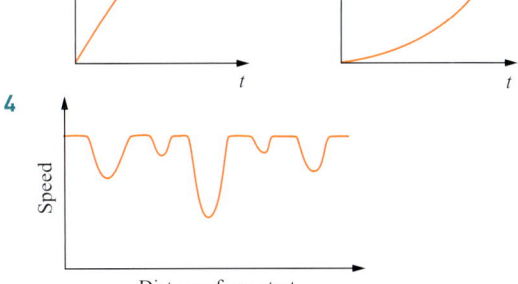

b h

t

4

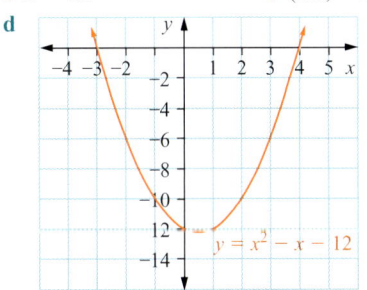

Speed

Distance from start

5 a $x = -3, x = 4; (0, -12)$
   b $x = 0.5$ **c** $(0.5, -12.25)$
   d

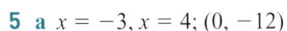

$y = x^2 - x - 12$

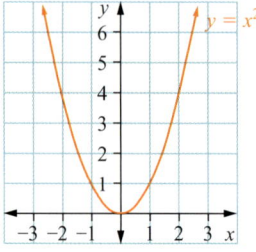

6 a i

ii

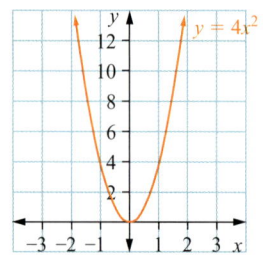

iii

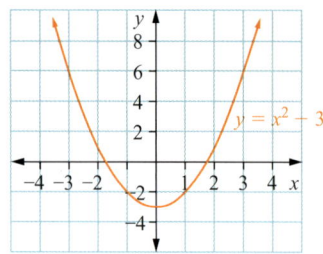

iv

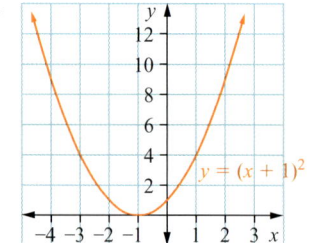

v

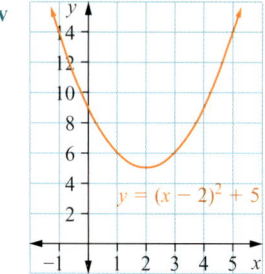

b i $(0, 0)$ **ii** $(0, 0)$ **iii** $(0, -3)$
iv $(-1, 0)$ **v** $(2, 5)$

7 $y = 2x^2 - 3$

8 a $x = 2, y = 3$
b $y = x + 1, y = -x + 5$

9 a $x^2 + y^2 = 8$
b $x^2 + y^2 - 10x + 12y - 39 = 0$

10 $(4, -2), r = 3$

11 a

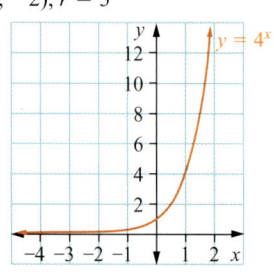

b

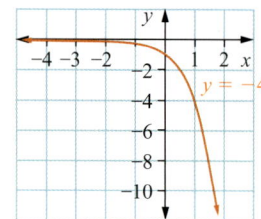

c

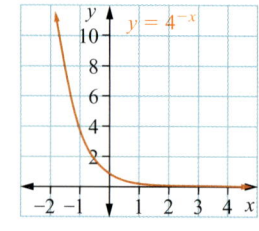

d

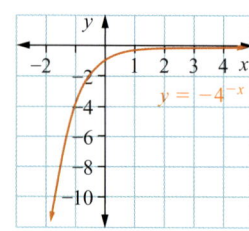

12 a B **b** C **c** D **d** A
13 a $x = -1, x = -2, x = -4, y = 8$
b

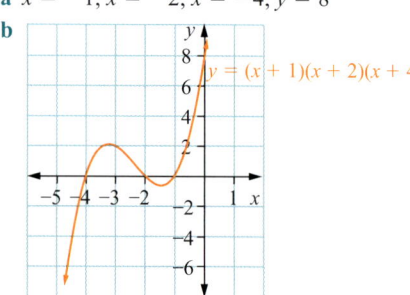

14 $(6, 4), (-4, -6)$

Review set 12B

1 C

2 a

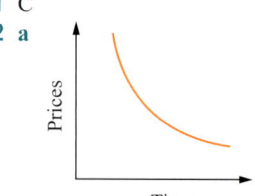

b

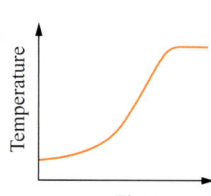

3 a

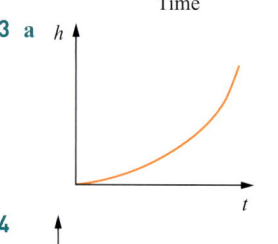

b h

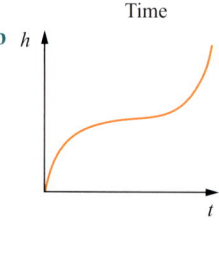

4

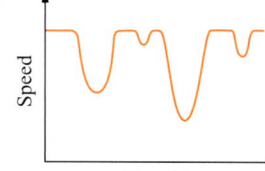

5 a $y = 2$ **b** $x = -2\frac{1}{2}$

c $(-2\frac{1}{2}), (-4\frac{1}{4})$

d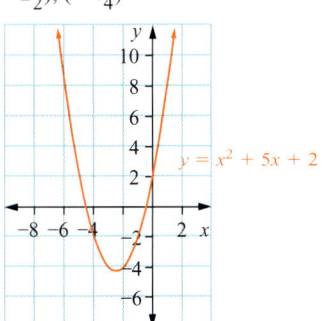

6 a C   b B   c A   d D

7 a i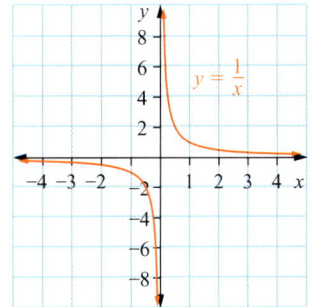

ii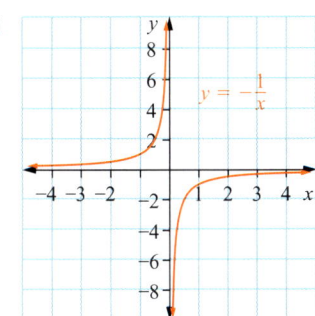

iii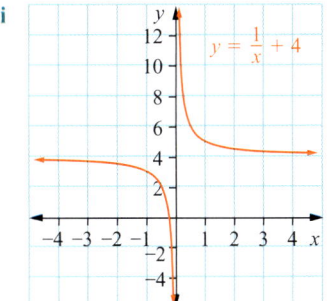

iv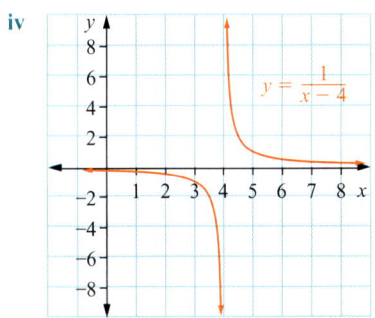

b i $x = 0, y = 0$ ii $x = 0, y = 0$
   iii $x = 0, y = 4$ iv $x = 4, y = 0$

8 a $(0, 0), r = \sqrt{8}$ b $(-5, 2), r = 3$
   c $(-5, 6), r = 1$

9 It lies inside the circle.   10 A, C
11 a C   b A   c B   d D
12 a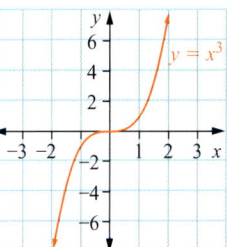

b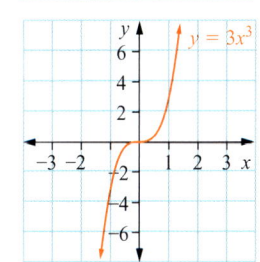

c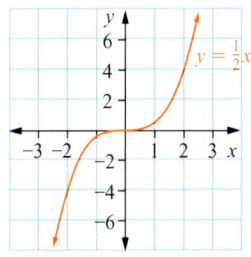

d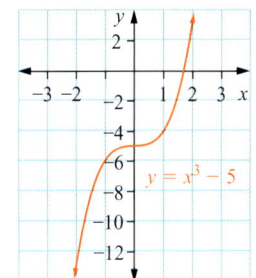

e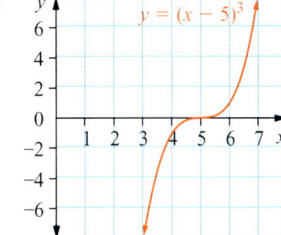

13 a $x = -1, x = -2, x = -3, y = 6$
   b

14 $(-7, 49), (4, 16)$

Review set 12C

1 B

2 a 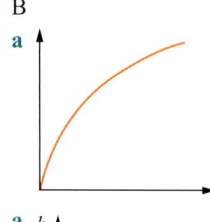 **b**

3 a h 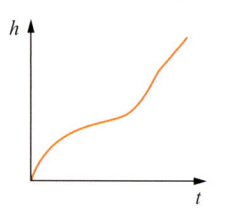 **b** h

4 a $x = -7, x = 4, y = 28$
 b $x = -1.5$
 c $\left(-\frac{3}{2}, \frac{121}{4}\right)$

d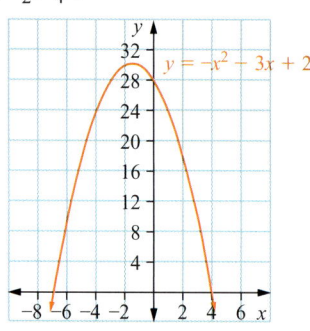
$y = -x^2 - 3x + 28$

5 a i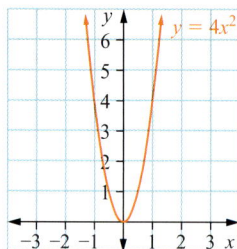
$y = 4x^2$

ii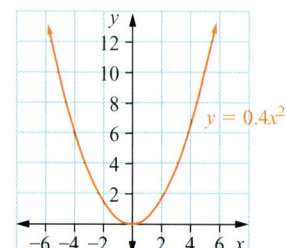
$y = 0.4x^2$

iii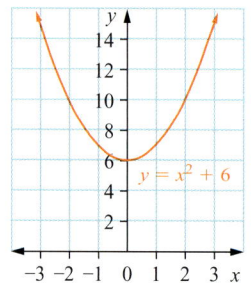
$y = x^2 + 6$

iv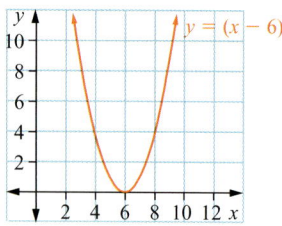
$y = (x - 6)^2$

v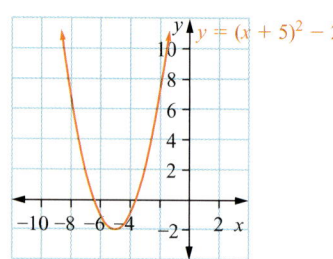
$y = (x + 5)^2 - 2$

b i $(0, 0)$ **ii** $(0, 0)$ **iii** $(0, 6)$
  iv $(6, 0)$ **v** $(-5, -2)$

6 $y = x^2 - 2x + 3$

7 a $x = -2, y = -7$
 b $y = -x - 9, y = x - 5$

8 a $x^2 + y^2 = \frac{9}{4}$
 b $x^2 + y^2 - 8x + 12y + 47 = 0$

9 $\left(-2, \frac{3}{2}\right), r = 2$

10 a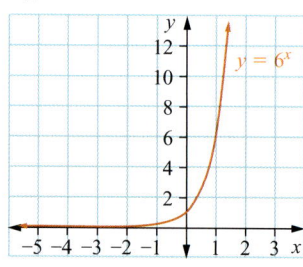
$y = 6^x$

b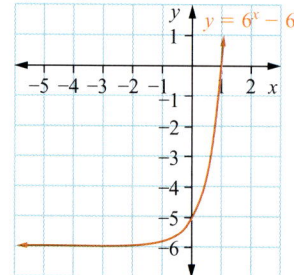
$y = 6^x - 6$

c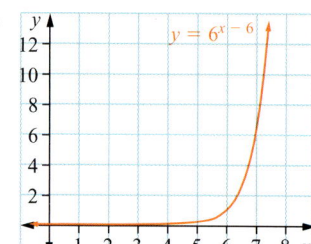
$y = 6^{x-6}$

11 a D **b** A **c** C **d** B

12 a Circle **b** Parabola
  c Straight line **d** Hyperbola
  e Exponential

13 a $x = 0, x = -2, x = 5, y = 0$

b

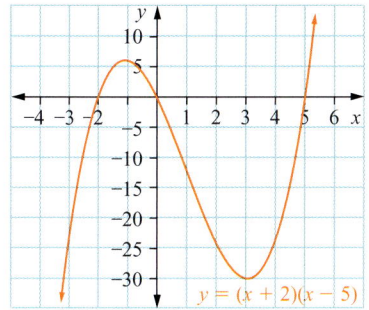

14 $(-4, -11)$ and $(\frac{3}{2}, 0)$

Review set 12D

1 D

2 a

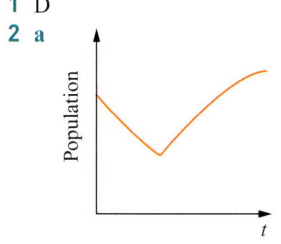

b

3

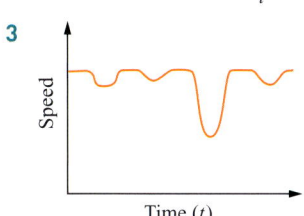

4 a $y = -7$　　　　**b** $x = -1$

c $(-1, -6)$

d

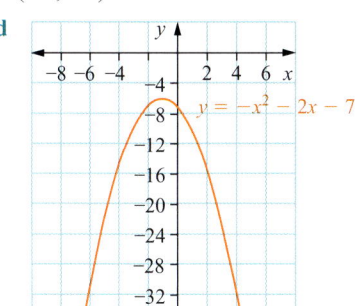

5 a D　　　**b** B　　　**c** A　　　**d** C

6 a i

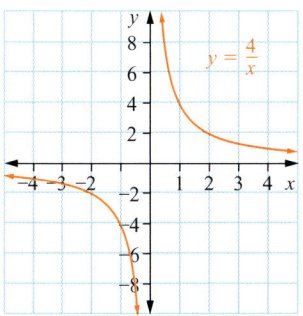

ii

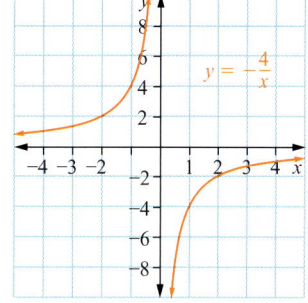

iii

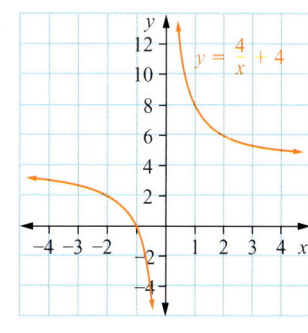

iv

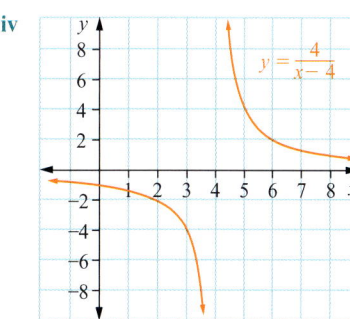

b i $x = 0, y = 0$　　　**ii** $x = 0, y = 0$

iii $x = 0, y = 4$　　　**iv** $x = 4, y = 0$

7 a $(0, 0), r = \sqrt{6}$　　　**b** $(8, -7), r = \sqrt{13}$

c $(-5, 0), r = 7$

8 It lies on the circle.

9 B, C

10 a C　　　**b** B　　　**c** D　　　**d** A

11 a

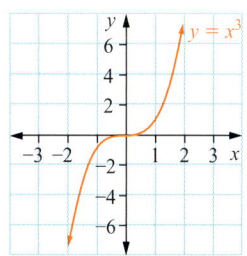

b

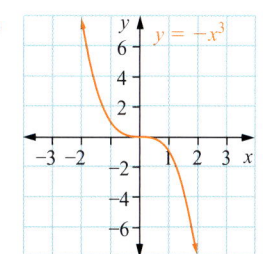

c
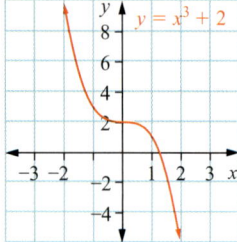
$y = x^3 + 2$

d
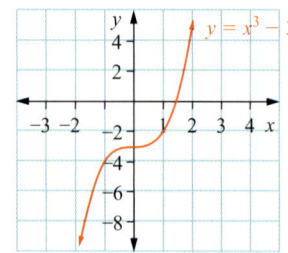
$y = x^3 - 3$

e
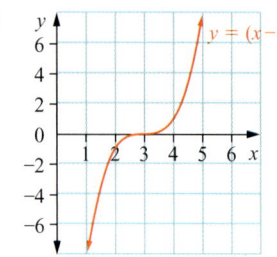
$y = (x-3)^3$

12 a Exponential **b** Straight line
c Parabola **d** Hyperbola
e Circle

13 a $x = 2, x = -2, x = -4, y = -16$

b
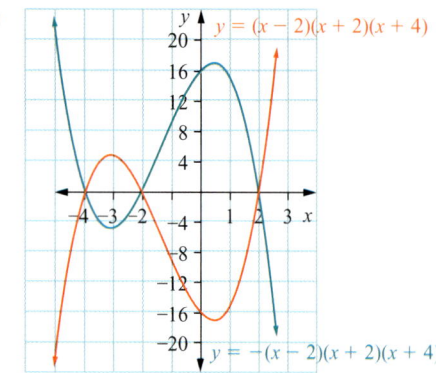
$y = (x-2)(x+2)(x+4)$
$y = -(x-2)(x+2)(x+4)$

14 $(-0.29, -0.29)$ and $(-1.71, -1.71)$

CHAPTER 13 PROPERTIES OF GEOMETRICAL FIGURES

Diagnostic test

1 B **2** D **3** C **4** B **5** D
6 B **7** A **8** D

Exercise 13A

1 a In $\triangle ABC$ and $\triangle EDC$:
$\angle ABC = \angle EDC$ (given)
$\angle ACB = \angle ECD$ (Vertically opposite $\angle$s are equal.)
$\therefore \triangle ABC \,|||\, \triangle EDC$ (Two angles of one $\triangle$ are equal to two angles of the other $\triangle$.)

b In $\triangle PQT$ and $\triangle RQS$:
$\angle PQT = \angle RQS$ (Vertically opposite $\angle$s are equal.)
$\angle PTQ = \angle RSQ$ (Alternate $\angle$s and $PT \parallel SR$.)
$\therefore \triangle PQT \,|||\, \triangle RQS$ (Two angles of one $\triangle$ are equal to two angles of the other $\triangle$.)

c In $\triangle XYZ$ and $\triangle WUV$:
$\frac{YZ}{UV} = \frac{XZ}{WV} = \frac{XY}{WU} \left(= \frac{5}{2}\right)$
$\therefore \triangle XYZ \,|||\, \triangle WUV$ (Three pairs of sides are in proportion.)

d In $\triangle NKL$ and $\triangle MNL$:
$\frac{NL}{ML} = \frac{NK}{MN} = \frac{KL}{NL} \left(= \frac{2}{3}\right)$
$\therefore \triangle NKL \,|||\, \triangle MNL$ (Three pairs of sides are in proportion.)

e In $\triangle ABE$ and $\triangle CBD$:
$\frac{AE}{CD} = \frac{AB}{CB} \left(= \frac{3}{1}\right)$
$\angle ABE = \angle CBD$ ($= 90°$ given)
$\therefore \triangle ABE \,|||\, \triangle CBD$ (In the right-angled $\triangle$s the hypotenuses and another pair of sides are in proportion.)

f
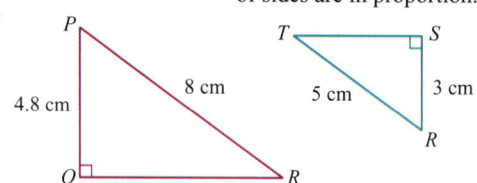

In $\triangle PQR$ and $\triangle RST$:
$\frac{PR}{RT} = \frac{PQ}{RS} \left(= \frac{8}{5}\right)$
$\angle PQR = \angle TSR$ ($= 90°$, given)
$\therefore \triangle PQR \,|||\, \triangle RST$ (In the right-angled $\triangle$s, the hypotenuse and another pair of sides are in proportion.)

g In $\triangle ABC$ and $\triangle EDF$:
$\frac{AC}{EF} = \frac{BC}{DF} \left(= \frac{1}{2}\right)$
$\angle ACB = \angle EFD$ ($= 70°$, given)
$\therefore \triangle ABC \,|||\, \triangle RST$ (Two pairs of sides are in proportion and the angles included by the sides are equal.)

h In $\triangle KLO$ and $\triangle MLN$:
$\frac{KL}{ML} = \frac{OL}{NL} \left(= \frac{3}{2}\right)$
$\angle KLO = \angle MLN$ (Vertically opposite angles are equal.)
$\therefore \triangle KLO \,|||\, \triangle MLN$ (Two pairs of sides are in proportion and the angles included by the sides are equal.)

2 a In $\triangle STU$ and $\triangle WTV$:
$\angle STU = \angle WTV$ (Vertically opposite angles are equal.)
$\angle UST = \angle VWT$ (Alternate angles and $SU \parallel VW$.)
$\therefore \triangle STU \,|||\, \triangle WTV$ (Two angles of one $\triangle$ equal two angles of the other $\triangle$.)
$\frac{x}{5} = \frac{4}{3}$ (Matching sides of similar $\triangle$s are in proportion.)
$x = 6\frac{2}{3}$ cm

b In $\triangle ABC$ and $\triangle DEC$:

$\angle ACB = \angle DCE$	(Vertically opposite angles are equal.)
$\angle ABC = \angle DEC$	($= 90°$, given)
$\therefore \triangle ABC \parallel\!\parallel\!\parallel \triangle DEC$	(Two angles of one $\triangle$ equal two angles of the other $\triangle$.)

$\dfrac{x}{3} = \dfrac{5}{7}$ (Matching sides of similar $\triangle$s are in proportion.)

$x = 2\frac{1}{7}$ cm

c In $\triangle UXV$ and $\triangle YXZ$:

$\angle UVX = \angle YZX$	(given)
$\angle UXV = \angle YXZ$	(Vertically opposite angles are equal.)
$\therefore \triangle UXV \parallel\!\parallel\!\parallel \triangle YXZ$	(Two angles of one $\triangle$ equal two angles of the other $\triangle$.)

$\dfrac{x}{4} = \dfrac{8}{7}$ (Matching sides of similar $\triangle$s are in proportion.)

$x = 4\frac{4}{7}$ cm

d In $\triangle PQR$ and $\triangle STR$:

$\angle PQR = \angle STR$	(given)
$\angle PRQ = \angle SRT$	(Vertically opposite angles are equal.)
$\therefore \triangle PQR \parallel\!\parallel\!\parallel \triangle STR$	(Two angles of one $\triangle$ equal two angles of the other $\triangle$.)

$\dfrac{x}{6} = \dfrac{7}{4}$ (Matching sides of similar $\triangle$s are in proportion.)

$x = 10.5$ cm

3 a In $\triangle ADE$ and $\triangle ABC$:

$\angle ADE = \angle ABC$	(Corresponding angles and $DE \parallel BC$.)
$\angle DAE = \angle BAC$	(common angle)
$\therefore \triangle ADE \parallel\!\parallel\!\parallel \triangle ABC$	(Two angles of one $\triangle$ equal two angles of the other $\triangle$.)

$\dfrac{x}{x+5} = \dfrac{2}{8}$ (Matching sides of similar $\triangle$s are in proportion.)

$8x = 2(x+5)$

$8x = 2x + 10$

$6x = 10$

$x = \dfrac{10}{6}$

$ = 1\frac{2}{3}$ cm

b In $\triangle ADE$ and $\triangle ABC$:

$\angle ADE = \angle ABC$	($= 90°$, given)
$\angle DAE = \angle BAC$	(common angle)
$\therefore \triangle ADE \parallel\!\parallel\!\parallel \triangle ABC$	(Two angles of one $\triangle$ equal two angles of the other $\triangle$.)

$\dfrac{4}{4+x} = \dfrac{5}{6}$ (Matching sides of similar $\triangle$s are in proportion.)

$24 = 5(4 + x)$

$24 = 20 + 5x$

$4 = 5x$

$x = \dfrac{4}{5}$ or 0.8 cm

4 a In $\triangle ABC$ and $\triangle EBD$:

$\angle ACB = \angle EDB$	($= 90°$, given)
$\angle ABC = \angle EBD$	(common angle)
$\therefore \triangle ABC \parallel\!\parallel\!\parallel \triangle EBD$	(Two angles of one $\triangle$ equal two angles of the other $\triangle$.)

$\dfrac{x}{x+4} = \dfrac{5}{8}$ (Matching sides of similar $\triangle$s are in proportion.)

$8x = 5(x + 4)$

$8x = 5x + 20$

$3x = 20$

$x = 6\frac{2}{3}$ cm

b In $\triangle KLM$ and $\triangle PLQ$:

$\angle MKL = \angle QPL$	($= 70°$, given)
$\angle KLM = \angle PLQ$	(common angle)
$\therefore \triangle KLM \parallel\!\parallel\!\parallel \triangle PLQ$	(Two angles of one $\triangle$ equal two angles of the other $\triangle$.)

$\dfrac{x}{6} = \dfrac{4}{7}$ (Matching sides of similar $\triangle$s are in proportion.)

$7x = 24$

$x = 3\frac{3}{7}$ cm

c In $\triangle XVU$ and $\triangle XZY$:

$\angle XVU = \angle XZY$	($= 50°$, given)
$\angle VXU = \angle ZXY$	(common angle)
$\therefore \triangle XVU \parallel\!\parallel\!\parallel \triangle XZY$	(Two angles of one $\triangle$ equal two angles of the other $\triangle$.)

$\dfrac{x}{6} = \dfrac{3}{7}$ (Matching sides of similar $\triangle$s are in proportion.)

$7x = 18$

$x = 2\frac{4}{7}$ cm

d In $\triangle ABC$ and $\triangle EBD$:

$\angle ABC = \angle EBD$	(common angle)
$\dfrac{CB}{DB} = \dfrac{AB}{EB}\left(= \dfrac{5}{2}\right)$	
$\therefore \triangle ABC \parallel\!\parallel\!\parallel \triangle EBD$	(Two pairs of sides are in proportion and the angles included by the sides are equal.)

$\dfrac{x}{2} = \dfrac{5}{2}$ (Matching sides of similar $\triangle$s are in proportion.)

$2x = 10$

$x = 5$ cm

e

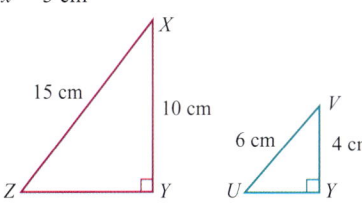

In $\triangle VYU$ and $\triangle XYZ$:

$\angle VYU = \angle XYZ$	($= 90°$, given)
$\dfrac{VU}{XZ} = \dfrac{VY}{XY}\left(= \dfrac{2}{5}\right)$	
$\therefore \triangle VYU \parallel\!\parallel\!\parallel \triangle XYZ$	(In the right-angled $\triangle$s the hypotenuses and another pair of sides are in proportion.)

In $\triangle VYU$, $6^2 = 4^2 + UY^2$

$\therefore UY = \sqrt{20} = 2\sqrt{5}$

$\therefore ZY = x + 2\sqrt{5}$

$\dfrac{UY}{ZY} = \dfrac{2}{5}$ (Matching sides of similar $\triangle$s are in proportion.)

$\dfrac{2\sqrt{5}}{x + 2\sqrt{5}} = \dfrac{2}{5}$

$10\sqrt{5} = 2(x + 2\sqrt{5})$

$10\sqrt{5} = 2x + 4\sqrt{5}$

$6\sqrt{5} = 2x$

$x = 3\sqrt{5}$

f In $\triangle PQR$ and $\triangle STR$:

$\angle PRQ = \angle SRT$ ($= 40°$, given)

$\dfrac{PQ}{SR} = \dfrac{RQ}{RT} \left(= \dfrac{3}{1}\right)$

$\therefore \triangle PRQ \,|||\, \triangle SRT$ (Two pairs of sides are in proportion and the angles included by the sides are equal.)

$\dfrac{x}{6} = \dfrac{1}{3}$ (Matching sides of similar $\triangle$s are in proportion.)

$x = 2$ cm

5 a In $\triangle ADE$ and $\triangle ACB$:

$\dfrac{AD}{AC} = \dfrac{AE}{AB} = \dfrac{1}{2}$ (D and E are midpoints of AC and AB respectively.)

$\angle DAE = \angle CAB$ (common angle)

$\therefore \triangle ADE \,|||\, \triangle ACB$ (Two pairs of sides are in proportion and the angles included by the sides are equal.)

b i $\angle ADE = \angle ACB$ (Matching angles of similar $\triangle$s are equal.)

    $\therefore DE \,\|\, CB$ (A pair of corresponding angles are equal.)

ii $\dfrac{DE}{CB} = \dfrac{AD}{AC} = \dfrac{1}{2}$ (Matching sides of similar $\triangle$s are in proportion.)

    $\therefore DE = \frac{1}{2}CB$

6 a In $\triangle ADE$ and $\triangle ACB$:

$\angle ADE = \angle ACB$ (Corresponding angles and $DE \,\|\, CB$.)

$\angle AED = \angle ABC$ (Corresponding angles and $DE \,\|\, CB$.)

$\therefore \triangle ADE \,|||\, \triangle ACB$ (Two angles of one $\triangle$ equal two angles of the other $\triangle$.)

b $\dfrac{AE}{AB} = \dfrac{AD}{AC}$ (Matching sides of similar $\triangle$s are in proportion.)

but $\dfrac{AD}{AC} = \dfrac{1}{2}$ (D is the midpoint of AC.)

$\therefore \dfrac{AE}{AB} = \dfrac{1}{2}$ or $AE = \frac{1}{2}AB$

E is the midpoint of AB.

7 a $\angle SPR = (90 - \alpha)°$ (Angle sum of a $\triangle$ is 180°.)

$\angle RPQ = 90° - (90 - \alpha)°$ ($\angle SPQ = 90°$)

$\angle RPQ = \alpha$

$\angle PQR = (90 - \alpha)$ (Angle sum of a $\triangle$ is 180°.)

In $\triangle SRP$ and $\triangle PRQ$:

$\angle SPR = \angle PQR$ ($= 90° - \alpha$)

$\angle SRP = \angle PRQ$ ($= 90°$)

$\therefore \triangle SRP \,|||\, \triangle PRQ$ (Two angles of one $\triangle$ equal two angles of the other $\triangle$.)

In $\triangle SRP$ and $\triangle SPQ$:

$\angle SRP = \angle SPQ$ ($= 90°$)

$\angle RSP = \angle PSQ$ ($= \alpha$)

$\therefore \triangle SRP \,|||\, \triangle SPQ$ (Two angles of one $\triangle$ equal two angles of the other $\triangle$.)

$\therefore \triangle SRP \,|||\, \triangle PRQ \,|||\, \triangle SPQ$

8 a $\dfrac{x}{4} = \dfrac{4}{5}$ (Matching sides of similar $\triangle$s are in proportion.)

$x = 3.2$ cm

b $\dfrac{x}{8} = \dfrac{3}{x}$ (Matching sides of similar $\triangle$s are in proportion.)

$x = \sqrt{24}$ or $2\sqrt{6}$ cm

c $\dfrac{x}{2\sqrt{6}} = \dfrac{7}{5}$ (Matching sides of similar $\triangle$s are in proportion.)

$\therefore x = 14\sqrt{\dfrac{6}{5}}$ cm

d $\dfrac{x}{5} = \dfrac{4}{x}$ (Matching sides of similar $\triangle$s are in proportion.)

$x^2 = 20$

$x = \sqrt{20}$ or $2\sqrt{5}$ cm

Exercise 13B

1 a 216 cm²   **b** 37.5 cm²
    c 13.5 cm²   **d** 116.16 cm²

2 a $k = 2.5$ **b** 500 cm²

3 a 24 cm²   **b** 42.67 cm²
    c 600 cm²   **d** 9.09 cm²

4 $\dfrac{\text{Area } \triangle DEF}{\text{Area } \triangle ABC} = \dfrac{\frac{1}{2} \times DE \times FE \times \sin E}{\frac{1}{2} \times AB \times CB \times \sin B}$

$\qquad = \dfrac{DE \times FE}{AB \times CB}$ ($\angle E = \angle B$)

$\qquad = \dfrac{(k \times AB) \times (k \times CB)}{AB \times CB}$

$\qquad = \dfrac{k^2}{1}$ ($DE = k \times AB$ and $FE = k \times CB$)

Or area $\triangle DEF = k^2 \times$ area $\triangle ABC$

5 a 117 cm²   **b** 53.76 cm²
    c 51.84 cm²   **d** 36.45 cm²
    e 12.8 cm²   **f** 180.56 cm²

6 a 360 cm²   **b** 9600 m² or 0.96 ha

7 a 432 cm³   **b** 7.5 m³
    c 343 cm³   **d** 666.8 cm³
    e 97.03 cm³   **f** 63.37 cm³

8 a i $k = 2.5$ **ii** 984.38 cm³
    b i $k = \frac{3}{4}$ **ii** 162 cm³

9 Surface area = 1134 cm²
    Volume = 2799.36 cm³

10 a 750 cm²   **b** 1875 cm³

11 a 0.0045 m² or 45 cm²   **b** 0.000 015 m³ or 15 cm³

12 2880   **13** 1 : 50

14 a 3 : 1   **b** 9 : 1

15 125   **16** 64

17 a 1000   **b** 100
    c 10
    d Not able to regulate body temperature.

Exercise 13C

1 a When it has a right angle.
    b When two adjacent sides are equal.
    c When two adjacent sides are equal.
    d When it has a right angle.

2 a True   **b** False   **c** False
    d True   **e** True   **f** True
    g False   **h** False   **i** True

3 a A square is a rhombus because it has two adjacent sides equal in length. A rhombus is not always a square because it does not always have 90° angles.
    b A rhombus is a parallelogram because opposite sides are parallel. A parallelogram is not always a rhombus as it does not always have two adjacent sides equal.

4 a For parallelogram *ABCD*
construct line *BD*.
In △*ABD* and △*CBD*:
BD is common.

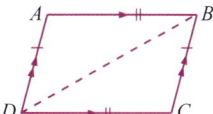

∠*ABD* = ∠*CDB*   (Alternate angles and *AB* ∥ *CD*.)
∠*ADB* = ∠*CBD*   (Alternate angles and *AD* ∥ *CB*.)
△*ABD* ≡ △*CDB*   (AAS)
AB = *CD*, *AD* = *CB*   (Matching sides in congruent
△s are equal.)
∴ Opposite sides of a parallelogram are equal.

b △*ABD* ≡ △*CDB*   (from part **a**)
∠*DAB* = ∠*BCD*   (Matching angles in congruent
△s are equal.)
∠*ABC* = ∠*ADC*   (Matching angles in congruent
△s are equal.)
∴ Opposite angles of a parallelogram are equal.

c Construct line *AC* so that *AC* and *DB* meet at point *E*.
In △*ABE* and △*CDE*:
AB = *CD*   (from part **a**)
∠*ABE* = ∠*CDE*   (Alternate angles and *AB* ∥ *CD*.)
∠*AEB* = ∠*CED*   (Vertically opposite angles
are equal.)
△*ABE* ≡ △*CDE*   (AAS)
AE = *CE*, *BE* = *DE*   (Matching sides in congruent
△s are equal.)
∴ The diagonals of a parallelogram bisect each other.

5 a A rectangle is a parallelogram
with one 90° angle (∠*C*).

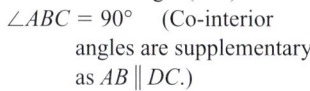

∠*ABC* = 90°   (Co-interior
angles are supplementary
as *AB* ∥ *DC*.)
∠*DAB* = 90°   (Opposite angles of a
parallelogram are equal.)
∠*CDA* = 90°   (Co-interior angles are
supplementary as *AB* ∥ *DC*.)
∴ All angles in a rectangle are 90°.

b In △*ADC* and △*BCD*:

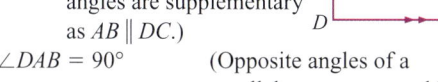

AD = *BC*.   (Opposite sides of
a parallelogram are equal.)
DC is common.
∠*ADC* = ∠*BCD*   (= 90°)
△*ADC* ≡ △*BCD*   (SAS)
AC = *BD*   (Matching sides in congruent
△s are equal.)
∴ The diagonals of a rectangle are equal.

6 a *AD* = *BC*   (Opposite sides of
a parallelogram
are equal.)

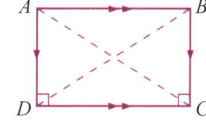

AB = *DC*   (Opposite sides of
a parallelogram
are equal.)
But *AD* = *DC*   (Adjacent sides of a rhombus
are equal.)
∴ *AD* = *BC* = *DC* = *AB*
∴ All the sides of a rhombus are equal.

b Let *AC* and *BD* intersect at point *E*.
In △*ABE* and △*CBE*:
AB = *BC*   (Adjacent
sides of a rhombus are equal.)

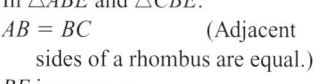

BE is common.
AE = *CE*   (The diagonals in a
parallelogram bisect each other.)
∴ △*ABE* ≡ △*CBE*   (SSS)
∠*AEB* = ∠*CEB*   (Matching angles in congruent
△s are equal.)
∠*AEB* + ∠*CEB* = 180°   (*AC* is a straight angle
and equals 180°.)
∴ ∠*AEB* = ∠*CEB* = 90°
Similarly △*ADE* ≡ △*CDE*   (SSS)
∴ ∠*AED* = ∠*CED* = 90°
∴ The diagonals of a rhombus intersect at right angles.

c From part **b** △*ABE* ≡ △*CBE*   (SSS)
∠*ABE* = ∠*CBE*   (Matching angles in congruent
△s are equal.)
Diagonal *DB* bisects ∠*ABC*.
Similarly △*ADE* ≡ △*CDE*   (SSS)
∠*ADE* = ∠*CDE*   (Matching angles in congruent
△s are equal.)
Diagonal *DB* bisects ∠*ADC*.
Similarly △*ADE* ≡ △*ABE*   (SSS)
∠*DAE* = ∠*BAE*   (Matching angles in congruent
△s are equal.)
Diagonal *AC* bisects ∠*BAD*.
Similarly △*BEC* ≡ △*DEC*   (SSS)
∠*BCE* = ∠*DCE*   (Matching angles in congruent
△s are equal.)
Diagonal *AC* bisects ∠*BCD*.
∴ The diagonals of a rhombus bisect the angles.

7 A rhombus has all of its sides equal. A square is a
rhombus, so it also has all of its sides equal.

8

	Parallelogram	Rhombus	Rectangle	Square
Both pairs of opposite sides parallel	√	√	√	√
Both pairs of opposite sides equal	√	√	√	√
Both pairs of opposite angles equal	√	√	√	√
All angles 90°			√	√
All sides equal		√		√
Diagonals bisect each other	√	√	√	√
Diagonals intersect at right angles		√		√
Diagonals equal			√	√
Diagonals bisect angles of quadrilateral		√		√

9 a $QS = 15$ cm (given)

$2(2x + 3) = 15$ (The diagonals in a parallelogram bisect each other.)

$4x + 6 = 15$

$4x = 9$

$x = 2.25$ cm

$3y = 2y + 5$ (The diagonals of a rhombus bisect each other.)

$y = 5$ cm

b $AD = BC = 8$ cm (Opposite sides of a rectangle are equal.)

$x = \sqrt{15^2 + 8^2}$

$= 17$ cm

$AC = BD$ (The diagonals of a rectangle are equal.)

$2y = 17$

$y = 8.5$ cm

c $x = \sqrt{3^2 + 5^2}$

$= 5.83$ cm (The diagonals of a rhombus intersect at right angles.)

$y = 5.83$ cm (Adjacent sides are equal.)

d The diagonals in a square are equal and bisect each other at right angles.

$x^2 = 4^2 + 4^2$

$x = \sqrt{32} = 4\sqrt{2}$

e $\angle DAB = 110°$ (given)

$\angle DCB = 110°$ (Opposite angles of a parallelogram are equal.)

$\angle PCB = 70°$ (Angles on a straight line equal $180°$.)

$\angle CBP = 70°$ (The base angles of isosceles $\triangle PBC$ are equal.)

$x + 70° + 70° = 180°$ (Angle sum of a $\triangle$ is $180°$.)

$x = 40°$

f $\angle QSR = 40°$ (Alternate angles and $PQ \parallel SR$.)

$\angle SQR = 40°$ (The diagonals of a rhombus bisect the angles they pass through.)

$\angle QRX = \angle QSR + \angle SQR$ (The exterior angle of a $\triangle$ equals the sum of the interior opposite angles.)

$\angle QRX = 40° + 40° = 80°$

$\angle RQX = x$ (The base angles of isosceles $\triangle QRX$ are equal.)

$x + x + 80° = 180°$ (Angle sum of a $\triangle$ is $180°$.)

$x = 50°$

10 a Let $\angle A = x$ and $\angle B = y$ then:

$\angle C = \angle A = x$

$\angle D = \angle B = y$

$x + y + x + y = 360°$ (Angle sum of a quadrilateral is $360°$.)

$2x + 2y = 360°$

$2(x + y) = 360°$

$x + y = 180°$

$\angle A + \angle D = 180°$

Hence $AB \parallel DC$ (A pair of co-interior angles are supplementary.)

Also $\angle A + \angle B = 180°$

Hence $AD \parallel BC$ (A pair of co-interior angles are supplementary.)

$\therefore ABCD$ is a parallelogram.

(Both pairs of opposite sides are parallel.)

b In $\triangle ACD$ and $\triangle CAB$:

$AD = CB$ (given)

$CD = AB$ (given)

AC is common.

$\triangle ACD \equiv \triangle CAB$ (SSS)

$\angle DAC = \angle BCA$ (Matching angles in congruent $\triangle$s are equal.)

$AD \parallel BC$ (A pair of alternate angles are equal.)

$\angle DCA = \angle BAC$ (Matching angles in congruent $\triangle$s are equal.)

$AB \parallel DC$ (A pair of alternate angles are equal.)

$\therefore ABCD$ is a parallelogram.

(Both pairs of opposite sides are parallel.)

c Let $ABCD$ be a quadrilateral with all sides equal.

Draw the diagonal BD.

In $\triangle ABD$ and $\triangle CDB$:

$AB = BC = CD = DA$ (given)

BD is common.

$\triangle ABD \equiv \triangle CDB$ (SSS)

$\angle ABD = \angle CDB$ (Matching angles in congruent $\triangle$s are equal.)

$AB \parallel DC$ (A pair of alternate angles are equal.)

$\angle BDA = \angle DBC$ (Matching angles in congruent $\triangle$s are equal.)

$AD \parallel BC$ (A pair of alternate angles are equal.)

$\therefore ABCD$ is a parallelogram.

(Both pairs of opposite sides are parallel.)

Any two adjacent equal sides are equal. (given)

$\therefore ABCD$ is a rhombus.

11 In $\triangle RQP$ and $\triangle PSR$:

$PQ = RS$ (given)

$\angle QPR = \angle SRP$ (Alternate angles and $PQ \parallel RS$.)

PR is common.

$\triangle RQP \equiv \triangle PSR$ (SAS)

$\angle QRP = \angle SPR$ (Matching angles in congruent $\triangle$s are equal.)

$PS \parallel QR$ (A pair of alternate angles are equal.)

$\therefore PQRS$ is a parallelogram.

(It is a quadrilateral with both pairs of opposite sides parallel.)

12 In $\triangle PXS$ and $\triangle RYQ$:

$PX = RY$ (given)

$\angle SPX = \angle QRY$ (Alternate angles and $PS \parallel QR$.)

$PS = QR$ (Opposite sides are equal.)

$\triangle PXS \equiv \triangle RYQ$ (SAS)

$\therefore SX = QY$ (Matching sides in congruent $\triangle$s are equal.)

13 $PQ = SR$ (Opposite sides are equal.)

As $QX = SY$ then $PX = RY$ since $PQ = SR$

In $\triangle PXS$ and $\triangle RYQ$:

$PX = RY$ (proven above)

$PS = RQ$ (Opposite sides are equal.)

$\angle SPX = \angle QRY$ (Opposite angles are equal.)

$\triangle PXS \equiv \triangle RYQ$ (SAS)

$\therefore SX = QY$ (Matching sides in congruent $\triangle$s are equal.)

14 $\angle YAB = 180° - \angle BAC$ ($\angle YAC$ is a straight angle and equals 180°.)

$\angle XCD = 180° - \angle DCA$ ($\angle XCA$ is a straight angle and equals 180°.)

But $\angle BAC = \angle DCA$ (Alternate angles and $AB \parallel DC$.)

$\angle YAB = \angle XCD$

In $\triangle YAB$ and $\triangle XCD$:

$\angle YAB = \angle XCD$	(proven above)
$AB = DC$	(Opposite sides in a parallelogram are equal.)
$YA = XC$	(given)
$\triangle YAB \equiv \triangle XCD$	(SAS)
$\angle AYB = \angle CXD$	(Matching angles in congruent $\triangle$s are equal.)
$YB \parallel DX$	(A pair of alternate angles are equal.)

Similarly $\triangle YAD \equiv \triangle XCB$ and $YD \parallel BX$.

$\therefore YBXD$ is a parallelogram.

(Both pairs of opposite sides are parallel.)

15 Draw the diagonals AC and BD.

In $\triangle ABE$ and $\triangle CDE$:

$AE = CE$	(The diagonals bisect each other.)
$BE = DE$	(The diagonals bisect each other.)
$\angle AEB = \angle CED$	(Vertically opposite angles are equal.)
$\triangle ABE \equiv \triangle CDE$	(SAS)
$\angle ABE = \angle CDE$	(Matching angles in congruent $\triangle$s are equal.)
$AB \parallel DC$	(A pair of alternate angles are equal.)

Similarly $\triangle AED \equiv \triangle CEB$ and $AD \parallel BC$.

$\therefore ABCD$ is a parallelogram.   (Both pairs of opposite sides are parallel.)

Since the diagonals are equal and bisect each other:

$EA = EB = EC = ED$

Let $\angle ABE = x$

$\angle BAE = x$	(The base angles of isosceles $\triangle ABE$ are equal.)
$\angle CDE = x$	(Alternate angles and $AB \parallel DC$.)
$\angle DCE = x$	(The base angles of isosceles $\triangle CDE$ are equal.)

Similarly let $\angle CBE = y$ then

$\angle BCE = y$, $\angle ADE = y$, $\angle DAE = y$

In the quadrilateral $ABCD$: $\angle A + \angle B + \angle C + \angle D$

$= (x + y) + (x + y) + (x + y) + (x + y)$

$4(x + y) = 360°$

$x + y = 90°$

$\angle A (= \angle B = \angle C = \angle D) = 90°$

$\therefore ABCD$ is a rectangle.   (A parallelogram that has at least one right angle.)

Language in mathematics

1 Two triangles are similar if:
- two angles of one triangle are equal to two angles of the other triangle
- three pairs of sides are in proportion
- two pairs of sides are in proportion and the angles included by these sides are equal
- the hypotenuse and one pair of sides of right-angled triangles are in proportion.

2 If a matching pair of sides of two similar figures are in the ratio $k : 1$ then:
- the areas of these two figures are in the ratio $k^2 : 1$
- the volumes of these two figures are in the ratio $k^3 : 1$.

3 a A rhombus has two pairs of opposite sides parallel, making it a parallelogram, but a parallelogram does not necessarily have a pair of adjacent sides equal so it is not a rhombus.

  b A square is a parallelogram with a pair of adjacent sides equal, making it a rhombus, but a rhombus does not necessarily contain a right angle.

4 a Bisect each other

  b Bisect each other, equal

  c Bisect each other at right angles, bisect the angles of the rhombus

  d Bisect each other at right angles, equal, bisect the angles of the square

5

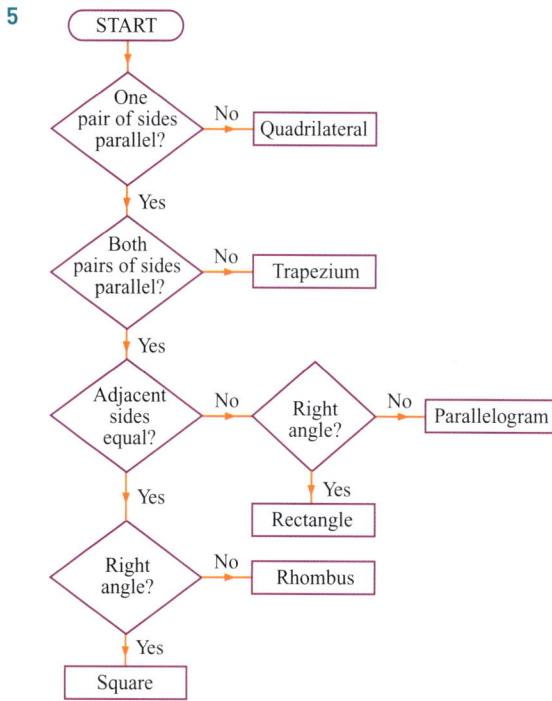

Check your skills

1 B	**2** B	**3** C	**4** C	**5** A
6 D	**7** B	**8** D		

Review set 13A

1 a $\angle RPQ = \angle UST$ (Matching angles of similar $\triangle$s are equal.)

$\angle RPX = \frac{1}{2} \times \angle RPQ$ (given)

$\angle USY = \frac{1}{2} \times \angle UST$ (given)

$\therefore \angle RPX = \angle USY$

In $\triangle PXR$ and $\triangle SYU$:

$\angle RPX = \angle USY$	(proven above)
$\angle PRX = \angle SUY$	($\triangle PQR \parallel\!\parallel\!\parallel \triangle STU$)
$\therefore \triangle PXR \parallel\!\parallel\!\parallel \triangle SYU$	(Two angles of one $\triangle$ equal two angles of the other $\triangle$.)

b $\frac{PX}{SY} = \frac{PR}{SU}$ (Matching sides of similar △s are in proportion.)

$\frac{PR}{SU} = \frac{PQ}{ST}$ (Matching sides of similar △s are in proportion.)

$\therefore \frac{PX}{SY} = \frac{PQ}{ST}$

2 a $\angle BEF = \angle CDF$ (given)

$\angle EFB = \angle DFC$ (Vertically opposite angles are equal.)

$\triangle EFB \;|||\; \triangle DFC$ (Two angles of one △ equal two angles of the other △.)
   (Matching sides of similar △s are in proportion.)

b $\frac{x}{4} = \frac{7}{3}$

$x = 9\frac{1}{3}$

3 a 220.32 cm²

   b i $k = 2.2$ **ii** 766.656 cm³

4 a True   **b** False

5 $x = 3$, $y = 3$

6 a In △ABD and △CBD:

$AB = CB$ (given)

$AD = CD$ (given)

BD is common.

$\therefore \triangle ABD \equiv \triangle CBD$ (SSS)

b In △ABK and △CBK:

$\angle ABK = \angle CBK$ (Matching angles in congruent △s are equal.)

$BA = BC$ (given)

BK is common.

$\triangle ABK \equiv \triangle CBK$ (SAS)

c $AK = CK$ (Matching sides in congruent △s are equal.)

$\angle BKA = \angle BKC$ (Matching angles in congruent △s are equal.)

$\angle BKA = \angle BKC = 90°$ ($\angle AKC = 180°$)

$\therefore BD$ bisects AC at right angles.

Review set 13B

1 a $\angle A$ is common.

$\frac{BA}{DA} = \frac{6}{2} = 3$

$\frac{CA}{EA} = \frac{9}{3} = 3$

$\triangle ADE \;|||\; \triangle ABC$ (Two pairs of sides are in proportion and the included angles are equal.)

b $\angle ADE = \angle ABC$ (Matching angles in similar △s are equal.)

$\therefore DE \parallel BC$ (A pair of corresponding angles are equal.)

2 a $\angle ADE = \angle ABC$ (given)

$\angle A$ is common.

$\therefore \triangle ADE \;|||\; \triangle ABC$ (Two angles of one △ equal two angles of the other △.)

b $\frac{AC}{AE} = \frac{AB}{AD}$ (Matching sides of similar △s are in proportion.)

$\frac{x+4}{6} = \frac{12}{4}$

$x = 14$ cm

Also $\frac{BC}{DE} = \frac{AB}{AD}$ (Matching sides of similar △s are in proportion.)

$\frac{y}{9} = 3$

$y = 27$ cm

3 a 1359.36 cm²   **b** 4354.56 cm³

4 a True   **b** False

   c True

5 $y = 55°$, $x = 35°$, $z = 3.6$ cm

6 a In △ABC and △CDA:

$\angle BAC = \angle DCA$ (Alternate angles and $AB \parallel DC$.)

$\angle BCA = \angle DAC$ (Alternate angles and $AD \parallel BC$.)

AC is common.

$\triangle ABC \equiv \triangle CDA$ (AAS)

$\angle ABC = \angle CDA$ (Matching angles in congruent △s are equal.)

Similarly $\triangle ABD \equiv \triangle CDB$

and $\angle DAB = \angle BCD$

$\therefore$ Opposite angles in a parallelogram are equal.

b Let $\angle A = x$ and $\angle B = y$

then $\angle C = x$ and $\angle D = y$ (Opposite angles are equal, given.)

$x + y + x + y = 360°$ (Angle sum of a quadrilateral is 360°.)

$2(x + y) = 360°$

$x + y = 180°$

$\therefore \angle A + \angle D = 180°$

$\therefore AB \parallel DC$ (A pair of co-interior angles are supplementary.)

Also $\angle A + \angle B = 180°$

$\therefore AD \parallel BC$ (A pair of co-interior angles are supplementary.)

$\therefore ABCD$ is a parallelogram.
     (Both pairs of opposite sides are parallel.)

Review set 13C

1 a In △DBE and △ABC:

$\angle BDE = \angle BAC$ (given)

$\angle B$ is common.

$\triangle DBE \;|||\; \triangle ABC$ (Two angles of one △ equal two angles of the other △.)

b $\frac{EB}{CB} = \frac{ED}{CA}$ (Matching sides of similar △s are in proportion.)

$\frac{x}{9} = \frac{5}{8}$

$x = 5.625$ cm

2 a In △ADE and △ABC:

$\frac{AD}{AB} = \frac{AE}{AC} = \frac{1}{2}$ (D and E are midpoints of AB and AC respectively)

$\angle A$ is common.

$\triangle ADE \;|||\; \triangle ABC$ (Two pairs of sides are in proportion and the included angles are equal.)

$\therefore \angle ADE = \angle ABC$ (Matching angles in similar △s are equal.)

$\therefore DE \parallel BC$ (A pair of corresponding angles are equal.)

b $\frac{DE}{BC} = \frac{AD}{AB}$ (Matching sides of similar △s are in proportion.)

$\frac{DE}{BC} = \frac{1}{2}$

$\therefore DE = \frac{1}{2}BC$

3 a $1 : 3$ **b** 0.024 m²

4 $x = 80°$

5 In $\triangle AEF$ and $\triangle BDC$:

$AE = BD$	(Opposite sides in a rectangle are equal.)
$EF = DC$	(given)
As $\angle AED = 90°$	(Angles in a rectangle are 90°.)
$\angle AEF = 180° - 90° = 90°$	($\angle DEF$ is a straight angle.)
Similarly $\angle BDC = 90°$	
$\triangle AEF \equiv \triangle BDC$	(SAS)
$\therefore AF = BC$	(Matching sides in congruent $\triangle$s are equal.)

6 $AX = \frac{1}{2}AB$ (given)

$BY = \frac{1}{2}BC$ (given)

As $AB = BC$ (A square has equal sides.)

then $AX = BY$

In $\triangle AXD$ and $\triangle BYA$:

$AX = BY$	(proven above)
$\angle XAD = \angle YBA$	($= 90°$, angles of a square)
$AD = BA$	(A square has equal sides.)
$\triangle AXD \equiv \triangle BYA$	(SAS)
$\therefore XD = YA$	(Matching sides in congruent $\triangle$s are equal.)

Review set 13D

1 a $\angle Q$ is common.

$\angle PRQ = \angle TSQ$ ($= 90°$, given)

$\therefore \triangle PQR \,|||\, \triangle TQS$ (Two angles of one $\triangle$ equal two angles of the other $\triangle$.)

b $\dfrac{PQ}{TQ} = \dfrac{RQ}{SQ}$ (Matching sides of similar $\triangle$s are in proportion.)

$\dfrac{x+5}{5} = \dfrac{7}{4}$

$4x + 20 = 35$

$x = 3.75$ cm

2 In $\triangle ADE$ and $\triangle ABC$:

$\angle A$ is common.

$\angle ADE = \angle ABC$ (Corresponding angles and $DE \parallel BC$.)

$\triangle ADE \,|||\, \triangle ABC$ (Two angles of one $\triangle$ equal two angles of the other $\triangle$.)

$\dfrac{AD}{AB} = \dfrac{AE}{AC}$ (Matching sides of similar $\triangle$s are in proportion.)

But $\dfrac{AD}{AB} = \dfrac{1}{2}$ (D is the midpoint of AB.)

$\therefore \dfrac{AE}{AC} = \dfrac{1}{2}$

$AE = \frac{1}{2}AC$

$\therefore E$ is the midpoint of AC.

3 4800 ball bearings

4 $\angle SQK = x$ (QK bisects SQR.)

$\angle SQR = 2x$ and

$\angle PQR = 4x$ (Diagonals of a rhombus bisect the angles.)

$\angle QSR = 2x$ (Base angle of isosceles $\triangle QRS$ are equal.)

$\angle QKR = 3x$ (Exterior angle of $\triangle SQK$ equals the sum of interior opposite angles.)

5 $x = 35°$, $y = 8$ cm

6 a $\angle ABE = \angle FEG$ (Corresponding angles and $AB \parallel FE$.)

$\angle CBE = \angle DEG$ (Corresponding angles and $BC \parallel ED$.)

$\angle ABE + \angle CBE = \angle FEG + \angle DEG$

$\therefore \angle ABC = \angle FED$

b In $\triangle ABC$ and $\triangle FED$:

$AB = FE$	(The opposite sides of parallelogram $ABEF$ are equal.)
$BC = ED$	(The opposite sides of parallelogram $BCDE$ are equal.)
$\angle ABC = \angle FED$	(part **a**)
$\triangle ABC \equiv \triangle FED$	(SAS)

c In quadrilateral $ACDF$:

$AC = FD$	(Matching sides in congruent $\triangle$s are equal, from part **a**.)
$AF = BE$	(Opposite sides in a parallelogram are equal.)
$BE = CD$	(Opposite sides in a parallelogram are equal.)
$\therefore AF = CD$	

Draw the diagonal AD in quadrilateral $ACDF$.

In $\triangle ACD$ and $\triangle DFA$:

$AF = CD$	(proven above)
$AC = FD$	(proven above)
AD is common.	
$\triangle ACD \equiv \triangle DFA$	(SSS)
$\angle CAD = \angle FDA$	(Matching angles in congruent $\triangle$s are equal.)
$AC \parallel FD$	(A pair of alternate angles are equal.)
$\angle CDA = \angle FAD$	(Matching angles in congruent $\triangle$s are equal.)
$AF \parallel CD$	(A pair of alternate angles are equal.)

$\therefore ACDF$ is a parallelogram.

(Both pairs of opposite sides are parallel.)

CUMULATIVE REVIEW: 10–13

1 a i $x = \frac{3}{4}$ **ii** $x = \frac{27}{25} = 1\frac{2}{25}$

   iii $x = -\frac{5}{19}$ **iv** $x = -\frac{35}{9} = -3\frac{8}{9}$

b i $9x^2 - 12x + 4$ **ii** $x^2 - 16$

   iii $9x^2 - 49$

c i $(x + 8)(x - 8)$ **ii** $(r + t)(r - t)$

   iii $(9p + 5q)(9p - 5q)$ **iv** $(x - 7)(x - 1)$

   v $(x + 5)(x - 2)$ **vi** $(3x - 5)(2x + 1)$

d i $x = \dfrac{4}{\sqrt[3]{5}}$ **ii** $x = \pm 1, \pm\sqrt{10}$

e $x = 4 \pm \sqrt{23}$

f $x = -5, y = 54$ or $x = -1\frac{1}{2}, y = 11$

g i $x = \dfrac{p - qy - l}{m}$ **ii** $x = \dfrac{p - b}{e + 1}$

2 a i $\sqrt{149}$ cm   **ii** $26°$

b i

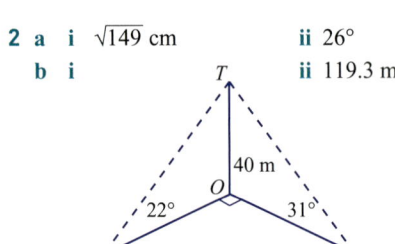

ii 119.3 m

c i

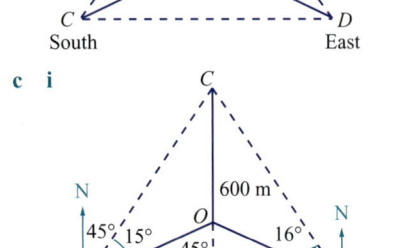

ii $315° - 270° = 45°$, $45° + 45° = 90°$

iii $AO = 2239$ m, $OB = 2092$ m, $AB = 3065$ m

iv $\angle AOB = 43°$, bearing $088°$T

d i $\theta = 127°51'$ **ii** $\theta = 140°48'$

e

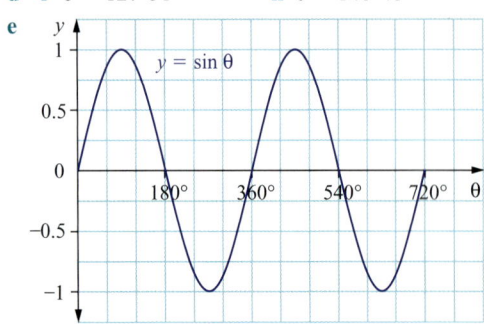

f i $-\dfrac{\sqrt{3}}{2}$ **ii** $-\dfrac{1}{2}$ **iii** $-\dfrac{1}{\sqrt{3}}$

3 a Graph C

b i   **b ii**

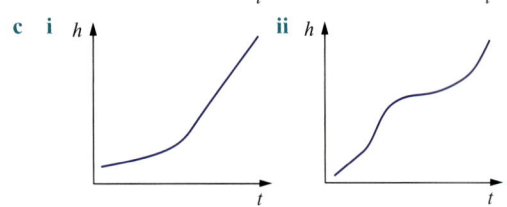

c i   **c ii**

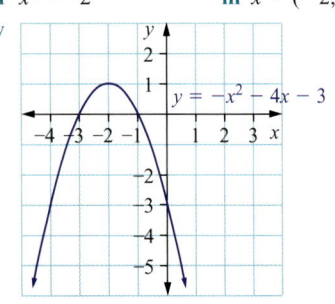

d i x-intercepts: $x = -1$, $x = -3$
  y-intercepts: $y = -3$

ii $x = -2$ **iii** $x = (-2, 1)$

iv

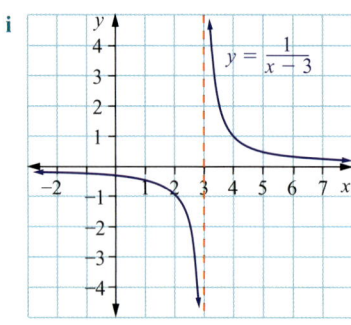

e i

ii

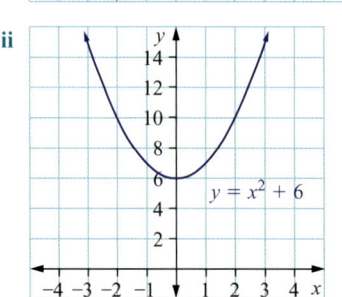

iii $(x + 3)^2 + (y - 1)^2 = 16$

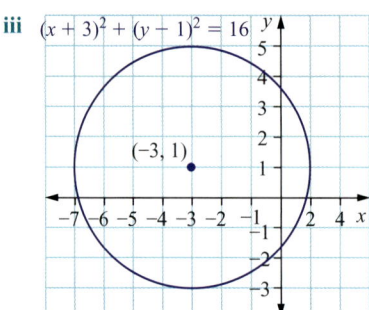

iv $y = (x - 4)^2 + 2$

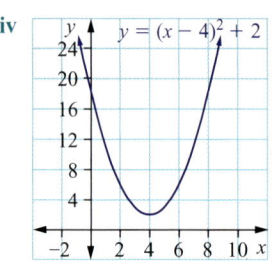

v $y = 5^x$

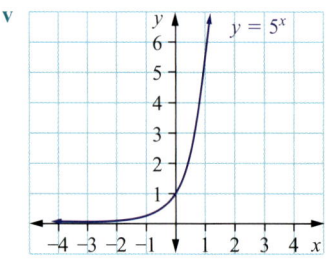

vi $y = \dfrac{5}{x} + 5$

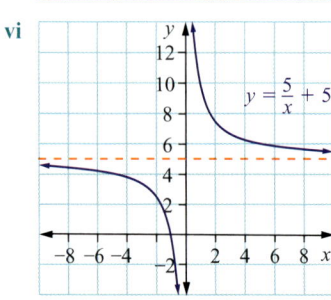

f Centre $(3, -2)$ and radius $= 5$

g **i** x-intercepts at $x = 4, -3, 1$
y-intercept at $y = 12$

ii

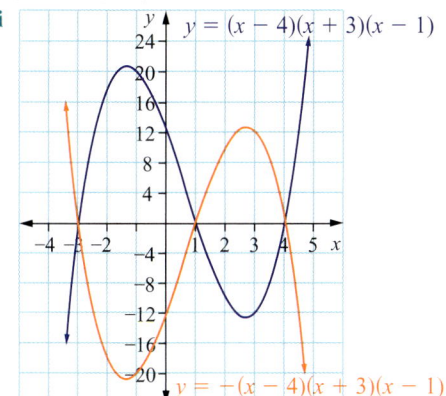

h $(5, 25)$ and $(7, 49)$

4 a i $\angle PRQ = \angle TSQ$ $(= 90°,$ given)
$RP \parallel ST$ (A pair of corresponding angles are equal.)
In $\triangle PQR$ and $\triangle TQS$:
$\angle RPQ = \angle STQ$ (Corresponding angles and $RP \parallel ST$.)
$\angle PQR = \angle TQS$ (common)
$\therefore \triangle PQR \parallel\parallel \triangle TQS$ (Two angles of one $\triangle$ equal two angles of the other $\triangle$.)

ii $x = \frac{24}{5} = 4\frac{4}{5}$ cm

b i In $\triangle ADE$ and $\triangle ABC$:
$\angle DAE = \angle BAC$ (common)
$\angle ADE = \angle ABC$ (Corresponding angles and $DE \parallel BC$.)
$\triangle ADE \parallel\parallel \triangle ABC$ (Two angles of one $\triangle$ equal two angles of the other $\triangle$.)

ii $\dfrac{AD}{AB} = \dfrac{DE}{BC}$ (Matching sides of similar $\triangle$s are in proportion.)

$AD = DB$ so $\dfrac{AD}{AB} = \dfrac{1}{2}$

$\therefore \dfrac{DE}{BC} = \dfrac{1}{2}$ or $DE = \dfrac{1}{2}BC$

c i $1 : 10$ **ii** 2.2 m^2
d $x = 116°, y = 64°$
e $\angle AED = \angle BDE$ $(= 90°, ABDE$ is a rectangle.)
$\angle AEF = \angle BDC = 90°$ $(FEDC$ is a straight line.)
In $\triangle AEF$ and $\triangle BDC$:
$AF = BC$ (given)
$AE = BD$ (Opposite sides of a rectangle are equal.)
$\angle AEF = \angle BDC$ (proven above)
$\triangle AEF \equiv \triangle BDC$ (RHS)
$\therefore EF = DC$ (Matching sides in congruent $\triangle$s are equal.)

CHAPTER 14 DATA ANALYSIS

Diagnostic test

1 B	**2** C	**3** A	**4** A	**5** D
6 D	**7** C	**8** D	**9** B	**10** C
11 C	**12** B	**13** A	**14** B	

Exercise 14A

1 a $\sigma_n = 0.632$ **b** $\sigma_n = 2.828$
   c $\sigma_n = 2.332$ **d** $\sigma_n = 1.732$
2 a $\sigma_n = 2.58$ **b** $\sigma_n = 1.41$
   c $\sigma_n = 5.57$ **d** $\sigma_n = 2.52$
3 a $\bar{x} = 6.6, \sigma_n = 2.2$ **b** $\bar{x} = 39.6, \sigma_n = 2.4$
4 a $\bar{x} = 25, \sigma_n = 3.12$
   b i $\bar{x} = 25, \sigma_n = 2.92$
     ii The mean stays the same but the standard deviation decreases.
   c i $\bar{x} = 24.63, \sigma_n = 3.08$
     ii The mean and standard deviation decrease.
   d i $\bar{x} = 25.38, \sigma_n = 3.08$
     ii The mean increases and the standard deviation decreases.
   e i $\bar{x} = 30.63, \sigma_n = 15.17$
     ii The mean and standard deviation increase.
   f i $\bar{x} = 22, \sigma_n = 8.46$
     ii The mean decreases and the standard deviation increases.
If a score less than the mean is added, the original mean is always decreased but the standard deviation can increase or decrease depending on how far the added score is below the mean. A similar comment applies when a score greater than the mean is added.
5 a $\bar{x} = 9.65, \sigma_n = 1.5$ **b** $\bar{x} = 122.64, \sigma_n = 1.02$
6 a $\bar{x} = 13.38, \sigma_n = 6.19$ **b** $\bar{x} = 24.91, \sigma_n = 12.43$
   c $\bar{x} = 25.98, \sigma_n = 11.29$ **d** $\bar{x} = 31.82, \sigma_n = 6.72$
7 a Range $= 6, \bar{x} = 17, \sigma_n = 1.85$
   b Range $= 6, \bar{x} = 22, \sigma_n = 1.85$
   c Range $= 6, \bar{x} = 9, \sigma_n = 1.85$
   d The range is unchanged, the mean is increased or decreased by that amount, and the standard deviation is unchanged.
8 a Range $= 5, \bar{x} = 10.3, \sigma_n = 1.62$
   b Range $= 15, \bar{x} = 30.9, \sigma_n = 4.85$
   c Range $= 1, \bar{x} = 2.06, \sigma_n = 0.32$
   d All are multiplied or divided by the constant.
9 $\bar{x} = 12.6, \sigma_n = 0.52$
10 a i C   **ii** A   **iii** A
   b i A   **ii** C   **iii** C
11 a i Data set F   **ii** Data set F   **iii** Data set D
   b All have a symmetrical distribution centred at 4.
   c i Range $= 4$ **ii** No
     iii Range $= 2$ **iv** No   **v** No
   d No
12 a i Range $= 4, \bar{x} = 14, \sigma_n = 1.41$
     ii Range $= 4, \bar{x} = 14, \sigma_n = 1.60$
     iii Range $= 4, \bar{x} = 14, \sigma_n = 1.15$
   b The range is the same.
   c The mean is the same.
   d The standard deviation is smallest for set **iii** and largest for set **ii**.
   e i

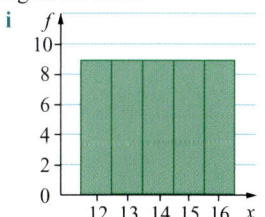

ii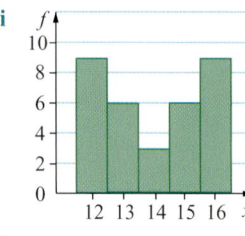

iii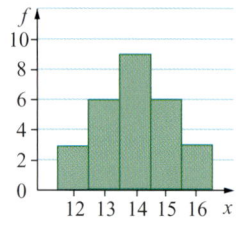

13 a The mean of data set 1 is equal to the mean of data set 2.
  b The range of data set 1 is equal to the range of data set 2.
  c The standard deviation of data set 1 is greater than the standard deviation of data set 2.

14 a $\bar{x} = 13.43$, $\sigma_n = 4.24$ **b** $\bar{x} = 21.91$
  c $\bar{x} = 4.95$ **d** Only the score of 4

15 a $\bar{x} = 29$, $\sigma_n = 6.28$ **b** $\bar{x} = 35.28$
  c $\bar{x} = 22.72$ **d** 70%

Exercise 14B

1 a Sydney: $\bar{x} = 26.99$, $\sigma_n = 0.63$
  Melbourne: $\bar{x} = 27.19$, $\sigma_n = 1.05$
  b Sydney; it has a smaller standard deviation.
2 a Brisbane: $\bar{x} = 30.10$, $\sigma_n = 0.84$
  Adelaide: $\bar{x} = 30.3$, $\sigma_n = 1.71$
  b Brisbane; it has a smaller standard deviation.
  c Brisbane: Range = 2.8, IQR = 1.0
  Adelaide: Range = 6.1, IQR = 1.8
  Brisbane's temperatures are more consistent (less variable) than Adelaide's temperatures.
3 a List 1: $\bar{x} = 7$, list 2: $\bar{x} = 7$. Both have the same mean.
  b List 1: $\sigma_n = 2.38$, list 2: $\sigma_n = 3.74$
  List 1
  c List 1: range = 7, list 2: range = 12
  List 1 is more consistent.
  d List 1: IQR = 4, list 2: IQR = 4
  The middle 50% of both lists have the same spread.
4 a School A:
    i 25.47   **ii** 32   **iii** 9.03
  School B:
    i 35.47   **ii** 33   **iii** 9.93
  b School A as the mean travel time is lower.
  c The range for both schools is about the same, but the spread of times across the range is more consistent for school A as its standard deviation is smaller.
5 a Stuart:
    i $\bar{x} = 5$ **ii** $\sigma_n = 1.76$
    iii Range = 5   **iv** IQR = 3.5
  Greg:
    i $\bar{x} = 5.1$ **ii** $\sigma_n = 3.45$
    iii Range = 12   **iv** IQR = 3

  b Stuart's standard deviation is much lower than Greg's, hence Stuart is more consistent.
  c i Outlier   **ii** Interquartile range
  d i Greg   **ii** No
6 a Lleyton 661, Rodger 679
  b Lleyton: $\bar{x} = 82.625$, $\sigma_n = 10.66$
  Rodger: $\bar{x} = 84.875$, $\sigma_n = 4.78$
  c 6
  d i Lleyton: Range = 37, Roger: Range = 16
    ii Lleyton: IQR = 8, Roger: IQR = 6.5
  e Rodger
  f i Lleyton scored higher marks than Rodger in 6 out of 8 tests.
    ii Rodger's average mark was higher and his scores were more consistent.
7 a English
  b English: Alicia's score was higher above the mean.
  c Mathematics: Alicia's score in English is 0.5 standard deviations above the mean whereas in Mathematics her score is 1 standard deviation above the mean.
  d When standard deviations were equal.
8 a Benjamin's class was more consistent.
  b

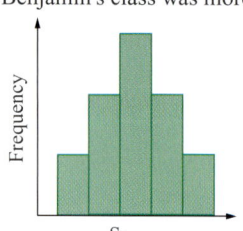

  Scores are grouped together as they are more consistent.

Exercise 14C

1 a, b

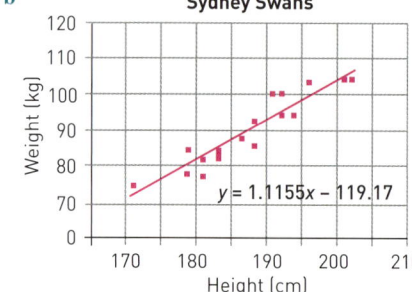

  c 90 kg   **d** 115 kg   **e** 174 cm
2 a, b

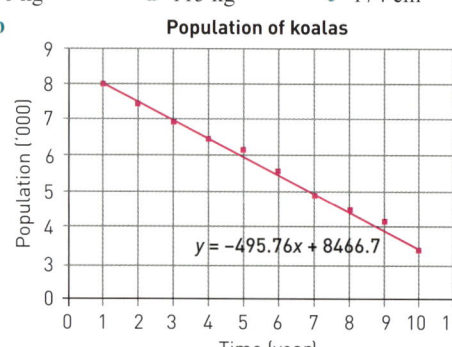

  c 6700   **d** 7.5 years   **e** About 17 years

3 a, b

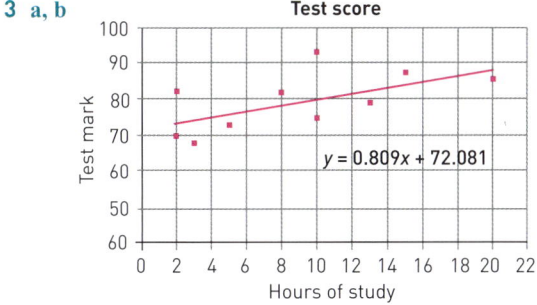

Test score graph

$y = 0.809x + 72.081$

c 86 marks   **d** 22 hours

e The score will be affected by the student's ability as well as time spent studying.

4 a, b

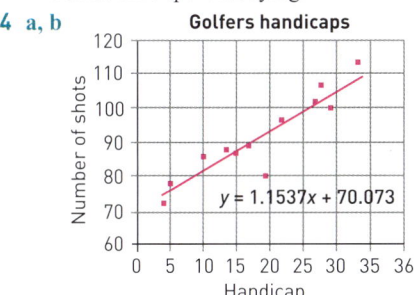

Golfers handicaps graph

$y = 1.1537x + 70.073$

c 93 shots   **d** Handicap of 10

e 93 shots, handicap of 10.3. Using the graph involves some estimation, but the values are close.

5 a $y = 61.93 + 0.2482x$
  b $y = 6.821 + 0.4421x$
  c $y = 521.1 - 4.692x$

6 a, b i

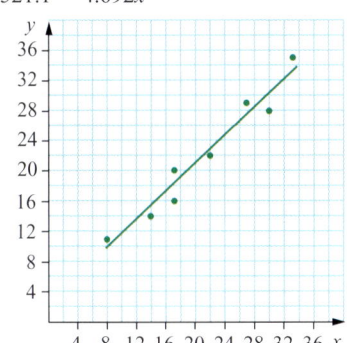

b ii $y = x + 2.2$

c $y = 2.064 + 0.9434x$

d i When $x = 18$, $y = 20.2$ (using equation in part **b**),
    $y = 19.0452$ (using equation in part **c**)
  ii When $x = 45$, $y = 47.2$ (using equation in part **b**),
    $y = 44.517$ (using equation in part **c**)

e i When $x = 18$, $y = 17.8$
  ii When $x = 45$, $y = 42.1$

f The y-values are similar for small values of x. As x increases, the differences in the y-values get larger.

7 a, b i

y-axis graph

b ii $y = 0.38x + 7$

c $y = 7.624 + 0.3626x$

d i When $x = 18$, $y = 13.84$ (using equation in part **b**),
    $y = 14.1508$ (using equation in part **c**)
  ii When $x = 45$, $y = 24.1$ (using equation in part **b**),
    $y = 23.941$ (using equation in part **c**)

e i When $x = 18$, $y = 14$
  ii When $x = 45$, $y = 24.8$

f The values are very similar using all three equations.

Language in mathematics

1 a Range = highest score − lowest score
    Interquartile range = upper quartile − lower quartile
  b Interpolation: predict values within the data range
    Extrapolation: extending a line of best fit to predict value beyond given data values

3 Adding a data value equal to the mean reduces the standard deviation, while adding data values more than one standard deviation from the mean increases the standard deviation.

4 Adding or subtracting the same number to each score does not alter the standard deviation. Multiplying or dividing all scores by the same number multiplies or divides the standard deviation by the same amount.

Check your skills

| **1** C | **2** D | **3** B | **4** A | **5** C |
| **6** D | **7** C | **8** B | | |

Review set 14A

1 a i $\bar{x} = 9.14$ **ii** $\sigma_n = 2.59$
    iii Range = 8   **iv** IQR = 4
  b i $\bar{x} = 14.14$ **ii** $\sigma_n = 2.59$
    iii Range = 8   **iv** IQR = 4
  c i $\bar{x} = 45.71$ **ii** $\sigma_n = 12.94$
    iii Range = 40   **iv** IQR = 20

2 a All means equal   **b** Equal ranges (4)
  c Data set C

3 a Data set C   **b** Data set C
  c Data set B

4 a, b

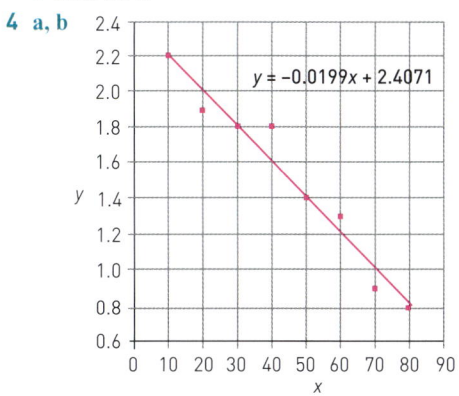

$y = -0.0199x + 2.4071$

c i $y = 1.7$ **ii** $x = 71$

Review set 14B

1 a i $\bar{x} = 11.725$ **ii** $\sigma_n = 2.608$
    iii Range = 16   **iv** IQR = 2
  b i $\bar{x} = 11.475$ **ii** $\sigma_n = 1.612$
    iii Range = 6   **iv** IQR = 2
  c The mean, standard deviation and range have been affected by the outlier.

2 a C   **b** A   **c** B

3 a less than   **b** greater than   **c** greater than

4 a, b

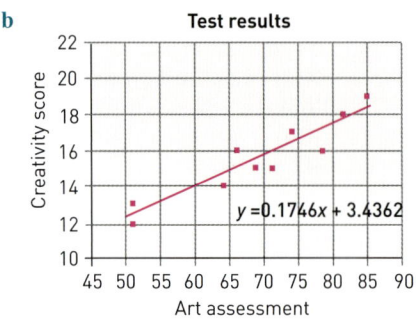

Test results

$y = 0.1746x + 3.4362$

c Creativity score of 14

Review set 14C

1 a i $\bar{x} = 5.25$ **ii** $\sigma_n = 1.79$
   iii Range = 6   **iv** IQR = 2.5
  b i $\bar{x} = 1.25$ **ii** $\sigma_n = 1.79$
   iii Range = 6   **iv** IQR = 2.5
  c i $\bar{x} = 2.625$ **ii** $\sigma_n = 0.89$
   iii Range = 3   **iv** IQR = 1.25

2 a B   **b** C   **c** A

3 a, b

Money spent

$y = 0.062x + 1.9591$

c i $3199   **ii** $44 208

Review set 14D

1 a i $\bar{x} = 20.81$ **ii** $\sigma_n = 13.06$
   iii Range = 55   **iv** IQR = 12.5
  b i $\bar{x} = 18.13$ **ii** $\sigma_n = 8.19$
   iii Range = 29   **iv** IQR = 12

2 a B   **b** A   **c** A

3 a, b

Cost of guests

$y = 0.08x + 4.9667$

c i $10 200   **ii** 88 guests

CHAPTER 15 POLYNOMIALS

Diagnostic test

1 D	**2** C	**3** A	**4** B	**5** C
6 B	**7** A	**8** C	**9** B	**10** B
11 A	**12** C	**13** B	**14** C	**15** B
16 A				

Exercise 15A

1 a

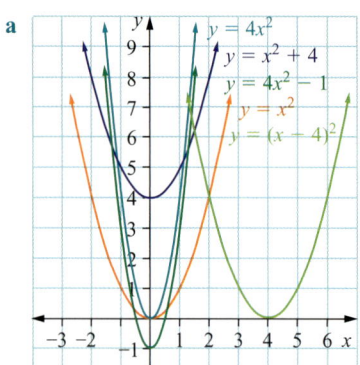

$y = 4x^2$
$y = x^2 + 4$
$y = 4x^2 - 1$
$y = x^2$
$y = (x - 4)^2$

b

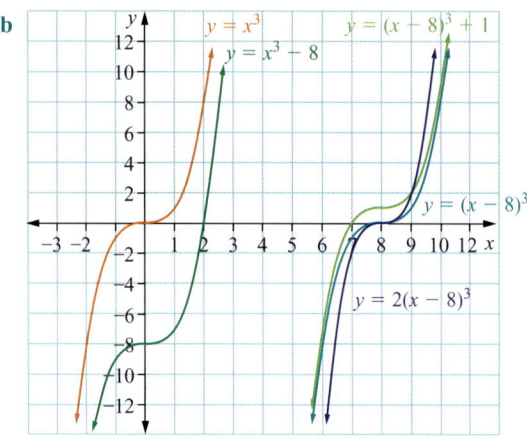

$y = x^3$
$y = (x - 8)^3 + 1$
$y = x^3 - 8$
$y = (x - 8)^3$
$y = 2(x - 8)^3$

c

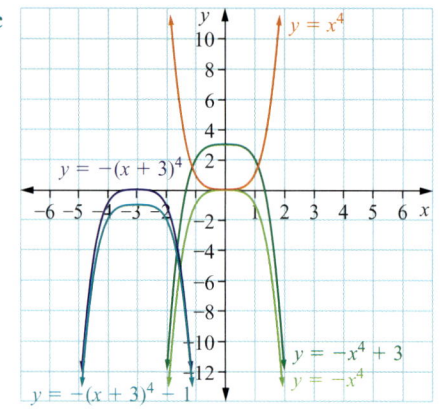

$y = x^4$
$y = -(x + 3)^4$
$y = -x^4 + 3$
$y = -x^4$
$y = -(x + 3)^4 + 1$

d

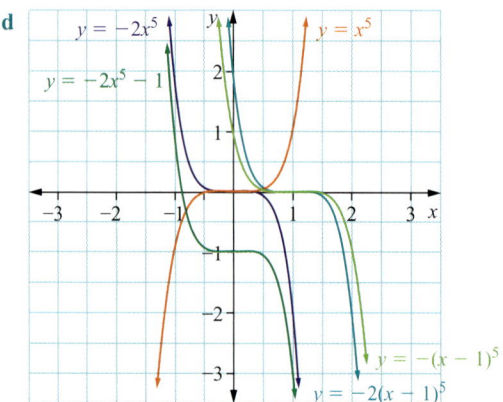

$y = -2x^5$
$y = x^5$
$y = -2x^5 - 1$
$y = -(x - 1)^5$
$y = -2(x - 1)^5$

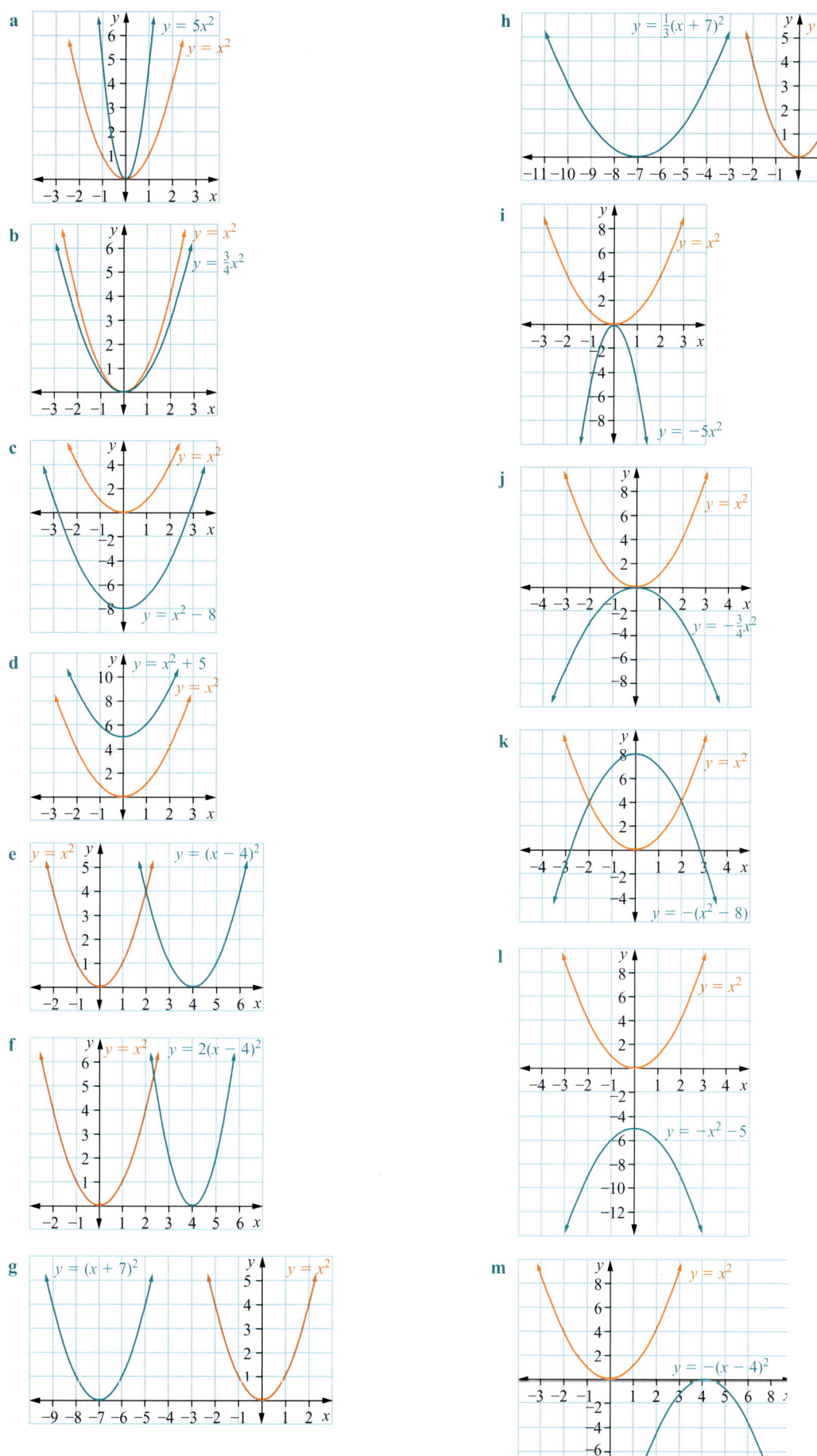

n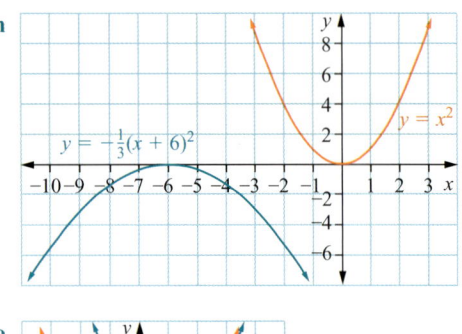

o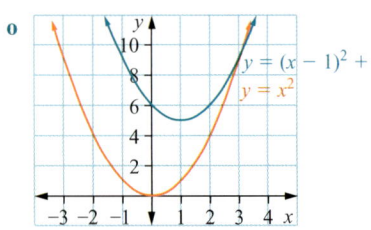

p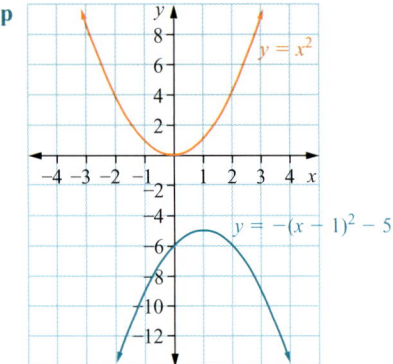

q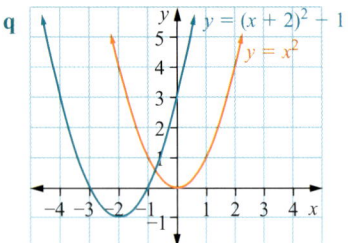

r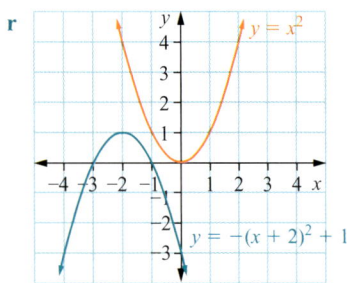

s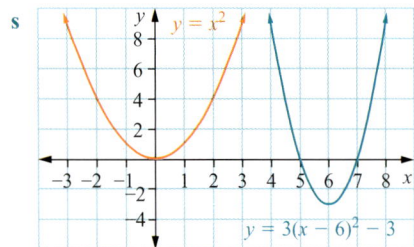

t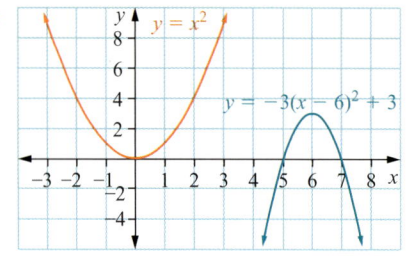

3 a D **b** B **c** C **d** D **e** A

4 a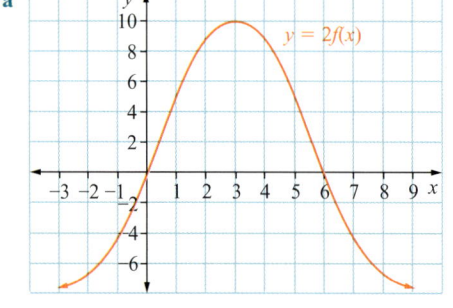

b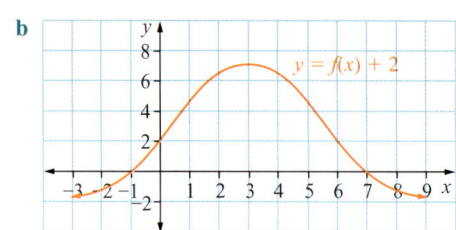

c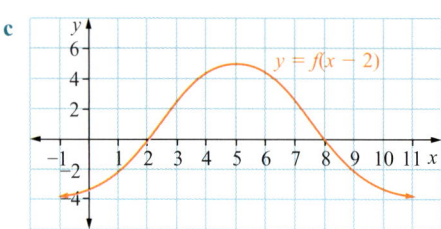

d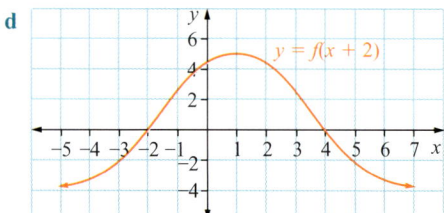

e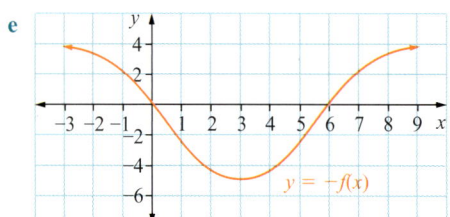

4 a

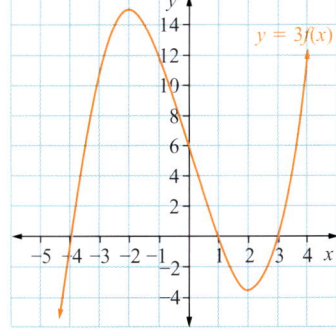

b

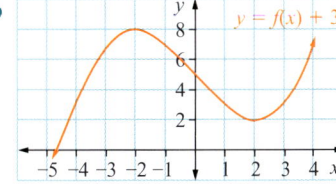

c

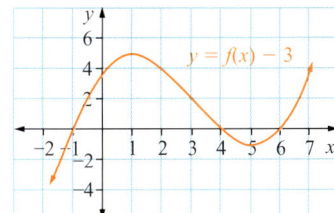

d

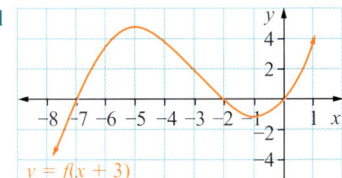

e

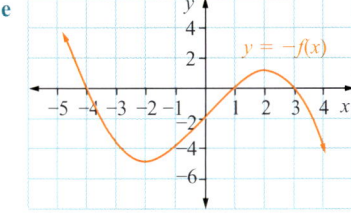

6 The curves are identical except the second curve is moved up one unit.

Exercise 15B

1 a

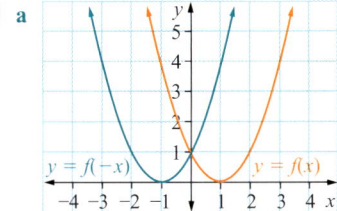

b

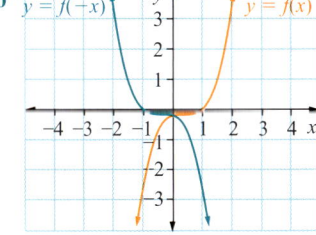

c

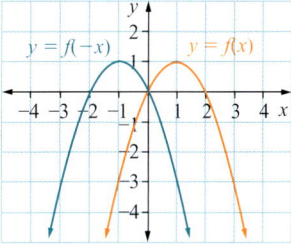

d

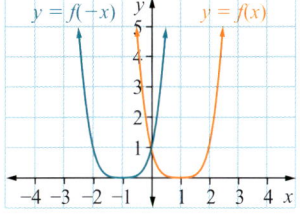

2 a

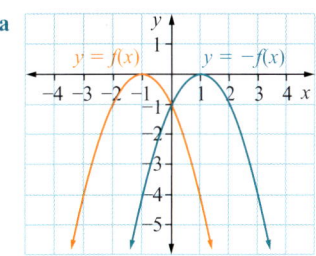

b

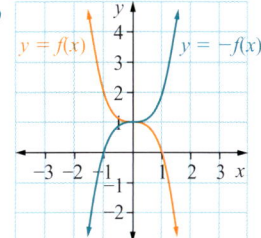

c

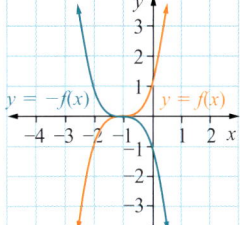

d

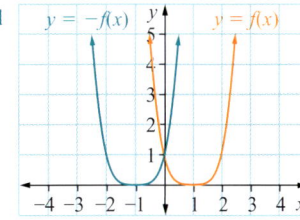

3 a Yes   **b** No   **c** Yes   **d** Yes
   e Yes   **f** No   **g** No   **h** Yes
   i No   **j** Yes

Exercise 15C

1 a Yes   **b** No   **c** Yes
   d No   **e** No   **f** No

8

ANSWERS

2 a i 5 **ii** $3x^5$ **iii** 3 **iv** 11 **v** no
b i 2 **ii** x^2 **iii** 1 **iv** -7 **v** yes
c i 3 **ii** $\frac{1}{3}x^3$ **iii** $\frac{1}{3}$ **iv** -1 **v** no
d i 3 **ii** $-2x^3$ **iii** -2 **iv** -1 **v** no
e i 1 **ii** $3x$ **iii** 3 **iv** 2 **v** no
f i 0 **ii** 5 **iii** 5 **iv** 5 **v** no

3 a $P(0) = 1, P(1) = -3, P(-2) = 27$
b $Q(-1) = -52, Q(1) = -2, Q(0) = -27$
c $R(2) = 192, R(-3) = 2187, R(0) = 0$

4 a 73 **b** 856 **c** 2461
d 32 459 **e** 976 584 **f** 5203
g 10 300 **h** 1011

5 a i $P(1) = 1, P(2) = 3, P(3) = 5, P(4) = 7, \ldots$
ii Odd numbers
b 1, 4, 9 **c** 2, 16, 54

6 a $P(x) = 2x$ **b** $P(x) = x^2 + 1$
c $P(x) = x^3$ **d** $P(x) = 3x - 1$
e $P(x) = 3x + 2$ **f** $P(x) = x^2$

7 a $P(x) = 3x + 5$ **b** $P(x) = 2x + 1$
c $P(x) = x^2 + 4x + 1$ **d** $P(x) = 4x^3 + x^2 + 3x + 1$
e $P(x) = 2x^3 - 5x^2 + 2x + 1$

Exercise 15D

1 a i $4x^2 + 2x - 1, 2x^2 - 12x + 5$
ii $3x^3 + x^2 - 2x + 9, -x^3 - 5x^2 + 8x + 5$
iii $2x^3 + 15x^2 + 3x - 2, 2x^3 + 3x^2 + 13x + 4$
iv $5x^4 + 5x^3 - 10x^2 + 9x - 13,$
$x^4 - x^3 + 4x^2 - x + 9$
v $x^4 + 13x^3 - x^2 - 4x - 6,$
$x^4 + 5x^3 + 15x^2 - 4x + 24$
b The degree of $P(x) \pm Q(x)$ is equal to the degree of $P(x)$ or $Q(x)$, whichever is the greater.
c No, provided the leading coefficients do not have the same magnitude.

2 a $2x^3 - 7x^2 - 12x - 7$ **b** $x^2 + 32x - 15$
c $-23x^2 + 2x - 13$ **d** $-x^2 - 32x + 15$
e $-2x^3 - 17x^2 - 18x + 9$ **f** $2x^3 + 17x^2 + 18x - 9$

3 a $x^3 + 2x^2 - 8x + 35$
b $2x^4 + 3x^3 + 5x^2 + 8x + 3$
c $-35x^3 - 98x^2 + 36x - 3$
d $8x^4 + 26x^3 - 13x^2 - 17x + 3$
e $-6x^4 + 13x^3 - 26x^2 + 58x - 9$

4 The degree of $P(x) \times Q(x)$
= degree of $P(x)$ + degree of $Q(x)$.

5 a $x^5 + 3x^4 - 6x^2 - 8x - 5$
b $6x^5 - x^4 + 14x^2 + 3x - 4$
c $x^4 + 6x^3 + 13x^2 + 12x + 4$
d $2x^4 - 11x^3 + 4x^2 + 29x + 12$
e $12x^4 + 31x^3 - 138x^2 + 41x + 30$
f $6x^4 - 41x^3 + 52x^2 + 17x - 10$

Exercise 15E

1 a
$$\begin{array}{r} 2\ 5\ 7 \\ 15\overline{)\ 3\ 8\ 6\ 4} \\ -\ 3\ 0 \\ \hline 8\ 6 \\ -\ 7\ 5 \\ \hline 1\ 1\ 4 \\ -\ 1\ 0\ 5 \\ \hline 9 \end{array}$$

b
$$\begin{array}{r} 2x^2 - x\ + 2 \\ 3x - 2\overline{)\ 6x^3 - 7x^2 + 8x - 5} \\ -(6x^3 - 4x^2) \\ \hline -3x^2 + 8x \\ -\ (-3x^2 + 2x) \\ \hline 6x - 5 \\ -\ (6x - 4) \\ \hline -1 \end{array}$$

2 a $12\ 564 = 28 \times 448 + 20$
b $92\ 156 = 18 \times 5119 + 14$
c $3x^2 - 11x - 10 = (x + 5)(3x - 26) + 120$
d $-2x^2 + 10x - 3 = (x + 1)(-2x + 12) - 15$
e $x^3 + 2x^2 - 8x - 6 = (x - 2)(x^2 + 4x) - 6$
f $3x^3 - 4x^2 + 3x + 2$
$= (x + 3)(3x^2 - 13x + 42) - 124$
g $x^4 + 4x^3 - 3x^2 + 2x - 1$
$= (x - 1)(x^3 + 5x^2 + 2x + 4) + 3$
h $2x^3 + x^2 - 4x - 7 = (2x - 3)(x^2 + 2x + 1) - 4$
i $3x^3 + 4x^2 - x + 7 = (3x - 2)(x^2 + 2x + 1) + 9$
j $2x^4 - 3x^3 + 6x^2 + 2x + 5$
$= (2x + 1)(x^3 - 2x^2 + 4x - 1) + 6$

4 a $(x - 1)(x + 2)(x + 3)$
b $(2x - 3)(x - 2)(x + 1)$
c $(x - 5)(2x + 1)(x - 3)$
d $(x + 3)(2x + 1)(2x - 1)$
e $(2x + 3)^3$ **f** $(2x - 1)^3$

5 a $x^2 - 9, -36$ **b** $-3x^2 + 2x + 1, 2$
c $5x^2 + 15x + 52, 152$ **d** $x^2 - x + 1, -2$
e $3x^2 - x - \frac{1}{2}, -2\frac{1}{2}$ **f** $x^3 + ax^2 + a^2x + a^3, 0$
g $4x - 15, 36x - 18$ **h** $2x + 7, 12x - 22$

Exercise 15F

1 a 5 **b** -13 **c** 5 **d** -7 **e** 197
f 82 **g** 27 **h** 11 **i** -6 **j** 35
2 a $a = 2$ **b** $k = -6$ **c** $a = 2, b = -5$
3 a $R = 0$ **b** $R = 0$
c $g(x)$ is a factor of $P(x)$

Exercise 15G

2 a $(x + 1)(x - 2)(x + 4)$ **b** $(x - 1)(x + 3)(x - 2)$
c $(x - 1)(x - 2)(x + 6)$ **d** $(x + 2)^3$
e $(x - 1)(x + 1)(x + 6)$ **f** $(x + 2)(x + 4)(x - 3)$
g $(x + 2)(x - 3)(x - 6)$
h $(x - 2)(x + 2)(x^2 + x + 1)$
i $(x - 1)^2(x + 2)^2$ **j** $(x + 2)(x - 7)(2x - 3)$

3 a $k = -19$ **b** $a = 2, b = -5$
c $m = -1, n = -5$ **d** $a = 6, b = -1$
e $k = 5, m = -36$

Exercise 15H

1 a $x = -3, 2, 4$ **b** $x = -5, -3, 1$
c $x = -12, 0, 2$ **d** $x = -4, -3, -2$
e $x = -2, \frac{1}{2}, 3$ **f** $x = 1$
g $x = -1, \dfrac{-5 \pm \sqrt{33}}{2}$ **h** $x = 2, -2 \pm \sqrt{2}$
i $x = -2, 2$ **j** $x = -1, 2, \dfrac{-3 \pm \sqrt{5}}{2}$

2 a $V = x^3 + 2x^2$ **b** $x^3 + 2x^2 - 45 = 0$
c $3 \times 3 \times 5$
3 a $V = x(10 - 2x)(8 - 2x)$
b $x = 1, 2$ ($x = 6$ is not possible.)
c $8 \times 6 \times 1, 6 \times 4 \times 2$

Exercise 15I

1 a

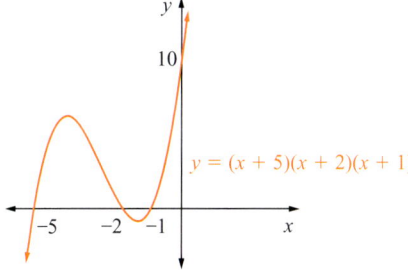

$y = (x + 5)(x + 2)(x + 1)$

b

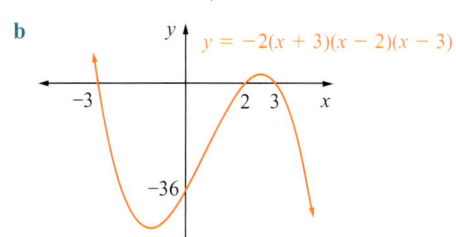

$y = -2(x + 3)(x - 2)(x - 3)$

c

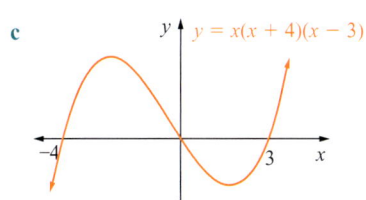

$y = x(x + 4)(x - 3)$

d

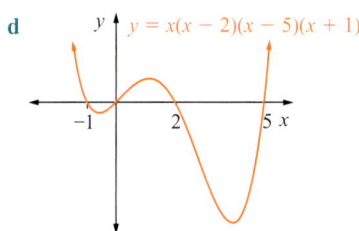

$y = x(x - 2)(x - 5)(x + 1)$

e

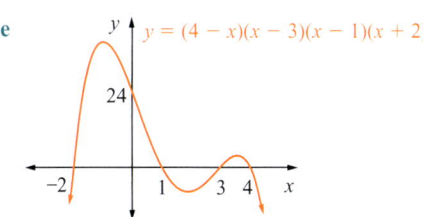

$y = (4 - x)(x - 3)(x - 1)(x + 2)$

2 a

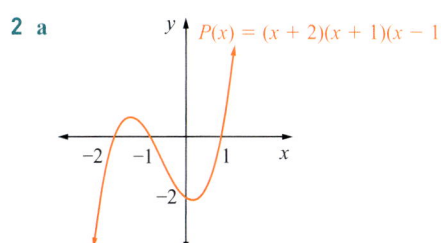

$P(x) = (x + 2)(x + 1)(x - 1)$

b

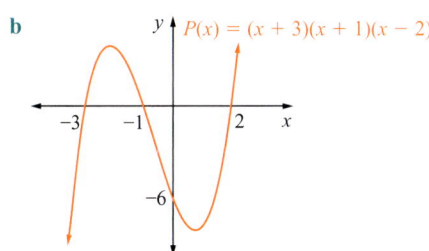

$P(x) = (x + 3)(x + 1)(x - 2)$

c

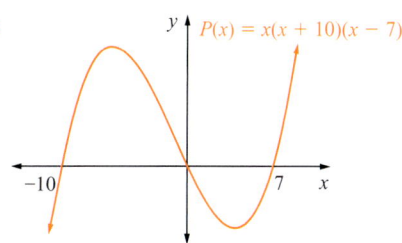

$P(x) = x(x + 10)(x - 7)$

d

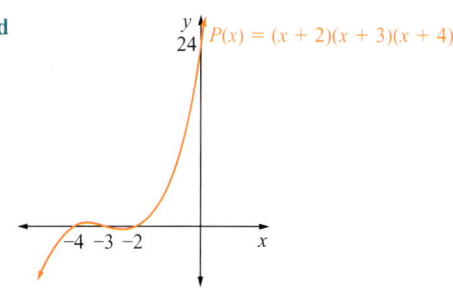

$P(x) = (x + 2)(x + 3)(x + 4)$

e

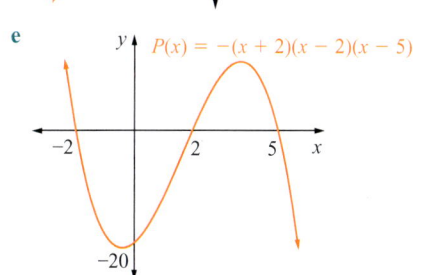

$P(x) = -(x + 2)(x - 2)(x - 5)$

f

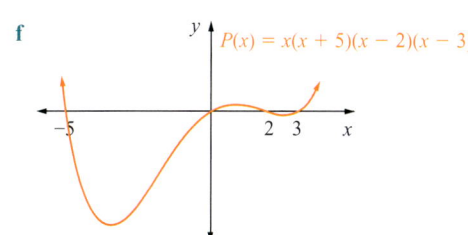

$P(x) = x(x + 5)(x - 2)(x - 3)$

g

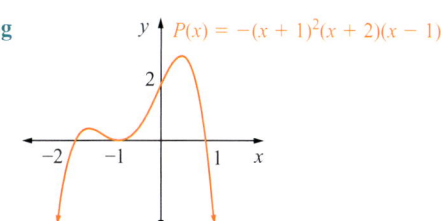

$P(x) = -(x + 1)^2(x + 2)(x - 1)$

h

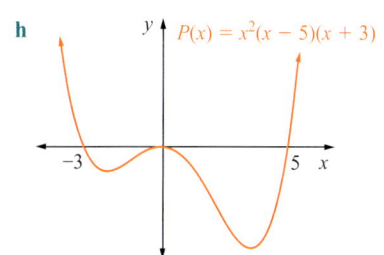

$P(x) = x^2(x - 5)(x + 3)$

Exercise 15J

2 d No
3 a 2
4 a 3   **b** No

5 a

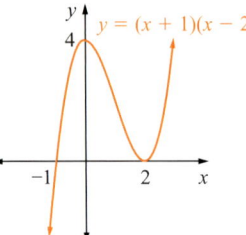

$y = (x + 1)(x - 2)^2$

b

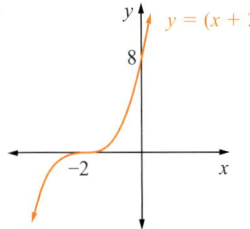

$y = (x + 2)^3$

c

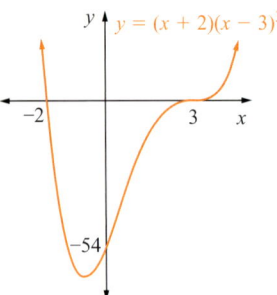

$y = (x + 2)(x - 3)^3$

d

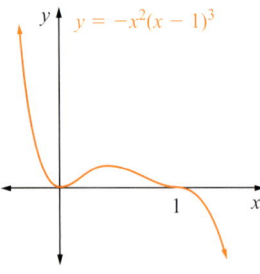

$y = -x^2(x - 1)^3$

e

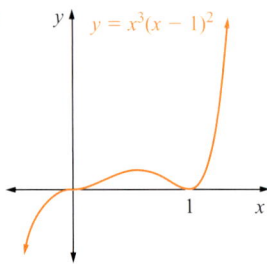

$y = x^3(x - 1)^2$

f

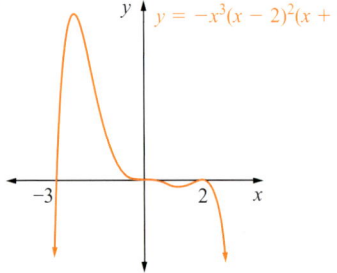

$y = -x^3(x - 2)^2(x + 3)$

6 a

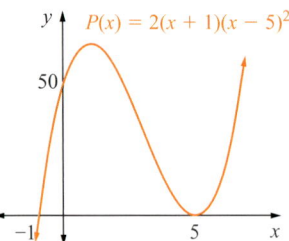

$P(x) = 2(x + 1)(x - 5)^2$

b

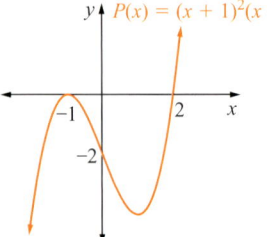

$P(x) = (x + 1)^2(x - 2)$

c

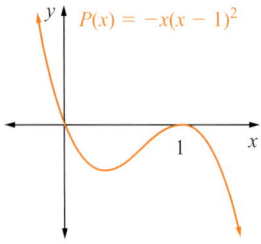

$P(x) = -x(x - 1)^2$

d

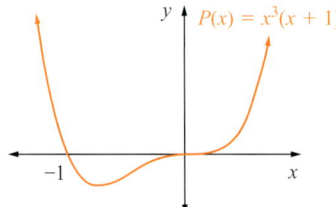

$P(x) = x^3(x + 1)$

e

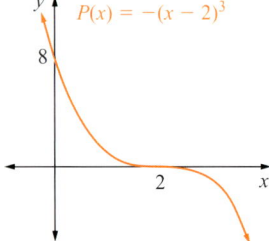

$P(x) = -(x - 2)^3$

f

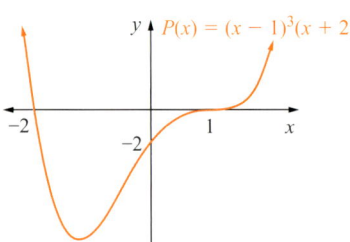

$P(x) = (x - 1)^3(x + 2)$

7 a i

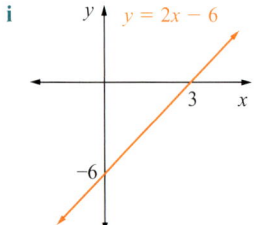

$y = 2x - 6$

ii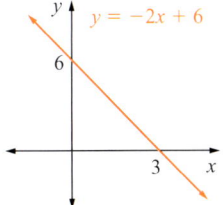

b i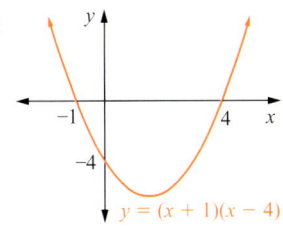

ii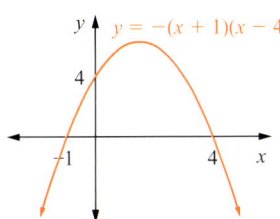

c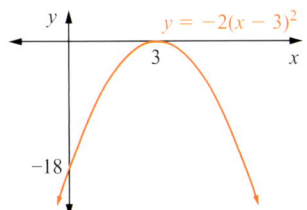

d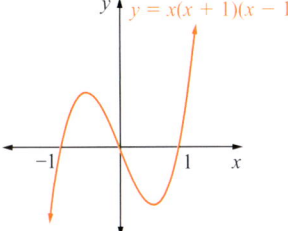

e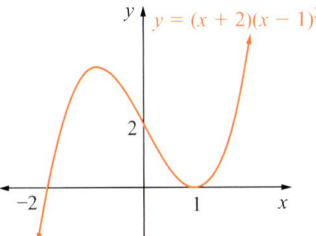

f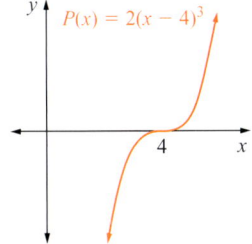

g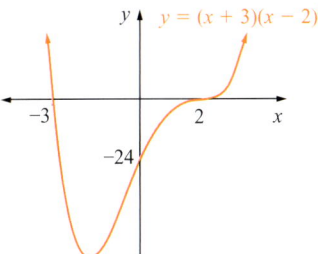

h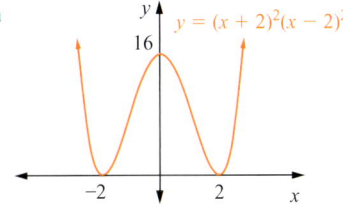

9 a, b i, ii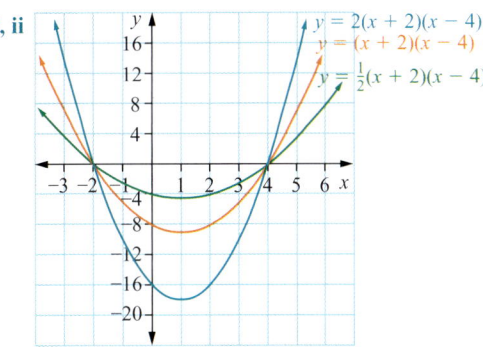

iii, iv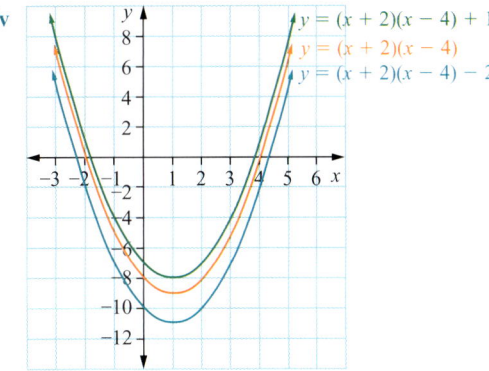

v, vi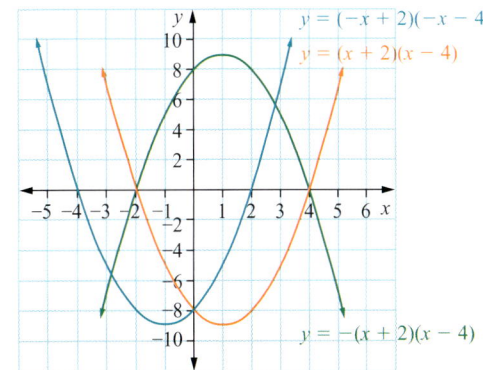

10 a i, ii

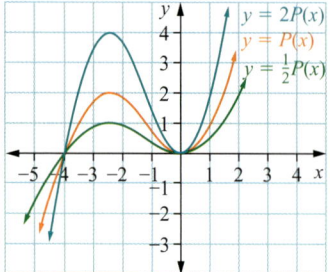

iii, iv

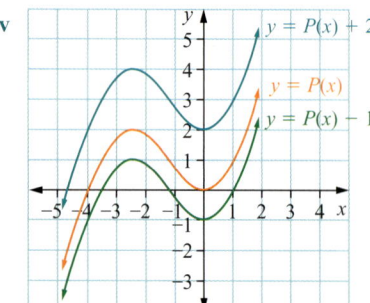

v, vi

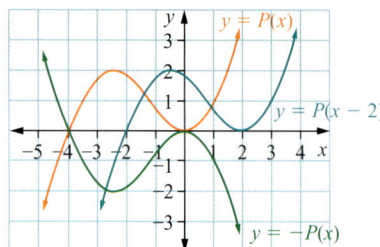

vii

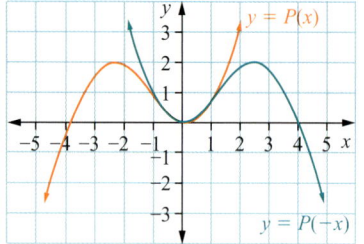

Language in mathematics

1 a The graph is steeper and narrower.
  b The graph is moved up k units if $k > 0$.
    The graph is moved down k units if $k < 0$.
  c The graph is moved to the right by k units if $k > 0$.
    The graph is moved to the left by k units if $k < 0$.
2 If n is even, the graph is symmetrical about the y-axis (reflects onto itself). If n is odd, the graph has point symmetry about the origin (rotates $180°$ about the origin onto itself).
3 a They are reflections in the x-axis.
  b They are reflections in the y-axis.
8 factor, algebraically, sketch

Check your skills

1 A	**2** C	**3** A	**4** C	**5** B
6 D	**7** A	**8** B	**9** D	**10** D
11 A	**12** C	**13** B	**14** B	**15** C

Review set 15A

1 a

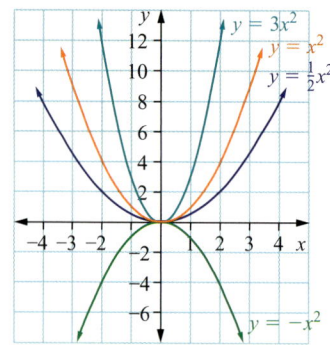

b

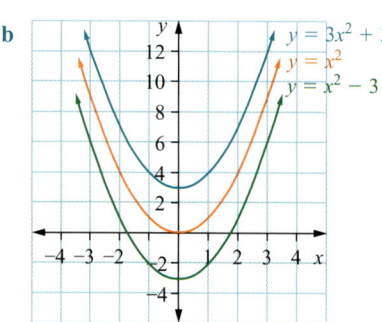

c

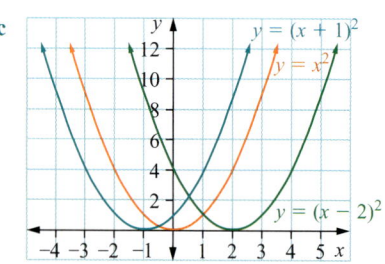

d

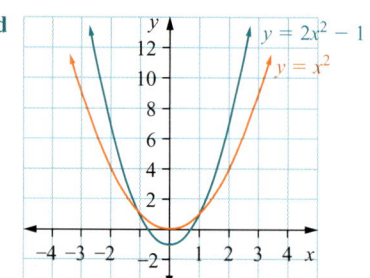

e

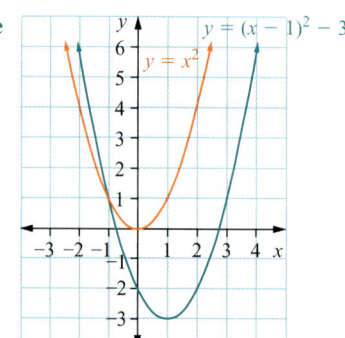

f

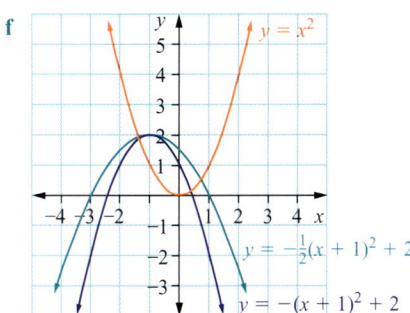

2 a

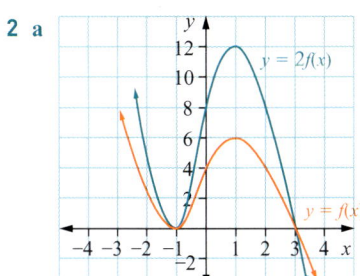

b $y = f(x)$ translated 2 units up.

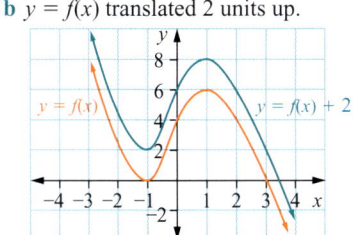

c $y = f(x)$ translated 2 units to the right.

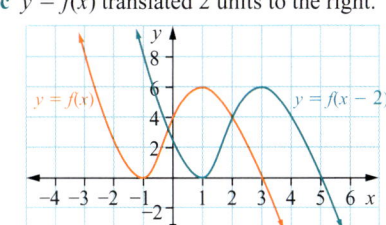

d $y = f(x)$ translated 2 units to the left.

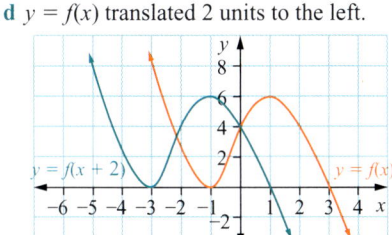

e $y = f(x)$ reflected in the x-axis.

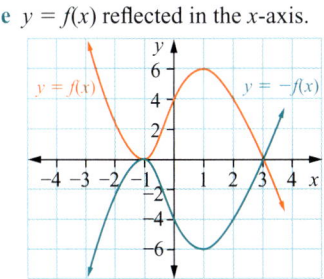

f $y = f(x)$ reflected in the y-axis.

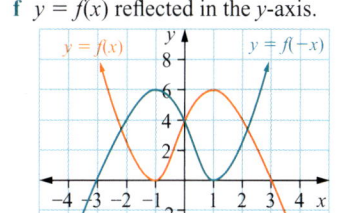

3 a Yes   **b** No   **c** No

4 a Yes   **b** No   **c** Yes   **d** No

5 a i 3   **ii** $2x^3$ **iii** 2   **iv** -2 **v** No

   b i 5   **ii** $-2x^5$ **iii** -2 **iv** 0   **v** No

6 a $3x^3 + 2x^2 - 4x + 5$ **b** $x^3 - 4x^2 + 4x + 9$

7 B

8 a $4x^4 - 2x^3 - 5x^2 + 8x - 5$

   b $4x^3 + 2x^2 - 3x + 5 = (x - 1)(4x^2 + 6x + 3) + 8$

9 a -9 **b** $k = 12$

10 a $P(2) = 0$ **b** $P(x) = (x - 2)(x + 2)(x + 3)$

   c $2, -2, -3$

   d

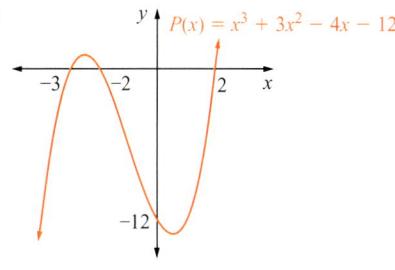

11 a

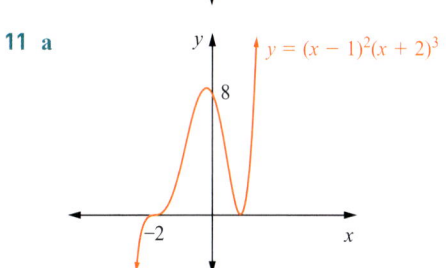

   b

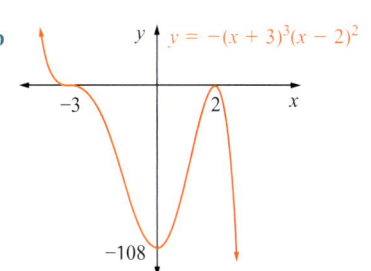

Review set 15B

1 a

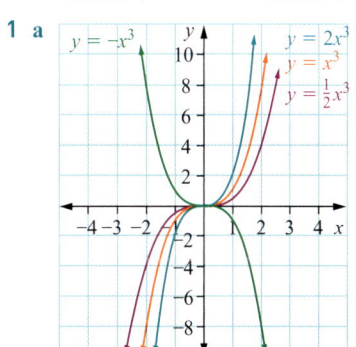

b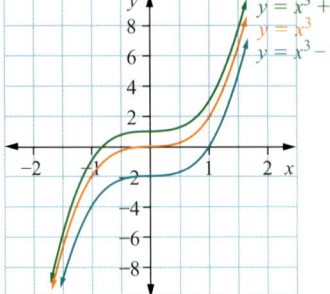

c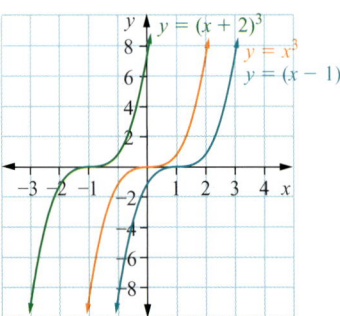

d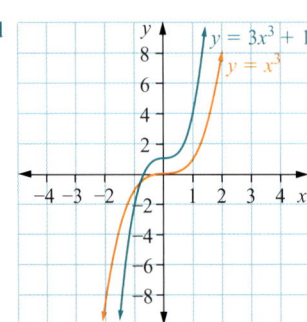

e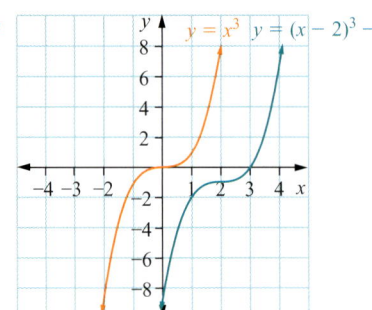

f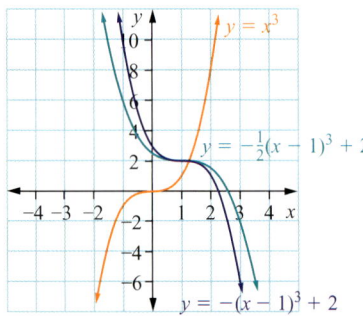

2 a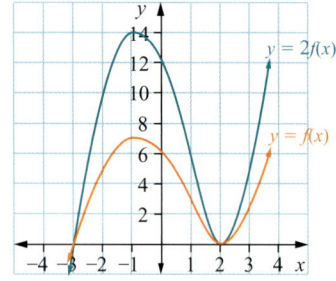

b $y = f(x)$ translated 2 units up.

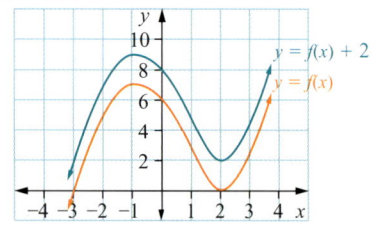

c $y = f(x)$ translated 2 units to the right.

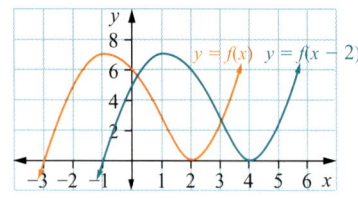

d $y = f(x)$ translated 2 units to the left.

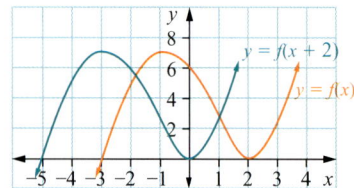

e Reflection of $y = f(x)$ in x-axis.

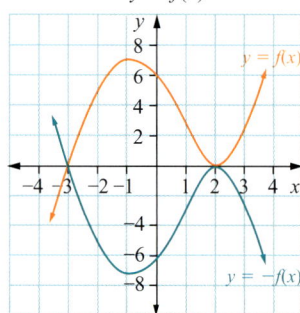

f Reflection of $y = f(x)$ in y-axis.

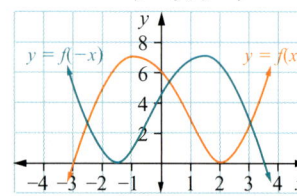

3 a No   **b** Yes   **c** Yes

4 a Yes   **b** No   **c** Yes   **d** No

5 a i 3   **ii** $5x^3$ **iii** 5   **iv** 3   **v** No

   b i 4   **ii** x^4 **iii** 1   **iv** 5   **v** Yes

6 a $2x^3 + 8x^2 + 5x + 7$

   b $6x^3 + 6x^2 - 9x + 15$

7 The degree of $P(x) \pm Q(x)$ equals the degree of $P(x)$ or $Q(x)$, whichever is the greater, unless the leading terms of $P(x)$ and $Q(x)$ are opposites or equal.

8 a $x^4 + 8x^3 + 8x^2 - 3x + 10$

  b $x^3 + 6x^2 - 4x + 5 = (x + 2)(x^2 + 4x - 12) + 29$

9 a 16   **b** $k = \frac{3}{4}$

10 a $P(-1) = 0$ **b** $(x + 1)(x + 4)(x - 3)$

  c $-1, -4, 3$

  d

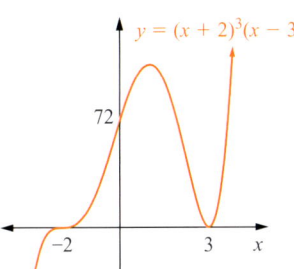

$y = x^3 + 2x^2 - 11x - 12$

11 a

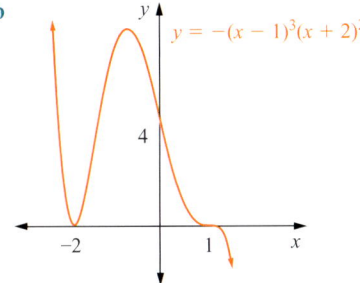

$y = (x + 2)^3(x - 3)^2$

  b

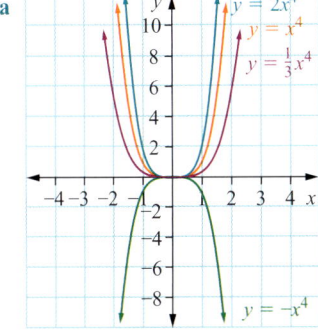

$y = -(x - 1)^3(x + 2)^2$

Review set 15C

1 a

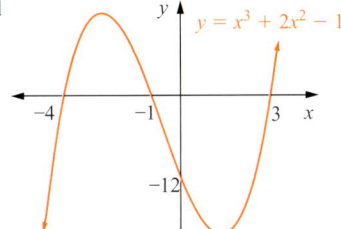

$y = 2x^4$, $y = x^4$, $y = \frac{1}{3}x^4$, $y = -x^4$

  b

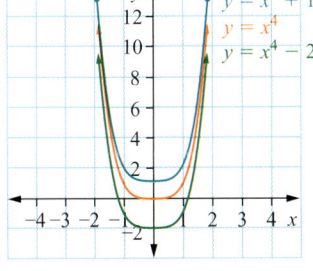

$y = x^4 + 1$, $y = x^4$, $y = x^4 - 2$

c

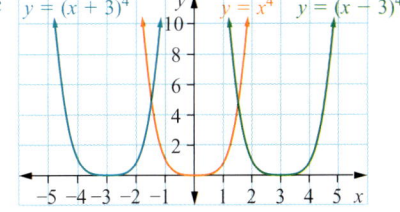

$y = (x + 3)^4$, $y = x^4$, $y = (x - 3)^4$

d

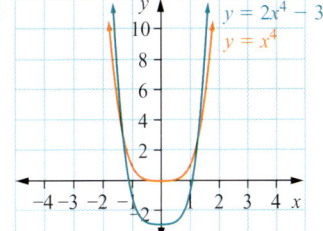

$y = 2x^4 - 3$, $y = x^4$

e

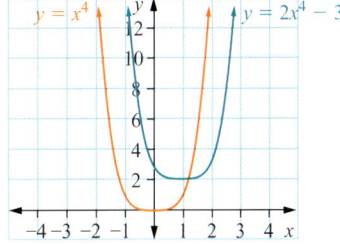

$y = x^4$, $y = 2x^4 - 3$

f

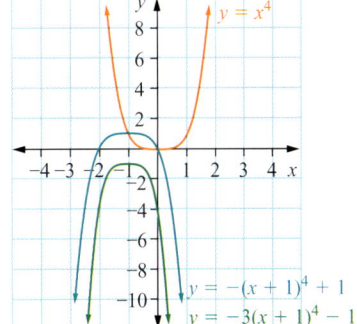

$y = x^4$, $y = -(x + 1)^4 + 1$, $y = -3(x + 1)^4 - 1$

2 a

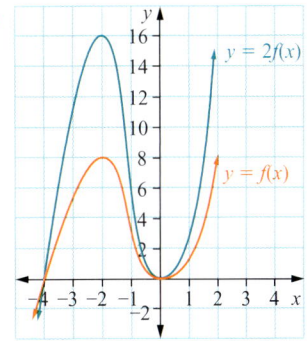

$y = 2f(x)$, $y = f(x)$

  b $y = f(x)$ translated 2 units up.

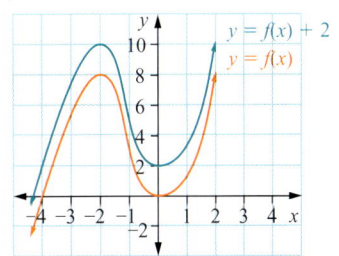

$y = f(x) + 2$, $y = f(x)$

c $y = f(x)$ translated 2 units to the right.

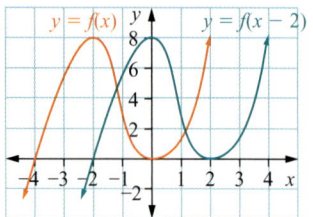

d $y = f(x)$ translated 2 units left.

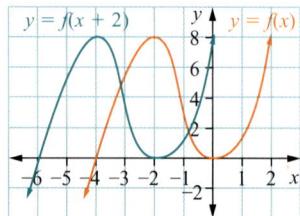

e Reflection of $y = f(x)$ in x-axis.

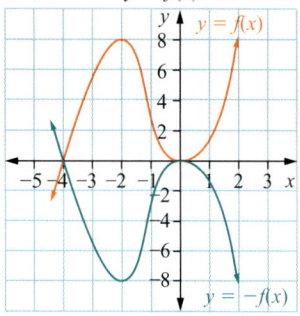

f Reflection of $y = f(x)$ in y-axis.

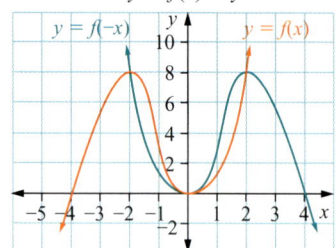

3 a Yes   **b** No   **c** Yes
4 a No   **b** Yes   **c** No   **d** Yes
5 a i 3   ii $-2x^3$ iii -2 iv 1   v No
   b i 4   ii x^4 iii 1   iv 3   v Yes
6 a $7x^3 - 6x^2 - 16x - 5$
   b $x^3 + 8x^2 + 6x + 19$
7 B (If the degree of $P(x)$ or $Q(x)$ is zero.)=
8 a $3x^4 - 10x^3 + 17x^2 - 21x + 6$
   b $3x^3 - 4x^2 + 9x - 3 = (x - 2)(3x^2 + 2x + 13) + 23$
9 a 47   **b** $k = -8$
10 a $P(-3) = 0$ **b** $P(x) = (x + 3)(x + 1)(x - 4)$
   c $-3, -1, 4$
   d

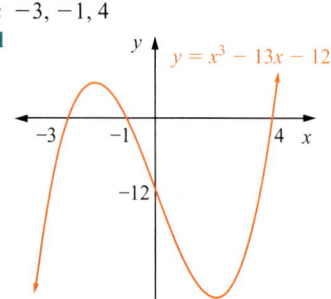

11 a

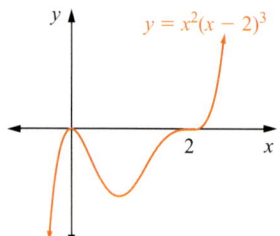

b

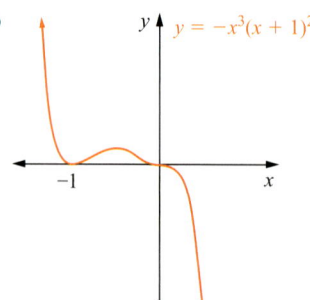

Review set 15D

1 a

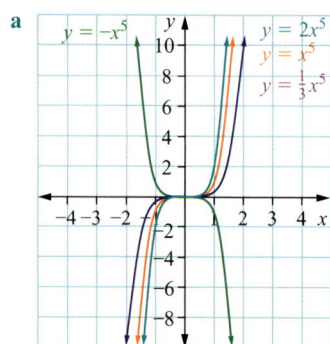

b

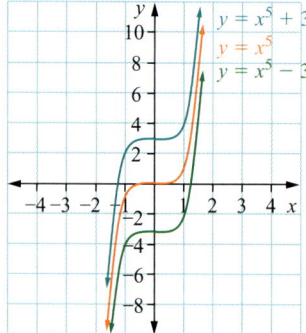

c

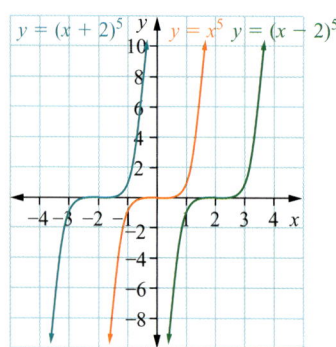

d

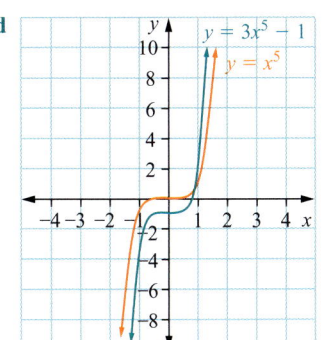

$y = 3x^5 - 1$
$y = x^5$

e

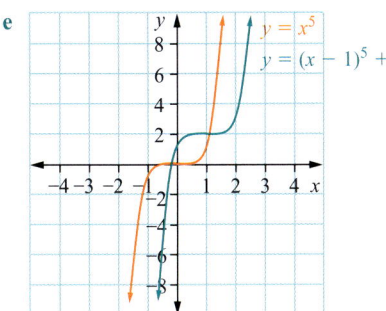

$y = x^5$
$y = (x - 1)^5 + 2$

f

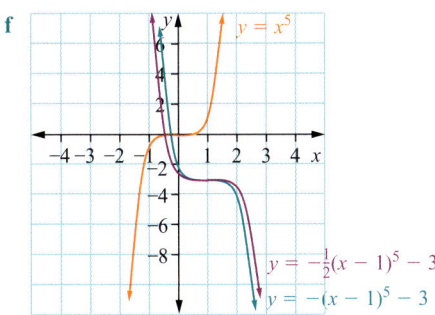

$y = x^5$
$y = -\frac{1}{2}(x - 1)^5 - 3$
$y = -(x - 1)^5 - 3$

2 a

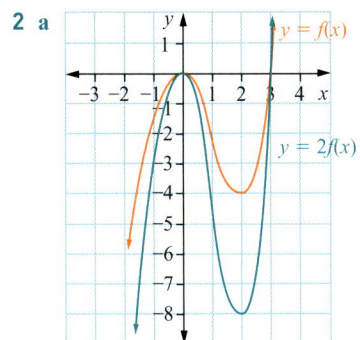

$y = f(x)$
$y = 2f(x)$

b $y = f(x)$ translated 2 units up.

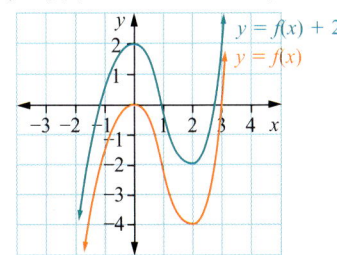

$y = f(x) + 2$
$y = f(x)$

c $y = f(x)$ translated 2 units right.

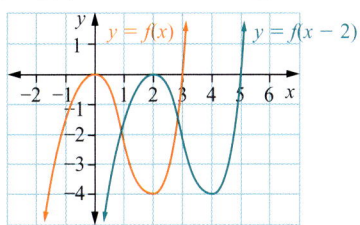

$y = f(x)$
$y = f(x - 2)$

d $y = f(x)$ translated 2 units left.

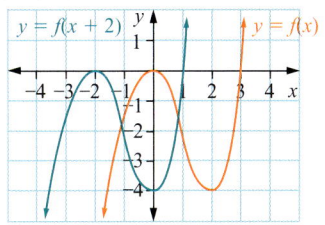

$y = f(x + 2)$
$y = f(x)$

e Reflection of $y = f(x)$ in x-axis.

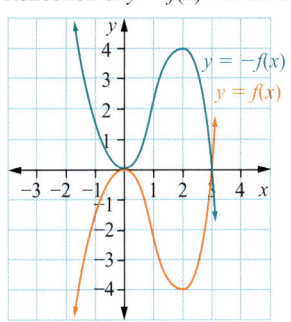

$y = -f(x)$
$y = f(x)$

f Reflection of $y = f(x)$ in y-axis.

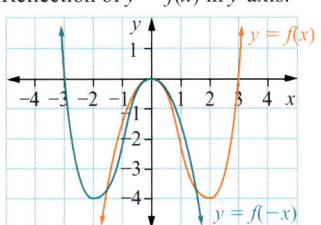

$y = f(x)$
$y = f(-x)$

3 a Yes   **b** Yes   **c** Yes

4 a Yes   **b** No   **c** No   **d** Yes

5 a i 4   **ii** x^4 **iii** 1   **iv** -1 **v** Yes

   b i 3   **ii** $-4x^3$ **iii** -4 **iv** 1   **v** No

6 a $x^4 + x^3 - x^2 - x - 1$

   b $x^4 + 5x^3 - 3x^2 + 7x - 21$

7 A (Unless the degrees of $P(x)$ and $Q(x)$ are both zero.)

8 a $x^4 - 9x^3 - 31x^2 + 12x - 9$

   b $x^3 - 12x^2 + 5x - 3 = (x + 3)(x^2 - 15x + 50) - 153$

9 a -70 **b** $k = -\frac{13}{8}$

10 a $P(-3) = 0$

    b $P(x) = (x + 3)(x - 2)(x - 3)$

    c $-3, 2, 3$

    d

$y = x^3 - 2x^2 - 9x + 18$

11 a

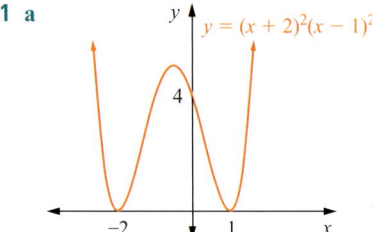
$y = (x + 2)^2(x - 1)^2$

b

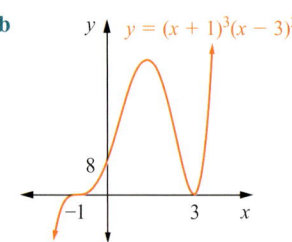
$y = (x + 1)^3(x - 3)^2$

CHAPTER 16 CIRCLE GEOMETRY

Diagnostic test

1 C	**2** D	**3** A	**4** A	**5** B
6 A	**7** D	**8** C	**9** B	**10** A
11 C	**12** A	**13** D	**14** D	**15** D
16 D	**17** B	**18** A	**19** C	**20** A
21 D				

Exercise 16A

1 a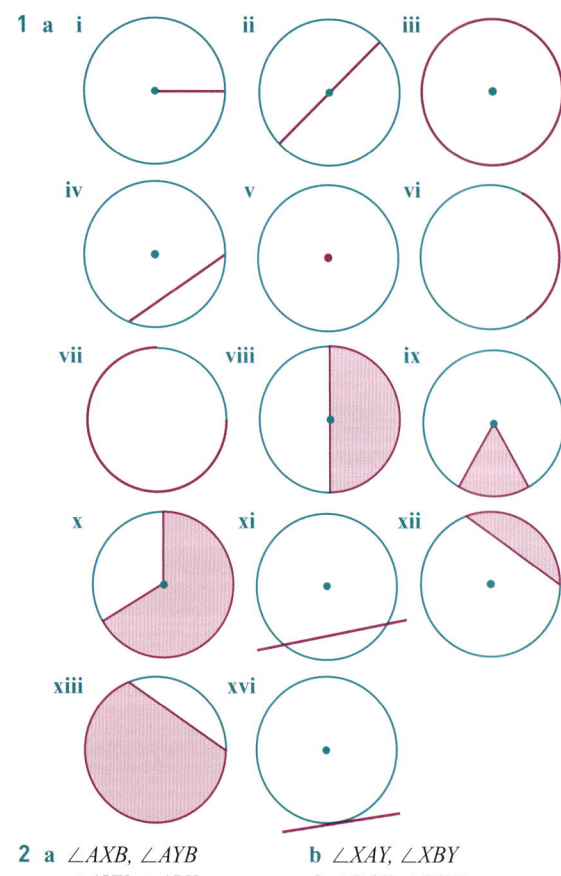
i   ii   iii
iv   v   vi
vii   viii   ix
x   xi   xii
xiii   xvi

2 a $\angle AXB$, $\angle AYB$ **b** $\angle XAY$, $\angle XBY$
c $\angle AXY$, $\angle ABY$ **d** $\angle BAX$, $\angle BYX$
3 a $\angle AOB$ **b** $\angle COD$ **c** $\angle EOF$
4 a ED **b** CB **c** AC
d EA **e** EC

5 a $\angle APB$ **b** $\angle AQB$
6 a $\angle XRY$, $\angle XSY$ **b** $\angle XPY$, $\angle XQY$
7 a $\angle POS$ **b** $\angle PQS$ (or $\angle PRS$)
c $\angle QPR$, $\angle QSR$
8 a $\angle ATB$, $\angle ASB$ **b** $\angle APB$, $\angle AQB$, $\angle ARB$
c $\angle APB$, $\angle ARB$ **d** $\angle ASB$
9 a minor arc BC **b** minor arc EC
c minor arc AE **d** major arc EB
e minor arc EA

Exercise 16B

2 a *Data:* $AB = CD$, O is the centre of the circle.
   Aim: To prove $\angle AOB = \angle COD$.
   Proof: In $\triangle AOB$ and $\triangle COD$:

$$AB = AC \qquad \text{(given)}$$
$$AO = CO \qquad \text{(radii)}$$
$$BO = DO \qquad \text{(radii)}$$
$$\therefore \triangle AOB \equiv \triangle COD \qquad \text{(SSS)}$$

   Hence $\angle AOB = \angle COD$ (Matching angles in
                         congruent $\triangle$s are equal.)
   Also $\angle ABO = \angle CDO$ (Matching angles in
                         congruent $\triangle$s are equal.)

b *Data:* $AB = CD$ and OP and OQ are perpendiculars
        from O to AB and CD respectively.
   Aim: To prove $OP = OQ$.
   Proof: In $\triangle OPB$ and $\triangle OQD$:

$$\angle OPB = \angle OQD = 90° \quad \text{(given)}$$
$$\angle OBP = \angle ODQ \qquad \text{(from part } \mathbf{a})$$
$$BO = DO \qquad \text{(radii)}$$
$$\therefore \triangle OPB \equiv \triangle OQD \qquad \text{(AAS)}$$
$$\therefore OP = OQ \qquad \text{(Matching sides in}$$

                         congruent $\triangle$s are equal.)

5 b *Data:* A, B and C are three non-collinear points.
        PQ and MN are the perpendicular bisectors
        of AB and BC respectively. X is the point of
        intersection of PQ and MN.
   Aim: To prove that X is the centre of the circle which
        passes through A, B and C.
   Proof: As X is on the perpendicular bisector of AB and
        BC, then $XA = XB$ and $XB = XC$; that is,
        $XA = XB = XC$.
        $\therefore A$, B, C are equidistant from X so X is the centre
        of the circle that passes through A, B and C.

9 a i *Proof:* In $\triangle PAQ$ and $\triangle PBQ$:

$$AP = BP \qquad \text{(equal radii)}$$
$$AQ = BQ \qquad \text{(equal radii)}$$
$$PQ \text{ is common.}$$
$$\therefore \triangle PAQ \equiv \triangle PBQ \qquad \text{(SSS)}$$

  ii $\angle APQ = \angle BPQ$
      $\angle PAQ = \angle PBQ$
      $\angle AQP = \angle BQP$

b i *Proof:* In $\triangle XAQ$ and $\triangle XBQ$:

$$AQ = BQ \qquad \text{(equal radii)}$$
$$\angle AQX = \angle BQX \qquad \text{(from part } \mathbf{a})$$
$$XQ \text{ is common.}$$
$$\therefore \triangle XAQ \equiv \triangle XBQ \qquad \text{(SAS)}$$

  ii $AX = BX$ (Matching sides in
                     congruent $\triangle$s are equal.)
      $\angle AXQ = \angle BXQ$ (Matching angles in
                     congruent $\triangle$s are equal.)
      But $\angle AXQ + \angle BXQ = 180°$
              (Angles on a straight line equal $180°$.)
      $\therefore \angle AXB = \angle BXQ = 90°$

Exercise 16C

1 a $x = 50°$ **b** $x = 55°$
   c $x = 125°$ **d** $x = 30$ cm
   e $x = 6$ cm, $y = 5$ cm, $z = 4$ cm
   f $x = 5$ cm   **g** $x = 12$ cm
   h $x = 108°$ **i** $x = 45°$
   j $x = 7$ cm   **k** $x = 10$ cm
   l $x = 10$ cm
2 a $y = 10$ cm, $x = 50°$ **b** $x = 12$ cm
3 $PQ = 24$ cm   **4** $KN = 18$ cm
5 8 cm   **6** 25 cm
7 130 mm   **8** $2\sqrt{5}$ cm ≈ 4.5 cm

Exercise 16D

1 a i $35°$ **ii** $70°$
   b i $121°$ **ii** $242°$
   c i $26°$ **ii** $52°$
3 a *Data:* O is the centre of the circle.
     Aim: To prove $\angle AOB = 2 \times \angle ACB$.
     Proof: Let $\angle ACO = x$ and $\angle OCB = y$.
     In $\triangle AOC$:
          $\angle OAC = \angle OCA$ (Base angles of an isosceles
                            $\triangle$ are equal; equal radii.)
                 $= x$
     Now $\angle POA = \angle OAC + \angle OCA$
                 (The exterior angle of a $\triangle$
                 equals the sum of the interior
                 opposite angles.)
                 $= 2x$
     Similarly $\angle POB = 2y$
          $\therefore \angle AOB = 2x + 2y = 2(x + y)$
                 $= 2 \times \angle ACB$
   b *Data:* O is the centre of the circle.
     Aim: To prove $\angle AOB = 2 \times \angle ACB$.
     Proof: Let $\angle ACO = x$ and $\angle OCB = y$.
            Show that $\angle POA = 2x$ and $\angle POB = 2y$.
            Now $\angle AOB = \angle POB - \angle POA$
                       $= 2y - 2x = 2(y - x)$
            But $\angle ACB = y - x$
               $\therefore \angle AOB = 2 \times \angle ACB$
4 a $x = 96°$ **b** $x = 46°$
   c $x = 70°$ **d** $x = 220°$
   e $x = 43°$ **f** $x = 50°$
5 a $x = 36°$ **b** $x = 128°$
   c $x = 30°$ **d** $x = 52°$
   e $x = 130°$ **f** $x = 68°$
6 b *Data:* O is the centre of the circle.
     Aim: To prove $\angle APB = \angle AQB$.
     Proof: $\angle APB = \frac{1}{2} \times \angle AOB$ and
     (The angle at the centre of a circle is double the angle
     at the circumference, standing on the same arc.)
             $\angle AQB = \frac{1}{2} \times \angle AOB$
     (The angle at the centre of a circle is double the angle
     at the circumference, standing on the same arc.)
         $\therefore \angle APB = \angle AQB$
7 a $x = 35°$, $y = 25°$ **b** $x = 140°$
   c $x = 40°$
   d $w = 30°$, $x = 35°$, $y = 35°$, $z = 40°$
   e $x = 40°$ **f** $x = 20°$

8 b i $\angle AOB$ **ii** $180°$
     iii $\angle ACB$ **iv** $90°$
   c *Data:* AB is a diameter and O is the centre.
     Aim: To prove $\angle ACB = 90°$.
     Proof: $\angle AOB = 2 \times \angle ACB$
     (The angle at the centre of a circle is double the angle
     at the circumference, standing on the same arc.)
     But $\angle AOB = 180°$ (Angles on a straight line
                             equal $180°$.)
         $2 \times \angle ACB = 180°$
         $\therefore \angle ACB = 90°$
9 a $x = 27°$, $y = 62°$ **b** $x = 8$ cm
11 b i $110°$ **ii** $250°$ **iii** $125°$
     iv $180°$ **v** $180°$
   c *Data:* $ABCD$ is a cyclic quadrilateral.
     Aim: To prove **i** $\angle ADC + \angle ABC = 180°$.
                   ii $\angle DAB + \angle DCB = 180°$
     Proof: **i** $\angle AOC = 2 \times \angle ADC$
     (The angle at the centre of a circle is double the angle
     at the circumference, standing on the same arc.)
     reflex $\angle AOC = 2 \times \angle ABC$
     (The angle at the centre of a circle is double the angle
     at the circumference, standing on the same arc.)
     But $\angle AOC +$ reflex $\angle AOC = 360°$
                   (Angles at a point equal $360°$.)
         $2 \times (\angle ADC + \angle ABC) = 360°$
         $\therefore \angle ADC + \angle ABC = 180°$
     ii $\angle ABC + \angle BCD + \angle CDA + \angle DAB = 360°$
                (Angle sum of a rectangle is $360°$.)
     $\therefore \angle BCD + \angle DAB + 180° = 360°$
             $\angle BCD + \angle DAB = 180°$
12 a $x = 126°$, $y = 75°$ **b** $x = 72°$
13 b $x = 55°$, $y = 125°$
   c *Data:* $ABCD$ is a cyclic quadrilateral. CB is produced
     to P.
     Aim: To prove $\angle ABP = \angle ADC$.
     Proof: Let $\angle ABP = x$
            $\angle ABC = 180° - x$ (CBP is a straight line.)
            $\angle ADC = x$ (Opposite angles in a cyclic
                        quadrilateral are supplementary.)
         $\therefore \angle ABP = \angle ADC$.
14 a $x = 152°$ **b** $x = 47°$
15 a $x = 25°$ **b** $y = 20°$
   c $x = 130°$ **d** $x = 45°$
   e $z = 116°$ **f** $w = 70°$
   g $z = 78°$ **h** $x = 76°$
   i $y = 40°$
16 a *Proof:* In $\triangle ABP$:
            $\angle PAB = 90°$ (The angle in a semicircle is
                         a right angle.)
     $\therefore \sin \angle APB = \dfrac{c}{PB}$
                $= \dfrac{c}{2r}$
     $\therefore 2r \times \sin \angle APB = c$
             $\therefore r = \dfrac{c}{2 \sin \angle APB}$
     But $\angle APB = \angle ACB$ (Angles in the same
                         segment are equal.)
               $= \angle C$
         $\therefore R = \dfrac{c}{2 \sin C}$
17 b i Yes   **ii** No   **iii** Yes   **iv** Yes
   c Rectangle, square

Exercise 16E

2 a $20°$ **b** 10 cm
c $25°$ **d** $14°$
e $x = 54°, y = 54°, z = 72°$ **f** $x = 50°, y = 40°$
g $50°$ **h** $x = 40°, y = 40°$
i $35°$ **j** $AB = 4\sqrt{7}$
4 a 13.7 cm **b** 23.7 cm **c** 33.5 cm
6 a i $x = 21$ cm, $y = 75°$
  ii $x = 50°, y = 15$ cm
  iii $x = 25°, y = 54$ cm
  iv $x = 122°$
 b $\angle P = 100°, \angle Q = 95°, \angle R = 80°, \angle S = 85°$
 c $PQ = 11$ cm **d** $RB = 5$ cm
7 a i $x = 52°, y = 52°, z = 76°, w = 38°$
  ii $x = 34°, y = 112°, z = 56°$
  iii $x = 156°, y = 78°$
  iv $x = 80°$
  v $x = 60°, y = 60°, z = 60°, w = 300°, v = 150°$
  vi $x = 126°$
 b *Data:* PQ is a tangent to the circle centre O.
  Aim: To prove $\angle BCQ = \angle CAB$.
  Proof: Join CO and BO. Let $\angle BCQ = x$.
  $\angle OCB = 90° - x$ (A tangent to a circle is perpendicular to the radius at the point of contact.)
  $\angle OBC = 90° - x$ (Base angles of an isosceles $\triangle$ are equal)
  $\angle COB = 180° - 2x$ (Angle sum of a $\triangle$ is $180°$.)
  $\angle BAC = 90° - x$ (The angle at the centre of a circle is double the angle at the circumference, standing on the same arc.)
  $\therefore \angle BCQ = \angle CAB$
8 a $x = 55°$ **b** $x = 136°$
 c $x = 50°, y = 50°$ **d** $x = 110°$
 e $x = 44°$ **f** $x = 75°, y = 49°$
 g $x = 138°$ **h** $x = 25°$
 i $x = 60°$
9 12 cm
10 b *Data:* KPL is the common tangent to two circles with centres O and C that touch externally at P.
  Aim: To prove C, P and O are collinear.
  Proof: $\angle KPO = 90°$ (A tangent to a circle is perpendicular to the radius at the point of contact.)
  $\angle KPC = 90°$ (A tangent to a circle is perpendicular to the radius at the point of contact.)
  $\therefore \angle CPO = 180°$
11 b i *Proof:* In $\triangle APD$ and $\triangle CPB$:
  $\angle APD = \angle CPB$ (Vertically opposite angles are equal.)
  $\angle DAP = \angle BCP$ (Angles at the circumfence of a circle, standing on same arc, are equal.)
  $\therefore \triangle APD \parallel\parallel \triangle CPB$ (Two angles of one $\triangle$ equal two angles of the other $\triangle$.)
  ii $\dfrac{AP}{CP} = \dfrac{PD}{PB} = \dfrac{AD}{CB}$
  iii $\dfrac{AP}{CP} = \dfrac{PD}{PB}$
  $\therefore AP \times PB = DP \times PC$

12 a $x = 4$ cm **b** $x = 6.7$ cm
 c $x = 7.5$ cm **d** $KX = 12.8$ cm
 e $x = 16$ cm **f** $x = 10$ cm
13 b *Data:* PT is a tangent to the circle.
  Aim: To prove $TP^2 = TA \times TB$.
  Proof: In $\triangle PTB$ and $\triangle ATP$:
  $\angle TPB = \angle PAB$ (The angle between a tangent and a chord is equal to the angle in the alternate segment.)
  $\angle PTB = \angle ATP$ (common)
  $\triangle PTB$ is similar to $\triangle ATP$. (Two angles of one $\triangle$ equal two angles of the other $\triangle$.)
  $\dfrac{AP}{PB} = \dfrac{TP}{TB} = \dfrac{TA}{TP}$
  $\therefore TP^2 = TA \times TB$.
14 a $TP = 4$ cm **b** $CD = 6$ cm
 c $QS = 20$ cm, $RS = 15$ cm
 d $LM = 9$ cm, $MN = 7$ cm
 e $x = 6$ cm **f** $x = 21$ cm
 g $x = 4$ cm
15 a $d^2 = h(h + 2R)$ **b** $4800.000\ 338$ m
 c 4.8 km
 d h^2 is extremely small compared with $2hR$.
16 b $TA = 24$ cm, $TD = 8$ cm
 c $SW = 25$ cm, yes
 d *Data:* AB and CD are two secants that meet at T.
  Aim: To prove $TB \times TA = TD \times TC$.
  Construction: Draw the tangent TP.
  Proof: $PT^2 = TB \times TA$ and $PT^2 = TD \times TC$
  (The square of the length of a tangent from an external point equals the product of the intercepts of any secant from the point.)
  $\therefore TB \times TA = TD \times TC$
17 a $x = 3$ cm **b** $x = 2$ cm
 c $x = 4$ cm
 d $w = 12$ cm, $x = 8$ cm, $y = 12$ cm, $z = 7$ cm

Exercise 16F

1 *Data:* AB and CD are chords.
  $\angle AOB = \angle COD$
  Proof: In $\triangle AOB$ and $\triangle COD$:
  $OA = OB = OC = OD$ (radii)
  $\angle AOB = \angle COD$ (given)
  $\therefore \triangle AOB \equiv \triangle COD$ (SAS)
  Hence $AB = CD$ (Matching sides in congruent $\triangle$s are equal.)
2 *Data:* AB and CD are chords.
  $OE = OF$
  Proof: In $\triangle EOB$ and $\triangle FOC$:
  $EO = FO$ (given)
  $\angle BEO = \angle CFO$
  $\quad = 90°$ (given)
  $BO = CO$ (radii)
  $\therefore \triangle EOB \equiv \triangle FOC$ (RHS)
  $\therefore EB = FC$ (Matching sides in congruent $\triangle$s are equal.)
  $\therefore \triangle EOA \equiv \triangle FOD$
  Hence $EA = FD$
  $\therefore AB = CD$

3 a *Proof:* In $\triangle CTA$ and $\triangle BTD$:

$\angle T$ is common.

$\angle TAC = \angle TDB$ (The exterior angle of a cyclic quadrilateral equals the interior opposite angle.)

Hence $\angle TCA = \angle TBD$

$\therefore \triangle CTA \,|||\, \triangle BTD$ ($\triangle$s have equal angles.)

b $\dfrac{AT}{DT} = \dfrac{TC}{TB} = \dfrac{AC}{DB}$

$\therefore TA \times TB = TC \times TD$

4 *Proof:* OF bisects BC.

The perpendicular from the centre to a chord bisects the chord.

Similarly OF bisects AD.

$AB = AF - BF$

$CD = DF - CF$

But $AF = DF$ and $BF = CF$

$\therefore AB = CD$

5 *Proof:* In $\triangle PKL$ and $\triangle RLK$:

$PQ = RS$ (given)

$\angle OKP = \angle OLR = 90°$

(The perpendicular from the centre to a chord bisects the chord.)

$\angle OKL = \angle OLK$ (Base angles of an isosceles $\triangle$ are equal.)

$\angle PKL = 90° + \angle OKL$ and

$\angle RLK = 90° + \angle OLK$

$\therefore \angle PKL = \angle RLK$

6 *Proof:* $AJ = JK$ (A perpendicular from the centre to a chord bisects the chord.)

Similarly $KM = MC$

$AC = AJ + JK + KM + MC = AJ + AJ + KM + KM$

$= 2(AJ + KM)$

But $PQ = JK + KM = AJ + KM$

$\therefore AC = 2 \times PQ$

7 a *Proof:* $\angle BCP = 180° - \angle BOD$ (Opposite angles of a cyclic quadrilateral are supplementary.)

$\angle ADQ = 180° - \angle BAD$ (Co-interior angles and $AB \parallel DC$.)

$\therefore \angle ADQ = \angle BCP$

Join AQ and BP.

In $\triangle ADQ$ and $\triangle BPC$:

$\angle AQP = \angle BPQ$ (The diagonals of a rectangle bisect each other giving the base angles of an isosceles triangle.)

$AQ = BP$ (The diagonals of a rectangle are equal.)

$\therefore \triangle AQD \equiv \triangle BPC$ (AAS)

Hence $CP = QD$ (Matching sides in congruent $\triangle$s are equal.)

b *Proof:* In $\triangle APD$ and $\triangle BQC$:

$\angle ADP = \angle BCQ$ (part **a**)

$\angle APD = \angle BQC$ ($= 90°$, given)

$AD = BC$ (part **a**)

$AP = BQ$ (Opposite sides of a rectangle are equal.)

$\therefore \triangle APD \equiv \triangle BQC$ (RHS)

Hence $AC = BD$ (Matching sides in congruent $\triangle$s are equal.)

8 *Proof:* Join OA.

In $\triangle COA$ and $\triangle BOA$:

$\angle OCA = \angle OAC$ (Base angles of an isosceles triangle are equal, equal radii.)

Similarly $\angle OAB = \angle OBA$

$OC = OB$ and OA is common.

$\therefore \triangle COA = \triangle BOA$ (SSS)

$\therefore \angle OCA = \angle OAC = \angle OAB = \angle OBA$

$\angle COB = 2 \times \angle CAB$ (The angle at the centre is double the angle at the circumference, standing on the same arc.)

Hence $\angle COB = 2 \times (2 \times \angle OBA)$

$= 4 \times \angle OBA$

9 *Proof:* PQRS is a parallelogram

$\angle TQR = \angle PSR$ (The exterior angle of a cyclic quadrilateral is equal to the interior opposite angle.)

$\angle PSR = \angle PTR$ (The opposite angles of a parallelogram are equal.)

$\therefore \angle TQR = \angle PTR$

Hence $\triangle QRT$ is isosceles as the base angles are equal.

10 *Proof:* $\angle BCD = \angle CAB$ (The angle between a tangent and a chord is equal to the angle in the alternate segment.)

$\angle CAB = \angle ABC$ (Base angles of an isosceles triangle are equal, $CA = CB$.)

$\therefore \angle ABC = \angle BCD$

Hence $AB \parallel CD$ (Alternate angles are equal.)

11 *Proof:* $\angle NQR = \angle QTR$ (The angle between a tangent and a chord is equal to the angle in the alternate segment.)

$\angle NQR = \angle QRS$ (Alternate angles and $QP \parallel RS$.)

Hence $\angle QRS = \angle QTR$

12 *Proof:* $\angle CDB = \angle BAC$ (Angles at the circumference, standing on the same arc, are equal.)

$\angle BAC = \angle ABD$ (Alternate angles and $CA \parallel BD$.)

$\therefore \angle BDC = \angle ABD$

$\angle CPB = (\angle BDC + \angle ABD$ (Exterior angle of a $\triangle$ equals the sum of interior opposite angles.)

Hence $\angle CPB = 2 \times \angle BDC$

13 *Proof:* $\angle PAB = \angle PQB$ (Angles at the circumference, standing on the same arc, are equal.)

Similarly $\angle APQ = \angle ABQ$

Hence $AP \parallel QB$ (Alternate angles are equal.)

14 *Proof:* $\angle DAB = \angle BCD$ (Angles at the circumference, standing on the same arc, are equal.)

Similarly $\angle ADC = \angle CBA$

$\angle PAD = \angle PDA$ (Base angles of an isosceles triangle are equal.)

$\therefore \angle PCB = \angle PBC$

Hence $\triangle PCB$ is isosceles.

$\therefore CP = BP$

15 *Proof:* $\angle KLR = \angle KSR$ (Angles at the circumference, standing on the same arc, are equal.)

$\angle KSM = 180° - \angle KSR$ (Angles on a straight line equal $180°$.)

$\angle RLM = 180° - \angle KLR$

Hence $\angle KSM = \angle RLM$

ANSWERS

16 *Proof:* ∠DAC = ∠BEC   (The exterior angle of a cyclic quadrilateral is equal to the interior opposite angle.)

  ∠BEC = ∠ADC   (Corresponding angles and AD ∥ BE.)

∴ ∠DAC = ∠ADC

Hence CA = CD   (Base angles of an isosceles triangle are equal.)

17 *Proof:* Let ∠PQS = ∠RQS = x and ∠PSQ = ∠RSQ = y

∴ ∠QRS = 180° − (x + y) and ∠QPS = 180° − (x + y)

But ∠QRS = 180° − ∠QPS   (The opposite angles of a cyclic quadrilateral are supplementary.)

Hence 180° − (x + y) = 180° − (180° − (x + y))

2(x + y) = 180°

x + y = 90°

Hence ∠QRS = ∠QPS = 90°

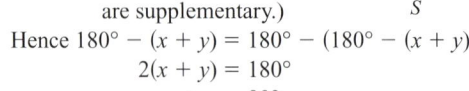

18 *Proof:* ∠ADB = 90°   (The angle at a semicircle is a right angle.)

∠BDE + ∠ADB = 180°   (Angles on a straight line equal 180°.)

∴ ∠BDE = 90°

∠BCE = 180° − ∠BDE   (The opposite angles of a cyclic quadrilateral are supplementary.)

Hence ∠ACE = 90°

19 *Proof:* ∠OPX = 90°   (The angle at a semicircle is a right angle.)

OP ⊥ to XY

∴ P bisects XY   (The perpendicular drawn from the centre to a chord bisects the chord.)

Hence XP = PY

20 *Proof:* Let ∠OPQ = x

Then ∠PRQ = x   (given)

∠POQ = 2x   (The angle at the centre is double the angle at the circumference standing on the same arc.)

∠OPQ = ∠OQP = x   (Base angles of an isosceles triangle are equal.)

In △POQ angle sum = 180°

x + x + 2x = 180°

∴ x = 45°

Hence ∠POQ = 90°

21 *Proof:* Join OB.

∠OBC = 90°   (The angle between a tangent and a radius is a right angle.)

∴ B bisects AC (The perpendicular drawn from the centre to a chord bisects the chord.)

Hence AB = BC

22 *Proof:* Join OD.

Let ∠CDB = x

Then ∠BDO = 90° − x   (The tangent and radius are perpendicular.)

∠OAB = ∠BDO = 90° − x   (△AOD is isosceles. AO = OD as radii are equal.)

∠OBA = x   (The angle sum of a △ is 180°.)

∠DBC = ∠OBA = x   (Vertically opposite angles are equal.)

∴ ∠CDB = ∠CBD = x

Hence △CDB is isosceles.

∴ CD = CB

23 *Proof:* ∠TQR = ∠QPR   (The angle between a tangent and a chord is equal to the angle in the alternate segment.)

Similarly ∠TRQ = ∠QPR

∴ ∠TQR = ∠TRQ

Hence △QRT is isosceles.

∴ RT = QT

24 *Proof:* Join AP.

Let ∠PBQ = x

Then ∠PBA = x   (PB bisects ∠QBA.)

∠APB = 90°   (The angle at a semicircle is a right angle.)

∴ ∠PAB = 90° − x

∠QPB = ∠PAB   (The angle between a tangent and a chord is equal to the angle in the alternate segment.)

∴ ∠QPB = 90° − x

In △PQB:

∠PQB + x + 90° − x = 180°   (The angle sum of a △ is 180°.)

Hence ∠PQB = 90°

25 *Proof:* PQ = PX   (Tangents from a common point are equal.)

Similarly PT = PX

Hence PQ = PT

26 *Proof:* ∠PQR = ∠PRQ   (Base angles of an isosceles triangle are equal.)

∠PQR = ∠PVW   (Corresponding angles and VW ∥ QR.)

∴ ∠PWV = ∠PQR

Hence VWRQ is cyclic.   (The exterior angle of a cyclic quadrilateral is equal to the interior opposite angle.)

27 *Proof:* PT² = PA × PB

(The square of the length of a tangent from an external point equals the product of the intercepts of any secant from the point.)

$\left(\dfrac{PA}{3}\right)^2 = PA \times PB$

PA² = 9(PA × PB)

PA = 9PB

But PA = PB + AB

PB + AB = 9PB

Hence AB = 8PB

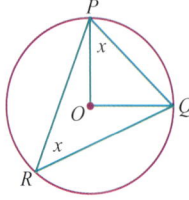

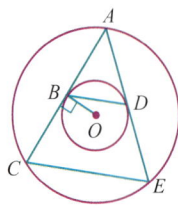

530   Insight Mathematics 10 stages 5.2/5.3 Australian Curriculum

Language in mathematics

1 a $\angle PSQ$ **b** $\angle QOR$ **c** $\angle STR$
d $\angle QPS$ **e** $\angle QRS$ **f** $\angle PSQ$

2 a **b** **c**
d **e** **f**

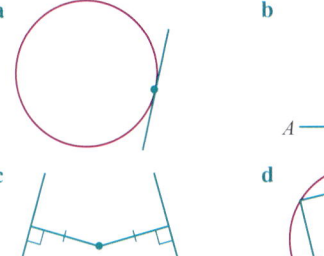

3 a Collinear points are points on the same straight line.
b Concyclic points are points through which a circle can be drawn.
c A cyclic quadrilateral is one that has its four vertices on the circumference of a circle.

4 a A sector joins two points on the circumference through the centre of the circle. A segment is formed when two points on the circumference are joined.
b Supplementary angles add to 180°. Complementary angle add to 90°.
c Alternate angles are on opposite sides of a transversal that cuts a pair of parallel lines. Alternative means different.

5 a **b**
c **d**

6 diameter, circumference, intersect

Check your skills

1 D		**2** A		**3** D		**4** B		**5** C	
6 A		**7** B		**8** C		**9** C		**10** C	
11 A		**12** B		**13** B		**14** C		**15** C	
16 B		**17** A							

Review set 16A

2 a $\angle ACB$ **b** $\angle AOB$
c $\angle BAC$ **d** $\angle CDE$
3 a $x = 70°$ **b** $x = 7.5$ cm
c $r = 13$ cm
4 $x = 5$ cm, $y = 40°$
5 a $x = 30°, y = 40°$ **b** $x = 70°$
c $x = 70°$ **d** $x = 110°$
e $x = 100°, y = 60°$ **f** $x = 100°$
6 a $x = 55°$ **b** $x = 62°$
c $x = 75°$ **d** $x = 98°$
e $x = 5.6$ cm **f** $x = 7$ cm

Review set 16B

2 a $\angle BEA$ **b** $\angle AOB$
c $\angle EBD$ **d** $\angle DCB$
3 a $x = 130°$ **b** $x = 8$ cm **c** $x = 50°$
4 $x = 6$ cm, $y = 55°$
5 a $x = 42°$ **b** $x = 70°, y = 10°$
c $x = \sqrt{39}$ cm **d** $x = 230°$
e $x = 100°, y = 110°$ **f** $x = 47°$
6 a $x = 8$ cm **b** $x = 52°$
c $x = 110°$ **d** $x = 5\frac{1}{3}$ cm
e $x = 4$ cm **f** $x = 5.5$ cm

Review set 16C

2 a $\angle PRQ$ **b** $\angle QOR$
c $\angle RPS$ **d** $\angle STP$
3 a $x = 7$ cm **b** $x = 3$ cm **c** $x = 8$ cm
4 $x = 5$ cm, $y = 13$ cm
5 a $x = 25°, y = 45°$ **b** $x = 70°$
c $x = 45°$ **d** $x = 100°, y = 30°$
e $x = 40°$ **f** $x = 125°$
6 a $x = 30°$ **b** $x = 80°$
c $x = 50°$ **d** $x = 70°$
e $x = 5$ cm **f** $x = 1$ cm
g $x = 3$ cm

Review set 16D

2 a $\angle JNK$ **b** $\angle JOK$
c $\angle MKN$ **d** $\angle KLM$
3 a $x = 5$ cm **b** $x = 4$ cm **c** $x = 40°$
4 $x = 8$ cm, $y = 30$ cm
5 a $x = 50°, y = 70°$ **b** $x = 27.5°$
c $x = 30°$ **d** $x = 120°$
e $x = 40°, y = 80°, z = 90°$
f $x = 20°$
6 a $x = 15$ cm **b** $x = 12$ cm, $y = 55°$
c $w = 48°, x = 42°, y = 42°, z = 96°$
d $x = 37°$ **e** $x = 5\frac{5}{7}$ cm ≈ 5.7 cm
f $x = 2.5$ cm **g** $x = 3$ cm

CUMULATIVE REVIEW: 14–16

1 a i $\bar{x} = 6.25$ **ii** $\sigma_n = 1.79$
iii Range $= 6$ **iv** IQR $= 2.5$
b i $\bar{x} = 4.25$ **ii** $\sigma_n = 1.79$
iii Range $= 6$ **iv** IQR $= 2.5$
c i $\bar{x} = 18.75$ **ii** $\sigma_n = 5.36$
iii Range $= 18$ **iv** IQR $= 7.5$

2 a, b

Income versus entertainment

$y = 0.0779x + 1.4729$

c i $3031 **ii** $32 440

3 a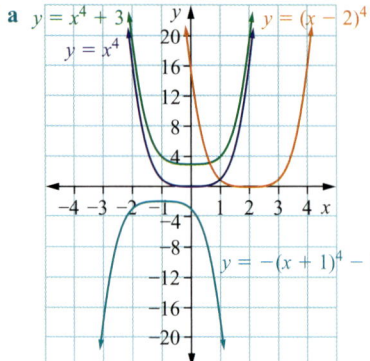

$y = x^4 + 3$, $y = x^4$, $y = (x - 2)^4$, $y = -(x + 1)^4 - 2$

b i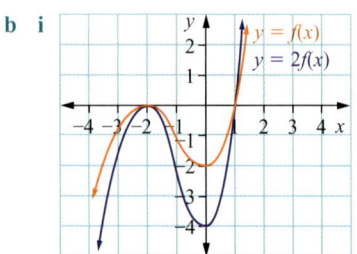

$y = f(x)$, $y = 2f(x)$

ii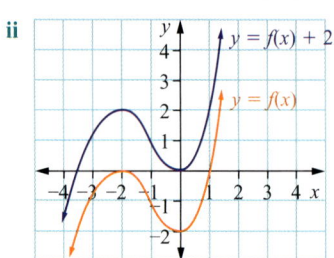

$y = f(x) + 2$, $y = f(x)$

iii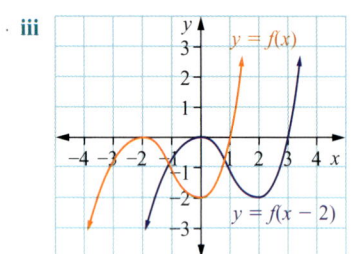

$y = f(x)$, $y = f(x - 2)$

vi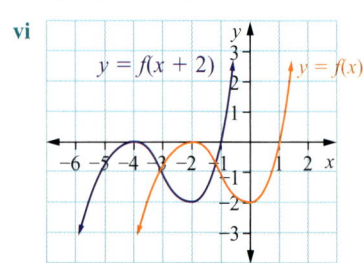

$y = f(x + 2)$, $y = f(x)$

v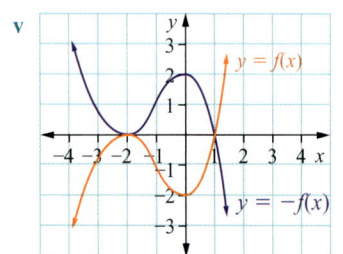

$y = f(x)$, $y = -f(x)$

vi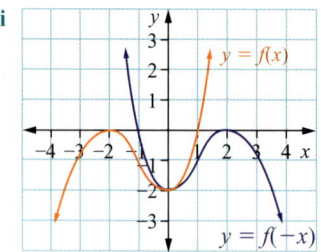

$y = f(x)$, $y = f(-x)$

c i Yes   **ii** No   **iii** No

d $\sqrt{x} = x^{\frac{1}{2}} \therefore$ not an integer power

e i 7   **ii** $2x^7$ **iii** 2   **iv** 1   **v** No

f i $2x^4 + 3x^3 - x^2 - 2x - 9$

  ii $2x^4 - 3x^3 - 5x^2 + 12x + 7$

g i $x^4 - 10x^3 + 23x^2 - 12x - 4$

  ii $x^2 - 6x - 5$ remainder -8

  iii $Q(x) = (x - 2)(x^2 - 6x - 5) - 8$

h 41

i i $P(-5) = 0 \therefore (x + 5)$ is a factor.

  ii $P(x) = (x + 5)(x - 3)(x + 2)$

  iii $x = -5, 3, -2$

  vi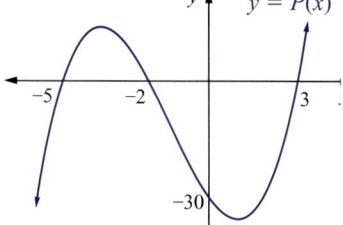

$y = P(x)$

j i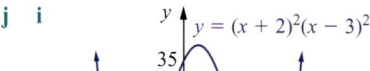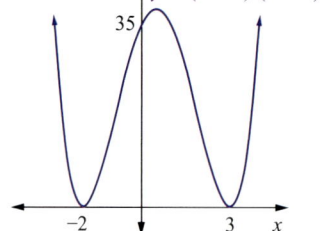

$y = (x + 2)^2(x - 3)^2$

  ii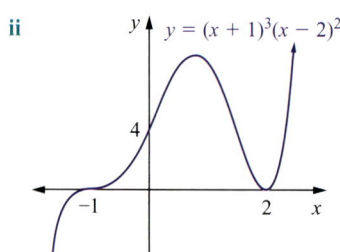

$y = (x + 1)^3(x - 2)^2$

  iii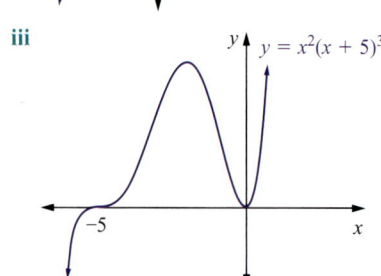

$y = x^2(x + 5)^3$

4 a i ii iii iv v vi vii viii ix

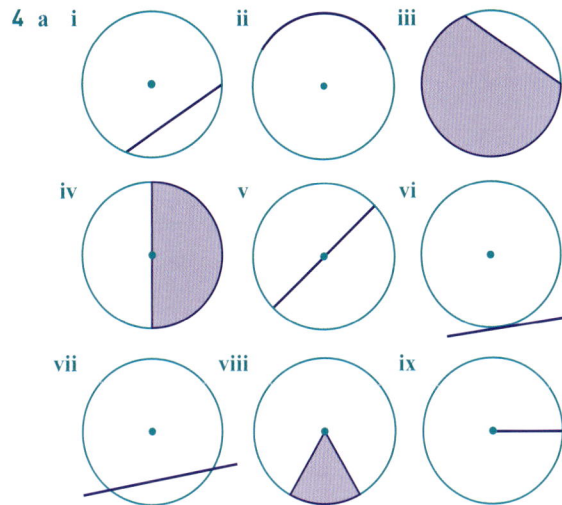

b i $x = 8$ cm (Equal angles subtend equal arcs. The $\triangle$s are congruent.)

ii $x = 7$ cm (The chords equidistant from the centre are equal.)

iii $x = 50°$, $y = 80°$ (Angles in the same segment are equal.)

iv $x = 50°$ (The angle at the circumference is half the angle at centre.)

v $x = 10$ cm (The angle between a tangent and a radius is 90°, Pythagoras' theorem.)

vi $x = 50°$ ($\triangle OAP \equiv \triangle OBP$ (SSS) The angle sum of a $\triangle$ is 180°. The tangent and radius are perpendicular.)

$y = 15$ cm (Tangents from a fixed point are equal.)

vii $x = 6\frac{3}{4}$ cm (The products of the intercepts of two chords are equal.)

viii $x = 2.4$ cm (The angle between a tangent and a radius is 90°, Pythagoras theorem.)

INDEX

Acknowledgements

The author and the publisher wish to thank the following copyright holders for reproduction of their material.

Corbis/Henry Horenstein, front & back cover, title page, p. vi.

Chapter 1: Shutterstock/Eric Isselee, p. 1; Istock.com/George Clerk, p. 3; Shutterstock/Angela Waye, p. 5; Shutterstock/Henryk Sadura, p. 11; Fotolia/Olga D. van de Veer, p. 15 left; **Chapter 2:** Shutterstock/Wassana Mathipikhai, p. 21; Lindsay Edwards, pp. 26, 32; **Chapter 3:** Shutterstock/Boonchuay PromJiam, p. 39; Lindsay Edwards, pp. 50, 56; **Chapter 4:** Shutterstock/kamnuan, p. 67; Lindsay Edwards, p. 78; Shutterstock/Eric Gevaert, p. 88 bottom; Shutterstock/Volosina, p. 91; Lindsay Edwards, p. 93; Istock.com/urbancow, p. 88 top; **Chapter 5:** Shutterstock/Ivan Kuzmin, p. 107; Shutterstock/everything possible, p. 109; Shutterstock/RyFlip, p. 113; Shutterstock/Zurijeta, p. 120; istock.com/AP, p. 123; **Chapter 6:** Shutterstock/gopause, p. 131; Shutterstock/alexskopje, p. 135; Shutterstock/Valua Vitaly, p. 138; Shutterstock/stefan11, p. 143; Shutterstock/06photo, p. 144; Shutterstock/marijaf, p. 145 top; Shutterstock/ChameleonsEye, p. 145 bottom; **Chapter 7:** Shutterstock/gopause, p. 151; Lindsay Edwards, pp. 157, 160, 170; **Chapter 8:** Shutterstock/gallimaufry, p. 177; Shutterstock, p. 181; Shutterstock/Mitch Gunn, p. 182; Shutterstock/Neale Cousland, p. 183; Lindsay Edwards, p. 189; Shutterstock/SurangaSL, p. 193; Shutterstock/wavebreakmedia, p. 194;

Shutterstock/jannoon028, p. 198; Shutterstock/Aaron Amat, p. 187; **Chapter 9:** Shutterstock/Hugh Lansdown, p. 205; Shutterstock/Taras Vyshnya, p. 209; Shutterstock/Steve Buckley, p. 216; **Chapter 10:** Shutterstock/tanaphongpict, p. 225; Lindsay Edwards, p. 229; Shutterstock/Irina Schmidt, p. 244; Lindsay Edwards, pp. 248, 251, 233; **Chapter 11:** Shutterstock/ArtTomCat, p. 257; Shutterstock/tungtopgun, p. 260; istock.com/photoquest7, p. 263; istock.com/elleran, p. 269; **Chapter 12:** Shutterstock/Andrew Burgess, p. 277; Shutterstock/simone mescolini, p. 279; Shutterstock/Monkey Business Images, p. 280; Shutterstock/CreativeNature.nl, p. 283; Shutterstock/Pablo77, p. 287 bottom; Shutterstock/nikkytok, p. 287 top; Lindsay Edwards, pp. 288, 296; istock.com/supertrader, p. 312; **Chapter 13:** Shutterstock/Ivan Kuzmin, p. 323; Shutterstock/Jack schiffer, p. 331; Shutterstock/Jasiek03, p. 333 top; Shutterstock/Boris Sosnovyy, p. 333 bottom; Shutterstock/Soloviova Liudmyla, p. 334; Lindsay Edwards, p. 337; **Chapter 14:** Shutterstock/John Carnemolla, p. 345; Lindsay Edwards, p. 349; Shutterstock/Peter Bernik, p. 351; Shutterstock/karelnoppe, p. 359; **Chapter 15:** istock.com/Craig Dingle, p. 365; Lindsay Edwards, pp. 382, 384; **Chapter 16:** Shutterstock/Eric Isselee, p. 401; Shutterstock/littleredshark, p. 408; istock.com/TheLaborShed, p. 419; Shutterstock/Olga Danylenko, p. 428; Shutterstock/rickyd, p. 357; Shutterstock/DenisNata, p. 15 right; Shutterstock/Andresr, p. 353.

Every effort has been made to trace the original source of copyright material contained in this book. The publisher will be pleased to hear from copyright holders to rectify any errors or omissions.